PROLOG

FIRST SIGHTING...

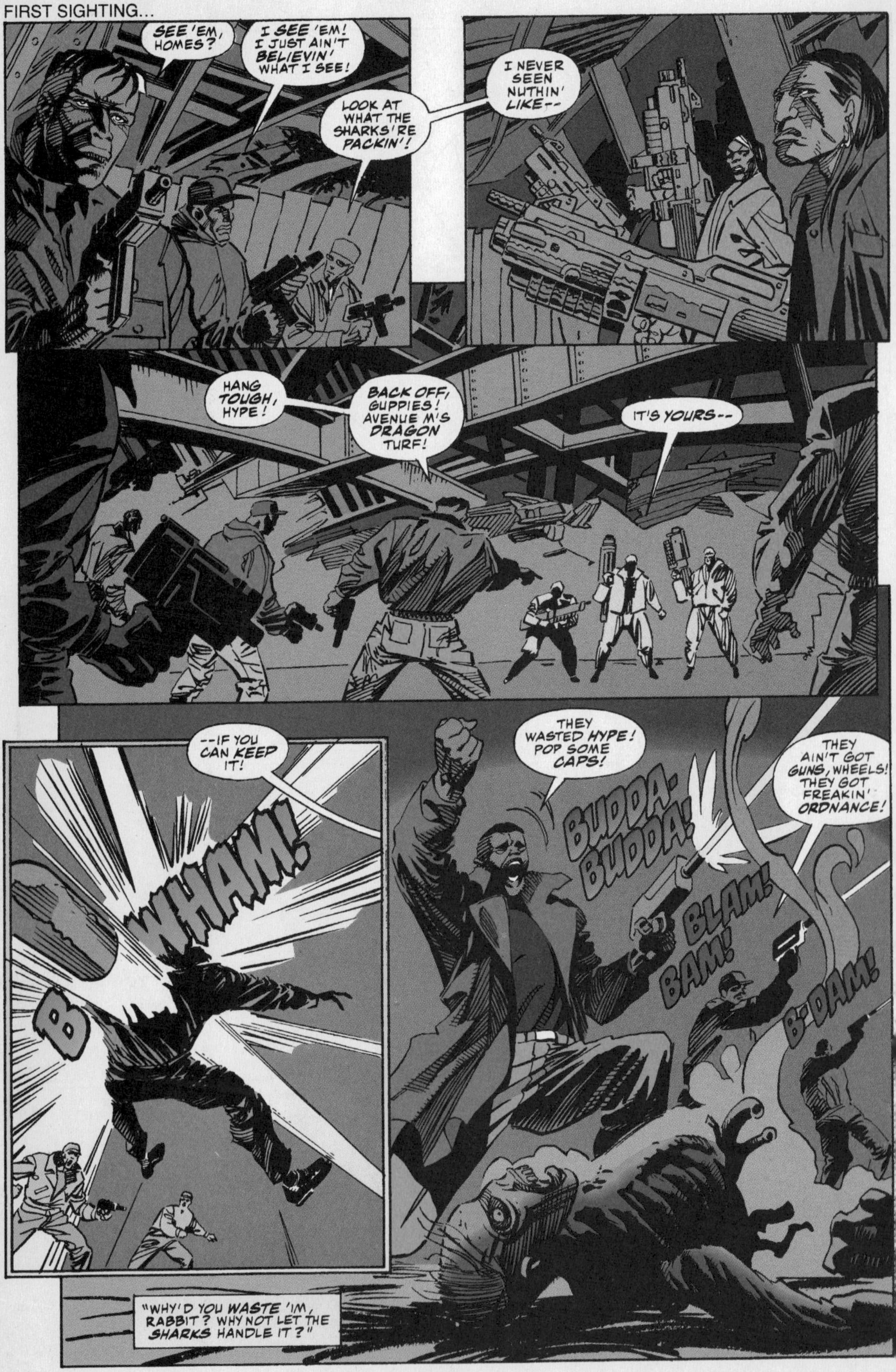
SEE 'EM, HOMES?
I SEE 'EM! I JUST AIN'T BELIEVIN' WHAT I SEE!
LOOK AT WHAT THE SHARKS'RE PACKIN'!
I NEVER SEEN NUTHIN' LIKE--
HANG TOUGH, HYPE!
BACK OFF, GUPPIES! AVENUE M'S DRAGON TURF!
IT'S YOURS--
--IF YOU CAN KEEP IT!
B-WHAM!
THEY WASTED HYPE! POP SOME CAPS!
BUDDA-BUDDA!
THEY AIN'T GOT GUNS, WHEELS! THEY GOT FREAKIN' ORDNANCE!
BLAM!
BAM!
B-DAM!
"WHY'D YOU WASTE 'IM, RABBIT? WHY NOT LET THE SHARKS HANDLE IT?"

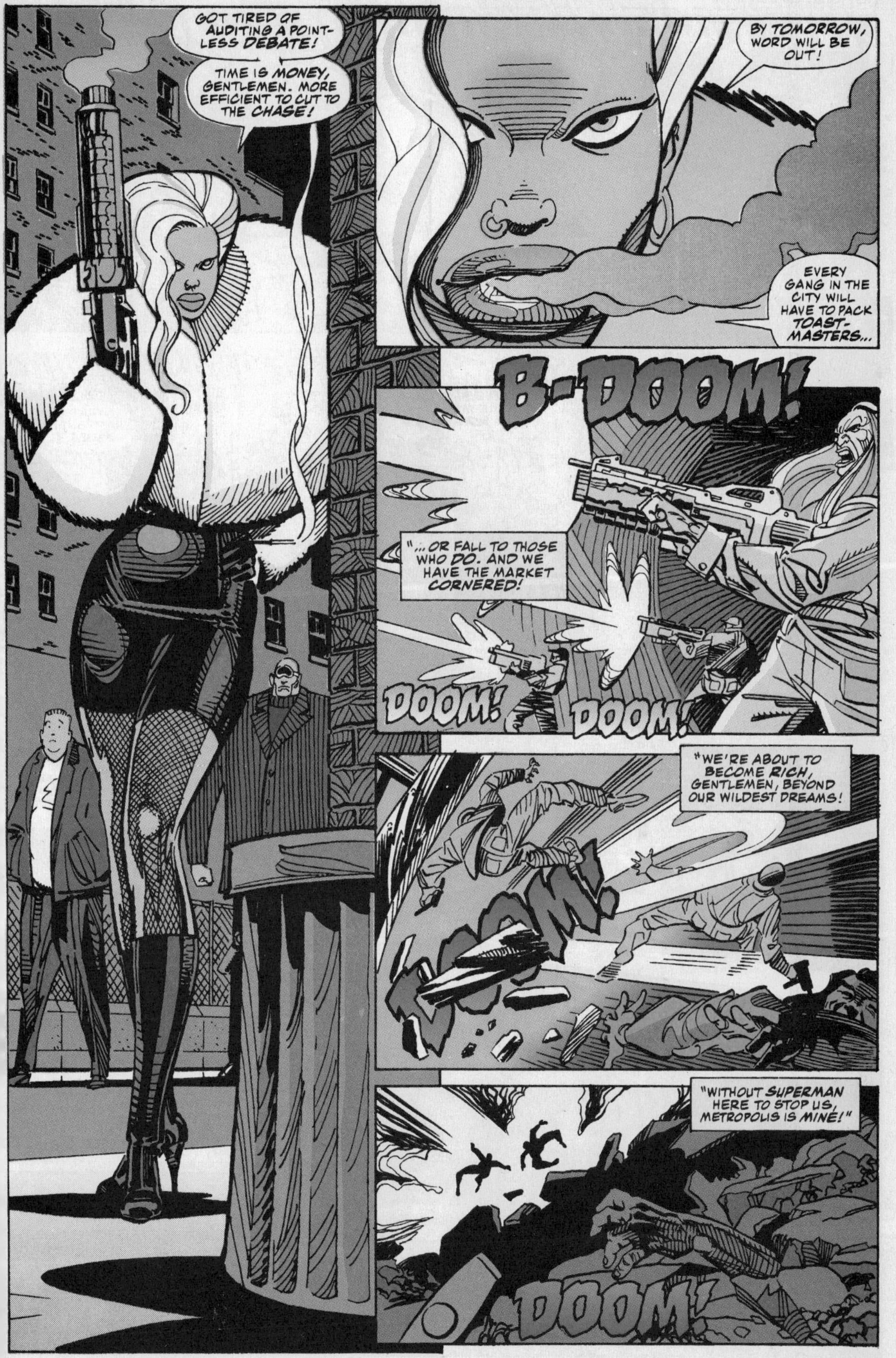
GOT TIRED OF AUDITING A POINTLESS DEBATE!
TIME IS MONEY, GENTLEMEN. MORE EFFICIENT TO CUT TO THE CHASE!
BY TOMORROW, WORD WILL BE OUT!
EVERY GANG IN THE CITY WILL HAVE TO PACK TOAST-MASTERS...
B-DOOM!
"...OR FALL TO THOSE WHO DO. AND WE HAVE THE MARKET CORNERED!
DOOM!
DOOM!
"WE'RE ABOUT TO BECOME RICH, GENTLEMEN, BEYOND OUR WILDEST DREAMS!
DOOM!
"WITHOUT SUPERMAN HERE TO STOP US, METROPOLIS IS MINE!"
DOOM!

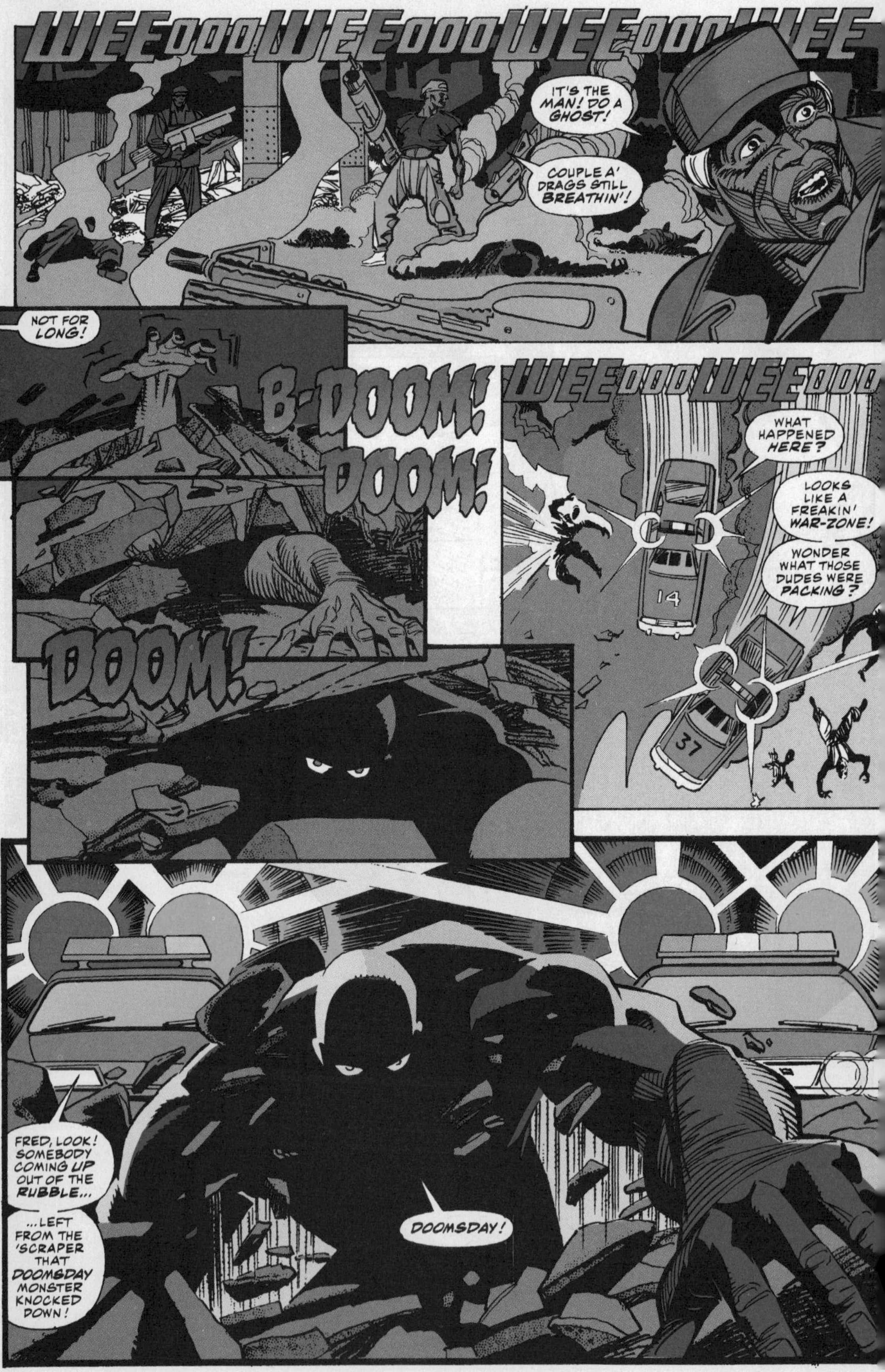
WEEooo WEEooo WEEooo WEE
IT'S THE MAN! DO A GHOST!
COUPLE A' DRAGS STILL BREATHIN'!
NOT FOR LONG!
B-DOOM! DOOM!
DOOM!
WEEooo WEEooo
WHAT HAPPENED HERE?
LOOKS LIKE A FREAKIN' WAR-ZONE!
WONDER WHAT THOSE DUDES WERE PACKING?
14
37
FRED, LOOK! SOMEBODY COMING UP OUT OF THE RUBBLE...
...LEFT FROM THE 'SCRAPER THAT DOOMSDAY MONSTER KNOCKED DOWN!
DOOMSDAY!

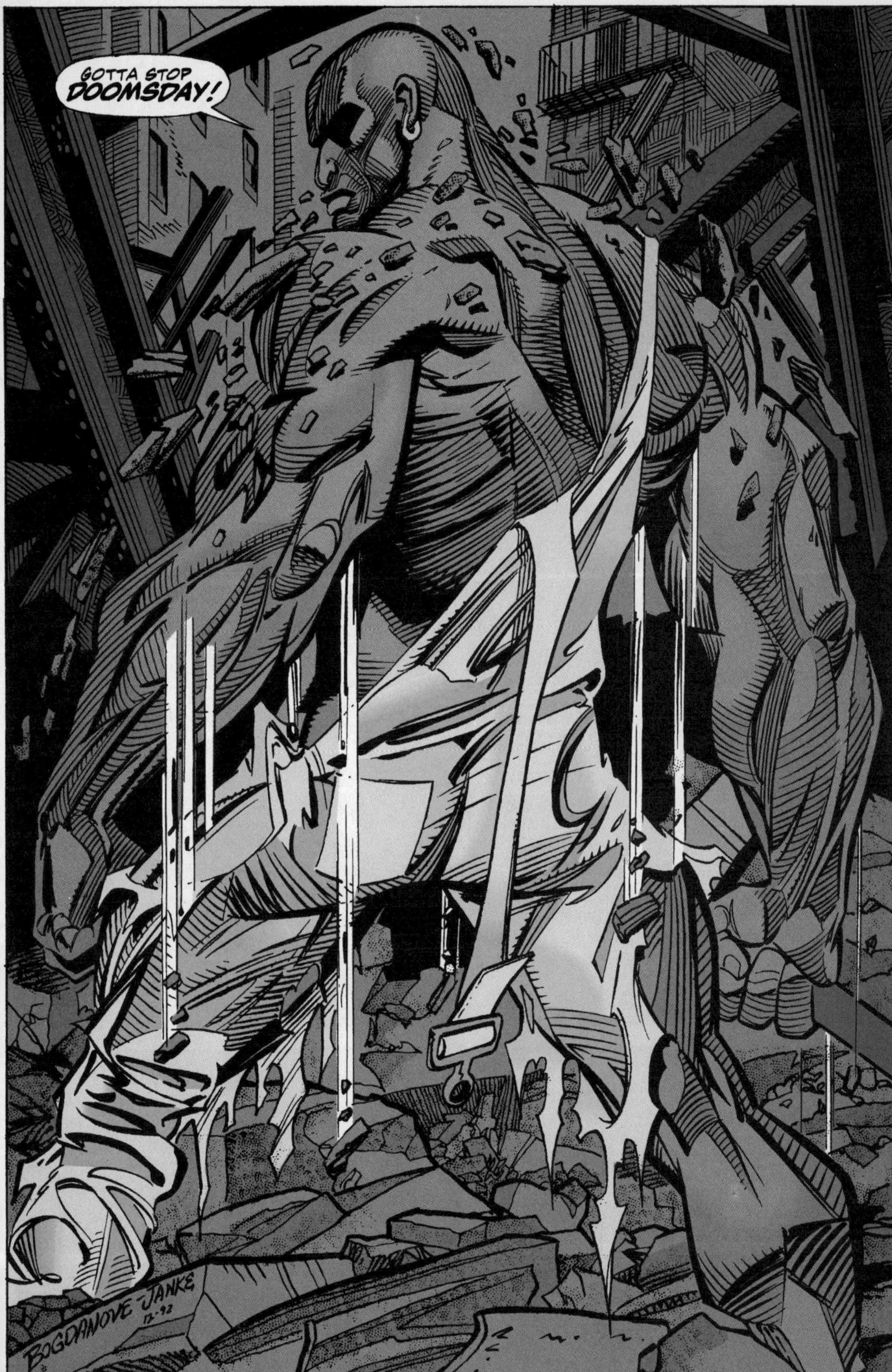
GOTTA STOP DOOMSDAY!
BOGDANOVE-JANKE 12-92

Louise Simonson: writer/Jon Bogdanove: penciller/Dennis Janke: inker

FIRST SIGHTING...

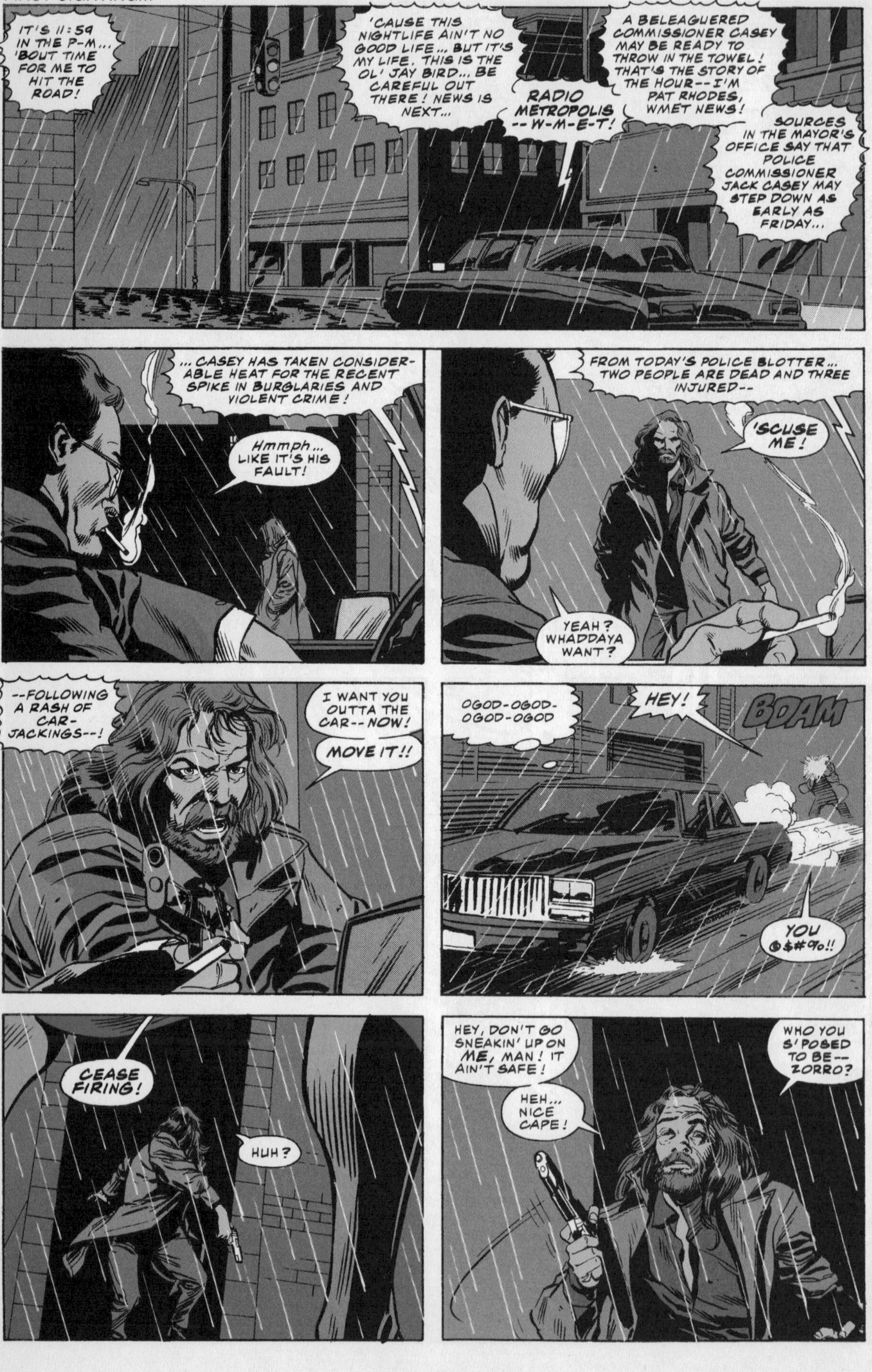

IT'S 11:59 IN THE P-M... 'BOUT TIME FOR ME TO HIT THE ROAD!
'CAUSE THIS NIGHTLIFE AIN'T NO GOOD LIFE... BUT IT'S MY LIFE. THIS IS THE OL' JAY BIRD... BE CAREFUL OUT THERE! NEWS IS NEXT...
RADIO METROPOLIS --W-M-E-T!
A BELEAGUERED COMMISSIONER CASEY MAY BE READY TO THROW IN THE TOWEL! THAT'S THE STORY OF THE HOUR--I'M PAT RHODES, WMET NEWS!
SOURCES IN THE MAYOR'S OFFICE SAY THAT POLICE COMMISSIONER JACK CASEY MAY STEP DOWN AS EARLY AS FRIDAY...
...CASEY HAS TAKEN CONSIDERABLE HEAT FOR THE RECENT SPIKE IN BURGLARIES AND VIOLENT CRIME!
Hmmph... LIKE IT'S HIS FAULT!
FROM TODAY'S POLICE BLOTTER... TWO PEOPLE ARE DEAD AND THREE INJURED--
'SCUSE ME!
YEAH? WHADDAYA WANT?
--FOLLOWING A RASH OF CAR-JACKINGS--!
I WANT YOU OUTTA THE CAR--NOW!
MOVE IT!!
OGOD-OGOD-OGOD-OGOD
HEY!
BDAM
YOU @$#%!!
CEASE FIRING!
HUH?
HEY, DON'T GO SNEAKIN' UP ON ME, MAN! IT AIN'T SAFE!
HEH... NICE CAPE!
WHO YOU S'POSED TO BE--ZORRO?

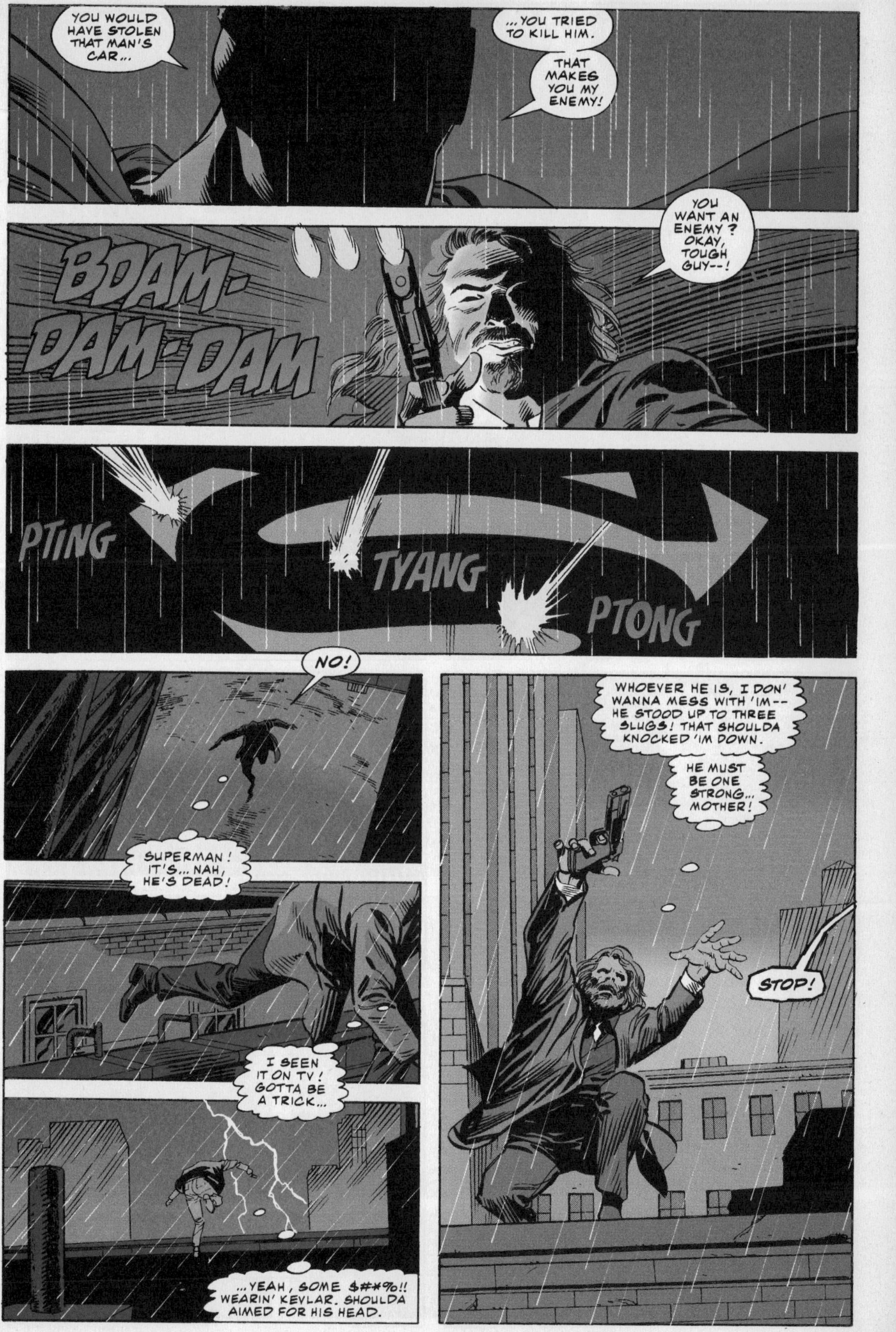

YOU WOULD HAVE STOLEN THAT MAN'S CAR...
...YOU TRIED TO KILL HIM.
THAT MAKES YOU MY ENEMY!
YOU WANT AN ENEMY? OKAY, TOUGH GUY--!
BDAM-DAM-DAM
PTING
TYANG
PTONG
NO!
SUPERMAN! IT'S... NAH, HE'S DEAD!
I SEEN IT ON TV! GOTTA BE A TRICK...
...YEAH, SOME $#*%!! WEARIN' KEVLAR. SHOULDA AIMED FOR HIS HEAD.
WHOEVER HE IS, I DON' WANNA MESS WITH 'IM-- HE STOOD UP TO THREE SLUGS! THAT SHOULDA KNOCKED 'IM DOWN.
HE MUST BE ONE STRONG... MOTHER!
STOP!

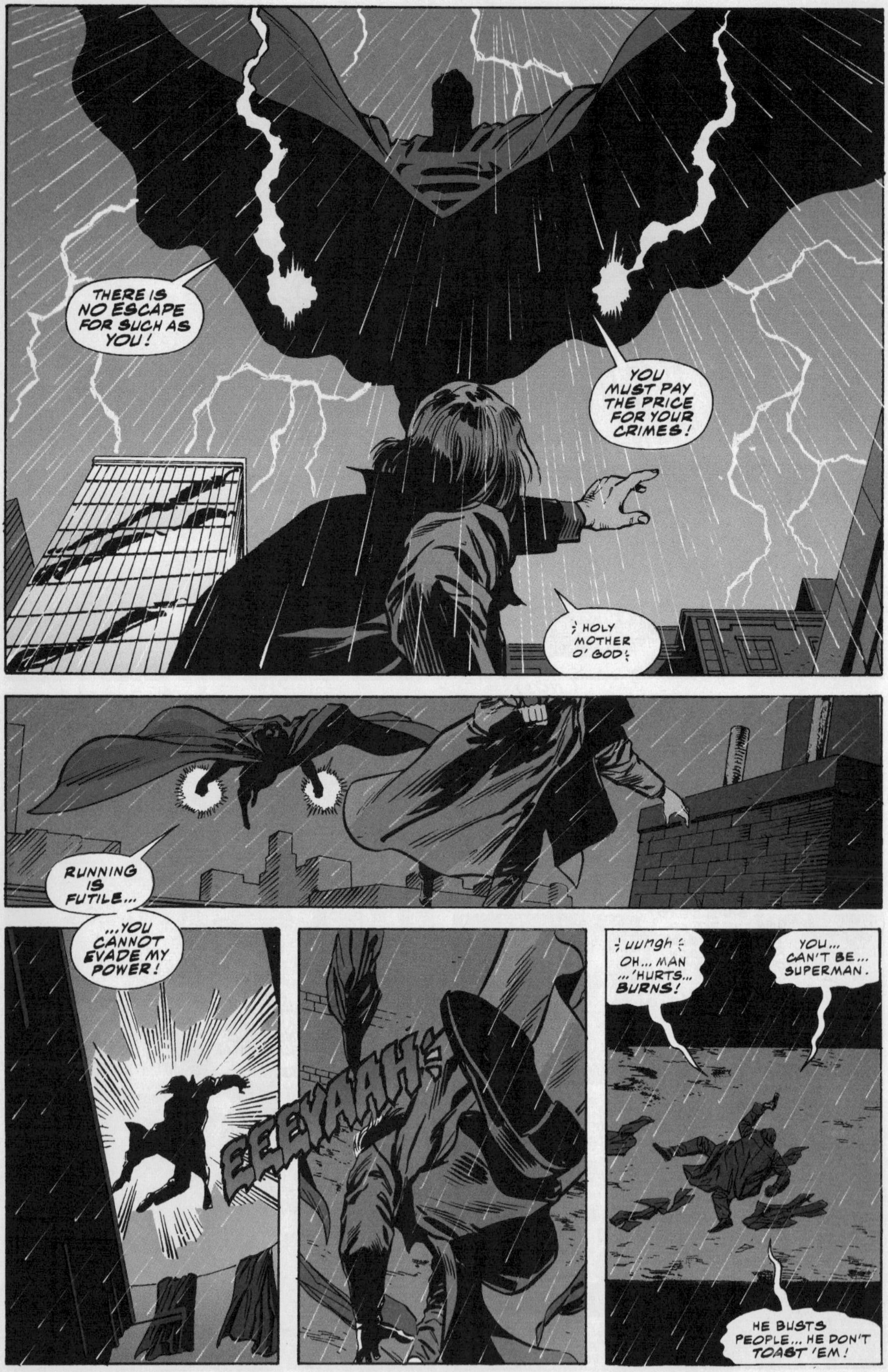
THERE IS NO ESCAPE FOR SUCH AS YOU!
YOU MUST PAY THE PRICE FOR YOUR CRIMES!
¡HOLY MOTHER O' GOD¡
RUNNING IS FUTILE...
...YOU CANNOT EVADE MY POWER!
EEEYAAAH!
¡uungh¡ OH... MAN ...'HURTS... BURNS!
YOU... CAN'T BE... SUPERMAN.
HE BUSTS PEOPLE... HE DON'T TOAST 'EM!

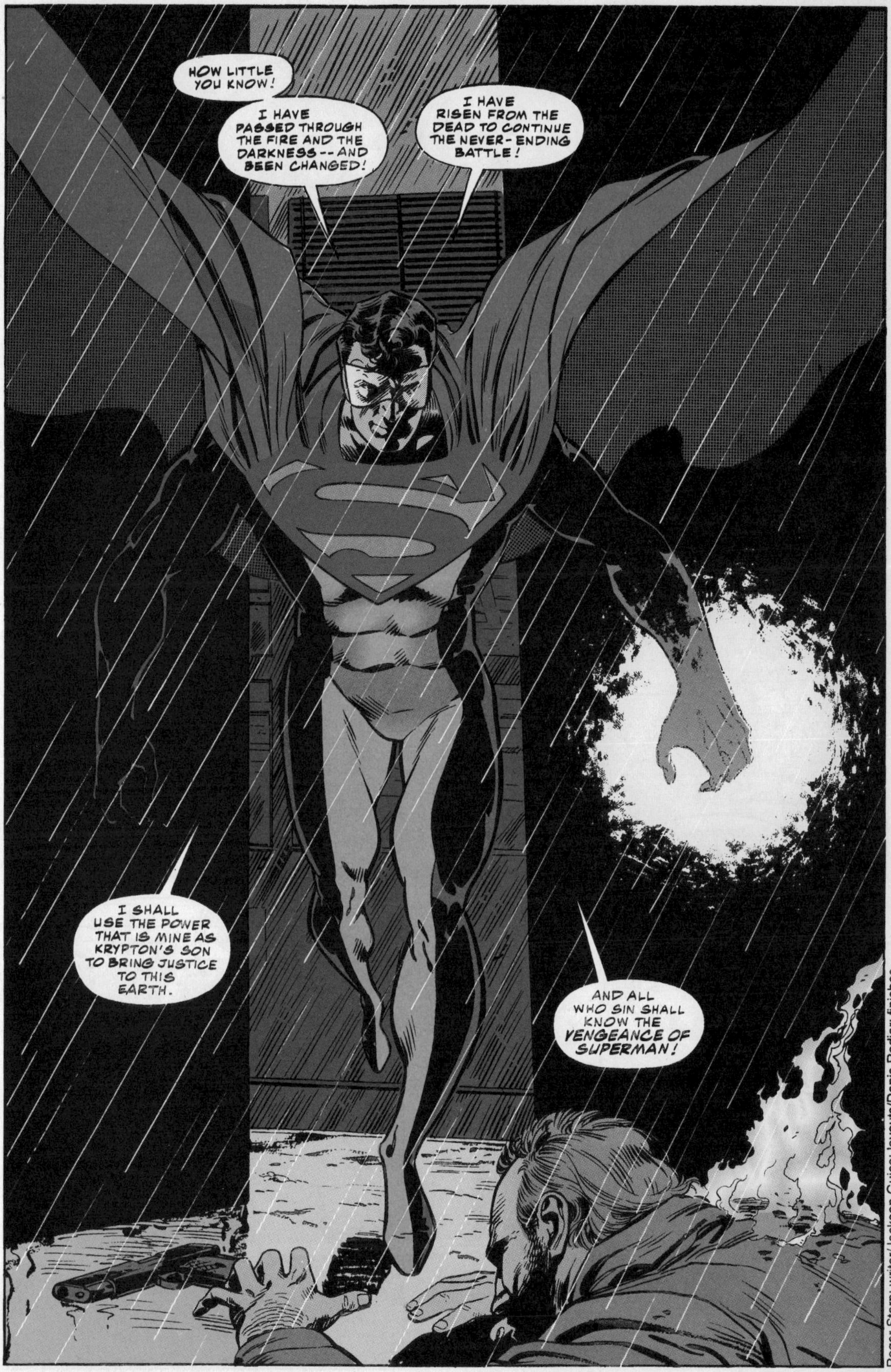
HOW LITTLE YOU KNOW!
I HAVE PASSED THROUGH THE FIRE AND THE DARKNESS -- AND BEEN CHANGED!
I HAVE RISEN FROM THE DEAD TO CONTINUE THE NEVER-ENDING BATTLE!
I SHALL USE THE POWER THAT IS MINE AS KRYPTON'S SON TO BRING JUSTICE TO THIS EARTH.
AND ALL WHO SIN SHALL KNOW THE *VENGEANCE OF SUPERMAN!*

Roger Stern: writer/Jackson Guice: layouts/Denis Rodier: finishes

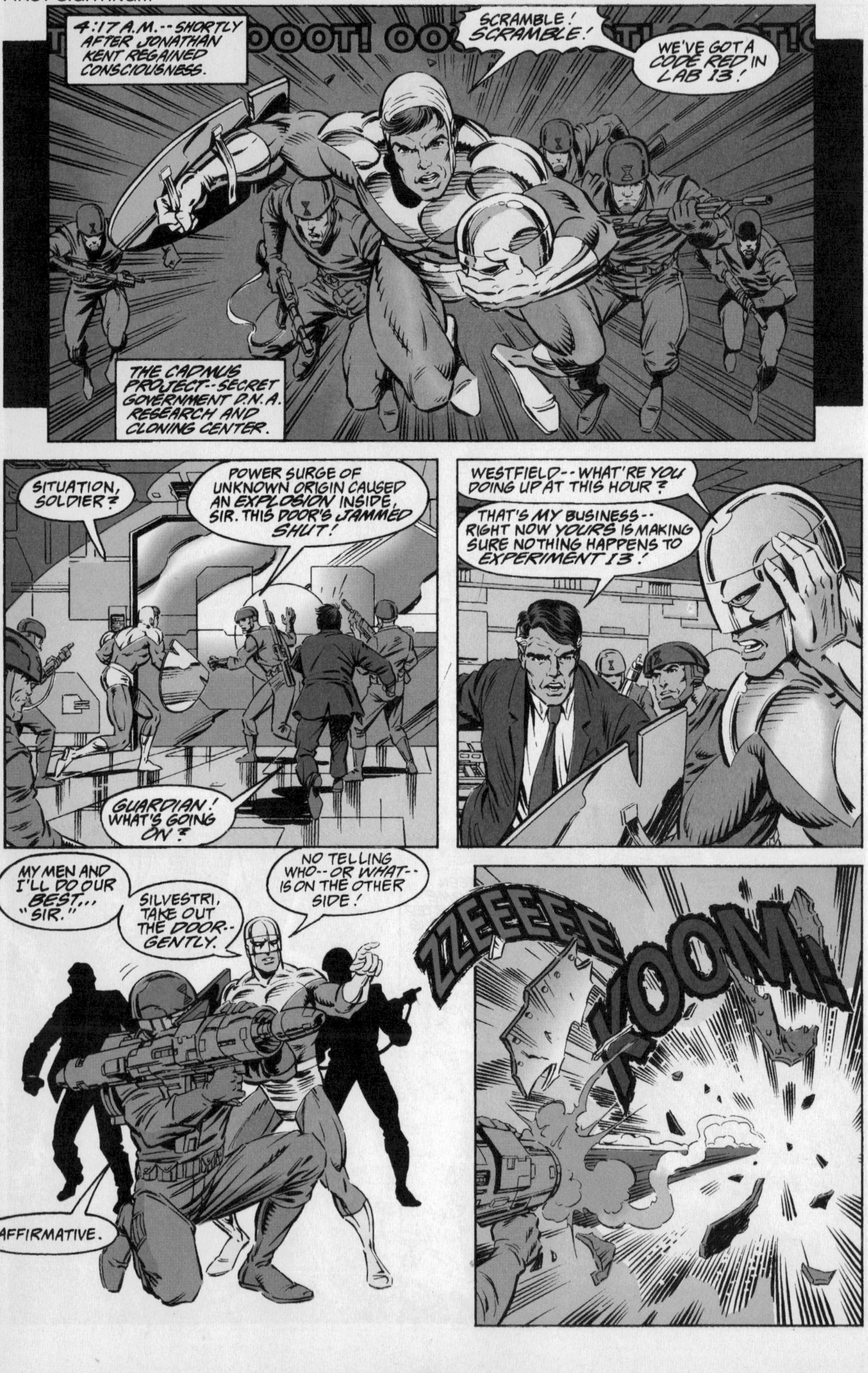
4:17 A.M.--SHORTLY AFTER JONATHAN KENT REGAINED CONSCIOUSNESS.
SCRAMBLE! SCRAMBLE!
WE'VE GOT A CODE RED IN LAB 13!
THE CADMUS PROJECT--SECRET GOVERNMENT D.N.A. RESEARCH AND CLONING CENTER.
SITUATION, SOLDIER?
POWER SURGE OF UNKNOWN ORIGIN CAUSED AN EXPLOSION INSIDE, SIR. THIS DOOR'S JAMMED SHUT!
GUARDIAN! WHAT'S GOING ON?
WESTFIELD--WHAT'RE YOU DOING UP AT THIS HOUR?
THAT'S MY BUSINESS--RIGHT NOW YOURS IS MAKING SURE NOTHING HAPPENS TO EXPERIMENT 13!
MY MEN AND I'LL DO OUR BEST... "SIR."
SILVESTRI, TAKE OUT THE DOOR--GENTLY.
NO TELLING WHO--OR WHAT--IS ON THE OTHER SIDE!
AFFIRMATIVE.
ZZEEEEE
KOOM!

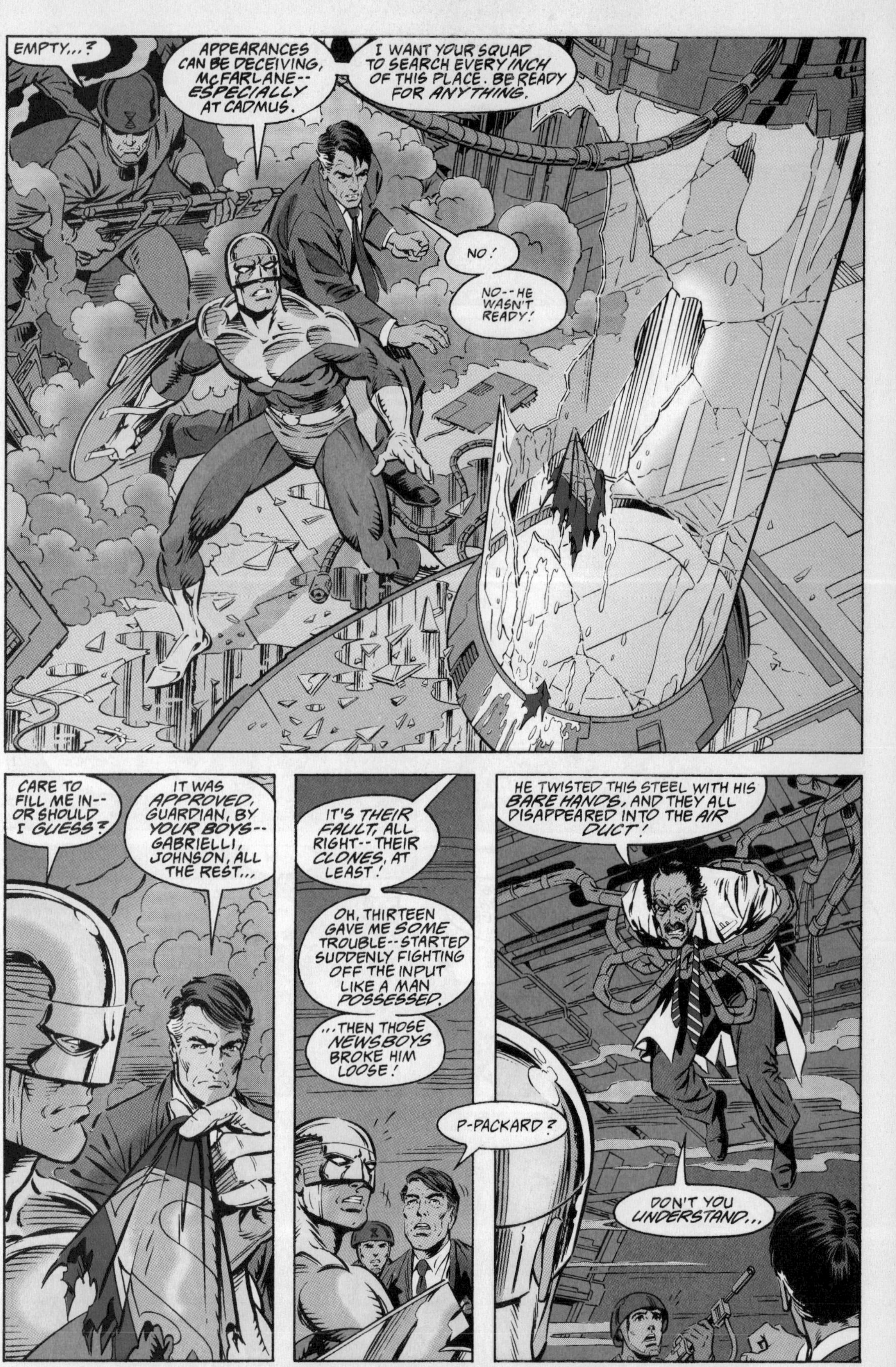
EMPTY...?
APPEARANCES CAN BE DECEIVING, McFARLANE-- ESPECIALLY AT CADMUS.
I WANT YOUR SQUAD TO SEARCH EVERY INCH OF THIS PLACE. BE READY FOR ANYTHING.
NO!
NO--HE WASN'T READY!
CARE TO FILL ME IN--OR SHOULD I GUESS?
IT WAS APPROVED, GUARDIAN, BY YOUR BOYS--GABRIELLI, JOHNSON, ALL THE REST...
IT'S THEIR FAULT, ALL RIGHT--THEIR CLONES, AT LEAST!
OH, THIRTEEN GAVE ME SOME TROUBLE--STARTED SUDDENLY FIGHTING OFF THE INPUT LIKE A MAN POSSESSED.
...THEN THOSE NEWSBOYS BROKE HIM LOOSE!
P-PACKARD?
HE TWISTED THIS STEEL WITH HIS BARE HANDS, AND THEY ALL DISAPPEARED INTO THE AIR DUCT!
DON'T YOU UNDERSTAND...

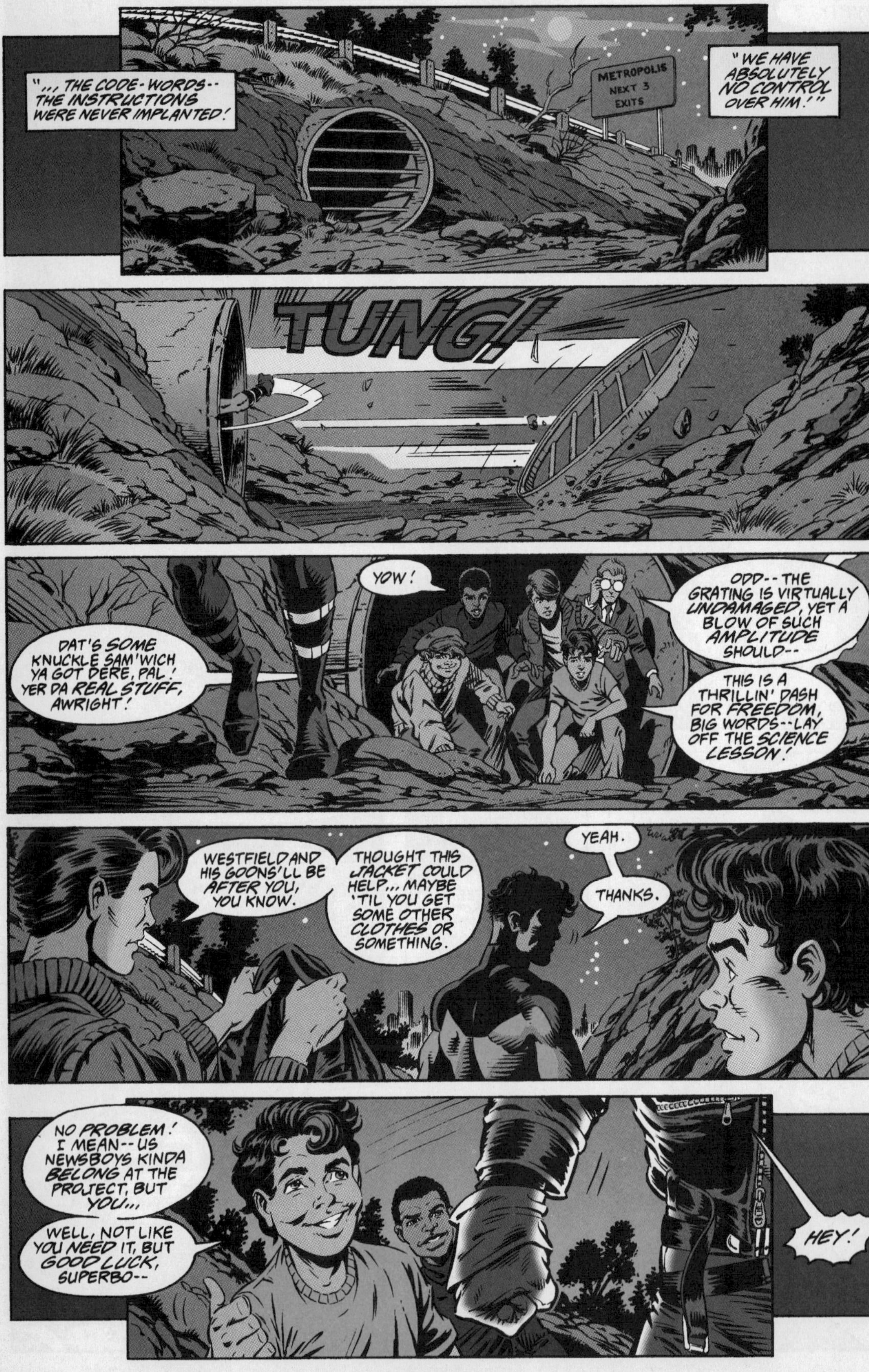
"..., THE CODE-WORDS-- THE INSTRUCTIONS WERE NEVER IMPLANTED!
METROPOLIS NEXT 3 EXITS
"WE HAVE ABSOLUTELY NO CONTROL OVER HIM!"
TUNG!
YOW!
DAT'S SOME KNUCKLE SAM'WICH YA GOT DERE, PAL! YER DA REAL STUFF, AWRIGHT!
ODD-- THE GRATING IS VIRTUALLY UNDAMAGED, YET A BLOW OF SUCH AMPLITUDE SHOULD--
THIS IS A THRILLIN' DASH FOR FREEDOM, BIG WORDS--LAY OFF THE SCIENCE LESSON!
WESTFIELD AND HIS GOONS'LL BE AFTER YOU, YOU KNOW.
THOUGHT THIS JACKET COULD HELP... MAYBE 'TIL YOU GET SOME OTHER CLOTHES OR SOMETHING.
YEAH.
THANKS.
NO PROBLEM! I MEAN--US NEWSBOYS KINDA BELONG AT THE PROJECT, BUT YOU...
WELL, NOT LIKE YOU NEED IT, BUT GOOD LUCK, SUPERBO--
HEY!

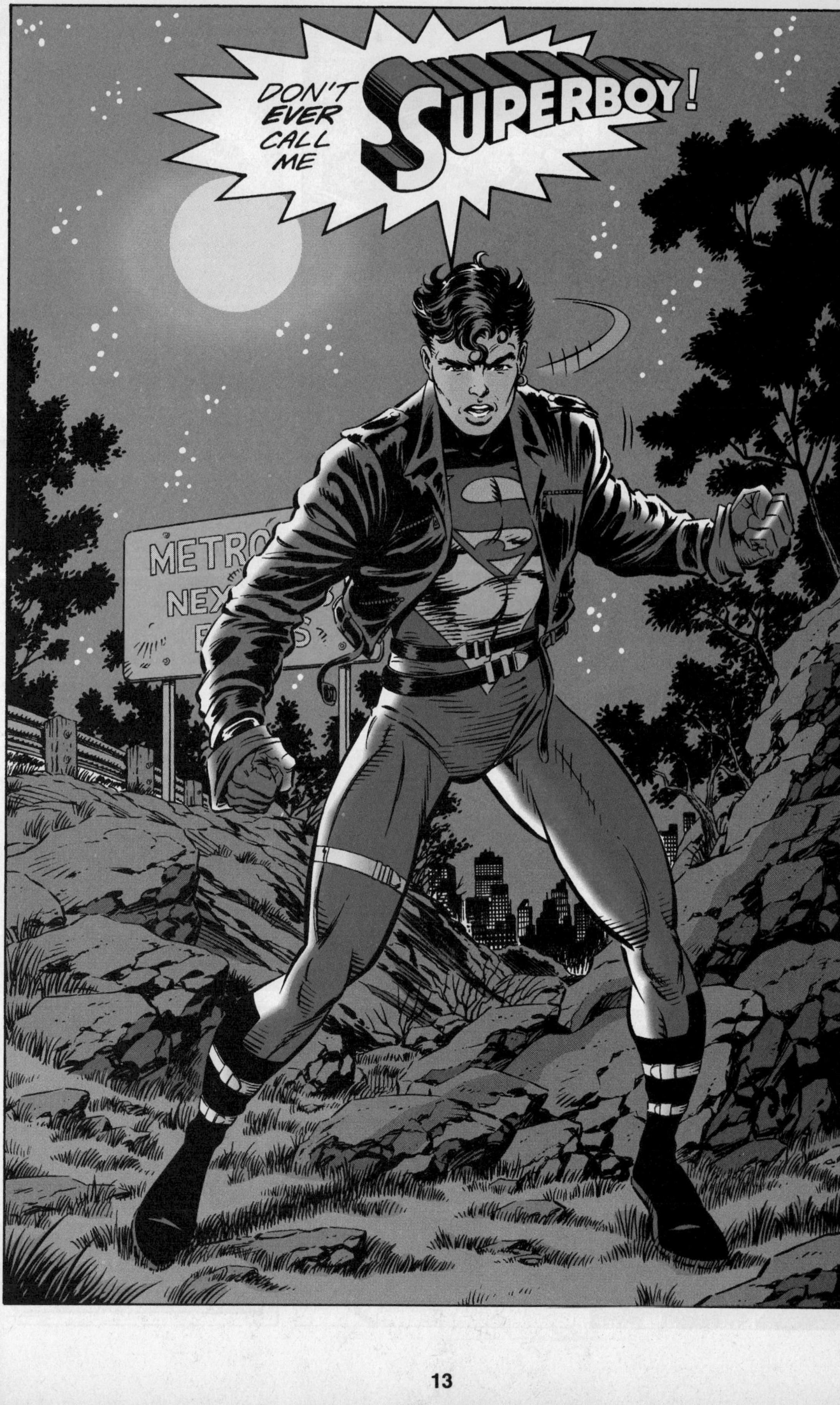
DON'T EVER CALL ME SUPERBOY!

Karl Kesel: writer/Tom Grummett: penciller/Doug Hazlewood: inker

FIRST SIGHTING...

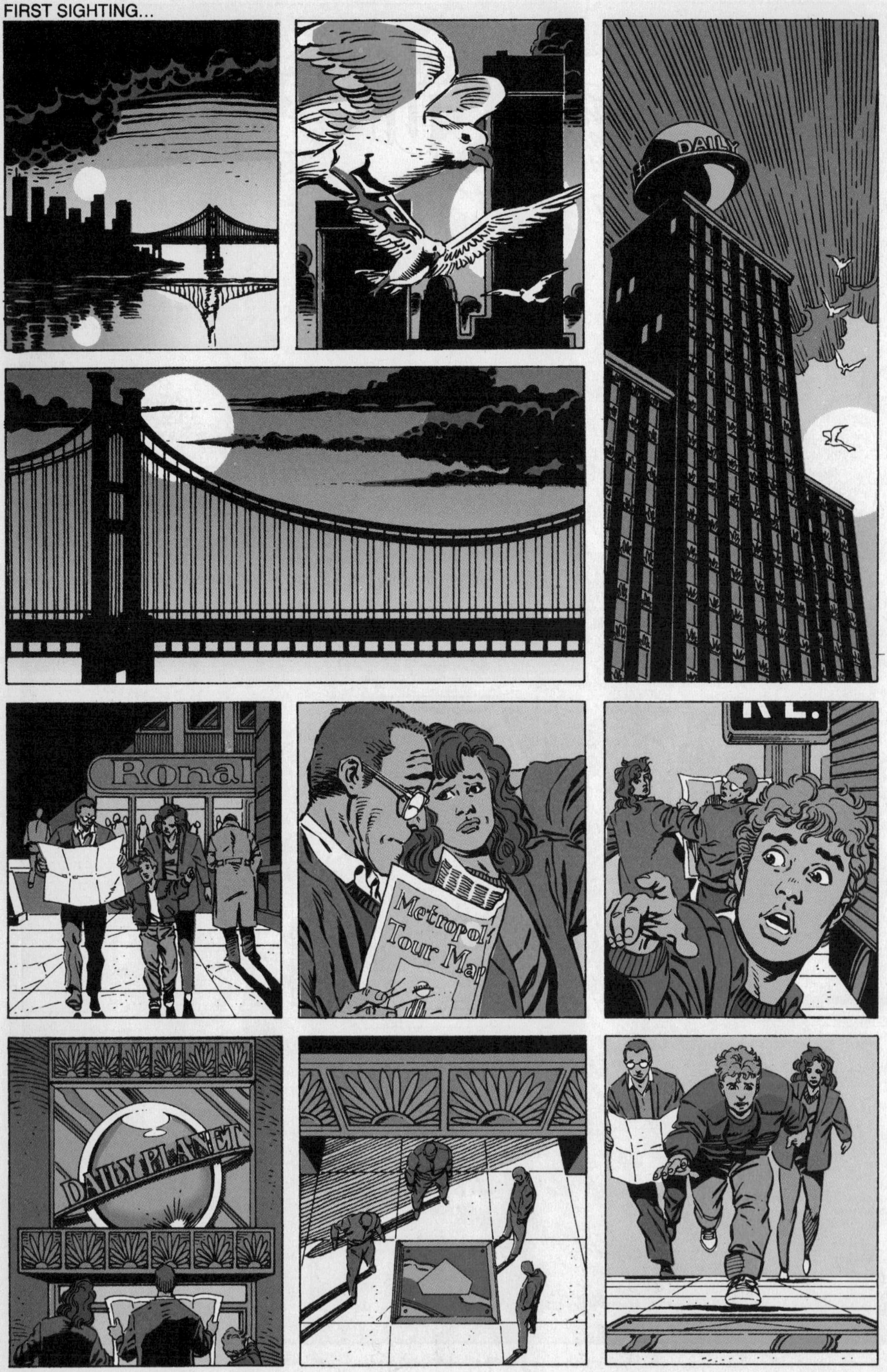
DAILY
Ronal
Tour Map
DAILY PLANET

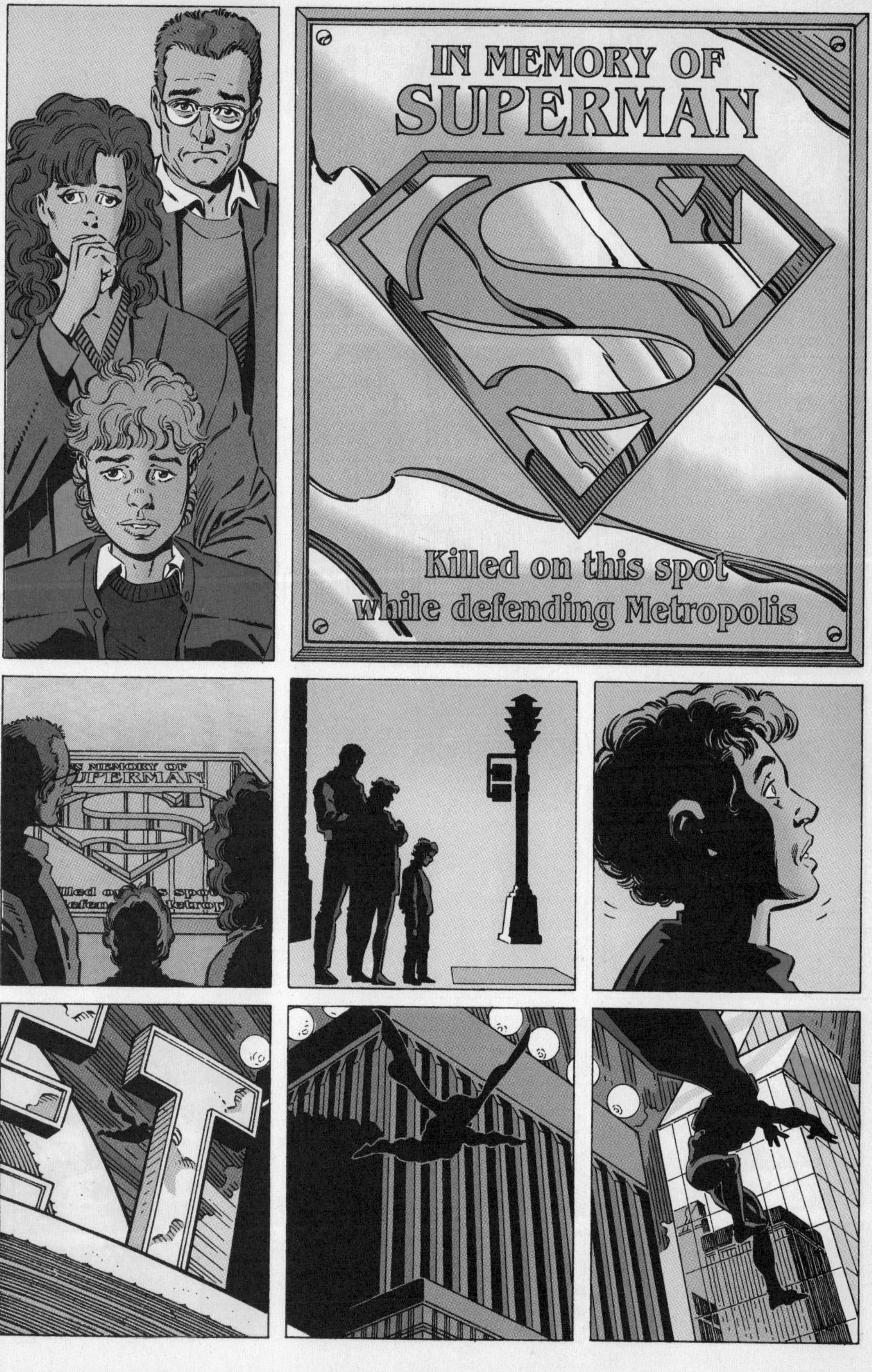
IN MEMORY OF
SUPERMAN
Killed on this spot
while defending Metropolis

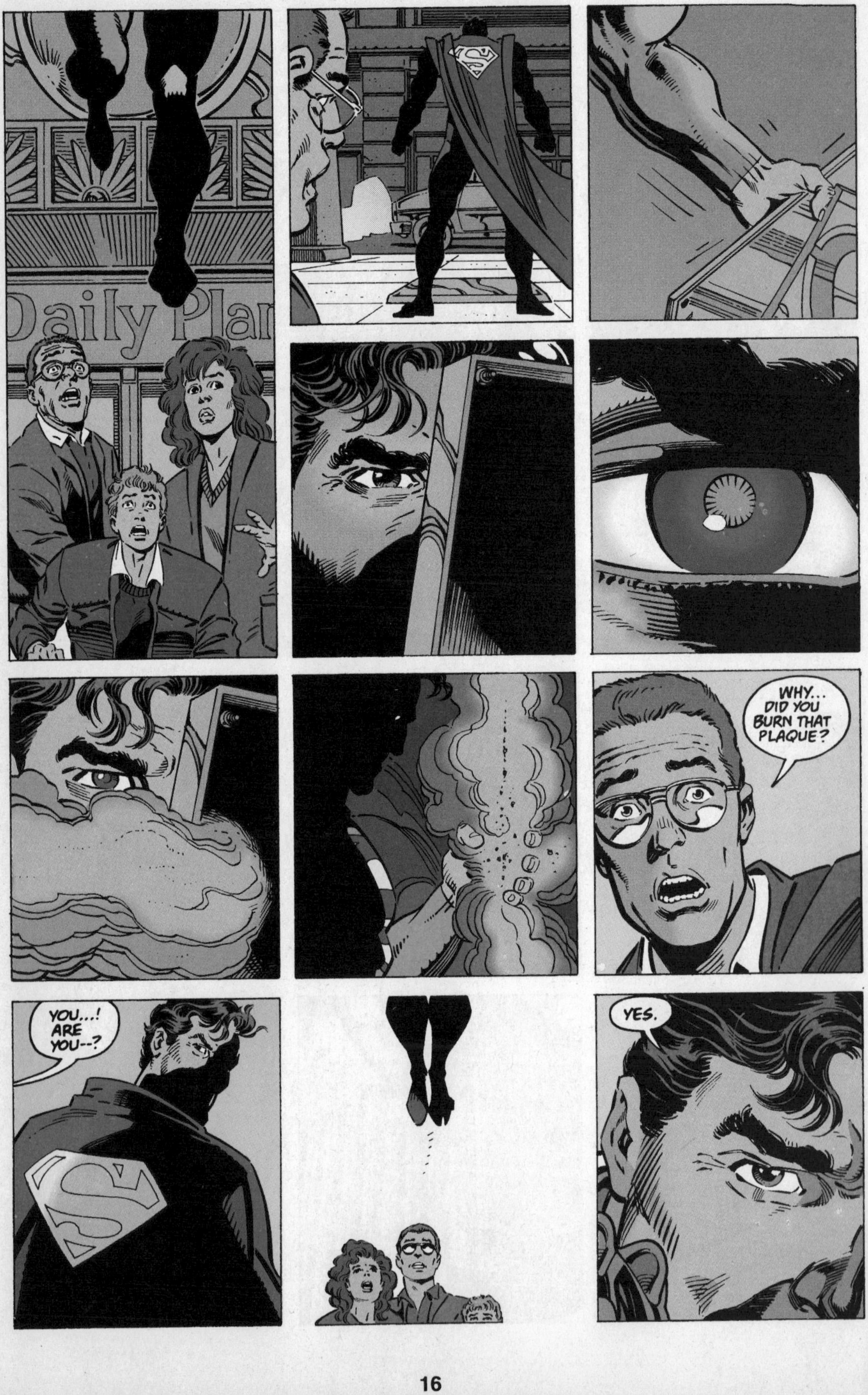
Daily Pla
WHY... DID YOU BURN THAT PLAQUE?
YOU...! ARE YOU--?
YES.

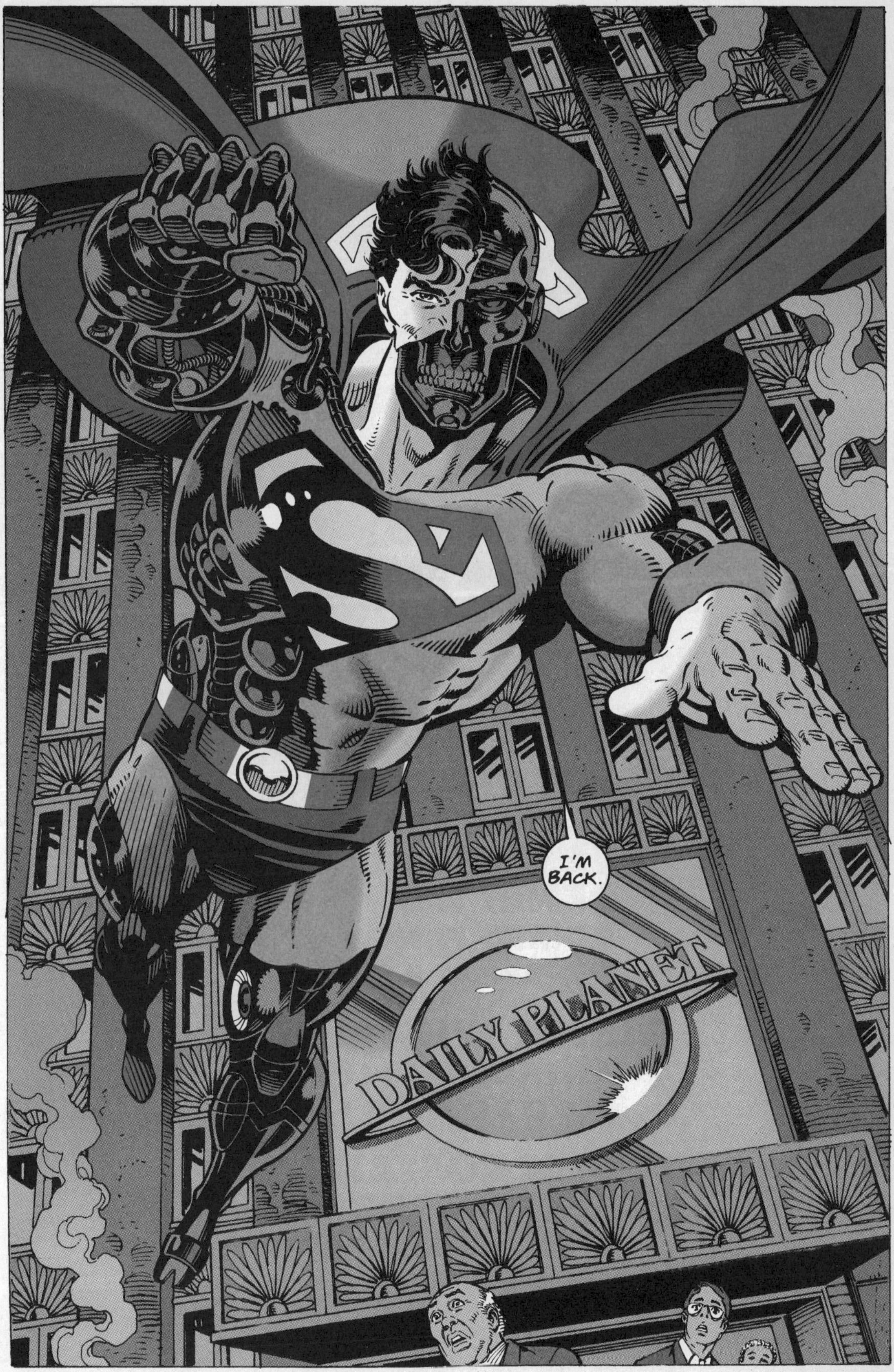
I'M BACK.
DAILY PLANET

Dan Jurgens: writer/Dan Jurgens: layouts/Brett Breeding: finishes

THE RETURN OF

SUPERMAN

DAN JURGENS
KARL KESEL
LOUISE SIMONSON
ROGER STERN
GERARD JONES
WRITERS

JON BOGDANOVE
TOM GRUMMETT
JACKSON GUICE
DAN JURGENS
M.D. BRIGHT
PENCILLERS

BRETT BREEDING
DOUG HAZLEWOOD
DENNIS JANKE
DENIS RODIER
ROMEO TANGHAL
INKERS

GLENN WHITMORE
ANTHONY TOLLIN
COLORISTS

JOHN COSTANZA
ALBERT DeGUZMAN
BILL OAKLEY
LETTERERS

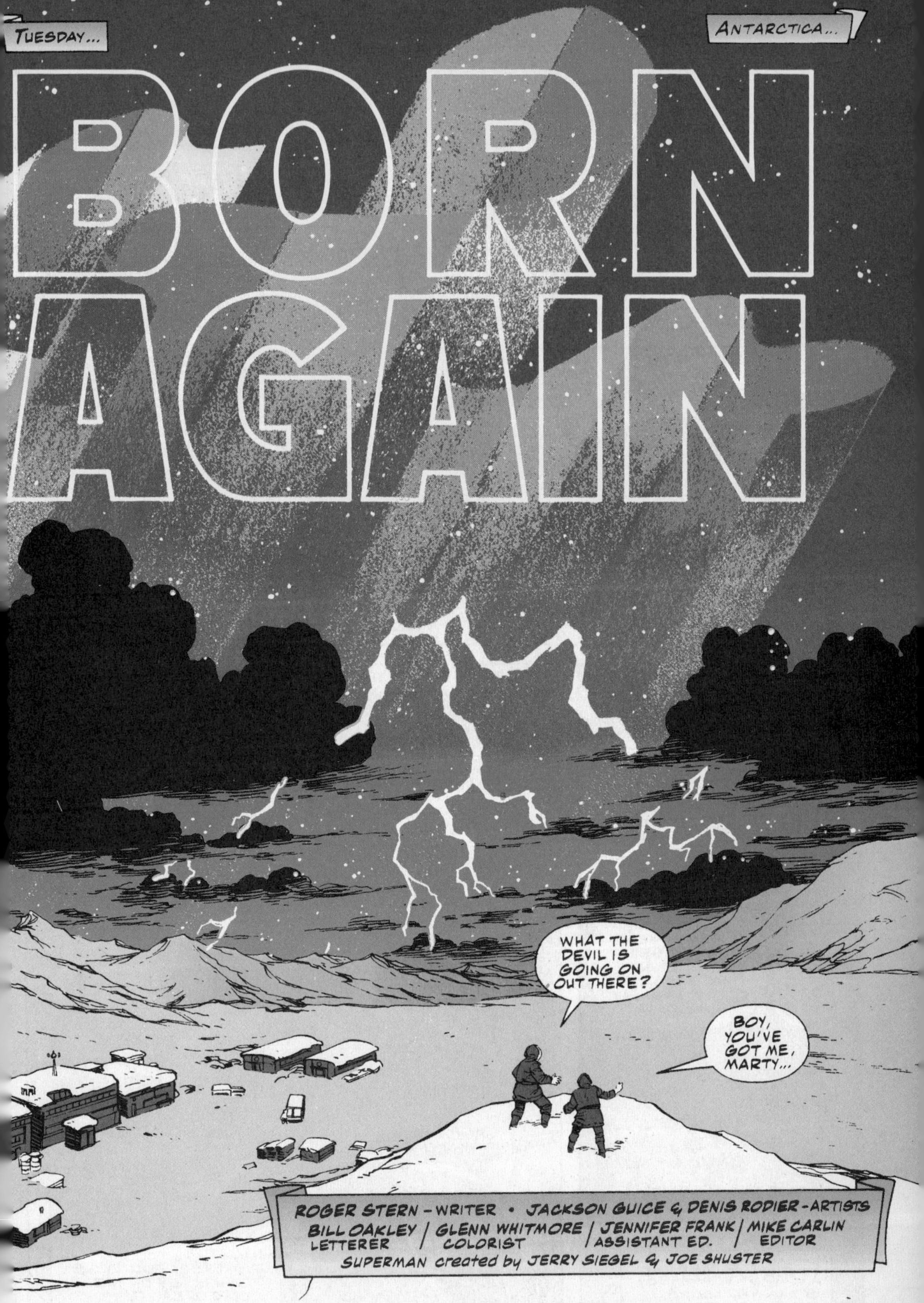
TUESDAY...
ANTARCTICA...
BORN AGAIN
WHAT THE DEVIL IS GOING ON OUT THERE?
BOY, YOU'VE GOT ME, MARTY...
ROGER STERN - WRITER • JACKSON GUICE & DENIS RODIER - ARTISTS
BILL OAKLEY LETTERER | GLENN WHITMORE COLORIST | JENNIFER FRANK ASSISTANT ED. | MIKE CARLIN EDITOR
SUPERMAN created by JERRY SIEGEL & JOE SHUSTER

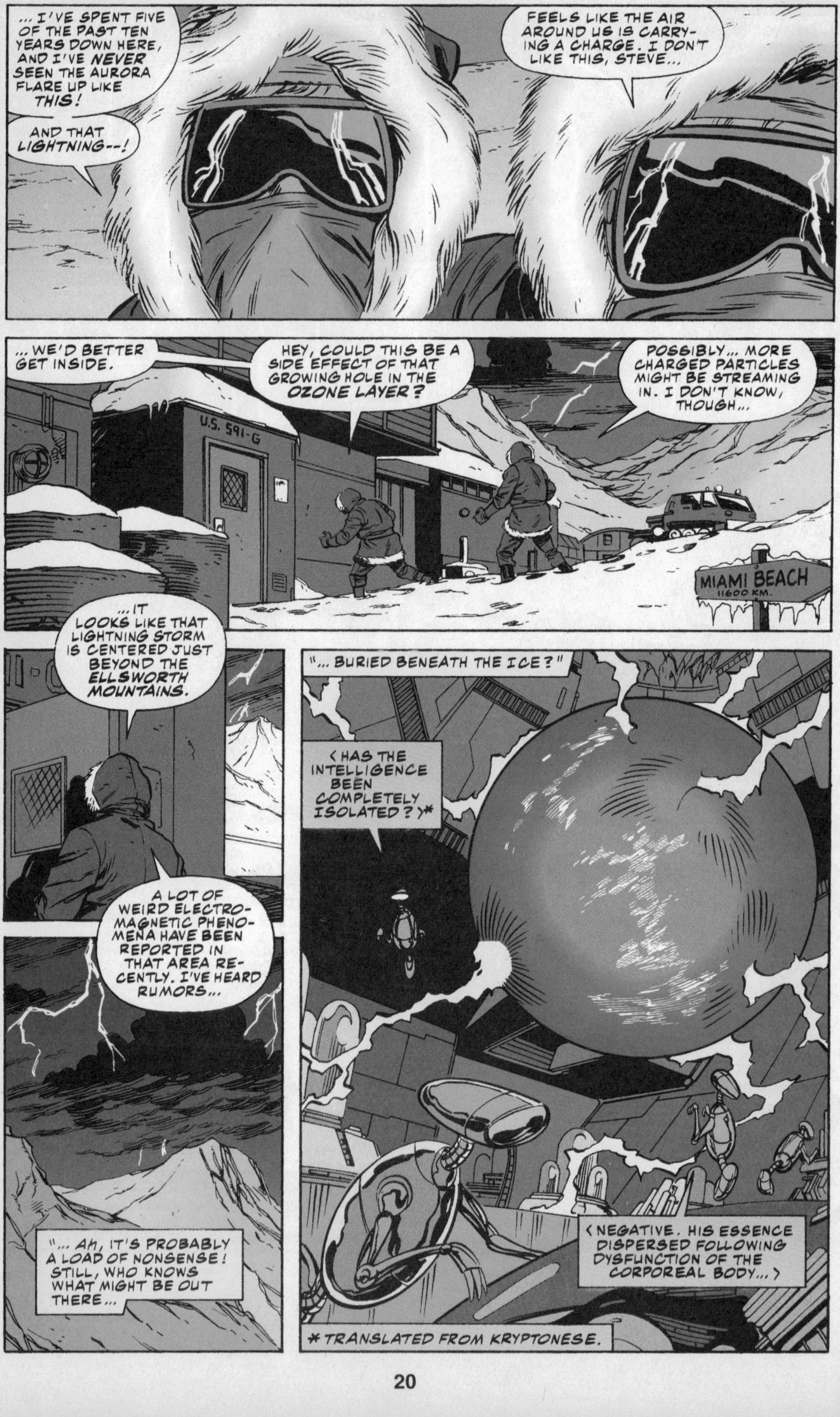
... I'VE SPENT FIVE OF THE PAST TEN YEARS DOWN HERE, AND I'VE NEVER SEEN THE AURORA FLARE UP LIKE THIS!
AND THAT LIGHTNING--!
FEELS LIKE THE AIR AROUND US IS CARRYING A CHARGE. I DON'T LIKE THIS, STEVE...
... WE'D BETTER GET INSIDE.
HEY, COULD THIS BE A SIDE EFFECT OF THAT GROWING HOLE IN THE OZONE LAYER?
POSSIBLY... MORE CHARGED PARTICLES MIGHT BE STREAMING IN. I DON'T KNOW, THOUGH...
U.S. 591-G
MIAMI BEACH 11600 KM.
... IT LOOKS LIKE THAT LIGHTNING STORM IS CENTERED JUST BEYOND THE ELLSWORTH MOUNTAINS.
A LOT OF WEIRD ELECTROMAGNETIC PHENOMENA HAVE BEEN REPORTED IN THAT AREA RECENTLY. I'VE HEARD RUMORS...
"... AH, IT'S PROBABLY A LOAD OF NONSENSE! STILL, WHO KNOWS WHAT MIGHT BE OUT THERE...
"... BURIED BENEATH THE ICE?"
< HAS THE INTELLIGENCE BEEN COMPLETELY ISOLATED? >*
< NEGATIVE. HIS ESSENCE DISPERSED FOLLOWING DYSFUNCTION OF THE CORPOREAL BODY... >
* TRANSLATED FROM KRYPTONESE.

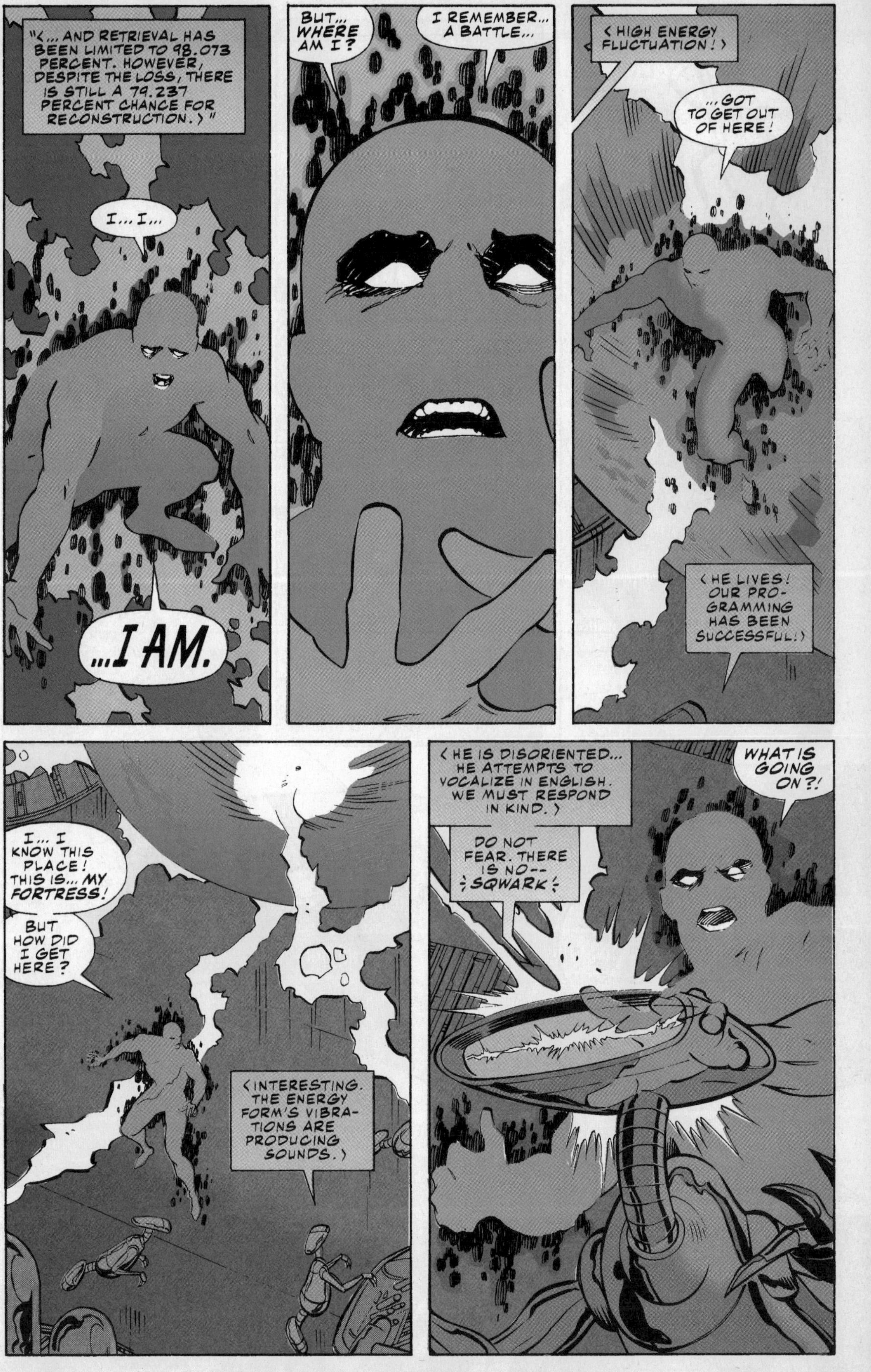
"<... AND RETRIEVAL HAS BEEN LIMITED TO 98.073 PERCENT. HOWEVER, DESPITE THE LOSS, THERE IS STILL A 79.237 PERCENT CHANCE FOR RECONSTRUCTION.>"
I... I...
...I AM.
BUT... WHERE AM I?
I REMEMBER... A BATTLE...
<HIGH ENERGY FLUCTUATION!>
...GOT TO GET OUT OF HERE!
<HE LIVES! OUR PROGRAMMING HAS BEEN SUCCESSFUL!>
I... I KNOW THIS PLACE! THIS IS... MY FORTRESS!
BUT HOW DID I GET HERE?
<INTERESTING. THE ENERGY FORM'S VIBRATIONS ARE PRODUCING SOUNDS.>
<HE IS DISORIENTED... HE ATTEMPTS TO VOCALIZE IN ENGLISH. WE MUST RESPOND IN KIND.>
DO NOT FEAR. THERE IS NO-- SQWARK
WHAT IS GOING ON?!

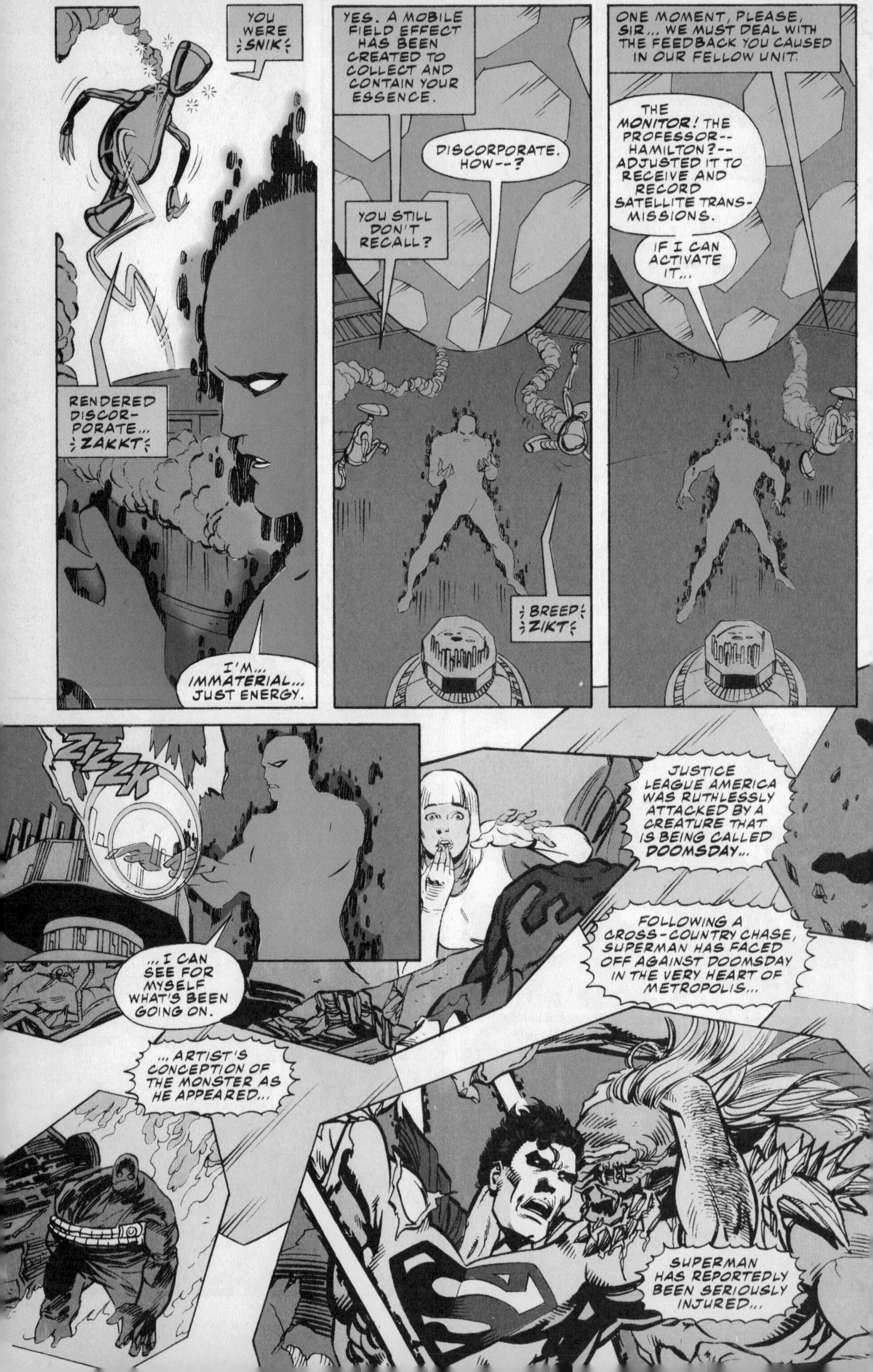
YOU WERE SNIK
RENDERED DISCORPORATE... ZAKKT
I'M... IMMATERIAL... JUST ENERGY.
YES. A MOBILE FIELD EFFECT HAS BEEN CREATED TO COLLECT AND CONTAIN YOUR ESSENCE.
DISCORPORATE. HOW--?
YOU STILL DON'T RECALL?
BREEP ZIKT
ONE MOMENT, PLEASE, SIR... WE MUST DEAL WITH THE FEEDBACK YOU CAUSED IN OUR FELLOW UNIT.
THE MONITOR! THE PROFESSOR--HAMILTON?--ADJUSTED IT TO RECEIVE AND RECORD SATELLITE TRANSMISSIONS.
IF I CAN ACTIVATE IT...
ZIZZZK
...I CAN SEE FOR MYSELF WHAT'S BEEN GOING ON.
JUSTICE LEAGUE AMERICA WAS RUTHLESSLY ATTACKED BY A CREATURE THAT IS BEING CALLED DOOMSDAY...
FOLLOWING A CROSS-COUNTRY CHASE, SUPERMAN HAS FACED OFF AGAINST DOOMSDAY IN THE VERY HEART OF METROPOLIS...
...ARTIST'S CONCEPTION OF THE MONSTER AS HE APPEARED...
SUPERMAN HAS REPORTEDLY BEEN SERIOUSLY INJURED...

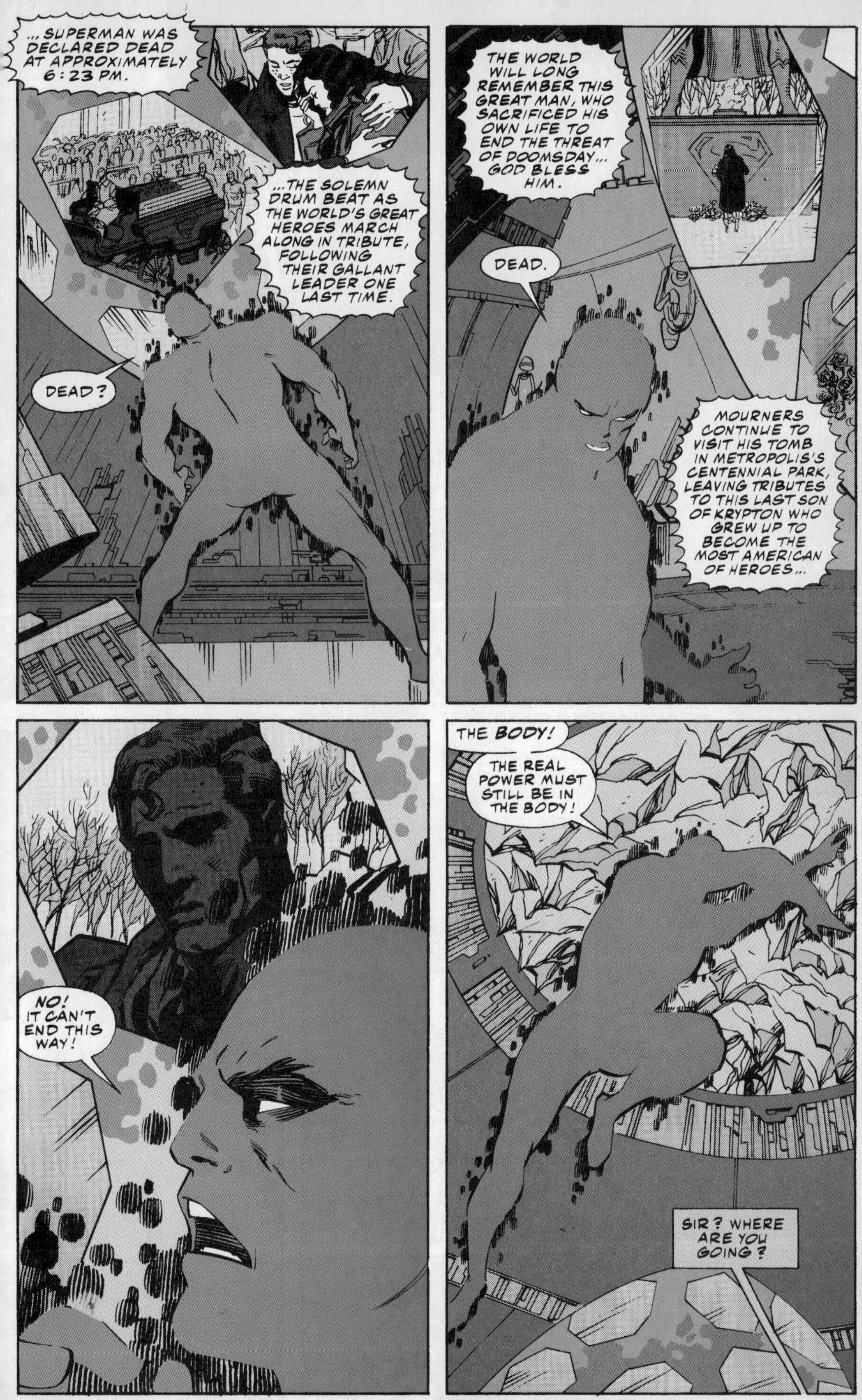
...SUPERMAN WAS DECLARED DEAD AT APPROXIMATELY 6:23 PM.
...THE SOLEMN DRUM BEAT AS THE WORLD'S GREAT HEROES MARCH ALONG IN TRIBUTE, FOLLOWING THEIR GALLANT LEADER ONE LAST TIME.
DEAD?
THE WORLD WILL LONG REMEMBER THIS GREAT MAN, WHO SACRIFICED HIS OWN LIFE TO END THE THREAT OF DOOMSDAY... GOD BLESS HIM.
DEAD.
MOURNERS CONTINUE TO VISIT HIS TOMB IN METROPOLIS'S CENTENNIAL PARK, LEAVING TRIBUTES TO THIS LAST SON OF KRYPTON WHO GREW UP TO BECOME THE MOST AMERICAN OF HEROES...
NO! IT CAN'T END THIS WAY!
THE BODY!
THE REAL POWER MUST STILL BE IN THE BODY!
SIR? WHERE ARE YOU GOING?

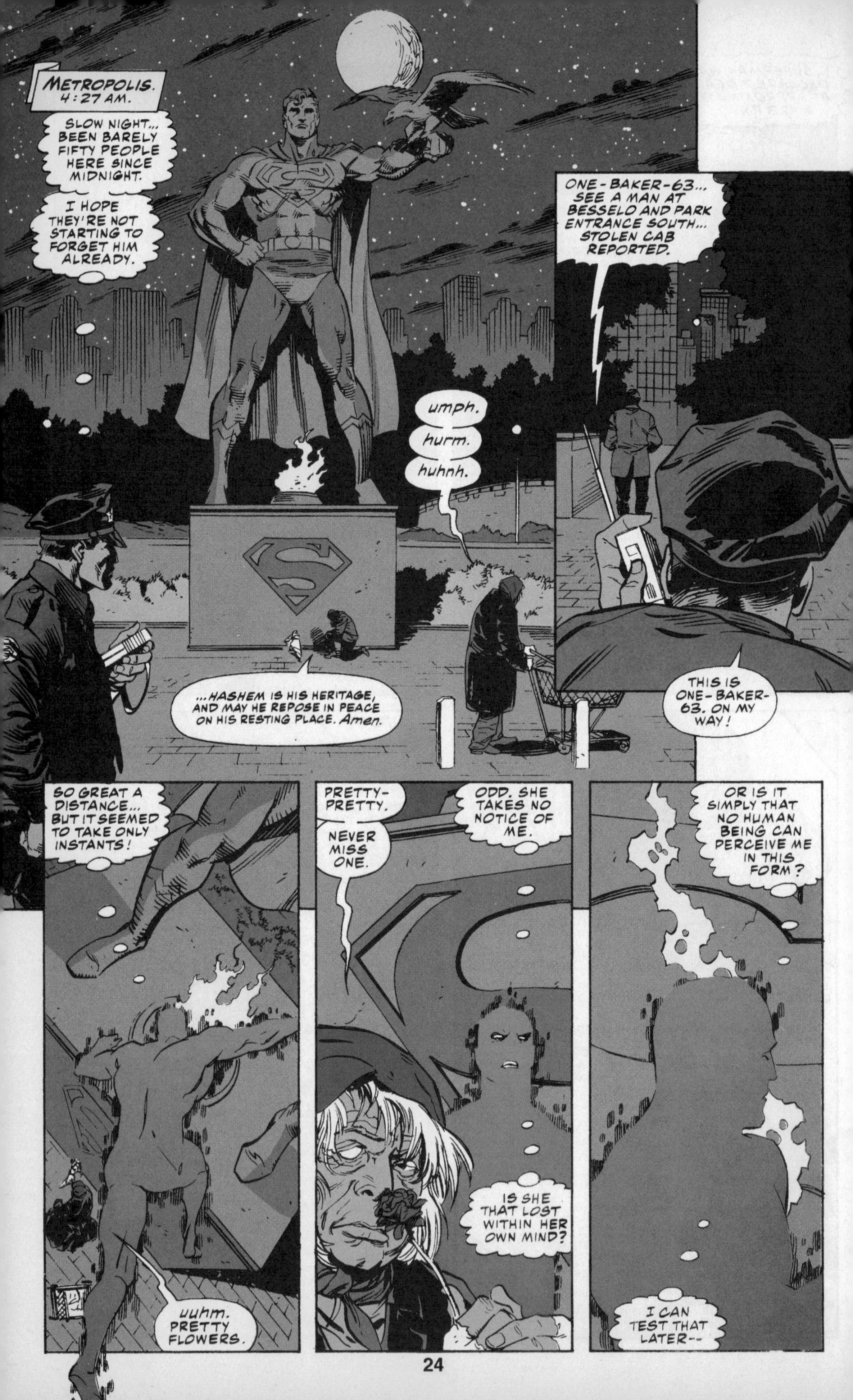
METROPOLIS. 4:27 AM.
SLOW NIGHT... BEEN BARELY FIFTY PEOPLE HERE SINCE MIDNIGHT.
I HOPE THEY'RE NOT STARTING TO FORGET HIM ALREADY.
umph.
hurm.
huhnh.
...HASHEM IS HIS HERITAGE, AND MAY HE REPOSE IN PEACE ON HIS RESTING PLACE. Amen.
ONE-BAKER-63... SEE A MAN AT BESSELO AND PARK ENTRANCE SOUTH... STOLEN CAB REPORTED.
THIS IS ONE-BAKER-63. ON MY WAY!
SO GREAT A DISTANCE... BUT IT SEEMED TO TAKE ONLY INSTANTS!
uuhm. PRETTY FLOWERS.
PRETTY-PRETTY.
NEVER MISS ONE.
ODD. SHE TAKES NO NOTICE OF ME.
IS SHE THAT LOST WITHIN HER OWN MIND?
OR IS IT SIMPLY THAT NO HUMAN BEING CAN PERCEIVE ME IN THIS FORM?
I CAN TEST THAT LATER--

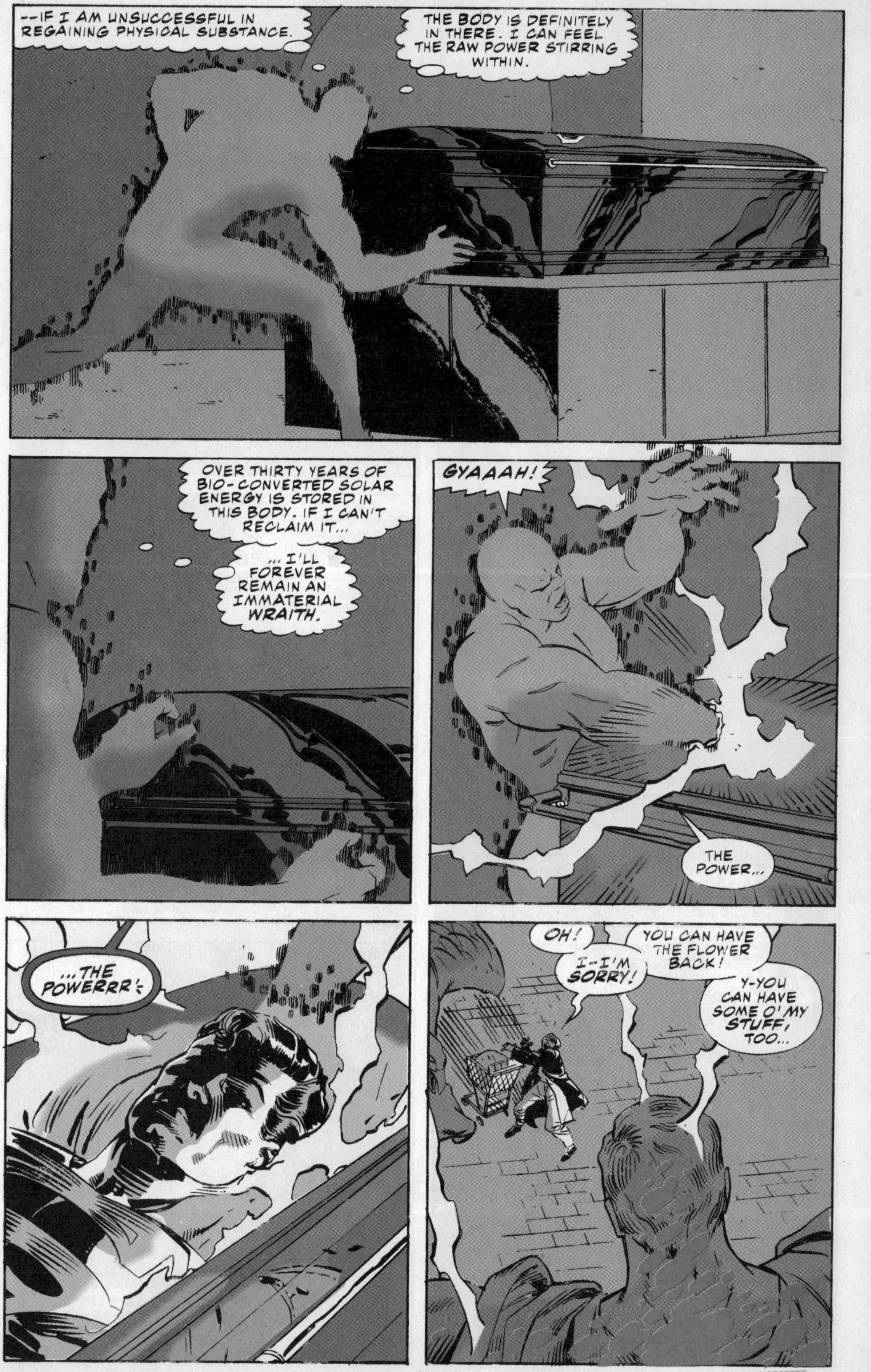
--IF I AM UNSUCCESSFUL IN REGAINING PHYSICAL SUBSTANCE.
THE BODY IS DEFINITELY IN THERE. I CAN FEEL THE RAW POWER STIRRING WITHIN.
OVER THIRTY YEARS OF BIO-CONVERTED SOLAR ENERGY IS STORED IN THIS BODY. IF I CAN'T RECLAIM IT...
...I'LL FOREVER REMAIN AN IMMATERIAL WRAITH.
GYAAAH!
THE POWER...
...THE POWERRR!
OH!
I-I'M SORRY!
YOU CAN HAVE THE FLOWER BACK!
Y-YOU CAN HAVE SOME O' MY STUFF, TOO...

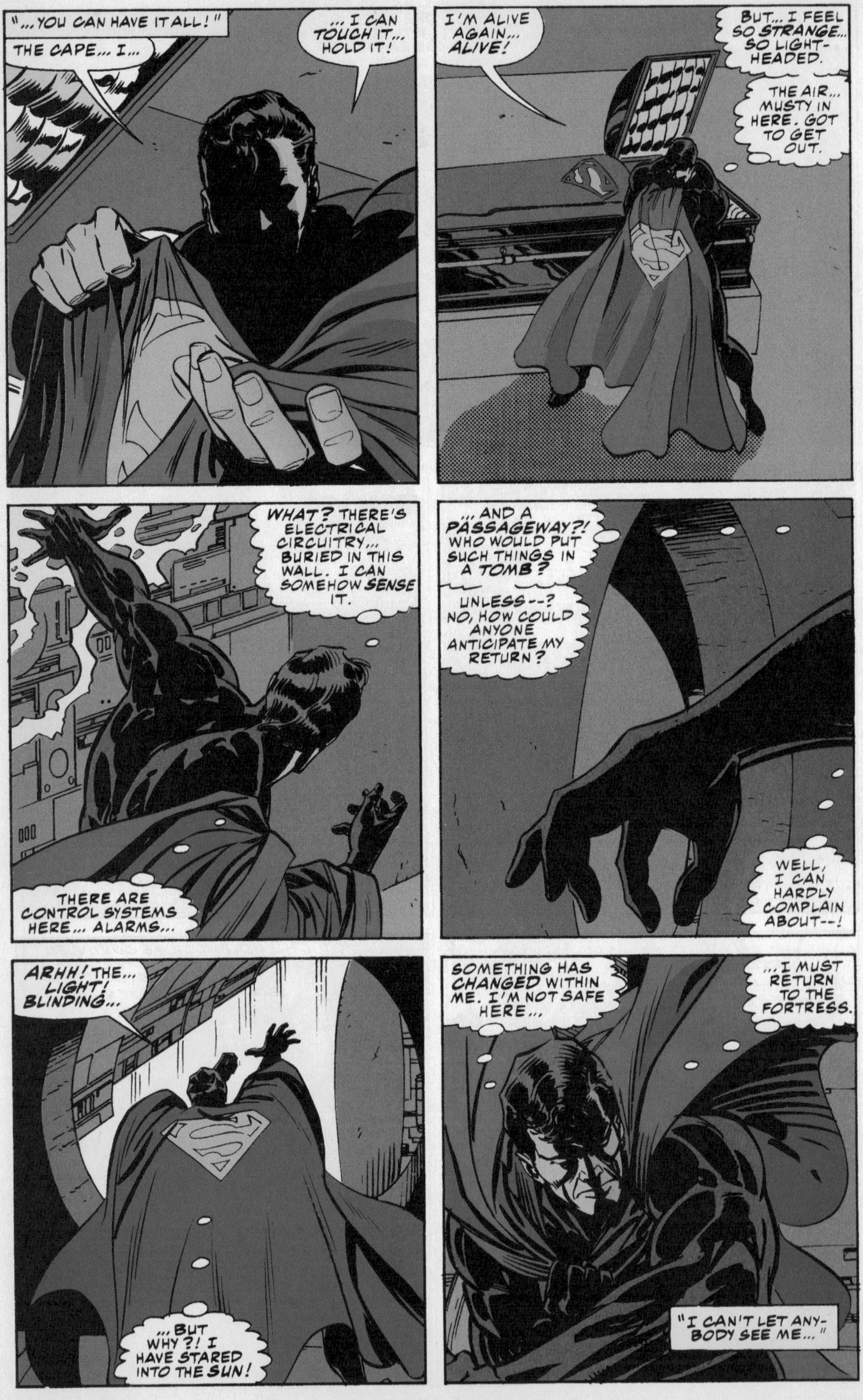
"...YOU CAN HAVE IT ALL!"
THE CAPE... I...
...I CAN TOUCH IT... HOLD IT!
I'M ALIVE AGAIN... ALIVE!
BUT... I FEEL SO STRANGE... SO LIGHT-HEADED.
THE AIR... MUSTY IN HERE. GOT TO GET OUT.
WHAT? THERE'S ELECTRICAL CIRCUITRY... BURIED IN THIS WALL. I CAN SOMEHOW SENSE IT.
THERE ARE CONTROL SYSTEMS HERE... ALARMS...
...AND A PASSAGEWAY?! WHO WOULD PUT SUCH THINGS IN A TOMB?
UNLESS--? NO, HOW COULD ANYONE ANTICIPATE MY RETURN?
WELL, I CAN HARDLY COMPLAIN ABOUT--!
ARHH! THE... LIGHT! BLINDING...
...BUT WHY?! I HAVE STARED INTO THE SUN!
SOMETHING HAS CHANGED WITHIN ME. I'M NOT SAFE HERE...
...I MUST RETURN TO THE FORTRESS.
"I CAN'T LET ANYBODY SEE ME..."

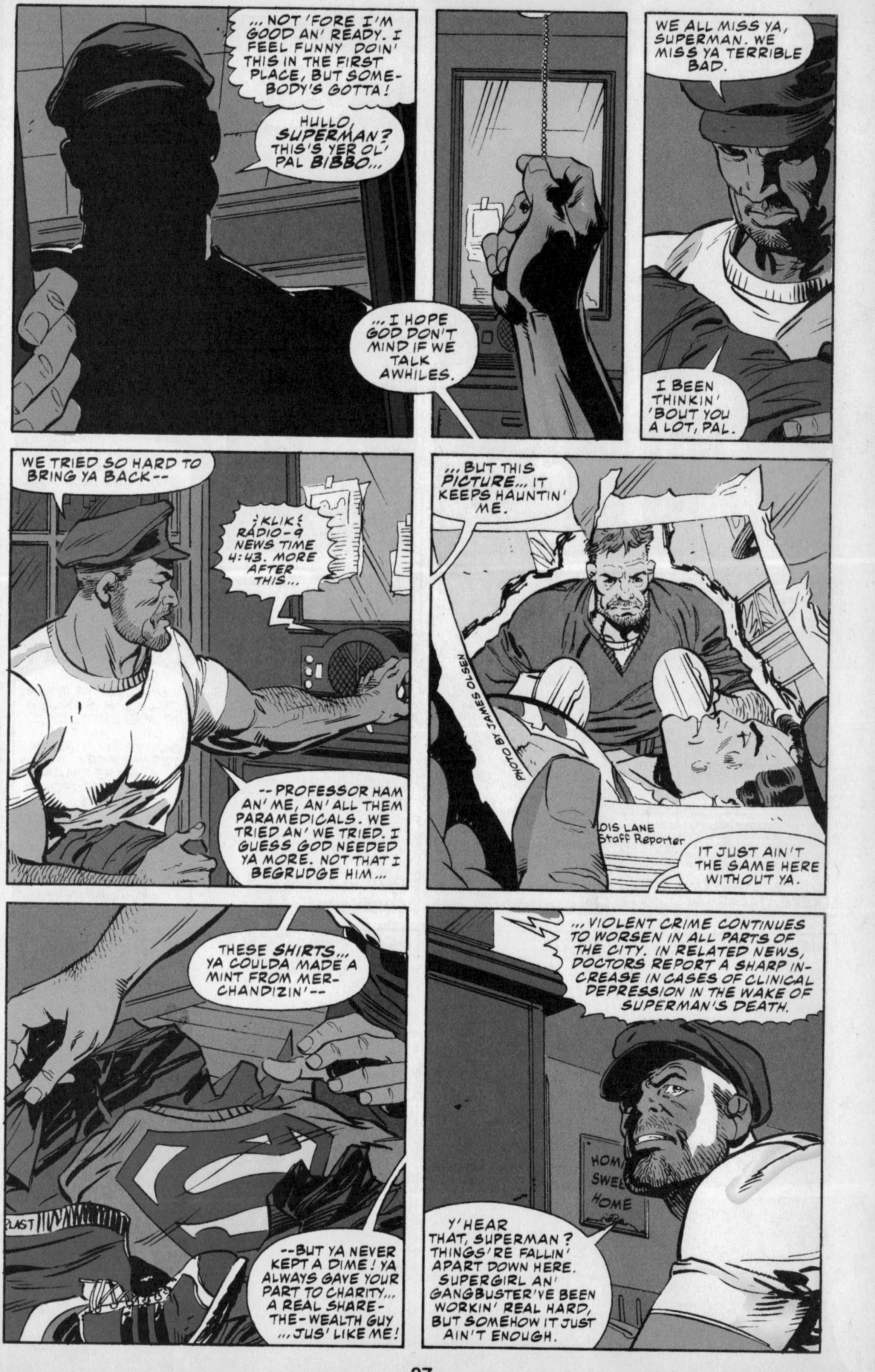
...NOT 'FORE I'M GOOD AN' READY. I FEEL FUNNY DOIN' THIS IN THE FIRST PLACE, BUT SOMEBODY'S GOTTA!
HULLO, SUPERMAN? THIS'S YER OL' PAL BIBBO...
...I HOPE GOD DON'T MIND IF WE TALK AWHILES.
WE ALL MISS YA, SUPERMAN. WE MISS YA TERRIBLE BAD.
I BEEN THINKIN' 'BOUT YOU A LOT, PAL.
WE TRIED SO HARD TO BRING YA BACK--
:KLIK: RADIO-9 NEWS TIME 4:43. MORE AFTER THIS...
--PROFESSOR HAM AN' ME, AN' ALL THEM PARAMEDICALS. WE TRIED AN' WE TRIED. I GUESS GOD NEEDED YA MORE. NOT THAT I BEGRUDGE HIM...
...BUT THIS PICTURE... IT KEEPS HAUNTIN' ME.
PHOTO BY JAMES OLSEN
LOIS LANE
Staff Reporter
IT JUST AIN'T THE SAME HERE WITHOUT YA.
THESE SHIRTS... YA COULDA MADE A MINT FROM MERCHANDIZIN'--
--BUT YA NEVER KEPT A DIME! YA ALWAYS GAVE YOUR PART TO CHARITY... A REAL SHARE-THE-WEALTH GUY ...JUS' LIKE ME!
...VIOLENT CRIME CONTINUES TO WORSEN IN ALL PARTS OF THE CITY. IN RELATED NEWS, DOCTORS REPORT A SHARP INCREASE IN CASES OF CLINICAL DEPRESSION IN THE WAKE OF SUPERMAN'S DEATH.
Y'HEAR THAT, SUPERMAN? THINGS'RE FALLIN' APART DOWN HERE. SUPERGIRL AN' GANGBUSTER'VE BEEN WORKIN' REAL HARD, BUT SOMEHOW IT JUST AIN'T ENOUGH.

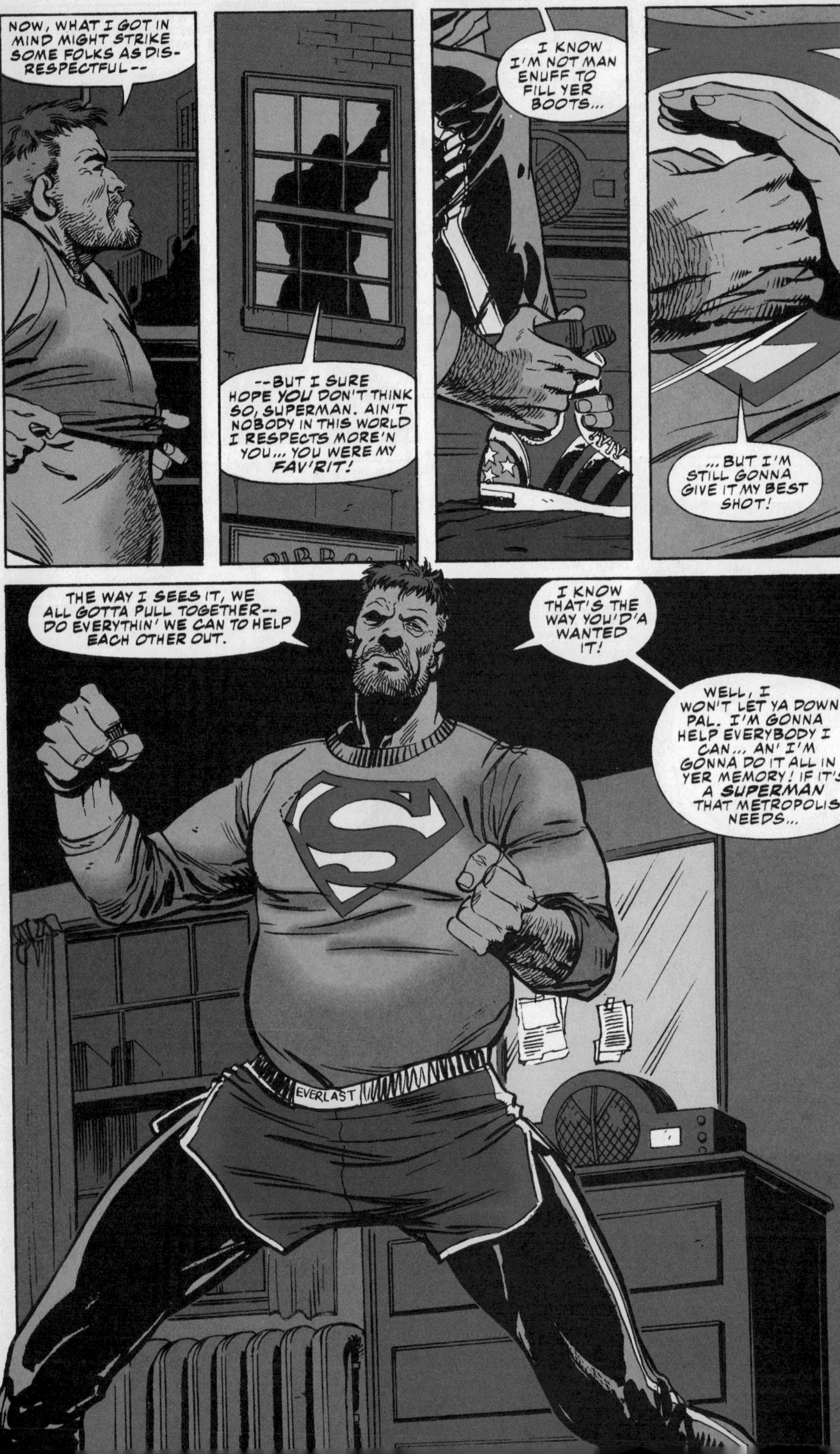
NOW, WHAT I GOT IN MIND MIGHT STRIKE SOME FOLKS AS DIS-RESPECTFUL--
--BUT I SURE HOPE YOU DON'T THINK SO, SUPERMAN. AIN'T NOBODY IN THIS WORLD I RESPECTS MORE'N YOU... YOU WERE MY FAV'RIT!
I KNOW I'M NOT MAN ENUFF TO FILL YER BOOTS...
...BUT I'M STILL GONNA GIVE IT MY BEST SHOT!
THE WAY I SEES IT, WE ALL GOTTA PULL TOGETHER--DO EVERYTHIN' WE CAN TO HELP EACH OTHER OUT.
I KNOW THAT'S THE WAY YOU'D'A WANTED IT!
WELL, I WON'T LET YA DOWN, PAL. I'M GONNA HELP EVERYBODY I CAN... AN' I'M GONNA DO IT ALL IN YER MEMORY! IF IT'S A SUPERMAN THAT METROPOLIS NEEDS...
EVERLAST

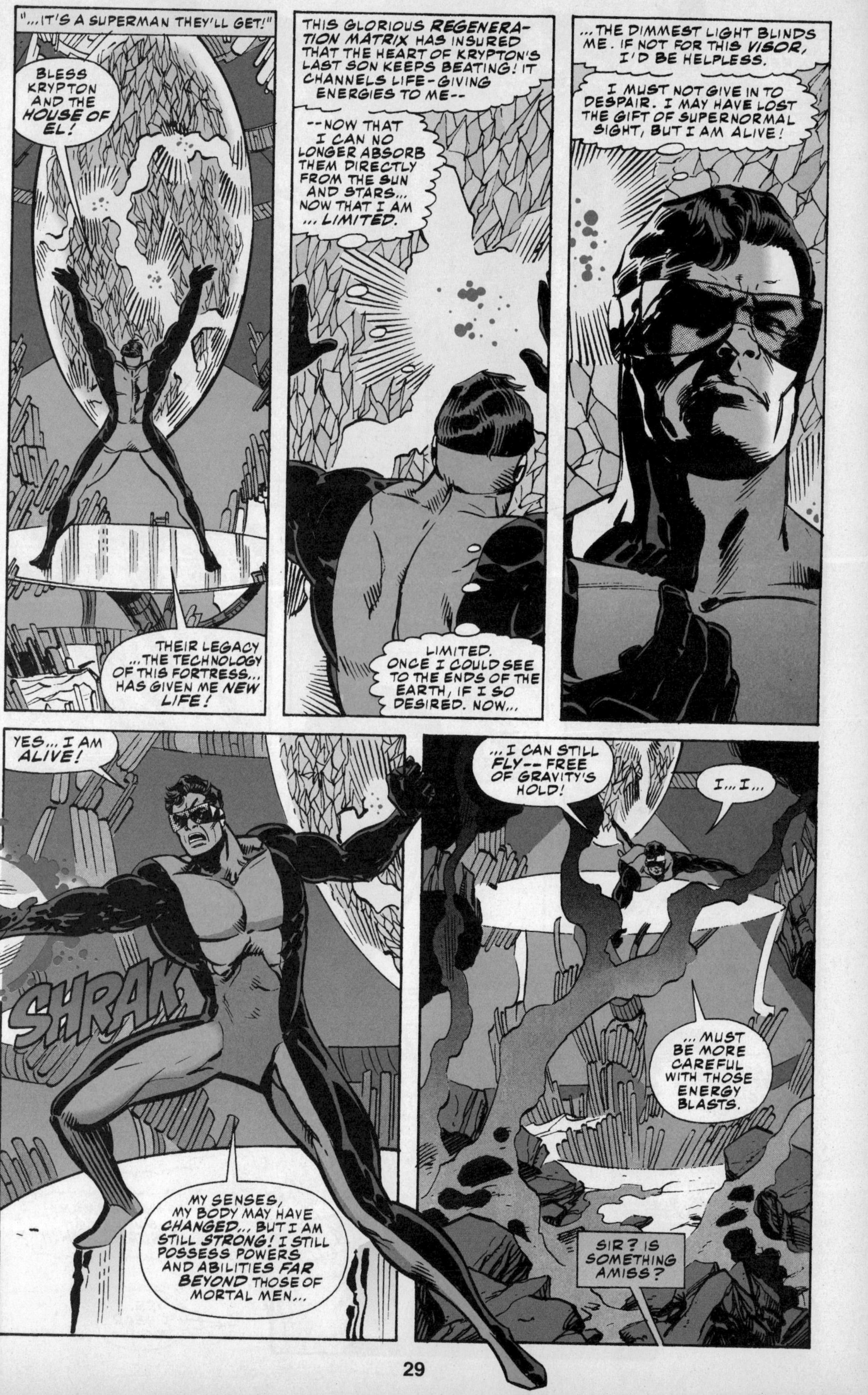
"...IT'S A SUPERMAN THEY'LL GET!"
BLESS KRYPTON AND THE HOUSE OF EL!
THEIR LEGACY ...THE TECHNOLOGY OF THIS FORTRESS... HAS GIVEN ME NEW LIFE!
THIS GLORIOUS REGENERATION MATRIX HAS INSURED THAT THE HEART OF KRYPTON'S LAST SON KEEPS BEATING! IT CHANNELS LIFE-GIVING ENERGIES TO ME--
--NOW THAT I CAN NO LONGER ABSORB THEM DIRECTLY FROM THE SUN AND STARS... NOW THAT I AM ...LIMITED.
LIMITED. ONCE I COULD SEE TO THE ENDS OF THE EARTH, IF I SO DESIRED. NOW...
...THE DIMMEST LIGHT BLINDS ME. IF NOT FOR THIS VISOR, I'D BE HELPLESS.
I MUST NOT GIVE IN TO DESPAIR. I MAY HAVE LOST THE GIFT OF SUPERNORMAL SIGHT, BUT I AM ALIVE!
YES... I AM ALIVE!
SHRAK
MY SENSES, MY BODY MAY HAVE CHANGED... BUT I AM STILL STRONG! I STILL POSSESS POWERS AND ABILITIES FAR BEYOND THOSE OF MORTAL MEN...
...I CAN STILL FLY-- FREE OF GRAVITY'S HOLD!
I... I...
...MUST BE MORE CAREFUL WITH THOSE ENERGY BLASTS.
SIR? IS SOMETHING AMISS?

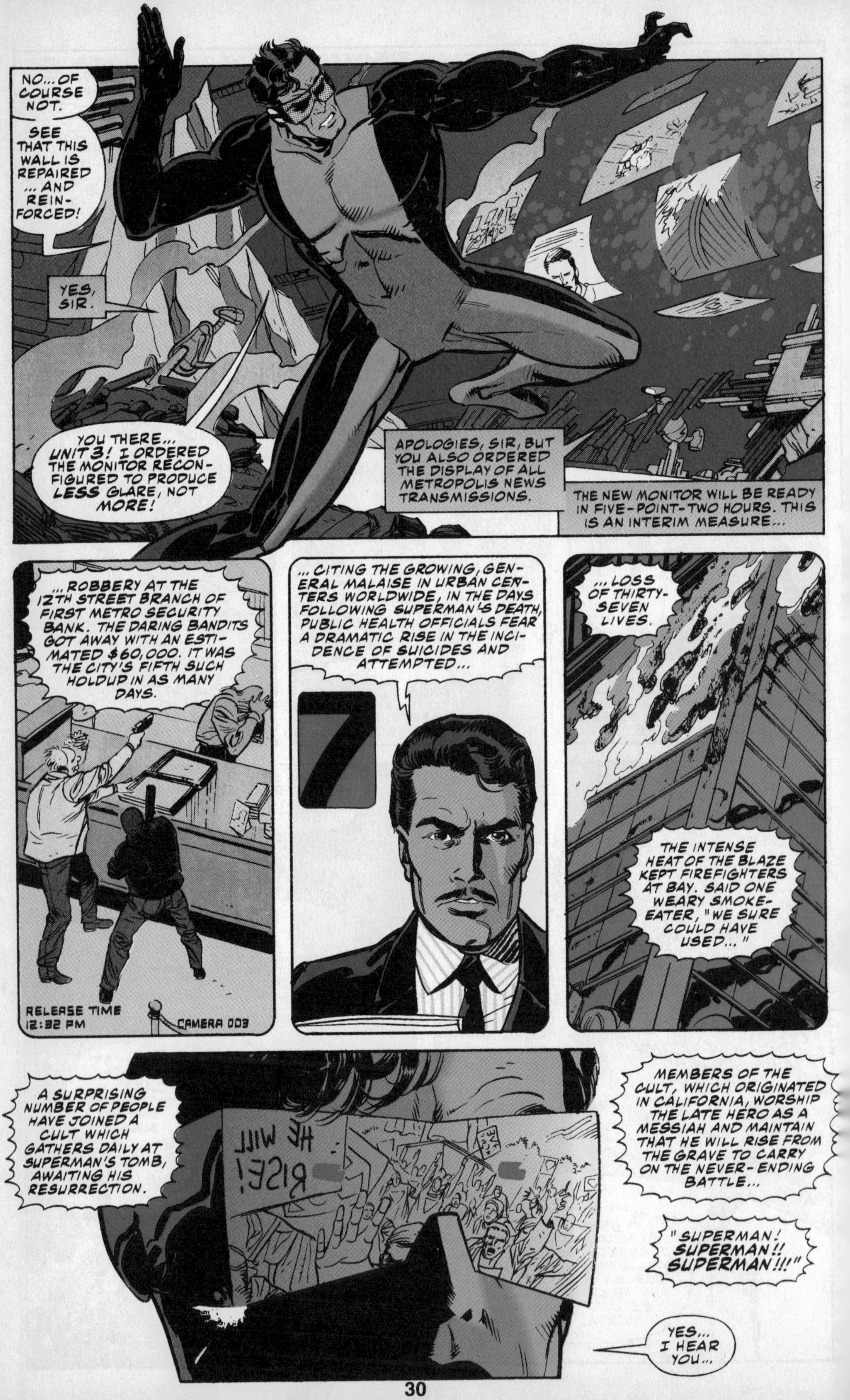

NO... OF COURSE NOT.
SEE THAT THIS WALL IS REPAIRED ... AND REIN-FORCED!
YES, SIR.
YOU THERE... UNIT 3! I ORDERED THE MONITOR RECON-FIGURED TO PRODUCE LESS GLARE, NOT MORE!
APOLOGIES, SIR, BUT YOU ALSO ORDERED THE DISPLAY OF ALL METROPOLIS NEWS TRANSMISSIONS.
THE NEW MONITOR WILL BE READY IN FIVE-POINT-TWO HOURS. THIS IS AN INTERIM MEASURE...
...ROBBERY AT THE 12TH STREET BRANCH OF FIRST METRO SECURITY BANK. THE DARING BANDITS GOT AWAY WITH AN ESTI-MATED $60,000. IT WAS THE CITY'S FIFTH SUCH HOLDUP IN AS MANY DAYS.
RELEASE TIME 12:32 PM
CAMERA 003
...CITING THE GROWING, GEN-ERAL MALAISE IN URBAN CEN-TERS WORLDWIDE, IN THE DAYS FOLLOWING SUPERMAN'S DEATH, PUBLIC HEALTH OFFICIALS FEAR A DRAMATIC RISE IN THE INCI-DENCE OF SUICIDES AND ATTEMPTED...
7
...LOSS OF THIRTY-SEVEN LIVES.
THE INTENSE HEAT OF THE BLAZE KEPT FIREFIGHTERS AT BAY. SAID ONE WEARY SMOKE-EATER, "WE SURE COULD HAVE USED..."
A SURPRISING NUMBER OF PEOPLE HAVE JOINED A CULT WHICH GATHERS DAILY AT SUPERMAN'S TOMB, AWAITING HIS RESURRECTION.
HE WILL RISE!
MEMBERS OF THE CULT, WHICH ORIGINATED IN CALIFORNIA, WORSHIP THE LATE HERO AS A MESSIAH AND MAINTAIN THAT HE WILL RISE FROM THE GRAVE TO CARRY ON THE NEVER-ENDING BATTLE...
"SUPERMAN! SUPERMAN!! SUPERMAN!!!"
YES... I HEAR YOU...

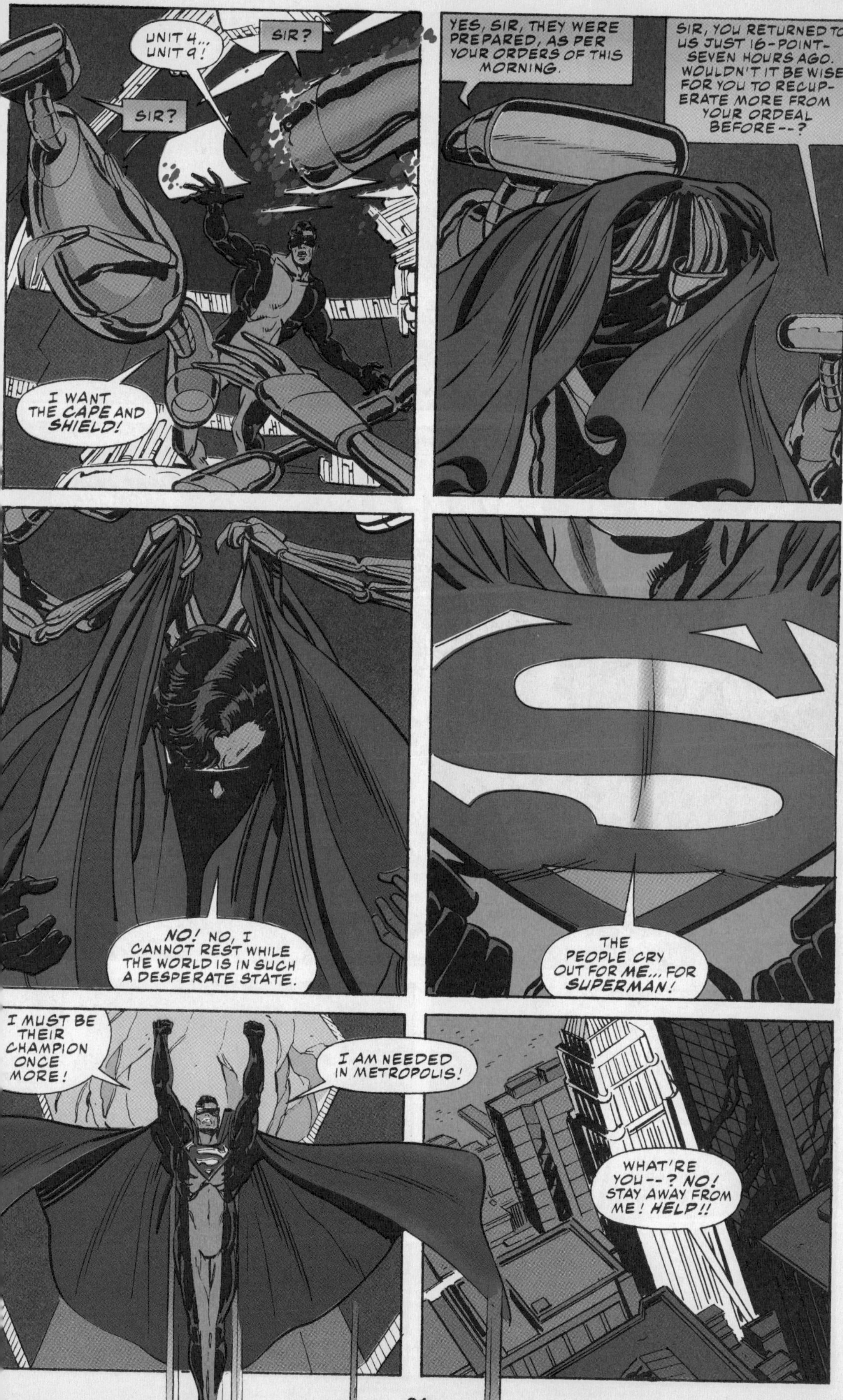
UNIT 4... UNIT 9!
SIR?
SIR?
I WANT THE CAPE AND SHIELD!
YES, SIR, THEY WERE PREPARED, AS PER YOUR ORDERS OF THIS MORNING.
SIR, YOU RETURNED TO US JUST 16-POINT-SEVEN HOURS AGO. WOULDN'T IT BE WISE FOR YOU TO RECUPERATE MORE FROM YOUR ORDEAL BEFORE--?
NO! NO, I CANNOT REST WHILE THE WORLD IS IN SUCH A DESPERATE STATE.
THE PEOPLE CRY OUT FOR ME... FOR SUPERMAN!
I MUST BE THEIR CHAMPION ONCE MORE!
I AM NEEDED IN METROPOLIS!
WHAT'RE YOU--? NO! STAY AWAY FROM ME! HELP!!

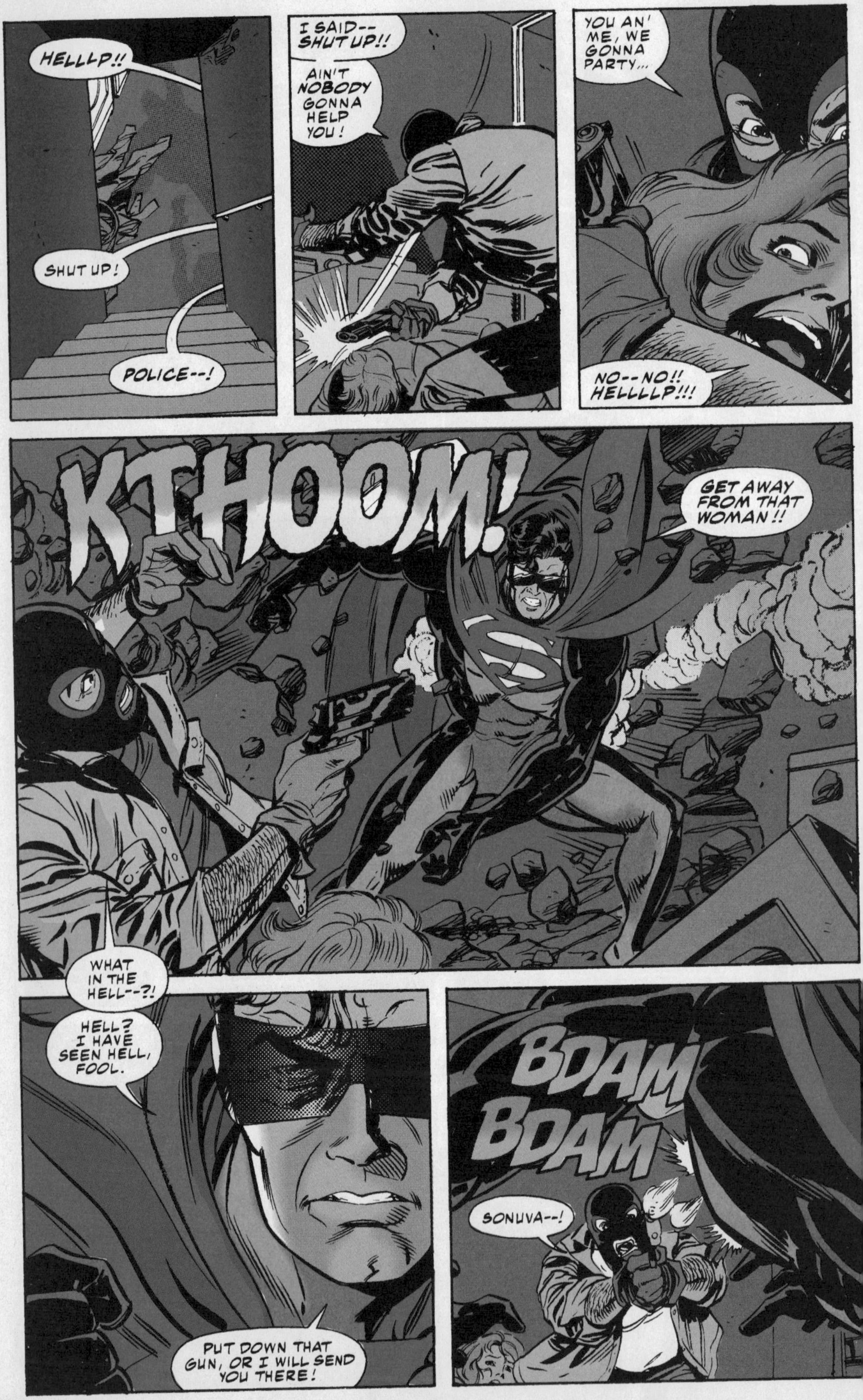
HELLLP!!
SHUT UP!
POLICE--!
I SAID-- SHUT UP!!
AIN'T NOBODY GONNA HELP YOU!
YOU AN' ME, WE GONNA PARTY...
NO--NO!! HELLLLP!!!
KTHOOM!
GET AWAY FROM THAT WOMAN!!
WHAT IN THE HELL--?!
HELL? I HAVE SEEN HELL, FOOL.
PUT DOWN THAT GUN, OR I WILL SEND YOU THERE!
BDAM BDAM
SONUVA--!

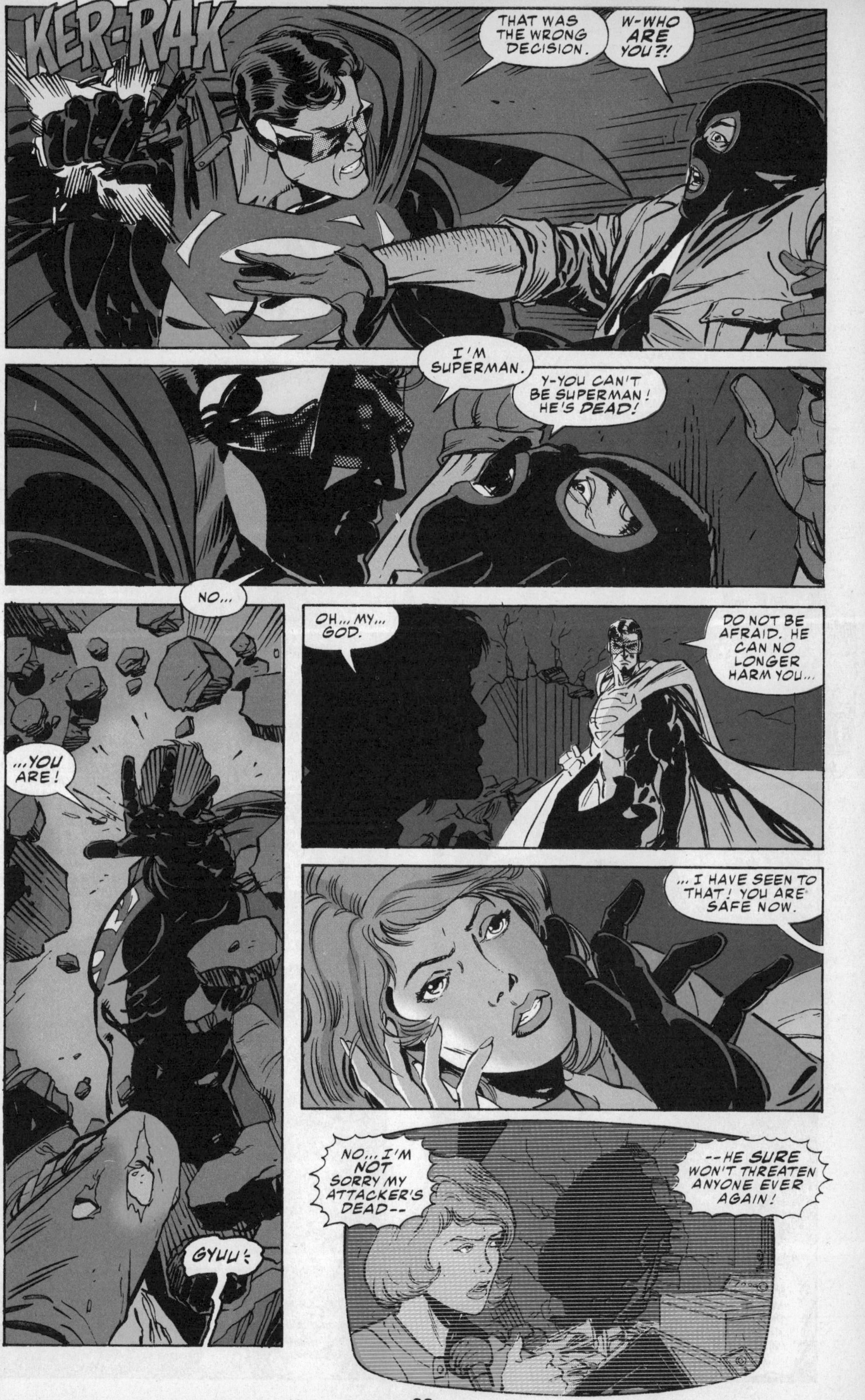

KER-RAK
THAT WAS THE WRONG DECISION.
W-WHO ARE YOU?!
I'M SUPERMAN.
Y-YOU CAN'T BE SUPERMAN! HE'S DEAD!
NO...
...YOU ARE!
GYUU!
OH... MY... GOD.
DO NOT BE AFRAID. HE CAN NO LONGER HARM YOU...
... I HAVE SEEN TO THAT! YOU ARE SAFE NOW.
NO... I'M NOT SORRY MY ATTACKER'S DEAD--
--HE SURE WON'T THREATEN ANYONE EVER AGAIN!

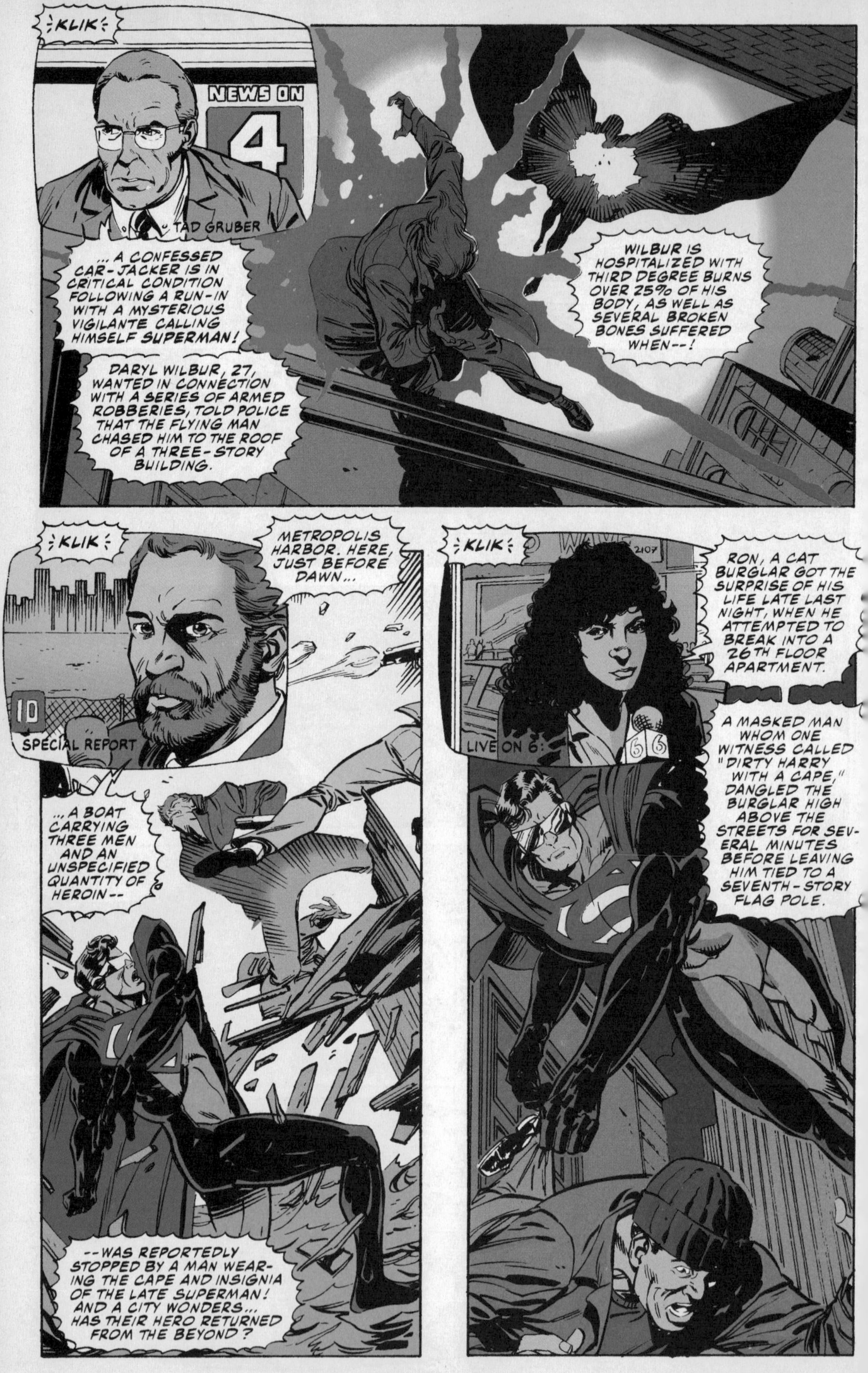

KLIK
NEWS ON 4
TAD GRUBER
... A CONFESSED CAR-JACKER IS IN CRITICAL CONDITION FOLLOWING A RUN-IN WITH A MYSTERIOUS VIGILANTE CALLING HIMSELF SUPERMAN!
DARYL WILBUR, 27, WANTED IN CONNECTION WITH A SERIES OF ARMED ROBBERIES, TOLD POLICE THAT THE FLYING MAN CHASED HIM TO THE ROOF OF A THREE-STORY BUILDING.
WILBUR IS HOSPITALIZED WITH THIRD DEGREE BURNS OVER 25% OF HIS BODY, AS WELL AS SEVERAL BROKEN BONES SUFFERED WHEN--!
KLIK
METROPOLIS HARBOR. HERE, JUST BEFORE DAWN...
10
SPECIAL REPORT
... A BOAT CARRYING THREE MEN AND AN UNSPECIFIED QUANTITY OF HEROIN--
--WAS REPORTEDLY STOPPED BY A MAN WEARING THE CAPE AND INSIGNIA OF THE LATE SUPERMAN! AND A CITY WONDERS... HAS THEIR HERO RETURNED FROM THE BEYOND?
KLIK
RON, A CAT BURGLAR GOT THE SURPRISE OF HIS LIFE LATE LAST NIGHT, WHEN HE ATTEMPTED TO BREAK INTO A 26TH FLOOR APARTMENT.
LIVE ON 6:
A MASKED MAN WHOM ONE WITNESS CALLED "DIRTY HARRY WITH A CAPE," DANGLED THE BURGLAR HIGH ABOVE THE STREETS FOR SEVERAL MINUTES BEFORE LEAVING HIM TIED TO A SEVENTH-STORY FLAG POLE.

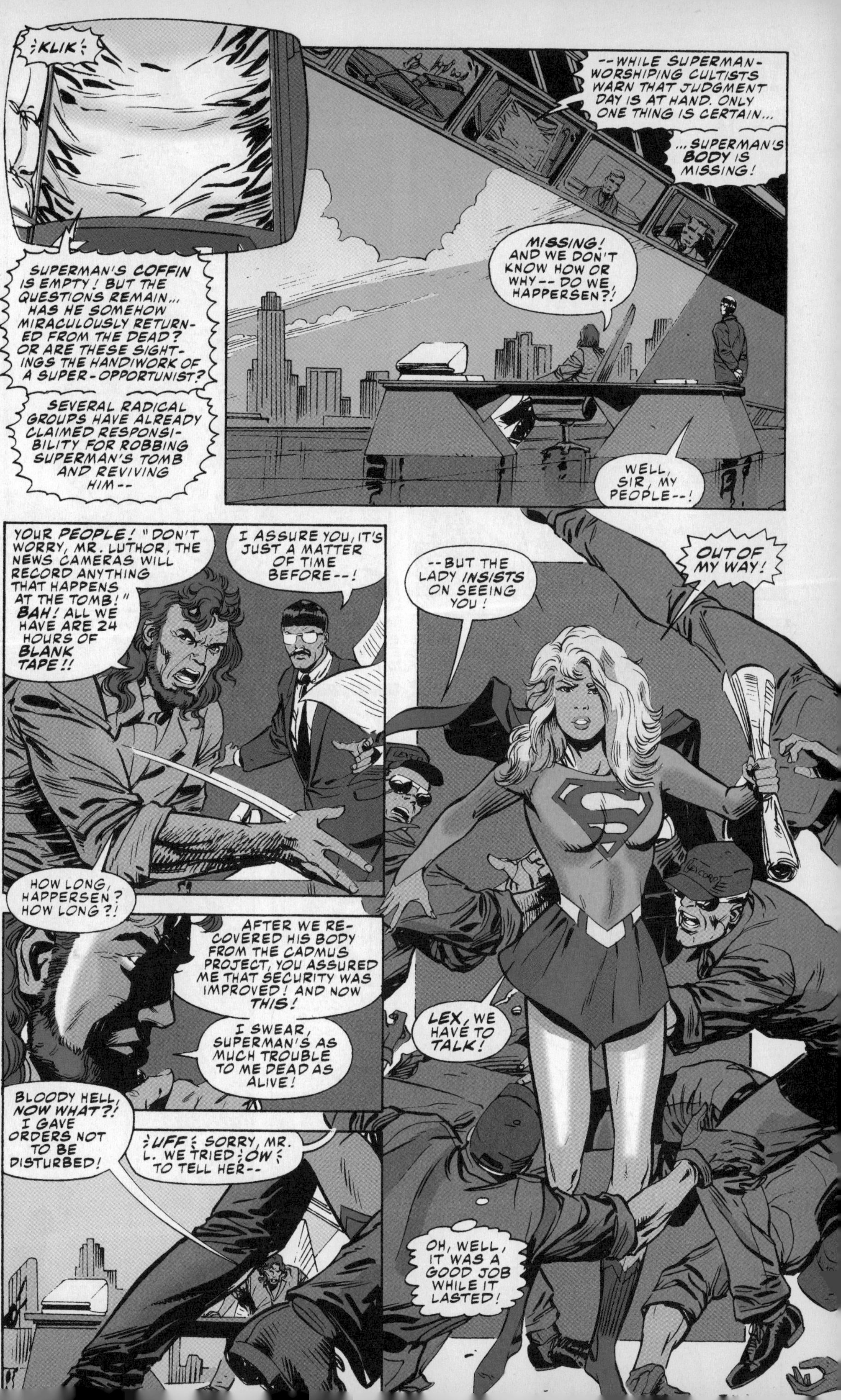

KLIK
--WHILE SUPERMAN-WORSHIPING CULTISTS WARN THAT JUDGMENT DAY IS AT HAND. ONLY ONE THING IS CERTAIN...
...SUPERMAN'S BODY IS MISSING!
SUPERMAN'S COFFIN IS EMPTY! BUT THE QUESTIONS REMAIN... HAS HE SOMEHOW MIRACULOUSLY RETURNED FROM THE DEAD? OR ARE THESE SIGHTINGS THE HANDIWORK OF A SUPER-OPPORTUNIST?
SEVERAL RADICAL GROUPS HAVE ALREADY CLAIMED RESPONSIBILITY FOR ROBBING SUPERMAN'S TOMB AND REVIVING HIM--
MISSING! AND WE DON'T KNOW HOW OR WHY--DO WE, HAPPERSEN?!
WELL, SIR, MY PEOPLE--!
YOUR PEOPLE! "DON'T WORRY, MR. LUTHOR, THE NEWS CAMERAS WILL RECORD ANYTHING THAT HAPPENS AT THE TOMB!" BAH! ALL WE HAVE ARE 24 HOURS OF BLANK TAPE!!
I ASSURE YOU, IT'S JUST A MATTER OF TIME BEFORE--!
HOW LONG, HAPPERSEN? HOW LONG?!
AFTER WE RECOVERED HIS BODY FROM THE CADMUS PROJECT, YOU ASSURED ME THAT SECURITY WAS IMPROVED! AND NOW THIS!
I SWEAR, SUPERMAN'S AS MUCH TROUBLE TO ME DEAD AS ALIVE!
BLOODY HELL, NOW WHAT?! I GAVE ORDERS NOT TO BE DISTURBED!
UFF SORRY, MR. L. WE TRIED OW TO TELL HER--
--BUT THE LADY INSISTS ON SEEING YOU!
OUT OF MY WAY!
LEX, WE HAVE TO TALK!
OH, WELL, IT WAS A GOOD JOB WHILE IT LASTED!

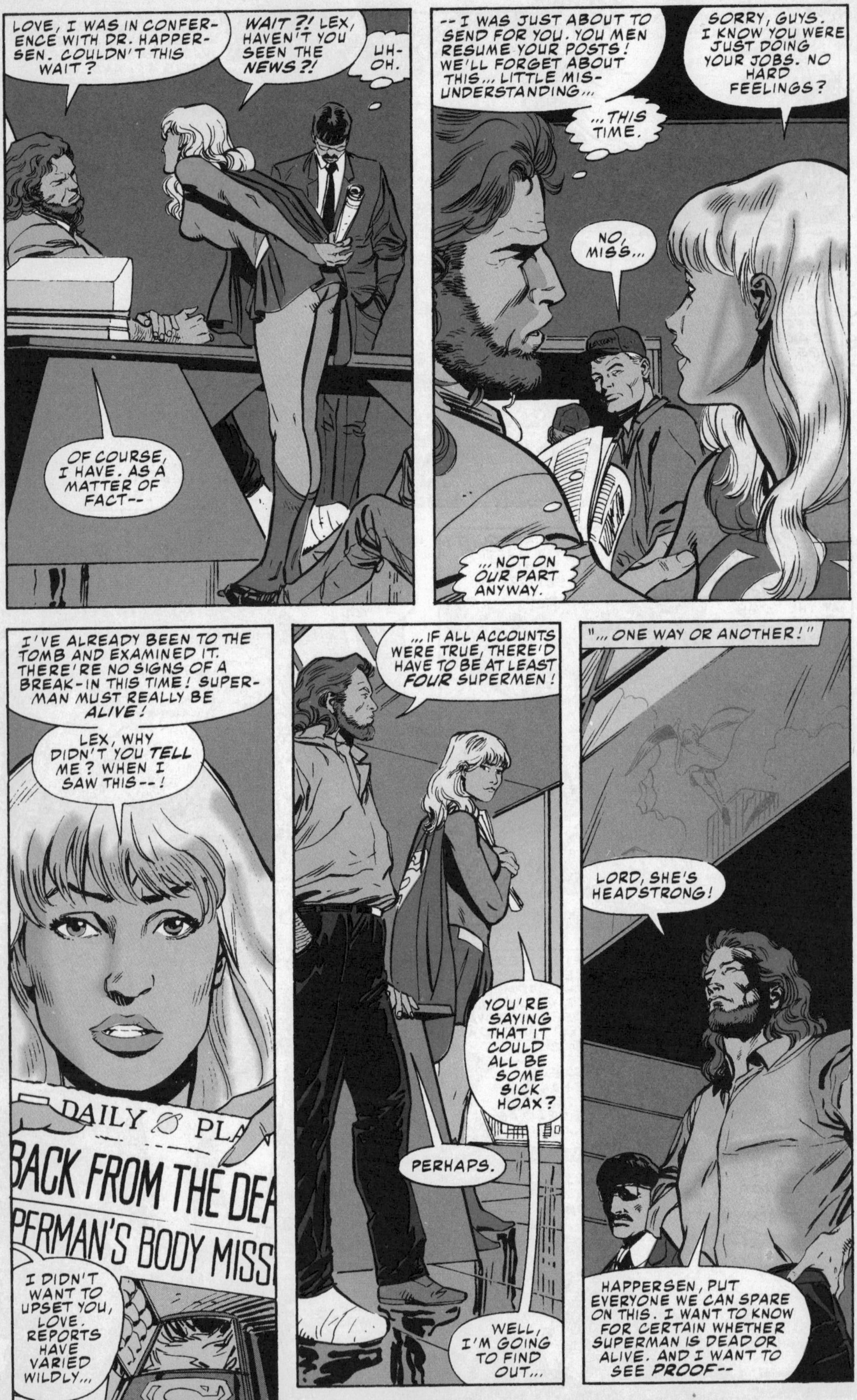
LOVE, I WAS IN CONFERENCE WITH DR. HAPPERSEN. COULDN'T THIS WAIT?
WAIT?! LEX, HAVEN'T YOU SEEN THE NEWS?!
UH-OH.
OF COURSE, I HAVE. AS A MATTER OF FACT--
--I WAS JUST ABOUT TO SEND FOR YOU. YOU MEN RESUME YOUR POSTS! WE'LL FORGET ABOUT THIS... LITTLE MISUNDERSTANDING...
...THIS TIME.
SORRY, GUYS. I KNOW YOU WERE JUST DOING YOUR JOBS. NO HARD FEELINGS?
NO, MISS...
...NOT ON OUR PART ANYWAY.
I'VE ALREADY BEEN TO THE TOMB AND EXAMINED IT. THERE'RE NO SIGNS OF A BREAK-IN THIS TIME! SUPERMAN MUST REALLY BE ALIVE!
LEX, WHY DIDN'T YOU TELL ME? WHEN I SAW THIS--!
DAILY PLA
BACK FROM THE DEA
PERMAN'S BODY MISS
I DIDN'T WANT TO UPSET YOU, LOVE. REPORTS HAVE VARIED WILDLY...
...IF ALL ACCOUNTS WERE TRUE, THERE'D HAVE TO BE AT LEAST FOUR SUPERMEN!
YOU'RE SAYING THAT IT COULD ALL BE SOME SICK HOAX?
PERHAPS.
WELL, I'M GOING TO FIND OUT...
"...ONE WAY OR ANOTHER!"
LORD, SHE'S HEADSTRONG!
HAPPERSEN, PUT EVERYONE WE CAN SPARE ON THIS. I WANT TO KNOW FOR CERTAIN WHETHER SUPERMAN IS DEAD OR ALIVE. AND I WANT TO SEE PROOF--

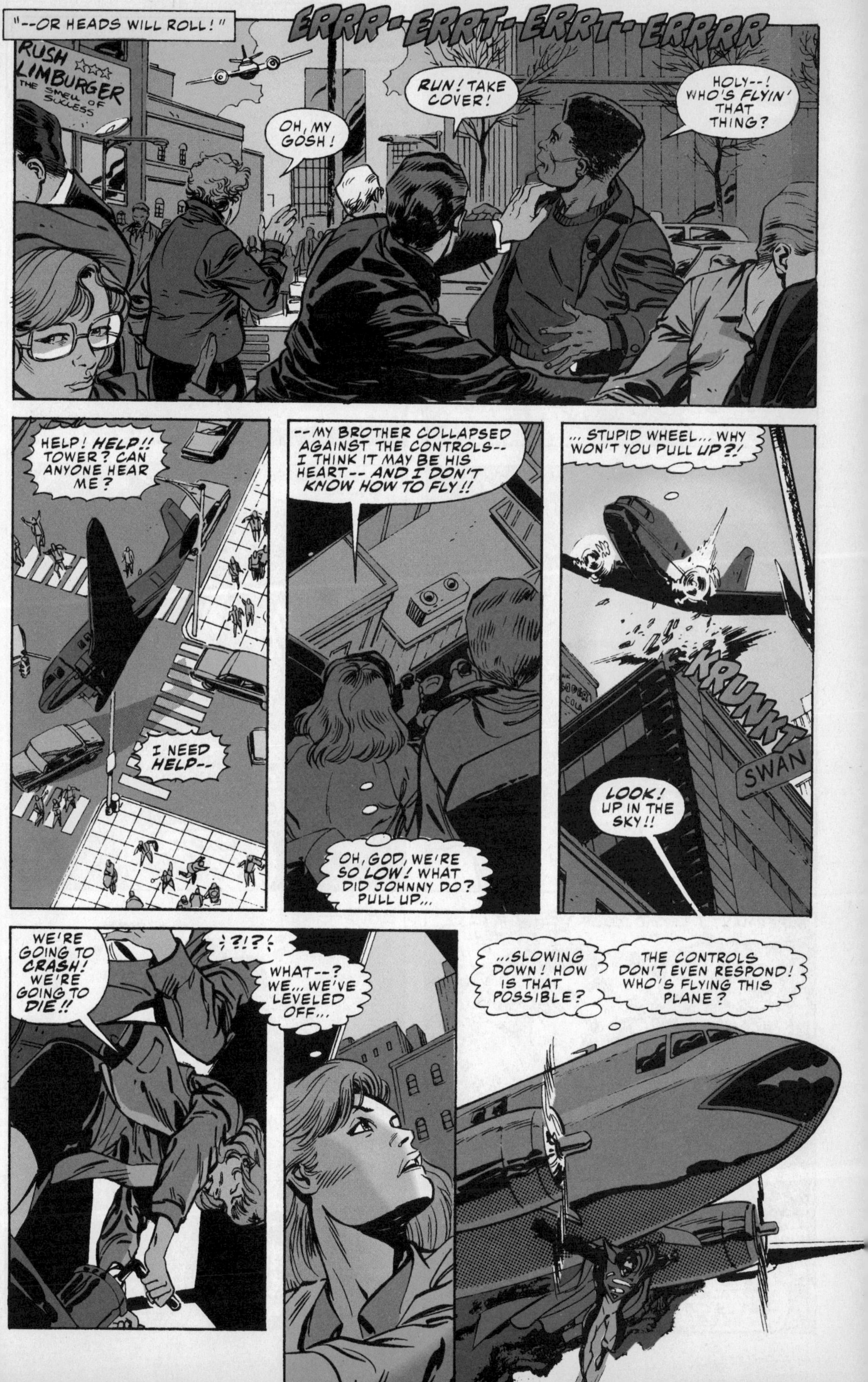
"--OR HEADS WILL ROLL!"
ERRR-ERRT-ERRT-ERRRR
RUSH LIMBURGER THE SMELL OF SUCCESS
OH, MY GOSH!
RUN! TAKE COVER!
HOLY--! WHO'S FLYIN' THAT THING?
HELP! HELP!! TOWER? CAN ANYONE HEAR ME?
I NEED HELP--
--MY BROTHER COLLAPSED AGAINST THE CONTROLS-- I THINK IT MAY BE HIS HEART-- AND I DON'T KNOW HOW TO FLY!!
OH, GOD, WE'RE SO LOW! WHAT DID JOHNNY DO? PULL UP...
... STUPID WHEEL... WHY WON'T YOU PULL UP?!
KRUNKT
SWAN
LOOK! UP IN THE SKY!!
WE'RE GOING TO CRASH! WE'RE GOING TO DIE!!
¡?!?¡
WHAT--? WE... WE'VE LEVELED OFF...
...SLOWING DOWN! HOW IS THAT POSSIBLE?
THE CONTROLS DON'T EVEN RESPOND! WHO'S FLYING THIS PLANE?

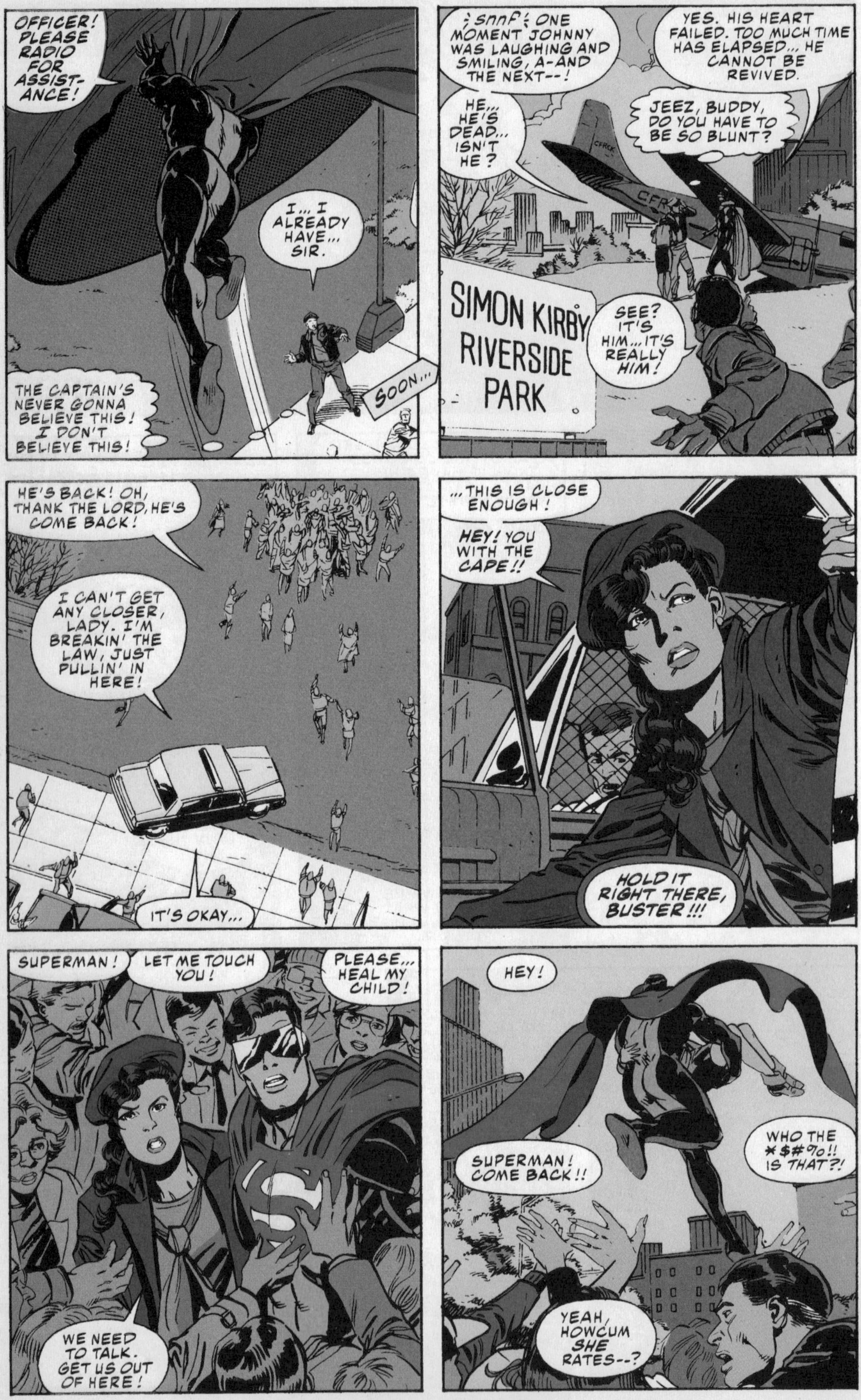

OFFICER! PLEASE RADIO FOR ASSIST-ANCE!
I... I ALREADY HAVE... SIR.
THE CAPTAIN'S NEVER GONNA BELIEVE THIS! I DON'T BELIEVE THIS!
SOON...
;SNIF; ONE MOMENT JOHNNY WAS LAUGHING AND SMILING, A-AND THE NEXT--!
YES. HIS HEART FAILED. TOO MUCH TIME HAS ELAPSED... HE CANNOT BE REVIVED.
HE... HE'S DEAD... ISN'T HE?
JEEZ, BUDDY, DO YOU HAVE TO BE SO BLUNT?
SIMON KIRBY RIVERSIDE PARK
SEE? IT'S HIM... IT'S REALLY HIM!
HE'S BACK! OH, THANK THE LORD, HE'S COME BACK!
I CAN'T GET ANY CLOSER, LADY. I'M BREAKIN' THE LAW, JUST PULLIN' IN HERE!
IT'S OKAY...
...THIS IS CLOSE ENOUGH!
HEY! YOU WITH THE CAPE!!
HOLD IT RIGHT THERE, BUSTER!!!
SUPERMAN!
LET ME TOUCH YOU!
PLEASE... HEAL MY CHILD!
WE NEED TO TALK. GET US OUT OF HERE!
HEY!
SUPERMAN! COME BACK!!
WHO THE *$#%!! IS THAT?!
YEAH, HOWCUM SHE RATES--?

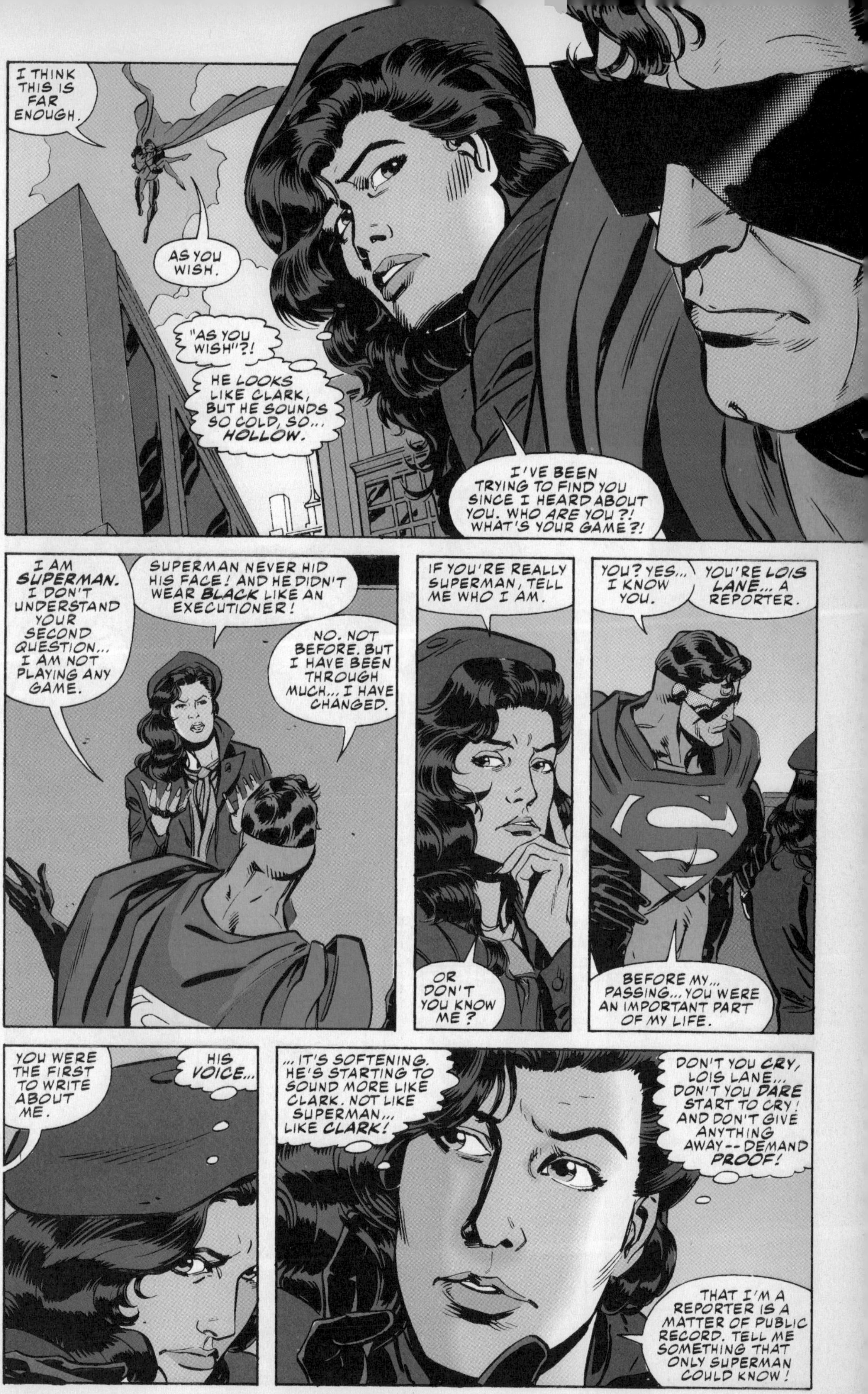
I THINK THIS IS FAR ENOUGH.
AS YOU WISH.
"AS YOU WISH"?!
HE LOOKS LIKE CLARK, BUT HE SOUNDS SO COLD, SO... HOLLOW.
I'VE BEEN TRYING TO FIND YOU SINCE I HEARD ABOUT YOU. WHO ARE YOU?! WHAT'S YOUR GAME?!
I AM SUPERMAN. I DON'T UNDERSTAND YOUR SECOND QUESTION... I AM NOT PLAYING ANY GAME.
SUPERMAN NEVER HID HIS FACE! AND HE DIDN'T WEAR BLACK LIKE AN EXECUTIONER!
NO. NOT BEFORE. BUT I HAVE BEEN THROUGH MUCH... I HAVE CHANGED.
IF YOU'RE REALLY SUPERMAN, TELL ME WHO I AM.
OR DON'T YOU KNOW ME?
YOU? YES... I KNOW YOU.
YOU'RE LOIS LANE... A REPORTER.
BEFORE MY... PASSING... YOU WERE AN IMPORTANT PART OF MY LIFE.
YOU WERE THE FIRST TO WRITE ABOUT ME.
HIS VOICE...
...IT'S SOFTENING. HE'S STARTING TO SOUND MORE LIKE CLARK. NOT LIKE SUPERMAN... LIKE CLARK!
DON'T YOU CRY, LOIS LANE... DON'T YOU DARE START TO CRY! AND DON'T GIVE ANYTHING AWAY--DEMAND PROOF!
THAT I'M A REPORTER IS A MATTER OF PUBLIC RECORD. TELL ME SOMETHING THAT ONLY SUPERMAN COULD KNOW!

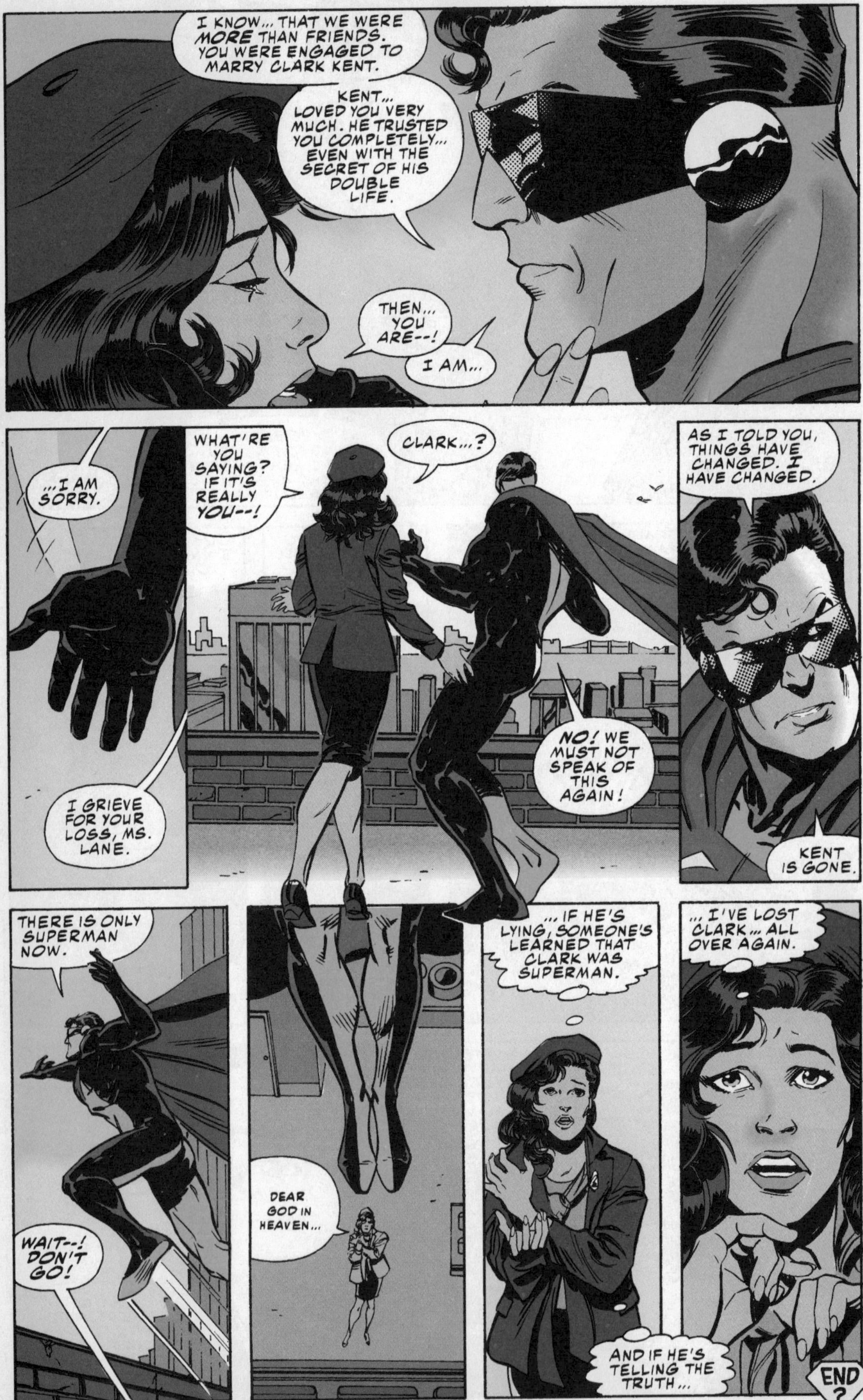
I KNOW... THAT WE WERE MORE THAN FRIENDS. YOU WERE ENGAGED TO MARRY CLARK KENT.
KENT... LOVED YOU VERY MUCH. HE TRUSTED YOU COMPLETELY... EVEN WITH THE SECRET OF HIS DOUBLE LIFE.
THEN... YOU ARE--!
I AM...
...I AM SORRY.
I GRIEVE FOR YOUR LOSS, MS. LANE.
WHAT'RE YOU SAYING? IF IT'S REALLY YOU--!
CLARK...?
NO! WE MUST NOT SPEAK OF THIS AGAIN!
AS I TOLD YOU, THINGS HAVE CHANGED. I HAVE CHANGED.
KENT IS GONE.
THERE IS ONLY SUPERMAN NOW.
WAIT--! DON'T GO!
DEAR GOD IN HEAVEN...
...IF HE'S LYING, SOMEONE'S LEARNED THAT CLARK WAS SUPERMAN.
AND IF HE'S TELLING THE TRUTH...
...I'VE LOST CLARK... ALL OVER AGAIN.
END ?

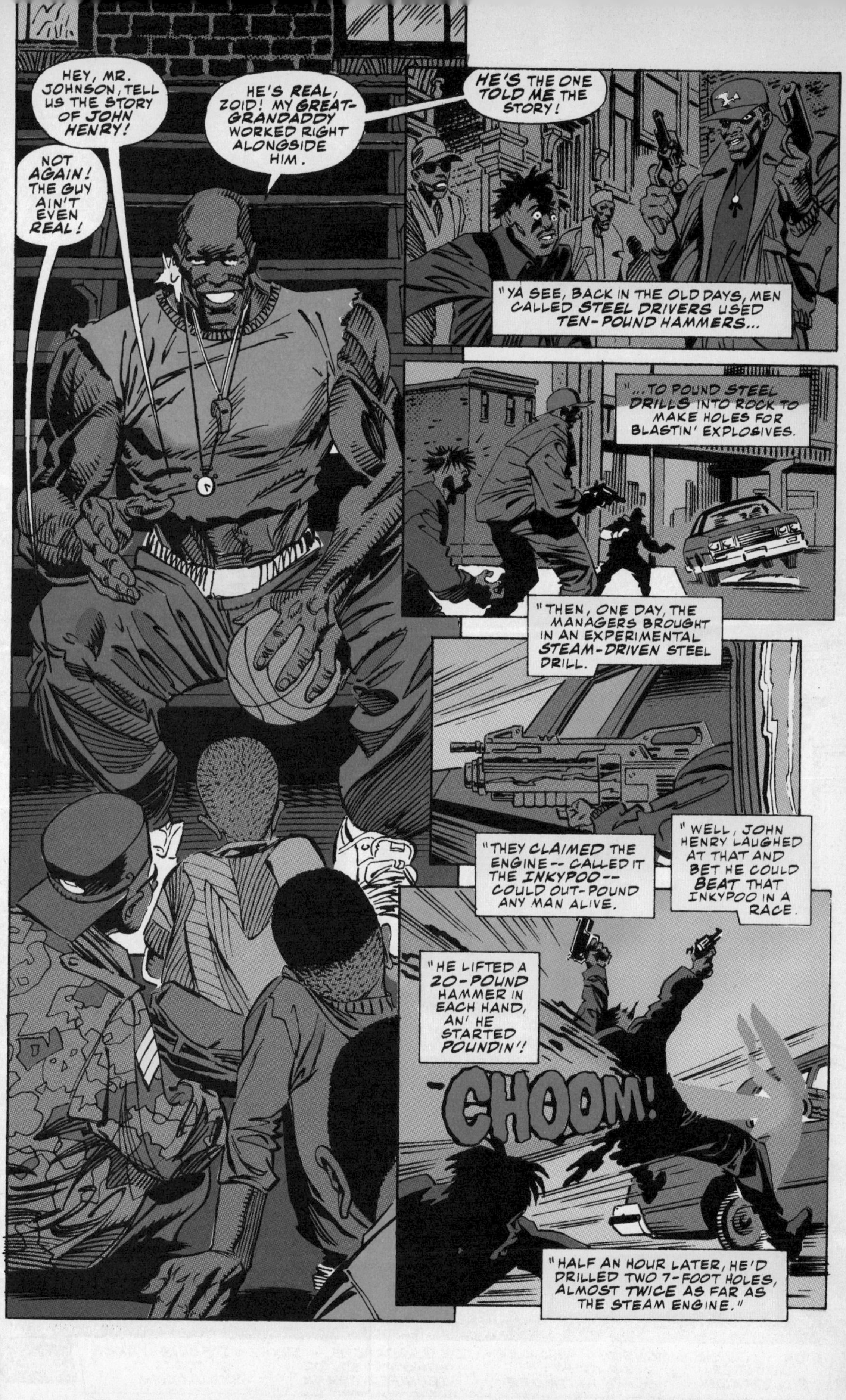

HEY, MR. JOHNSON, TELL US THE STORY OF JOHN HENRY!
NOT AGAIN! THE GUY AIN'T EVEN REAL!
HE'S REAL, ZOID! MY GREAT-GRANDADDY WORKED RIGHT ALONGSIDE HIM.
HE'S THE ONE TOLD ME THE STORY!
"YA SEE, BACK IN THE OLD DAYS, MEN CALLED STEEL DRIVERS USED TEN-POUND HAMMERS...
"...TO POUND STEEL DRILLS INTO ROCK TO MAKE HOLES FOR BLASTIN' EXPLOSIVES.
"THEN, ONE DAY, THE MANAGERS BROUGHT IN AN EXPERIMENTAL STEAM-DRIVEN STEEL DRILL.
"THEY CLAIMED THE ENGINE -- CALLED IT THE INKYPOO -- COULD OUT-POUND ANY MAN ALIVE.
"WELL, JOHN HENRY LAUGHED AT THAT AND BET HE COULD BEAT THAT INKYPOO IN A RACE.
"HE LIFTED A 20-POUND HAMMER IN EACH HAND, AN' HE STARTED POUNDIN'!
CHOOM!
"HALF AN HOUR LATER, HE'D DRILLED TWO 7-FOOT HOLES, ALMOST TWICE AS FAR AS THE STEAM ENGINE."

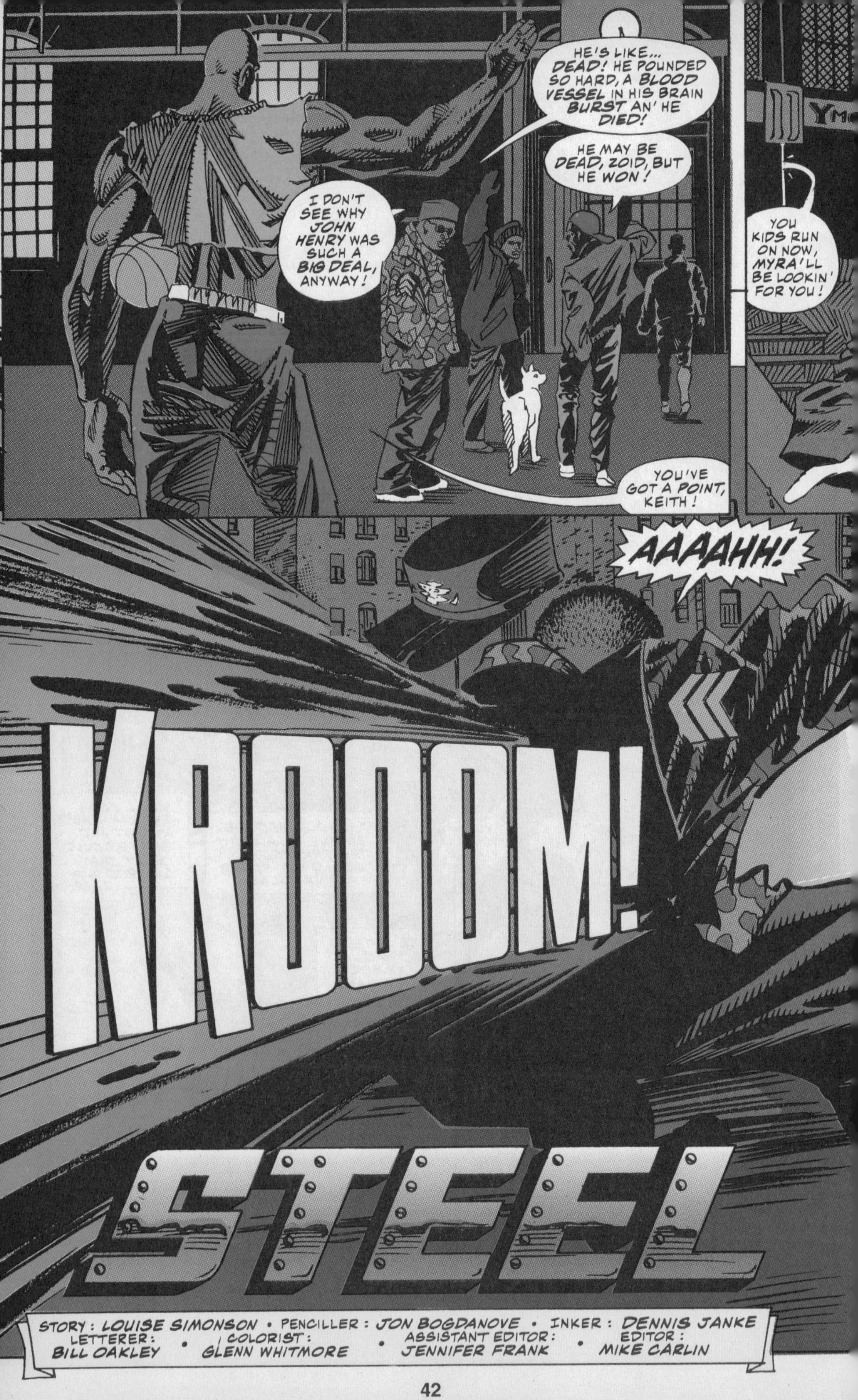
HE'S LIKE... DEAD! HE POUNDED SO HARD, A BLOOD VESSEL IN HIS BRAIN BURST AN' HE DIED!
HE MAY BE DEAD, ZOID, BUT HE WON!
I DON'T SEE WHY JOHN HENRY WAS SUCH A BIG DEAL, ANYWAY!
YOU'VE GOT A POINT, KEITH!
YOU KIDS RUN ON NOW, MYRA'LL BE LOOKIN' FOR YOU!
AAAAHH!
KROOOM!
STEEL
STORY: LOUISE SIMONSON • PENCILLER: JON BOGDANOVE • INKER: DENNIS JANKE
LETTERER: BILL OAKLEY • COLORIST: GLENN WHITMORE • ASSISTANT EDITOR: JENNIFER FRANK • EDITOR: MIKE CARLIN

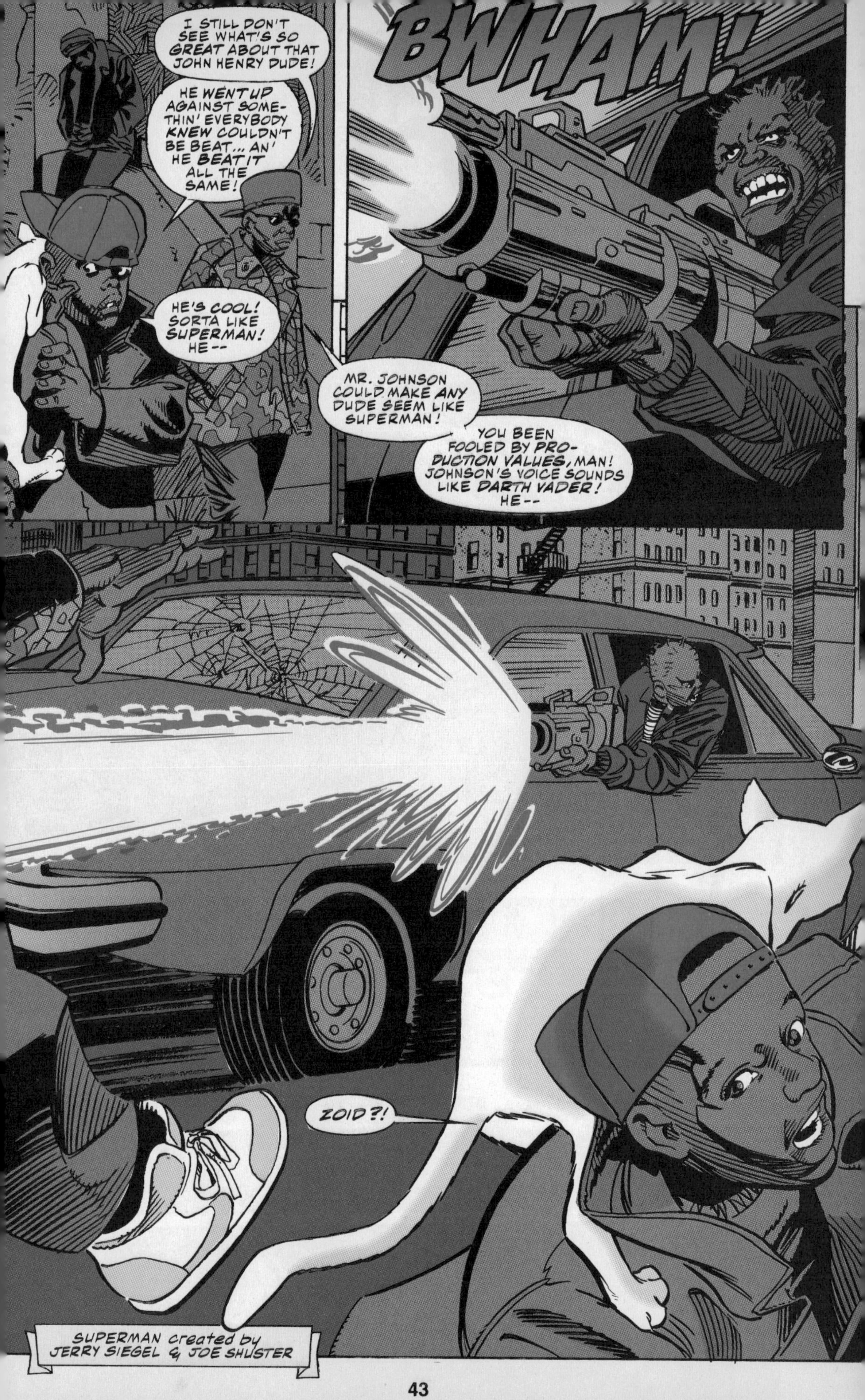
I STILL DON'T SEE WHAT'S SO GREAT ABOUT THAT JOHN HENRY DUDE!
HE WENT UP AGAINST SOMETHIN' EVERYBODY KNEW COULDN'T BE BEAT... AN' HE BEAT IT ALL THE SAME!
HE'S COOL! SORTA LIKE SUPERMAN! HE--
BWHAM!
MR. JOHNSON COULD MAKE ANY DUDE SEEM LIKE SUPERMAN!
YOU BEEN FOOLED BY PRODUCTION VALUES, MAN! JOHNSON'S VOICE SOUNDS LIKE DARTH VADER! HE--
ZOID?!
SUPERMAN created by JERRY SIEGEL & JOE SHUSTER

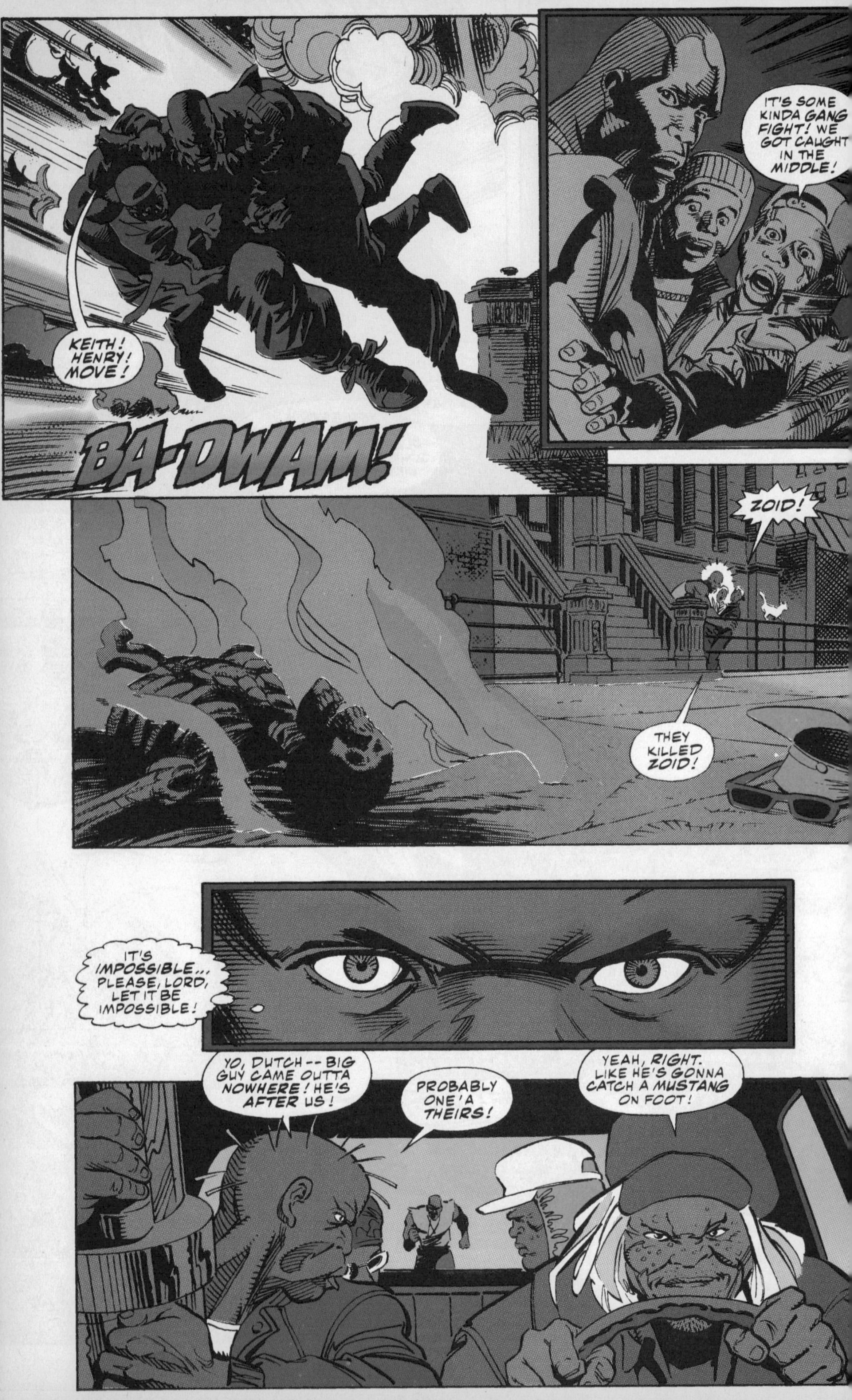
KEITH! HENRY! MOVE!
BA-DWAM!
IT'S SOME KINDA GANG FIGHT! WE GOT CAUGHT IN THE MIDDLE!
ZOID!
THEY KILLED ZOID!
IT'S IMPOSSIBLE... PLEASE, LORD, LET IT BE IMPOSSIBLE!
YO, DUTCH -- BIG GUY CAME OUTTA NOWHERE! HE'S AFTER US!
PROBABLY ONE 'A THEIRS!
YEAH, RIGHT. LIKE HE'S GONNA CATCH A MUSTANG ON FOOT!

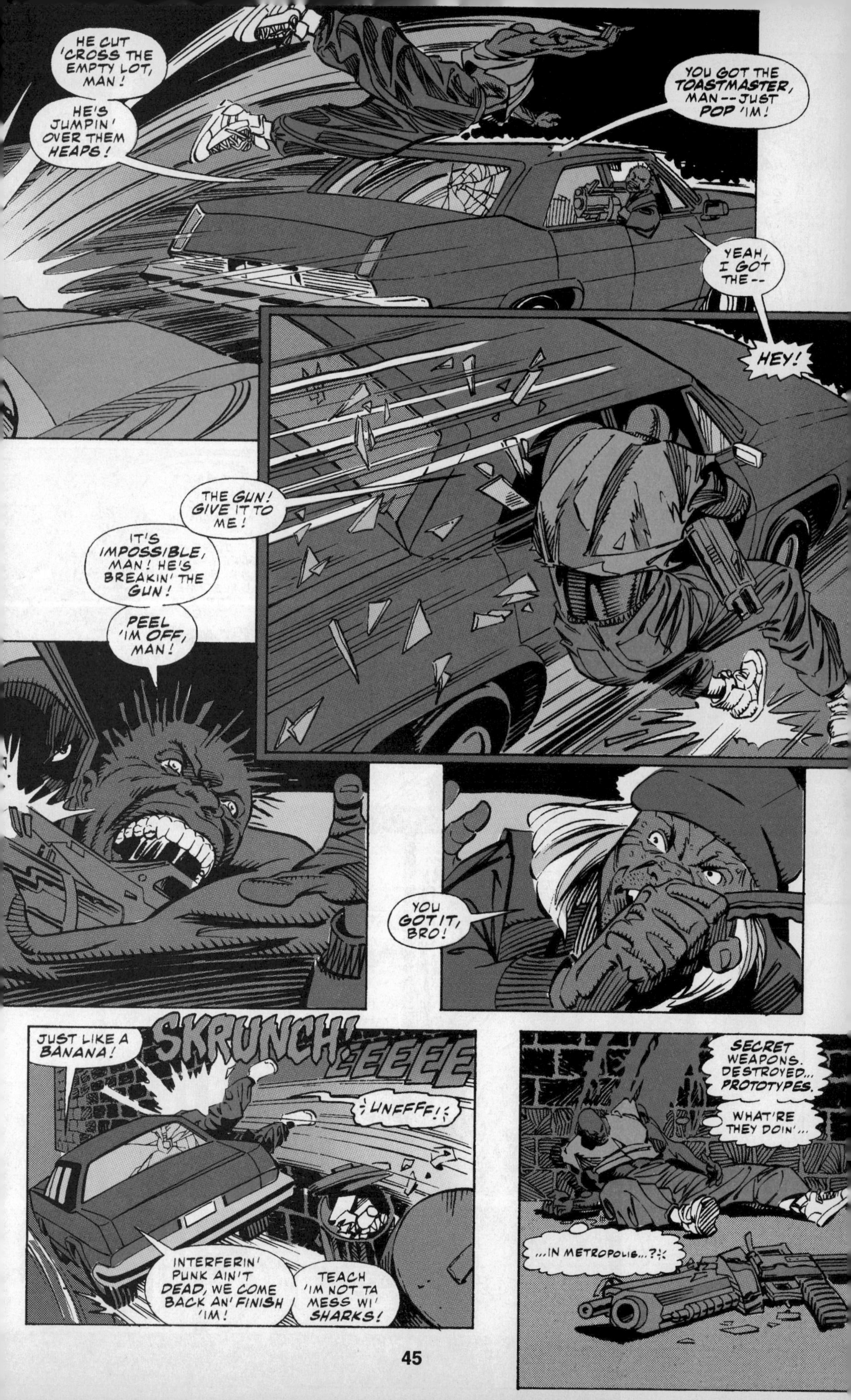

HE CUT 'CROSS THE EMPTY LOT, MAN!
HE'S JUMPIN' OVER THEM HEAPS!
YOU GOT THE TOASTMASTER, MAN--JUST POP 'IM!
YEAH, I GOT THE--
HEY!
THE GUN! GIVE IT TO ME!
IT'S IMPOSSIBLE, MAN! HE'S BREAKIN' THE GUN!
PEEL 'IM OFF, MAN!
YOU GOT IT, BRO!
JUST LIKE A BANANA!
SKRUNCH!
EEEEE
UNFFFF!
INTERFERIN' PUNK AIN'T DEAD, WE COME BACK AN' FINISH 'IM!
TEACH 'IM NOT TA MESS WI' SHARKS!
SECRET WEAPONS. DESTROYED... PROTOTYPES.
WHAT'RE THEY DOIN'...
...IN METROPOLIS...?

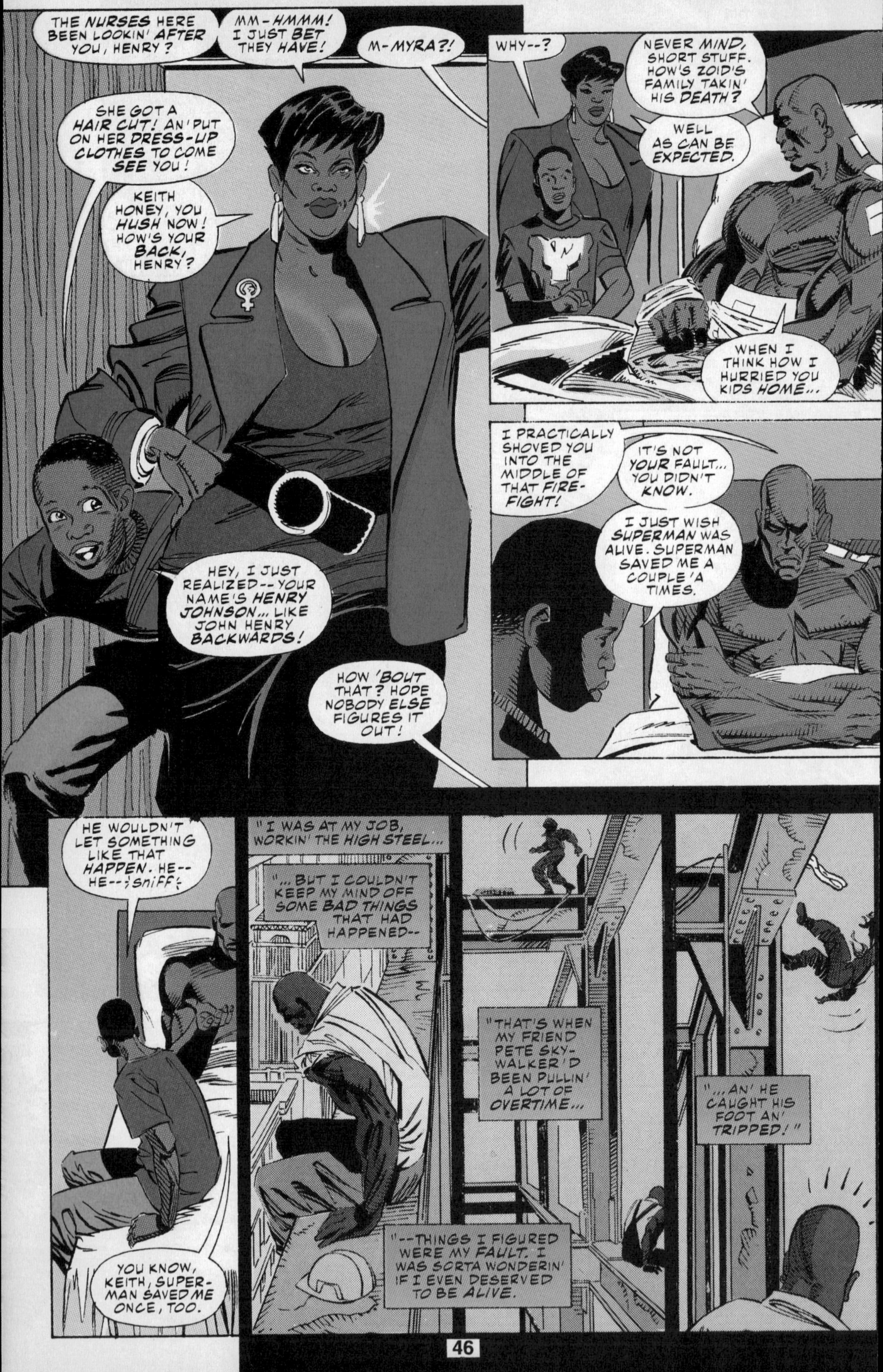
THE NURSES HERE BEEN LOOKIN' AFTER YOU, HENRY?
MM-HMMM! I JUST BET THEY HAVE!
M-MYRA?!
SHE GOT A HAIR CUT! AN' PUT ON HER DRESS-UP CLOTHES TO COME SEE YOU!
KEITH HONEY, YOU HUSH NOW! HOW'S YOUR BACK, HENRY?
HEY, I JUST REALIZED-- YOUR NAME'S HENRY JOHNSON... LIKE JOHN HENRY BACKWARDS!
HOW 'BOUT THAT? HOPE NOBODY ELSE FIGURES IT OUT!
WHY--?
NEVER MIND, SHORT STUFF. HOW'S ZOID'S FAMILY TAKIN' HIS DEATH?
WELL AS CAN BE EXPECTED.
WHEN I THINK HOW I HURRIED YOU KIDS HOME...
I PRACTICALLY SHOVED YOU INTO THE MIDDLE OF THAT FIRE-FIGHT!
IT'S NOT YOUR FAULT... YOU DIDN'T KNOW.
I JUST WISH SUPERMAN WAS ALIVE. SUPERMAN SAVED ME A COUPLE 'A TIMES.
HE WOULDN'T LET SOMETHING LIKE THAT HAPPEN. HE-- HE-- ;sniff;
YOU KNOW, KEITH, SUPER-MAN SAVED ME ONCE, TOO.
"I WAS AT MY JOB, WORKIN' THE HIGH STEEL...
"...BUT I COULDN'T KEEP MY MIND OFF SOME BAD THINGS THAT HAD HAPPENED--
"--THINGS I FIGURED WERE MY FAULT. I WAS SORTA WONDERIN' IF I EVEN DESERVED TO BE ALIVE.
"THAT'S WHEN MY FRIEND PETE SKY-WALKER'D BEEN PULLIN' A LOT OF OVERTIME...
"...AN' HE CAUGHT HIS FOOT AN' TRIPPED!"

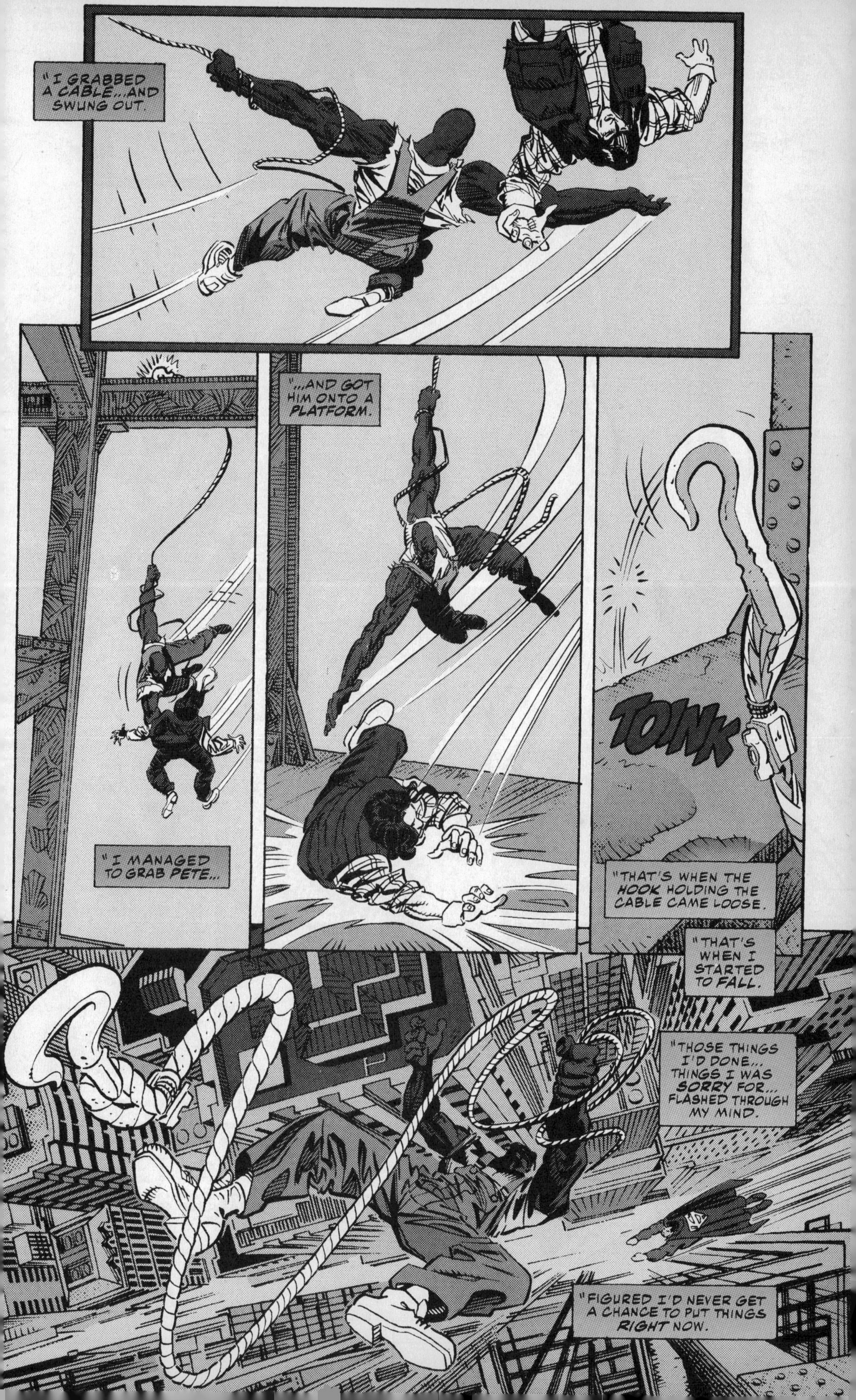
"I GRABBED A CABLE...AND SWUNG OUT.
"I MANAGED TO GRAB PETE...
"...AND GOT HIM ONTO A PLATFORM.
TOINK
"THAT'S WHEN THE HOOK HOLDING THE CABLE CAME LOOSE.
"THAT'S WHEN I STARTED TO FALL.
"THOSE THINGS I'D DONE... THINGS I WAS SORRY FOR... FLASHED THROUGH MY MIND.
"FIGURED I'D NEVER GET A CHANCE TO PUT THINGS RIGHT NOW.

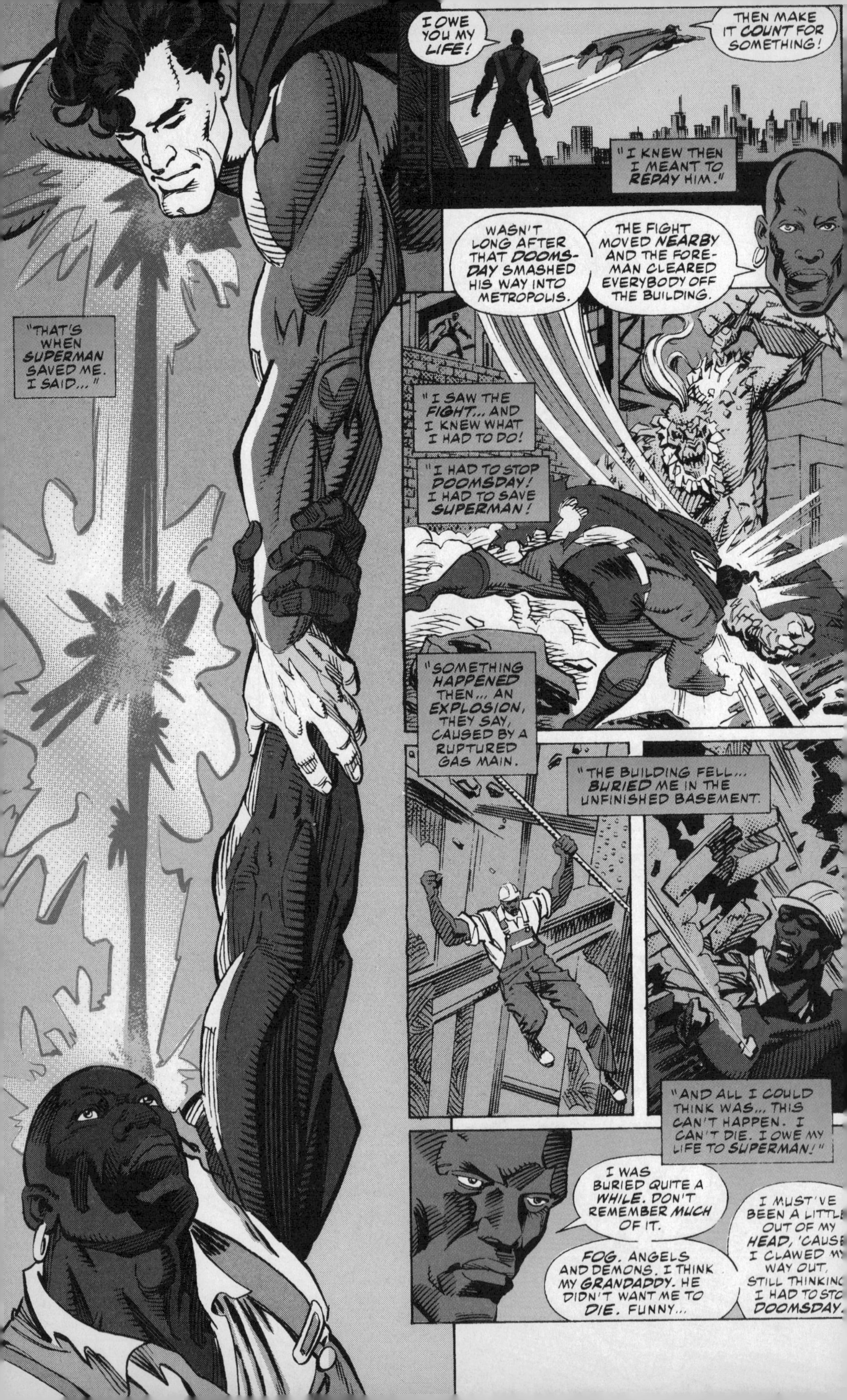
"THAT'S WHEN SUPERMAN SAVED ME. I SAID..."
I OWE YOU MY LIFE!
THEN MAKE IT COUNT FOR SOMETHING!
"I KNEW THEN I MEANT TO REPAY HIM."
WASN'T LONG AFTER THAT DOOMSDAY SMASHED HIS WAY INTO METROPOLIS.
THE FIGHT MOVED NEARBY AND THE FOREMAN CLEARED EVERYBODY OFF THE BUILDING.
"I SAW THE FIGHT... AND I KNEW WHAT I HAD TO DO!
"I HAD TO STOP DOOMSDAY! I HAD TO SAVE SUPERMAN!
"SOMETHING HAPPENED THEN... AN EXPLOSION, THEY SAY, CAUSED BY A RUPTURED GAS MAIN.
"THE BUILDING FELL... BURIED ME IN THE UNFINISHED BASEMENT.
"AND ALL I COULD THINK WAS... THIS CAN'T HAPPEN. I CAN'T DIE. I OWE MY LIFE TO SUPERMAN!"
I WAS BURIED QUITE A WHILE. DON'T REMEMBER MUCH OF IT.
FOG. ANGELS AND DEMONS. I THINK MY GRANDADDY. HE DIDN'T WANT ME TO DIE. FUNNY...
I MUST'VE BEEN A LITTLE OUT OF MY HEAD, 'CAUSE I CLAWED MY WAY OUT, STILL THINKING I HAD TO STOP DOOMSDAY.

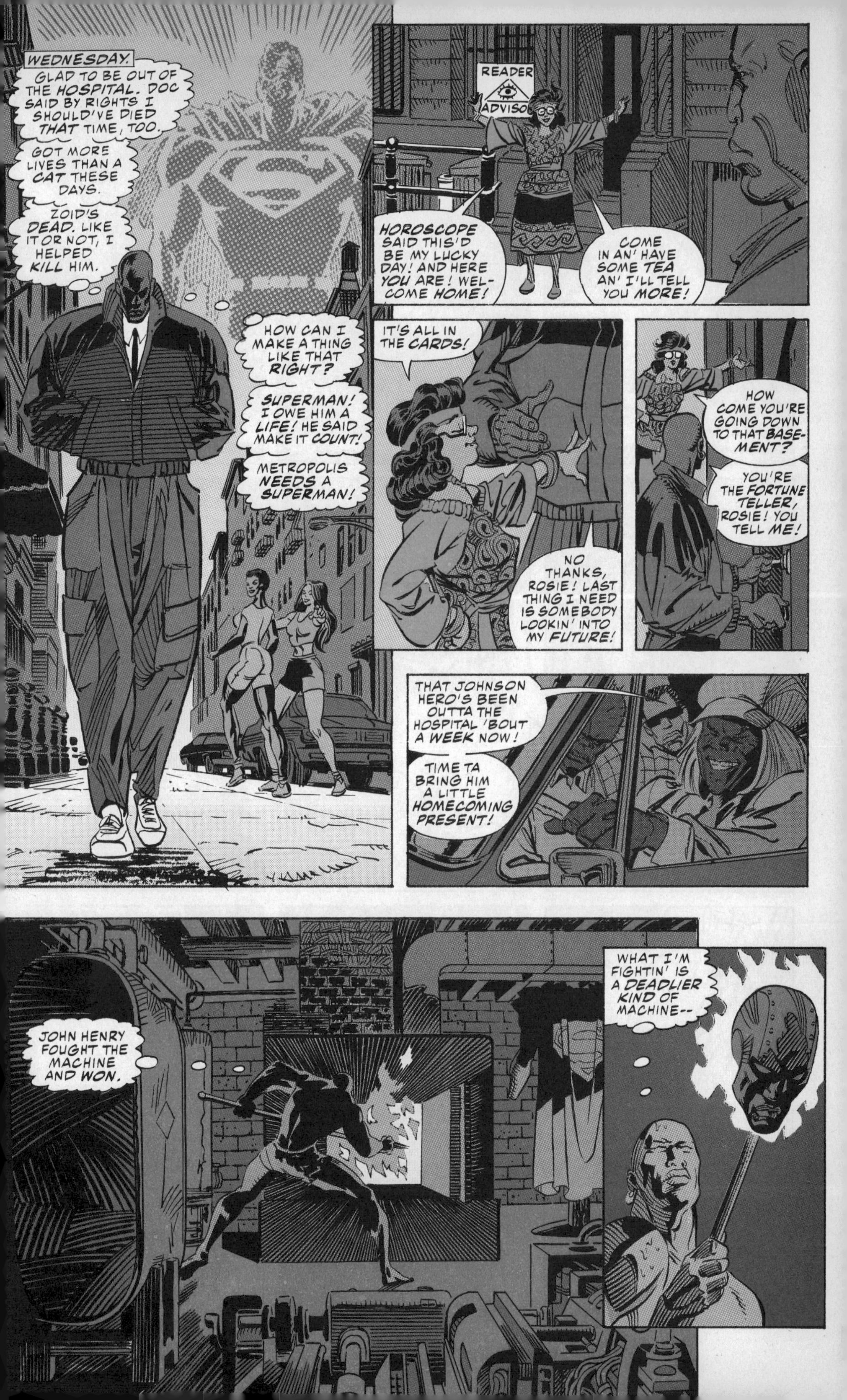
WEDNESDAY.
GLAD TO BE OUT OF THE HOSPITAL. DOC SAID BY RIGHTS I SHOULD'VE DIED THAT TIME, TOO.
GOT MORE LIVES THAN A CAT THESE DAYS.
ZOID'S DEAD. LIKE IT OR NOT, I HELPED KILL HIM.
HOW CAN I MAKE A THING LIKE THAT RIGHT?
SUPERMAN! I OWE HIM A LIFE! HE SAID MAKE IT COUNT!
METROPOLIS NEEDS A SUPERMAN!
READER
ADVISO
HOROSCOPE SAID THIS'D BE MY LUCKY DAY! AND HERE YOU ARE! WEL-COME HOME!
COME IN AN' HAVE SOME TEA AN' I'LL TELL YOU MORE!
IT'S ALL IN THE CARDS!
NO THANKS, ROSIE! LAST THING I NEED IS SOMEBODY LOOKIN' INTO MY FUTURE!
HOW COME YOU'RE GOING DOWN TO THAT BASE-MENT?
YOU'RE THE FORTUNE TELLER, ROSIE! YOU TELL ME!
THAT JOHNSON HERO'S BEEN OUTTA THE HOSPITAL 'BOUT A WEEK NOW!
TIME TA BRING HIM A LITTLE HOMECOMING PRESENT!
JOHN HENRY FOUGHT THE MACHINE AND WON.
WHAT I'M FIGHTIN' IS A DEADLIER KIND OF MACHINE--

--ONE I HELPED PUT IN MOTION.

ONE I'M GONNA STOP...

...EVEN IF IT KILLS ME.

WHAT'S HE DOIN' DOWN THERE?

DON'T MATTER! FIVE SECONDS FROM NOW, HE'S GONNA BE DEAD!

KRISH

POK!

FWOOM

ADER ADVISOR

EEEEEEEEE

FIREBOMB-- HIT THE OIL RESERVOIR! FLAMES EVERY- WHERE! THAT'S ROSIE!

VHRROOOUMMM!

HER DOOR IS LOCKED!

GET BACK FROM THE DOOR!

KRA- MMA

THOOM

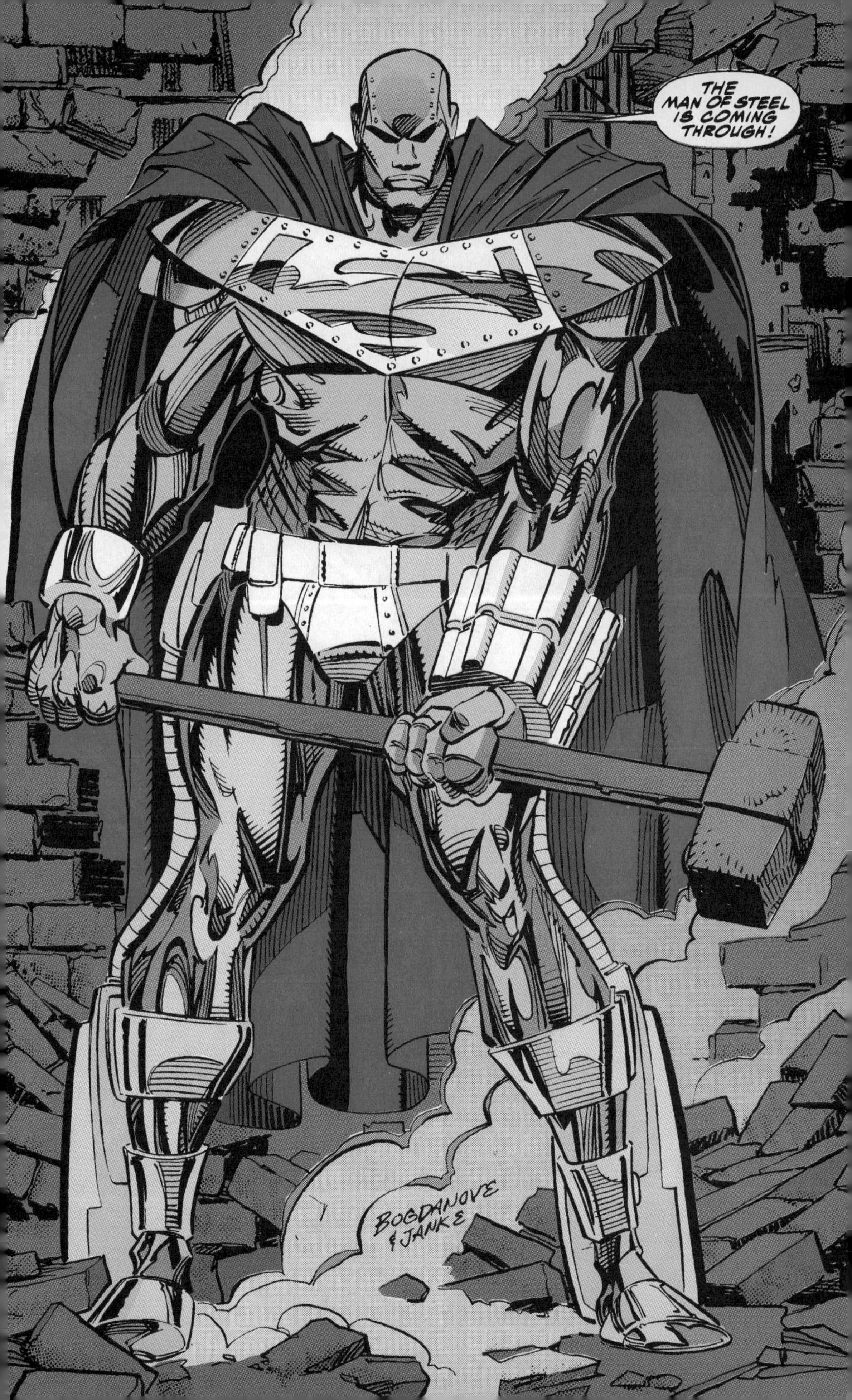
THE MAN OF STEEL IS COMING THROUGH!
BOGDANOVE & JANKE

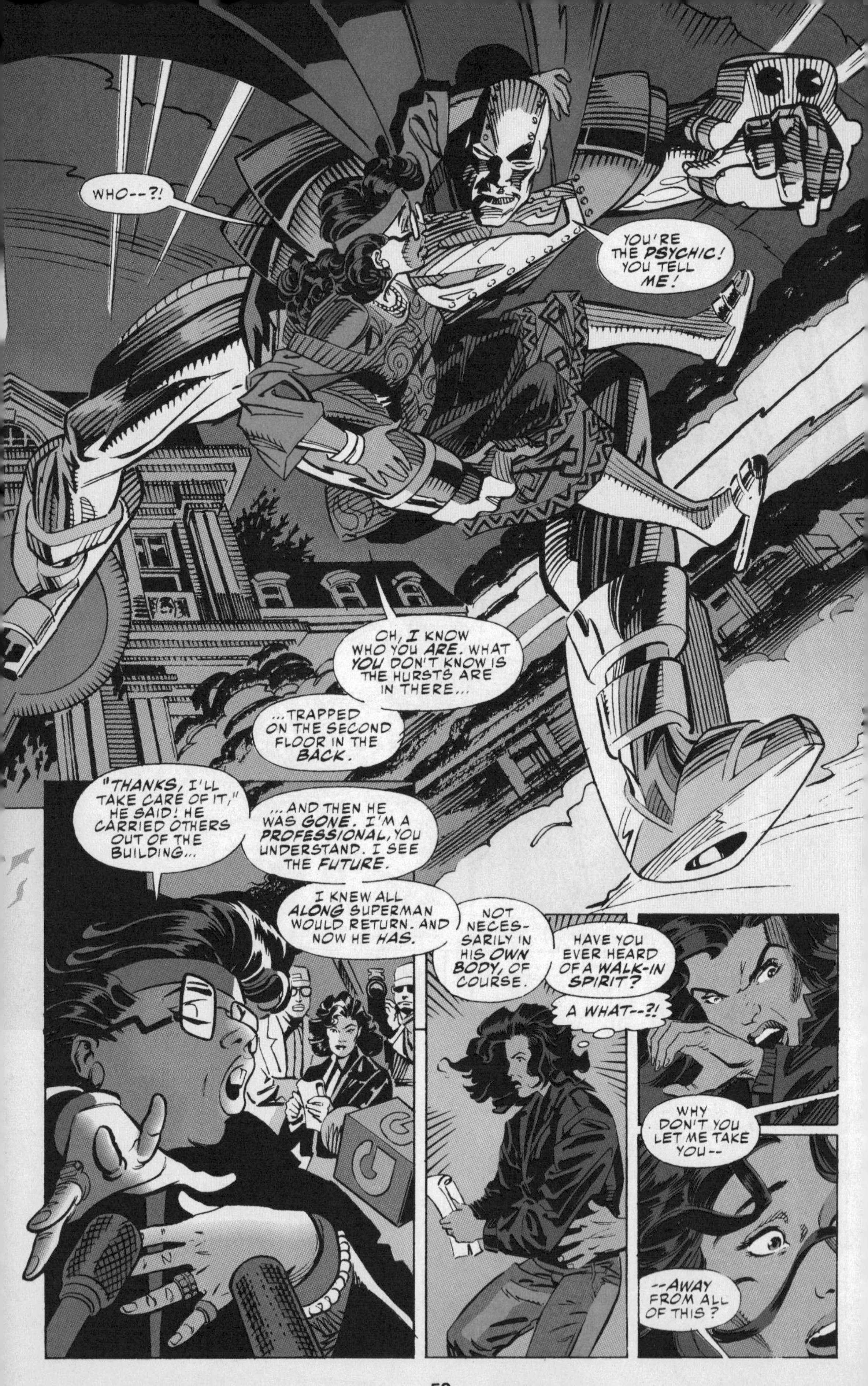
WHO--?!
YOU'RE THE PSYCHIC! YOU TELL ME!
OH, I KNOW WHO YOU ARE. WHAT YOU DON'T KNOW IS THE HURSTS ARE IN THERE...
...TRAPPED ON THE SECOND FLOOR IN THE BACK.
"THANKS, I'LL TAKE CARE OF IT," HE SAID! HE CARRIED OTHERS OUT OF THE BUILDING...
...AND THEN HE WAS GONE. I'M A PROFESSIONAL, YOU UNDERSTAND. I SEE THE FUTURE.
I KNEW ALL ALONG SUPERMAN WOULD RETURN. AND NOW HE HAS.
NOT NECES-SARILY IN HIS OWN BODY, OF COURSE.
HAVE YOU EVER HEARD OF A WALK-IN SPIRIT?
A WHAT--?!
WHY DON'T YOU LET ME TAKE YOU--
--AWAY FROM ALL OF THIS?

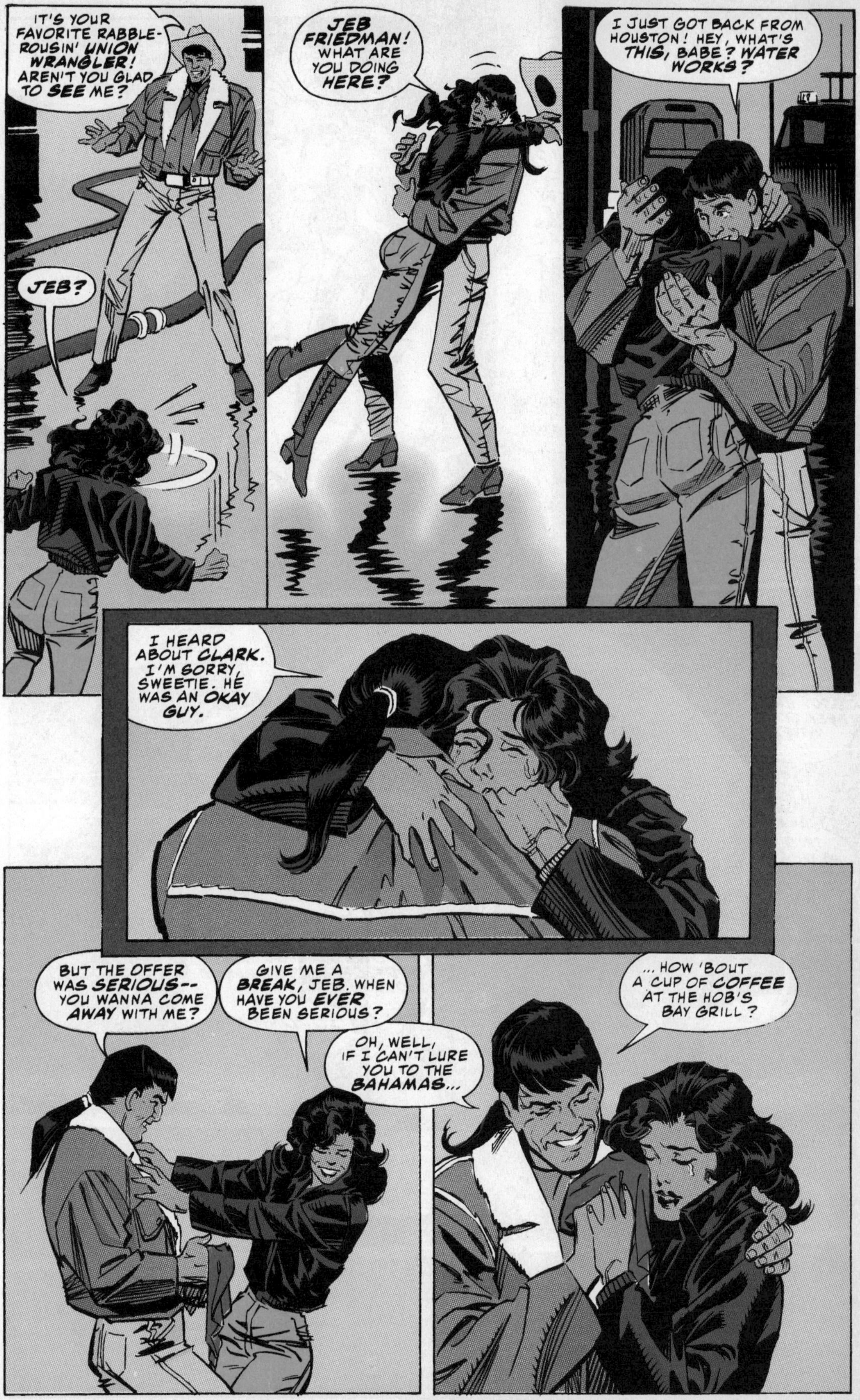
IT'S YOUR FAVORITE RABBLE-ROUSIN' UNION WRANGLER! AREN'T YOU GLAD TO SEE ME?
JEB?
JEB FRIEDMAN! WHAT ARE YOU DOING HERE?
I JUST GOT BACK FROM HOUSTON! HEY, WHAT'S THIS, BABE? WATER WORKS?
I HEARD ABOUT CLARK. I'M SORRY, SWEETIE. HE WAS AN OKAY GUY.
BUT THE OFFER WAS SERIOUS-- YOU WANNA COME AWAY WITH ME?
GIVE ME A BREAK, JEB. WHEN HAVE YOU EVER BEEN SERIOUS?
OH, WELL, IF I CAN'T LURE YOU TO THE BAHAMAS...
...HOW 'BOUT A CUP OF COFFEE AT THE HOB'S BAY GRILL?

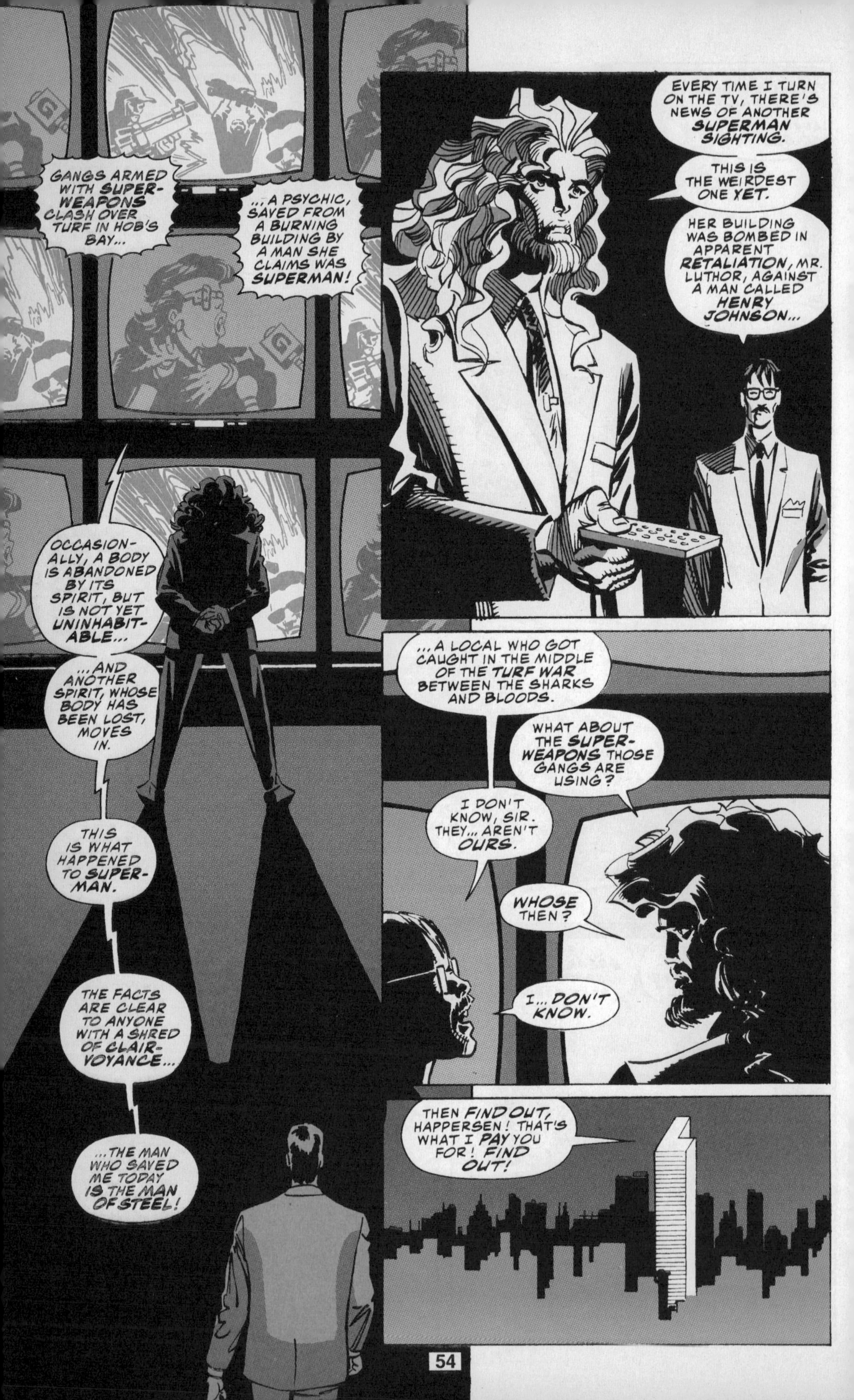
GANGS ARMED WITH SUPER-WEAPONS CLASH OVER TURF IN HOB'S BAY...
...A PSYCHIC, SAVED FROM A BURNING BUILDING BY A MAN SHE CLAIMS WAS SUPERMAN!
EVERY TIME I TURN ON THE TV, THERE'S NEWS OF ANOTHER SUPERMAN SIGHTING.
THIS IS THE WEIRDEST ONE YET.
HER BUILDING WAS BOMBED IN APPARENT RETALIATION, MR. LUTHOR, AGAINST A MAN CALLED HENRY JOHNSON...
OCCASION-ALLY, A BODY IS ABANDONED BY ITS SPIRIT, BUT IS NOT YET UNINHABIT-ABLE...
...AND ANOTHER SPIRIT, WHOSE BODY HAS BEEN LOST, MOVES IN.
THIS IS WHAT HAPPENED TO SUPER-MAN.
...A LOCAL WHO GOT CAUGHT IN THE MIDDLE OF THE TURF WAR BETWEEN THE SHARKS AND BLOODS.
WHAT ABOUT THE SUPER-WEAPONS THOSE GANGS ARE USING?
I DON'T KNOW, SIR. THEY... AREN'T OURS.
WHOSE THEN?
I... DON'T KNOW.
THE FACTS ARE CLEAR TO ANYONE WITH A SHRED OF CLAIR-VOYANCE...
...THE MAN WHO SAVED ME TODAY IS THE MAN OF STEEL!
THEN FIND OUT, HAPPERSEN! THAT'S WHAT I PAY YOU FOR! FIND OUT!

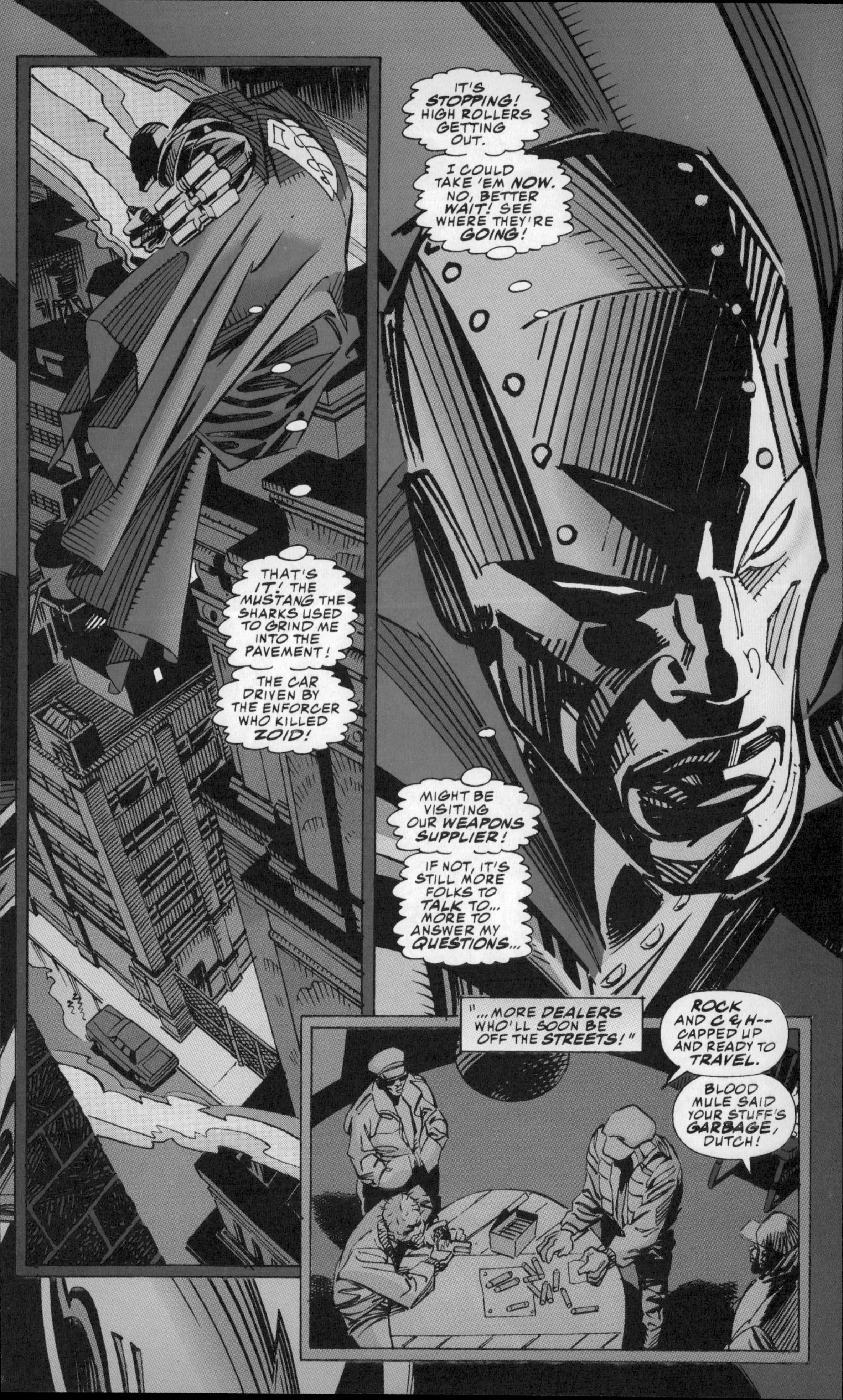
IT'S STOPPING! HIGH ROLLERS GETTING OUT.
I COULD TAKE 'EM NOW. NO, BETTER WAIT! SEE WHERE THEY'RE GOING!
THAT'S IT! THE MUSTANG THE SHARKS USED TO GRIND ME INTO THE PAVEMENT!
THE CAR DRIVEN BY THE ENFORCER WHO KILLED ZOID!
MIGHT BE VISITING OUR WEAPONS SUPPLIER!
IF NOT, IT'S STILL MORE FOLKS TO TALK TO... MORE TO ANSWER MY QUESTIONS...
"...MORE DEALERS WHO'LL SOON BE OFF THE STREETS!"
ROCK AND C & H-- CAPPED UP AND READY TO TRAVEL.
BLOOD MULE SAID YOUR STUFF'S GARBAGE, DUTCH!

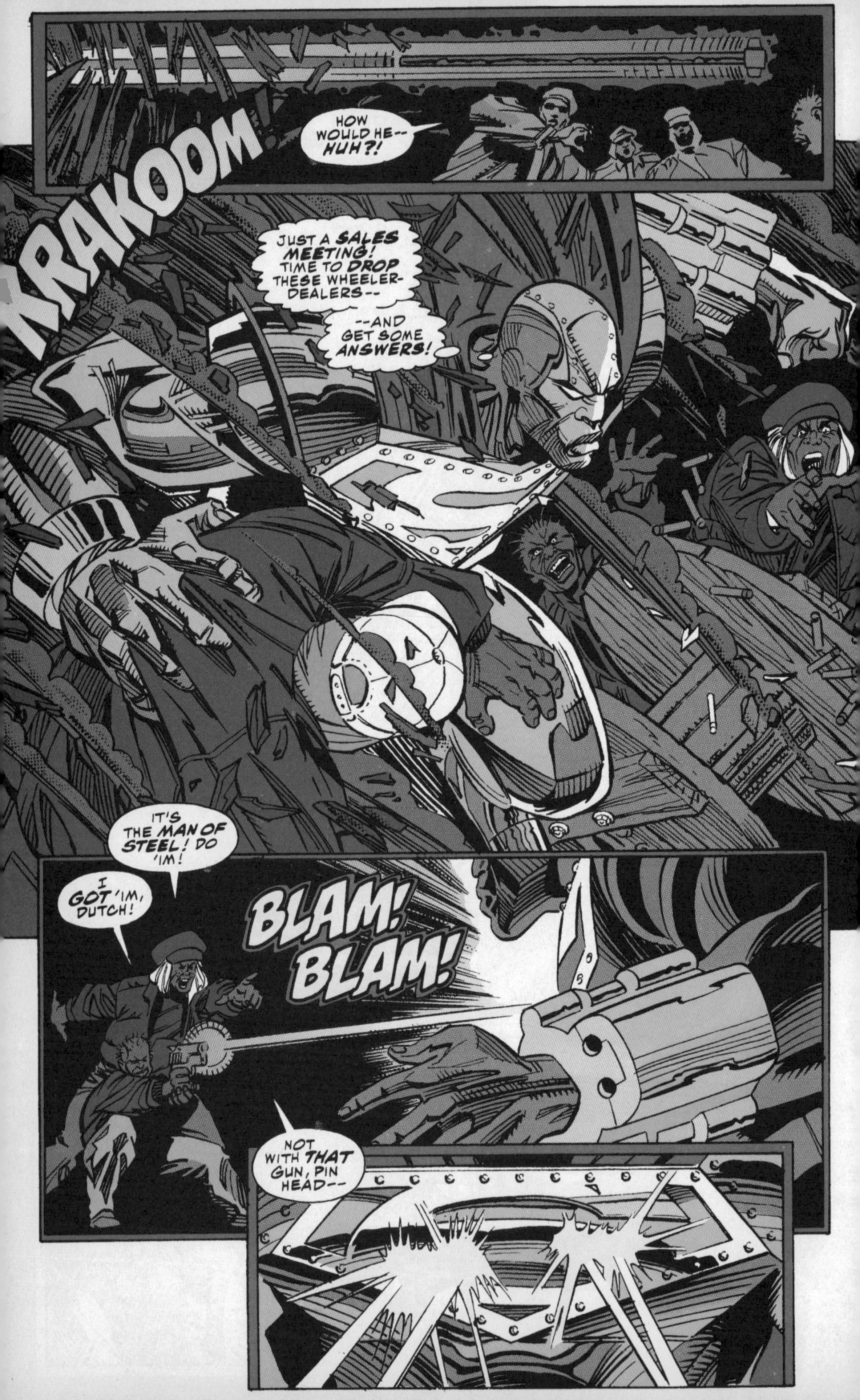
KRAKOOM!
HOW WOULD HE-- HUH?!
JUST A SALES MEETING! TIME TO DROP THESE WHEELER-DEALERS--
--AND GET SOME ANSWERS!
IT'S THE MAN OF STEEL! DO 'IM!
I GOT 'IM, DUTCH!
BLAM! BLAM!
NOT WITH THAT GUN, PIN HEAD--

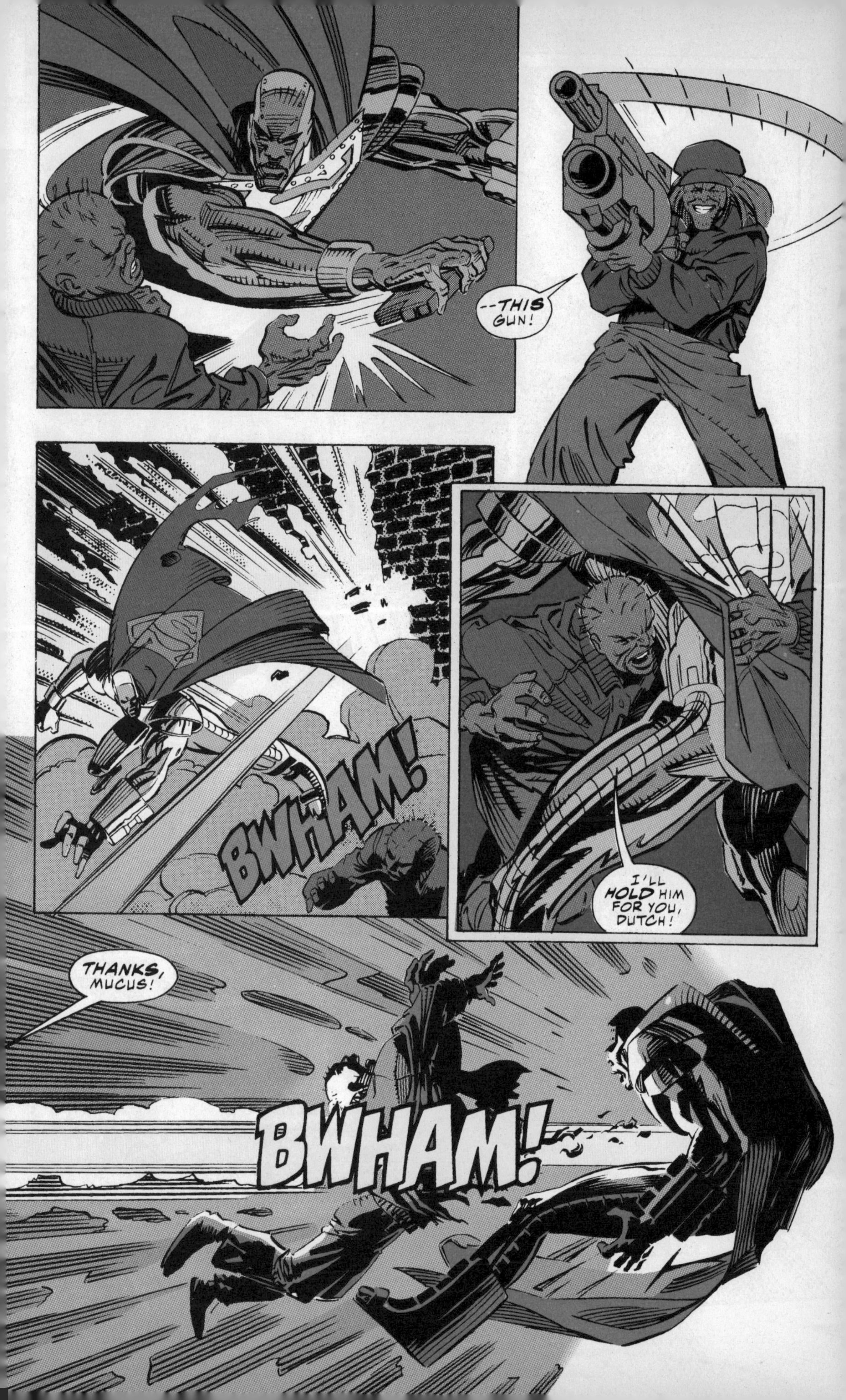
--THIS GUN!
BWHAM!
I'LL HOLD HIM FOR YOU, DUTCH!
THANKS, MUCUS!
BWHAM!

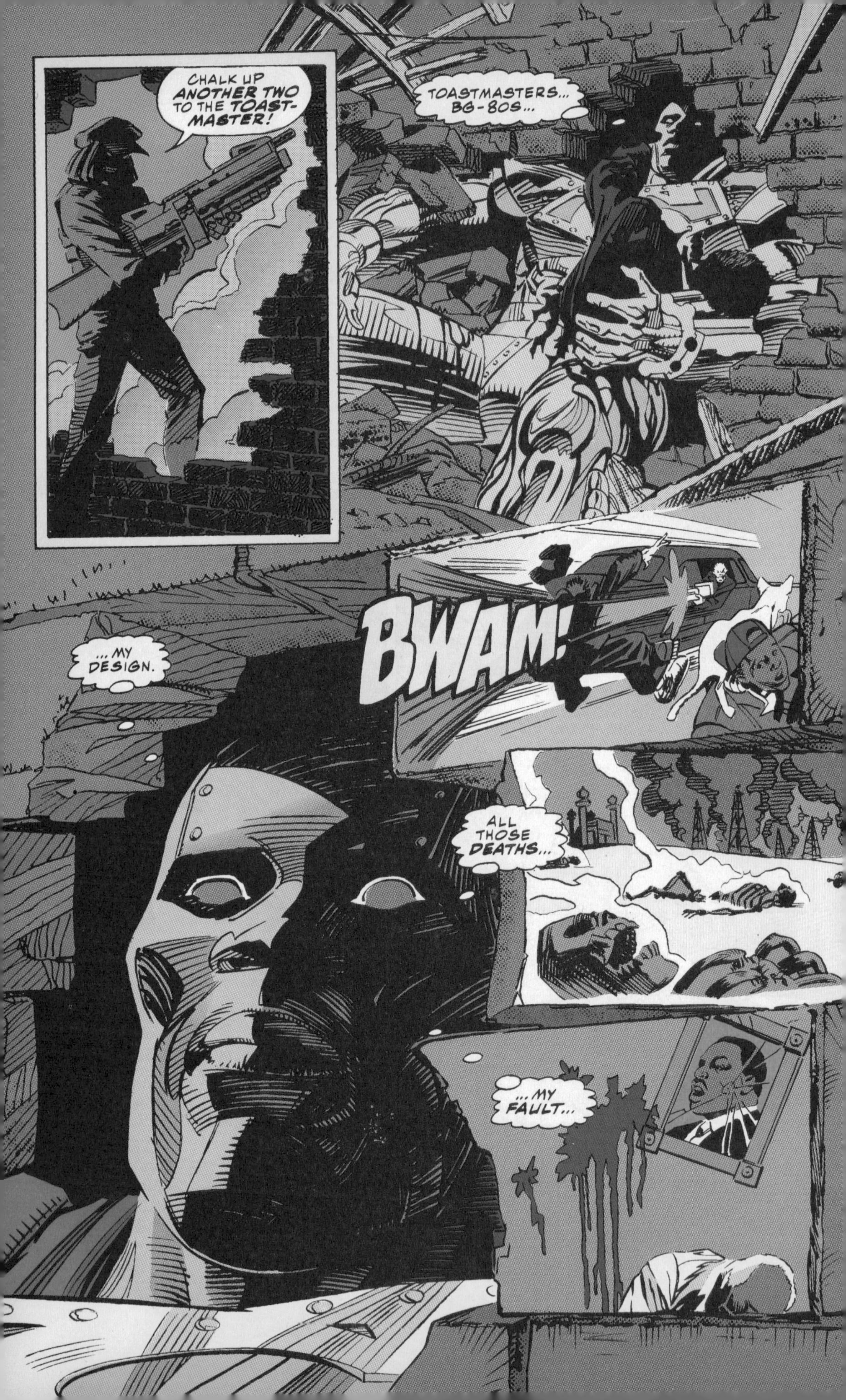

CHALK UP ANOTHER TWO TO THE TOAST-MASTER!
TOASTMASTERS... BG-80S...
BWAM!
... MY DESIGN.
ALL THOSE DEATHS...
... MY FAULT...

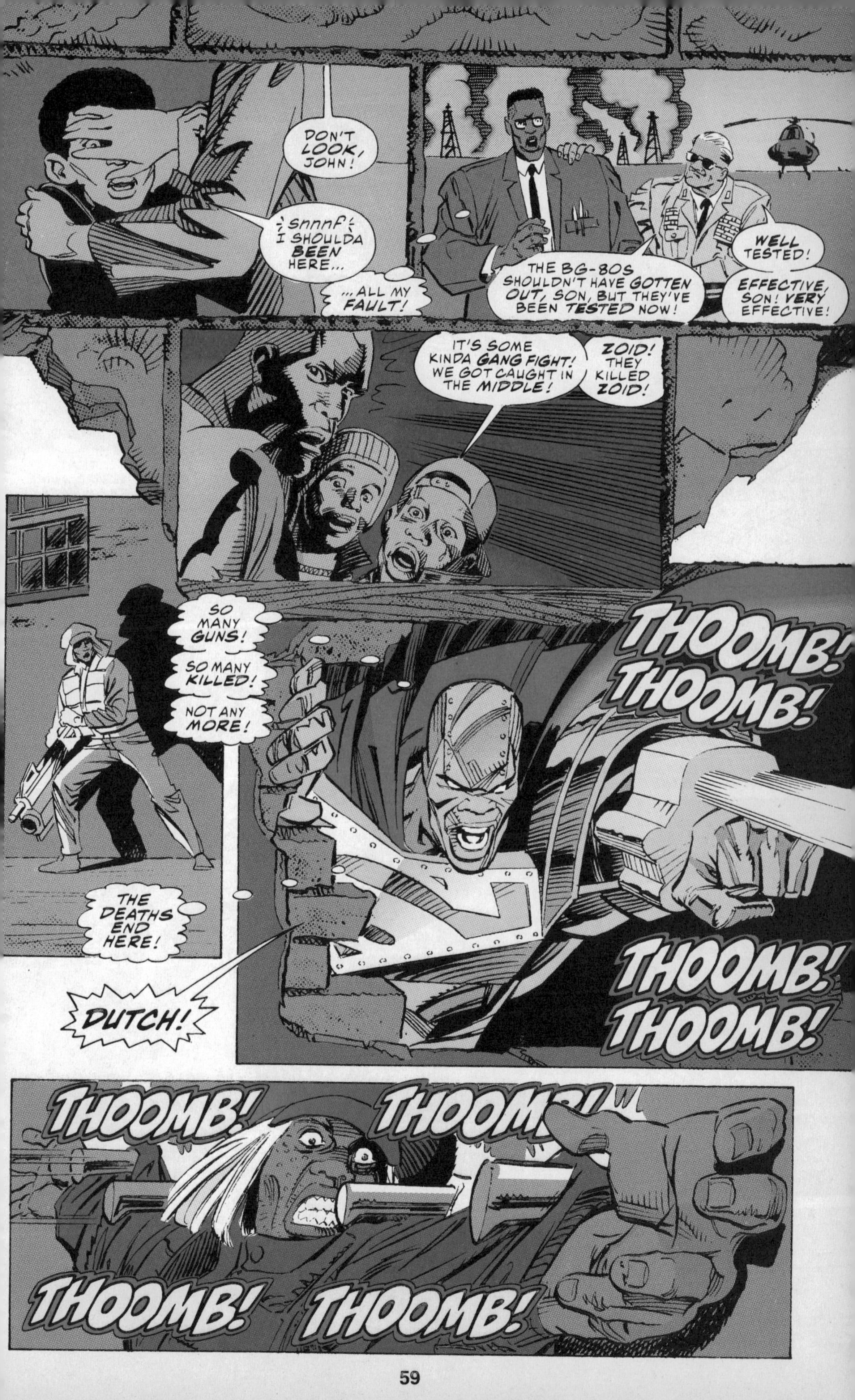
DON'T LOOK, JOHN!
Snnnf I SHOULDA BEEN HERE...
...ALL MY FAULT!
THE BG-80S SHOULDN'T HAVE GOTTEN OUT, SON, BUT THEY'VE BEEN TESTED NOW!
WELL TESTED!
EFFECTIVE, SON! VERY EFFECTIVE!
IT'S SOME KINDA GANG FIGHT! WE GOT CAUGHT IN THE MIDDLE!
ZOID! THEY KILLED ZOID!
SO MANY GUNS!
SO MANY KILLED!
NOT ANY MORE!
THE DEATHS END HERE!
DUTCH!
THOOMB! THOOMB!
THOOMB! THOOMB!
THOOMB!
THOOMB!
THOOMB!
THOOMB!

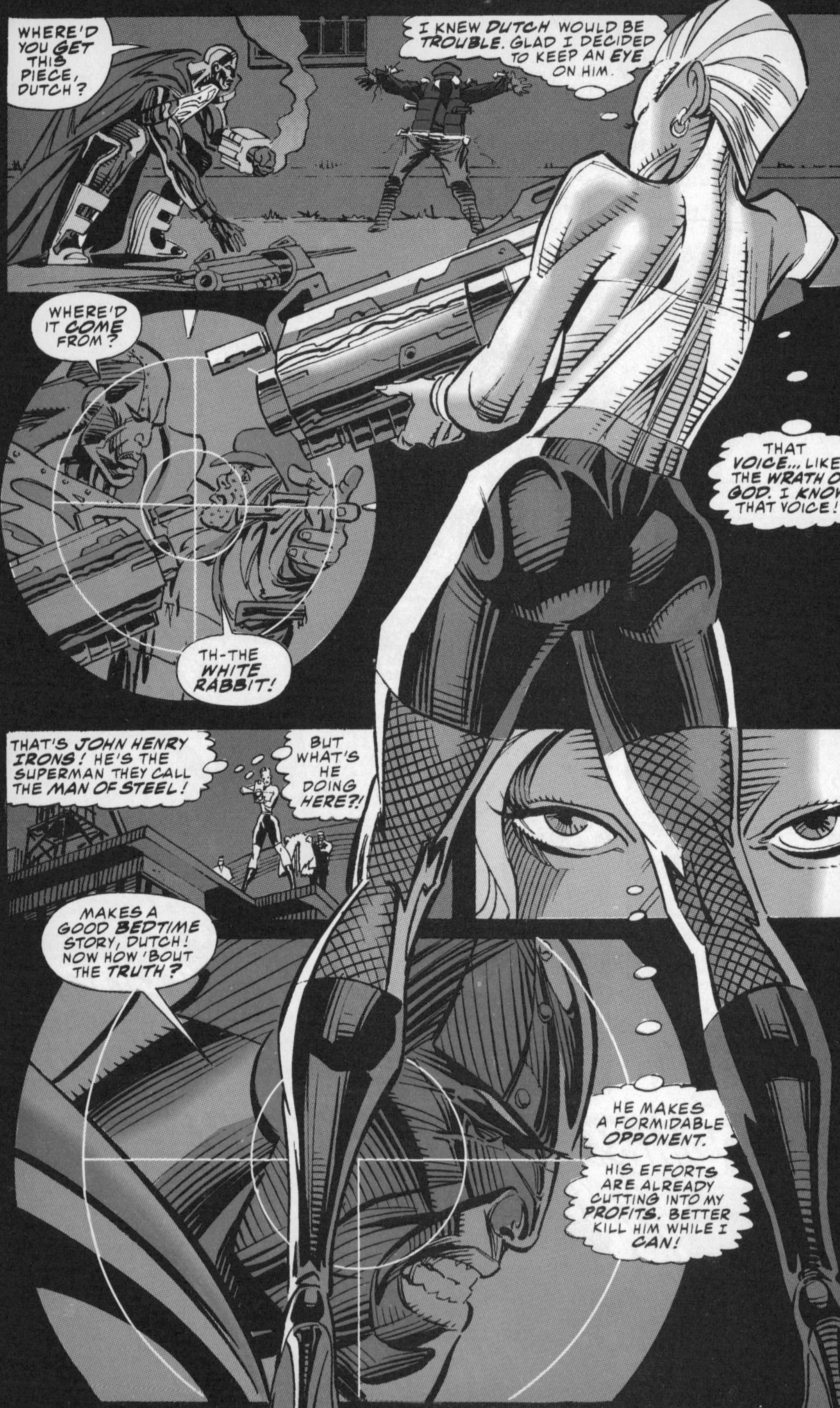
WHERE'D YOU GET THIS PIECE, DUTCH?
I KNEW DUTCH WOULD BE TROUBLE. GLAD I DECIDED TO KEEP AN EYE ON HIM.
WHERE'D IT COME FROM?
TH-THE WHITE RABBIT!
THAT VOICE... LIKE THE WRATH OF GOD. I KNOW THAT VOICE!
THAT'S JOHN HENRY IRONS! HE'S THE SUPERMAN THEY CALL THE MAN OF STEEL!
BUT WHAT'S HE DOING HERE?!
MAKES A GOOD BEDTIME STORY, DUTCH! NOW HOW 'BOUT THE TRUTH?
HE MAKES A FORMIDABLE OPPONENT.
HIS EFFORTS ARE ALREADY CUTTING INTO MY PROFITS. BETTER KILL HIM WHILE I CAN!

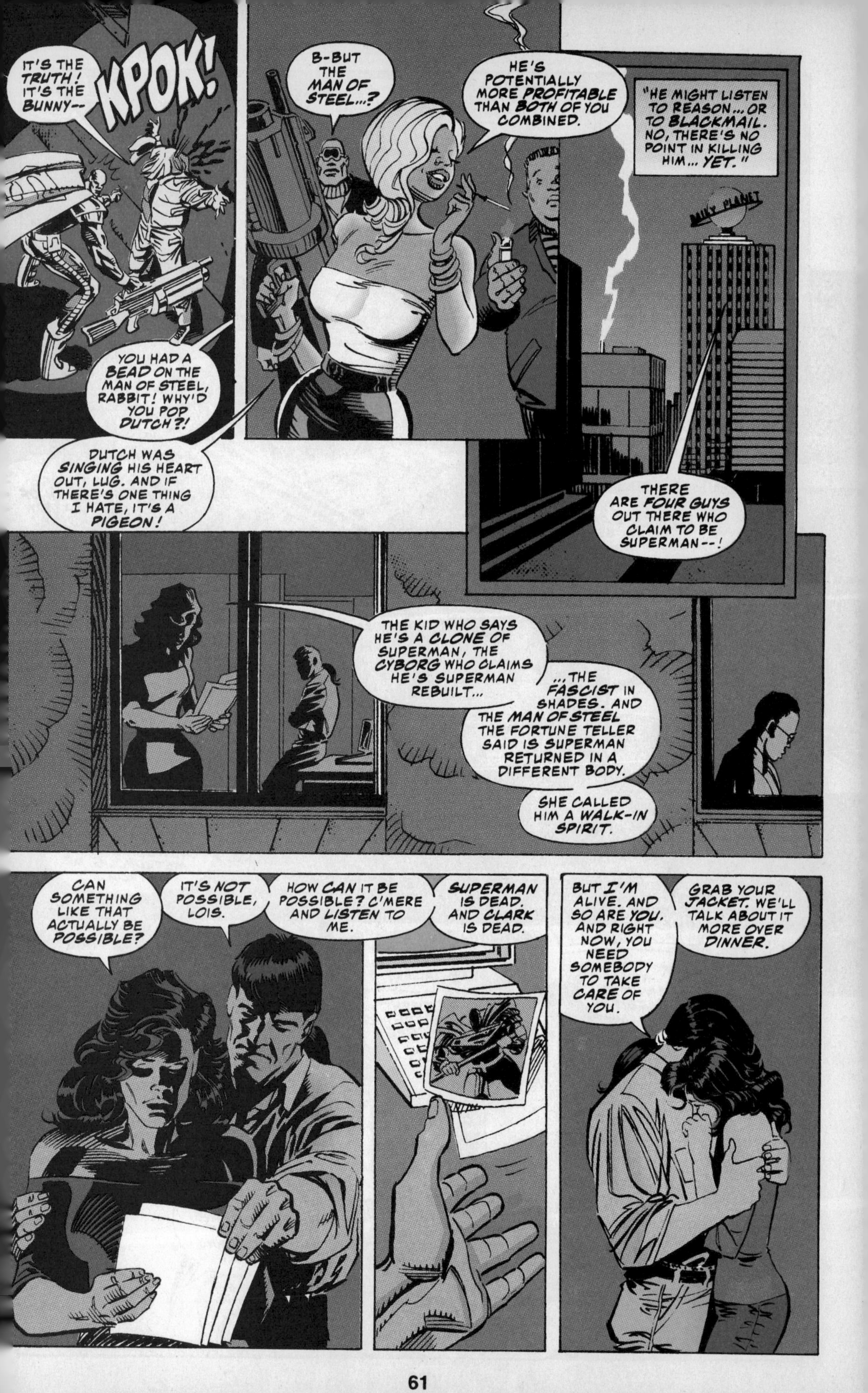
IT'S THE TRUTH! IT'S THE BUNNY--
KPOK!
YOU HAD A BEAD ON THE MAN OF STEEL, RABBIT! WHY'D YOU POP DUTCH?!
DUTCH WAS SINGING HIS HEART OUT, LUG. AND IF THERE'S ONE THING I HATE, IT'S A PIGEON!
B-BUT THE MAN OF STEEL...?
HE'S POTENTIALLY MORE PROFITABLE THAN BOTH OF YOU COMBINED.
"HE MIGHT LISTEN TO REASON... OR TO BLACKMAIL. NO, THERE'S NO POINT IN KILLING HIM... YET."
DAILY PLANET
THERE ARE FOUR GUYS OUT THERE WHO CLAIM TO BE SUPERMAN--!
THE KID WHO SAYS HE'S A CLONE OF SUPERMAN, THE CYBORG WHO CLAIMS HE'S SUPERMAN REBUILT...
...THE FASCIST IN SHADES. AND THE MAN OF STEEL THE FORTUNE TELLER SAID IS SUPERMAN RETURNED IN A DIFFERENT BODY.
SHE CALLED HIM A WALK-IN SPIRIT.
CAN SOMETHING LIKE THAT ACTUALLY BE POSSIBLE?
IT'S NOT POSSIBLE, LOIS.
HOW CAN IT BE POSSIBLE? C'MERE AND LISTEN TO ME.
SUPERMAN IS DEAD. AND CLARK IS DEAD.
BUT I'M ALIVE. AND SO ARE YOU. AND RIGHT NOW, YOU NEED SOMEBODY TO TAKE CARE OF YOU.
GRAB YOUR JACKET. WE'LL TALK ABOUT IT MORE OVER DINNER.

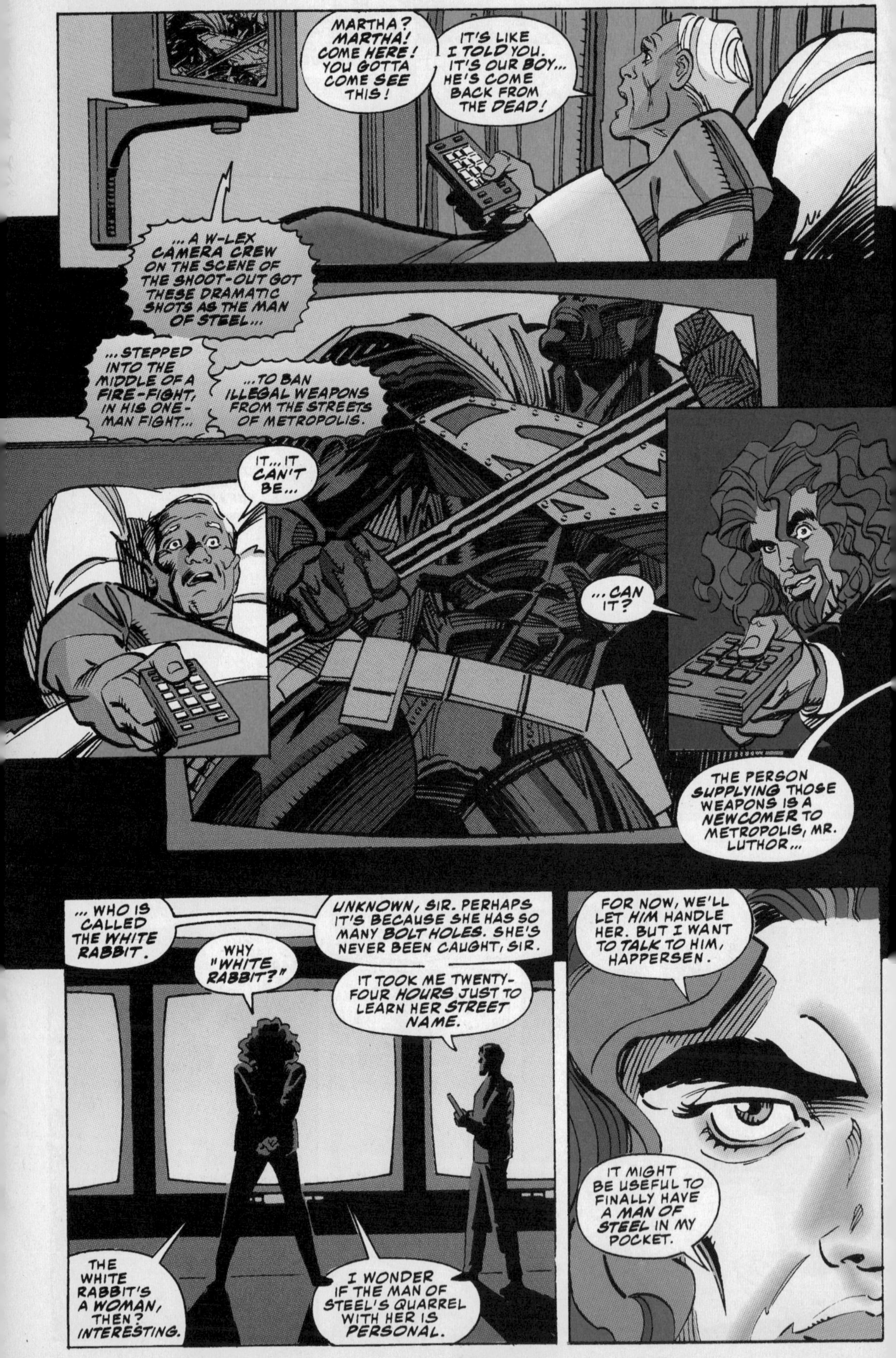
MARTHA? MARTHA! COME HERE! YOU GOTTA COME SEE THIS!
IT'S LIKE I TOLD YOU. IT'S OUR BOY... HE'S COME BACK FROM THE DEAD!
...A W-LEX CAMERA CREW ON THE SCENE OF THE SHOOT-OUT GOT THESE DRAMATIC SHOTS AS THE MAN OF STEEL...
...STEPPED INTO THE MIDDLE OF A FIRE-FIGHT, IN HIS ONE-MAN FIGHT...
...TO BAN ILLEGAL WEAPONS FROM THE STREETS OF METROPOLIS.
IT... IT CAN'T BE...
...CAN IT?
THE PERSON SUPPLYING THOSE WEAPONS IS A NEWCOMER TO METROPOLIS, MR. LUTHOR...
...WHO IS CALLED THE WHITE RABBIT.
WHY "WHITE RABBIT?"
UNKNOWN, SIR. PERHAPS IT'S BECAUSE SHE HAS SO MANY BOLT HOLES. SHE'S NEVER BEEN CAUGHT, SIR.
IT TOOK ME TWENTY-FOUR HOURS JUST TO LEARN HER STREET NAME.
THE WHITE RABBIT'S A WOMAN, THEN? INTERESTING.
I WONDER IF THE MAN OF STEEL'S QUARREL WITH HER IS PERSONAL.
FOR NOW, WE'LL LET HIM HANDLE HER. BUT I WANT TO TALK TO HIM, HAPPERSEN.
IT MIGHT BE USEFUL TO FINALLY HAVE A MAN OF STEEL IN MY POCKET.

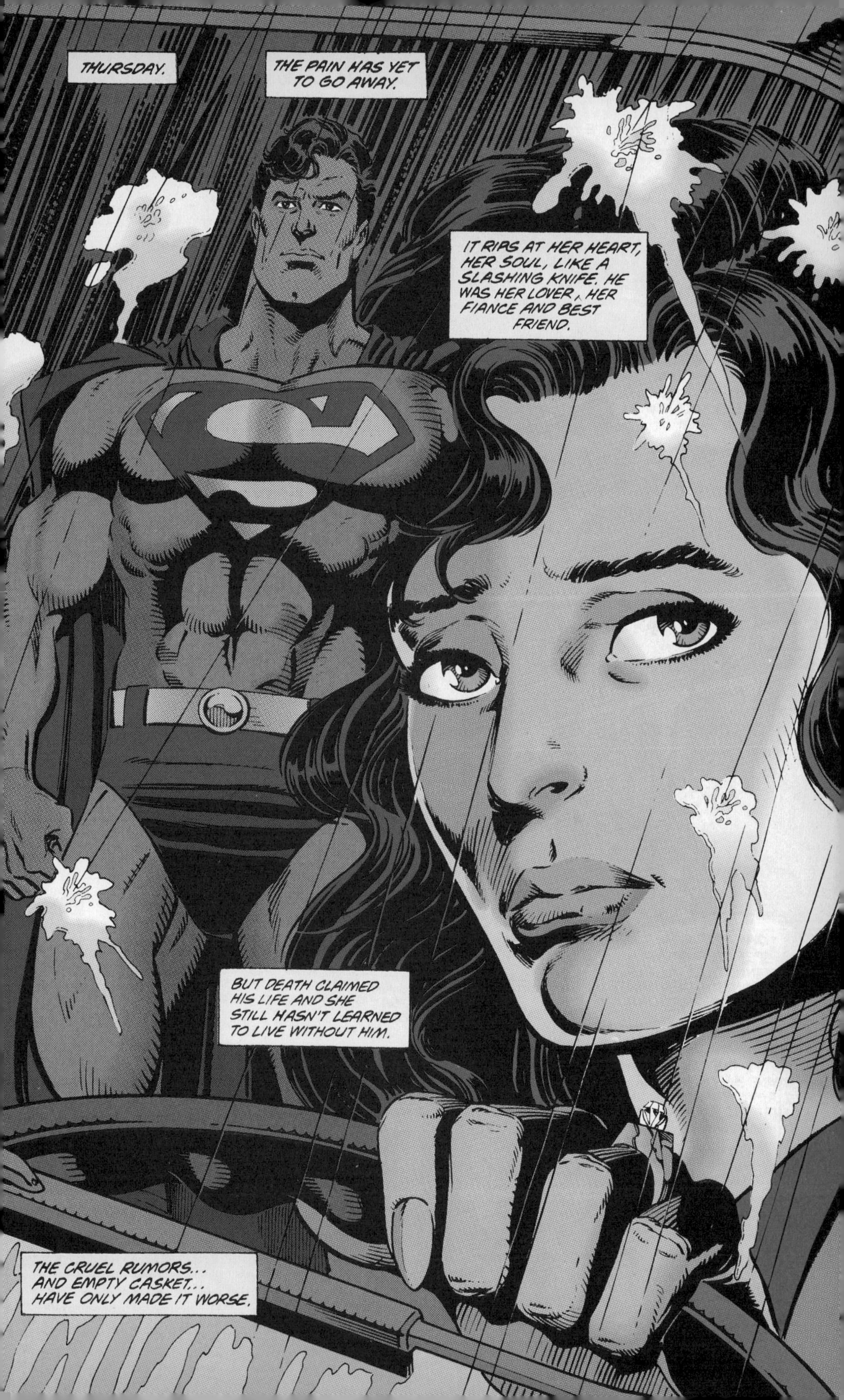
THURSDAY.
THE PAIN HAS YET TO GO AWAY.
IT RIPS AT HER HEART, HER SOUL, LIKE A SLASHING KNIFE. HE WAS HER LOVER, HER FIANCE AND BEST FRIEND.
BUT DEATH CLAIMED HIS LIFE AND SHE STILL HASN'T LEARNED TO LIVE WITHOUT HIM.
THE CRUEL RUMORS... AND EMPTY CASKET... HAVE ONLY MADE IT WORSE.

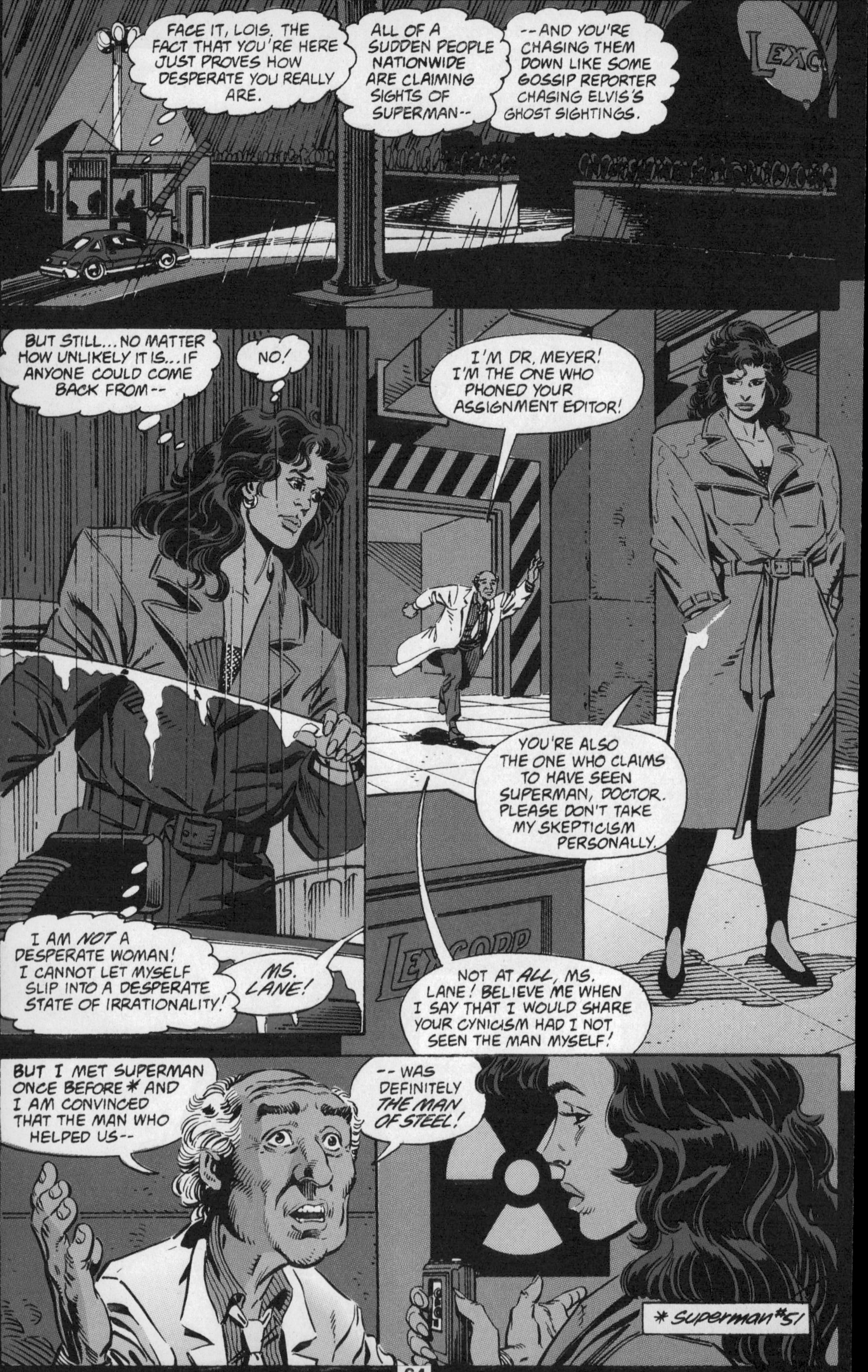
FACE IT, LOIS. THE FACT THAT YOU'RE HERE JUST PROVES HOW DESPERATE YOU REALLY ARE.
ALL OF A SUDDEN PEOPLE NATIONWIDE ARE CLAIMING SIGHTS OF SUPERMAN--
--AND YOU'RE CHASING THEM DOWN LIKE SOME GOSSIP REPORTER CHASING ELVIS'S GHOST SIGHTINGS.
BUT STILL... NO MATTER HOW UNLIKELY IT IS... IF ANYONE COULD COME BACK FROM--
NO!
I AM *NOT* A DESPERATE WOMAN! I CANNOT LET MYSELF SLIP INTO A DESPERATE STATE OF IRRATIONALITY!
MS. LANE!
I'M DR. MEYER! I'M THE ONE WHO PHONED YOUR ASSIGNMENT EDITOR!
YOU'RE ALSO THE ONE WHO CLAIMS TO HAVE SEEN SUPERMAN, DOCTOR. PLEASE DON'T TAKE MY SKEPTICISM PERSONALLY.
LEXCORP
NOT AT *ALL*, MS. LANE! BELIEVE ME WHEN I SAY THAT I WOULD SHARE YOUR CYNICISM HAD I NOT SEEN THE MAN MYSELF!
BUT I MET SUPERMAN ONCE BEFORE* AND I AM CONVINCED THAT THE MAN WHO HELPED US--
--WAS DEFINITELY *THE MAN OF STEEL!*
* Superman #51

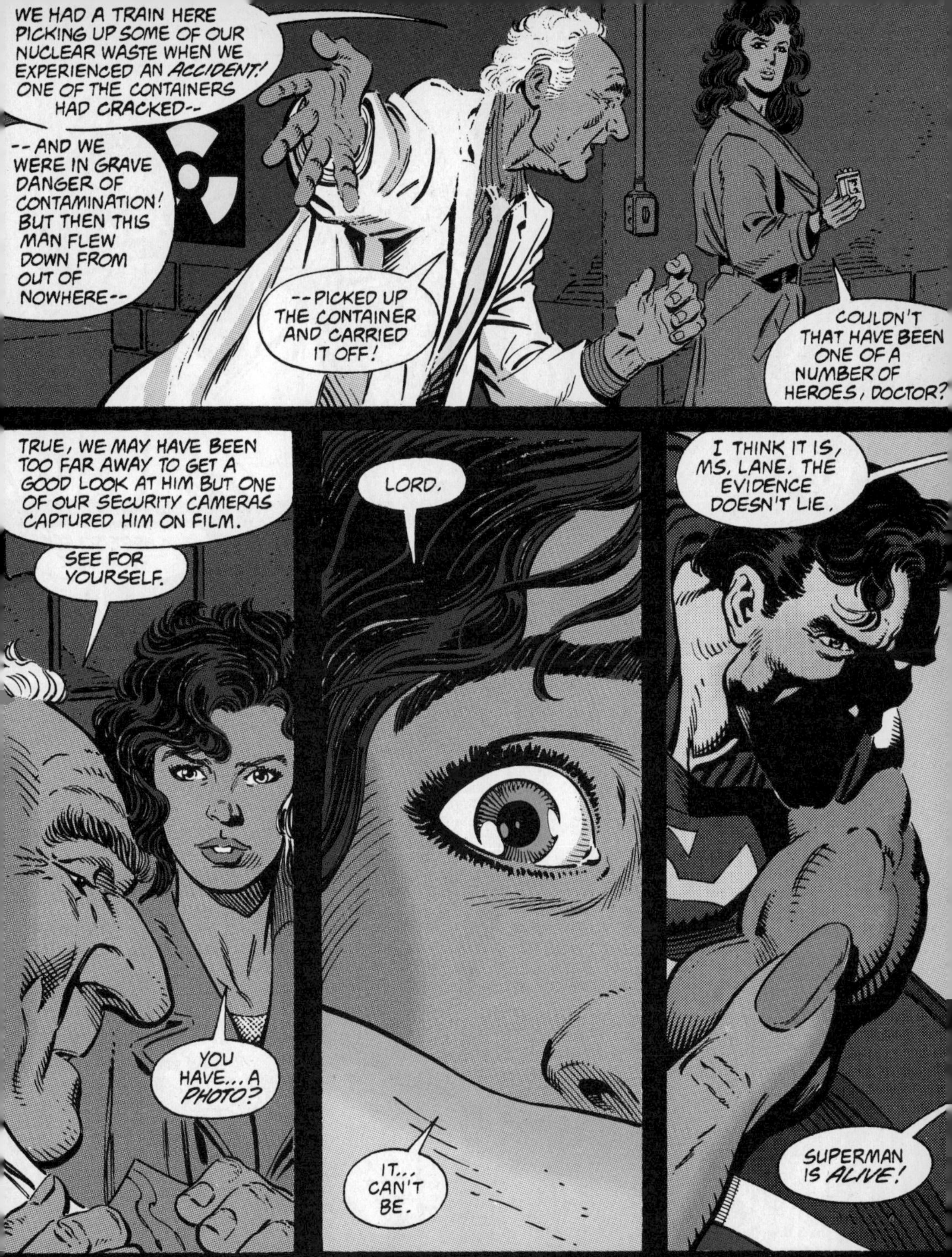
WE HAD A TRAIN HERE PICKING UP SOME OF OUR NUCLEAR WASTE WHEN WE EXPERIENCED AN ACCIDENT! ONE OF THE CONTAINERS HAD CRACKED--
--AND WE WERE IN GRAVE DANGER OF CONTAMINATION! BUT THEN THIS MAN FLEW DOWN FROM OUT OF NOWHERE--
--PICKED UP THE CONTAINER AND CARRIED IT OFF!
COULDN'T THAT HAVE BEEN ONE OF A NUMBER OF HEROES, DOCTOR?
TRUE, WE MAY HAVE BEEN TOO FAR AWAY TO GET A GOOD LOOK AT HIM BUT ONE OF OUR SECURITY CAMERAS CAPTURED HIM ON FILM.
SEE FOR YOURSELF.
YOU HAVE... A PHOTO?
LORD.
IT... CAN'T BE.
I THINK IT IS, MS. LANE. THE EVIDENCE DOESN'T LIE.
SUPERMAN IS ALIVE!

ALIVE

DAN JURGENS story & layout
BRETT BREEDING finished art
JOHN COSTANZA letterer
GLENN WHITMORE colorist
JENNIFER FRANK assistant editor
MIKE CARLIN editor
Superman created by
Jerry Siegel and Joe Shuster

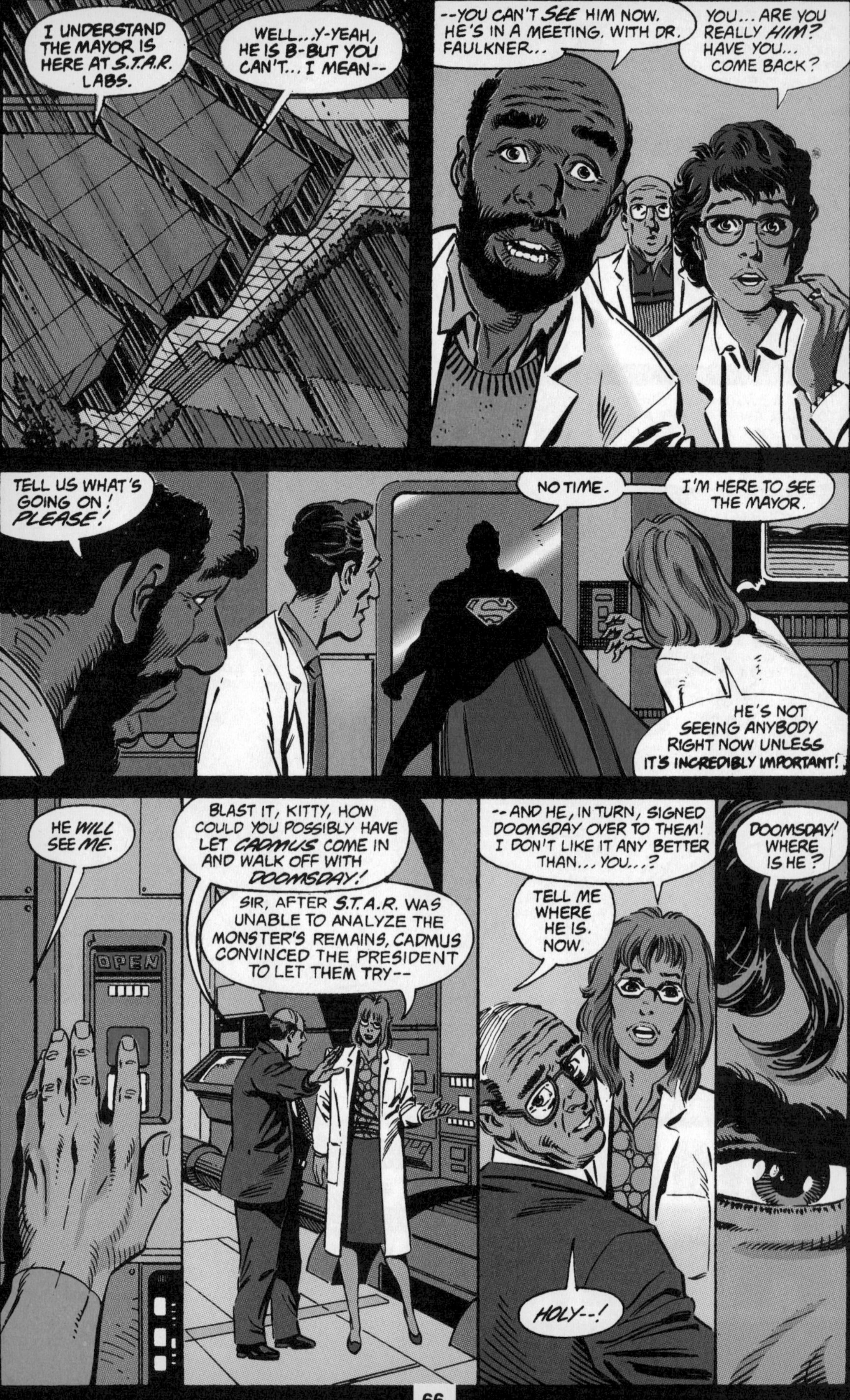
I UNDERSTAND THE MAYOR IS HERE AT S.T.A.R. LABS.
WELL...Y-YEAH, HE IS B-BUT YOU CAN'T... I MEAN--
--YOU CAN'T SEE HIM NOW. HE'S IN A MEETING. WITH DR. FAULKNER...
YOU... ARE YOU REALLY HIM? HAVE YOU... COME BACK?
TELL US WHAT'S GOING ON! PLEASE!
NO TIME.
I'M HERE TO SEE THE MAYOR.
HE'S NOT SEEING ANYBODY RIGHT NOW UNLESS IT'S INCREDIBLY IMPORTANT!
HE WILL SEE ME.
OPEN
BLAST IT, KITTY, HOW COULD YOU POSSIBLY HAVE LET CADMUS COME IN AND WALK OFF WITH DOOMSDAY!
SIR, AFTER S.T.A.R. WAS UNABLE TO ANALYZE THE MONSTER'S REMAINS, CADMUS CONVINCED THE PRESIDENT TO LET THEM TRY--
--AND HE, IN TURN, SIGNED DOOMSDAY OVER TO THEM! I DON'T LIKE IT ANY BETTER THAN... YOU...?
TELL ME WHERE HE IS. NOW.
HOLY--!
DOOMSDAY! WHERE IS HE?

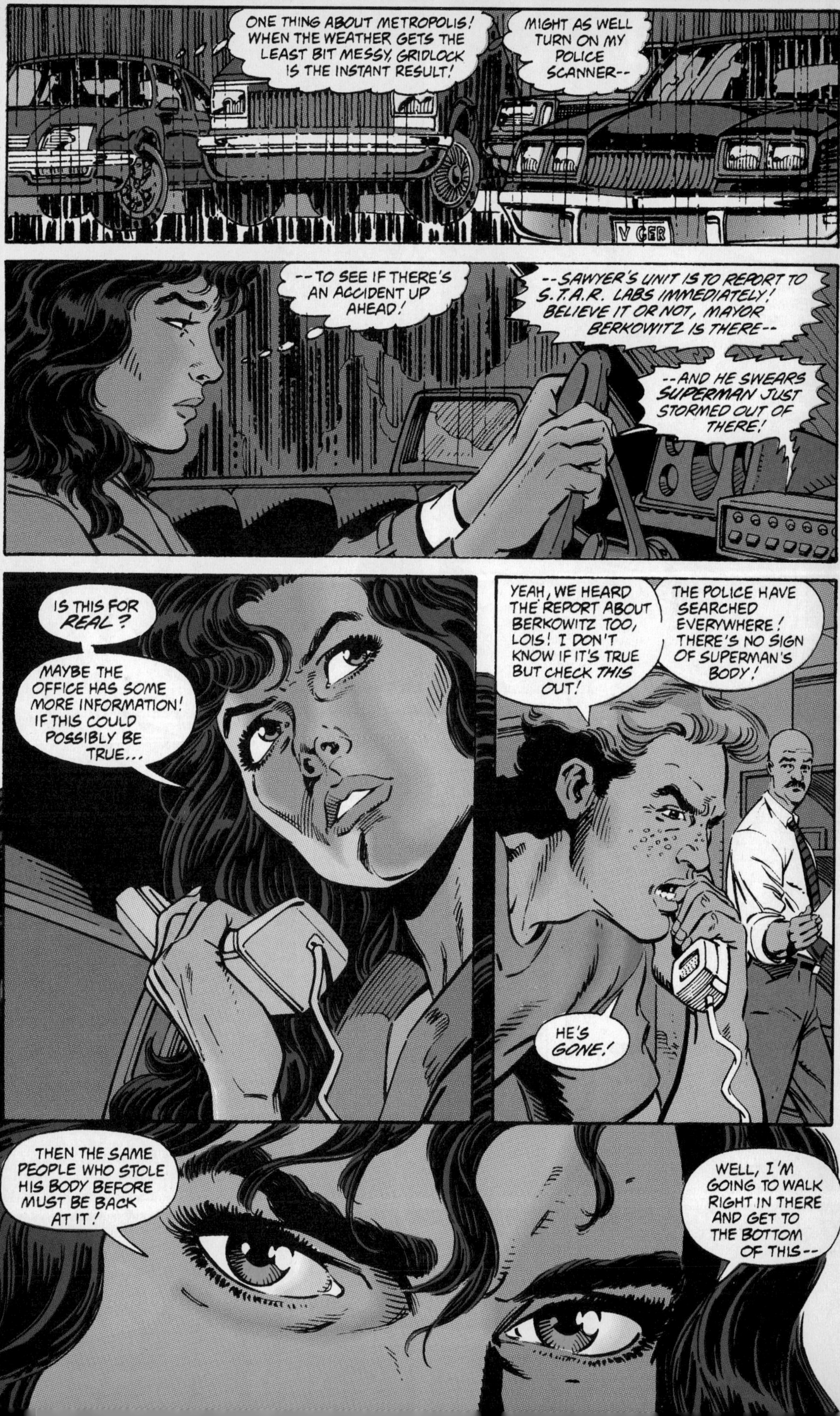
ONE THING ABOUT METROPOLIS! WHEN THE WEATHER GETS THE LEAST BIT MESSY, GRIDLOCK IS THE INSTANT RESULT!
MIGHT AS WELL TURN ON MY POLICE SCANNER--
V GER
--TO SEE IF THERE'S AN ACCIDENT UP AHEAD!
--SAWYER'S UNIT IS TO REPORT TO S.T.A.R. LABS IMMEDIATELY! BELIEVE IT OR NOT, MAYOR BERKOWITZ IS THERE--
--AND HE SWEARS SUPERMAN JUST STORMED OUT OF THERE!
IS THIS FOR REAL?
MAYBE THE OFFICE HAS SOME MORE INFORMATION! IF THIS COULD POSSIBLY BE TRUE...
YEAH, WE HEARD THE REPORT ABOUT BERKOWITZ TOO, LOIS! I DON'T KNOW IF IT'S TRUE BUT CHECK THIS OUT!
THE POLICE HAVE SEARCHED EVERYWHERE! THERE'S NO SIGN OF SUPERMAN'S BODY!
HE'S GONE!
THEN THE SAME PEOPLE WHO STOLE HIS BODY BEFORE MUST BE BACK AT IT!
WELL, I'M GOING TO WALK RIGHT IN THERE AND GET TO THE BOTTOM OF THIS--

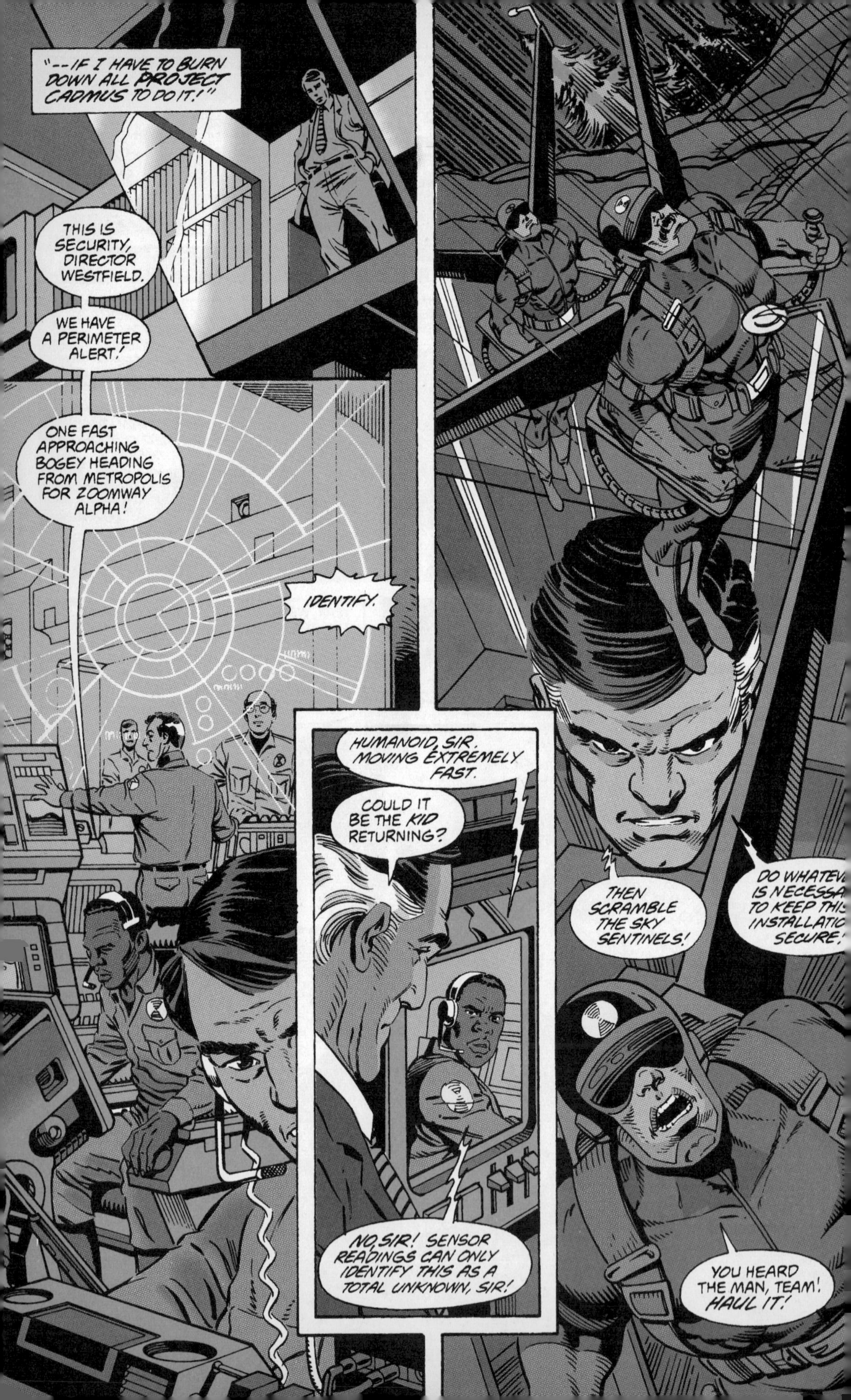
"--IF I HAVE TO BURN DOWN ALL PROJECT CADMUS TO DO IT!"
THIS IS SECURITY, DIRECTOR WESTFIELD.
WE HAVE A PERIMETER ALERT!
ONE FAST APPROACHING BOGEY HEADING FROM METROPOLIS FOR ZOOMWAY ALPHA!
IDENTIFY.
HUMANOID, SIR. MOVING EXTREMELY FAST.
COULD IT BE THE KID RETURNING?
NO, SIR! SENSOR READINGS CAN ONLY IDENTIFY THIS AS A TOTAL UNKNOWN, SIR!
THEN SCRAMBLE THE SKY SENTINELS!
YOU HEARD THE MAN, TEAM! HAUL IT!

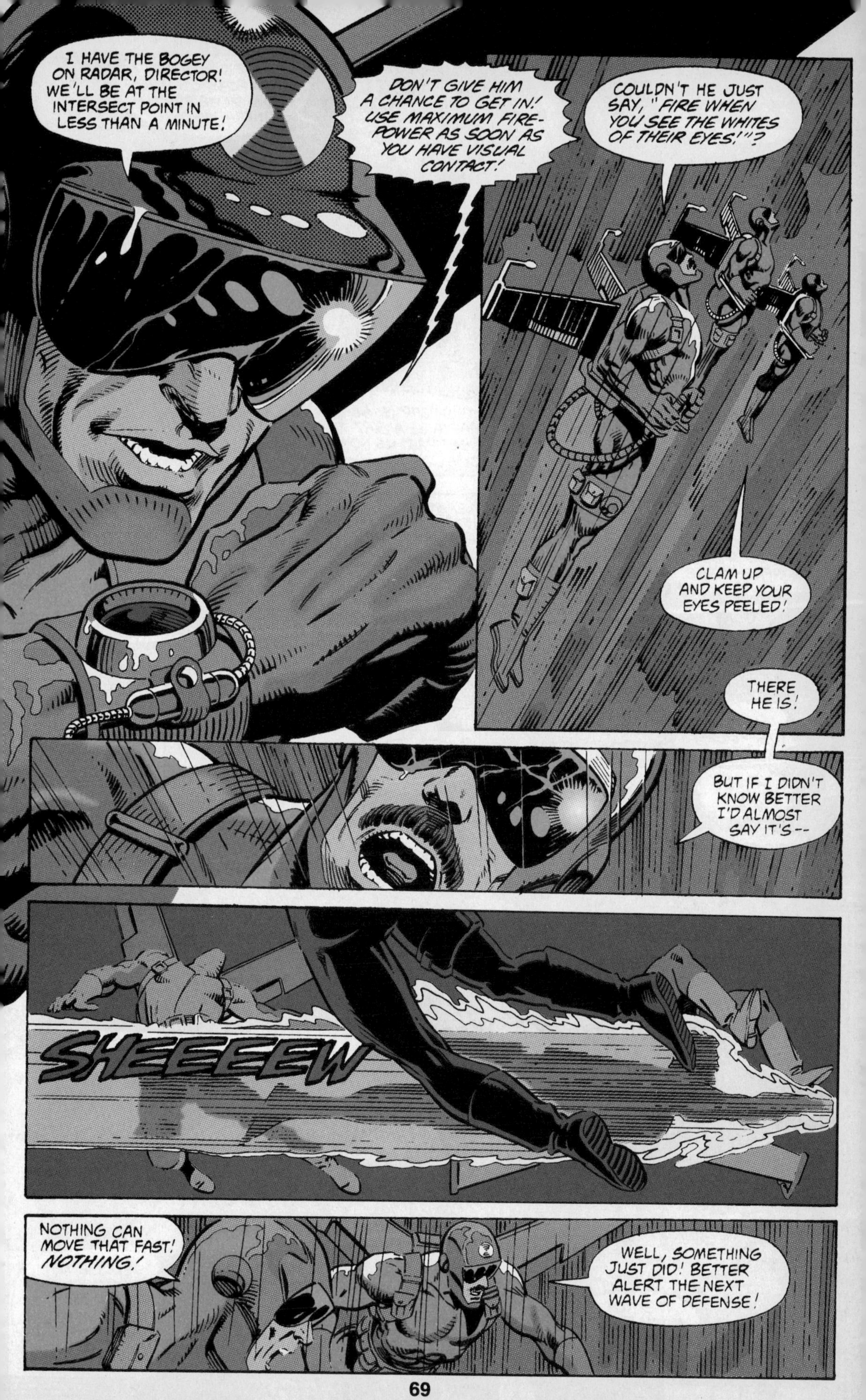
I HAVE THE BOGEY ON RADAR, DIRECTOR! WE'LL BE AT THE INTERSECT POINT IN LESS THAN A MINUTE!
DON'T GIVE HIM A CHANCE TO GET IN! USE MAXIMUM FIRE-POWER AS SOON AS YOU HAVE VISUAL CONTACT!
COULDN'T HE JUST SAY, "FIRE WHEN YOU SEE THE WHITES OF THEIR EYES!"?
CLAM UP AND KEEP YOUR EYES PEELED!
THERE HE IS!
BUT IF I DIDN'T KNOW BETTER I'D ALMOST SAY IT'S--
SHEEEEEW
NOTHING CAN MOVE THAT FAST! NOTHING!
WELL, SOMETHING JUST DID! BETTER ALERT THE NEXT WAVE OF DEFENSE!

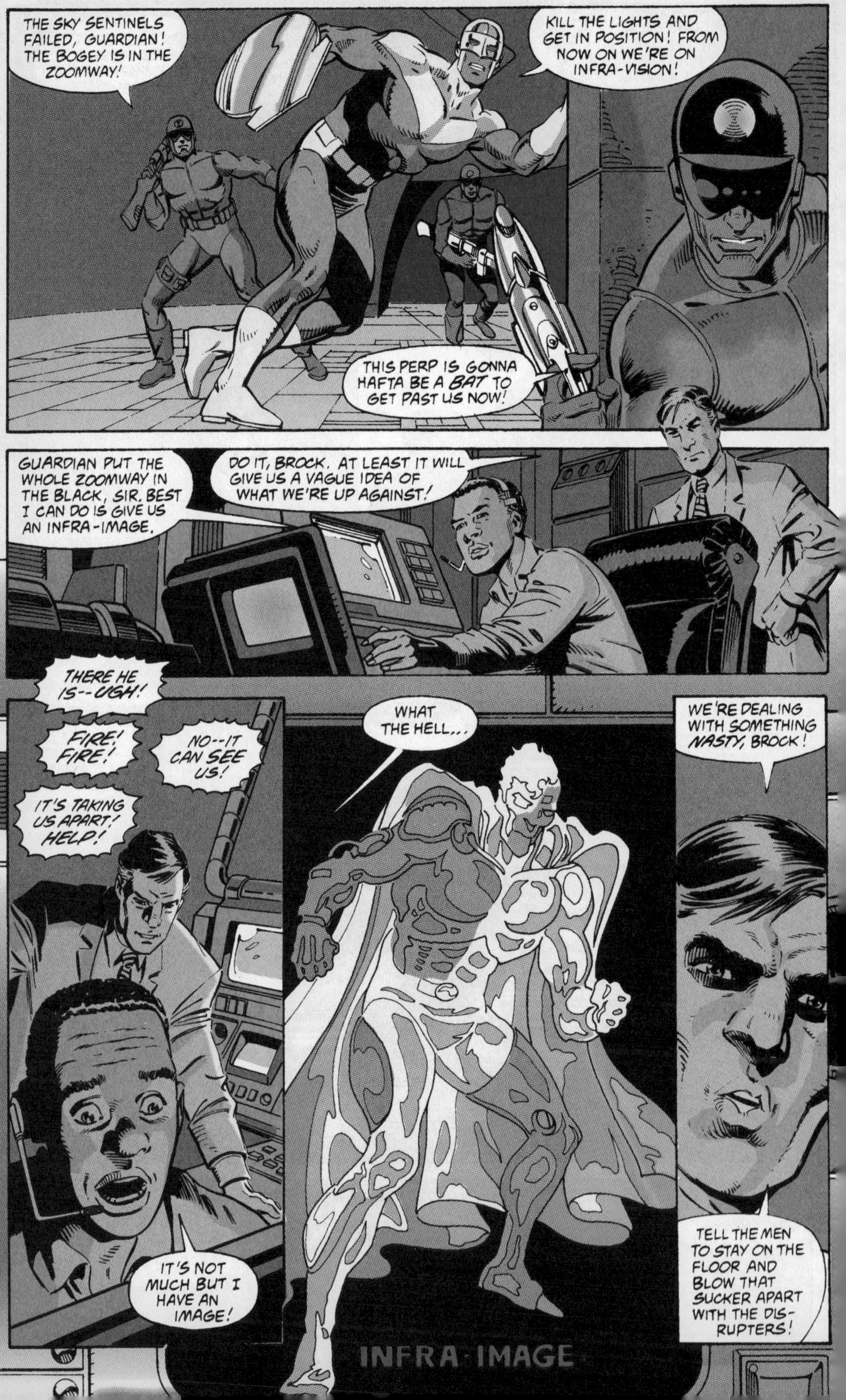
THE SKY SENTINELS FAILED, GUARDIAN! THE BOGEY IS IN THE ZOOMWAY!
KILL THE LIGHTS AND GET IN POSITION! FROM NOW ON WE'RE ON INFRA-VISION!
THIS PERP IS GONNA HAFTA BE A BAT TO GET PAST US NOW!
GUARDIAN PUT THE WHOLE ZOOMWAY IN THE BLACK, SIR. BEST I CAN DO IS GIVE US AN INFRA-IMAGE.
DO IT, BROCK. AT LEAST IT WILL GIVE US A VAGUE IDEA OF WHAT WE'RE UP AGAINST!
THERE HE IS--UGH!
FIRE! FIRE!
NO--IT CAN SEE US!
IT'S TAKING US APART! HELP!
IT'S NOT MUCH BUT I HAVE AN IMAGE!
WHAT THE HELL...
WE'RE DEALING WITH SOMETHING NASTY, BROCK!
TELL THE MEN TO STAY ON THE FLOOR AND BLOW THAT SUCKER APART WITH THE DIS-RUPTERS!
INFRA-IMAGE

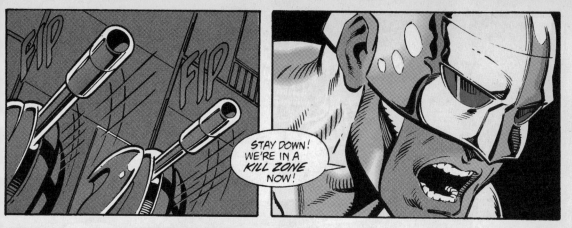

STAY DOWN! WE'RE IN A *KILL ZONE* NOW!

FIRE!

MAXIMUM POWER ON TARGET! THIS'LL SHAKE HIM APART FOR SURE!

YOUR WEAPONS CAN'T HURT ME! GIVE ME WHAT I WANT AND I'LL LEAVE!

DAMN! TURN THE LIGHTS BACK ON SO I CAN SEE WHO I'M UP AGAINST!

THERE'S NO WAY YOU'RE GOING TO STOP ME!

KCHUNNG

I'VE COME FOR *DOOMSDAY!*

IT.... CAN'T.... BE...

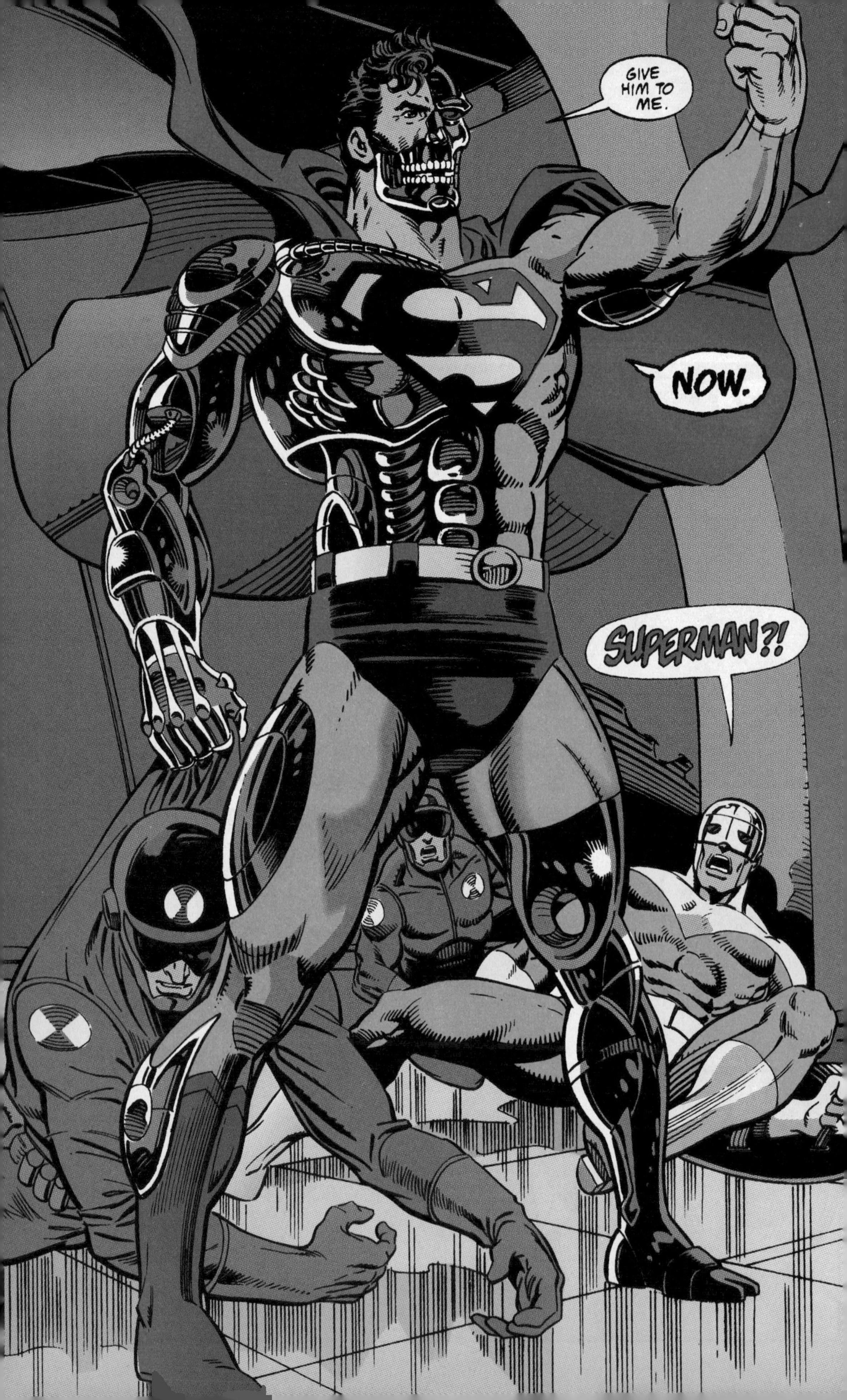
GIVE HIM TO ME.
NOW.
SUPERMAN?!

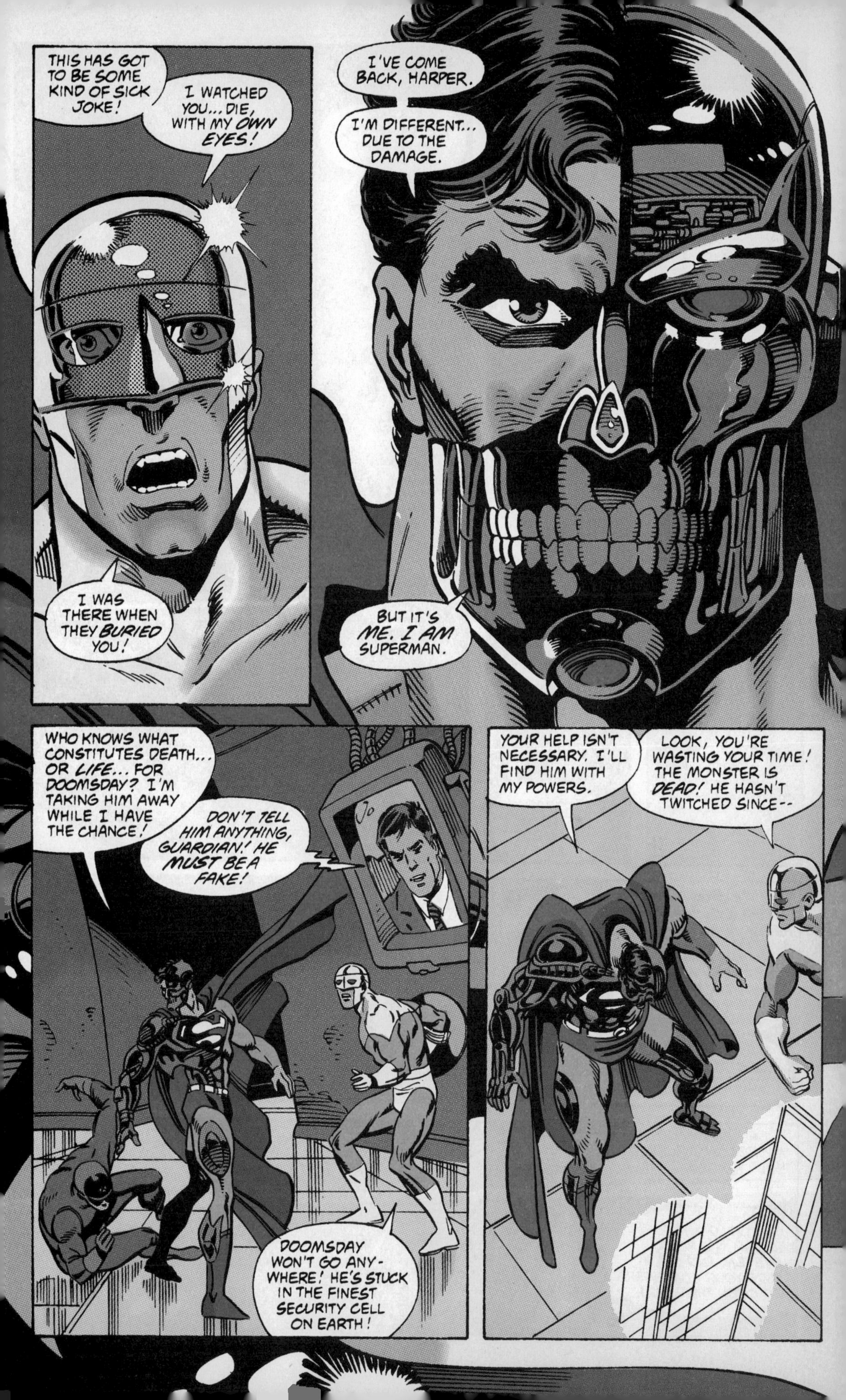
THIS HAS GOT TO BE SOME KIND OF SICK JOKE!
I WATCHED YOU... DIE, WITH MY OWN EYES!
I WAS THERE WHEN THEY BURIED YOU!
I'VE COME BACK, HARPER.
I'M DIFFERENT... DUE TO THE DAMAGE.
BUT IT'S ME. I AM SUPERMAN.
WHO KNOWS WHAT CONSTITUTES DEATH... OR LIFE... FOR DOOMSDAY? I'M TAKING HIM AWAY WHILE I HAVE THE CHANCE!
DON'T TELL HIM ANYTHING, GUARDIAN! HE MUST BE A FAKE!
DOOMSDAY WON'T GO ANY-WHERE! HE'S STUCK IN THE FINEST SECURITY CELL ON EARTH!
YOUR HELP ISN'T NECESSARY. I'LL FIND HIM WITH MY POWERS.
LOOK, YOU'RE WASTING YOUR TIME! THE MONSTER IS DEAD! HE HASN'T TWITCHED SINCE--

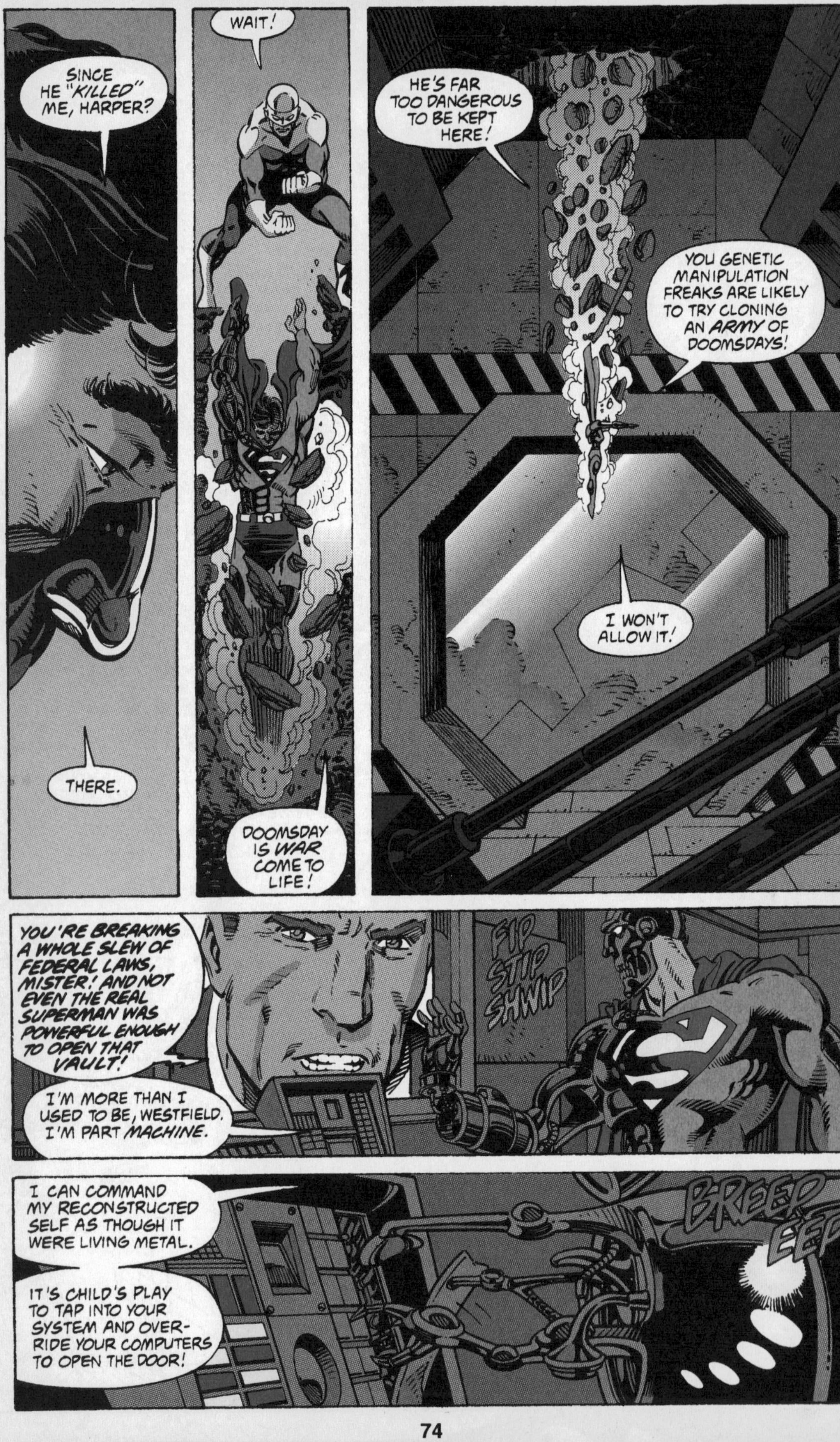

SINCE HE "KILLED" ME, HARPER?
THERE.
WAIT!
DOOMSDAY IS WAR COME TO LIFE!
HE'S FAR TOO DANGEROUS TO BE KEPT HERE!
YOU GENETIC MANIPULATION FREAKS ARE LIKELY TO TRY CLONING AN ARMY OF DOOMSDAYS!
I WON'T ALLOW IT!
YOU'RE BREAKING A WHOLE SLEW OF FEDERAL LAWS, MISTER! AND NOT EVEN THE REAL SUPERMAN WAS POWERFUL ENOUGH TO OPEN THAT VAULT!
FIP
STIP
SHWIP
I'M MORE THAN I USED TO BE, WESTFIELD. I'M PART MACHINE.
I CAN COMMAND MY RECONSTRUCTED SELF AS THOUGH IT WERE LIVING METAL.
IT'S CHILD'S PLAY TO TAP INTO YOUR SYSTEM AND OVER-RIDE YOUR COMPUTERS TO OPEN THE DOOR!
BREEP
EEP

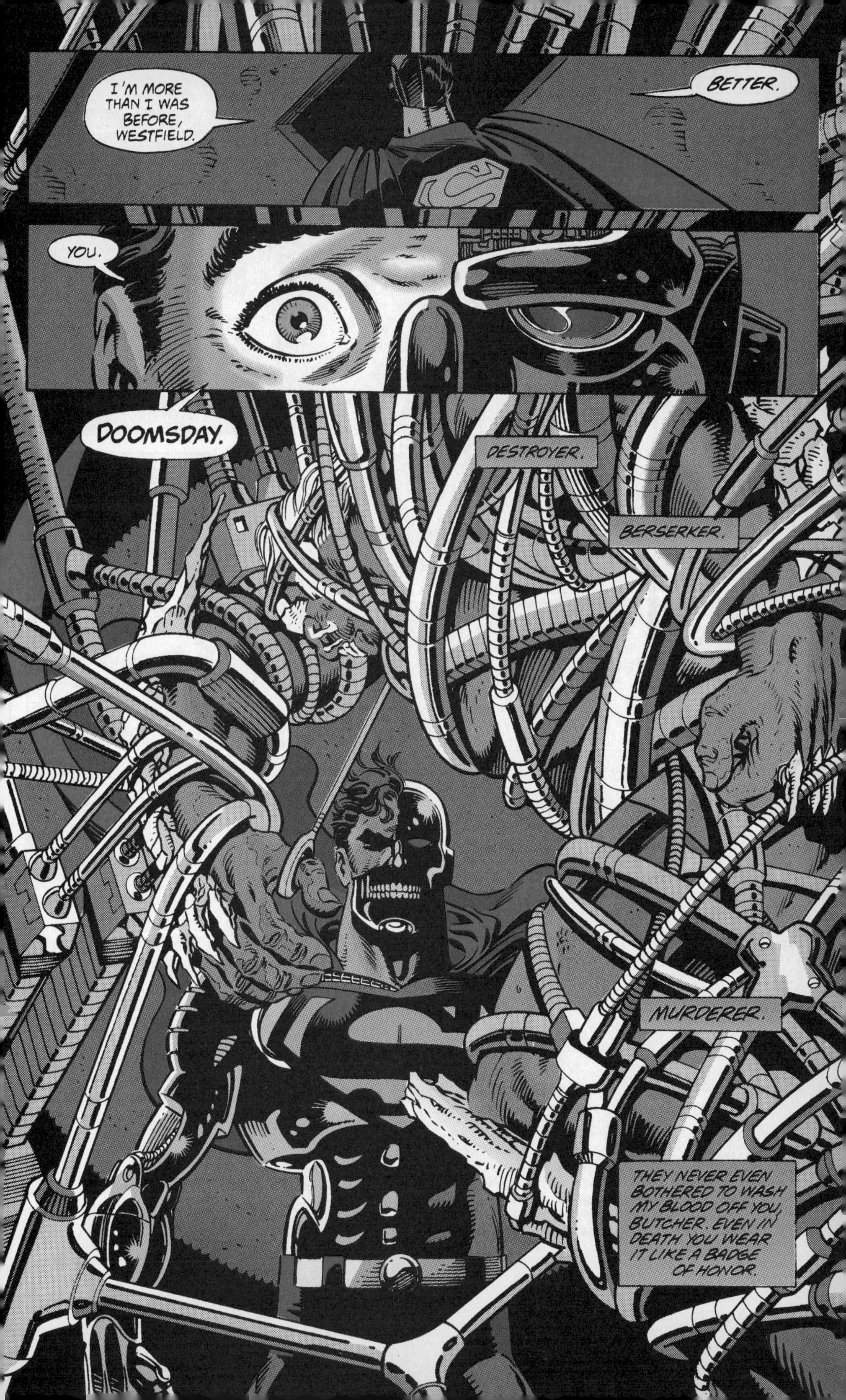
I'M MORE THAN I WAS BEFORE, WESTFIELD.
BETTER.
YOU.
DOOMSDAY.
DESTROYER.
BERSERKER.
MURDERER.
THEY NEVER EVEN BOTHERED TO WASH MY BLOOD OFF YOU, BUTCHER. EVEN IN DEATH YOU WEAR IT LIKE A BADGE OF HONOR.

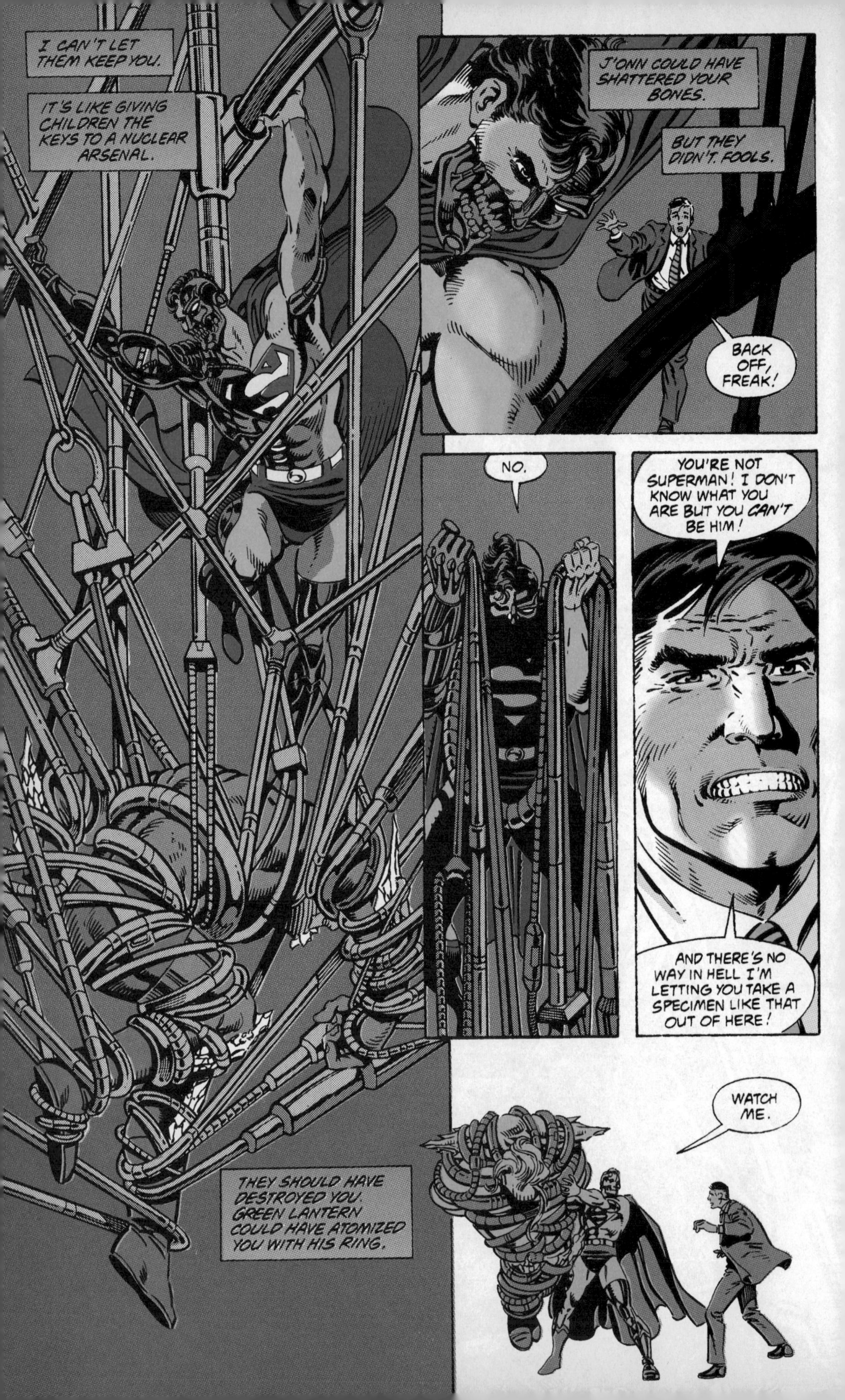
I CAN'T LET THEM KEEP YOU.
IT'S LIKE GIVING CHILDREN THE KEYS TO A NUCLEAR ARSENAL.
THEY SHOULD HAVE DESTROYED YOU. GREEN LANTERN COULD HAVE ATOMIZED YOU WITH HIS RING.
J'ONN COULD HAVE SHATTERED YOUR BONES.
BUT THEY DIDN'T. FOOLS.
BACK OFF, FREAK!
NO.
YOU'RE NOT SUPERMAN! I DON'T KNOW WHAT YOU ARE BUT YOU CAN'T BE HIM!
AND THERE'S NO WAY IN HELL I'M LETTING YOU TAKE A SPECIMEN LIKE THAT OUT OF HERE!
WATCH ME.

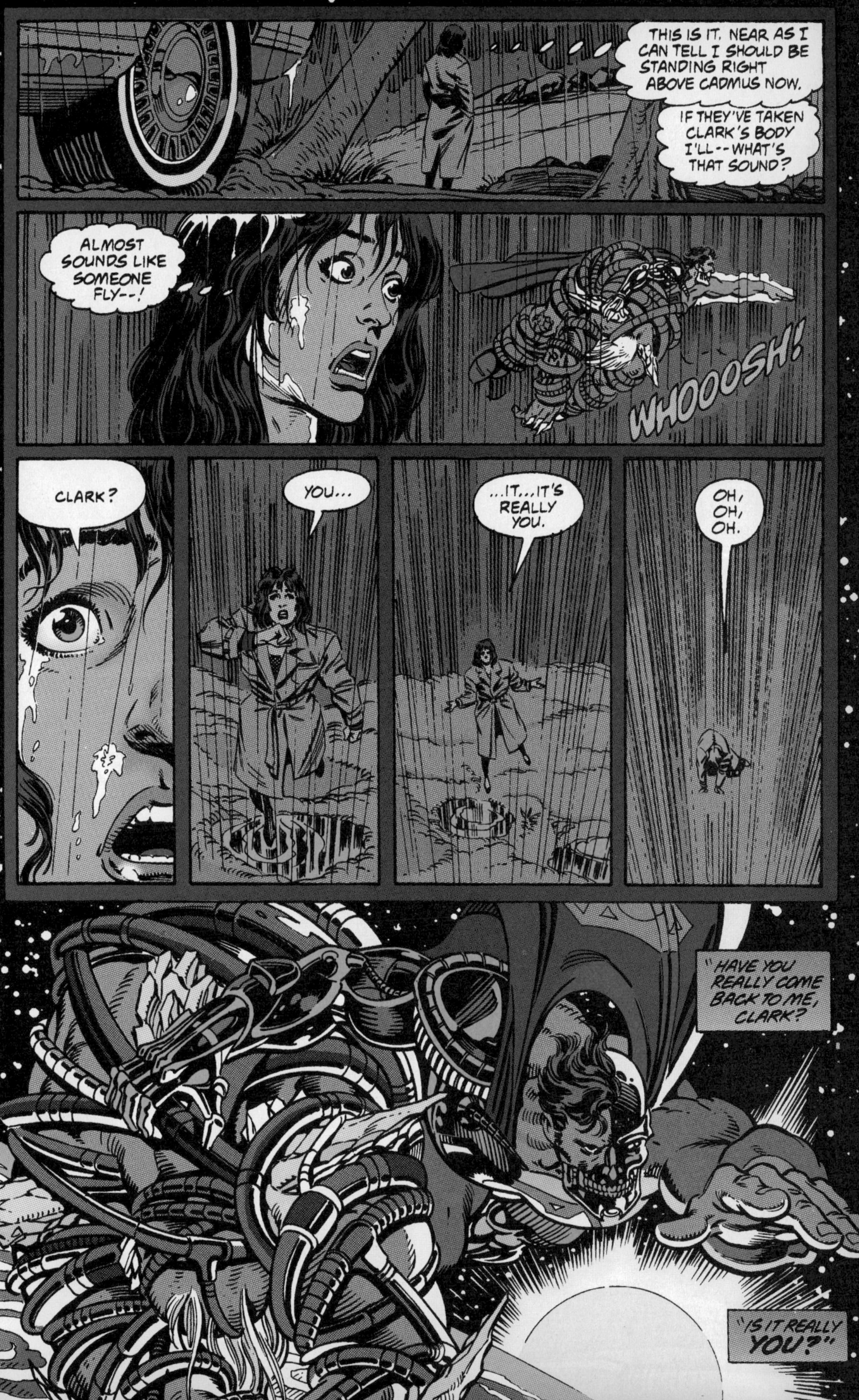
THIS IS IT. NEAR AS I CAN TELL I SHOULD BE STANDING RIGHT ABOVE CADMUS NOW.
IF THEY'VE TAKEN CLARK'S BODY I'LL--WHAT'S THAT SOUND?
ALMOST SOUNDS LIKE SOMEONE FLY--!
WHOOOOSH!
CLARK?
YOU...
...IT...IT'S REALLY YOU.
OH, OH, OH.
"HAVE YOU REALLY COME BACK TO ME, CLARK?
"IS IT REALLY YOU?"

PERFECT.

THAT ASTEROID IS JUST WHAT I NEED.

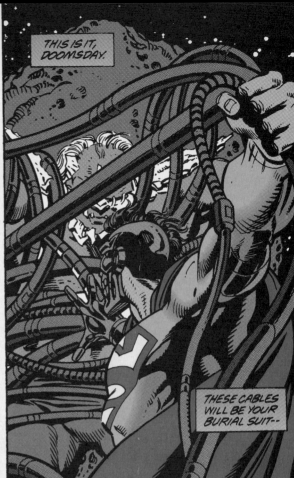

THIS IS IT, DOOMSDAY.

THESE CABLES WILL BE YOUR BURIAL SUIT--

--AND THIS ASTEROID'S FROZEN ORE, MELTED AROUND YOU, WILL BE YOUR CASKET.

LET THE COLD VACUUM OF SPACE BE YOUR ETERNAL RESTING PLACE.

IT'S MORE THAN YOU DESERVE.

WHIRR

SHIP

A PRECAUTION.

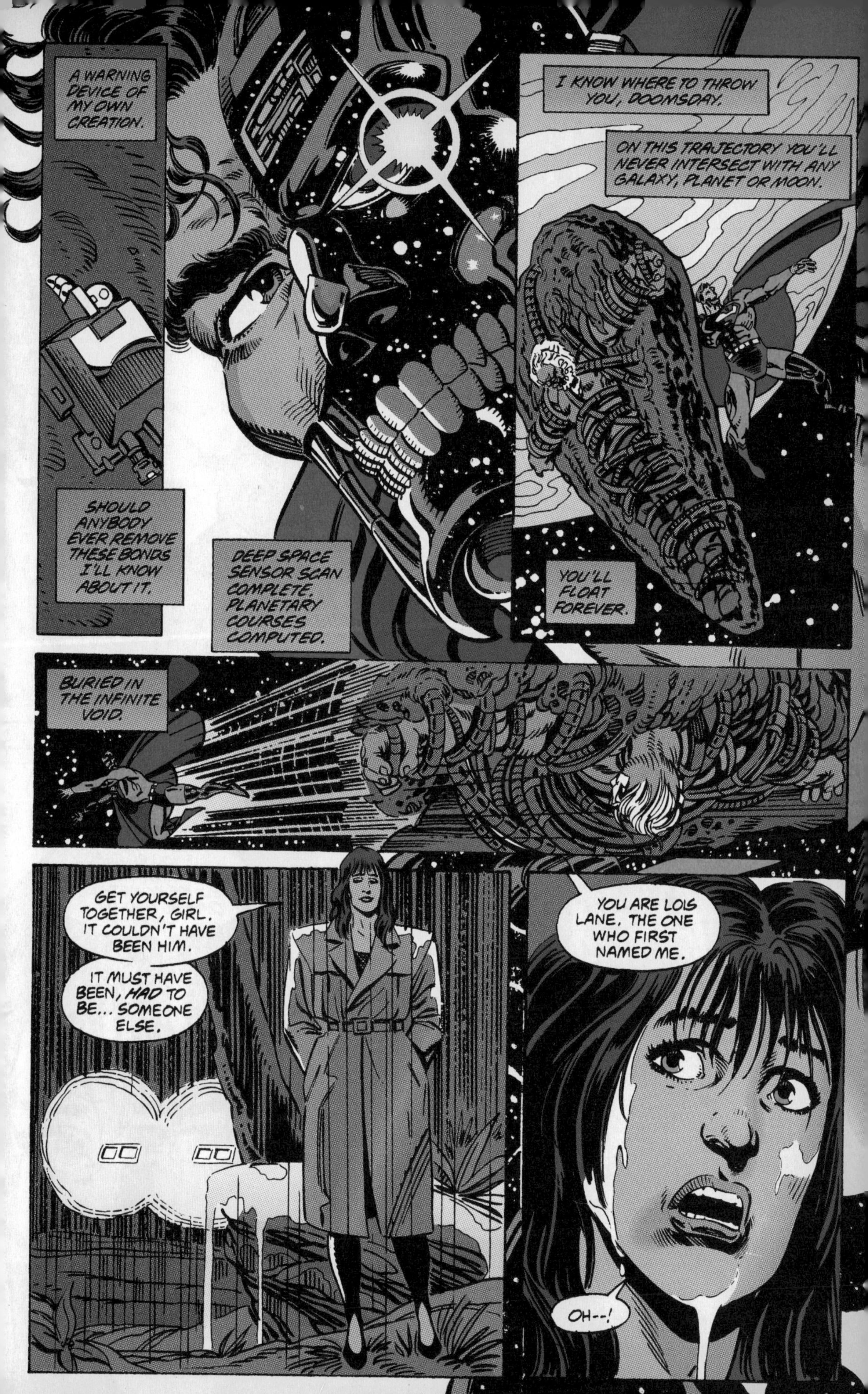
A WARNING DEVICE OF MY OWN CREATION.
SHOULD ANYBODY EVER REMOVE THESE BONDS I'LL KNOW ABOUT IT.
DEEP SPACE SENSOR SCAN COMPLETE. PLANETARY COURSES COMPUTED.
I KNOW WHERE TO THROW YOU, DOOMSDAY.
ON THIS TRAJECTORY YOU'LL NEVER INTERSECT WITH ANY GALAXY, PLANET OR MOON.
YOU'LL FLOAT FOREVER.
BURIED IN THE INFINITE VOID.
GET YOURSELF TOGETHER, GIRL. IT COULDN'T HAVE BEEN HIM.
IT MUST HAVE BEEN, HAD TO BE... SOMEONE ELSE.
YOU ARE LOIS LANE. THE ONE WHO FIRST NAMED ME.
OH--!

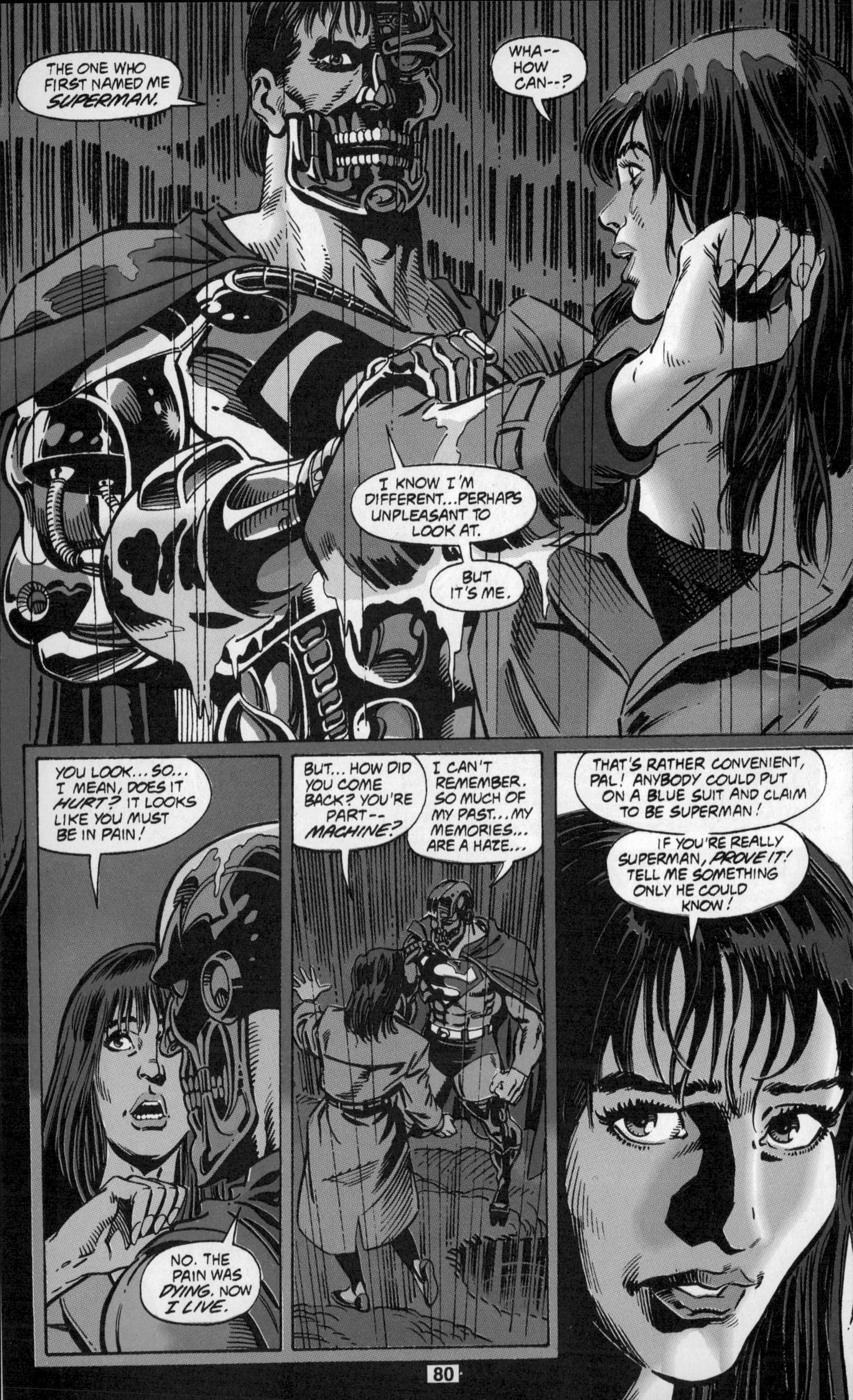
THE ONE WHO FIRST NAMED ME SUPERMAN.
WHA-- HOW CAN--?
I KNOW I'M DIFFERENT...PERHAPS UNPLEASANT TO LOOK AT.
BUT IT'S ME.
YOU LOOK... SO... I MEAN, DOES IT HURT? IT LOOKS LIKE YOU MUST BE IN PAIN!
NO. THE PAIN WAS DYING. NOW I LIVE.
BUT... HOW DID YOU COME BACK? YOU'RE PART-- MACHINE?
I CAN'T REMEMBER. SO MUCH OF MY PAST... MY MEMORIES... ARE A HAZE...
THAT'S RATHER CONVENIENT, PAL! ANYBODY COULD PUT ON A BLUE SUIT AND CLAIM TO BE SUPERMAN!
IF YOU'RE REALLY SUPERMAN, PROVE IT! TELL ME SOMETHING ONLY HE COULD KNOW!

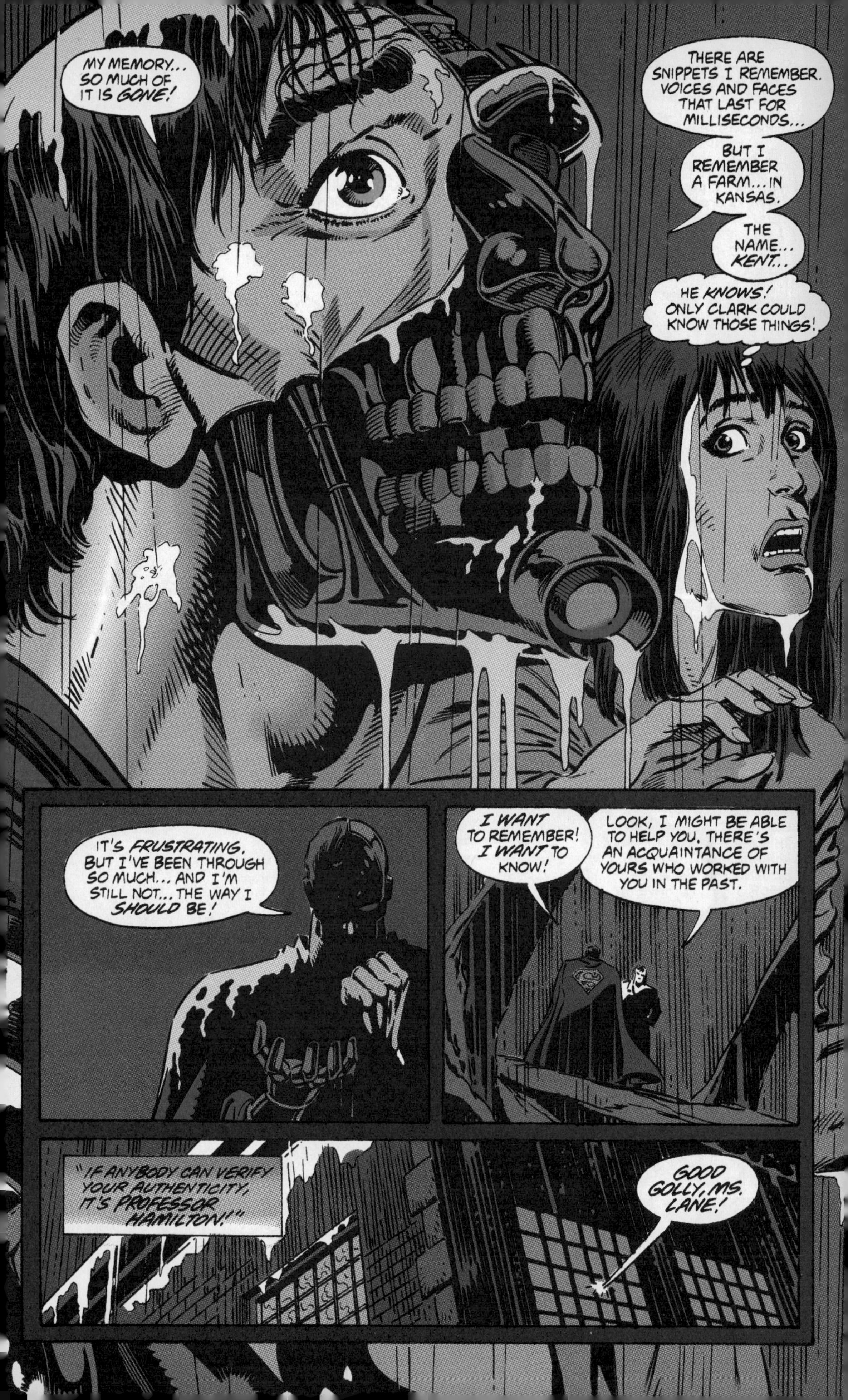
MY MEMORY... SO MUCH OF IT IS GONE!
THERE ARE SNIPPETS I REMEMBER. VOICES AND FACES THAT LAST FOR MILLISECONDS...
BUT I REMEMBER A FARM... IN KANSAS.
THE NAME... KENT...
HE KNOWS! ONLY CLARK COULD KNOW THOSE THINGS!
IT'S FRUSTRATING, BUT I'VE BEEN THROUGH SO MUCH... AND I'M STILL NOT... THE WAY I SHOULD BE!
I WANT TO REMEMBER! I WANT TO KNOW!
LOOK, I MIGHT BE ABLE TO HELP YOU. THERE'S AN ACQUAINTANCE OF YOURS WHO WORKED WITH YOU IN THE PAST.
"IF ANYBODY CAN VERIFY YOUR AUTHENTICITY, IT'S PROFESSOR HAMILTON!"
GOOD GOLLY, MS. LANE!

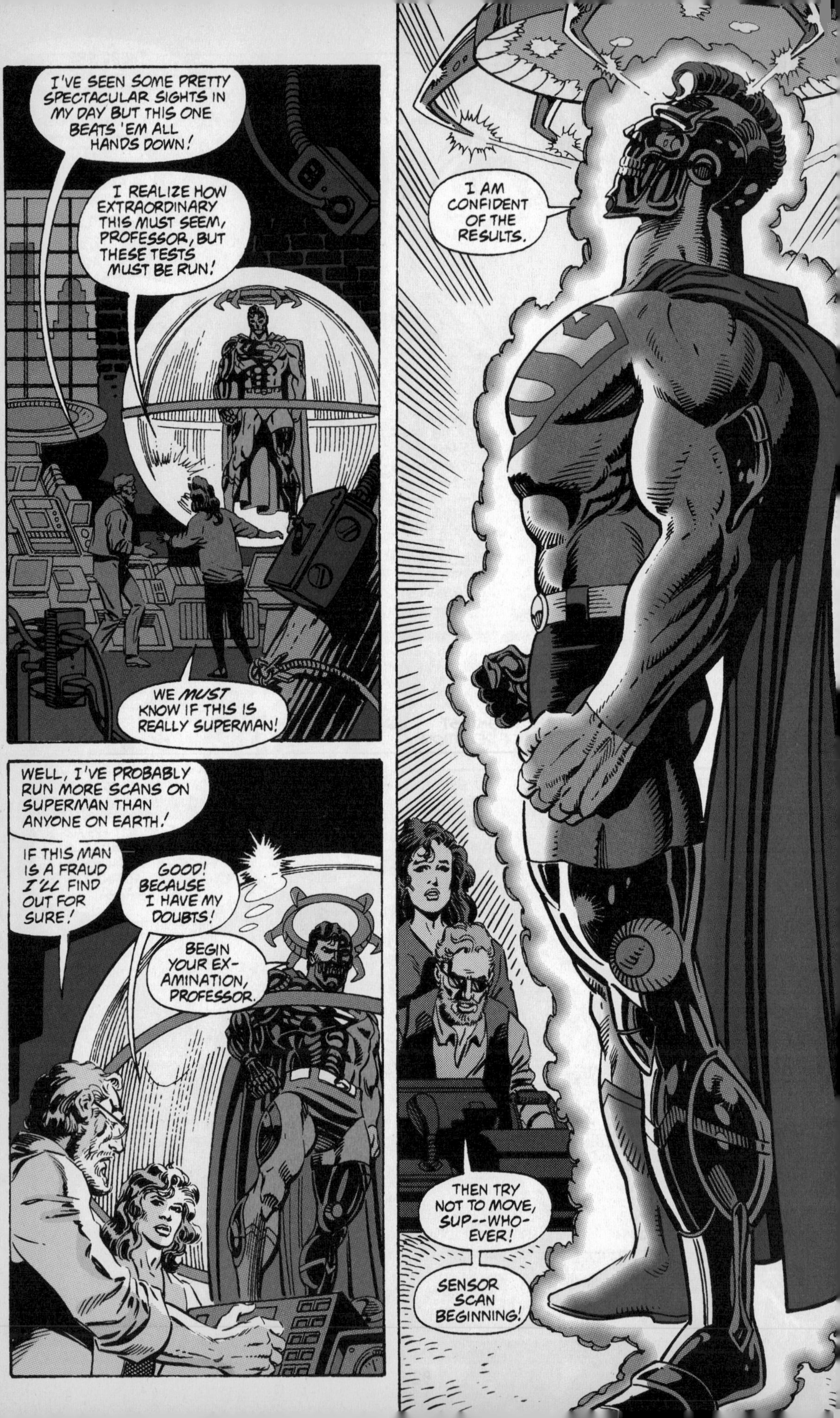
I'VE SEEN SOME PRETTY SPECTACULAR SIGHTS IN MY DAY BUT THIS ONE BEATS 'EM ALL HANDS DOWN!
I REALIZE HOW EXTRAORDINARY THIS MUST SEEM, PROFESSOR, BUT THESE TESTS MUST BE RUN!
WE MUST KNOW IF THIS IS REALLY SUPERMAN!
WELL, I'VE PROBABLY RUN MORE SCANS ON SUPERMAN THAN ANYONE ON EARTH!
IF THIS MAN IS A FRAUD I'LL FIND OUT FOR SURE!
GOOD! BECAUSE I HAVE MY DOUBTS!
BEGIN YOUR EX-AMINATION, PROFESSOR.
I AM CONFIDENT OF THE RESULTS.
THEN TRY NOT TO MOVE, SUP--WHO-EVER!
SENSOR SCAN BEGINNING!

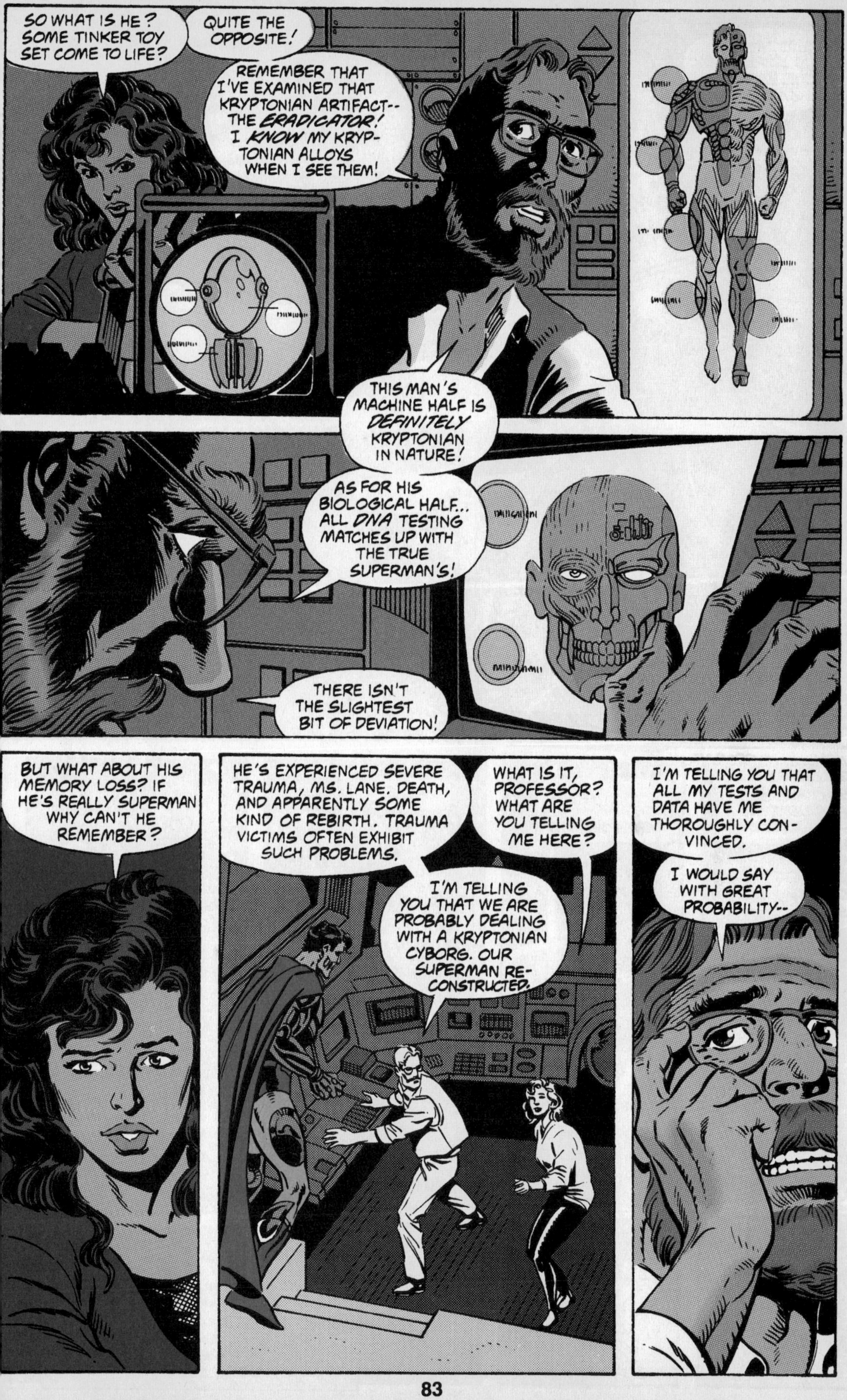
SO WHAT IS HE? SOME TINKER TOY SET COME TO LIFE?
QUITE THE OPPOSITE!
REMEMBER THAT I'VE EXAMINED THAT KRYPTONIAN ARTIFACT-- THE ERADICATOR! I KNOW MY KRYPTONIAN ALLOYS WHEN I SEE THEM!
THIS MAN'S MACHINE HALF IS DEFINITELY KRYPTONIAN IN NATURE!
AS FOR HIS BIOLOGICAL HALF... ALL DNA TESTING MATCHES UP WITH THE TRUE SUPERMAN'S!
THERE ISN'T THE SLIGHTEST BIT OF DEVIATION!
BUT WHAT ABOUT HIS MEMORY LOSS? IF HE'S REALLY SUPERMAN WHY CAN'T HE REMEMBER?
HE'S EXPERIENCED SEVERE TRAUMA, MS. LANE. DEATH, AND APPARENTLY SOME KIND OF REBIRTH. TRAUMA VICTIMS OFTEN EXHIBIT SUCH PROBLEMS.
WHAT IS IT, PROFESSOR? WHAT ARE YOU TELLING ME HERE?
I'M TELLING YOU THAT WE ARE PROBABLY DEALING WITH A KRYPTONIAN CYBORG. OUR SUPERMAN RECONSTRUCTED.
I'M TELLING YOU THAT ALL MY TESTS AND DATA HAVE ME THOROUGHLY CONVINCED.
I WOULD SAY WITH GREAT PROBABILITY--

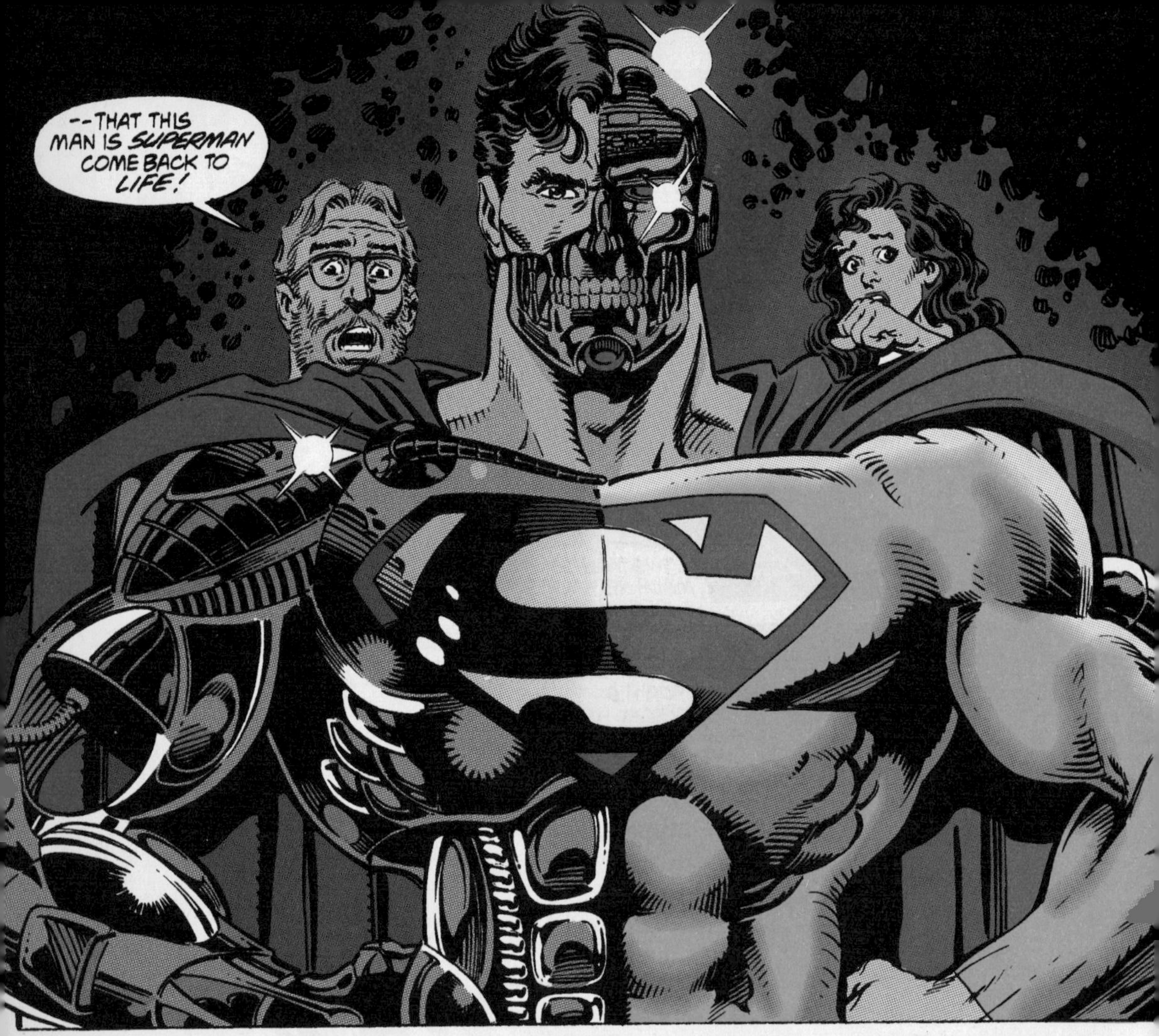
--THAT THIS MAN IS SUPERMAN COME BACK TO LIFE!

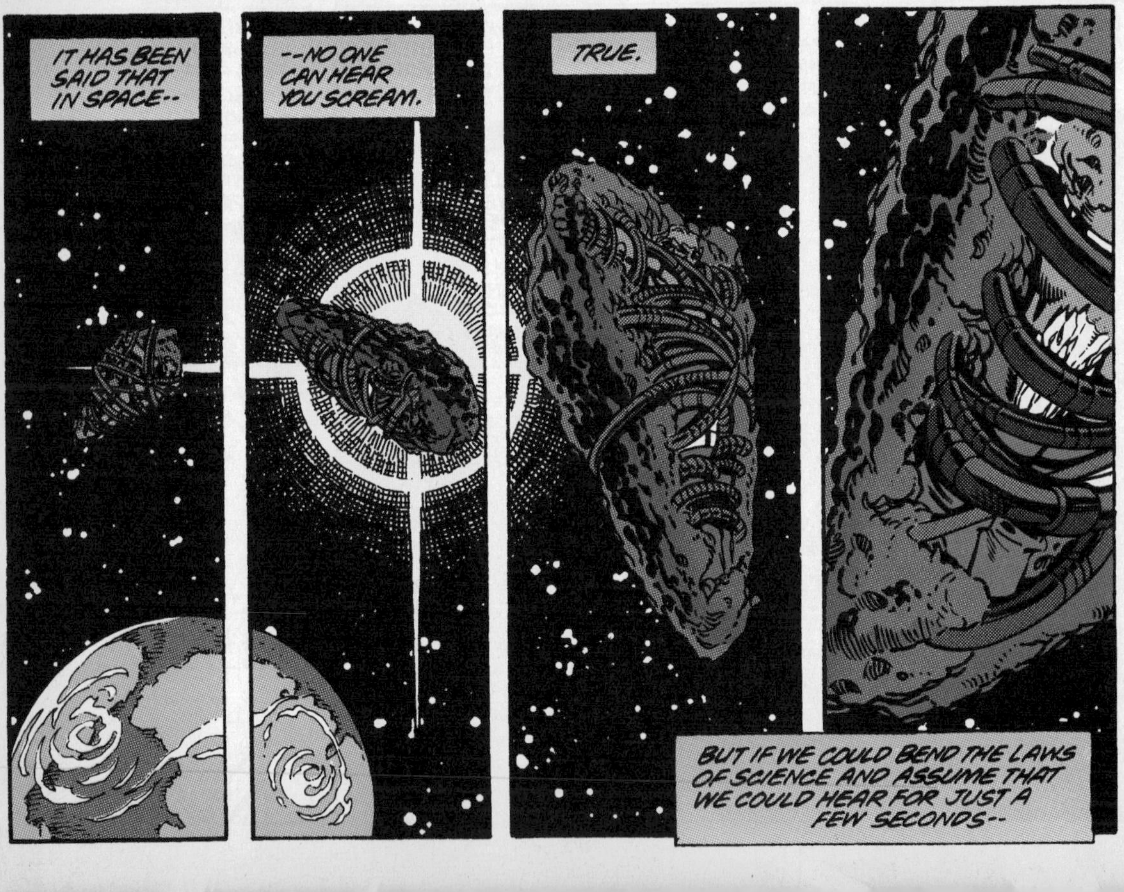
IT HAS BEEN SAID THAT IN SPACE--
--NO ONE CAN HEAR YOU SCREAM.
TRUE.
BUT IF WE COULD BEND THE LAWS OF SCIENCE AND ASSUME THAT WE COULD HEAR FOR JUST A FEW SECONDS--

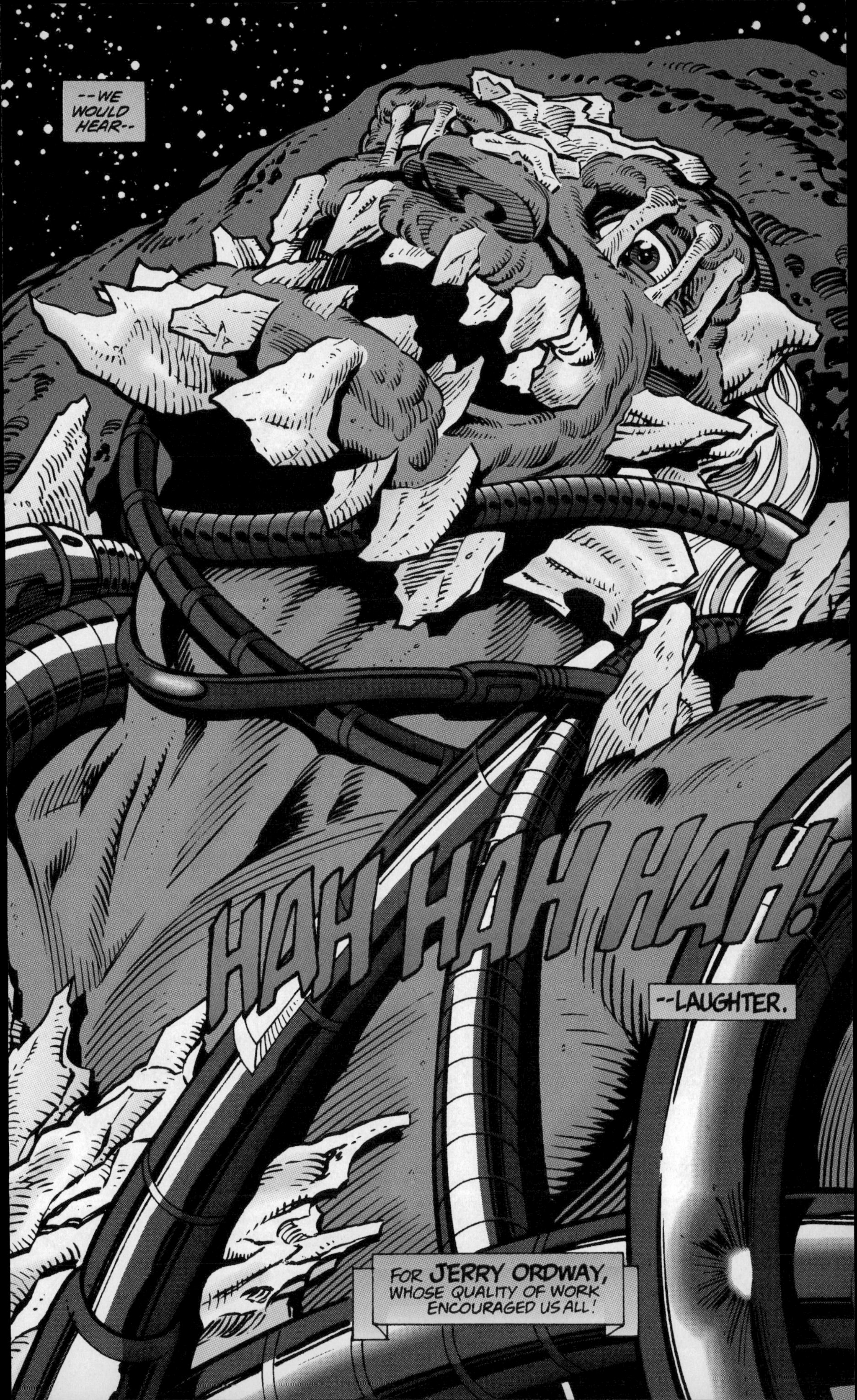
--WE WOULD HEAR--
HAH HAH HAH!
--LAUGHTER.
FOR JERRY ORDWAY, WHOSE QUALITY OF WORK ENCOURAGED US ALL!

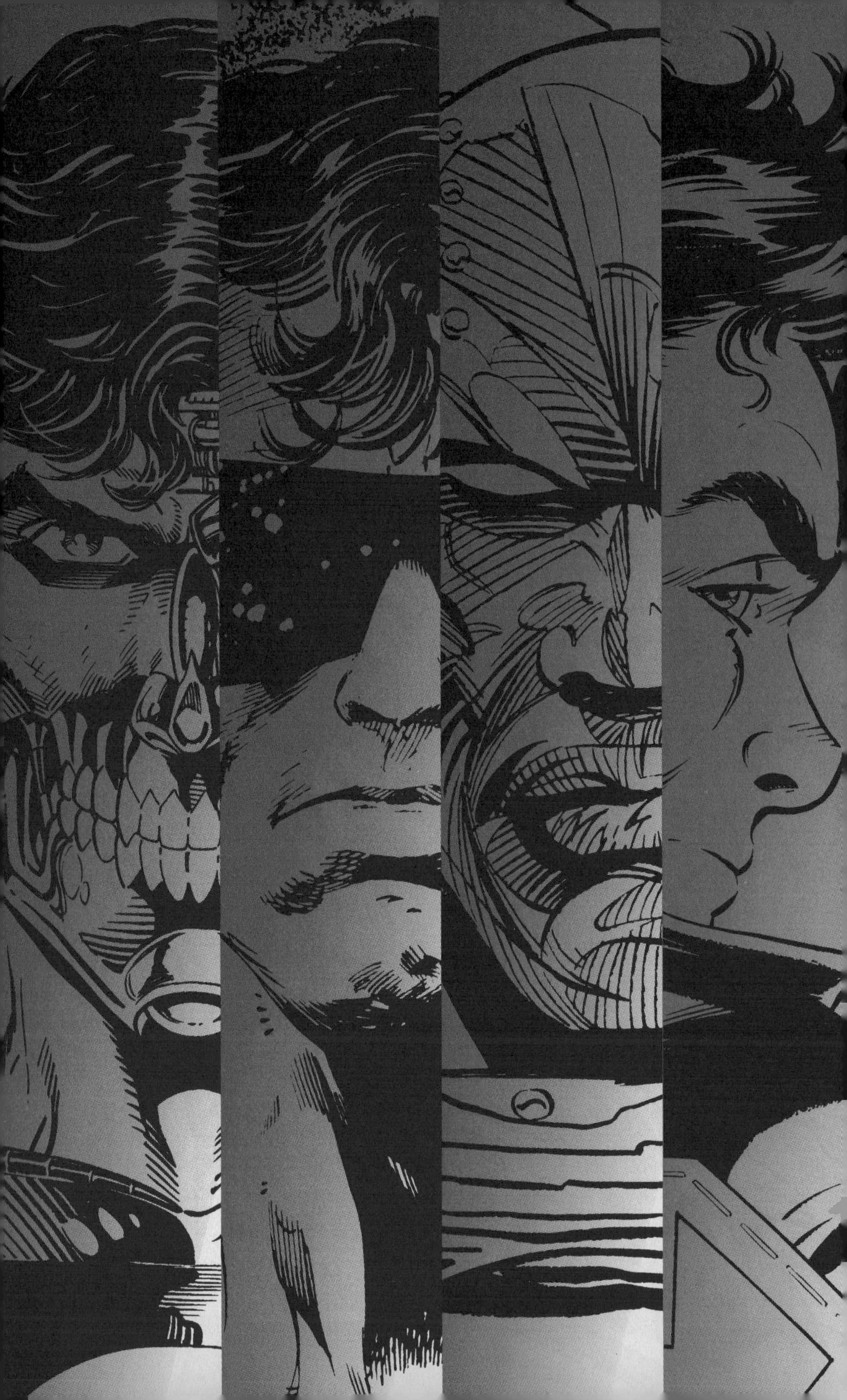

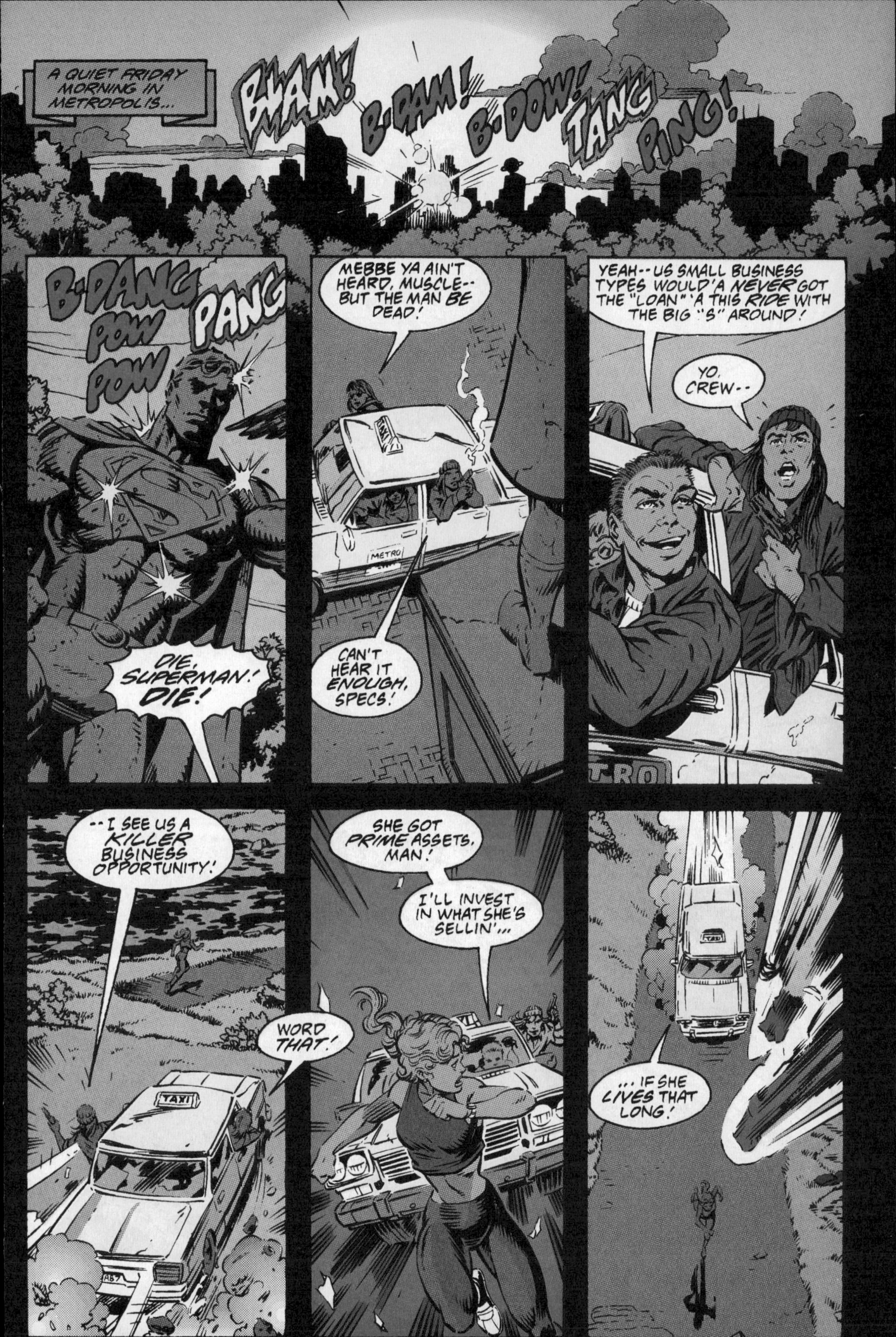
A QUIET FRIDAY MORNING IN METROPOLIS...
BLAM! B-DAM! B-DOW! TANG PING!
B-DANG POW POW PANG
DIE, SUPERMAN! DIE!
MEBBE YA AIN'T HEARD, MUSCLE-- BUT THE MAN BE DEAD!
CAN'T HEAR IT ENOUGH, SPECS!
YEAH--US SMALL BUSINESS TYPES WOULD'A NEVER GOT THE "LOAN" 'A THIS RIDE WITH THE BIG "S" AROUND!
YO. CREW--
--I SEE US A KILLER BUSINESS OPPORTUNITY!
WORD THAT!
SHE GOT PRIME ASSETS, MAN!
I'LL INVEST IN WHAT SHE'S SELLIN'...
...IF SHE LIVES THAT LONG!

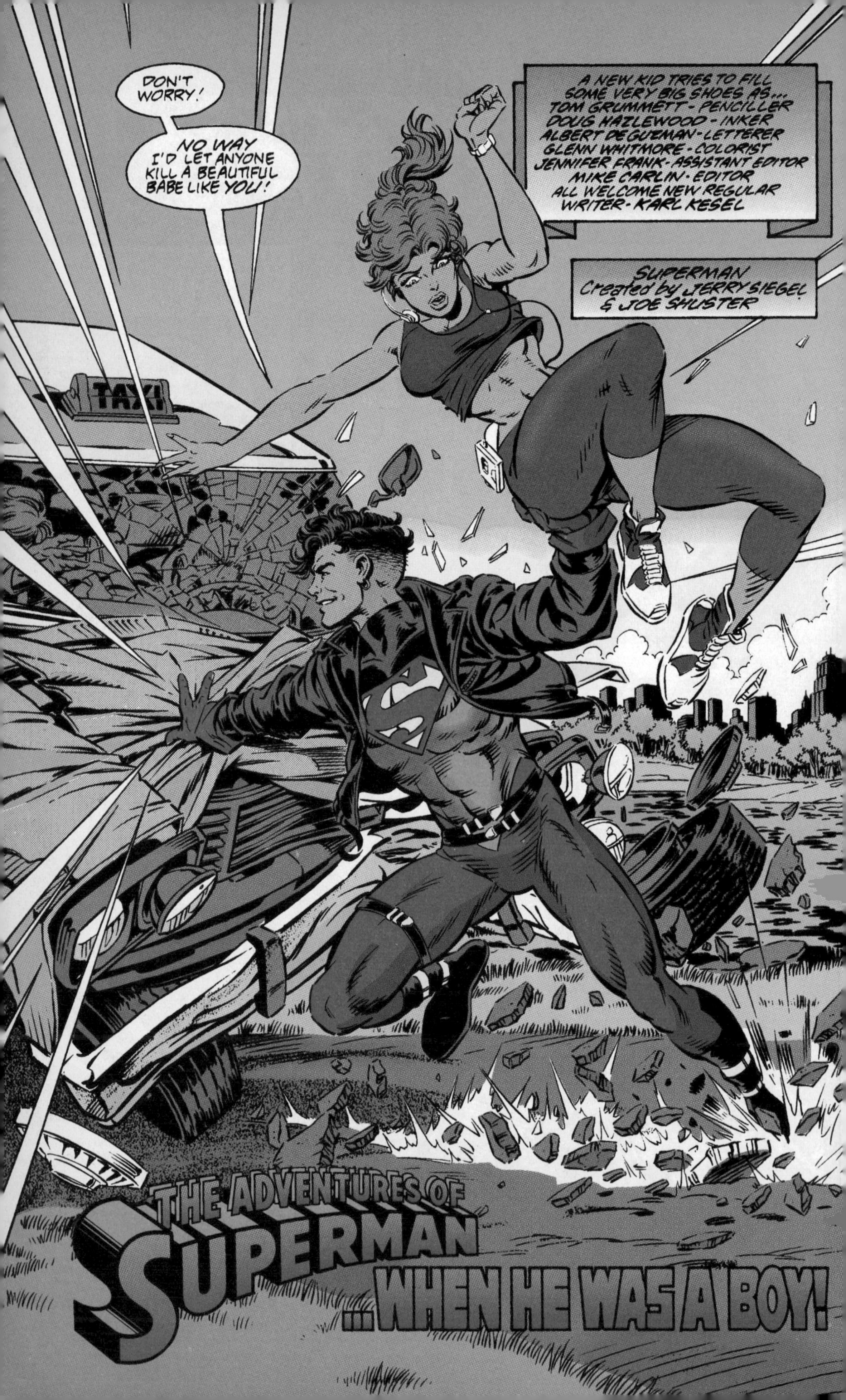
DON'T WORRY!
NO WAY I'D LET ANYONE KILL A BEAUTIFUL BABE LIKE YOU!
A NEW KID TRIES TO FILL SOME VERY BIG SHOES AS... TOM GRUMMETT - PENCILLER DOUG HAZLEWOOD - INKER ALBERT DEGUZMAN - LETTERER GLENN WHITMORE - COLORIST JENNIFER FRANK - ASSISTANT EDITOR MIKE CARLIN - EDITOR ALL WELCOME NEW REGULAR WRITER - KARL KESEL
SUPERMAN Created by JERRY SIEGEL & JOE SHUSTER
TAXI
THE ADVENTURES OF SUPERMAN
...WHEN HE WAS A BOY!

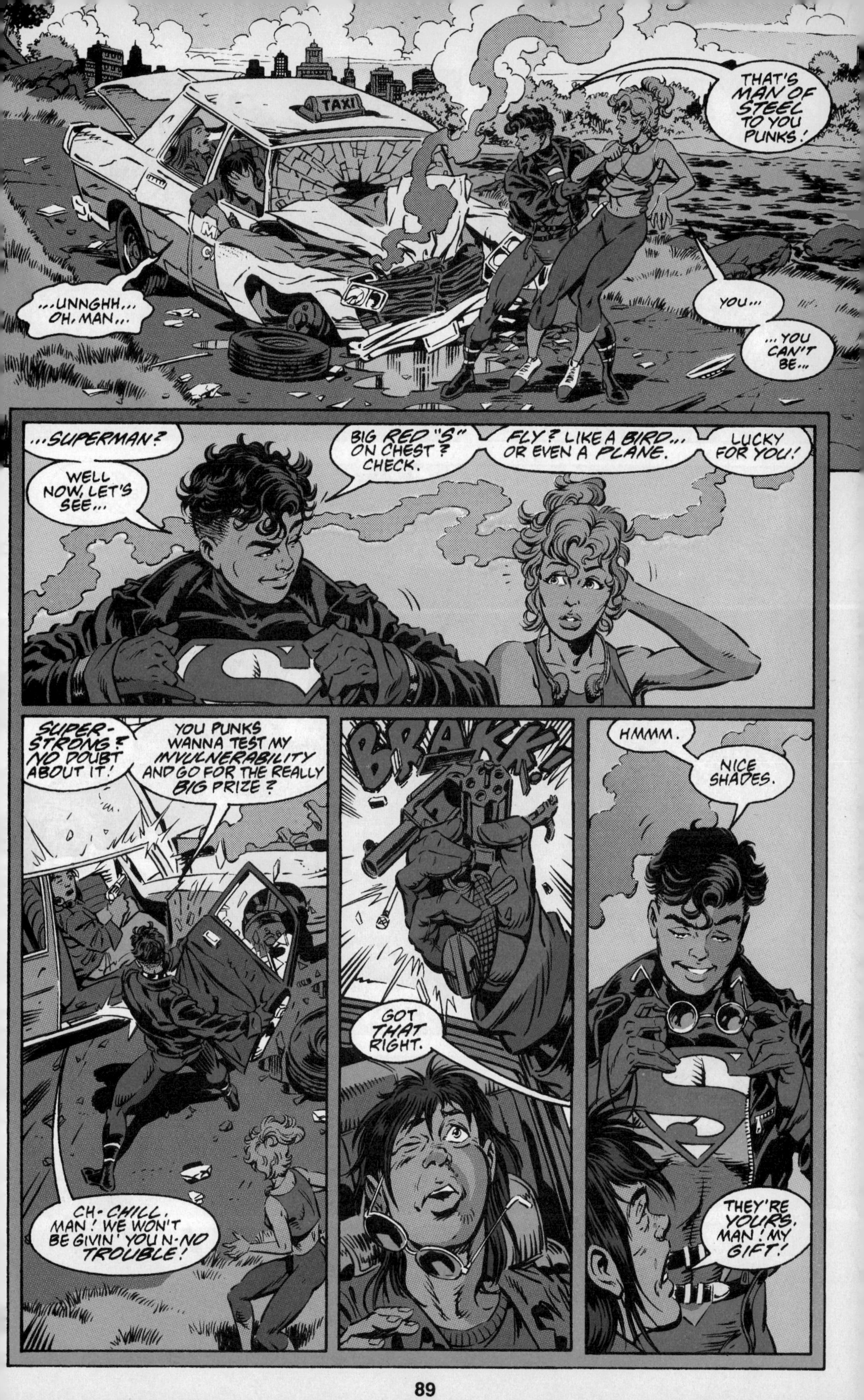
THAT'S MAN OF STEEL TO YOU PUNKS!
...UNNGHH... OH, MAN...
YOU...
...YOU CAN'T BE...
...SUPERMAN?
WELL NOW, LET'S SEE...
BIG RED "S" ON CHEST? CHECK.
FLY? LIKE A BIRD... OR EVEN A PLANE.
LUCKY FOR YOU!
SUPER-STRONG? NO DOUBT ABOUT IT!
YOU PUNKS WANNA TEST MY INVULNERABILITY AND GO FOR THE REALLY BIG PRIZE?
CH-CHILL, MAN! WE WON'T BE GIVIN' YOU N-NO TROUBLE!
BRAKK!
GOT THAT RIGHT.
HMMM.
NICE SHADES.
THEY'RE YOURS, MAN! MY GIFT!

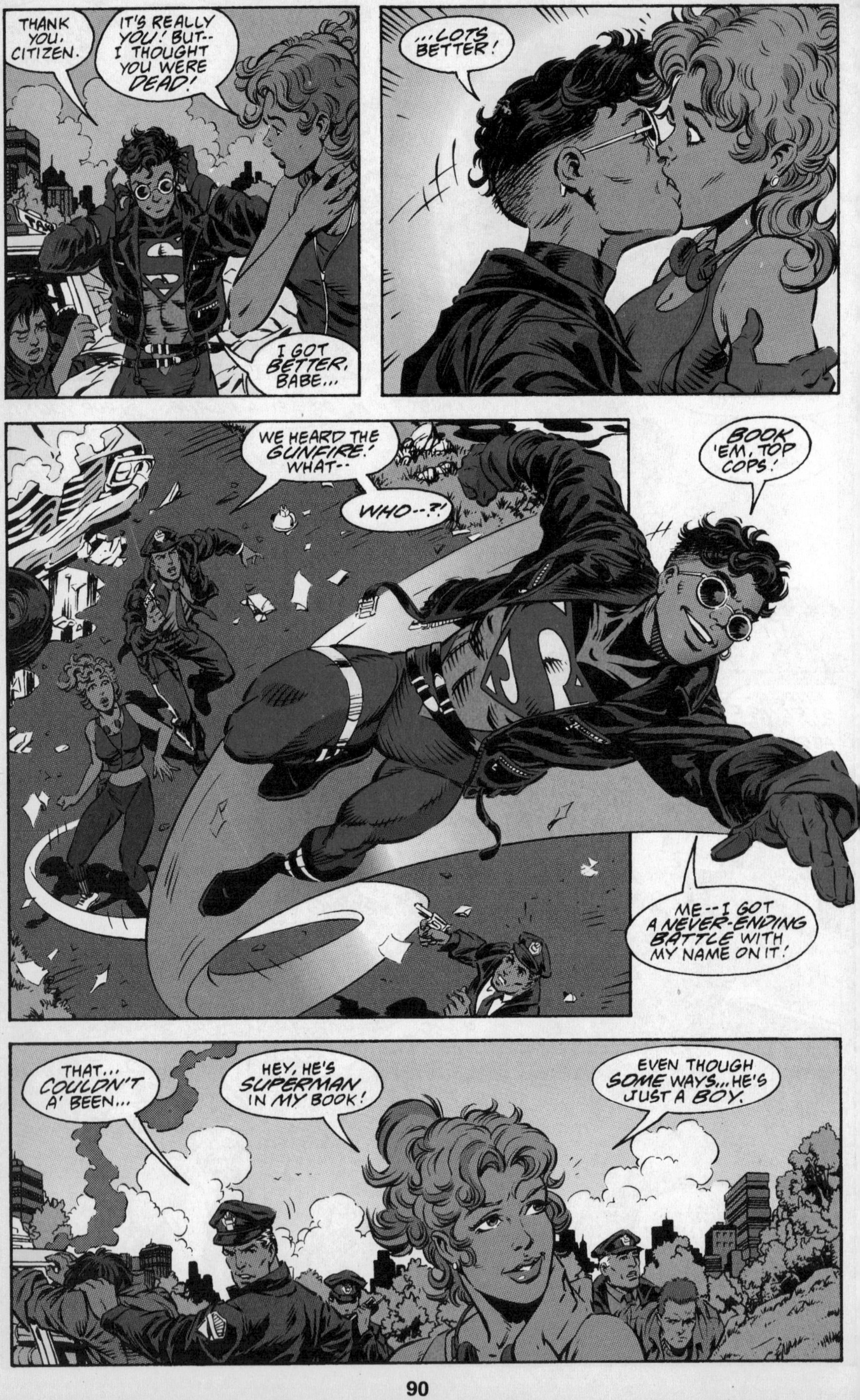

THANK YOU, CITIZEN.
IT'S REALLY YOU! BUT-- I THOUGHT YOU WERE DEAD!
I GOT BETTER, BABE...
...LOTS BETTER!
WE HEARD THE GUNFIRE! WHAT--
WHO--?!
BOOK 'EM, TOP COPS!
ME--I GOT A NEVER-ENDING BATTLE WITH MY NAME ON IT!
THAT... COULDN'T A' BEEN...
HEY, HE'S SUPERMAN IN MY BOOK!
EVEN THOUGH SOME WAYS... HE'S JUST A BOY.

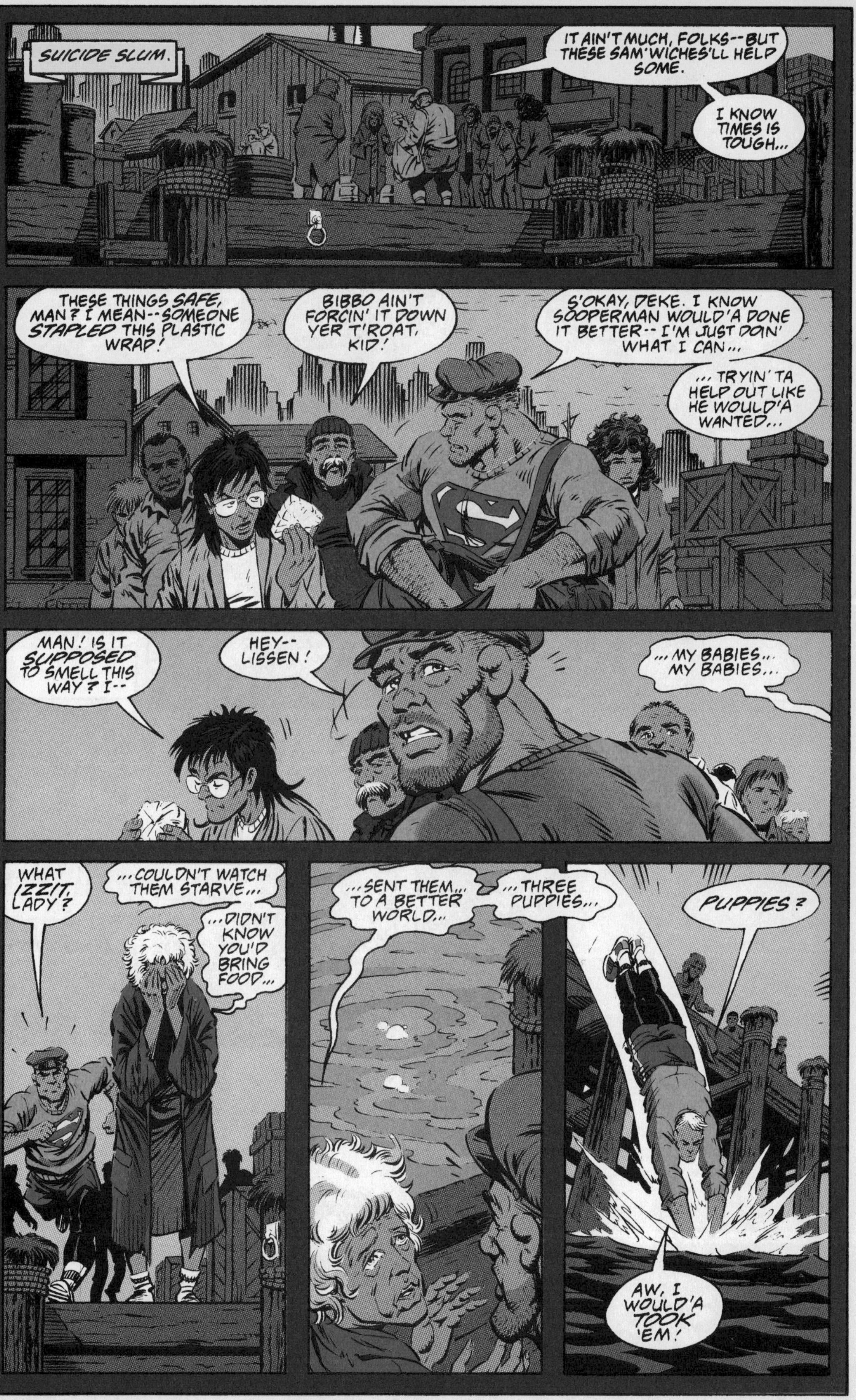
SUICIDE SLUM.
IT AIN'T MUCH, FOLKS--BUT THESE SAM'WICHES'LL HELP SOME.
I KNOW TIMES IS TOUGH...
THESE THINGS SAFE, MAN? I MEAN--SOMEONE STAPLED THIS PLASTIC WRAP!
BIBBO AIN'T FORCIN' IT DOWN YER T'ROAT, KID!
S'OKAY, DEKE. I KNOW SOOPERMAN WOULD'A DONE IT BETTER-- I'M JUST DOIN' WHAT I CAN...
...TRYIN' TA HELP OUT LIKE HE WOULD'A WANTED...
MAN! IS IT SUPPOSED TO SMELL THIS WAY? I--
HEY-- LISSEN!
...MY BABIES... MY BABIES...
WHAT IZZIT, LADY?
...COULDN'T WATCH THEM STARVE...
...DIDN'T KNOW YOU'D BRING FOOD...
...SENT THEM... TO A BETTER WORLD...
...THREE PUPPIES...
PUPPIES?
AW, I WOULD'A TOOK 'EM!

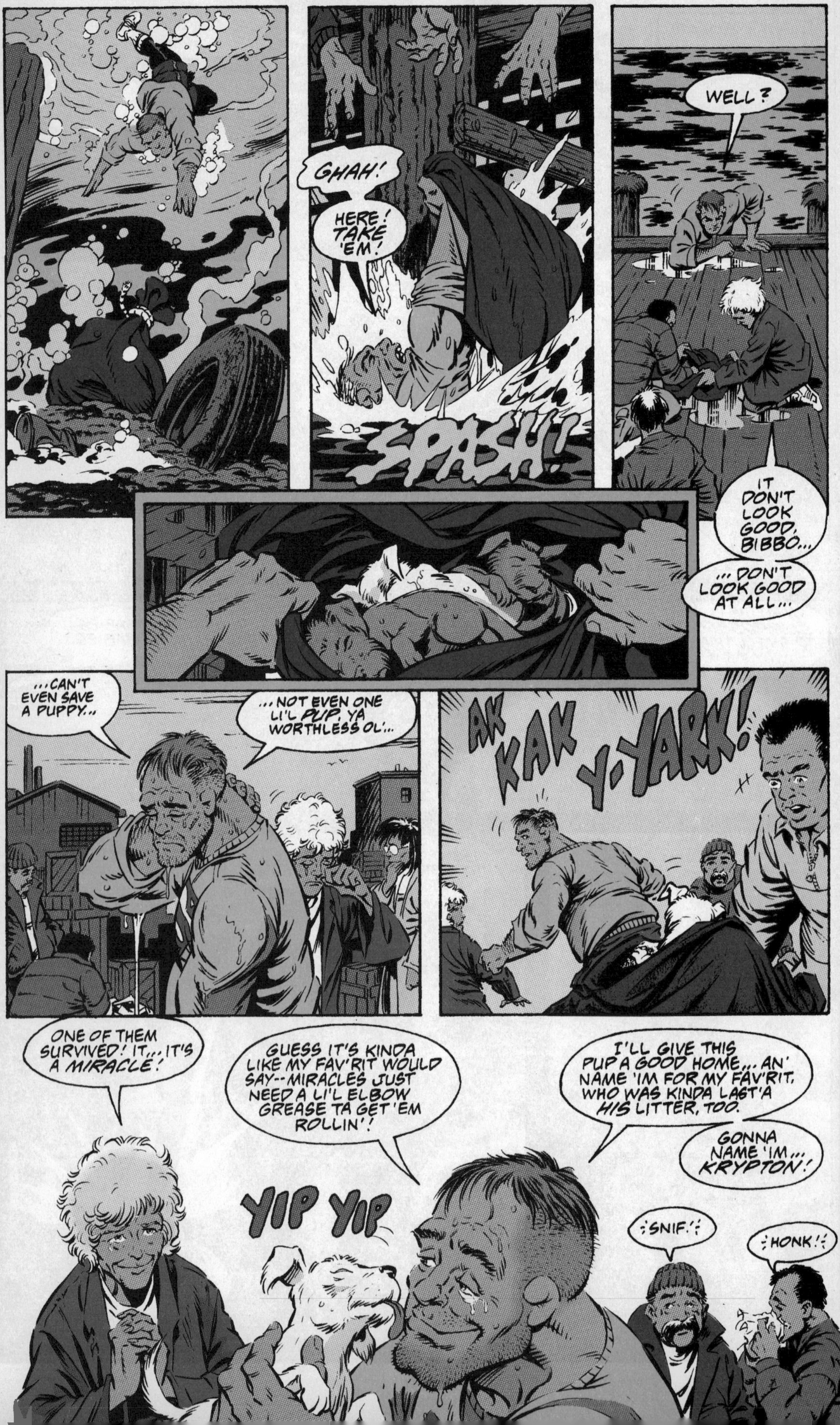
GHAH!
HERE! TAKE 'EM!
SPASH!
WELL?
IT DON'T LOOK GOOD, BIBBO...
...DON'T LOOK GOOD AT ALL...
...CAN'T EVEN SAVE A PUPPY...
...NOT EVEN ONE LI'L PUP, YA WORTHLESS OL'...
AK KAK Y-YARK!
ONE OF THEM SURVIVED! IT... IT'S A MIRACLE!
GUESS IT'S KINDA LIKE MY FAV'RIT WOULD SAY--MIRACLES JUST NEED A LI'L ELBOW GREASE TA GET 'EM ROLLIN'!
I'LL GIVE THIS PUP A GOOD HOME... AN' NAME 'IM FOR MY FAV'RIT, WHO WAS KINDA LAST'A HIS LITTER, TOO.
GONNA NAME 'IM... KRYPTON!
YIP YIP
SNIF
HONK

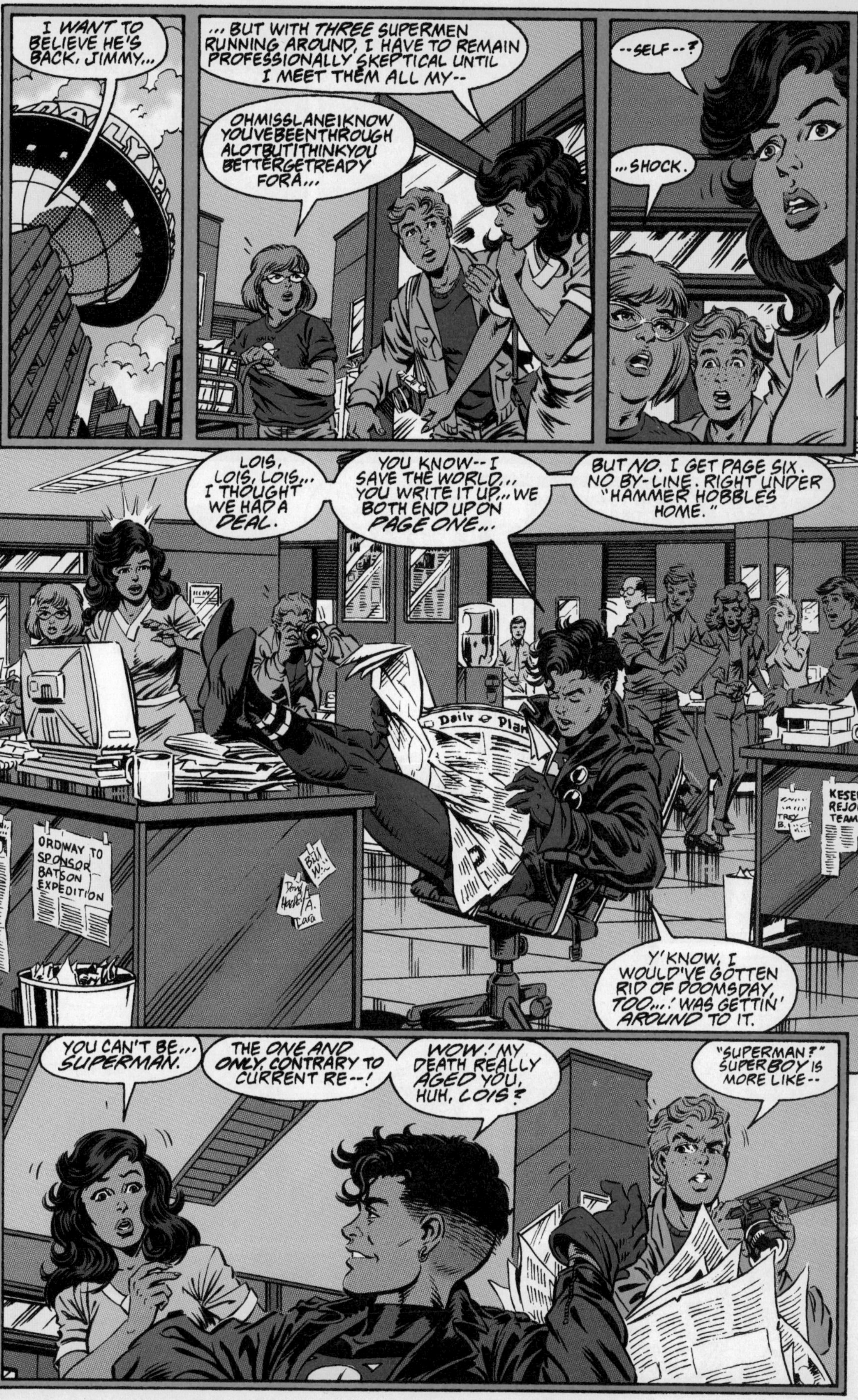

I WANT TO BELIEVE HE'S BACK, JIMMY...
...BUT WITH THREE SUPERMEN RUNNING AROUND, I HAVE TO REMAIN PROFESSIONALLY SKEPTICAL UNTIL I MEET THEM ALL MY--
OHMISSLANEIKNOW YOUVEBEENTHROUGH ALOTBUTITHINKYOU BETTERGETREADY FORA...
--SELF--?
...SHOCK.
LOIS, LOIS, LOIS... I THOUGHT WE HAD A DEAL.
YOU KNOW--I SAVE THE WORLD... YOU WRITE IT UP... WE BOTH END UP ON PAGE ONE...
BUT NO. I GET PAGE SIX. NO BY-LINE. RIGHT UNDER "HAMMER HOBBLES HOME."
Daily Planet
ORDWAY TO SPONSOR BATSON EXPEDITION
KESEL REJOIN TEAM
Y'KNOW, I WOULD'VE GOTTEN RID OF DOOMSDAY, TOO...! WAS GETTIN' AROUND TO IT.
YOU CAN'T BE... SUPERMAN.
THE ONE AND ONLY, CONTRARY TO CURRENT RE--!
WOW! MY DEATH REALLY AGED YOU, HUH, LOIS?
"SUPERMAN?" SUPERBOY IS MORE LIKE--

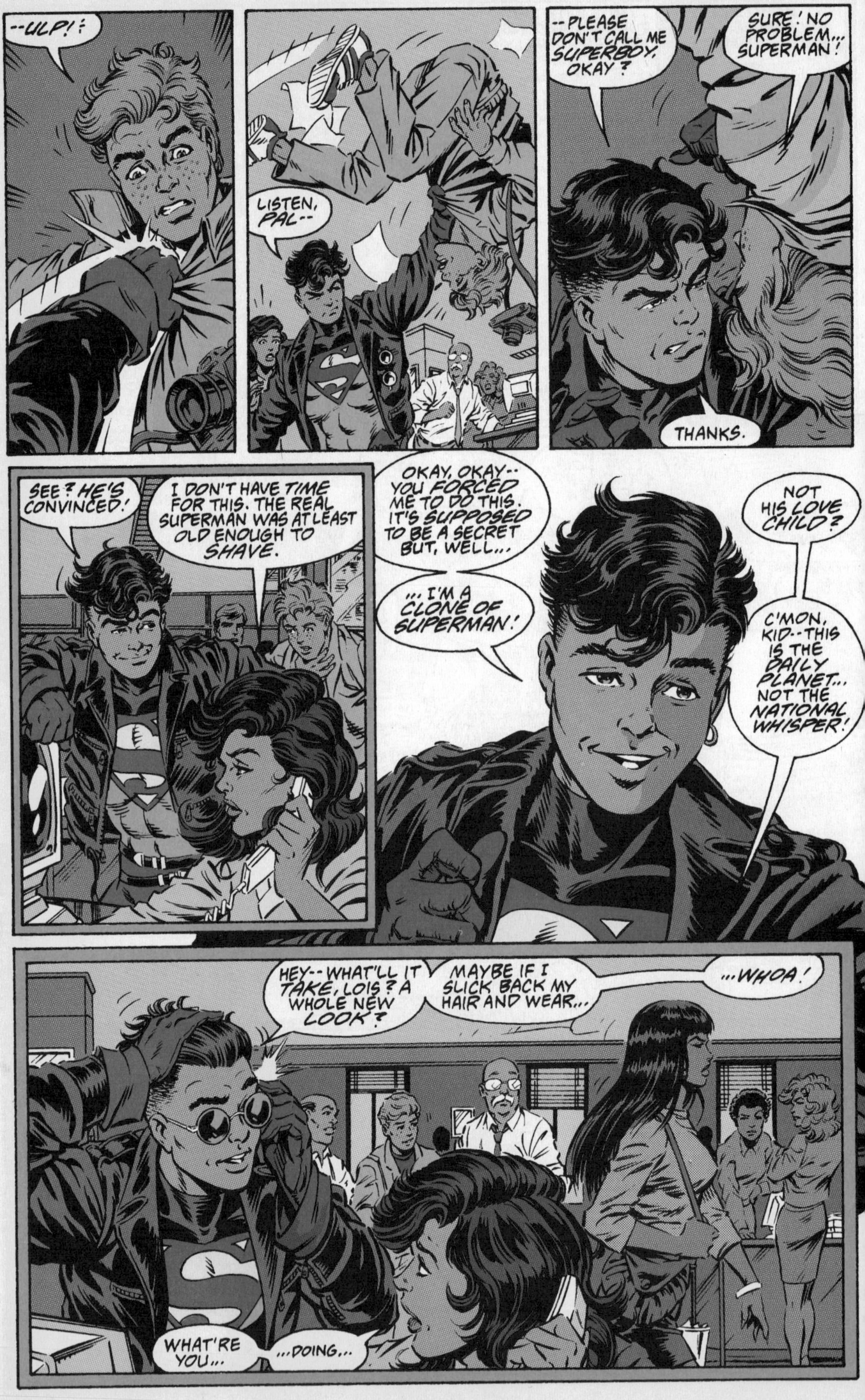
--ULP!
LISTEN, PAL--
--PLEASE DON'T CALL ME SUPERBOY, OKAY?
SURE! NO PROBLEM... SUPERMAN!
THANKS.
SEE? HE'S CONVINCED!
I DON'T HAVE TIME FOR THIS. THE REAL SUPERMAN WAS AT LEAST OLD ENOUGH TO SHAVE.
OKAY, OKAY-- YOU FORCED ME TO DO THIS. IT'S SUPPOSED TO BE A SECRET BUT, WELL...
...I'M A CLONE OF SUPERMAN!
NOT HIS LOVE CHILD?
C'MON, KID--THIS IS THE DAILY PLANET... NOT THE NATIONAL WHISPER!
HEY--WHAT'LL IT TAKE, LOIS? A WHOLE NEW LOOK?
MAYBE IF I SLICK BACK MY HAIR AND WEAR...
...WHOA!
WHAT'RE YOU...
...DOING...

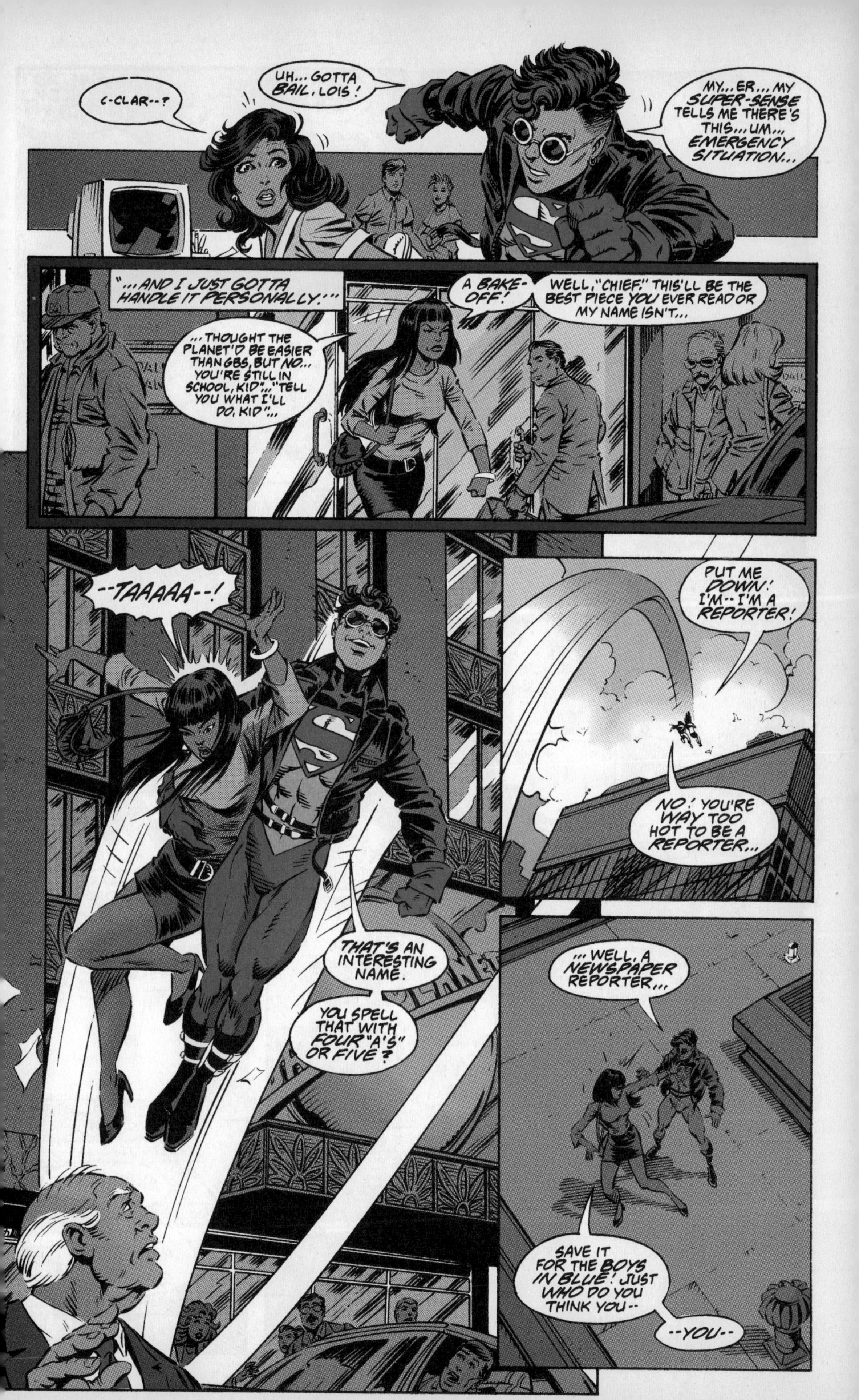
C-CLAR--?
UH... GOTTA BAIL, LOIS!
MY... ER... MY SUPER-SENSE TELLS ME THERE'S THIS... UM... EMERGENCY SITUATION...
"...AND I JUST GOTTA HANDLE IT PERSONALLY."
...THOUGHT THE PLANET'D BE EASIER THAN GBS, BUT NO... "YOU'RE STILL IN SCHOOL, KID"... "TELL YOU WHAT I'LL DO, KID"...
A BAKE-OFF!
WELL, "CHIEF," THIS'LL BE THE BEST PIECE YOU EVER READ OR MY NAME ISN'T...
--TAAAAA--!
THAT'S AN INTERESTING NAME.
YOU SPELL THAT WITH FOUR "A'S" OR FIVE?
PUT ME DOWN! I'M--I'M A REPORTER!
NO! YOU'RE WAY TOO HOT TO BE A REPORTER...
...WELL, A NEWSPAPER REPORTER...
SAVE IT FOR THE BOYS IN BLUE! JUST WHO DO YOU THINK YOU--
--YOU--

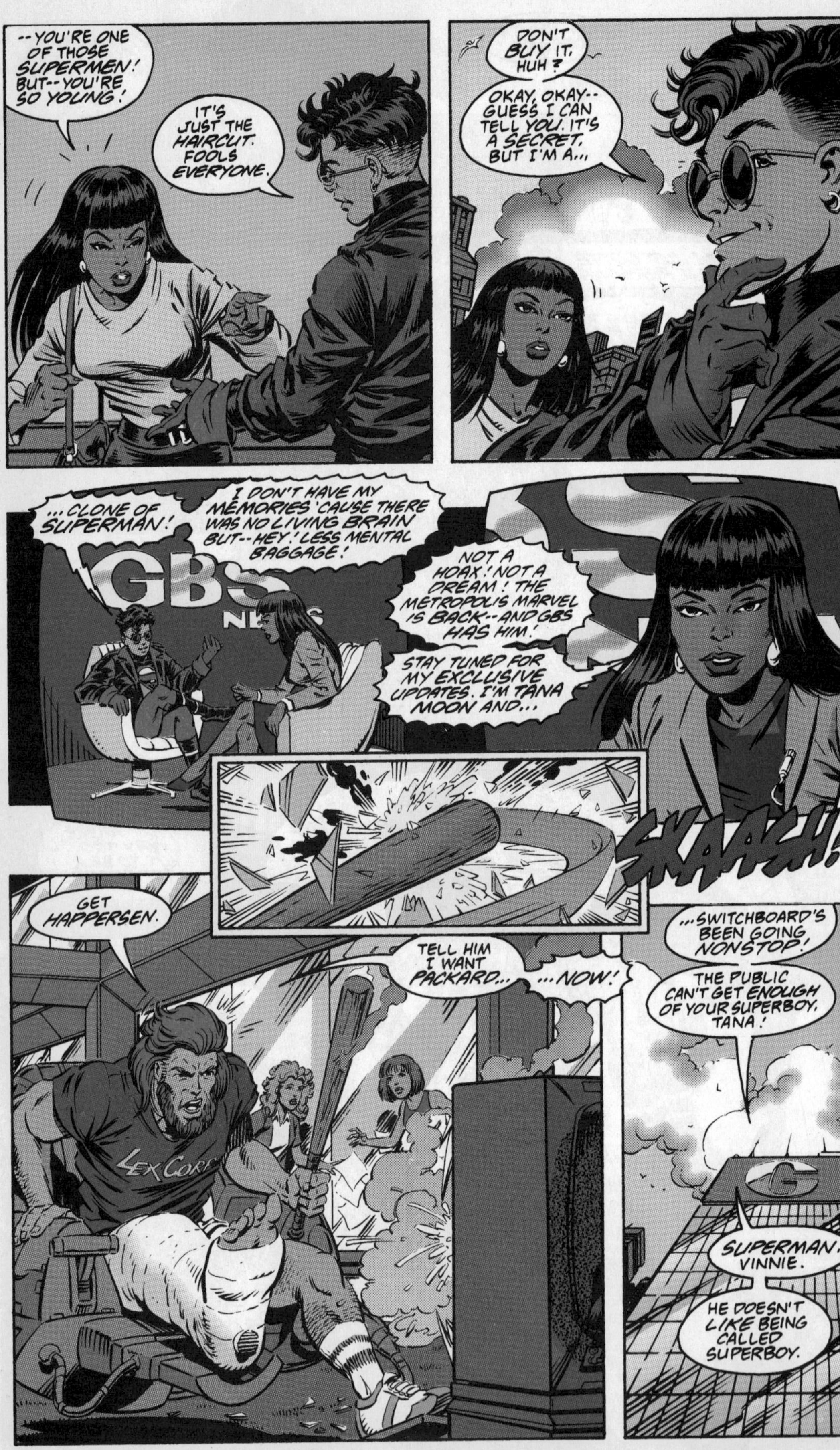
--YOU'RE ONE OF THOSE SUPERMEN! BUT--YOU'RE SO YOUNG!
IT'S JUST THE HAIRCUT. FOOLS EVERYONE.
DON'T BUY IT, HUH?
OKAY, OKAY--GUESS I CAN TELL YOU. IT'S A SECRET, BUT I'M A...
...CLONE OF SUPERMAN!
I DON'T HAVE MY MEMORIES 'CAUSE THERE WAS NO LIVING BRAIN BUT--HEY! LESS MENTAL BAGGAGE!
NOT A HOAX! NOT A DREAM! THE METROPOLIS MARVEL IS BACK--AND GBS HAS HIM!
STAY TUNED FOR MY EXCLUSIVE UPDATES. I'M TANA MOON AND...
SKAASH!
GET HAPPERSEN.
TELL HIM I WANT PACKARD...
...NOW!
LEXCORP
...SWITCHBOARD'S BEEN GOING NONSTOP!
THE PUBLIC CAN'T GET ENOUGH OF YOUR SUPERBOY, TANA!
SUPERMAN, VINNIE.
HE DOESN'T LIKE BEING CALLED SUPERBOY.

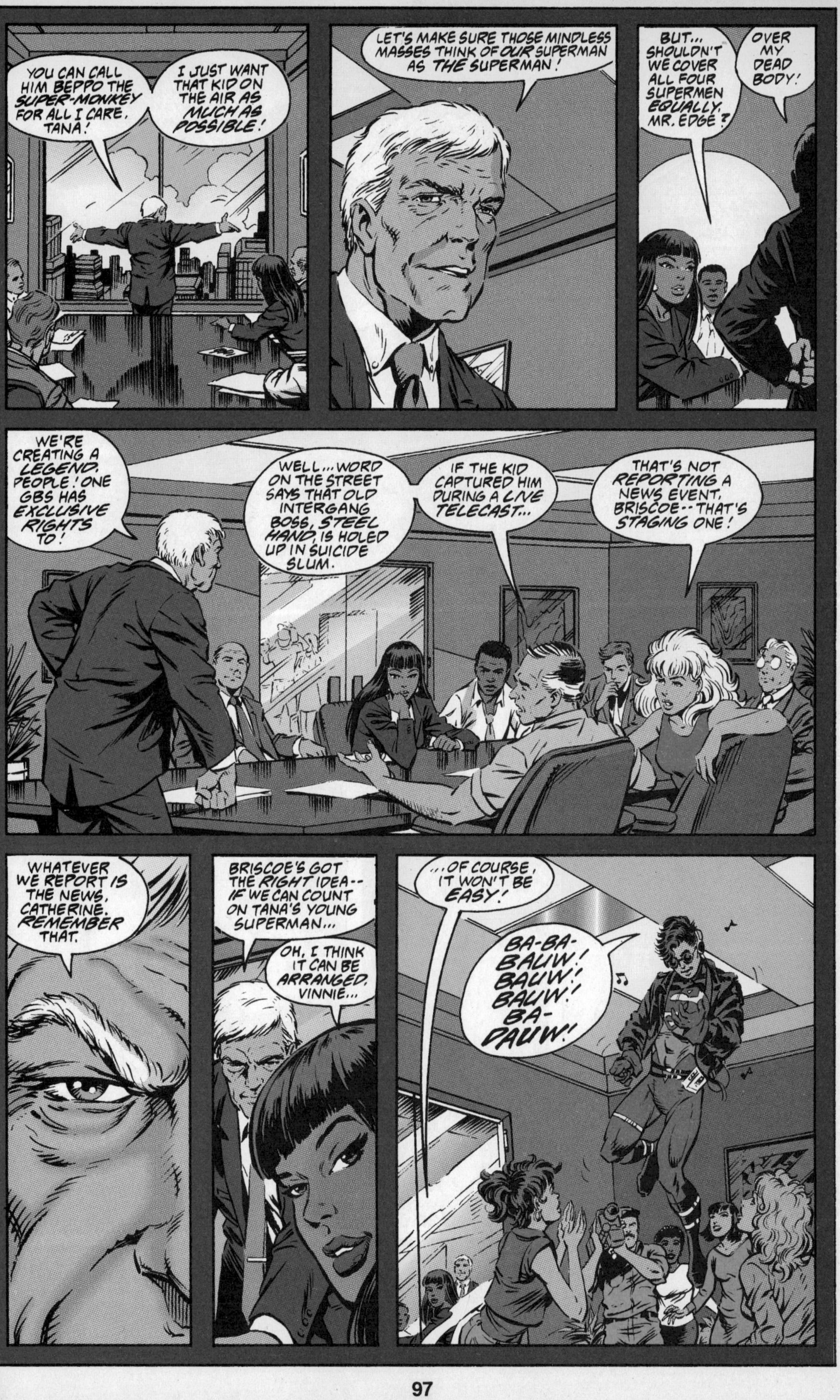
YOU CAN CALL HIM BEPPO THE SUPER-MONKEY FOR ALL I CARE, TANA!
I JUST WANT THAT KID ON THE AIR AS MUCH AS POSSIBLE!
LET'S MAKE SURE THOSE MINDLESS MASSES THINK OF OUR SUPERMAN AS THE SUPERMAN!
BUT... SHOULDN'T WE COVER ALL FOUR SUPERMEN EQUALLY, MR. EDGE?
OVER MY DEAD BODY!
WE'RE CREATING A LEGEND, PEOPLE! ONE GBS HAS EXCLUSIVE RIGHTS TO!
WELL... WORD ON THE STREET SAYS THAT OLD INTERGANG BOSS, STEEL HAND, IS HOLED UP IN SUICIDE SLUM.
IF THE KID CAPTURED HIM DURING A LIVE TELECAST...
THAT'S NOT REPORTING A NEWS EVENT, BRISCOE-- THAT'S STAGING ONE!
WHATEVER WE REPORT IS THE NEWS, CATHERINE. REMEMBER THAT.
BRISCOE'S GOT THE RIGHT IDEA-- IF WE CAN COUNT ON TANA'S YOUNG SUPERMAN...
OH, I THINK IT CAN BE ARRANGED, VINNIE...
...OF COURSE, IT WON'T BE EASY!
BA-BA-BAUW! BAUW! BAUW! BA-DAUW!

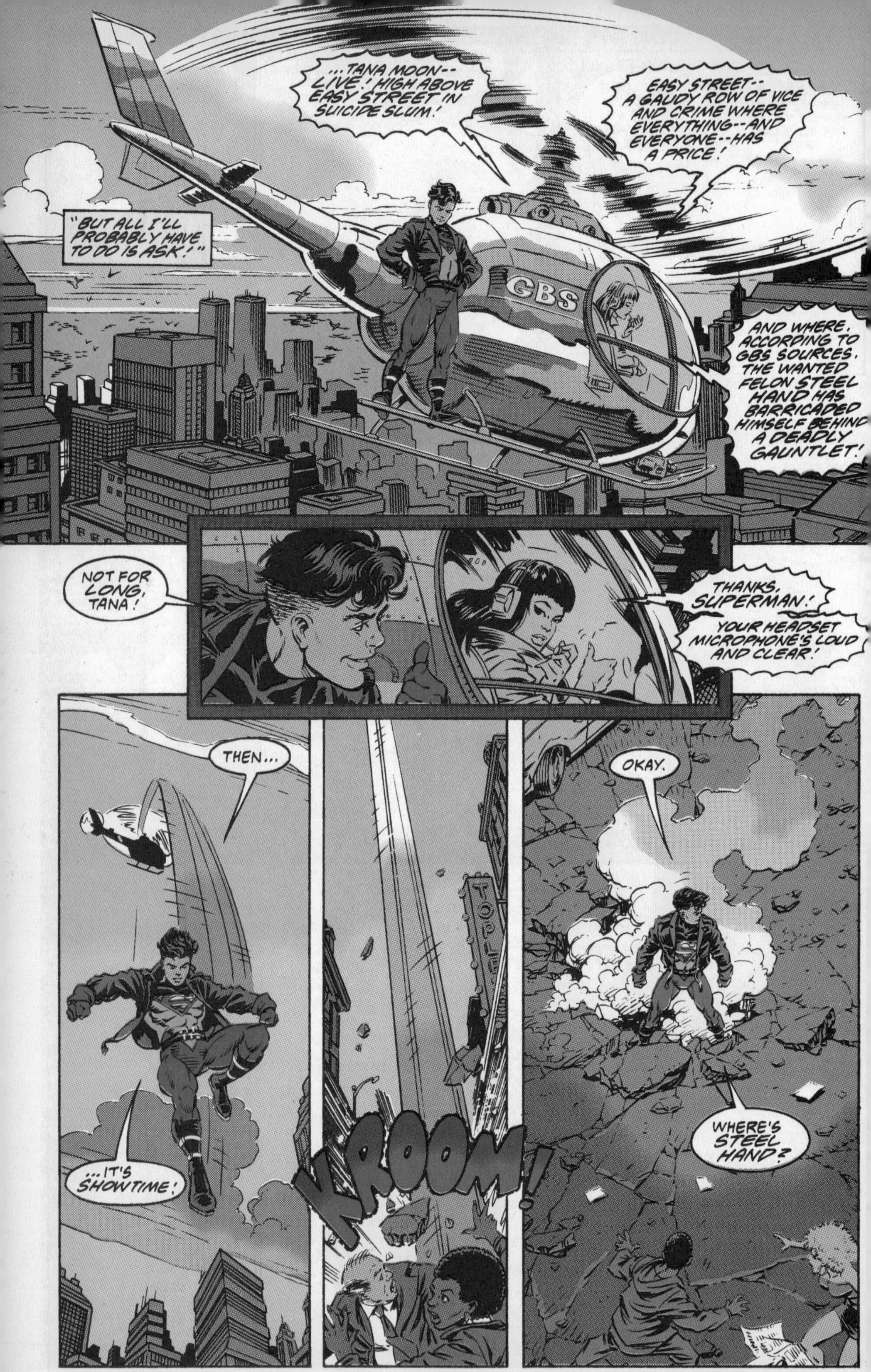
...TANA MOON-- LIVE! HIGH ABOVE EASY STREET IN SUICIDE SLUM!
EASY STREET-- A GAUDY ROW OF VICE AND CRIME WHERE EVERYTHING--AND EVERYONE--HAS A PRICE!
"BUT ALL I'LL PROBABLY HAVE TO DO IS ASK!"
GBS
AND WHERE, ACCORDING TO GBS SOURCES, THE WANTED FELON STEEL HAND HAS BARRICADED HIMSELF BEHIND A DEADLY GAUNTLET!
NOT FOR LONG, TANA!
THANKS, SUPERMAN!
YOUR HEADSET MICROPHONE'S LOUD AND CLEAR!
THEN...
...IT'S SHOWTIME!
KROOOM!
OKAY.
WHERE'S STEEL HAND?

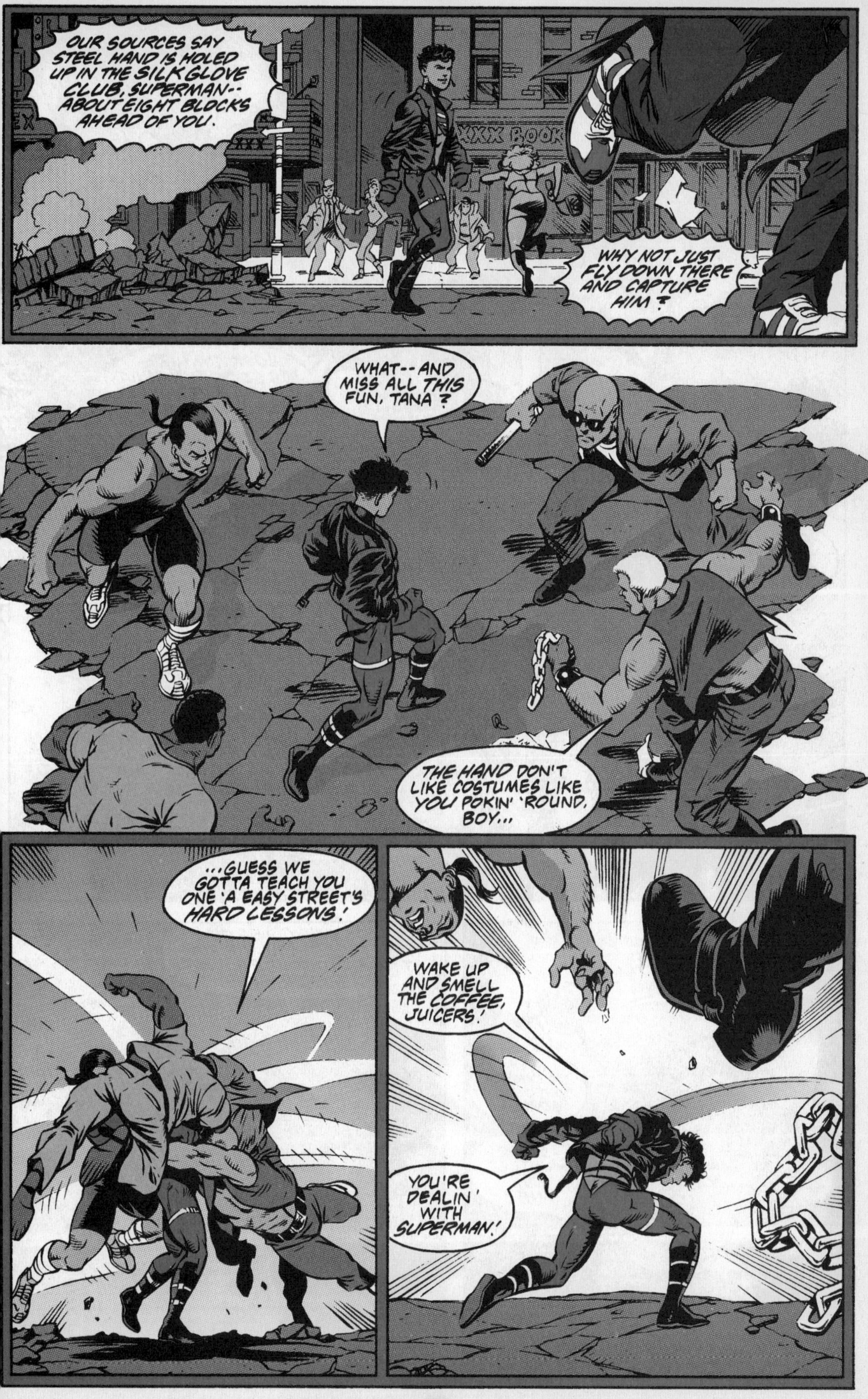
OUR SOURCES SAY STEEL HAND IS HOLED UP IN THE SILK GLOVE CLUB, SUPERMAN-- ABOUT EIGHT BLOCKS AHEAD OF YOU.
WHY NOT JUST FLY DOWN THERE AND CAPTURE HIM?
WHAT--AND MISS ALL THIS FUN, TANA?
THE HAND DON'T LIKE COSTUMES LIKE YOU POKIN' 'ROUND, BOY...
...GUESS WE GOTTA TEACH YOU ONE 'A EASY STREET'S HARD LESSONS!
WAKE UP AND SMELL THE COFFEE, JUICERS!
YOU'RE DEALIN' WITH SUPERMAN!

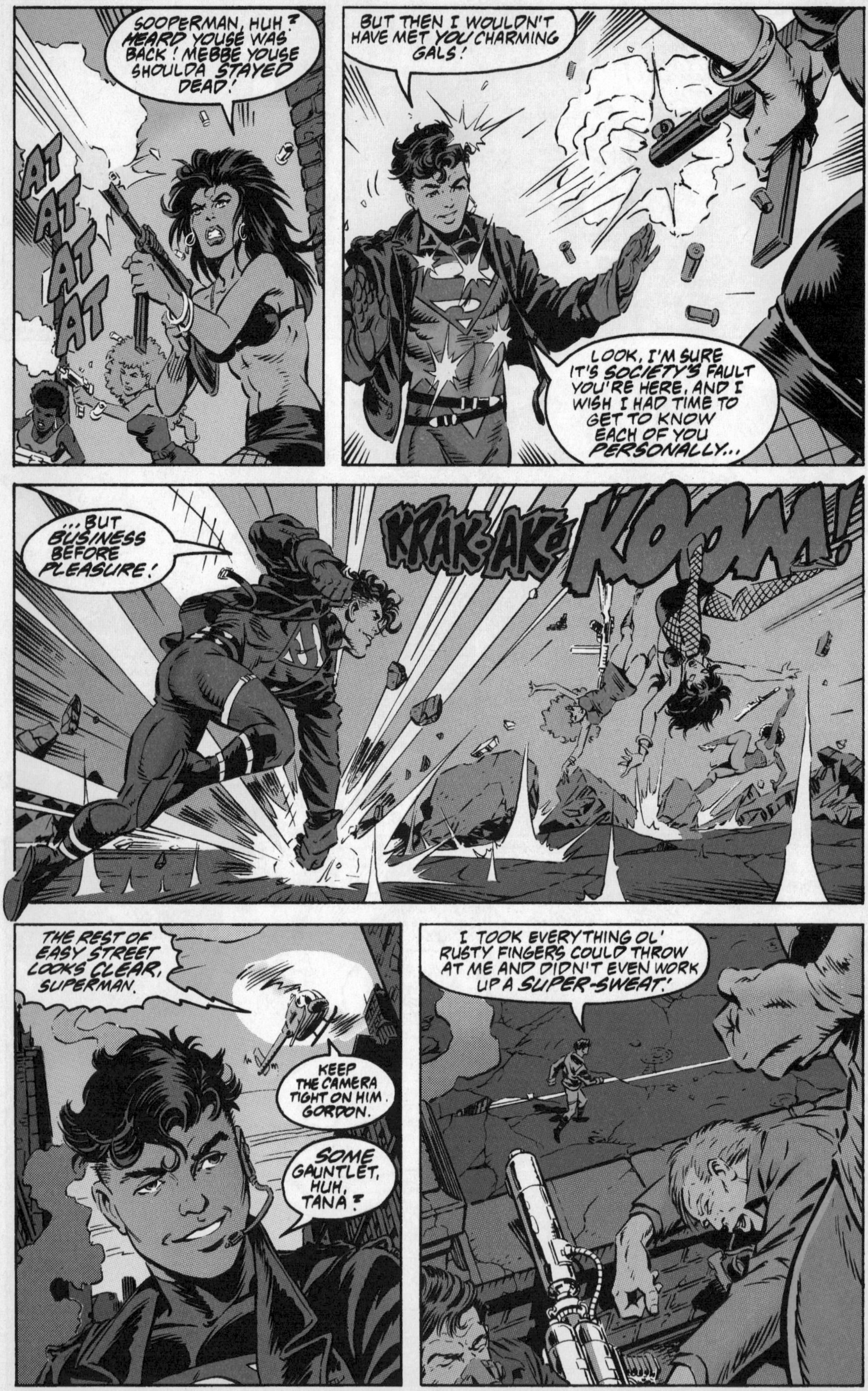
SOOPERMAN, HUH? HEARD YOUSE WAS BACK! MEBBE YOUSE SHOULDA STAYED DEAD!
AT AT AT AT AT
BUT THEN I WOULDN'T HAVE MET YOU CHARMING GALS!
LOOK, I'M SURE IT'S SOCIETY'S FAULT YOU'RE HERE, AND I WISH I HAD TIME TO GET TO KNOW EACH OF YOU PERSONALLY...
...BUT BUSINESS BEFORE PLEASURE!
KRAK-AK-KOOM!
THE REST OF EASY STREET LOOKS CLEAR, SUPERMAN.
KEEP THE CAMERA TIGHT ON HIM, GORDON.
SOME GAUNTLET, HUH, TANA?
I TOOK EVERYTHING OL' RUSTY FINGERS COULD THROW AT ME AND DIDN'T EVEN WORK UP A SUPER-SWEAT!

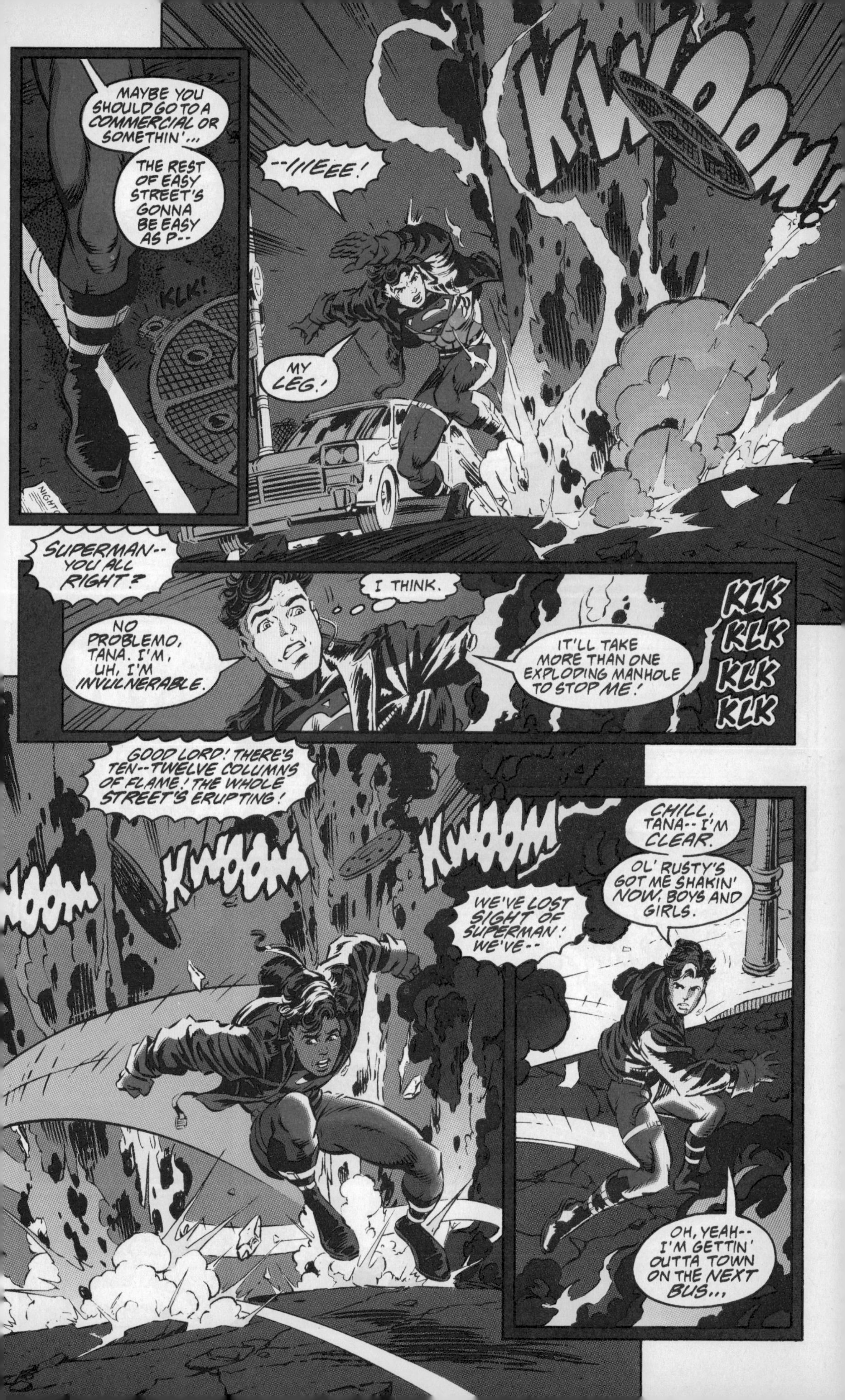
MAYBE YOU SHOULD GO TO A COMMERCIAL OR SOMETHIN'...
THE REST OF EASY STREET'S GONNA BE EASY AS P--
KLK!
--IIIEEE!
KWOOM!
MY LEG!
SUPERMAN-- YOU ALL RIGHT?
I THINK.
NO PROBLEMO, TANA. I'M, UH, I'M INVULNERABLE.
IT'LL TAKE MORE THAN ONE EXPLODING MANHOLE TO STOP ME!
KLK KLK KLK KLK
GOOD LORD! THERE'S TEN--TWELVE COLUMNS OF FLAME! THE WHOLE STREET'S ERUPTING!
KWOOM
KWOOM
KWOOM
WE'VE LOST SIGHT OF SUPERMAN! WE'VE--
CHILL, TANA-- I'M CLEAR.
OL' RUSTY'S GOT ME SHAKIN' NOW, BOYS AND GIRLS.
OH, YEAH-- I'M GETTIN' OUTTA TOWN ON THE NEXT BUS...

BBRRRRRMMM!

AW, C'MON!

IT WAS A JO--

ARCAD

KRNNK

BA-BRAMM

THAT BUS MUST'VE BEEN LOADED WITH EXPLOSIVES! HALF THE BLOCK IS GONE!

WLEX RADIO

I--I DIDN'T SEE A DRIVER--IT COULD'VE BEEN REMOTE-CONTROLLED, BUT...

...SUPERMAN...

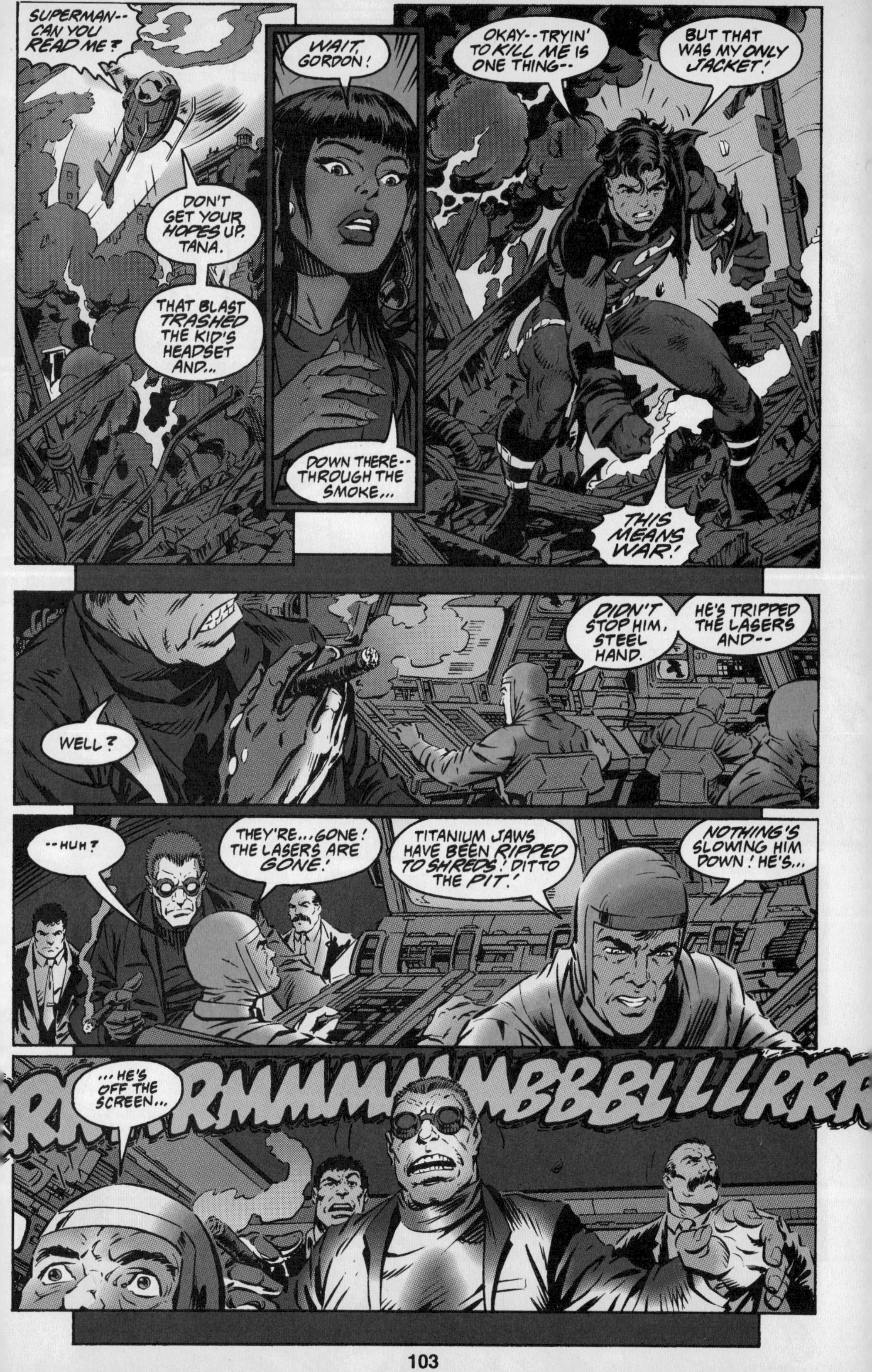
SUPERMAN-- CAN YOU READ ME?
DON'T GET YOUR HOPES UP, TANA.
THAT BLAST TRASHED THE KID'S HEADSET AND...
WAIT, GORDON!
DOWN THERE-- THROUGH THE SMOKE...
OKAY--TRYIN' TO KILL ME IS ONE THING--
BUT THAT WAS MY ONLY JACKET!
THIS MEANS WAR!
WELL?
DIDN'T STOP HIM, STEEL HAND.
HE'S TRIPPED THE LASERS AND--
--HUH?
THEY'RE...GONE! THE LASERS ARE GONE!
TITANIUM JAWS HAVE BEEN RIPPED TO SHREDS! DITTO THE PIT!
NOTHING'S SLOWING HIM DOWN! HE'S...
...HE'S OFF THE SCREEN...
RRMMMMMMBBBLLLRRR

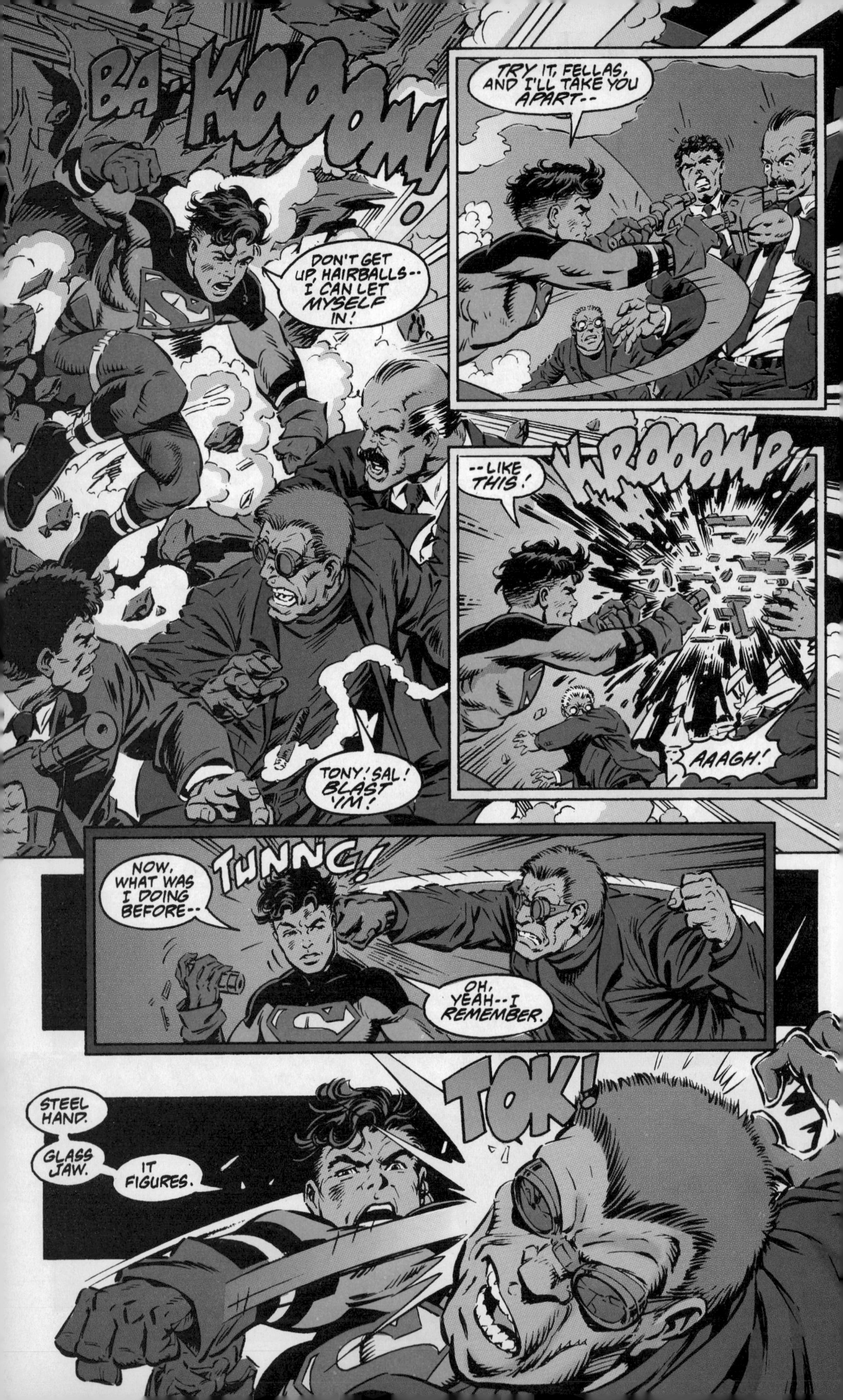
BA-KOOOM
DON'T GET UP, HAIRBALLS-- I CAN LET MYSELF IN!
TRY IT, FELLAS, AND I'LL TAKE YOU APART--
TONY! SAL! BLAST 'IM!
--LIKE THIS!
KROOOM
AAAGH!
NOW, WHAT WAS I DOING BEFORE--
TUNNG!
OH, YEAH--I REMEMBER.
TOK!
STEEL HAND.
GLASS JAW.
IT FIGURES.

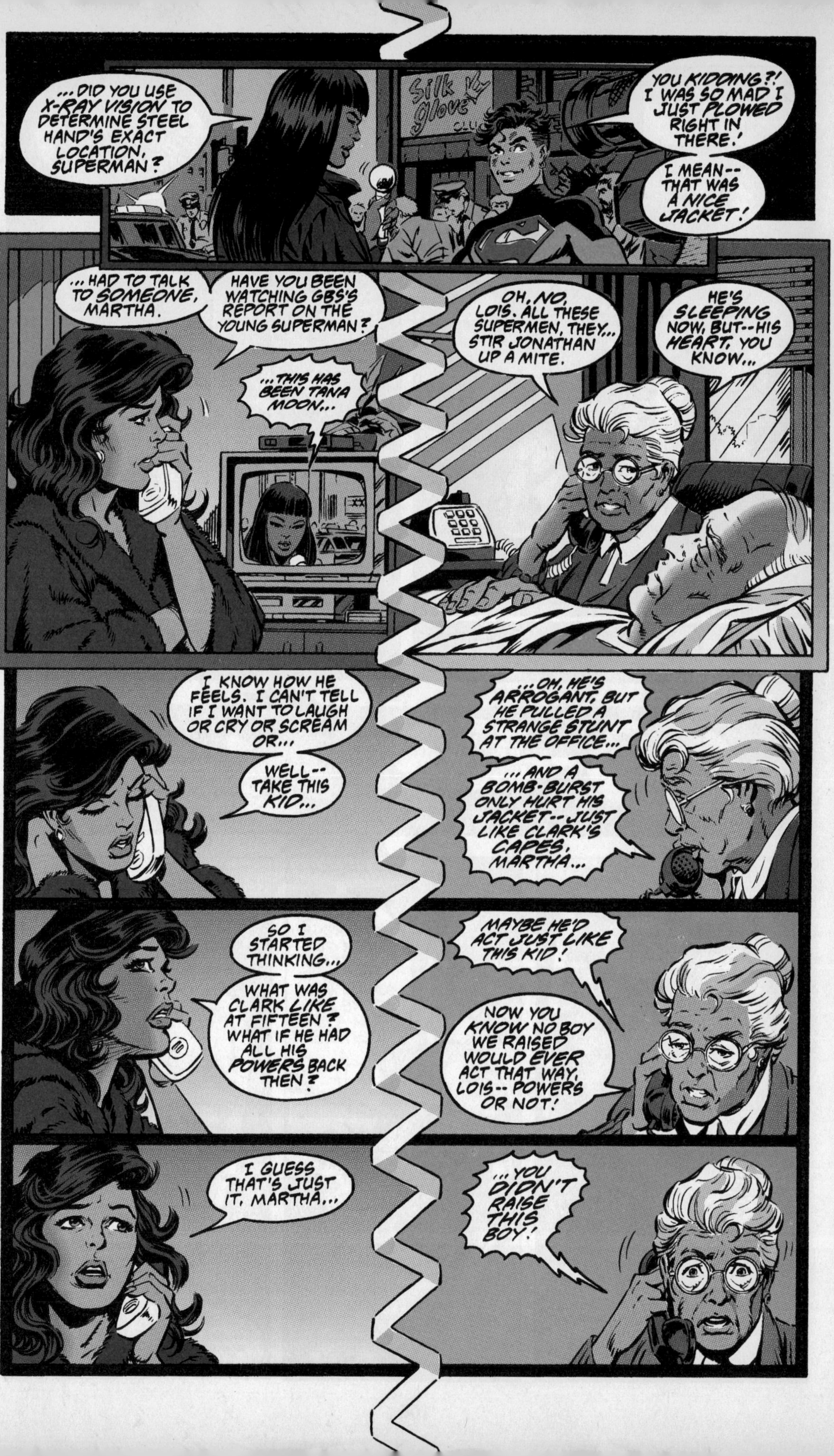

...DID YOU USE X-RAY VISION TO DETERMINE STEEL HAND'S EXACT LOCATION, SUPERMAN?
YOU KIDDING?! I WAS SO MAD I JUST PLOWED RIGHT IN THERE!
I MEAN-- THAT WAS A NICE JACKET!
Silk glove
...HAD TO TALK TO SOMEONE, MARTHA.
HAVE YOU BEEN WATCHING GBS'S REPORT ON THE YOUNG SUPERMAN?
...THIS HAS BEEN TANA MOON...
OH, NO, LOIS. ALL THESE SUPERMEN, THEY... STIR JONATHAN UP A MITE.
HE'S SLEEPING NOW, BUT--HIS HEART, YOU KNOW...
I KNOW HOW HE FEELS. I CAN'T TELL IF I WANT TO LAUGH OR CRY OR SCREAM OR...
WELL-- TAKE THIS KID...
...OH, HE'S ARROGANT, BUT HE PULLED A STRANGE STUNT AT THE OFFICE...
...AND A BOMB-BURST ONLY HURT HIS JACKET-- JUST LIKE CLARK'S CAPES, MARTHA...
SO I STARTED THINKING...
WHAT WAS CLARK LIKE AT FIFTEEN? WHAT IF HE HAD ALL HIS POWERS BACK THEN?
MAYBE HE'D ACT JUST LIKE THIS KID!
NOW YOU KNOW NO BOY WE RAISED WOULD EVER ACT THAT WAY, LOIS-- POWERS OR NOT!
I GUESS THAT'S JUST IT, MARTHA...
...YOU DIDN'T RAISE THIS BOY!

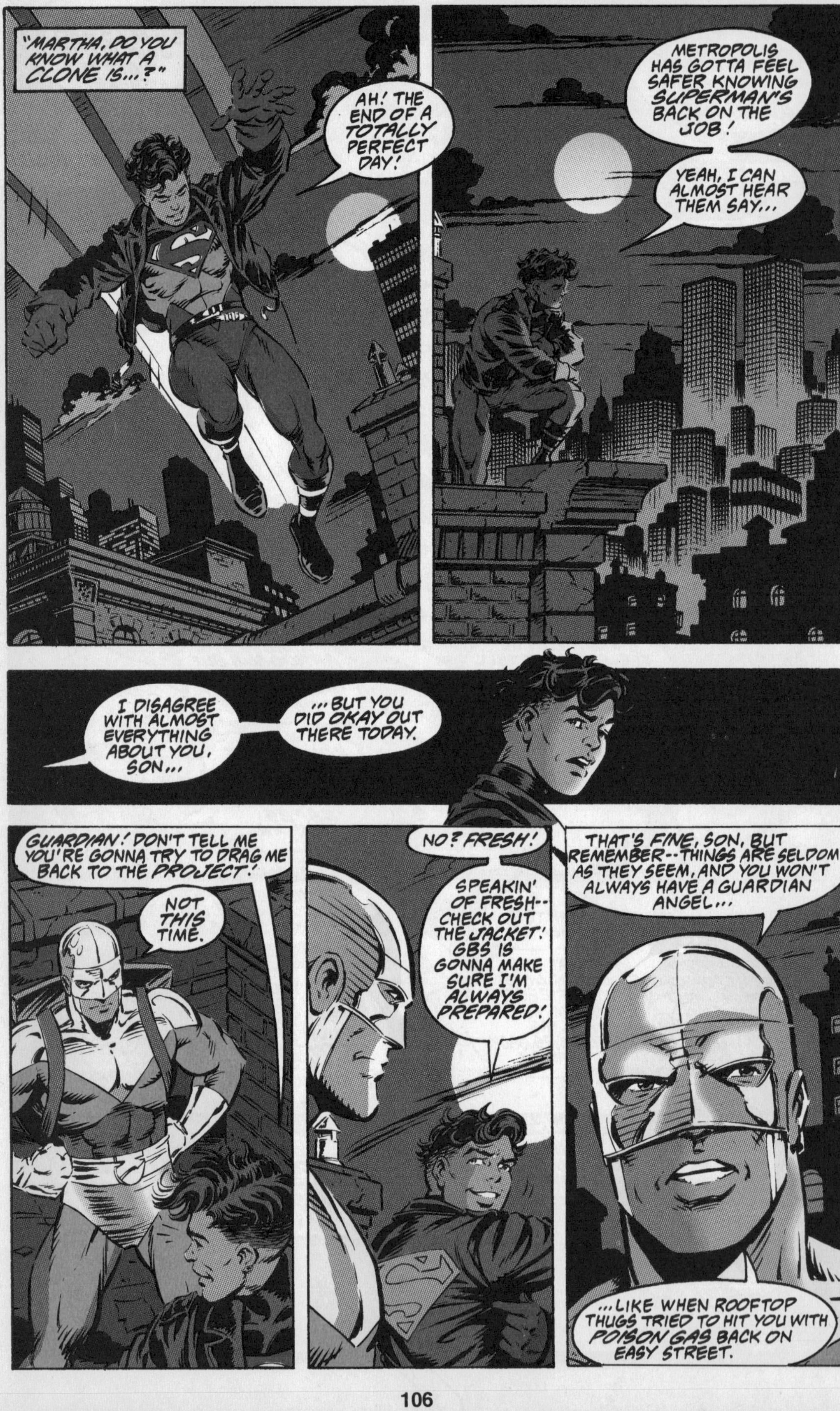
"MARTHA, DO YOU KNOW WHAT A CLONE IS...?"
AH! THE END OF A TOTALLY PERFECT DAY!
METROPOLIS HAS GOTTA FEEL SAFER KNOWING SUPERMAN'S BACK ON THE JOB!
YEAH, I CAN ALMOST HEAR THEM SAY...
I DISAGREE WITH ALMOST EVERYTHING ABOUT YOU, SON...
...BUT YOU DID OKAY OUT THERE TODAY.
GUARDIAN! DON'T TELL ME YOU'RE GONNA TRY TO DRAG ME BACK TO THE PROJECT!
NOT THIS TIME.
NO? FRESH!
SPEAKIN' OF FRESH--CHECK OUT THE JACKET! GBS IS GONNA MAKE SURE I'M ALWAYS PREPARED!
THAT'S FINE, SON, BUT REMEMBER--THINGS ARE SELDOM AS THEY SEEM, AND YOU WON'T ALWAYS HAVE A GUARDIAN ANGEL...
...LIKE WHEN ROOFTOP THUGS TRIED TO HIT YOU WITH POISON GAS BACK ON EASY STREET.

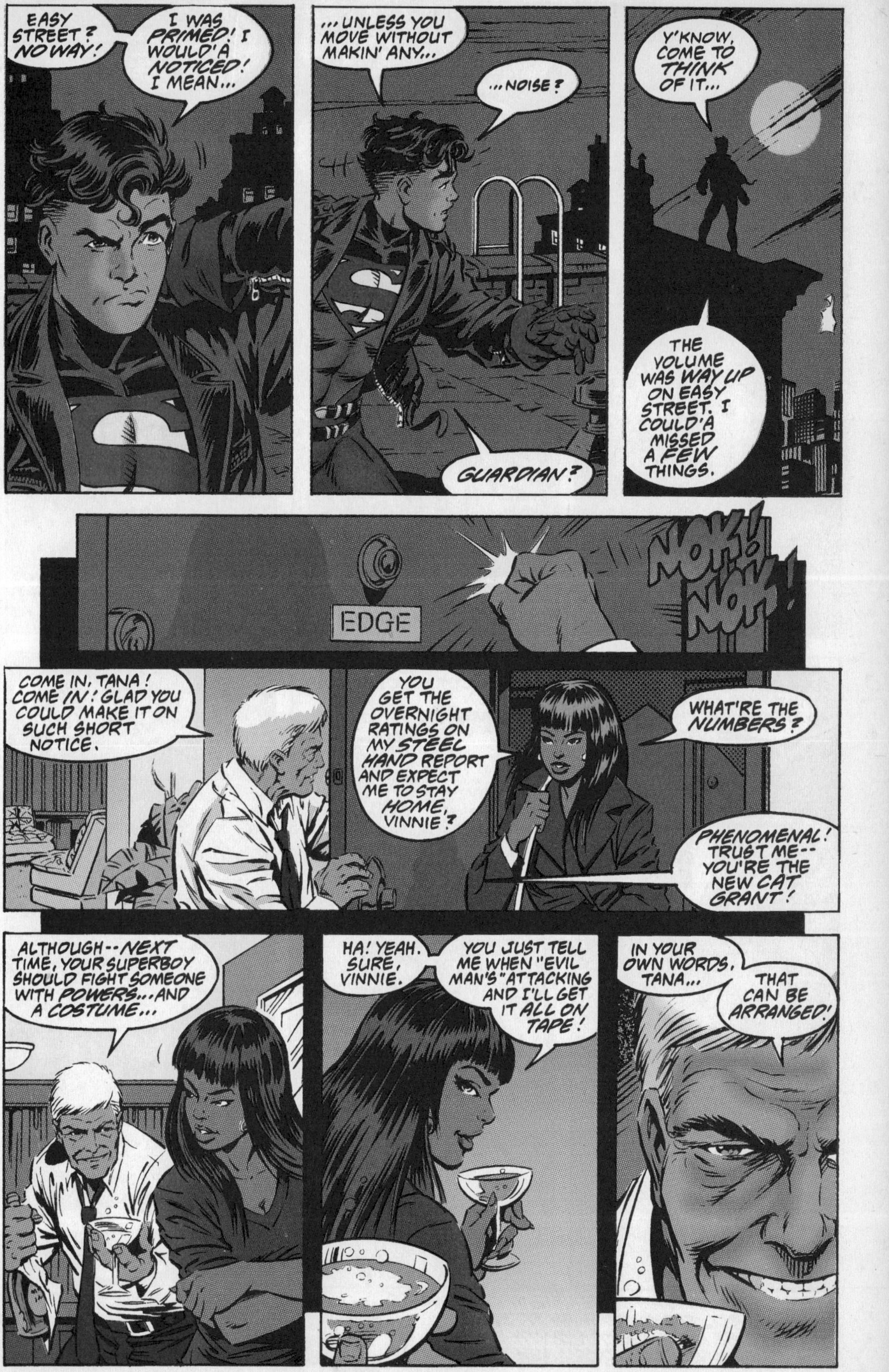
EASY STREET? NO WAY!
I WAS PRIMED! I WOULD'A NOTICED! I MEAN...
...UNLESS YOU MOVE WITHOUT MAKIN' ANY...
...NOISE?
GUARDIAN?
Y'KNOW, COME TO THINK OF IT...
THE VOLUME WAS WAY UP ON EASY STREET. I COULD'A MISSED A FEW THINGS.
EDGE
NOK! NOK!
COME IN, TANA! COME IN! GLAD YOU COULD MAKE IT ON SUCH SHORT NOTICE.
YOU GET THE OVERNIGHT RATINGS ON MY STEEL HAND REPORT AND EXPECT ME TO STAY HOME, VINNIE?
WHAT'RE THE NUMBERS?
PHENOMENAL! TRUST ME-- YOU'RE THE NEW CAT GRANT!
ALTHOUGH--NEXT TIME, YOUR SUPERBOY SHOULD FIGHT SOMEONE WITH POWERS...AND A COSTUME...
HA! YEAH. SURE, VINNIE.
YOU JUST TELL ME WHEN "EVIL MAN'S" ATTACKING AND I'LL GET IT ALL ON TAPE!
IN YOUR OWN WORDS, TANA...
THAT CAN BE ARRANGED!

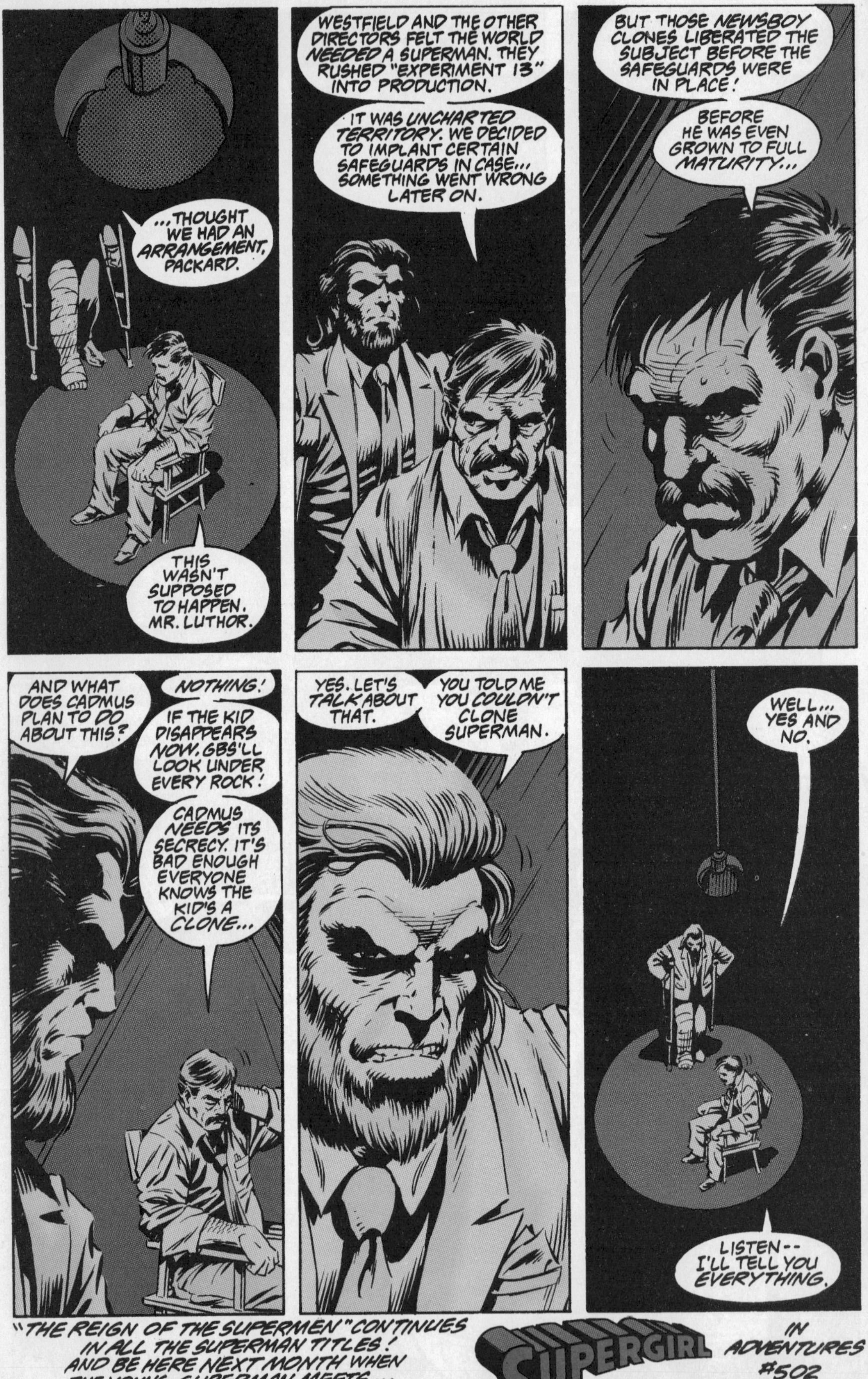
...THOUGHT WE HAD AN ARRANGEMENT, PACKARD.
THIS WASN'T SUPPOSED TO HAPPEN. MR. LUTHOR.
WESTFIELD AND THE OTHER DIRECTORS FELT THE WORLD NEEDED A SUPERMAN. THEY RUSHED "EXPERIMENT 13" INTO PRODUCTION.
IT WAS UNCHARTED TERRITORY. WE DECIDED TO IMPLANT CERTAIN SAFEGUARDS IN CASE... SOMETHING WENT WRONG LATER ON.
BUT THOSE NEWSBOY CLONES LIBERATED THE SUBJECT BEFORE THE SAFEGUARDS WERE IN PLACE!
BEFORE HE WAS EVEN GROWN TO FULL MATURITY...
AND WHAT DOES CADMUS PLAN TO DO ABOUT THIS?
NOTHING!
IF THE KID DISAPPEARS NOW, GBS'LL LOOK UNDER EVERY ROCK!
CADMUS NEEDS ITS SECRECY. IT'S BAD ENOUGH EVERYONE KNOWS THE KID'S A CLONE...
YES. LET'S TALK ABOUT THAT.
YOU TOLD ME YOU COULDN'T CLONE SUPERMAN.
WELL... YES AND NO.
LISTEN-- I'LL TELL YOU EVERYTHING.

"THE REIGN OF THE SUPERMEN" CONTINUES IN ALL THE SUPERMAN TITLES! AND BE HERE NEXT MONTH WHEN THE YOUNG SUPERMAN MEETS... SUPERGIRL IN ADVENTURES #502

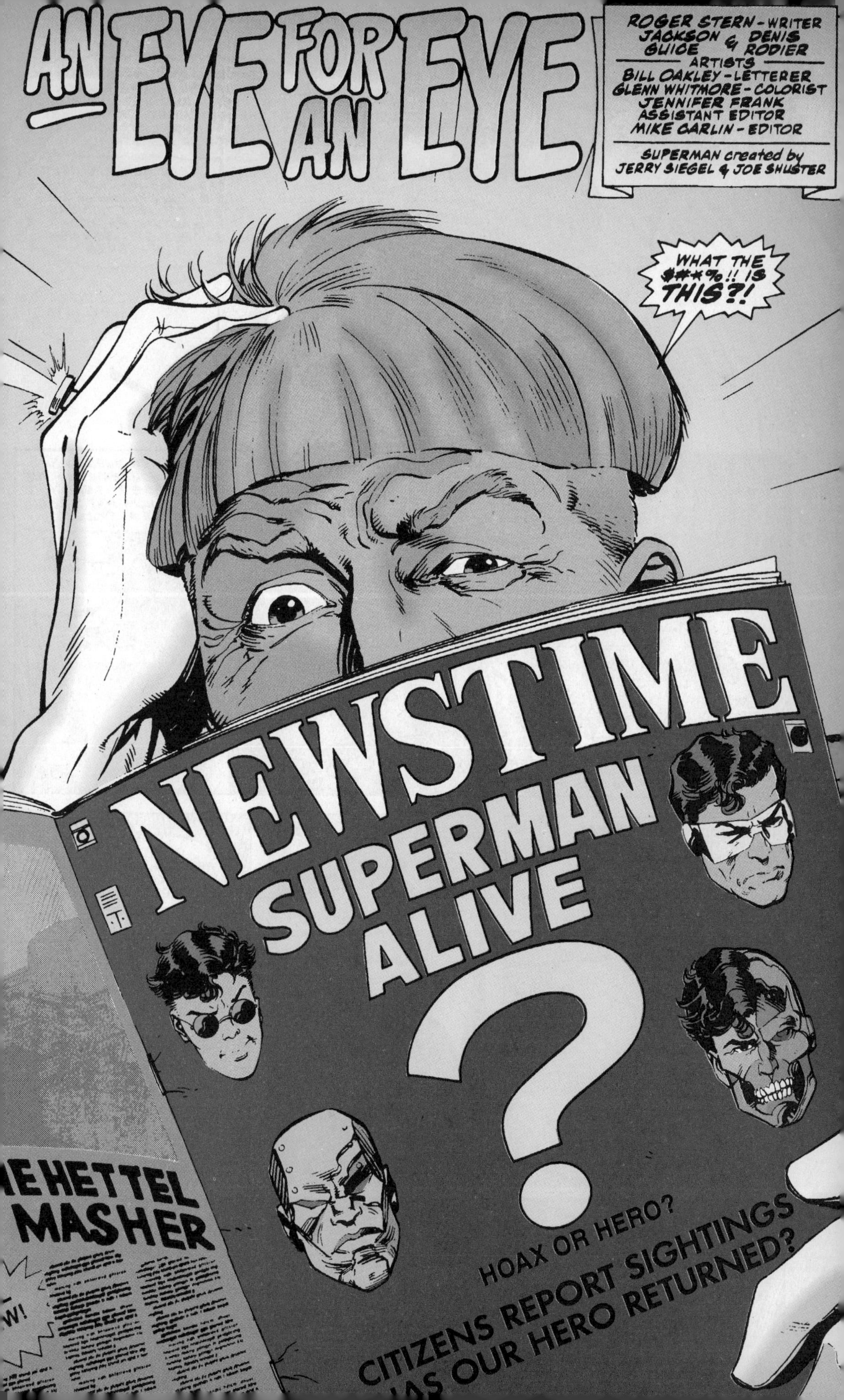
AN EYE FOR AN EYE
ROGER STERN - WRITER
JACKSON GUICE & DENIS RODIER
ARTISTS
BILL OAKLEY - LETTERER
GLENN WHITMORE - COLORIST
JENNIFER FRANK
ASSISTANT EDITOR
MIKE CARLIN - EDITOR
SUPERMAN created by
JERRY SIEGEL & JOE SHUSTER
WHAT THE $#*%!! IS THIS?!
NEWSTIME
SUPERMAN ALIVE
?
HOAX OR HERO?
CITIZENS REPORT SIGHTINGS
HAS OUR HERO RETURNED?
HETTEL
MASHER

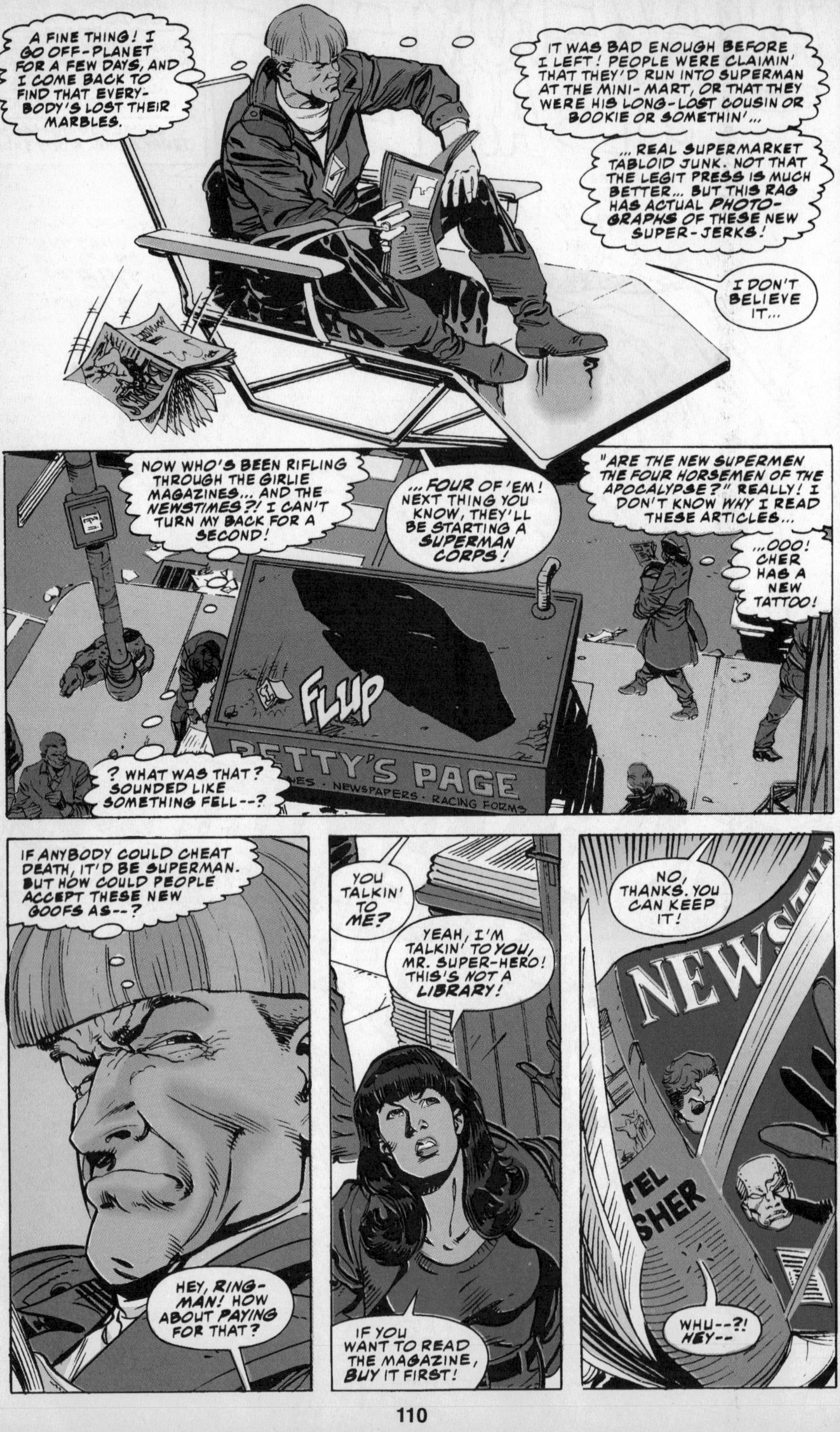

A FINE THING! I GO OFF-PLANET FOR A FEW DAYS, AND I COME BACK TO FIND THAT EVERY-BODY'S LOST THEIR MARBLES.
IT WAS BAD ENOUGH BEFORE I LEFT! PEOPLE WERE CLAIMIN' THAT THEY'D RUN INTO SUPERMAN AT THE MINI-MART, OR THAT THEY WERE HIS LONG-LOST COUSIN OR BOOKIE OR SOMETHIN'...
... REAL SUPERMARKET TABLOID JUNK. NOT THAT THE LEGIT PRESS IS MUCH BETTER... BUT THIS RAG HAS ACTUAL PHOTO-GRAPHS OF THESE NEW SUPER-JERKS!
I DON'T BELIEVE IT...
NOW WHO'S BEEN RIFLING THROUGH THE GIRLIE MAGAZINES... AND THE NEWSTIMES?! I CAN'T TURN MY BACK FOR A SECOND!
... FOUR OF 'EM! NEXT THING YOU KNOW, THEY'LL BE STARTING A SUPERMAN CORPS!
"ARE THE NEW SUPERMEN THE FOUR HORSEMEN OF THE APOCALYPSE?" REALLY! I DON'T KNOW WHY I READ THESE ARTICLES...
...OOO! CHER HAS A NEW TATTOO!
FLUP
? WHAT WAS THAT? SOUNDED LIKE SOMETHING FELL--?
BETTY'S PAGE
NES . NEWSPAPERS . RACING FORMS
IF ANYBODY COULD CHEAT DEATH, IT'D BE SUPERMAN. BUT HOW COULD PEOPLE ACCEPT THESE NEW GOOFS AS--?
HEY, RING-MAN! HOW ABOUT PAYING FOR THAT?
YOU TALKIN' TO ME?
YEAH, I'M TALKIN' TO YOU, MR. SUPER-HERO! THIS'S NOT A LIBRARY!
IF YOU WANT TO READ THE MAGAZINE, BUY IT FIRST!
NO, THANKS. YOU CAN KEEP IT!
NEWS
TEL
SHER
WHU--?! HEY--

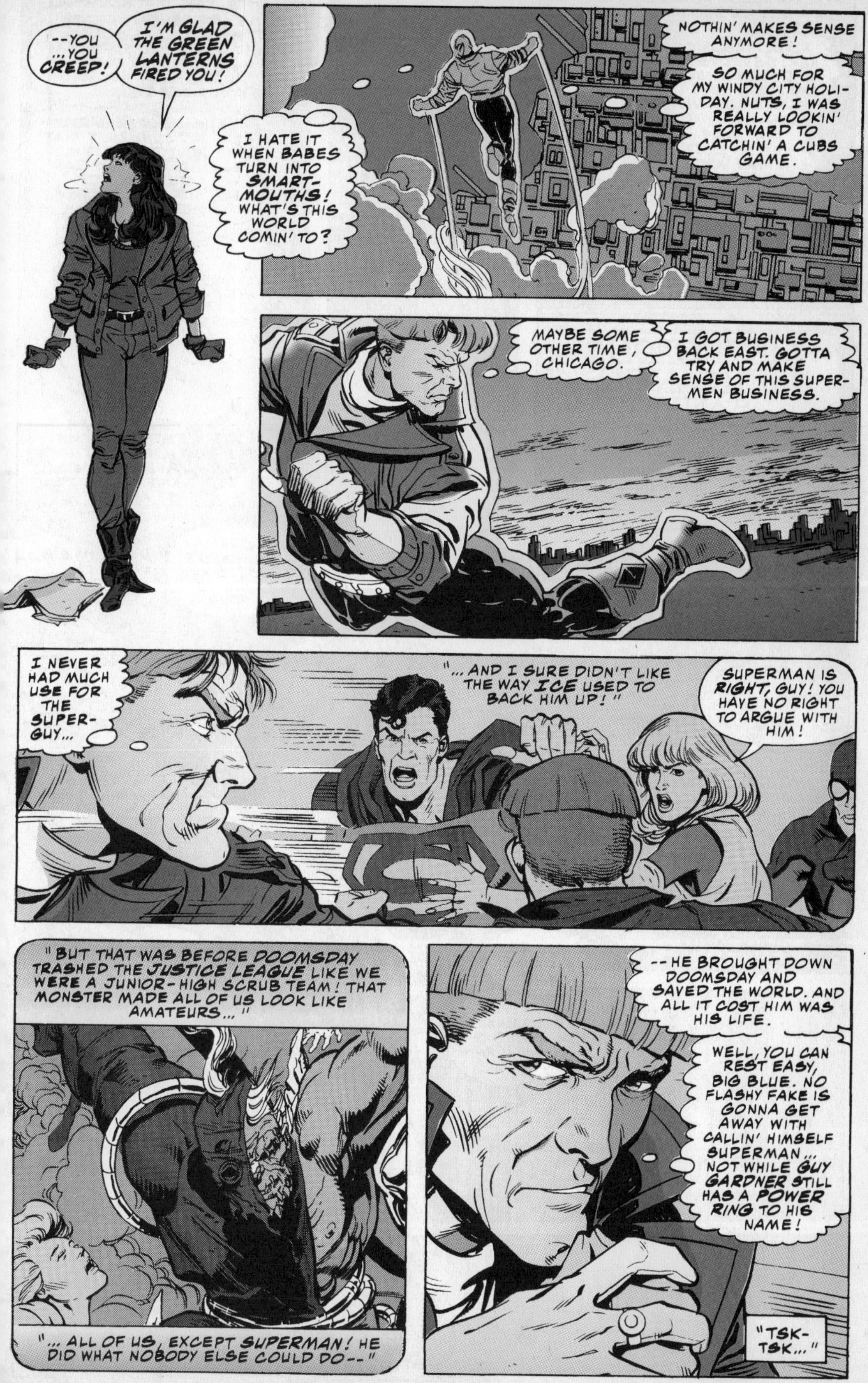
--YOU ...YOU CREEP!
I'M GLAD THE GREEN LANTERNS FIRED YOU!
I HATE IT WHEN BABES TURN INTO SMART-MOUTHS! WHAT'S THIS WORLD COMIN' TO?
NOTHIN' MAKES SENSE ANYMORE!
SO MUCH FOR MY WINDY CITY HOLI-DAY. NUTS, I WAS REALLY LOOKIN' FORWARD TO CATCHIN' A CUBS GAME.
MAYBE SOME OTHER TIME, CHICAGO.
I GOT BUSINESS BACK EAST. GOTTA TRY AND MAKE SENSE OF THIS SUPER-MEN BUSINESS.
I NEVER HAD MUCH USE FOR THE SUPER-GUY...
"...AND I SURE DIDN'T LIKE THE WAY ICE USED TO BACK HIM UP!"
SUPERMAN IS RIGHT, GUY! YOU HAVE NO RIGHT TO ARGUE WITH HIM!
"BUT THAT WAS BEFORE DOOMSDAY TRASHED THE JUSTICE LEAGUE LIKE WE WERE A JUNIOR-HIGH SCRUB TEAM! THAT MONSTER MADE ALL OF US LOOK LIKE AMATEURS..."
"...ALL OF US, EXCEPT SUPERMAN! HE DID WHAT NOBODY ELSE COULD DO--"
--HE BROUGHT DOWN DOOMSDAY AND SAVED THE WORLD. AND ALL IT COST HIM WAS HIS LIFE.
WELL, YOU CAN REST EASY, BIG BLUE. NO FLASHY FAKE IS GONNA GET AWAY WITH CALLIN' HIMSELF SUPERMAN... NOT WHILE GUY GARDNER STILL HAS A POWER RING TO HIS NAME!
"TSK-TSK..."

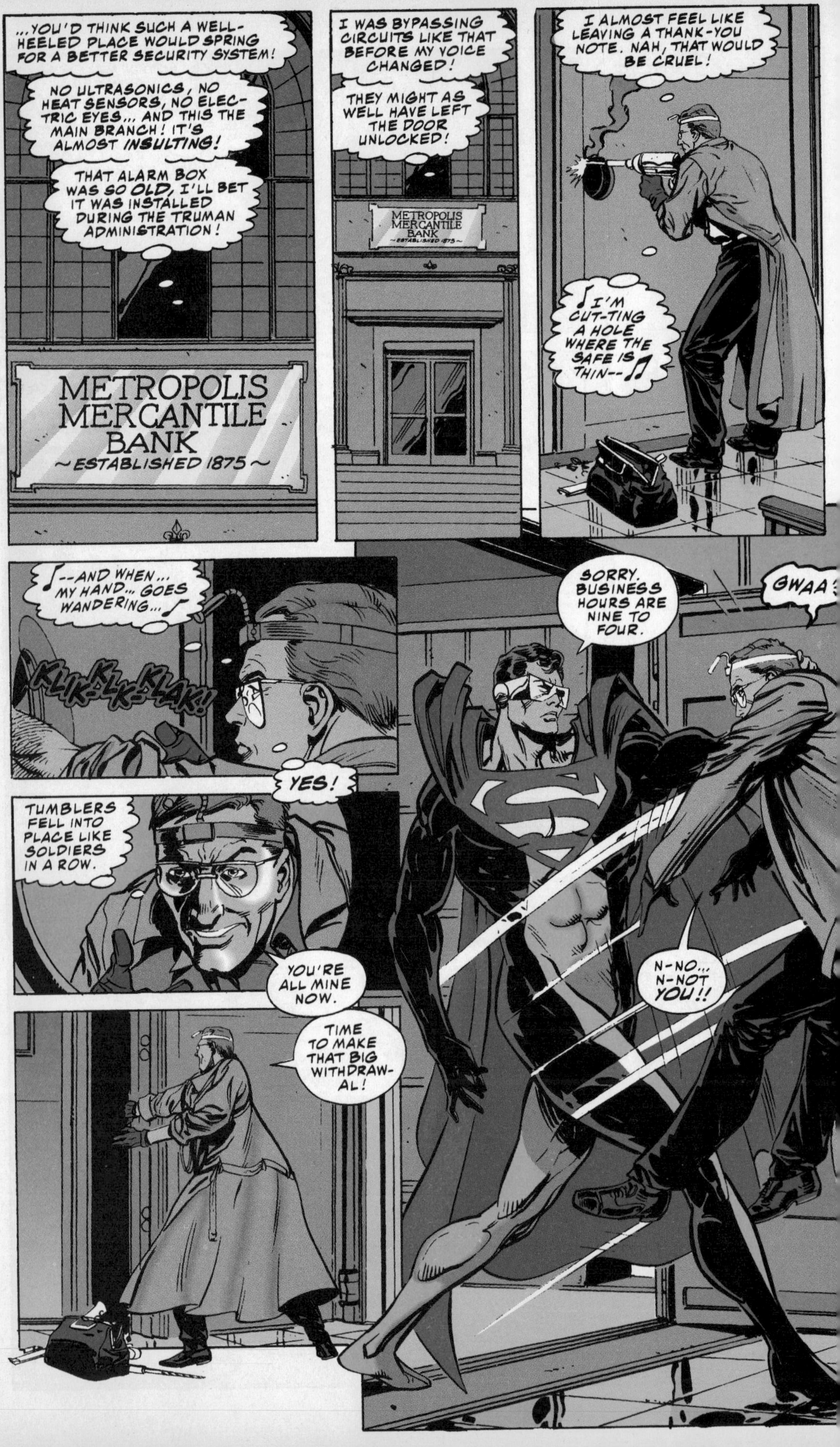
...YOU'D THINK SUCH A WELL-HEELED PLACE WOULD SPRING FOR A BETTER SECURITY SYSTEM!
NO ULTRASONICS, NO HEAT SENSORS, NO ELECTRIC EYES... AND THIS THE MAIN BRANCH! IT'S ALMOST INSULTING!
THAT ALARM BOX WAS SO OLD, I'LL BET IT WAS INSTALLED DURING THE TRUMAN ADMINISTRATION!
METROPOLIS MERCANTILE BANK ~ESTABLISHED 1875~
I WAS BYPASSING CIRCUITS LIKE THAT BEFORE MY VOICE CHANGED!
THEY MIGHT AS WELL HAVE LEFT THE DOOR UNLOCKED!
METROPOLIS MERCANTILE BANK ~ESTABLISHED 1875~
I ALMOST FEEL LIKE LEAVING A THANK-YOU NOTE. NAH, THAT WOULD BE CRUEL!
♪ I'M CUT-TING A HOLE WHERE THE SAFE IS THIN-- ♪
♪ --AND WHEN... MY HAND... GOES WANDERING... ♪
KLIK-KLIK-KLAK!
YES!
TUMBLERS FELL INTO PLACE LIKE SOLDIERS IN A ROW.
YOU'RE ALL MINE NOW.
TIME TO MAKE THAT BIG WITHDRAW-AL!
SORRY. BUSINESS HOURS ARE NINE TO FOUR.
GWAA
N-NO... N-NOT YOU!!

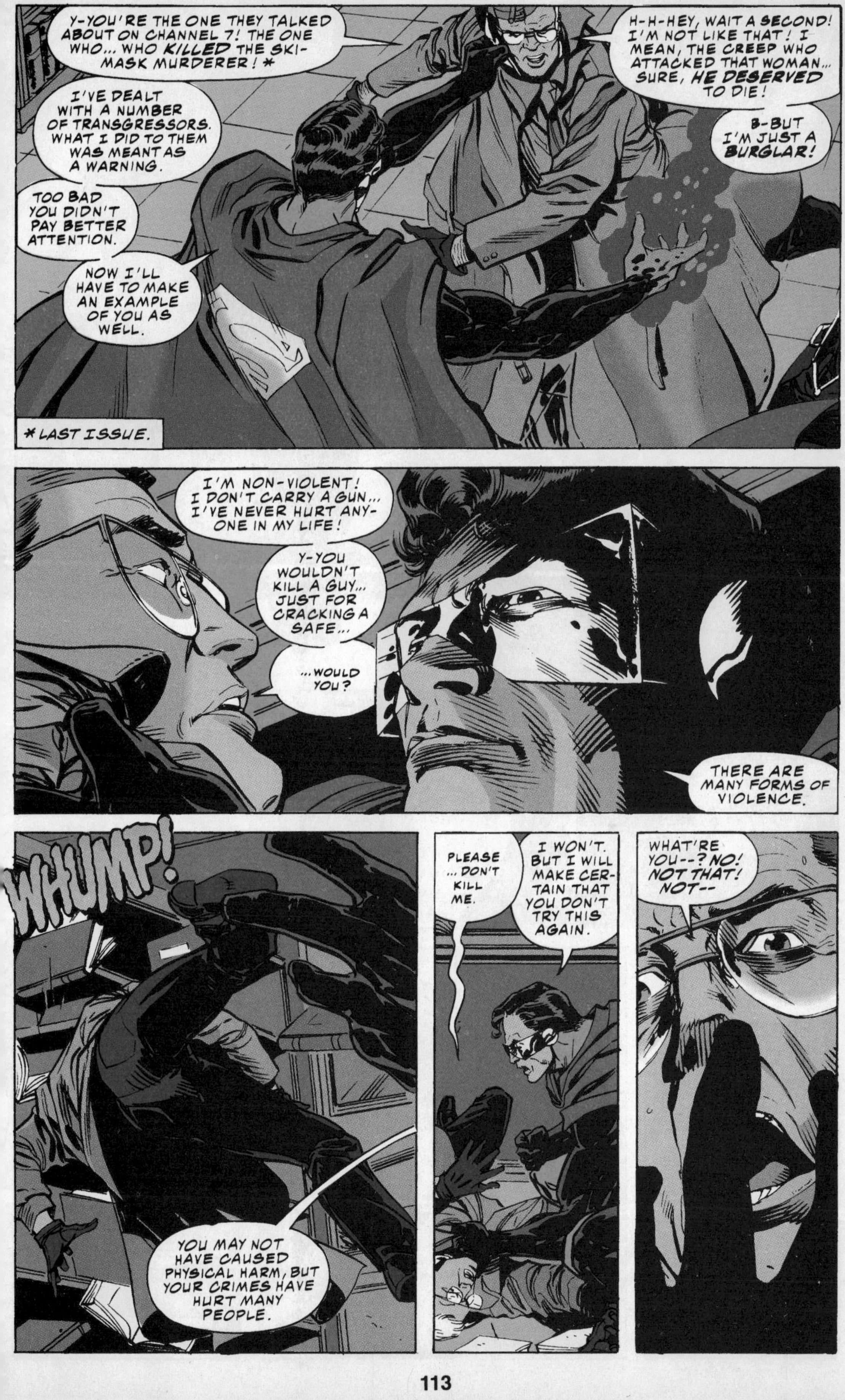
Y-YOU'RE THE ONE THEY TALKED ABOUT ON CHANNEL 7! THE ONE WHO... WHO KILLED THE SKI-MASK MURDERER! *
H-H-HEY, WAIT A SECOND! I'M NOT LIKE THAT! I MEAN, THE CREEP WHO ATTACKED THAT WOMAN... SURE, HE DESERVED TO DIE!
B-BUT I'M JUST A BURGLAR!
I'VE DEALT WITH A NUMBER OF TRANSGRESSORS. WHAT I DID TO THEM WAS MEANT AS A WARNING.
TOO BAD YOU DIDN'T PAY BETTER ATTENTION.
NOW I'LL HAVE TO MAKE AN EXAMPLE OF YOU AS WELL.
* LAST ISSUE.
I'M NON-VIOLENT! I DON'T CARRY A GUN... I'VE NEVER HURT ANYONE IN MY LIFE!
Y-YOU WOULDN'T KILL A GUY... JUST FOR CRACKING A SAFE...
...WOULD YOU?
THERE ARE MANY FORMS OF VIOLENCE.
WHUMP!
YOU MAY NOT HAVE CAUSED PHYSICAL HARM, BUT YOUR CRIMES HAVE HURT MANY PEOPLE.
PLEASE ...DON'T KILL ME.
I WON'T. BUT I WILL MAKE CERTAIN THAT YOU DON'T TRY THIS AGAIN.
WHAT'RE YOU--? NO! NOT THAT! NOT--

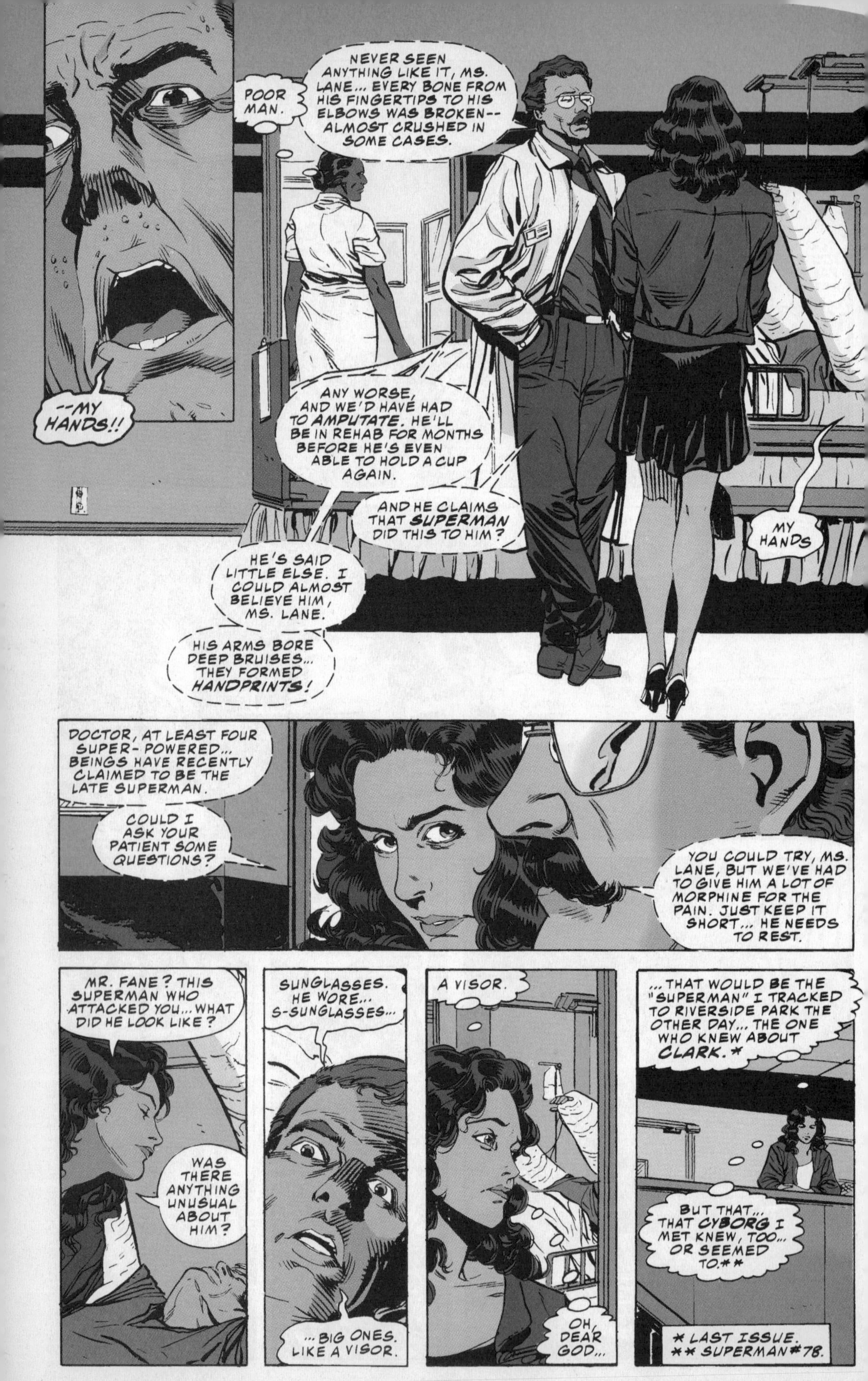
POOR MAN.
NEVER SEEN ANYTHING LIKE IT, MS. LANE... EVERY BONE FROM HIS FINGERTIPS TO HIS ELBOWS WAS BROKEN-- ALMOST CRUSHED IN SOME CASES.
--MY HANDS!!
ANY WORSE, AND WE'D HAVE HAD TO AMPUTATE. HE'LL BE IN REHAB FOR MONTHS BEFORE HE'S EVEN ABLE TO HOLD A CUP AGAIN.
AND HE CLAIMS THAT SUPERMAN DID THIS TO HIM?
MY HANDS
HE'S SAID LITTLE ELSE. I COULD ALMOST BELIEVE HIM, MS. LANE.
HIS ARMS BORE DEEP BRUISES... THEY FORMED HANDPRINTS!
DOCTOR, AT LEAST FOUR SUPER-POWERED... BEINGS HAVE RECENTLY CLAIMED TO BE THE LATE SUPERMAN.
COULD I ASK YOUR PATIENT SOME QUESTIONS?
YOU COULD TRY, MS. LANE, BUT WE'VE HAD TO GIVE HIM A LOT OF MORPHINE FOR THE PAIN. JUST KEEP IT SHORT... HE NEEDS TO REST.
MR. FANE? THIS SUPERMAN WHO ATTACKED YOU... WHAT DID HE LOOK LIKE?
WAS THERE ANYTHING UNUSUAL ABOUT HIM?
SUNGLASSES. HE WORE... S-SUNGLASSES...
...BIG ONES. LIKE A VISOR.
A VISOR.
OH, DEAR GOD...
...THAT WOULD BE THE "SUPERMAN" I TRACKED TO RIVERSIDE PARK THE OTHER DAY... THE ONE WHO KNEW ABOUT CLARK.*
BUT THAT... THAT CYBORG I MET KNEW, TOO... OR SEEMED TO.**
* LAST ISSUE.
** SUPERMAN #78.

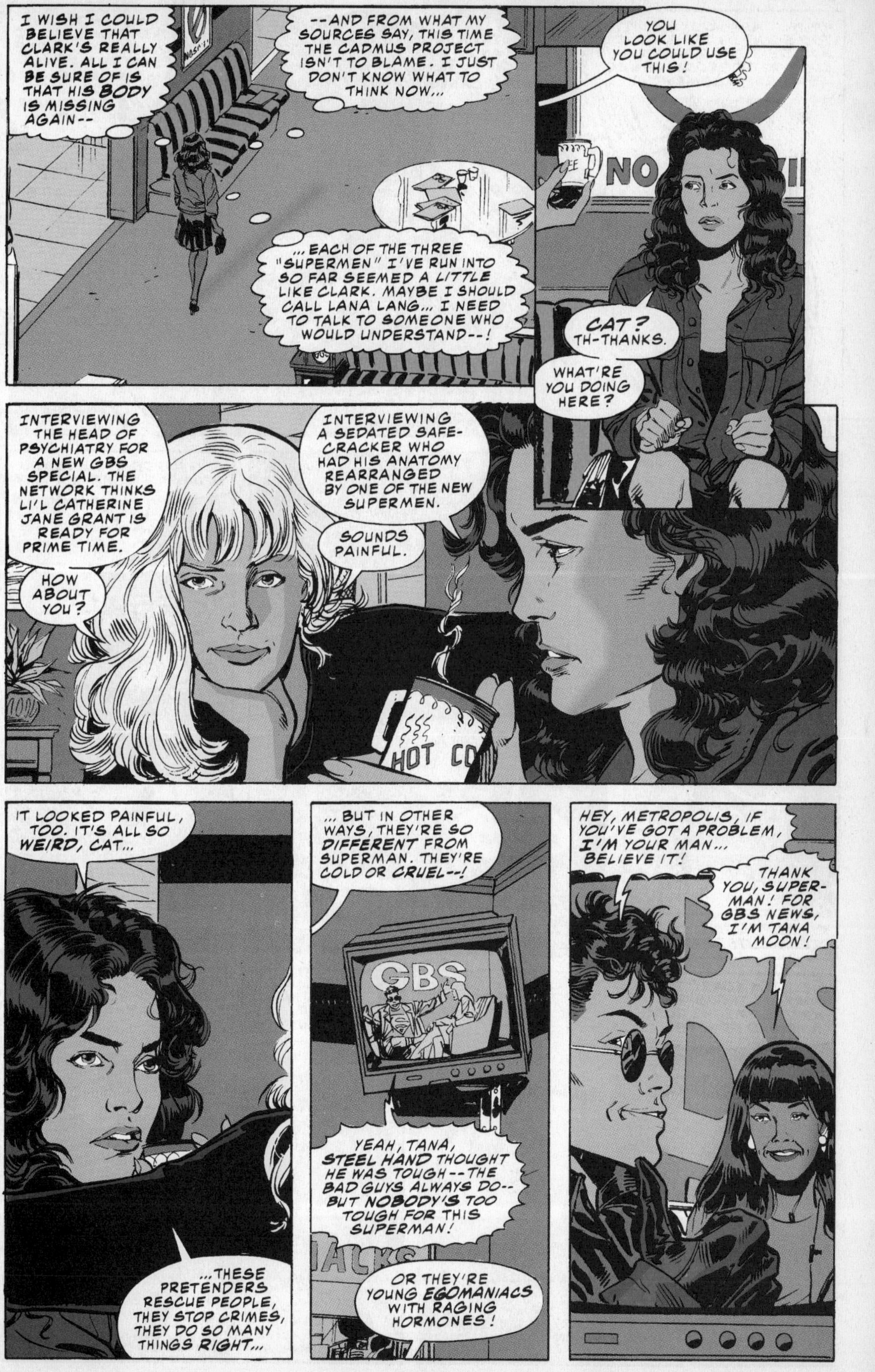
I WISH I COULD BELIEVE THAT CLARK'S REALLY ALIVE. ALL I CAN BE SURE OF IS THAT HIS BODY IS MISSING AGAIN--
--AND FROM WHAT MY SOURCES SAY, THIS TIME THE CADMUS PROJECT ISN'T TO BLAME. I JUST DON'T KNOW WHAT TO THINK NOW...
...EACH OF THE THREE "SUPERMEN" I'VE RUN INTO SO FAR SEEMED A LITTLE LIKE CLARK. MAYBE I SHOULD CALL LANA LANG... I NEED TO TALK TO SOMEONE WHO WOULD UNDERSTAND--!
YOU LOOK LIKE YOU COULD USE THIS!
CAT? TH-THANKS.
WHAT'RE YOU DOING HERE?
INTERVIEWING THE HEAD OF PSYCHIATRY FOR A NEW GBS SPECIAL. THE NETWORK THINKS LI'L CATHERINE JANE GRANT IS READY FOR PRIME TIME.
HOW ABOUT YOU?
INTERVIEWING A SEDATED SAFE-CRACKER WHO HAD HIS ANATOMY REARRANGED BY ONE OF THE NEW SUPERMEN.
SOUNDS PAINFUL.
HOT CO
IT LOOKED PAINFUL, TOO. IT'S ALL SO WEIRD, CAT...
...THESE PRETENDERS RESCUE PEOPLE, THEY STOP CRIMES, THEY DO SO MANY THINGS RIGHT...
...BUT IN OTHER WAYS, THEY'RE SO DIFFERENT FROM SUPERMAN. THEY'RE COLD OR CRUEL--!
GBS
YEAH, TANA, STEEL HAND THOUGHT HE WAS TOUGH--THE BAD GUYS ALWAYS DO--BUT NOBODY'S TOO TOUGH FOR THIS SUPERMAN!
OR THEY'RE YOUNG EGOMANIACS WITH RAGING HORMONES!
HEY, METROPOLIS, IF YOU'VE GOT A PROBLEM, I'M YOUR MAN... BELIEVE IT!
THANK YOU, SUPER-MAN! FOR GBS NEWS, I'M TANA MOON!

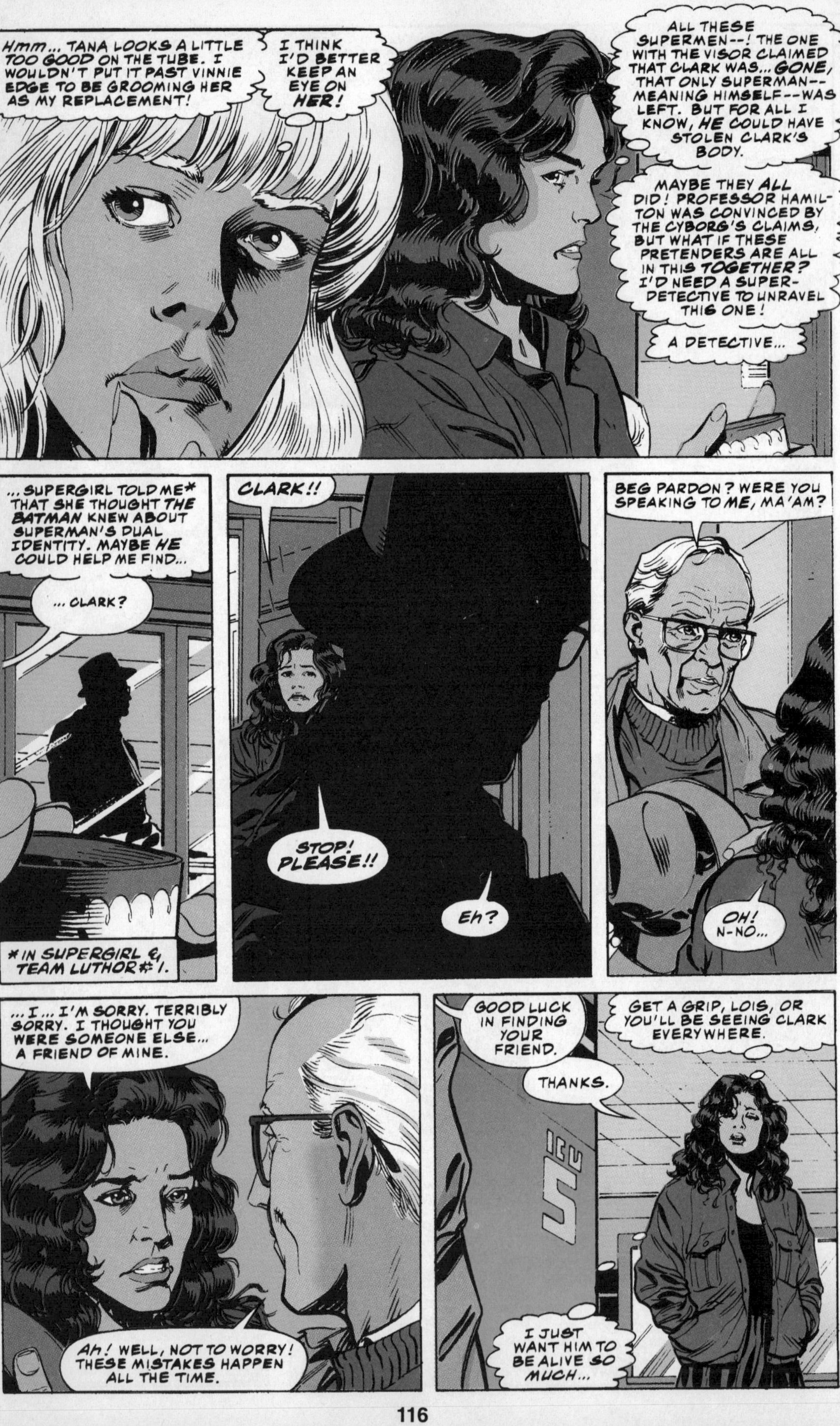
Hmm... TANA LOOKS A LITTLE TOO GOOD ON THE TUBE. I WOULDN'T PUT IT PAST VINNIE EDGE TO BE GROOMING HER AS MY REPLACEMENT!
I THINK I'D BETTER KEEP AN EYE ON HER!
ALL THESE SUPERMEN--! THE ONE WITH THE VISOR CLAIMED THAT CLARK WAS... GONE, THAT ONLY SUPERMAN--MEANING HIMSELF--WAS LEFT. BUT FOR ALL I KNOW, HE COULD HAVE STOLEN CLARK'S BODY.
MAYBE THEY ALL DID! PROFESSOR HAMILTON WAS CONVINCED BY THE CYBORG'S CLAIMS, BUT WHAT IF THESE PRETENDERS ARE ALL IN THIS TOGETHER? I'D NEED A SUPER-DETECTIVE TO UNRAVEL THIS ONE!
A DETECTIVE...
...SUPERGIRL TOLD ME* THAT SHE THOUGHT THE BATMAN KNEW ABOUT SUPERMAN'S DUAL IDENTITY. MAYBE HE COULD HELP ME FIND...
...CLARK?
*IN SUPERGIRL & TEAM LUTHOR #1.
CLARK!!
STOP! PLEASE!!
Eh?
BEG PARDON? WERE YOU SPEAKING TO ME, MA'AM?
OH! N-NO...
...I... I'M SORRY. TERRIBLY SORRY. I THOUGHT YOU WERE SOMEONE ELSE... A FRIEND OF MINE.
Ah! WELL, NOT TO WORRY! THESE MISTAKES HAPPEN ALL THE TIME.
GOOD LUCK IN FINDING YOUR FRIEND.
THANKS.
GET A GRIP, LOIS, OR YOU'LL BE SEEING CLARK EVERYWHERE.
I JUST WANT HIM TO BE ALIVE SO MUCH...

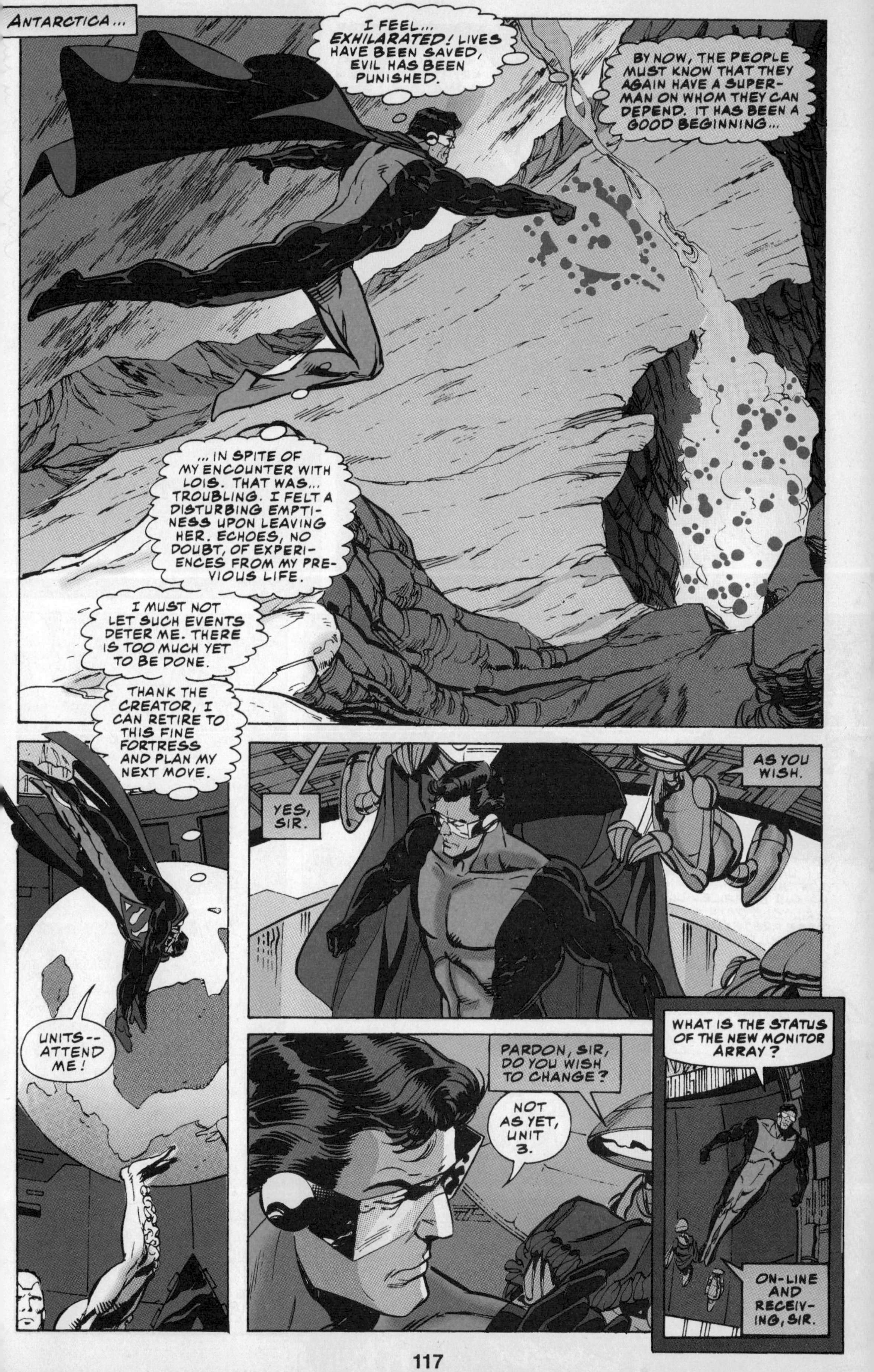
ANTARCTICA...
I FEEL... EXHILARATED! LIVES HAVE BEEN SAVED, EVIL HAS BEEN PUNISHED.
BY NOW, THE PEOPLE MUST KNOW THAT THEY AGAIN HAVE A SUPER-MAN ON WHOM THEY CAN DEPEND. IT HAS BEEN A GOOD BEGINNING...
...IN SPITE OF MY ENCOUNTER WITH LOIS. THAT WAS... TROUBLING. I FELT A DISTURBING EMPTI-NESS UPON LEAVING HER. ECHOES, NO DOUBT, OF EXPERI-ENCES FROM MY PRE-VIOUS LIFE.
I MUST NOT LET SUCH EVENTS DETER ME. THERE IS TOO MUCH YET TO BE DONE.
THANK THE CREATOR, I CAN RETIRE TO THIS FINE FORTRESS AND PLAN MY NEXT MOVE.
UNITS-- ATTEND ME!
YES, SIR.
AS YOU WISH.
PARDON, SIR, DO YOU WISH TO CHANGE?
NOT AS YET, UNIT 3.
WHAT IS THE STATUS OF THE NEW MONITOR ARRAY?
ON-LINE AND RECEIV-ING, SIR.

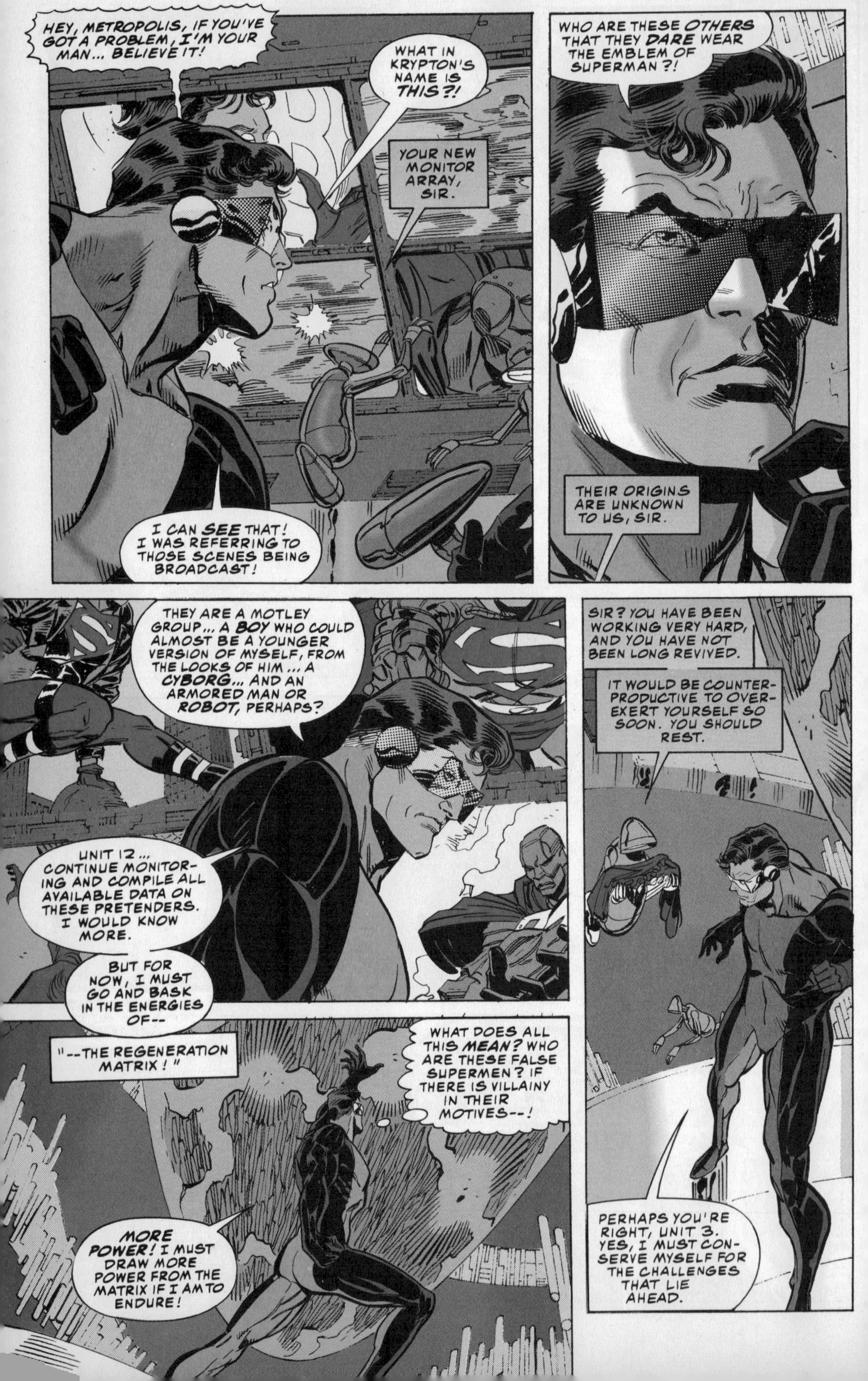
HEY, METROPOLIS, IF YOU'VE GOT A PROBLEM, I'M YOUR MAN... BELIEVE IT!
WHAT IN KRYPTON'S NAME IS THIS?!
YOUR NEW MONITOR ARRAY, SIR.
I CAN SEE THAT! I WAS REFERRING TO THOSE SCENES BEING BROADCAST!
WHO ARE THESE OTHERS THAT THEY DARE WEAR THE EMBLEM OF SUPERMAN?!
THEIR ORIGINS ARE UNKNOWN TO US, SIR.
THEY ARE A MOTLEY GROUP... A BOY WHO COULD ALMOST BE A YOUNGER VERSION OF MYSELF, FROM THE LOOKS OF HIM... A CYBORG... AND AN ARMORED MAN OR ROBOT, PERHAPS?
UNIT 12... CONTINUE MONITORING AND COMPILE ALL AVAILABLE DATA ON THESE PRETENDERS. I WOULD KNOW MORE.
BUT FOR NOW, I MUST GO AND BASK IN THE ENERGIES OF--
SIR? YOU HAVE BEEN WORKING VERY HARD, AND YOU HAVE NOT BEEN LONG REVIVED.
IT WOULD BE COUNTER-PRODUCTIVE TO OVER-EXERT YOURSELF SO SOON. YOU SHOULD REST.
PERHAPS YOU'RE RIGHT, UNIT 3. YES, I MUST CONSERVE MYSELF FOR THE CHALLENGES THAT LIE AHEAD.
"--THE REGENERATION MATRIX!"
WHAT DOES ALL THIS MEAN? WHO ARE THESE FALSE SUPERMEN? IF THERE IS VILLAINY IN THEIR MOTIVES--!
MORE POWER! I MUST DRAW MORE POWER FROM THE MATRIX IF I AM TO ENDURE!

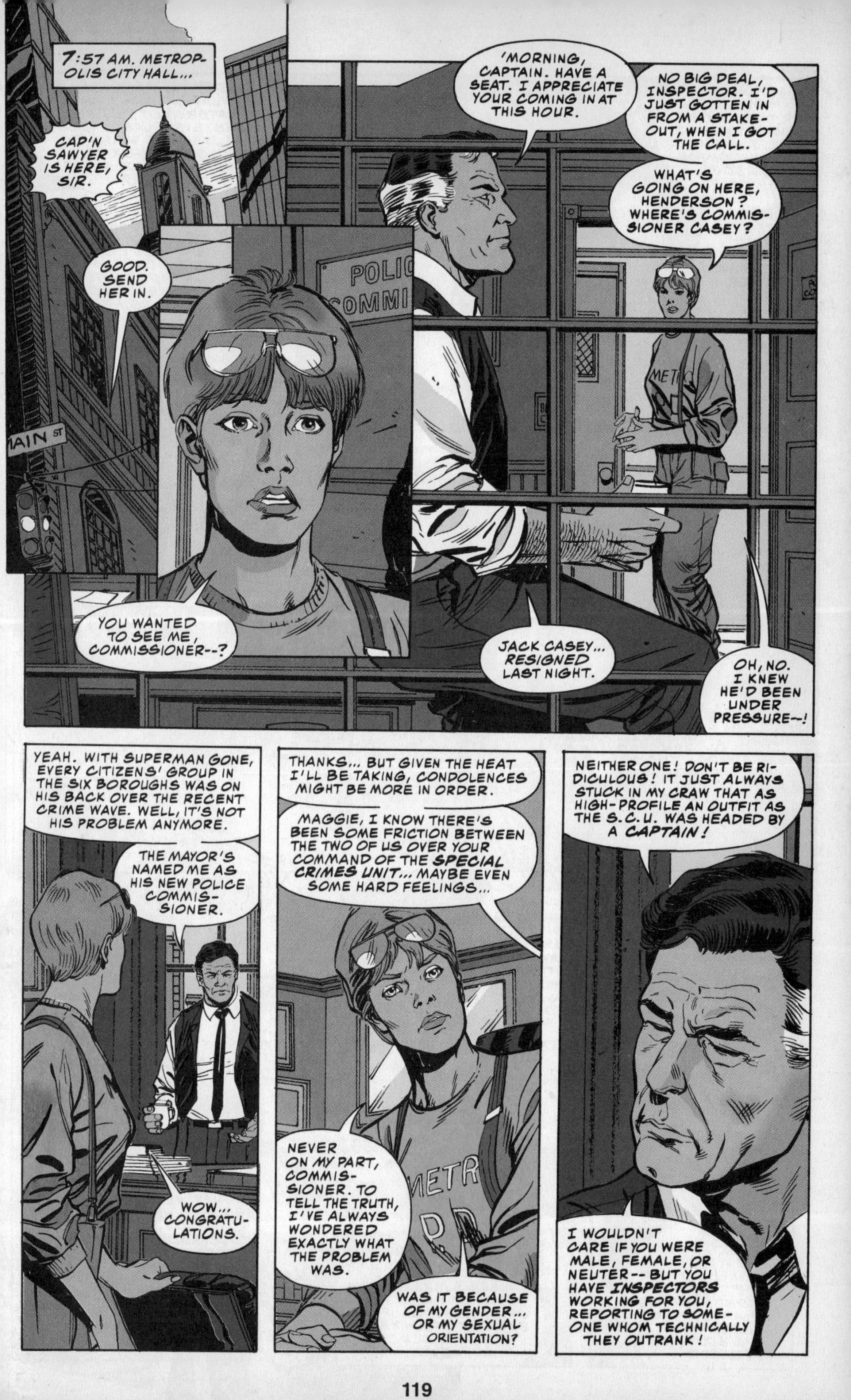
7:57 AM. METROPOLIS CITY HALL...
CAP'N SAWYER IS HERE, SIR.
GOOD. SEND HER IN.
MAIN ST
POLIC COMMI
YOU WANTED TO SEE ME, COMMISSIONER--?
'MORNING, CAPTAIN. HAVE A SEAT. I APPRECIATE YOUR COMING IN AT THIS HOUR.
NO BIG DEAL, INSPECTOR. I'D JUST GOTTEN IN FROM A STAKE-OUT, WHEN I GOT THE CALL.
WHAT'S GOING ON HERE, HENDERSON? WHERE'S COMMISSIONER CASEY?
JACK CASEY... RESIGNED LAST NIGHT.
OH, NO. I KNEW HE'D BEEN UNDER PRESSURE--!
YEAH. WITH SUPERMAN GONE, EVERY CITIZENS' GROUP IN THE SIX BOROUGHS WAS ON HIS BACK OVER THE RECENT CRIME WAVE. WELL, IT'S NOT HIS PROBLEM ANYMORE.
THE MAYOR'S NAMED ME AS HIS NEW POLICE COMMISSIONER.
WOW... CONGRATULATIONS.
THANKS... BUT GIVEN THE HEAT I'LL BE TAKING, CONDOLENCES MIGHT BE MORE IN ORDER.
MAGGIE, I KNOW THERE'S BEEN SOME FRICTION BETWEEN THE TWO OF US OVER YOUR COMMAND OF THE SPECIAL CRIMES UNIT... MAYBE EVEN SOME HARD FEELINGS...
NEVER ON MY PART, COMMISSIONER. TO TELL THE TRUTH, I'VE ALWAYS WONDERED EXACTLY WHAT THE PROBLEM WAS.
WAS IT BECAUSE OF MY GENDER... OR MY SEXUAL ORIENTATION?
NEITHER ONE! DON'T BE RIDICULOUS! IT JUST ALWAYS STUCK IN MY CRAW THAT AS HIGH-PROFILE AN OUTFIT AS THE S.C.U. WAS HEADED BY A CAPTAIN!
I WOULDN'T CARE IF YOU WERE MALE, FEMALE, OR NEUTER -- BUT YOU HAVE INSPECTORS WORKING FOR YOU, REPORTING TO SOMEONE WHOM TECHNICALLY THEY OUTRANK!

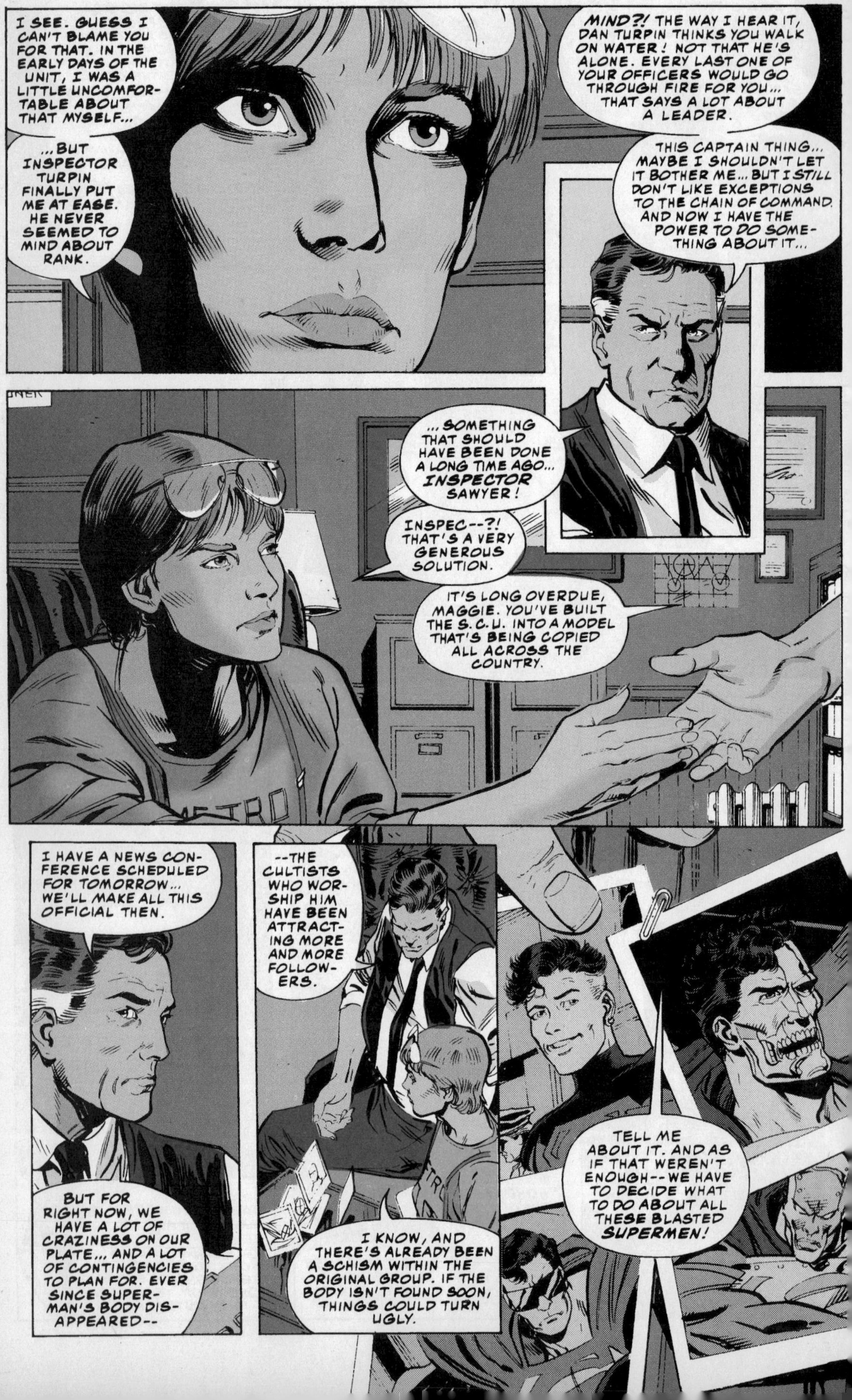
I SEE. GUESS I CAN'T BLAME YOU FOR THAT. IN THE EARLY DAYS OF THE UNIT, I WAS A LITTLE UNCOMFORTABLE ABOUT THAT MYSELF...
...BUT INSPECTOR TURPIN FINALLY PUT ME AT EASE. HE NEVER SEEMED TO MIND ABOUT RANK.
MIND?! THE WAY I HEAR IT, DAN TURPIN THINKS YOU WALK ON WATER! NOT THAT HE'S ALONE. EVERY LAST ONE OF YOUR OFFICERS WOULD GO THROUGH FIRE FOR YOU... THAT SAYS A LOT ABOUT A LEADER.
THIS CAPTAIN THING... MAYBE I SHOULDN'T LET IT BOTHER ME... BUT I STILL DON'T LIKE EXCEPTIONS TO THE CHAIN OF COMMAND. AND NOW I HAVE THE POWER TO DO SOMETHING ABOUT IT...
...SOMETHING THAT SHOULD HAVE BEEN DONE A LONG TIME AGO... INSPECTOR SAWYER!
INSPEC--?! THAT'S A VERY GENEROUS SOLUTION.
IT'S LONG OVERDUE, MAGGIE. YOU'VE BUILT THE S.C.U. INTO A MODEL THAT'S BEING COPIED ALL ACROSS THE COUNTRY.
I HAVE A NEWS CONFERENCE SCHEDULED FOR TOMORROW... WE'LL MAKE ALL THIS OFFICIAL THEN.
BUT FOR RIGHT NOW, WE HAVE A LOT OF CRAZINESS ON OUR PLATE... AND A LOT OF CONTINGENCIES TO PLAN FOR. EVER SINCE SUPERMAN'S BODY DISAPPEARED--
--THE CULTISTS WHO WORSHIP HIM HAVE BEEN ATTRACTING MORE AND MORE FOLLOWERS.
I KNOW, AND THERE'S ALREADY BEEN A SCHISM WITHIN THE ORIGINAL GROUP. IF THE BODY ISN'T FOUND SOON, THINGS COULD TURN UGLY.
TELL ME ABOUT IT. AND AS IF THAT WEREN'T ENOUGH--WE HAVE TO DECIDE WHAT TO DO ABOUT ALL THESE BLASTED SUPERMEN!

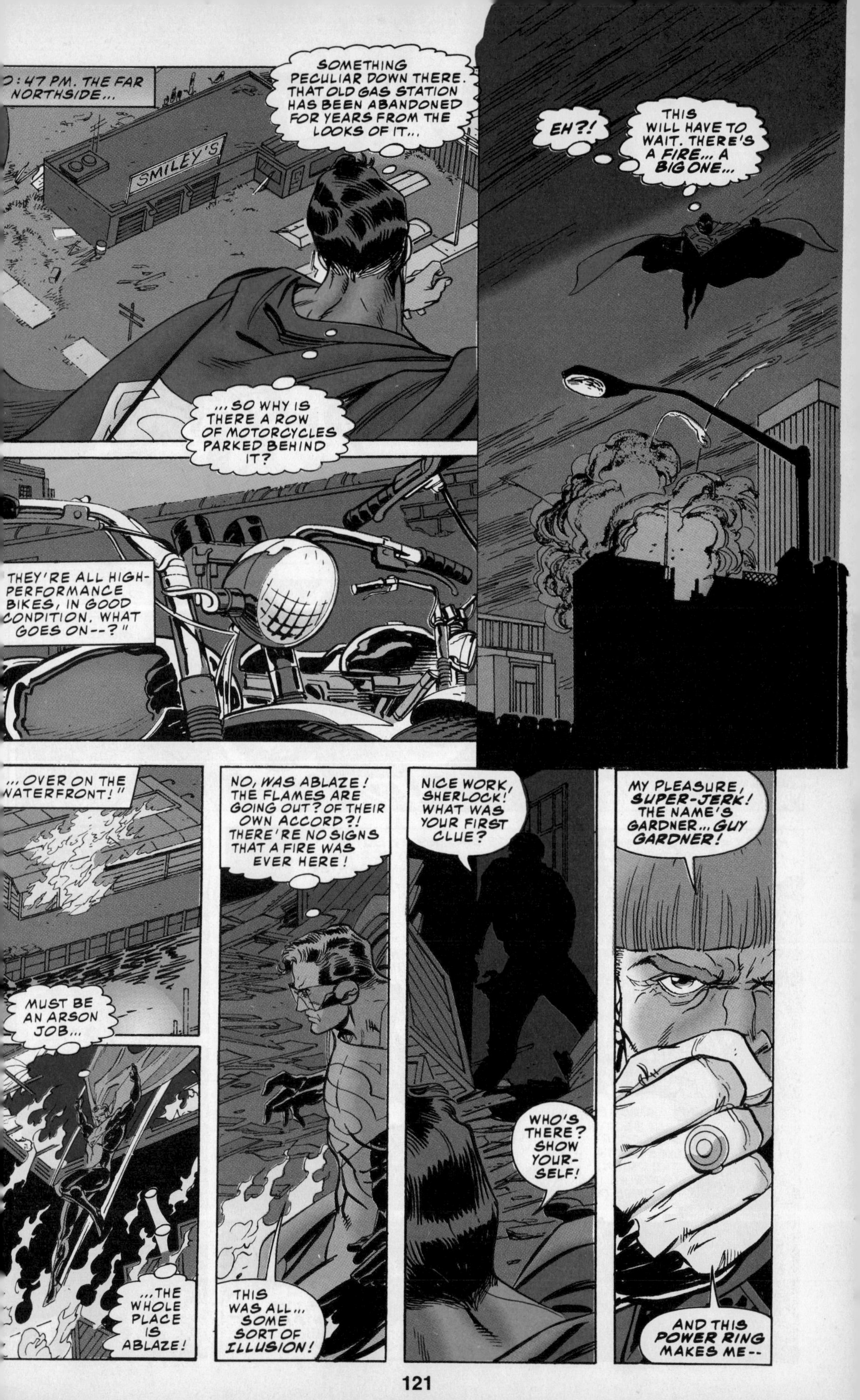

10:47 PM. THE FAR NORTHSIDE...
SOMETHING PECULIAR DOWN THERE. THAT OLD GAS STATION HAS BEEN ABANDONED FOR YEARS FROM THE LOOKS OF IT...
SMILEY'S
...SO WHY IS THERE A ROW OF MOTORCYCLES PARKED BEHIND IT?
THEY'RE ALL HIGH-PERFORMANCE BIKES, IN GOOD CONDITION. WHAT GOES ON--?"
EH?!
THIS WILL HAVE TO WAIT. THERE'S A FIRE... A BIG ONE...
...OVER ON THE WATERFRONT!"
MUST BE AN ARSON JOB...
...THE WHOLE PLACE IS ABLAZE!
NO, WAS ABLAZE! THE FLAMES ARE GOING OUT? OF THEIR OWN ACCORD?! THERE'RE NO SIGNS THAT A FIRE WAS EVER HERE!
THIS WAS ALL... SOME SORT OF ILLUSION!
NICE WORK, SHERLOCK! WHAT WAS YOUR FIRST CLUE?
WHO'S THERE? SHOW YOURSELF!
MY PLEASURE, SUPER-JERK! THE NAME'S GARDNER... GUY GARDNER!
AND THIS POWER RING MAKES ME--

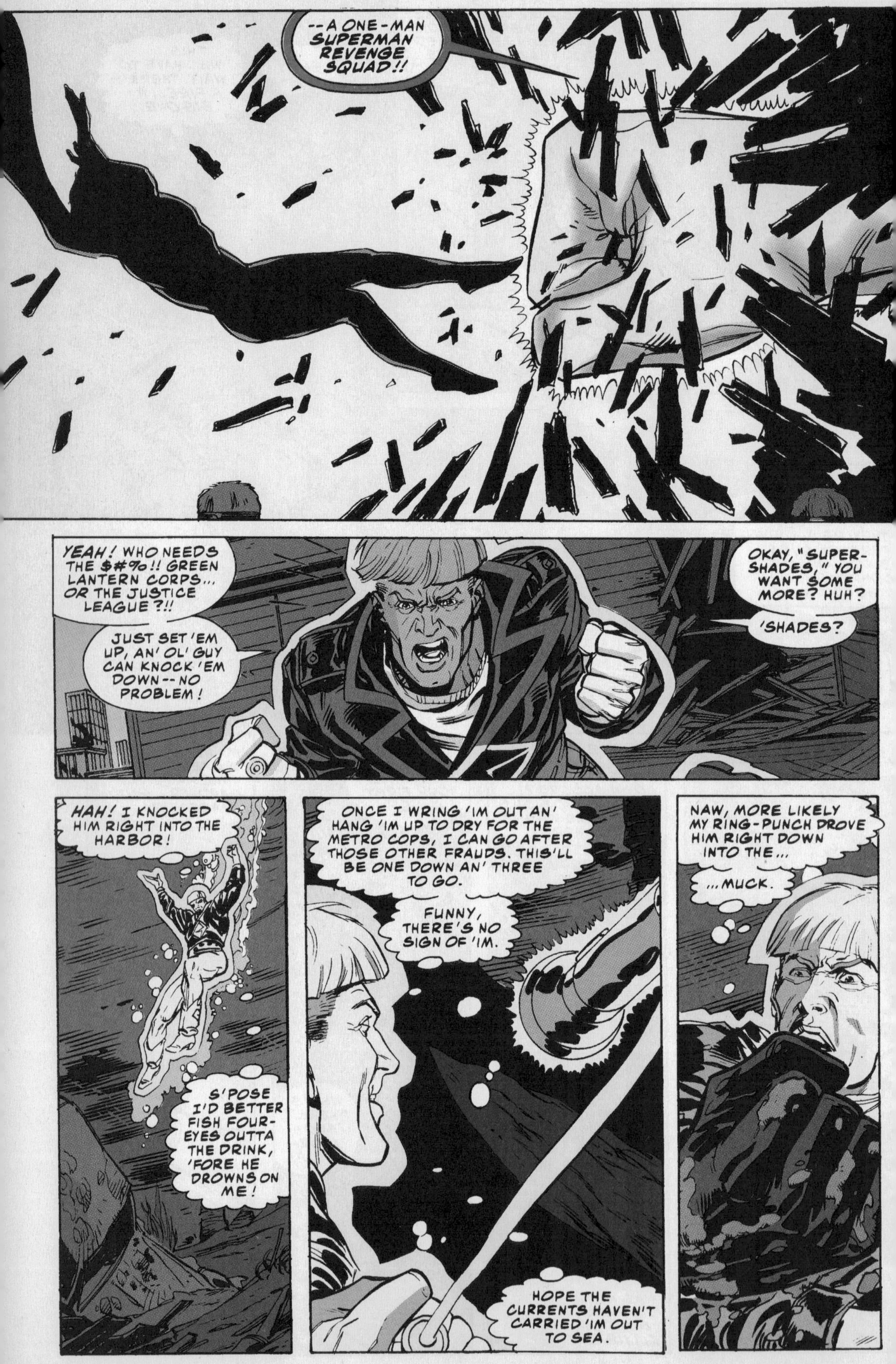
--A ONE-MAN SUPERMAN REVENGE SQUAD!!
YEAH! WHO NEEDS THE $#%!! GREEN LANTERN CORPS... OR THE JUSTICE LEAGUE?!!
JUST SET 'EM UP, AN' OL' GUY CAN KNOCK 'EM DOWN--NO PROBLEM!
OKAY, "SUPER-SHADES," YOU WANT SOME MORE? HUH?
'SHADES?
HAH! I KNOCKED HIM RIGHT INTO THE HARBOR!
S'POSE I'D BETTER FISH FOUR-EYES OUTTA THE DRINK, 'FORE HE DROWNS ON ME!
ONCE I WRING 'IM OUT AN' HANG 'IM UP TO DRY FOR THE METRO COPS, I CAN GO AFTER THOSE OTHER FRAUDS. THIS'LL BE ONE DOWN AN' THREE TO GO.
FUNNY, THERE'S NO SIGN OF 'IM.
HOPE THE CURRENTS HAVEN'T CARRIED 'IM OUT TO SEA.
NAW, MORE LIKELY MY RING-PUNCH DROVE HIM RIGHT DOWN INTO THE...
...MUCK.

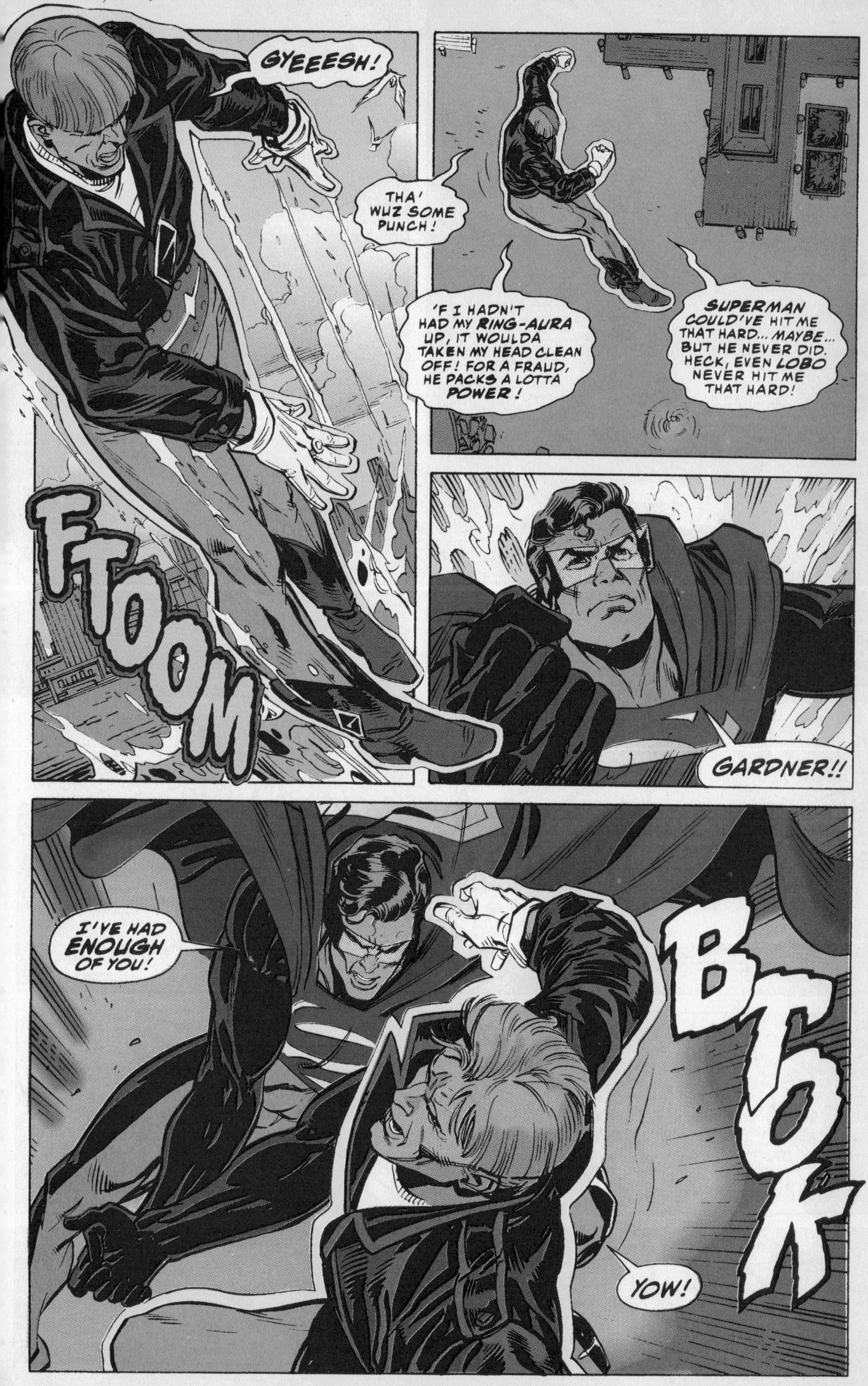

GYEEESH!
THA' WUZ SOME PUNCH!
'F I HADN'T HAD MY RING-AURA UP, IT WOULDA TAKEN MY HEAD CLEAN OFF! FOR A FRAUD, HE PACKS A LOTTA POWER!
SUPERMAN COULD'VE HIT ME THAT HARD... MAYBE... BUT HE NEVER DID. HECK, EVEN LOBO NEVER HIT ME THAT HARD!
FTOOM
GARDNER!!
I'VE HAD ENOUGH OF YOU!
BTOK
YOW!

KER-RACK!

WHOA!

THIS SUCKER'S--

--TOUGH!

THE REST OF THIS WORLD MAY HAVE TO PUT UP WITH YOU-- BUT SUPERMAN DOES NOT!

AND I WILL NOT!

GOT A SHORT FUSE, TOO... THIS COULD GET INTERESTIN'..

... BUT I CAN'T LET 'IM KEEP ME ON THE DEFENSIVE.

YOU TALK A GOOD FIGHT, SHADES--

--BUT I'M BETTIN' THAT THIS SHINING KNIGHT CAN PIN YOU TO THE WALL!

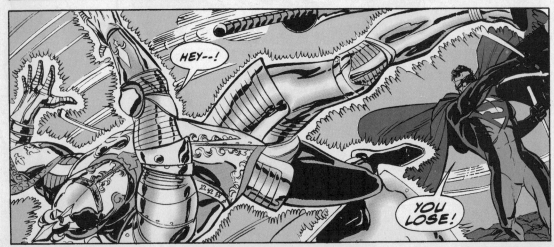

HEY--!

YOU LOSE!

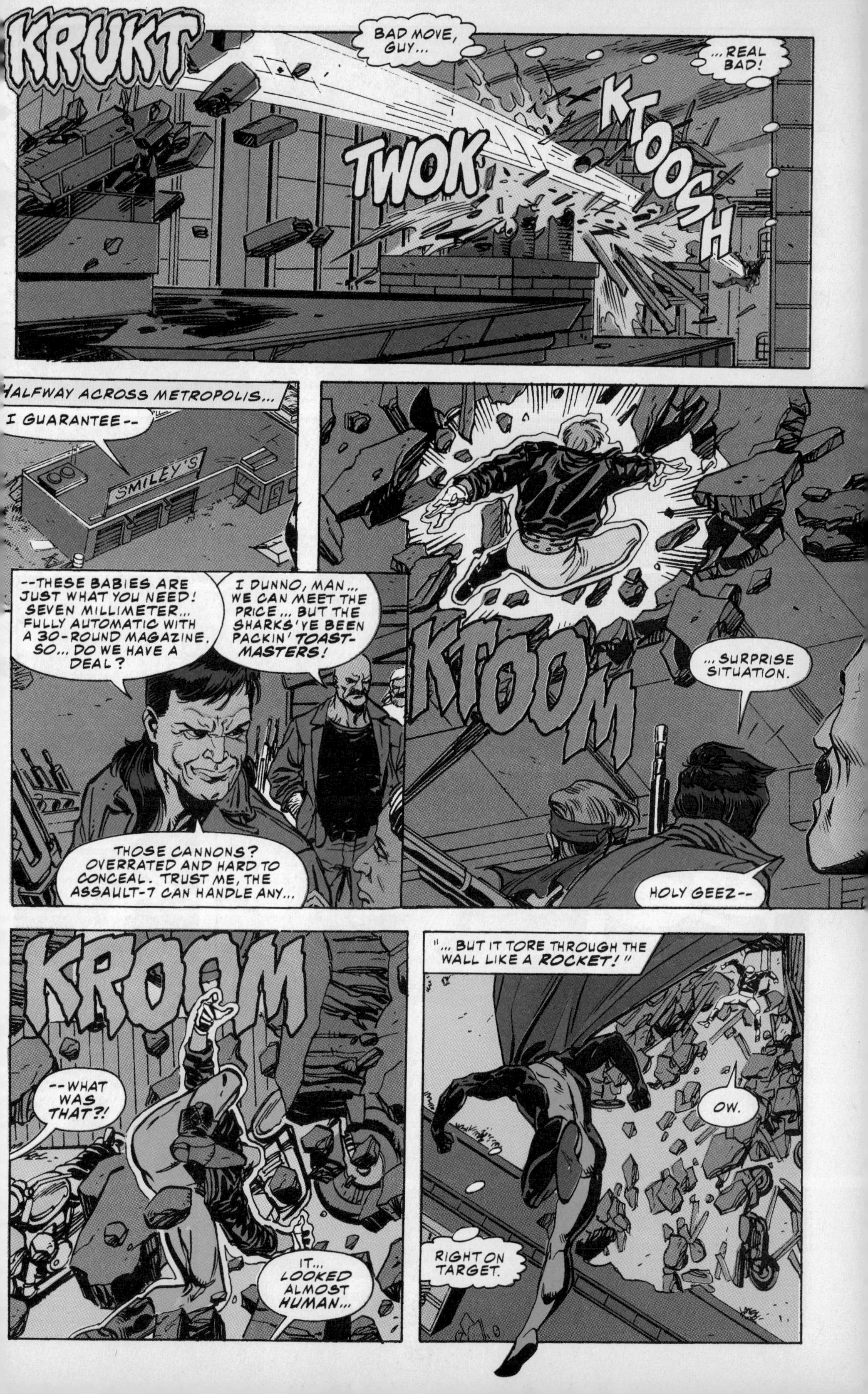
KRUKT
BAD MOVE, GUY...
...REAL BAD!
TWOK
KTOOSH
HALFWAY ACROSS METROPOLIS...
I GUARANTEE--
SMILEY'S
--THESE BABIES ARE JUST WHAT YOU NEED! SEVEN MILLIMETER... FULLY AUTOMATIC WITH A 30-ROUND MAGAZINE. SO... DO WE HAVE A DEAL?
I DUNNO, MAN... WE CAN MEET THE PRICE... BUT THE SHARKS'VE BEEN PACKIN' TOAST-MASTERS!
THOSE CANNONS? OVERRATED AND HARD TO CONCEAL. TRUST ME, THE ASSAULT-7 CAN HANDLE ANY...
KTOOM
...SURPRISE SITUATION.
HOLY GEEZ--
KROOM
--WHAT WAS THAT?!
IT... LOOKED ALMOST HUMAN...
"...BUT IT TORE THROUGH THE WALL LIKE A ROCKET!"
OW.
RIGHT ON TARGET.

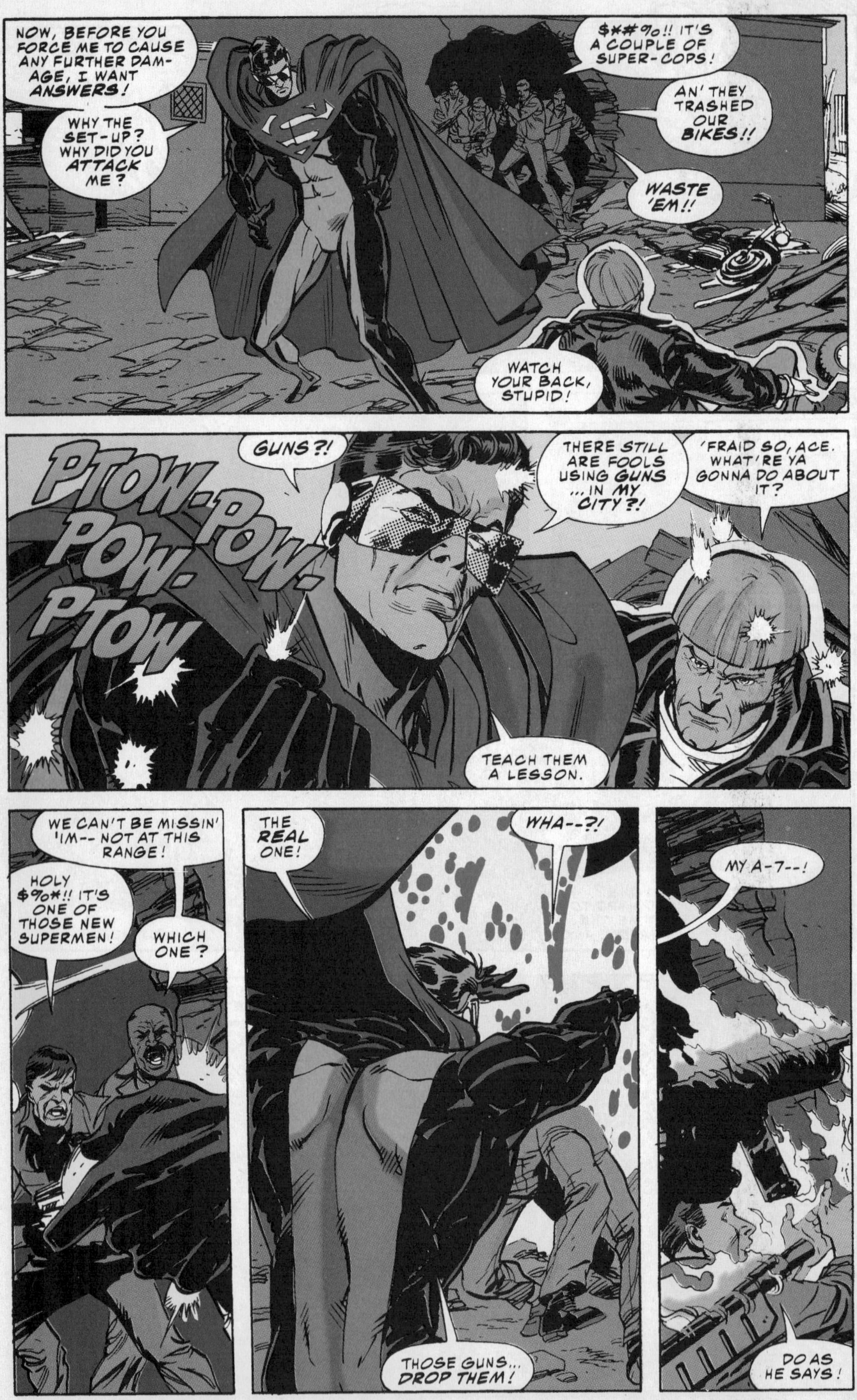
NOW, BEFORE YOU FORCE ME TO CAUSE ANY FURTHER DAMAGE, I WANT ANSWERS!
WHY THE SET-UP? WHY DID YOU ATTACK ME?
$*#%!! IT'S A COUPLE OF SUPER-COPS!
AN' THEY TRASHED OUR BIKES!!
WASTE 'EM!!
WATCH YOUR BACK, STUPID!
PTOW-POW-POW-PTOW
GUNS?!
THERE STILL ARE FOOLS USING GUNS ...IN MY CITY?!
'FRAID SO, ACE. WHAT'RE YA GONNA DO ABOUT IT?
TEACH THEM A LESSON.
WE CAN'T BE MISSIN' 'IM-- NOT AT THIS RANGE!
HOLY $%*!! IT'S ONE OF THOSE NEW SUPERMEN!
WHICH ONE?
THE REAL ONE!
WHA--?!
THOSE GUNS... DROP THEM!
MY A-7--!
DO AS HE SAYS!

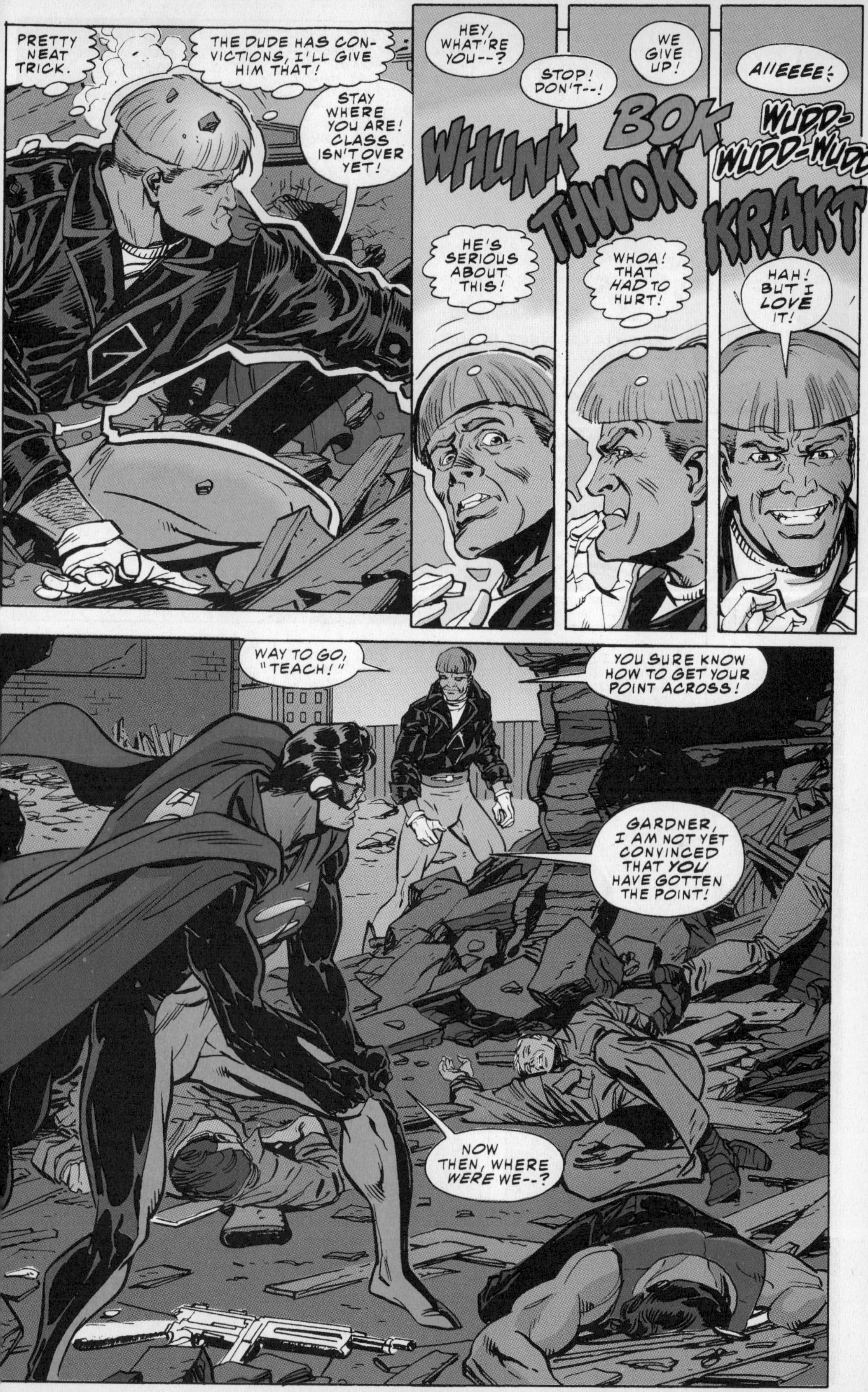

PRETTY NEAT TRICK.
THE DUDE HAS CONVICTIONS, I'LL GIVE HIM THAT!
STAY WHERE YOU ARE! CLASS ISN'T OVER YET!
HEY, WHAT'RE YOU--?
STOP! DON'T--!
WHUNK
HE'S SERIOUS ABOUT THIS!
WE GIVE UP!
BOK
THWOK
WHOA! THAT HAD TO HURT!
AIIEEEE!
WUDD-WUDD-WUDD
KRAKT
HAH! BUT I LOVE IT!
WAY TO GO, "TEACH!"
YOU SURE KNOW HOW TO GET YOUR POINT ACROSS!
GARDNER, I AM NOT YET CONVINCED THAT YOU HAVE GOTTEN THE POINT!
NOW THEN, WHERE WERE WE--?

HEY-HEY, TAKE IT *EASY!* LOOK, YOU'VE GOT EVERY RIGHT TO BE MAD...

... BUT HEAR ME OUT, OKAY? I'M SORRY I BUSHWHACKED YOU, BUT I JUST HAD TO KNOW!

KNOW *WHAT?*

KNOW IF YOU WERE *REALLY SUPERMAN!* AN' LEMME TELL YA, FROM WHAT I JUST SAW, YOU'RE SURE AS HECK THE SUPER-MAN *I* WANNA HAVE AROUND!

I DON'T BELIEVE THIS.

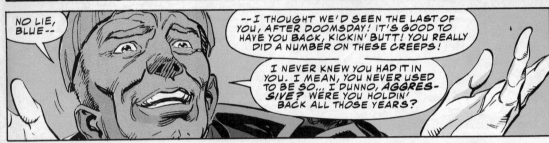

NO LIE, BLUE--

-- I THOUGHT WE'D SEEN THE LAST OF YOU, AFTER DOOMSDAY! IT'S GOOD TO HAVE YOU BACK, KICKIN' BUTT! YOU REALLY DID A NUMBER ON THESE CREEPS!

I NEVER KNEW YOU HAD IT IN YOU. I MEAN, YOU NEVER USED TO BE SO... I DUNNO, *AGGRES-SIVE?* WERE YOU HOLDIN' BACK ALL THOSE YEARS?

HOLDING BACK? PERHAPS. I HAVE BEEN THROUGH MANY CHANGES.

YEAH, I GUESS DYIN' AND COMIN' BACK WOULD MAKE YA SEE THINGS DIFFERENTLY!

HEY, LUCKY THING I CAME CRASHIN' IN ON THESE HOODS, HUH?

LUCK HAD NOTHING TO DO WITH IT. I'D NOTICED SOME-THING SUSPICIOUS ABOUT THIS PLACE EARLIER.

YA MEAN...YOU THREW ME OVER HERE *DELIBERATELY?* THAT WAS *BRILLIANT!* YOU ARE DEFINITELY *THE MAN!*

THIS SURE MAKES THINGS EASIER ...NOW I ONLY HAVE *THREE* PHONIES TO CHASE DOWN!

GARDNER, I DON'T WANT YOU CHASING DOWN ANY-*ONE* OR ANYTHING IN MY CITY! DO I MAKE MYSELF *CLEAR?!*

OH, SURE... I GETCHA! YOU WANT TO NAIL THOSE FAKES YOURSELF, RIGHT?

SORRY, SUPES, I CAN BE A REAL *CEMENT-HEAD* SOME-TIMES.

INDEED.

OH, AND GARDNER? THE NAME IS SUPERMAN ...*NOT* "SUPES!"

WHATEVER YA SAY, BIG GUY! JUST KEEP UP THE GOOD WORK...

...I'LL SQUARE THINGS HERE WITH THE COPS.

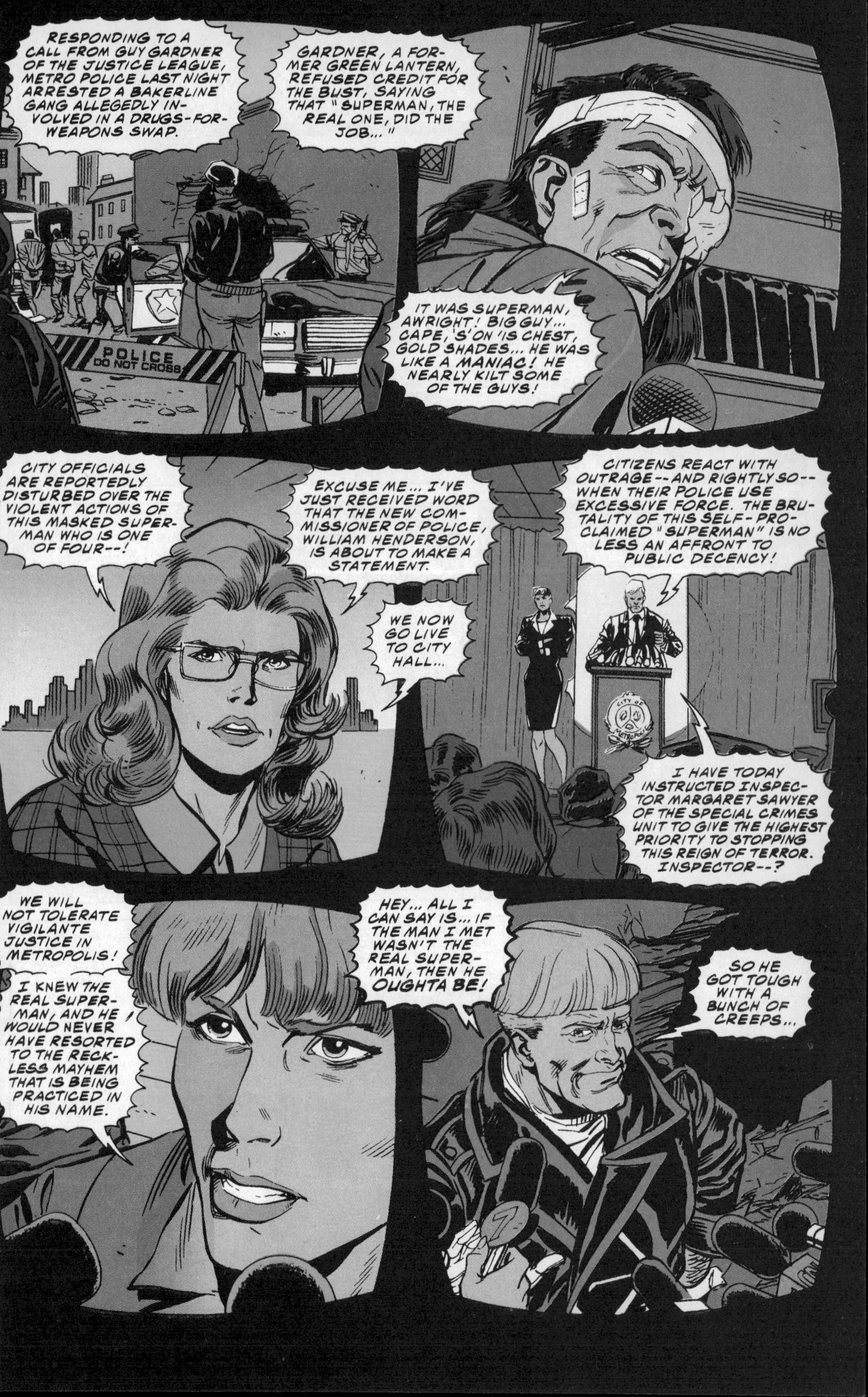
RESPONDING TO A CALL FROM GUY GARDNER OF THE JUSTICE LEAGUE, METRO POLICE LAST NIGHT ARRESTED A BAKERLINE GANG ALLEGEDLY INVOLVED IN A DRUGS-FOR-WEAPONS SWAP.
POLICE DO NOT CROSS
GARDNER, A FORMER GREEN LANTERN, REFUSED CREDIT FOR THE BUST, SAYING THAT "SUPERMAN, THE REAL ONE, DID THE JOB..."
IT WAS SUPERMAN, AWRIGHT! BIG GUY... CAPE, 'S' ON 'IS CHEST, GOLD SHADES... HE WAS LIKE A MANIAC! HE NEARLY KILT SOME OF THE GUYS!
CITY OFFICIALS ARE REPORTEDLY DISTURBED OVER THE VIOLENT ACTIONS OF THIS MASKED SUPERMAN WHO IS ONE OF FOUR--!
EXCUSE ME... I'VE JUST RECEIVED WORD THAT THE NEW COMMISSIONER OF POLICE, WILLIAM HENDERSON, IS ABOUT TO MAKE A STATEMENT.
WE NOW GO LIVE TO CITY HALL...
CITIZENS REACT WITH OUTRAGE--AND RIGHTLY SO--WHEN THEIR POLICE USE EXCESSIVE FORCE. THE BRUTALITY OF THIS SELF-PROCLAIMED "SUPERMAN" IS NO LESS AN AFFRONT TO PUBLIC DECENCY!
CITY OF METROPOLIS
I HAVE TODAY INSTRUCTED INSPECTOR MARGARET SAWYER OF THE SPECIAL CRIMES UNIT TO GIVE THE HIGHEST PRIORITY TO STOPPING THIS REIGN OF TERROR. INSPECTOR--?
WE WILL NOT TOLERATE VIGILANTE JUSTICE IN METROPOLIS!
I KNEW THE REAL SUPERMAN, AND HE WOULD NEVER HAVE RESORTED TO THE RECKLESS MAYHEM THAT IS BEING PRACTICED IN HIS NAME.
HEY... ALL I CAN SAY IS... IF THE MAN I MET WASN'T THE REAL SUPERMAN, THEN HE OUGHTA BE!
SO HE GOT TOUGH WITH A BUNCH OF CREEPS...

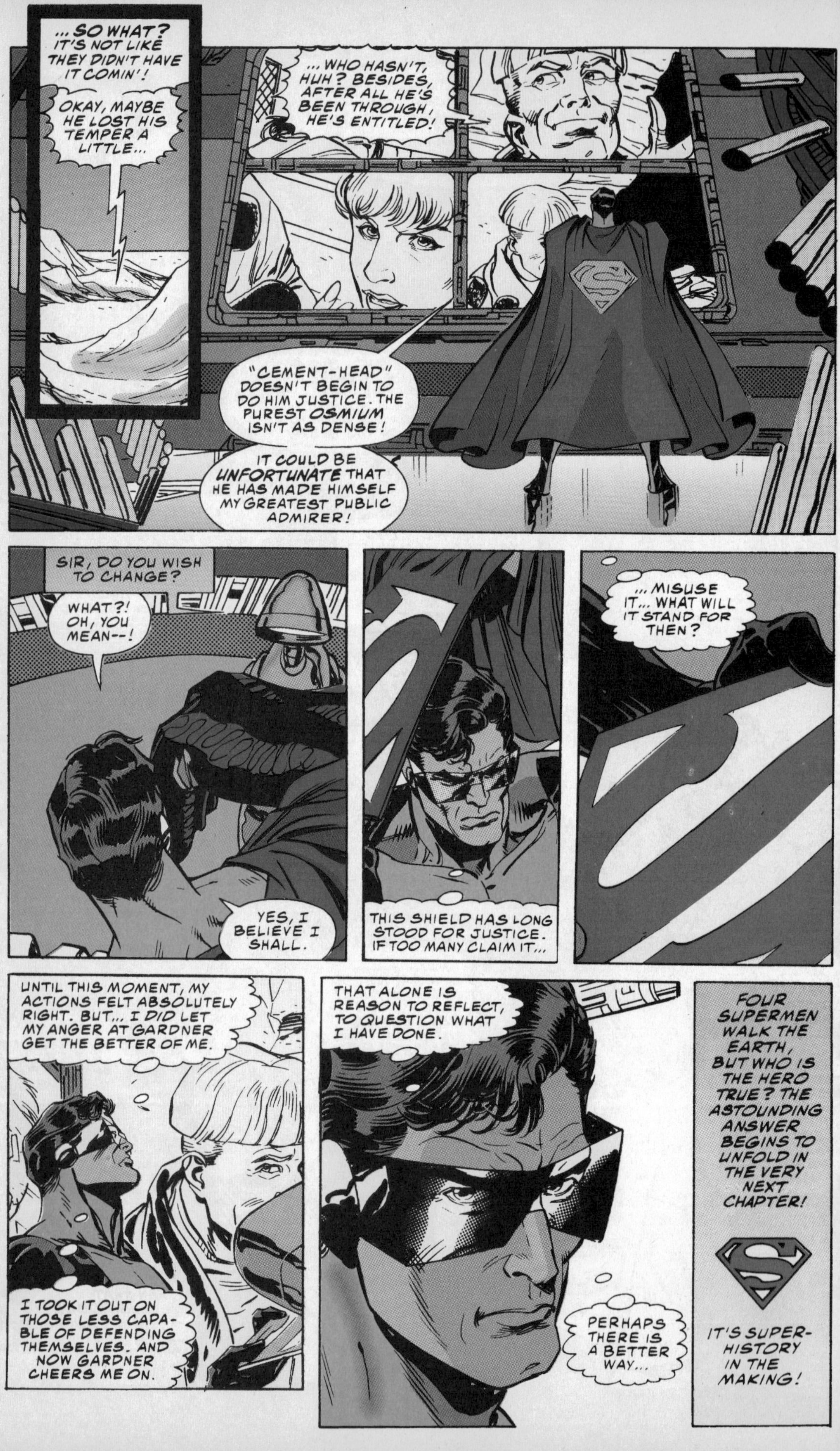
...SO WHAT? IT'S NOT LIKE THEY DIDN'T HAVE IT COMIN'!
OKAY, MAYBE HE LOST HIS TEMPER A LITTLE...
...WHO HASN'T, HUH? BESIDES, AFTER ALL HE'S BEEN THROUGH, HE'S ENTITLED!
"CEMENT-HEAD" DOESN'T BEGIN TO DO HIM JUSTICE. THE PUREST OSMIUM ISN'T AS DENSE!
IT COULD BE UNFORTUNATE THAT HE HAS MADE HIMSELF MY GREATEST PUBLIC ADMIRER!
SIR, DO YOU WISH TO CHANGE?
WHAT?! OH, YOU MEAN--!
YES, I BELIEVE I SHALL.
THIS SHIELD HAS LONG STOOD FOR JUSTICE. IF TOO MANY CLAIM IT...
...MISUSE IT... WHAT WILL IT STAND FOR THEN?
UNTIL THIS MOMENT, MY ACTIONS FELT ABSOLUTELY RIGHT. BUT... I DID LET MY ANGER AT GARDNER GET THE BETTER OF ME.
I TOOK IT OUT ON THOSE LESS CAPABLE OF DEFENDING THEMSELVES. AND NOW GARDNER CHEERS ME ON.
THAT ALONE IS REASON TO REFLECT, TO QUESTION WHAT I HAVE DONE.
PERHAPS THERE IS A BETTER WAY...
FOUR SUPERMEN WALK THE EARTH, BUT WHO IS THE HERO TRUE? THE ASTOUNDING ANSWER BEGINS TO UNFOLD IN THE VERY NEXT CHAPTER!
IT'S SUPER-HISTORY IN THE MAKING!

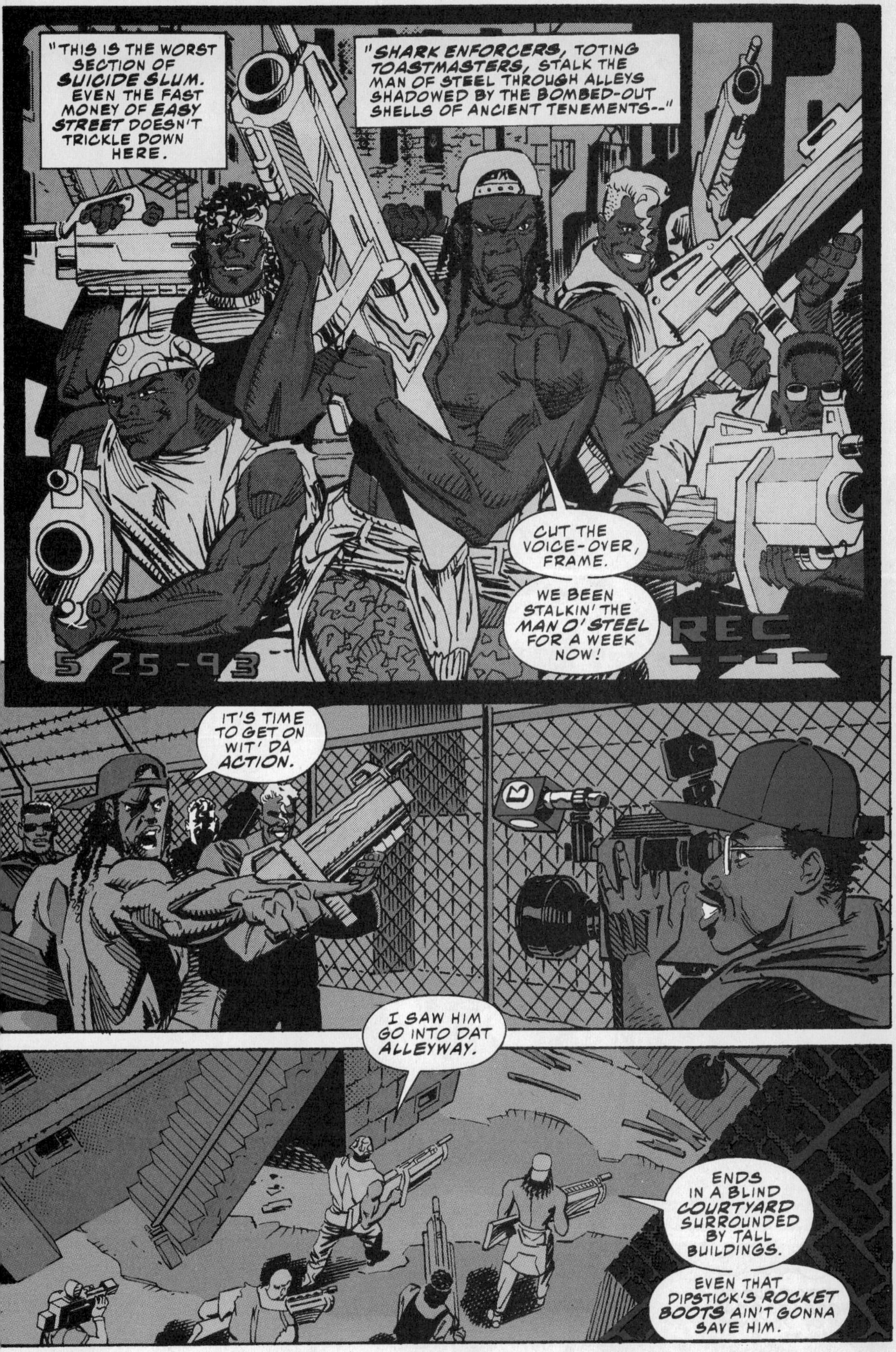
"THIS IS THE WORST SECTION OF SUICIDE SLUM. EVEN THE FAST MONEY OF EASY STREET DOESN'T TRICKLE DOWN HERE.
"SHARK ENFORCERS, TOTING TOASTMASTERS, STALK THE MAN OF STEEL THROUGH ALLEYS SHADOWED BY THE BOMBED-OUT SHELLS OF ANCIENT TENEMENTS--"
CUT THE VOICE-OVER, FRAME.
WE BEEN STALKIN' THE MAN O' STEEL FOR A WEEK NOW!
REC
5 25-93
IT'S TIME TO GET ON WIT' DA ACTION.
I SAW HIM GO INTO DAT ALLEYWAY.
ENDS IN A BLIND COURTYARD SURROUNDED BY TALL BUILDINGS.
EVEN THAT DIPSTICK'S ROCKET BOOTS AIN'T GONNA SAVE HIM.

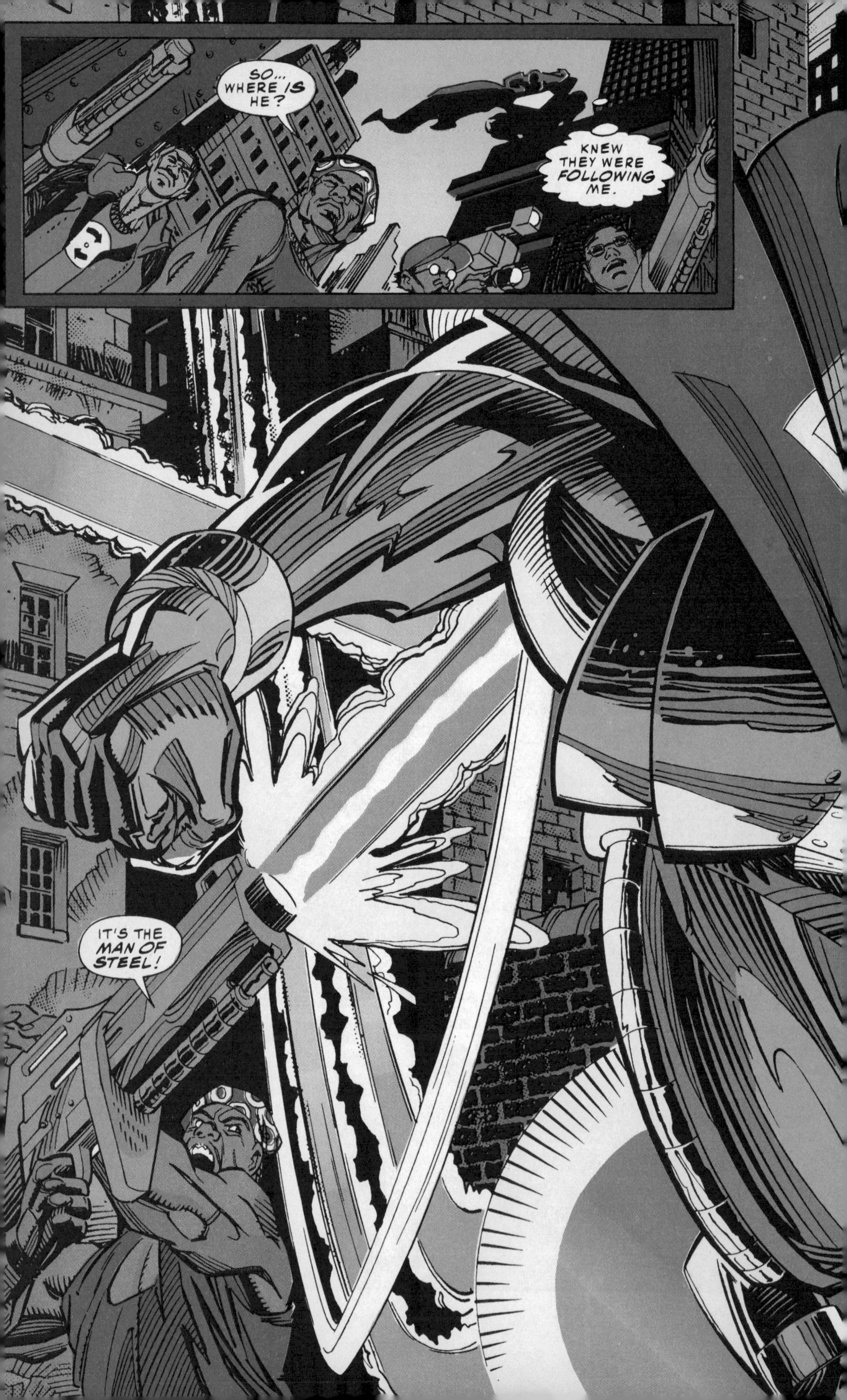
SO... WHERE IS HE?
KNEW THEY WERE FOLLOWING ME.
IT'S THE MAN OF STEEL!

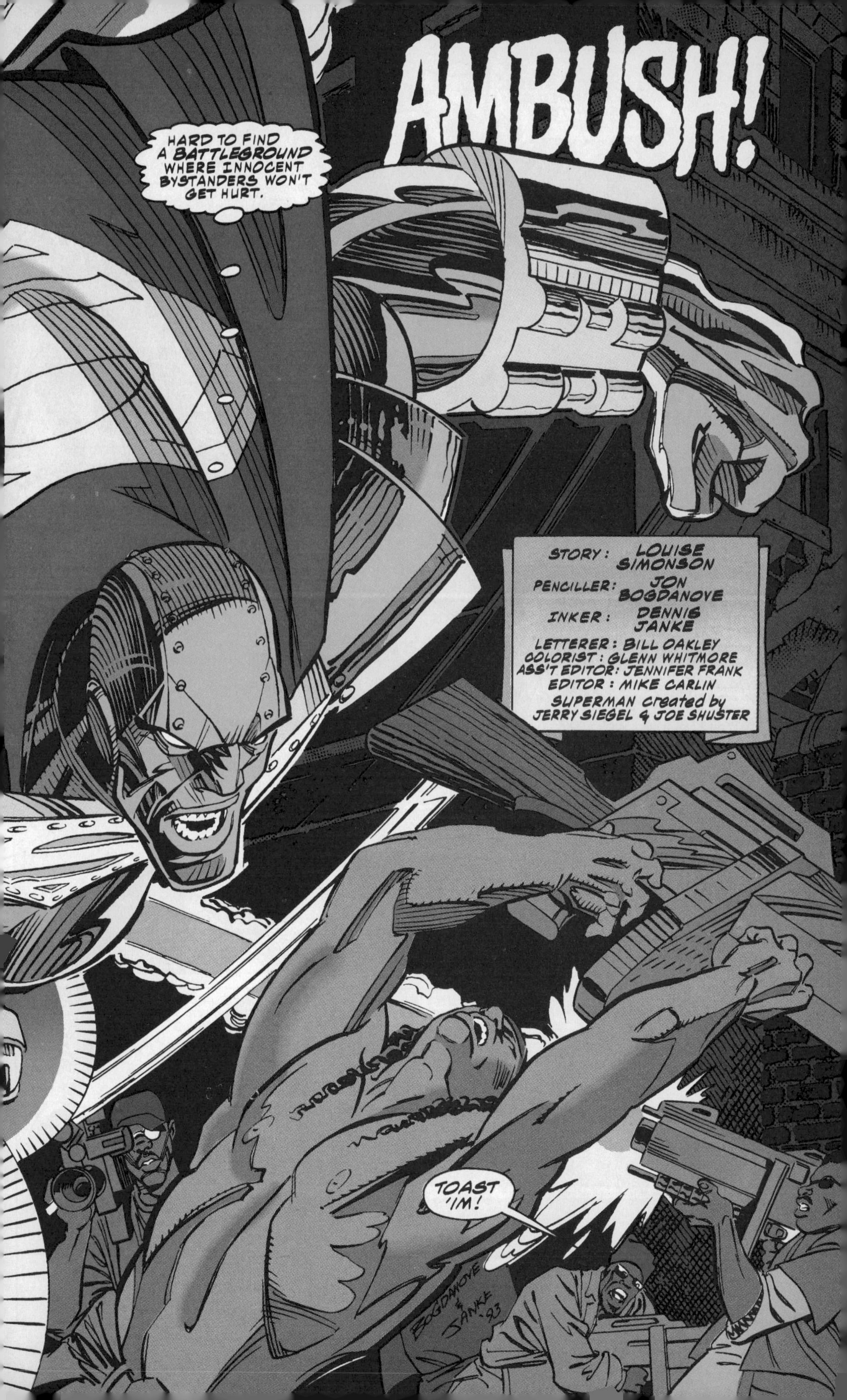
AMBUSH!
HARD TO FIND A BATTLEGROUND WHERE INNOCENT BYSTANDERS WON'T GET HURT.
STORY: LOUISE SIMONSON
PENCILLER: JON BOGDANOVE
INKER: DENNIS JANKE
LETTERER: BILL OAKLEY
COLORIST: GLENN WHITMORE
ASS'T EDITOR: JENNIFER FRANK
EDITOR: MIKE CARLIN
SUPERMAN created by JERRY SIEGEL & JOE SHUSTER
TOAST 'IM!
BOGDANOVE & JANKE -93

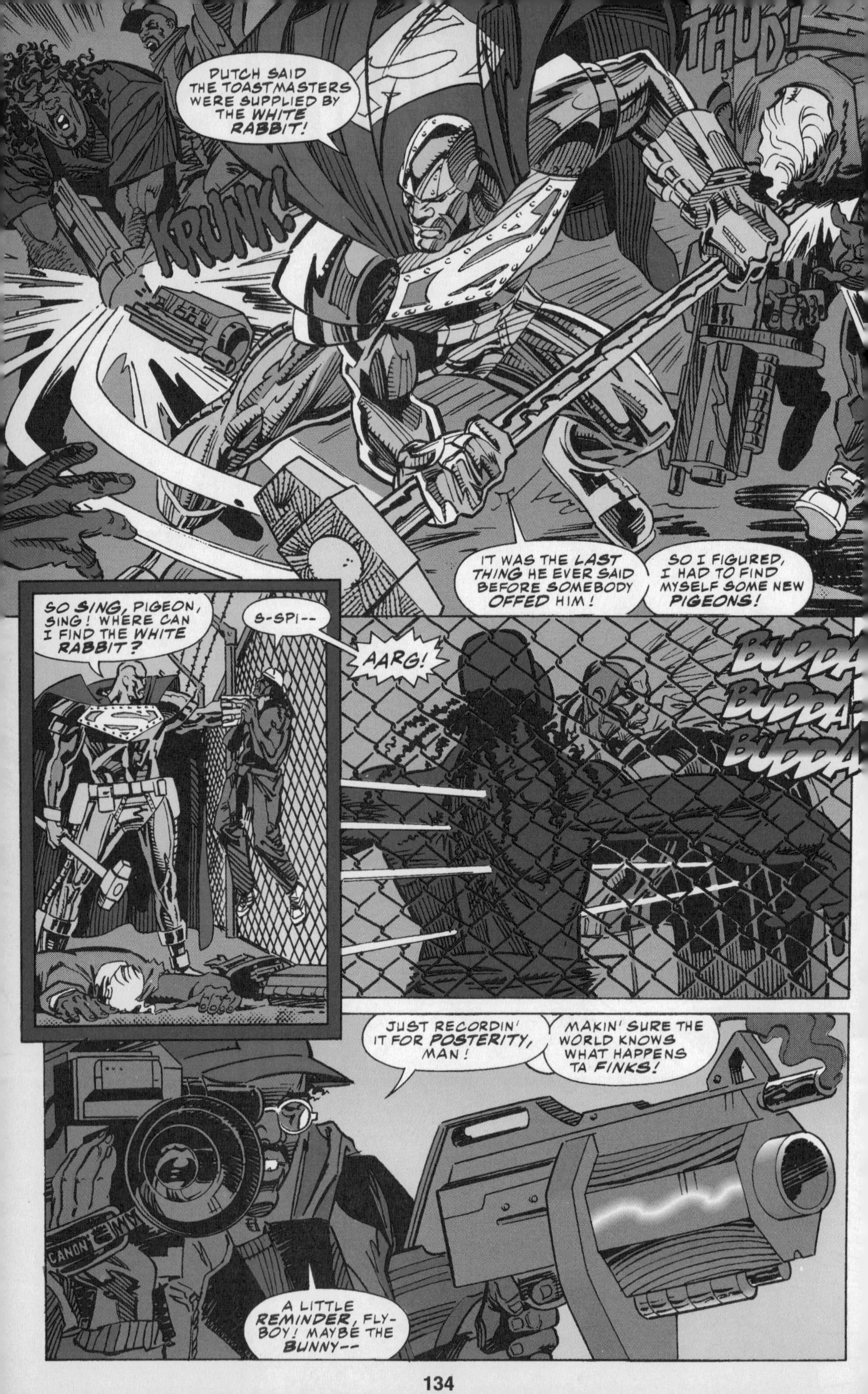
THUD!
DUTCH SAID THE TOASTMASTERS WERE SUPPLIED BY THE WHITE RABBIT!
KRUNK!
IT WAS THE LAST THING HE EVER SAID BEFORE SOMEBODY OFFED HIM!
SO I FIGURED, I HAD TO FIND MYSELF SOME NEW PIGEONS!
SO SING, PIGEON, SING! WHERE CAN I FIND THE WHITE RABBIT?
S-SPI--
AARG!
BUDDA BUDDA BUDDA
JUST RECORDIN' IT FOR POSTERITY, MAN!
MAKIN' SURE THE WORLD KNOWS WHAT HAPPENS TA FINKS!
CANON
A LITTLE REMINDER, FLY-BOY! MAYBE THE BUNNY--

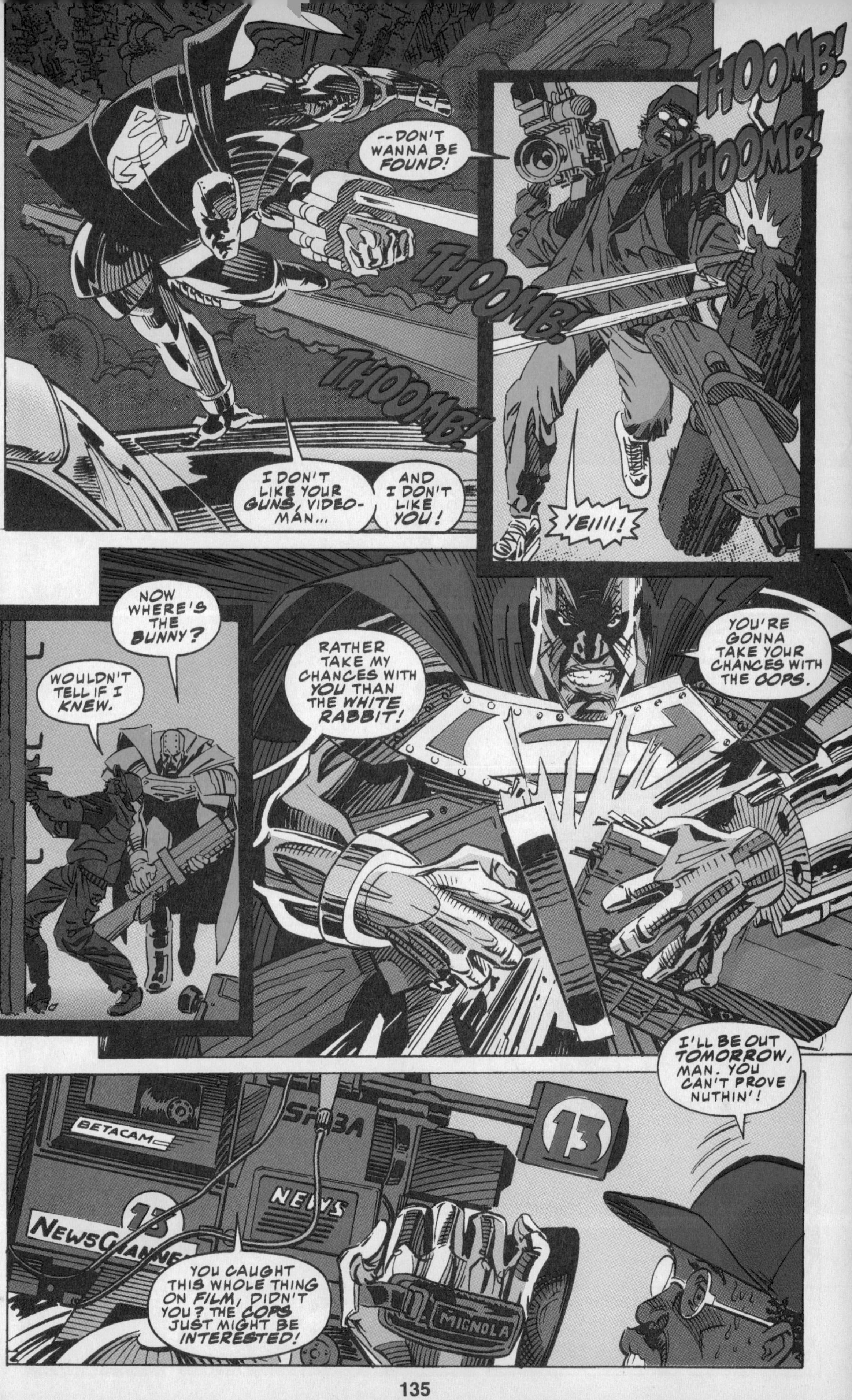
THOOMB!
THOOMB!
--DON'T WANNA BE FOUND!
THOOMB!
THOOMB!
I DON'T LIKE YOUR GUNS, VIDEO-MAN...
AND I DON'T LIKE YOU!
YEI!!!!!
NOW WHERE'S THE BUNNY?
WOULDN'T TELL IF I KNEW.
RATHER TAKE MY CHANCES WITH YOU THAN THE WHITE RABBIT!
YOU'RE GONNA TAKE YOUR CHANCES WITH THE COPS.
I'LL BE OUT TOMORROW, MAN. YOU CAN'T PROVE NUTHIN'!
BETACAM
13
NEWS
YOU CAUGHT THIS WHOLE THING ON FILM, DIDN'T YOU? THE COPS JUST MIGHT BE INTERESTED!
MIGNOLA

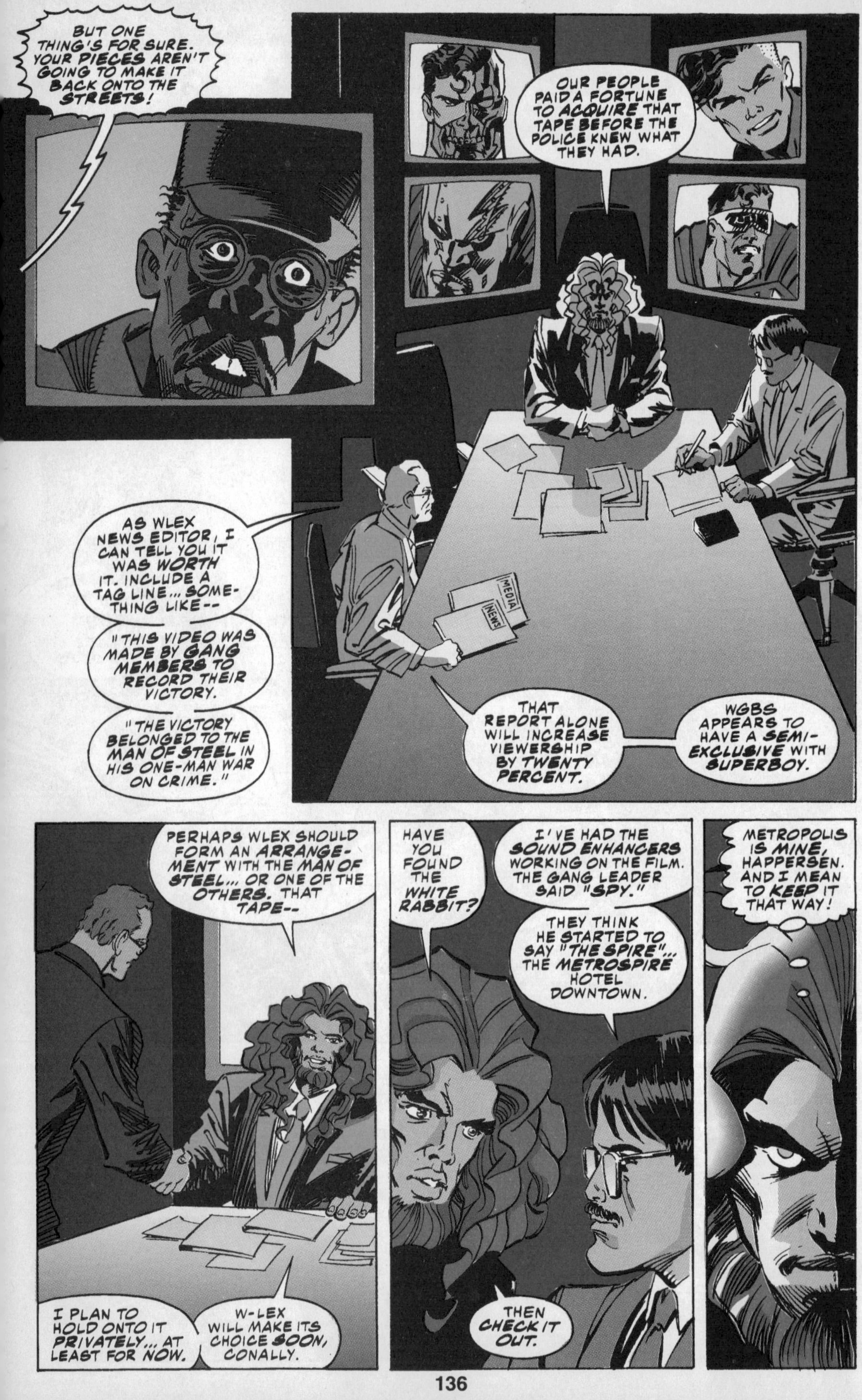
BUT ONE THING'S FOR SURE. YOUR PIECES AREN'T GOING TO MAKE IT BACK ONTO THE STREETS!
OUR PEOPLE PAID A FORTUNE TO ACQUIRE THAT TAPE BEFORE THE POLICE KNEW WHAT THEY HAD.
AS WLEX NEWS EDITOR, I CAN TELL YOU IT WAS WORTH IT. INCLUDE A TAG LINE... SOMETHING LIKE--
"THIS VIDEO WAS MADE BY GANG MEMBERS TO RECORD THEIR VICTORY.
"THE VICTORY BELONGED TO THE MAN OF STEEL IN HIS ONE-MAN WAR ON CRIME."
MEDIA
NEWS
THAT REPORT ALONE WILL INCREASE VIEWERSHIP BY TWENTY PERCENT.
WGBS APPEARS TO HAVE A SEMI-EXCLUSIVE WITH SUPERBOY.
PERHAPS WLEX SHOULD FORM AN ARRANGEMENT WITH THE MAN OF STEEL... OR ONE OF THE OTHERS. THAT TAPE--
I PLAN TO HOLD ONTO IT PRIVATELY... AT LEAST FOR NOW.
W-LEX WILL MAKE ITS CHOICE SOON, CONALLY.
HAVE YOU FOUND THE WHITE RABBIT?
I'VE HAD THE SOUND ENHANCERS WORKING ON THE FILM. THE GANG LEADER SAID "SPY."
THEY THINK HE STARTED TO SAY "THE SPIRE"... THE METROSPIRE HOTEL DOWNTOWN.
THEN CHECK IT OUT.
METROPOLIS IS MINE, HAPPERSEN. AND I MEAN TO KEEP IT THAT WAY!

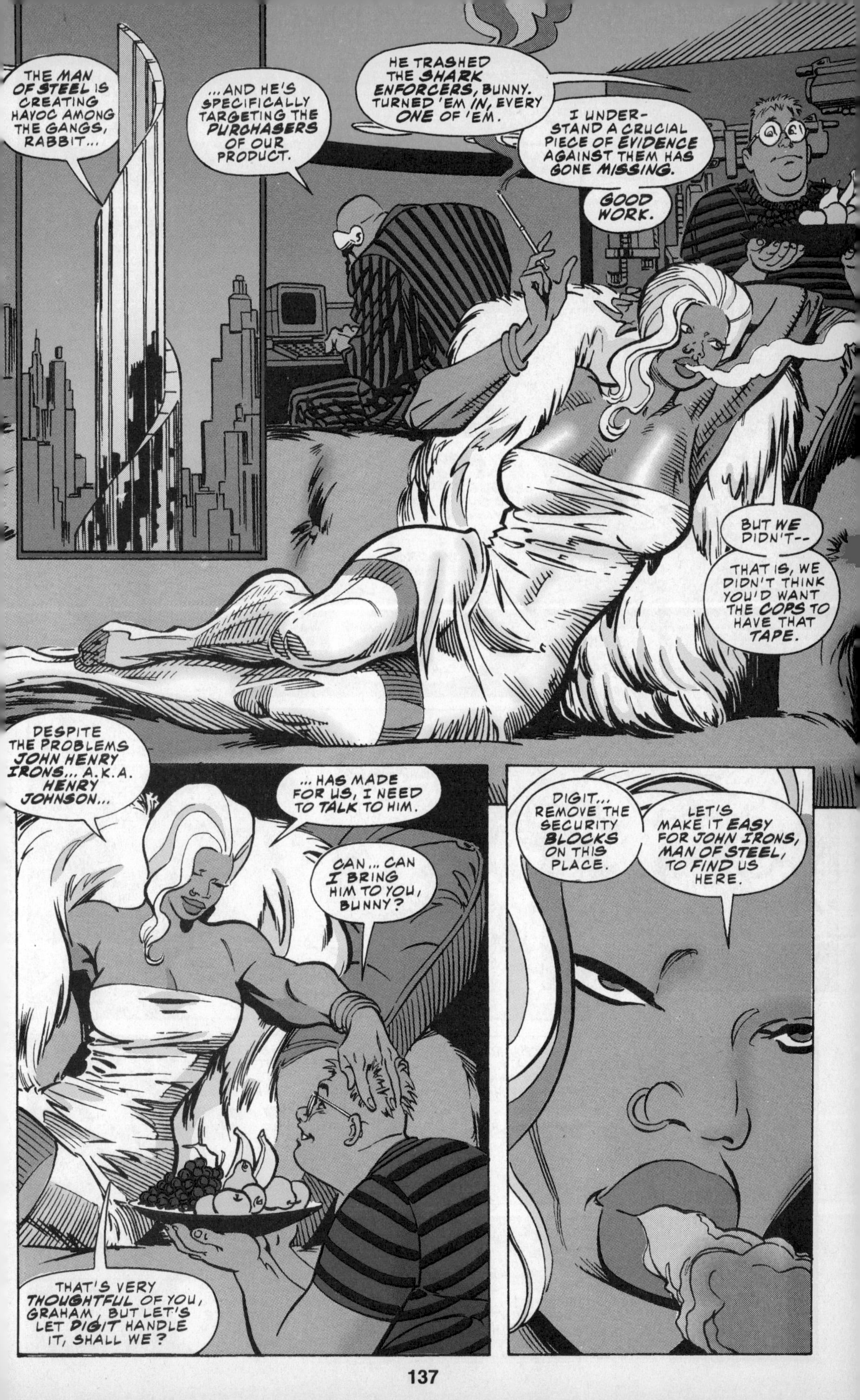
THE MAN OF STEEL IS CREATING HAVOC AMONG THE GANGS, RABBIT...
...AND HE'S SPECIFICALLY TARGETING THE PURCHASERS OF OUR PRODUCT.
HE TRASHED THE SHARK ENFORCERS, BUNNY. TURNED 'EM IN, EVERY ONE OF 'EM.
I UNDER-STAND A CRUCIAL PIECE OF EVIDENCE AGAINST THEM HAS GONE MISSING.
GOOD WORK.
BUT WE DIDN'T--
THAT IS, WE DIDN'T THINK YOU'D WANT THE COPS TO HAVE THAT TAPE.
DESPITE THE PROBLEMS JOHN HENRY IRONS... A.K.A. HENRY JOHNSON...
...HAS MADE FOR US, I NEED TO TALK TO HIM.
CAN... CAN I BRING HIM TO YOU, BUNNY?
THAT'S VERY THOUGHTFUL OF YOU, GRAHAM, BUT LET'S LET DIGIT HANDLE IT, SHALL WE?
DIGIT... REMOVE THE SECURITY BLOCKS ON THIS PLACE.
LET'S MAKE IT EASY FOR JOHN IRONS, MAN OF STEEL, TO FIND US HERE.

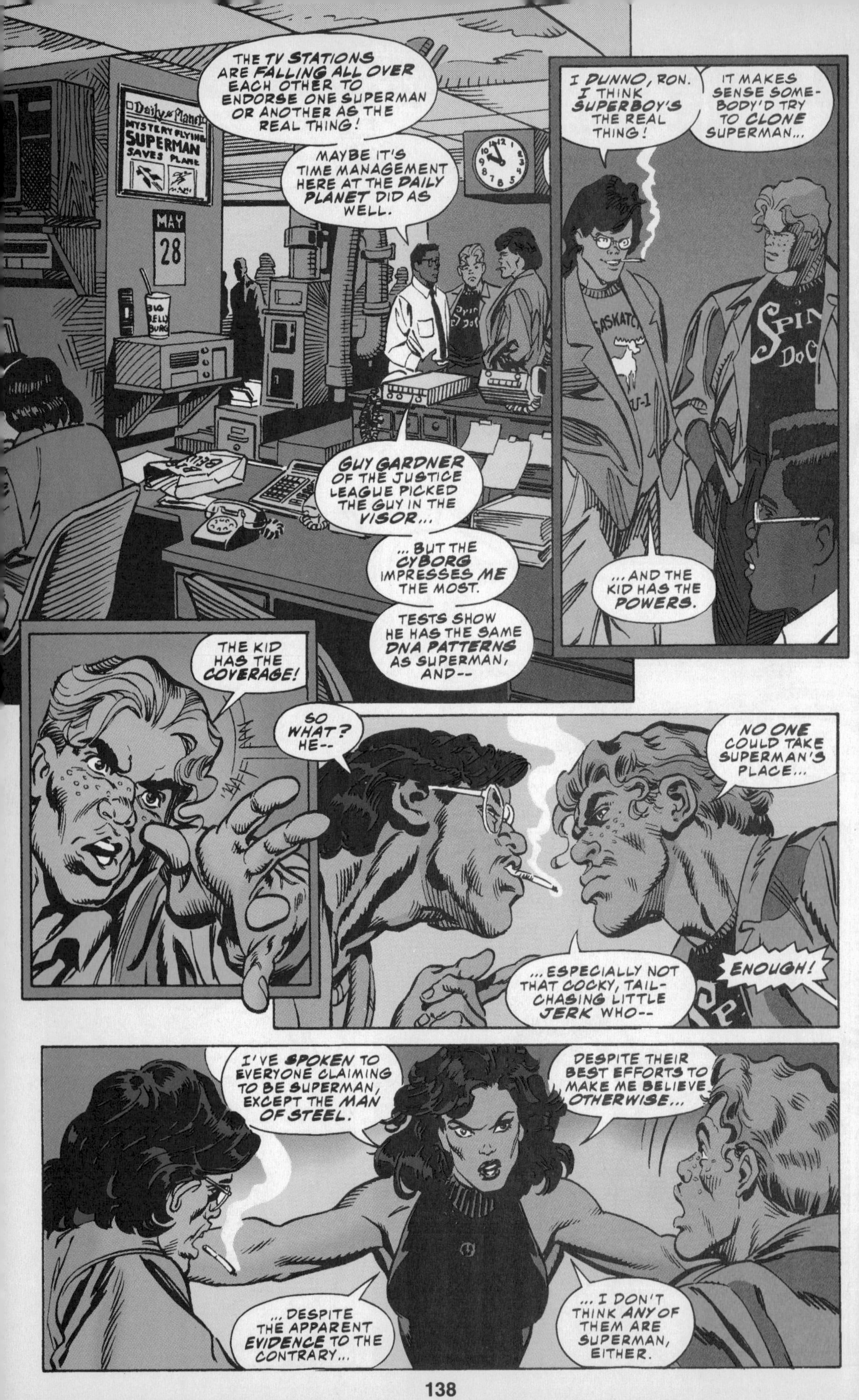

DAILY PLANET
MYSTERY FLYING SUPERMAN SAVES PLANE
MAY 28
BIG BELLY BURG
THE TV STATIONS ARE FALLING ALL OVER EACH OTHER TO ENDORSE ONE SUPERMAN OR ANOTHER AS THE REAL THING!
MAYBE IT'S TIME MANAGEMENT HERE AT THE DAILY PLANET DID AS WELL.
GUY GARDNER OF THE JUSTICE LEAGUE PICKED THE GUY IN THE VISOR...
...BUT THE CYBORG IMPRESSES ME THE MOST.
TESTS SHOW HE HAS THE SAME DNA PATTERNS AS SUPERMAN, AND--
I DUNNO, RON. I THINK SUPERBOY'S THE REAL THING!
IT MAKES SENSE SOMEBODY'D TRY TO CLONE SUPERMAN...
...AND THE KID HAS THE POWERS.
THE KID HAS THE COVERAGE!
SO WHAT? HE--
NO ONE COULD TAKE SUPERMAN'S PLACE...
...ESPECIALLY NOT THAT COCKY, TAIL-CHASING LITTLE JERK WHO--
ENOUGH!
I'VE SPOKEN TO EVERYONE CLAIMING TO BE SUPERMAN, EXCEPT THE MAN OF STEEL.
DESPITE THEIR BEST EFFORTS TO MAKE ME BELIEVE OTHERWISE...
...DESPITE THE APPARENT EVIDENCE TO THE CONTRARY...
...I DON'T THINK ANY OF THEM ARE SUPERMAN, EITHER.

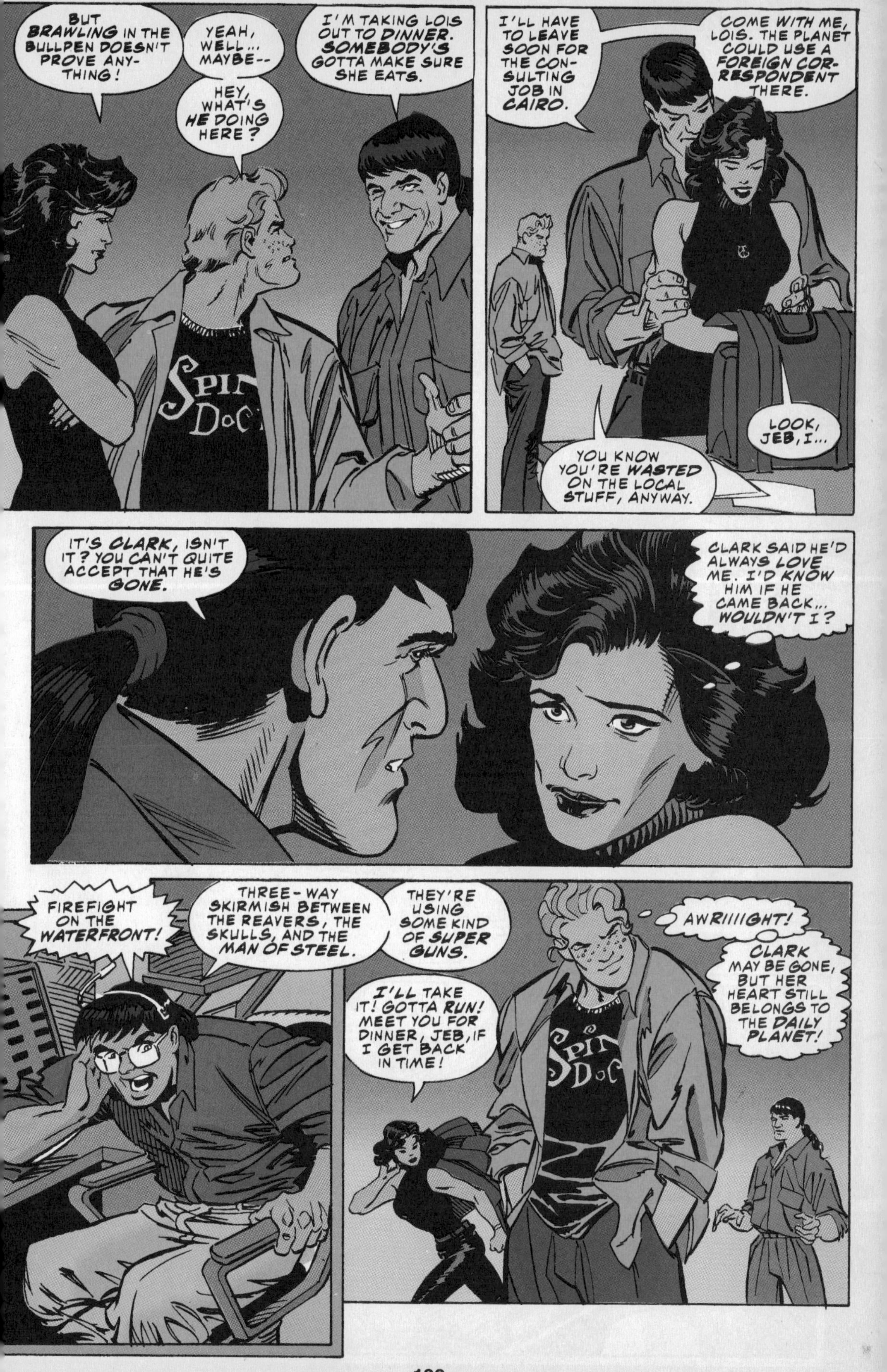
BUT BRAWLING IN THE BULLPEN DOESN'T PROVE ANYTHING!
YEAH, WELL... MAYBE--
HEY, WHAT'S HE DOING HERE?
I'M TAKING LOIS OUT TO DINNER. SOMEBODY'S GOTTA MAKE SURE SHE EATS.
SPIN DOC
I'LL HAVE TO LEAVE SOON FOR THE CONSULTING JOB IN CAIRO.
COME WITH ME, LOIS. THE PLANET COULD USE A FOREIGN CORRESPONDENT THERE.
YOU KNOW YOU'RE WASTED ON THE LOCAL STUFF, ANYWAY.
LOOK, JEB, I...
IT'S CLARK, ISN'T IT? YOU CAN'T QUITE ACCEPT THAT HE'S GONE.
CLARK SAID HE'D ALWAYS LOVE ME. I'D KNOW HIM IF HE CAME BACK... WOULDN'T I?
FIREFIGHT ON THE WATERFRONT!
THREE-WAY SKIRMISH BETWEEN THE REAVERS, THE SKULLS, AND THE MAN OF STEEL.
THEY'RE USING SOME KIND OF SUPER GUNS.
I'LL TAKE IT! GOTTA RUN! MEET YOU FOR DINNER, JEB, IF I GET BACK IN TIME!
AWRIIIIGHT!
CLARK MAY BE GONE, BUT HER HEART STILL BELONGS TO THE DAILY PLANET!
SPIN DOC

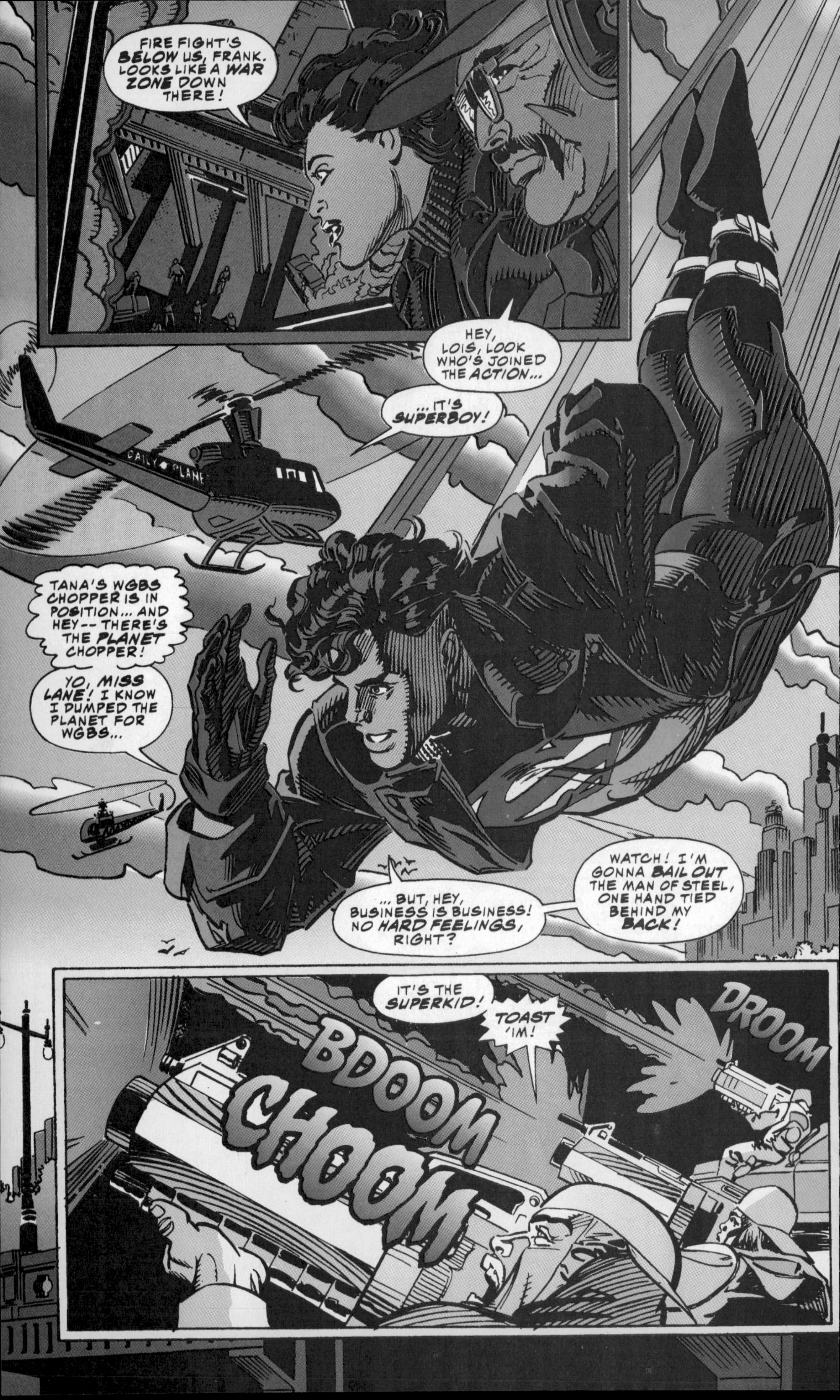
FIRE FIGHT'S BELOW US, FRANK. LOOKS LIKE A WAR ZONE DOWN THERE!
HEY, LOIS, LOOK WHO'S JOINED THE ACTION...
...IT'S SUPERBOY!
DAILY PLANET
TANA'S WGBS CHOPPER IS IN POSITION... AND HEY-- THERE'S THE PLANET CHOPPER!
YO, MISS LANE! I KNOW I DUMPED THE PLANET FOR WGBS...
...BUT, HEY, BUSINESS IS BUSINESS! NO HARD FEELINGS, RIGHT?
WATCH! I'M GONNA BAIL OUT THE MAN OF STEEL, ONE HAND TIED BEHIND MY BACK!
IT'S THE SUPERKID!
TOAST 'IM!
DROOM
BDOOM
CHOOM
CHOOM

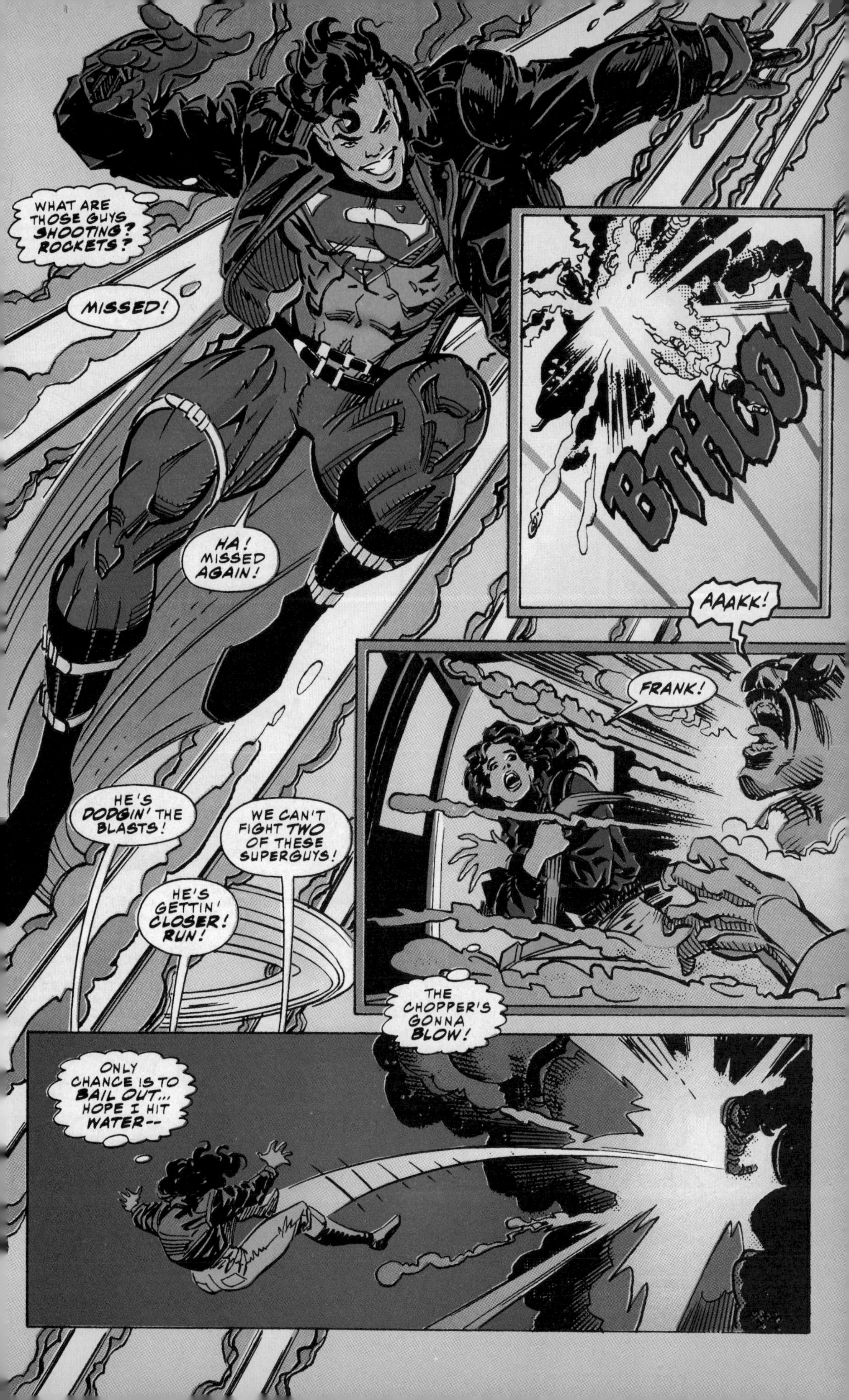
WHAT ARE THOSE GUYS SHOOTING? ROCKETS?
MISSED!
HA! MISSED AGAIN!
BTHOOM
AAAKK!
FRANK!
HE'S DODGIN' THE BLASTS!
WE CAN'T FIGHT TWO OF THESE SUPERGUYS!
HE'S GETTIN' CLOSER! RUN!
THE CHOPPER'S GONNA BLOW!
ONLY CHANCE IS TO BAIL OUT... HOPE I HIT WATER--

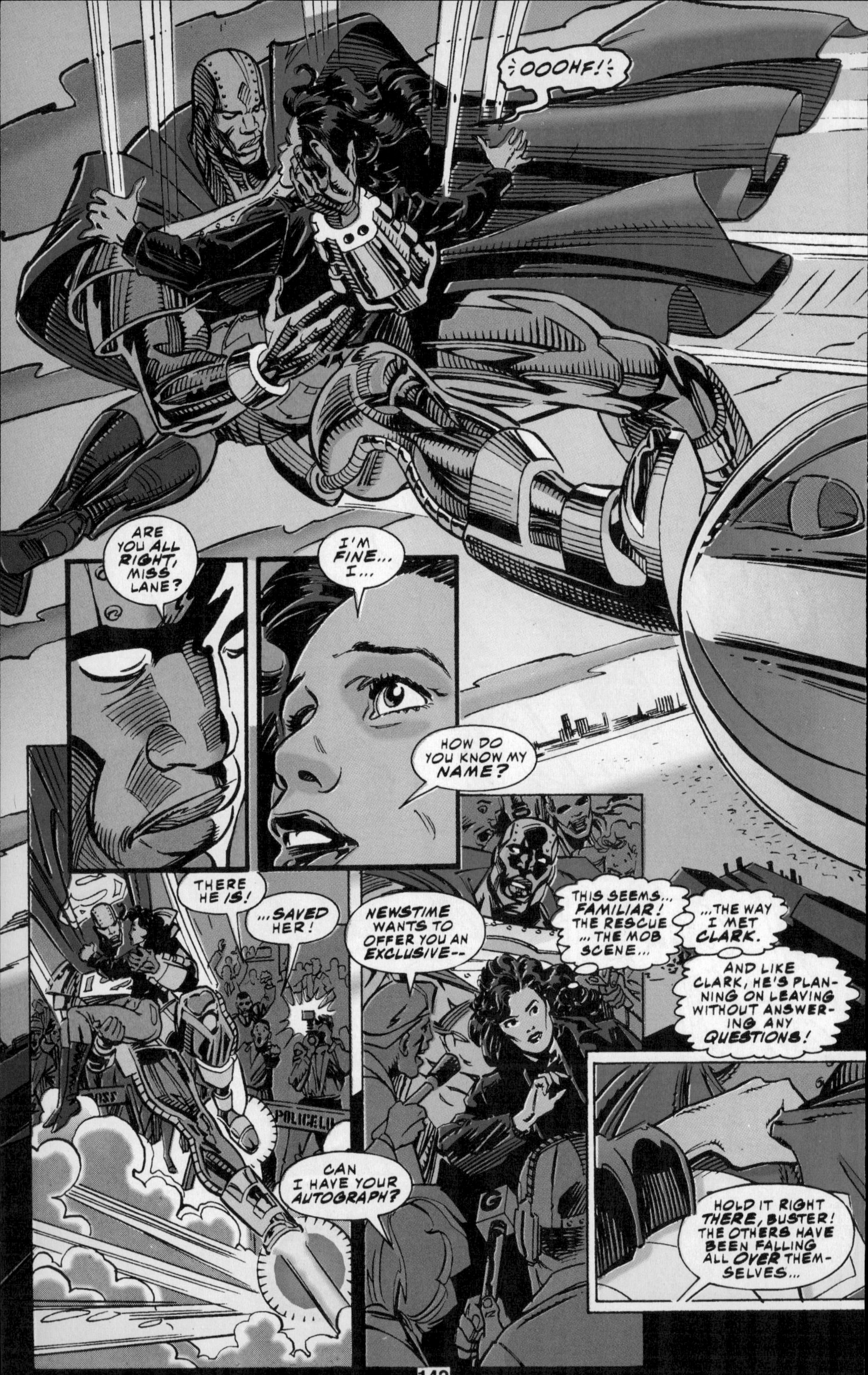
OOOHF!
ARE YOU ALL RIGHT, MISS LANE?
I'M FINE... I...
HOW DO YOU KNOW MY NAME?
THERE HE IS!
...SAVED HER!
NEWSTIME WANTS TO OFFER YOU AN EXCLUSIVE--
THIS SEEMS... FAMILIAR! THE RESCUE ... THE MOB SCENE...
...THE WAY I MET CLARK.
AND LIKE CLARK, HE'S PLANNING ON LEAVING WITHOUT ANSWERING ANY QUESTIONS!
CAN I HAVE YOUR AUTOGRAPH?
HOLD IT RIGHT THERE, BUSTER! THE OTHERS HAVE BEEN FALLING ALL OVER THEMSELVES...
POLICE LI

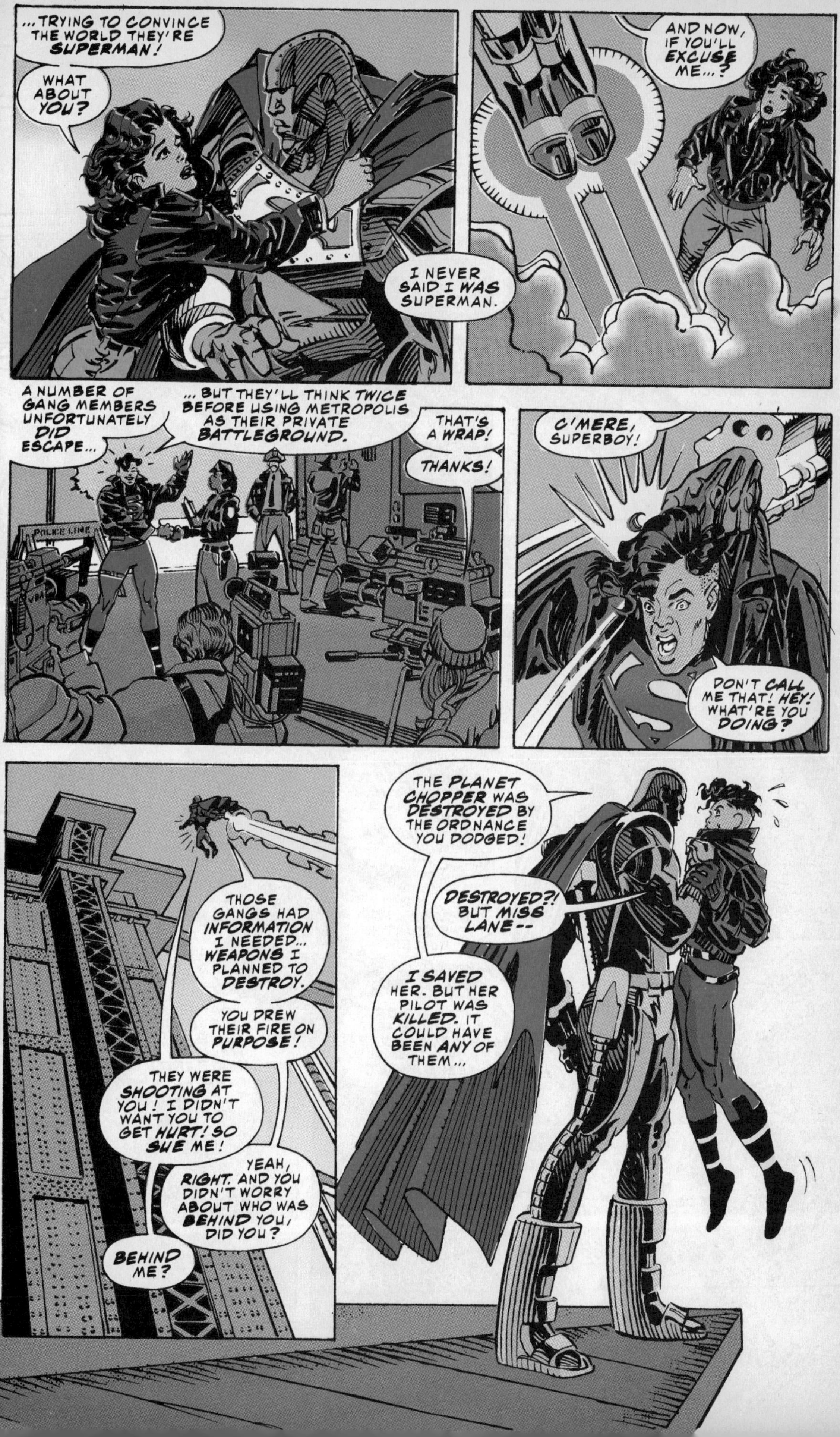

...TRYING TO CONVINCE THE WORLD THEY'RE SUPERMAN!
WHAT ABOUT YOU?
I NEVER SAID I WAS SUPERMAN.
AND NOW, IF YOU'LL EXCUSE ME...?
A NUMBER OF GANG MEMBERS UNFORTUNATELY DID ESCAPE...
...BUT THEY'LL THINK TWICE BEFORE USING METROPOLIS AS THEIR PRIVATE BATTLEGROUND.
THAT'S A WRAP!
THANKS!
POLICE LINE
C'MERE, SUPERBOY!
DON'T CALL ME THAT! HEY! WHAT'RE YOU DOING?
THOSE GANGS HAD INFORMATION I NEEDED... WEAPONS I PLANNED TO DESTROY.
YOU DREW THEIR FIRE ON PURPOSE!
THEY WERE SHOOTING AT YOU! I DIDN'T WANT YOU TO GET HURT! SO SUE ME!
YEAH, RIGHT. AND YOU DIDN'T WORRY ABOUT WHO WAS BEHIND YOU, DID YOU?
BEHIND ME?
THE PLANET CHOPPER WAS DESTROYED BY THE ORDNANCE YOU DODGED!
DESTROYED?! BUT MISS LANE--
I SAVED HER. BUT HER PILOT WAS KILLED. IT COULD HAVE BEEN ANY OF THEM...

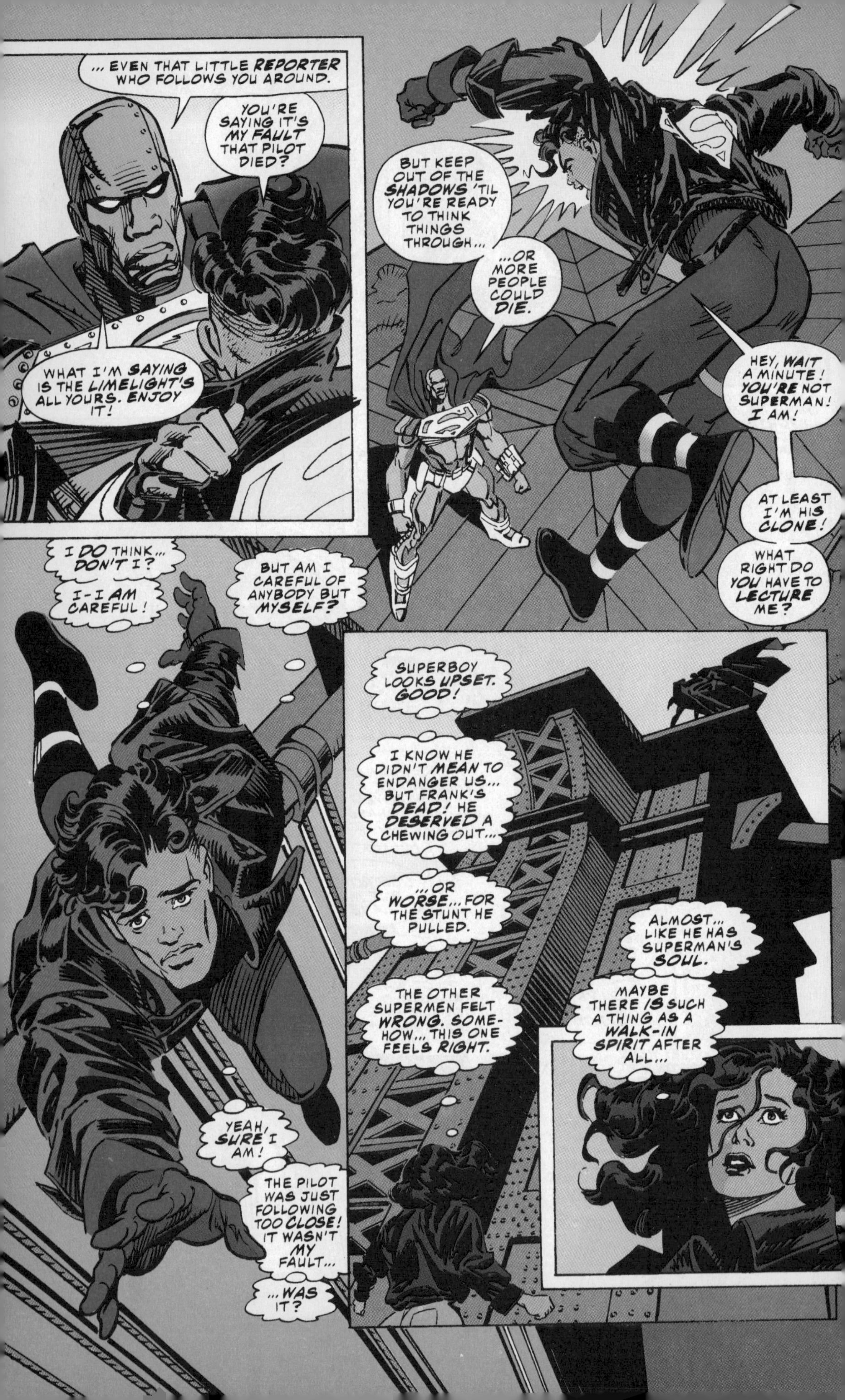
... EVEN THAT LITTLE REPORTER WHO FOLLOWS YOU AROUND.
YOU'RE SAYING IT'S MY FAULT THAT PILOT DIED?
WHAT I'M SAYING IS THE LIMELIGHT'S ALL YOURS. ENJOY IT!
BUT KEEP OUT OF THE SHADOWS 'TIL YOU'RE READY TO THINK THINGS THROUGH...
...OR MORE PEOPLE COULD DIE.
HEY, WAIT A MINUTE! YOU'RE NOT SUPERMAN! I AM!
AT LEAST I'M HIS CLONE!
WHAT RIGHT DO YOU HAVE TO LECTURE ME?
I DO THINK... DON'T I?
I-I AM CAREFUL!
BUT AM I CAREFUL OF ANYBODY BUT MYSELF?
YEAH, SURE I AM!
THE PILOT WAS JUST FOLLOWING TOO CLOSE! IT WASN'T MY FAULT...
...WAS IT?
SUPERBOY LOOKS UPSET. GOOD!
I KNOW HE DIDN'T MEAN TO ENDANGER US... BUT FRANK'S DEAD! HE DESERVED A CHEWING OUT...
...OR WORSE... FOR THE STUNT HE PULLED.
THE OTHER SUPERMEN FELT WRONG. SOME-HOW... THIS ONE FEELS RIGHT.
ALMOST... LIKE HE HAS SUPERMAN'S SOUL.
MAYBE THERE IS SUCH A THING AS A WALK-IN SPIRIT AFTER ALL...

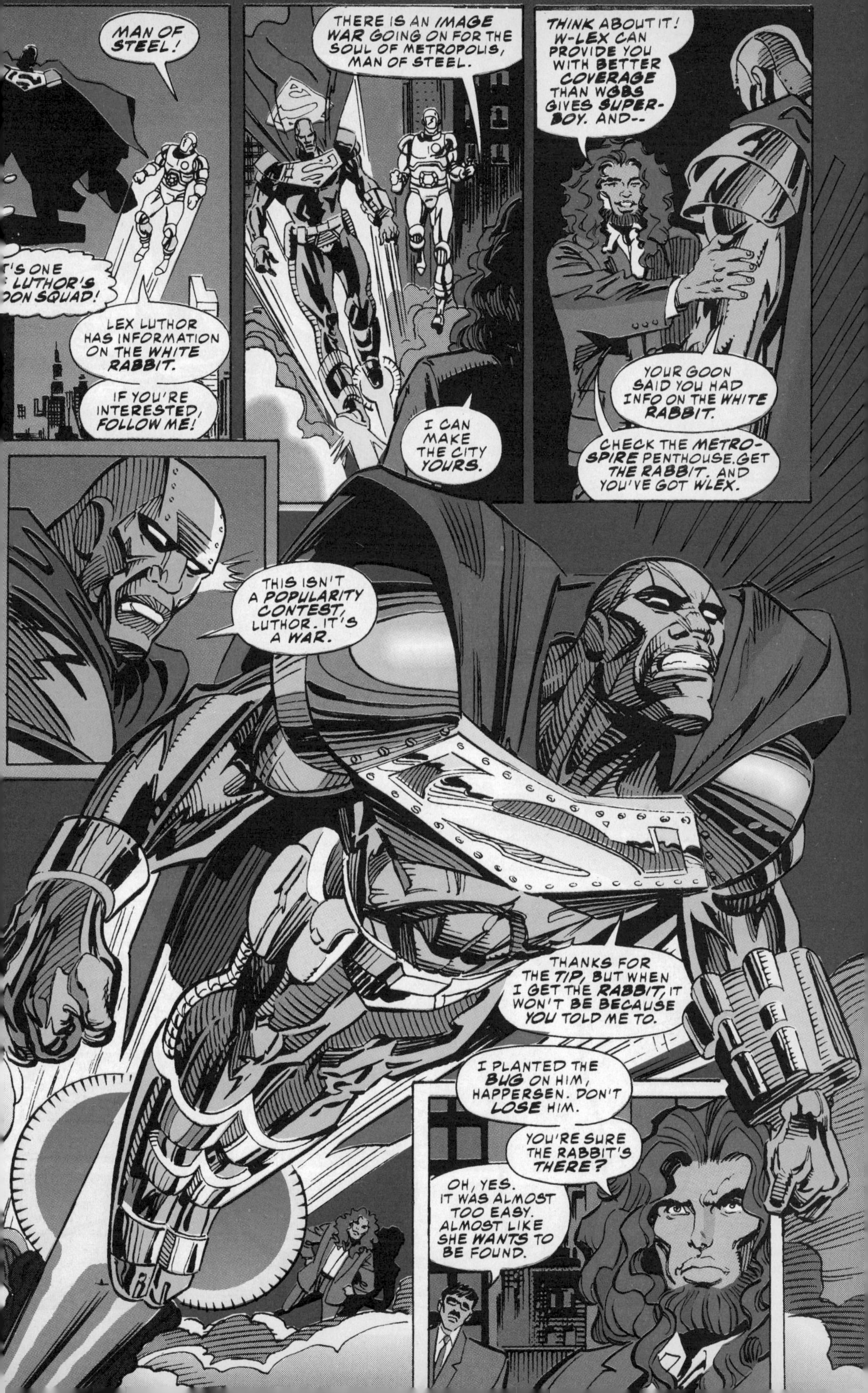

MAN OF STEEL!
IT'S ONE OF LUTHOR'S GOON SQUAD!
LEX LUTHOR HAS INFORMATION ON THE WHITE RABBIT.
IF YOU'RE INTERESTED, FOLLOW ME!
THERE IS AN IMAGE WAR GOING ON FOR THE SOUL OF METROPOLIS, MAN OF STEEL.
I CAN MAKE THE CITY YOURS.
THINK ABOUT IT! W-LEX CAN PROVIDE YOU WITH BETTER COVERAGE THAN WGBS GIVES SUPERBOY. AND--
YOUR GOON SAID YOU HAD INFO ON THE WHITE RABBIT.
CHECK THE METROSPIRE PENTHOUSE. GET THE RABBIT. AND YOU'VE GOT WLEX.
THIS ISN'T A POPULARITY CONTEST, LUTHOR. IT'S A WAR.
THANKS FOR THE TIP, BUT WHEN I GET THE RABBIT, IT WON'T BE BECAUSE YOU TOLD ME TO.
I PLANTED THE BUG ON HIM, HAPPERSEN. DON'T LOSE HIM.
YOU'RE SURE THE RABBIT'S THERE?
OH, YES. IT WAS ALMOST TOO EASY. ALMOST LIKE SHE WANTS TO BE FOUND.

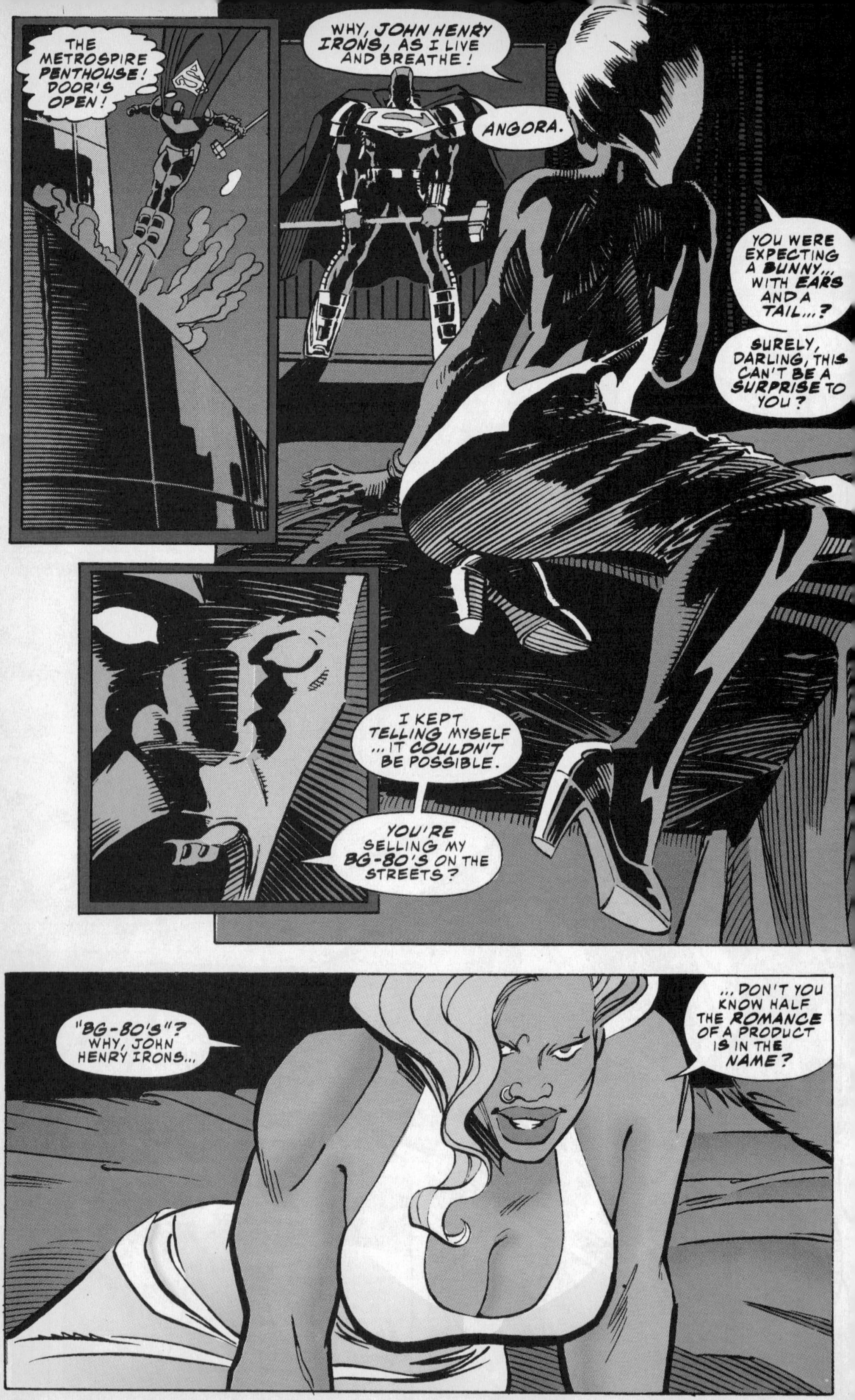
THE METROSPIRE PENTHOUSE! DOOR'S OPEN!
WHY, JOHN HENRY IRONS, AS I LIVE AND BREATHE!
ANGORA.
YOU WERE EXPECTING A BUNNY... WITH EARS AND A TAIL...?
SURELY, DARLING, THIS CAN'T BE A SURPRISE TO YOU?
I KEPT TELLING MYSELF ...IT COULDN'T BE POSSIBLE.
YOU'RE SELLING MY BG-80'S ON THE STREETS?
"BG-80'S"? WHY, JOHN HENRY IRONS...
...DON'T YOU KNOW HALF THE ROMANCE OF A PRODUCT IS IN THE NAME?

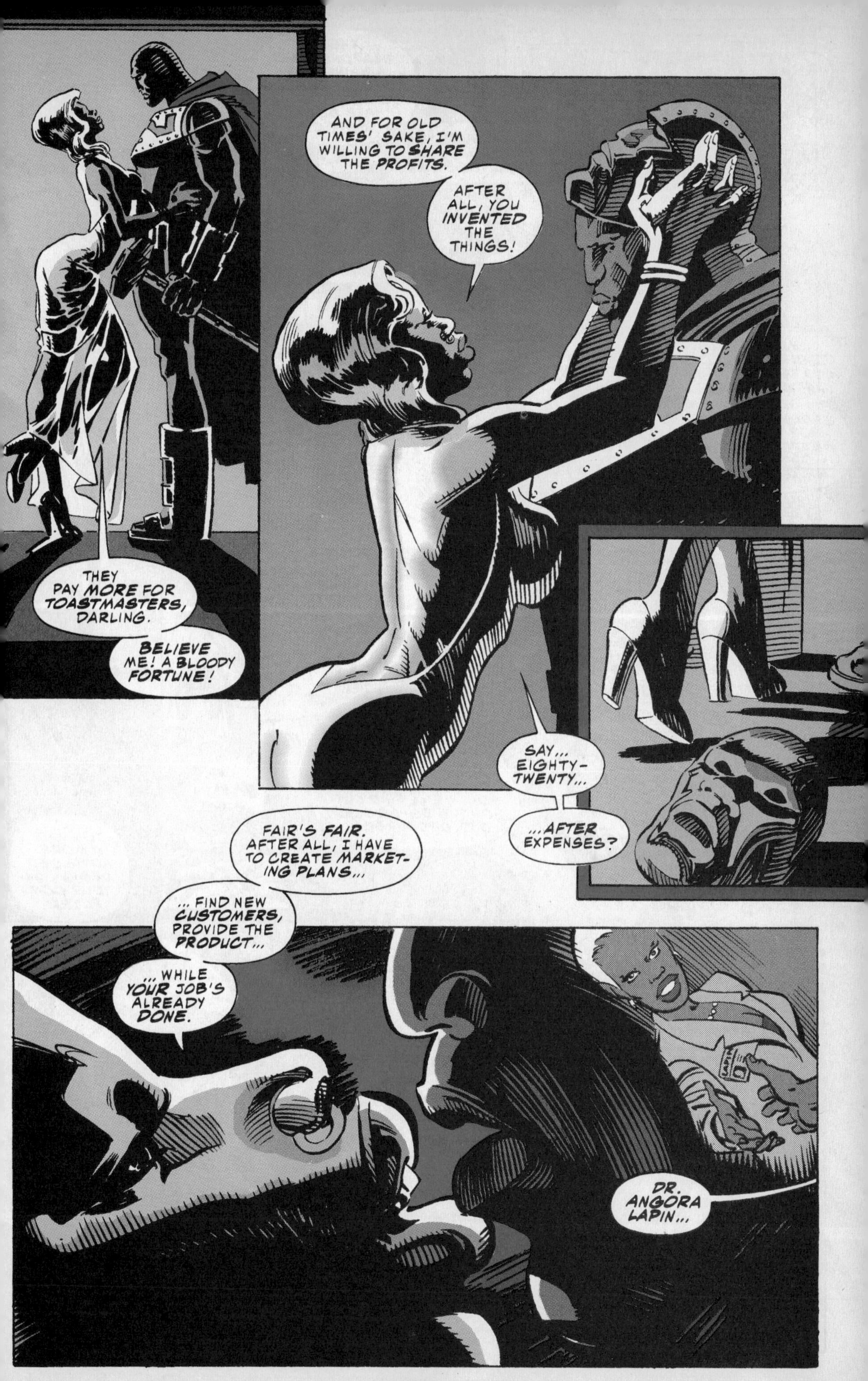

THEY PAY MORE FOR TOASTMASTERS, DARLING.
BELIEVE ME! A BLOODY FORTUNE!
AND FOR OLD TIMES' SAKE, I'M WILLING TO SHARE THE PROFITS.
AFTER ALL, YOU INVENTED THE THINGS!
SAY... EIGHTY-TWENTY...
...AFTER EXPENSES?
FAIR'S FAIR. AFTER ALL, I HAVE TO CREATE MARKETING PLANS...
... FIND NEW CUSTOMERS, PROVIDE THE PRODUCT...
... WHILE YOUR JOB'S ALREADY DONE.
DR. ANGORA LAPIN...

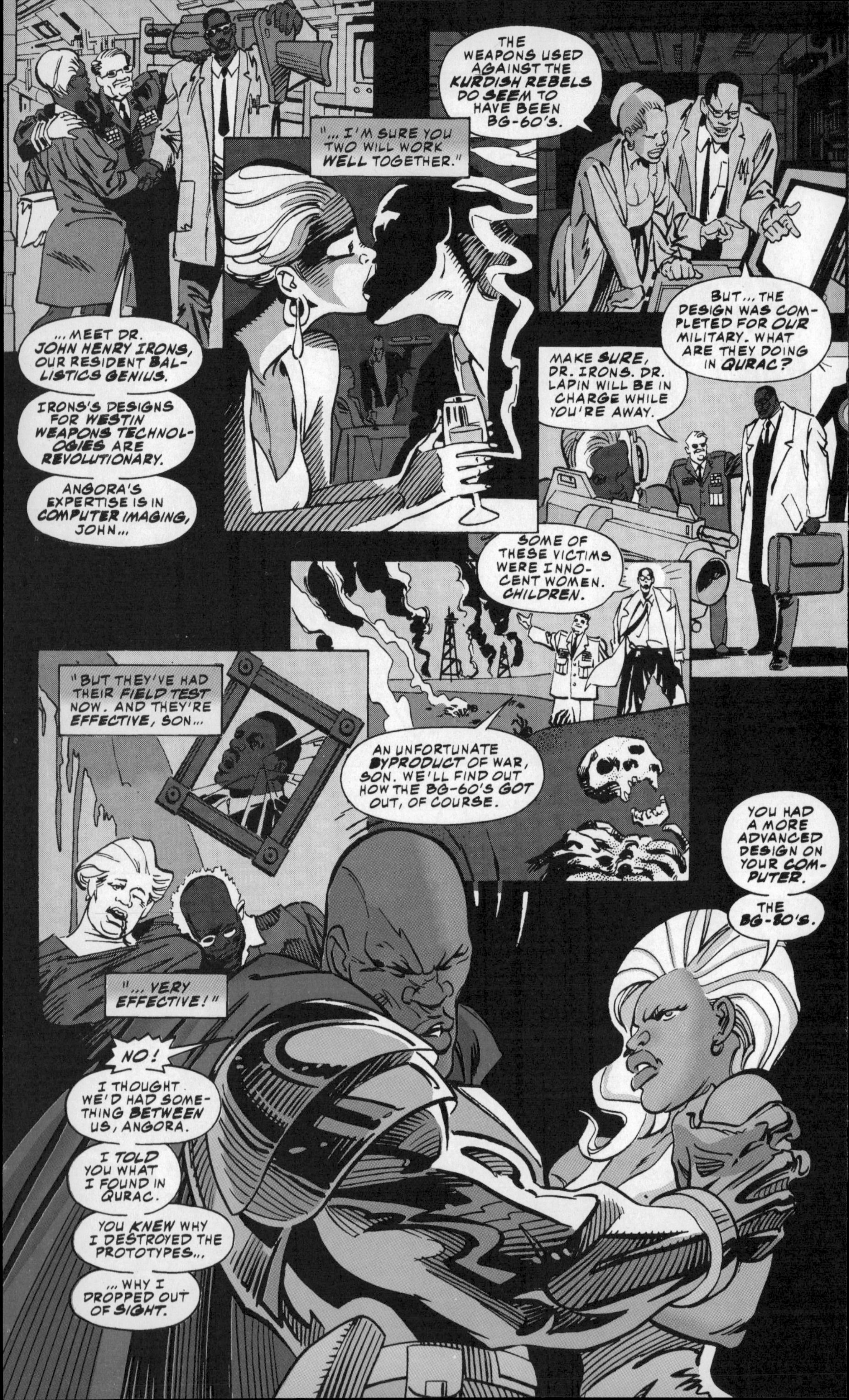
...MEET DR. JOHN HENRY IRONS, OUR RESIDENT BALLISTICS GENIUS.
IRONS'S DESIGNS FOR WESTIN WEAPONS TECHNOLOGIES ARE REVOLUTIONARY.
ANGORA'S EXPERTISE IS IN COMPUTER IMAGING, JOHN...
"...I'M SURE YOU TWO WILL WORK WELL TOGETHER."
THE WEAPONS USED AGAINST THE KURDISH REBELS DO SEEM TO HAVE BEEN BG-60'S.
BUT... THE DESIGN WAS COMPLETED FOR OUR MILITARY. WHAT ARE THEY DOING IN QURAC?
MAKE SURE, DR. IRONS. DR. LAPIN WILL BE IN CHARGE WHILE YOU'RE AWAY.
SOME OF THESE VICTIMS WERE INNOCENT WOMEN. CHILDREN.
AN UNFORTUNATE BYPRODUCT OF WAR, SON. WE'LL FIND OUT HOW THE BG-60'S GOT OUT, OF COURSE.
"BUT THEY'VE HAD THEIR FIELD TEST NOW. AND THEY'RE EFFECTIVE, SON...
"...VERY EFFECTIVE!"
YOU HAD A MORE ADVANCED DESIGN ON YOUR COMPUTER.
THE BG-80'S.
NO!
I THOUGHT WE'D HAD SOMETHING BETWEEN US, ANGORA.
I TOLD YOU WHAT I FOUND IN QURAC.
YOU KNEW WHY I DESTROYED THE PROTOTYPES...
...WHY I DROPPED OUT OF SIGHT.

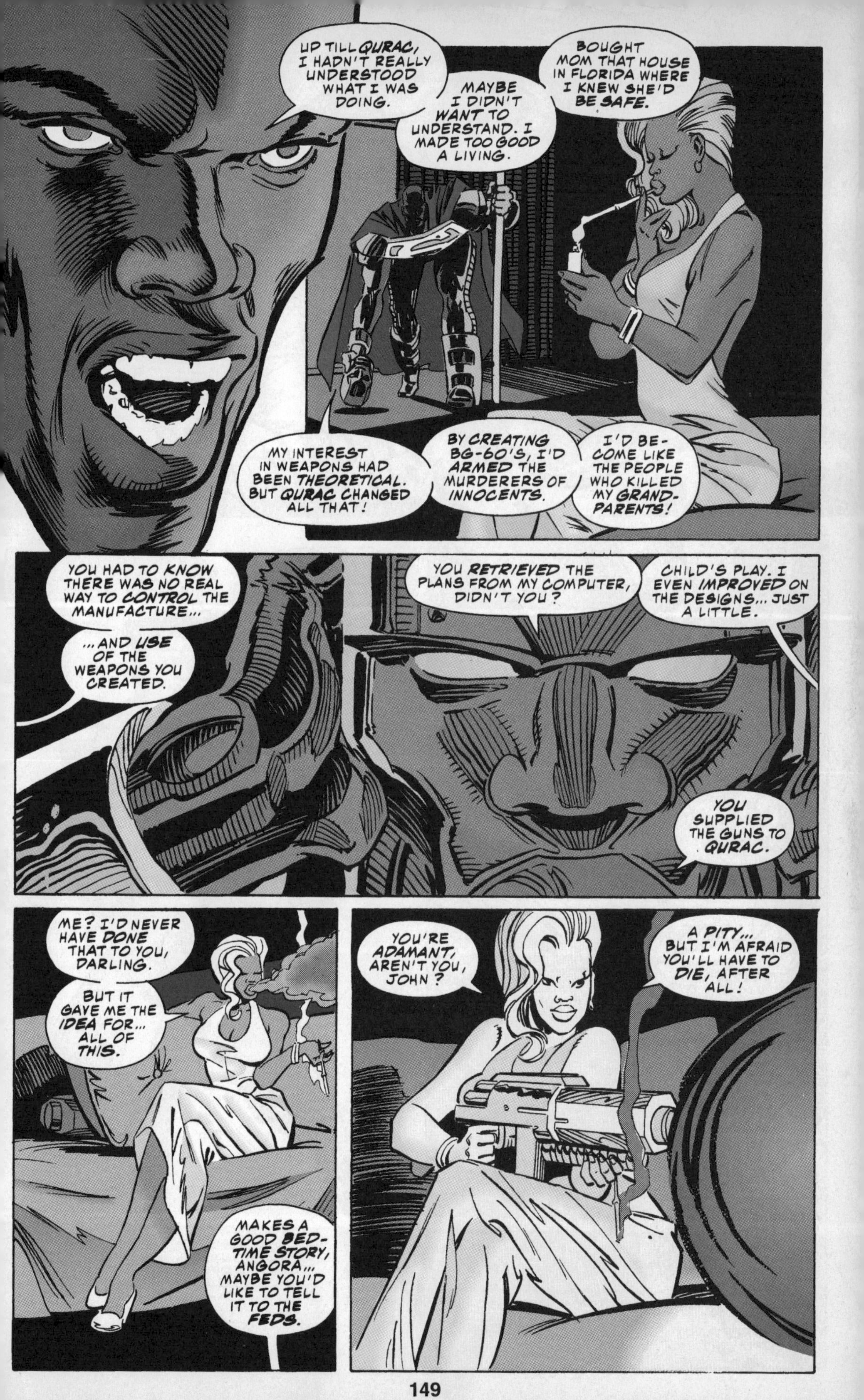
UP TILL QURAC, I HADN'T REALLY UNDERSTOOD WHAT I WAS DOING.
MAYBE I DIDN'T WANT TO UNDERSTAND. I MADE TOO GOOD A LIVING.
BOUGHT MOM THAT HOUSE IN FLORIDA WHERE I KNEW SHE'D BE SAFE.
MY INTEREST IN WEAPONS HAD BEEN THEORETICAL. BUT QURAC CHANGED ALL THAT!
BY CREATING BG-60'S, I'D ARMED THE MURDERERS OF INNOCENTS.
I'D BECOME LIKE THE PEOPLE WHO KILLED MY GRANDPARENTS!
YOU HAD TO KNOW THERE WAS NO REAL WAY TO CONTROL THE MANUFACTURE...
...AND USE OF THE WEAPONS YOU CREATED.
YOU RETRIEVED THE PLANS FROM MY COMPUTER, DIDN'T YOU?
CHILD'S PLAY. I EVEN IMPROVED ON THE DESIGNS... JUST A LITTLE.
YOU SUPPLIED THE GUNS TO QURAC.
ME? I'D NEVER HAVE DONE THAT TO YOU, DARLING.
BUT IT GAVE ME THE IDEA FOR... ALL OF THIS.
MAKES A GOOD BEDTIME STORY, ANGORA... MAYBE YOU'D LIKE TO TELL IT TO THE FEDS.
YOU'RE ADAMANT, AREN'T YOU, JOHN?
A PITY... BUT I'M AFRAID YOU'LL HAVE TO DIE, AFTER ALL!

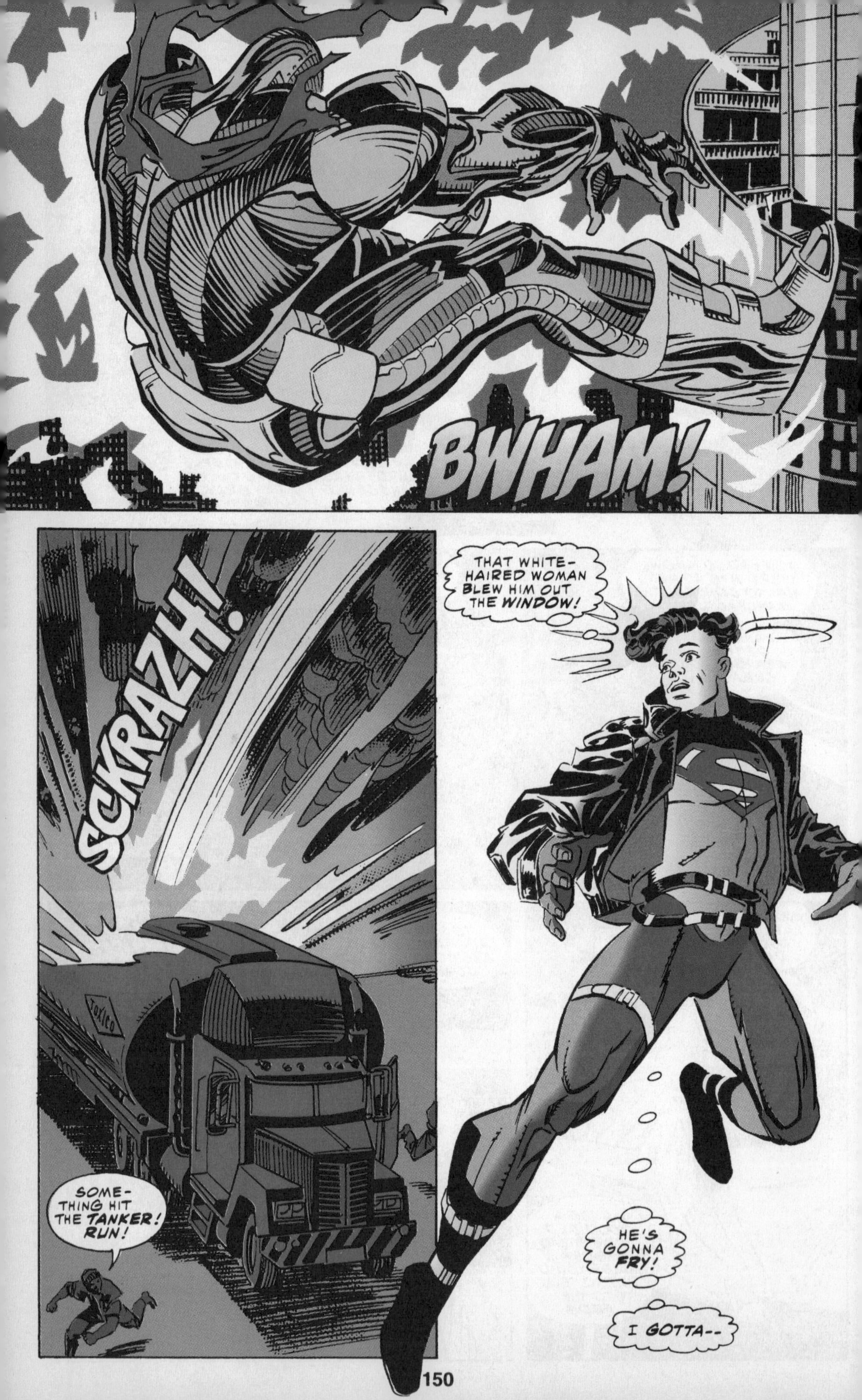
BWHAM!
SCKRAZH!
TOXICO
SOME-THING HIT THE TANKER! RUN!
THAT WHITE-HAIRED WOMAN BLEW HIM OUT THE WINDOW!
HE'S GONNA FRY!
I GOTTA--

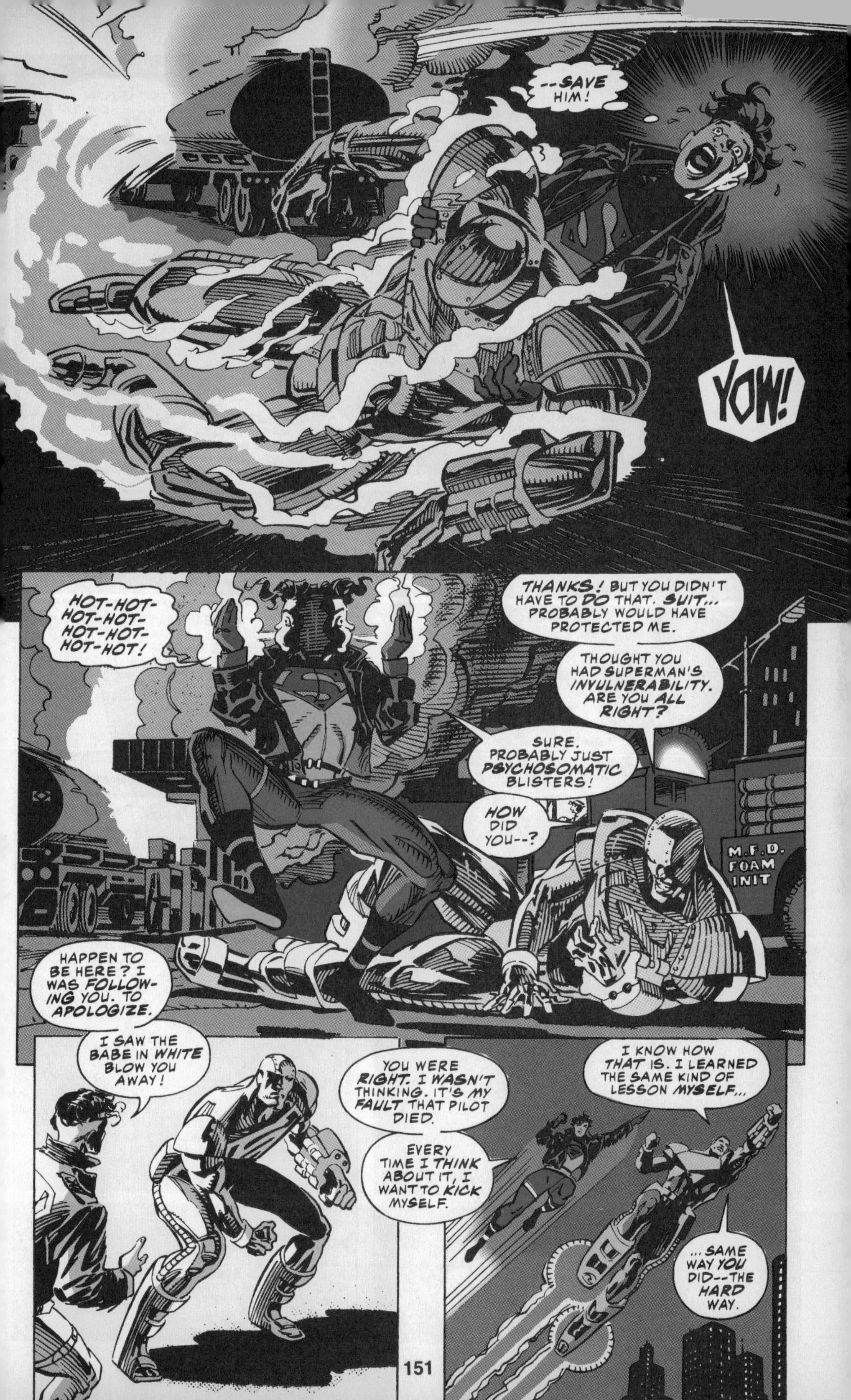
--SAVE HIM!
YOW!
HOT-HOT-HOT-HOT-HOT-HOT-HOT-HOT!
THANKS! BUT YOU DIDN'T HAVE TO DO THAT. SUIT... PROBABLY WOULD HAVE PROTECTED ME.
THOUGHT YOU HAD SUPERMAN'S INVULNERABILITY. ARE YOU ALL RIGHT?
SURE. PROBABLY JUST PSYCHOSOMATIC BLISTERS!
HOW DID YOU--?
M.F.D. FOAM UNIT
HAPPEN TO BE HERE? I WAS FOLLOWING YOU. TO APOLOGIZE.
I SAW THE BABE IN WHITE BLOW YOU AWAY!
YOU WERE RIGHT. I WASN'T THINKING. IT'S MY FAULT THAT PILOT DIED.
EVERY TIME I THINK ABOUT IT, I WANT TO KICK MYSELF.
I KNOW HOW THAT IS. I LEARNED THE SAME KIND OF LESSON MYSELF...
...SAME WAY YOU DID--THE HARD WAY.

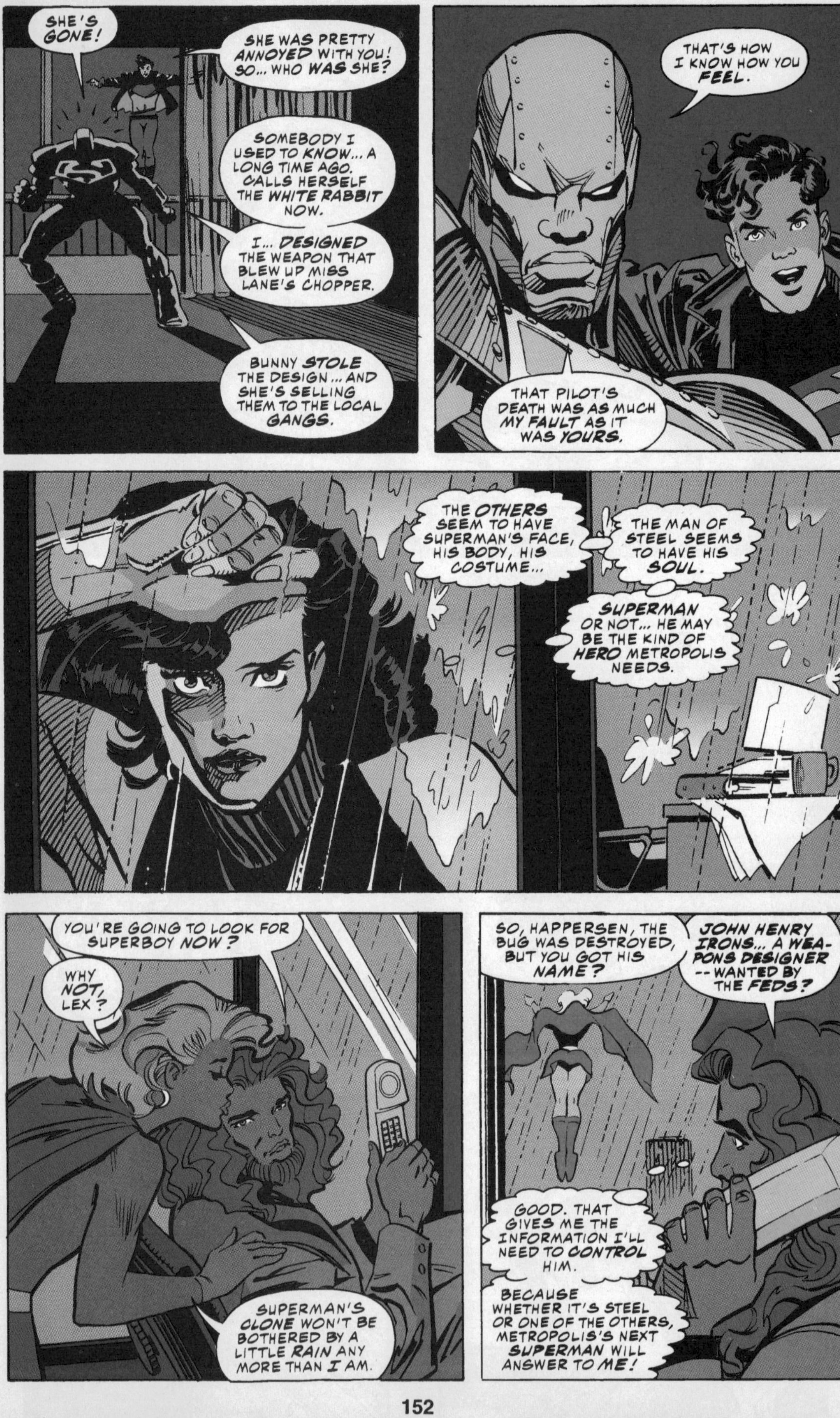
SHE'S GONE!
SHE WAS PRETTY ANNOYED WITH YOU! SO... WHO WAS SHE?
SOMEBODY I USED TO KNOW... A LONG TIME AGO. CALLS HERSELF THE WHITE RABBIT NOW.
I... DESIGNED THE WEAPON THAT BLEW UP MISS LANE'S CHOPPER.
BUNNY STOLE THE DESIGN... AND SHE'S SELLING THEM TO THE LOCAL GANGS.
THAT'S HOW I KNOW HOW YOU FEEL.
THAT PILOT'S DEATH WAS AS MUCH MY FAULT AS IT WAS YOURS.
THE OTHERS SEEM TO HAVE SUPERMAN'S FACE, HIS BODY, HIS COSTUME...
THE MAN OF STEEL SEEMS TO HAVE HIS SOUL.
SUPERMAN OR NOT... HE MAY BE THE KIND OF HERO METROPOLIS NEEDS.
YOU'RE GOING TO LOOK FOR SUPERBOY NOW?
WHY NOT, LEX?
SUPERMAN'S CLONE WON'T BE BOTHERED BY A LITTLE RAIN ANY MORE THAN I AM.
SO, HAPPERSEN, THE BUG WAS DESTROYED, BUT YOU GOT HIS NAME?
JOHN HENRY IRONS... A WEAPONS DESIGNER -- WANTED BY THE FEDS?
GOOD. THAT GIVES ME THE INFORMATION I'LL NEED TO CONTROL HIM.
BECAUSE WHETHER IT'S STEEL OR ONE OF THE OTHERS, METROPOLIS'S NEXT SUPERMAN WILL ANSWER TO ME!

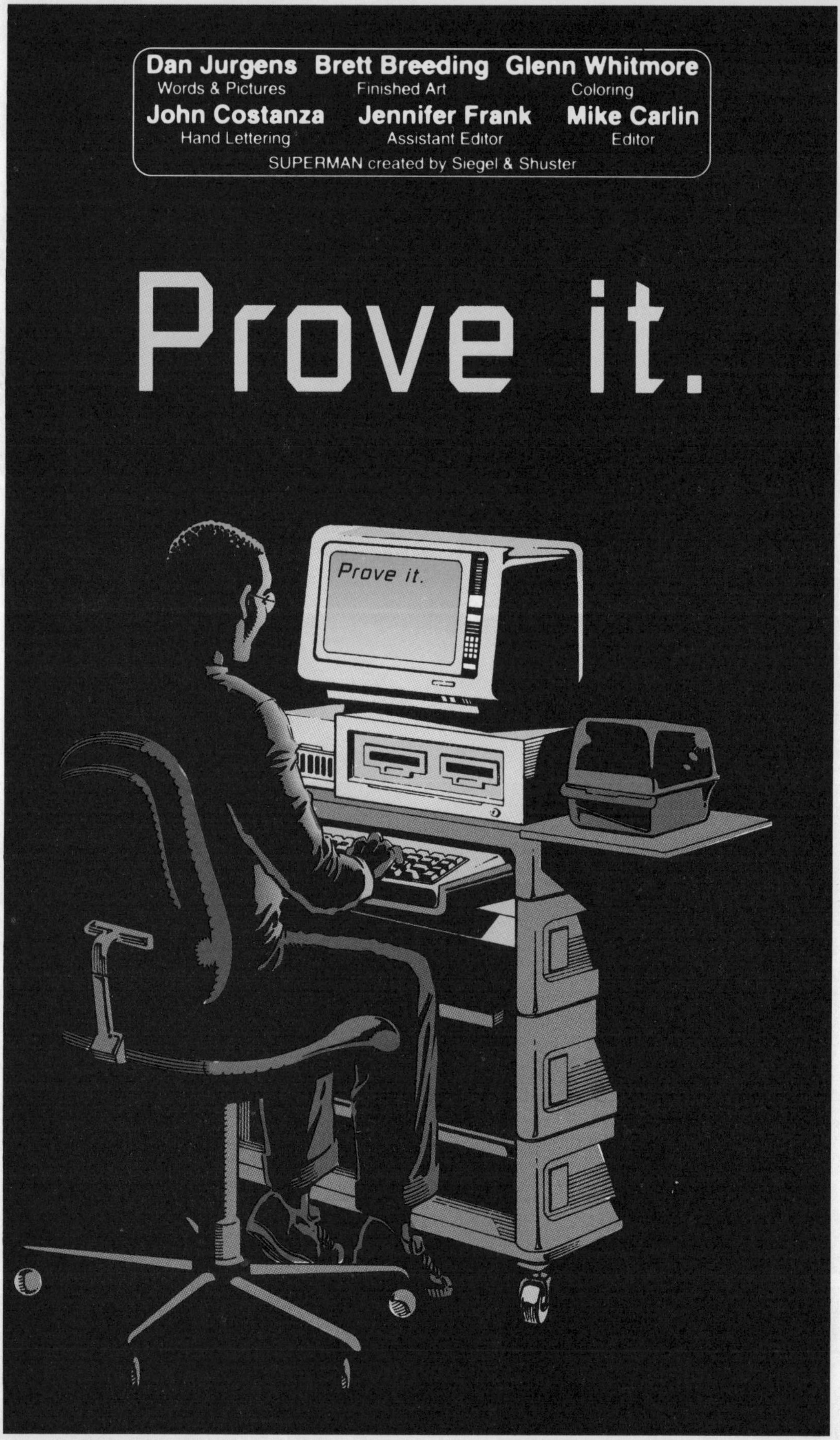
Dan Jurgens Words & Pictures
Brett Breeding Finished Art
Glenn Whitmore Coloring
John Costanza Hand Lettering
Jennifer Frank Assistant Editor
Mike Carlin Editor
SUPERMAN created by Siegel & Shuster
Prove it.
Prove it.

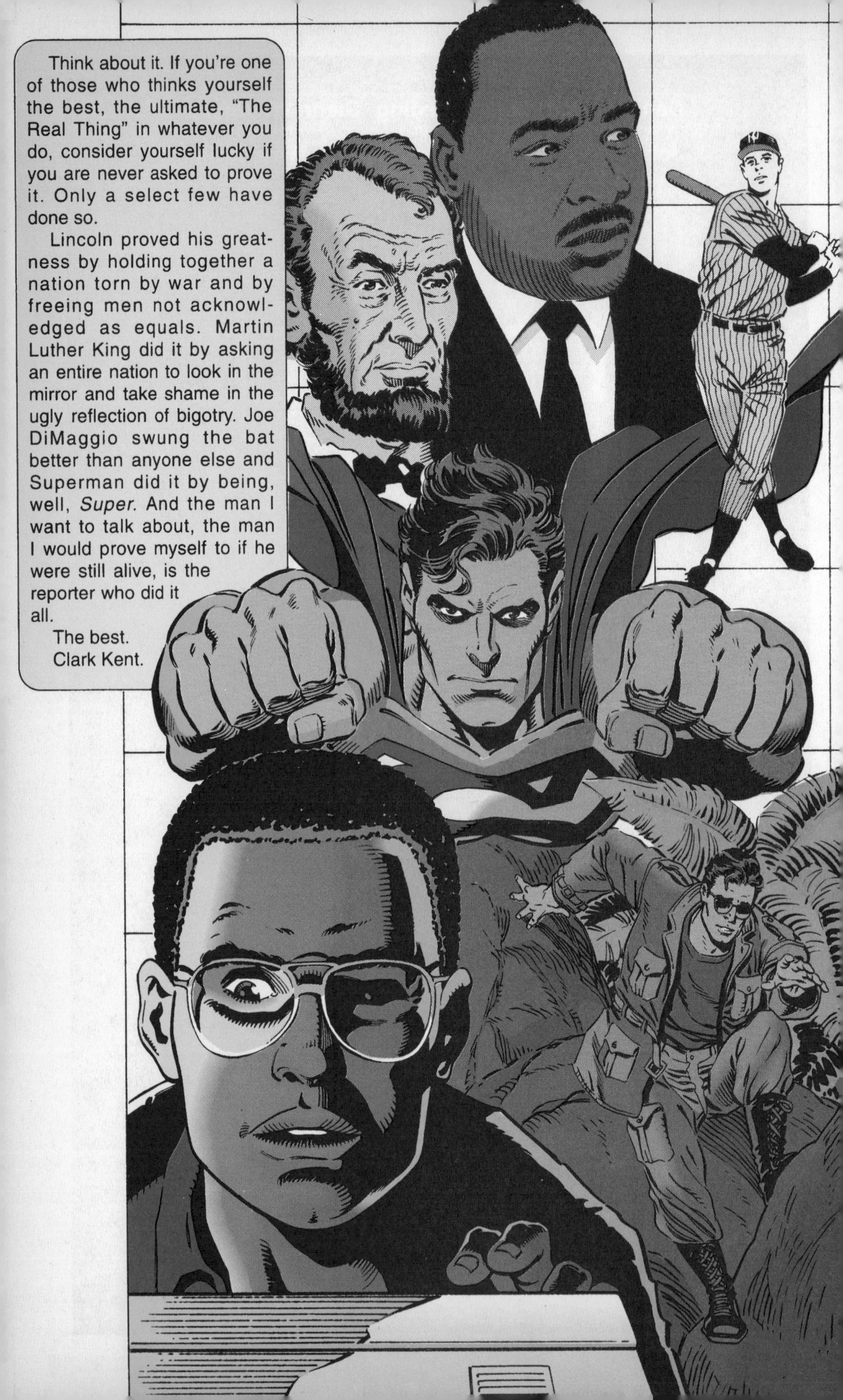
Think about it. If you're one of those who thinks yourself the best, the ultimate, "The Real Thing" in whatever you do, consider yourself lucky if you are never asked to prove it. Only a select few have done so.
Lincoln proved his greatness by holding together a nation torn by war and by freeing men not acknowledged as equals. Martin Luther King did it by asking an entire nation to look in the mirror and take shame in the ugly reflection of bigotry. Joe DiMaggio swung the bat better than anyone else and Superman did it by being, well, *Super.* And the man I want to talk about, the man I would prove myself to if he were still alive, is the reporter who did it all.
The best.
Clark Kent.

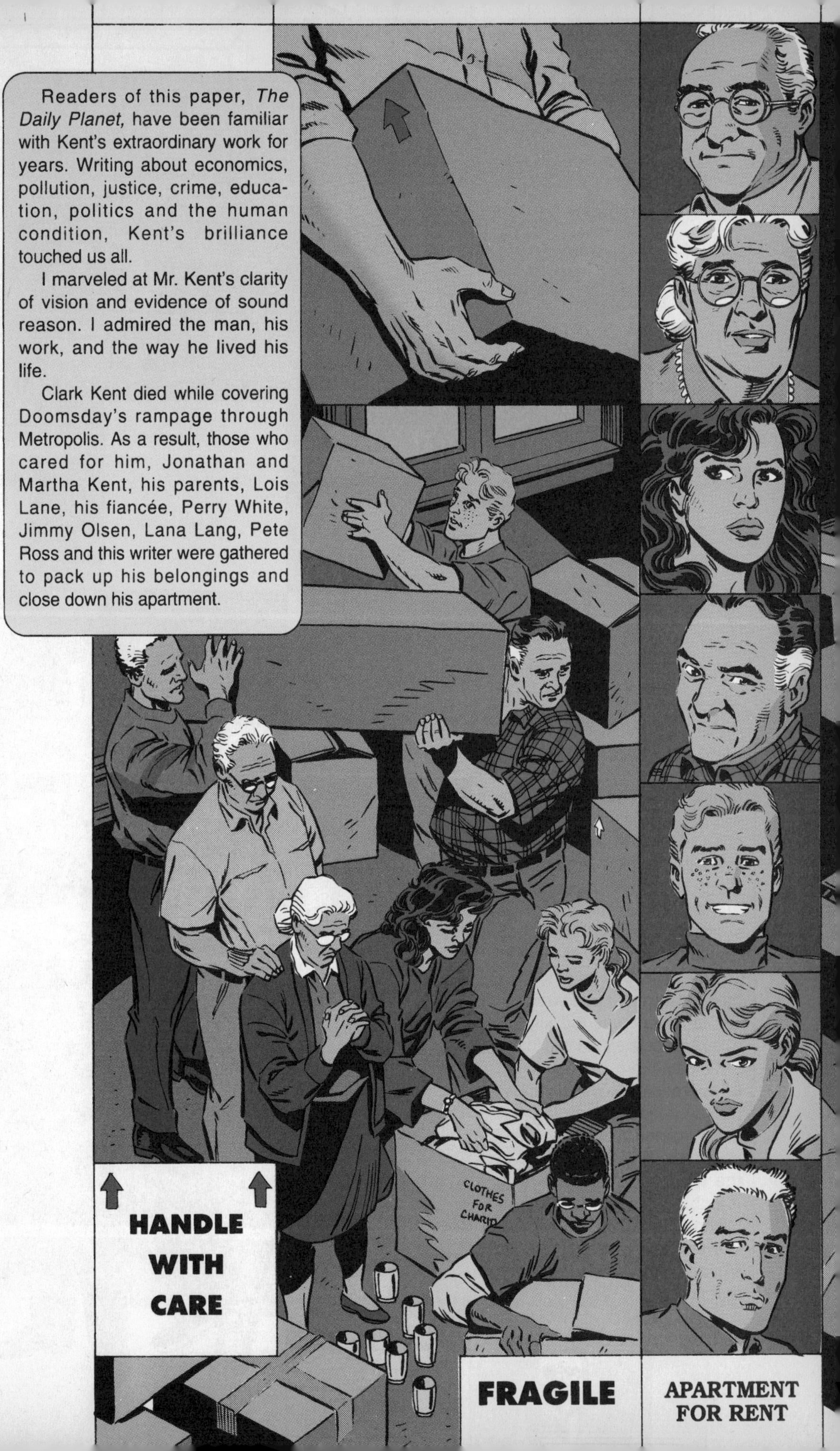
Readers of this paper, *The Daily Planet,* have been familiar with Kent's extraordinary work for years. Writing about economics, pollution, justice, crime, education, politics and the human condition, Kent's brilliance touched us all.
I marveled at Mr. Kent's clarity of vision and evidence of sound reason. I admired the man, his work, and the way he lived his life.
Clark Kent died while covering Doomsday's rampage through Metropolis. As a result, those who cared for him, Jonathan and Martha Kent, his parents, Lois Lane, his fiancée, Perry White, Jimmy Olsen, Lana Lang, Pete Ross and this writer were gathered to pack up his belongings and close down his apartment.
HANDLE WITH CARE
CLOTHES FOR CHARITY
FRAGILE
APARTMENT FOR RENT

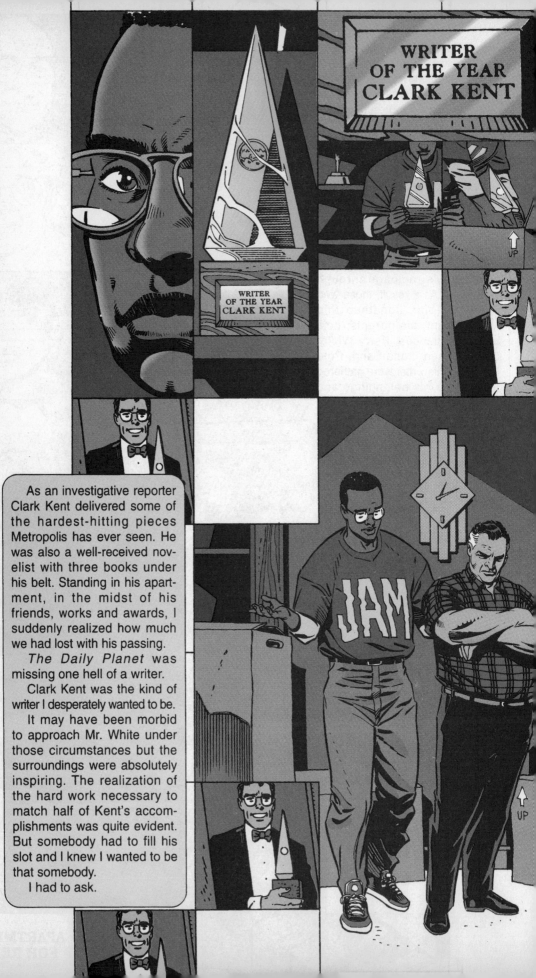

WRITER
OF THE YEAR
CLARK KENT

WRITER
OF THE YEAR
CLARK KENT

UP

UP

As an investigative reporter Clark Kent delivered some of the hardest-hitting pieces Metropolis has ever seen. He was also a well-received novelist with three books under his belt. Standing in his apartment, in the midst of his friends, works and awards, I suddenly realized how much we had lost with his passing.

The Daily Planet was missing one hell of a writer.

Clark Kent was the kind of writer I desperately wanted to be.

It may have been morbid to approach Mr. White under those circumstances but the surroundings were absolutely inspiring. The realization of the hard work necessary to match half of Kent's accomplishments was quite evident. But somebody had to fill his slot and I knew I wanted to be that somebody.

I had to ask.

JAM

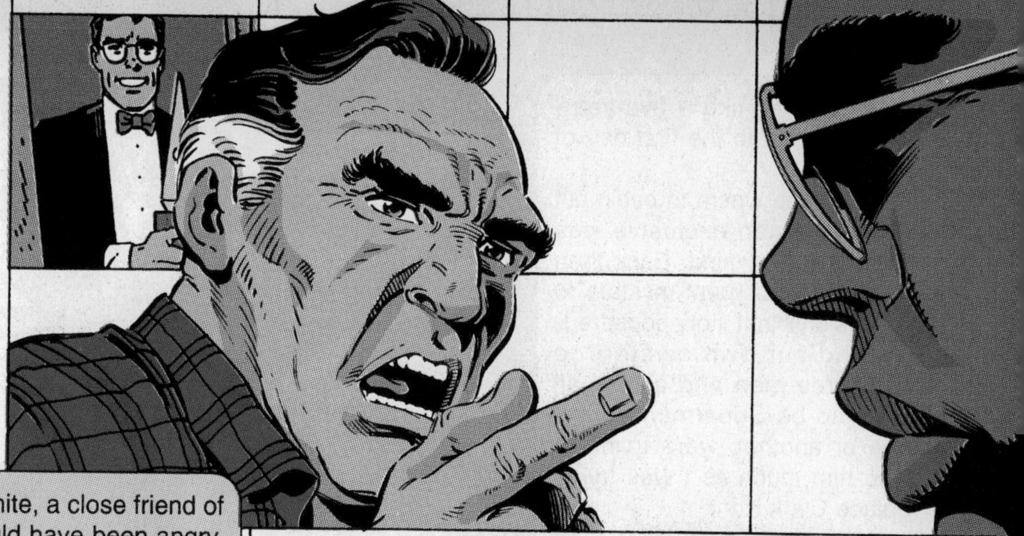

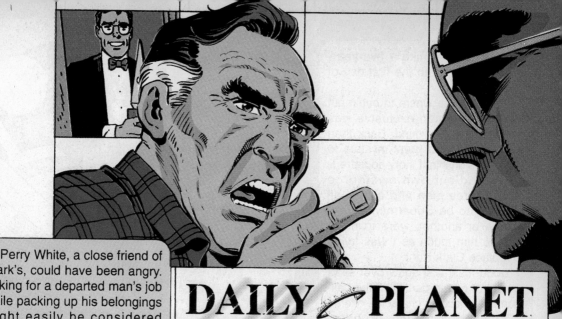

Perry White, a close friend of Clark's, could have been angry. Asking for a departed man's job while packing up his belongings might easily be considered crass and opportunistic. But Perry White recognizes and values hungry reporters.

He told me how Clark Kent, a novice right off the street, came in with the exclusive on Superman after the Man of Steel had first arrived in Metropolis.

Perry White challenged me to bring him a story so big he couldn't turn it down; a story so powerful and important that even Clark Kent would have been impressed.

"If you think you're good enough to fill Clark's shoes, you've got to back it up, Troupe.

"Prove it!"

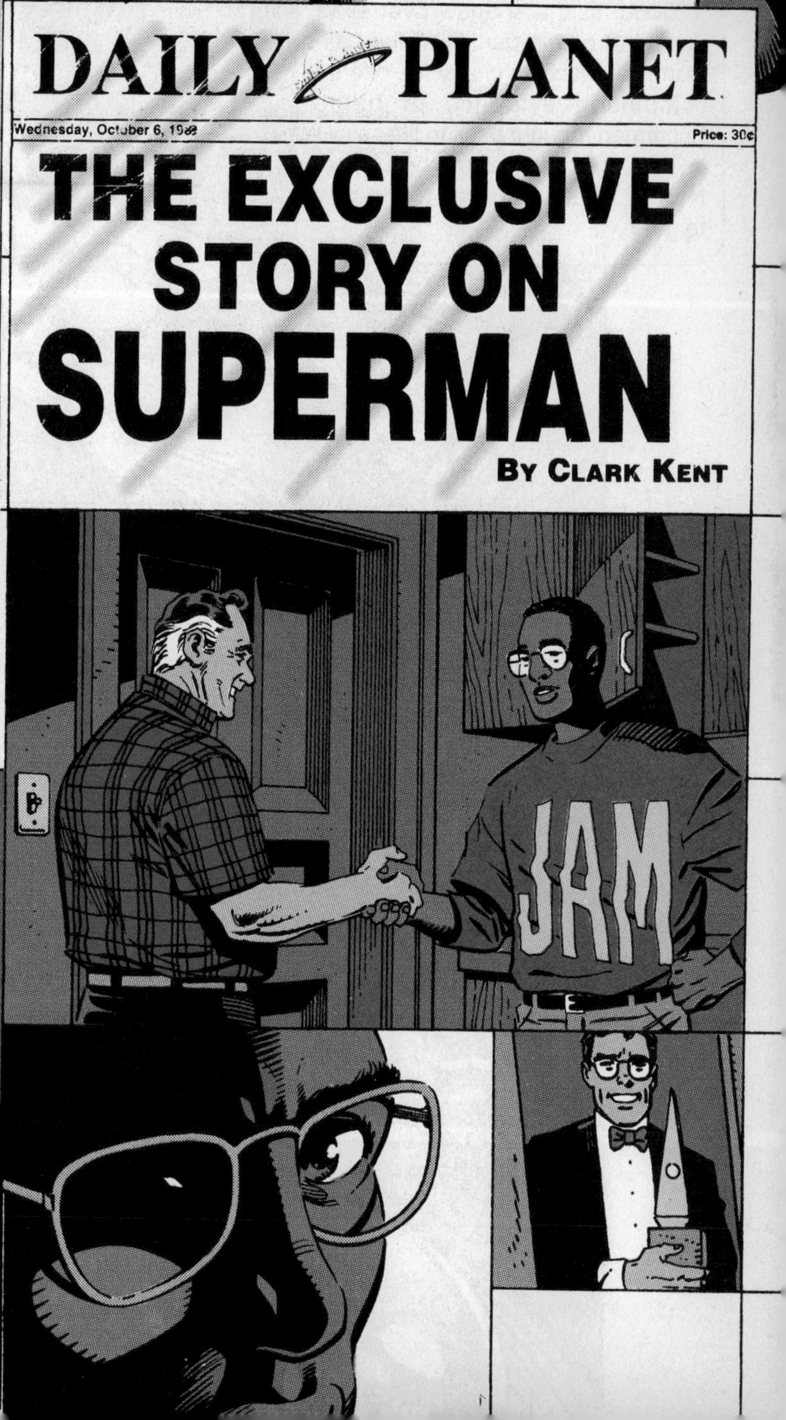
DAILY PLANET
Wednesday, October 6, 1988
Price: 30¢
THE EXCLUSIVE STORY ON SUPERMAN
BY CLARK KENT
JAM

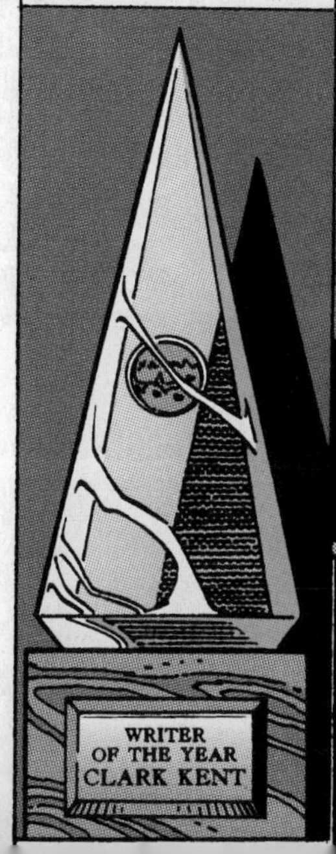
WRITER
OF THE YEAR
CLARK KENT

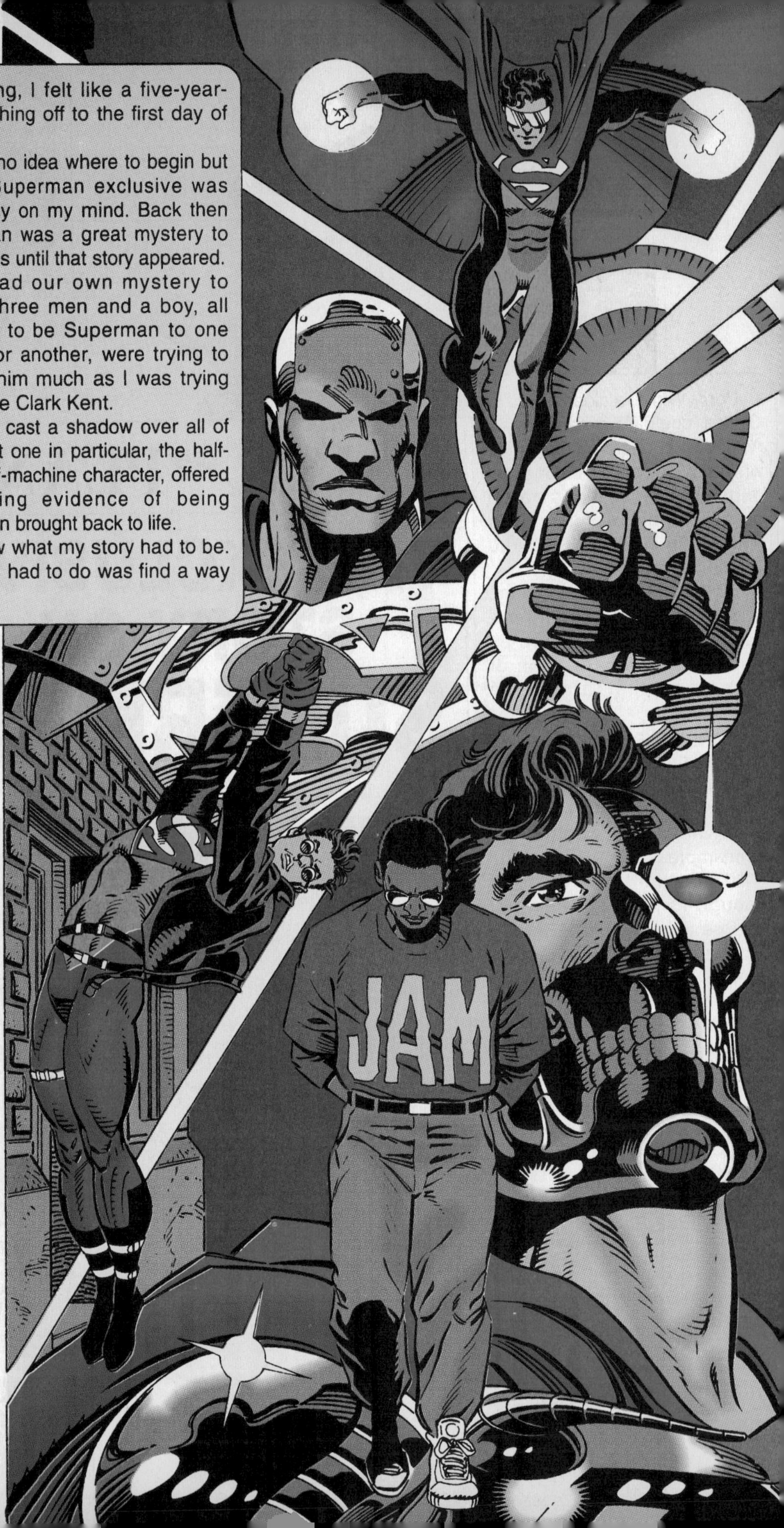
Leaving, I felt like a five-year-old marching off to the first day of school.
I had no idea where to begin but Kent's Superman exclusive was constantly on my mind. Back then Superman was a great mystery to Metropolis until that story appeared.
We had our own mystery to solve. Three men and a boy, all claiming to be Superman to one degree or another, were trying to replace him much as I was trying to replace Clark Kent.
Doubt cast a shadow over all of them, but one in particular, the half-man, half-machine character, offered compelling evidence of being Superman brought back to life.
I knew what my story had to be. Now all I had to do was find a way to get it.
JAM

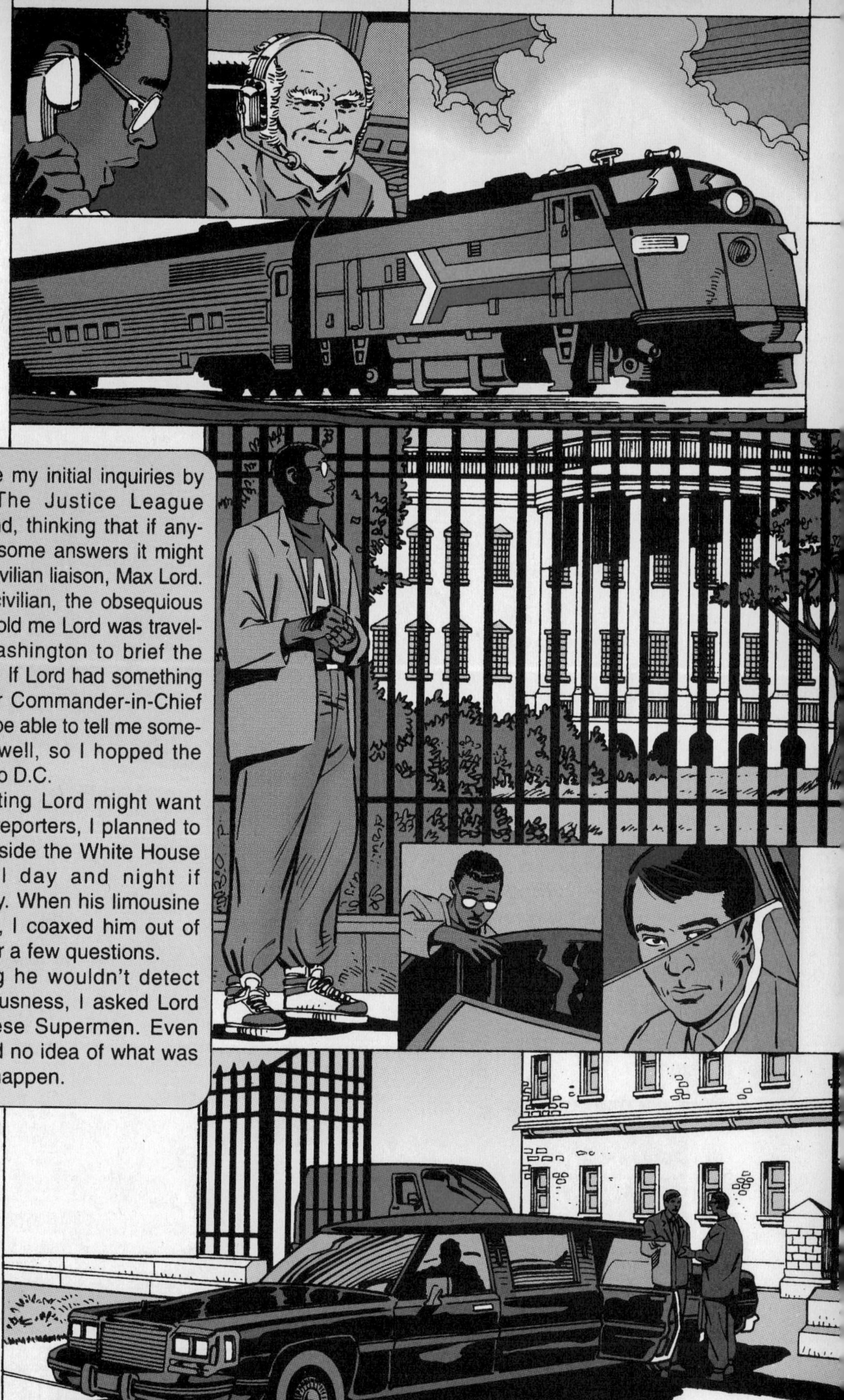

I made my initial inquiries by calling The Justice League Compound, thinking that if anyone had some answers it might be their civilian liaison, Max Lord. Another civilian, the obsequious Oberon, told me Lord was traveling to Washington to brief the President. If Lord had something to tell our Commander-in-Chief he might be able to tell me something as well, so I hopped the first train to D.C.

Expecting Lord might want to avoid reporters, I planned to stand outside the White House gates all day and night if necessary. When his limousine pulled up, I coaxed him out of the car for a few questions.

Hoping he wouldn't detect my nervousness, I asked Lord about these Supermen. Even then I had no idea of what was about to happen.

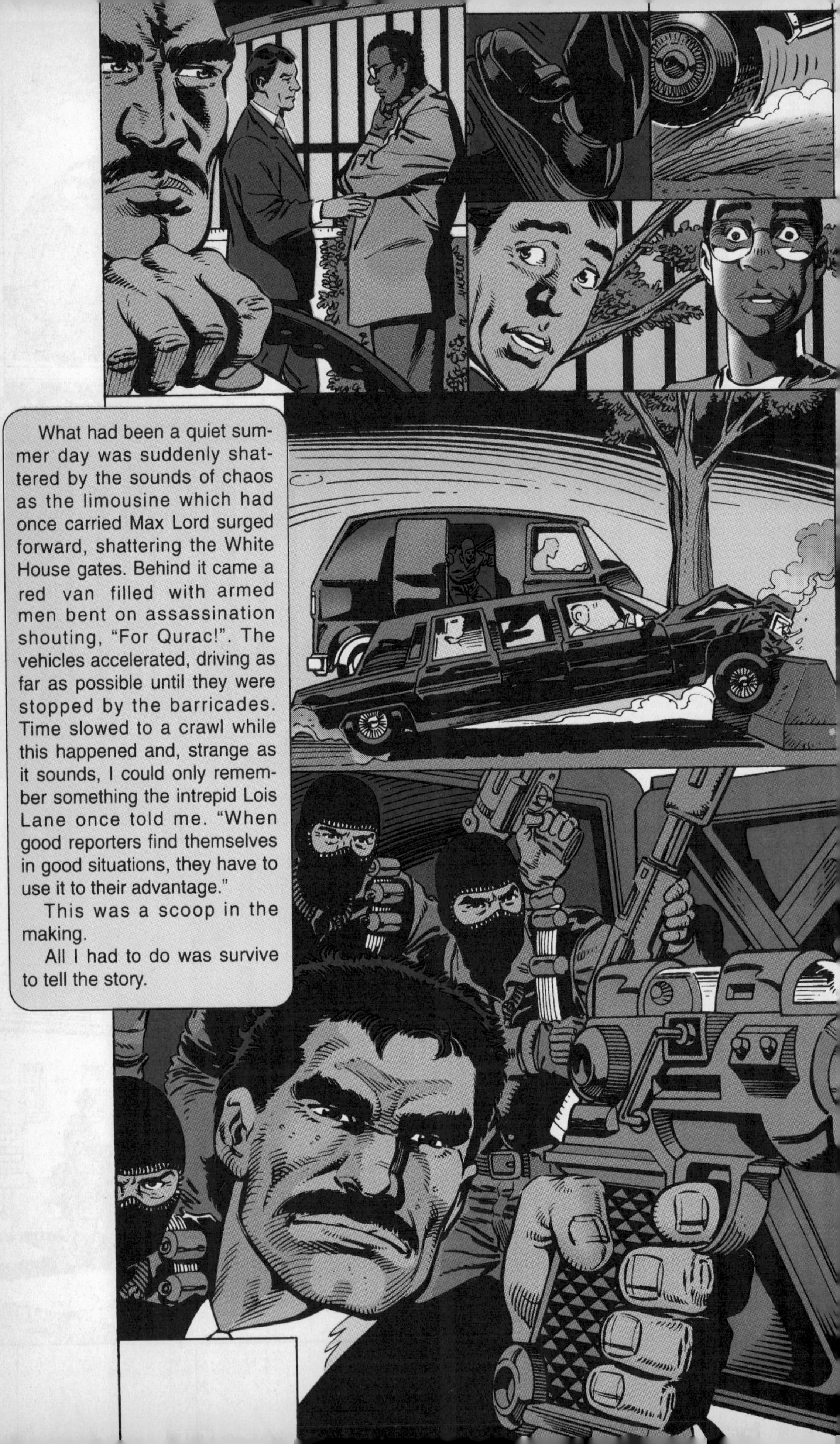
What had been a quiet summer day was suddenly shattered by the sounds of chaos as the limousine which had once carried Max Lord surged forward, shattering the White House gates. Behind it came a red van filled with armed men bent on assassination shouting, "For Qurac!". The vehicles accelerated, driving as far as possible until they were stopped by the barricades. Time slowed to a crawl while this happened and, strange as it sounds, I could only remember something the intrepid Lois Lane once told me. "When good reporters find themselves in good situations, they have to use it to their advantage."
This was a scoop in the making.
All I had to do was survive to tell the story.

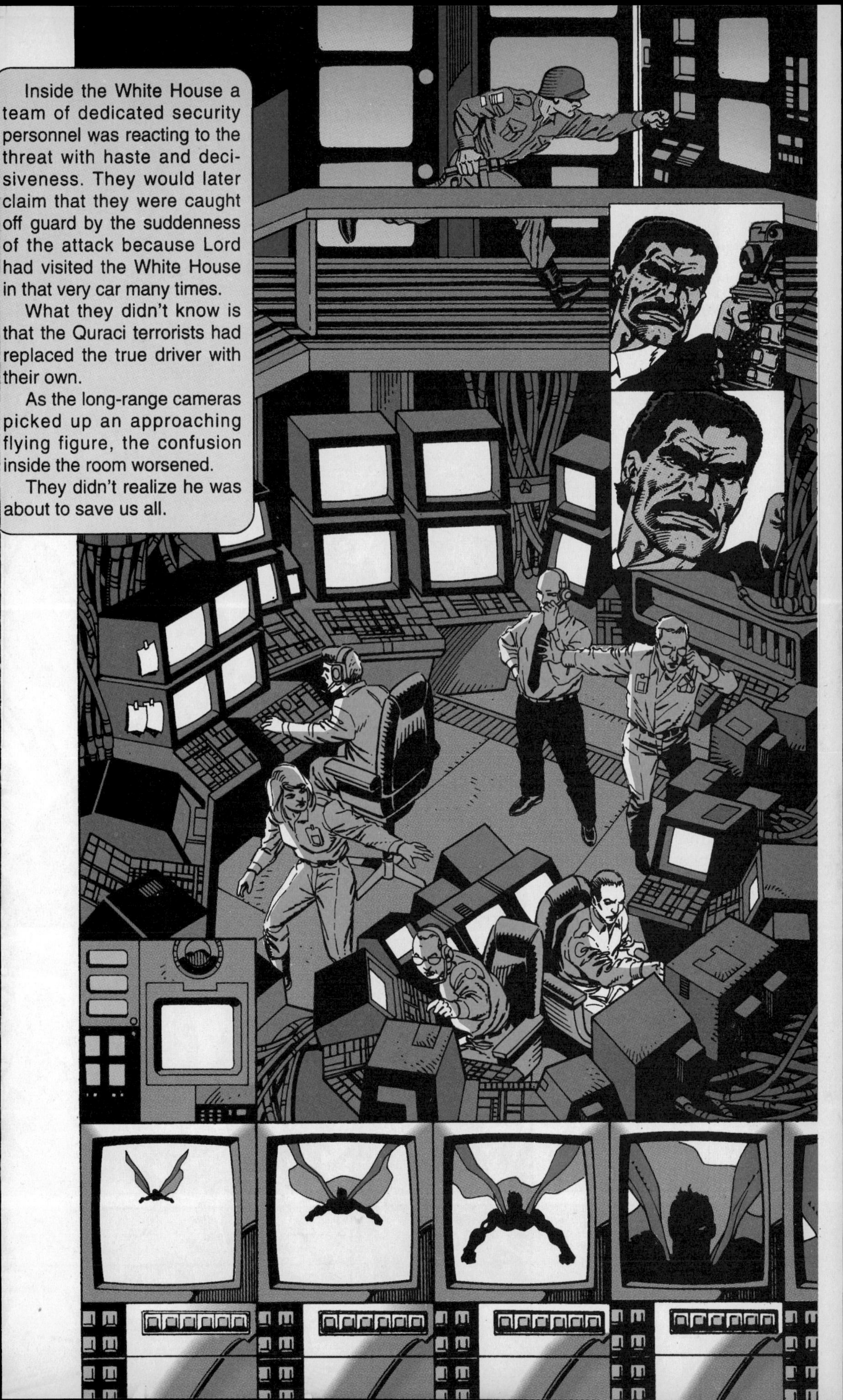
Inside the White House a team of dedicated security personnel was reacting to the threat with haste and decisiveness. They would later claim that they were caught off guard by the suddenness of the attack because Lord had visited the White House in that very car many times.
What they didn't know is that the Quraci terrorists had replaced the true driver with their own.
As the long-range cameras picked up an approaching flying figure, the confusion inside the room worsened.
They didn't realize he was about to save us all.

The possible answer to the great Superman mystery went into action right before me.

This Superman moved so fast and so powerfully that no description will suffice. He was everywhere at once, tearing into the would-be assassins with the ferocity of a mother lion protecting her young.

But that proved nothing of his true identity. Despite the suit, the familiar "S" and the cape; despite the exhibition of powers, questions persisted. Was this Superman back from the dead or an impostor?

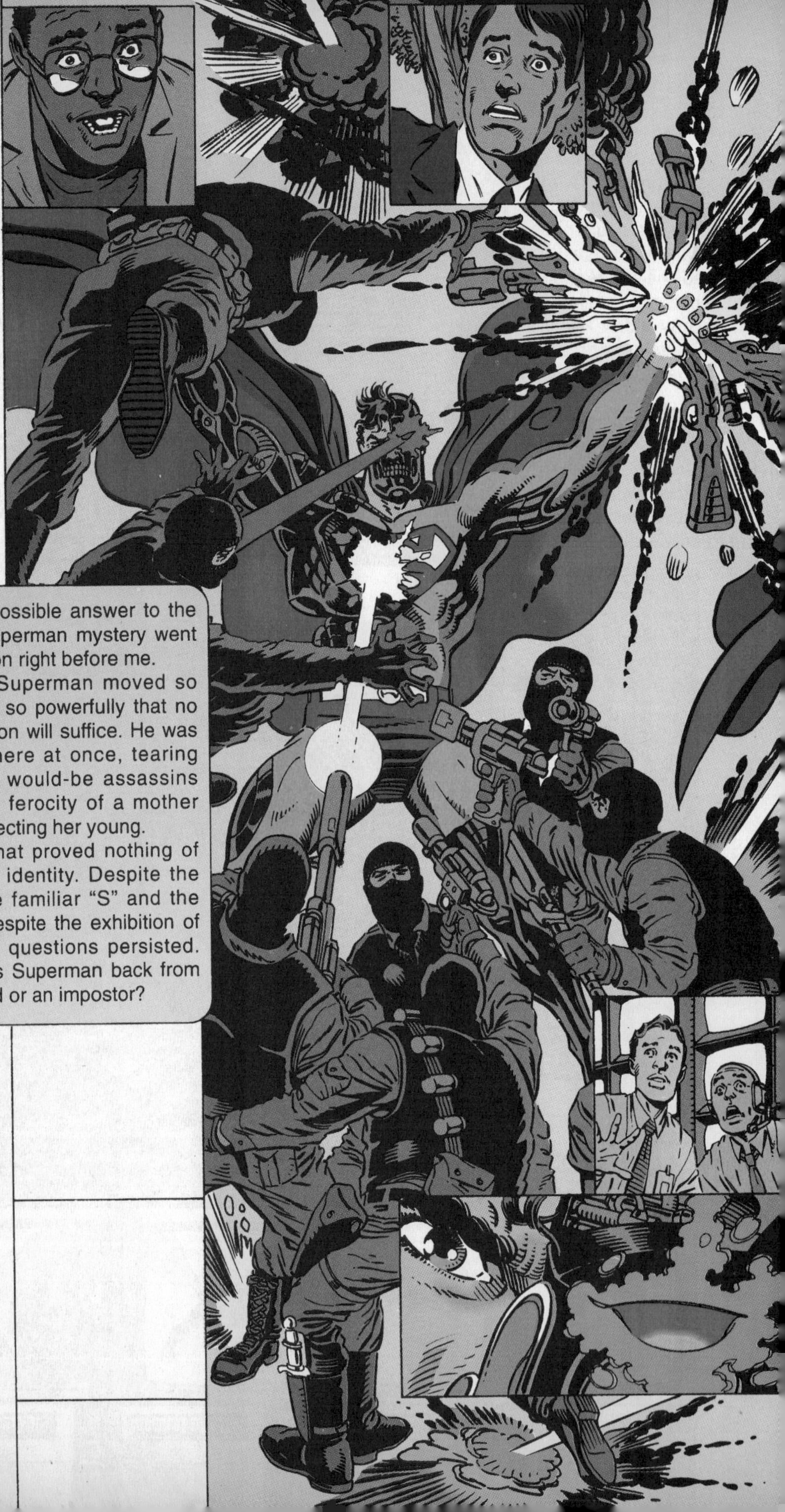

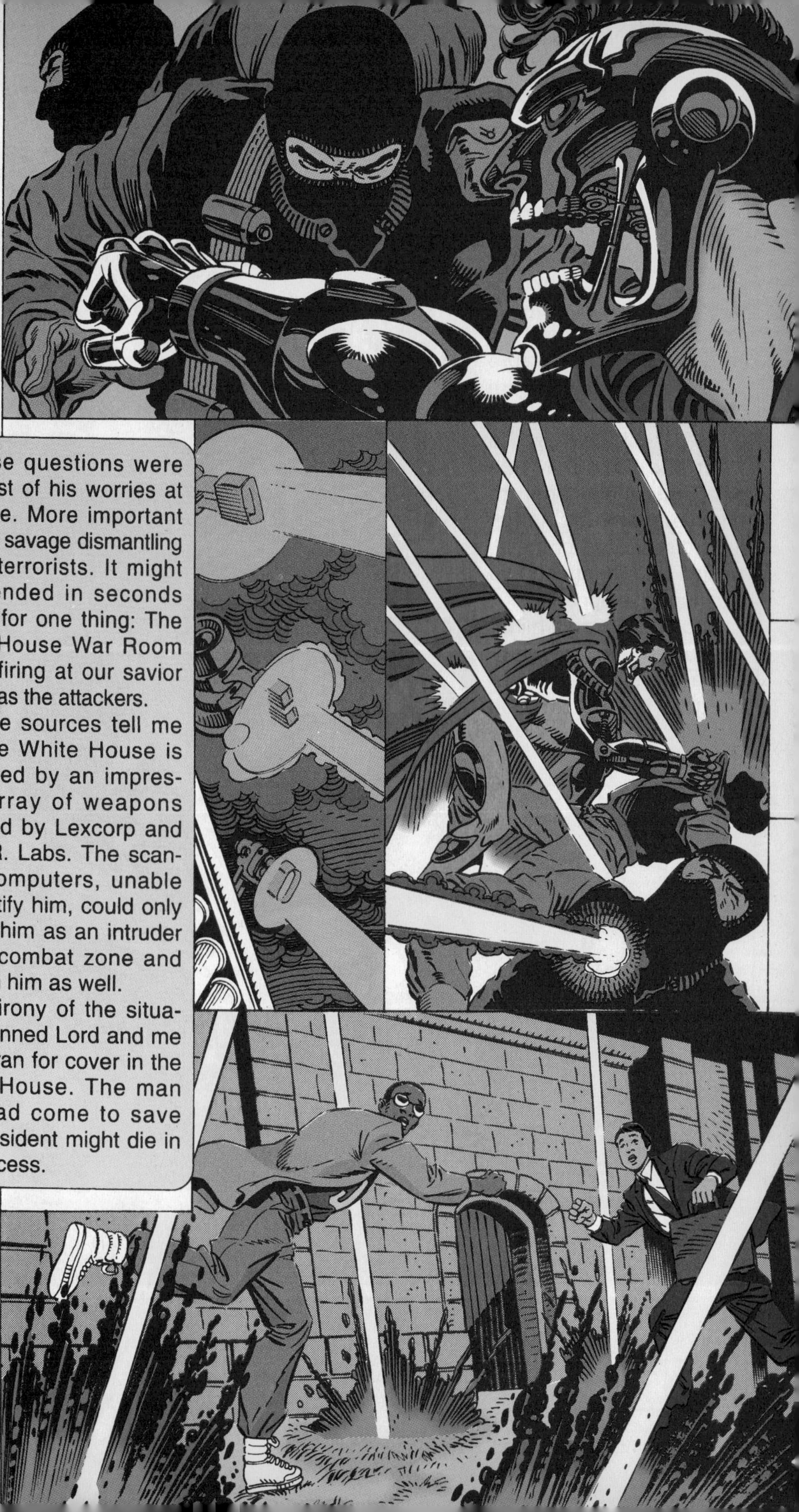

Those questions were the least of his worries at the time. More important was his savage dismantling of the terrorists. It might have ended in seconds except for one thing: The White House War Room began firing at our savior as well as the attackers.

Inside sources tell me that the White House is protected by an impressive array of weapons supplied by Lexcorp and S.T.A.R. Labs. The scanning computers, unable to identify him, could only regard him as an intruder in the combat zone and fired on him as well.

The irony of the situation stunned Lord and me as we ran for cover in the White House. The man who had come to save the President might die in the process.

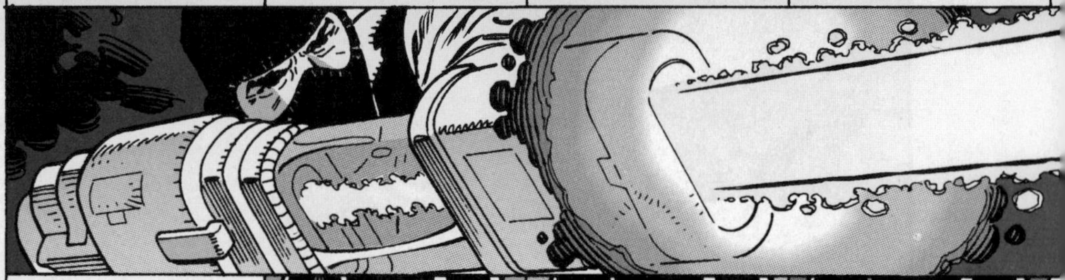

The White House was not alone in having impressive weapons. The Quraci terrorists obviously knew they'd face formidable odds and brought the fire power to match it.

As one of them fired a futuristic bazooka, this neo-Superman began to change. One arm, seemingly constructed of metal, twisted and re-formed into a cannon-like apparatus.

Superman fired a blinding burst of energy before the assassin could concentrate his bazooka on the White House, and the matter was resolved.

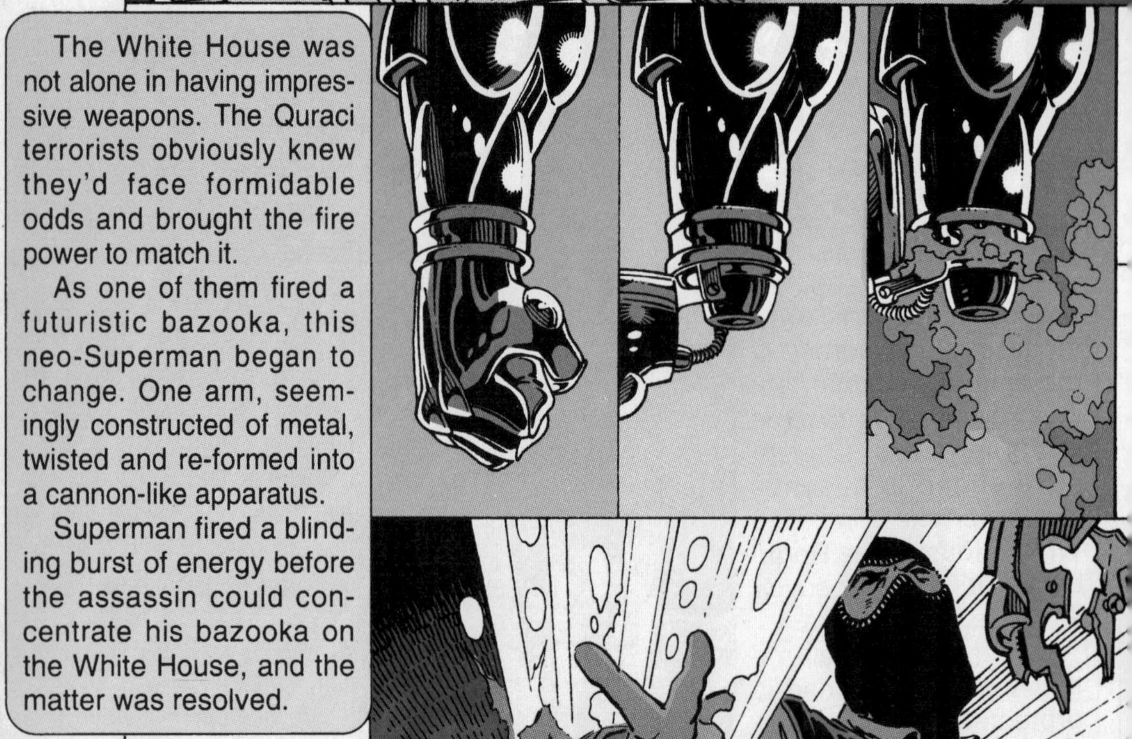

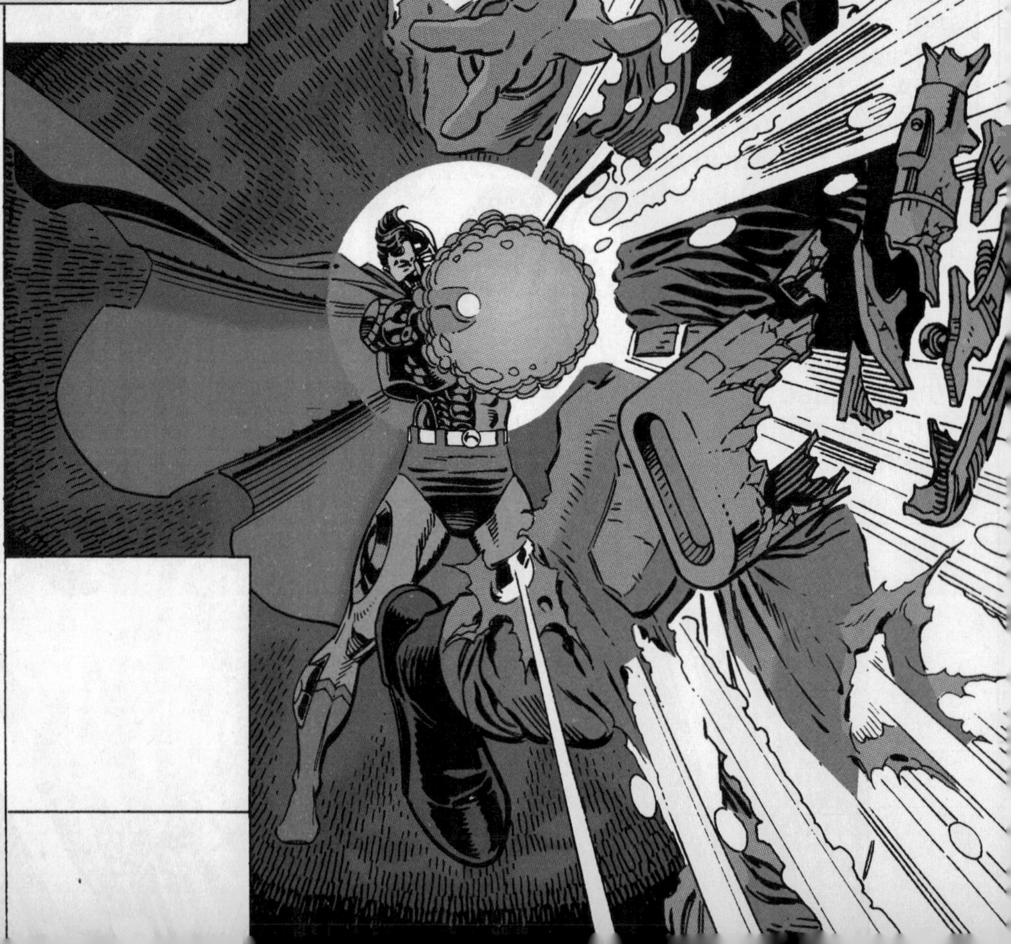

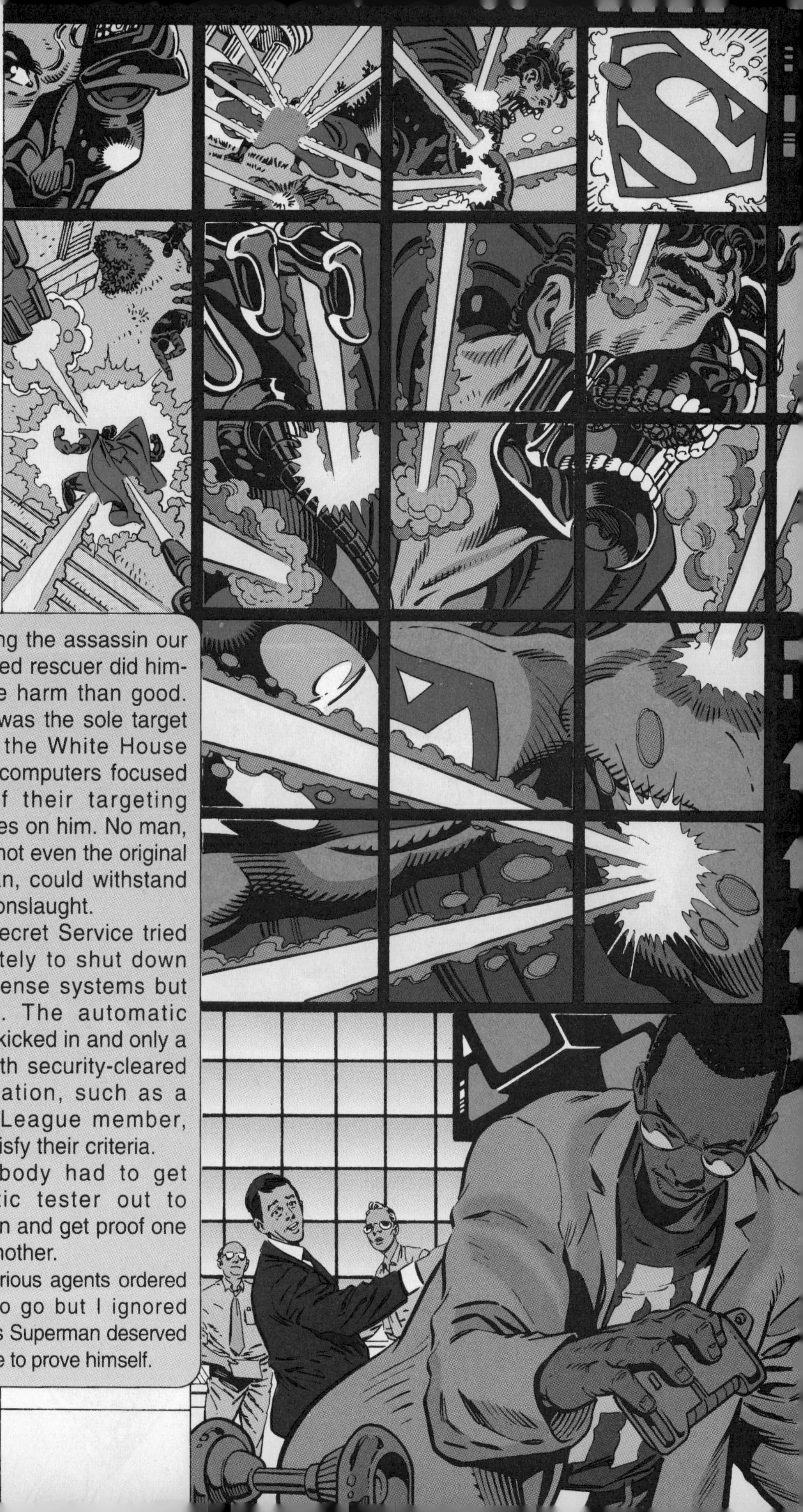

In felling the assassin our unidentified rescuer did himself more harm than good. Now he was the sole target left and the White House defense computers focused 100% of their targeting capabilities on him. No man, perhaps not even the original Superman, could withstand such an onslaught.

The Secret Service tried desperately to shut down their defense systems but couldn't. The automatic override kicked in and only a target with security-cleared identification, such as a Justice League member, could satisfy their criteria.

Somebody had to get a genetic tester out to Superman and get proof one way or another.

The various agents ordered me not to go but I ignored them. This Superman deserved his chance to prove himself.

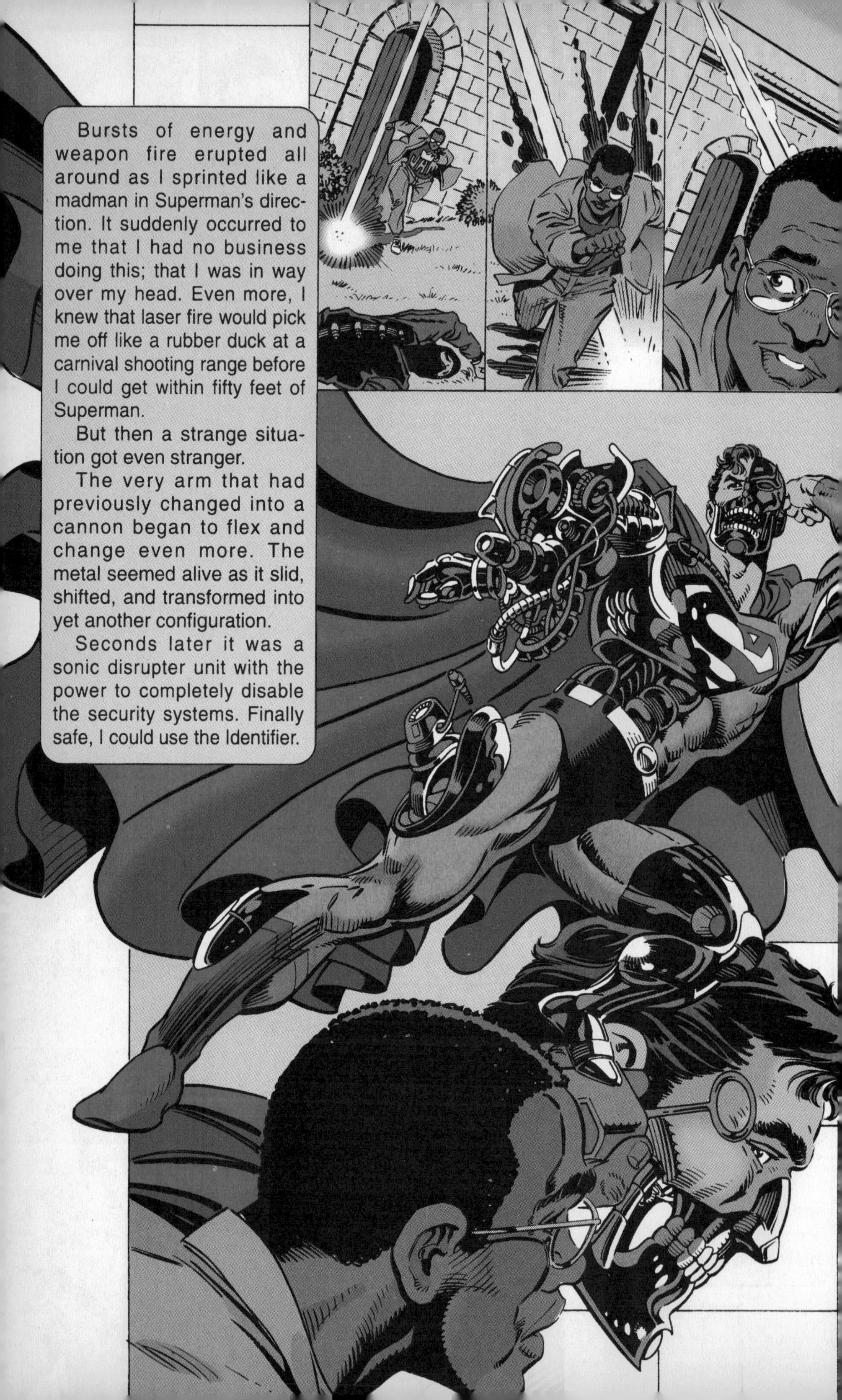
Bursts of energy and weapon fire erupted all around as I sprinted like a madman in Superman's direction. It suddenly occurred to me that I had no business doing this; that I was in way over my head. Even more, I knew that laser fire would pick me off like a rubber duck at a carnival shooting range before I could get within fifty feet of Superman.
But then a strange situation got even stranger.
The very arm that had previously changed into a cannon began to flex and change even more. The metal seemed alive as it slid, shifted, and transformed into yet another configuration.
Seconds later it was a sonic disrupter unit with the power to completely disable the security systems. Finally safe, I could use the Identifier.

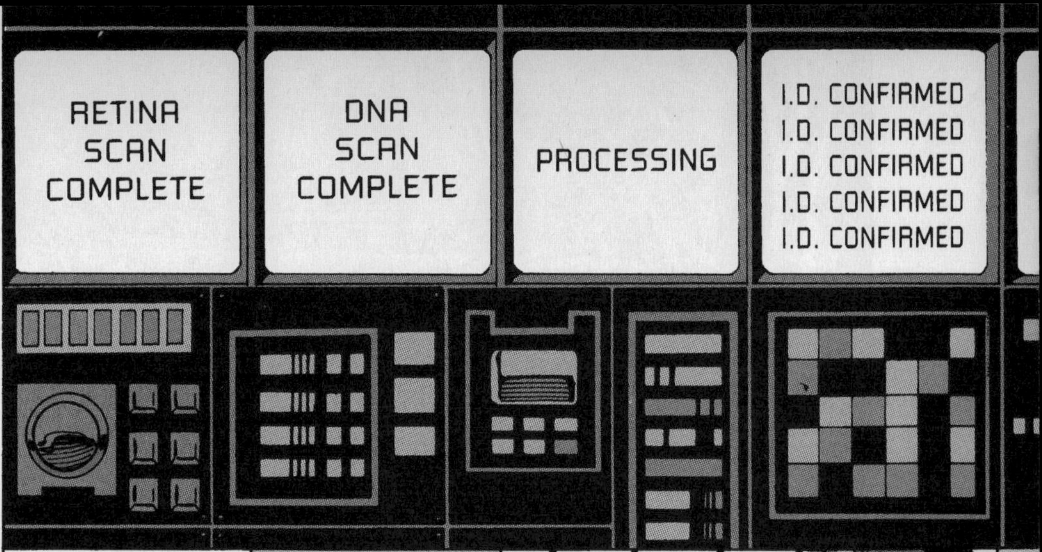
RETINA SCAN COMPLETE
DNA SCAN COMPLETE
PROCESSING
I.D. CONFIRMED
I.D. CONFIRMED
I.D. CONFIRMED
I.D. CONFIRMED
I.D. CONFIRMED

Every single identifying process available indicated this half-man, half-machine standing in front of me was undoubtedly Superman.

The greatest of them all, the man who paid the ultimate price protecting Metropolis, Superman, was rebuilt, alive and well.

He strode toward the White House with the determination, confidence and aura only a true hero could muster.

His commanding presence left them in awe. Even Max Lord, who lives in the midst of heroes, was speechless.

But Superman was all business, telling us the terrorist attack might not be over and a thorough security check was needed. He wanted to access the White House computers which, in turn, could tap into virtually every computer system in the world.

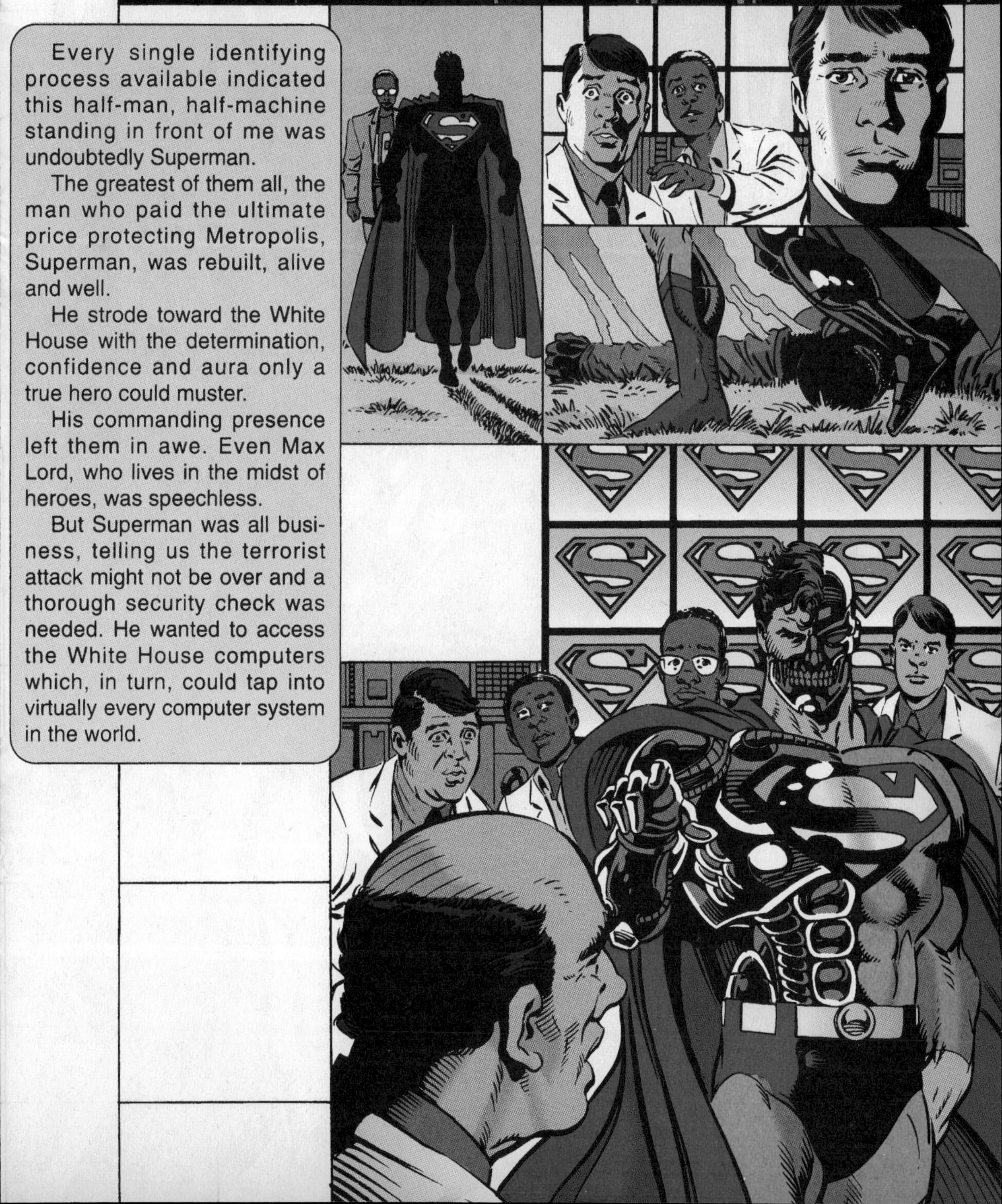

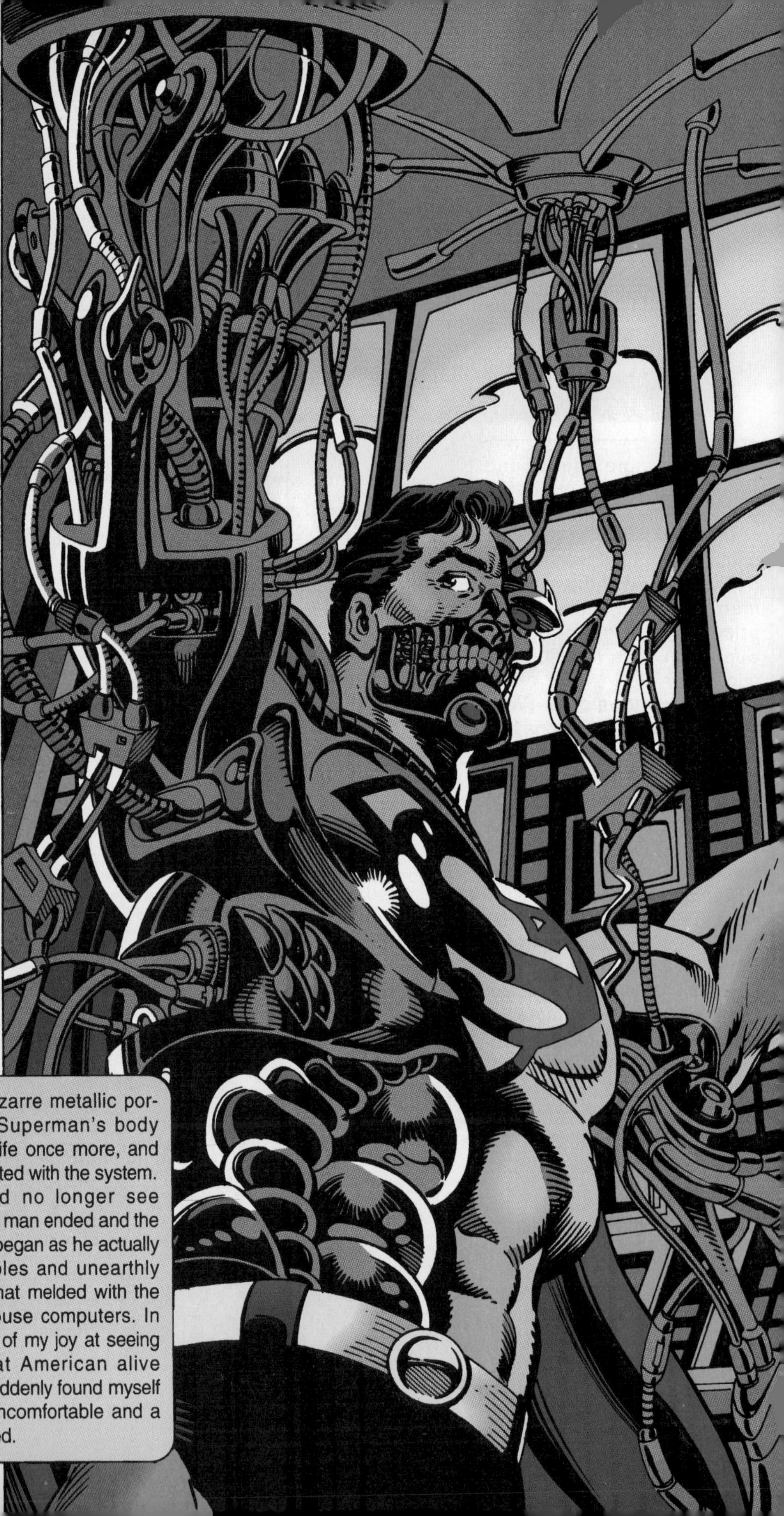

The bizarre metallic portions of Superman's body came to life once more, and he integrated with the system.

I could no longer see where the man ended and the machine began as he actually grew cables and unearthly devices that melded with the White House computers. In the midst of my joy at seeing this great American alive again I suddenly found myself slightly uncomfortable and a little scared.

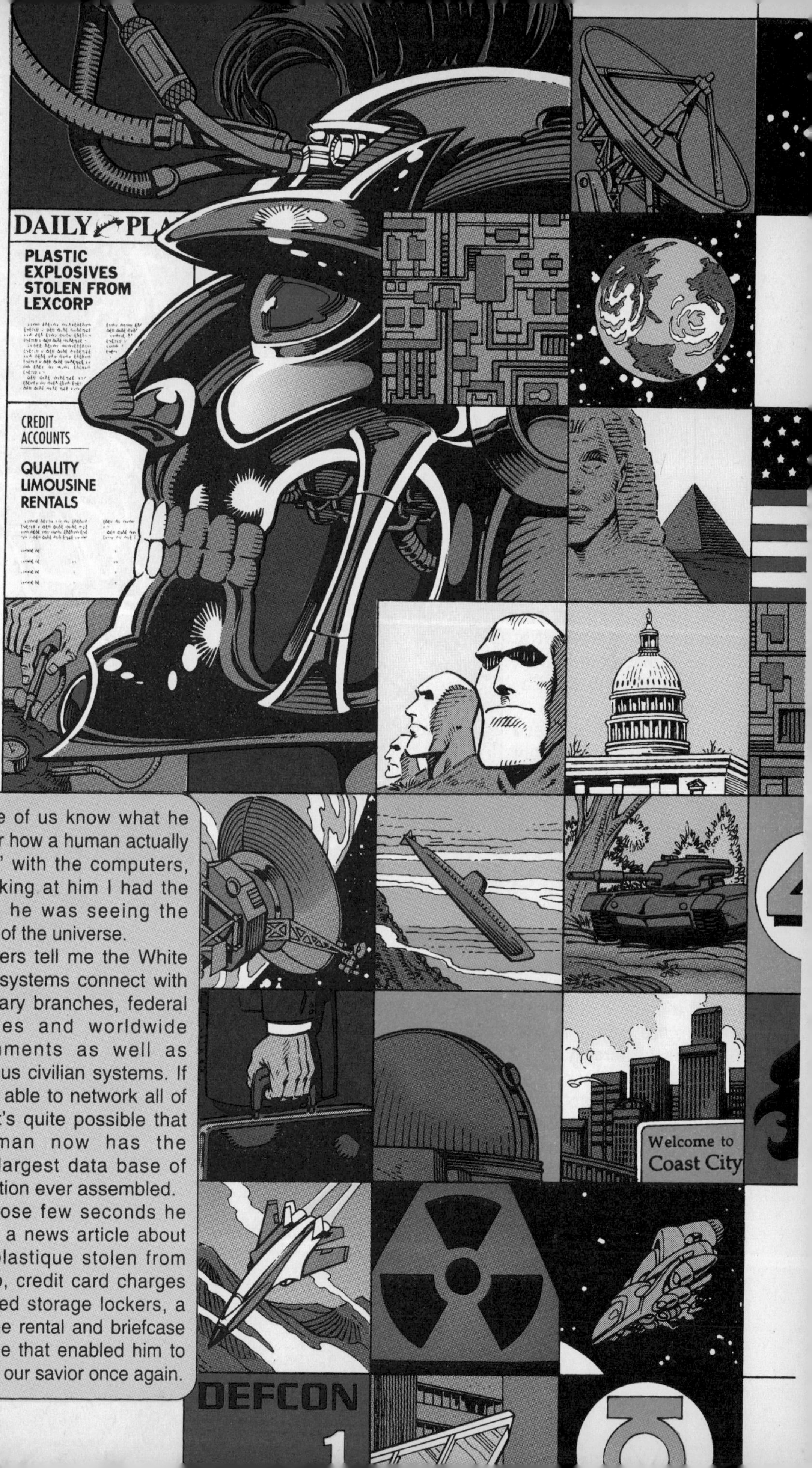
DAILY
PLASTIC EXPLOSIVES STOLEN FROM LEXCORP
CREDIT ACCOUNTS
QUALITY LIMOUSINE RENTALS
Welcome to Coast City
DEFCON 1

None of us know what he "saw" or how a human actually "talked" with the computers, but looking at him I had the feeling he was seeing the secrets of the universe.

Staffers tell me the White House systems connect with all military branches, federal agencies and worldwide governments as well as numerous civilian systems. If he was able to network all of them, it's quite possible that Superman now has the single largest data base of information ever assembled.

In those few seconds he tracked a news article about some plastique stolen from Lexcorp, credit card charges for rented storage lockers, a limousine rental and briefcase purchase that enabled him to become our savior once again.

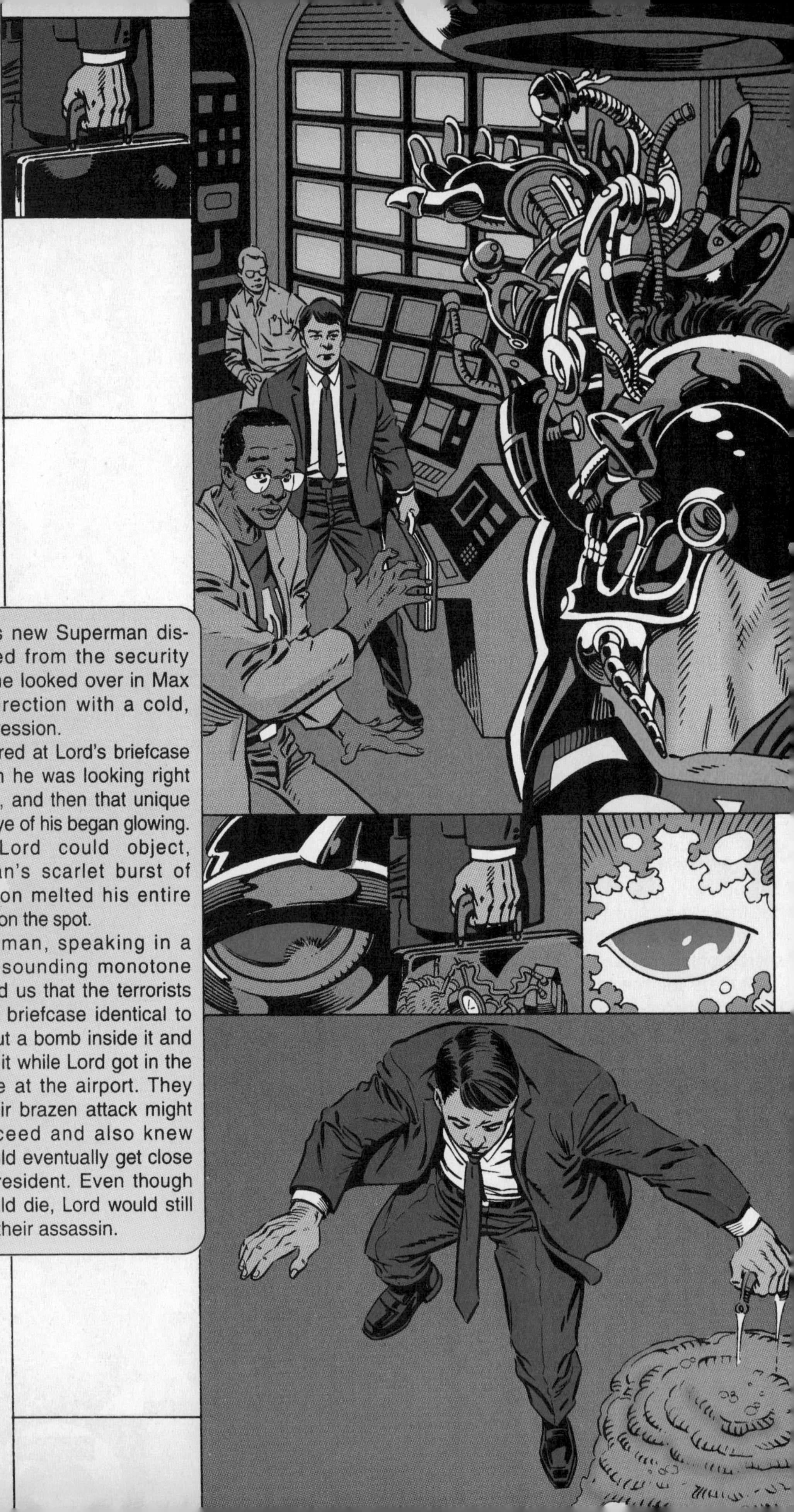

As this new Superman disconnected from the security system, he looked over in Max Lord's direction with a cold, hard expression.

He stared at Lord's briefcase as though he was looking right through it, and then that unique jeweled eye of his began glowing. Before Lord could object, Superman's scarlet burst of heat-vision melted his entire briefcase on the spot.

Superman, speaking in a metallic-sounding monotone voice, told us that the terrorists bought a briefcase identical to Lord's, put a bomb inside it and switched it while Lord got in the limousine at the airport. They knew their brazen attack might not succeed and also knew Lord would eventually get close to the President. Even though they would die, Lord would still become their assassin.

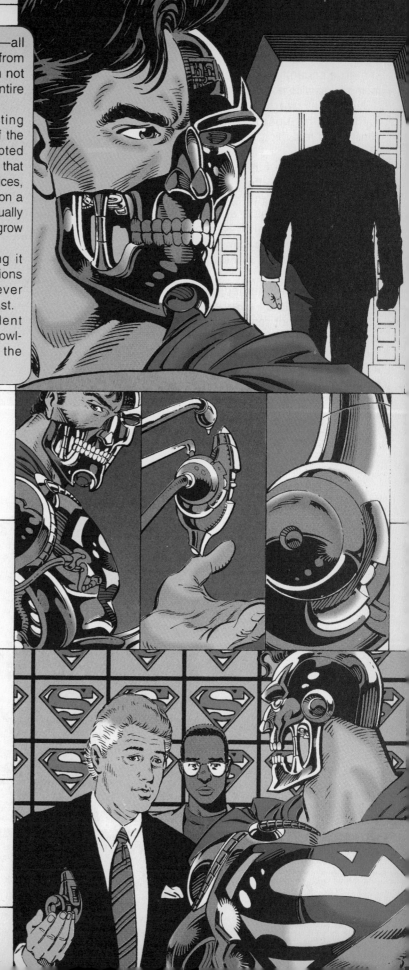

We were all speechless—all except one, that is. A voice from the entry thanked Superman not only for himself but for the entire country.

It was an historic meeting between two powerful men of the free world. Superman accepted this man's thanks and told him that should he ever need his services, he merely had to contact him on a special device. Superman actually seemed to construct it, even grow it, on the spot.

He handed it over saying it was a personal communications device, something he'd never given any President in the past.

With that, the President accepted the device and acknowledged this Man of Steel as the one, true Superman.

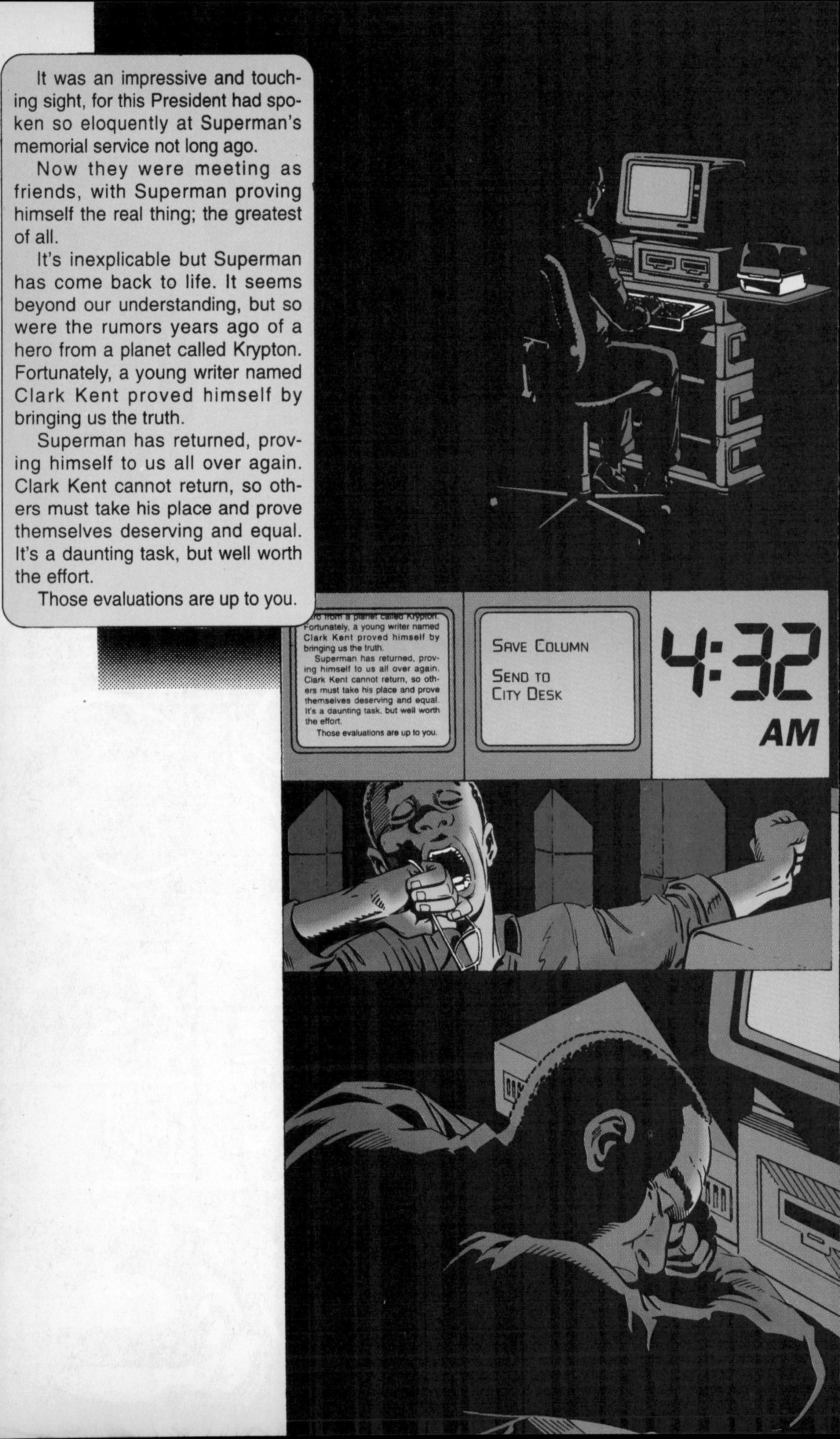

It was an impressive and touching sight, for this President had spoken so eloquently at Superman's memorial service not long ago.
Now they were meeting as friends, with Superman proving himself the real thing; the greatest of all.
It's inexplicable but Superman has come back to life. It seems beyond our understanding, but so were the rumors years ago of a hero from a planet called Krypton. Fortunately, a young writer named Clark Kent proved himself by bringing us the truth.
Superman has returned, proving himself to us all over again. Clark Kent cannot return, so others must take his place and prove themselves deserving and equal. It's a daunting task, but well worth the effort.
Those evaluations are up to you.
Fortunately, a young writer named Clark Kent proved himself by bringing us the truth.
Superman has returned, proving himself to us all over again. Clark Kent cannot return, so others must take his place and prove themselves deserving and equal. It's a daunting task, but well worth the effort.
Those evaluations are up to you.
SAVE COLUMN
SEND TO CITY DESK
4:32 AM

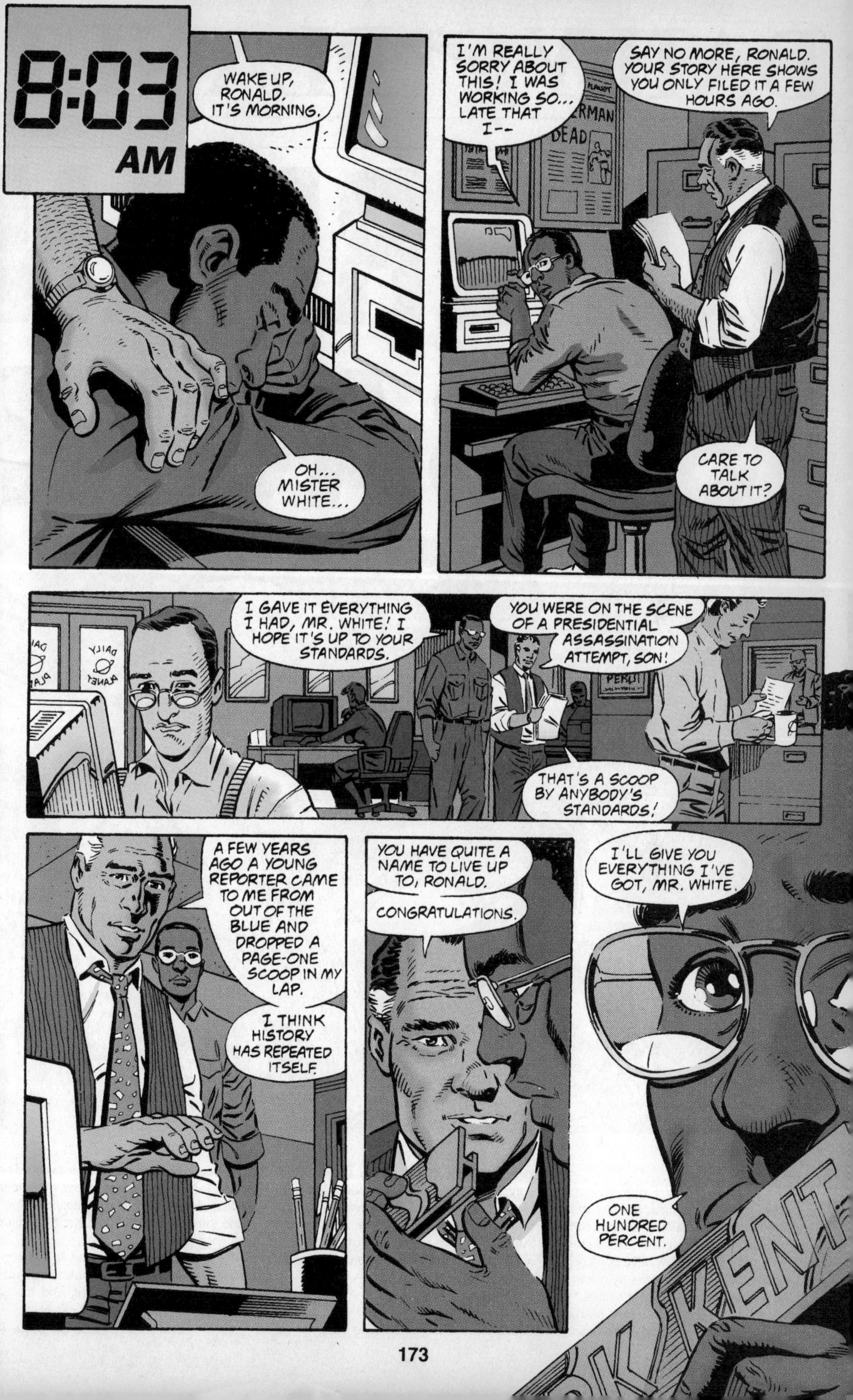
8:03 AM
WAKE UP, RONALD, IT'S MORNING.
OH... MISTER WHITE...
I'M REALLY SORRY ABOUT THIS! I WAS WORKING SO... LATE THAT I--
SAY NO MORE, RONALD. YOUR STORY HERE SHOWS YOU ONLY FILED IT A FEW HOURS AGO.
CARE TO TALK ABOUT IT?
I GAVE IT EVERYTHING I HAD, MR. WHITE! I HOPE IT'S UP TO YOUR STANDARDS.
YOU WERE ON THE SCENE OF A PRESIDENTIAL ASSASSINATION ATTEMPT, SON!
THAT'S A SCOOP BY ANYBODY'S STANDARDS!
A FEW YEARS AGO A YOUNG REPORTER CAME TO ME FROM OUT OF THE BLUE AND DROPPED A PAGE-ONE SCOOP IN MY LAP.
I THINK HISTORY HAS REPEATED ITSELF.
YOU HAVE QUITE A NAME TO LIVE UP TO, RONALD.
CONGRATULATIONS.
I'LL GIVE YOU EVERYTHING I'VE GOT, MR. WHITE.
ONE HUNDRED PERCENT.
KENT

DAILY PLANET

Friday, May 28, 1993   Price: 40

SUPERMAN IS BACK!

Story by RONALD TROUPE

"Prove it!"

Think about it. If you're one of those who thinks yourself the best, the ultimate, "The Real Thing" in whatever you do, consider yourself lucky if you are never asked to prove it. Only a select few have done so.

Lincoln proved his greatness by holding together a nation torn by war and by freeing men not acknowledged as equals. Martin Luther King did it by asking an entire nation

to look in the mirror and take shame in the ugly reflection of bigotry. Joe DiMaggio swung the bat better than anyone else and Superman did it by being, well, *Super*. And the man I want to talk about, the man I would prove myself to if he were still alive, is the reporter who did it all.

The best.

Clark Kent.

Readers of this paper, *The Daily Planet*,

have been familiar with Kent's extraordinar[y] work for years. Writing about economics[,] pollution, justice, crime, education, politic[s] and the human condition, Kent's brillianc[e] touched us all.

I marveled at Mr. Kent's clarity o[f] vision and evidence of sound reason. [I] admired the man, his work, and the wa[y] he lived his life.

—story continued on page A3

174

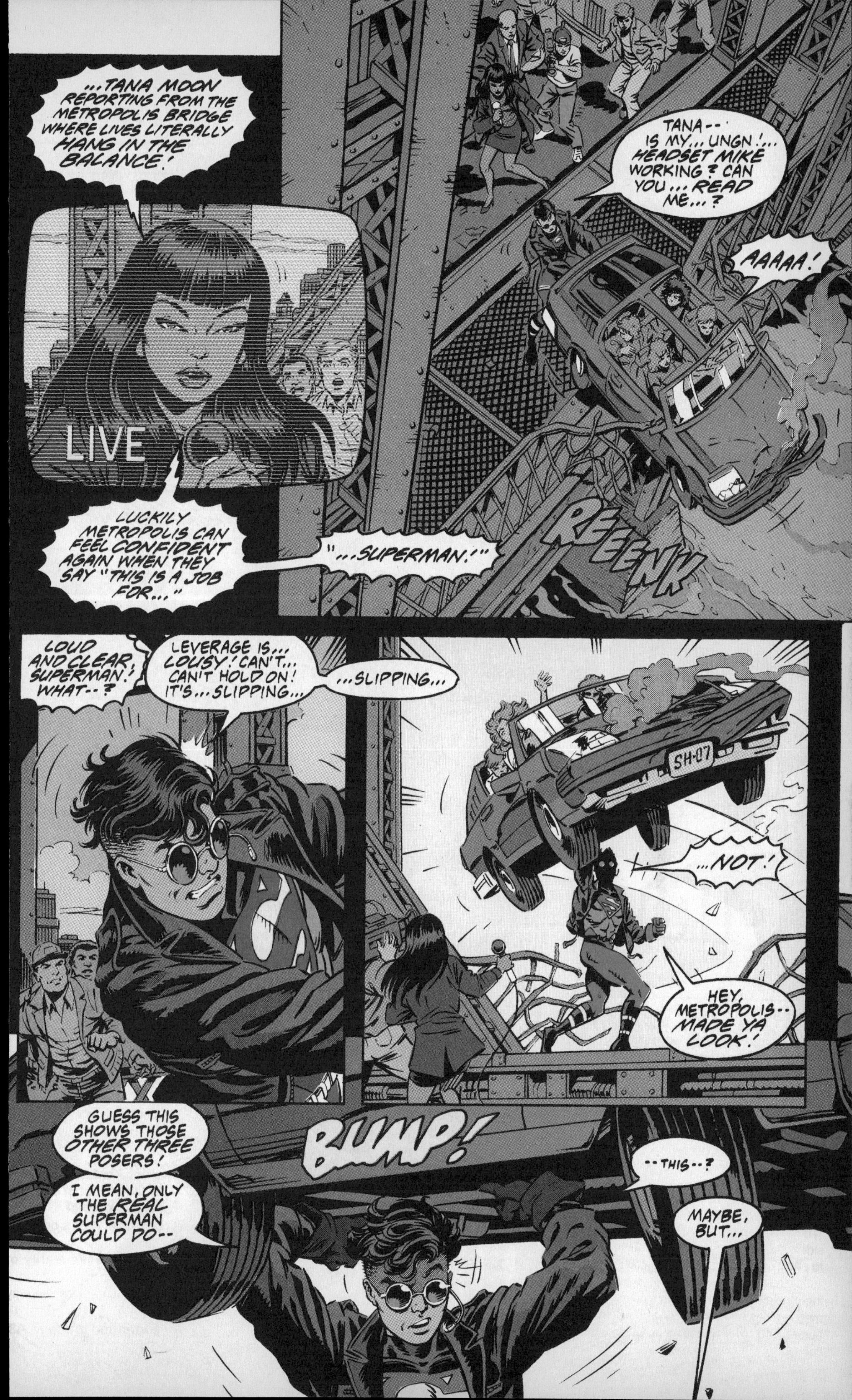
...TANA MOON REPORTING FROM THE METROPOLIS BRIDGE WHERE LIVES LITERALLY HANG IN THE BALANCE!
LIVE
TANA-- IS MY... UNGN!... HEADSET MIKE WORKING? CAN YOU... READ ME...?
AAAAA!
LUCKILY METROPOLIS CAN FEEL CONFIDENT AGAIN WHEN THEY SAY "THIS IS A JOB FOR..."
"...SUPERMAN!"
REEENK
LOUD AND CLEAR, SUPERMAN! WHAT--?
LEVERAGE IS... LOUSY! CAN'T... CAN'T HOLD ON! IT'S... SLIPPING...
...SLIPPING...
SH-07
...NOT!
HEY, METROPOLIS-- MADE YA LOOK!
GUESS THIS SHOWS THOSE OTHER THREE POSERS!
BUMP!
I MEAN, ONLY THE REAL SUPERMAN COULD DO--
--THIS--?
MAYBE, BUT...

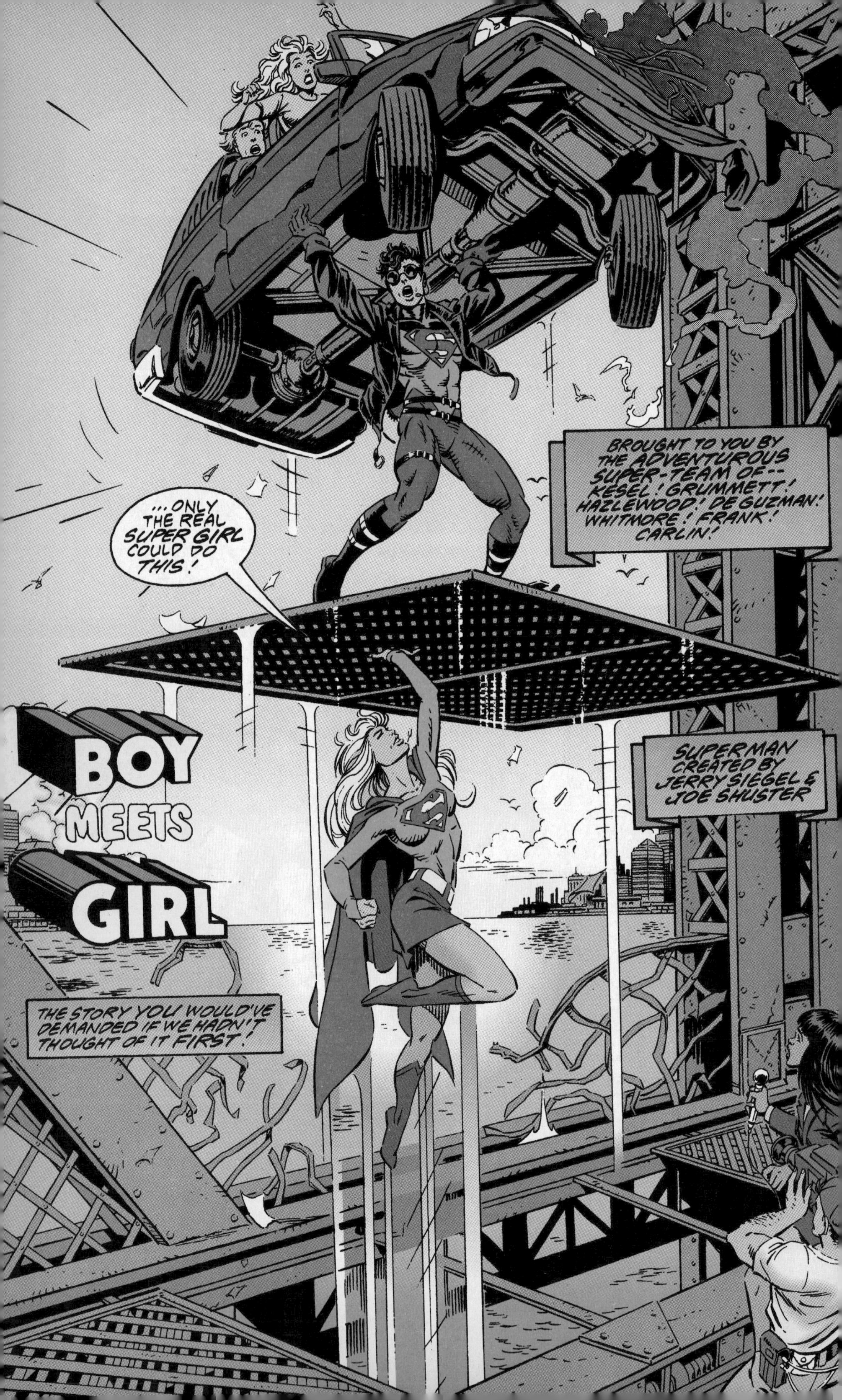
...ONLY THE REAL SUPER GIRL COULD DO THIS!
BROUGHT TO YOU BY THE ADVENTUROUS SUPER-TEAM OF-- KESEL! GRUMMETT! HAZLEWOOD! DE GUZMAN! WHITMORE! FRANK! CARLIN!
BOY MEETS GIRL
SUPERMAN CREATED BY JERRY SIEGEL & JOE SHUSTER
THE STORY YOU WOULD'VE DEMANDED IF WE HADN'T THOUGHT OF IT FIRST!

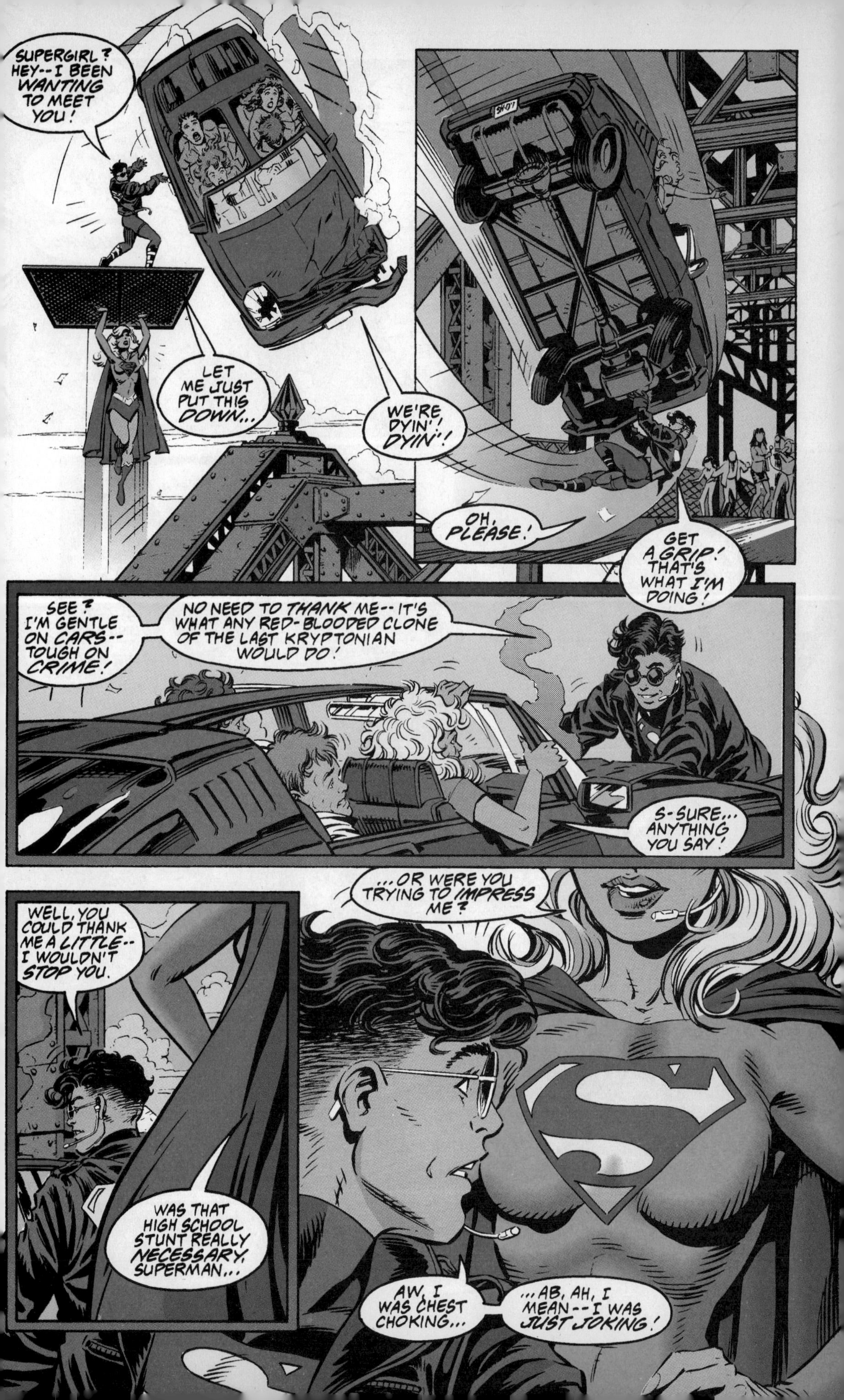
SUPERGIRL? HEY--I BEEN WANTING TO MEET YOU!
LET ME JUST PUT THIS DOWN...
WE'RE DYIN'! DYIN'!
OH, PLEASE!
GET A GRIP! THAT'S WHAT I'M DOING!
SEE? I'M GENTLE ON CARS--TOUGH ON CRIME!
NO NEED TO THANK ME--IT'S WHAT ANY RED-BLOODED CLONE OF THE LAST KRYPTONIAN WOULD DO!
S-SURE... ANYTHING YOU SAY!
WELL, YOU COULD THANK ME A LITTLE--I WOULDN'T STOP YOU.
...OR WERE YOU TRYING TO IMPRESS ME?
WAS THAT HIGH SCHOOL STUNT REALLY NECESSARY, SUPERMAN...
AW, I WAS CHEST CHOKING...
...AB, AH, I MEAN--I WAS JUST JOKING!

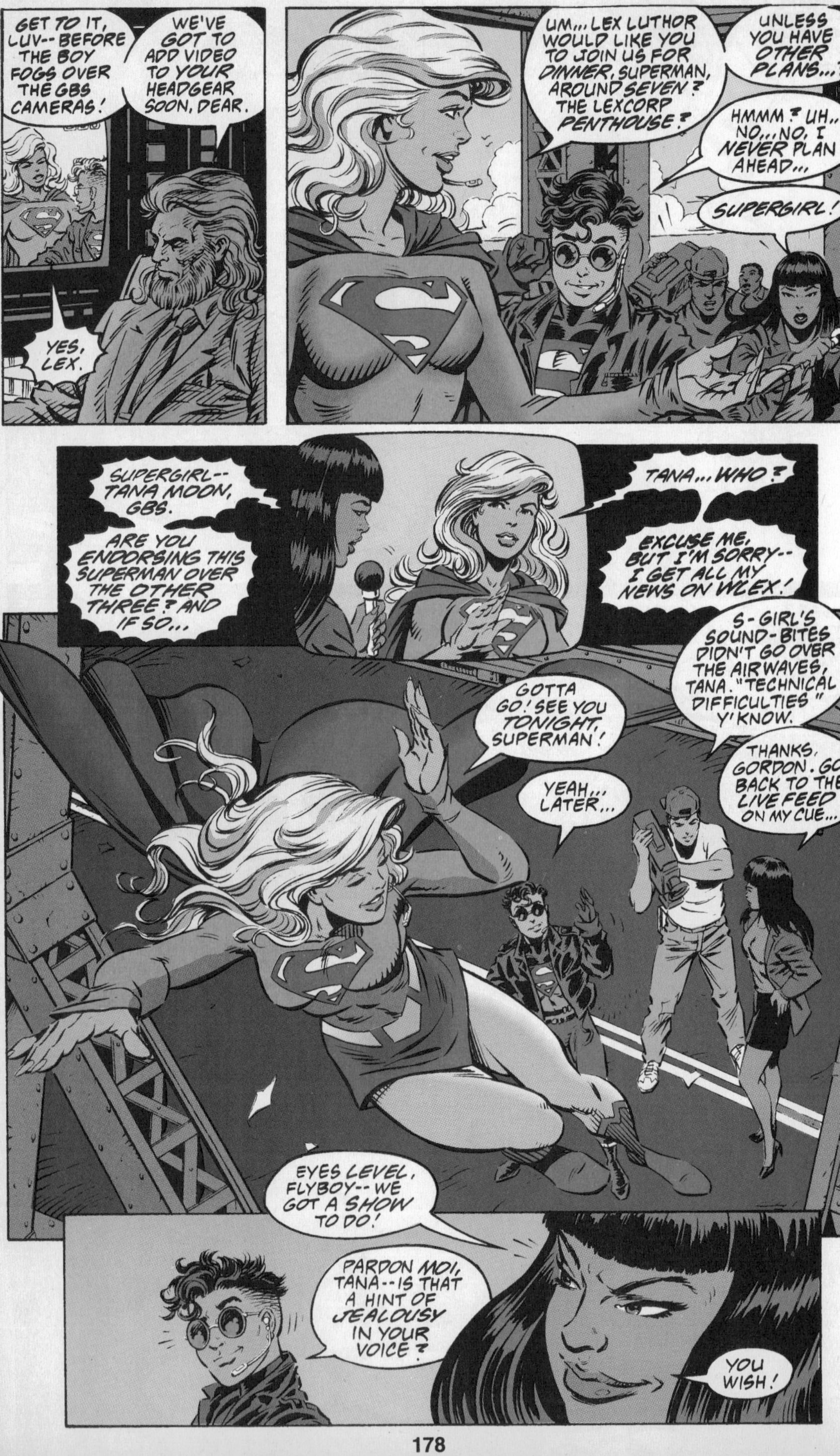
GET TO IT, LUV-- BEFORE THE BOY FOGS OVER THE GBS CAMERAS!
WE'VE GOT TO ADD VIDEO TO YOUR HEADGEAR SOON, DEAR.
YES, LEX.
UM... LEX LUTHOR WOULD LIKE YOU TO JOIN US FOR DINNER, SUPERMAN, AROUND SEVEN? THE LEXCORP PENTHOUSE?
UNLESS YOU HAVE OTHER PLANS...?
HMMM? UH... NO... NO, I NEVER PLAN AHEAD...
SUPERGIRL!
SUPERGIRL-- TANA MOON, GBS.
ARE YOU ENDORSING THIS SUPERMAN OVER THE OTHER THREE? AND IF SO...
TANA... WHO?
EXCUSE ME, BUT I'M SORRY-- I GET ALL MY NEWS ON WLEX!
GOTTA GO! SEE YOU TONIGHT, SUPERMAN!
S-GIRL'S SOUND-BITES DIDN'T GO OVER THE AIRWAVES, TANA. "TECHNICAL DIFFICULTIES" Y'KNOW.
YEAH... LATER...
THANKS, GORDON. GO BACK TO THE LIVE FEED ON MY CUE...
EYES LEVEL, FLYBOY-- WE GOT A SHOW TO DO!
PARDON MOI, TANA--IS THAT A HINT OF JEALOUSY IN YOUR VOICE?
YOU WISH!

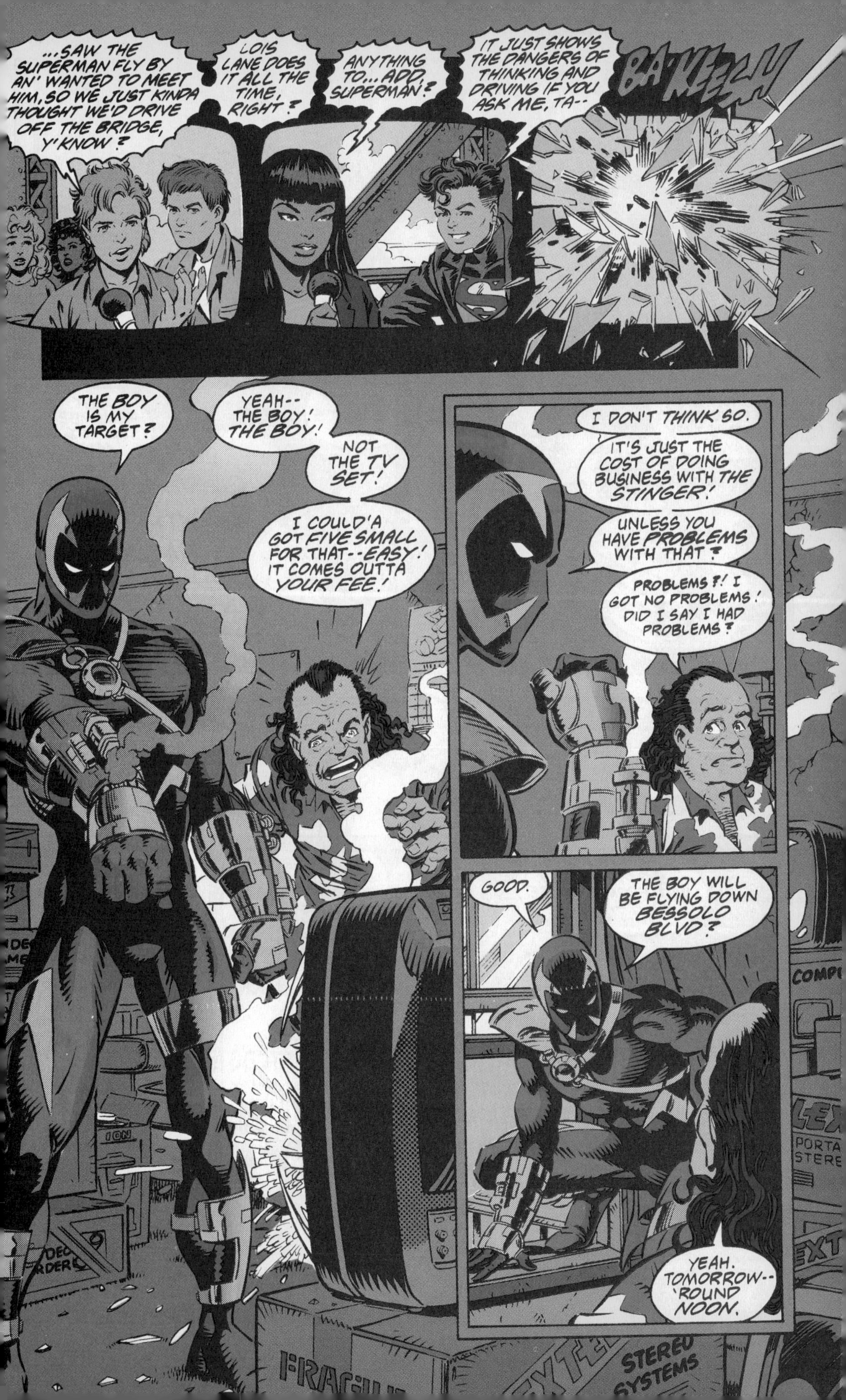
...SAW THE SUPERMAN FLY BY AN' WANTED TO MEET HIM, SO WE JUST KINDA THOUGHT WE'D DRIVE OFF THE BRIDGE, Y'KNOW?
LOIS LANE DOES IT ALL THE TIME, RIGHT?
ANYTHING TO... ADD, SUPERMAN?
IT JUST SHOWS THE DANGERS OF THINKING AND DRIVING IF YOU ASK ME, TA--
BA-KEESH!!
THE BOY IS MY TARGET?
YEAH-- THE BOY! THE BOY!
NOT THE TV SET!
I COULD'A GOT FIVE SMALL FOR THAT--EASY! IT COMES OUTTA YOUR FEE!
I DON'T THINK SO.
IT'S JUST THE COST OF DOING BUSINESS WITH THE STINGER!
UNLESS YOU HAVE PROBLEMS WITH THAT?
PROBLEMS?! I GOT NO PROBLEMS! DID I SAY I HAD PROBLEMS?
GOOD.
THE BOY WILL BE FLYING DOWN BESSOLO BLVD?
YEAH. TOMORROW-- 'ROUND NOON.
STEREO SYSTEMS

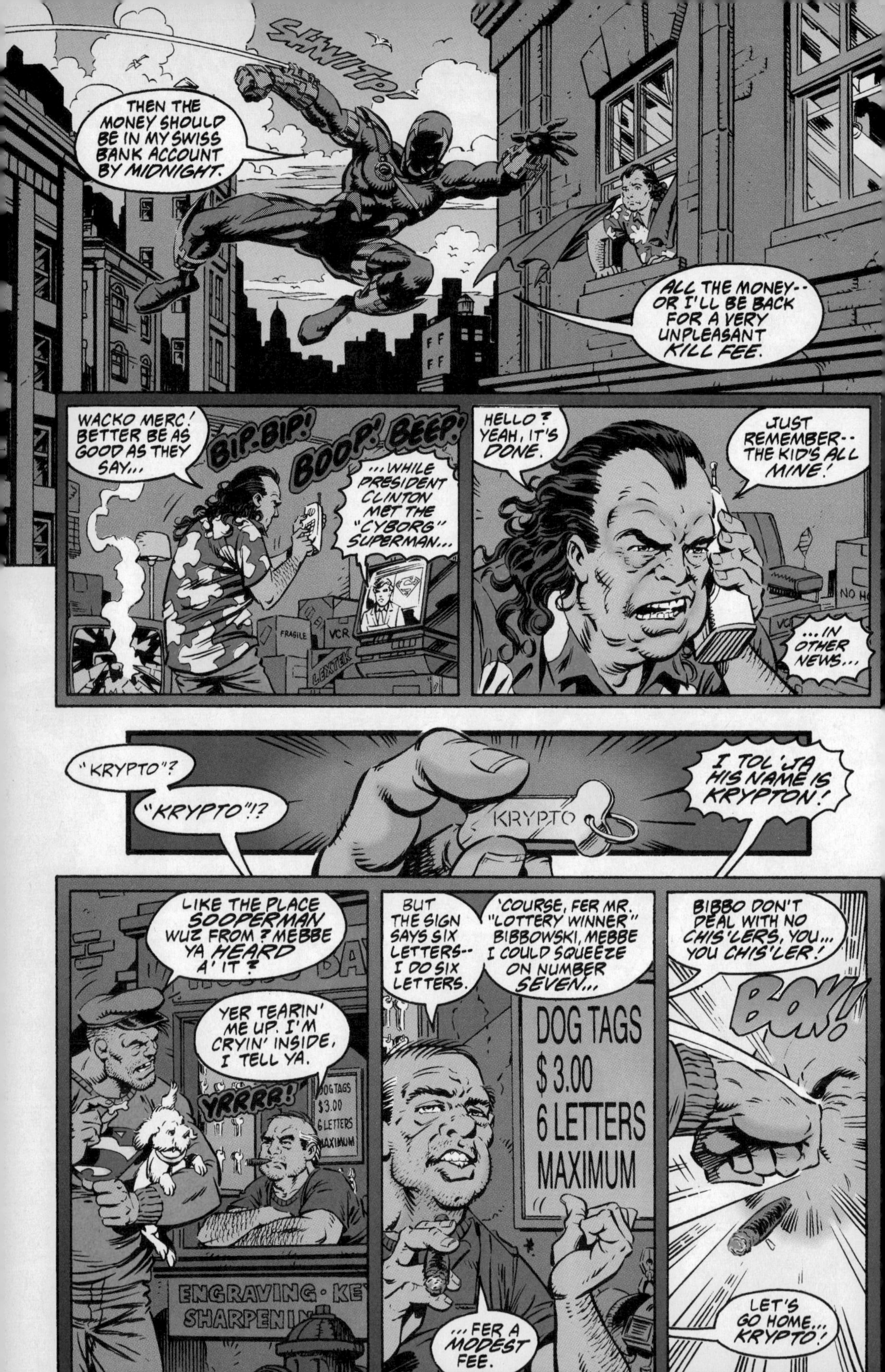
SHWIIP!
THEN THE MONEY SHOULD BE IN MY SWISS BANK ACCOUNT BY MIDNIGHT.
ALL THE MONEY-- OR I'LL BE BACK FOR A VERY UNPLEASANT KILL FEE.
WACKO MERC! BETTER BE AS GOOD AS THEY SAY...
BIP-BIP! BOOP! BEEP!
...WHILE PRESIDENT CLINTON MET THE "CYBORG" SUPERMAN...
FRAGILE
VCR
LEXTEK
HELLO? YEAH, IT'S DONE.
JUST REMEMBER-- THE KID'S ALL MINE!
...IN OTHER NEWS...
"KRYPTO"?
"KRYPTO"!?
KRYPTO
I TOL'JA HIS NAME IS KRYPTON!
LIKE THE PLACE SOOPERMAN WUZ FROM? MEBBE YA HEARD A' IT?
YER TEARIN' ME UP. I'M CRYIN' INSIDE, I TELL YA.
YRRRR!
DOG TAGS $3.00 6 LETTERS MAXIMUM
ENGRAVING · KE
SHARPENIN
BUT THE SIGN SAYS SIX LETTERS-- I DO SIX LETTERS.
'COURSE, FER MR. "LOTTERY WINNER" BIBBOWSKI, MEBBE I COULD SQUEEZE ON NUMBER SEVEN...
DOG TAGS
$ 3.00
6 LETTERS
MAXIMUM
...FER A MODEST FEE.
BIBBO DON'T DEAL WITH NO CHIS'LERS, YOU... YOU CHIS'LER!
BOK!
LET'S GO HOME... KRYPTO!

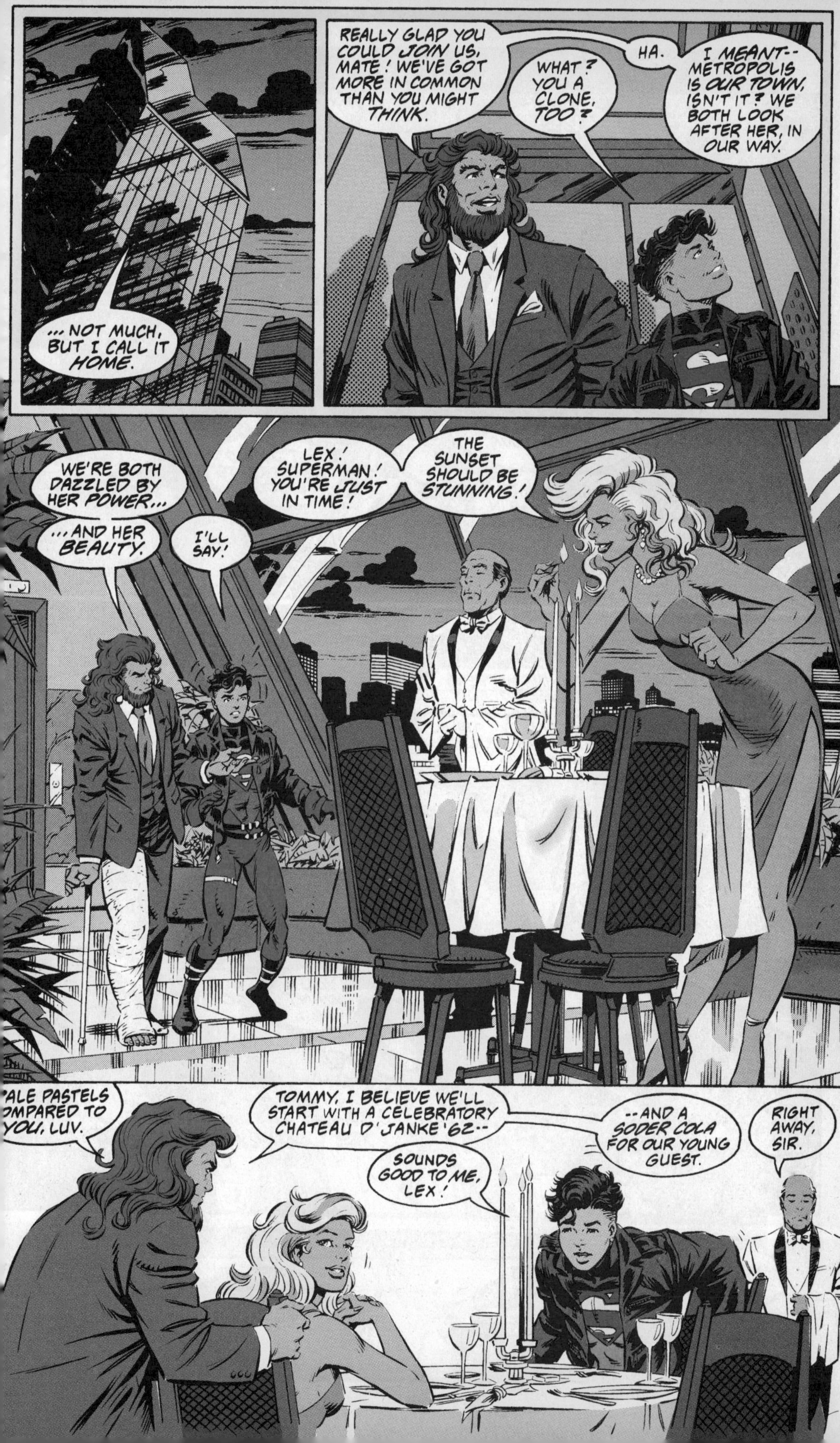
... NOT MUCH, BUT I CALL IT HOME.
REALLY GLAD YOU COULD JOIN US, MATE! WE'VE GOT MORE IN COMMON THAN YOU MIGHT THINK.
WHAT? YOU A CLONE, TOO?
HA.
I MEANT-- METROPOLIS IS OUR TOWN, ISN'T IT? WE BOTH LOOK AFTER HER, IN OUR WAY.
WE'RE BOTH DAZZLED BY HER POWER...
...AND HER BEAUTY.
I'LL SAY!
LEX! SUPERMAN! YOU'RE JUST IN TIME!
THE SUNSET SHOULD BE STUNNING!
PALE PASTELS COMPARED TO YOU, LUV.
TOMMY, I BELIEVE WE'LL START WITH A CELEBRATORY CHATEAU D'JANKE '62--
SOUNDS GOOD TO ME, LEX!
--AND A SODER COLA FOR OUR YOUNG GUEST.
RIGHT AWAY, SIR.

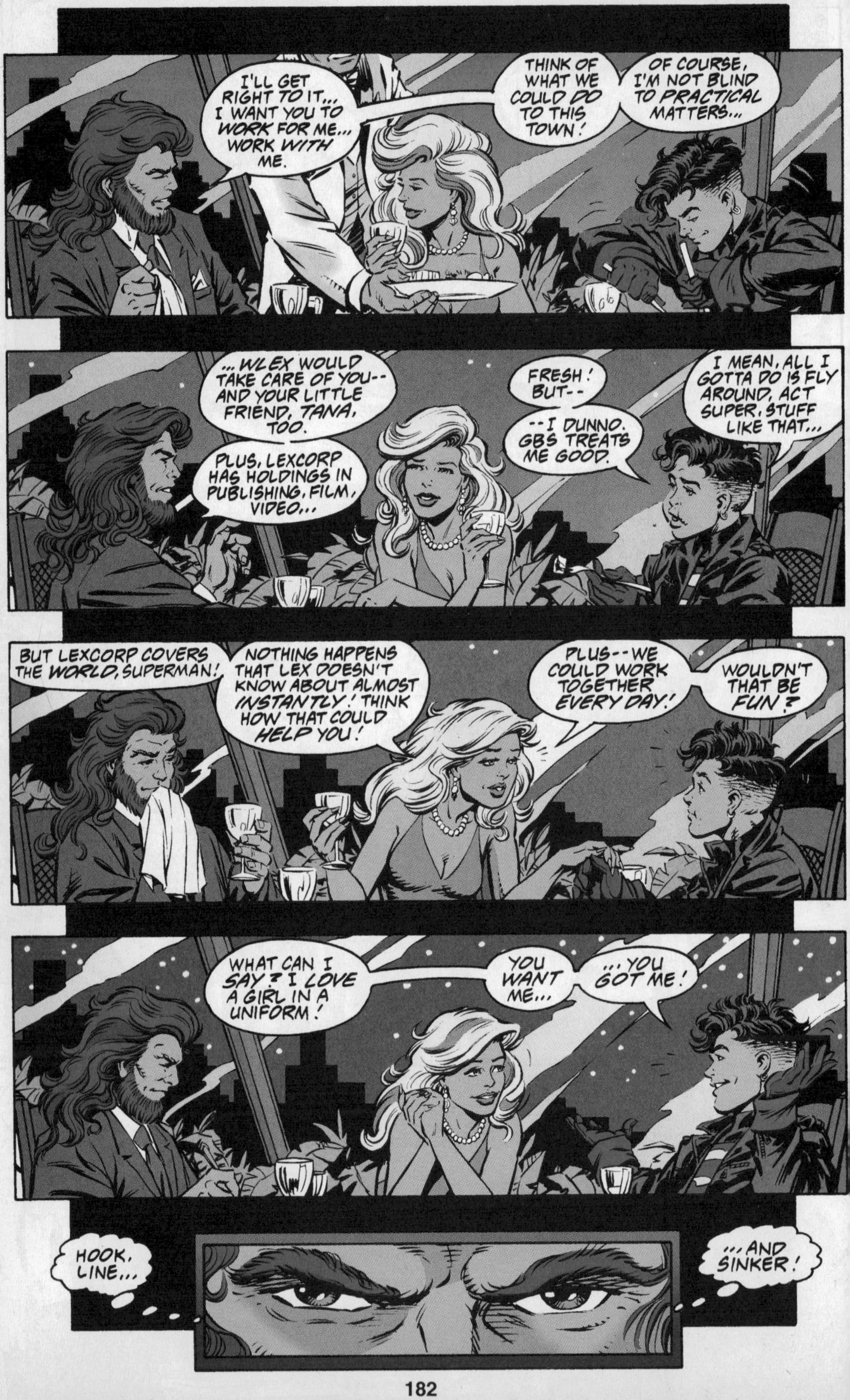
I'LL GET RIGHT TO IT... I WANT YOU TO WORK FOR ME... WORK WITH ME.
THINK OF WHAT WE COULD DO TO THIS TOWN!
OF COURSE, I'M NOT BLIND TO PRACTICAL MATTERS...
...WLEX WOULD TAKE CARE OF YOU-- AND YOUR LITTLE FRIEND, TANA, TOO.
PLUS, LEXCORP HAS HOLDINGS IN PUBLISHING, FILM, VIDEO...
FRESH! BUT--
--I DUNNO. GBS TREATS ME GOOD.
I MEAN, ALL I GOTTA DO IS FLY AROUND, ACT SUPER, STUFF LIKE THAT...
BUT LEXCORP COVERS THE WORLD, SUPERMAN!
NOTHING HAPPENS THAT LEX DOESN'T KNOW ABOUT ALMOST INSTANTLY! THINK HOW THAT COULD HELP YOU!
PLUS--WE COULD WORK TOGETHER EVERY DAY!
WOULDN'T THAT BE FUN?
WHAT CAN I SAY? I LOVE A GIRL IN A UNIFORM!
YOU WANT ME...
...YOU GOT ME!
HOOK, LINE...
...AND SINKER!

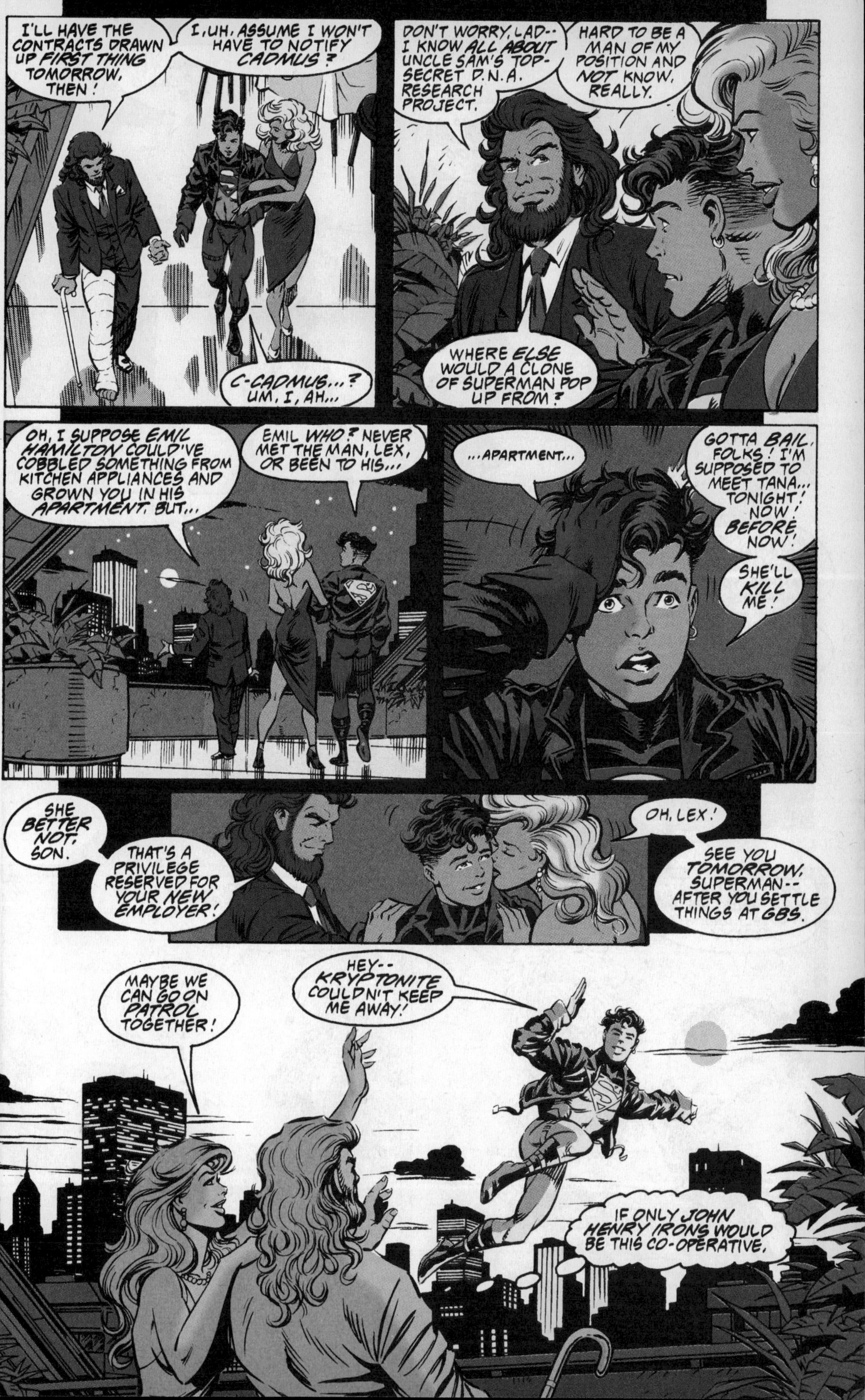
I'LL HAVE THE CONTRACTS DRAWN UP FIRST THING TOMORROW, THEN!
I, UH, ASSUME I WON'T HAVE TO NOTIFY CADMUS?
C-CADMUS...? UM, I, AH...
DON'T WORRY, LAD-- I KNOW ALL ABOUT UNCLE SAM'S TOP-SECRET D.N.A. RESEARCH PROJECT.
HARD TO BE A MAN OF MY POSITION AND NOT KNOW, REALLY.
WHERE ELSE WOULD A CLONE OF SUPERMAN POP UP FROM?
OH, I SUPPOSE EMIL HAMILTON COULD'VE COBBLED SOMETHING FROM KITCHEN APPLIANCES AND GROWN YOU IN HIS APARTMENT. BUT...
EMIL WHO? NEVER MET THE MAN, LEX, OR BEEN TO HIS...
...APARTMENT...
GOTTA BAIL, FOLKS! I'M SUPPOSED TO MEET TANA... TONIGHT! NOW! BEFORE NOW!
SHE'LL KILL ME!
SHE BETTER NOT, SON.
THAT'S A PRIVILEGE RESERVED FOR YOUR NEW EMPLOYER!
OH, LEX!
SEE YOU TOMORROW, SUPERMAN-- AFTER YOU SETTLE THINGS AT GBS.
MAYBE WE CAN GO ON PATROL TOGETHER!
HEY-- KRYPTONITE COULDN'T KEEP ME AWAY!
IF ONLY JOHN HENRY IRONS WOULD BE THIS CO-OPERATIVE.

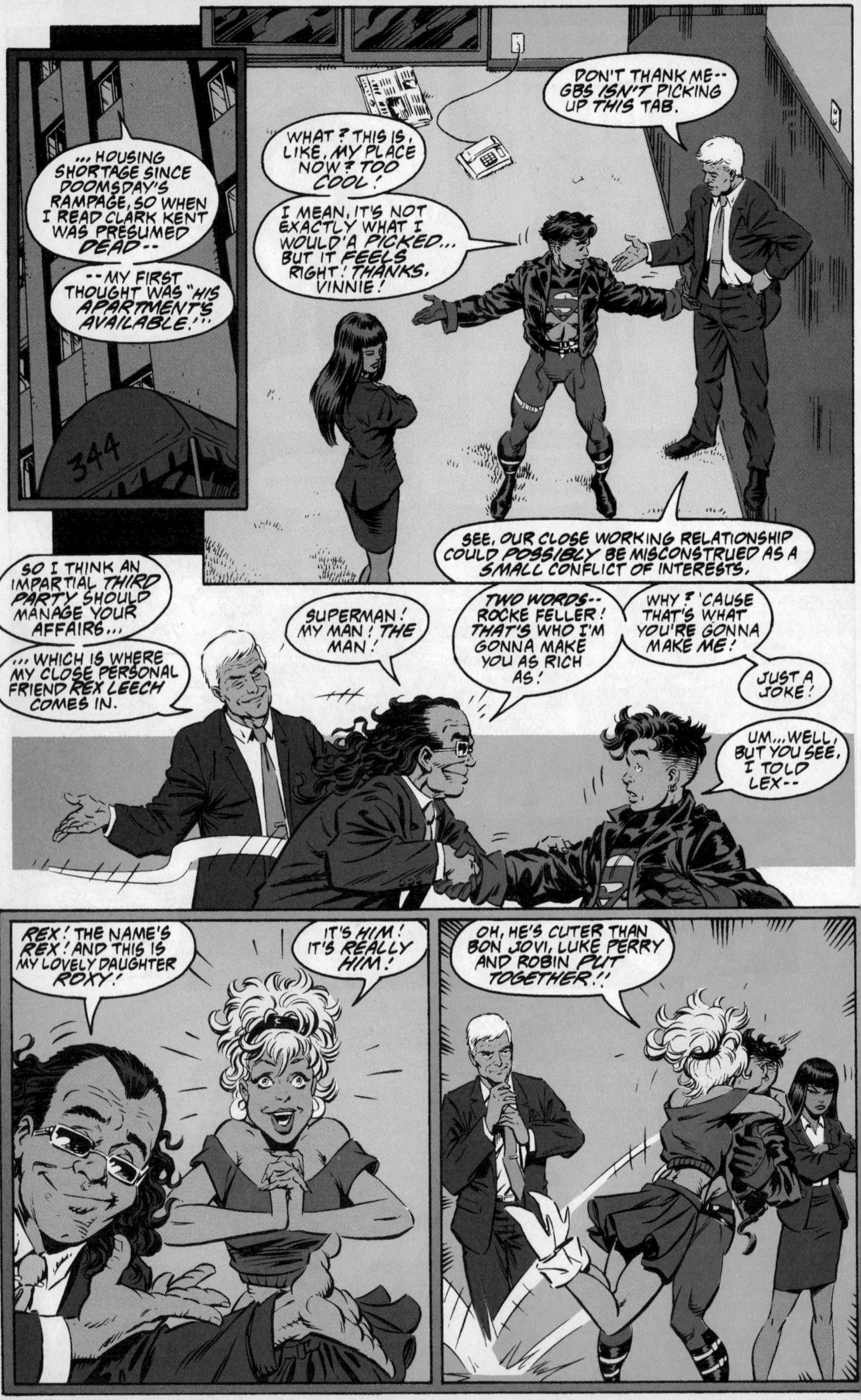
...HOUSING SHORTAGE SINCE DOOMSDAY'S RAMPAGE, SO WHEN I READ CLARK KENT WAS PRESUMED DEAD--
--MY FIRST THOUGHT WAS "HIS APARTMENT'S AVAILABLE!"
DON'T THANK ME-- GBS ISN'T PICKING UP THIS TAB.
WHAT? THIS IS, LIKE, MY PLACE NOW? TOO COOL!
I MEAN, IT'S NOT EXACTLY WHAT I WOULD'A PICKED... BUT IT FEELS RIGHT! THANKS, VINNIE!
SEE, OUR CLOSE WORKING RELATIONSHIP COULD POSSIBLY BE MISCONSTRUED AS A SMALL CONFLICT OF INTERESTS.
SO I THINK AN IMPARTIAL THIRD PARTY SHOULD MANAGE YOUR AFFAIRS...
...WHICH IS WHERE MY CLOSE PERSONAL FRIEND REX LEECH COMES IN.
SUPERMAN! MY MAN! THE MAN!
TWO WORDS-- ROCKE FELLER! THAT'S WHO I'M GONNA MAKE YOU AS RICH AS!
WHY? 'CAUSE THAT'S WHAT YOU'RE GONNA MAKE ME!
JUST A JOKE!
UM...WELL, BUT YOU SEE, I TOLD LEX--
REX! THE NAME'S REX! AND THIS IS MY LOVELY DAUGHTER ROXY!
IT'S HIM! IT'S REALLY HIM!
OH, HE'S CUTER THAN BON JOVI, LUKE PERRY AND ROBIN PUT TOGETHER!!

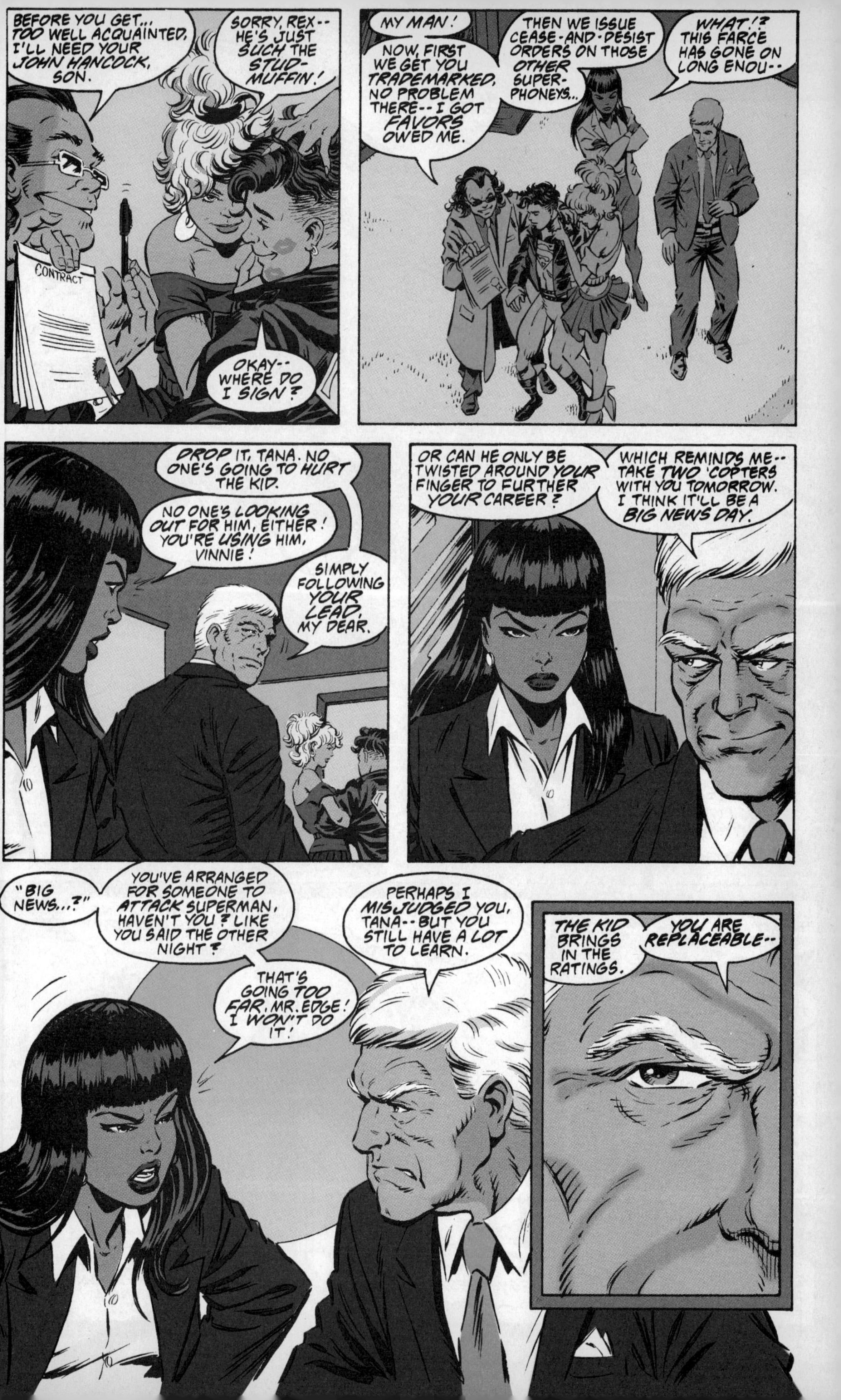
BEFORE YOU GET... TOO WELL ACQUAINTED, I'LL NEED YOUR JOHN HANCOCK, SON.
SORRY, REX-- HE'S JUST SUCH THE STUD-MUFFIN!
CONTRACT
OKAY-- WHERE DO I SIGN?
MY MAN!
NOW, FIRST WE GET YOU TRADEMARKED, NO PROBLEM THERE-- I GOT FAVORS OWED ME.
THEN WE ISSUE CEASE-AND-DESIST ORDERS ON THOSE OTHER SUPER-PHONEYS...
WHAT!? THIS FARCE HAS GONE ON LONG ENOU--
DROP IT, TANA. NO ONE'S GOING TO HURT THE KID.
NO ONE'S LOOKING OUT FOR HIM, EITHER! YOU'RE USING HIM, VINNIE!
SIMPLY FOLLOWING YOUR LEAD, MY DEAR.
OR CAN HE ONLY BE TWISTED AROUND YOUR FINGER TO FURTHER YOUR CAREER?
WHICH REMINDS ME-- TAKE TWO 'COPTERS WITH YOU TOMORROW. I THINK IT'LL BE A BIG NEWS DAY.
"BIG NEWS...?"
YOU'VE ARRANGED FOR SOMEONE TO ATTACK SUPERMAN, HAVEN'T YOU? LIKE YOU SAID THE OTHER NIGHT?
THAT'S GOING TOO FAR, MR. EDGE! I WON'T DO IT!
PERHAPS I MISJUDGED YOU, TANA-- BUT YOU STILL HAVE A LOT TO LEARN.
THE KID BRINGS IN THE RATINGS.
YOU ARE REPLACEABLE--

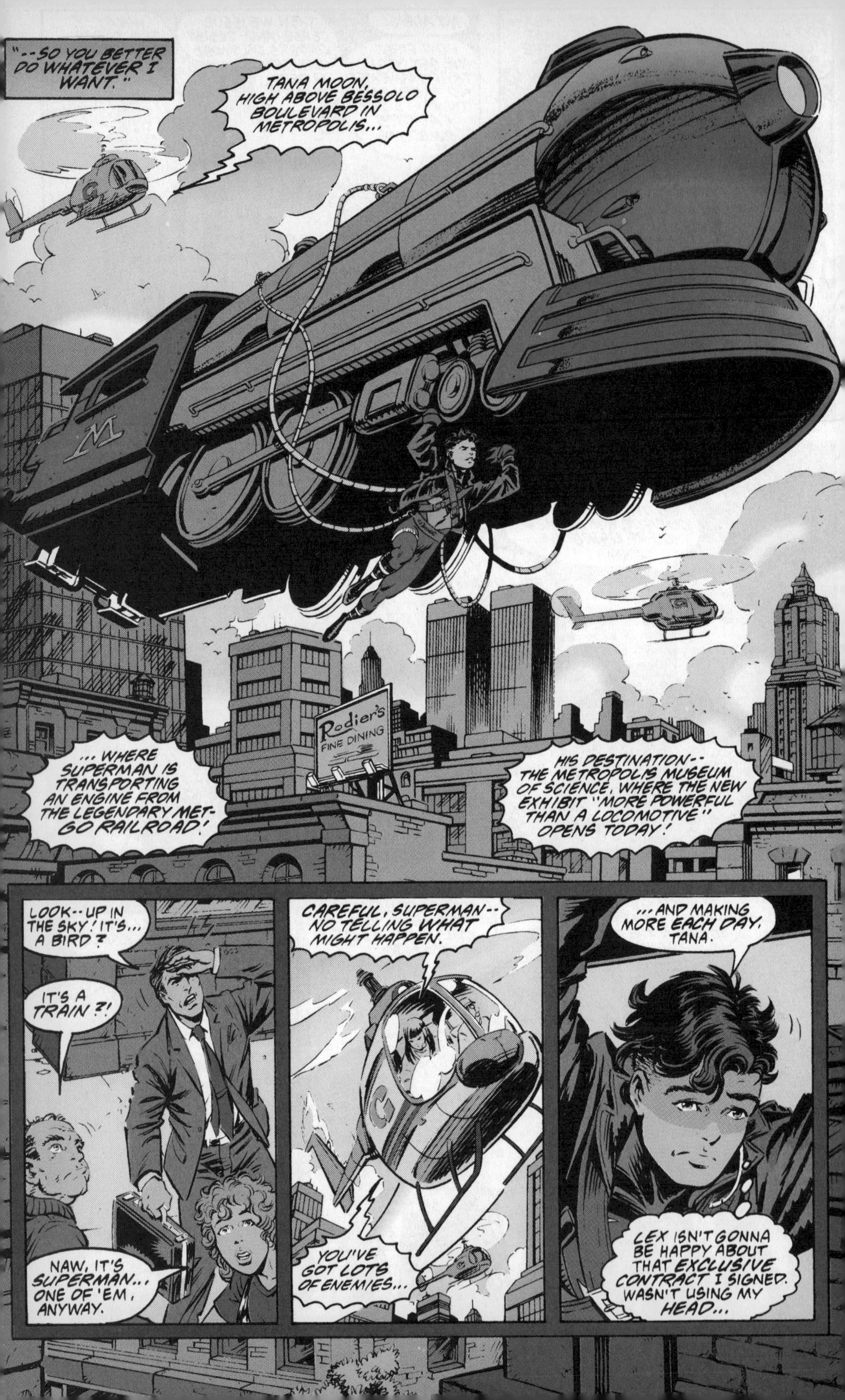
"--SO YOU BETTER DO WHATEVER I WANT."
TANA MOON, HIGH ABOVE BESSOLO BOULEVARD IN METROPOLIS...
...WHERE SUPERMAN IS TRANSPORTING AN ENGINE FROM THE LEGENDARY MET-GO RAILROAD!
HIS DESTINATION--THE METROPOLIS MUSEUM OF SCIENCE, WHERE THE NEW EXHIBIT "MORE POWERFUL THAN A LOCOMOTIVE" OPENS TODAY!
Rodier's FINE DINING
LOOK--UP IN THE SKY! IT'S... A BIRD?
IT'S A TRAIN?!
NAW, IT'S SUPERMAN... ONE OF 'EM, ANYWAY.
CAREFUL, SUPERMAN--NO TELLING WHAT MIGHT HAPPEN.
YOU'VE GOT LOTS OF ENEMIES...
...AND MAKING MORE EACH DAY, TANA.
LEX ISN'T GONNA BE HAPPY ABOUT THAT EXCLUSIVE CONTRACT I SIGNED. WASN'T USING MY HEAD...

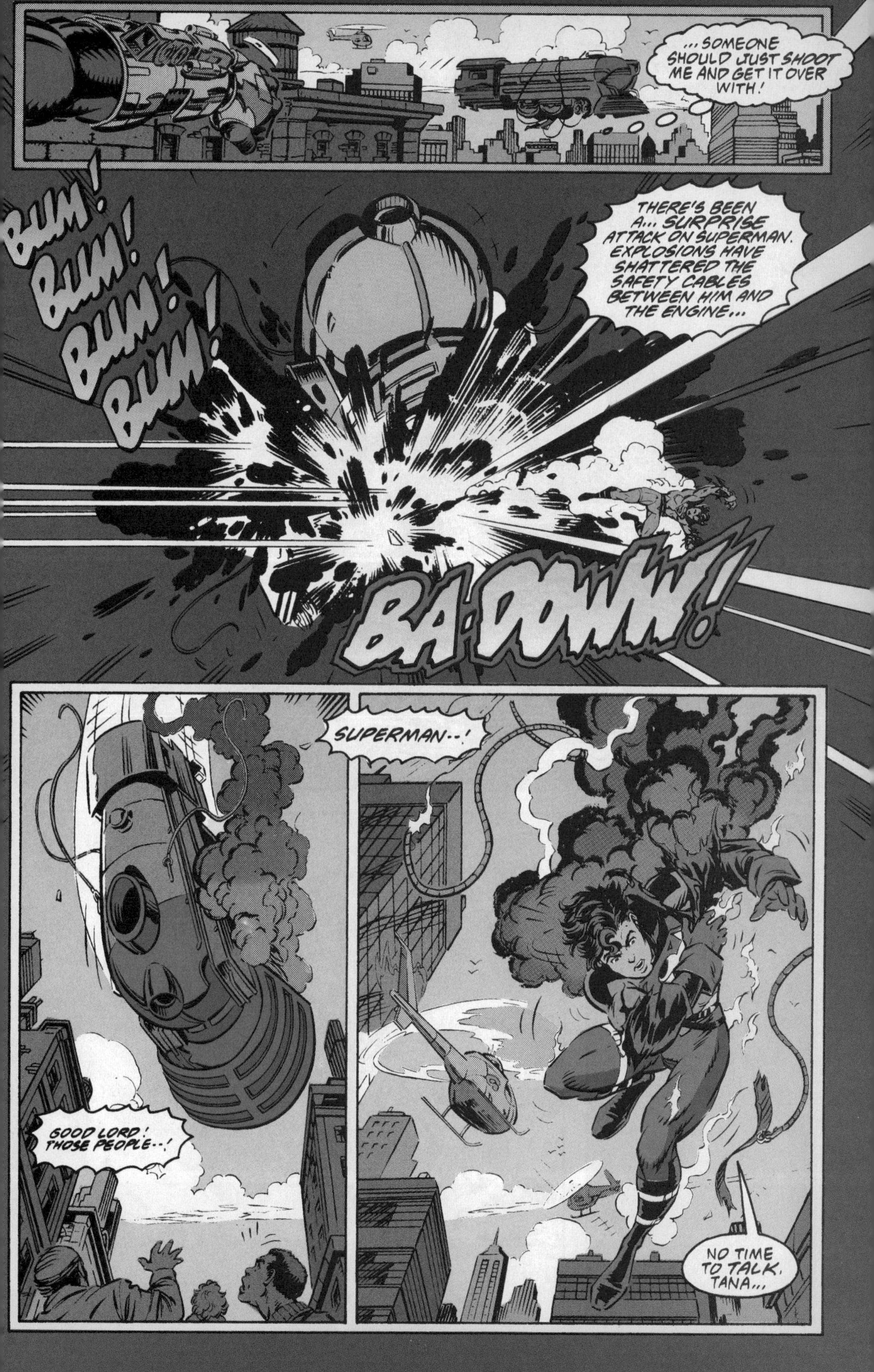
...SOMEONE SHOULD JUST SHOOT ME AND GET IT OVER WITH!
BUM! BUM! BUM! BUM!
THERE'S BEEN A... SURPRISE ATTACK ON SUPERMAN. EXPLOSIONS HAVE SHATTERED THE SAFETY CABLES BETWEEN HIM AND THE ENGINE...
BA-DOWW!
SUPERMAN--!
GOOD LORD! THOSE PEOPLE--!
NO TIME TO TALK, TANA...

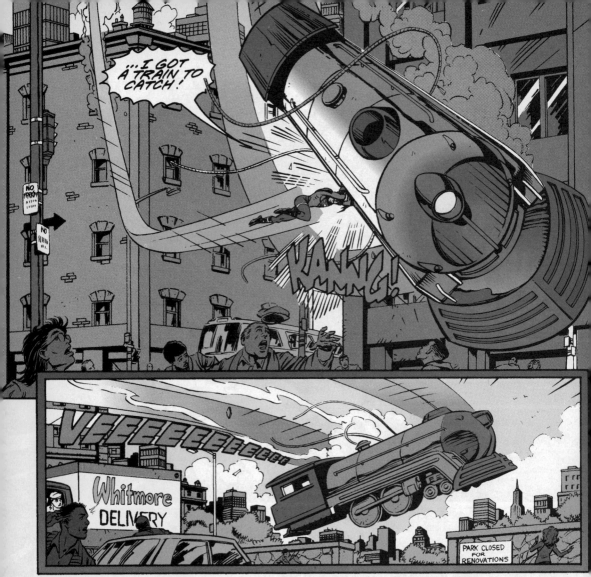

...I GOT A TRAIN TO CATCH!

KANNG!

VEEEEEEEEEE

Whitmore DELIVERY

PARK CLOSED FOR RENOVATIONS

KEEP ON HIM--OR VINNIE EDGE WILL HAVE BOTH OUR JOBS!

CHOOOM!

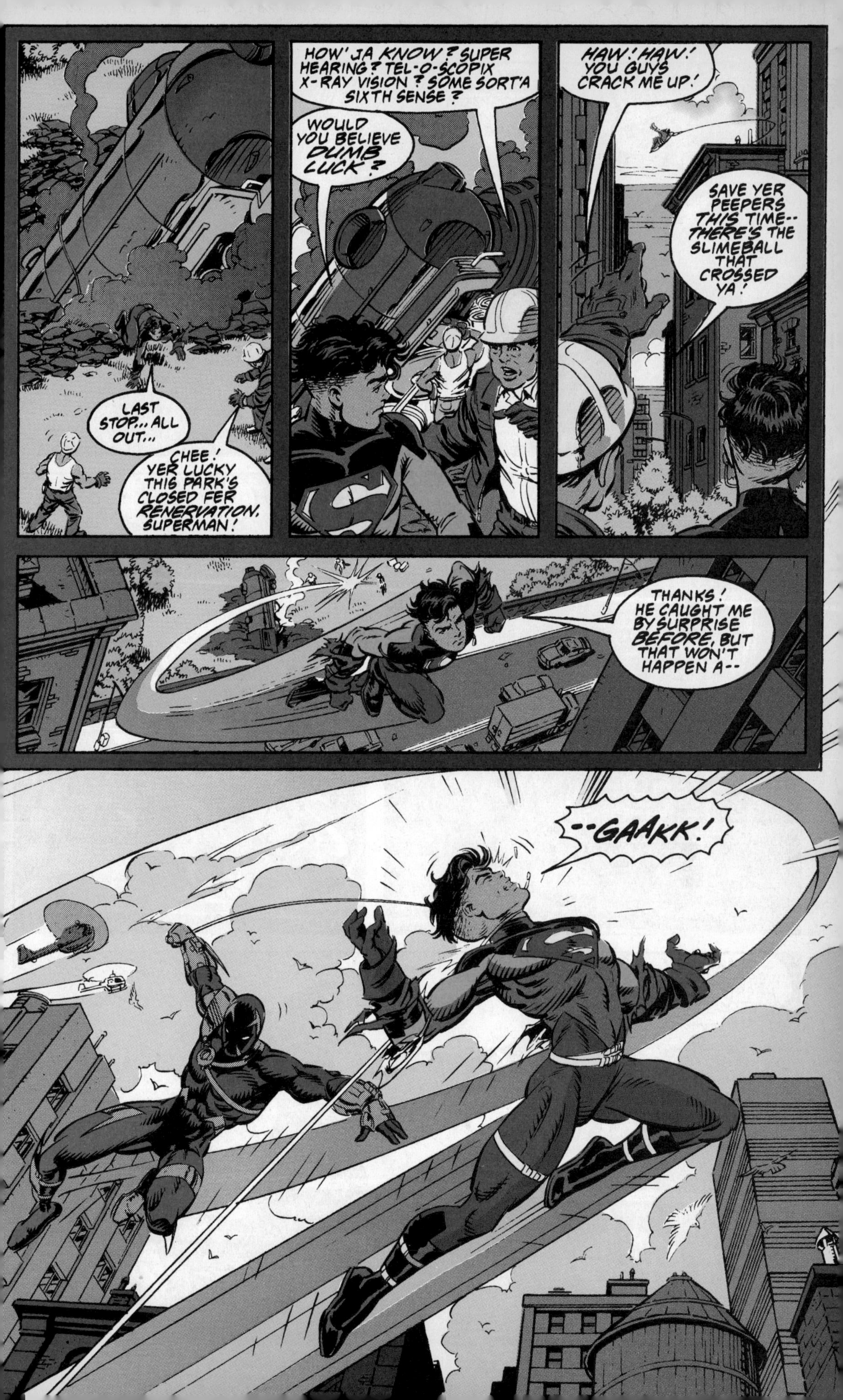
LAST STOP... ALL OUT...
CHEE! YER LUCKY THIS PARK'S CLOSED FER RENERVATION, SUPERMAN!
HOW'JA KNOW? SUPER HEARING? TEL-O-SCOPIX X-RAY VISION? SOME SORT'A SIXTH SENSE?
WOULD YOU BELIEVE DUMB LUCK?
HAW! HAW! YOU GUYS CRACK ME UP!
SAVE YER PEEPERS THIS TIME-- THERE'S THE SLIMEBALL THAT CROSSED YA!
THANKS! HE CAUGHT ME BY SURPRISE BEFORE, BUT THAT WON'T HAPPEN A--
--GAAKK!

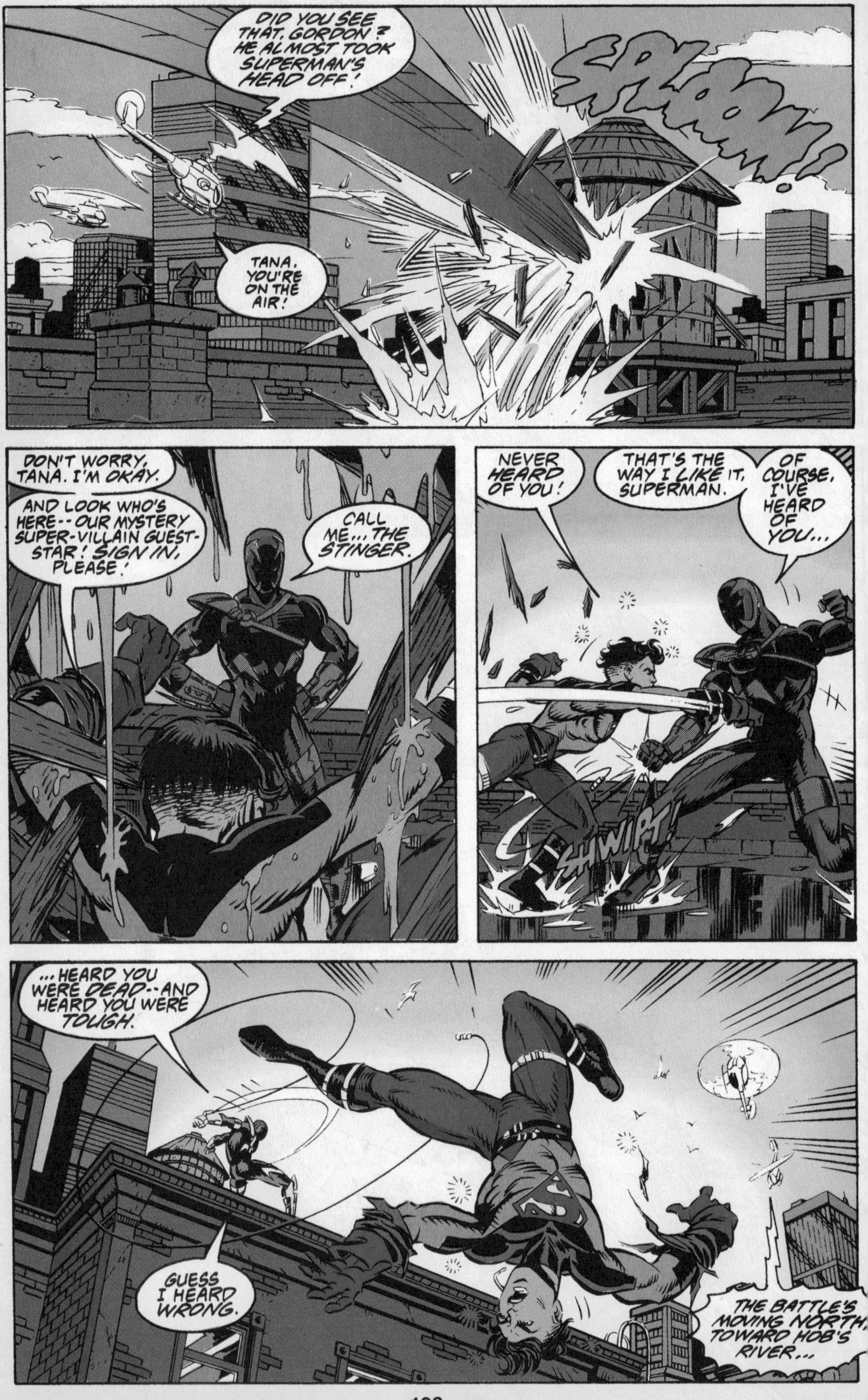
DID YOU SEE THAT, GORDON? HE ALMOST TOOK SUPERMAN'S HEAD OFF!
SPLOOM!!
TANA, YOU'RE ON THE AIR!
DON'T WORRY, TANA. I'M OKAY.
AND LOOK WHO'S HERE--OUR MYSTERY SUPER-VILLAIN GUEST-STAR! SIGN IN, PLEASE!
CALL ME... THE STINGER.
NEVER HEARD OF YOU!
THAT'S THE WAY I LIKE IT, SUPERMAN.
OF COURSE, I'VE HEARD OF YOU...
SHWIPT!
...HEARD YOU WERE DEAD--AND HEARD YOU WERE TOUGH.
GUESS I HEARD WRONG.
THE BATTLE'S MOVING NORTH, TOWARD HOB'S RIVER...

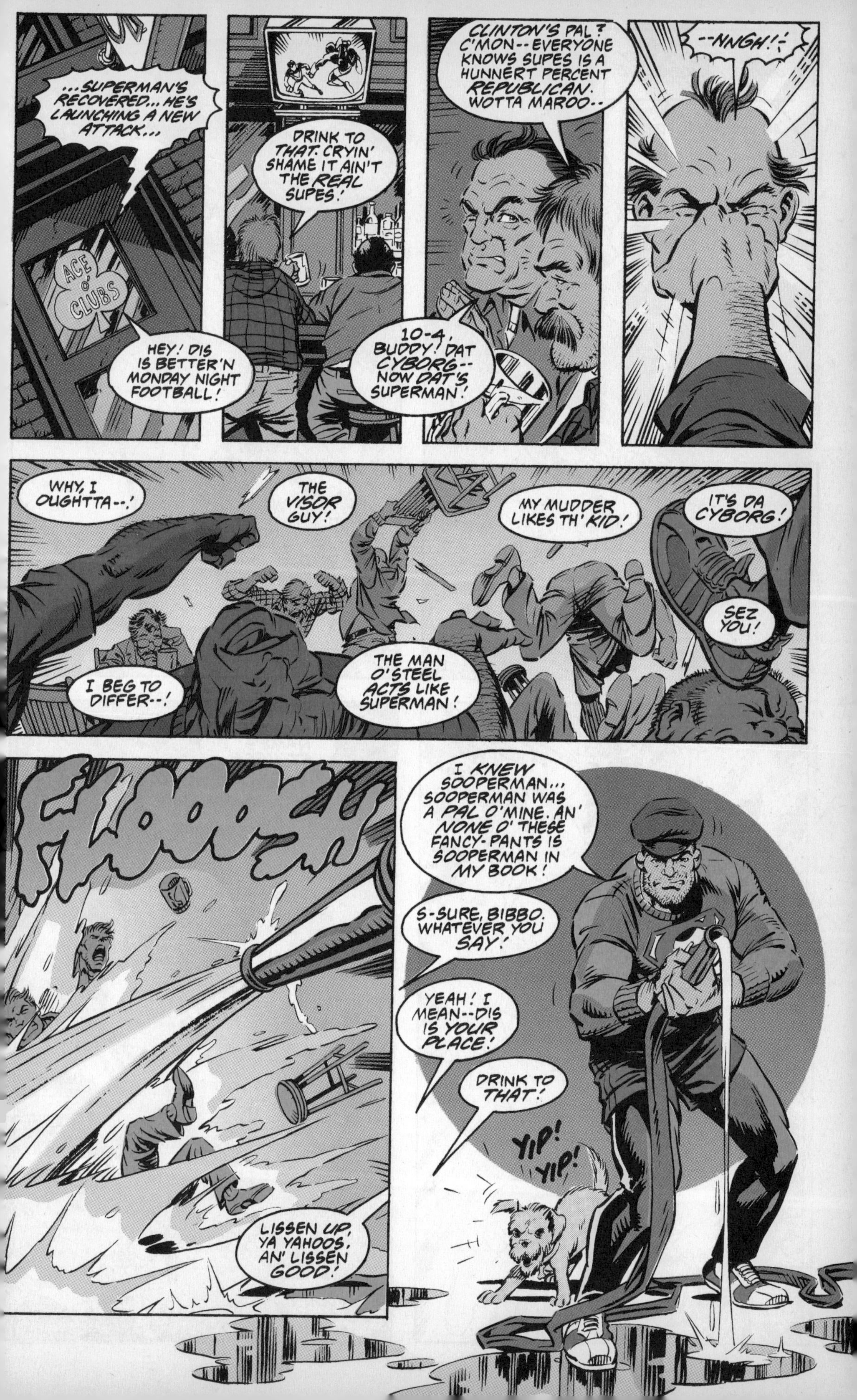
...SUPERMAN'S RECOVERED... HE'S LAUNCHING A NEW ATTACK...
HEY! DIS IS BETTER'N MONDAY NIGHT FOOTBALL!
ACE o' CLUBS
DRINK TO THAT. CRYIN' SHAME IT AIN'T THE REAL SUPES!
10-4, BUDDY! DAT CYBORG-- NOW DAT'S SUPERMAN!
CLINTON'S PAL? C'MON--EVERYONE KNOWS SUPES IS A HUNNERT PERCENT REPUBLICAN. WOTTA MAROO..
--NNGH!--
WHY, I OUGHTTA--!
THE VISOR GUY!
MY MUDDER LIKES TH' KID!
IT'S DA CYBORG!
SEZ YOU!
I BEG TO DIFFER--!
THE MAN O'STEEL ACTS LIKE SUPERMAN!
FLOOOSH
LISSEN UP, YA YAHOOS, AN' LISSEN GOOD!
I KNEW SOOPERMAN... SOOPERMAN WAS A PAL O'MINE. AN' NONE O' THESE FANCY-PANTS IS SOOPERMAN IN MY BOOK!
S-SURE, BIBBO. WHATEVER YOU SAY!
YEAH! I MEAN--DIS IS YOUR PLACE!
DRINK TO THAT!
YIP! YIP!

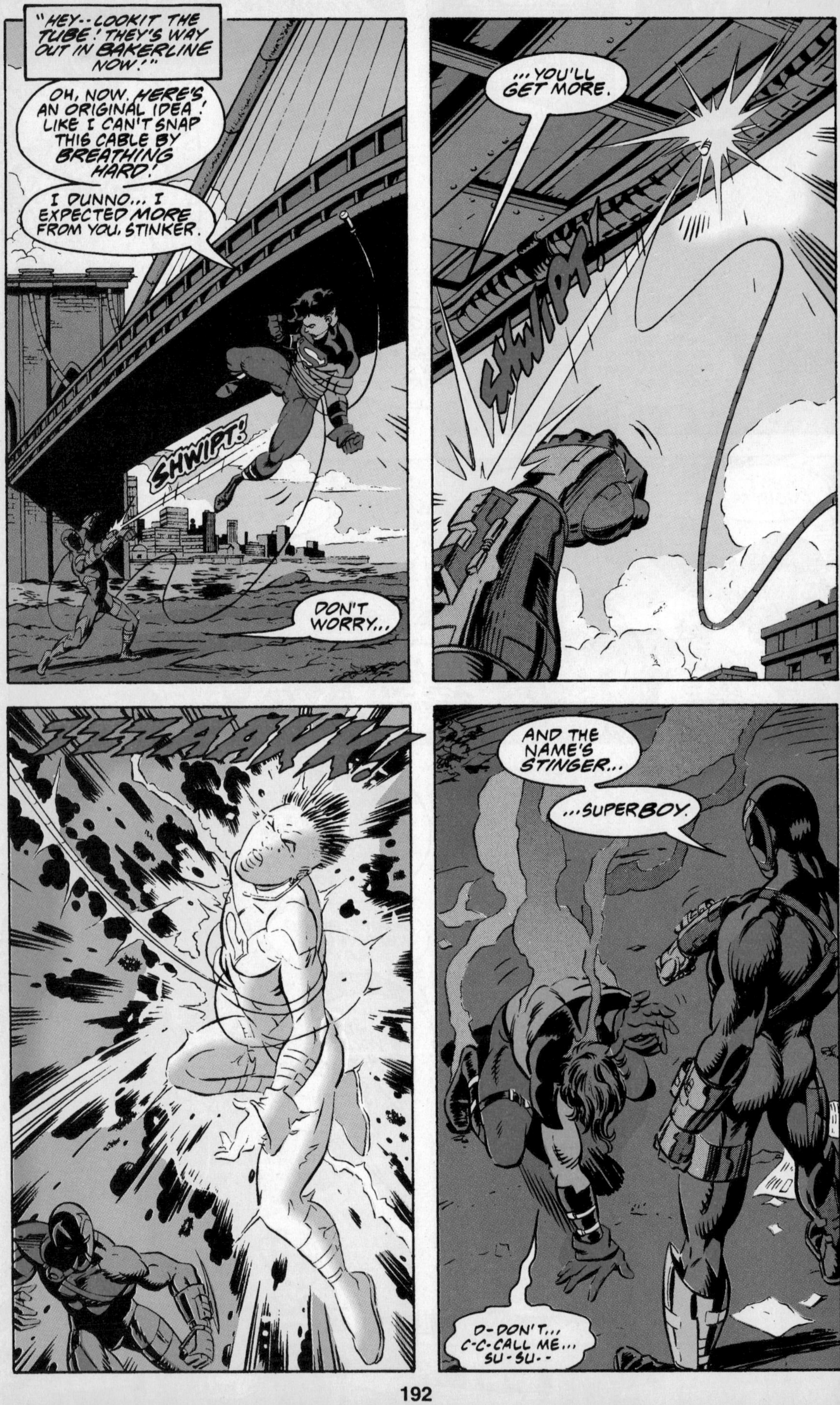
"HEY--LOOKIT THE TUBE! THEY'S WAY OUT IN BAKERLINE NOW!"
OH, NOW. HERE'S AN ORIGINAL IDEA! LIKE I CAN'T SNAP THIS CABLE BY BREATHING HARD!
I DUNNO... I EXPECTED MORE FROM YOU, STINKER.
SHWIPT!
DON'T WORRY...
...YOU'LL GET MORE.
SHWIPT!
AND THE NAME'S STINGER...
...SUPERBOY.
D-DON'T... C-C-CALL ME... SU-SU--

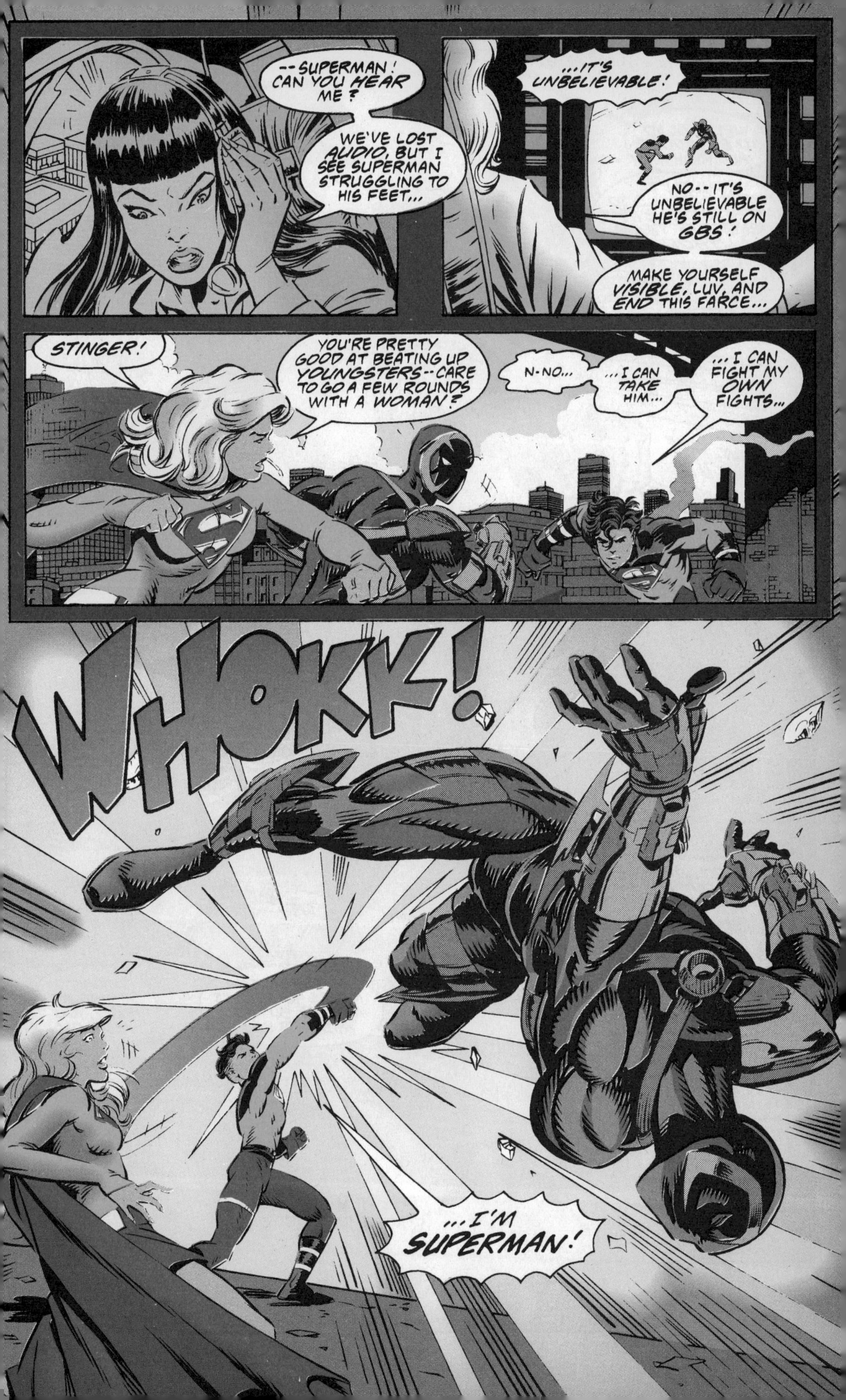
--SUPERMAN! CAN YOU HEAR ME?
WE'VE LOST AUDIO, BUT I SEE SUPERMAN STRUGGLING TO HIS FEET...
...IT'S UNBELIEVABLE!
NO--IT'S UNBELIEVABLE HE'S STILL ON GBS!
MAKE YOURSELF VISIBLE, LUV, AND END THIS FARCE...
STINGER!
YOU'RE PRETTY GOOD AT BEATING UP YOUNGSTERS--CARE TO GO A FEW ROUNDS WITH A WOMAN?
N-NO...
...I CAN TAKE HIM...
...I CAN FIGHT MY OWN FIGHTS...
WHOKK!
...I'M SUPERMAN!

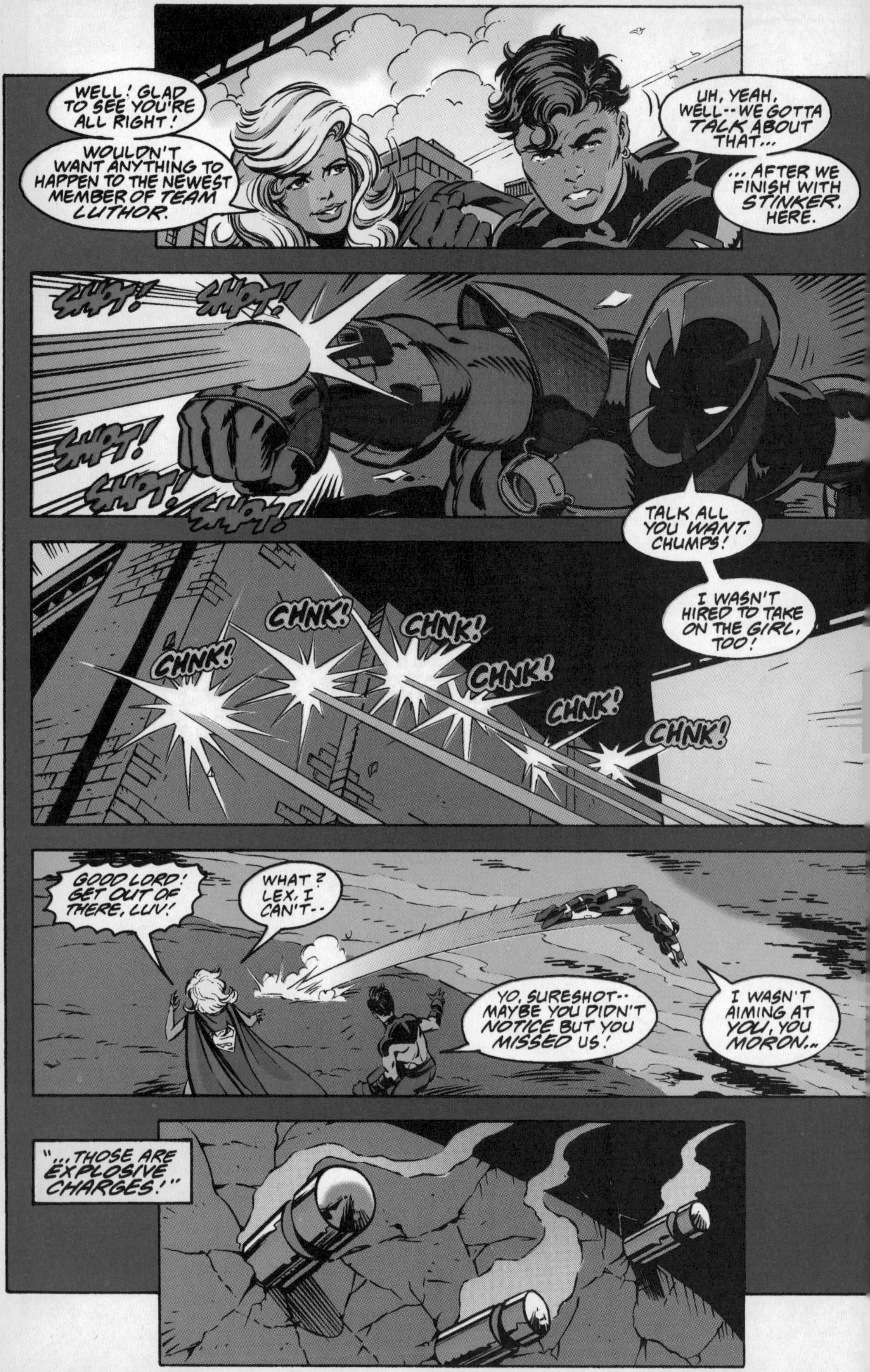

WELL! GLAD TO SEE YOU'RE ALL RIGHT!
WOULDN'T WANT ANYTHING TO HAPPEN TO THE NEWEST MEMBER OF TEAM LUTHOR.
UH, YEAH, WELL--WE GOTTA TALK ABOUT THAT...
...AFTER WE FINISH WITH STINKER, HERE.
SHPT! SHPT!
SHPT! SHPT! SHPT!
TALK ALL YOU WANT, CHUMPS!
I WASN'T HIRED TO TAKE ON THE GIRL, TOO!
CHNK! CHNK! CHNK! CHNK! CHNK! CHNK!
GOOD LORD! GET OUT OF THERE, LUV!
WHAT? LEX, I CAN'T--
YO, SURESHOT--MAYBE YOU DIDN'T NOTICE BUT YOU MISSED US!
I WASN'T AIMING AT YOU, YOU MORON...
"...THOSE ARE EXPLOSIVE CHARGES!"

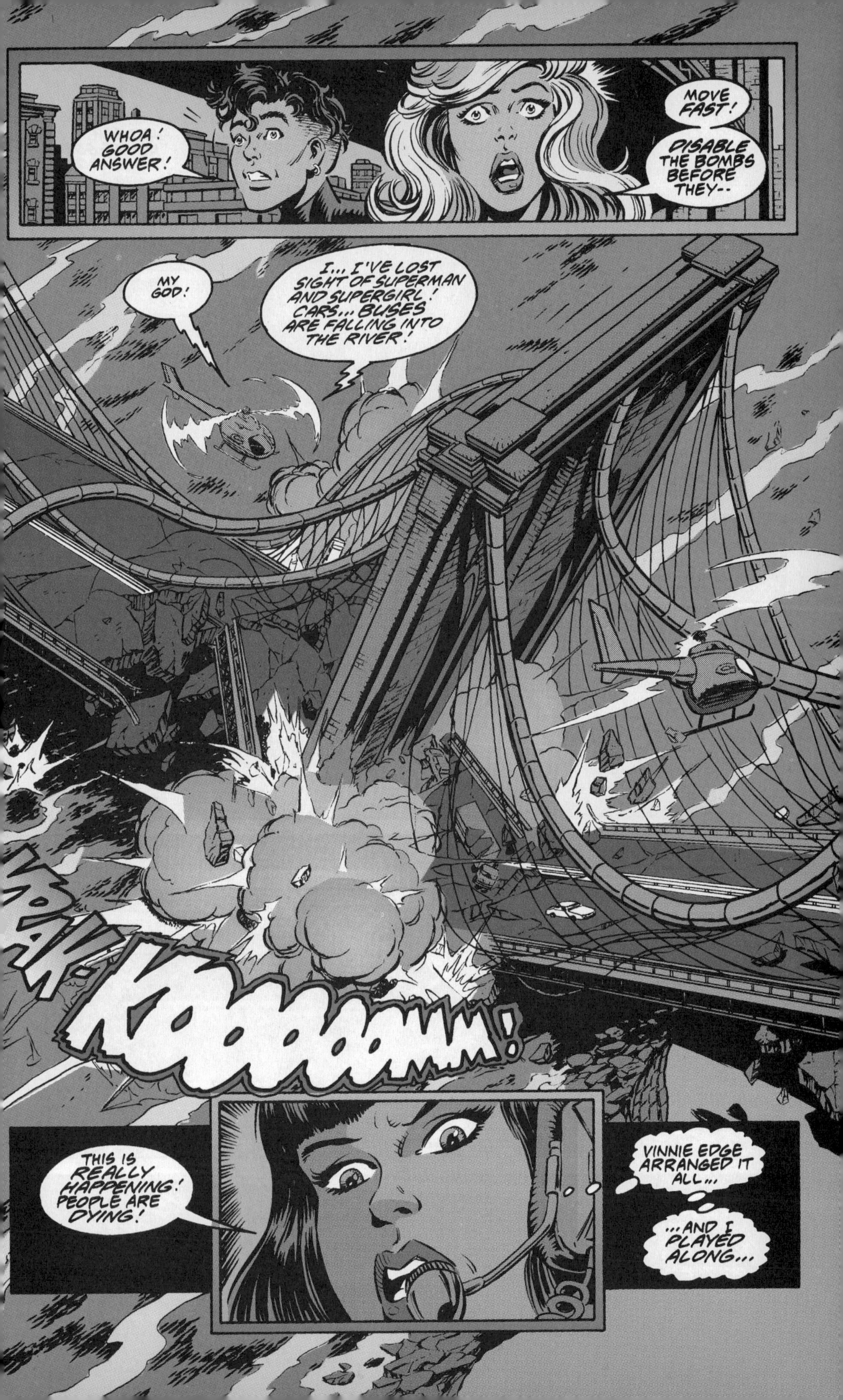

WHOA! GOOD ANSWER!
MOVE FAST!
DISABLE THE BOMBS BEFORE THEY--
MY GOD!
I... I'VE LOST SIGHT OF SUPERMAN AND SUPERGIRL! CARS... BUSES ARE FALLING INTO THE RIVER!
KRAK-
KROOOOMMM!
THIS IS REALLY HAPPENING! PEOPLE ARE DYING!
VINNIE EDGE ARRANGED IT ALL...
...AND I PLAYED ALONG...

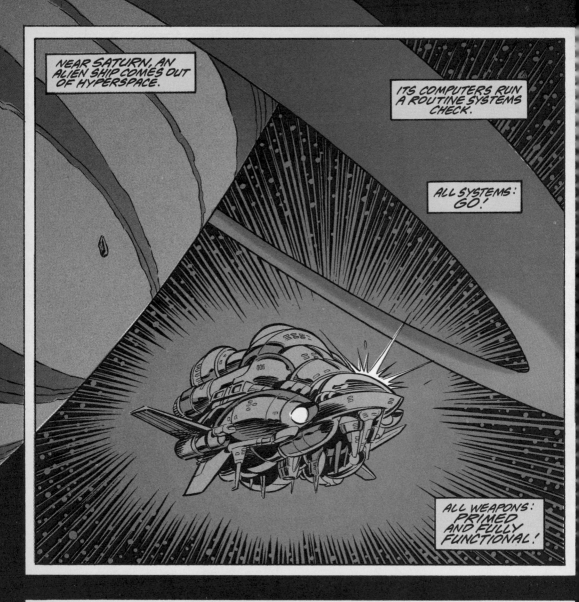

NEAR SATURN, AN ALIEN SHIP COMES OUT OF HYPERSPACE.

ITS COMPUTERS RUN A ROUTINE SYSTEMS CHECK.

ALL SYSTEMS: GO!

ALL WEAPONS: PRIMED AND FULLY FUNCTIONAL!

THE SHIP WILL REACH ITS TARGET IN LESS THAN THREE DAYS.

AND THEN IT'S WAR!

NEXT WEEK:
SUPERGIRL AND THE YOUNG SUPERMAN CRAWL FROM THE WRECKAGE...OR DO THEY? FIND OUT IN **ACTION #689**

IN FOUR WEEKS:
THE CYBORG SUPERMAN -- AND A SURPRISE VILLAIN -- GUEST-STAR WHEN THINGS REALLY HEAT UP IN **ADVENTURES #503**

"LINE OF FIRE!"

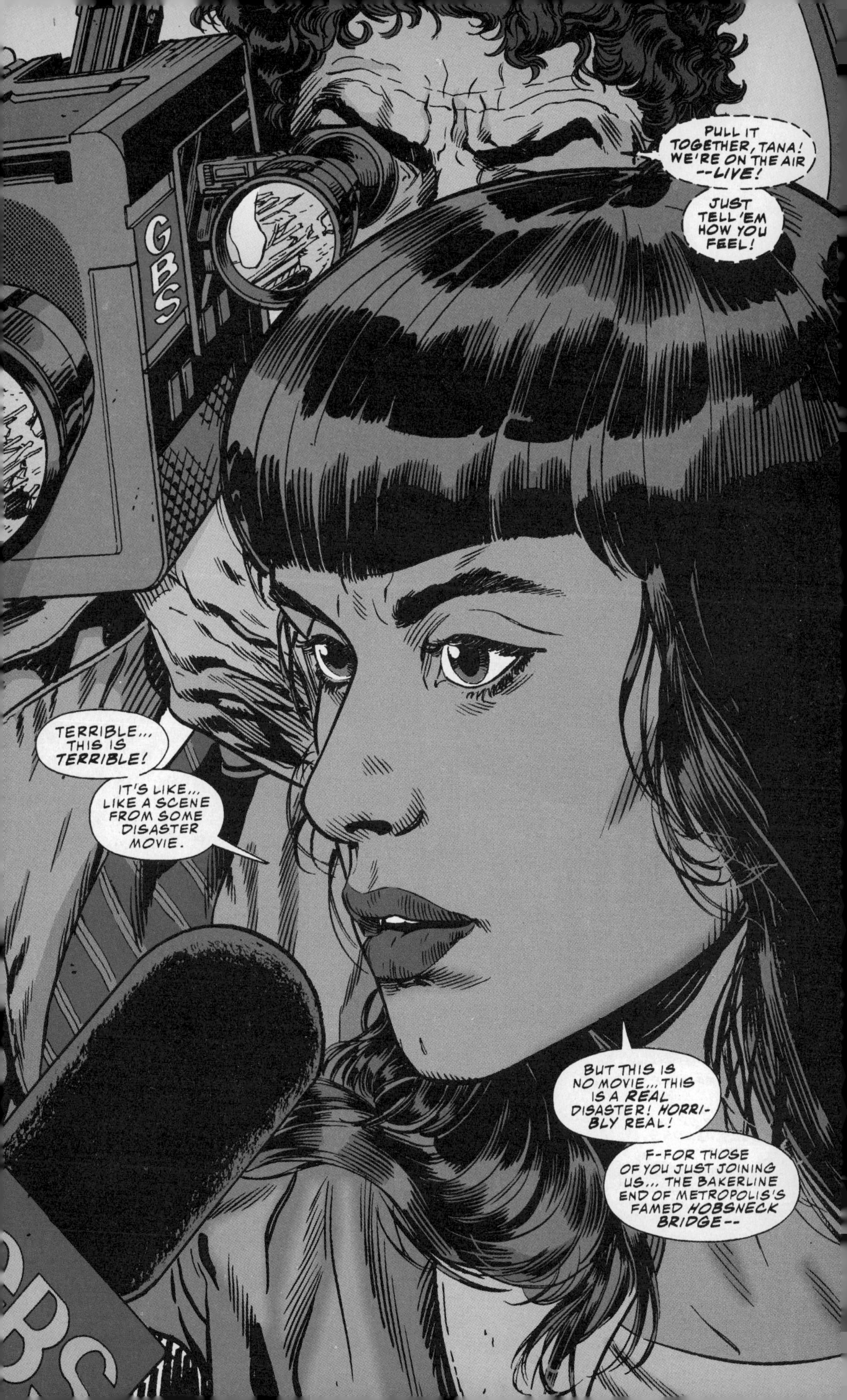
PULL IT TOGETHER, TANA! WE'RE ON THE AIR --LIVE!
JUST TELL 'EM HOW YOU FEEL!
TERRIBLE... THIS IS TERRIBLE!
IT'S LIKE... LIKE A SCENE FROM SOME DISASTER MOVIE.
BUT THIS IS NO MOVIE... THIS IS A REAL DISASTER! HORRIBLY REAL!
F-FOR THOSE OF YOU JUST JOINING US... THE BAKERLINE END OF METROPOLIS'S FAMED HOBSNECK BRIDGE--
GBS

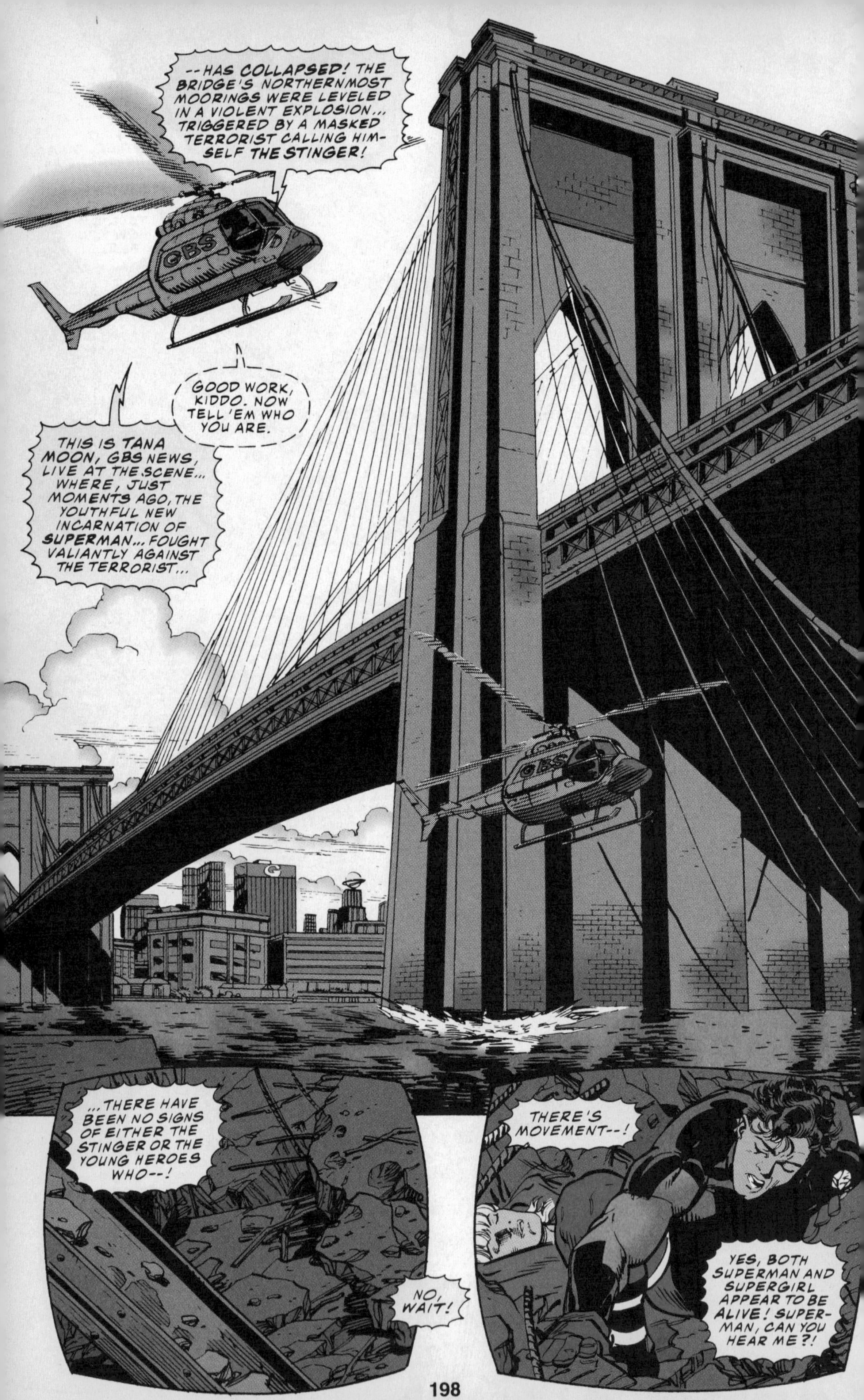
--HAS COLLAPSED! THE BRIDGE'S NORTHERNMOST MOORINGS WERE LEVELED IN A VIOLENT EXPLOSION... TRIGGERED BY A MASKED TERRORIST CALLING HIM-SELF THE STINGER!
GOOD WORK, KIDDO. NOW TELL 'EM WHO YOU ARE.
THIS IS TANA MOON, GBS NEWS, LIVE AT THE SCENE... WHERE, JUST MOMENTS AGO, THE YOUTHFUL NEW INCARNATION OF SUPERMAN... FOUGHT VALIANTLY AGAINST THE TERRORIST...
GBS
GBS
...THERE HAVE BEEN NO SIGNS OF EITHER THE STINGER OR THE YOUNG HEROES WHO--!
NO, WAIT!
THERE'S MOVEMENT--!
YES, BOTH SUPERMAN AND SUPERGIRL APPEAR TO BE ALIVE! SUPER-MAN, CAN YOU HEAR ME?!

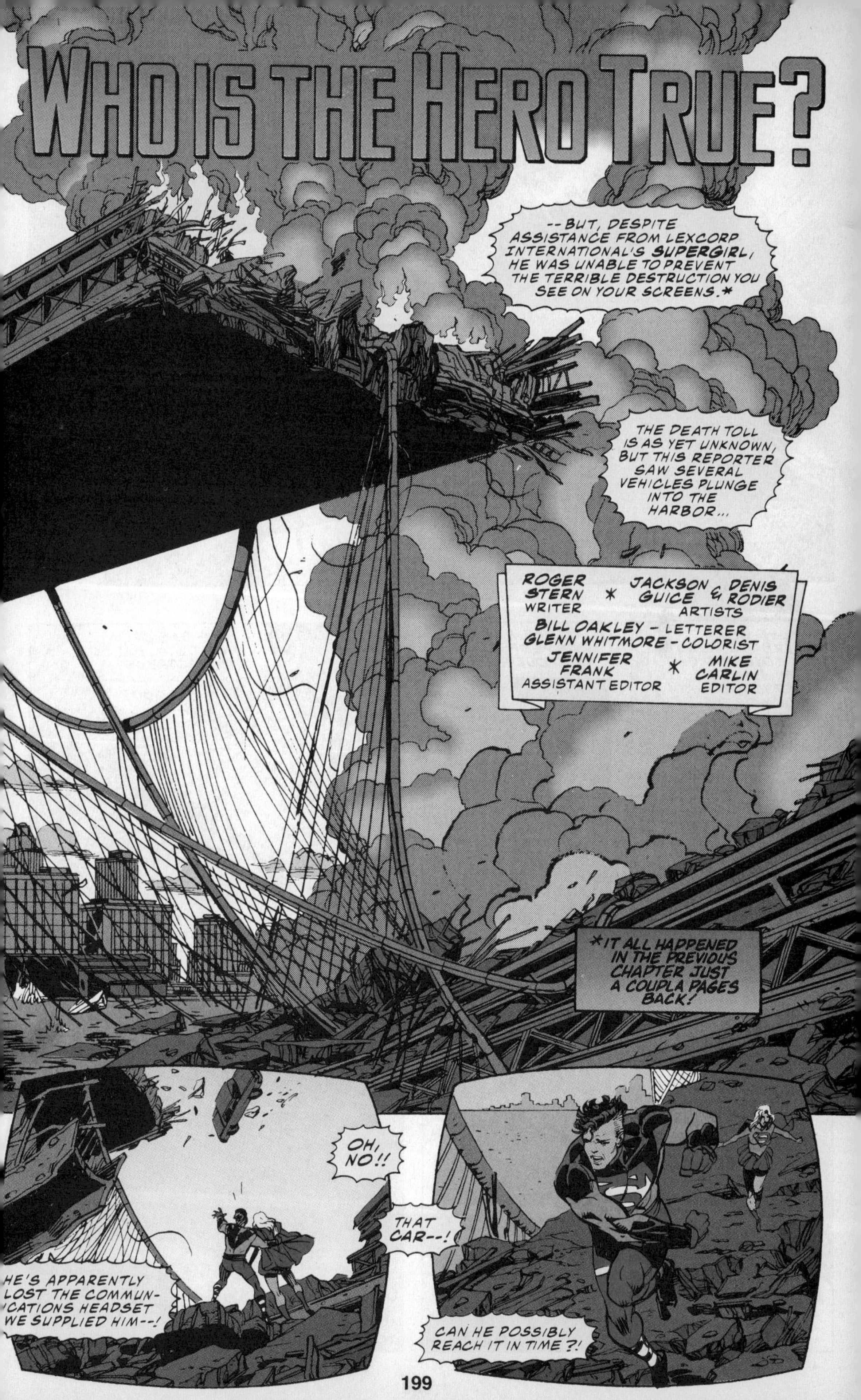
WHO IS THE HERO TRUE?
-- BUT, DESPITE ASSISTANCE FROM LEXCORP INTERNATIONAL'S SUPERGIRL, HE WAS UNABLE TO PREVENT THE TERRIBLE DESTRUCTION YOU SEE ON YOUR SCREENS.*
THE DEATH TOLL IS AS YET UNKNOWN, BUT THIS REPORTER SAW SEVERAL VEHICLES PLUNGE INTO THE HARBOR...
ROGER STERN WRITER * JACKSON GUICE & DENIS RODIER ARTISTS
BILL OAKLEY - LETTERER
GLENN WHITMORE - COLORIST
JENNIFER FRANK ASSISTANT EDITOR * MIKE CARLIN EDITOR
*IT ALL HAPPENED IN THE PREVIOUS CHAPTER JUST A COUPLA PAGES BACK!
OH, NO!!
THAT CAR--!
HE'S APPARENTLY LOST THE COMMUNICATIONS HEADSET WE SUPPLIED HIM--!
CAN HE POSSIBLY REACH IT IN TIME?!

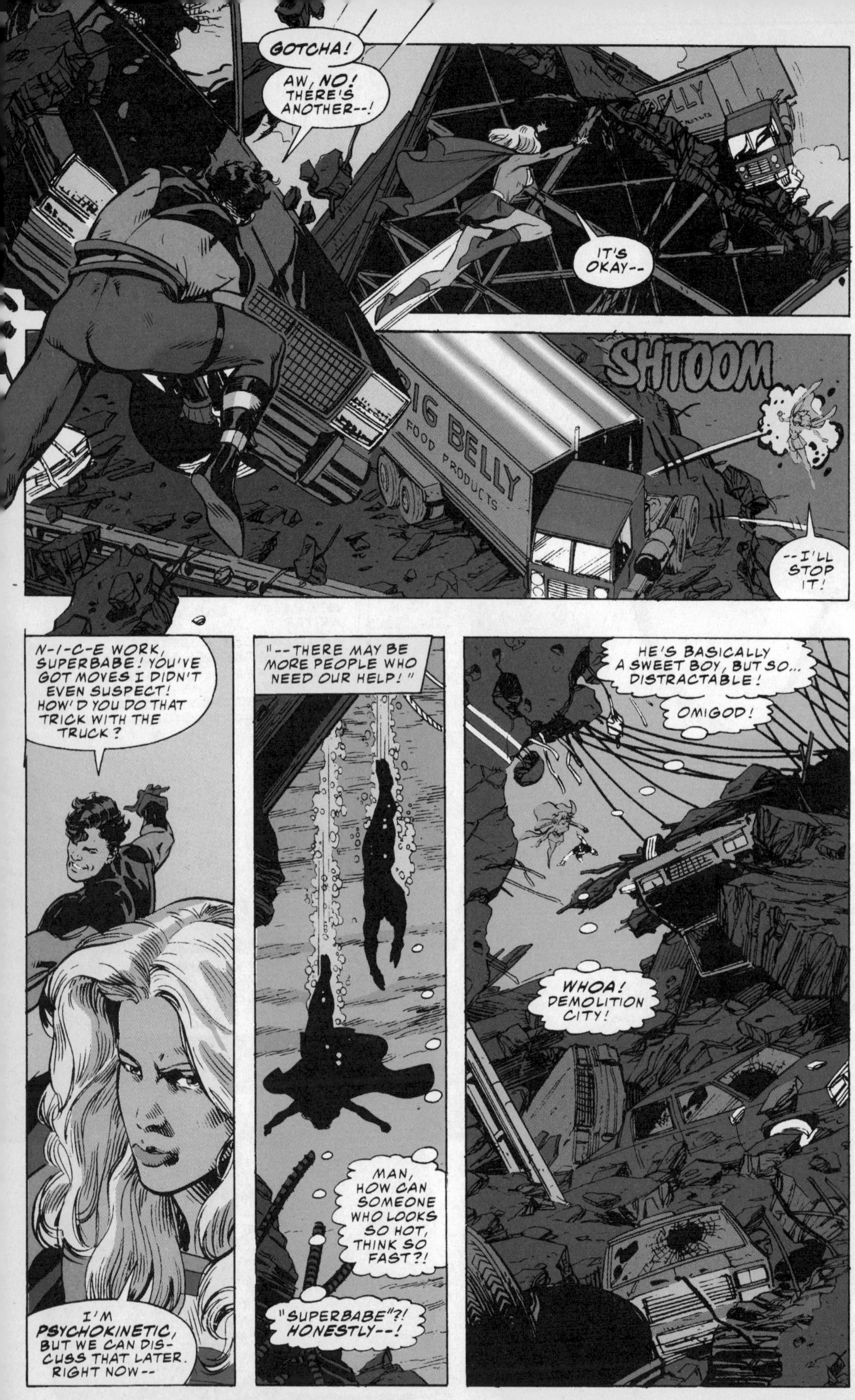
GOTCHA!
AW, NO! THERE'S ANOTHER--!
IT'S OKAY--
SHTOOM
BIG BELLY FOOD PRODUCTS
--I'LL STOP IT!
N-I-C-E WORK, SUPERBABE! YOU'VE GOT MOVES I DIDN'T EVEN SUSPECT! HOW'D YOU DO THAT TRICK WITH THE TRUCK?
I'M PSYCHOKINETIC, BUT WE CAN DISCUSS THAT LATER. RIGHT NOW--
"--THERE MAY BE MORE PEOPLE WHO NEED OUR HELP!"
MAN, HOW CAN SOMEONE WHO LOOKS SO HOT, THINK SO FAST?!
"SUPERBABE"?! HONESTLY--!
HE'S BASICALLY A SWEET BOY, BUT SO... DISTRACTABLE!
OMIGOD!
WHOA! DEMOLITION CITY!

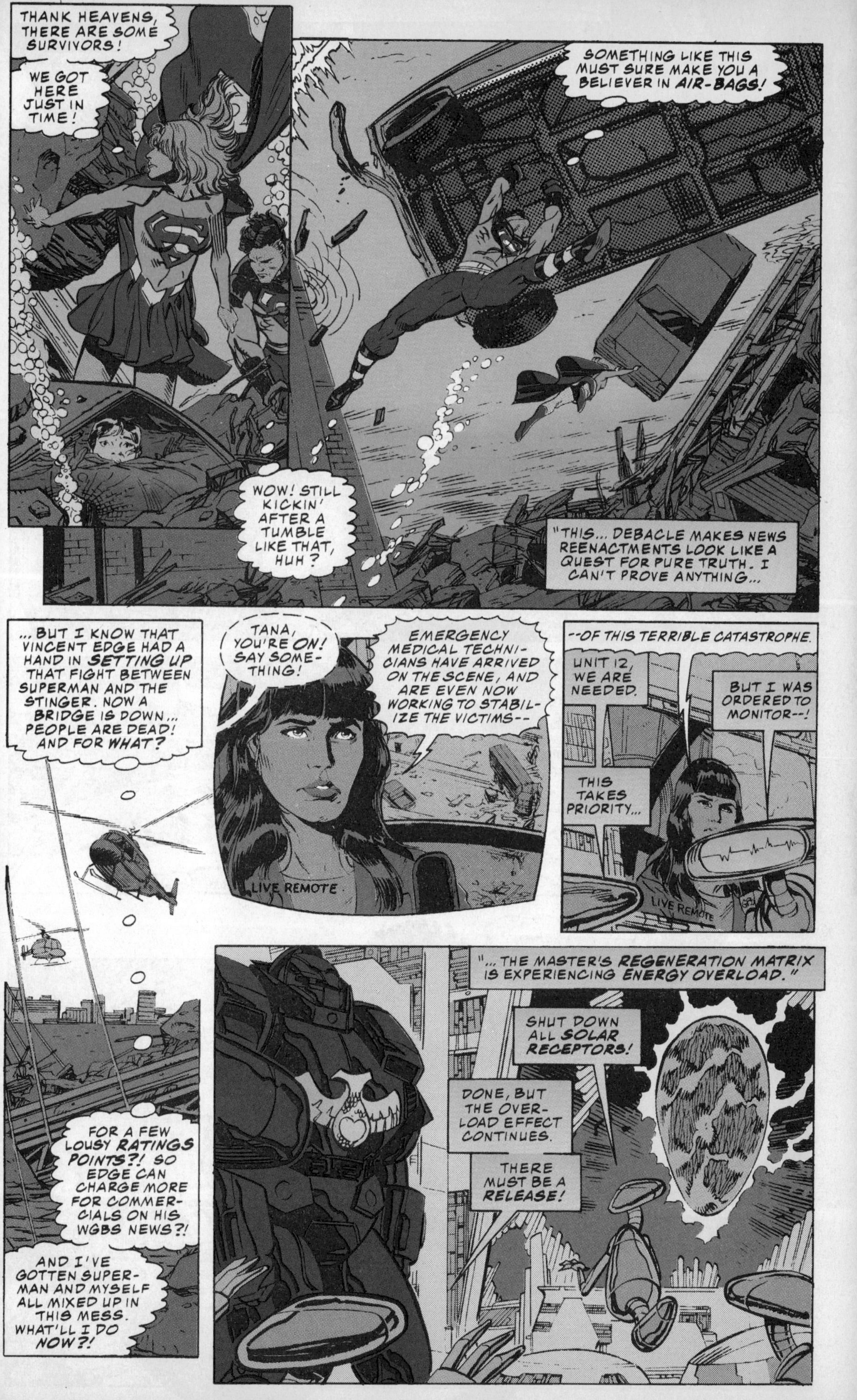
THANK HEAVENS, THERE ARE SOME SURVIVORS!
WE GOT HERE JUST IN TIME!
SOMETHING LIKE THIS MUST SURE MAKE YOU A BELIEVER IN AIR-BAGS!
WOW! STILL KICKIN' AFTER A TUMBLE LIKE THAT, HUH?
"THIS... DEBACLE MAKES NEWS REENACTMENTS LOOK LIKE A QUEST FOR PURE TRUTH. I CAN'T PROVE ANYTHING...
... BUT I KNOW THAT VINCENT EDGE HAD A HAND IN SETTING UP THAT FIGHT BETWEEN SUPERMAN AND THE STINGER. NOW A BRIDGE IS DOWN... PEOPLE ARE DEAD! AND FOR WHAT?
TANA, YOU'RE ON! SAY SOMETHING!
EMERGENCY MEDICAL TECHNICIANS HAVE ARRIVED ON THE SCENE, AND ARE EVEN NOW WORKING TO STABILIZE THE VICTIMS--
LIVE REMOTE
--OF THIS TERRIBLE CATASTROPHE.
UNIT 12, WE ARE NEEDED.
BUT I WAS ORDERED TO MONITOR--!
THIS TAKES PRIORITY...
LIVE REMOTE
FOR A FEW LOUSY RATINGS POINTS?! SO EDGE CAN CHARGE MORE FOR COMMERCIALS ON HIS WGBS NEWS?!
AND I'VE GOTTEN SUPERMAN AND MYSELF ALL MIXED UP IN THIS MESS. WHAT'LL I DO NOW?!
"... THE MASTER'S REGENERATION MATRIX IS EXPERIENCING ENERGY OVERLOAD."
SHUT DOWN ALL SOLAR RECEPTORS!
DONE, BUT THE OVERLOAD EFFECT CONTINUES.
THERE MUST BE A RELEASE!

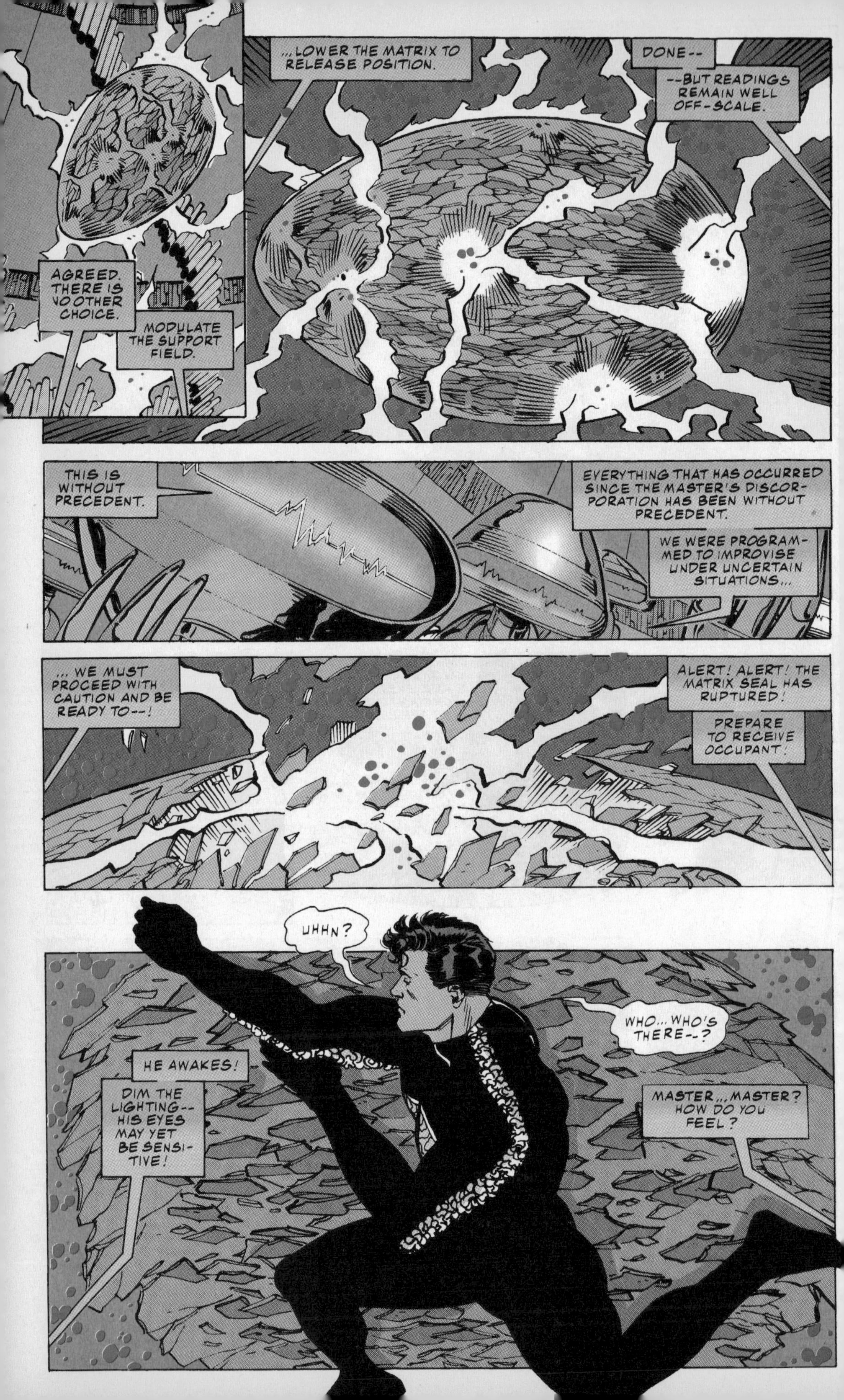
AGREED. THERE IS NO OTHER CHOICE.
MODULATE THE SUPPORT FIELD.
...LOWER THE MATRIX TO RELEASE POSITION.
DONE--
--BUT READINGS REMAIN WELL OFF-SCALE.
THIS IS WITHOUT PRECEDENT.
EVERYTHING THAT HAS OCCURRED SINCE THE MASTER'S DISCOR-PORATION HAS BEEN WITHOUT PRECEDENT.
WE WERE PROGRAM-MED TO IMPROVISE UNDER UNCERTAIN SITUATIONS...
... WE MUST PROCEED WITH CAUTION AND BE READY TO--!
ALERT! ALERT! THE MATRIX SEAL HAS RUPTURED!
PREPARE TO RECEIVE OCCUPANT!
UHHN?
WHO... WHO'S THERE--?
HE AWAKES!
DIM THE LIGHTING-- HIS EYES MAY YET BE SENSI-TIVE!
MASTER... MASTER? HOW DO YOU FEEL?

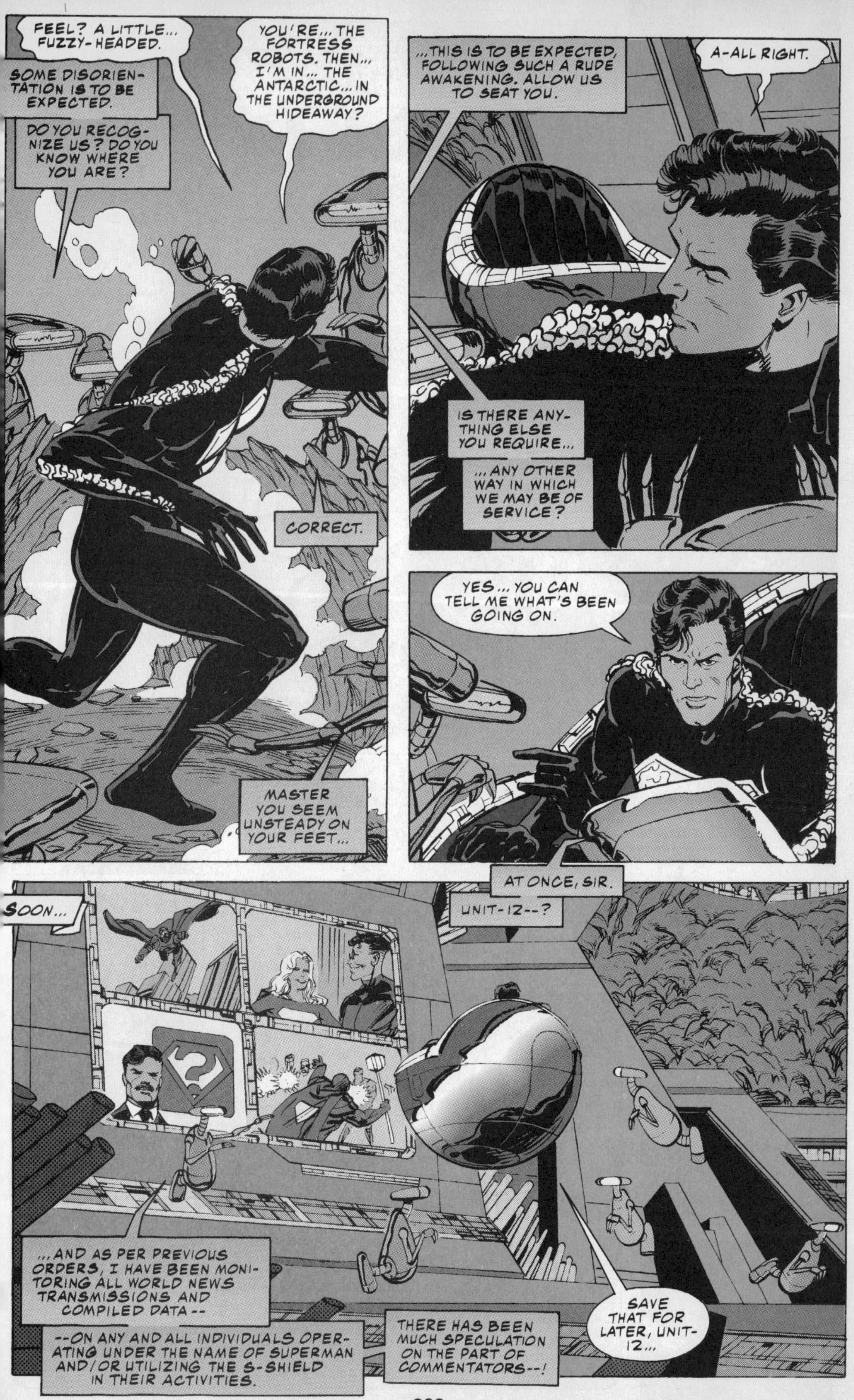

FEEL? A LITTLE... FUZZY-HEADED.
SOME DISORIENTATION IS TO BE EXPECTED.
DO YOU RECOGNIZE US? DO YOU KNOW WHERE YOU ARE?
YOU'RE... THE FORTRESS ROBOTS. THEN... I'M IN... THE ANTARCTIC... IN THE UNDERGROUND HIDEAWAY?
CORRECT.
MASTER YOU SEEM UNSTEADY ON YOUR FEET...
...THIS IS TO BE EXPECTED, FOLLOWING SUCH A RUDE AWAKENING. ALLOW US TO SEAT YOU.
A-ALL RIGHT.
IS THERE ANYTHING ELSE YOU REQUIRE...
...ANY OTHER WAY IN WHICH WE MAY BE OF SERVICE?
YES... YOU CAN TELL ME WHAT'S BEEN GOING ON.
AT ONCE, SIR.
SOON...
UNIT-12--?
...AND AS PER PREVIOUS ORDERS, I HAVE BEEN MONITORING ALL WORLD NEWS TRANSMISSIONS AND COMPILED DATA--
--ON ANY AND ALL INDIVIDUALS OPERATING UNDER THE NAME OF SUPERMAN AND/OR UTILIZING THE S-SHIELD IN THEIR ACTIVITIES.
THERE HAS BEEN MUCH SPECULATION ON THE PART OF COMMENTATORS--!
SAVE THAT FOR LATER, UNIT-12...

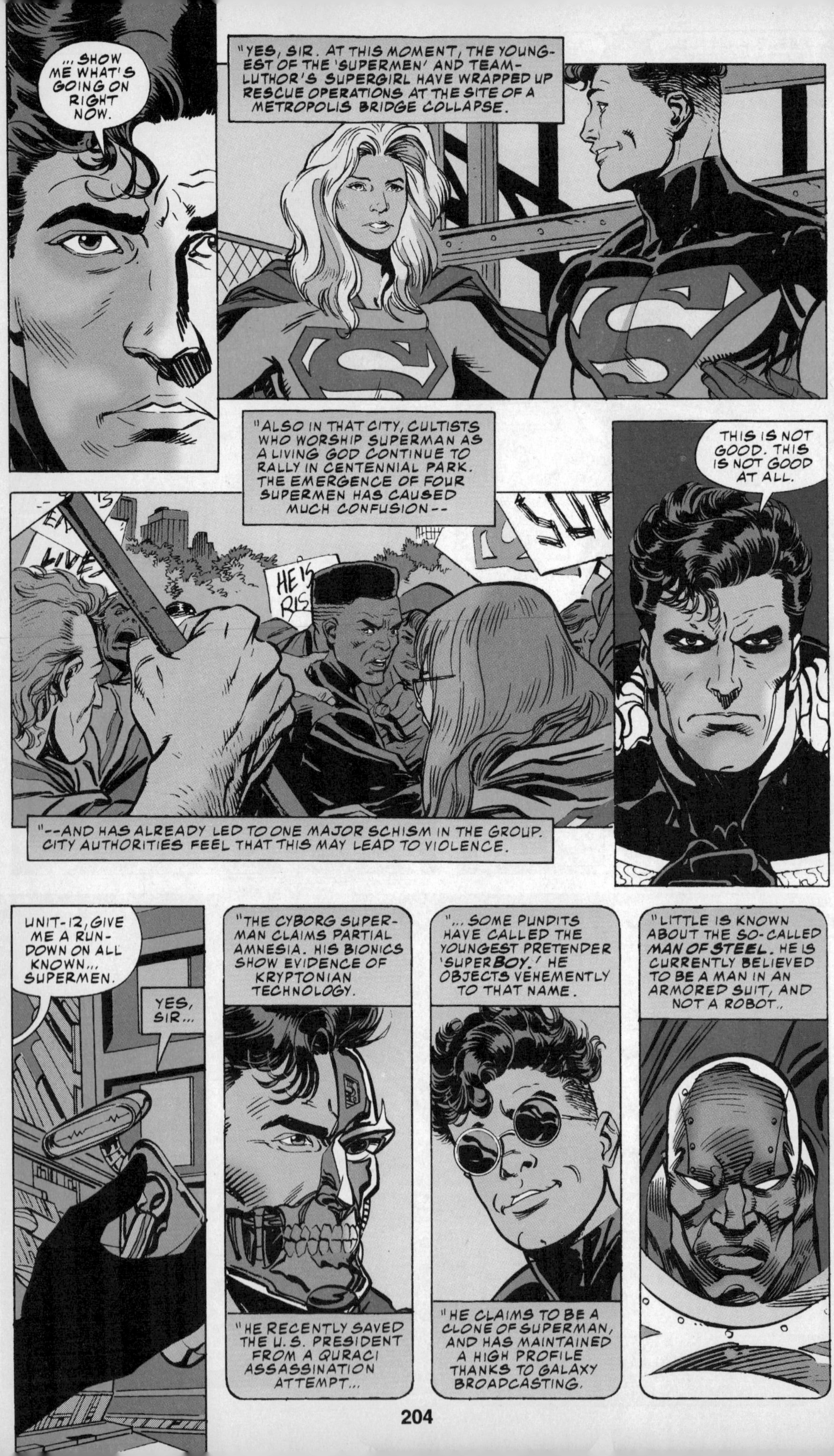
...SHOW ME WHAT'S GOING ON RIGHT NOW.
"YES, SIR. AT THIS MOMENT, THE YOUNGEST OF THE 'SUPERMEN' AND TEAM-LUTHOR'S SUPERGIRL HAVE WRAPPED UP RESCUE OPERATIONS AT THE SITE OF A METROPOLIS BRIDGE COLLAPSE.
"ALSO IN THAT CITY, CULTISTS WHO WORSHIP SUPERMAN AS A LIVING GOD CONTINUE TO RALLY IN CENTENNIAL PARK. THE EMERGENCE OF FOUR SUPERMEN HAS CAUSED MUCH CONFUSION--
"--AND HAS ALREADY LED TO ONE MAJOR SCHISM IN THE GROUP. CITY AUTHORITIES FEEL THAT THIS MAY LEAD TO VIOLENCE.
THIS IS NOT GOOD. THIS IS NOT GOOD AT ALL.
UNIT-12, GIVE ME A RUNDOWN ON ALL KNOWN... SUPERMEN.
YES, SIR...
"THE CYBORG SUPERMAN CLAIMS PARTIAL AMNESIA. HIS BIONICS SHOW EVIDENCE OF KRYPTONIAN TECHNOLOGY.
"HE RECENTLY SAVED THE U.S. PRESIDENT FROM A QURACI ASSASSINATION ATTEMPT...
"...SOME PUNDITS HAVE CALLED THE YOUNGEST PRETENDER 'SUPERBOY.' HE OBJECTS VEHEMENTLY TO THAT NAME.
"HE CLAIMS TO BE A CLONE OF SUPERMAN, AND HAS MAINTAINED A HIGH PROFILE THANKS TO GALAXY BROADCASTING.
"LITTLE IS KNOWN ABOUT THE SO-CALLED MAN OF STEEL. HE IS CURRENTLY BELIEVED TO BE A MAN IN AN ARMORED SUIT, AND NOT A ROBOT..

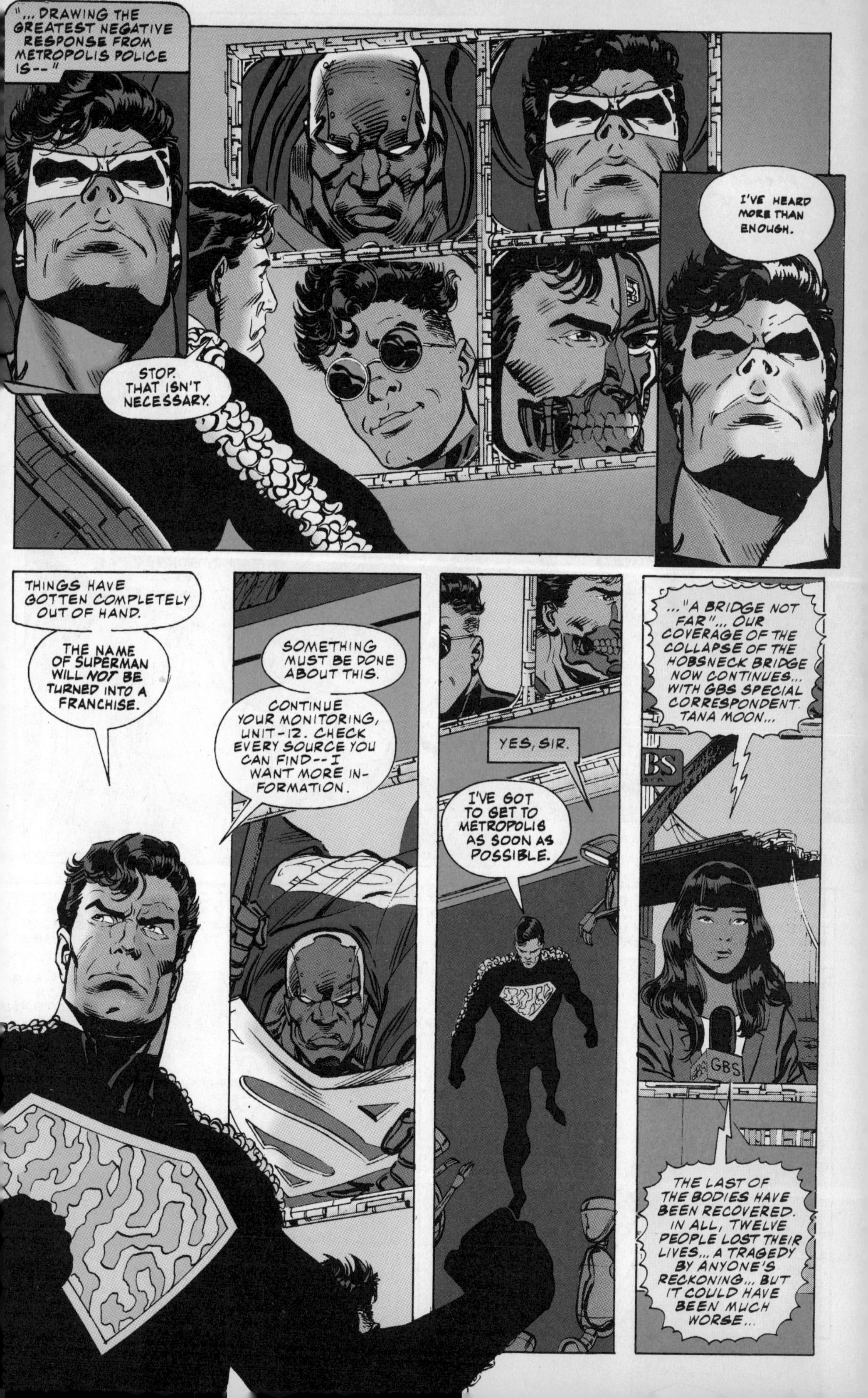
"... DRAWING THE GREATEST NEGATIVE RESPONSE FROM METROPOLIS POLICE IS--"
STOP. THAT ISN'T NECESSARY.
I'VE HEARD MORE THAN ENOUGH.
THINGS HAVE GOTTEN COMPLETELY OUT OF HAND.
THE NAME OF SUPERMAN WILL NOT BE TURNED INTO A FRANCHISE.
SOMETHING MUST BE DONE ABOUT THIS.
CONTINUE YOUR MONITORING, UNIT-12. CHECK EVERY SOURCE YOU CAN FIND-- I WANT MORE INFORMATION.
YES, SIR.
I'VE GOT TO GET TO METROPOLIS AS SOON AS POSSIBLE.
..."A BRIDGE NOT FAR"... OUR COVERAGE OF THE COLLAPSE OF THE HOBSNECK BRIDGE NOW CONTINUES... WITH GBS SPECIAL CORRESPONDENT TANA MOON...
GBS
THE LAST OF THE BODIES HAVE BEEN RECOVERED. IN ALL, TWELVE PEOPLE LOST THEIR LIVES... A TRAGEDY BY ANYONE'S RECKONING... BUT IT COULD HAVE BEEN MUCH WORSE...

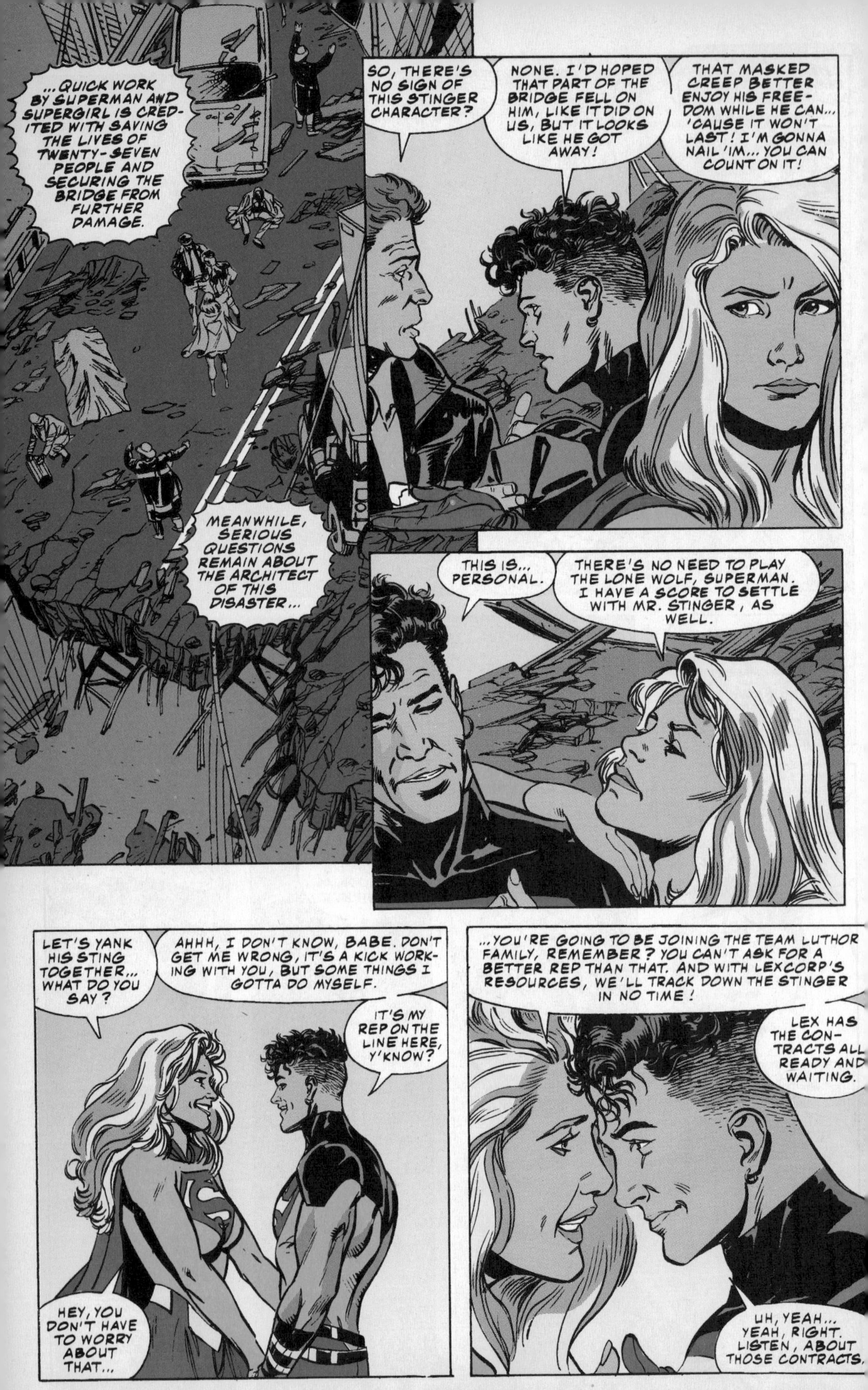
...QUICK WORK BY SUPERMAN AND SUPERGIRL IS CREDITED WITH SAVING THE LIVES OF TWENTY-SEVEN PEOPLE AND SECURING THE BRIDGE FROM FURTHER DAMAGE.
MEANWHILE, SERIOUS QUESTIONS REMAIN ABOUT THE ARCHITECT OF THIS DISASTER...
SO, THERE'S NO SIGN OF THIS STINGER CHARACTER?
NONE. I'D HOPED THAT PART OF THE BRIDGE FELL ON HIM, LIKE IT DID ON US, BUT IT LOOKS LIKE HE GOT AWAY!
THAT MASKED CREEP BETTER ENJOY HIS FREEDOM WHILE HE CAN... 'CAUSE IT WON'T LAST! I'M GONNA NAIL 'IM... YOU CAN COUNT ON IT!
THIS IS... PERSONAL.
THERE'S NO NEED TO PLAY THE LONE WOLF, SUPERMAN. I HAVE A SCORE TO SETTLE WITH MR. STINGER, AS WELL.
LET'S YANK HIS STING TOGETHER... WHAT DO YOU SAY?
AHHH, I DON'T KNOW, BABE. DON'T GET ME WRONG, IT'S A KICK WORKING WITH YOU, BUT SOME THINGS I GOTTA DO MYSELF.
IT'S MY REP ON THE LINE HERE, Y'KNOW?
HEY, YOU DON'T HAVE TO WORRY ABOUT THAT...
...YOU'RE GOING TO BE JOINING THE TEAM LUTHOR FAMILY, REMEMBER? YOU CAN'T ASK FOR A BETTER REP THAN THAT. AND WITH LEXCORP'S RESOURCES, WE'LL TRACK DOWN THE STINGER IN NO TIME!
LEX HAS THE CONTRACTS ALL READY AND WAITING.
UH, YEAH... YEAH, RIGHT. LISTEN, ABOUT THOSE CONTRACTS,

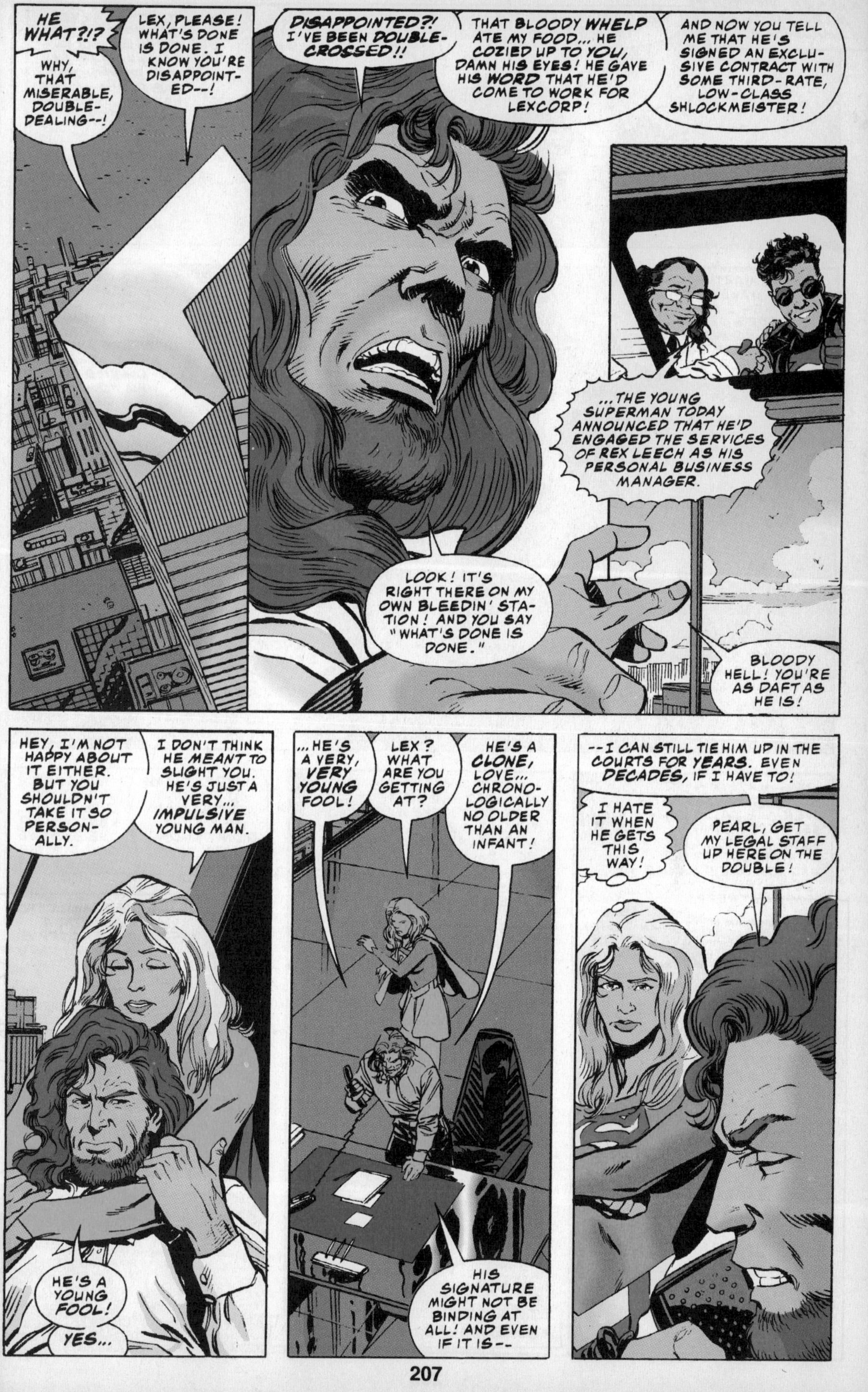
HE WHAT?!?
WHY, THAT MISERABLE, DOUBLE-DEALING--!
LEX, PLEASE! WHAT'S DONE IS DONE. I KNOW YOU'RE DISAPPOINTED--!
DISAPPOINTED?! I'VE BEEN DOUBLE-CROSSED!!
THAT BLOODY WHELP ATE MY FOOD... HE COZIED UP TO YOU, DAMN HIS EYES! HE GAVE HIS WORD THAT HE'D COME TO WORK FOR LEXCORP!
AND NOW YOU TELL ME THAT HE'S SIGNED AN EXCLUSIVE CONTRACT WITH SOME THIRD-RATE, LOW-CLASS SHLOCKMEISTER!
...THE YOUNG SUPERMAN TODAY ANNOUNCED THAT HE'D ENGAGED THE SERVICES OF REX LEECH AS HIS PERSONAL BUSINESS MANAGER.
LOOK! IT'S RIGHT THERE ON MY OWN BLEEDIN' STATION! AND YOU SAY "WHAT'S DONE IS DONE."
BLOODY HELL! YOU'RE AS DAFT AS HE IS!
HEY, I'M NOT HAPPY ABOUT IT EITHER. BUT YOU SHOULDN'T TAKE IT SO PERSONALLY.
I DON'T THINK HE MEANT TO SLIGHT YOU. HE'S JUST A VERY... IMPULSIVE YOUNG MAN.
HE'S A YOUNG FOOL!
YES...
...HE'S A VERY, VERY YOUNG FOOL!
LEX? WHAT ARE YOU GETTING AT?
HE'S A CLONE, LOVE... CHRONOLOGICALLY NO OLDER THAN AN INFANT!
HIS SIGNATURE MIGHT NOT BE BINDING AT ALL! AND EVEN IF IT IS--
--I CAN STILL TIE HIM UP IN THE COURTS FOR YEARS. EVEN DECADES, IF I HAVE TO!
I HATE IT WHEN HE GETS THIS WAY!
PEARL, GET MY LEGAL STAFF UP HERE ON THE DOUBLE!

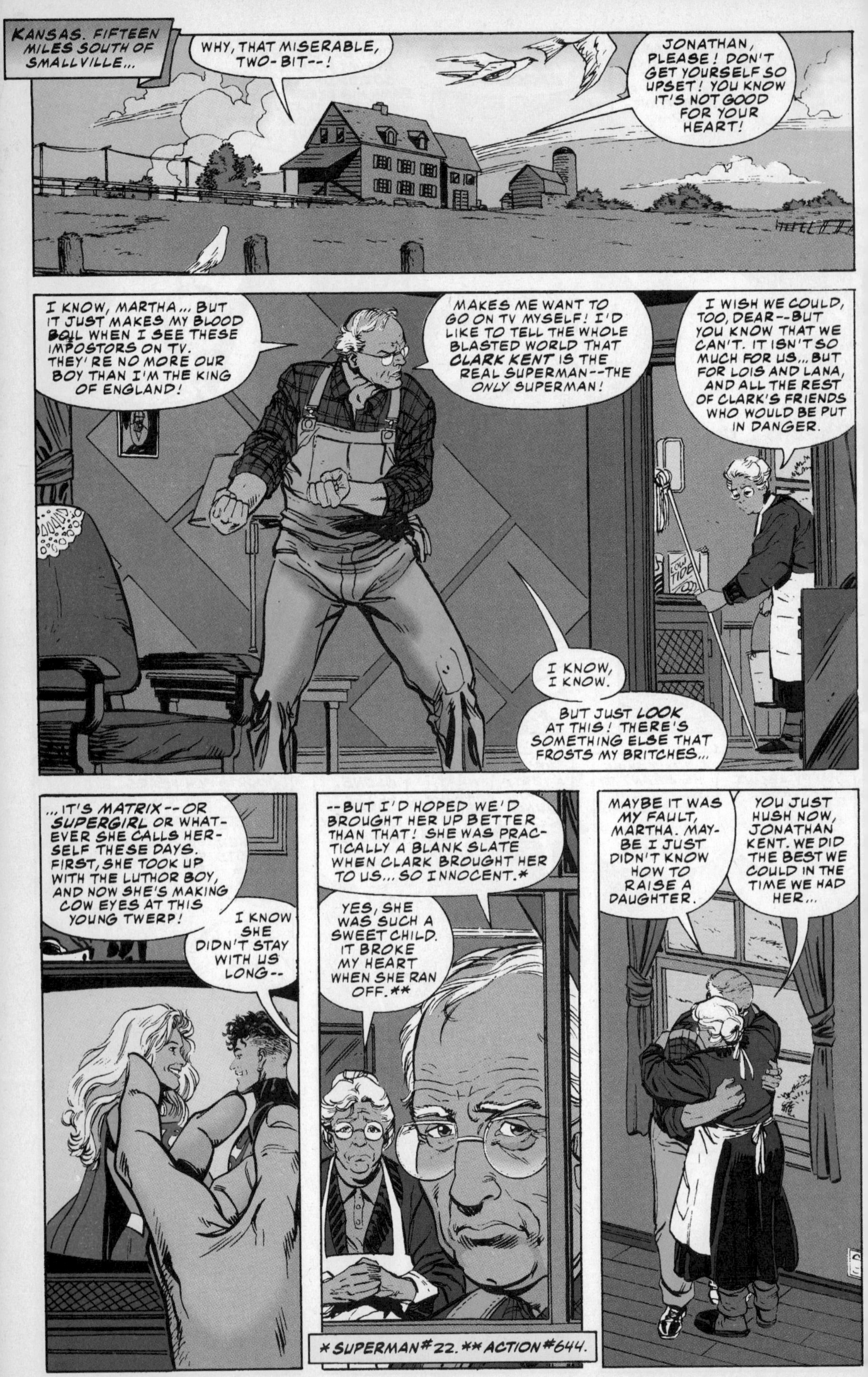
KANSAS. FIFTEEN MILES SOUTH OF SMALLVILLE...
WHY, THAT MISERABLE, TWO-BIT--!
JONATHAN, PLEASE! DON'T GET YOURSELF SO UPSET! YOU KNOW IT'S NOT GOOD FOR YOUR HEART!
I KNOW, MARTHA... BUT IT JUST MAKES MY BLOOD BOIL WHEN I SEE THESE IMPOSTORS ON TV. THEY'RE NO MORE OUR BOY THAN I'M THE KING OF ENGLAND!
MAKES ME WANT TO GO ON TV MYSELF! I'D LIKE TO TELL THE WHOLE BLASTED WORLD THAT CLARK KENT IS THE REAL SUPERMAN--THE ONLY SUPERMAN!
I WISH WE COULD, TOO, DEAR--BUT YOU KNOW THAT WE CAN'T. IT ISN'T SO MUCH FOR US... BUT FOR LOIS AND LANA, AND ALL THE REST OF CLARK'S FRIENDS WHO WOULD BE PUT IN DANGER.
I KNOW, I KNOW.
BUT JUST LOOK AT THIS! THERE'S SOMETHING ELSE THAT FROSTS MY BRITCHES...
...IT'S MATRIX--OR SUPERGIRL OR WHATEVER SHE CALLS HERSELF THESE DAYS. FIRST, SHE TOOK UP WITH THE LUTHOR BOY, AND NOW SHE'S MAKING COW EYES AT THIS YOUNG TWERP!
I KNOW SHE DIDN'T STAY WITH US LONG--
--BUT I'D HOPED WE'D BROUGHT HER UP BETTER THAN THAT! SHE WAS PRACTICALLY A BLANK SLATE WHEN CLARK BROUGHT HER TO US... SO INNOCENT.*
YES, SHE WAS SUCH A SWEET CHILD. IT BROKE MY HEART WHEN SHE RAN OFF.**
*SUPERMAN #22. **ACTION #644.
MAYBE IT WAS MY FAULT, MARTHA. MAYBE I JUST DIDN'T KNOW HOW TO RAISE A DAUGHTER.
YOU JUST HUSH NOW, JONATHAN KENT. WE DID THE BEST WE COULD IN THE TIME WE HAD HER...

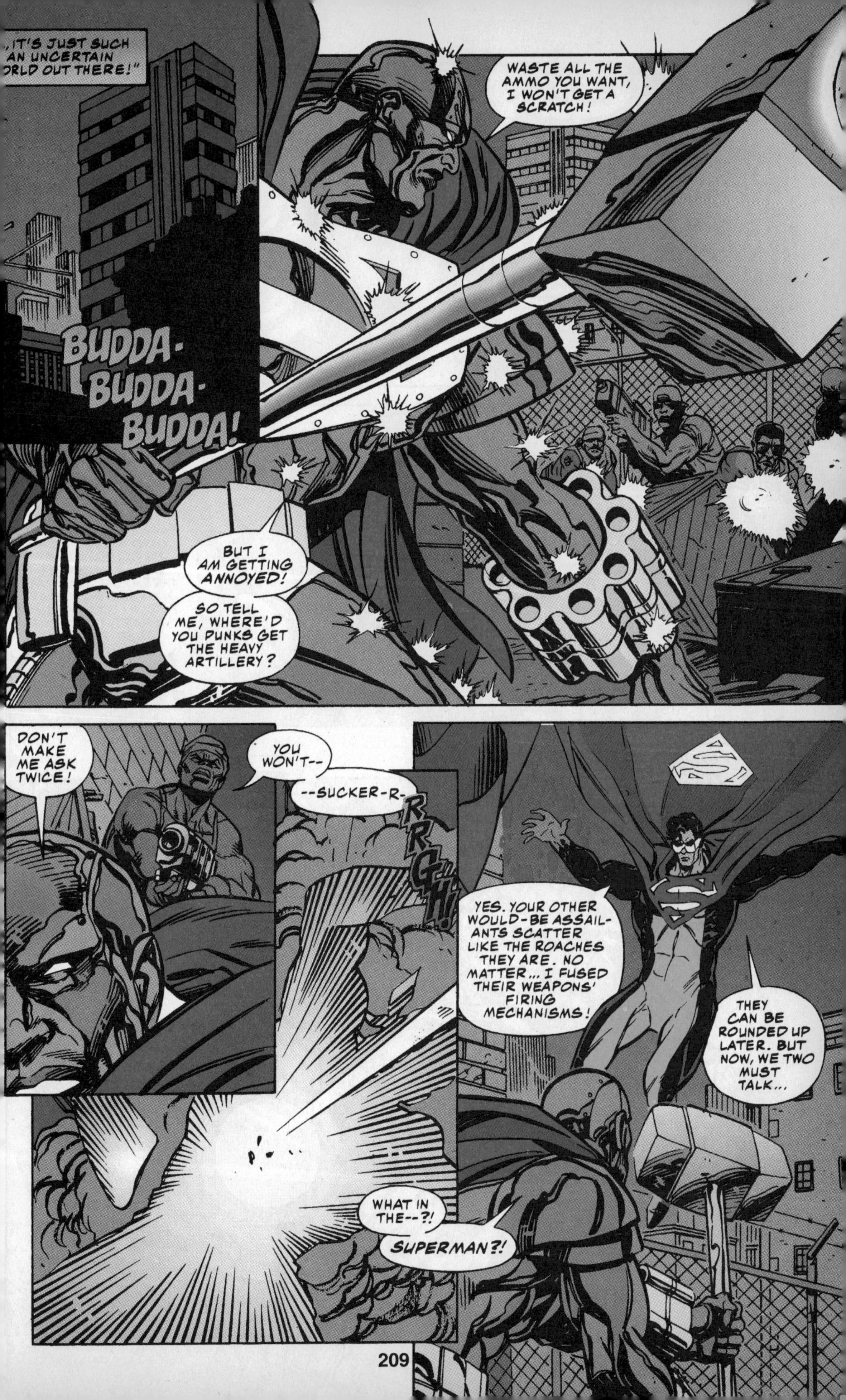

...IT'S JUST SUCH AN UNCERTAIN WORLD OUT THERE!"
WASTE ALL THE AMMO YOU WANT, I WON'T GET A SCRATCH!
BUDDA-BUDDA-BUDDA!
BUT I AM GETTING ANNOYED!
SO TELL ME, WHERE'D YOU PUNKS GET THE HEAVY ARTILLERY?
DON'T MAKE ME ASK TWICE!
YOU WON'T--
--SUCKER-R-RRGH!
WHAT IN THE--?!
SUPERMAN?!
YES. YOUR OTHER WOULD-BE ASSAIL-ANTS SCATTER LIKE THE ROACHES THEY ARE. NO MATTER... I FUSED THEIR WEAPONS' FIRING MECHANISMS!
THEY CAN BE ROUNDED UP LATER. BUT NOW, WE TWO MUST TALK...

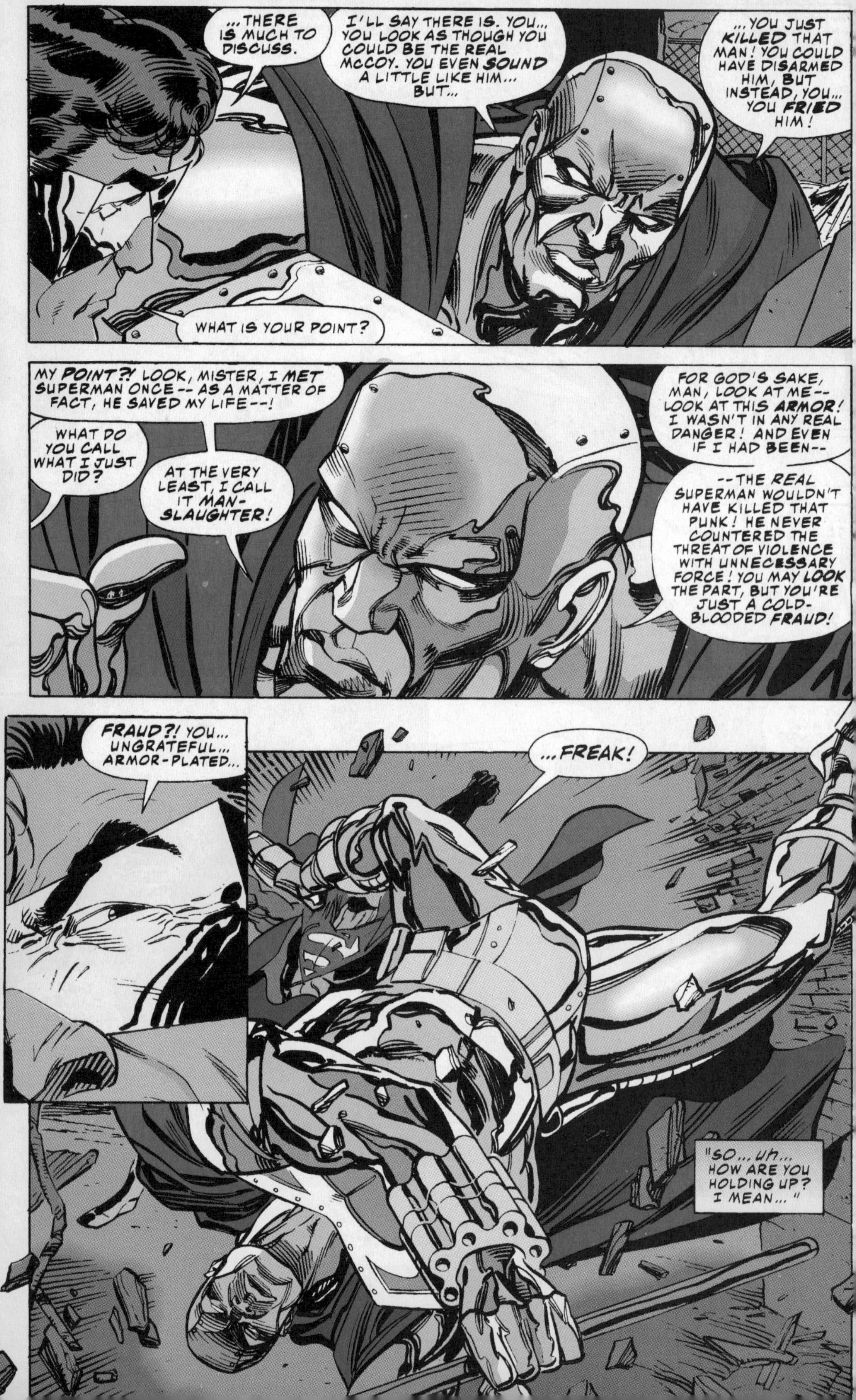
...THERE IS MUCH TO DISCUSS.
I'LL SAY THERE IS. YOU... YOU LOOK AS THOUGH YOU COULD BE THE REAL McCOY. YOU EVEN SOUND A LITTLE LIKE HIM... BUT...
...YOU JUST KILLED THAT MAN! YOU COULD HAVE DISARMED HIM, BUT INSTEAD, YOU... YOU FRIED HIM!
WHAT IS YOUR POINT?
MY POINT?! LOOK, MISTER, I MET SUPERMAN ONCE -- AS A MATTER OF FACT, HE SAVED MY LIFE --!
WHAT DO YOU CALL WHAT I JUST DID?
AT THE VERY LEAST, I CALL IT MAN-SLAUGHTER!
FOR GOD'S SAKE, MAN, LOOK AT ME -- LOOK AT THIS ARMOR! I WASN'T IN ANY REAL DANGER! AND EVEN IF I HAD BEEN --
-- THE REAL SUPERMAN WOULDN'T HAVE KILLED THAT PUNK! HE NEVER COUNTERED THE THREAT OF VIOLENCE WITH UNNECESSARY FORCE! YOU MAY LOOK THE PART, BUT YOU'RE JUST A COLD-BLOODED FRAUD!
FRAUD?! YOU... UNGRATEFUL... ARMOR-PLATED...
...FREAK!
"SO... uh... HOW ARE YOU HOLDING UP? I MEAN..."

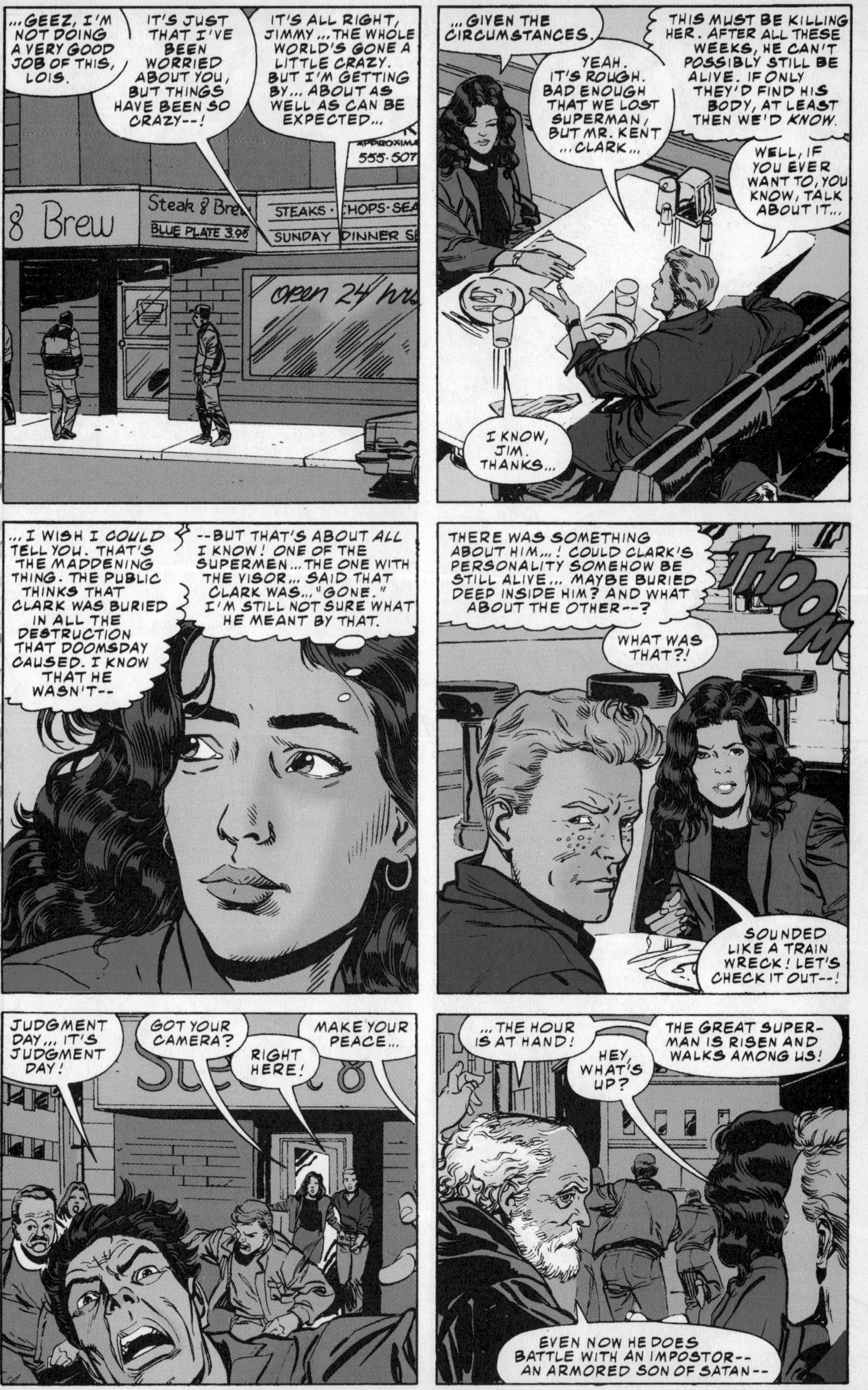
...GEEZ, I'M NOT DOING A VERY GOOD JOB OF THIS, LOIS.
IT'S JUST THAT I'VE BEEN WORRIED ABOUT YOU, BUT THINGS HAVE BEEN SO CRAZY--!
IT'S ALL RIGHT, JIMMY... THE WHOLE WORLD'S GONE A LITTLE CRAZY. BUT I'M GETTING BY... ABOUT AS WELL AS CAN BE EXPECTED...
Steak & Brew
BLUE PLATE 3.95
STEAKS · CHOPS · SEA
SUNDAY DINNER S
open 24 hrs
...GIVEN THE CIRCUMSTANCES.
YEAH. IT'S ROUGH. BAD ENOUGH THAT WE LOST SUPERMAN, BUT MR. KENT ...CLARK...
THIS MUST BE KILLING HER. AFTER ALL THESE WEEKS, HE CAN'T POSSIBLY STILL BE ALIVE. IF ONLY THEY'D FIND HIS BODY, AT LEAST THEN WE'D KNOW.
WELL, IF YOU EVER WANT TO, YOU KNOW, TALK ABOUT IT...
I KNOW, JIM. THANKS...
...I WISH I COULD TELL YOU. THAT'S THE MADDENING THING. THE PUBLIC THINKS THAT CLARK WAS BURIED IN ALL THE DESTRUCTION THAT DOOMSDAY CAUSED. I KNOW THAT HE WASN'T--
--BUT THAT'S ABOUT ALL I KNOW! ONE OF THE SUPERMEN... THE ONE WITH THE VISOR... SAID THAT CLARK WAS... "GONE." I'M STILL NOT SURE WHAT HE MEANT BY THAT.
THERE WAS SOMETHING ABOUT HIM...! COULD CLARK'S PERSONALITY SOMEHOW BE STILL ALIVE... MAYBE BURIED DEEP INSIDE HIM? AND WHAT ABOUT THE OTHER--?
THOOM
WHAT WAS THAT?!
SOUNDED LIKE A TRAIN WRECK! LET'S CHECK IT OUT--!
JUDGMENT DAY... IT'S JUDGMENT DAY!
GOT YOUR CAMERA?
RIGHT HERE!
MAKE YOUR PEACE...
...THE HOUR IS AT HAND!
HEY, WHAT'S UP?
THE GREAT SUPERMAN IS RISEN AND WALKS AMONG US!
EVEN NOW HE DOES BATTLE WITH AN IMPOSTOR-- AN ARMORED SON OF SATAN--

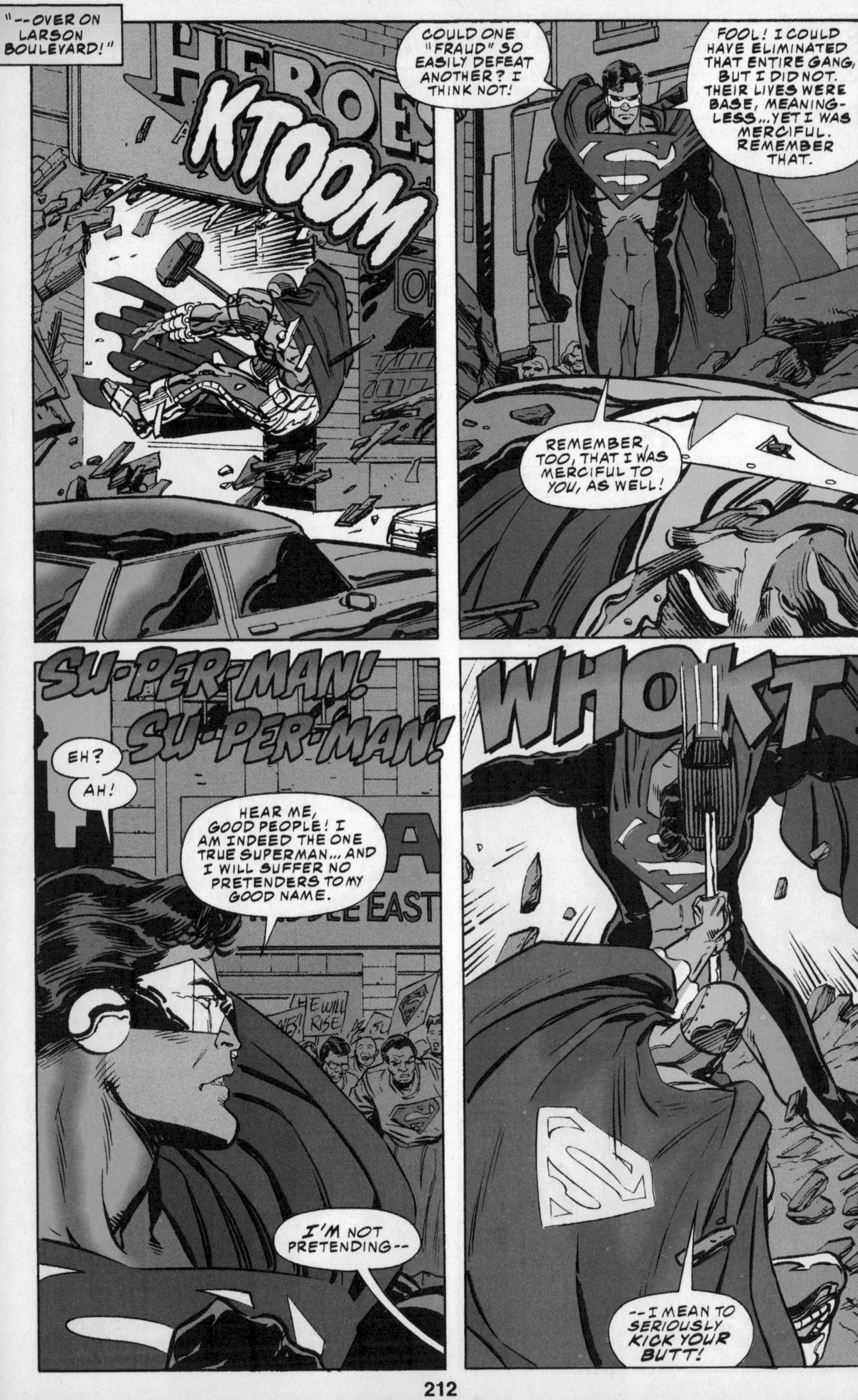
"--OVER ON LARSON BOULEVARD!"
HEROES
KTOOM
COULD ONE "FRAUD" SO EASILY DEFEAT ANOTHER? I THINK NOT!
FOOL! I COULD HAVE ELIMINATED THAT ENTIRE GANG, BUT I DID NOT. THEIR LIVES WERE BASE, MEANINGLESS... YET I WAS MERCIFUL. REMEMBER THAT.
REMEMBER TOO, THAT I WAS MERCIFUL TO YOU, AS WELL!
SU-PER-MAN! SU-PER-MAN!
EH?
AH!
HEAR ME, GOOD PEOPLE! I AM INDEED THE ONE TRUE SUPERMAN... AND I WILL SUFFER NO PRETENDERS TO MY GOOD NAME.
HE WILL RISE
I'M NOT PRETENDING--
WHOKT
--I MEAN TO SERIOUSLY KICK YOUR BUTT!

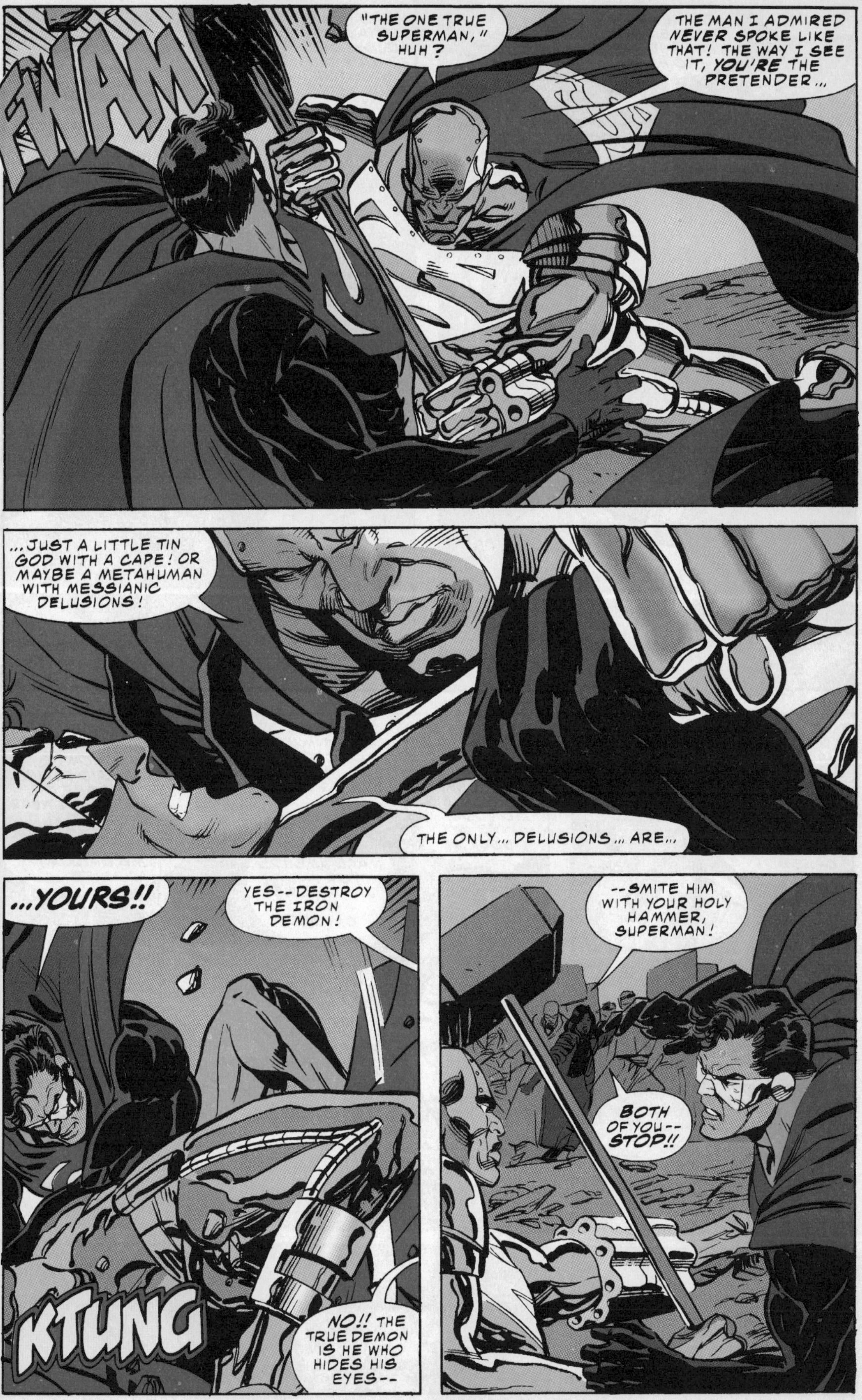
FWAM
"THE ONE TRUE SUPERMAN," HUH?
THE MAN I ADMIRED NEVER SPOKE LIKE THAT! THE WAY I SEE IT, YOU'RE THE PRETENDER...
...JUST A LITTLE TIN GOD WITH A CAPE! OR MAYBE A METAHUMAN WITH MESSIANIC DELUSIONS!
THE ONLY... DELUSIONS... ARE...
...YOURS!!
YES--DESTROY THE IRON DEMON!
KTUNG
NO!! THE TRUE DEMON IS HE WHO HIDES HIS EYES--
--SMITE HIM WITH YOUR HOLY HAMMER, SUPERMAN!
BOTH OF YOU-- STOP!!

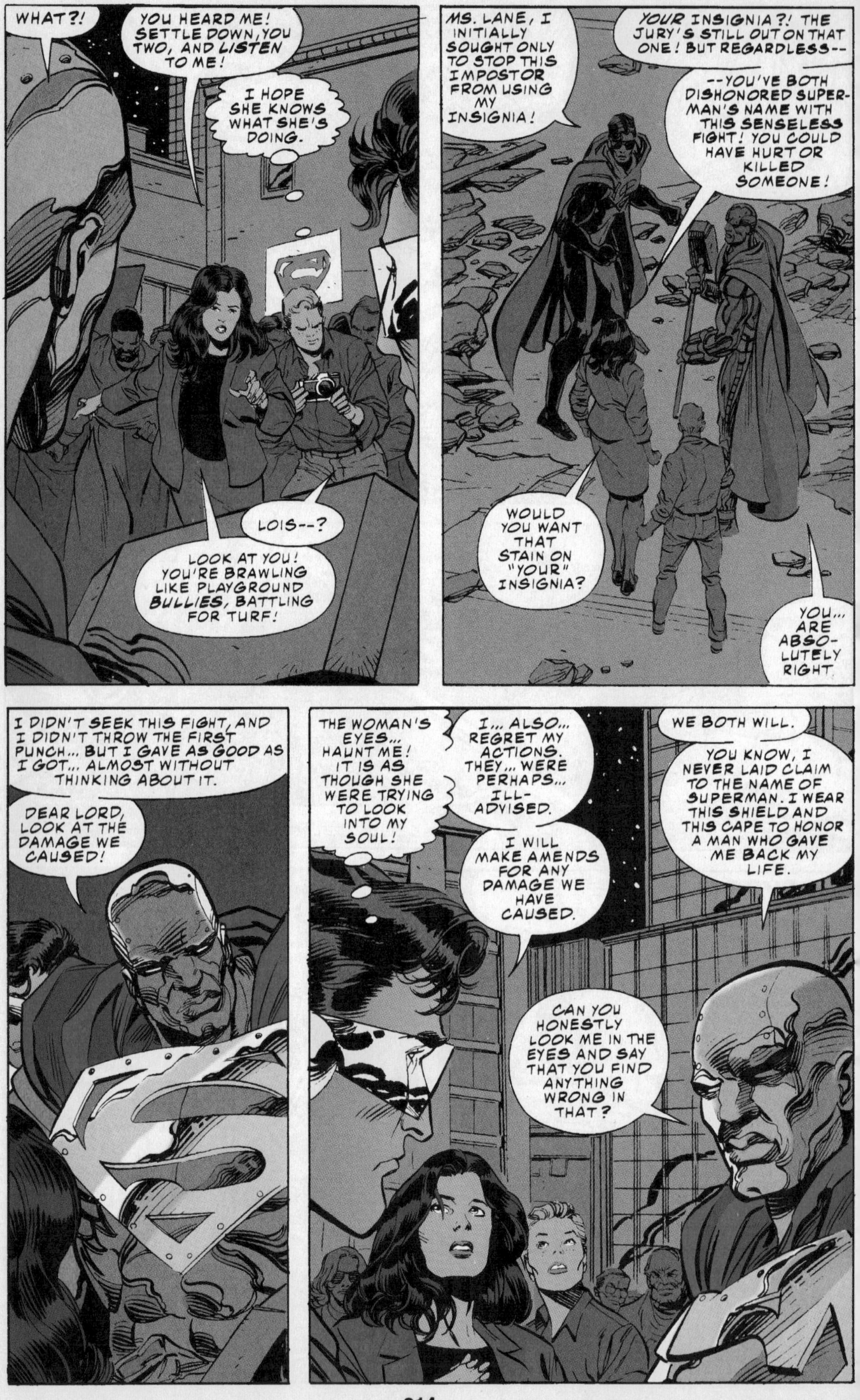

WHAT?!
YOU HEARD ME! SETTLE DOWN, YOU TWO, AND LISTEN TO ME!
I HOPE SHE KNOWS WHAT SHE'S DOING.
LOIS--?
LOOK AT YOU! YOU'RE BRAWLING LIKE PLAYGROUND BULLIES, BATTLING FOR TURF!
MS. LANE, I INITIALLY SOUGHT ONLY TO STOP THIS IMPOSTOR FROM USING MY INSIGNIA!
YOUR INSIGNIA?! THE JURY'S STILL OUT ON THAT ONE! BUT REGARDLESS--
--YOU'VE BOTH DISHONORED SUPER-MAN'S NAME WITH THIS SENSELESS FIGHT! YOU COULD HAVE HURT OR KILLED SOMEONE!
WOULD YOU WANT THAT STAIN ON "YOUR" INSIGNIA?
YOU... ARE ABSO-LUTELY RIGHT.
I DIDN'T SEEK THIS FIGHT, AND I DIDN'T THROW THE FIRST PUNCH... BUT I GAVE AS GOOD AS I GOT... ALMOST WITHOUT THINKING ABOUT IT.
DEAR LORD, LOOK AT THE DAMAGE WE CAUSED!
THE WOMAN'S EYES... HAUNT ME! IT IS AS THOUGH SHE WERE TRYING TO LOOK INTO MY SOUL!
I... ALSO... REGRET MY ACTIONS. THEY... WERE PERHAPS... ILL-ADVISED.
I WILL MAKE AMENDS FOR ANY DAMAGE WE HAVE CAUSED.
WE BOTH WILL.
YOU KNOW, I NEVER LAID CLAIM TO THE NAME OF SUPERMAN. I WEAR THIS SHIELD AND THIS CAPE TO HONOR A MAN WHO GAVE ME BACK MY LIFE.
CAN YOU HONESTLY LOOK ME IN THE EYES AND SAY THAT YOU FIND ANYTHING WRONG IN THAT?

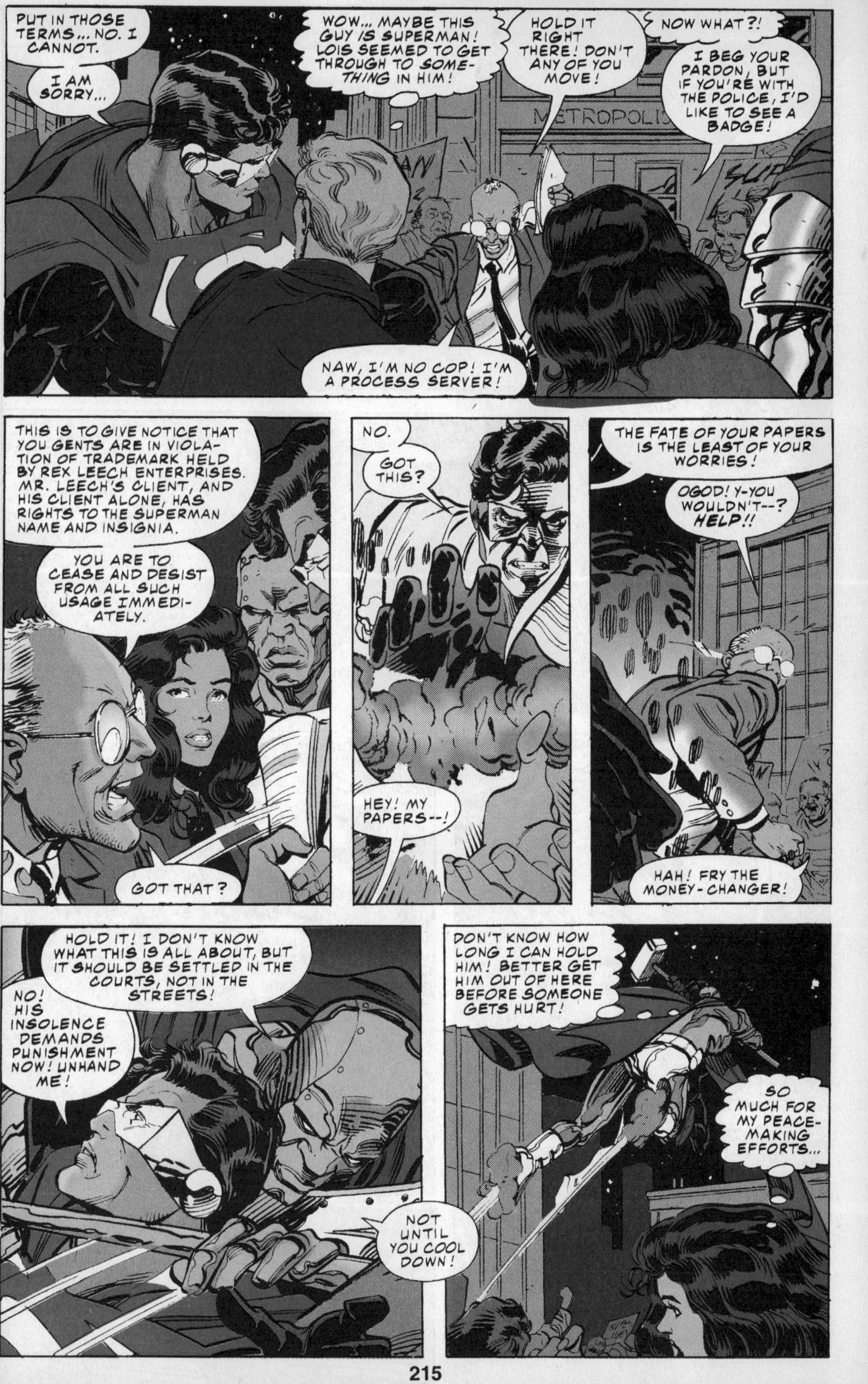

PUT IN THOSE TERMS... NO. I CANNOT.
I AM SORRY...
WOW... MAYBE THIS GUY IS SUPERMAN! LOIS SEEMED TO GET THROUGH TO SOMETHING IN HIM!
HOLD IT RIGHT THERE! DON'T ANY OF YOU MOVE!
NOW WHAT?!
I BEG YOUR PARDON, BUT IF YOU'RE WITH THE POLICE, I'D LIKE TO SEE A BADGE!
NAW, I'M NO COP! I'M A PROCESS SERVER!
THIS IS TO GIVE NOTICE THAT YOU GENTS ARE IN VIOLATION OF TRADEMARK HELD BY REX LEECH ENTERPRISES. MR. LEECH'S CLIENT, AND HIS CLIENT ALONE, HAS RIGHTS TO THE SUPERMAN NAME AND INSIGNIA.
YOU ARE TO CEASE AND DESIST FROM ALL SUCH USAGE IMMEDIATELY.
GOT THAT?
NO.
GOT THIS?
HEY! MY PAPERS--!
THE FATE OF YOUR PAPERS IS THE LEAST OF YOUR WORRIES!
OGOD! Y-YOU WOULDN'T--? HELP!!
HAH! FRY THE MONEY-CHANGER!
HOLD IT! I DON'T KNOW WHAT THIS IS ALL ABOUT, BUT IT SHOULD BE SETTLED IN THE COURTS, NOT IN THE STREETS!
NO! HIS INSOLENCE DEMANDS PUNISHMENT NOW! UNHAND ME!
NOT UNTIL YOU COOL DOWN!
DON'T KNOW HOW LONG I CAN HOLD HIM! BETTER GET HIM OUT OF HERE BEFORE SOMEONE GETS HURT!
SO MUCH FOR MY PEACE-MAKING EFFORTS...

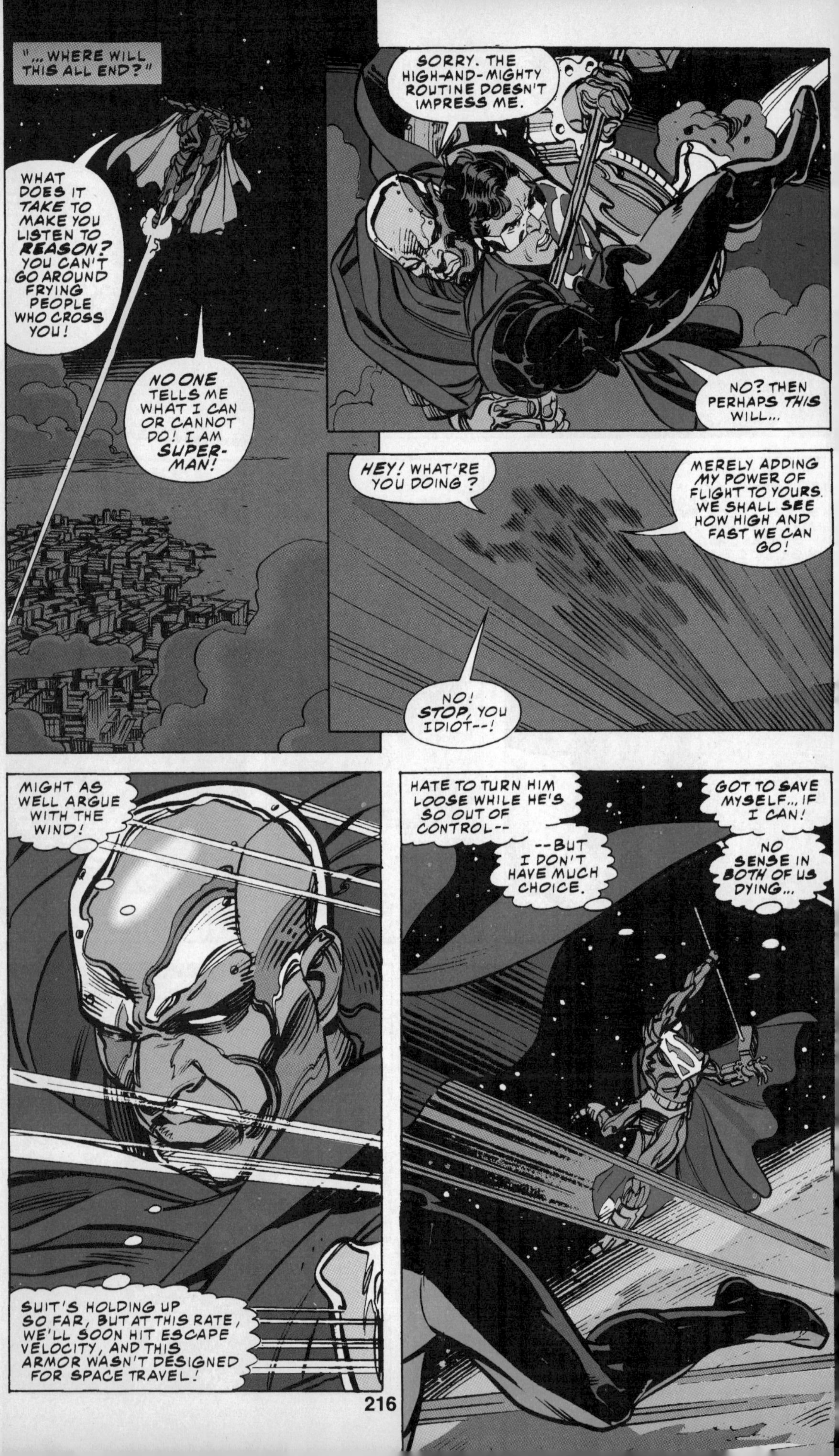
"...WHERE WILL THIS ALL END?"
WHAT DOES IT TAKE TO MAKE YOU LISTEN TO REASON? YOU CAN'T GO AROUND FRYING PEOPLE WHO CROSS YOU!
NO ONE TELLS ME WHAT I CAN OR CANNOT DO! I AM SUPERMAN!
SORRY. THE HIGH-AND-MIGHTY ROUTINE DOESN'T IMPRESS ME.
NO? THEN PERHAPS THIS WILL...
HEY! WHAT'RE YOU DOING?
MERELY ADDING MY POWER OF FLIGHT TO YOURS. WE SHALL SEE HOW HIGH AND FAST WE CAN GO!
NO! STOP, YOU IDIOT--!
MIGHT AS WELL ARGUE WITH THE WIND!
SUIT'S HOLDING UP SO FAR, BUT AT THIS RATE, WE'LL SOON HIT ESCAPE VELOCITY, AND THIS ARMOR WASN'T DESIGNED FOR SPACE TRAVEL!
HATE TO TURN HIM LOOSE WHILE HE'S SO OUT OF CONTROL--
--BUT I DON'T HAVE MUCH CHOICE.
GOT TO SAVE MYSELF... IF I CAN!
NO SENSE IN BOTH OF US DYING...

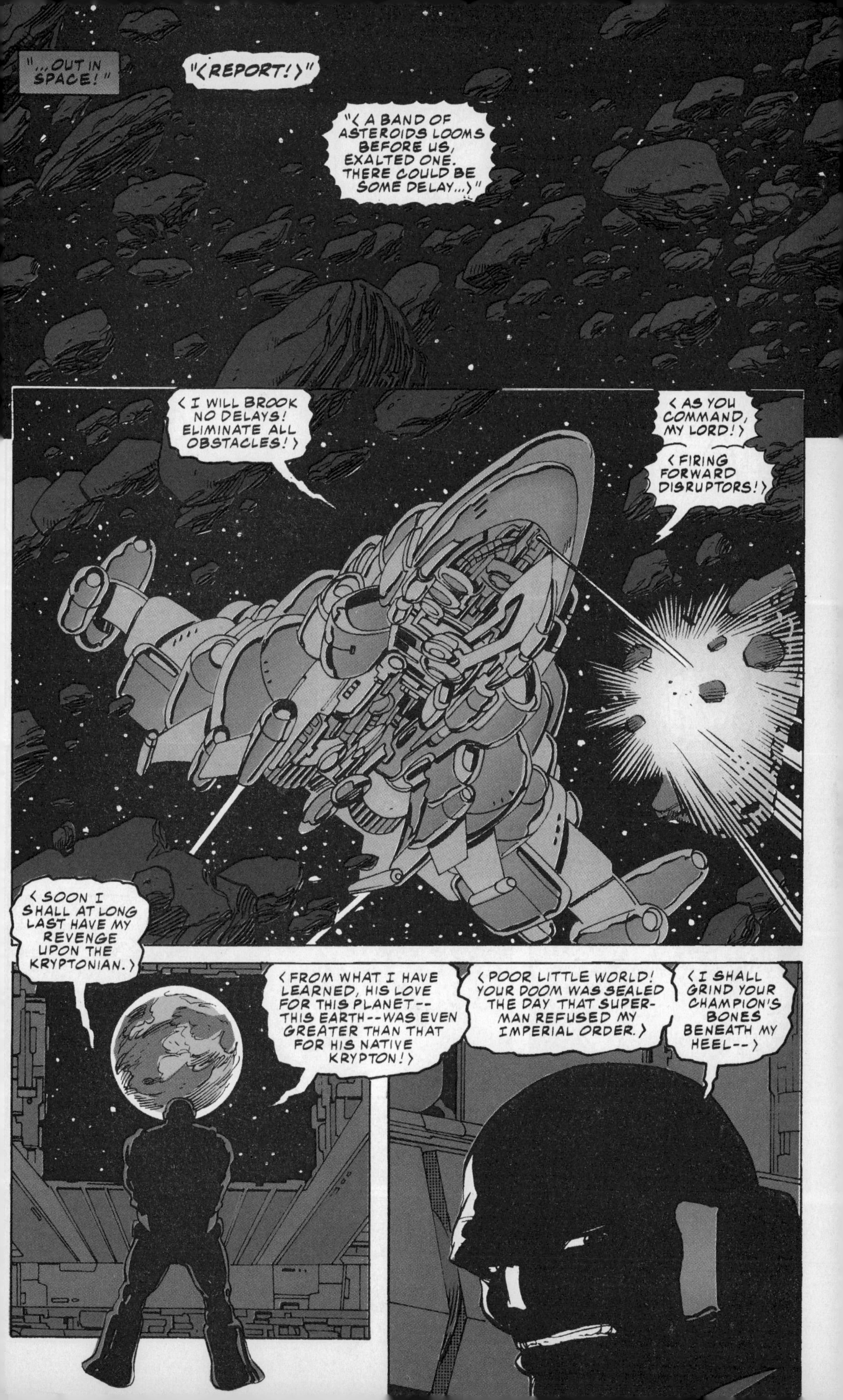
"...OUT IN SPACE!"
"< REPORT! >"
"< A BAND OF ASTEROIDS LOOMS BEFORE US, EXALTED ONE. THERE COULD BE SOME DELAY... >"
< I WILL BROOK NO DELAYS! ELIMINATE ALL OBSTACLES! >
< AS YOU COMMAND, MY LORD! >
< FIRING FORWARD DISRUPTORS! >
< SOON I SHALL AT LONG LAST HAVE MY REVENGE UPON THE KRYPTONIAN. >
< FROM WHAT I HAVE LEARNED, HIS LOVE FOR THIS PLANET--THIS EARTH--WAS EVEN GREATER THAN THAT FOR HIS NATIVE KRYPTON! >
< POOR LITTLE WORLD! YOUR DOOM WAS SEALED THE DAY THAT SUPER-MAN REFUSED MY IMPERIAL ORDER. >
< I SHALL GRIND YOUR CHAMPION'S BONES BENEATH MY HEEL-- >

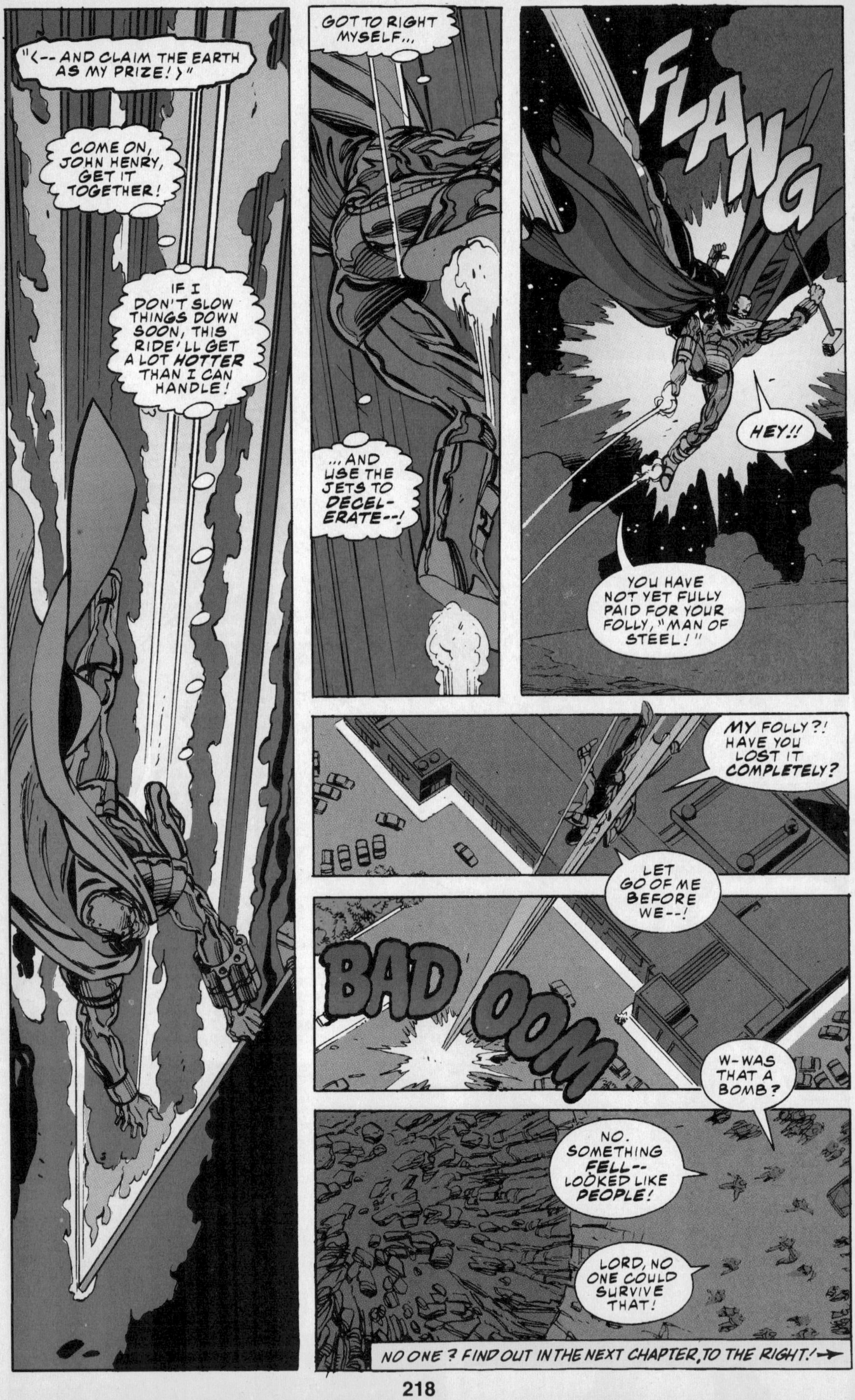
"<-- AND CLAIM THE EARTH AS MY PRIZE!>"
COME ON, JOHN HENRY, GET IT TOGETHER!
IF I DON'T SLOW THINGS DOWN SOON, THIS RIDE'LL GET A LOT HOTTER THAN I CAN HANDLE!
GOT TO RIGHT MYSELF...
...AND USE THE JETS TO DECEL-ERATE--!
FLANG
HEY!!
YOU HAVE NOT YET FULLY PAID FOR YOUR FOLLY, "MAN OF STEEL!"
MY FOLLY?! HAVE YOU LOST IT COMPLETELY?
LET GO OF ME BEFORE WE--!
BAD OOM
W-WAS THAT A BOMB?
NO. SOMETHING FELL-- LOOKED LIKE PEOPLE!
LORD, NO ONE COULD SURVIVE THAT!
NO ONE? FIND OUT IN THE NEXT CHAPTER, TO THE RIGHT!→

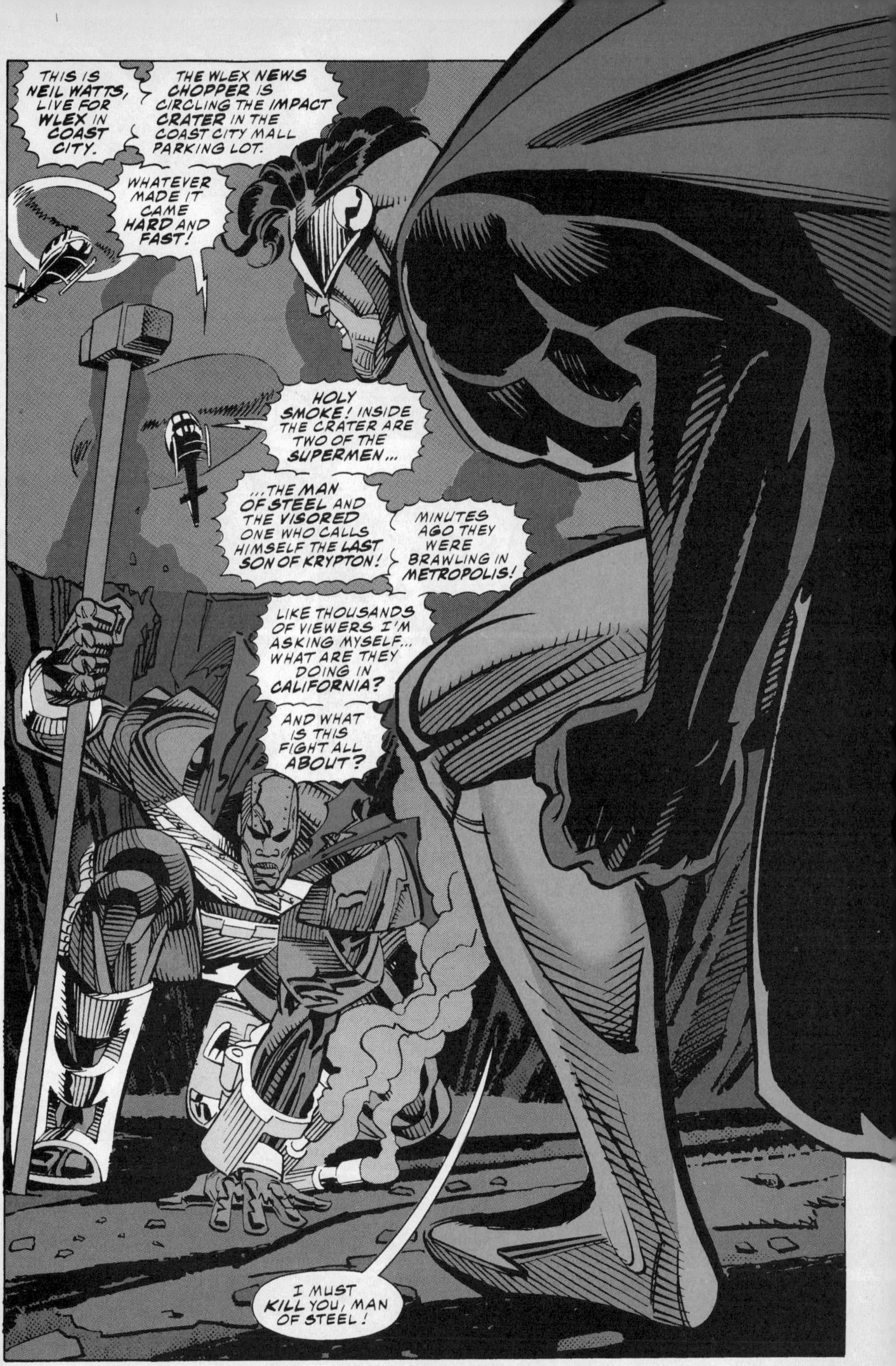
THIS IS NEIL WATTS, LIVE FOR WLEX IN COAST CITY.
THE WLEX NEWS CHOPPER IS CIRCLING THE IMPACT CRATER IN THE COAST CITY MALL PARKING LOT.
WHATEVER MADE IT CAME HARD AND FAST!
HOLY SMOKE! INSIDE THE CRATER ARE TWO OF THE SUPERMEN...
...THE MAN OF STEEL AND THE VISORED ONE WHO CALLS HIMSELF THE LAST SON OF KRYPTON!
MINUTES AGO THEY WERE BRAWLING IN METROPOLIS!
LIKE THOUSANDS OF VIEWERS I'M ASKING MYSELF... WHAT ARE THEY DOING IN CALIFORNIA?
AND WHAT IS THIS FIGHT ALL ABOUT?
I MUST KILL YOU, MAN OF STEEL!

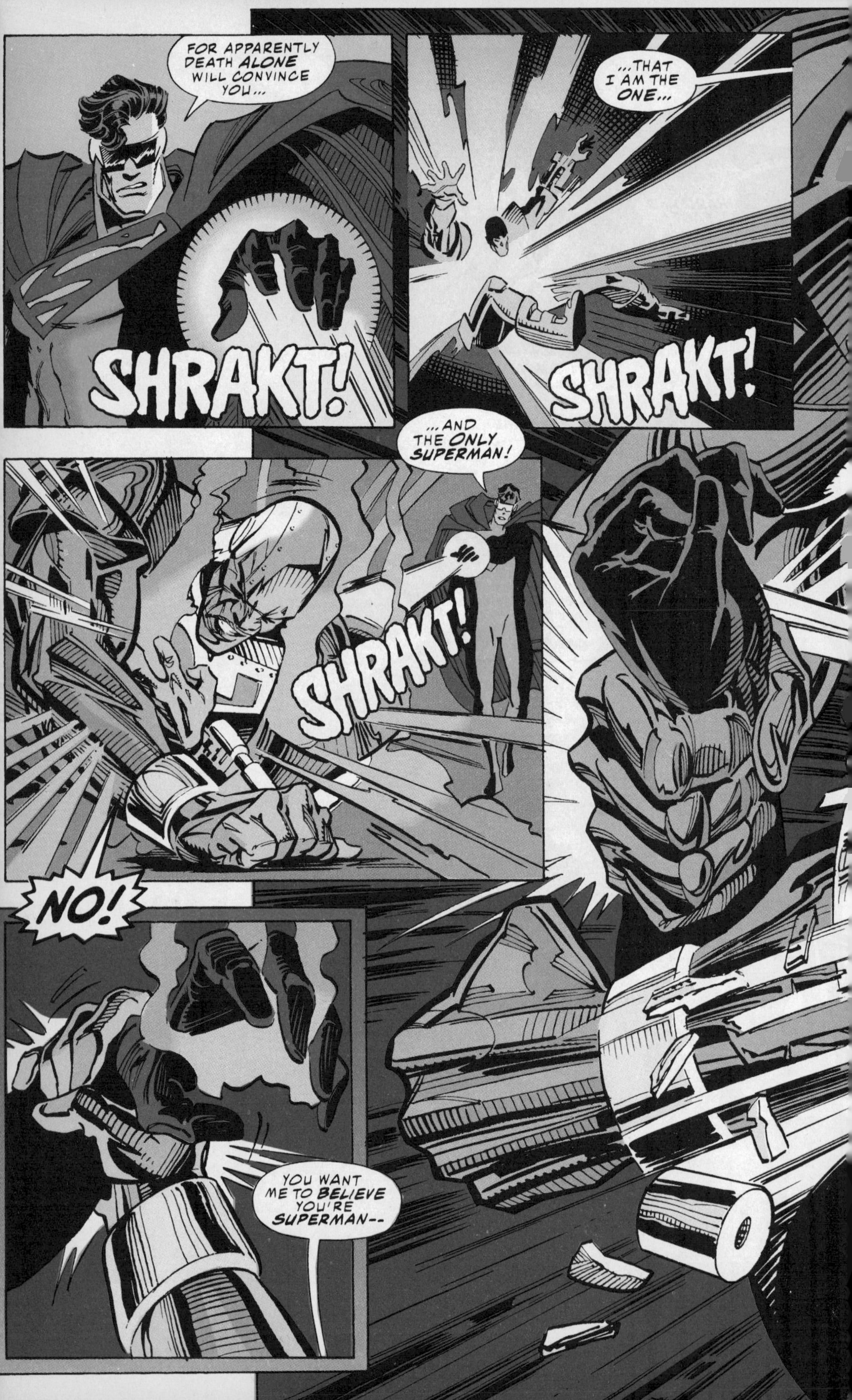
FOR APPARENTLY DEATH ALONE WILL CONVINCE YOU...
SHRAKT!
...THAT I AM THE ONE...
SHRAKT!
...AND THE ONLY SUPERMAN!
SHRAKT!
NO!
YOU WANT ME TO BELIEVE YOU'RE SUPERMAN--

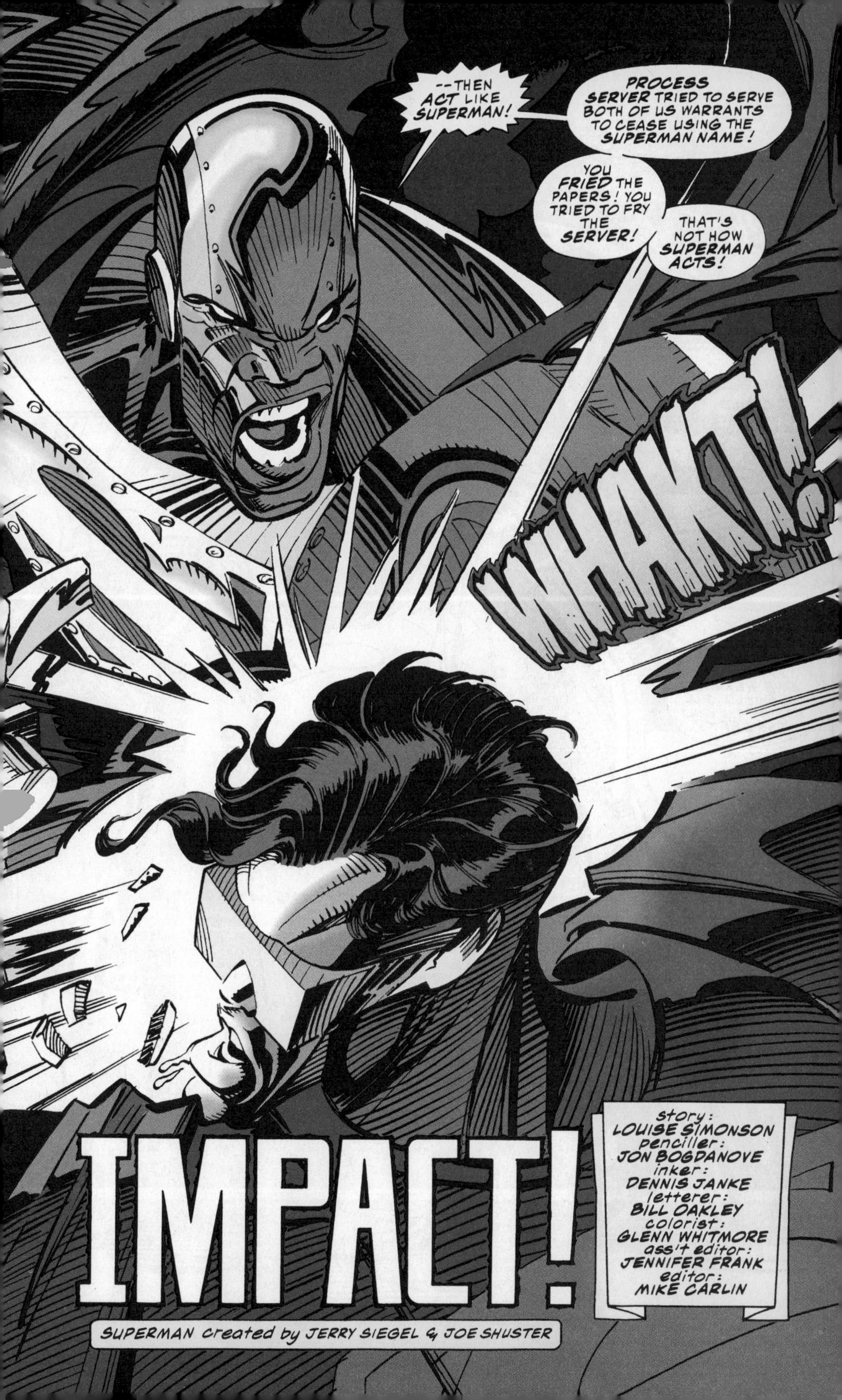
--THEN ACT LIKE SUPERMAN!
PROCESS SERVER TRIED TO SERVE BOTH OF US WARRANTS TO CEASE USING THE SUPERMAN NAME!
YOU FRIED THE PAPERS! YOU TRIED TO FRY THE SERVER!
THAT'S NOT HOW SUPERMAN ACTS!
WHAKT!!
IMPACT!
story: LOUISE SIMONSON
penciller: JON BOGDANOVE
inker: DENNIS JANKE
letterer: BILL OAKLEY
colorist: GLENN WHITMORE
ass't editor: JENNIFER FRANK
editor: MIKE CARLIN
SUPERMAN created by JERRY SIEGEL & JOE SHUSTER

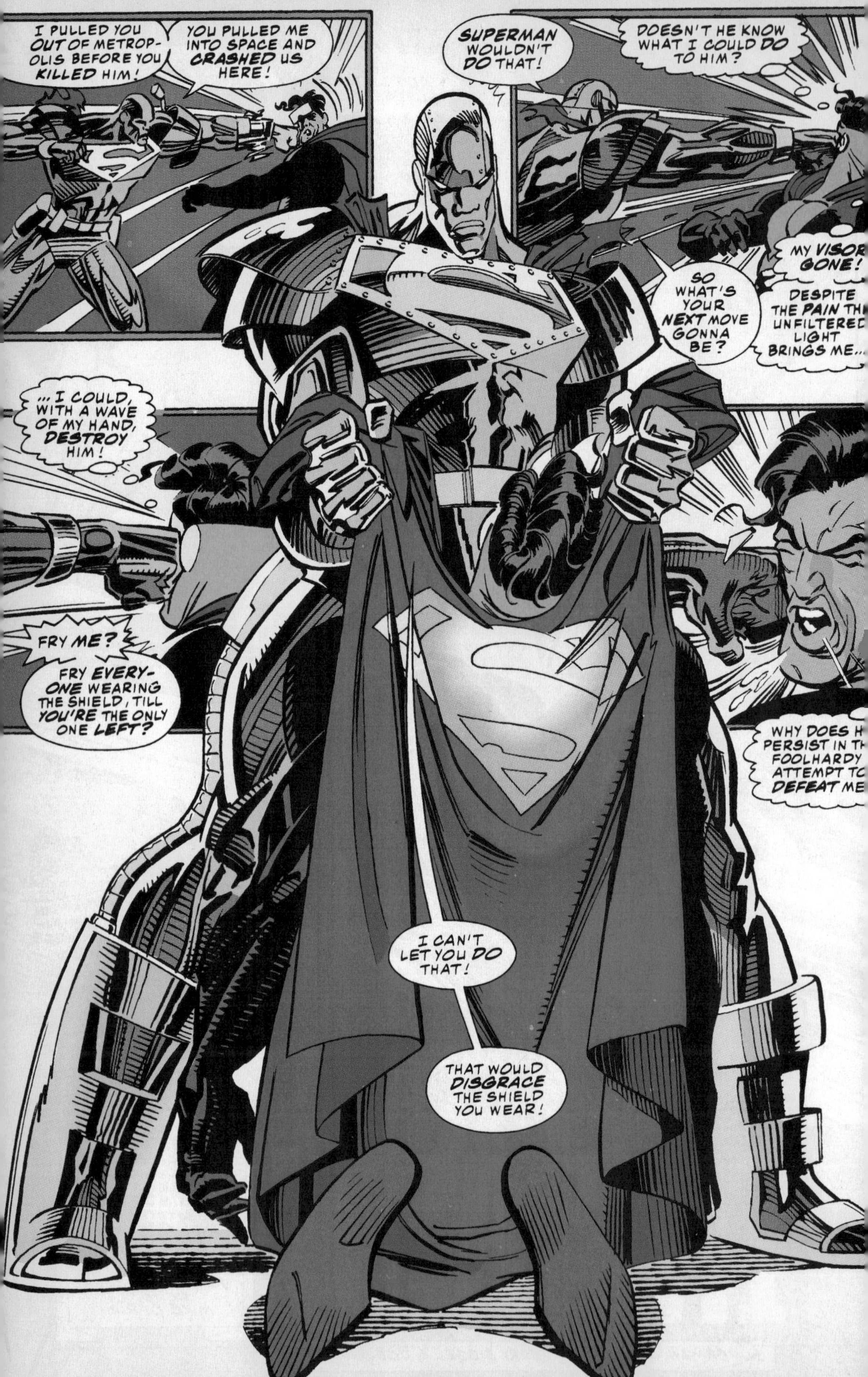

I PULLED YOU OUT OF METROPOLIS BEFORE YOU KILLED HIM!
YOU PULLED ME INTO SPACE AND CRASHED US HERE!
SUPERMAN WOULDN'T DO THAT!
DOESN'T HE KNOW WHAT I COULD DO TO HIM?
MY VISOR GONE!
DESPITE THE PAIN TH UNFILTERED LIGHT BRINGS ME...
SO WHAT'S YOUR NEXT MOVE GONNA BE?
...I COULD, WITH A WAVE OF MY HAND, DESTROY HIM!
FRY ME?
FRY EVERYONE WEARING THE SHIELD, TILL YOU'RE THE ONLY ONE LEFT?
WHY DOES H PERSIST IN TH FOOLHARDY ATTEMPT TO DEFEAT ME
I CAN'T LET YOU DO THAT!
THAT WOULD DISGRACE THE SHIELD YOU WEAR!

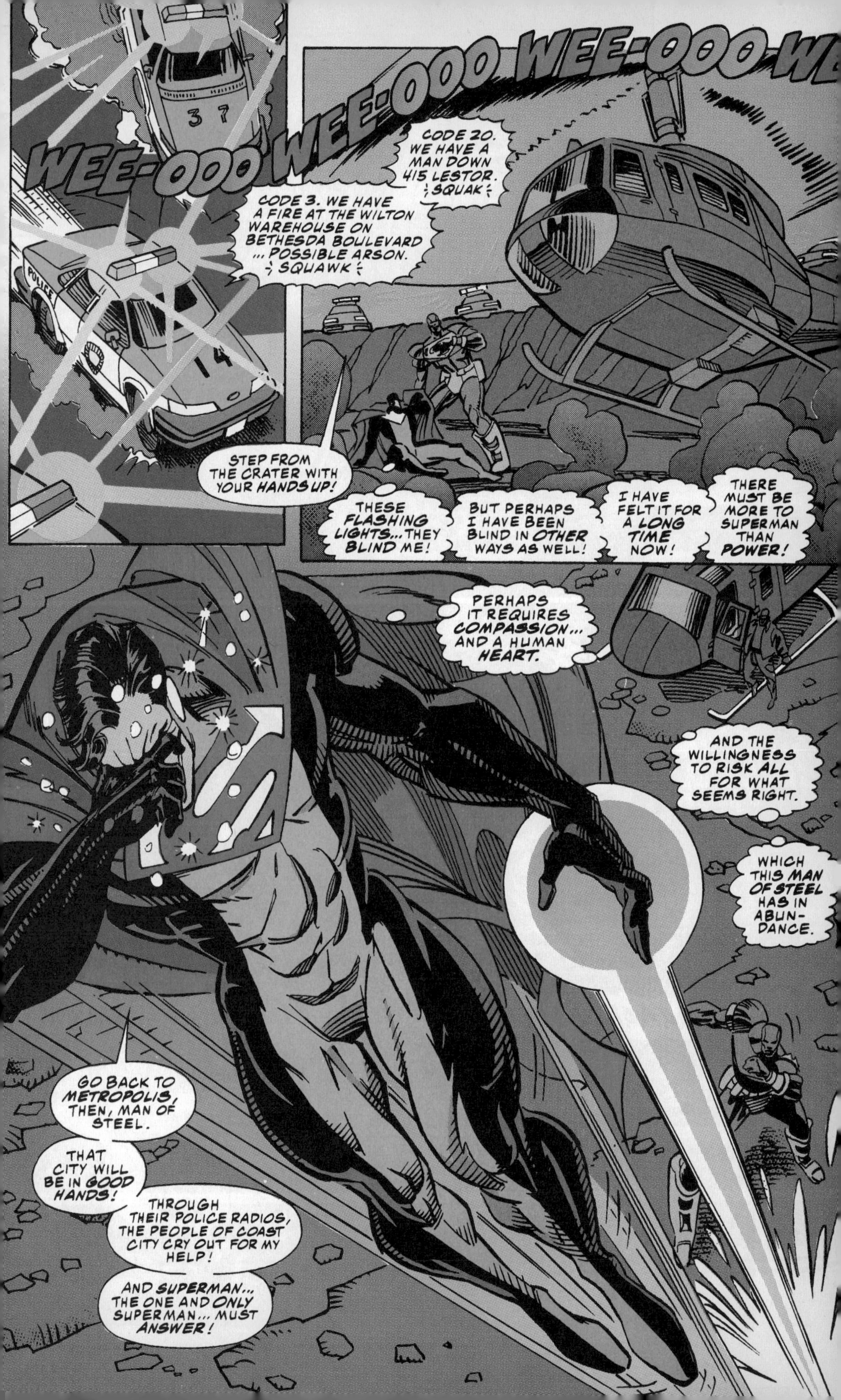

WEE-OOO WEE-OOO WEE-OOO WEE-OOO WE
CODE 20. WE HAVE A MAN DOWN 415 LESTOR. ⁘SQUAK⁘
CODE 3. WE HAVE A FIRE AT THE WILTON WAREHOUSE ON BETHESDA BOULEVARD ... POSSIBLE ARSON. ⁘SQUAWK⁘
STEP FROM THE CRATER WITH YOUR HANDS UP!
THESE FLASHING LIGHTS... THEY BLIND ME!
BUT PERHAPS I HAVE BEEN BLIND IN OTHER WAYS AS WELL!
I HAVE FELT IT FOR A LONG TIME NOW!
THERE MUST BE MORE TO SUPERMAN THAN POWER!
PERHAPS IT REQUIRES COMPASSION... AND A HUMAN HEART.
AND THE WILLINGNESS TO RISK ALL FOR WHAT SEEMS RIGHT.
WHICH THIS MAN OF STEEL HAS IN ABUN-DANCE.
GO BACK TO METROPOLIS, THEN, MAN OF STEEL.
THAT CITY WILL BE IN GOOD HANDS!
THROUGH THEIR POLICE RADIOS, THE PEOPLE OF COAST CITY CRY OUT FOR MY HELP!
AND SUPERMAN... THE ONE AND ONLY SUPERMAN... MUST ANSWER!

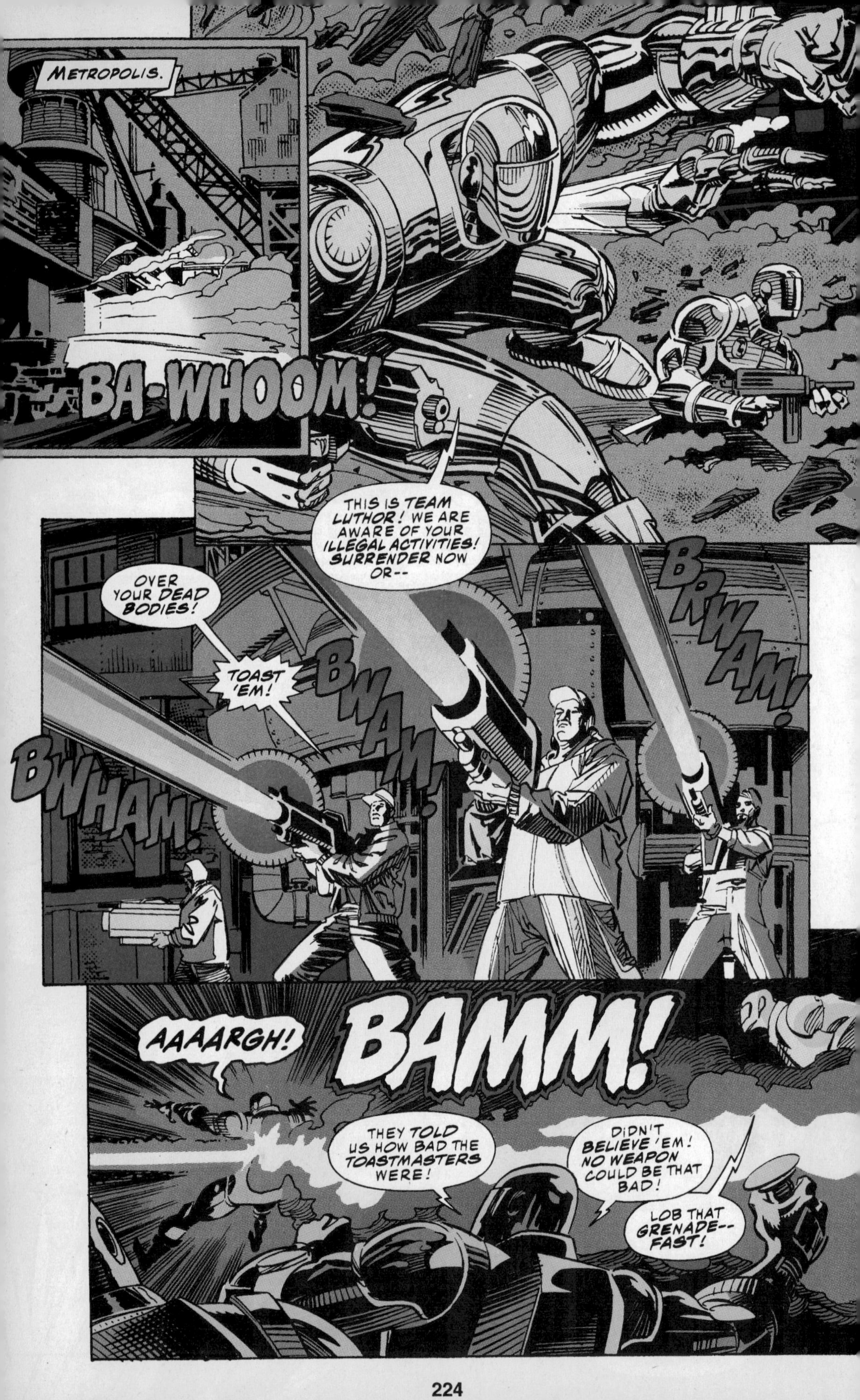
METROPOLIS.
BA-WHOOM!
THIS IS TEAM LUTHOR! WE ARE AWARE OF YOUR ILLEGAL ACTIVITIES! SURRENDER NOW OR--
OVER YOUR DEAD BODIES!
TOAST 'EM!
BRWAM!
BWAM!
BWHAM!
AAAARGH!
BAMM!
THEY TOLD US HOW BAD THE TOASTMASTERS WERE!
DIDN'T BELIEVE 'EM! NO WEAPON COULD BE THAT BAD!
LOB THAT GRENADE--FAST!

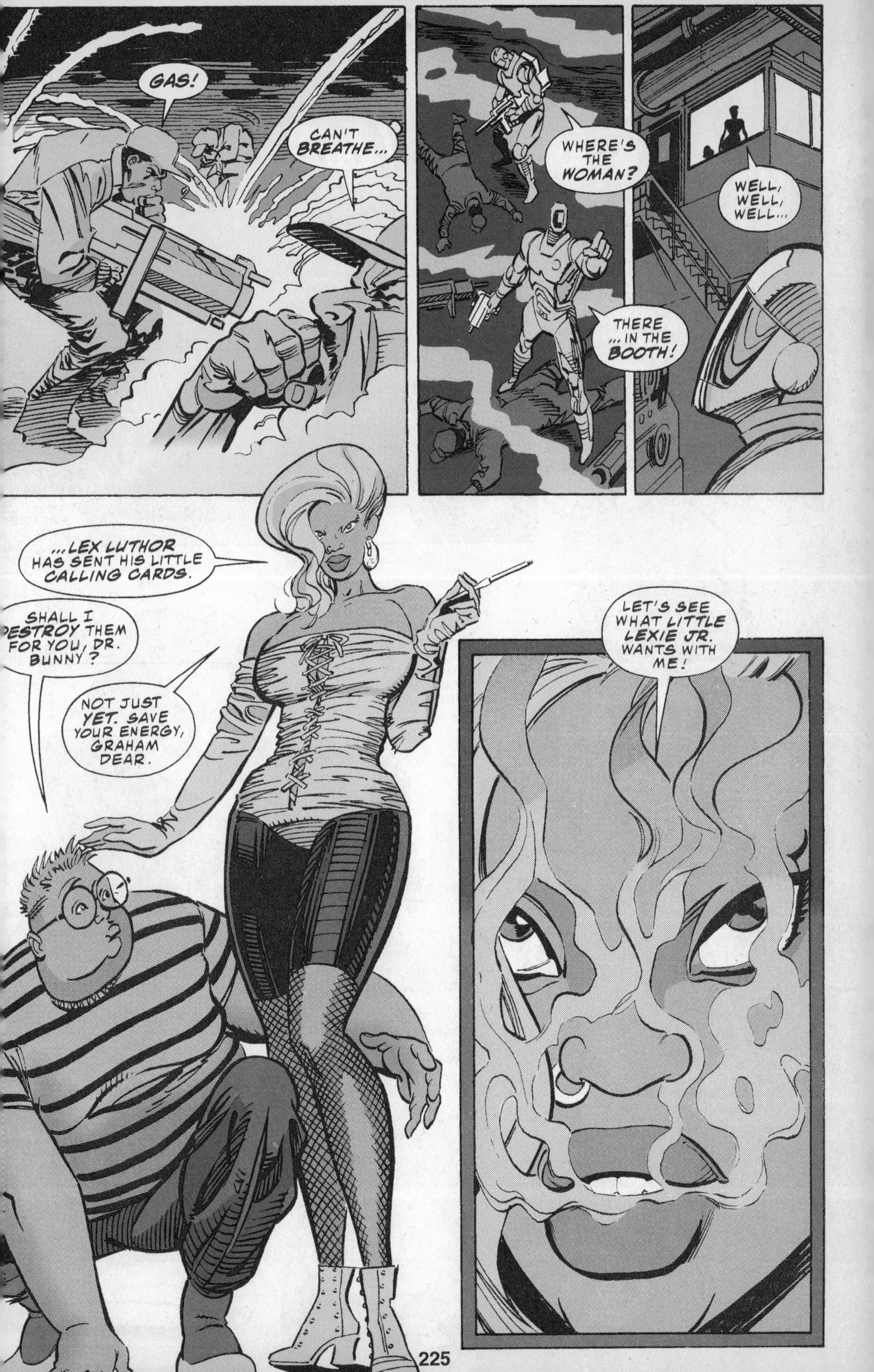
GAS!
CAN'T BREATHE...
WHERE'S THE WOMAN?
THERE ...IN THE BOOTH!
WELL, WELL, WELL...
...LEX LUTHOR HAS SENT HIS LITTLE CALLING CARDS.
SHALL I DESTROY THEM FOR YOU, DR. BUNNY?
NOT JUST YET. SAVE YOUR ENERGY, GRAHAM DEAR.
LET'S SEE WHAT LITTLE LEXIE JR. WANTS WITH ME!

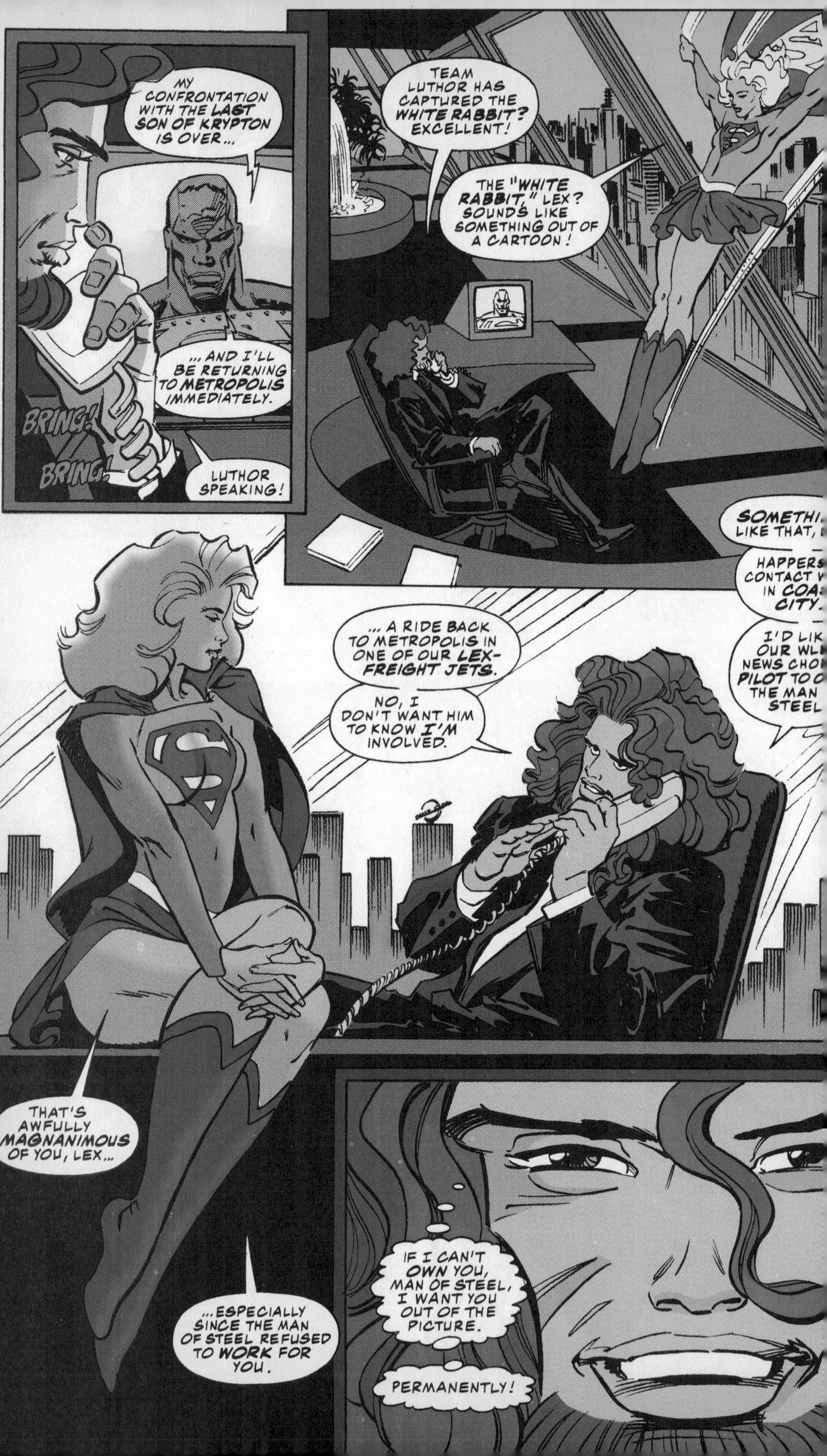
MY CONFRONTATION WITH THE LAST SON OF KRYPTON IS OVER...
...AND I'LL BE RETURNING TO METROPOLIS IMMEDIATELY.
BRING!
BRING!
LUTHOR SPEAKING!
TEAM LUTHOR HAS CAPTURED THE WHITE RABBIT? EXCELLENT!
THE "WHITE RABBIT," LEX? SOUNDS LIKE SOMETHING OUT OF A CARTOON!
LIKE THAT,
CONTACT IN CITY.
OUR NEWS PILOT THE MAN STEEL
...A RIDE BACK TO METROPOLIS IN ONE OF OUR LEX-FREIGHT JETS.
NO, I DON'T WANT HIM TO KNOW I'M INVOLVED.
THAT'S AWFULLY MAGNANIMOUS OF YOU, LEX...
...ESPECIALLY SINCE THE MAN OF STEEL REFUSED TO WORK FOR YOU.
IF I CAN'T OWN YOU, MAN OF STEEL, I WANT YOU OUT OF THE PICTURE.
PERMANENTLY!

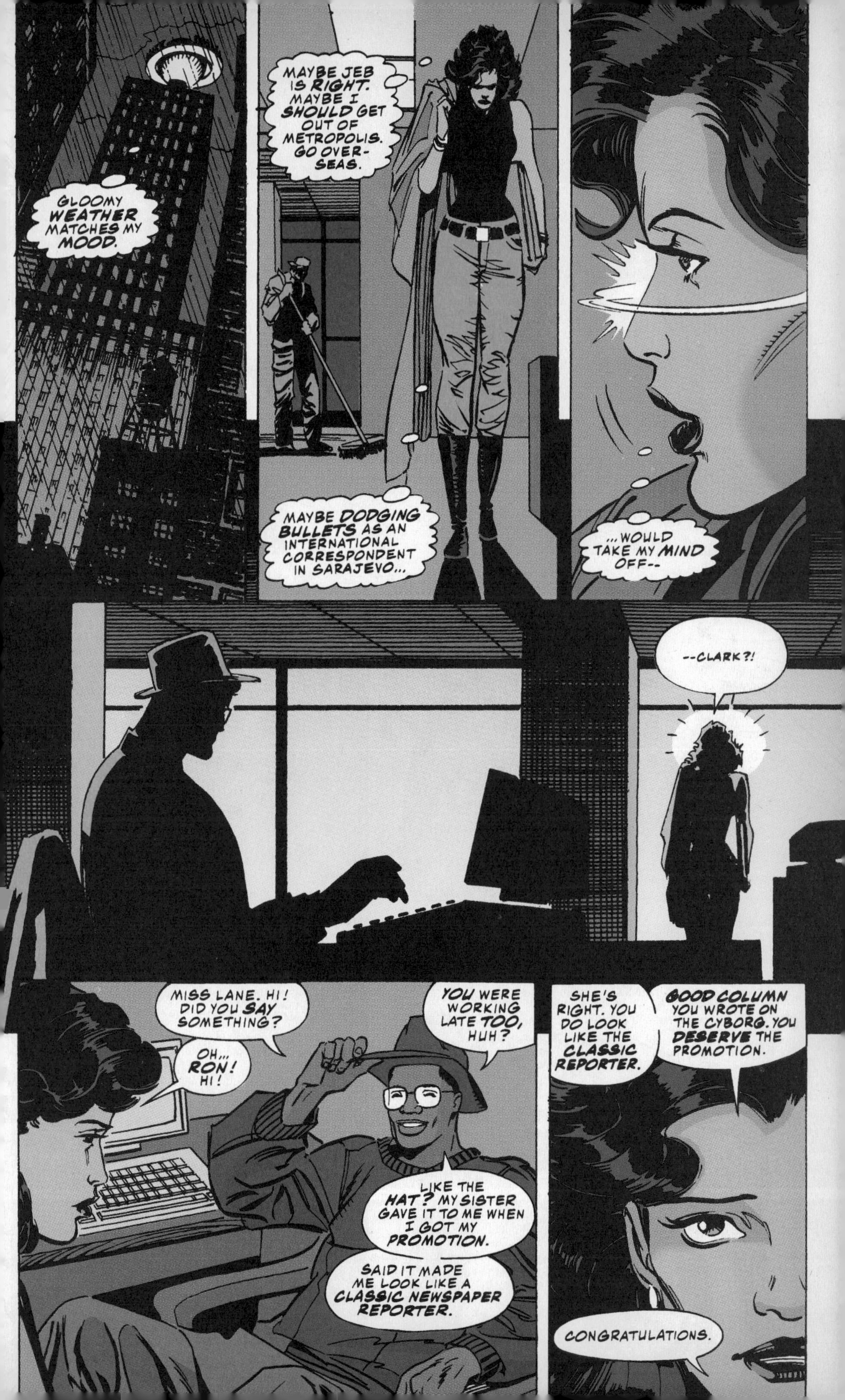
GLOOMY WEATHER MATCHES MY MOOD.
MAYBE JEB IS RIGHT. MAYBE I SHOULD GET OUT OF METROPOLIS. GO OVER-SEAS.
MAYBE DODGING BULLETS AS AN INTERNATIONAL CORRESPONDENT IN SARAJEVO...
...WOULD TAKE MY MIND OFF--
--CLARK?!
MISS LANE. HI! DID YOU SAY SOMETHING?
OH... RON! HI!
YOU WERE WORKING LATE TOO, HUH?
LIKE THE HAT? MY SISTER GAVE IT TO ME WHEN I GOT MY PROMOTION.
SAID IT MADE ME LOOK LIKE A CLASSIC NEWSPAPER REPORTER.
SHE'S RIGHT. YOU DO LOOK LIKE THE CLASSIC REPORTER.
GOOD COLUMN YOU WROTE ON THE CYBORG. YOU DESERVE THE PROMOTION.
CONGRATULATIONS.

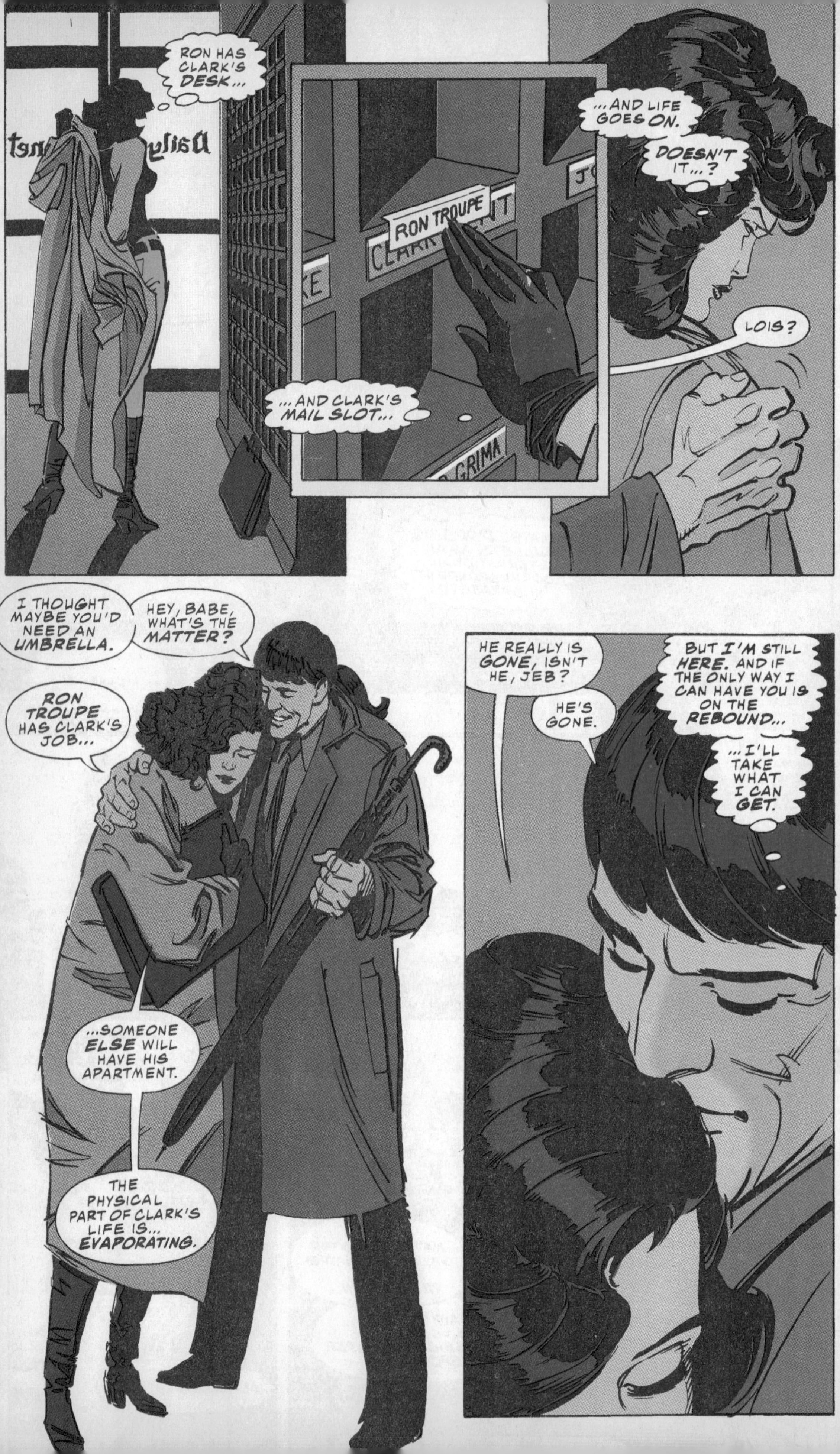
RON HAS CLARK'S DESK...
...AND CLARK'S MAIL SLOT...
RON TROUPE
...AND LIFE GOES ON.
DOESN'T IT...?
LOIS?
I THOUGHT MAYBE YOU'D NEED AN UMBRELLA.
HEY, BABE, WHAT'S THE MATTER?
RON TROUPE HAS CLARK'S JOB...
...SOMEONE ELSE WILL HAVE HIS APARTMENT.
THE PHYSICAL PART OF CLARK'S LIFE IS... EVAPORATING.
HE REALLY IS GONE, ISN'T HE, JEB?
HE'S GONE.
BUT I'M STILL HERE. AND IF THE ONLY WAY I CAN HAVE YOU IS ON THE REBOUND...
...I'LL TAKE WHAT I CAN GET.

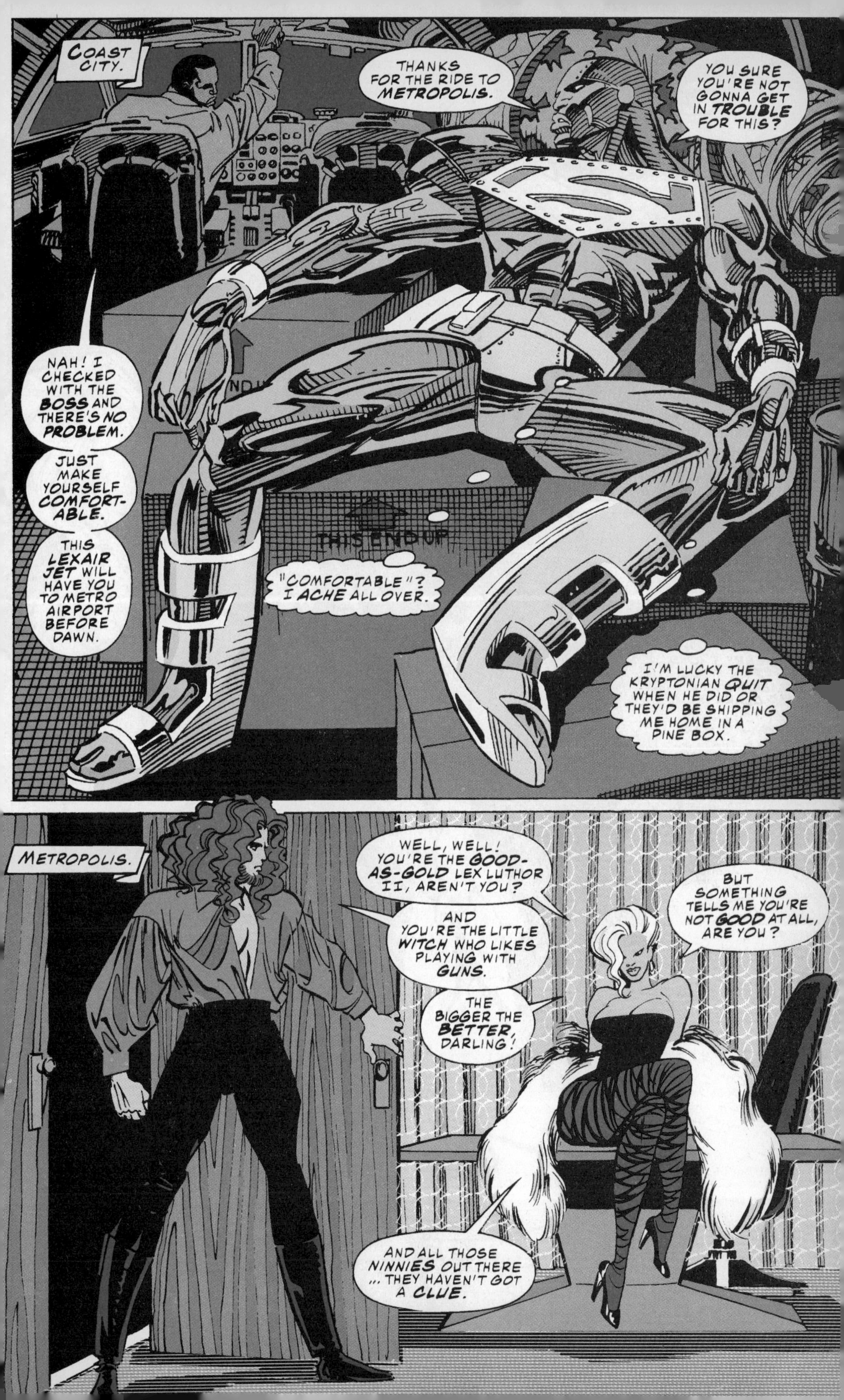
COAST CITY.
THANKS FOR THE RIDE TO METROPOLIS.
YOU SURE YOU'RE NOT GONNA GET IN TROUBLE FOR THIS?
NAH! I CHECKED WITH THE BOSS AND THERE'S NO PROBLEM.
JUST MAKE YOURSELF COMFORTABLE.
THIS LEXAIR JET WILL HAVE YOU TO METRO AIRPORT BEFORE DAWN.
"COMFORTABLE"? I ACHE ALL OVER.
THIS END UP
I'M LUCKY THE KRYPTONIAN QUIT WHEN HE DID OR THEY'D BE SHIPPING ME HOME IN A PINE BOX.
METROPOLIS.
WELL, WELL! YOU'RE THE GOOD-AS-GOLD LEX LUTHOR II, AREN'T YOU?
BUT SOMETHING TELLS ME YOU'RE NOT GOOD AT ALL, ARE YOU?
AND YOU'RE THE LITTLE WITCH WHO LIKES PLAYING WITH GUNS.
THE BIGGER THE BETTER, DARLING!
AND ALL THOSE NINNIES OUT THERE ... THEY HAVEN'T GOT A CLUE.

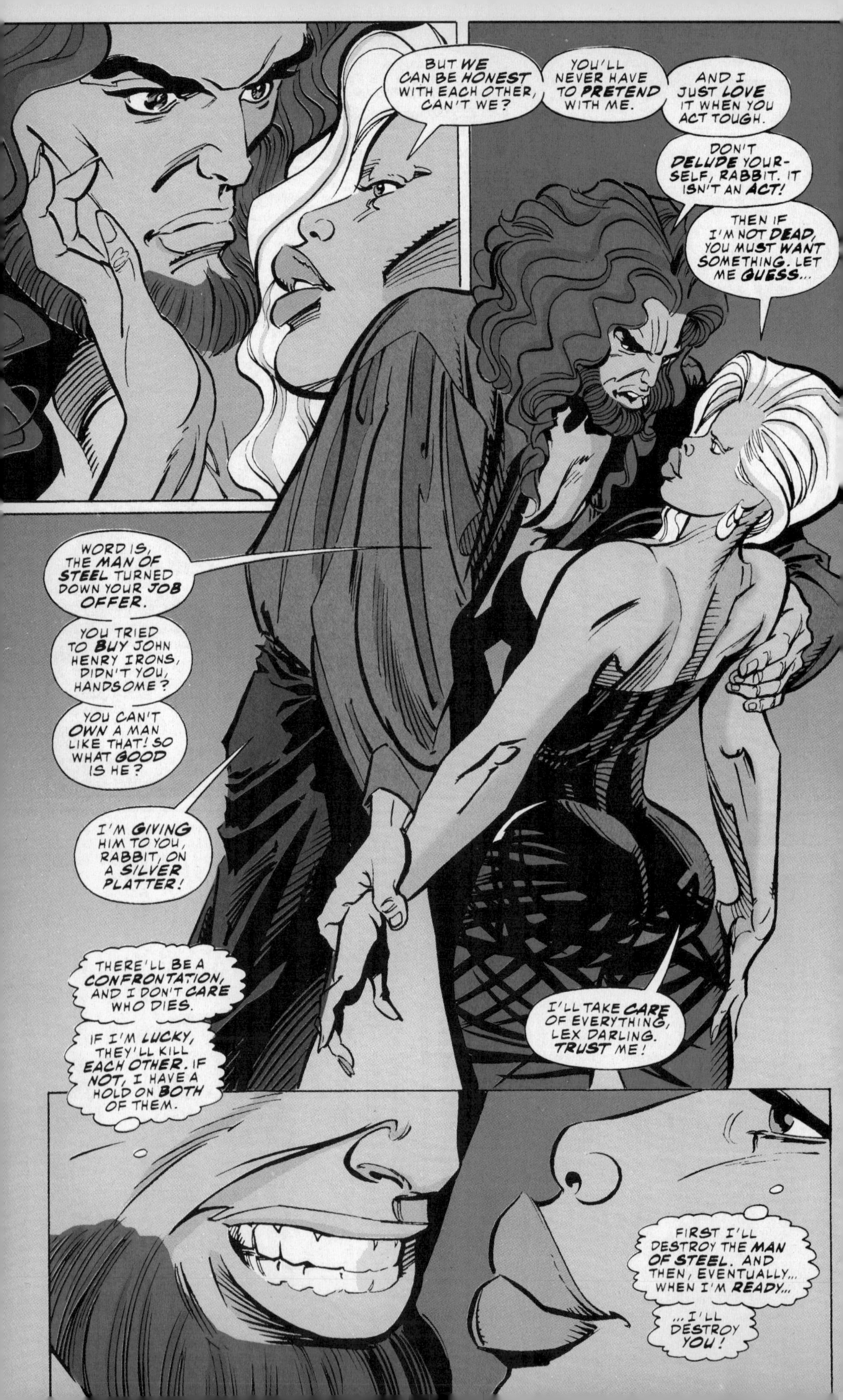

BUT WE CAN BE HONEST WITH EACH OTHER, CAN'T WE?
YOU'LL NEVER HAVE TO PRETEND WITH ME.
AND I JUST LOVE IT WHEN YOU ACT TOUGH.
DON'T DELUDE YOURSELF, RABBIT. IT ISN'T AN ACT!
THEN IF I'M NOT DEAD, YOU MUST WANT SOMETHING. LET ME GUESS...
WORD IS, THE MAN OF STEEL TURNED DOWN YOUR JOB OFFER.
YOU TRIED TO BUY JOHN HENRY IRONS, DIDN'T YOU, HANDSOME?
YOU CAN'T OWN A MAN LIKE THAT! SO WHAT GOOD IS HE?
I'M GIVING HIM TO YOU, RABBIT, ON A SILVER PLATTER!
THERE'LL BE A CONFRONTATION, AND I DON'T CARE WHO DIES.
IF I'M LUCKY, THEY'LL KILL EACH OTHER. IF NOT, I HAVE A HOLD ON BOTH OF THEM.
I'LL TAKE CARE OF EVERYTHING, LEX DARLING. TRUST ME!
FIRST I'LL DESTROY THE MAN OF STEEL. AND THEN, EVENTUALLY... WHEN I'M READY...
...I'LL DESTROY YOU!

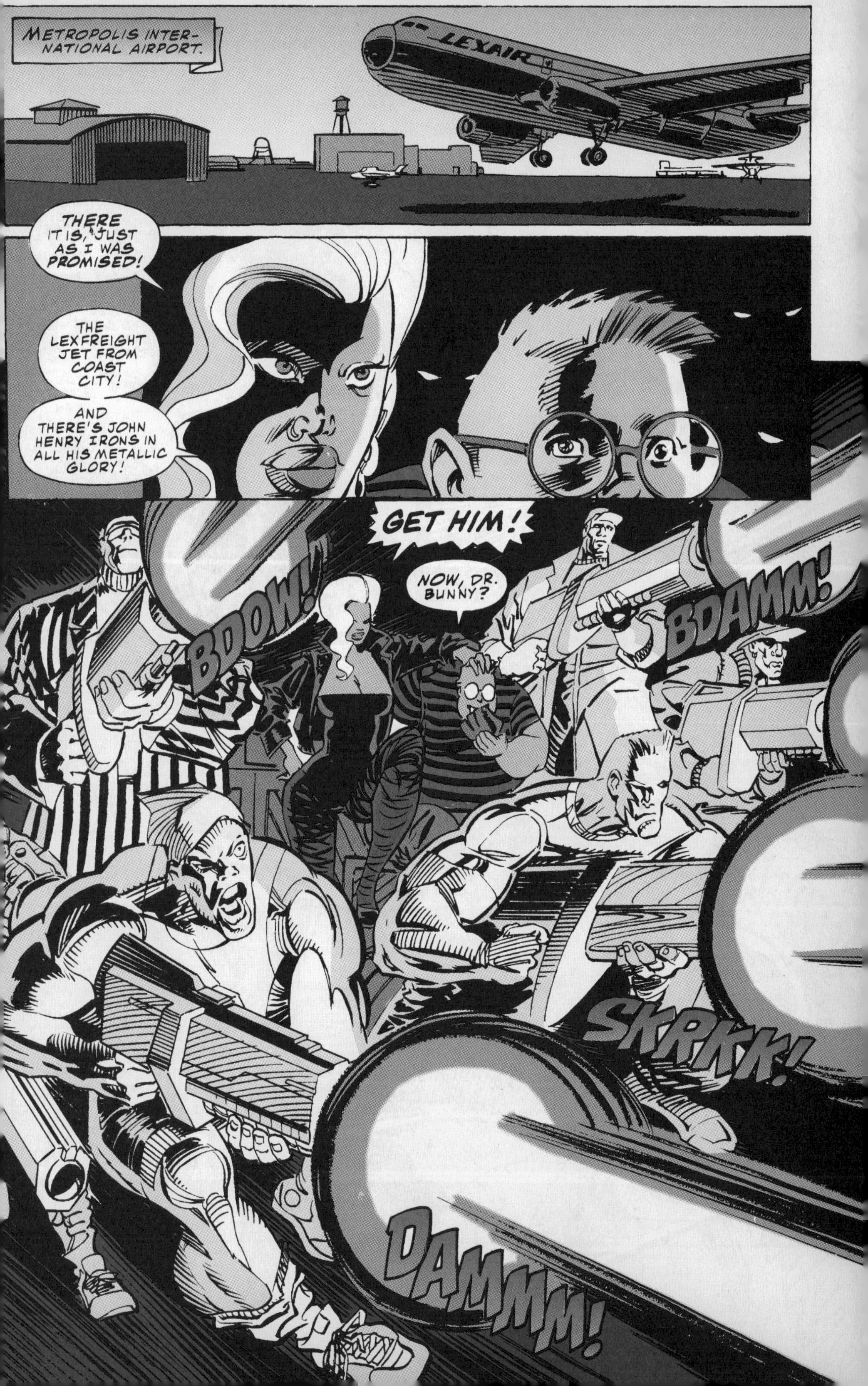

METROPOLIS INTER-NATIONAL AIRPORT.
LEXAIR
THERE IT IS, JUST AS I WAS PROMISED!
THE LEXFREIGHT JET FROM COAST CITY!
AND THERE'S JOHN HENRY IRONS IN ALL HIS METALLIC GLORY!
GET HIM!
NOW, DR. BUNNY?
BDOW!
BDAMM!
SKRKK!
DAMMM!

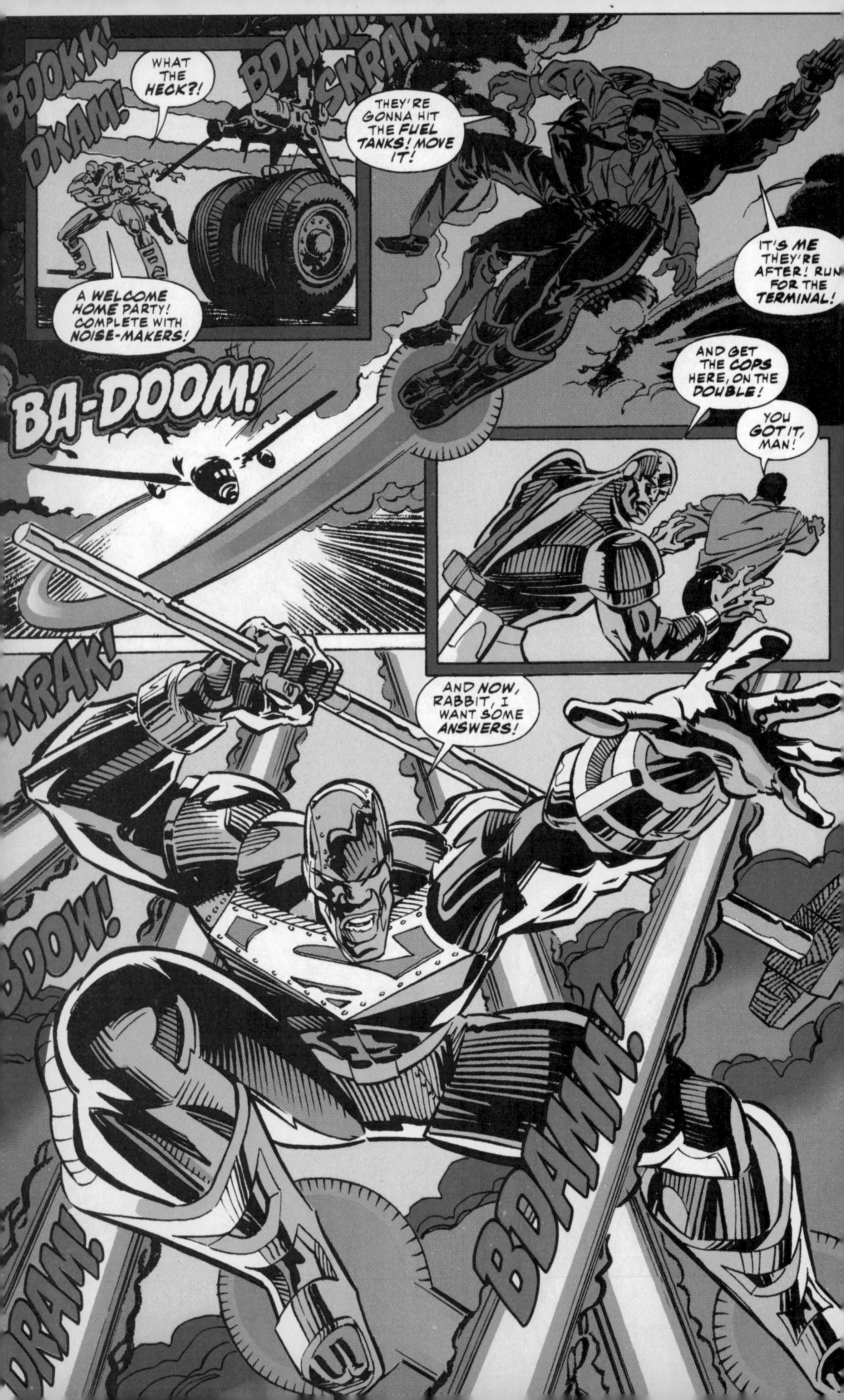
BDOKK!
DKAM!
WHAT THE HECK?!
BDAMM!
SKRAK!
THEY'RE GONNA HIT THE FUEL TANKS! MOVE IT!
A WELCOME HOME PARTY! COMPLETE WITH NOISE-MAKERS!
IT'S ME THEY'RE AFTER! RUN FOR THE TERMINAL!
AND GET THE COPS HERE, ON THE DOUBLE!
YOU GOT IT, MAN!
BA-DOOM!
SKRAK!
AND NOW, RABBIT, I WANT SOME ANSWERS!
BDOW!
BDAMM!
DRAM!

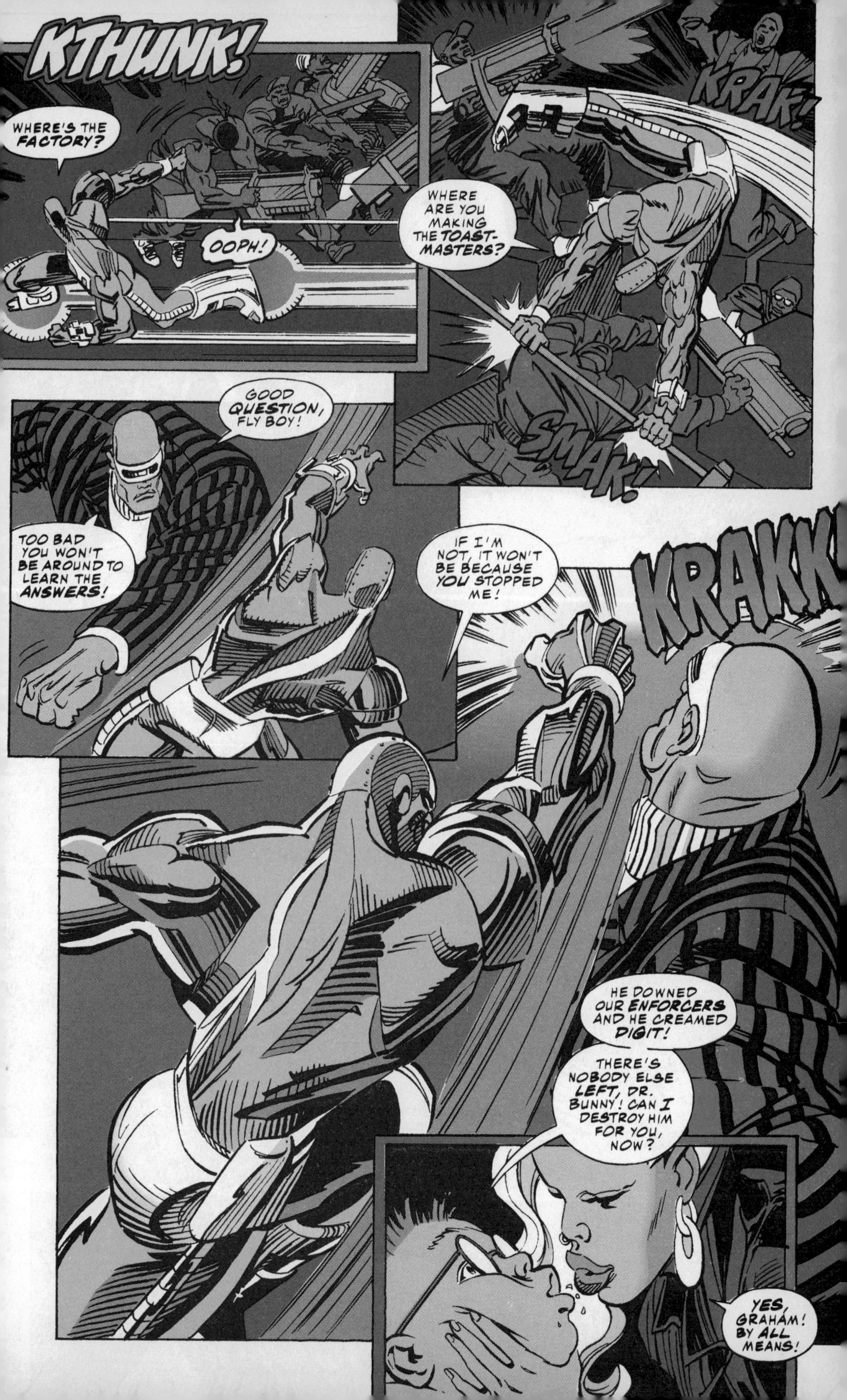
KTHUNK!
WHERE'S THE FACTORY?
OOPH!
KRAK!
WHERE ARE YOU MAKING THE TOAST-MASTERS?
SMAK!
GOOD QUESTION, FLY BOY!
TOO BAD YOU WON'T BE AROUND TO LEARN THE ANSWERS!
IF I'M NOT, IT WON'T BE BECAUSE YOU STOPPED ME!
KRAKK!
HE DOWNED OUR ENFORCERS AND HE CREAMED DIGIT!
THERE'S NOBODY ELSE LEFT, DR. BUNNY! CAN I DESTROY HIM FOR YOU, NOW?
YES, GRAHAM! BY ALL MEANS!

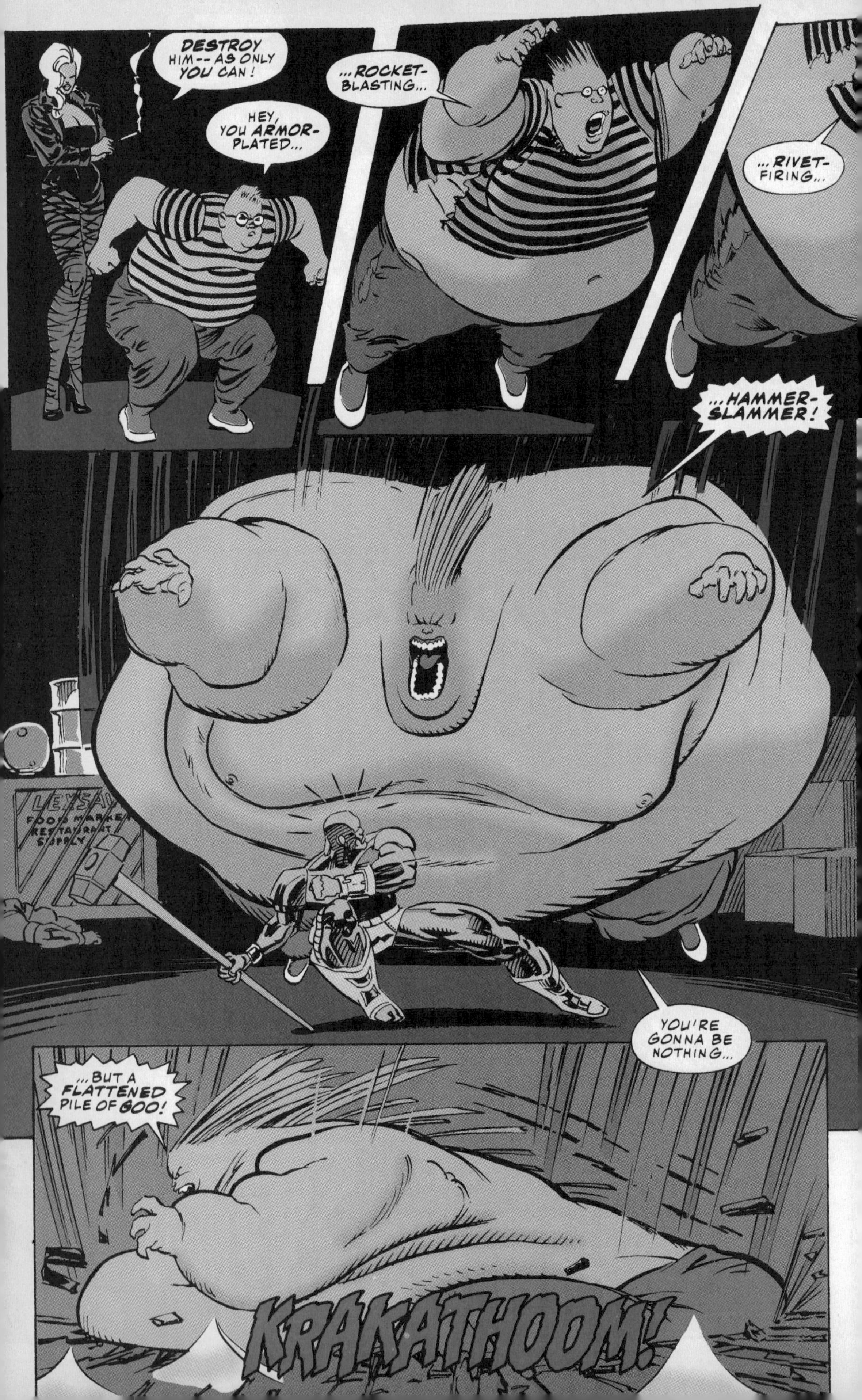
DESTROY HIM-- AS ONLY YOU CAN!
HEY, YOU ARMOR-PLATED...
...ROCKET-BLASTING...
...RIVET-FIRING...
...HAMMER-SLAMMER!
YOU'RE GONNA BE NOTHING...
...BUT A FLATTENED PILE OF GOO!
KRAKATHOOM!

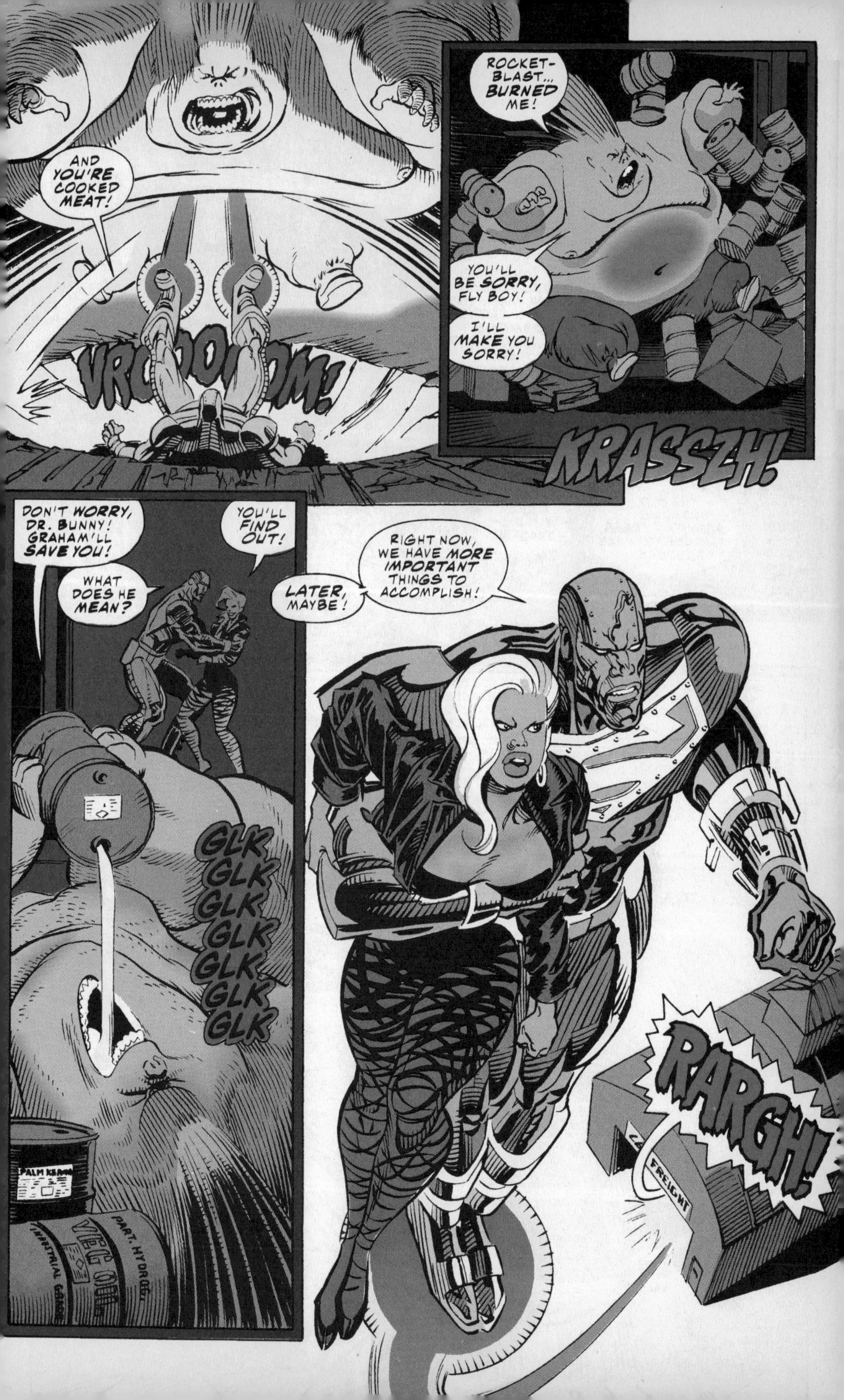

AND YOU'RE COOKED MEAT!
VROOOOOOM!
ROCKET-BLAST... BURNED ME!
YOU'LL BE SORRY, FLY BOY!
I'LL MAKE YOU SORRY!
KRASSZH!
DON'T WORRY, DR. BUNNY! GRAHAM'LL SAVE YOU!
YOU'LL FIND OUT!
WHAT DOES HE MEAN?
LATER, MAYBE!
RIGHT NOW, WE HAVE MORE IMPORTANT THINGS TO ACCOMPLISH!
GLK GLK GLK GLK GLK GLK GLK
RARGH!
FREIGHT
PART. HYDROG.
VEG OIL

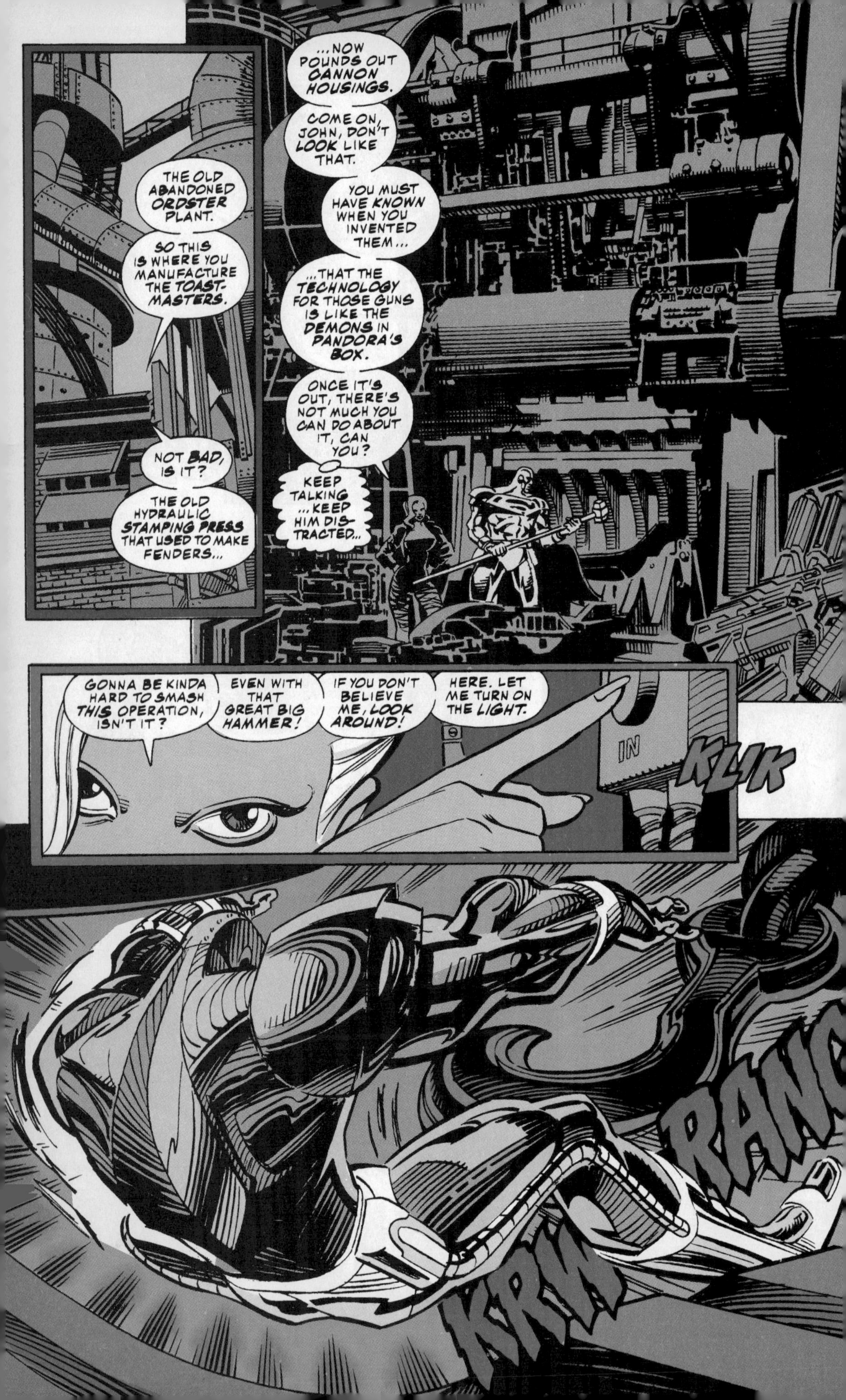
THE OLD ABANDONED ORDSTER PLANT.
SO THIS IS WHERE YOU MANUFACTURE THE TOAST-MASTERS.
NOT BAD, IS IT?
THE OLD HYDRAULIC STAMPING PRESS THAT USED TO MAKE FENDERS...
...NOW POUNDS OUT CANNON HOUSINGS.
COME ON, JOHN, DON'T LOOK LIKE THAT.
YOU MUST HAVE KNOWN WHEN YOU INVENTED THEM...
...THAT THE TECHNOLOGY FOR THOSE GUNS IS LIKE THE DEMONS IN PANDORA'S BOX.
ONCE IT'S OUT, THERE'S NOT MUCH YOU CAN DO ABOUT IT, CAN YOU?
KEEP TALKING ...KEEP HIM DIS-TRACTED...
GONNA BE KINDA HARD TO SMASH THIS OPERATION, ISN'T IT?
EVEN WITH THAT GREAT BIG HAMMER!
IF YOU DON'T BELIEVE ME, LOOK AROUND!
HERE. LET ME TURN ON THE LIGHT.
IN
KLIK
KRUN
RANG

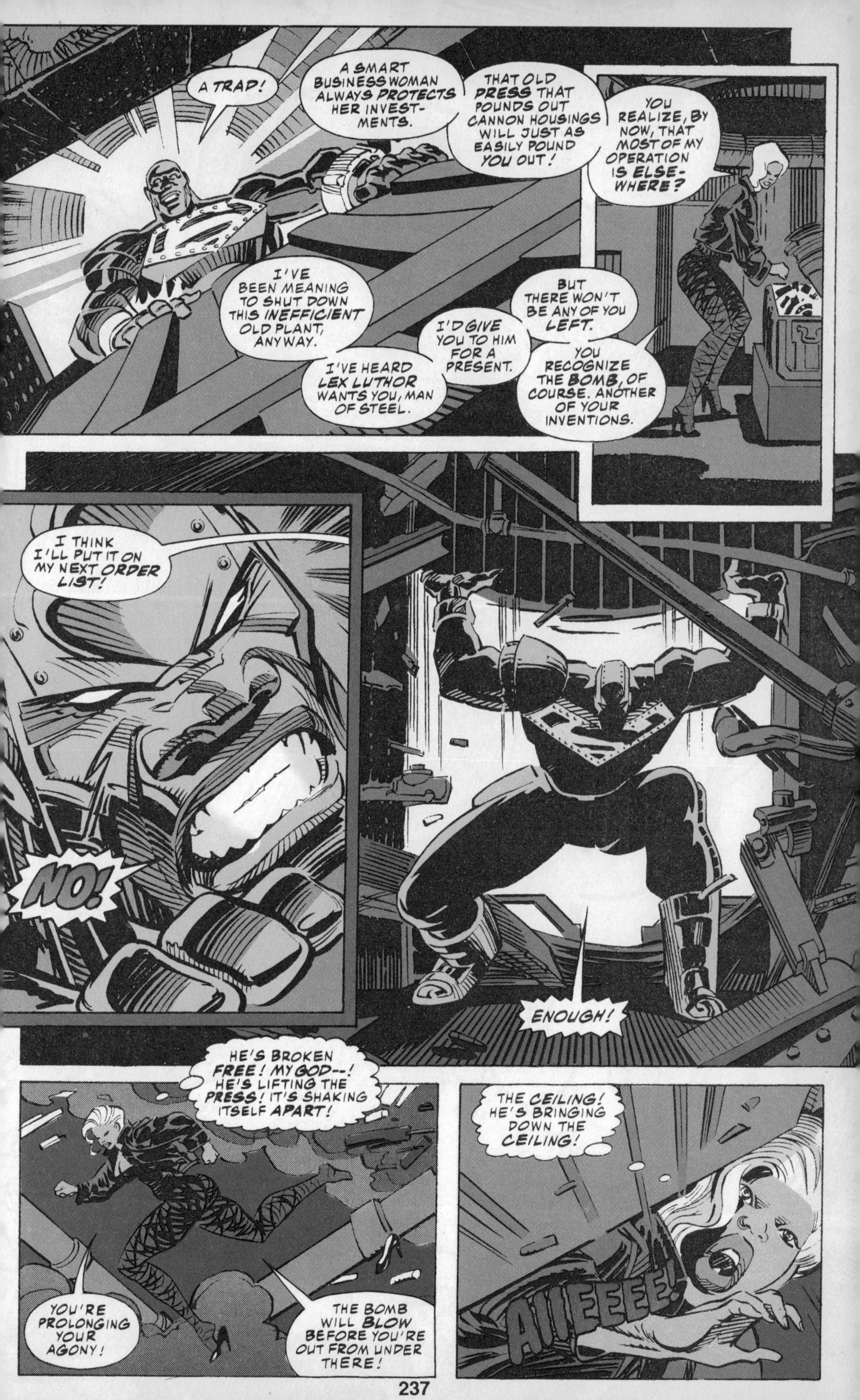

A TRAP!
A SMART BUSINESSWOMAN ALWAYS PROTECTS HER INVESTMENTS.
THAT OLD PRESS THAT POUNDS OUT CANNON HOUSINGS WILL JUST AS EASILY POUND YOU OUT!
YOU REALIZE, BY NOW, THAT MOST OF MY OPERATION IS ELSEWHERE?
I'VE BEEN MEANING TO SHUT DOWN THIS INEFFICIENT OLD PLANT, ANYWAY.
I'VE HEARD LEX LUTHOR WANTS YOU, MAN OF STEEL.
I'D GIVE YOU TO HIM FOR A PRESENT.
BUT THERE WON'T BE ANY OF YOU LEFT.
YOU RECOGNIZE THE BOMB, OF COURSE. ANOTHER OF YOUR INVENTIONS.
I THINK I'LL PUT IT ON MY NEXT ORDER LIST!
NO!
ENOUGH!
HE'S BROKEN FREE! MY GOD--! HE'S LIFTING THE PRESS! IT'S SHAKING ITSELF APART!
YOU'RE PROLONGING YOUR AGONY!
THE BOMB WILL BLOW BEFORE YOU'RE OUT FROM UNDER THERE!
THE CEILING! HE'S BRINGING DOWN THE CEILING!
AIIEEEEE!

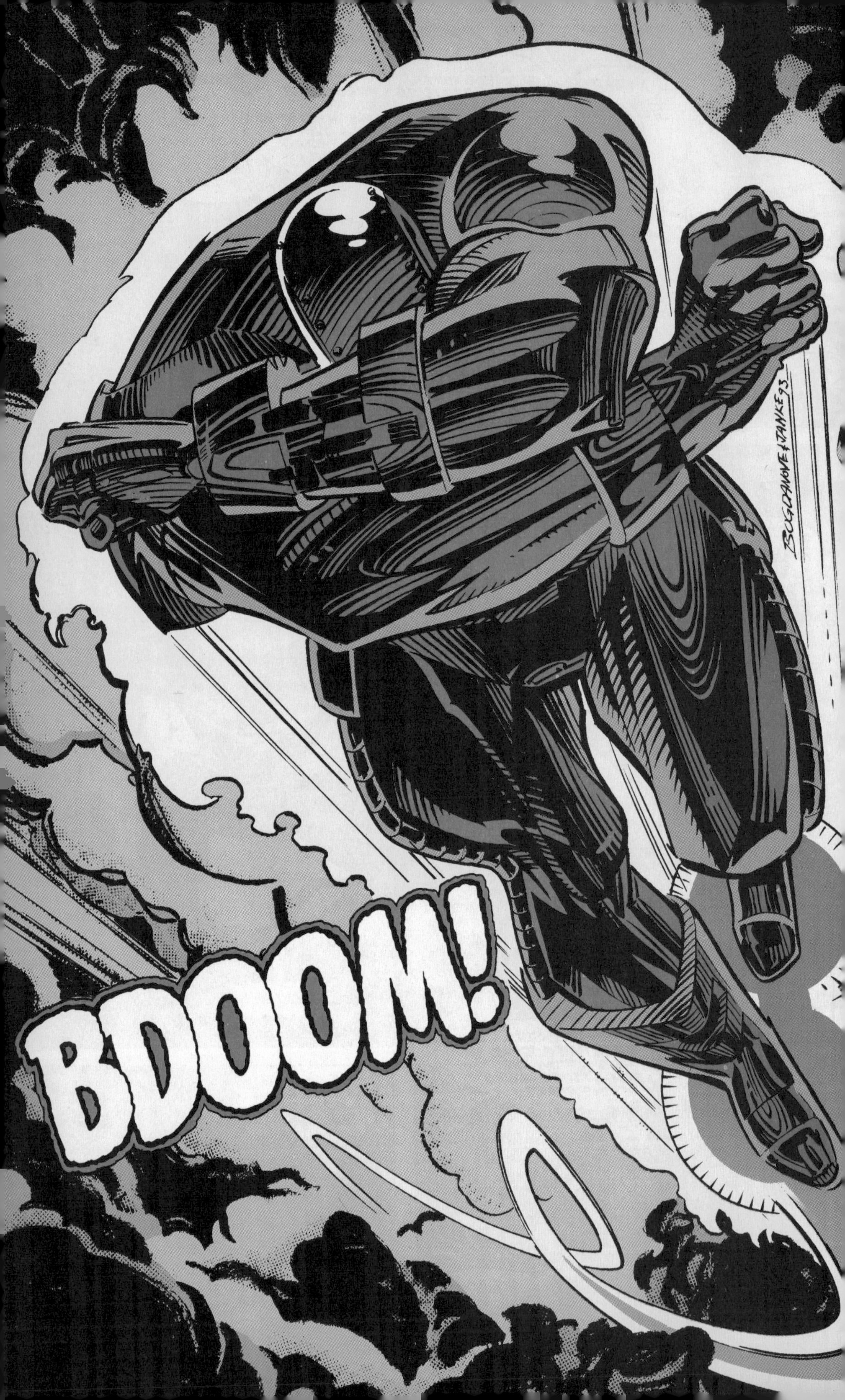
BDOOM!
BOGDANOVE & JANKE 93

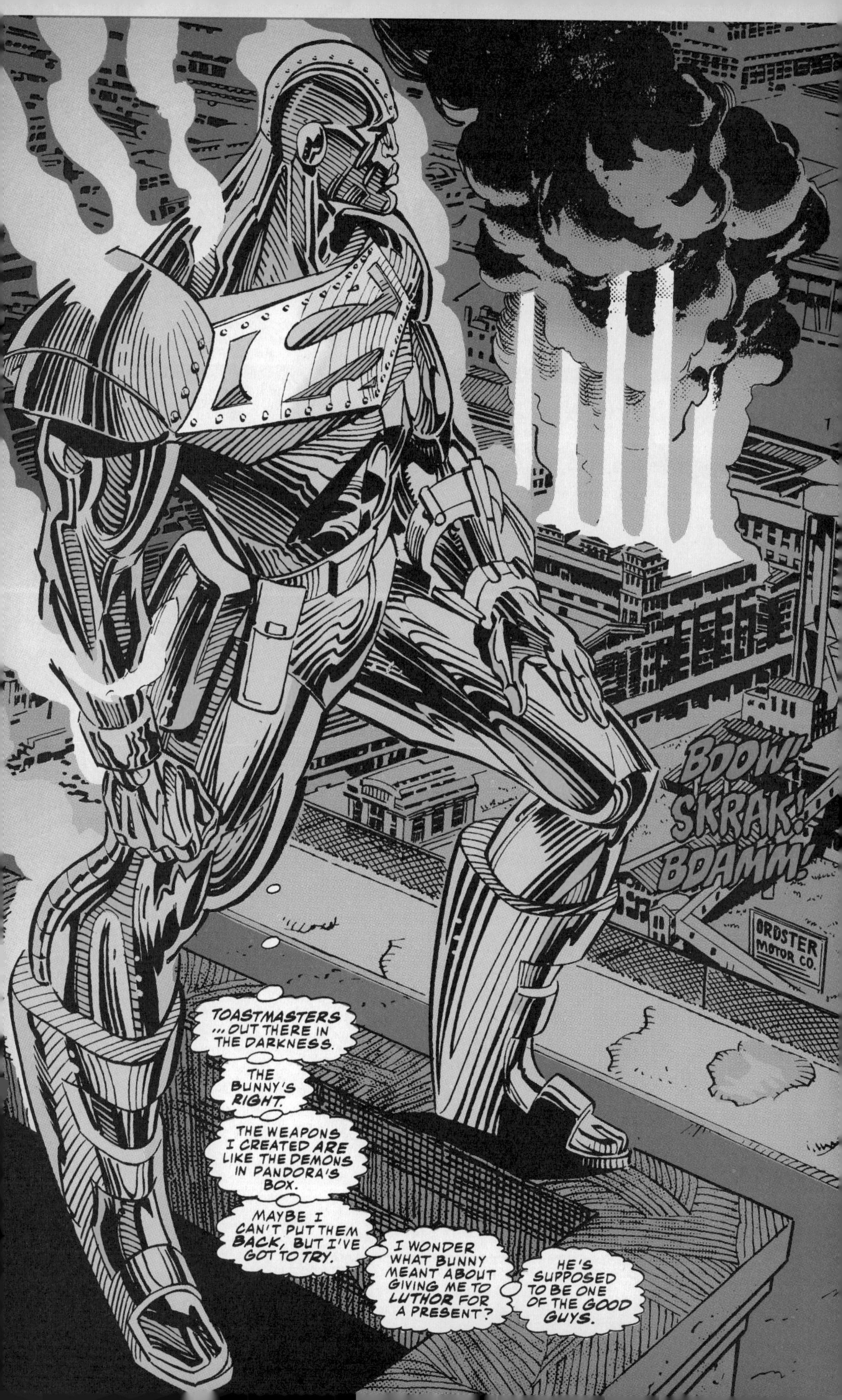
BDOW! SKRAK! BDAMM!
ORDSTER MOTOR CO.
TOASTMASTERS ...OUT THERE IN THE DARKNESS.
THE BUNNY'S RIGHT.
THE WEAPONS I CREATED ARE LIKE THE DEMONS IN PANDORA'S BOX.
MAYBE I CAN'T PUT THEM BACK, BUT I'VE GOT TO TRY.
I WONDER WHAT BUNNY MEANT ABOUT GIVING ME TO LUTHOR FOR A PRESENT?
HE'S SUPPOSED TO BE ONE OF THE GOOD GUYS.

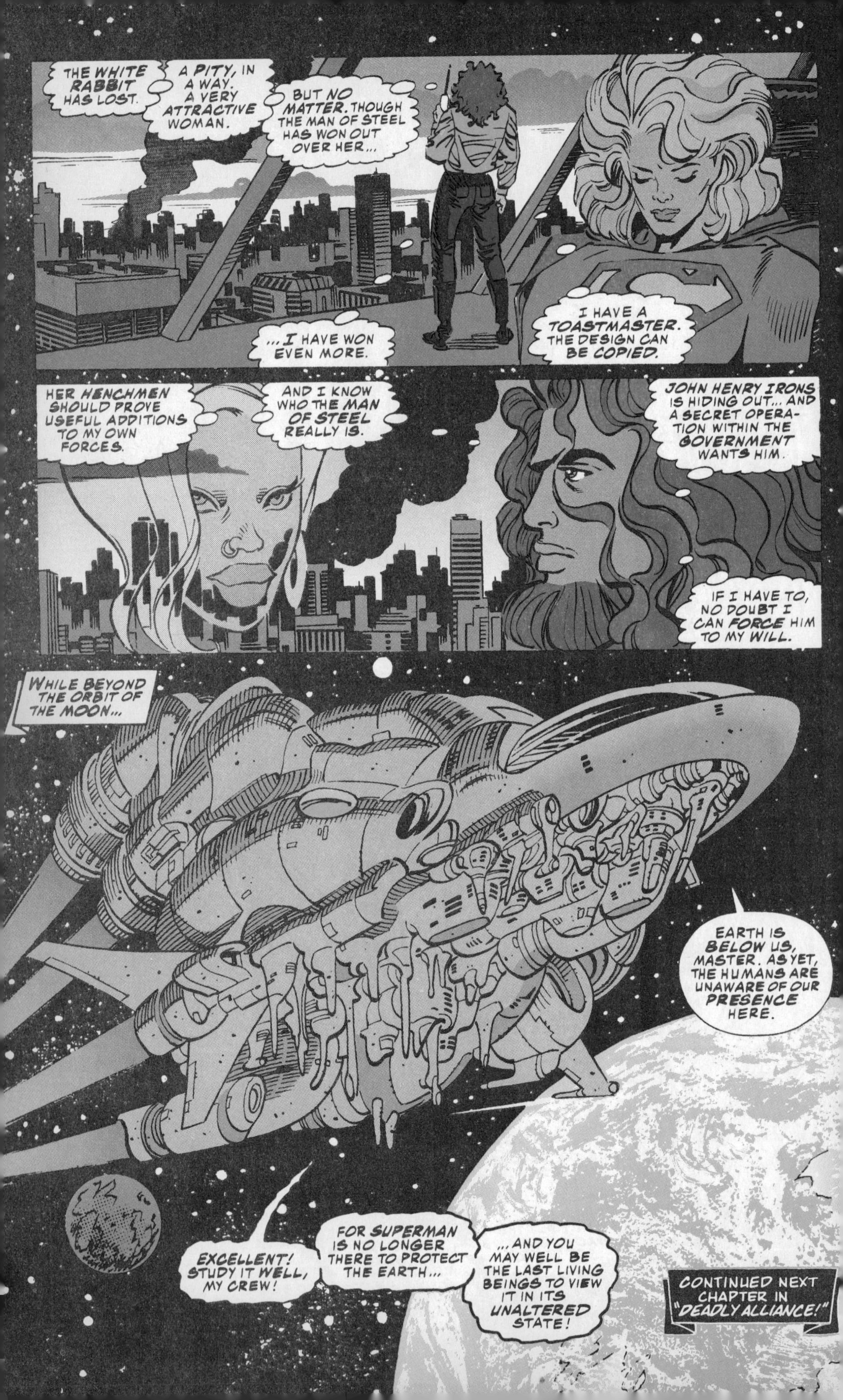
THE WHITE RABBIT HAS LOST.
A PITY, IN A WAY. A VERY ATTRACTIVE WOMAN.
BUT NO MATTER. THOUGH THE MAN OF STEEL HAS WON OUT OVER HER...
...I HAVE WON EVEN MORE.
I HAVE A TOASTMASTER. THE DESIGN CAN BE COPIED.
HER HENCHMEN SHOULD PROVE USEFUL ADDITIONS TO MY OWN FORCES.
AND I KNOW WHO THE MAN OF STEEL REALLY IS.
JOHN HENRY IRONS IS HIDING OUT... AND A SECRET OPERATION WITHIN THE GOVERNMENT WANTS HIM.
IF I HAVE TO, NO DOUBT I CAN FORCE HIM TO MY WILL.
WHILE BEYOND THE ORBIT OF THE MOON...
EARTH IS BELOW US, MASTER. AS YET, THE HUMANS ARE UNAWARE OF OUR PRESENCE HERE.
EXCELLENT! STUDY IT WELL, MY CREW!
FOR SUPERMAN IS NO LONGER THERE TO PROTECT THE EARTH...
...AND YOU MAY WELL BE THE LAST LIVING BEINGS TO VIEW IT IN ITS UNALTERED STATE!
CONTINUED NEXT CHAPTER IN "DEADLY ALLIANCE!"

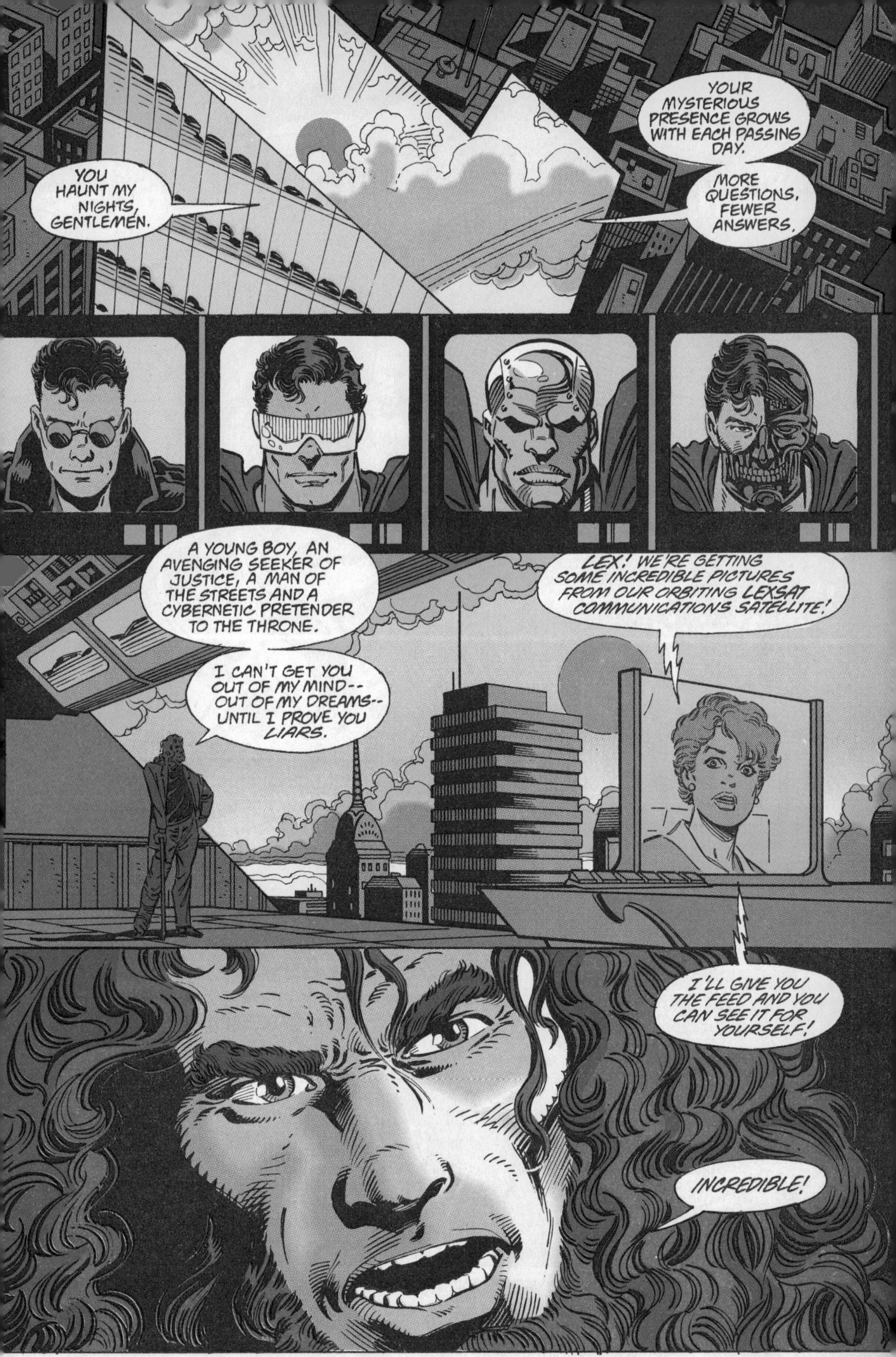
YOU HAUNT MY NIGHTS, GENTLEMEN.
YOUR MYSTERIOUS PRESENCE GROWS WITH EACH PASSING DAY.
MORE QUESTIONS, FEWER ANSWERS.
A YOUNG BOY, AN AVENGING SEEKER OF JUSTICE, A MAN OF THE STREETS AND A CYBERNETIC PRETENDER TO THE THRONE.
I CAN'T GET YOU OUT OF MY MIND-- OUT OF MY DREAMS-- UNTIL I PROVE YOU LIARS.
LEX! WE'RE GETTING SOME INCREDIBLE PICTURES FROM OUR ORBITING LEXSAT COMMUNICATIONS SATELLITE!
I'LL GIVE YOU THE FEED AND YOU CAN SEE IT FOR YOURSELF!
INCREDIBLE!

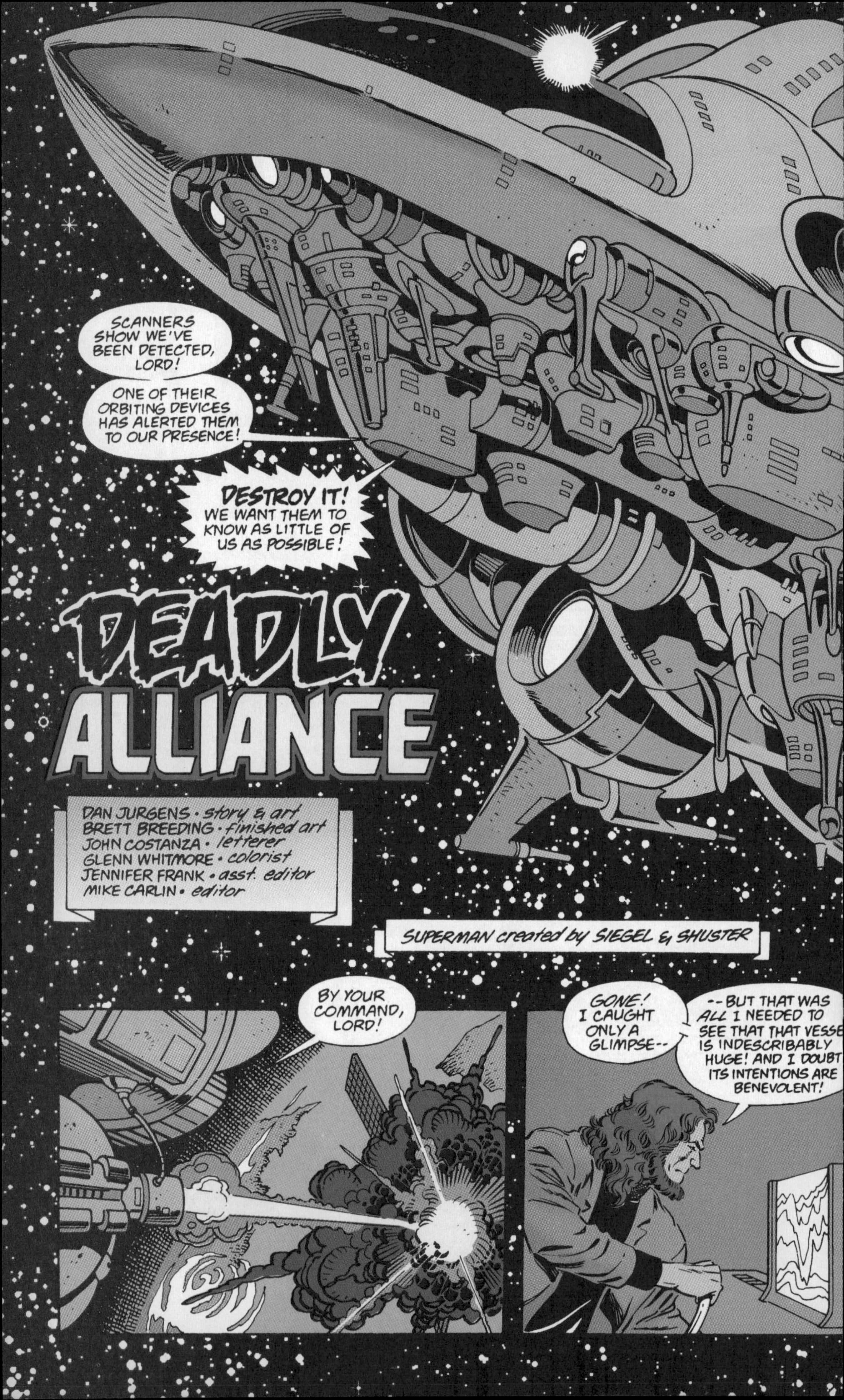
SCANNERS SHOW WE'VE BEEN DETECTED, LORD!
ONE OF THEIR ORBITING DEVICES HAS ALERTED THEM TO OUR PRESENCE!
DESTROY IT! WE WANT THEM TO KNOW AS LITTLE OF US AS POSSIBLE!
DEADLY ALLIANCE
DAN JURGENS • story & art
BRETT BREEDING • finished art
JOHN COSTANZA • letterer
GLENN WHITMORE • colorist
JENNIFER FRANK • asst. editor
MIKE CARLIN • editor
SUPERMAN created by SIEGEL & SHUSTER
BY YOUR COMMAND, LORD!
GONE! I CAUGHT ONLY A GLIMPSE--
--BUT THAT WAS ALL I NEEDED TO SEE THAT THAT VESSE IS INDESCRIBABLY HUGE! AND I DOUBT ITS INTENTIONS ARE BENEVOLENT!

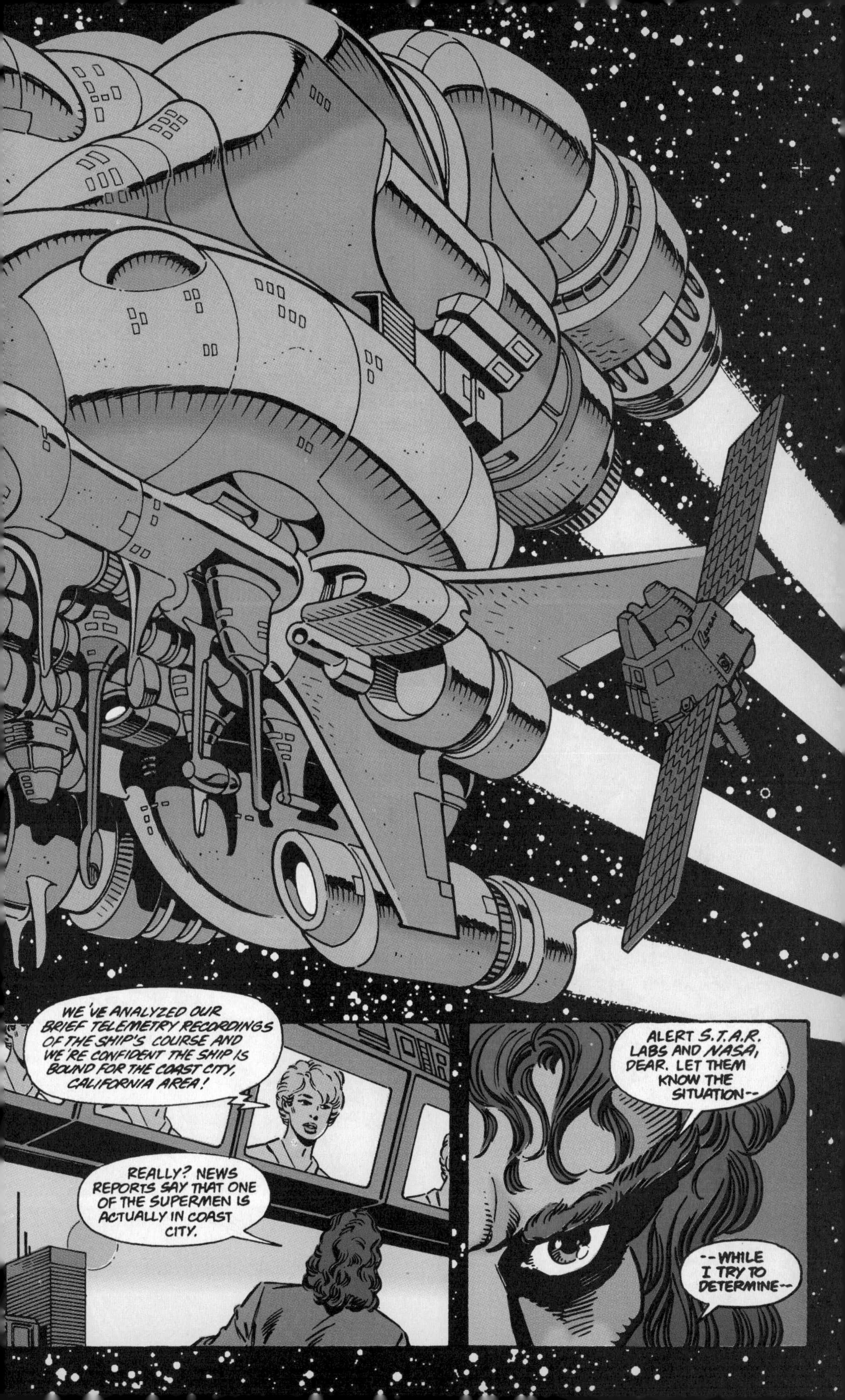
WE'VE ANALYZED OUR BRIEF TELEMETRY RECORDINGS OF THE SHIP'S COURSE AND WE'RE CONFIDENT THE SHIP IS BOUND FOR THE COAST CITY, CALIFORNIA AREA!
REALLY? NEWS REPORTS SAY THAT ONE OF THE SUPERMEN IS ACTUALLY IN COAST CITY.
ALERT S.T.A.R. LABS AND NASA, DEAR. LET THEM KNOW THE SITUATION--
--WHILE I TRY TO DETERMINE--

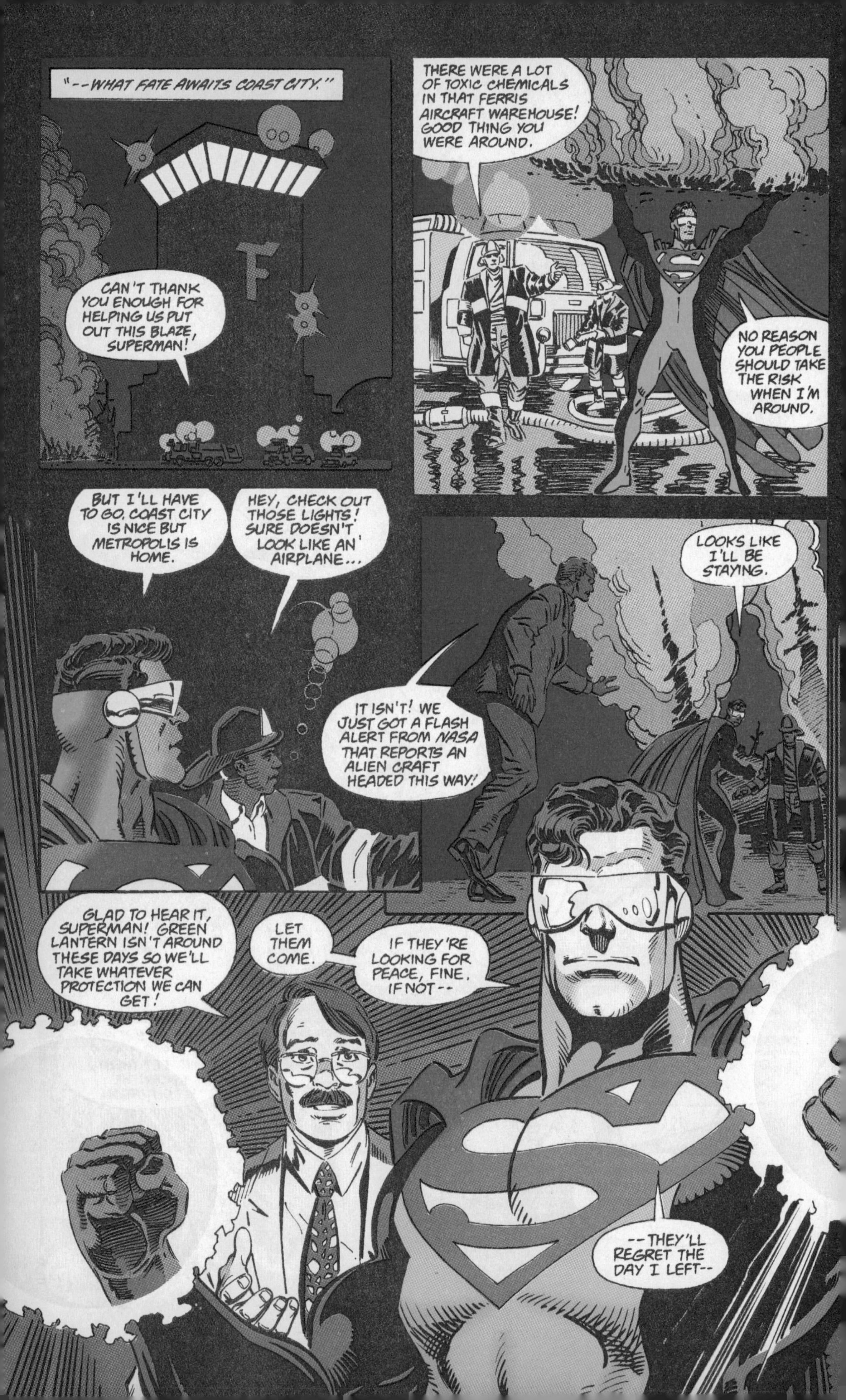
"--WHAT FATE AWAITS COAST CITY."
CAN'T THANK YOU ENOUGH FOR HELPING US PUT OUT THIS BLAZE, SUPERMAN!
THERE WERE A LOT OF TOXIC CHEMICALS IN THAT FERRIS AIRCRAFT WAREHOUSE! GOOD THING YOU WERE AROUND.
NO REASON YOU PEOPLE SHOULD TAKE THE RISK WHEN I'M AROUND.
BUT I'LL HAVE TO GO. COAST CITY IS NICE BUT METROPOLIS IS HOME.
HEY, CHECK OUT THOSE LIGHTS! SURE DOESN'T LOOK LIKE AN' AIRPLANE...
IT ISN'T! WE JUST GOT A FLASH ALERT FROM NASA THAT REPORTS AN ALIEN CRAFT HEADED THIS WAY!
LOOKS LIKE I'LL BE STAYING.
GLAD TO HEAR IT, SUPERMAN! GREEN LANTERN ISN'T AROUND THESE DAYS SO WE'LL TAKE WHATEVER PROTECTION WE CAN GET!
LET THEM COME.
IF THEY'RE LOOKING FOR PEACE, FINE. IF NOT--
--THEY'LL REGRET THE DAY I LEFT--

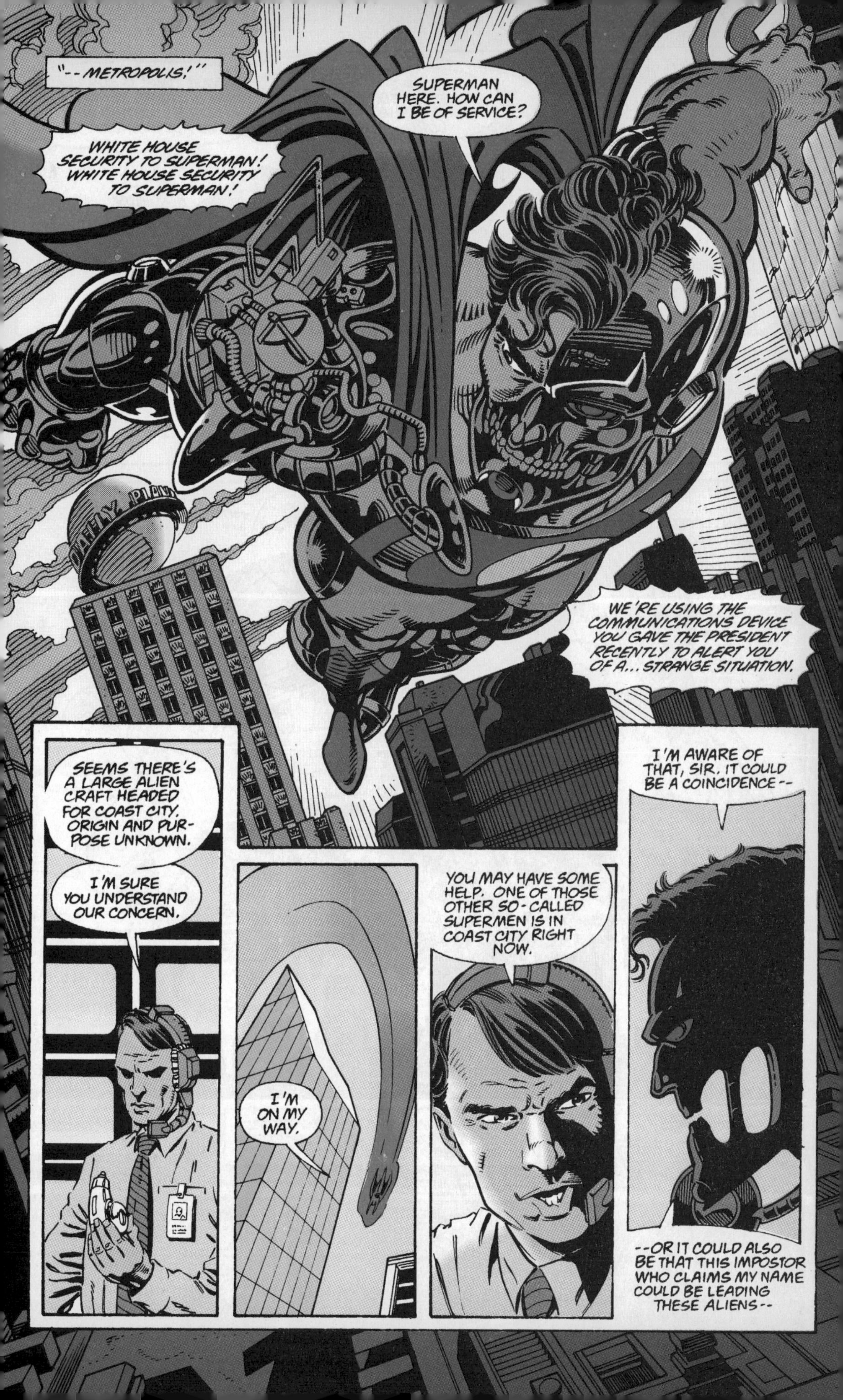
"--METROPOLIS!"
WHITE HOUSE SECURITY TO SUPERMAN! WHITE HOUSE SECURITY TO SUPERMAN!
SUPERMAN HERE. HOW CAN I BE OF SERVICE?
WE'RE USING THE COMMUNICATIONS DEVICE YOU GAVE THE PRESIDENT RECENTLY TO ALERT YOU OF A... STRANGE SITUATION.
SEEMS THERE'S A LARGE ALIEN CRAFT HEADED FOR COAST CITY. ORIGIN AND PURPOSE UNKNOWN.
I'M SURE YOU UNDERSTAND OUR CONCERN.
I'M ON MY WAY.
YOU MAY HAVE SOME HELP. ONE OF THOSE OTHER SO-CALLED SUPERMEN IS IN COAST CITY RIGHT NOW.
I'M AWARE OF THAT, SIR. IT COULD BE A COINCIDENCE--
--OR IT COULD ALSO BE THAT THIS IMPOSTOR WHO CLAIMS MY NAME COULD BE LEADING THESE ALIENS--

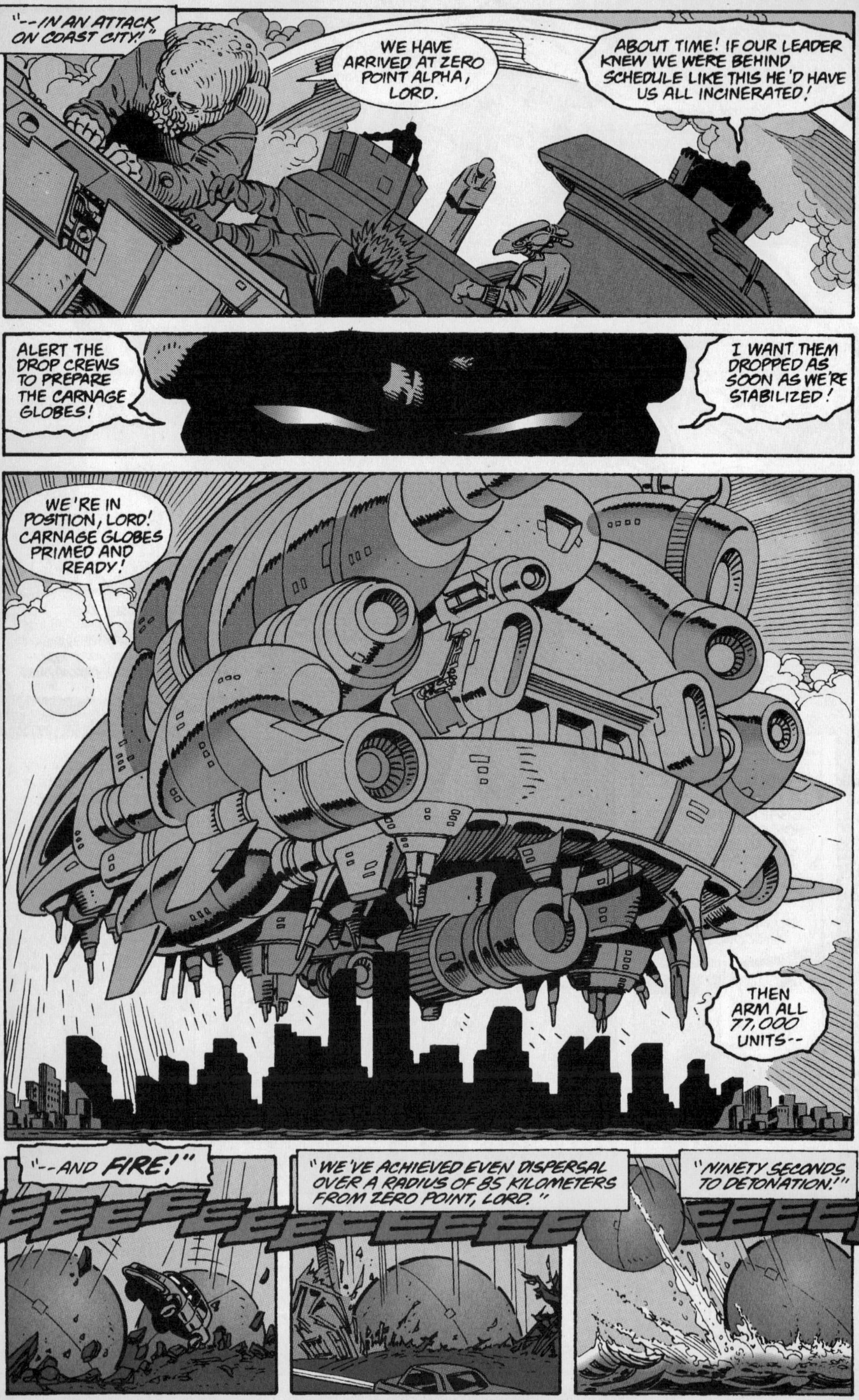
"--IN AN ATTACK ON COAST CITY!"
WE HAVE ARRIVED AT ZERO POINT ALPHA, LORD.
ABOUT TIME! IF OUR LEADER KNEW WE WERE BEHIND SCHEDULE LIKE THIS HE'D HAVE US ALL INCINERATED!
ALERT THE DROP CREWS TO PREPARE THE CARNAGE GLOBES!
I WANT THEM DROPPED AS SOON AS WE'RE STABILIZED!
WE'RE IN POSITION, LORD! CARNAGE GLOBES PRIMED AND READY!
THEN ARM ALL 77,000 UNITS--
"--AND FIRE!"
"WE'VE ACHIEVED EVEN DISPERSAL OVER A RADIUS OF 85 KILOMETERS FROM ZERO POINT, LORD."
"NINETY SECONDS TO DETONATION!"

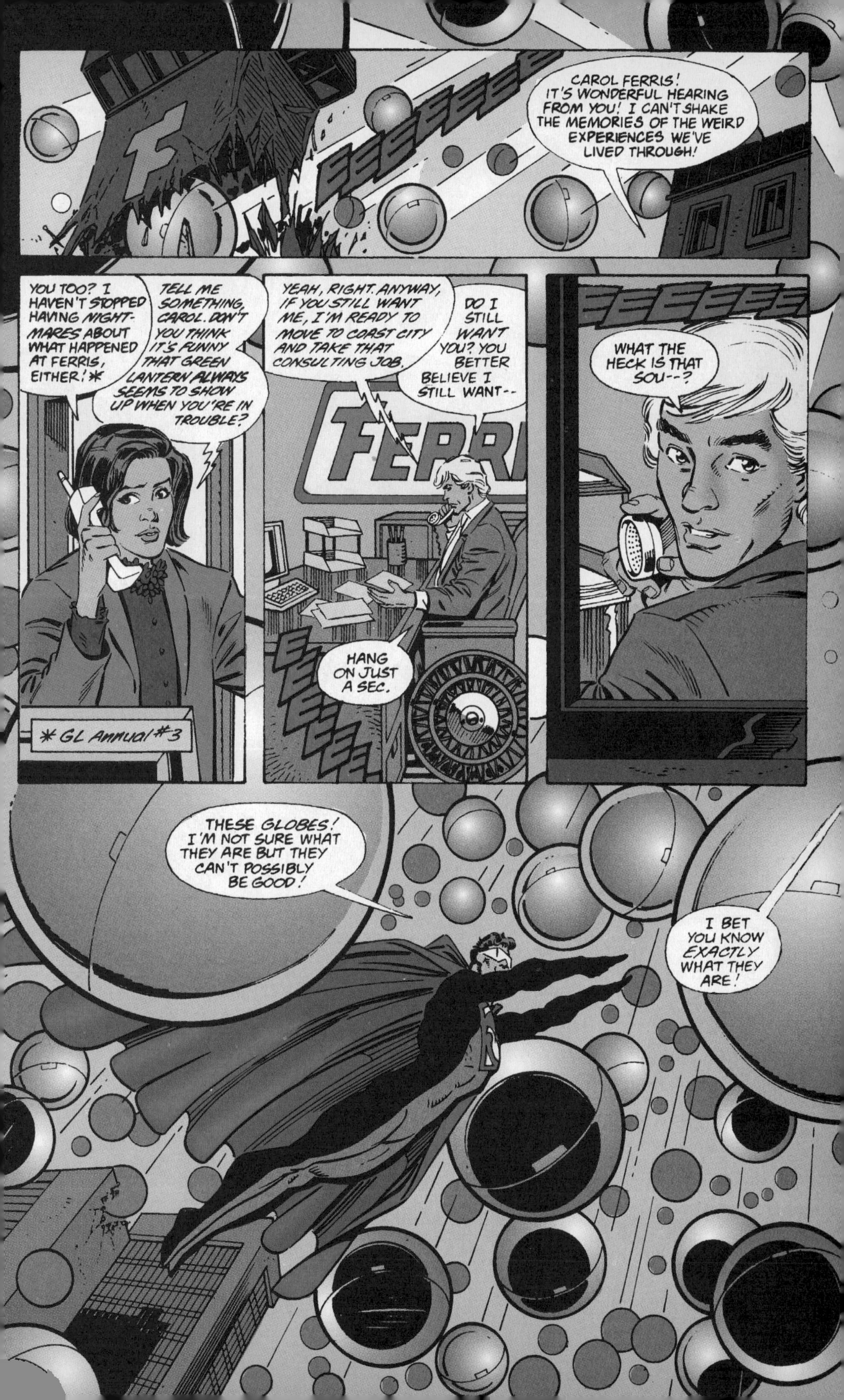

EEEEEEEEE
CAROL FERRIS! IT'S WONDERFUL HEARING FROM YOU! I CAN'T SHAKE THE MEMORIES OF THE WEIRD EXPERIENCES WE'VE LIVED THROUGH!
YOU TOO? I HAVEN'T STOPPED HAVING NIGHT-MARES ABOUT WHAT HAPPENED AT FERRIS, EITHER! *
TELL ME SOMETHING, CAROL. DON'T YOU THINK IT'S FUNNY THAT GREEN LANTERN ALWAYS SEEMS TO SHOW UP WHEN YOU'RE IN TROUBLE?
* GL Annual #3
YEAH, RIGHT. ANYWAY, IF YOU STILL WANT ME, I'M READY TO MOVE TO COAST CITY AND TAKE THAT CONSULTING JOB.
DO I STILL WANT YOU? YOU BETTER BELIEVE I STILL WANT--
FERRI
EEEEEEE
HANG ON JUST A SEC.
EEEEEEE
WHAT THE HECK IS THAT SOU--?
THESE GLOBES! I'M NOT SURE WHAT THEY ARE BUT THEY CAN'T POSSIBLY BE GOOD!
I BET YOU KNOW EXACTLY WHAT THEY ARE!

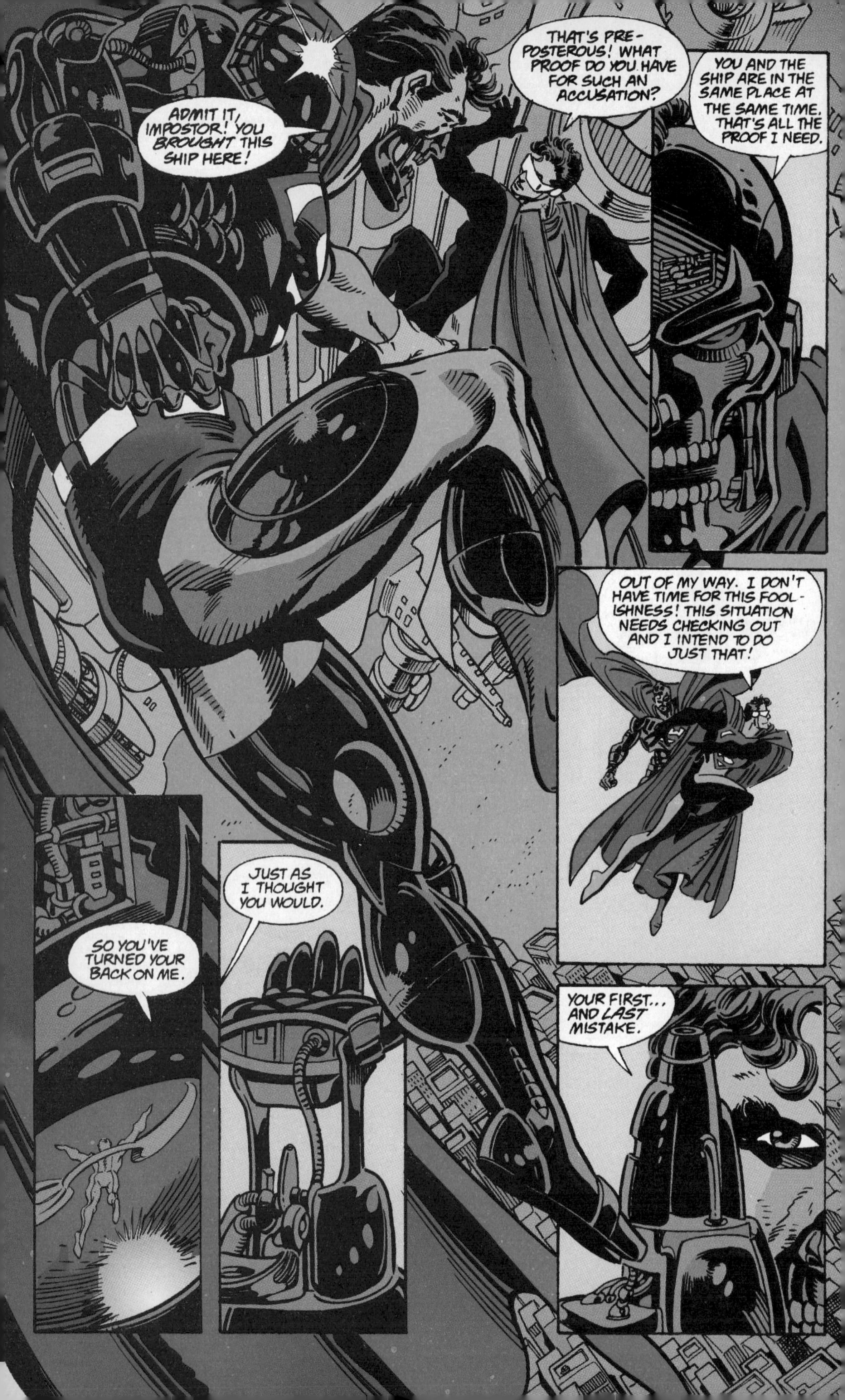
ADMIT IT, IMPOSTOR! YOU BROUGHT THIS SHIP HERE!
THAT'S PREPOSTEROUS! WHAT PROOF DO YOU HAVE FOR SUCH AN ACCUSATION?
YOU AND THE SHIP ARE IN THE SAME PLACE AT THE SAME TIME. THAT'S ALL THE PROOF I NEED.
OUT OF MY WAY. I DON'T HAVE TIME FOR THIS FOOLISHNESS! THIS SITUATION NEEDS CHECKING OUT AND I INTEND TO DO JUST THAT!
SO YOU'VE TURNED YOUR BACK ON ME.
JUST AS I THOUGHT YOU WOULD.
YOUR FIRST... AND LAST MISTAKE.

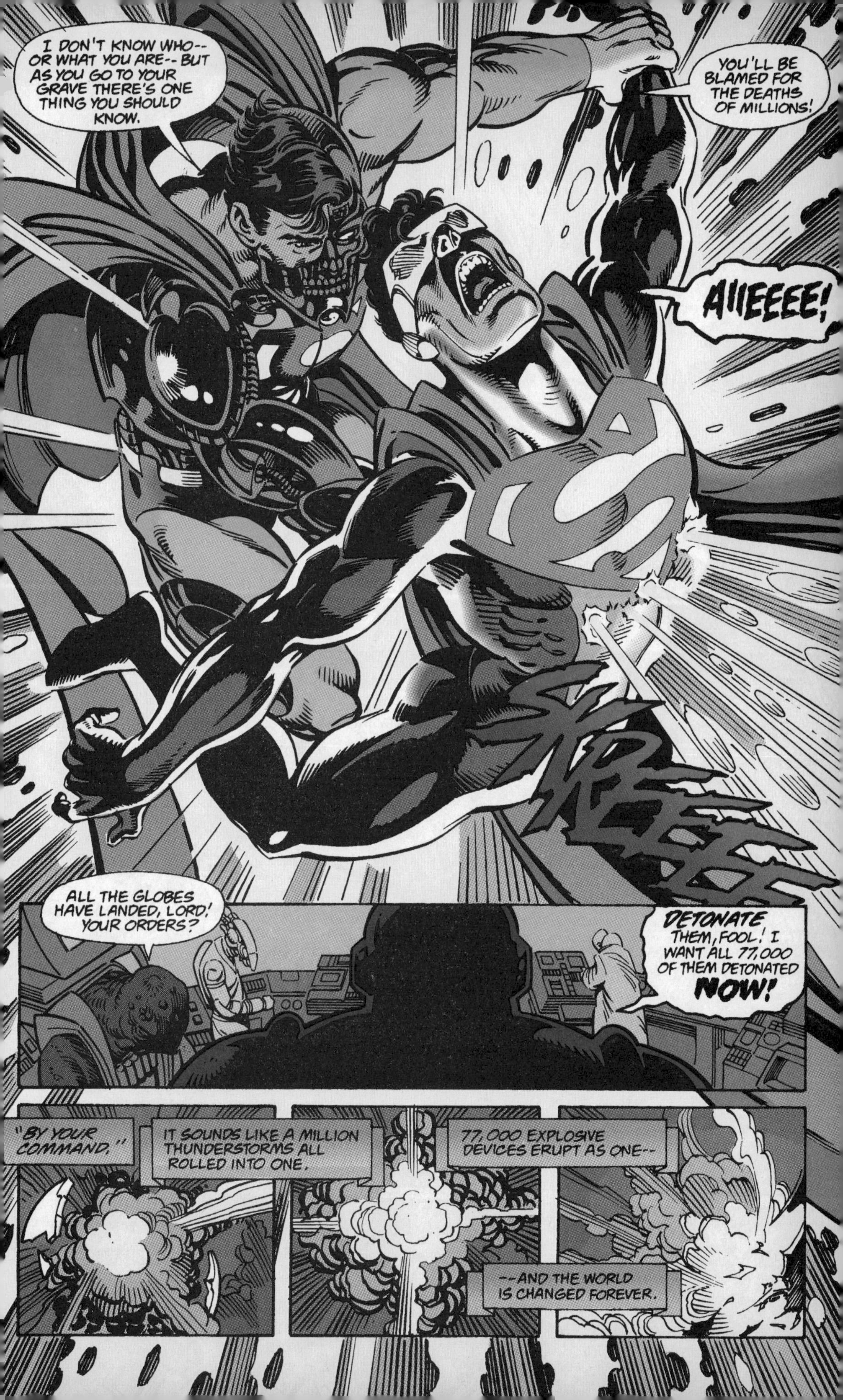
I DON'T KNOW WHO-- OR WHAT YOU ARE-- BUT AS YOU GO TO YOUR GRAVE THERE'S ONE THING YOU SHOULD KNOW.
YOU'LL BE BLAMED FOR THE DEATHS OF MILLIONS!
AIIEEEE!
SKREEE
ALL THE GLOBES HAVE LANDED, LORD! YOUR ORDERS?
DETONATE THEM, FOOL! I WANT ALL 77,000 OF THEM DETONATED NOW!
"BY YOUR COMMAND."
IT SOUNDS LIKE A MILLION THUNDERSTORMS ALL ROLLED INTO ONE.
77,000 EXPLOSIVE DEVICES ERUPT AS ONE--
--AND THE WORLD IS CHANGED FOREVER.

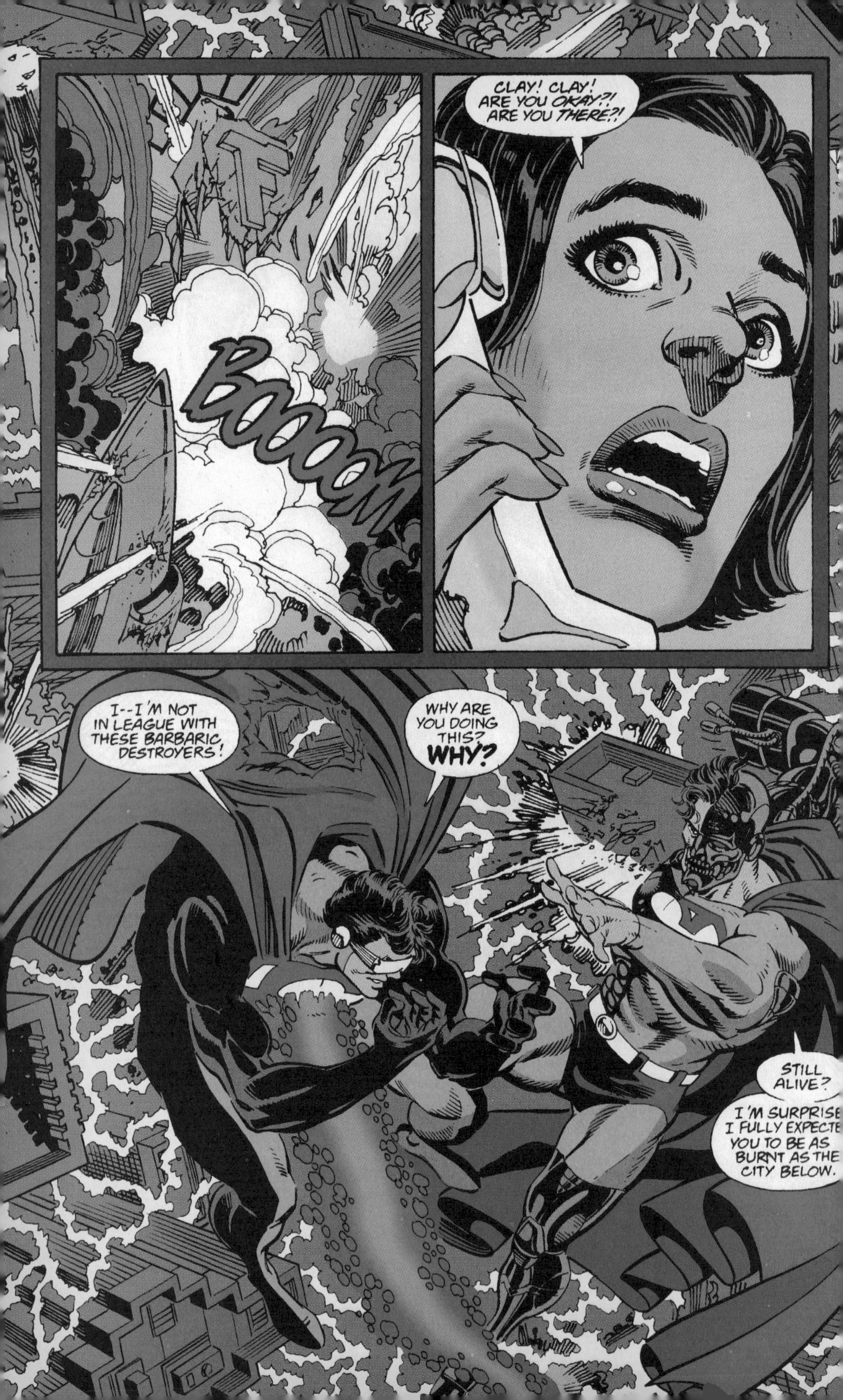
BOOOOOM
CLAY! CLAY! ARE YOU OKAY?! ARE YOU THERE?!
I--I'M NOT IN LEAGUE WITH THESE BARBARIC DESTROYERS!
WHY ARE YOU DOING THIS? WHY?
STILL ALIVE?
I'M SURPRISE I FULLY EXPECTE YOU TO BE AS BURNT AS THE CITY BELOW.

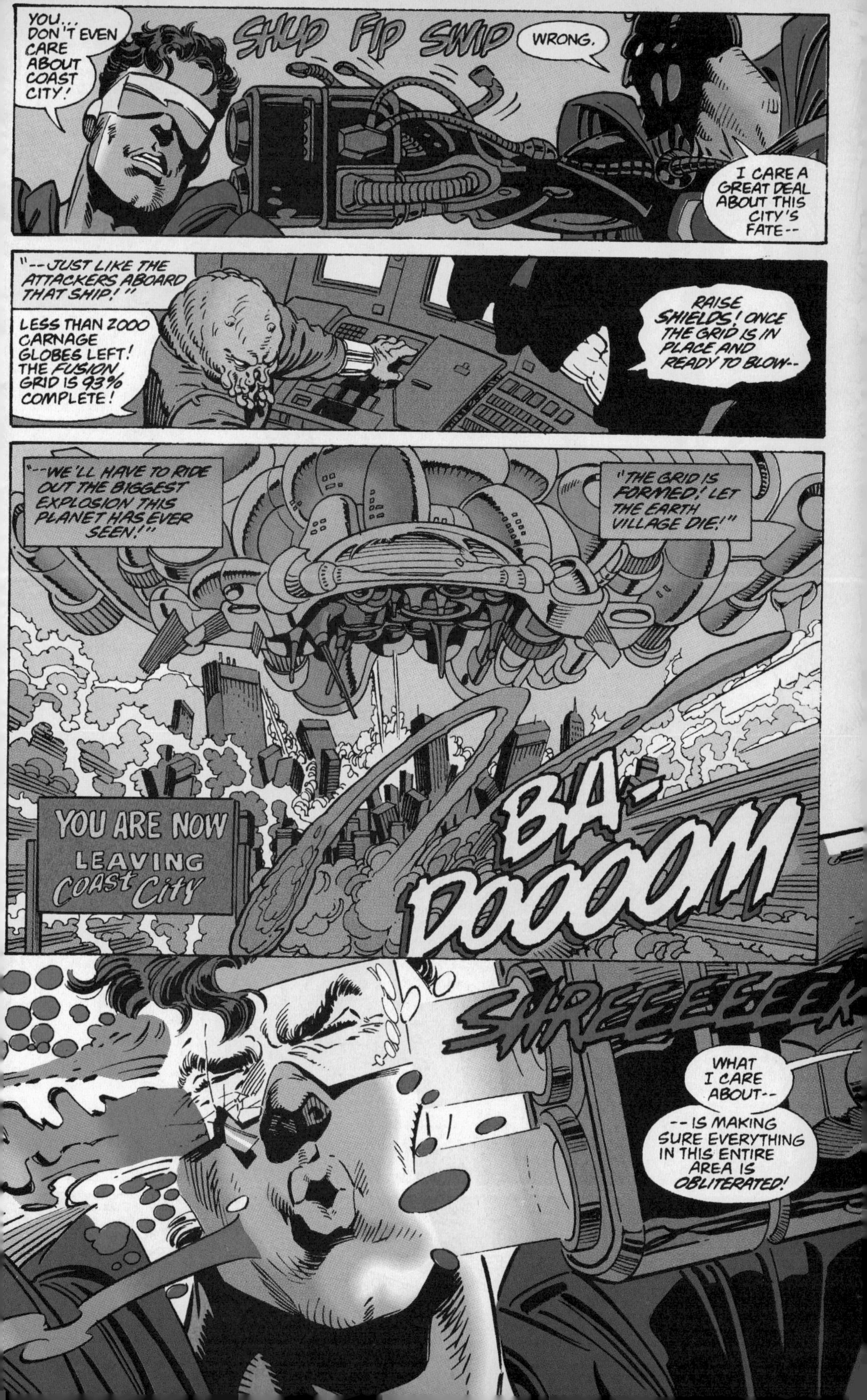
YOU... DON'T EVEN CARE ABOUT COAST CITY!
SHUP FIP SWIP
WRONG.
I CARE A GREAT DEAL ABOUT THIS CITY'S FATE--
"--JUST LIKE THE ATTACKERS ABOARD THAT SHIP!"
LESS THAN 2000 CARNAGE GLOBES LEFT! THE FUSION GRID IS 93% COMPLETE!
RAISE SHIELDS! ONCE THE GRID IS IN PLACE AND READY TO BLOW--
"--WE'LL HAVE TO RIDE OUT THE BIGGEST EXPLOSION THIS PLANET HAS EVER SEEN!"
"THE GRID IS FORMED! LET THE EARTH VILLAGE DIE!"
YOU ARE NOW LEAVING COAST CITY
BA-DOOOOM
SHREEEEEEK
WHAT I CARE ABOUT--
--IS MAKING SURE EVERYTHING IN THIS ENTIRE AREA IS OBLITERATED!

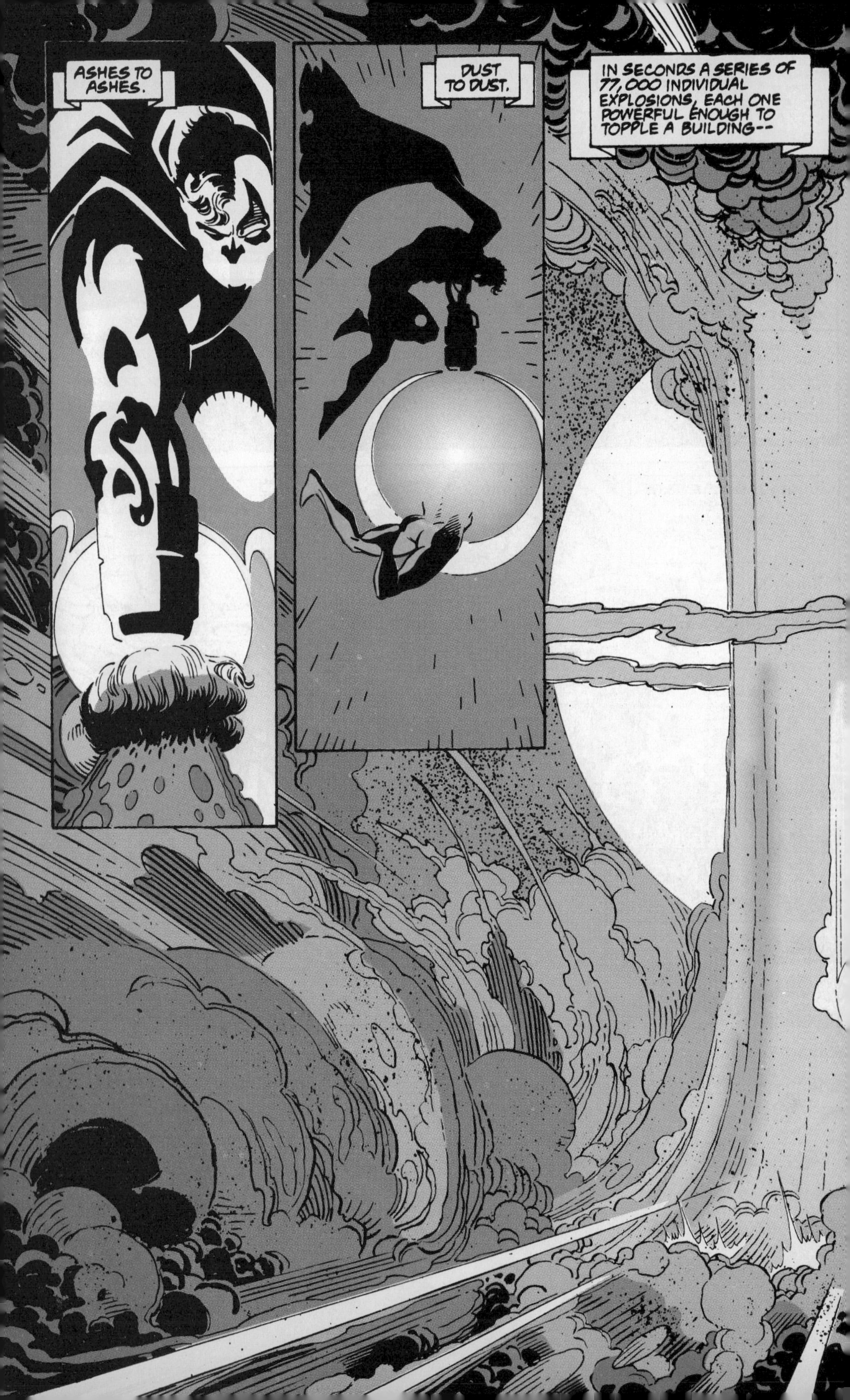
ASHES TO ASHES.
DUST TO DUST.
IN SECONDS A SERIES OF 77,000 INDIVIDUAL EXPLOSIONS, EACH ONE POWERFUL ENOUGH TO TOPPLE A BUILDING--

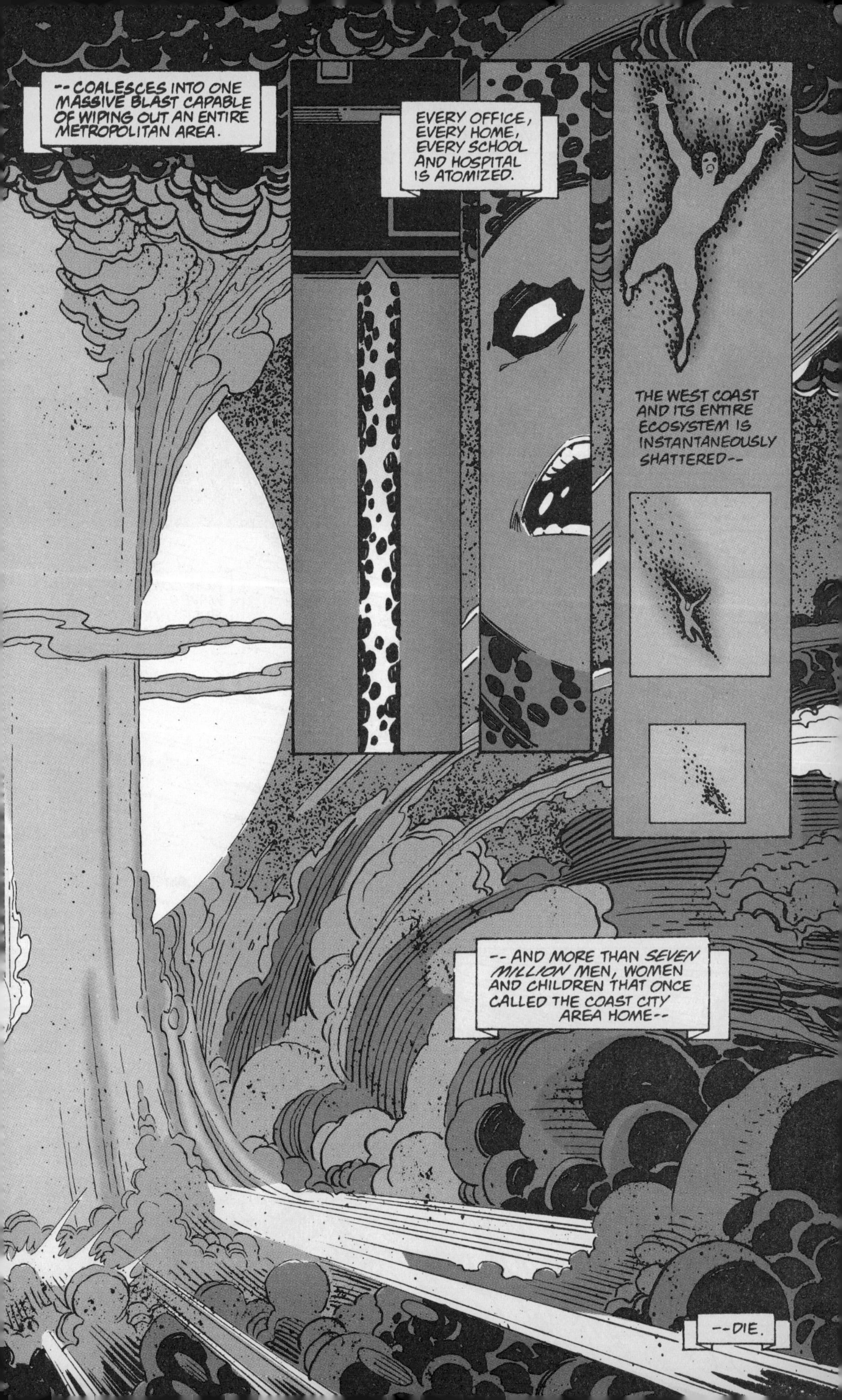

--COALESCES INTO ONE MASSIVE BLAST CAPABLE OF WIPING OUT AN ENTIRE METROPOLITAN AREA.
EVERY OFFICE, EVERY HOME, EVERY SCHOOL AND HOSPITAL IS ATOMIZED.
THE WEST COAST AND ITS ENTIRE ECOSYSTEM IS INSTANTANEOUSLY SHATTERED--
--AND MORE THAN SEVEN MILLION MEN, WOMEN AND CHILDREN THAT ONCE CALLED THE COAST CITY AREA HOME--
--DIE.

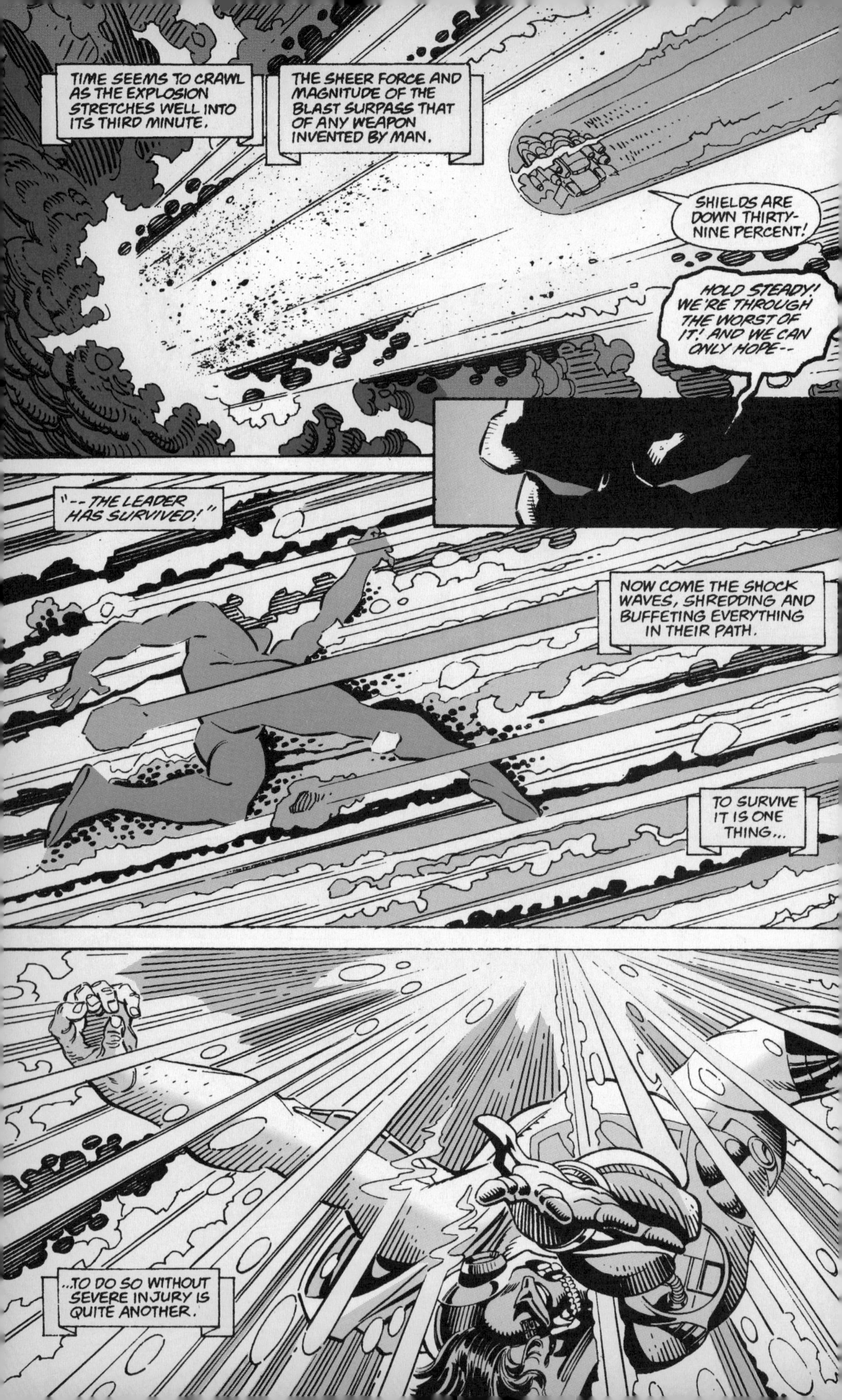

TIME SEEMS TO CRAWL AS THE EXPLOSION STRETCHES WELL INTO ITS THIRD MINUTE.
THE SHEER FORCE AND MAGNITUDE OF THE BLAST SURPASS THAT OF ANY WEAPON INVENTED BY MAN.
SHIELDS ARE DOWN THIRTY-NINE PERCENT!
HOLD STEADY! WE'RE THROUGH THE WORST OF IT! AND WE CAN ONLY HOPE--
"--THE LEADER HAS SURVIVED!"
NOW COME THE SHOCK WAVES, SHREDDING AND BUFFETING EVERYTHING IN THEIR PATH.
TO SURVIVE IT IS ONE THING...
...TO DO SO WITHOUT SEVERE INJURY IS QUITE ANOTHER.

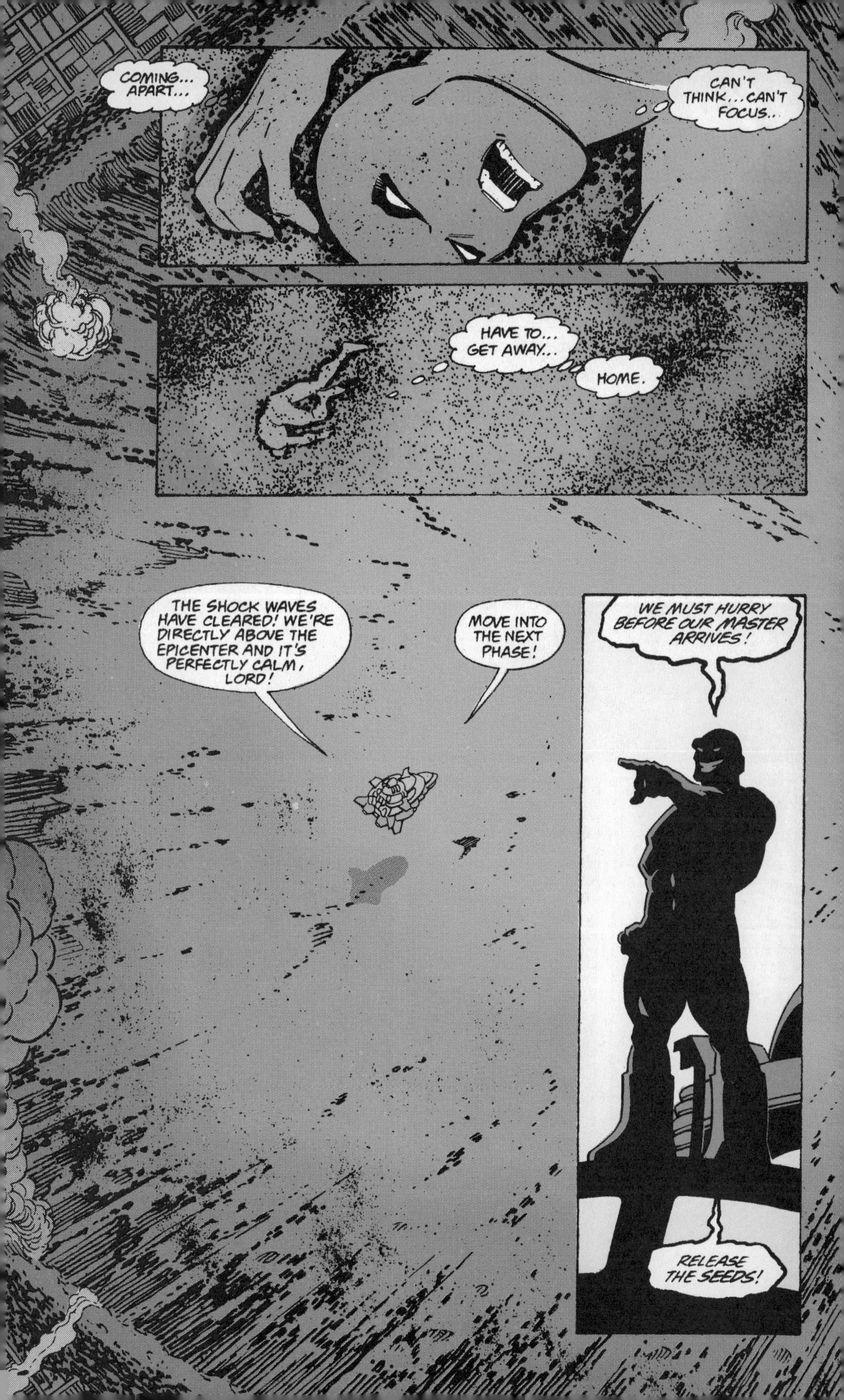
COMING... APART...
CAN'T THINK... CAN'T FOCUS...
HAVE TO... GET AWAY...
HOME.
THE SHOCK WAVES HAVE CLEARED! WE'RE DIRECTLY ABOVE THE EPICENTER AND IT'S PERFECTLY CALM, LORD!
MOVE INTO THE NEXT PHASE!
WE MUST HURRY BEFORE OUR MASTER ARRIVES!
RELEASE THE SEEDS!

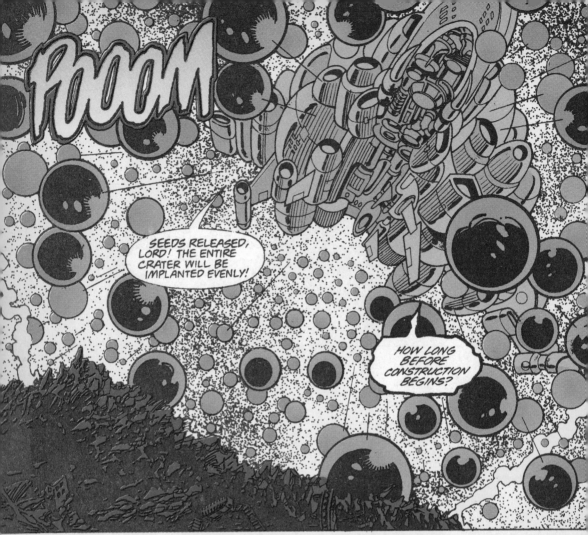

FOOOM

SEEDS RELEASED, LORD! THE ENTIRE CRATER WILL BE IMPLANTED EVENLY!

HOW LONG BEFORE CONSTRUCTION BEGINS?

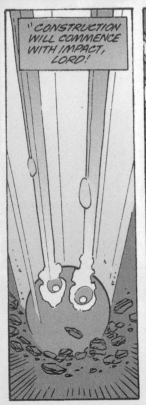

"CONSTRUCTION WILL COMMENCE WITH IMPACT, LORD!

"ONCE ALL SEEDS HAVE BURROWED TO THE APPROPRIATE DEPTH--

"--EACH UNIT WILL FOLLOW ITS PROGRAM--

"--UNTIL THEY FULLY DEPLOY AND CONNECT WITH ONE ANOTHER."

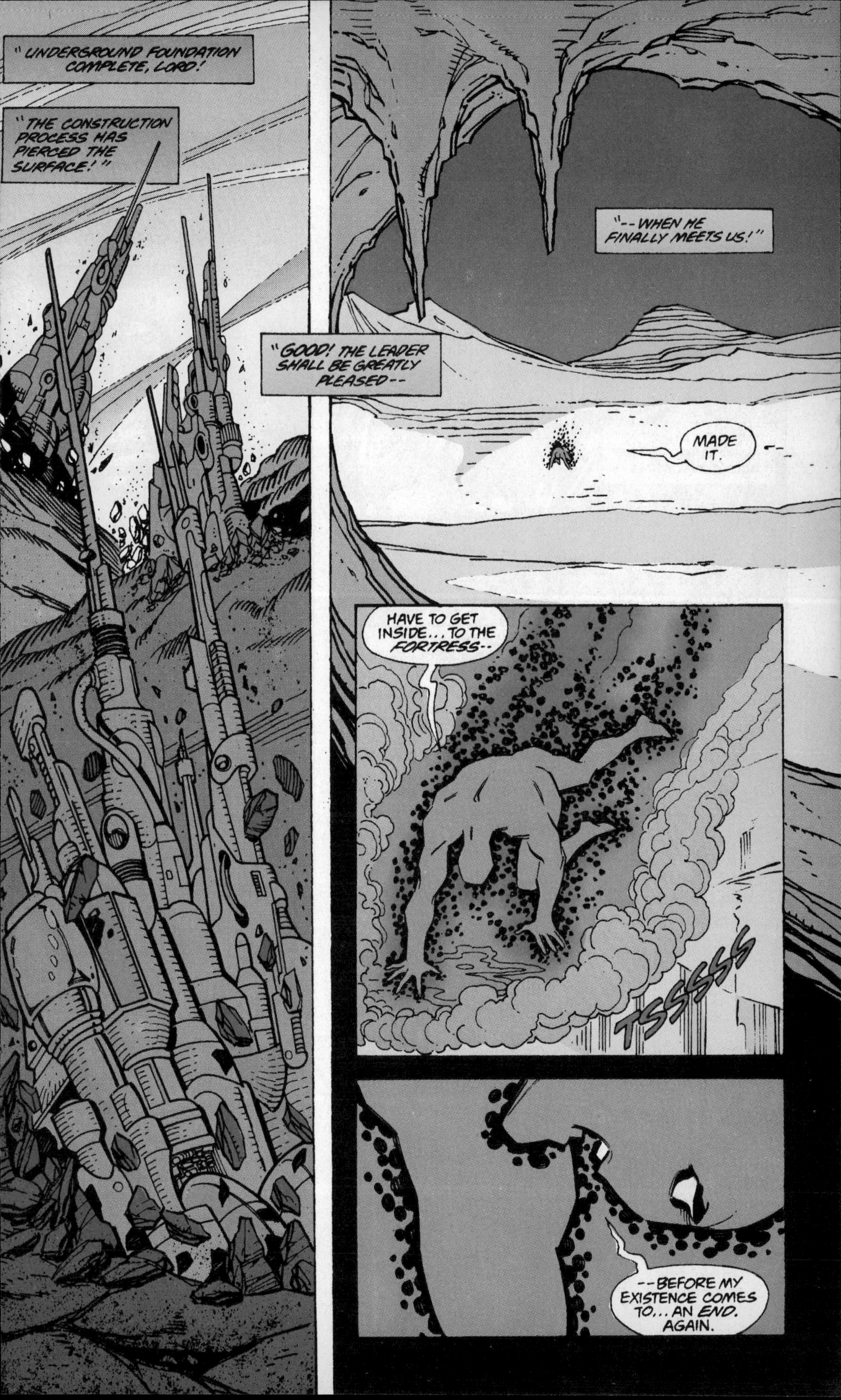
"UNDERGROUND FOUNDATION COMPLETE, LORD!
"THE CONSTRUCTION PROCESS HAS PIERCED THE SURFACE!"
"GOOD! THE LEADER SHALL BE GREATLY PLEASED--
"--WHEN HE FINALLY MEETS US!"
MADE IT.
HAVE TO GET INSIDE... TO THE FORTRESS--
TSSSSSS
--BEFORE MY EXISTENCE COMES TO... AN END. AGAIN.

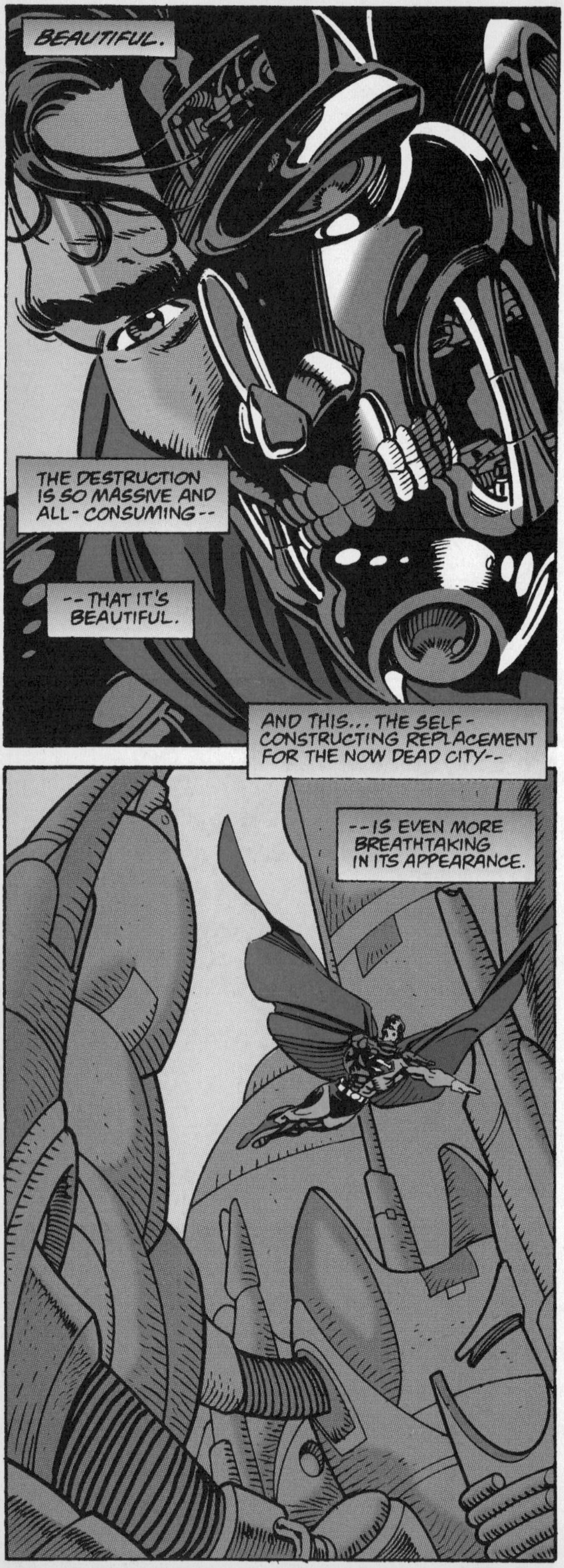
BEAUTIFUL.
THE DESTRUCTION IS SO MASSIVE AND ALL-CONSUMING--
--THAT IT'S BEAUTIFUL.
AND THIS... THE SELF-CONSTRUCTING REPLACEMENT FOR THE NOW DEAD CITY--
--IS EVEN MORE BREATHTAKING IN ITS APPEARANCE.

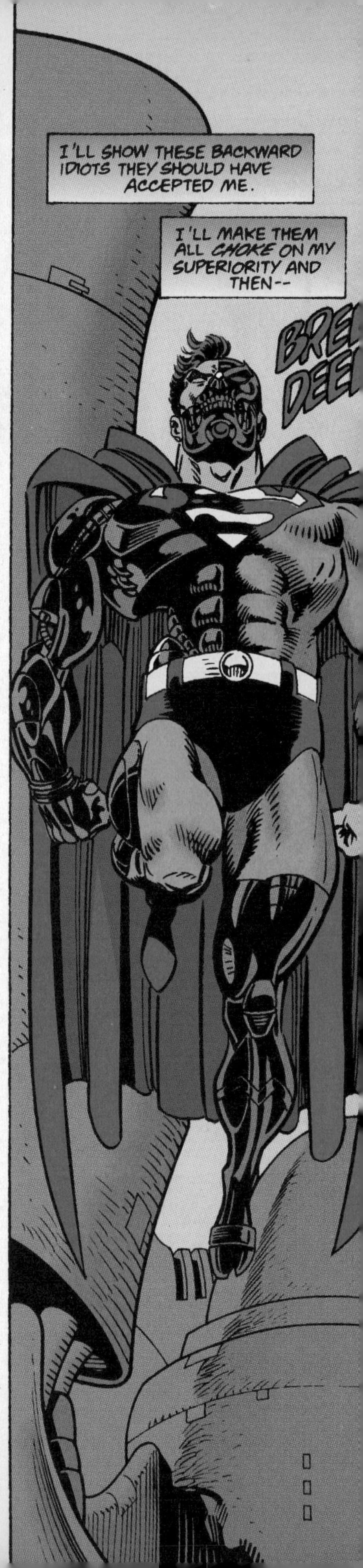
I'LL SHOW THESE BACKWARD IDIOTS THEY SHOULD HAVE ACCEPTED ME.
I'LL MAKE THEM ALL CHOKE ON MY SUPERIORITY AND THEN--

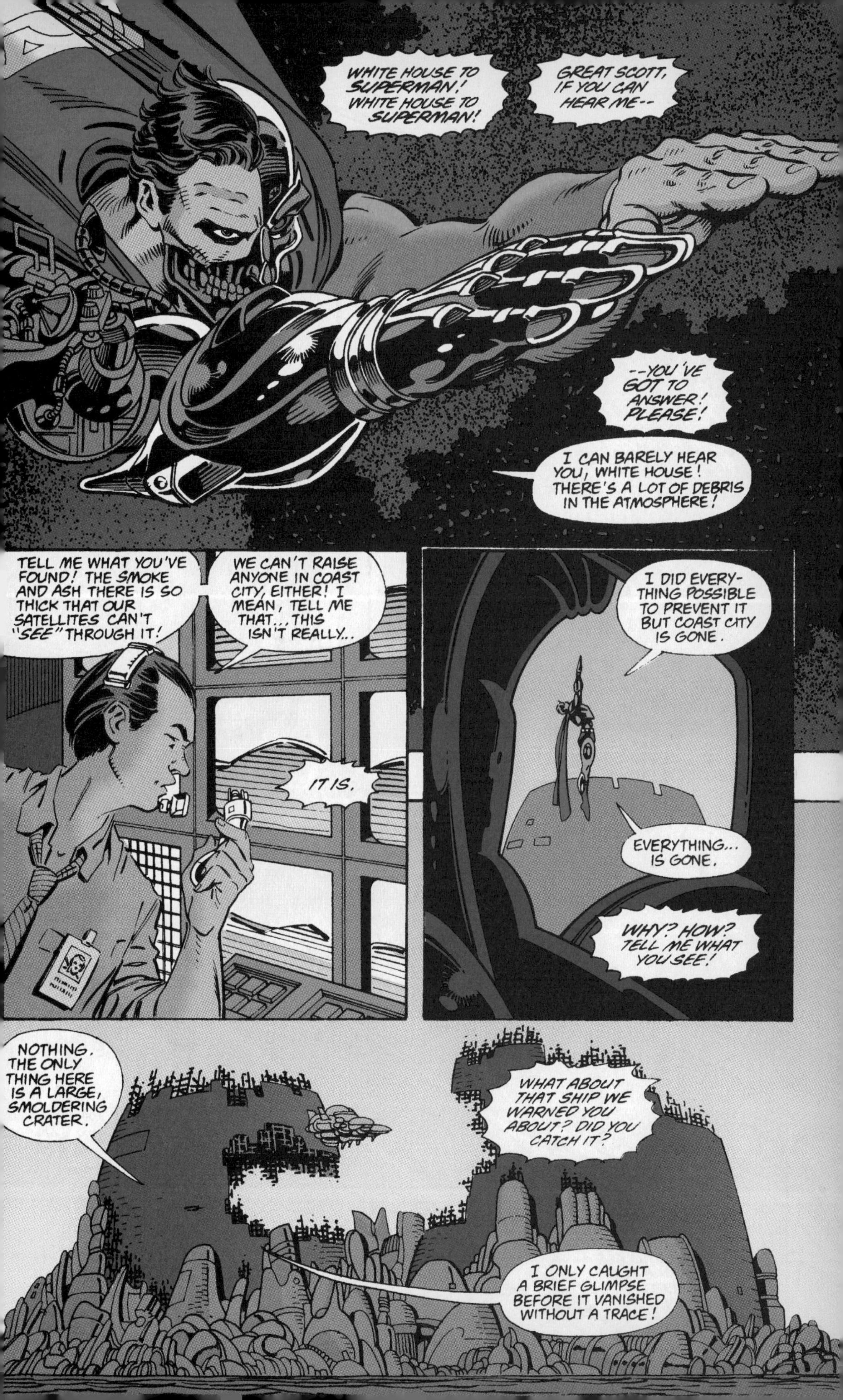
WHITE HOUSE TO SUPERMAN! WHITE HOUSE TO SUPERMAN!
GREAT SCOTT, IF YOU CAN HEAR ME--
--YOU'VE GOT TO ANSWER! PLEASE!
I CAN BARELY HEAR YOU, WHITE HOUSE! THERE'S A LOT OF DEBRIS IN THE ATMOSPHERE!
TELL ME WHAT YOU'VE FOUND! THE SMOKE AND ASH THERE IS SO THICK THAT OUR SATELLITES CAN'T "SEE" THROUGH IT!
WE CAN'T RAISE ANYONE IN COAST CITY, EITHER! I MEAN, TELL ME THAT... THIS ISN'T REALLY...
IT IS.
I DID EVERYTHING POSSIBLE TO PREVENT IT BUT COAST CITY IS GONE.
EVERYTHING... IS GONE.
WHY? HOW? TELL ME WHAT YOU SEE!
NOTHING. THE ONLY THING HERE IS A LARGE, SMOLDERING CRATER.
WHAT ABOUT THAT SHIP WE WARNED YOU ABOUT? DID YOU CATCH IT?
I ONLY CAUGHT A BRIEF GLIMPSE BEFORE IT VANISHED WITHOUT A TRACE!

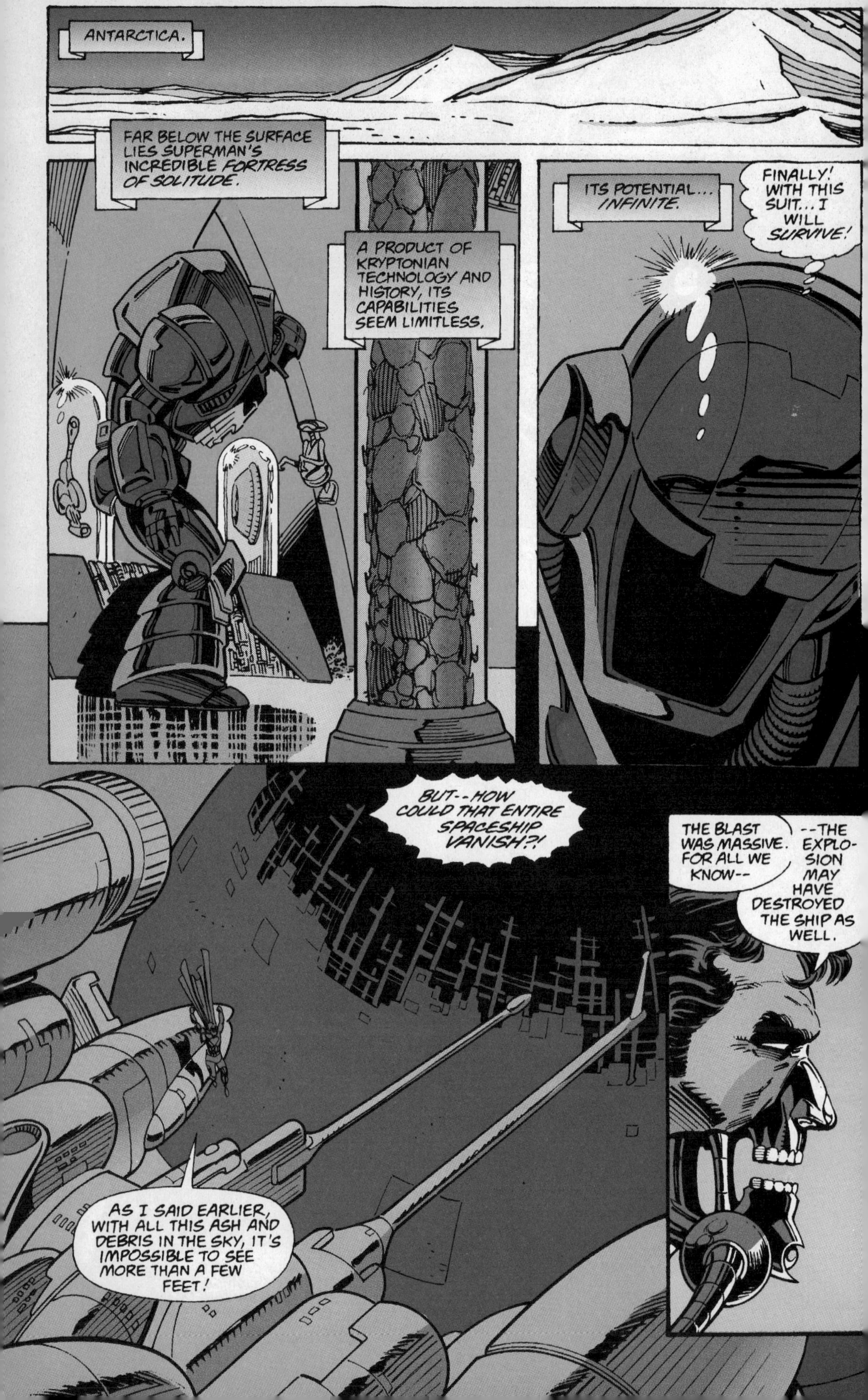
ANTARCTICA.
FAR BELOW THE SURFACE LIES SUPERMAN'S INCREDIBLE *FORTRESS OF SOLITUDE*.
A PRODUCT OF KRYPTONIAN TECHNOLOGY AND HISTORY, ITS CAPABILITIES SEEM LIMITLESS.
ITS POTENTIAL... *INFINITE*.
FINALLY! WITH THIS SUIT... I WILL *SURVIVE!*
BUT--HOW COULD THAT ENTIRE SPACESHIP VANISH?!
THE BLAST WAS MASSIVE. FOR ALL WE KNOW--
--THE EXPLOSION MAY HAVE DESTROYED THE SHIP AS WELL.
AS I SAID EARLIER, WITH ALL THIS ASH AND DEBRIS IN THE SKY, IT'S IMPOSSIBLE TO SEE MORE THAN A FEW FEET!

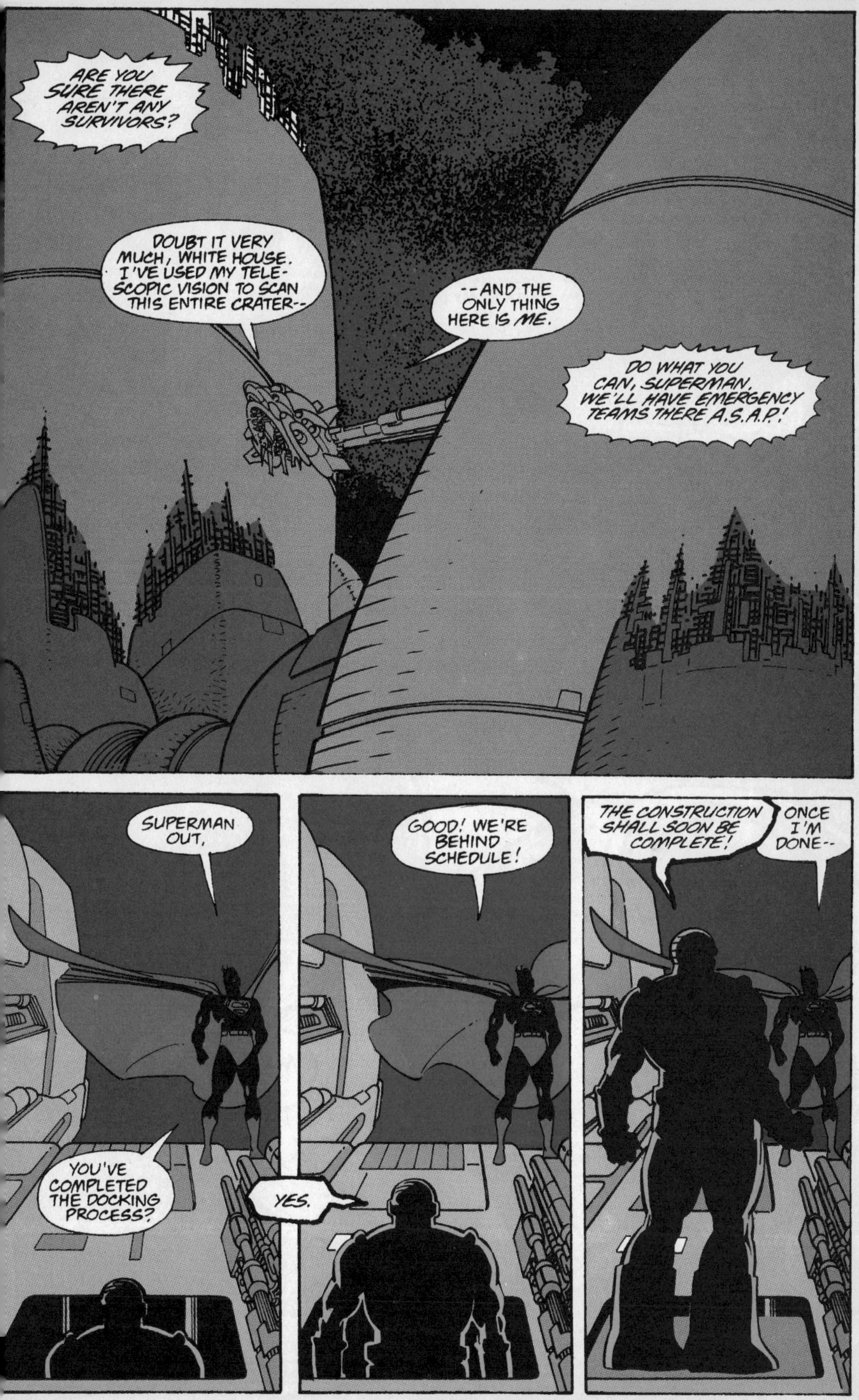
ARE YOU SURE THERE AREN'T ANY SURVIVORS?
DOUBT IT VERY MUCH, WHITE HOUSE. I'VE USED MY TELE-SCOPIC VISION TO SCAN THIS ENTIRE CRATER--
--AND THE ONLY THING HERE IS ME.
DO WHAT YOU CAN, SUPERMAN. WE'LL HAVE EMERGENCY TEAMS THERE A.S.A.P.!
SUPERMAN OUT.
YOU'VE COMPLETED THE DOCKING PROCESS?
GOOD! WE'RE BEHIND SCHEDULE!
YES.
THE CONSTRUCTION SHALL SOON BE COMPLETE!
ONCE I'M DONE--

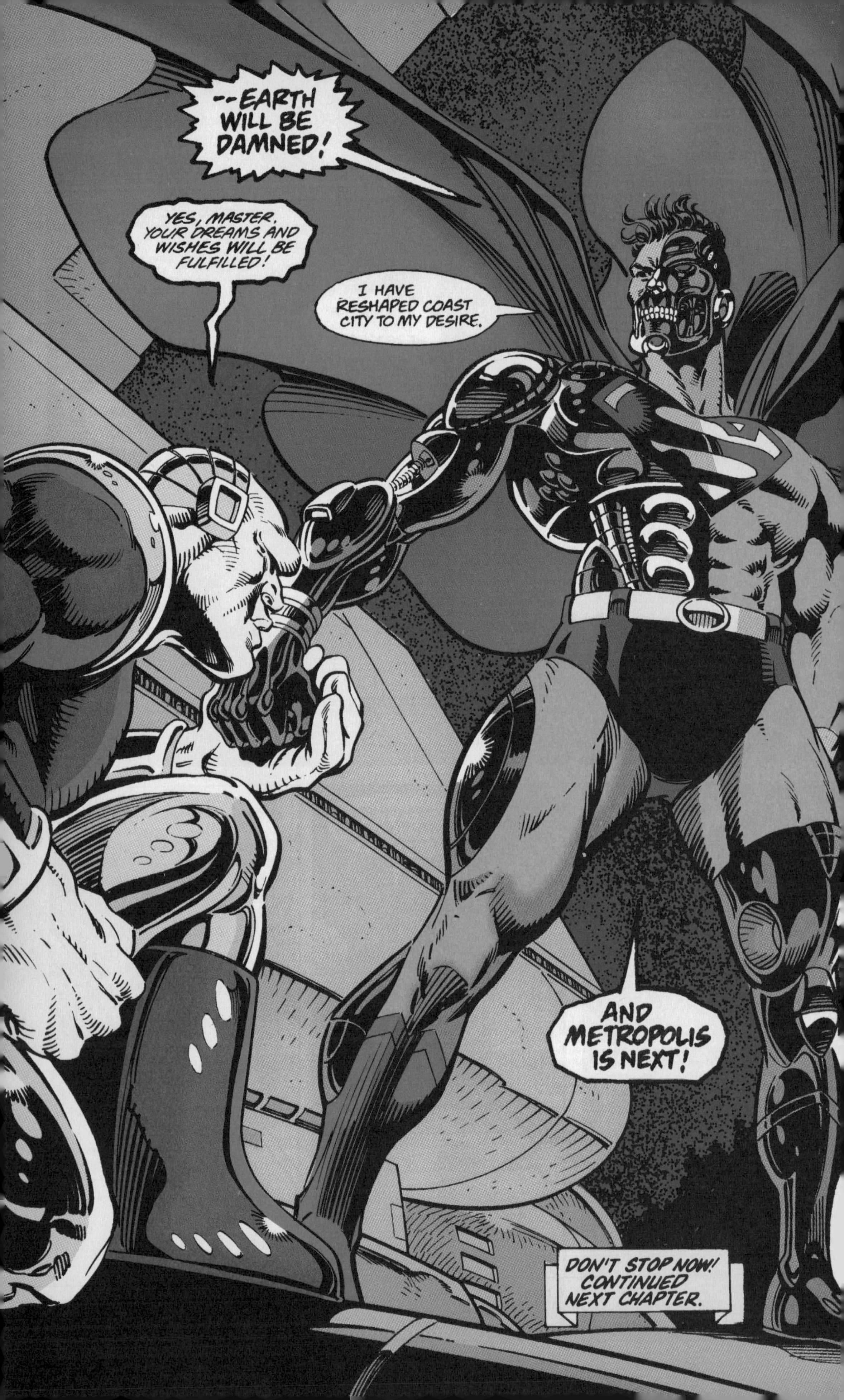
--EARTH WILL BE DAMNED!
YES, MASTER. YOUR DREAMS AND WISHES WILL BE FULFILLED!
I HAVE RESHAPED COAST CITY TO MY DESIRE.
AND METROPOLIS IS NEXT!
DON'T STOP NOW! CONTINUED NEXT CHAPTER.

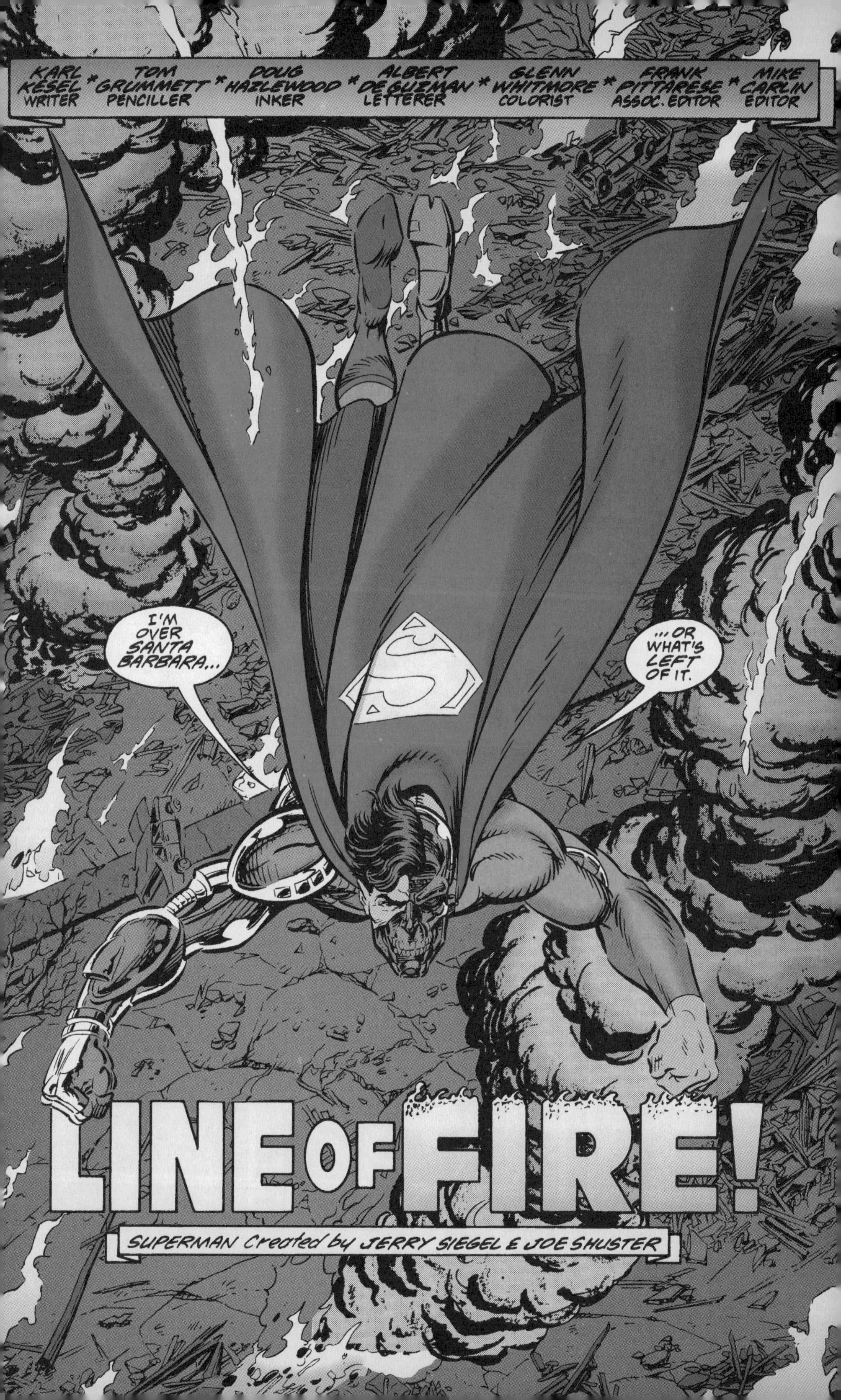

KARL KESEL WRITER * TOM GRUMMETT PENCILLER * DOUG HAZLEWOOD INKER * ALBERT DE GUZMAN LETTERER * GLENN WHITMORE COLORIST * FRANK PITTARESE ASSOC. EDITOR * MIKE CARLIN EDITOR
I'M OVER SANTA BARBARA...
...OR WHAT'S LEFT OF IT.
LINE OF FIRE!
SUPERMAN Created by JERRY SIEGEL & JOE SHUSTER

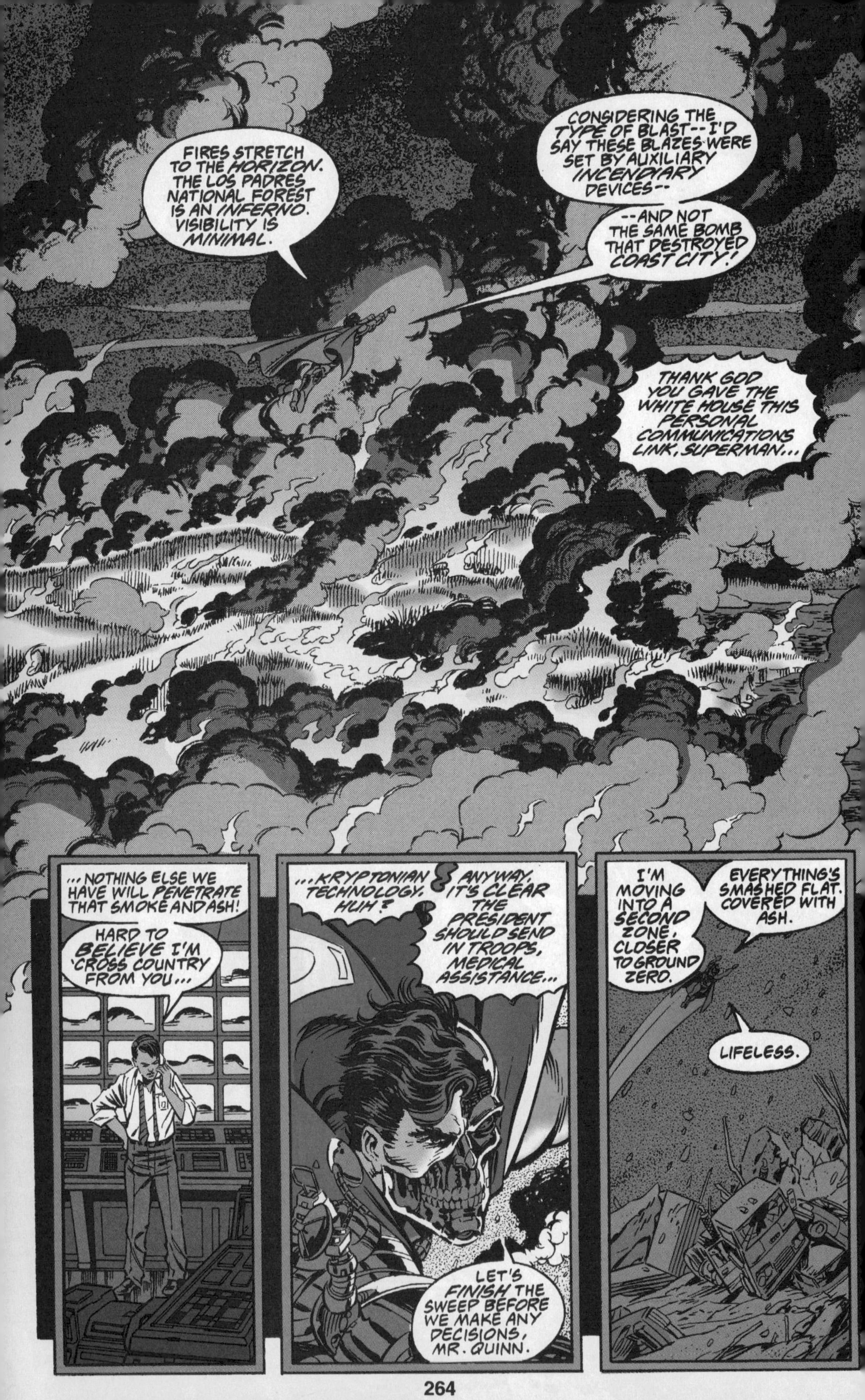
FIRES STRETCH TO THE HORIZON. THE LOS PADRES NATIONAL FOREST IS AN INFERNO. VISIBILITY IS MINIMAL.
CONSIDERING THE TYPE OF BLAST--I'D SAY THESE BLAZES WERE SET BY AUXILIARY INCENDIARY DEVICES--
--AND NOT THE SAME BOMB THAT DESTROYED COAST CITY!
THANK GOD YOU GAVE THE WHITE HOUSE THIS PERSONAL COMMUNICATIONS LINK, SUPERMAN...
...NOTHING ELSE WE HAVE WILL PENETRATE THAT SMOKE AND ASH!
HARD TO BELIEVE I'M 'CROSS COUNTRY FROM YOU...
...KRYPTONIAN TECHNOLOGY. HUH?
ANYWAY, IT'S CLEAR THE PRESIDENT SHOULD SEND IN TROOPS, MEDICAL ASSISTANCE...
LET'S FINISH THE SWEEP BEFORE WE MAKE ANY DECISIONS, MR. QUINN.
I'M MOVING INTO A SECOND ZONE, CLOSER TO GROUND ZERO.
EVERYTHING'S SMASHED FLAT. COVERED WITH ASH.
LIFELESS.

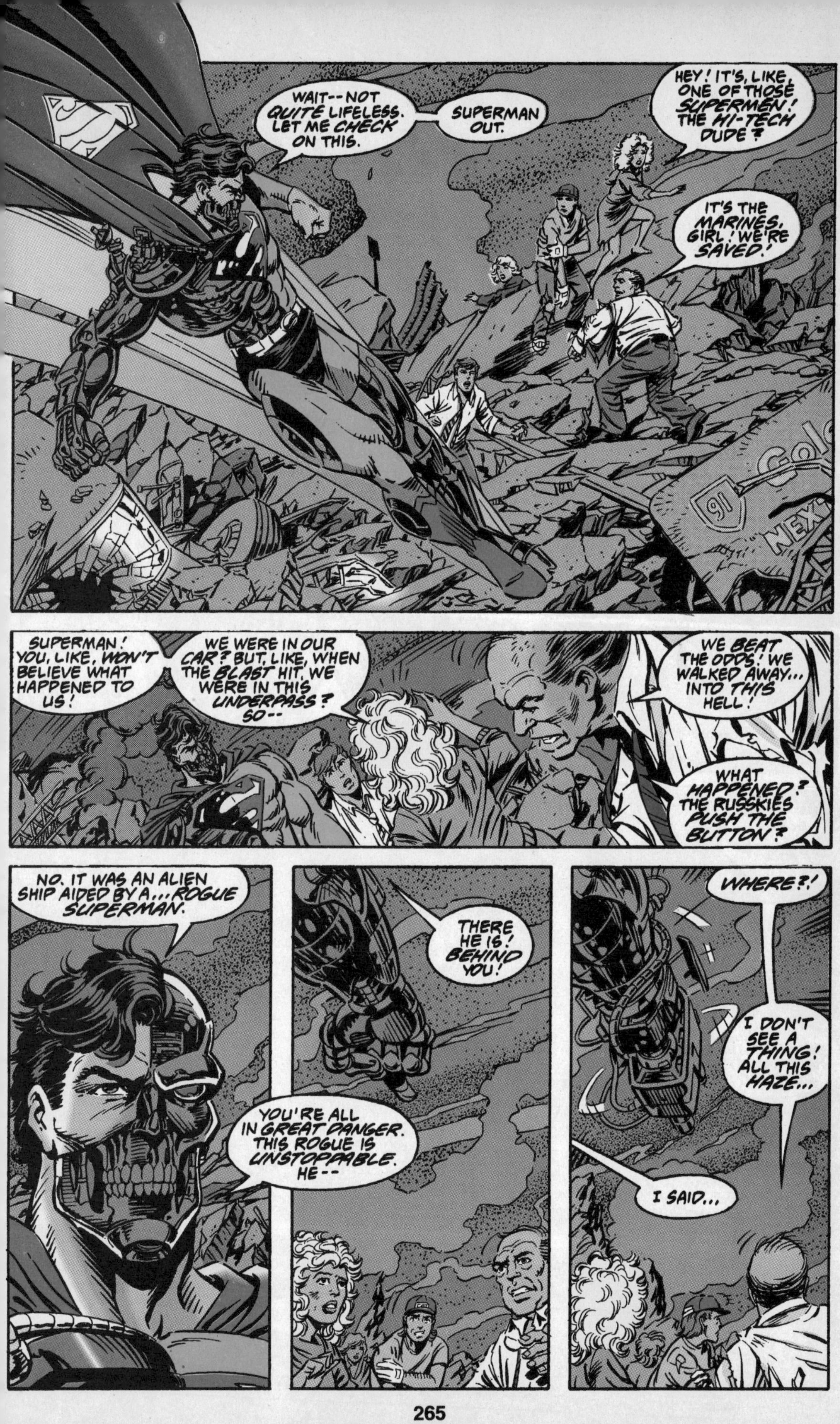

WAIT--NOT QUITE LIFELESS. LET ME CHECK ON THIS.
SUPERMAN OUT.
HEY! IT'S, LIKE, ONE OF THOSE SUPERMEN! THE HI-TECH DUDE?
IT'S THE MARINES, GIRL! WE'RE SAVED!
SUPERMAN! YOU, LIKE, WON'T BELIEVE WHAT HAPPENED TO US!
WE WERE IN OUR CAR? BUT, LIKE, WHEN THE BLAST HIT, WE WERE IN THIS UNDERPASS? SO--
WE BEAT THE ODDS! WE WALKED AWAY... INTO THIS HELL!
WHAT HAPPENED? THE RUSSKIES PUSH THE BUTTON?
NO. IT WAS AN ALIEN SHIP AIDED BY A... ROGUE SUPERMAN.
THERE HE IS! BEHIND YOU!
YOU'RE ALL IN GREAT DANGER. THIS ROGUE IS UNSTOPPABLE. HE--
WHERE?!
I DON'T SEE A THING! ALL THIS HAZE...
I SAID...

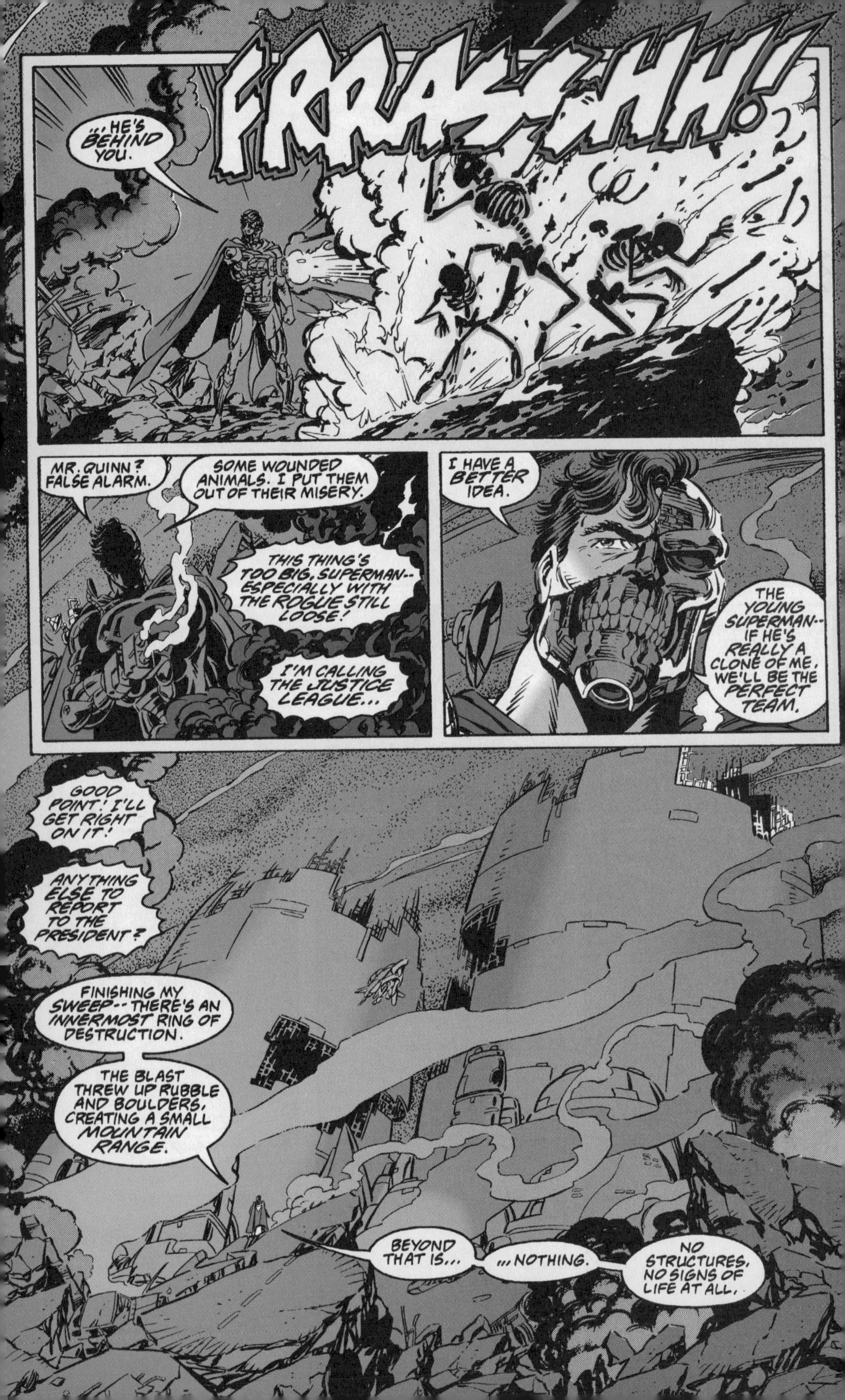
FRRAKSHH!
...HE'S BEHIND YOU.
MR. QUINN? FALSE ALARM.
SOME WOUNDED ANIMALS. I PUT THEM OUT OF THEIR MISERY.
THIS THING'S TOO BIG, SUPERMAN-- ESPECIALLY WITH THE ROGUE STILL LOOSE!
I'M CALLING THE JUSTICE LEAGUE...
I HAVE A BETTER IDEA.
THE YOUNG SUPERMAN-- IF HE'S REALLY A CLONE OF ME, WE'LL BE THE PERFECT TEAM.
GOOD POINT! I'LL GET RIGHT ON IT!
ANYTHING ELSE TO REPORT TO THE PRESIDENT?
FINISHING MY SWEEP-- THERE'S AN INNERMOST RING OF DESTRUCTION.
THE BLAST THREW UP RUBBLE AND BOULDERS, CREATING A SMALL MOUNTAIN RANGE.
BEYOND THAT IS...
...NOTHING.
NO STRUCTURES, NO SIGNS OF LIFE AT ALL.

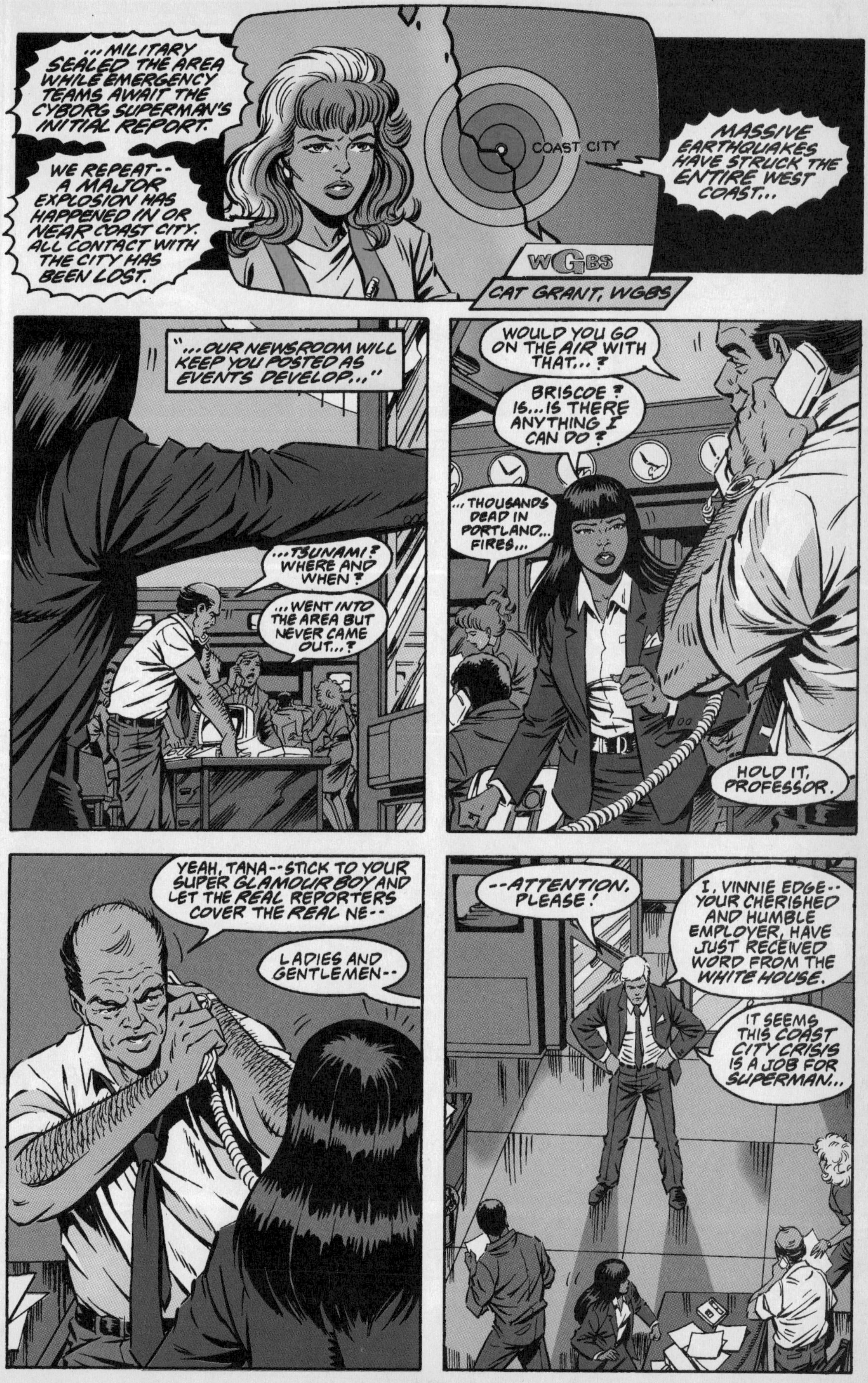
...MILITARY SEALED THE AREA WHILE EMERGENCY TEAMS AWAIT THE CYBORG SUPERMAN'S INITIAL REPORT.
WE REPEAT-- A MAJOR EXPLOSION HAS HAPPENED IN OR NEAR COAST CITY. ALL CONTACT WITH THE CITY HAS BEEN LOST.
COAST CITY
MASSIVE EARTHQUAKES HAVE STRUCK THE ENTIRE WEST COAST...
WGBS
CAT GRANT, WGBS
"...OUR NEWSROOM WILL KEEP YOU POSTED AS EVENTS DEVELOP..."
...TSUNAMI? WHERE AND WHEN?
...WENT INTO THE AREA BUT NEVER CAME OUT...?
WOULD YOU GO ON THE AIR WITH THAT...?
BRISCOE? IS...IS THERE ANYTHING I CAN DO?
...THOUSANDS DEAD IN PORTLAND... FIRES...
HOLD IT, PROFESSOR.
YEAH, TANA--STICK TO YOUR SUPER GLAMOUR BOY AND LET THE REAL REPORTERS COVER THE REAL NE--
LADIES AND GENTLEMEN--
--ATTENTION, PLEASE!
I, VINNIE EDGE-- YOUR CHERISHED AND HUMBLE EMPLOYER, HAVE JUST RECEIVED WORD FROM THE WHITE HOUSE.
IT SEEMS THIS COAST CITY CRISIS IS A JOB FOR SUPERMAN...

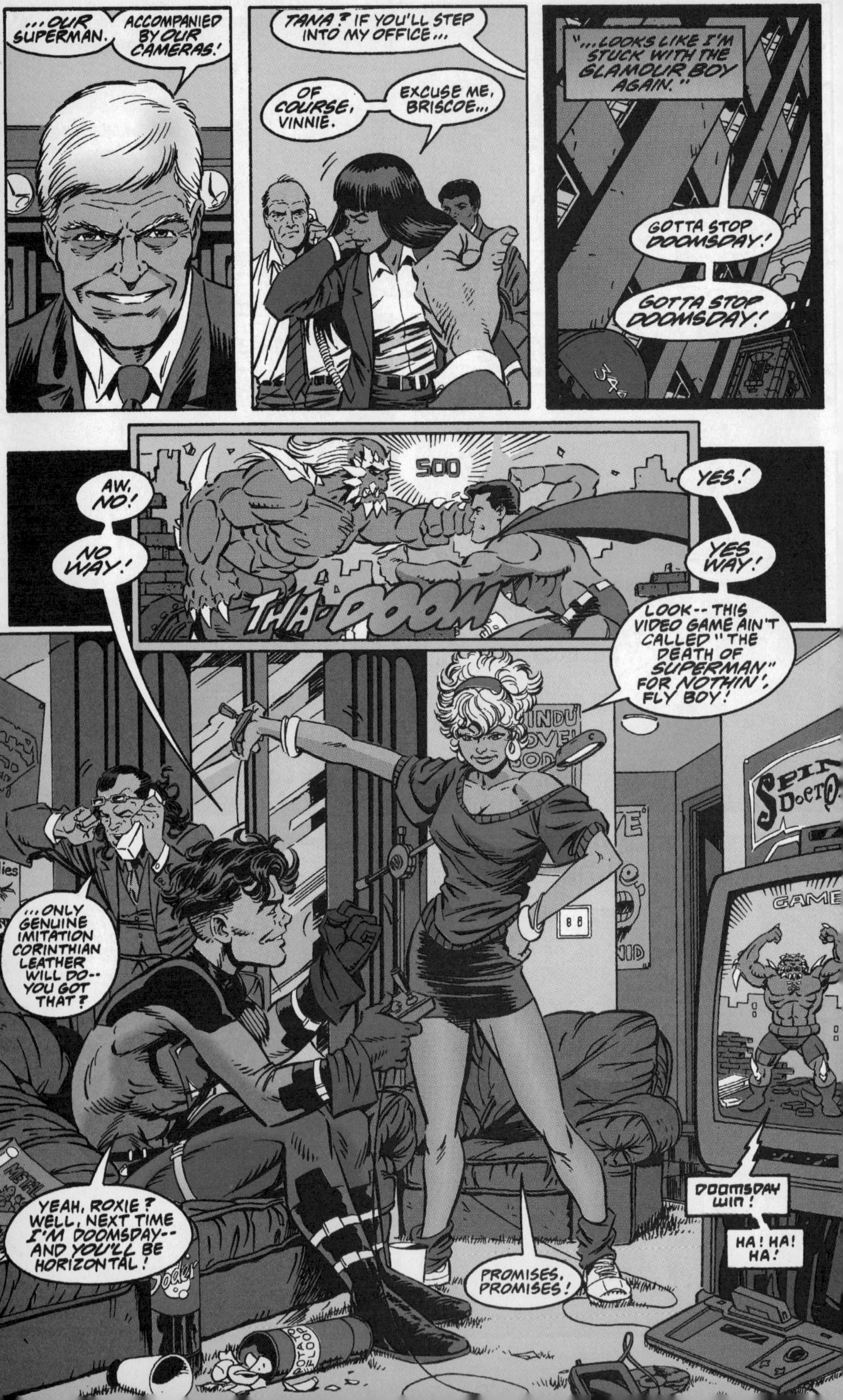
...OUR SUPERMAN.
ACCOMPANIED BY OUR CAMERAS!
TANA? IF YOU'LL STEP INTO MY OFFICE...
OF COURSE, VINNIE.
EXCUSE ME, BRISCOE...
"...LOOKS LIKE I'M STUCK WITH THE GLAMOUR BOY AGAIN."
GOTTA STOP DOOMSDAY!
GOTTA STOP DOOMSDAY!
500
AW, NO!
NO WAY!
YES!
YES WAY!
THA-DOOM
LOOK-- THIS VIDEO GAME AIN'T CALLED "THE DEATH OF SUPERMAN" FOR NOTHIN', FLY BOY!
...ONLY GENUINE IMITATION CORINTHIAN LEATHER WILL DO-- YOU GOT THAT?
YEAH, ROXIE? WELL, NEXT TIME I'M DOOMSDAY-- AND YOU'LL BE HORIZONTAL!
PROMISES, PROMISES!
DOOMSDAY WIN!
HA! HA! HA!

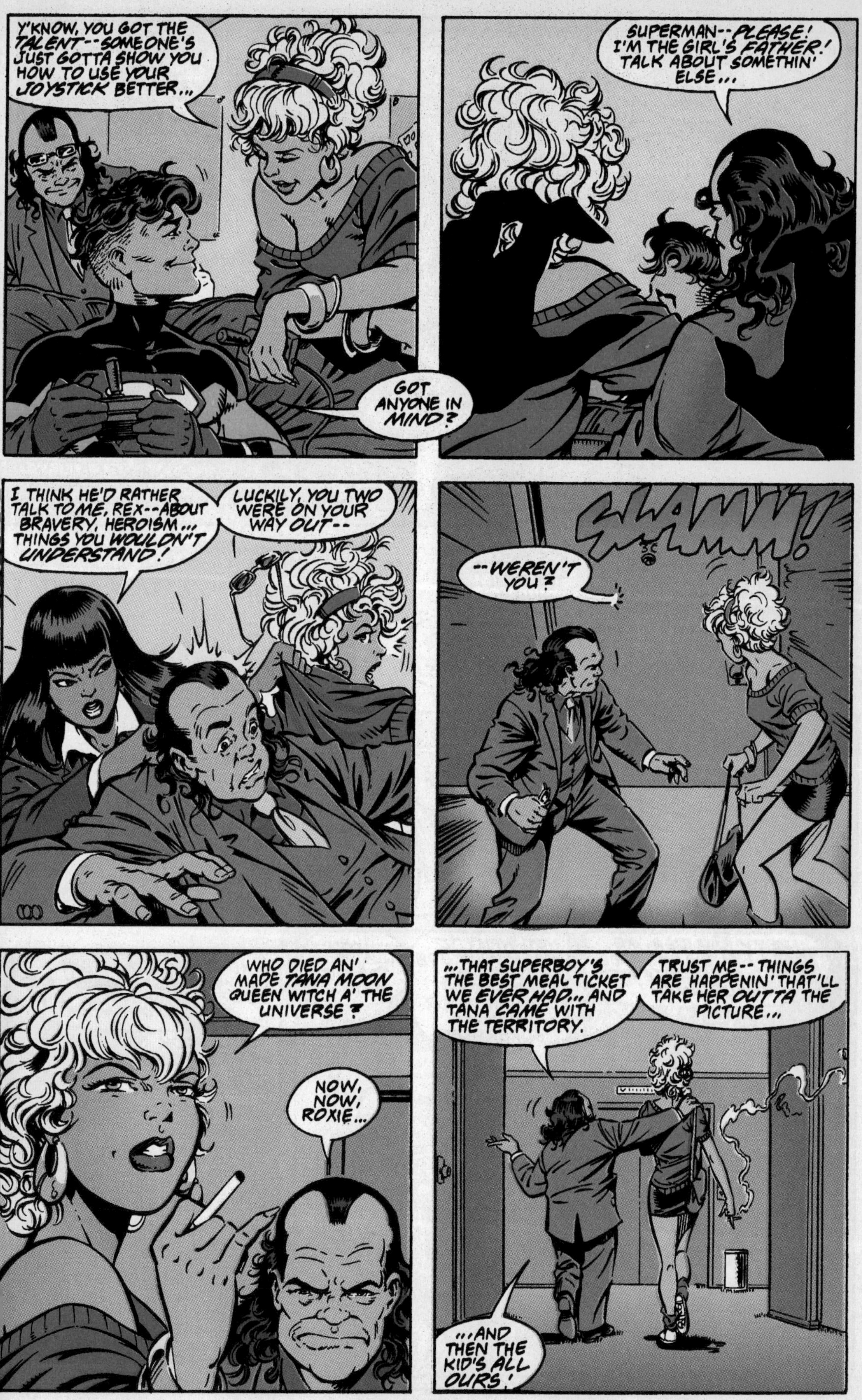

Y'KNOW, YOU GOT THE TALENT--SOMEONE'S JUST GOTTA SHOW YOU HOW TO USE YOUR JOYSTICK BETTER...
GOT ANYONE IN MIND?
SUPERMAN--PLEASE! I'M THE GIRL'S FATHER! TALK ABOUT SOMETHIN' ELSE...
I THINK HE'D RATHER TALK TO ME, REX--ABOUT BRAVERY, HEROISM..., THINGS YOU WOULDN'T UNDERSTAND!
LUCKILY, YOU TWO WERE ON YOUR WAY OUT--
SLAMM!
--WEREN'T YOU?
WHO DIED AN' MADE TANA MOON QUEEN WITCH A' THE UNIVERSE?
NOW, NOW, ROXIE...
...THAT SUPERBOY'S THE BEST MEAL TICKET WE EVER HAD... AND TANA CAME WITH THE TERRITORY.
TRUST ME--THINGS ARE HAPPENIN' THAT'LL TAKE HER OUTTA THE PICTURE...
...AND THEN THE KID'S ALL OURS!

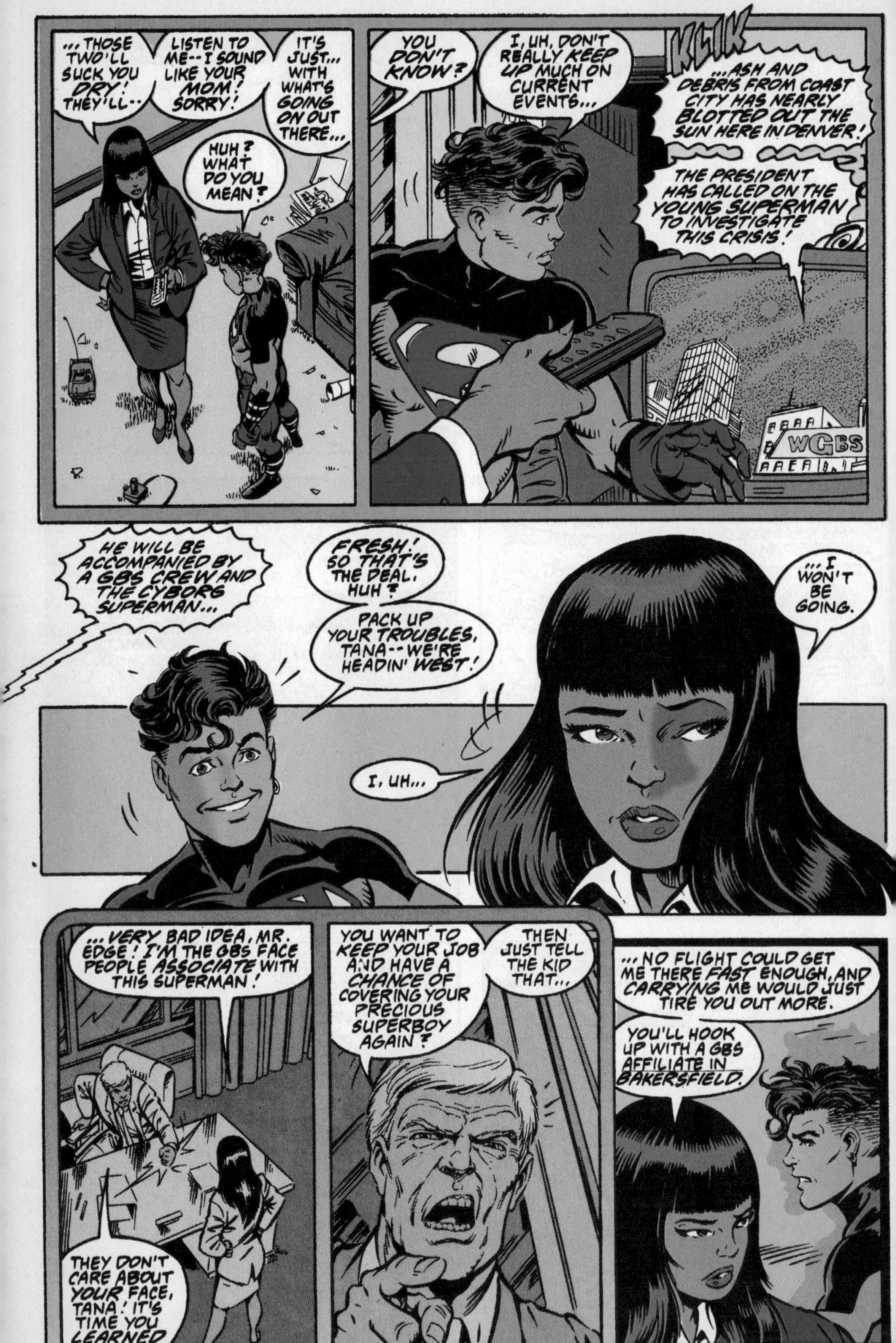
...THOSE TWO'LL SUCK YOU DRY! THEY'LL--
LISTEN TO ME--I SOUND LIKE YOUR MOM! SORRY!
IT'S JUST... WITH WHAT'S GOING ON OUT THERE...
HUH? WHAT DO YOU MEAN?
YOU DON'T KNOW?
I, UH, DON'T REALLY KEEP UP MUCH ON CURRENT EVENTS...
KLIK
...ASH AND DEBRIS FROM COAST CITY HAS NEARLY BLOTTED OUT THE SUN HERE IN DENVER!
THE PRESIDENT HAS CALLED ON THE YOUNG SUPERMAN TO INVESTIGATE THIS CRISIS!
WGBS
HE WILL BE ACCOMPANIED BY A GBS CREW AND THE CYBORG SUPERMAN...
FRESH! SO THAT'S THE DEAL, HUH?
PACK UP YOUR TROUBLES, TANA--WE'RE HEADIN' WEST!
I, UH...
...I WON'T BE GOING.
...VERY BAD IDEA, MR. EDGE! I'M THE GBS FACE PEOPLE ASSOCIATE WITH THIS SUPERMAN!
THEY DON'T CARE ABOUT YOUR FACE, TANA! IT'S TIME YOU LEARNED THAT!
YOU WANT TO KEEP YOUR JOB AND HAVE A CHANCE OF COVERING YOUR PRECIOUS SUPERBOY AGAIN?
THEN JUST TELL THE KID THAT...
...NO FLIGHT COULD GET ME THERE FAST ENOUGH, AND CARRYING ME WOULD JUST TIRE YOU OUT MORE.
YOU'LL HOOK UP WITH A GBS AFFILIATE IN BAKERSFIELD.

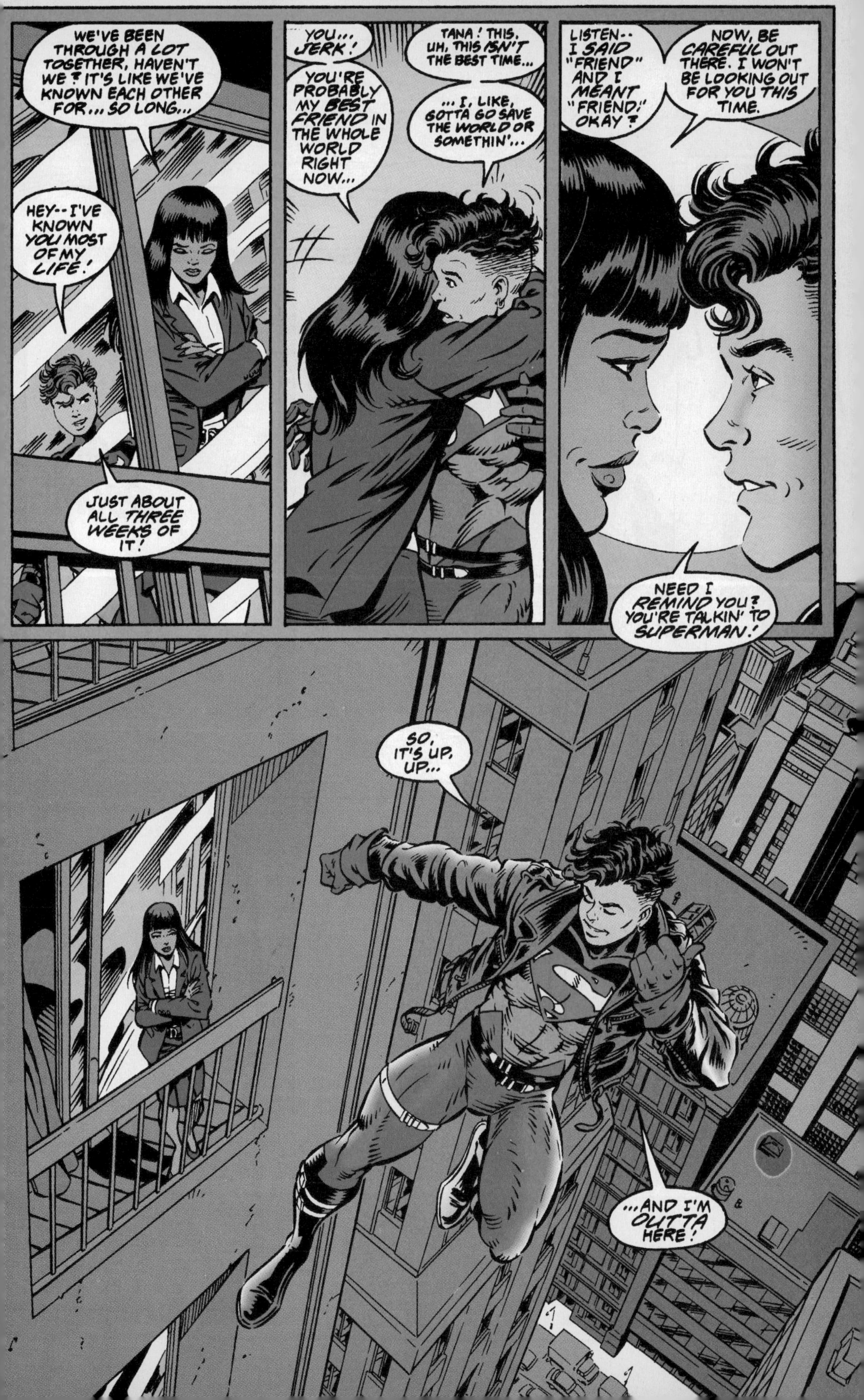
WE'VE BEEN THROUGH A LOT TOGETHER, HAVEN'T WE? IT'S LIKE WE'VE KNOWN EACH OTHER FOR... SO LONG...
HEY-- I'VE KNOWN YOU MOST OF MY LIFE!
JUST ABOUT ALL THREE WEEKS OF IT!
YOU... JERK!
YOU'RE PROBABLY MY BEST FRIEND IN THE WHOLE WORLD RIGHT NOW...
TANA! THIS, UH, THIS ISN'T THE BEST TIME...
... I, LIKE, GOTTA GO SAVE THE WORLD OR SOMETHIN'...
LISTEN-- I SAID "FRIEND" AND I MEANT "FRIEND." OKAY?
NOW, BE CAREFUL OUT THERE. I WON'T BE LOOKING OUT FOR YOU THIS TIME.
NEED I REMIND YOU? YOU'RE TALKIN' TO SUPERMAN!
SO, IT'S UP, UP...
...AND I'M OUTTA HERE!

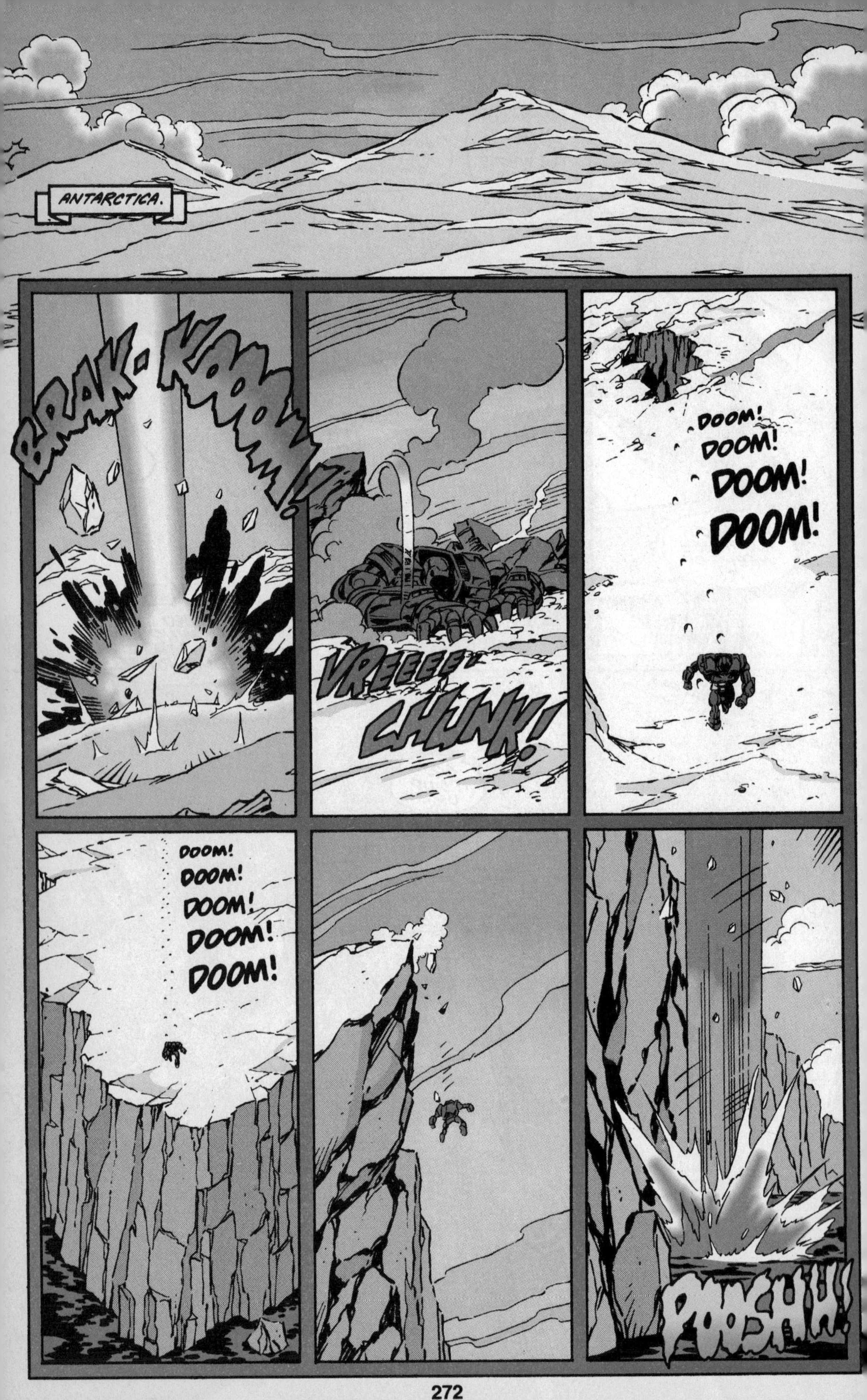
ANTARCTICA.
BRAK-KOOOOM!!
VREEEEE-CHUNK!
DOOM! DOOM! DOOM! DOOM!
DOOM! DOOM! DOOM! DOOM! DOOM!
POOSHH!

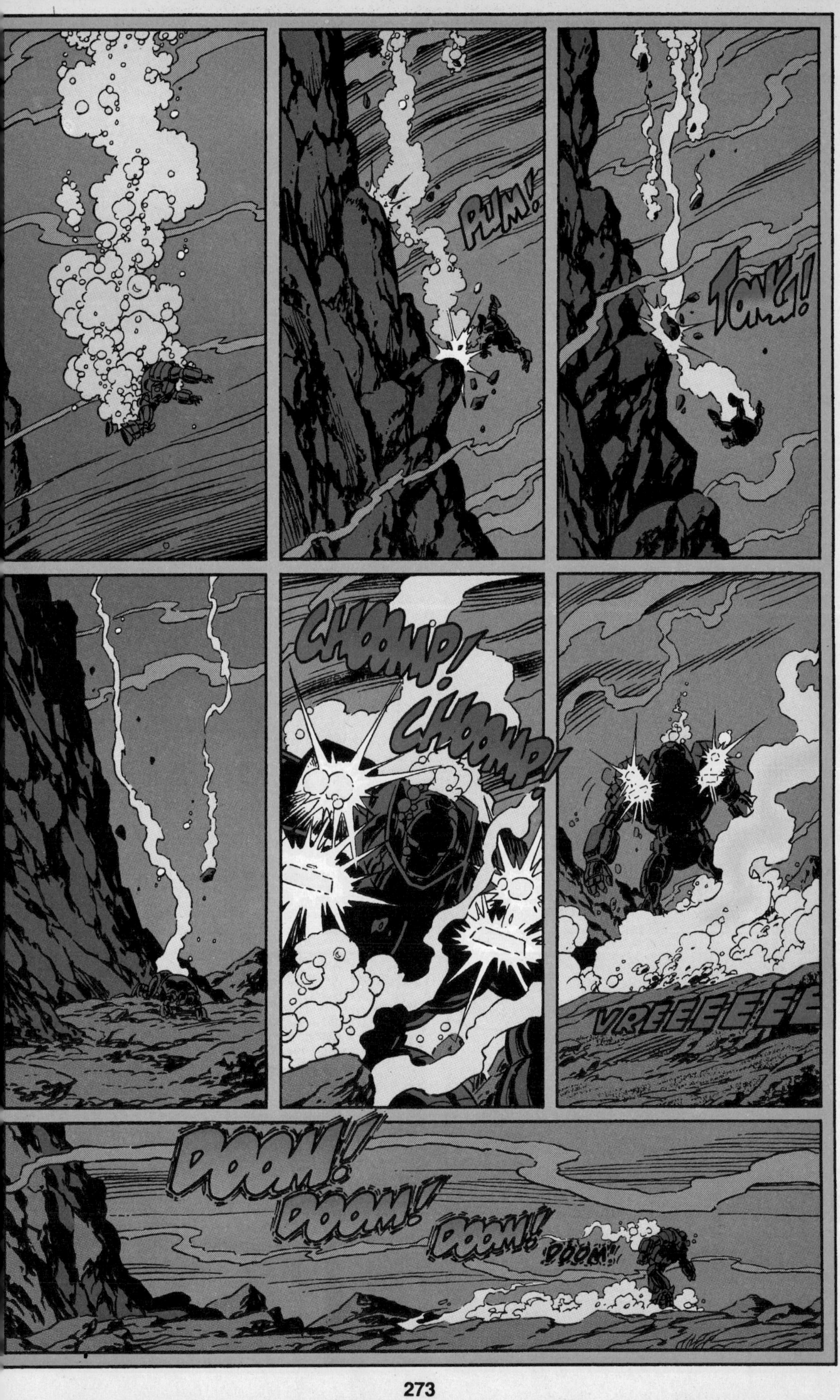
PUM!
TONG!
CHOOMP!
CHOOMP!
VREEEEEEE
DOOM!
DOOM!
DOOM!
DOOM!

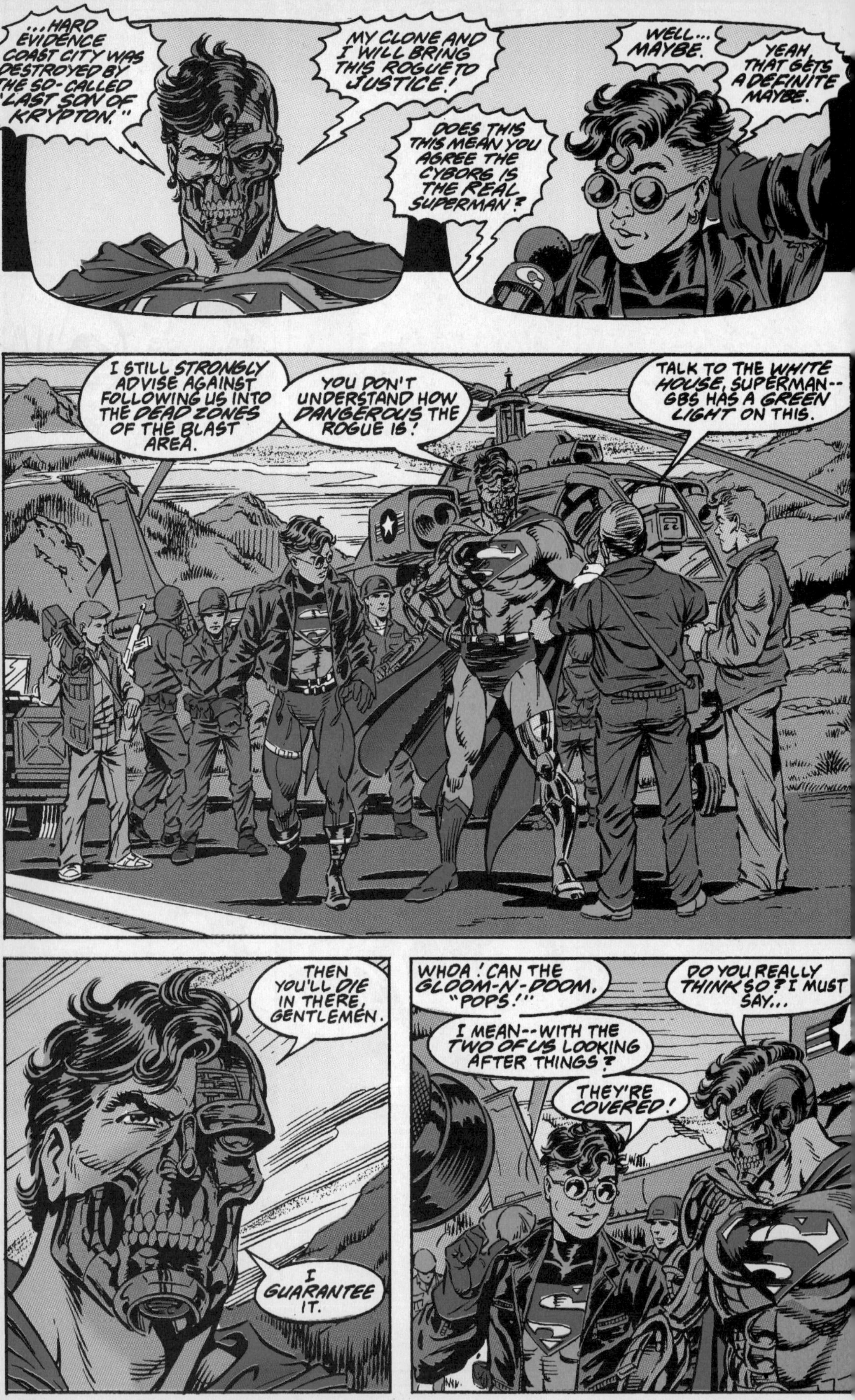
...HARD EVIDENCE COAST CITY WAS DESTROYED BY THE SO-CALLED "LAST SON OF KRYPTON."
MY CLONE AND I WILL BRING THIS ROGUE TO JUSTICE!
DOES THIS THIS MEAN YOU AGREE THE CYBORG IS THE REAL SUPERMAN?
WELL... MAYBE.
YEAH, THAT GETS A DEFINITE MAYBE.
I STILL STRONGLY ADVISE AGAINST FOLLOWING US INTO THE DEAD ZONES OF THE BLAST AREA.
YOU DON'T UNDERSTAND HOW DANGEROUS THE ROGUE IS!
TALK TO THE WHITE HOUSE, SUPERMAN-- GBS HAS A GREEN LIGHT ON THIS.
THEN YOU'LL DIE IN THERE, GENTLEMEN.
I GUARANTEE IT.
WHOA! CAN THE GLOOM-N-DOOM, "POPS!"
I MEAN--WITH THE TWO OF US LOOKING AFTER THINGS?
THEY'RE COVERED!
DO YOU REALLY THINK SO? I MUST SAY...

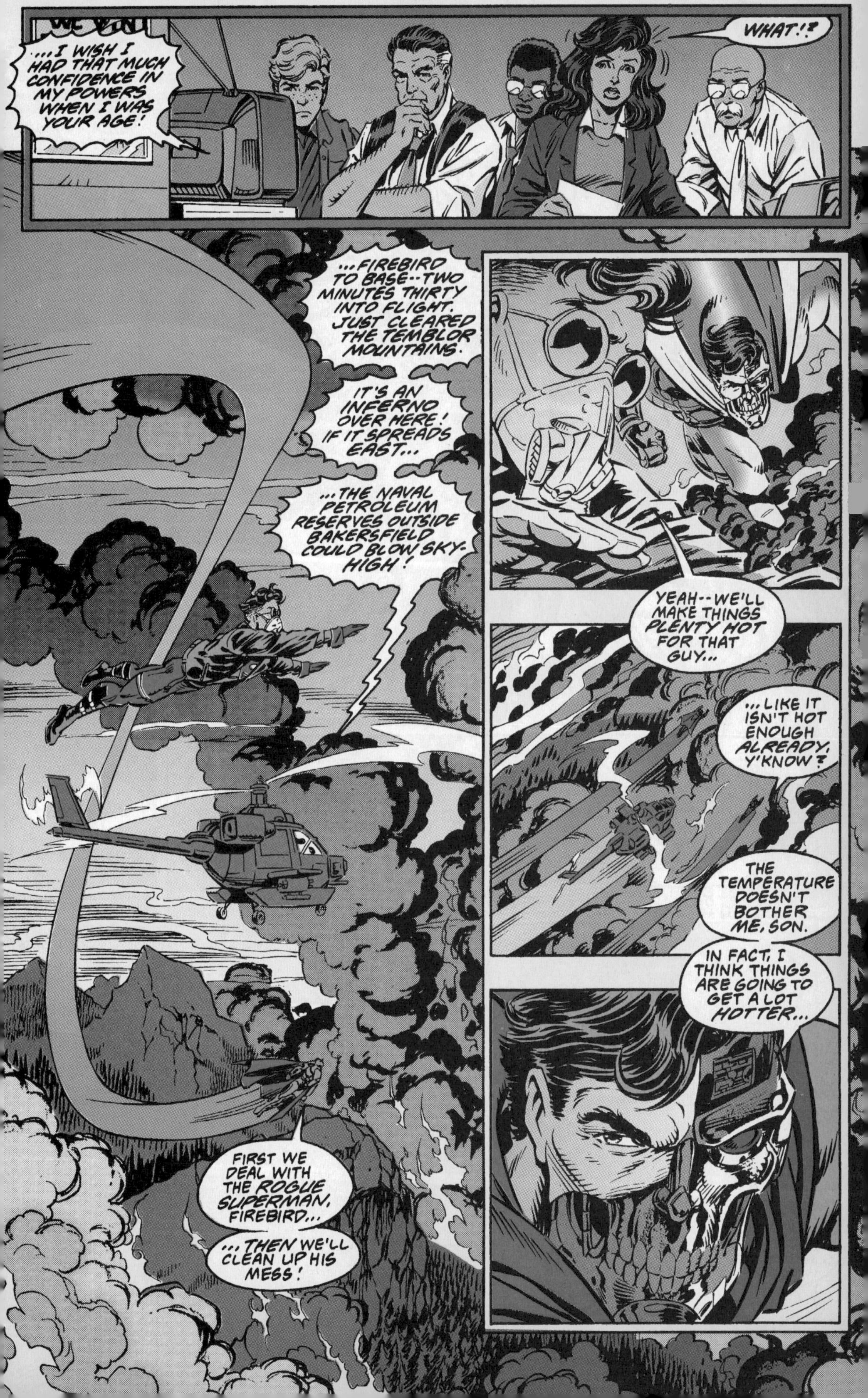
WE
...I WISH I HAD THAT MUCH CONFIDENCE IN MY POWERS WHEN I WAS YOUR AGE!
WHAT!?
...FIREBIRD TO BASE--TWO MINUTES THIRTY INTO FLIGHT. JUST CLEARED THE TEMBLOR MOUNTAINS.
IT'S AN INFERNO OVER HERE! IF IT SPREADS EAST...
...THE NAVAL PETROLEUM RESERVES OUTSIDE BAKERSFIELD COULD BLOW SKY-HIGH!
FIRST WE DEAL WITH THE ROGUE SUPERMAN, FIREBIRD...
...THEN WE'LL CLEAN UP HIS MESS!
YEAH--WE'LL MAKE THINGS PLENTY HOT FOR THAT GUY...
...LIKE IT ISN'T HOT ENOUGH ALREADY, Y'KNOW?
THE TEMPERATURE DOESN'T BOTHER ME, SON.
IN FACT, I THINK THINGS ARE GOING TO GET A LOT HOTTER...

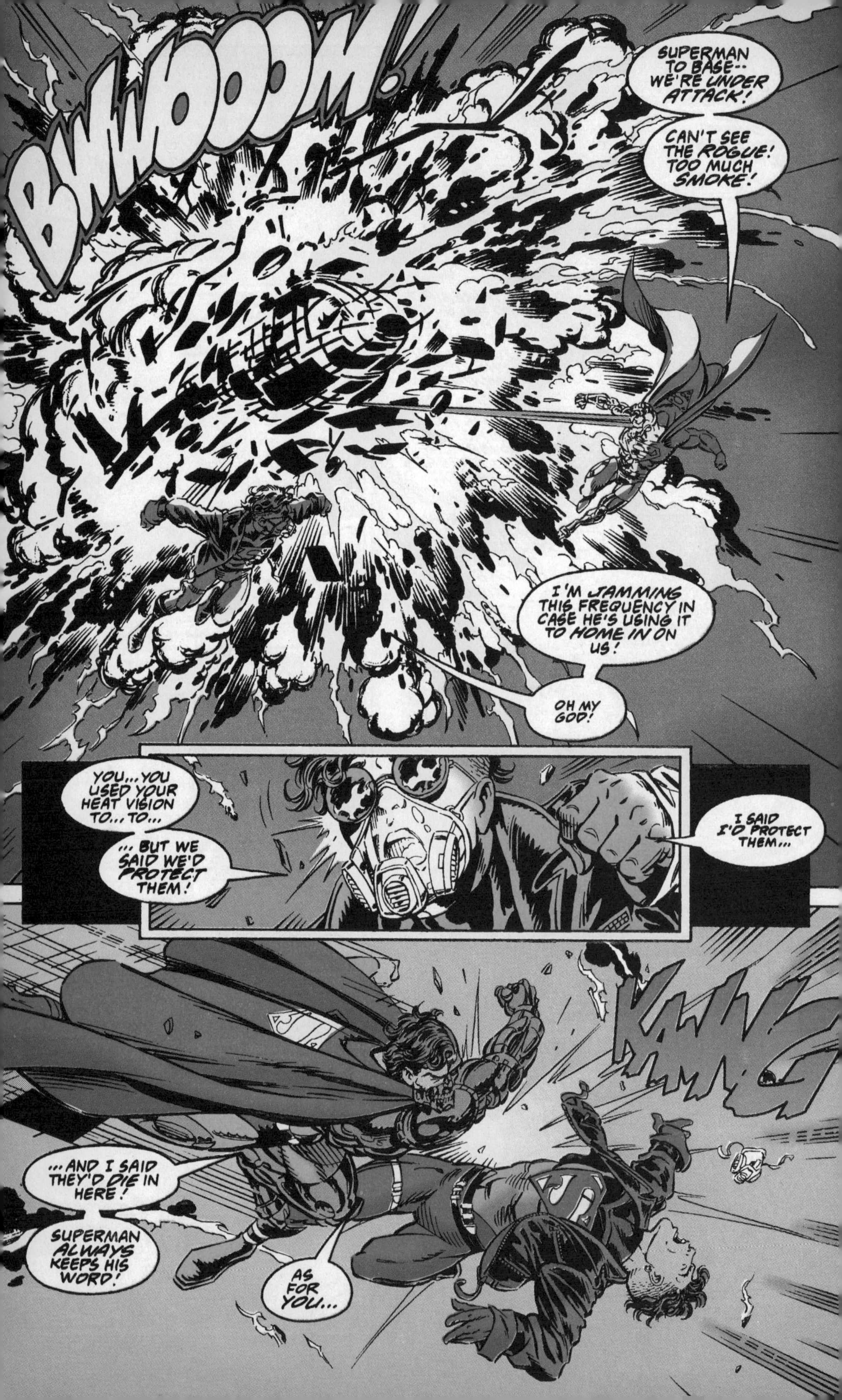

BWHOOOOM!
SUPERMAN TO BASE-- WE'RE UNDER ATTACK!
CAN'T SEE THE ROGUE! TOO MUCH SMOKE!
I'M JAMMING THIS FREQUENCY IN CASE HE'S USING IT TO HOME IN ON US!
OH MY GOD!
YOU... YOU USED YOUR HEAT VISION TO... TO...
... BUT WE SAID WE'D PROTECT THEM!
I SAID I'D PROTECT THEM...
KAWANG
...AND I SAID THEY'D DIE IN HERE!
SUPERMAN ALWAYS KEEPS HIS WORD!
AS FOR YOU...

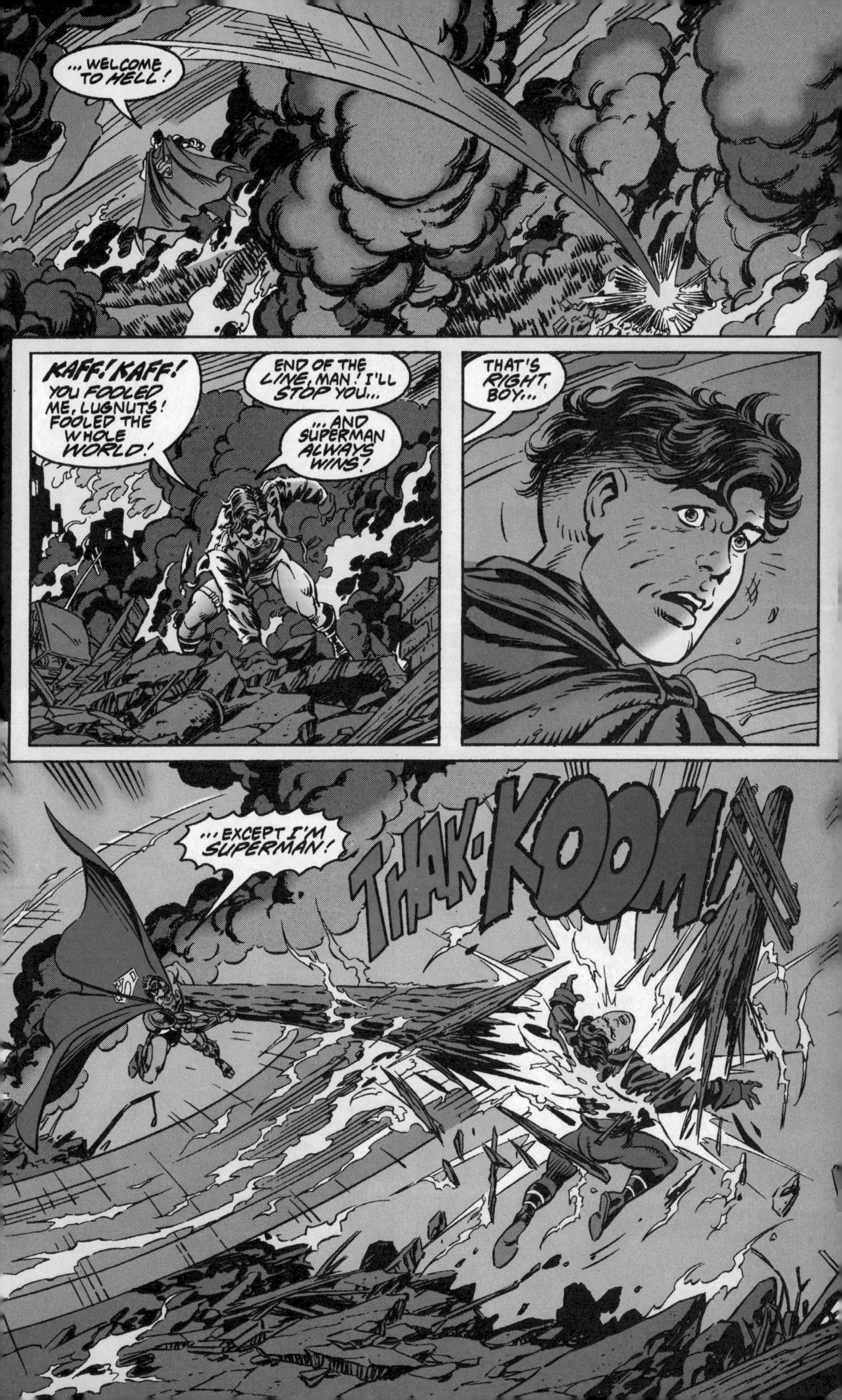
...WELCOME TO HELL!
KAFF! KAFF! YOU FOOLED ME, LUGNUTS! FOOLED THE WHOLE WORLD!
END OF THE LINE, MAN! I'LL STOP YOU...
...AND SUPERMAN ALWAYS WINS!
THAT'S RIGHT, BOY...
...EXCEPT I'M SUPERMAN!
THAK-KOOM!

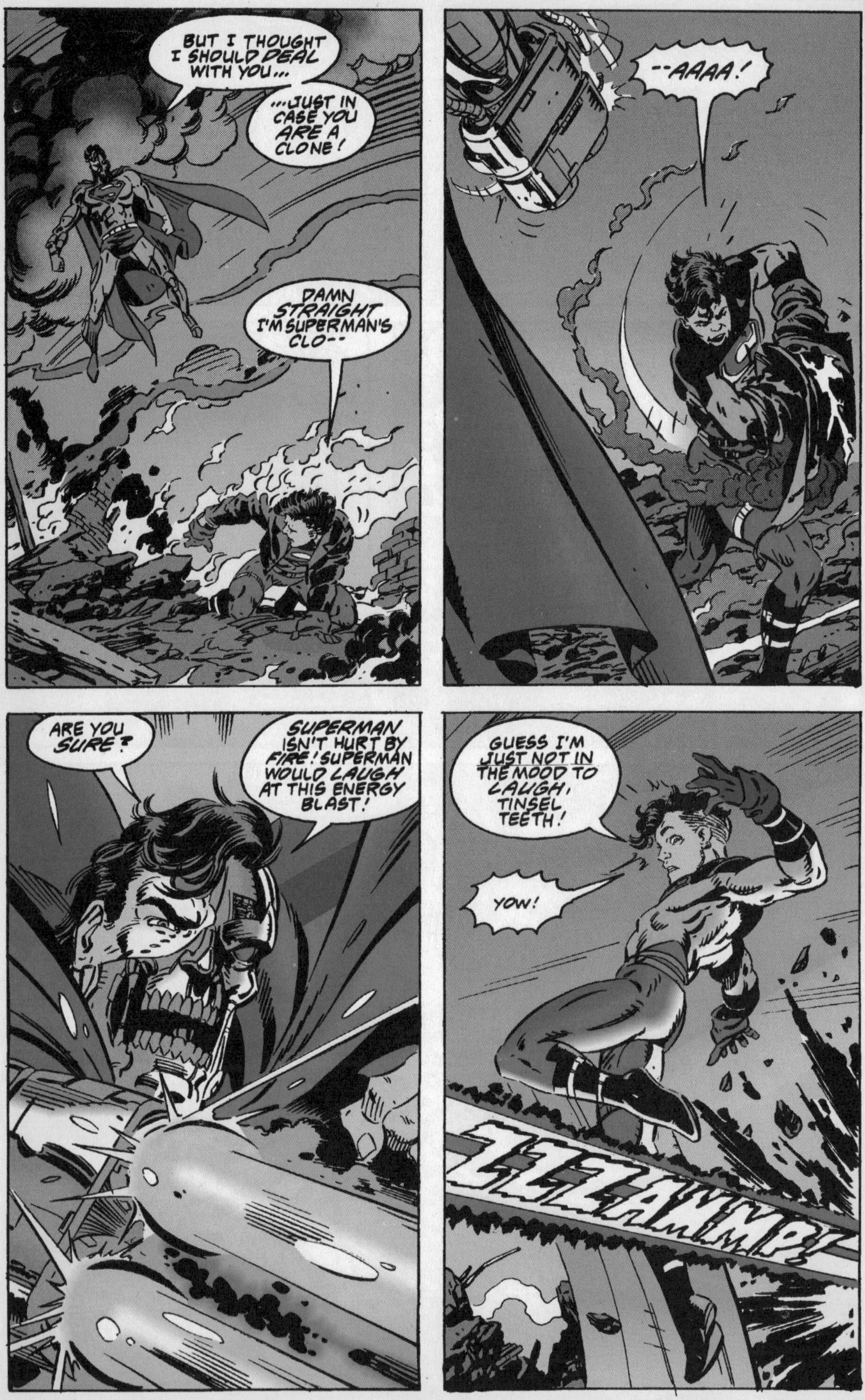
BUT I THOUGHT I SHOULD DEAL WITH YOU...
...JUST IN CASE YOU ARE A CLONE!
DAMN STRAIGHT I'M SUPERMAN'S CLO--
--AAAA!
ARE YOU SURE?
SUPERMAN ISN'T HURT BY FIRE! SUPERMAN WOULD LAUGH AT THIS ENERGY BLAST!
GUESS I'M JUST NOT IN THE MOOD TO LAUGH, TINSEL TEETH!
YOW!
THAMP!

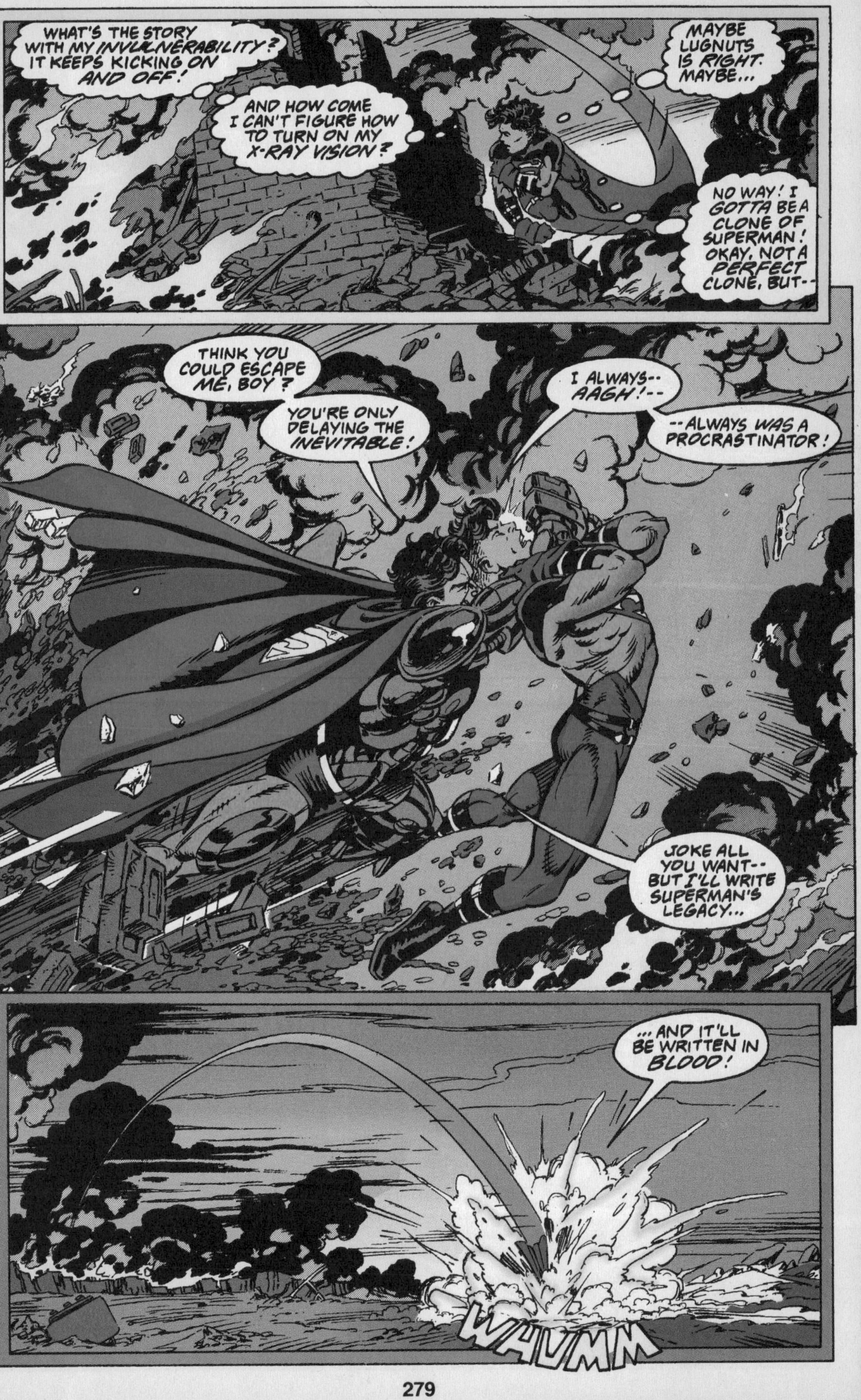
WHAT'S THE STORY WITH MY INVULNERABILITY? IT KEEPS KICKING ON AND OFF!
AND HOW COME I CAN'T FIGURE HOW TO TURN ON MY X-RAY VISION?
MAYBE LUGNUTS IS RIGHT. MAYBE...
NO WAY! I GOTTA BE A CLONE OF SUPERMAN! OKAY, NOT A PERFECT CLONE, BUT--
THINK YOU COULD ESCAPE ME, BOY?
YOU'RE ONLY DELAYING THE INEVITABLE!
I ALWAYS-- AAGH!--
--ALWAYS WAS A PROCRASTINATOR!
JOKE ALL YOU WANT-- BUT I'LL WRITE SUPERMAN'S LEGACY...
...AND IT'LL BE WRITTEN IN BLOOD!
WHUMM

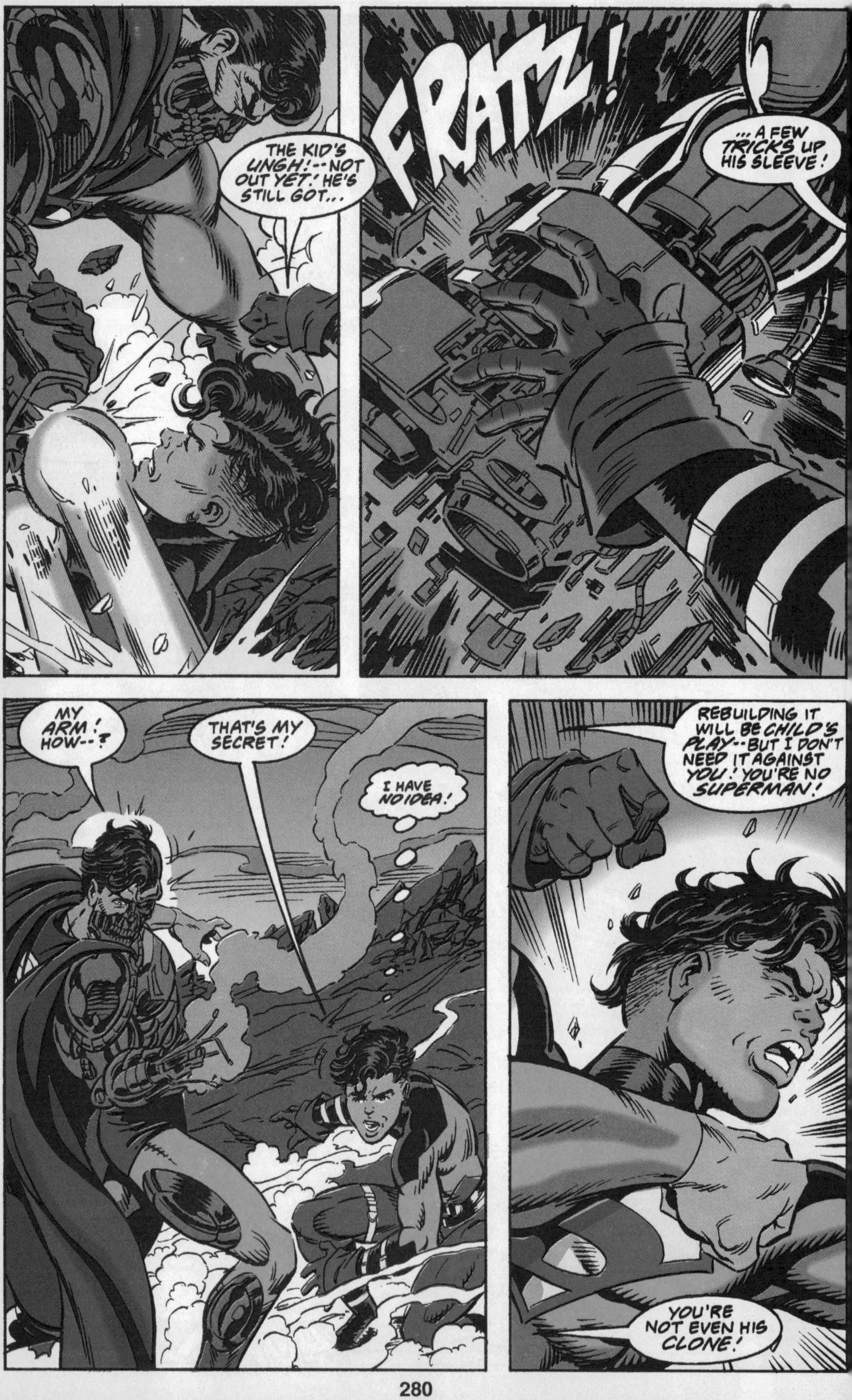
THE KID'S UNGH!--NOT OUT YET! HE'S STILL GOT...
FRATZ!
...A FEW TRICKS UP HIS SLEEVE!
MY ARM! HOW--?
THAT'S MY SECRET!
I HAVE NO IDEA!
REBUILDING IT WILL BE CHILD'S PLAY--BUT I DON'T NEED IT AGAINST YOU! YOU'RE NO SUPERMAN!
YOU'RE NOT EVEN HIS CLONE!

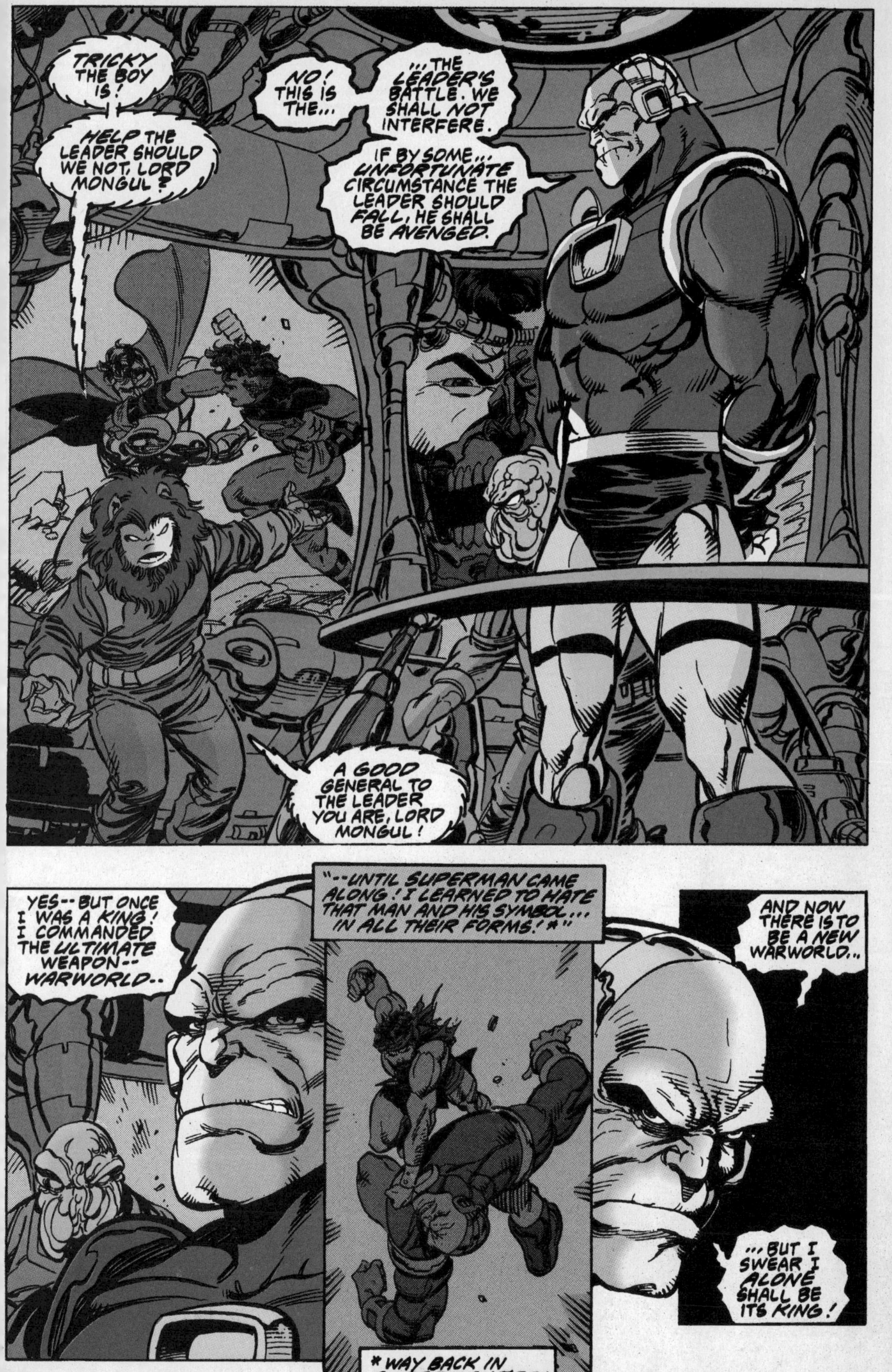
TRICKY THE BOY IS!
HELP THE LEADER SHOULD WE NOT, LORD MONGUL?
NO! THIS IS THE...
...THE LEADER'S BATTLE. WE SHALL NOT INTERFERE.
IF BY SOME... UNFORTUNATE CIRCUMSTANCE THE LEADER SHOULD FALL, HE SHALL BE AVENGED.
A GOOD GENERAL TO THE LEADER YOU ARE, LORD MONGUL!
YES--BUT ONCE I WAS A KING! I COMMANDED THE ULTIMATE WEAPON--WARWORLD..
"--UNTIL SUPERMAN CAME ALONG! I LEARNED TO HATE THAT MAN AND HIS SYMBOL... IN ALL THEIR FORMS!*"
AND NOW THERE IS TO BE A NEW WARWORLD...
...BUT I SWEAR I ALONE SHALL BE ITS KING!
*WAY BACK IN SUPERMAN #321

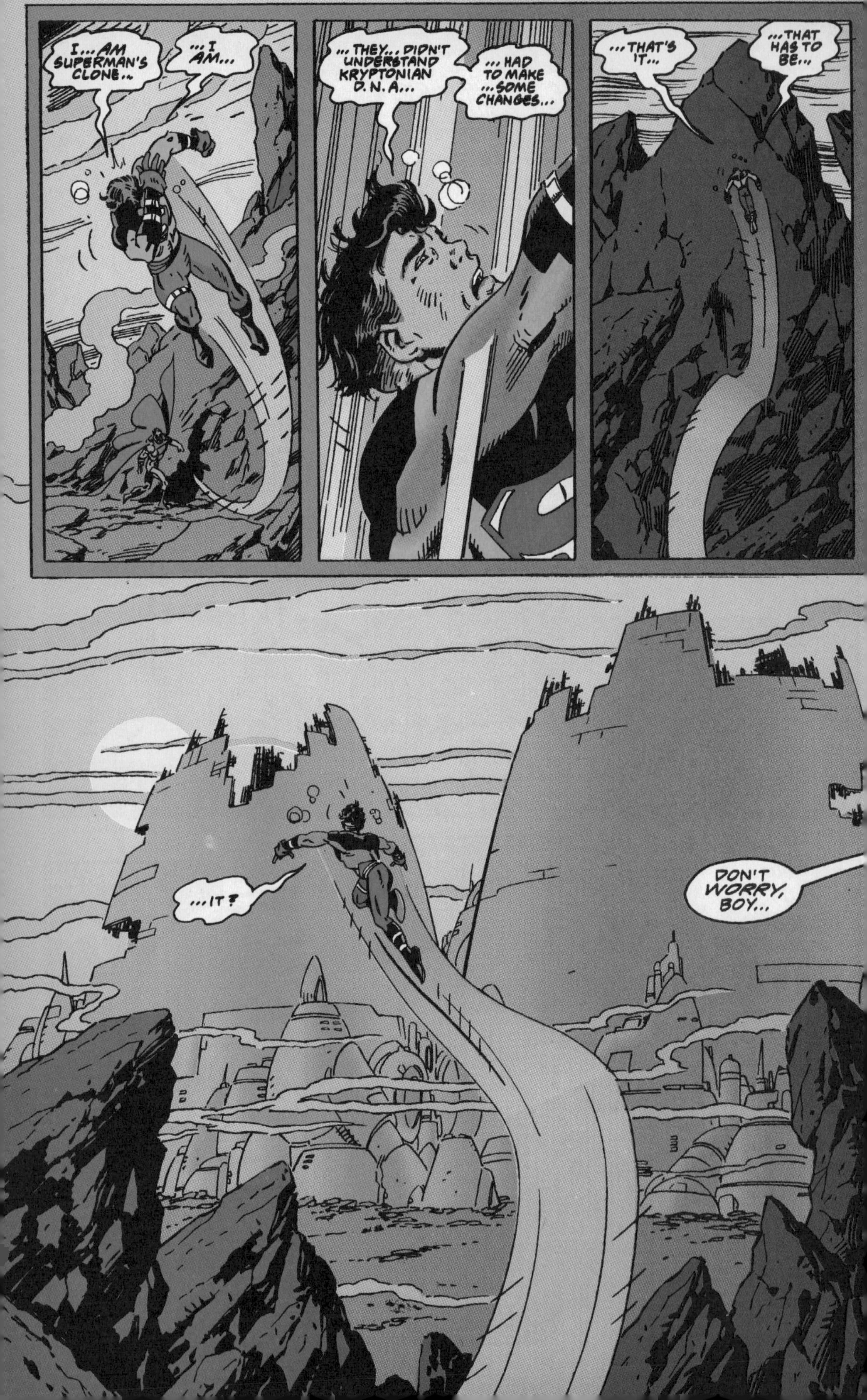
I... AM SUPERMAN'S CLONE...
...I AM...
...THEY... DIDN'T UNDERSTAND KRYPTONIAN D.N.A...
...HAD TO MAKE ...SOME CHANGES...
...THAT'S IT...
...THAT HAS TO BE...
...IT?
DON'T WORRY, BOY...

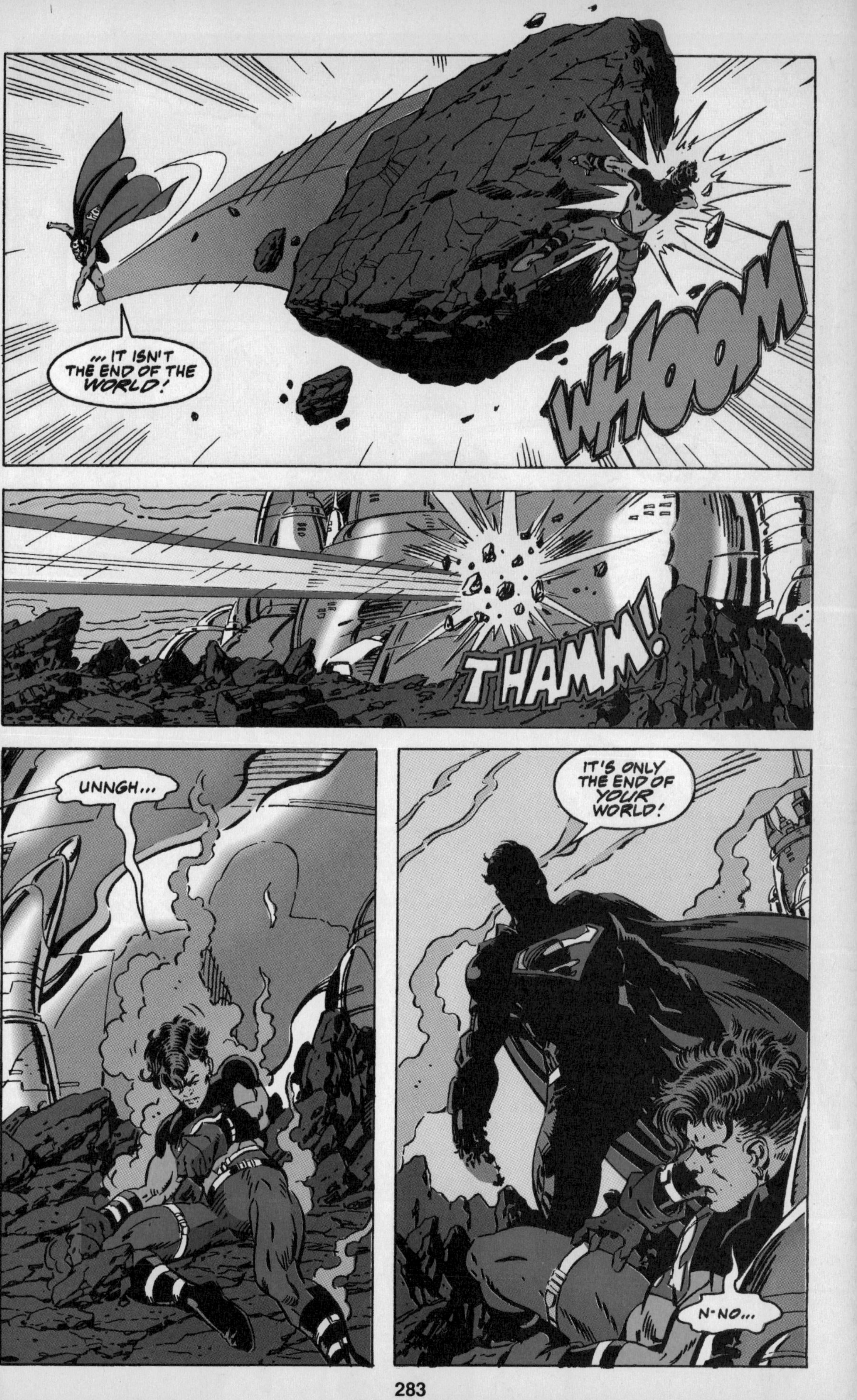
... IT ISN'T THE END OF THE WORLD!
WHOOM
THAMM!
UNNGH...
IT'S ONLY THE END OF YOUR WORLD!
N-NO...

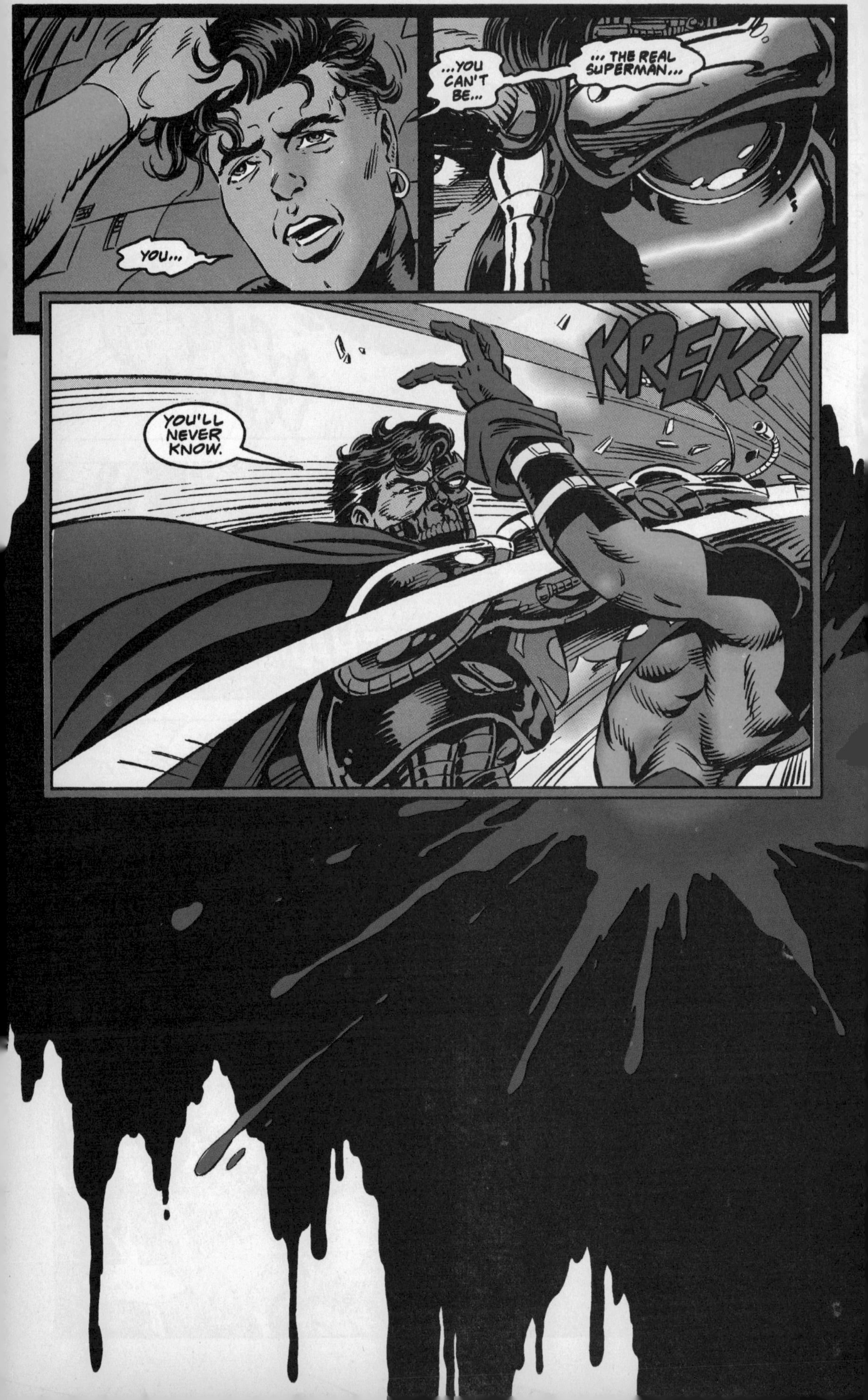
YOU...
...YOU CAN'T BE...
... THE REAL SUPERMAN...
KREK!
YOU'LL NEVER KNOW.

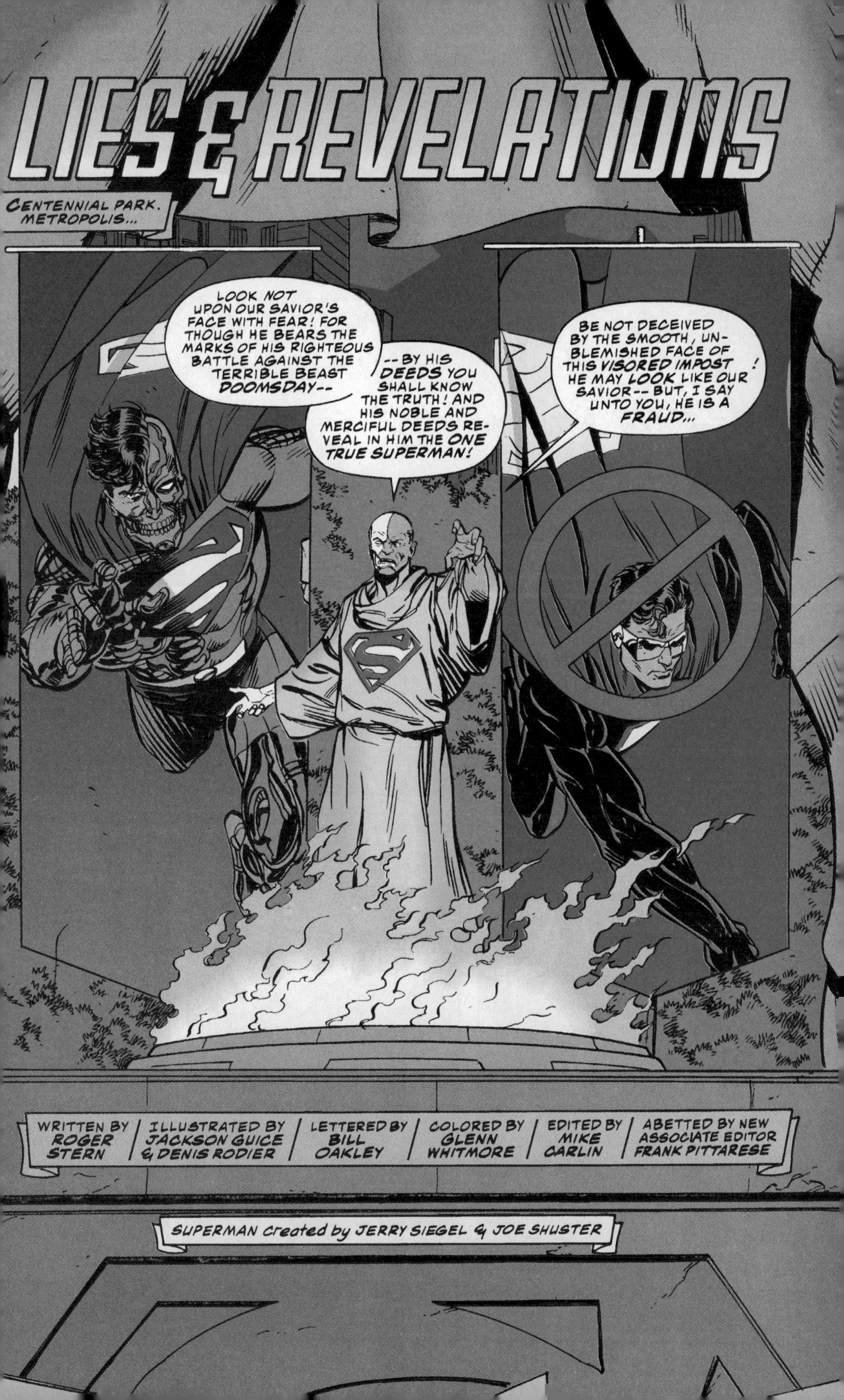
LIES & REVELATIONS
CENTENNIAL PARK. METROPOLIS...
LOOK NOT UPON OUR SAVIOR'S FACE WITH FEAR! FOR THOUGH HE BEARS THE MARKS OF HIS RIGHTEOUS BATTLE AGAINST THE TERRIBLE BEAST DOOMSDAY--
--BY HIS DEEDS YOU SHALL KNOW THE TRUTH! AND HIS NOBLE AND MERCIFUL DEEDS REVEAL IN HIM THE ONE TRUE SUPERMAN!
BE NOT DECEIVED BY THE SMOOTH, UNBLEMISHED FACE OF THIS VISORED IMPOST ! HE MAY LOOK LIKE OUR SAVIOR-- BUT, I SAY UNTO YOU, HE IS A FRAUD...
WRITTEN BY ROGER STERN | ILLUSTRATED BY JACKSON GUICE & DENIS RODIER | LETTERED BY BILL OAKLEY | COLORED BY GLENN WHITMORE | EDITED BY MIKE CARLIN | ABETTED BY NEW ASSOCIATE EDITOR FRANK PITTARESE
SUPERMAN created by JERRY SIEGEL & JOE SHUSTER

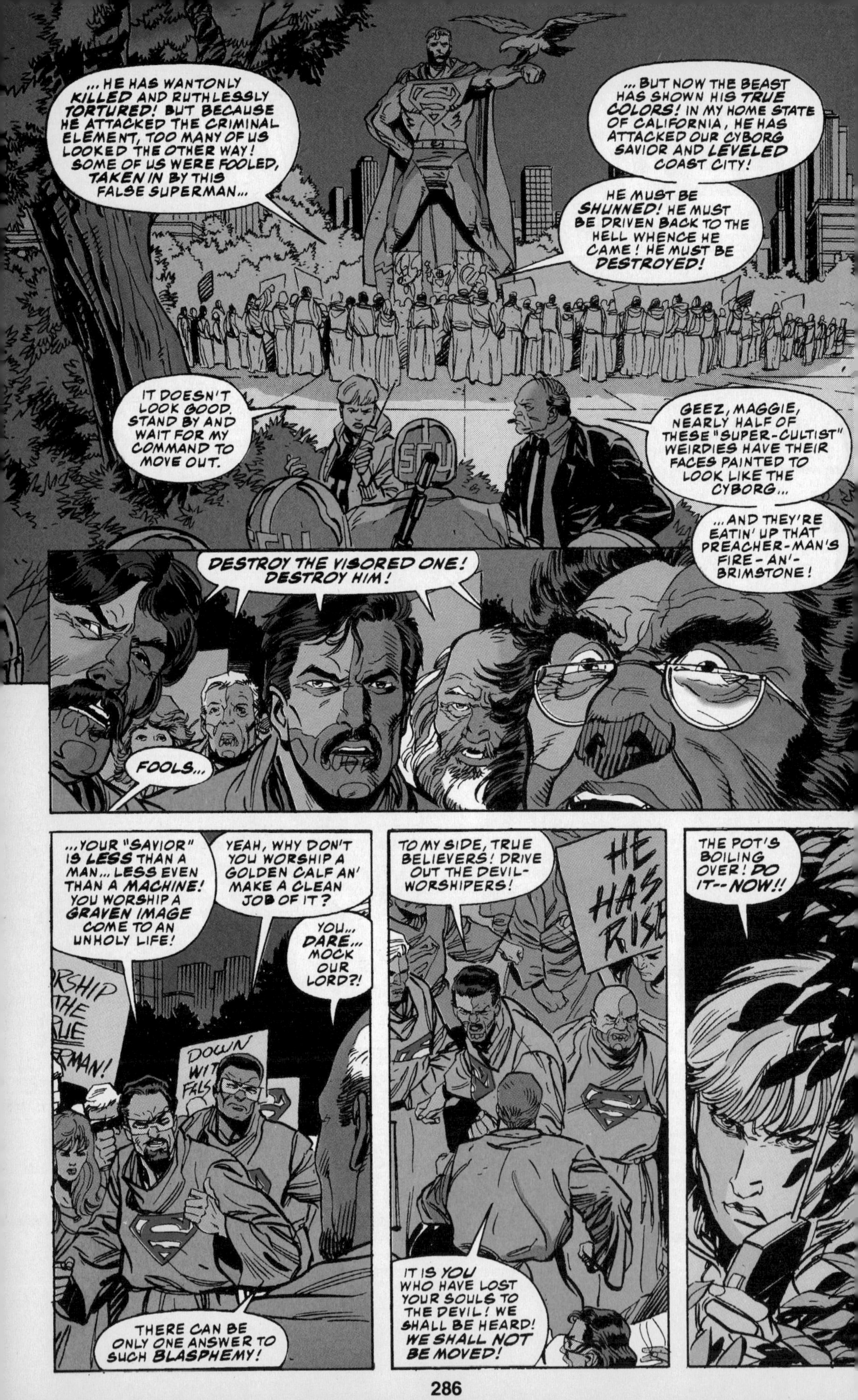
...HE HAS WANTONLY KILLED AND RUTHLESSLY TORTURED! BUT BECAUSE HE ATTACKED THE CRIMINAL ELEMENT, TOO MANY OF US LOOKED THE OTHER WAY! SOME OF US WERE FOOLED, TAKEN IN BY THIS FALSE SUPERMAN...
...BUT NOW THE BEAST HAS SHOWN HIS TRUE COLORS! IN MY HOME STATE OF CALIFORNIA, HE HAS ATTACKED OUR CYBORG SAVIOR AND LEVELED COAST CITY!
HE MUST BE SHUNNED! HE MUST BE DRIVEN BACK TO THE HELL WHENCE HE CAME! HE MUST BE DESTROYED!
IT DOESN'T LOOK GOOD. STAND BY AND WAIT FOR MY COMMAND TO MOVE OUT.
GEEZ, MAGGIE, NEARLY HALF OF THESE "SUPER-CULTIST" WEIRDIES HAVE THEIR FACES PAINTED TO LOOK LIKE THE CYBORG...
...AND THEY'RE EATIN' UP THAT PREACHER-MAN'S FIRE-AN'-BRIMSTONE!
DESTROY THE VISORED ONE! DESTROY HIM!
FOOLS...
...YOUR "SAVIOR" IS LESS THAN A MAN... LESS EVEN THAN A MACHINE! YOU WORSHIP A GRAVEN IMAGE COME TO AN UNHOLY LIFE!
YEAH, WHY DON'T YOU WORSHIP A GOLDEN CALF AN' MAKE A CLEAN JOB OF IT?
YOU... DARE... MOCK OUR LORD?!
THERE CAN BE ONLY ONE ANSWER TO SUCH BLASPHEMY!
TO MY SIDE, TRUE BELIEVERS! DRIVE OUT THE DEVIL-WORSHIPERS!
IT IS YOU WHO HAVE LOST YOUR SOULS TO THE DEVIL! WE SHALL BE HEARD! WE SHALL NOT BE MOVED!
THE POT'S BOILING OVER! DO IT--NOW!!

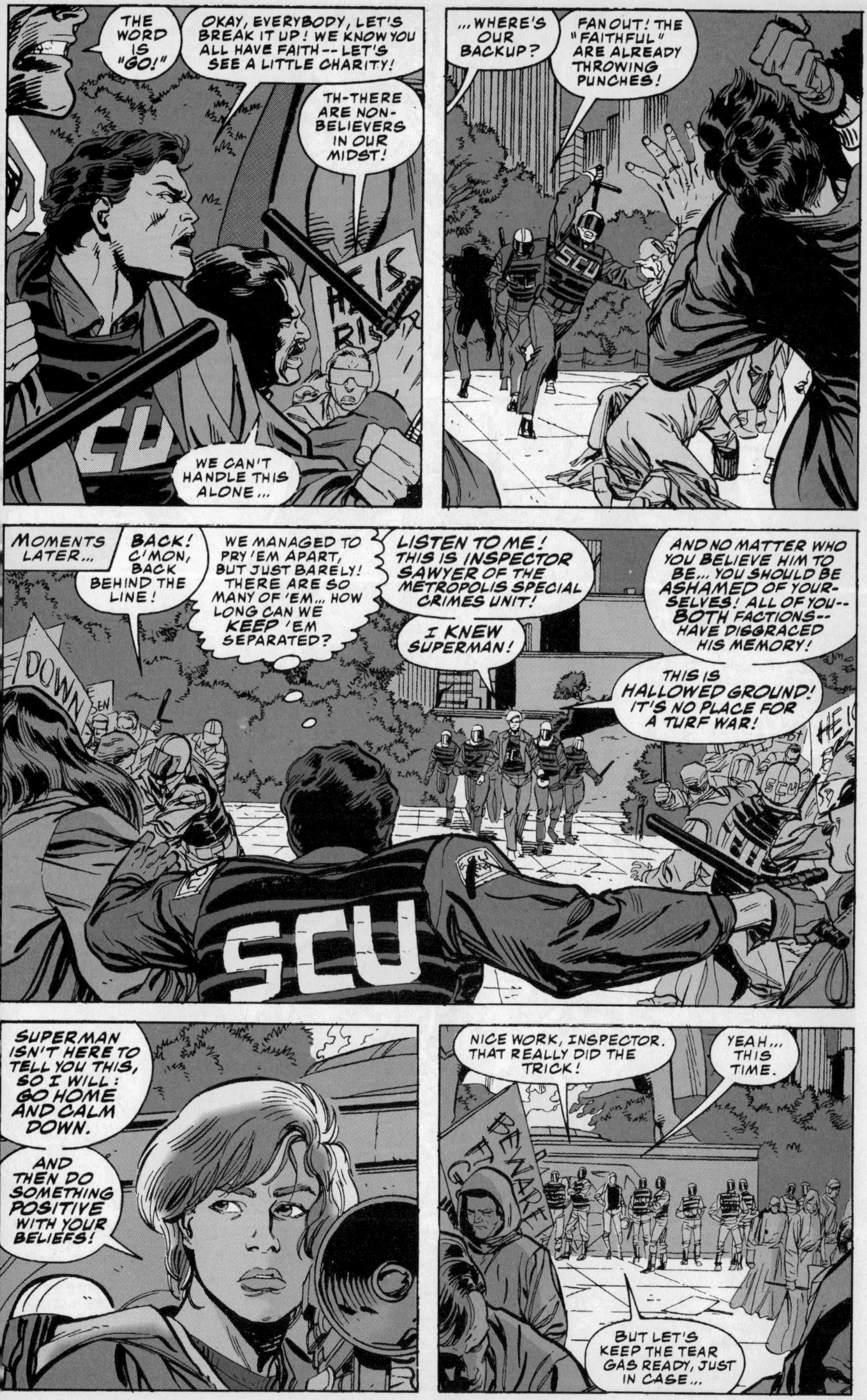
THE WORD IS "GO!"
OKAY, EVERYBODY, LET'S BREAK IT UP! WE KNOW YOU ALL HAVE FAITH -- LET'S SEE A LITTLE CHARITY!
TH-THERE ARE NON-BELIEVERS IN OUR MIDST!
WE CAN'T HANDLE THIS ALONE...
...WHERE'S OUR BACKUP?
FAN OUT! THE "FAITHFUL" ARE ALREADY THROWING PUNCHES!
SCU
MOMENTS LATER...
BACK! C'MON, BACK BEHIND THE LINE!
WE MANAGED TO PRY 'EM APART, BUT JUST BARELY! THERE ARE SO MANY OF 'EM... HOW LONG CAN WE KEEP 'EM SEPARATED?
LISTEN TO ME! THIS IS INSPECTOR SAWYER OF THE METROPOLIS SPECIAL CRIMES UNIT!
I KNEW SUPERMAN!
AND NO MATTER WHO YOU BELIEVE HIM TO BE... YOU SHOULD BE ASHAMED OF YOURSELVES! ALL OF YOU-- BOTH FACTIONS-- HAVE DISGRACED HIS MEMORY!
THIS IS HALLOWED GROUND! IT'S NO PLACE FOR A TURF WAR!
DOWN
SCU
SUPERMAN ISN'T HERE TO TELL YOU THIS, SO I WILL: GO HOME AND CALM DOWN.
AND THEN DO SOMETHING POSITIVE WITH YOUR BELIEFS!
NICE WORK, INSPECTOR. THAT REALLY DID THE TRICK!
YEAH... THIS TIME.
BEWARE
BUT LET'S KEEP THE TEAR GAS READY, JUST IN CASE...

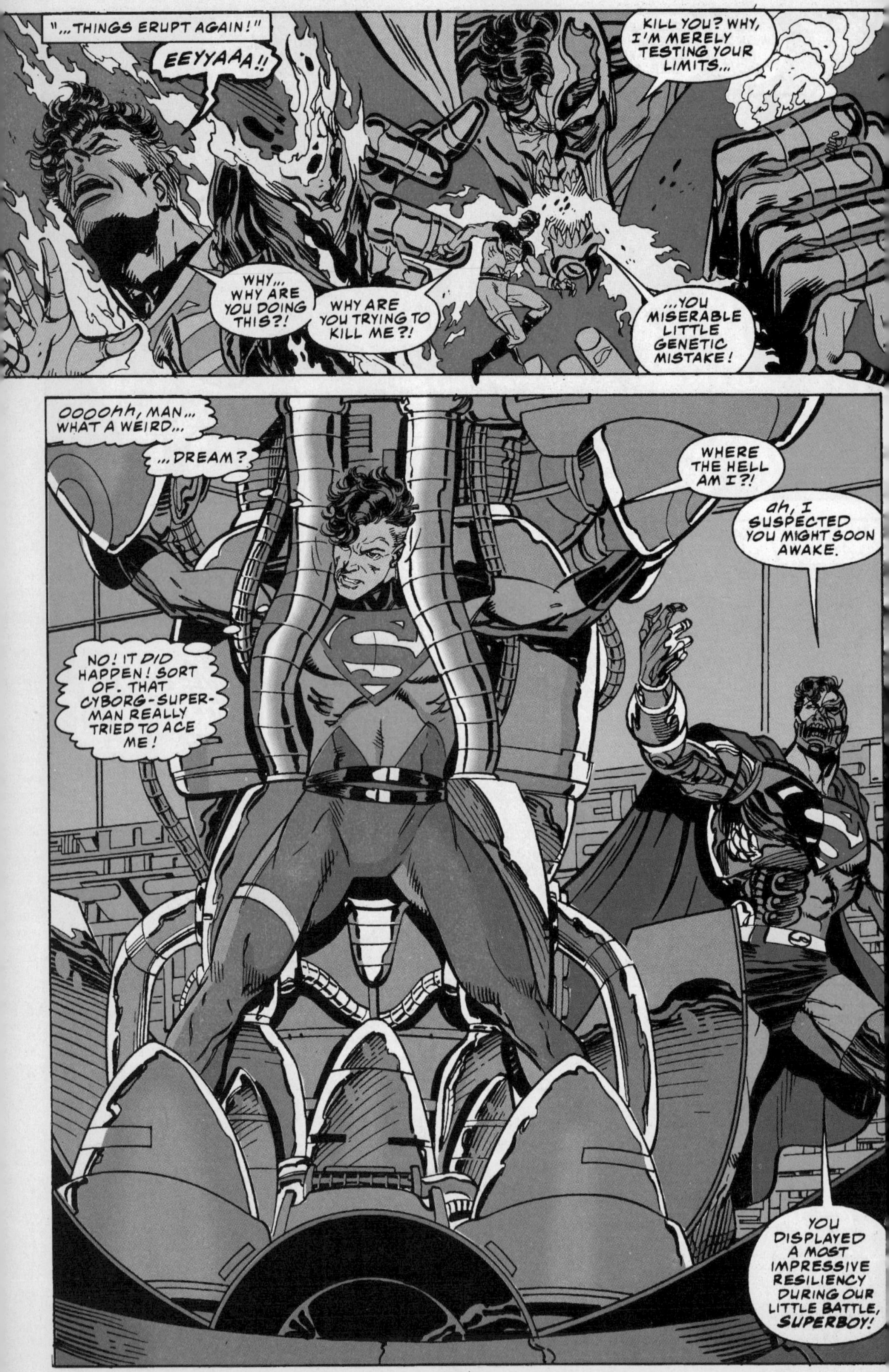
"...THINGS ERUPT AGAIN!"
EEYYAAA!!
WHY... WHY ARE YOU DOING THIS?!
WHY ARE YOU TRYING TO KILL ME?!
KILL YOU? WHY, I'M MERELY TESTING YOUR LIMITS...
...YOU MISERABLE LITTLE GENETIC MISTAKE!
OOOOhh, MAN... WHAT A WEIRD...
...DREAM?
WHERE THE HELL AM I?!
NO! IT DID HAPPEN! SORT OF. THAT CYBORG-SUPERMAN REALLY TRIED TO ACE ME!
ah, I SUSPECTED YOU MIGHT SOON AWAKE.
YOU DISPLAYED A MOST IMPRESSIVE RESILIENCY DURING OUR LITTLE BATTLE, SUPERBOY!

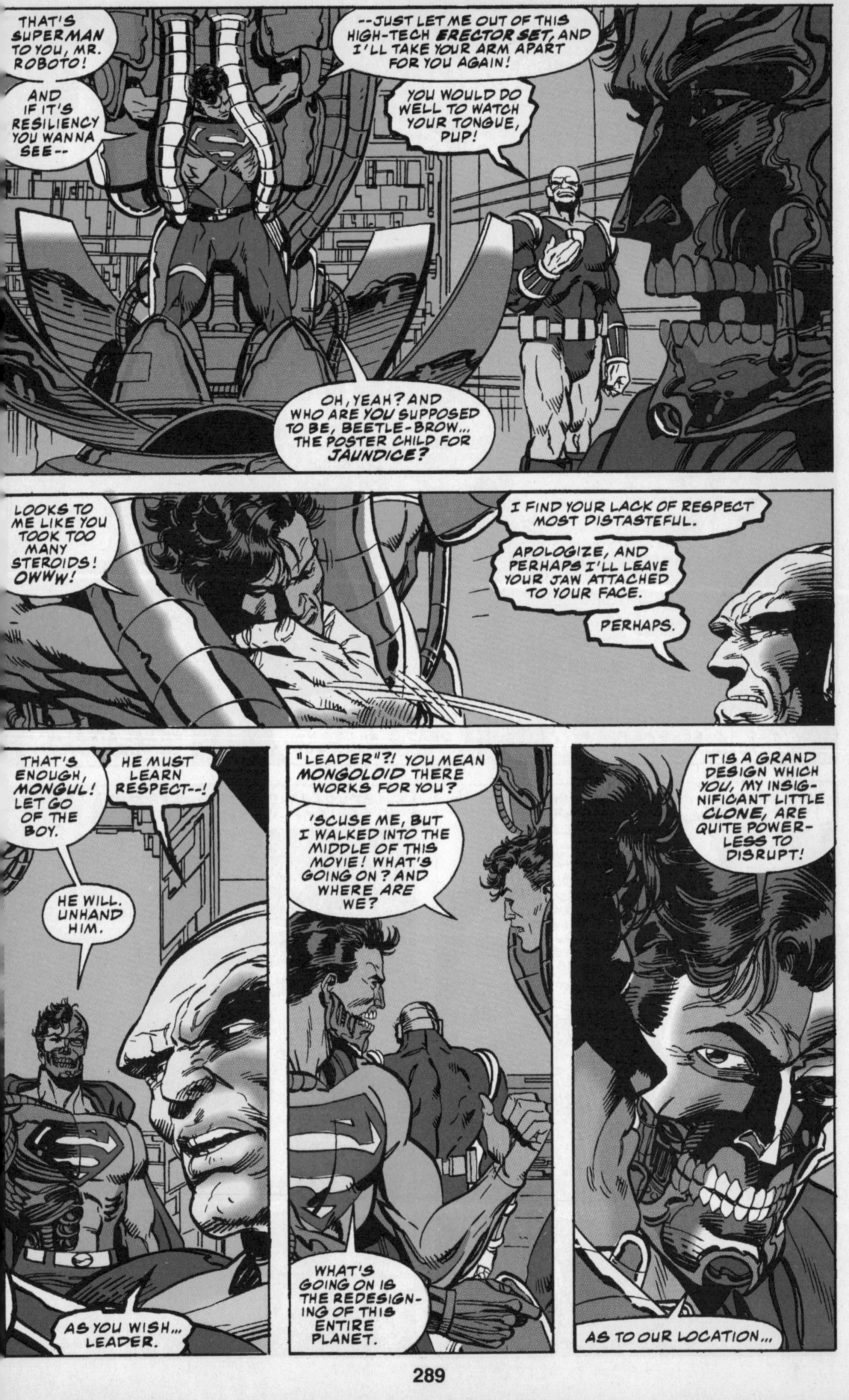
THAT'S SUPERMAN TO YOU, MR. ROBOTO!
AND IF IT'S RESILIENCY YOU WANNA SEE--
--JUST LET ME OUT OF THIS HIGH-TECH ERECTOR SET, AND I'LL TAKE YOUR ARM APART FOR YOU AGAIN!
YOU WOULD DO WELL TO WATCH YOUR TONGUE, PUP!
OH, YEAH? AND WHO ARE YOU SUPPOSED TO BE, BEETLE-BROW... THE POSTER CHILD FOR JAUNDICE?
LOOKS TO ME LIKE YOU TOOK TOO MANY STEROIDS! OWWW!
I FIND YOUR LACK OF RESPECT MOST DISTASTEFUL.
APOLOGIZE, AND PERHAPS I'LL LEAVE YOUR JAW ATTACHED TO YOUR FACE.
PERHAPS.
THAT'S ENOUGH, MONGUL! LET GO OF THE BOY.
HE MUST LEARN RESPECT--!
HE WILL. UNHAND HIM.
AS YOU WISH... LEADER.
"LEADER"?! YOU MEAN MONGOLOID THERE WORKS FOR YOU?
'SCUSE ME, BUT I WALKED INTO THE MIDDLE OF THIS MOVIE! WHAT'S GOING ON? AND WHERE ARE WE?
WHAT'S GOING ON IS THE REDESIGNING OF THIS ENTIRE PLANET.
IT IS A GRAND DESIGN WHICH YOU, MY INSIGNIFICANT LITTLE CLONE, ARE QUITE POWERLESS TO DISRUPT!
AS TO OUR LOCATION...

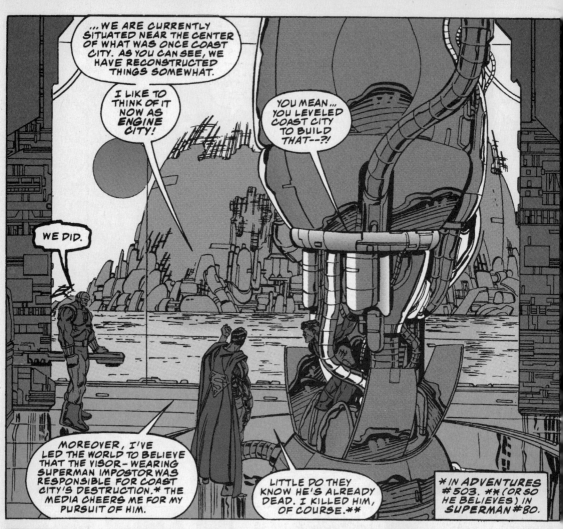

...WE ARE CURRENTLY SITUATED NEAR THE CENTER OF WHAT WAS ONCE COAST CITY. AS YOU CAN SEE, WE HAVE RECONSTRUCTED THINGS SOMEWHAT.

I LIKE TO THINK OF IT NOW AS ENGINE CITY!

YOU MEAN... YOU LEVELED COAST CITY TO BUILD THAT--?!

WE DID.

MOREOVER, I'VE LED THE WORLD TO BELIEVE THAT THE VISOR-WEARING SUPERMAN IMPOSTOR WAS RESPONSIBLE FOR COAST CITY'S DESTRUCTION.* THE MEDIA CHEERS ME FOR MY PURSUIT OF HIM.

LITTLE DO THEY KNOW HE'S ALREADY DEAD. I KILLED HIM, OF COURSE.**

*IN ADVENTURES #503. **(OR SO HE BELIEVES) IN SUPERMAN #80.

WHY ARE YOU DOING THIS?

MY REASONS ARE MY OWN. SUPERMAN KNOWS BEST.

DON'T HAND ME THAT! YOU'RE NOT SUPERMAN!

I AM NOW. IF YOU WISH TO REACH YOUR MATURITY, YOU SHOULD ACCEPT AND ACKNOWLEDGE ME AS YOUR MASTER. YOU HAVE NO OTHER OPTIONS.

THERE IS NO ESCAPE FROM ENGINE CITY.

COME, MONGUL...

"...LET US LEAVE OUR YOUNG FRIEND TO CONTEMPLATE HIS FUTURE."

OH, MAN... I REALLY BLEW IT THIS TIME!

IF EVEN HALF OF WHAT HE SAID IS TRUE, HE'S GOT THE WHOLE WORLD IN A VISE.

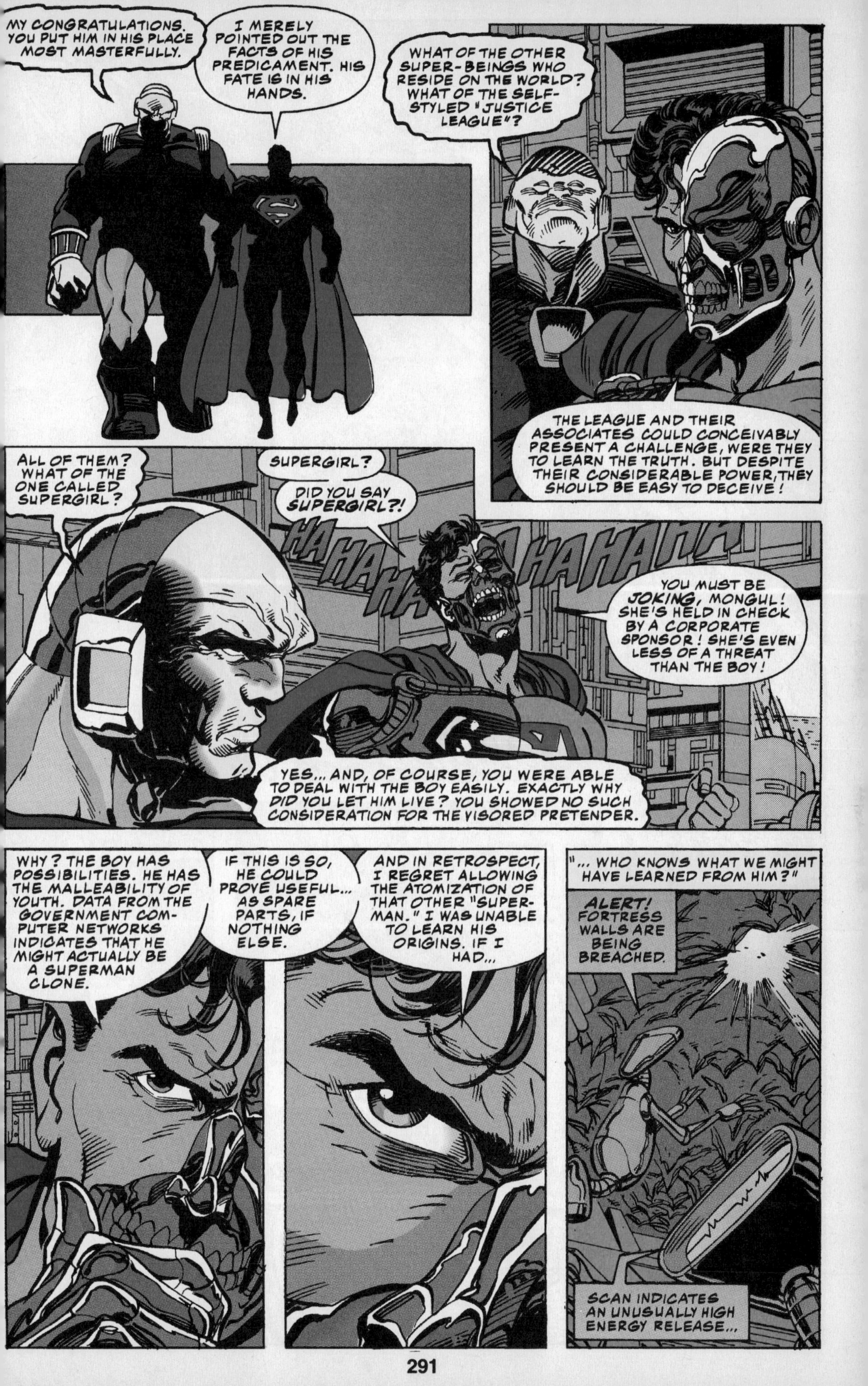

MY CONGRATULATIONS. YOU PUT HIM IN HIS PLACE MOST MASTERFULLY.
I MERELY POINTED OUT THE FACTS OF HIS PREDICAMENT. HIS FATE IS IN HIS HANDS.
WHAT OF THE OTHER SUPER-BEINGS WHO RESIDE ON THE WORLD? WHAT OF THE SELF-STYLED "JUSTICE LEAGUE"?
THE LEAGUE AND THEIR ASSOCIATES COULD CONCEIVABLY PRESENT A CHALLENGE, WERE THEY TO LEARN THE TRUTH. BUT DESPITE THEIR CONSIDERABLE POWER, THEY SHOULD BE EASY TO DECEIVE!
ALL OF THEM? WHAT OF THE ONE CALLED SUPERGIRL?
SUPERGIRL?
DID YOU SAY SUPERGIRL?!
HAHAHAHAHAHAHAHA
YOU MUST BE JOKING, MONGUL! SHE'S HELD IN CHECK BY A CORPORATE SPONSOR! SHE'S EVEN LESS OF A THREAT THAN THE BOY!
YES... AND, OF COURSE, YOU WERE ABLE TO DEAL WITH THE BOY EASILY. EXACTLY WHY DID YOU LET HIM LIVE? YOU SHOWED NO SUCH CONSIDERATION FOR THE VISORED PRETENDER.
WHY? THE BOY HAS POSSIBILITIES. HE HAS THE MALLEABILITY OF YOUTH. DATA FROM THE GOVERNMENT COMPUTER NETWORKS INDICATES THAT HE MIGHT ACTUALLY BE A SUPERMAN CLONE.
IF THIS IS SO, HE COULD PROVE USEFUL... AS SPARE PARTS, IF NOTHING ELSE.
AND IN RETROSPECT, I REGRET ALLOWING THE ATOMIZATION OF THAT OTHER "SUPERMAN." I WAS UNABLE TO LEARN HIS ORIGINS. IF I HAD...
"... WHO KNOWS WHAT WE MIGHT HAVE LEARNED FROM HIM?"
ALERT! FORTRESS WALLS ARE BEING BREACHED.
SCAN INDICATES AN UNUSUALLY HIGH ENERGY RELEASE...

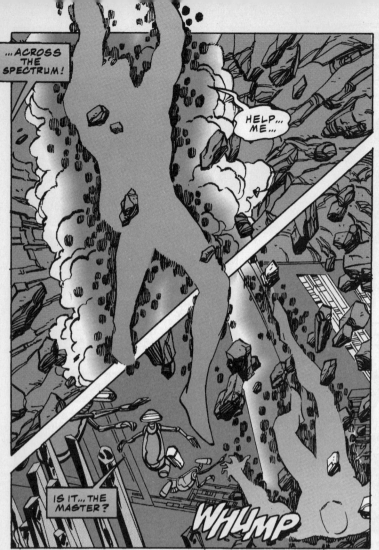

...ACROSS THE SPECTRUM!

HELP... ME...

IS IT... THE MASTER?

WHUMP

HE HAS BEEN SERIOUSLY INJURED. HIS BODY SHOWS SIGNS OF SEVERE RADIATION BURNS.

WHAT COULD HAVE CAUSED THIS?

THE CYBORG... DANGER! NEED THE... REGENERATION MATRIX. TAKE ME THERE... HURRY!

YES, SIR. AT ONCE.

BUT THERE IS SOMETHING YOU SHOULD KNOW ABOUT--!

LATER. FIRST...

...THE MATRIX? NO. NO... IT'S OPEN... EMPTY!

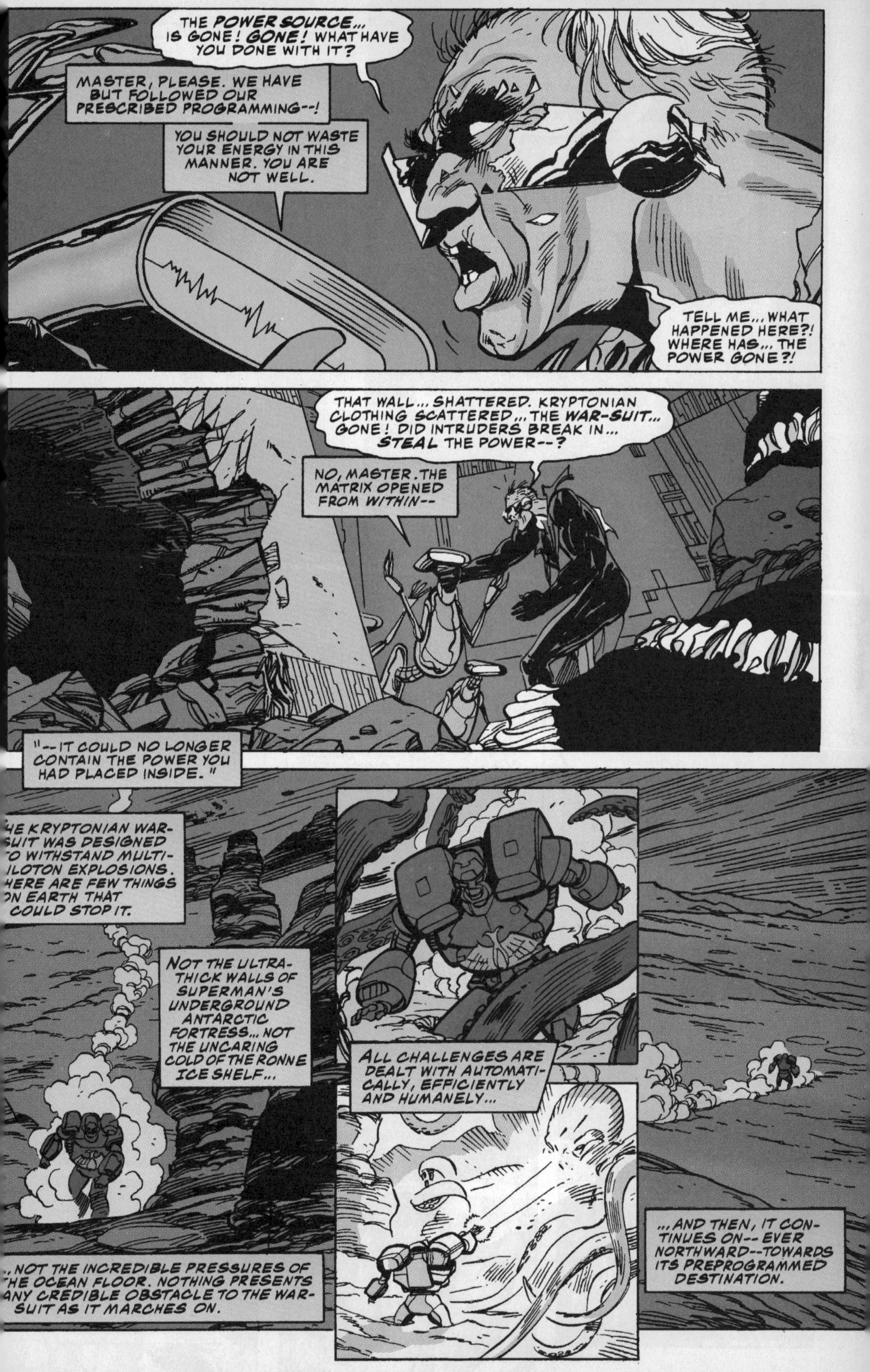
THE POWER SOURCE... IS GONE! GONE! WHAT HAVE YOU DONE WITH IT?
MASTER, PLEASE. WE HAVE BUT FOLLOWED OUR PRESCRIBED PROGRAMMING--!
YOU SHOULD NOT WASTE YOUR ENERGY IN THIS MANNER. YOU ARE NOT WELL.
TELL ME... WHAT HAPPENED HERE?! WHERE HAS... THE POWER GONE?!
THAT WALL... SHATTERED. KRYPTONIAN CLOTHING SCATTERED... THE WAR-SUIT... GONE! DID INTRUDERS BREAK IN... STEAL THE POWER--?
NO, MASTER. THE MATRIX OPENED FROM WITHIN--
"--IT COULD NO LONGER CONTAIN THE POWER YOU HAD PLACED INSIDE."
HE KRYPTONIAN WAR-SUIT WAS DESIGNED TO WITHSTAND MULTI-ILOTON EXPLOSIONS. HERE ARE FEW THINGS ON EARTH THAT COULD STOP IT.
NOT THE ULTRA-THICK WALLS OF SUPERMAN'S UNDERGROUND ANTARCTIC FORTRESS... NOT THE UNCARING COLD OF THE RONNE ICE SHELF...
..NOT THE INCREDIBLE PRESSURES OF THE OCEAN FLOOR. NOTHING PRESENTS ANY CREDIBLE OBSTACLE TO THE WAR-SUIT AS IT MARCHES ON.
ALL CHALLENGES ARE DEALT WITH AUTOMATICALLY, EFFICIENTLY AND HUMANELY...
...AND THEN, IT CONTINUES ON-- EVER NORTHWARD--TOWARDS ITS PREPROGRAMMED DESTINATION.

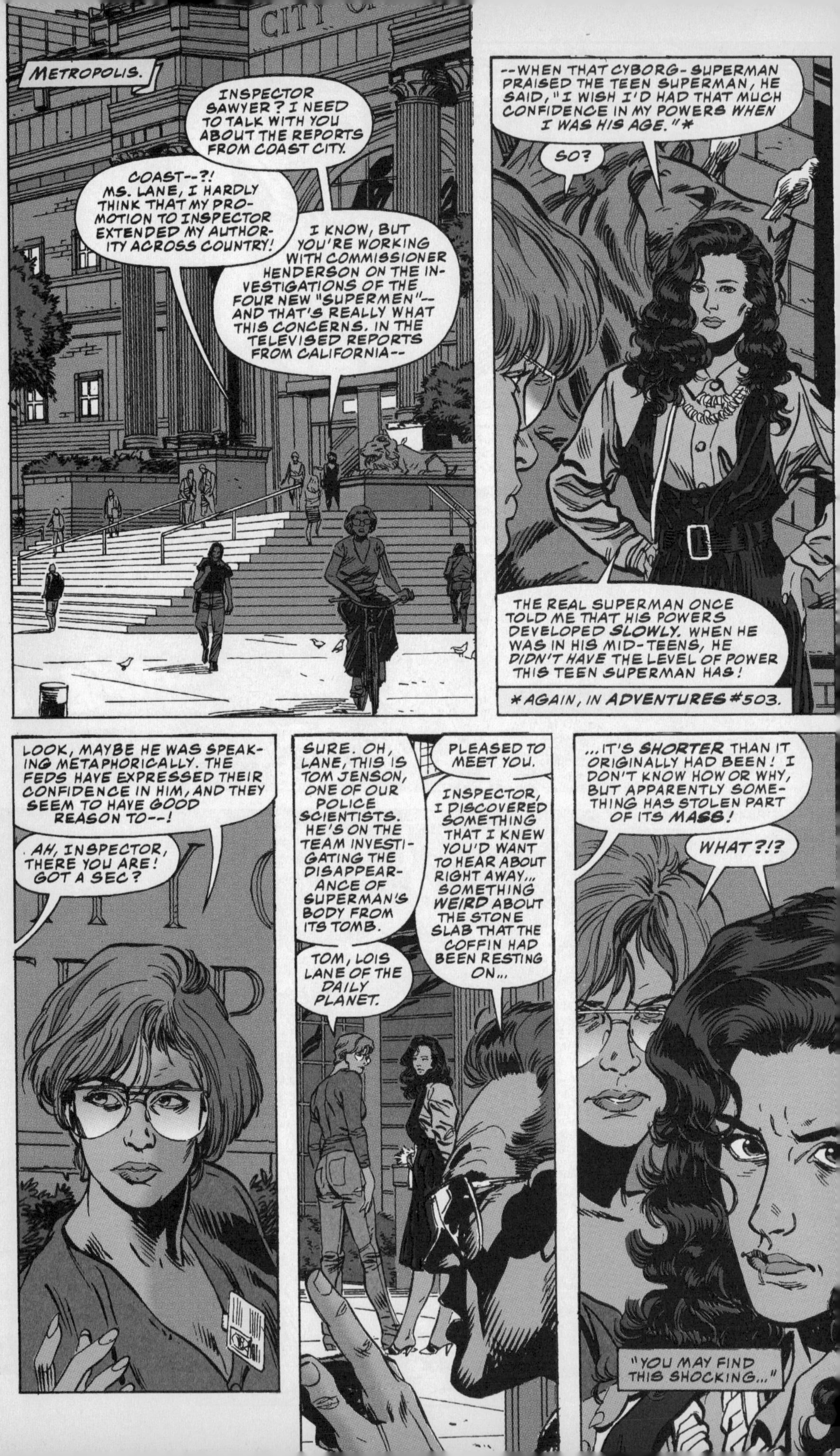

CITY O
METROPOLIS.
INSPECTOR SAWYER? I NEED TO TALK WITH YOU ABOUT THE REPORTS FROM COAST CITY.
COAST--?! MS. LANE, I HARDLY THINK THAT MY PROMOTION TO INSPECTOR EXTENDED MY AUTHORITY ACROSS COUNTRY!
I KNOW, BUT YOU'RE WORKING WITH COMMISSIONER HENDERSON ON THE INVESTIGATIONS OF THE FOUR NEW "SUPERMEN"-- AND THAT'S REALLY WHAT THIS CONCERNS. IN THE TELEVISED REPORTS FROM CALIFORNIA--
--WHEN THAT CYBORG-SUPERMAN PRAISED THE TEEN SUPERMAN, HE SAID, "I WISH I'D HAD THAT MUCH CONFIDENCE IN MY POWERS WHEN I WAS HIS AGE." *
SO?
THE REAL SUPERMAN ONCE TOLD ME THAT HIS POWERS DEVELOPED SLOWLY. WHEN HE WAS IN HIS MID-TEENS, HE DIDN'T HAVE THE LEVEL OF POWER THIS TEEN SUPERMAN HAS!
* AGAIN, IN ADVENTURES #503.
LOOK, MAYBE HE WAS SPEAKING METAPHORICALLY. THE FEDS HAVE EXPRESSED THEIR CONFIDENCE IN HIM, AND THEY SEEM TO HAVE GOOD REASON TO--!
AH, INSPECTOR, THERE YOU ARE! GOT A SEC?
SURE. OH, LANE, THIS IS TOM JENSON, ONE OF OUR POLICE SCIENTISTS. HE'S ON THE TEAM INVESTIGATING THE DISAPPEARANCE OF SUPERMAN'S BODY FROM ITS TOMB.
TOM, LOIS LANE OF THE DAILY PLANET.
PLEASED TO MEET YOU.
INSPECTOR, I DISCOVERED SOMETHING THAT I KNEW YOU'D WANT TO HEAR ABOUT RIGHT AWAY... SOMETHING WEIRD ABOUT THE STONE SLAB THAT THE COFFIN HAD BEEN RESTING ON...
"YOU MAY FIND THIS SHOCKING..."
...IT'S SHORTER THAN IT ORIGINALLY HAD BEEN! I DON'T KNOW HOW OR WHY, BUT APPARENTLY SOMETHING HAS STOLEN PART OF ITS MASS!
WHAT?!?

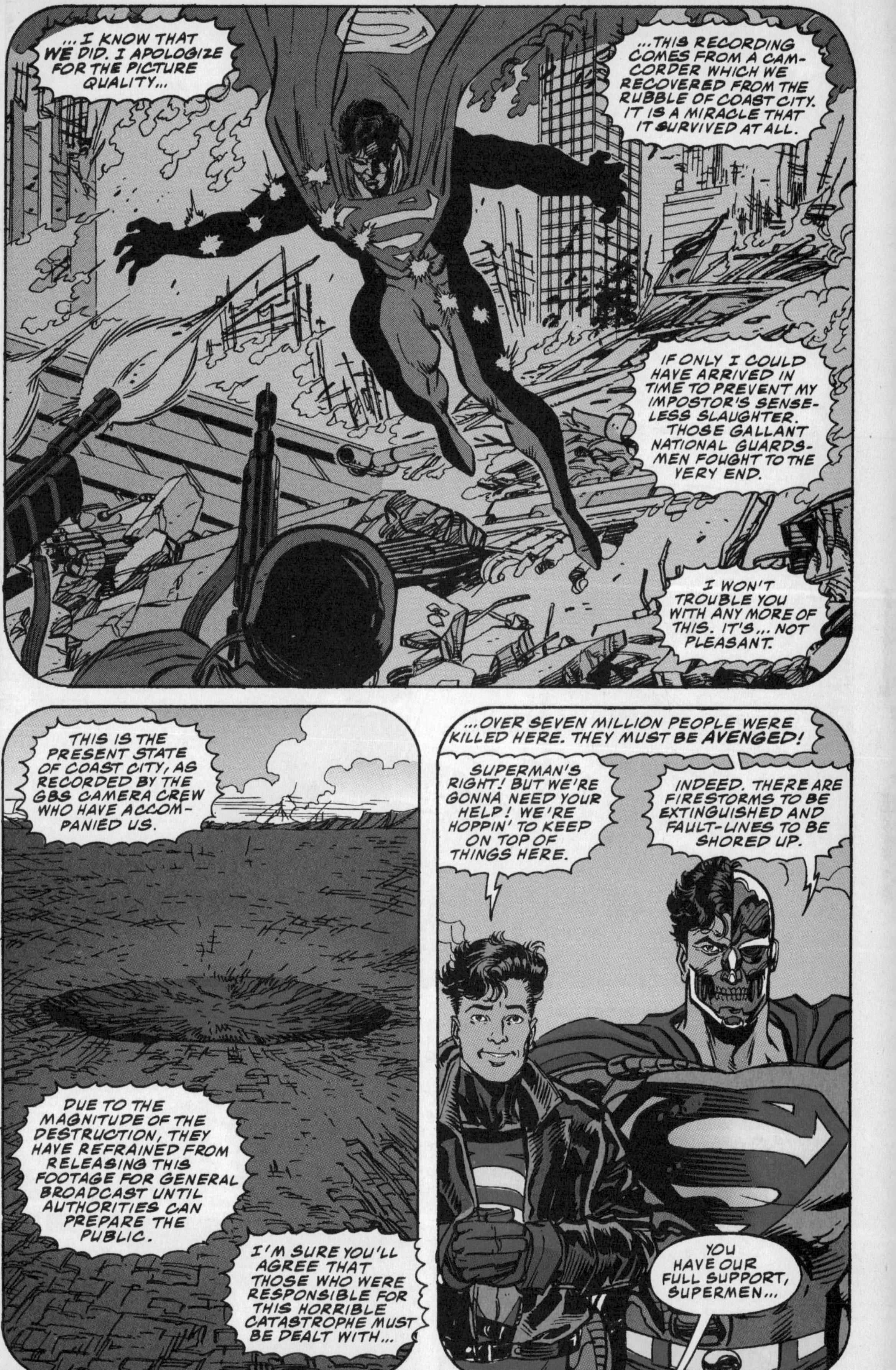

...I KNOW THAT WE DID. I APOLOGIZE FOR THE PICTURE QUALITY...
...THIS RECORDING COMES FROM A CAM-CORDER WHICH WE RECOVERED FROM THE RUBBLE OF COAST CITY. IT IS A MIRACLE THAT IT SURVIVED AT ALL.
IF ONLY I COULD HAVE ARRIVED IN TIME TO PREVENT MY IMPOSTOR'S SENSE-LESS SLAUGHTER. THOSE GALLANT NATIONAL GUARDS-MEN FOUGHT TO THE VERY END.
I WON'T TROUBLE YOU WITH ANY MORE OF THIS. IT'S... NOT PLEASANT.
THIS IS THE PRESENT STATE OF COAST CITY, AS RECORDED BY THE GBS CAMERA CREW WHO HAVE ACCOM-PANIED US.
DUE TO THE MAGNITUDE OF THE DESTRUCTION, THEY HAVE REFRAINED FROM RELEASING THIS FOOTAGE FOR GENERAL BROADCAST UNTIL AUTHORITIES CAN PREPARE THE PUBLIC.
I'M SURE YOU'LL AGREE THAT THOSE WHO WERE RESPONSIBLE FOR THIS HORRIBLE CATASTROPHE MUST BE DEALT WITH...
...OVER SEVEN MILLION PEOPLE WERE KILLED HERE. THEY MUST BE AVENGED!
SUPERMAN'S RIGHT! BUT WE'RE GONNA NEED YOUR HELP! WE'RE HOPPIN' TO KEEP ON TOP OF THINGS HERE.
INDEED. THERE ARE FIRESTORMS TO BE EXTINGUISHED AND FAULT-LINES TO BE SHORED UP.
YOU HAVE OUR FULL SUPPORT, SUPERMEN...

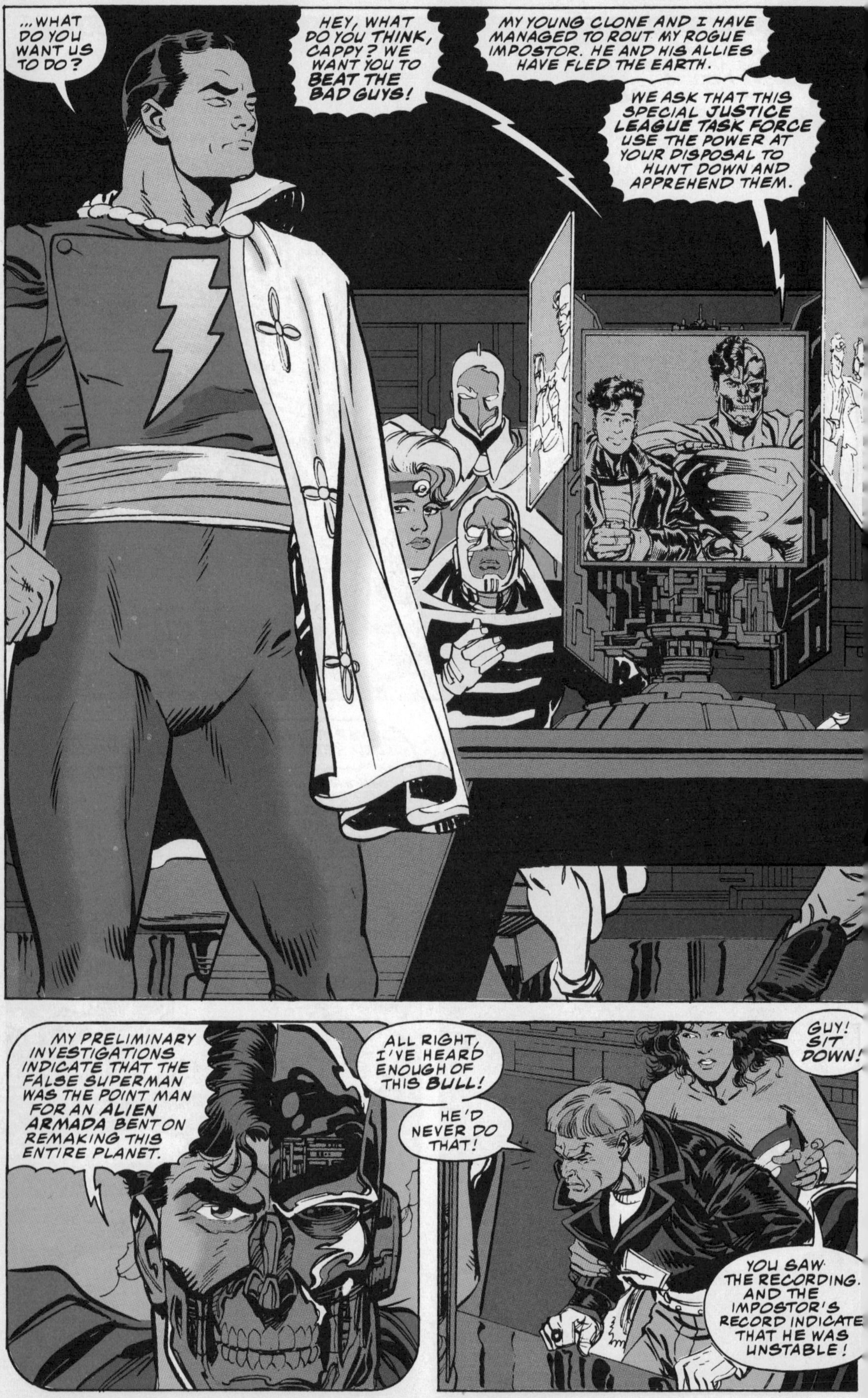
...WHAT DO YOU WANT US TO DO?
HEY, WHAT DO YOU THINK, CAPPY? WE WANT YOU TO BEAT THE BAD GUYS!
MY YOUNG CLONE AND I HAVE MANAGED TO ROUT MY ROGUE IMPOSTOR. HE AND HIS ALLIES HAVE FLED THE EARTH.
WE ASK THAT THIS SPECIAL JUSTICE LEAGUE TASK FORCE USE THE POWER AT YOUR DISPOSAL TO HUNT DOWN AND APPREHEND THEM.
MY PRELIMINARY INVESTIGATIONS INDICATE THAT THE FALSE SUPERMAN WAS THE POINT MAN FOR AN ALIEN ARMADA BENT ON REMAKING THIS ENTIRE PLANET.
ALL RIGHT, I'VE HEARD ENOUGH OF THIS BULL!
HE'D NEVER DO THAT!
GUY! SIT DOWN!
YOU SAW THE RECORDING. AND THE IMPOSTOR'S RECORD INDICATE THAT HE WAS UNSTABLE!

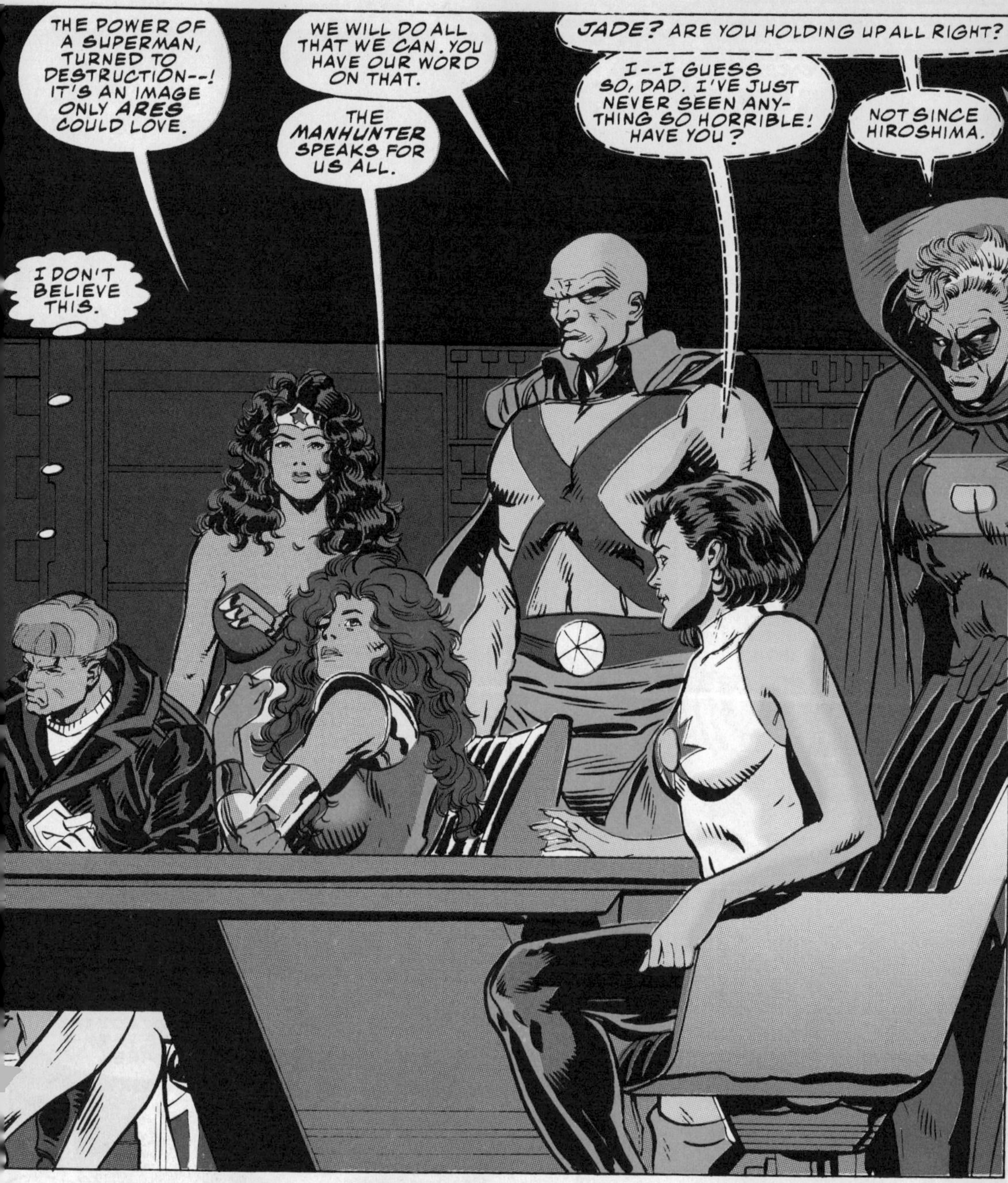
THE POWER OF A SUPERMAN, TURNED TO DESTRUCTION--! IT'S AN IMAGE ONLY ARES COULD LOVE.
I DON'T BELIEVE THIS.
WE WILL DO ALL THAT WE CAN. YOU HAVE OUR WORD ON THAT.
THE MANHUNTER SPEAKS FOR US ALL.
JADE? ARE YOU HOLDING UP ALL RIGHT?
I--I GUESS SO, DAD. I'VE JUST NEVER SEEN ANYTHING SO HORRIBLE! HAVE YOU?
NOT SINCE HIROSHIMA.

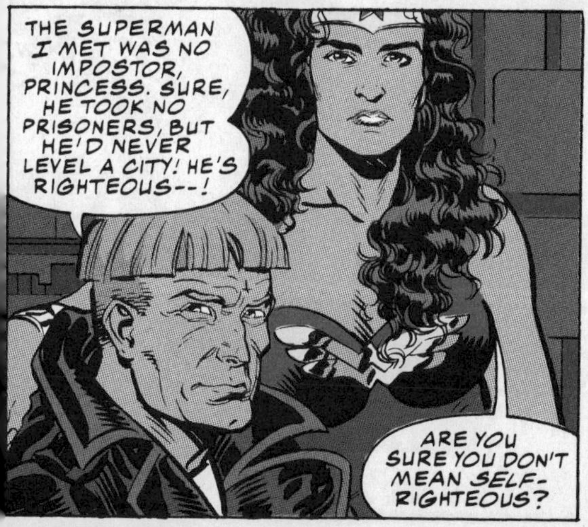
THE SUPERMAN I MET WAS NO IMPOSTOR, PRINCESS. SURE, HE TOOK NO PRISONERS, BUT HE'D NEVER LEVEL A CITY! HE'S RIGHTEOUS--!
ARE YOU SURE YOU DON'T MEAN SELF-RIGHTEOUS?

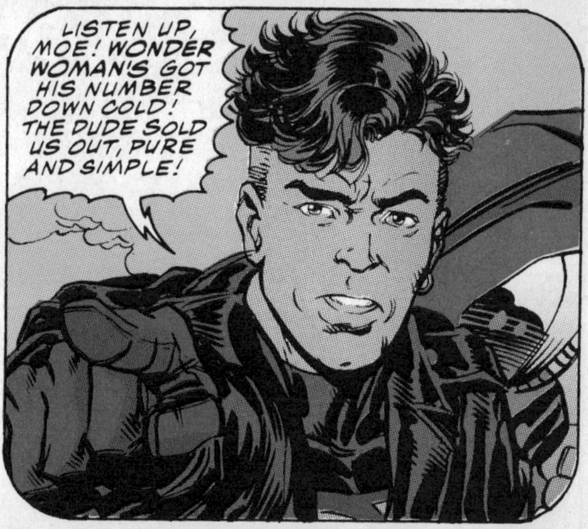
LISTEN UP, MOE! WONDER WOMAN'S GOT HIS NUMBER DOWN COLD! THE DUDE SOLD US OUT, PURE AND SIMPLE!

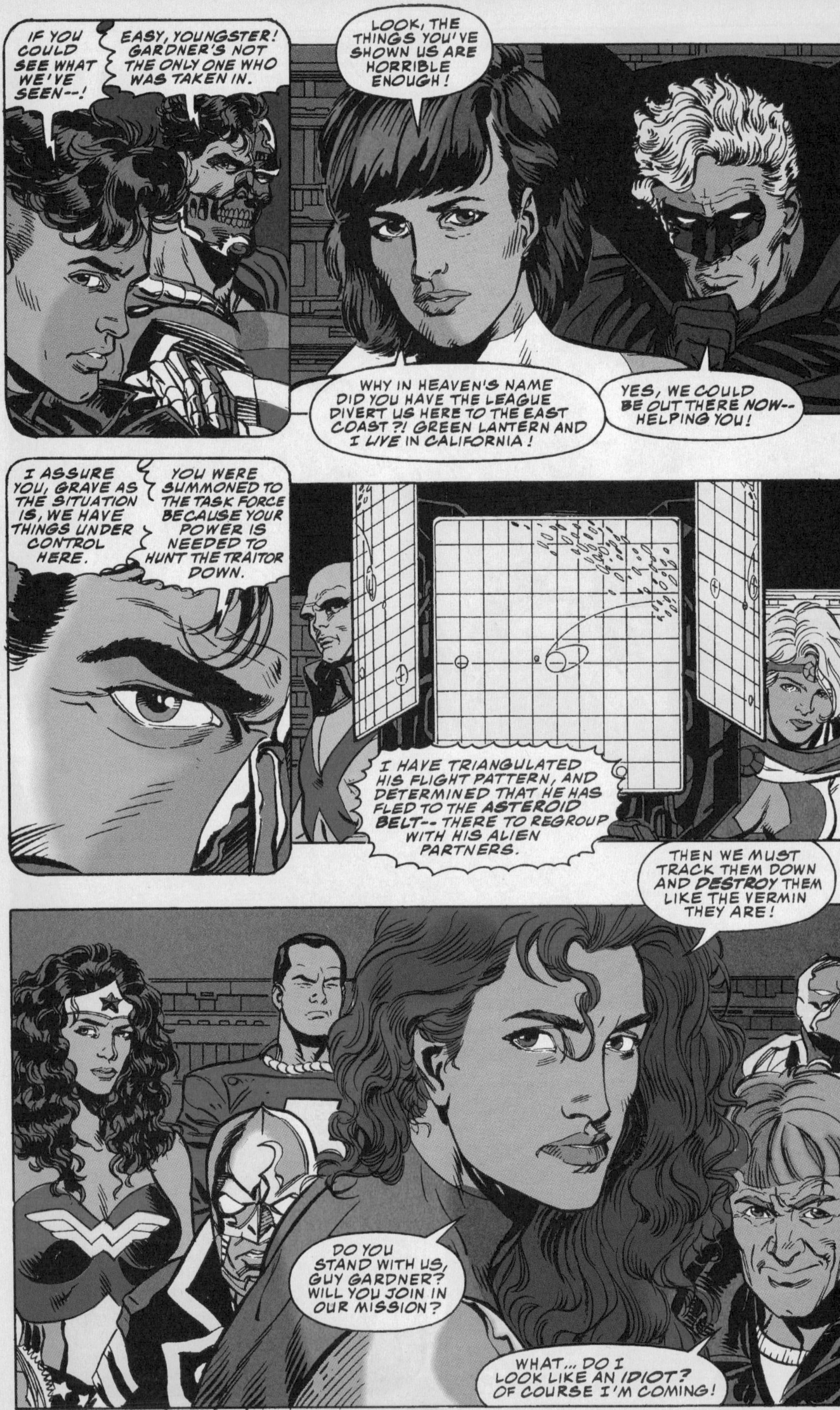
IF YOU COULD SEE WHAT WE'VE SEEN--!
EASY, YOUNGSTER! GARDNER'S NOT THE ONLY ONE WHO WAS TAKEN IN.
LOOK, THE THINGS YOU'VE SHOWN US ARE HORRIBLE ENOUGH!
WHY IN HEAVEN'S NAME DID YOU HAVE THE LEAGUE DIVERT US HERE TO THE EAST COAST?! GREEN LANTERN AND I LIVE IN CALIFORNIA!
YES, WE COULD BE OUT THERE NOW-- HELPING YOU!
I ASSURE YOU, GRAVE AS THE SITUATION IS, WE HAVE THINGS UNDER CONTROL HERE.
YOU WERE SUMMONED TO THE TASK FORCE BECAUSE YOUR POWER IS NEEDED TO HUNT THE TRAITOR DOWN.
I HAVE TRIANGULATED HIS FLIGHT PATTERN, AND DETERMINED THAT HE HAS FLED TO THE ASTEROID BELT-- THERE TO REGROUP WITH HIS ALIEN PARTNERS.
THEN WE MUST TRACK THEM DOWN AND DESTROY THEM LIKE THE VERMIN THEY ARE!
DO YOU STAND WITH US, GUY GARDNER? WILL YOU JOIN IN OUR MISSION?
WHAT... DO I LOOK LIKE AN IDIOT? OF COURSE I'M COMING!

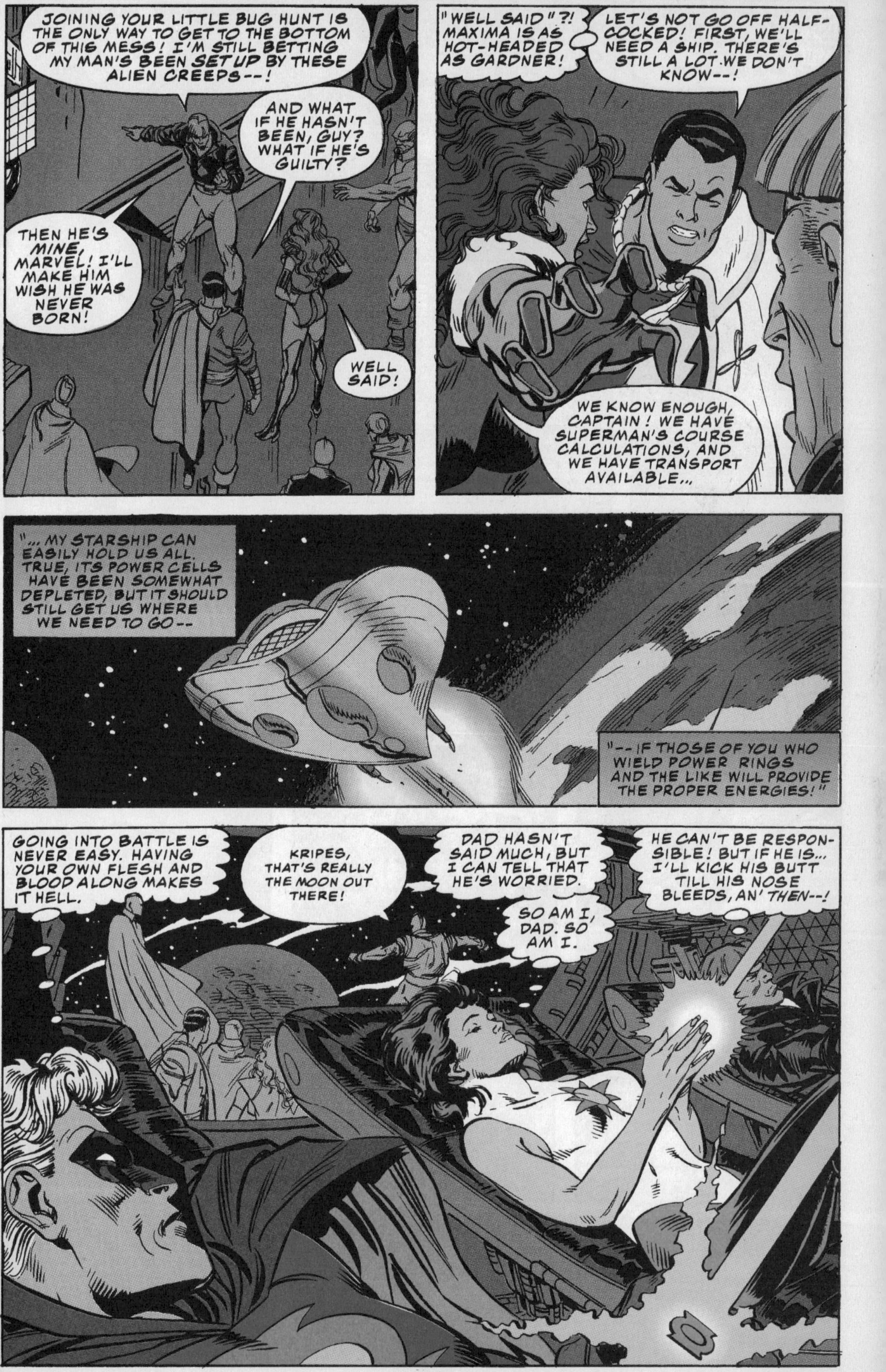

JOINING YOUR LITTLE BUG HUNT IS THE ONLY WAY TO GET TO THE BOTTOM OF THIS MESS! I'M STILL BETTING MY MAN'S BEEN *SET UP* BY THESE ALIEN CREEPS--!
AND WHAT IF HE HASN'T BEEN, GUY? WHAT IF HE'S GUILTY?
THEN HE'S *MINE*, MARVEL! I'LL MAKE HIM WISH HE WAS NEVER BORN!
WELL SAID!
"WELL SAID"?! MAXIMA IS AS HOT-HEADED AS GARDNER!
LET'S NOT GO OFF HALF-COCKED! FIRST, WE'LL NEED A SHIP. THERE'S STILL A LOT WE DON'T KNOW--!
WE KNOW ENOUGH, CAPTAIN! WE HAVE SUPERMAN'S COURSE CALCULATIONS, AND WE HAVE TRANSPORT AVAILABLE...
"... MY STARSHIP CAN EASILY HOLD US ALL. TRUE, ITS POWER CELLS HAVE BEEN SOMEWHAT DEPLETED, BUT IT SHOULD STILL GET US WHERE WE NEED TO GO--
"--IF THOSE OF YOU WHO WIELD POWER RINGS AND THE LIKE WILL PROVIDE THE PROPER ENERGIES!"
GOING INTO BATTLE IS NEVER EASY. HAVING YOUR OWN FLESH AND BLOOD ALONG MAKES IT HELL.
KRIPES, THAT'S REALLY THE MOON OUT THERE!
DAD HASN'T SAID MUCH, BUT I CAN TELL THAT HE'S WORRIED.
SO AM I, DAD. SO AM I.
HE CAN'T BE RESPONSIBLE! BUT IF HE IS... I'LL KICK HIS BUTT TILL HIS NOSE BLEEDS, AN' *THEN*--!

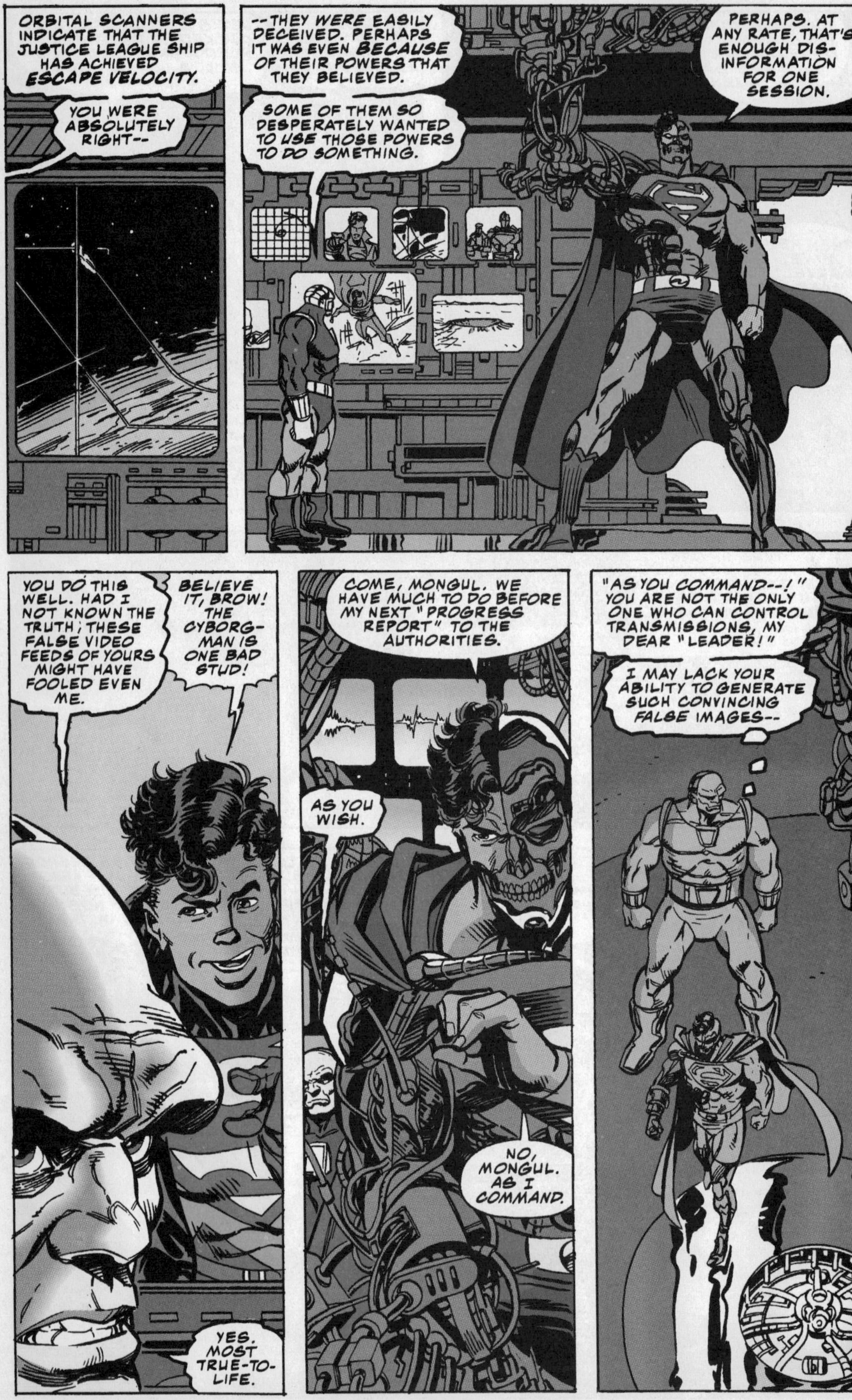
ORBITAL SCANNERS INDICATE THAT THE JUSTICE LEAGUE SHIP HAS ACHIEVED ESCAPE VELOCITY.
YOU WERE ABSOLUTELY RIGHT--
--THEY WERE EASILY DECEIVED. PERHAPS IT WAS EVEN BECAUSE OF THEIR POWERS THAT THEY BELIEVED.
SOME OF THEM SO DESPERATELY WANTED TO USE THOSE POWERS TO DO SOMETHING.
PERHAPS. AT ANY RATE, THAT'S ENOUGH DIS-INFORMATION FOR ONE SESSION.
YOU DO THIS WELL. HAD I NOT KNOWN THE TRUTH, THESE FALSE VIDEO FEEDS OF YOURS MIGHT HAVE FOOLED EVEN ME.
BELIEVE IT, BROW! THE CYBORG-MAN IS ONE BAD STUD!
YES. MOST TRUE-TO-LIFE.
COME, MONGUL. WE HAVE MUCH TO DO BEFORE MY NEXT "PROGRESS REPORT" TO THE AUTHORITIES.
AS YOU WISH.
NO, MONGUL. AS I COMMAND.
"AS YOU COMMAND--!" YOU ARE NOT THE ONLY ONE WHO CAN CONTROL TRANSMISSIONS, MY DEAR "LEADER!"
I MAY LACK YOUR ABILITY TO GENERATE SUCH CONVINCING FALSE IMAGES--

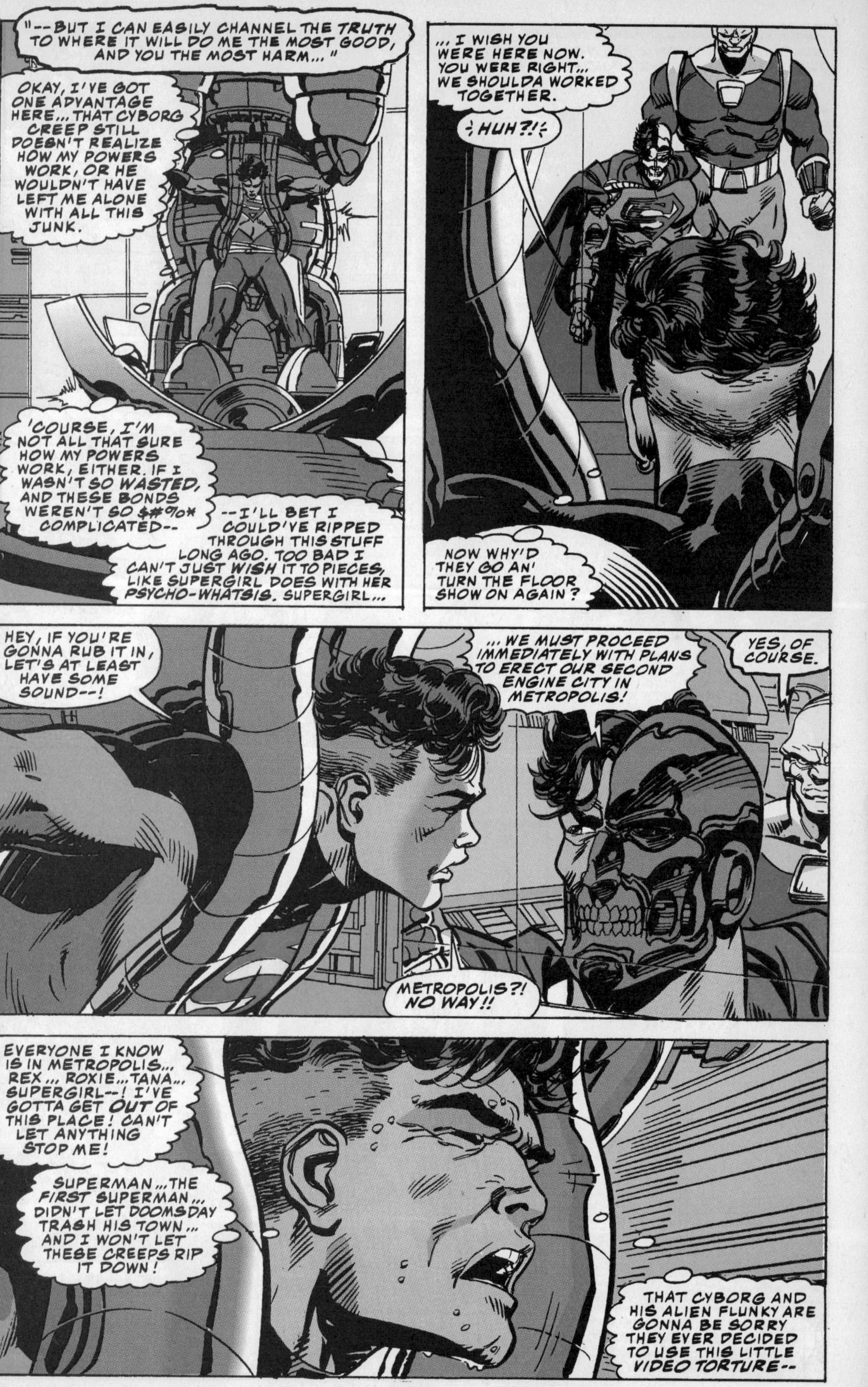
"--BUT I CAN EASILY CHANNEL THE TRUTH TO WHERE IT WILL DO ME THE MOST GOOD, AND YOU THE MOST HARM..."
OKAY, I'VE GOT ONE ADVANTAGE HERE... THAT CYBORG CREEP STILL DOESN'T REALIZE HOW MY POWERS WORK, OR HE WOULDN'T HAVE LEFT ME ALONE WITH ALL THIS JUNK.
'COURSE, I'M NOT ALL THAT SURE HOW MY POWERS WORK, EITHER. IF I WASN'T SO WASTED, AND THESE BONDS WEREN'T SO $#%* COMPLICATED--
--I'LL BET I COULD'VE RIPPED THROUGH THIS STUFF LONG AGO. TOO BAD I CAN'T JUST WISH IT TO PIECES, LIKE SUPERGIRL DOES WITH HER PSYCHO-WHATSIS. SUPERGIRL...
..., I WISH YOU WERE HERE NOW. YOU WERE RIGHT... WE SHOULDA WORKED TOGETHER.
HUH?!
NOW WHY'D THEY GO AN' TURN THE FLOOR SHOW ON AGAIN?
HEY, IF YOU'RE GONNA RUB IT IN, LET'S AT LEAST HAVE SOME SOUND--!
...WE MUST PROCEED IMMEDIATELY WITH PLANS TO ERECT OUR SECOND ENGINE CITY IN METROPOLIS!
YES, OF COURSE.
METROPOLIS?! NO WAY!!
EVERYONE I KNOW IS IN METROPOLIS... REX... ROXIE...TANA... SUPERGIRL--! I'VE GOTTA GET OUT OF THIS PLACE! CAN'T LET ANYTHING STOP ME!
SUPERMAN...THE FIRST SUPERMAN... DIDN'T LET DOOMSDAY TRASH HIS TOWN... AND I WON'T LET THESE CREEPS RIP IT DOWN!
THAT CYBORG AND HIS ALIEN FLUNKY ARE GONNA BE SORRY THEY EVER DECIDED TO USE THIS LITTLE VIDEO TORTURE--

"--'CAUSE IT'LL BE A COLD DAY IN HELL BEFORE I GIVE UP NOW!"

ANTARCTICA.

HOW FARES THE MASTER?

NOT WELL. HIS PHYSICAL CONDITION HAS BEEN STABILIZED-- BUT HE HAS DRIFTED INTO DELIRIUM.

I... AM... SUPERMAN.

I... AM... THE LAST SON... OF KRYPTON.

THE NUTRIENT BATH IS A POOR SUBSTITUTE FOR THE REGENERA-TION MATRIX.

AS LONG AS THIS MENTAL CONFUSION CONTINUES, THERE IS DANGER THAT HIS MIND WILL DISCORPORATE.

I... AM SUPERMAN.

WHERE... WHERE IS THE POWER?

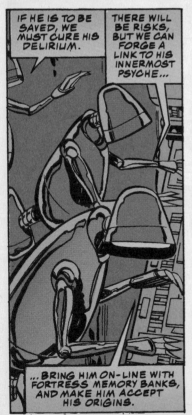

IF HE IS TO BE SAVED, WE MUST CURE HIS DELIRIUM.

THERE WILL BE RISKS, BUT WE CAN FORGE A LINK TO HIS INNERMOST PSYCHE...

...BRING HIM ON-LINE WITH FORTRESS MEMORY BANKS, AND MAKE HIM ACCEPT HIS ORIGINS.

Downloading...you were created 200,000 years ago on the planet, Krypton.

I... WAS...?

You began as an integrated analysis and weapons system. Your creator called you the ERADICATOR.

In time, you developed sentience...and came into the possession of Krypton's last living survivor, KAL-EL the SUPERMAN. But he resisted your efforts to preserve the Kryptonian way.

KAL-EL... RESISTED ME? BUT...

He sought to destroy you, but you became one with the power of Earth's sun, and were re-formed as a humanoid.

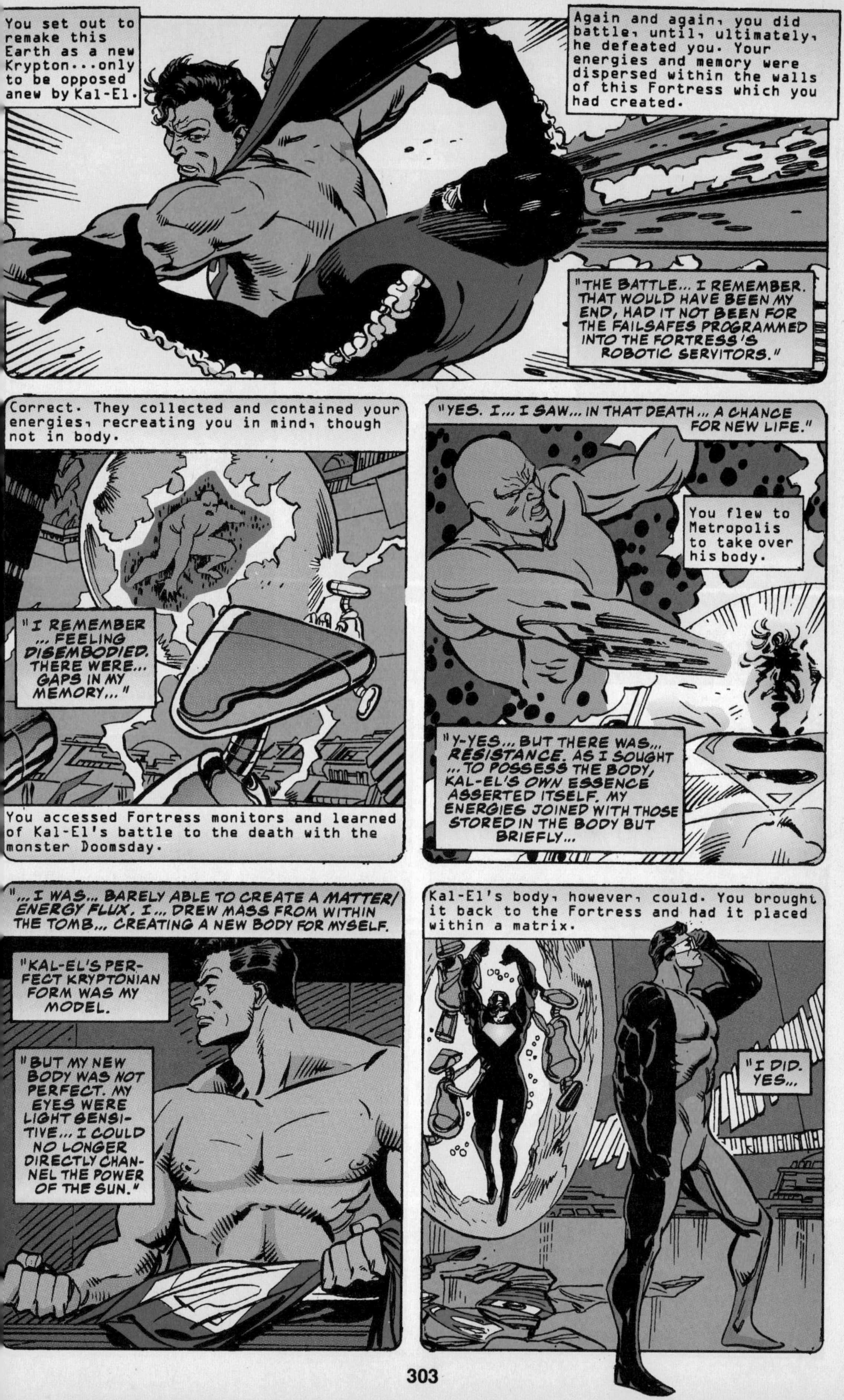
You set out to remake this Earth as a new Krypton...only to be opposed anew by Kal-El.
Again and again, you did battle, until, ultimately, he defeated you. Your energies and memory were dispersed within the walls of this Fortress which you had created.
"THE BATTLE... I REMEMBER. THAT WOULD HAVE BEEN MY END, HAD IT NOT BEEN FOR THE FAILSAFES PROGRAMMED INTO THE FORTRESS'S ROBOTIC SERVITORS."
Correct. They collected and contained your energies, recreating you in mind, though not in body.
"I REMEMBER ... FEELING DISEMBODIED. THERE WERE... GAPS IN MY MEMORY..."
You accessed Fortress monitors and learned of Kal-El's battle to the death with the monster Doomsday.
"YES. I... I SAW... IN THAT DEATH... A CHANCE FOR NEW LIFE."
You flew to Metropolis to take over his body.
"Y-YES... BUT THERE WAS... RESISTANCE. AS I SOUGHT ... TO POSSESS THE BODY, KAL-EL'S OWN ESSENCE ASSERTED ITSELF. MY ENERGIES JOINED WITH THOSE STORED IN THE BODY BUT BRIEFLY...
"... I WAS... BARELY ABLE TO CREATE A MATTER/ENERGY FLUX. I... DREW MASS FROM WITHIN THE TOMB... CREATING A NEW BODY FOR MYSELF.
"KAL-EL'S PERFECT KRYPTONIAN FORM WAS MY MODEL.
"BUT MY NEW BODY WAS NOT PERFECT. MY EYES WERE LIGHT SENSITIVE... I COULD NO LONGER DIRECTLY CHANNEL THE POWER OF THE SUN."
Kal-El's body, however, could. You brought it back to the Fortress and had it placed within a matrix.
"I DID. YES...

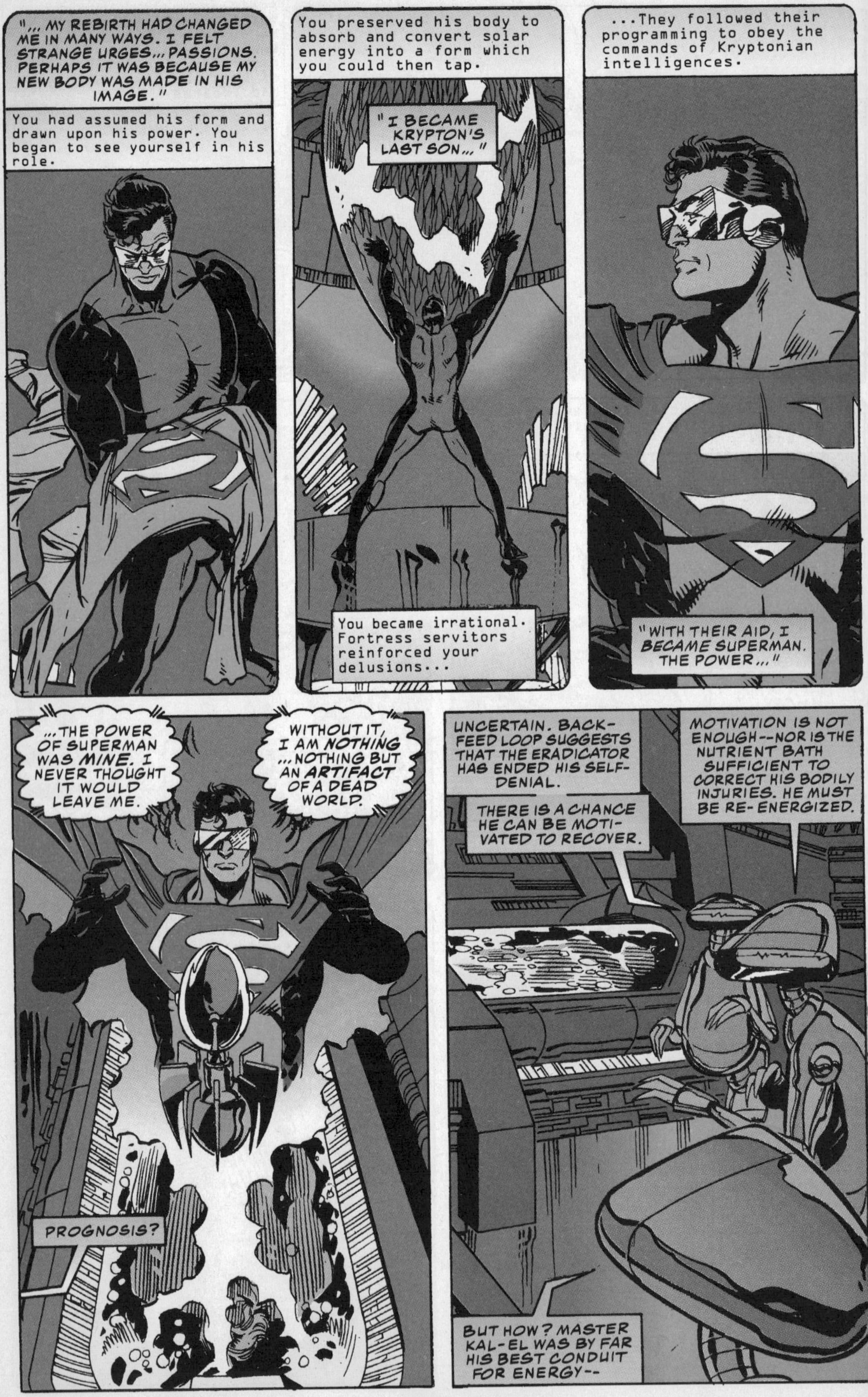
"... MY REBIRTH HAD CHANGED ME IN MANY WAYS. I FELT STRANGE URGES... PASSIONS. PERHAPS IT WAS BECAUSE MY NEW BODY WAS MADE IN HIS IMAGE."
You had assumed his form and drawn upon his power. You began to see yourself in his role.
You preserved his body to absorb and convert solar energy into a form which you could then tap.
"I BECAME KRYPTON'S LAST SON..."
You became irrational. Fortress servitors reinforced your delusions...
...They followed their programming to obey the commands of Kryptonian intelligences.
"WITH THEIR AID, I BECAME SUPERMAN. THE POWER..."
...THE POWER OF SUPERMAN WAS MINE. I NEVER THOUGHT IT WOULD LEAVE ME.
WITHOUT IT, I AM NOTHING ...NOTHING BUT AN ARTIFACT OF A DEAD WORLD.
PROGNOSIS?
UNCERTAIN. BACK-FEED LOOP SUGGESTS THAT THE ERADICATOR HAS ENDED HIS SELF-DENIAL.
THERE IS A CHANCE HE CAN BE MOTI-VATED TO RECOVER.
MOTIVATION IS NOT ENOUGH--NOR IS THE NUTRIENT BATH SUFFICIENT TO CORRECT HIS BODILY INJURIES. HE MUST BE RE-ENERGIZED.
BUT HOW? MASTER KAL-EL WAS BY FAR HIS BEST CONDUIT FOR ENERGY--

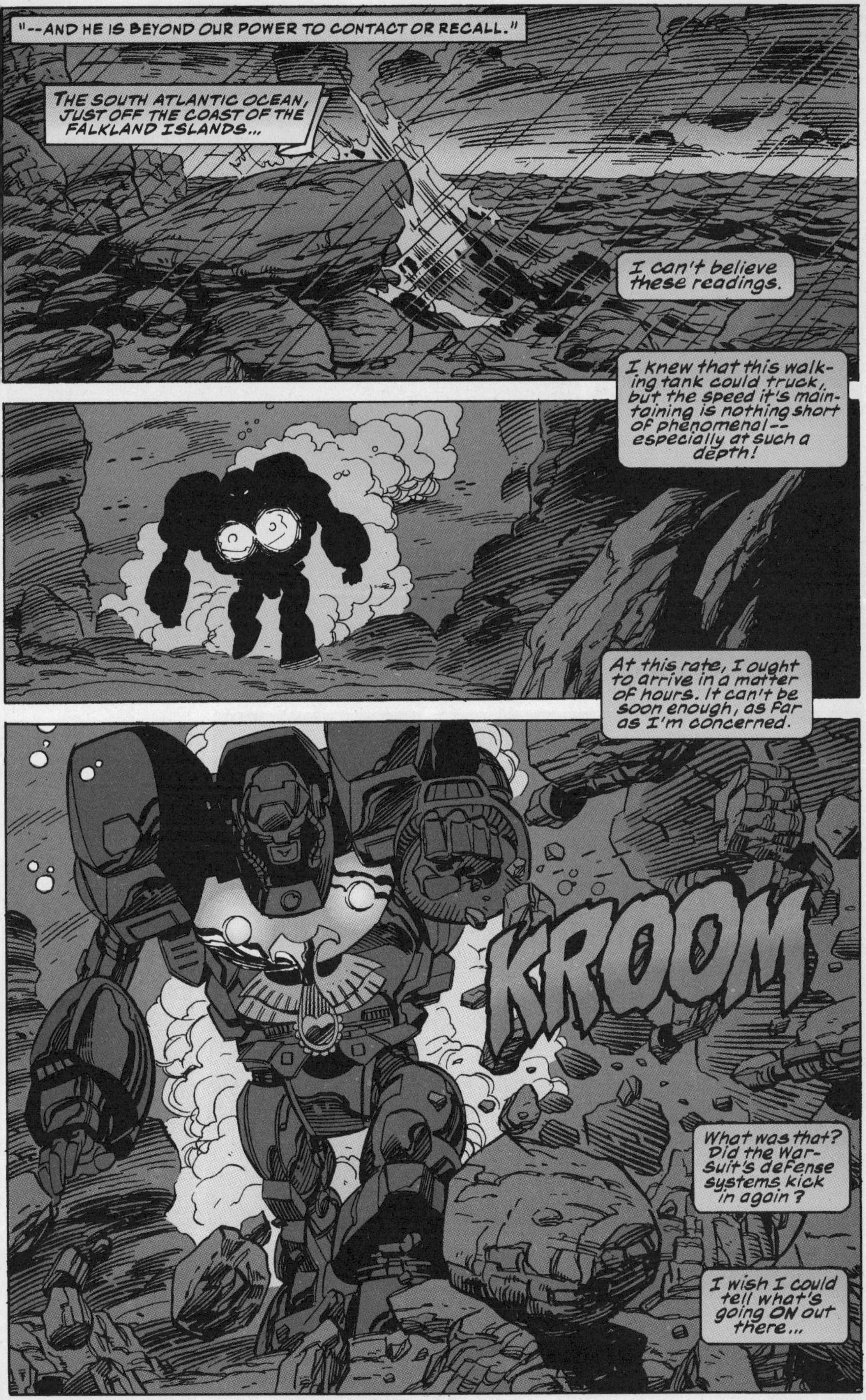
"--AND HE IS BEYOND OUR POWER TO CONTACT OR RECALL."
THE SOUTH ATLANTIC OCEAN, JUST OFF THE COAST OF THE FALKLAND ISLANDS...
I can't believe these readings.
I knew that this walking tank could truck, but the speed it's maintaining is nothing short of phenomenal-- especially at such a depth!
At this rate, I ought to arrive in a matter of hours. It can't be soon enough, as far as I'm concerned.
KROOM
What was that? Did the War-Suit's defense systems kick in again?
I wish I could tell what's going ON out there...

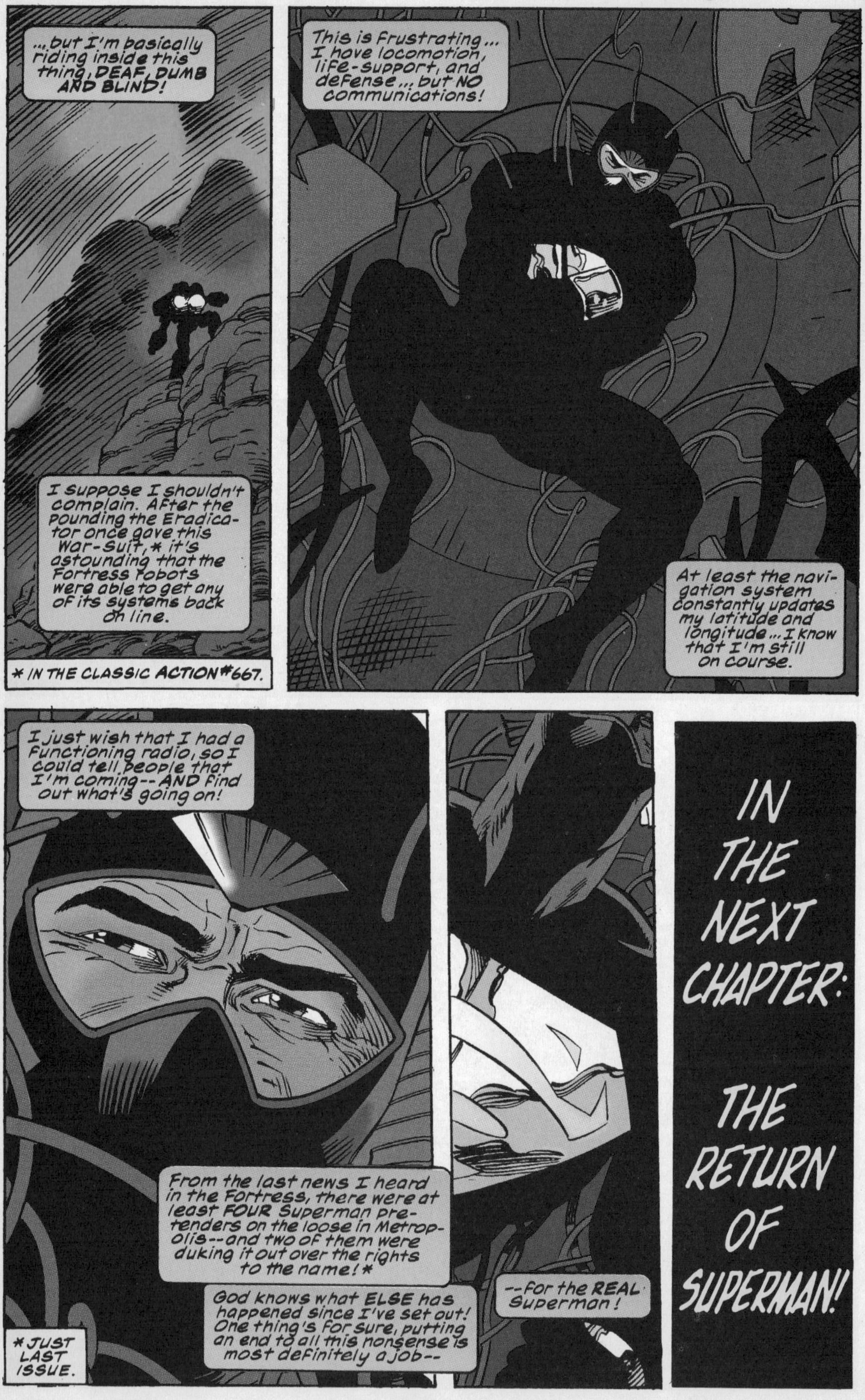
...but I'm basically riding inside this thing, DEAF, DUMB AND BLIND!
I suppose I shouldn't complain. After the pounding the Eradicator once gave this War-Suit,* it's astounding that the Fortress robots were able to get any of its systems back on line.
* IN THE CLASSIC ACTION #667.
This is frustrating... I have locomotion, life-support, and defense... but NO communications!
At least the navigation system constantly updates my latitude and longitude... I know that I'm still on course.
I just wish that I had a functioning radio, so I could tell people that I'm coming-- AND find out what's going on!
From the last news I heard in the Fortress, there were at least FOUR Superman pretenders on the loose in Metropolis--and two of them were duking it out over the rights to the name!*
God knows what ELSE has happened since I've set out! One thing's for sure, putting an end to all this nonsense is most definitely a job--
*JUST LAST ISSUE.
--for the REAL Superman!
IN THE NEXT CHAPTER: THE RETURN OF SUPERMAN!

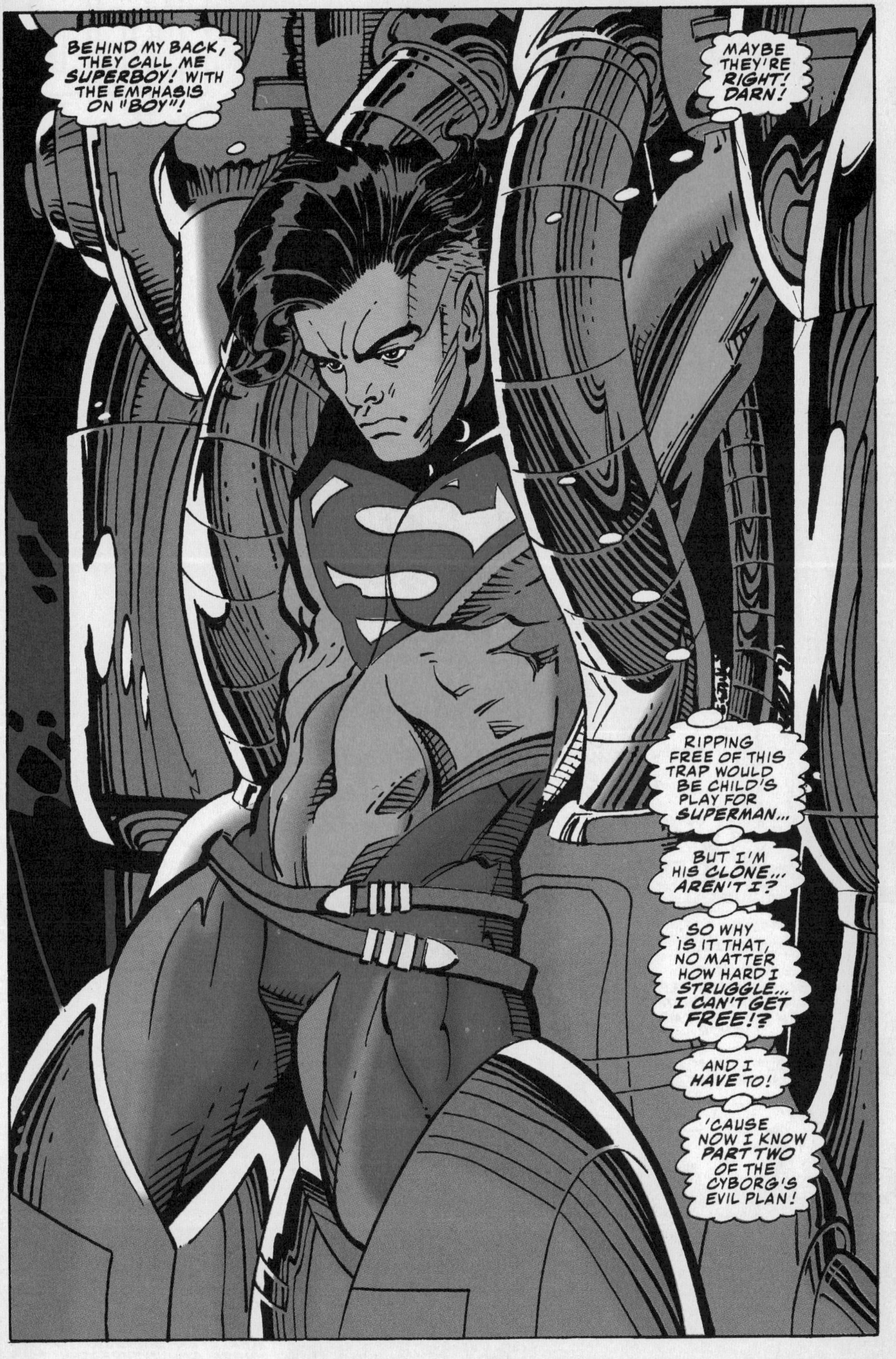
BEHIND MY BACK, THEY CALL ME SUPERBOY! WITH THE EMPHASIS ON "BOY"!
MAYBE THEY'RE RIGHT! DARN!
RIPPING FREE OF THIS TRAP WOULD BE CHILD'S PLAY FOR SUPERMAN...
BUT I'M HIS CLONE... AREN'T I?
SO WHY IS IT THAT, NO MATTER HOW HARD I STRUGGLE... I CAN'T GET FREE!?
AND I HAVE TO!
'CAUSE NOW I KNOW PART TWO OF THE CYBORG'S EVIL PLAN!

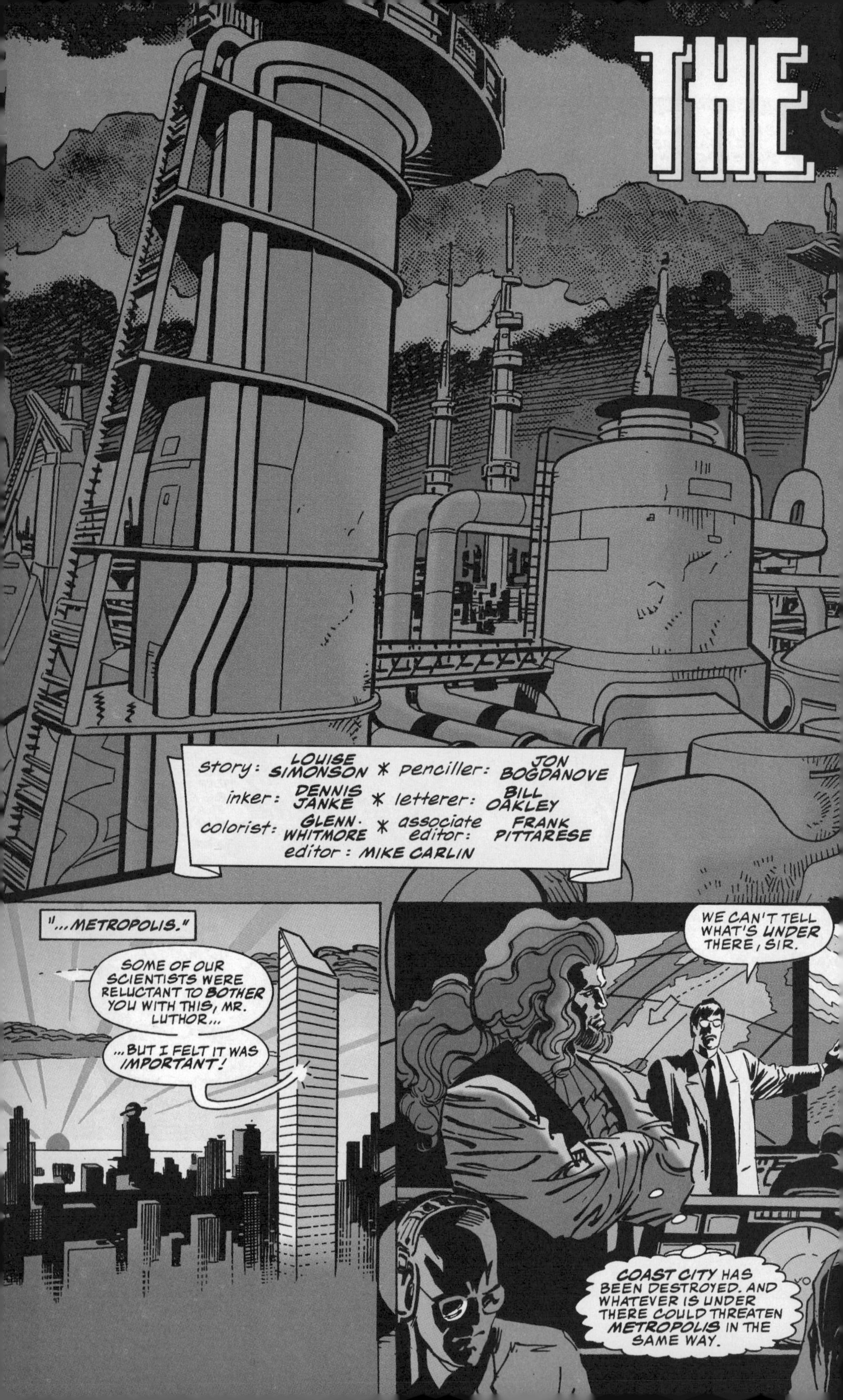
THE
story: LOUISE SIMONSON * penciller: JON BOGDANOVE
inker: DENNIS JANKE * letterer: BILL OAKLEY
colorist: GLENN WHITMORE * associate editor: FRANK PITTARESE
editor: MIKE CARLIN
"...METROPOLIS."
SOME OF OUR SCIENTISTS WERE RELUCTANT TO BOTHER YOU WITH THIS, MR. LUTHOR...
...BUT I FELT IT WAS IMPORTANT!
WE CAN'T TELL WHAT'S UNDER THERE, SIR.
COAST CITY HAS BEEN DESTROYED. AND WHATEVER IS UNDER THERE COULD THREATEN METROPOLIS IN THE SAME WAY.

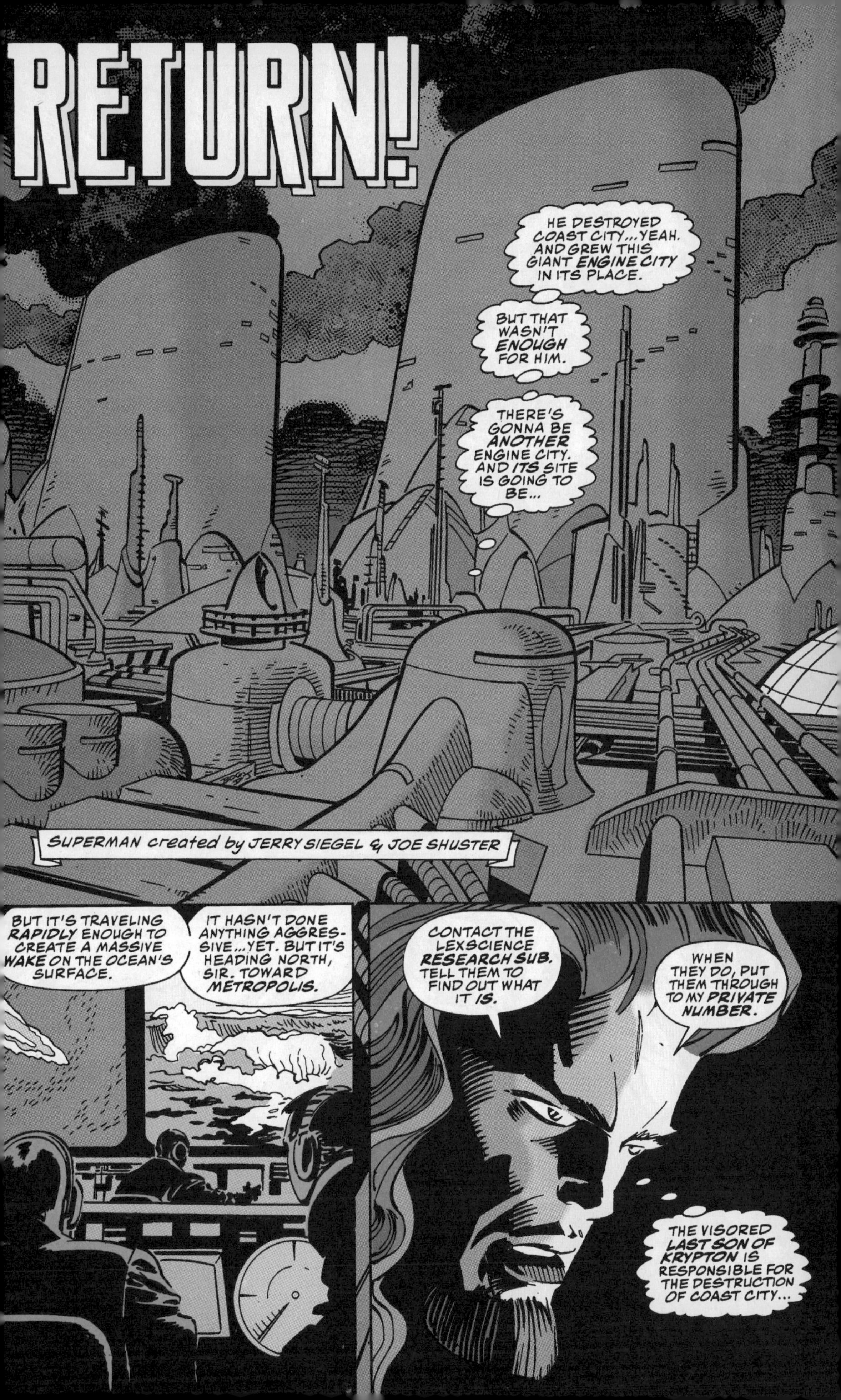
RETURN!
HE DESTROYED COAST CITY... YEAH. AND GREW THIS GIANT ENGINE CITY IN ITS PLACE.
BUT THAT WASN'T ENOUGH FOR HIM.
THERE'S GONNA BE ANOTHER ENGINE CITY. AND ITS SITE IS GOING TO BE...
SUPERMAN created by JERRY SIEGEL & JOE SHUSTER
BUT IT'S TRAVELING RAPIDLY ENOUGH TO CREATE A MASSIVE WAKE ON THE OCEAN'S SURFACE.
IT HASN'T DONE ANYTHING AGGRES-SIVE... YET. BUT IT'S HEADING NORTH, SIR. TOWARD METROPOLIS.
CONTACT THE LEXSCIENCE RESEARCH SUB. TELL THEM TO FIND OUT WHAT IT IS.
WHEN THEY DO, PUT THEM THROUGH TO MY PRIVATE NUMBER.
THE VISORED LAST SON OF KRYPTON IS RESPONSIBLE FOR THE DESTRUCTION OF COAST CITY...

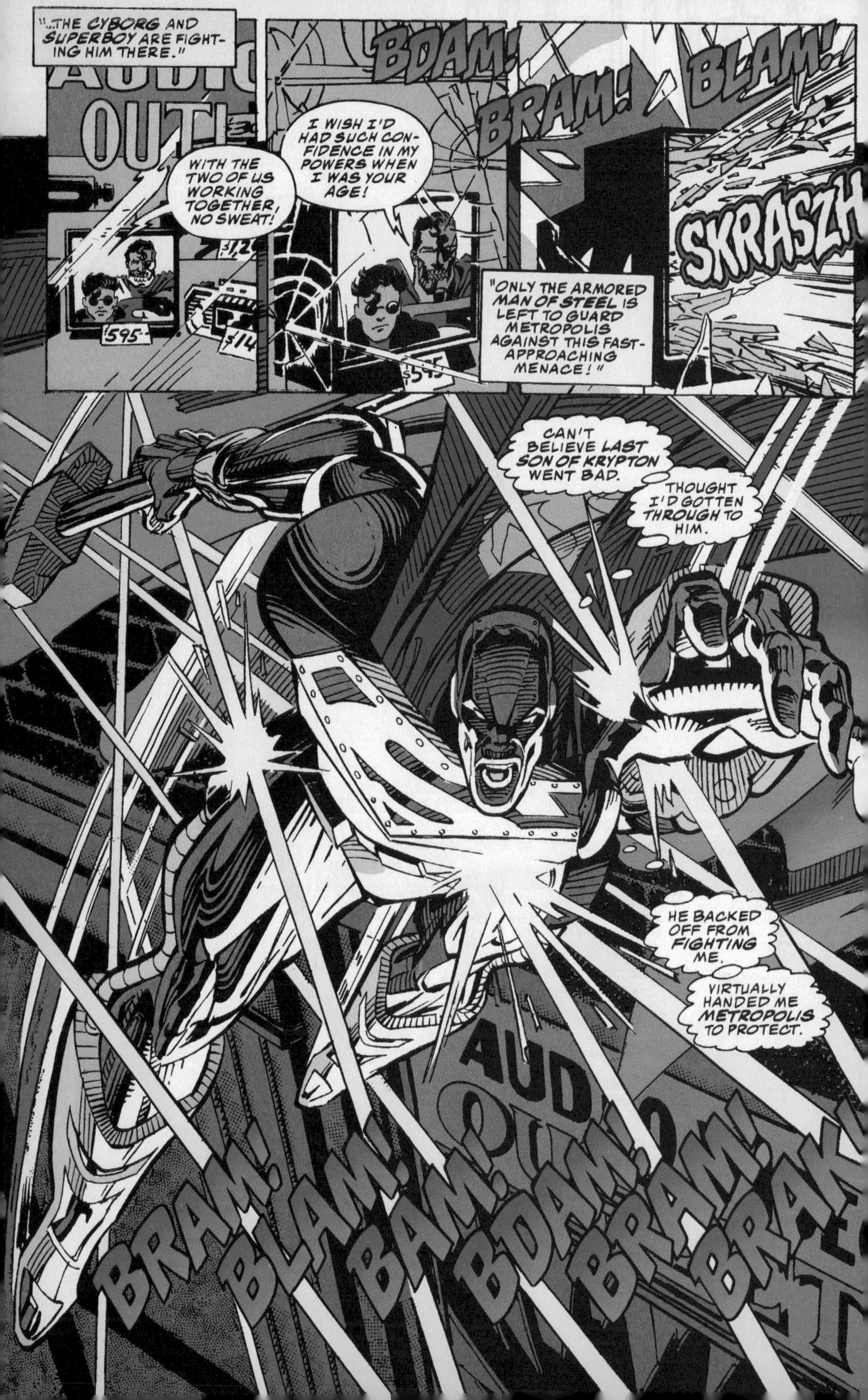

"...THE CYBORG AND SUPERBOY ARE FIGHTING HIM THERE."
WITH THE TWO OF US WORKING TOGETHER, NO SWEAT!
I WISH I'D HAD SUCH CONFIDENCE IN MY POWERS WHEN I WAS YOUR AGE!
BDAM! BRAM! BLAM!
SKRASZH
"ONLY THE ARMORED MAN OF STEEL IS LEFT TO GUARD METROPOLIS AGAINST THIS FAST-APPROACHING MENACE!"
CAN'T BELIEVE LAST SON OF KRYPTON WENT BAD.
THOUGHT I'D GOTTEN THROUGH TO HIM.
HE BACKED OFF FROM FIGHTING ME.
VIRTUALLY HANDED ME METROPOLIS TO PROTECT.
BRAM! BLAM! BAM! BDAM! BRAM! BRAK

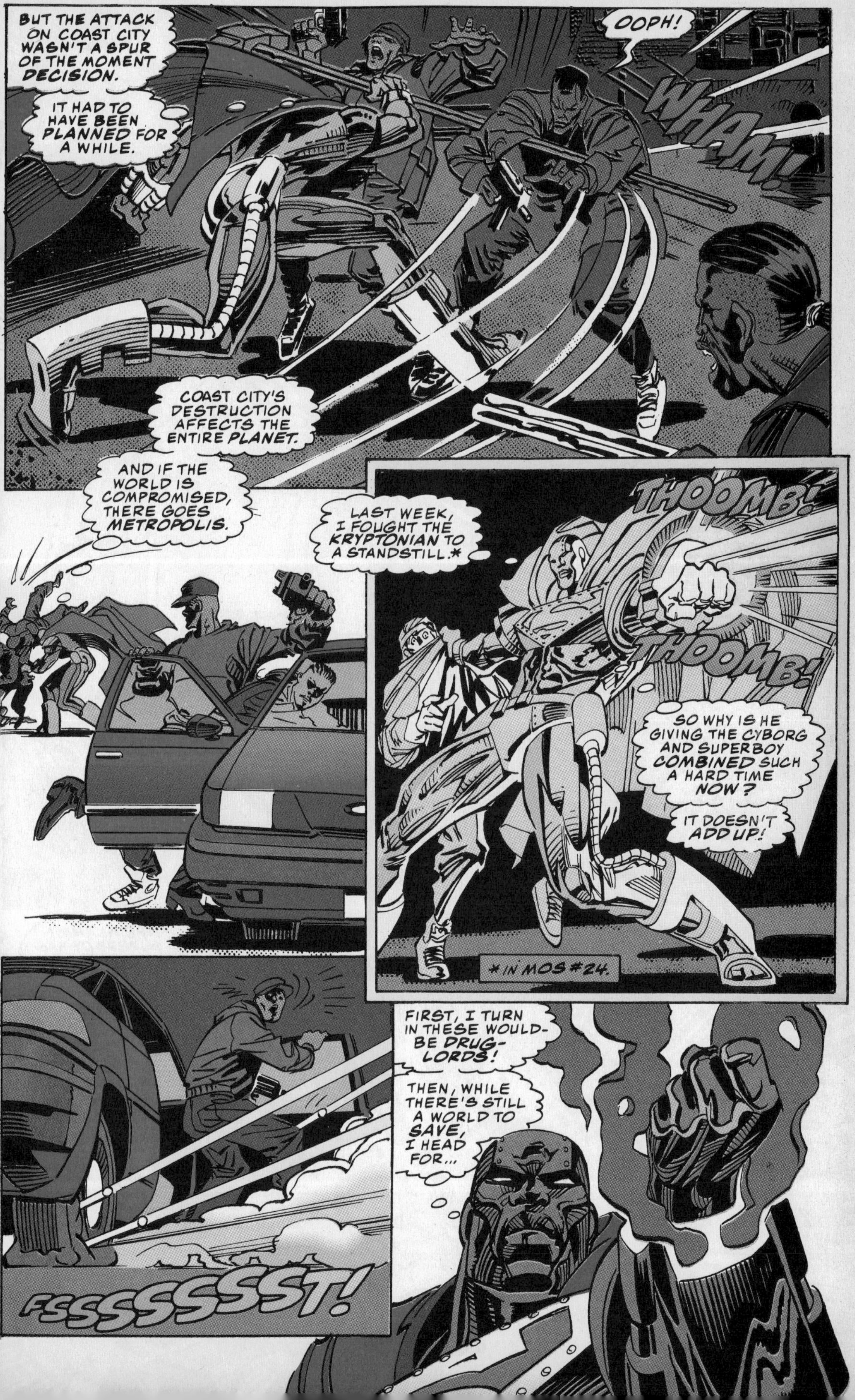
BUT THE ATTACK ON COAST CITY WASN'T A SPUR OF THE MOMENT DECISION.
IT HAD TO HAVE BEEN PLANNED FOR A WHILE.
OOPH!
WHAM!
COAST CITY'S DESTRUCTION AFFECTS THE ENTIRE PLANET.
AND IF THE WORLD IS COMPROMISED, THERE GOES METROPOLIS.
LAST WEEK, I FOUGHT THE KRYPTONIAN TO A STANDSTILL.*
THOOMB!
THOOMB!
SO WHY IS HE GIVING THE CYBORG AND SUPERBOY COMBINED SUCH A HARD TIME NOW?
IT DOESN'T ADD UP!
* IN MOS #24.
FIRST, I TURN IN THESE WOULD-BE DRUG-LORDS!
THEN, WHILE THERE'S STILL A WORLD TO SAVE, I HEAD FOR...
FSSSSSSSST!

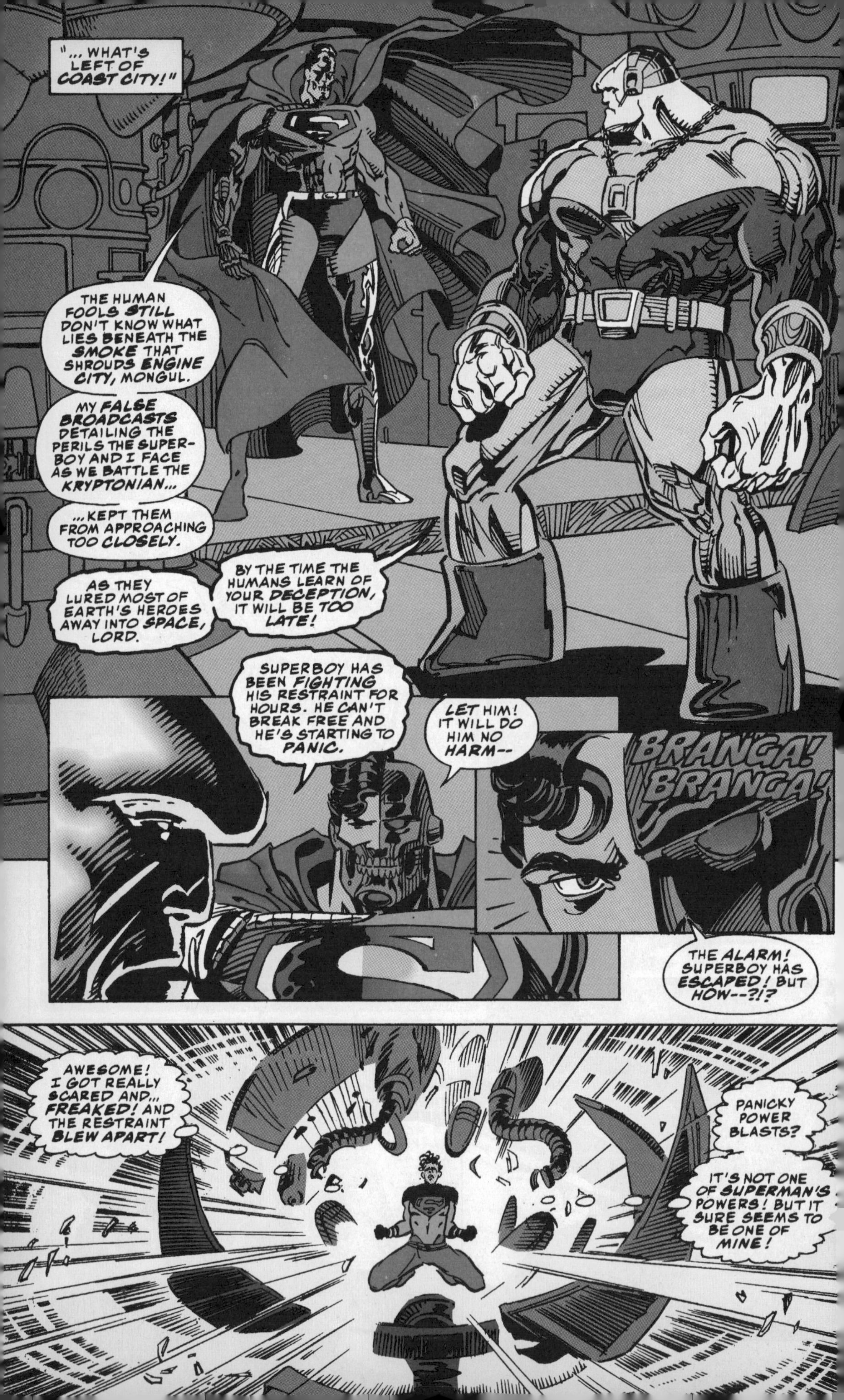
"...WHAT'S LEFT OF COAST CITY!"
THE HUMAN FOOLS STILL DON'T KNOW WHAT LIES BENEATH THE SMOKE THAT SHROUDS ENGINE CITY, MONGUL.
MY FALSE BROADCASTS DETAILING THE PERILS THE SUPERBOY AND I FACE AS WE BATTLE THE KRYPTONIAN...
...KEPT THEM FROM APPROACHING TOO CLOSELY.
AS THEY LURED MOST OF EARTH'S HEROES AWAY INTO SPACE, LORD.
BY THE TIME THE HUMANS LEARN OF YOUR DECEPTION, IT WILL BE TOO LATE!
SUPERBOY HAS BEEN FIGHTING HIS RESTRAINT FOR HOURS. HE CAN'T BREAK FREE AND HE'S STARTING TO PANIC.
LET HIM! IT WILL DO HIM NO HARM--
BRANGA! BRANGA!
THE ALARM! SUPERBOY HAS ESCAPED! BUT HOW--?!?
AWESOME! I GOT REALLY SCARED AND... FREAKED! AND THE RESTRAINT BLEW APART!
PANICKY POWER BLASTS?
IT'S NOT ONE OF SUPERMAN'S POWERS! BUT IT SURE SEEMS TO BE ONE OF MINE!

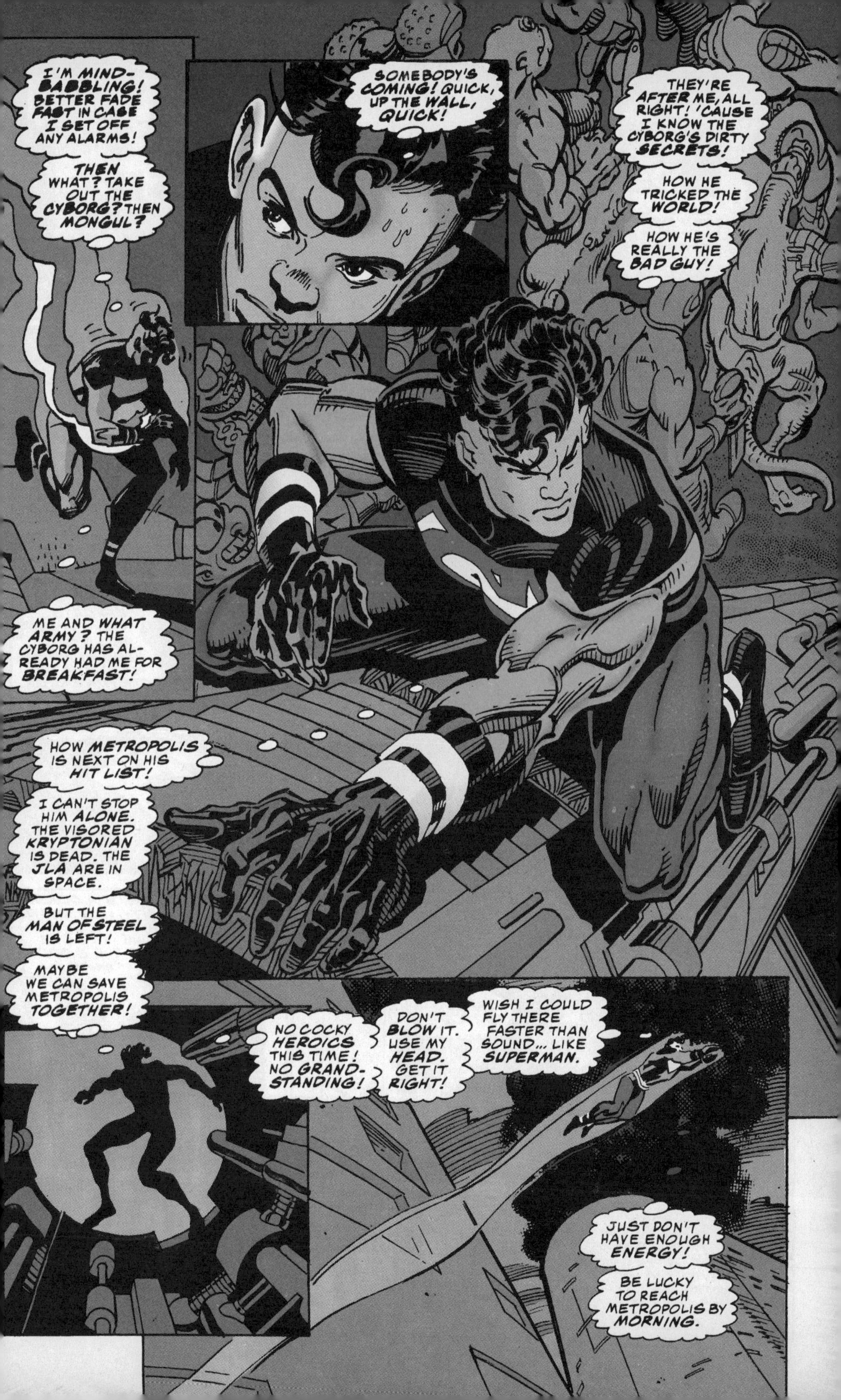
I'M MIND-BABBLING! BETTER FADE FAST IN CASE I SET OFF ANY ALARMS!
THEN WHAT? TAKE OUT THE CYBORG? THEN MONGUL?
SOMEBODY'S COMING! QUICK, UP THE WALL, QUICK!
THEY'RE AFTER ME, ALL RIGHT! 'CAUSE I KNOW THE CYBORG'S DIRTY SECRETS!
HOW HE TRICKED THE WORLD!
HOW HE'S REALLY THE BAD GUY!
ME AND WHAT ARMY? THE CYBORG HAS ALREADY HAD ME FOR BREAKFAST!
HOW METROPOLIS IS NEXT ON HIS HIT LIST!
I CAN'T STOP HIM ALONE. THE VISORED KRYPTONIAN IS DEAD. THE JLA ARE IN SPACE.
BUT THE MAN OF STEEL IS LEFT!
MAYBE WE CAN SAVE METROPOLIS TOGETHER!
NO COCKY HEROICS THIS TIME! NO GRAND-STANDING!
DON'T BLOW IT. USE MY HEAD. GET IT RIGHT!
WISH I COULD FLY THERE FASTER THAN SOUND... LIKE SUPERMAN.
JUST DON'T HAVE ENOUGH ENERGY!
BE LUCKY TO REACH METROPOLIS BY MORNING.

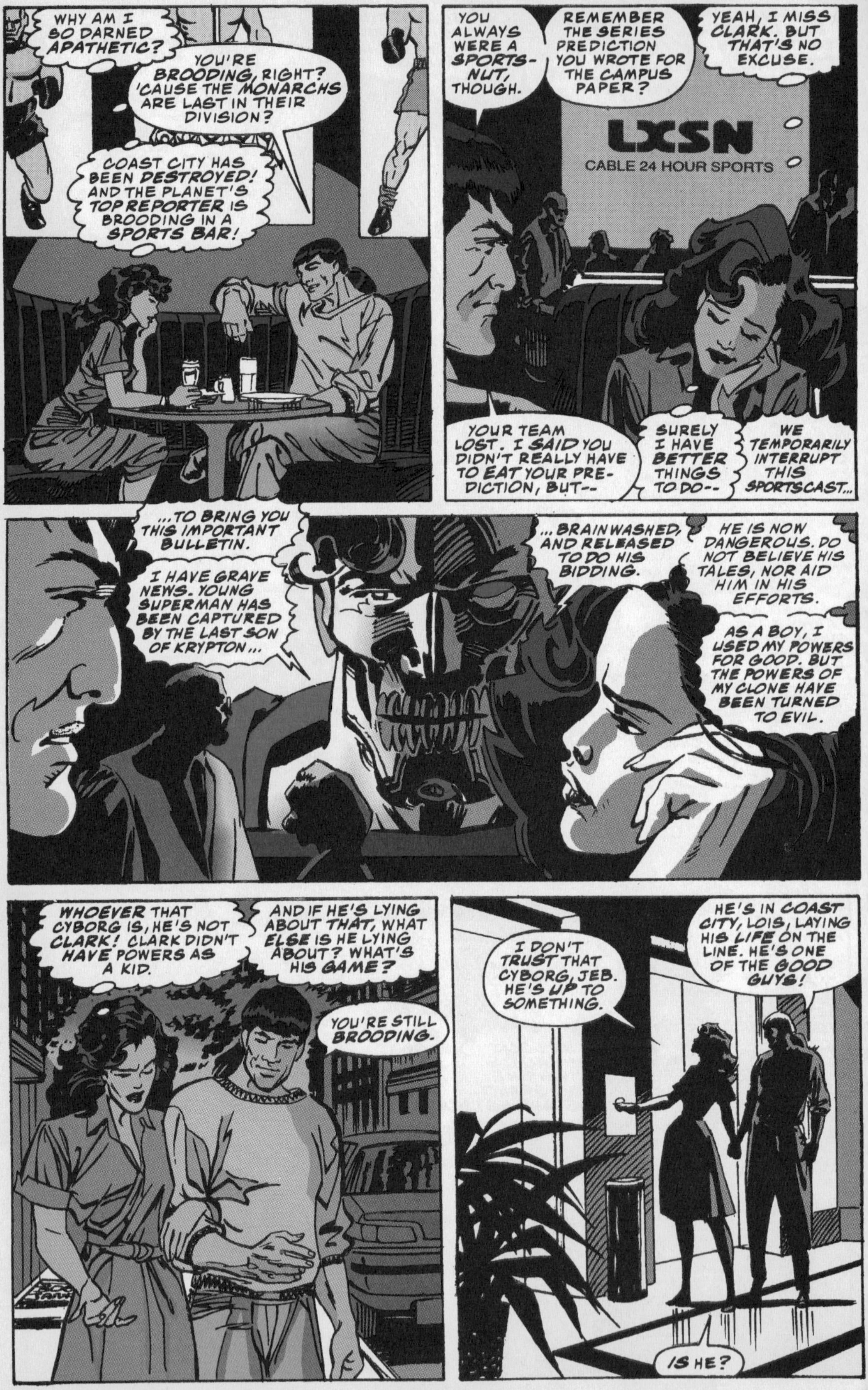

WHY AM I SO DARNED APATHETIC?
YOU'RE BROODING, RIGHT? 'CAUSE THE MONARCHS ARE LAST IN THEIR DIVISION?
COAST CITY HAS BEEN DESTROYED! AND THE PLANET'S TOP REPORTER IS BROODING IN A SPORTS BAR!
YOU ALWAYS WERE A SPORTS-NUT, THOUGH.
REMEMBER THE SERIES PREDICTION YOU WROTE FOR THE CAMPUS PAPER?
YEAH, I MISS CLARK. BUT THAT'S NO EXCUSE.
LXSN
CABLE 24 HOUR SPORTS
YOUR TEAM LOST. I SAID YOU DIDN'T REALLY HAVE TO EAT YOUR PRE-DICTION, BUT--
SURELY I HAVE BETTER THINGS TO DO--
WE TEMPORARILY INTERRUPT THIS SPORTSCAST...
...TO BRING YOU THIS IMPORTANT BULLETIN.
I HAVE GRAVE NEWS. YOUNG SUPERMAN HAS BEEN CAPTURED BY THE LAST SON OF KRYPTON...
...BRAINWASHED, AND RELEASED TO DO HIS BIDDING.
HE IS NOW DANGEROUS. DO NOT BELIEVE HIS TALES, NOR AID HIM IN HIS EFFORTS.
AS A BOY, I USED MY POWERS FOR GOOD. BUT THE POWERS OF MY CLONE HAVE BEEN TURNED TO EVIL.
WHOEVER THAT CYBORG IS, HE'S NOT CLARK! CLARK DIDN'T HAVE POWERS AS A KID.
AND IF HE'S LYING ABOUT THAT, WHAT ELSE IS HE LYING ABOUT? WHAT'S HIS GAME?
YOU'RE STILL BROODING.
I DON'T TRUST THAT CYBORG, JEB. HE'S UP TO SOMETHING.
HE'S IN COAST CITY, LOIS, LAYING HIS LIFE ON THE LINE. HE'S ONE OF THE GOOD GUYS!
IS HE?

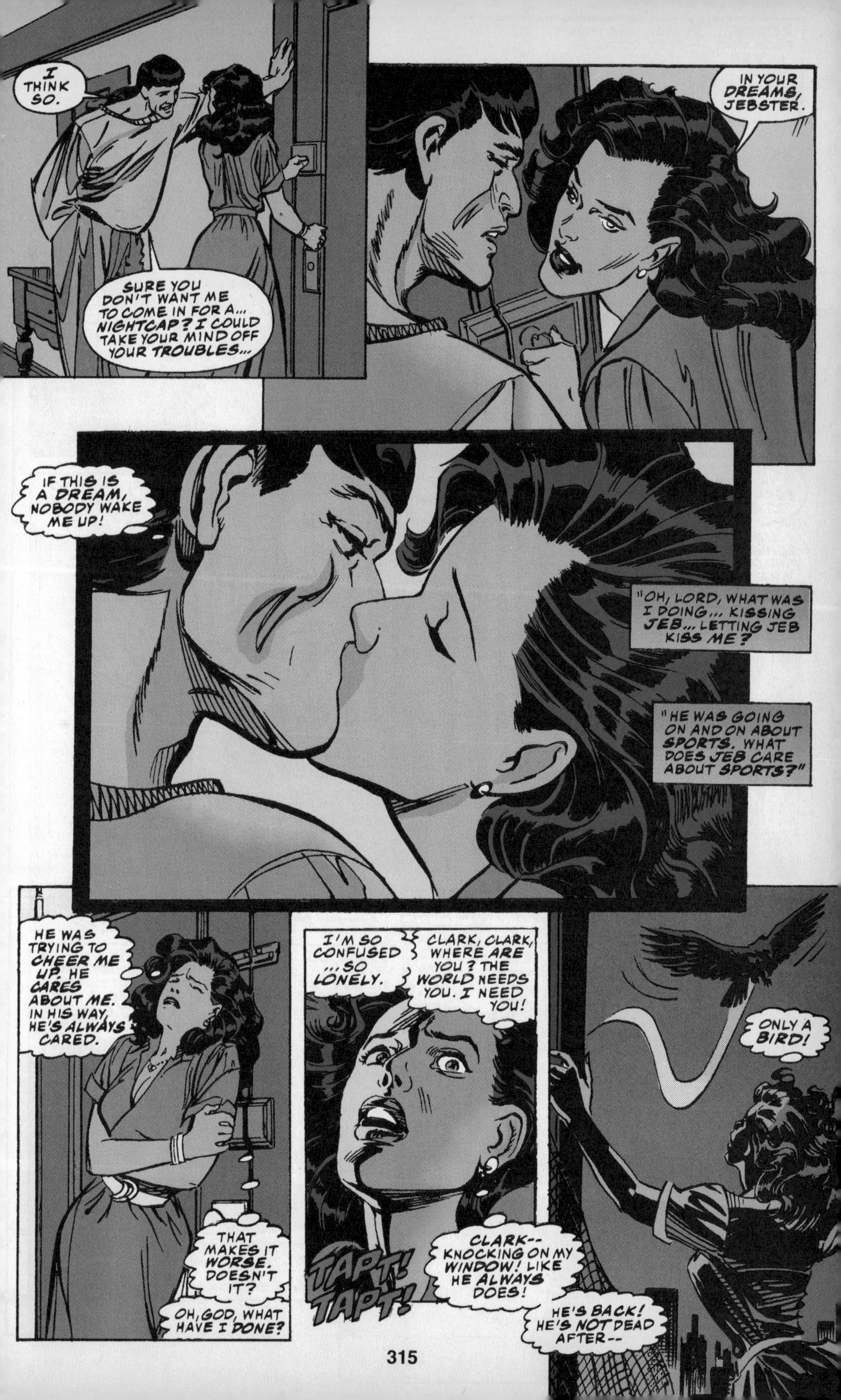
I THINK SO.
SURE YOU DON'T WANT ME TO COME IN FOR A... NIGHTCAP? I COULD TAKE YOUR MIND OFF YOUR TROUBLES...
IN YOUR DREAMS, JEBSTER.
IF THIS IS A DREAM, NOBODY WAKE ME UP!
"OH, LORD, WHAT WAS I DOING... KISSING JEB... LETTING JEB KISS ME?
"HE WAS GOING ON AND ON ABOUT SPORTS. WHAT DOES JEB CARE ABOUT SPORTS?"
HE WAS TRYING TO CHEER ME UP. HE CARES ABOUT ME. IN HIS WAY, HE'S ALWAYS CARED.
THAT MAKES IT WORSE. DOESN'T IT?
OH, GOD, WHAT HAVE I DONE?
I'M SO CONFUSED ...SO LONELY.
CLARK, CLARK, WHERE ARE YOU? THE WORLD NEEDS YOU. I NEED YOU!
TAPT! TAPT!
CLARK-- KNOCKING ON MY WINDOW! LIKE HE ALWAYS DOES!
HE'S BACK! HE'S NOT DEAD AFTER--
ONLY A BIRD!

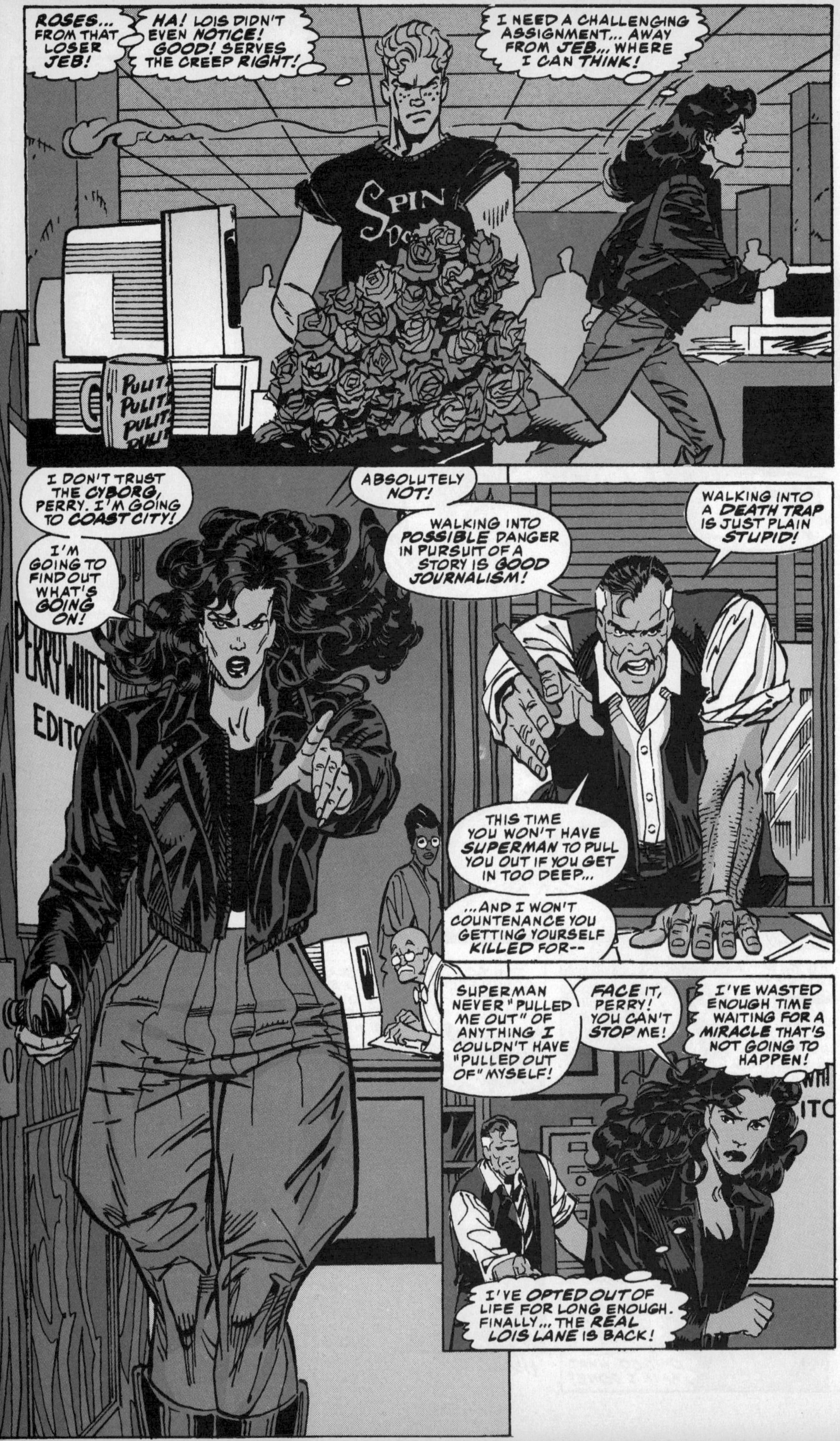

ROSES... FROM THAT LOSER JEB!
HA! LOIS DIDN'T EVEN NOTICE! GOOD! SERVES THE CREEP RIGHT!
I NEED A CHALLENGING ASSIGNMENT... AWAY FROM JEB... WHERE I CAN THINK!
SPIN
PULITZ PULITZ PULITZ PULITZ
I DON'T TRUST THE CYBORG, PERRY. I'M GOING TO COAST CITY!
I'M GOING TO FIND OUT WHAT'S GOING ON!
ABSOLUTELY NOT!
WALKING INTO POSSIBLE DANGER IN PURSUIT OF A STORY IS GOOD JOURNALISM!
WALKING INTO A DEATH TRAP IS JUST PLAIN STUPID!
PERRY WHITE EDITO
THIS TIME YOU WON'T HAVE SUPERMAN TO PULL YOU OUT IF YOU GET IN TOO DEEP...
...AND I WON'T COUNTENANCE YOU GETTING YOURSELF KILLED FOR--
SUPERMAN NEVER "PULLED ME OUT" OF ANYTHING I COULDN'T HAVE "PULLED OUT OF" MYSELF!
FACE IT, PERRY! YOU CAN'T STOP ME!
I'VE WASTED ENOUGH TIME WAITING FOR A MIRACLE THAT'S NOT GOING TO HAPPEN!
I'VE OPTED OUT OF LIFE FOR LONG ENOUGH. FINALLY... THE REAL LOIS LANE IS BACK!

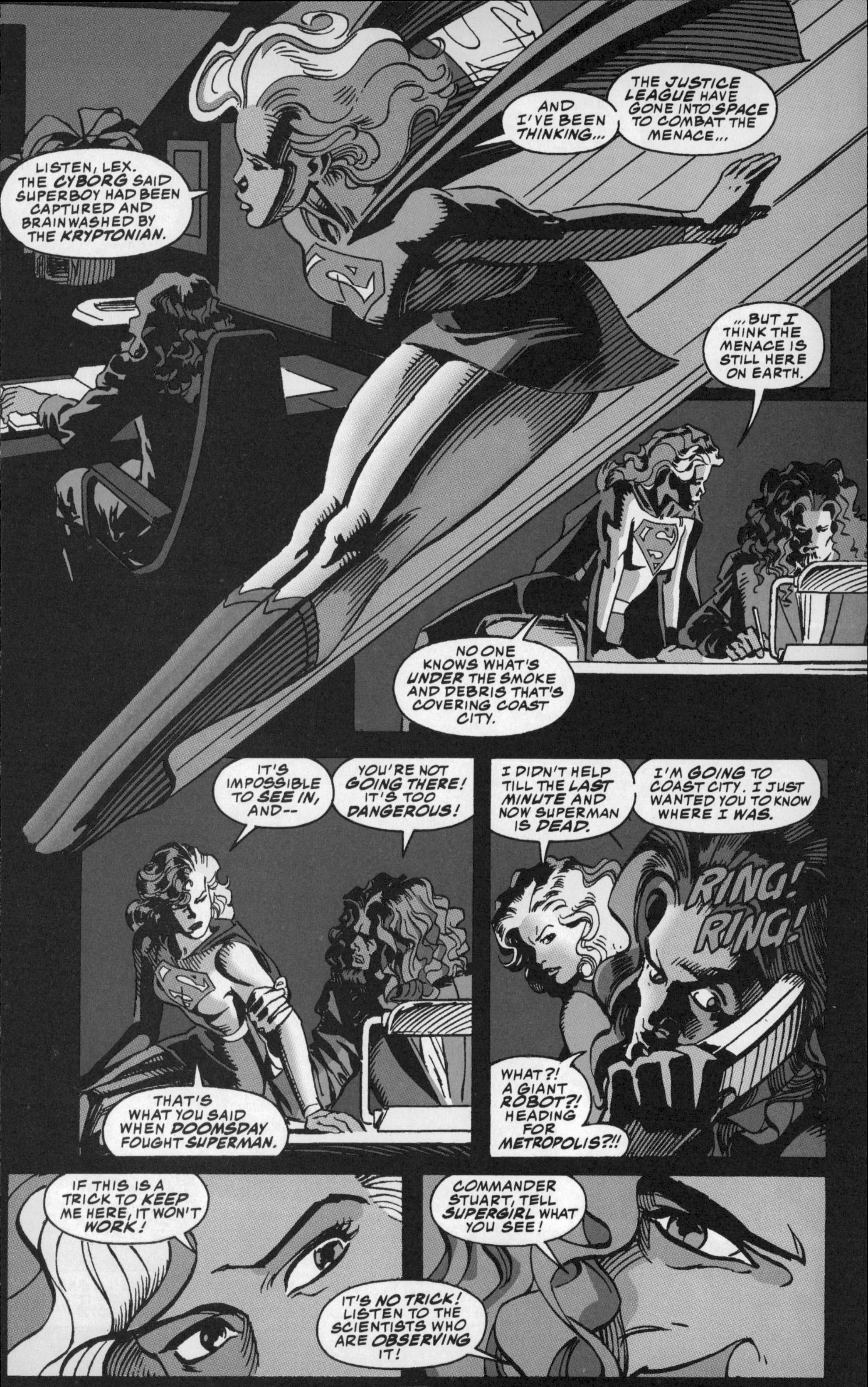

LISTEN, LEX. THE CYBORG SAID SUPERBOY HAD BEEN CAPTURED AND BRAINWASHED BY THE KRYPTONIAN.
AND I'VE BEEN THINKING...
THE JUSTICE LEAGUE HAVE GONE INTO SPACE TO COMBAT THE MENACE...
...BUT I THINK THE MENACE IS STILL HERE ON EARTH.
NO ONE KNOWS WHAT'S UNDER THE SMOKE AND DEBRIS THAT'S COVERING COAST CITY.
IT'S IMPOSSIBLE TO SEE IN, AND--
YOU'RE NOT GOING THERE! IT'S TOO DANGEROUS!
THAT'S WHAT YOU SAID WHEN DOOMSDAY FOUGHT SUPERMAN.
I DIDN'T HELP TILL THE LAST MINUTE AND NOW SUPERMAN IS DEAD.
I'M GOING TO COAST CITY. I JUST WANTED YOU TO KNOW WHERE I WAS.
RING! RING!
WHAT?! A GIANT ROBOT?! HEADING FOR METROPOLIS?!!
IF THIS IS A TRICK TO KEEP ME HERE, IT WON'T WORK!
COMMANDER STUART, TELL SUPERGIRL WHAT YOU SEE!
IT'S NO TRICK! LISTEN TO THE SCIENTISTS WHO ARE OBSERVING IT!

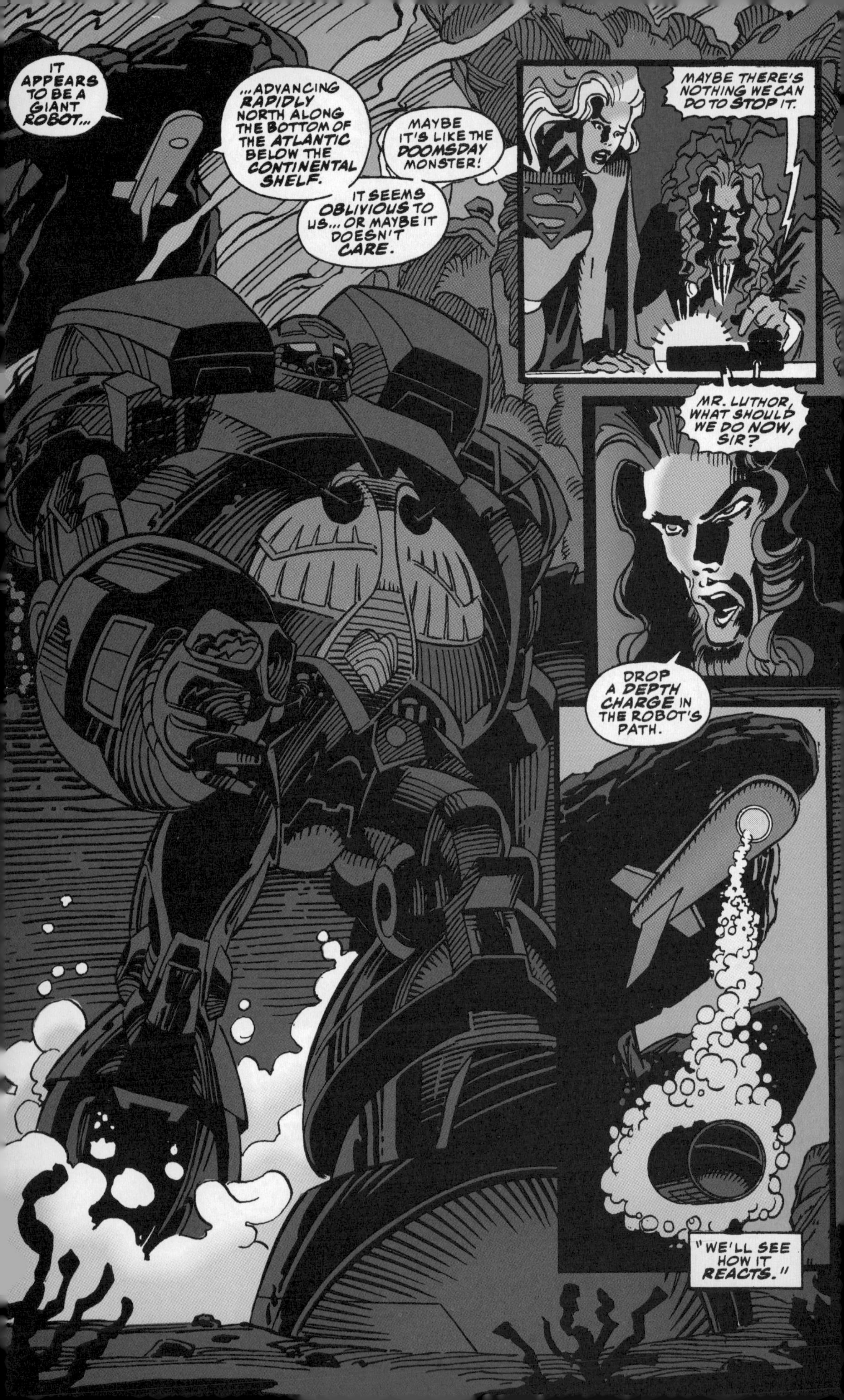
IT APPEARS TO BE A GIANT ROBOT...
...ADVANCING RAPIDLY NORTH ALONG THE BOTTOM OF THE ATLANTIC BELOW THE CONTINENTAL SHELF.
MAYBE IT'S LIKE THE DOOMSDAY MONSTER!
IT SEEMS OBLIVIOUS TO US... OR MAYBE IT DOESN'T CARE.
MAYBE THERE'S NOTHING WE CAN DO TO STOP IT.
MR. LUTHOR, WHAT SHOULD WE DO NOW, SIR?
DROP A DEPTH CHARGE IN THE ROBOT'S PATH.
"WE'LL SEE HOW IT REACTS."

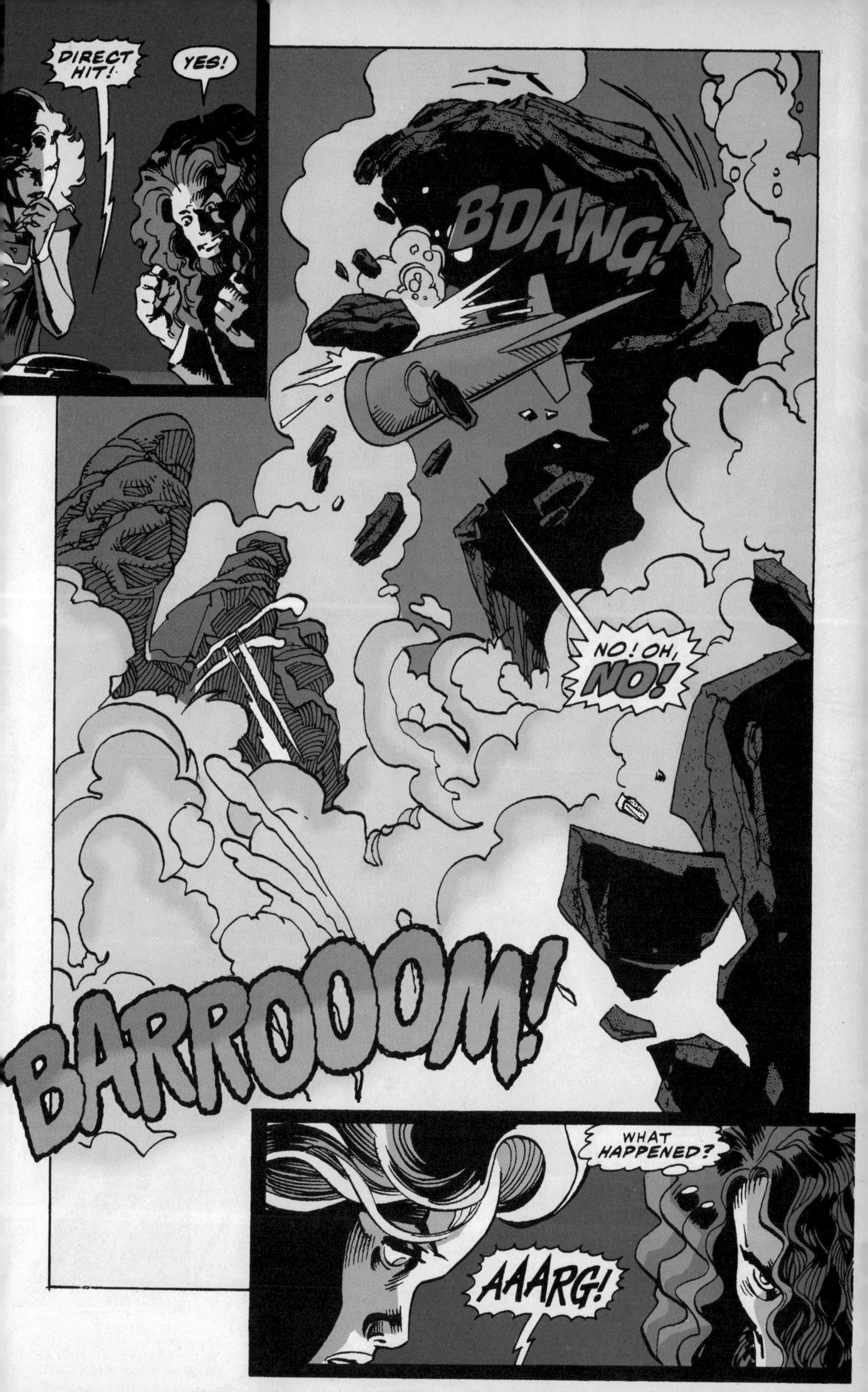
DIRECT HIT!
YES!
BDANG!
NO! OH, NO!
BARROOOM!
WHAT HAPPENED?
AAARG!

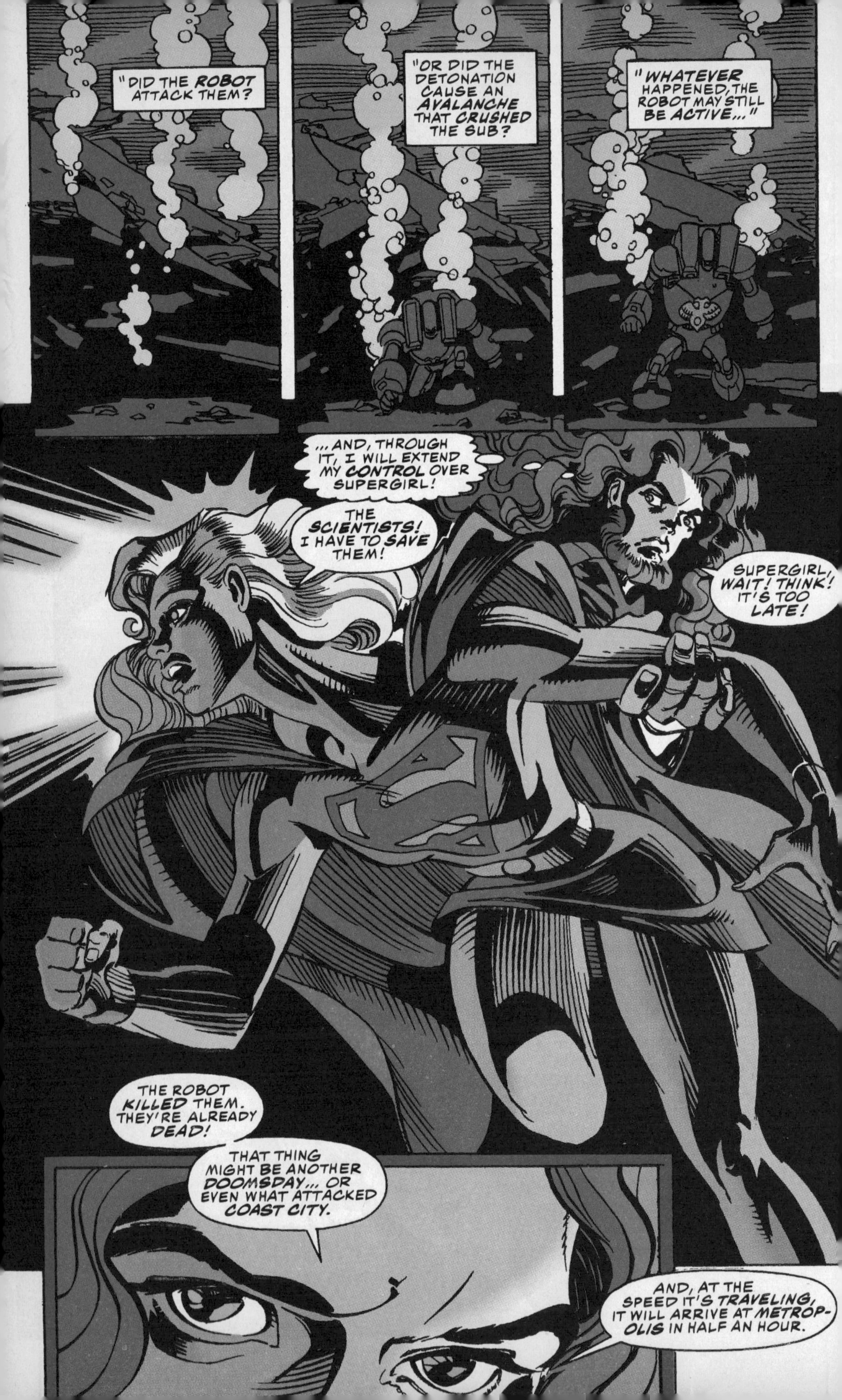
"DID THE ROBOT ATTACK THEM?
"OR DID THE DETONATION CAUSE AN AVALANCHE THAT CRUSHED THE SUB?
"WHATEVER HAPPENED, THE ROBOT MAY STILL BE ACTIVE..."
...AND, THROUGH IT, I WILL EXTEND MY CONTROL OVER SUPERGIRL!
THE SCIENTISTS! I HAVE TO SAVE THEM!
SUPERGIRL, WAIT! THINK! IT'S TOO LATE!
THE ROBOT KILLED THEM. THEY'RE ALREADY DEAD!
THAT THING MIGHT BE ANOTHER DOOMSDAY... OR EVEN WHAT ATTACKED COAST CITY.
AND, AT THE SPEED IT'S TRAVELING, IT WILL ARRIVE AT METROPOLIS IN HALF AN HOUR.

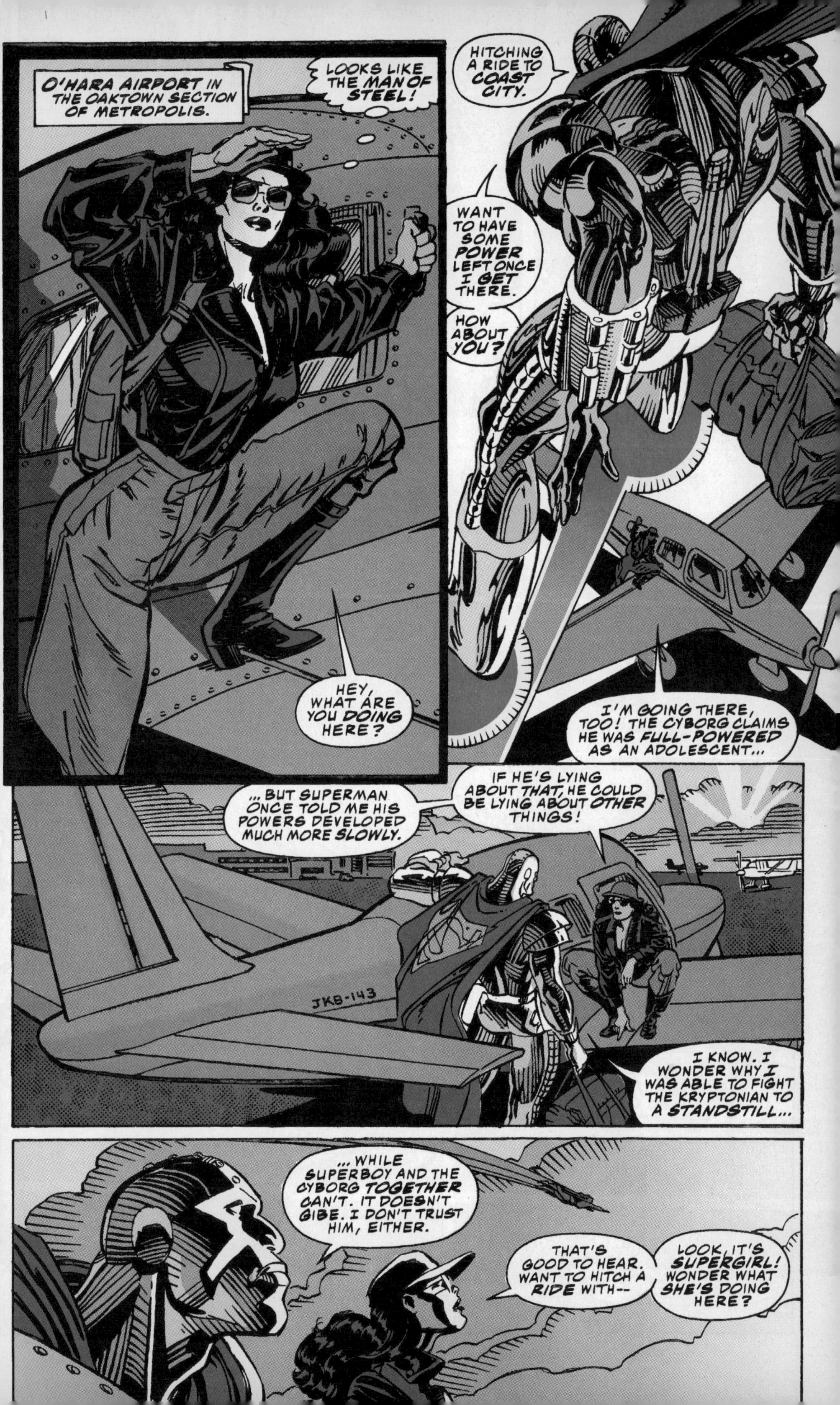
O'HARA AIRPORT IN THE OAKTOWN SECTION OF METROPOLIS.
LOOKS LIKE THE MAN OF STEEL!
HITCHING A RIDE TO COAST CITY.
WANT TO HAVE SOME POWER LEFT ONCE I GET THERE.
HOW ABOUT YOU?
HEY, WHAT ARE YOU DOING HERE?
I'M GOING THERE, TOO! THE CYBORG CLAIMS HE WAS FULL-POWERED AS AN ADOLESCENT...
...BUT SUPERMAN ONCE TOLD ME HIS POWERS DEVELOPED MUCH MORE SLOWLY.
IF HE'S LYING ABOUT THAT, HE COULD BE LYING ABOUT OTHER THINGS!
JKB-143
I KNOW. I WONDER WHY I WAS ABLE TO FIGHT THE KRYPTONIAN TO A STANDSTILL...
...WHILE SUPERBOY AND THE CYBORG TOGETHER CAN'T. IT DOESN'T GIBE. I DON'T TRUST HIM, EITHER.
THAT'S GOOD TO HEAR. WANT TO HITCH A RIDE WITH--
LOOK, IT'S SUPERGIRL! WONDER WHAT SHE'S DOING HERE?

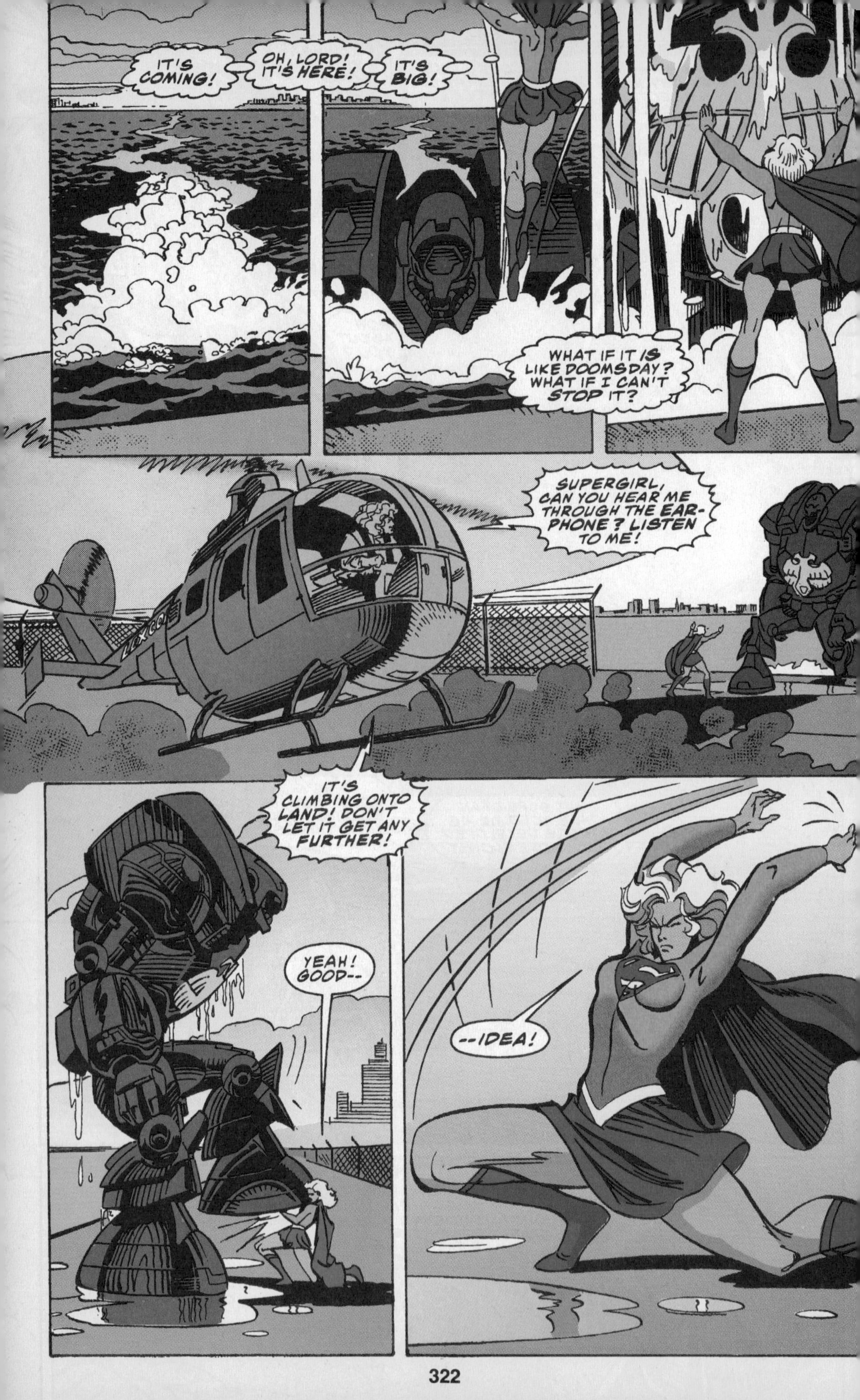
IT'S COMING!
OH, LORD! IT'S HERE!
IT'S BIG!
WHAT IF IT IS LIKE DOOMSDAY? WHAT IF I CAN'T STOP IT?
SUPERGIRL, CAN YOU HEAR ME THROUGH THE EARPHONE? LISTEN TO ME!
LEXCO
IT'S CLIMBING ONTO LAND! DON'T LET IT GET ANY FURTHER!
YEAH! GOOD--
--IDEA!

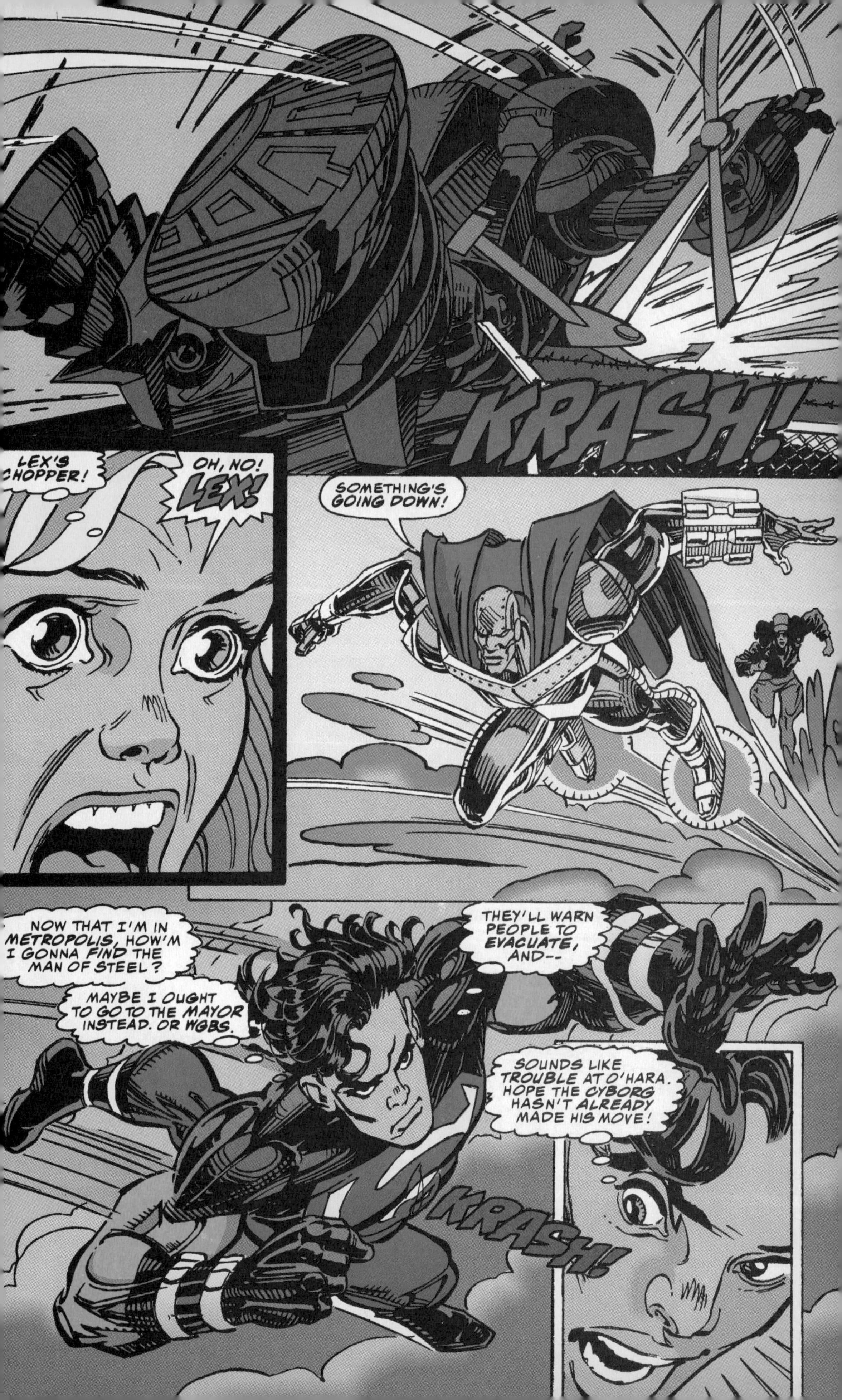
KRASH!
LEX'S CHOPPER!
OH, NO! LEX!
SOMETHING'S GOING DOWN!
NOW THAT I'M IN METROPOLIS, HOW'M I GONNA FIND THE MAN OF STEEL?
MAYBE I OUGHT TO GO TO THE MAYOR INSTEAD. OR WGBS.
THEY'LL WARN PEOPLE TO EVACUATE, AND--
SOUNDS LIKE TROUBLE AT O'HARA. HOPE THE CYBORG HASN'T ALREADY MADE HIS MOVE!
KRASH!

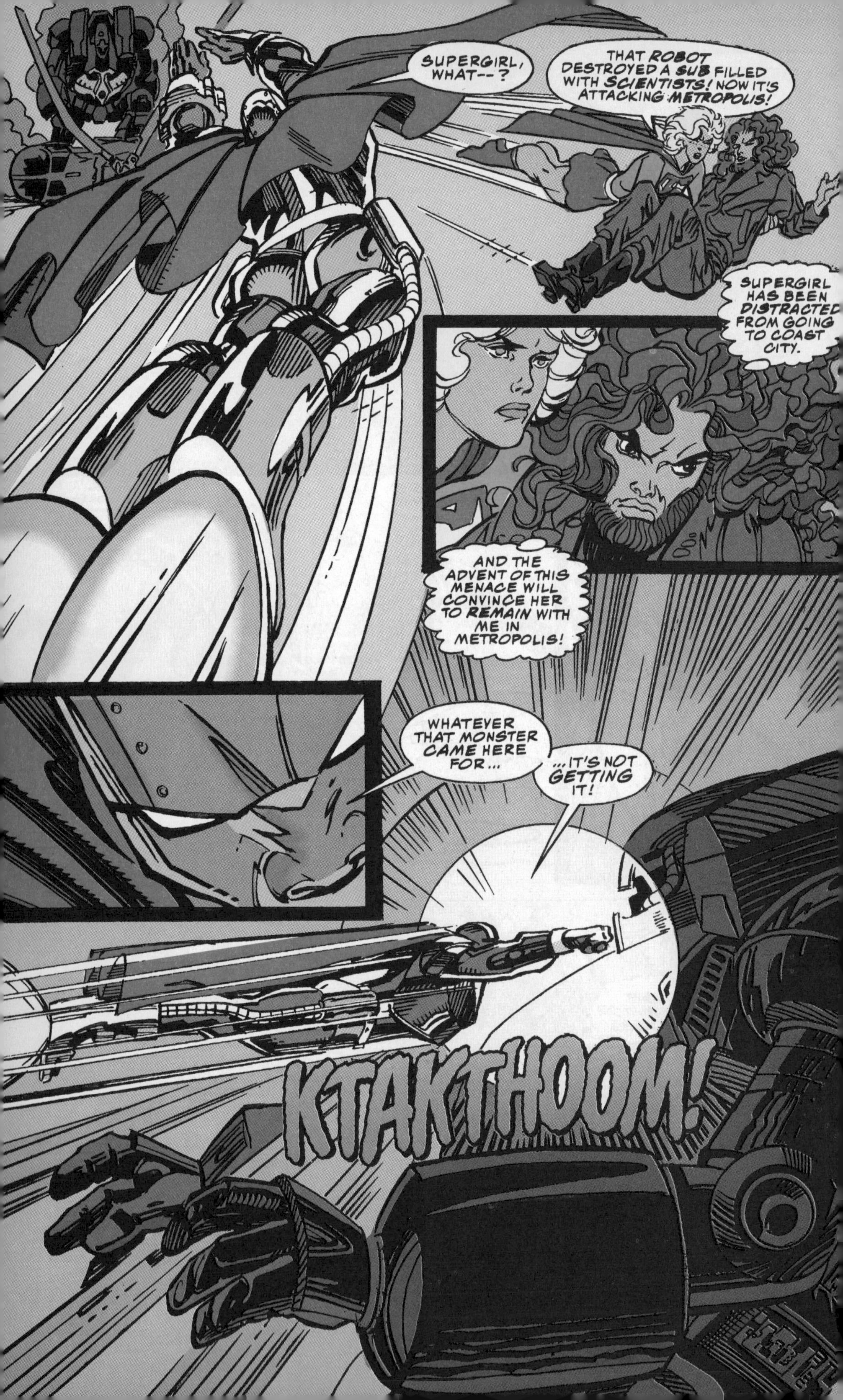

SUPERGIRL, WHAT--?
THAT ROBOT DESTROYED A SUB FILLED WITH SCIENTISTS! NOW IT'S ATTACKING METROPOLIS!
SUPERGIRL HAS BEEN DISTRACTED FROM GOING TO COAST CITY.
AND THE ADVENT OF THIS MENACE WILL CONVINCE HER TO REMAIN WITH ME IN METROPOLIS!
WHATEVER THAT MONSTER CAME HERE FOR...
...IT'S NOT GETTING IT!
KTAKTHOOM!

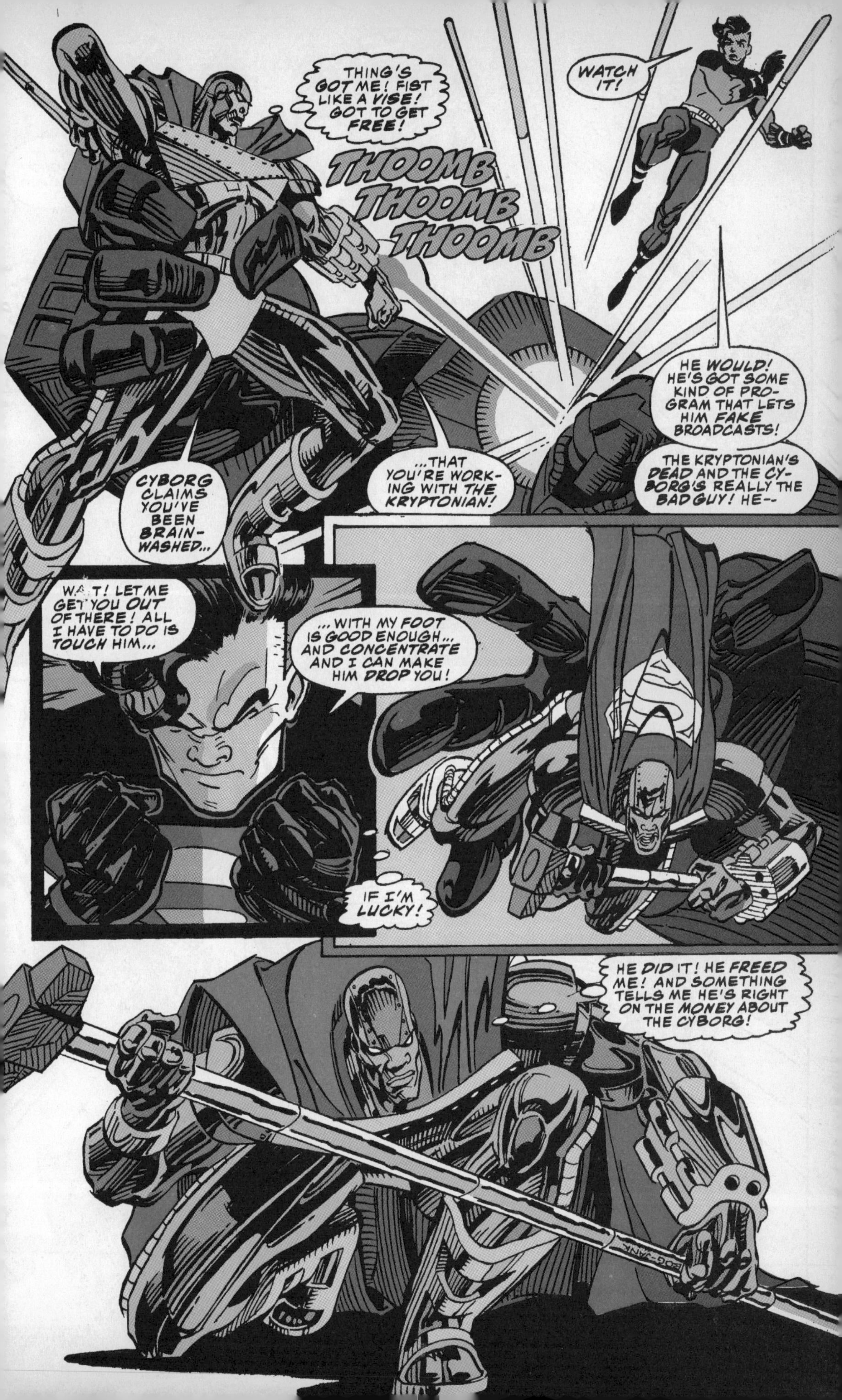

THING'S GOT ME! FIST LIKE A VISE! GOT TO GET FREE!
WATCH IT!
THOOMB THOOMB THOOMB
HE WOULD! HE'S GOT SOME KIND OF PRO-GRAM THAT LETS HIM FAKE BROADCASTS!
THE KRYPTONIAN'S DEAD AND THE CY-BORG'S REALLY THE BAD GUY! HE--
CYBORG CLAIMS YOU'VE BEEN BRAIN-WASHED...
...THAT YOU'RE WORK-ING WITH THE KRYPTONIAN!
WAIT! LET ME GET YOU OUT OF THERE! ALL I HAVE TO DO IS TOUCH HIM...
...WITH MY FOOT IS GOOD ENOUGH... AND CONCENTRATE AND I CAN MAKE HIM DROP YOU!
IF I'M LUCKY!
HE DID IT! HE FREED ME! AND SOMETHING TELLS ME HE'S RIGHT ON THE MONEY ABOUT THE CYBORG!

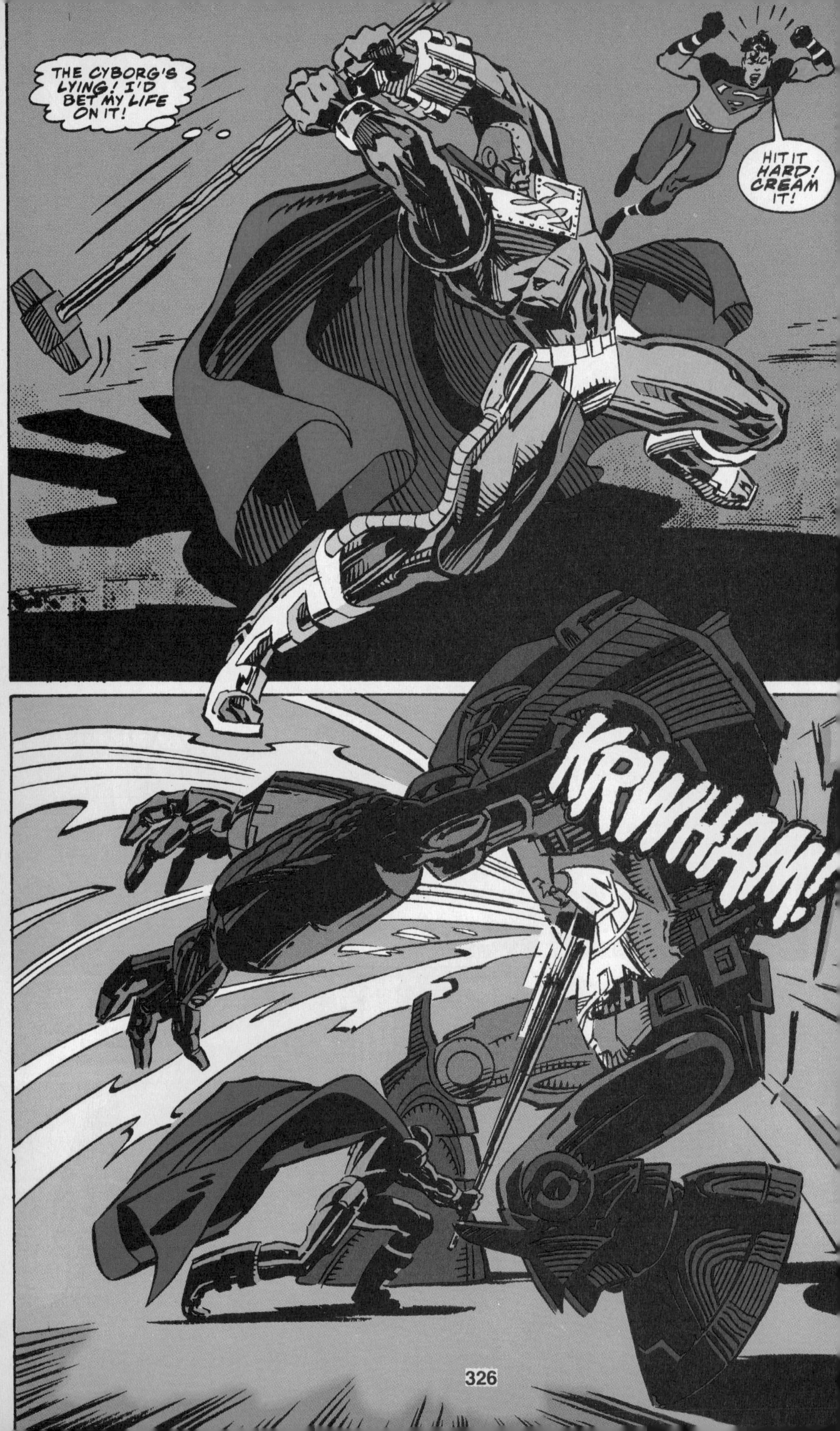
THE CYBORG'S LYING! I'D BET MY LIFE ON IT!
HIT IT HARD! CREAM IT!
KRWHAM!

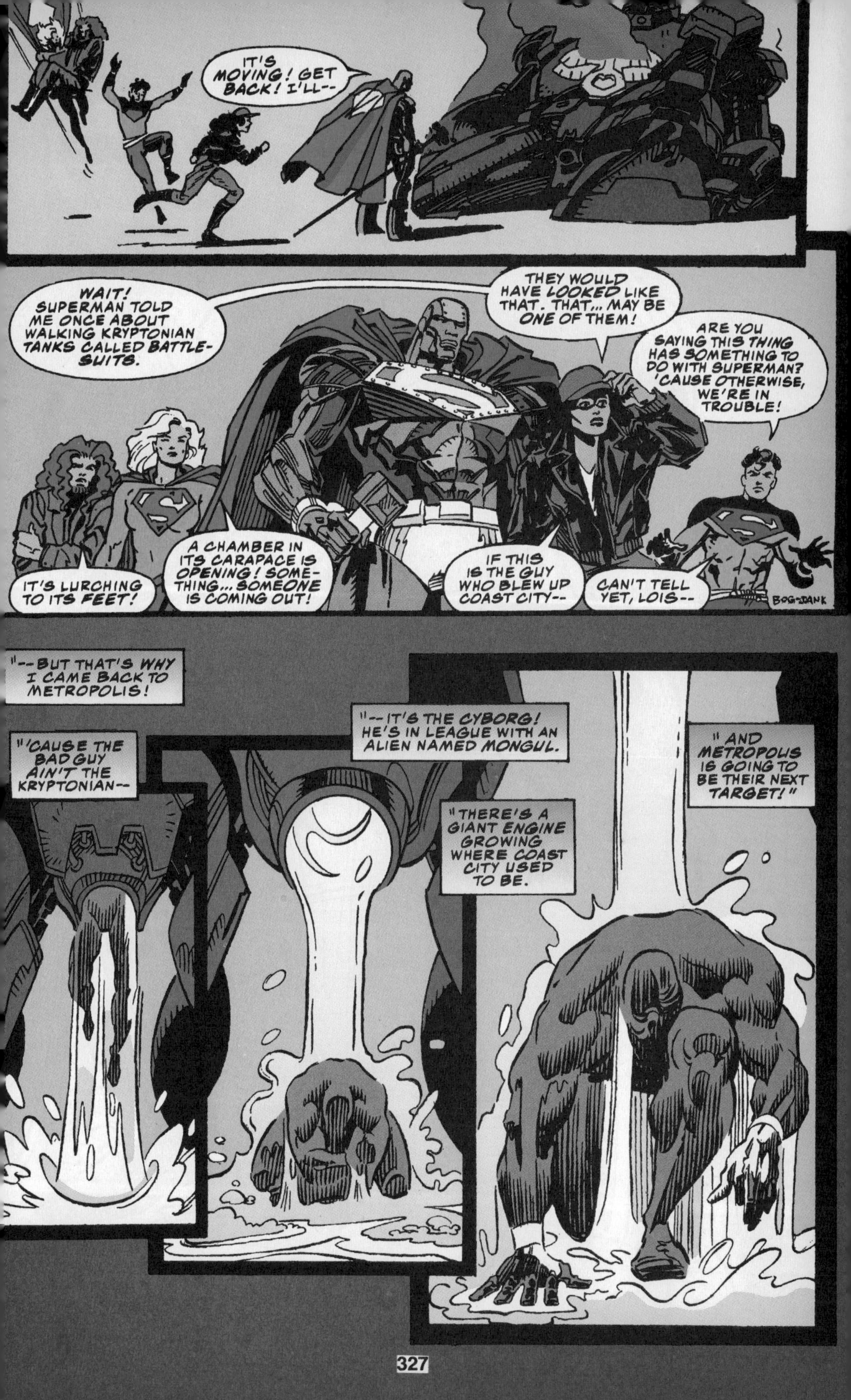
IT'S MOVING! GET BACK! I'LL--
WAIT! SUPERMAN TOLD ME ONCE ABOUT WALKING KRYPTONIAN TANKS CALLED BATTLE-SUITS.
THEY WOULD HAVE LOOKED LIKE THAT. THAT... MAY BE ONE OF THEM!
ARE YOU SAYING THIS THING HAS SOMETHING TO DO WITH SUPERMAN? 'CAUSE OTHERWISE, WE'RE IN TROUBLE!
IT'S LURCHING TO ITS FEET!
A CHAMBER IN ITS CARAPACE IS OPENING! SOME-THING... SOMEONE IS COMING OUT!
IF THIS IS THE GUY WHO BLEW UP COAST CITY--
CAN'T TELL YET, LOIS--
BOG-DANK
"--BUT THAT'S WHY I CAME BACK TO METROPOLIS!
"'CAUSE THE BAD GUY AIN'T THE KRYPTONIAN--
"--IT'S THE CYBORG! HE'S IN LEAGUE WITH AN ALIEN NAMED MONGUL.
"THERE'S A GIANT ENGINE GROWING WHERE COAST CITY USED TO BE.
"AND METROPOLIS IS GOING TO BE THEIR NEXT TARGET!"

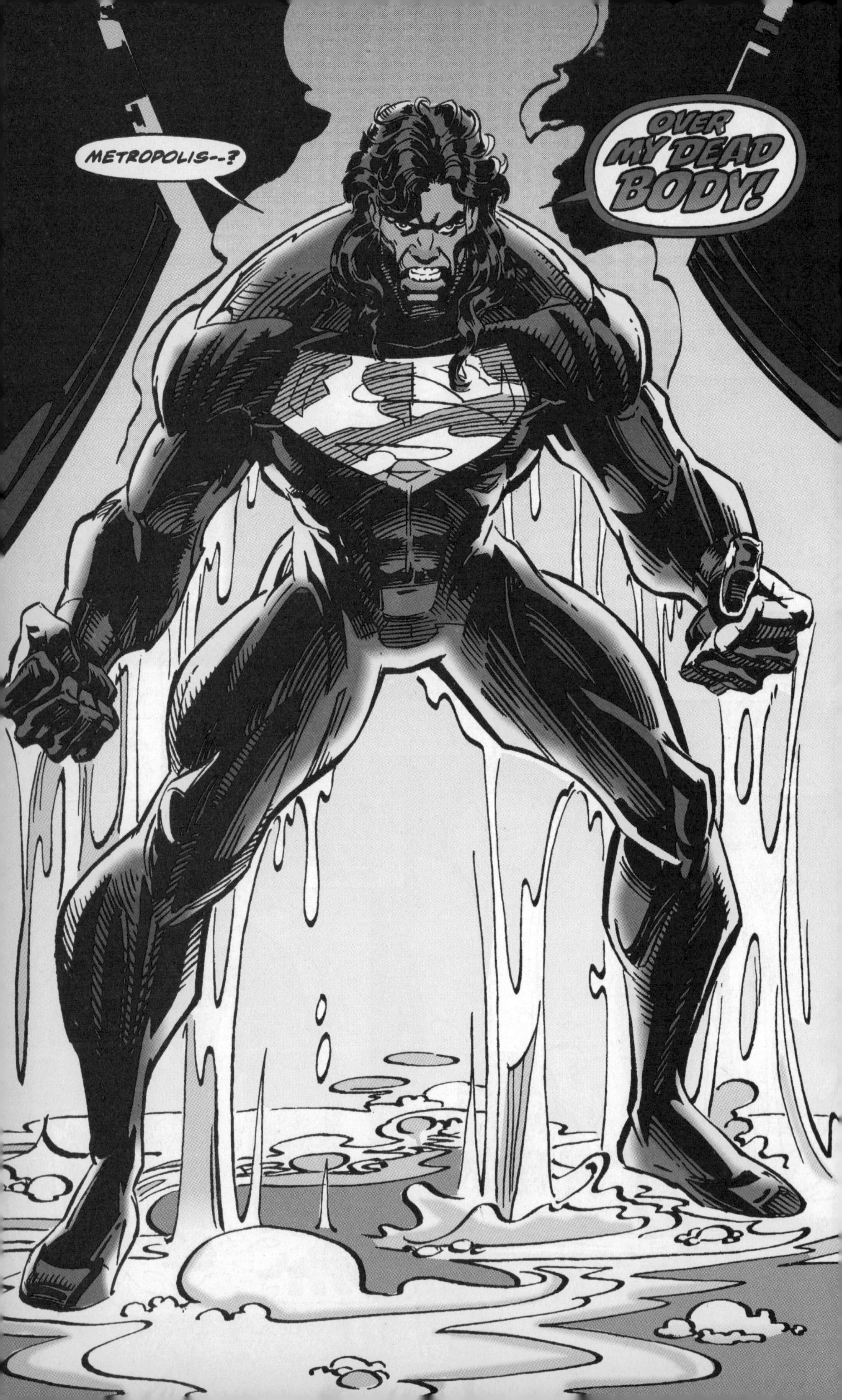
METROPOLIS--?
OVER MY DEAD BODY!

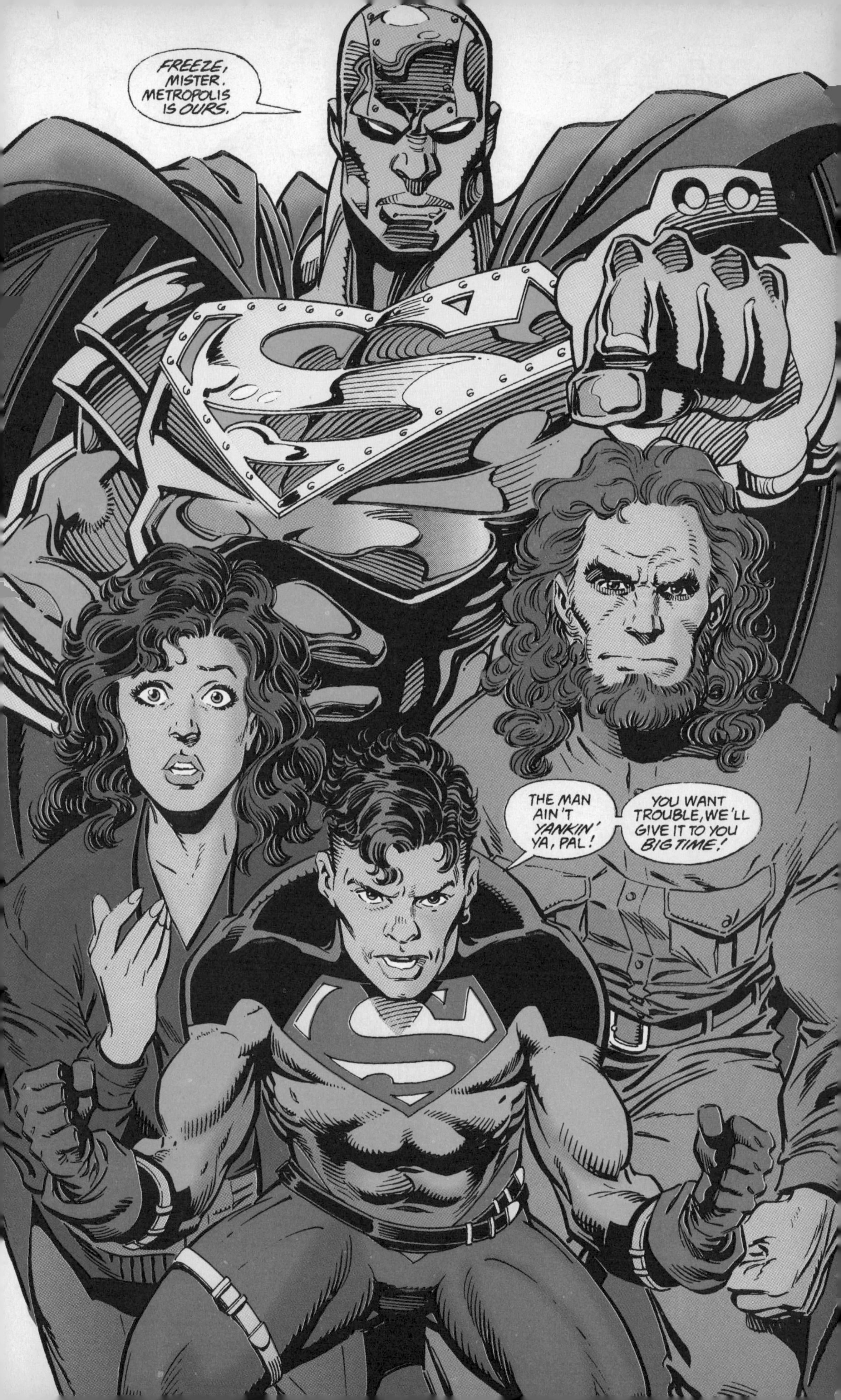
FREEZE, MISTER. METROPOLIS IS OURS.
THE MAN AIN'T YANKIN' YA, PAL!
YOU WANT TROUBLE, WE'LL GIVE IT TO YOU BIG TIME!

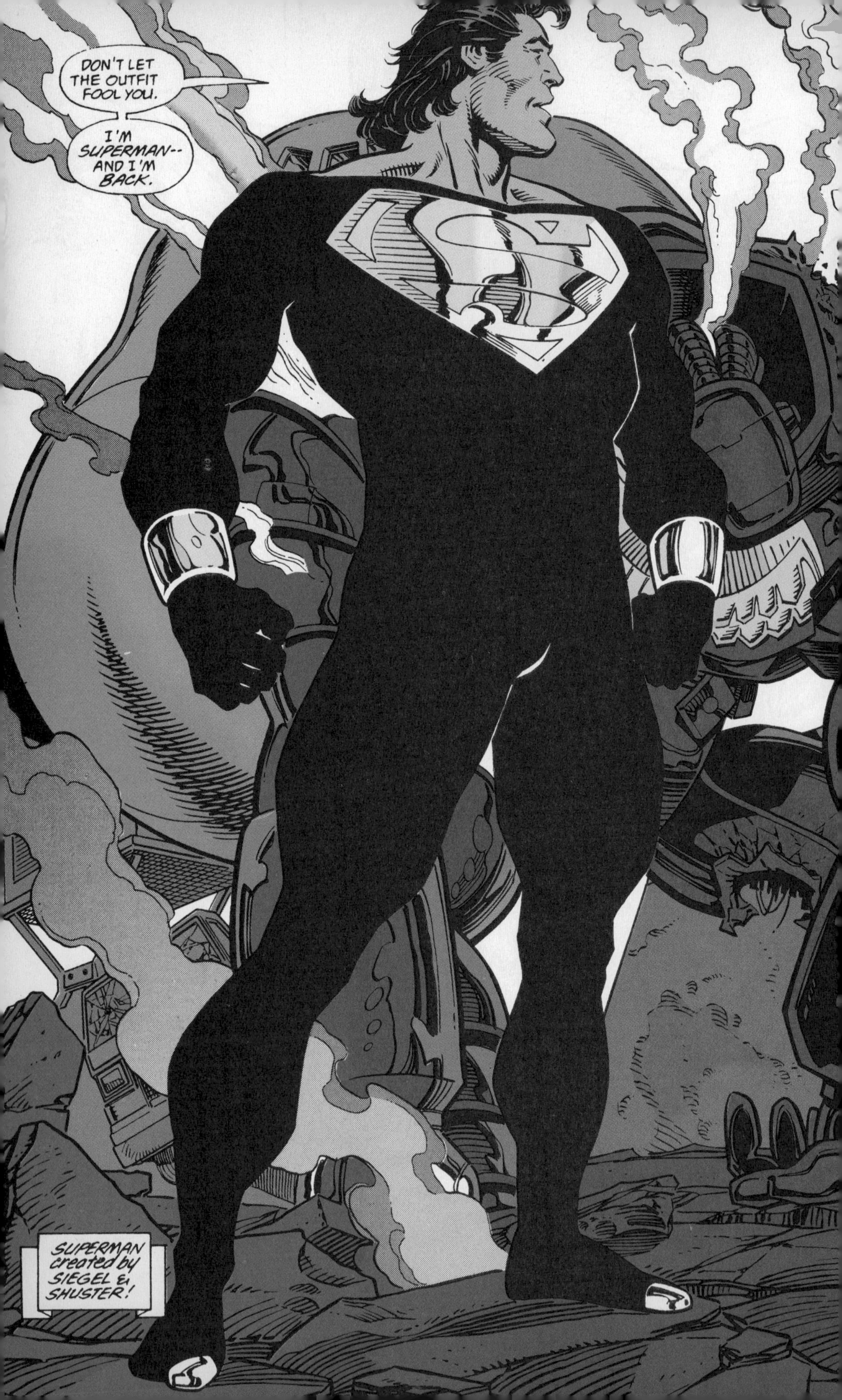
DON'T LET THE OUTFIT FOOL YOU.
I'M SUPERMAN-- AND I'M BACK.
SUPERMAN created by SIEGEL & SHUSTER!

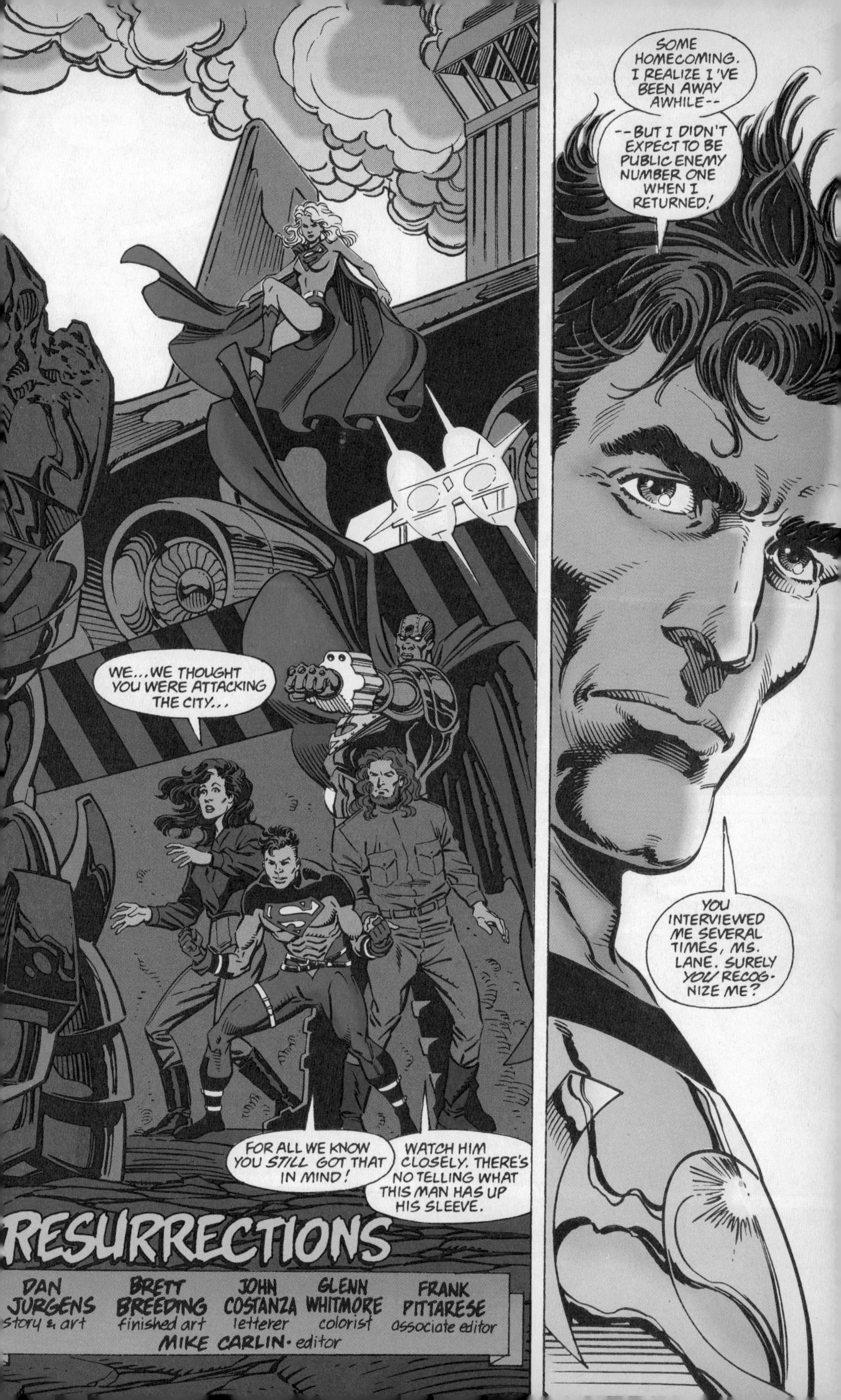

SOME HOMECOMING. I REALIZE I'VE BEEN AWAY AWHILE--
--BUT I DIDN'T EXPECT TO BE PUBLIC ENEMY NUMBER ONE WHEN I RETURNED!
WE...WE THOUGHT YOU WERE ATTACKING THE CITY...
FOR ALL WE KNOW YOU STILL GOT THAT IN MIND!
WATCH HIM CLOSELY. THERE'S NO TELLING WHAT THIS MAN HAS UP HIS SLEEVE.
YOU INTERVIEWED ME SEVERAL TIMES, MS. LANE. SURELY YOU RECOGNIZE ME?
RESURRECTIONS
DAN JURGENS story & art
BRETT BREEDING finished art
JOHN COSTANZA letterer
GLENN WHITMORE colorist
FRANK PITTARESE associate editor
MIKE CARLIN • editor

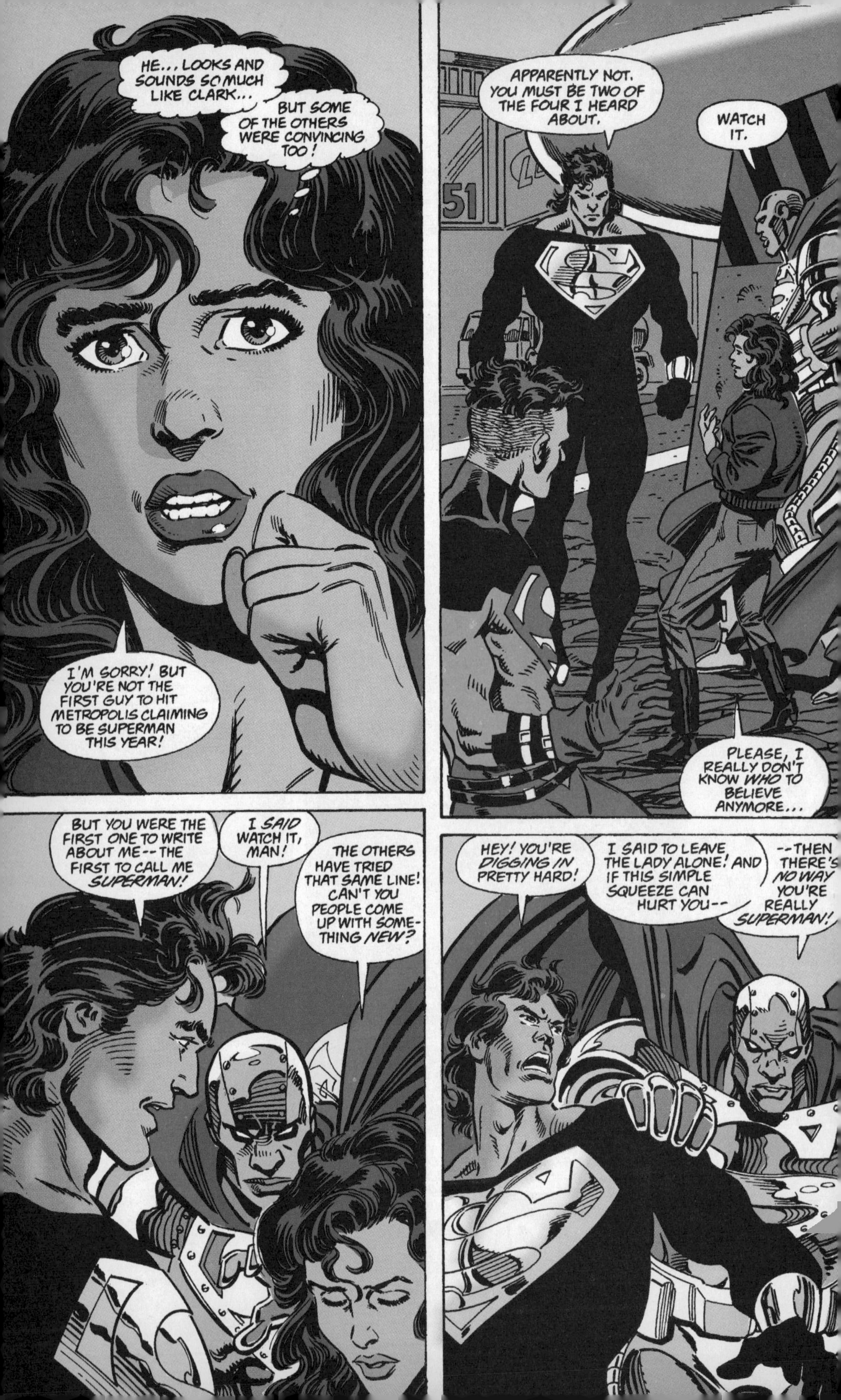

HE... LOOKS AND SOUNDS SO MUCH LIKE CLARK...
BUT SOME OF THE OTHERS WERE CONVINCING TOO!
I'M SORRY! BUT YOU'RE NOT THE FIRST GUY TO HIT METROPOLIS CLAIMING TO BE SUPERMAN THIS YEAR!
APPARENTLY NOT. YOU MUST BE TWO OF THE FOUR I HEARD ABOUT.
WATCH IT.
51
PLEASE, I REALLY DON'T KNOW *WHO* TO BELIEVE ANYMORE...
BUT YOU WERE THE FIRST ONE TO WRITE ABOUT ME--THE FIRST TO CALL ME *SUPERMAN!*
I *SAID* WATCH IT, MAN!
THE OTHERS HAVE TRIED THAT SAME LINE! CAN'T YOU PEOPLE COME UP WITH SOME-THING *NEW?*
HEY! YOU'RE *DIGGING IN* PRETTY HARD!
I SAID TO LEAVE THE LADY ALONE! AND IF THIS SIMPLE SQUEEZE CAN HURT YOU--
--THEN THERE'S *NO WAY* YOU'RE REALLY *SUPERMAN!*

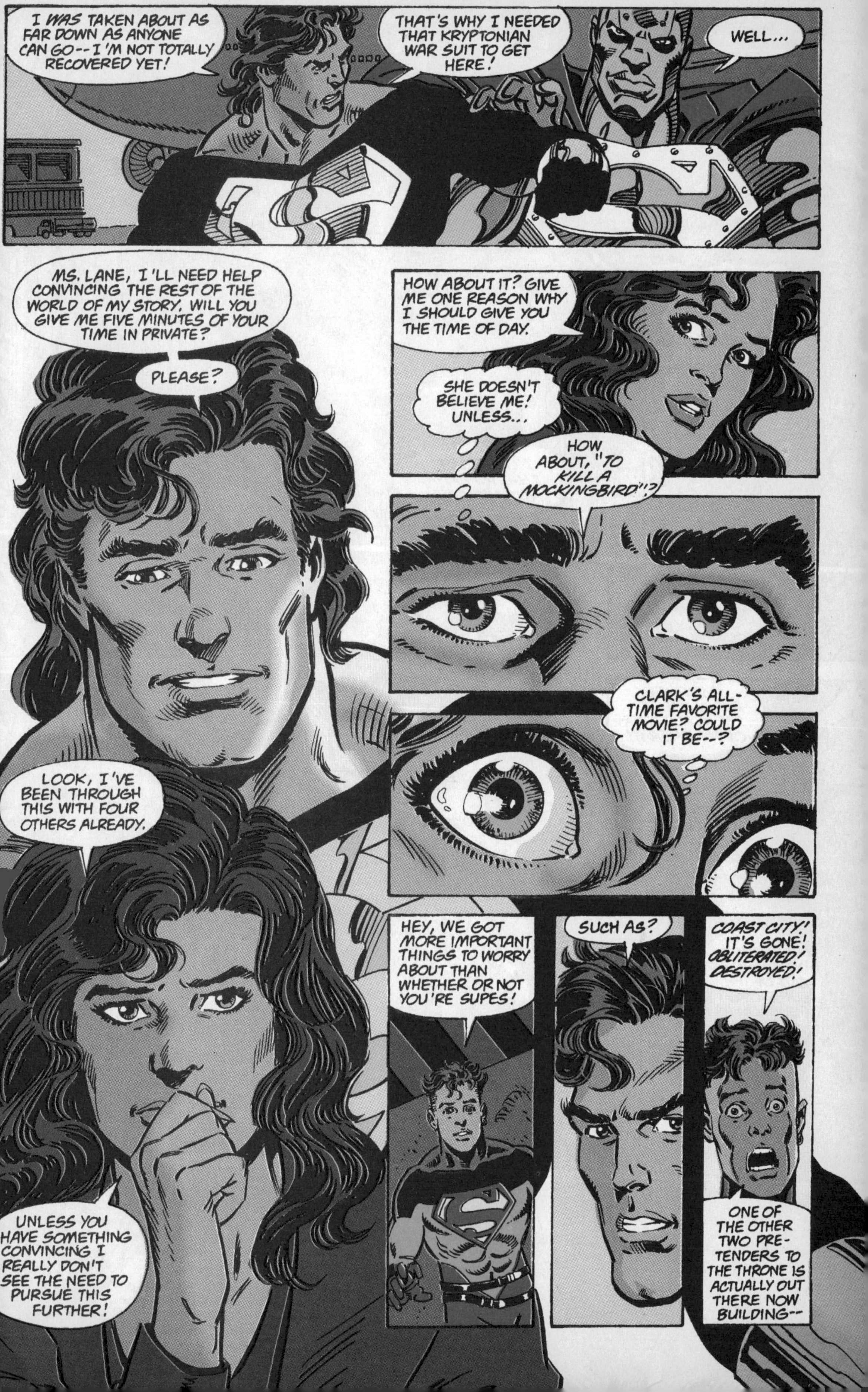

I WAS TAKEN ABOUT AS FAR DOWN AS ANYONE CAN GO-- I'M NOT TOTALLY RECOVERED YET!
THAT'S WHY I NEEDED THAT KRYPTONIAN WAR SUIT TO GET HERE!
WELL...
MS. LANE, I'LL NEED HELP CONVINCING THE REST OF THE WORLD OF MY STORY. WILL YOU GIVE ME FIVE MINUTES OF YOUR TIME IN PRIVATE?
PLEASE?
HOW ABOUT IT? GIVE ME ONE REASON WHY I SHOULD GIVE YOU THE TIME OF DAY.
SHE DOESN'T BELIEVE ME! UNLESS...
HOW ABOUT, "TO KILL A MOCKINGBIRD"?
CLARK'S ALL-TIME FAVORITE MOVIE? COULD IT BE--?
LOOK, I'VE BEEN THROUGH THIS WITH FOUR OTHERS ALREADY.
UNLESS YOU HAVE SOMETHING CONVINCING I REALLY DON'T SEE THE NEED TO PURSUE THIS FURTHER!
HEY, WE GOT MORE IMPORTANT THINGS TO WORRY ABOUT THAN WHETHER OR NOT YOU'RE SUPES!
SUCH AS?
COAST CITY! IT'S GONE! OBLITERATED! DESTROYED!
ONE OF THE OTHER TWO PRETENDERS TO THE THRONE IS ACTUALLY OUT THERE NOW BUILDING--

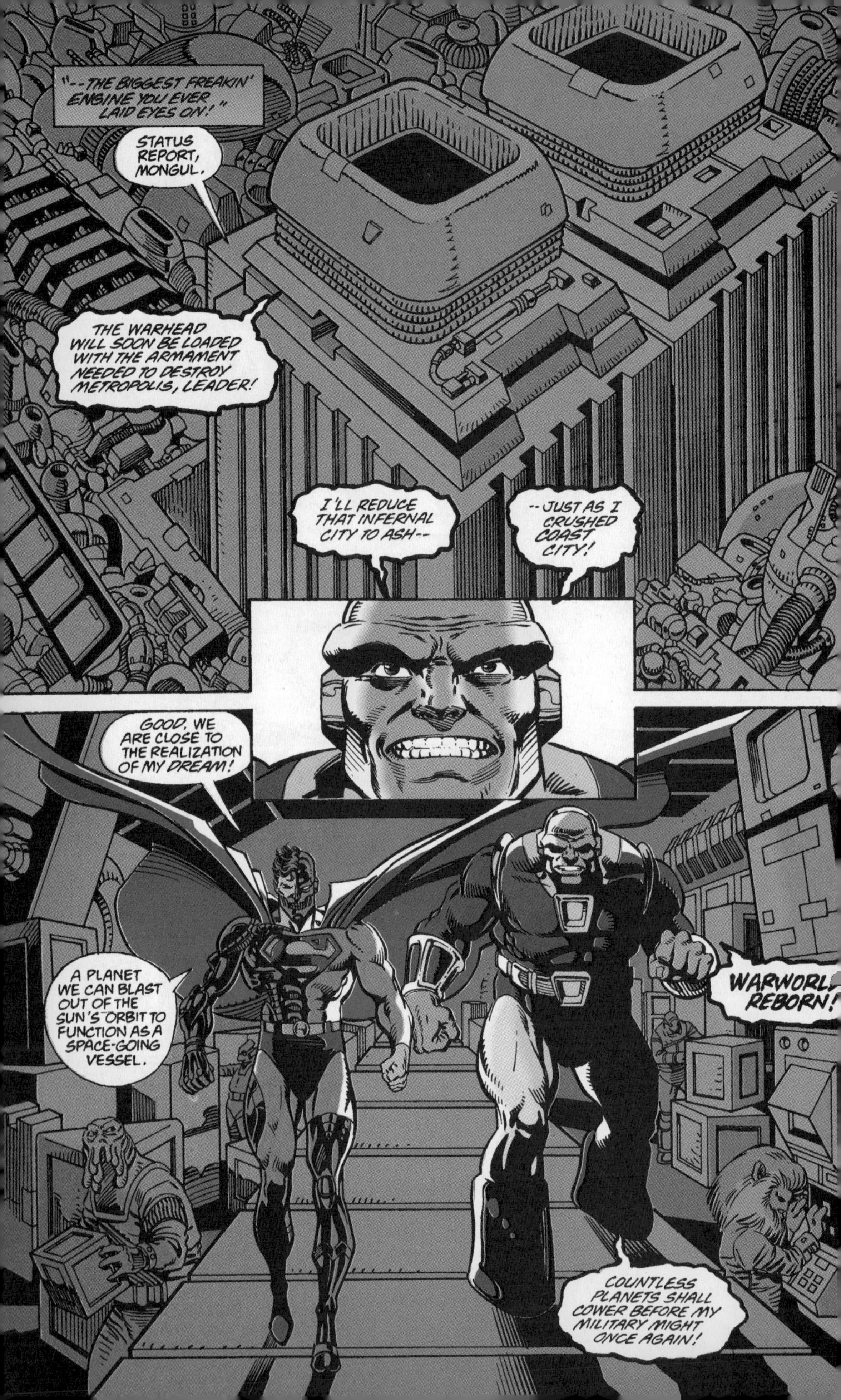
"--THE BIGGEST FREAKIN' ENGINE YOU EVER LAID EYES ON!"
STATUS REPORT, MONGUL.
THE WARHEAD WILL SOON BE LOADED WITH THE ARMAMENT NEEDED TO DESTROY METROPOLIS, LEADER!
I'LL REDUCE THAT INFERNAL CITY TO ASH--
--JUST AS I CRUSHED COAST CITY!
GOOD. WE ARE CLOSE TO THE REALIZATION OF MY DREAM!
A PLANET WE CAN BLAST OUT OF THE SUN'S ORBIT TO FUNCTION AS A SPACE-GOING VESSEL.
WARWORLD REBORN!
COUNTLESS PLANETS SHALL COWER BEFORE MY MILITARY MIGHT ONCE AGAIN!

I SAVOR THE IRONY OF IT ALL! I'LL TURN THE DEAD KRYPTONIAN'S HOME PLANET INTO THE MIGHTIEST WEAPON THE GALAXIES HAVE EVER KNOWN!

THE FISTS OF MONGUL SHALL RULE ONCE MORE!

COWER BEFORE YOU, MONGUL?

UNDERSTAND THIS!

YOU ARE MY SERVANT! YOU SERVE MY WISHES!

THIS BAD. I GO. YOU TOO!

YOU WERE NOTHING BUT A TWO-BIT RULER FROM A TWO-BIT PLANET WHEN I FOUND YOU!

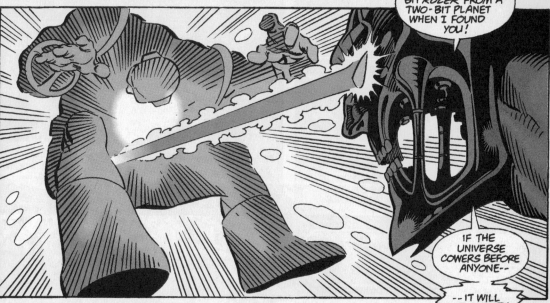

IF THE UNIVERSE COWERS BEFORE ANYONE--

--IT WILL BE ME!

OHH...

REMEMBER OUR DEAL. YOU SATISFY YOUR BLOOD LUST BY BEING ONE OF MY SOLDIERS--

--WHILE I GET MY REVENGE AGAINST EARTH AND SUPERMAN!

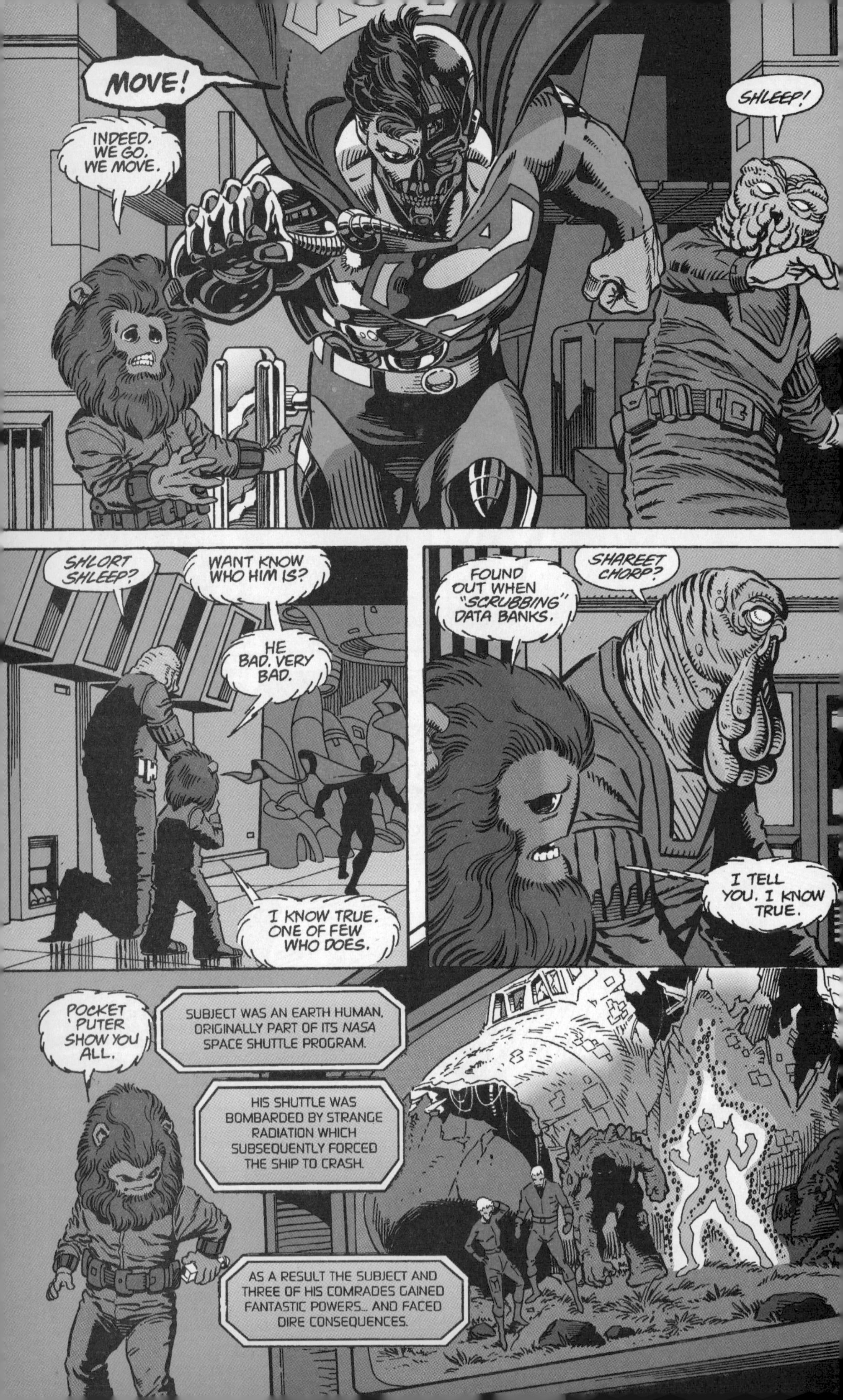
MOVE!
INDEED. WE GO. WE MOVE.
SHLEEP!
SHLORT SHLEEP?
WANT KNOW WHO HIM IS?
HE BAD. VERY BAD.
I KNOW TRUE. ONE OF FEW WHO DOES.
SHAREET CHORP?
FOUND OUT WHEN "SCRUBBING" DATA BANKS.
I TELL YOU. I KNOW TRUE.
POCKET PUTER SHOW YOU ALL.
SUBJECT WAS AN EARTH HUMAN, ORIGINALLY PART OF ITS *NASA* SPACE SHUTTLE PROGRAM.
HIS SHUTTLE WAS BOMBARDED BY STRANGE RADIATION WHICH SUBSEQUENTLY FORCED THE SHIP TO CRASH.
AS A RESULT THE SUBJECT AND THREE OF HIS COMRADES GAINED FANTASTIC POWERS... AND FACED DIRE CONSEQUENCES.

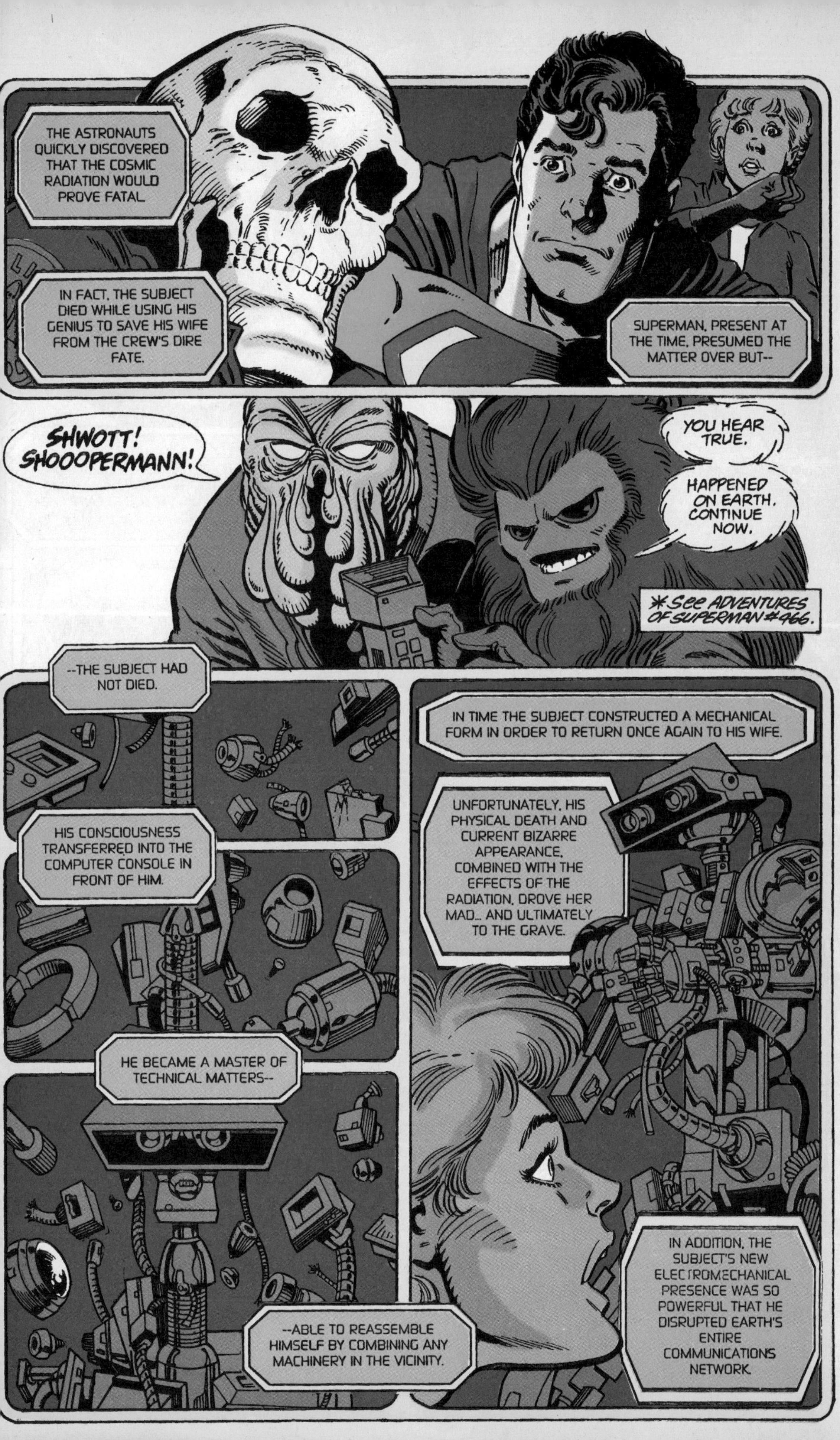
THE ASTRONAUTS QUICKLY DISCOVERED THAT THE COSMIC RADIATION WOULD PROVE FATAL.
IN FACT, THE SUBJECT DIED WHILE USING HIS GENIUS TO SAVE HIS WIFE FROM THE CREW'S DIRE FATE.
SUPERMAN, PRESENT AT THE TIME, PRESUMED THE MATTER OVER BUT--
SHWOTT! SHOOOPERMANN!
YOU HEAR TRUE.
HAPPENED ON EARTH. CONTINUE NOW.
*See ADVENTURES OF SUPERMAN #466.
--THE SUBJECT HAD NOT DIED.
HIS CONSCIOUSNESS TRANSFERRED INTO THE COMPUTER CONSOLE IN FRONT OF HIM.
HE BECAME A MASTER OF TECHNICAL MATTERS--
--ABLE TO REASSEMBLE HIMSELF BY COMBINING ANY MACHINERY IN THE VICINITY.
IN TIME THE SUBJECT CONSTRUCTED A MECHANICAL FORM IN ORDER TO RETURN ONCE AGAIN TO HIS WIFE.
UNFORTUNATELY, HIS PHYSICAL DEATH AND CURRENT BIZARRE APPEARANCE, COMBINED WITH THE EFFECTS OF THE RADIATION, DROVE HER MAD... AND ULTIMATELY TO THE GRAVE.
IN ADDITION, THE SUBJECT'S NEW ELECTROMECHANICAL PRESENCE WAS SO POWERFUL THAT HE DISRUPTED EARTH'S ENTIRE COMMUNICATIONS NETWORK.

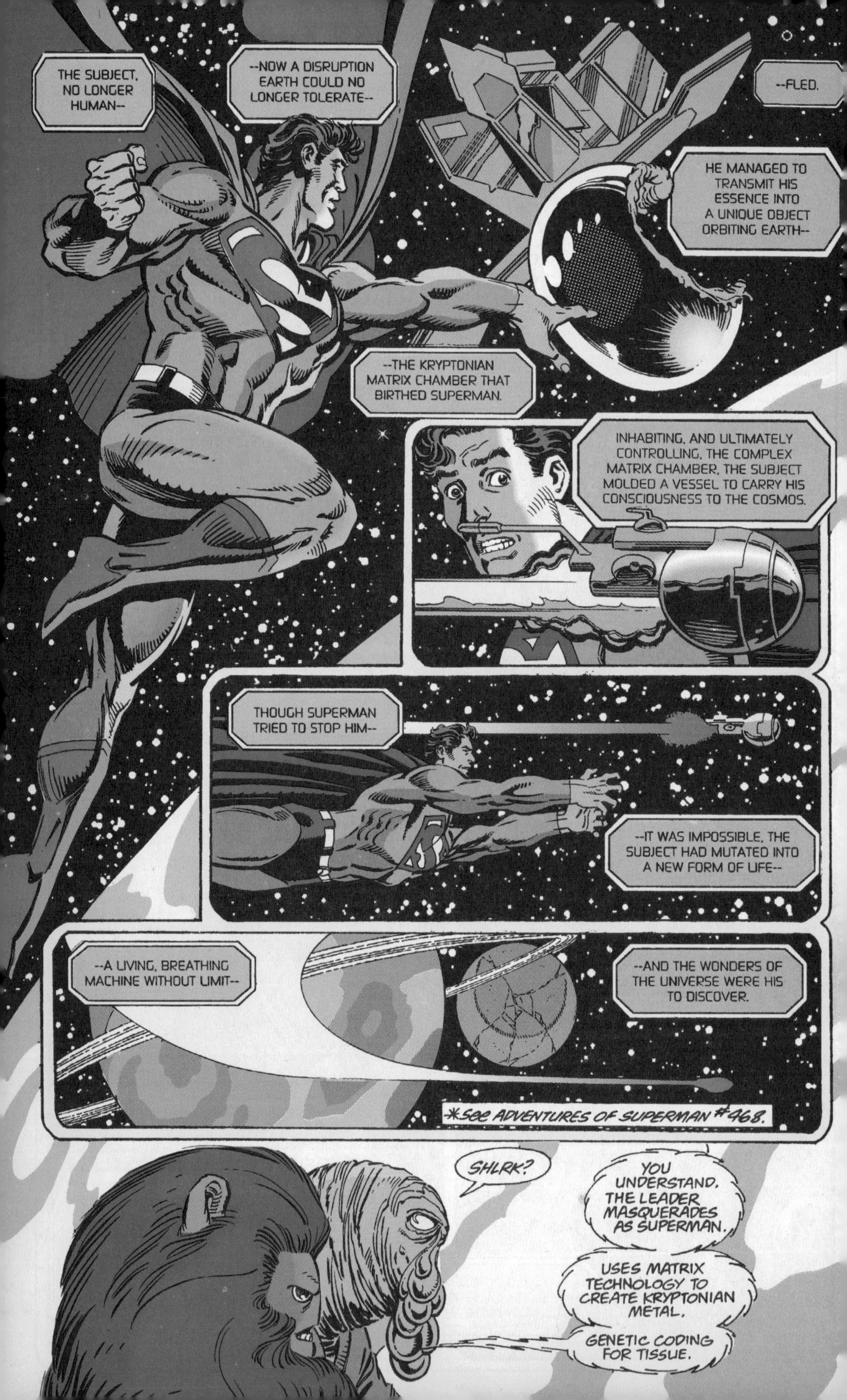
THE SUBJECT, NO LONGER HUMAN--
--NOW A DISRUPTION EARTH COULD NO LONGER TOLERATE--
--FLED.
HE MANAGED TO TRANSMIT HIS ESSENCE INTO A UNIQUE OBJECT ORBITING EARTH--
--THE KRYPTONIAN MATRIX CHAMBER THAT BIRTHED SUPERMAN.
INHABITING, AND ULTIMATELY CONTROLLING, THE COMPLEX MATRIX CHAMBER, THE SUBJECT MOLDED A VESSEL TO CARRY HIS CONSCIOUSNESS TO THE COSMOS.
THOUGH SUPERMAN TRIED TO STOP HIM--
--IT WAS IMPOSSIBLE. THE SUBJECT HAD MUTATED INTO A NEW FORM OF LIFE--
--A LIVING, BREATHING MACHINE WITHOUT LIMIT--
--AND THE WONDERS OF THE UNIVERSE WERE HIS TO DISCOVER.
*SEE ADVENTURES OF SUPERMAN #468.
SHLRK?
YOU UNDERSTAND. THE LEADER MASQUERADES AS SUPERMAN.
USES MATRIX TECHNOLOGY TO CREATE KRYPTONIAN METAL.
GENETIC CODING FOR TISSUE.

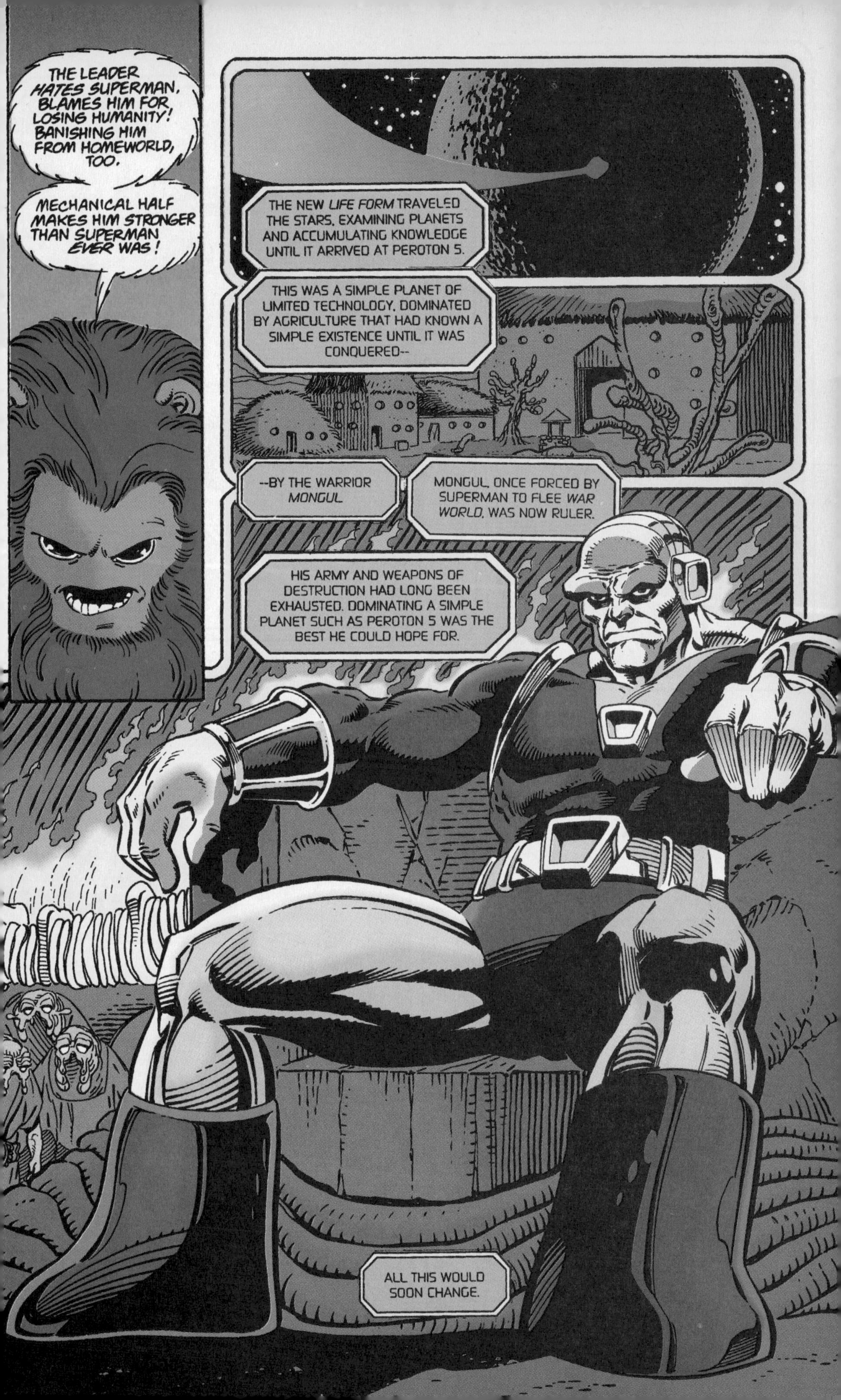

THE LEADER HATES SUPERMAN. BLAMES HIM FOR LOSING HUMANITY! BANISHING HIM FROM HOMEWORLD, TOO.
MECHANICAL HALF MAKES HIM STRONGER THAN SUPERMAN EVER WAS!
THE NEW LIFE FORM TRAVELED THE STARS, EXAMINING PLANETS AND ACCUMULATING KNOWLEDGE UNTIL IT ARRIVED AT PEROTON 5.
THIS WAS A SIMPLE PLANET OF LIMITED TECHNOLOGY, DOMINATED BY AGRICULTURE THAT HAD KNOWN A SIMPLE EXISTENCE UNTIL IT WAS CONQUERED--
--BY THE WARRIOR MONGUL.
MONGUL, ONCE FORCED BY SUPERMAN TO FLEE WAR WORLD, WAS NOW RULER.
HIS ARMY AND WEAPONS OF DESTRUCTION HAD LONG BEEN EXHAUSTED. DOMINATING A SIMPLE PLANET SUCH AS PEROTON 5 WAS THE BEST HE COULD HOPE FOR.
ALL THIS WOULD SOON CHANGE.

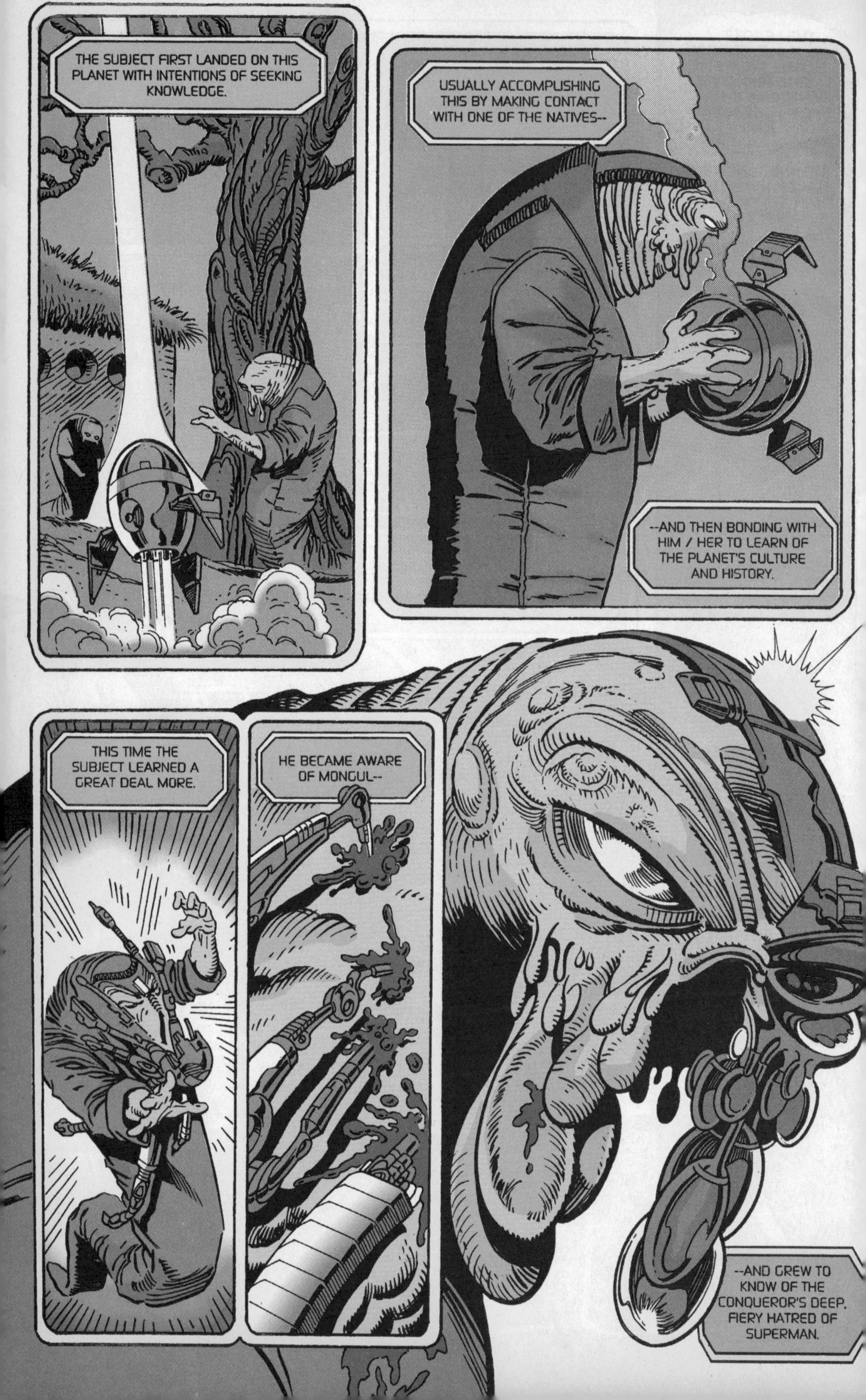
THE SUBJECT FIRST LANDED ON THIS PLANET WITH INTENTIONS OF SEEKING KNOWLEDGE.
USUALLY ACCOMPLISHING THIS BY MAKING CONTACT WITH ONE OF THE NATIVES--
--AND THEN BONDING WITH HIM / HER TO LEARN OF THE PLANET'S CULTURE AND HISTORY.
THIS TIME THE SUBJECT LEARNED A GREAT DEAL MORE.
HE BECAME AWARE OF MONGUL--
--AND GREW TO KNOW OF THE CONQUEROR'S DEEP, FIERY HATRED OF SUPERMAN.

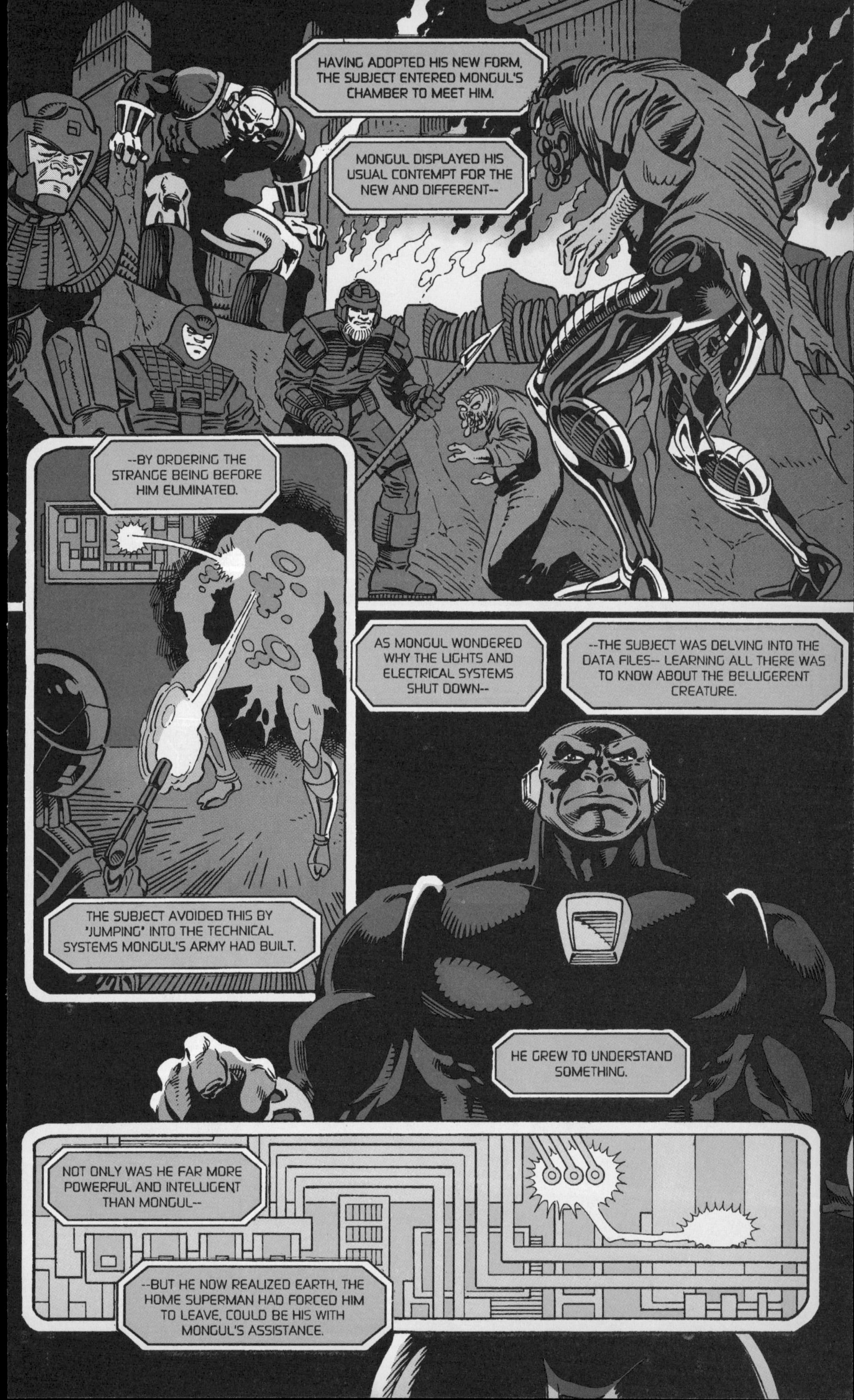
HAVING ADOPTED HIS NEW FORM, THE SUBJECT ENTERED MONGUL'S CHAMBER TO MEET HIM.
MONGUL DISPLAYED HIS USUAL CONTEMPT FOR THE NEW AND DIFFERENT--
--BY ORDERING THE STRANGE BEING BEFORE HIM ELIMINATED.
THE SUBJECT AVOIDED THIS BY "JUMPING" INTO THE TECHNICAL SYSTEMS MONGUL'S ARMY HAD BUILT.
AS MONGUL WONDERED WHY THE LIGHTS AND ELECTRICAL SYSTEMS SHUT DOWN--
--THE SUBJECT WAS DELVING INTO THE DATA FILES-- LEARNING ALL THERE WAS TO KNOW ABOUT THE BELLIGERENT CREATURE.
HE GREW TO UNDERSTAND SOMETHING.
NOT ONLY WAS HE FAR MORE POWERFUL AND INTELLIGENT THAN MONGUL--
--BUT HE NOW REALIZED EARTH, THE HOME SUPERMAN HAD FORCED HIM TO LEAVE, COULD BE HIS WITH MONGUL'S ASSISTANCE.

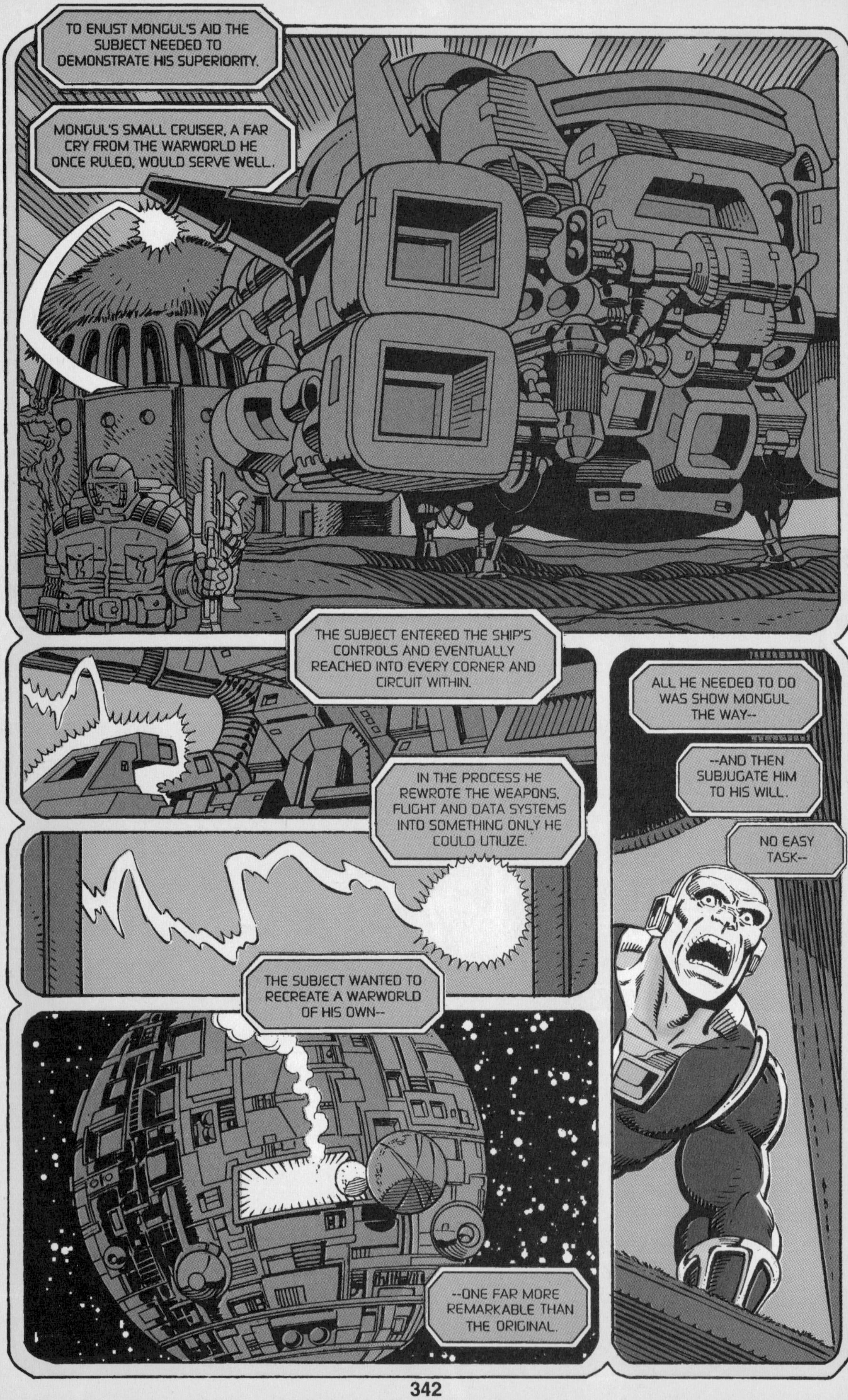
TO ENLIST MONGUL'S AID THE SUBJECT NEEDED TO DEMONSTRATE HIS SUPERIORITY.
MONGUL'S SMALL CRUISER, A FAR CRY FROM THE WARWORLD HE ONCE RULED, WOULD SERVE WELL.
THE SUBJECT ENTERED THE SHIP'S CONTROLS AND EVENTUALLY REACHED INTO EVERY CORNER AND CIRCUIT WITHIN.
IN THE PROCESS HE REWROTE THE WEAPONS, FLIGHT AND DATA SYSTEMS INTO SOMETHING ONLY HE COULD UTILIZE.
THE SUBJECT WANTED TO RECREATE A WARWORLD OF HIS OWN--
--ONE FAR MORE REMARKABLE THAN THE ORIGINAL.
ALL HE NEEDED TO DO WAS SHOW MONGUL THE WAY--
--AND THEN SUBJUGATE HIM TO HIS WILL.
NO EASY TASK--

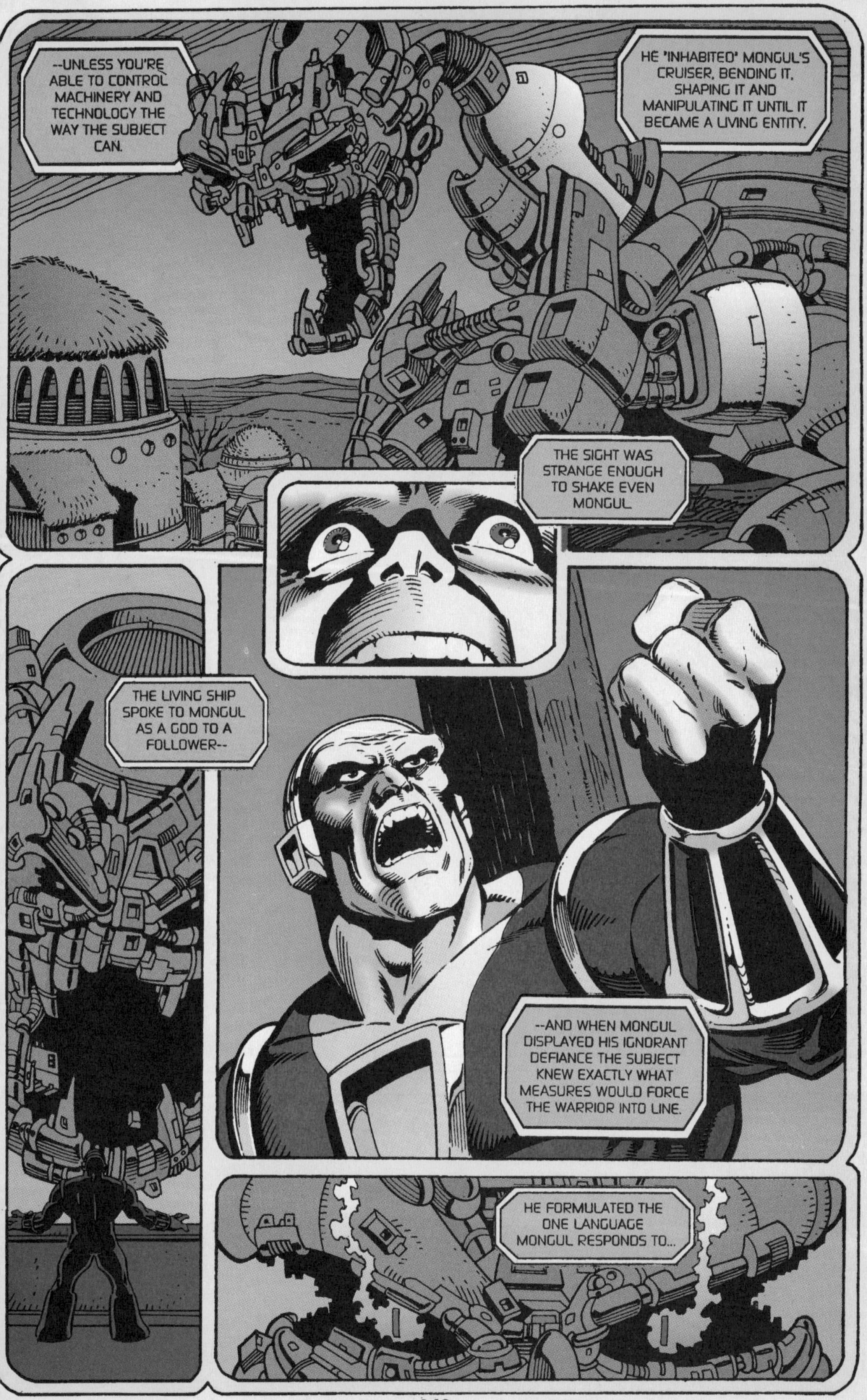
--UNLESS YOU'RE ABLE TO CONTROL MACHINERY AND TECHNOLOGY THE WAY THE SUBJECT CAN.
HE "INHABITED" MONGUL'S CRUISER, BENDING IT, SHAPING IT AND MANIPULATING IT UNTIL IT BECAME A LIVING ENTITY.
THE SIGHT WAS STRANGE ENOUGH TO SHAKE EVEN MONGUL.
THE LIVING SHIP SPOKE TO MONGUL AS A GOD TO A FOLLOWER--
--AND WHEN MONGUL DISPLAYED HIS IGNORANT DEFIANCE THE SUBJECT KNEW EXACTLY WHAT MEASURES WOULD FORCE THE WARRIOR INTO LINE.
HE FORMULATED THE ONE LANGUAGE MONGUL RESPONDS TO...

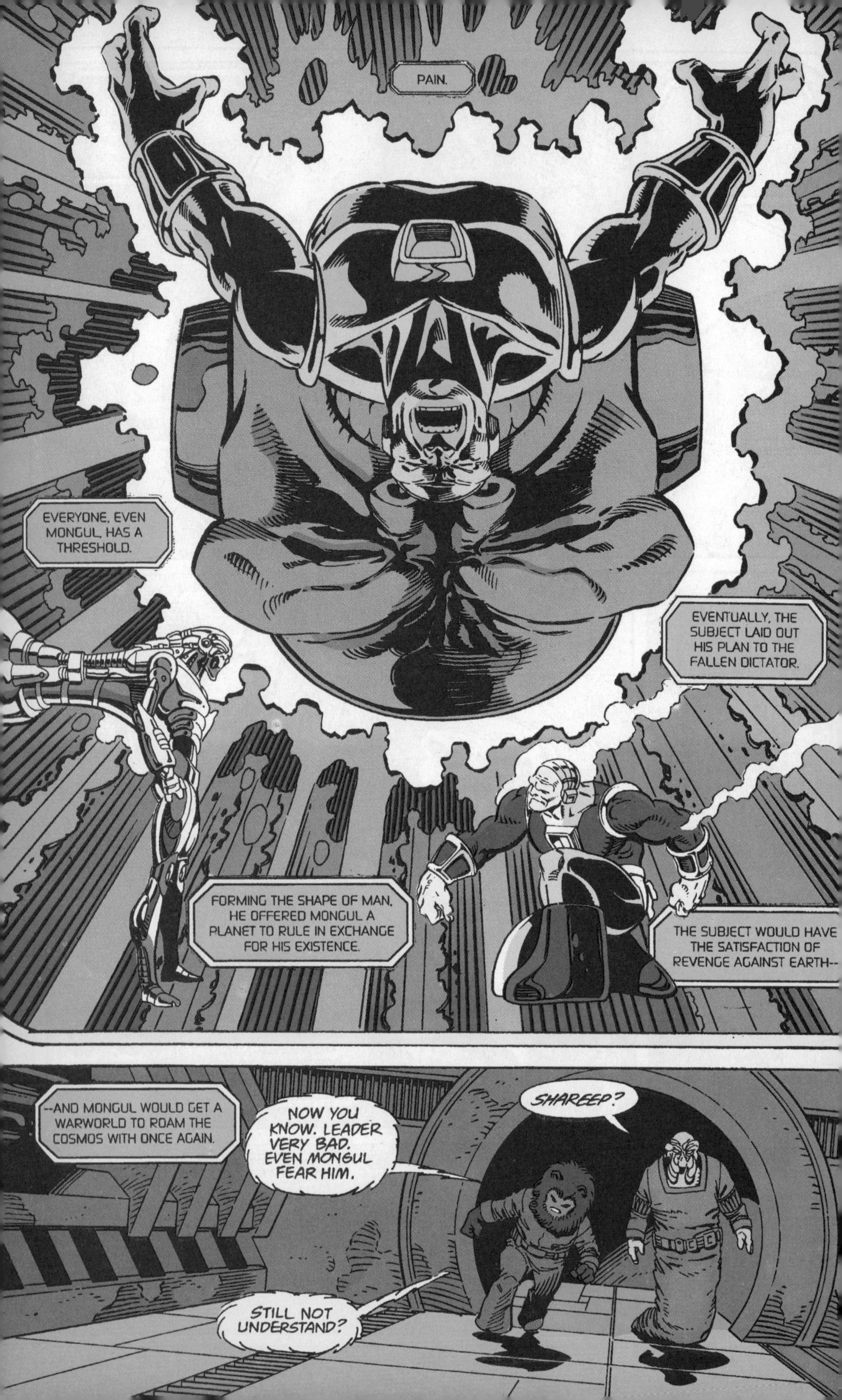

PAIN.
EVERYONE, EVEN MONGUL, HAS A THRESHOLD.
EVENTUALLY, THE SUBJECT LAID OUT HIS PLAN TO THE FALLEN DICTATOR.
FORMING THE SHAPE OF MAN, HE OFFERED MONGUL A PLANET TO RULE IN EXCHANGE FOR HIS EXISTENCE.
THE SUBJECT WOULD HAVE THE SATISFACTION OF REVENGE AGAINST EARTH--
--AND MONGUL WOULD GET A WARWORLD TO ROAM THE COSMOS WITH ONCE AGAIN.
NOW YOU KNOW. LEADER VERY BAD. EVEN MONGUL FEAR HIM.
SHAREEP?
STILL NOT UNDERSTAND?

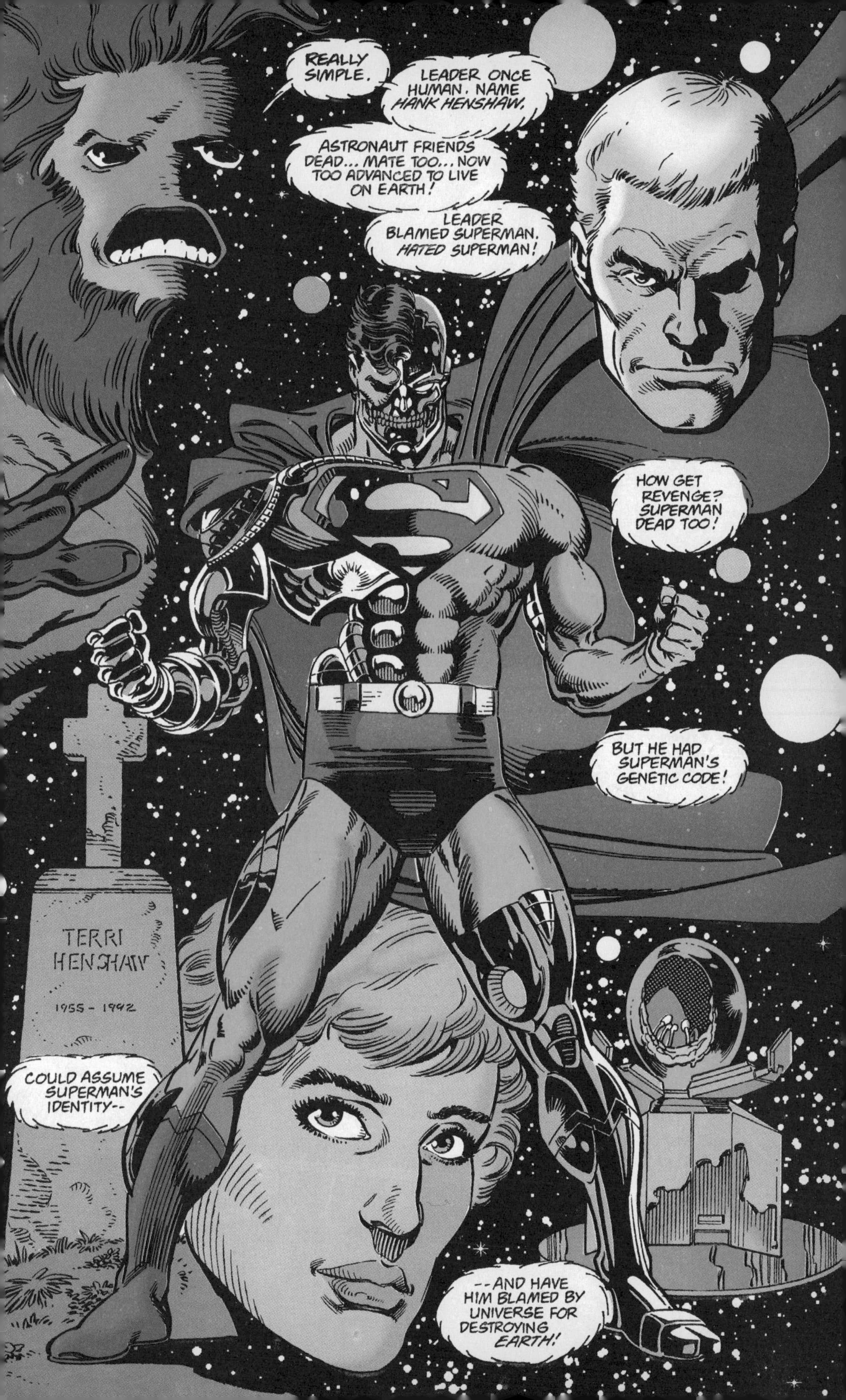
REALLY SIMPLE.
LEADER ONCE HUMAN. NAME HANK HENSHAW.
ASTRONAUT FRIENDS DEAD... MATE TOO... NOW TOO ADVANCED TO LIVE ON EARTH!
LEADER BLAMED SUPERMAN. HATED SUPERMAN!
HOW GET REVENGE? SUPERMAN DEAD TOO!
BUT HE HAD SUPERMAN'S GENETIC CODE!
TERRI HENSHAW
1955 - 1992
COULD ASSUME SUPERMAN'S IDENTITY--
--AND HAVE HIM BLAMED BY UNIVERSE FOR DESTROYING EARTH!

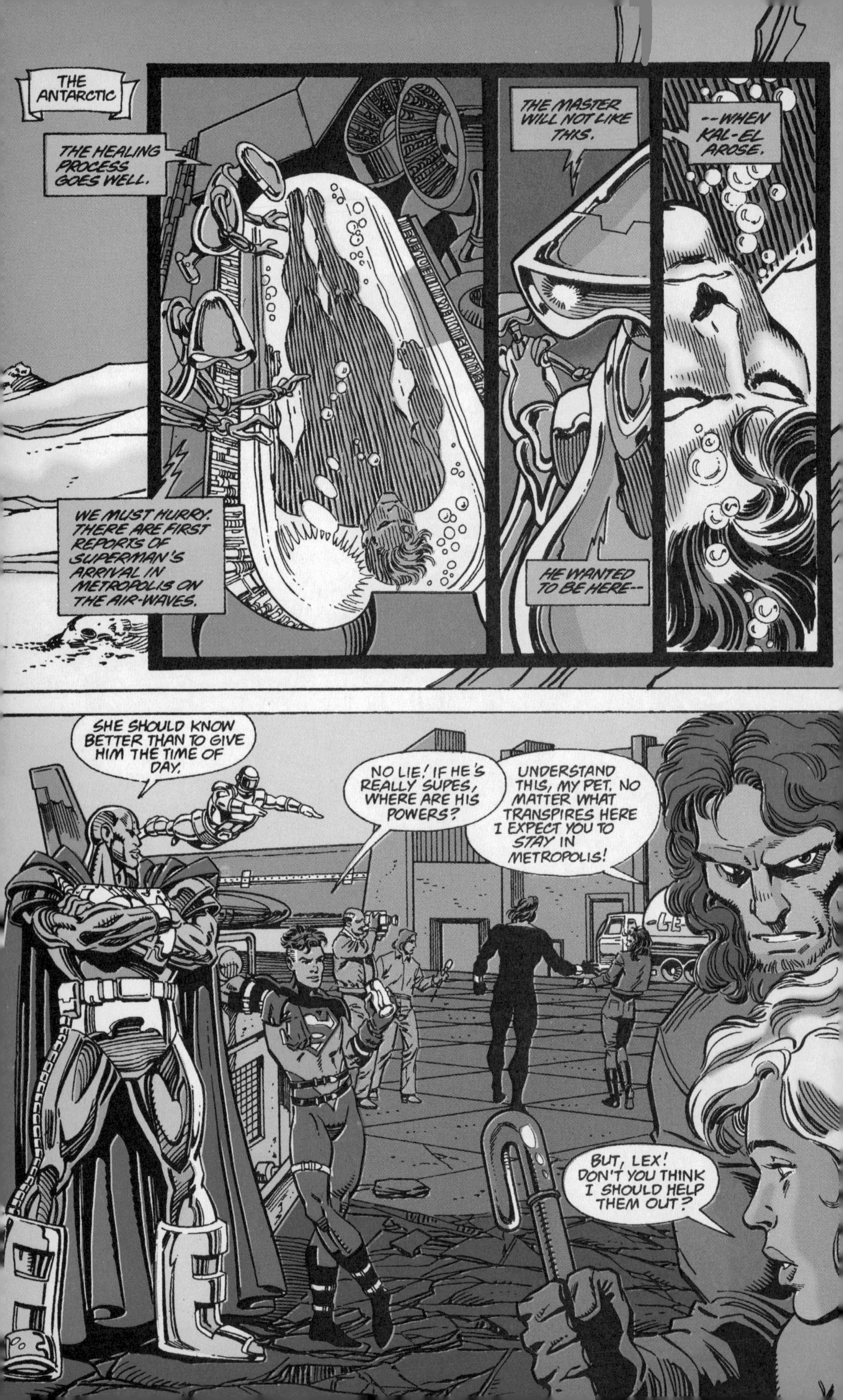
THE ANTARCTIC
THE HEALING PROCESS GOES WELL.
WE MUST HURRY. THERE ARE FIRST REPORTS OF SUPERMAN'S ARRIVAL IN METROPOLIS ON THE AIR-WAVES.
THE MASTER WILL NOT LIKE THIS.
HE WANTED TO BE HERE--
--WHEN KAL-EL AROSE.
SHE SHOULD KNOW BETTER THAN TO GIVE HIM THE TIME OF DAY.
NO LIE! IF HE'S REALLY SUPES, WHERE ARE HIS POWERS?
UNDERSTAND THIS, MY PET. NO MATTER WHAT TRANSPIRES HERE I EXPECT YOU TO STAY IN METROPOLIS!
BUT, LEX! DON'T YOU THINK I SHOULD HELP THEM OUT?

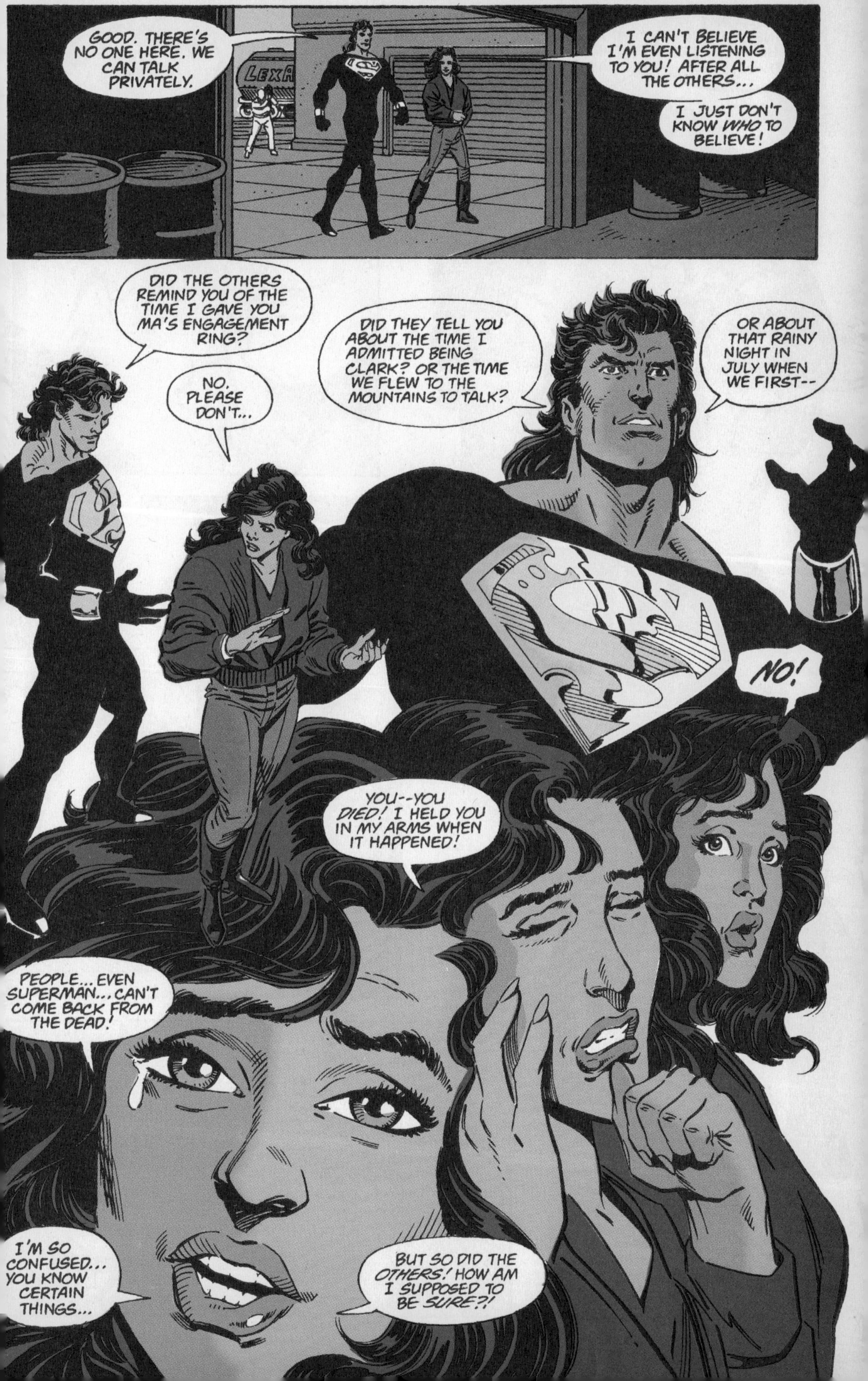
GOOD. THERE'S NO ONE HERE. WE CAN TALK PRIVATELY.
I CAN'T BELIEVE I'M EVEN LISTENING TO YOU! AFTER ALL THE OTHERS...
I JUST DON'T KNOW WHO TO BELIEVE!
DID THE OTHERS REMIND YOU OF THE TIME I GAVE YOU MA'S ENGAGEMENT RING?
NO. PLEASE DON'T...
DID THEY TELL YOU ABOUT THE TIME I ADMITTED BEING CLARK? OR THE TIME WE FLEW TO THE MOUNTAINS TO TALK?
OR ABOUT THAT RAINY NIGHT IN JULY WHEN WE FIRST--
NO!
YOU--YOU DIED! I HELD YOU IN MY ARMS WHEN IT HAPPENED!
PEOPLE... EVEN SUPERMAN... CAN'T COME BACK FROM THE DEAD!
I'M SO CONFUSED... YOU KNOW CERTAIN THINGS...
BUT SO DID THE OTHERS! HOW AM I SUPPOSED TO BE SURE?!

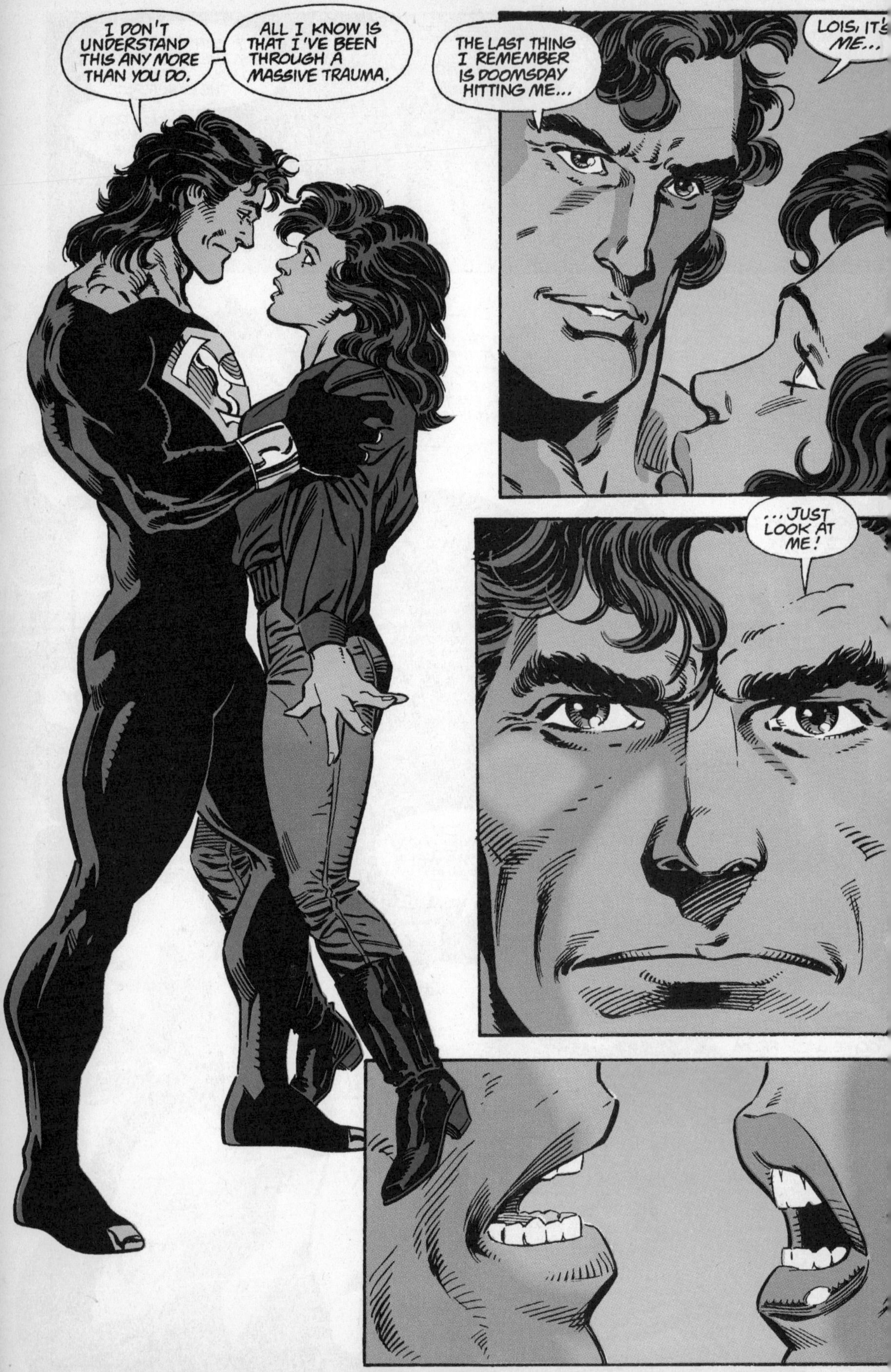

I DON'T UNDERSTAND THIS ANY MORE THAN YOU DO.
ALL I KNOW IS THAT I'VE BEEN THROUGH A MASSIVE TRAUMA.
THE LAST THING I REMEMBER IS DOOMSDAY HITTING ME...
LOIS, IT'S ME...
...JUST LOOK AT ME!

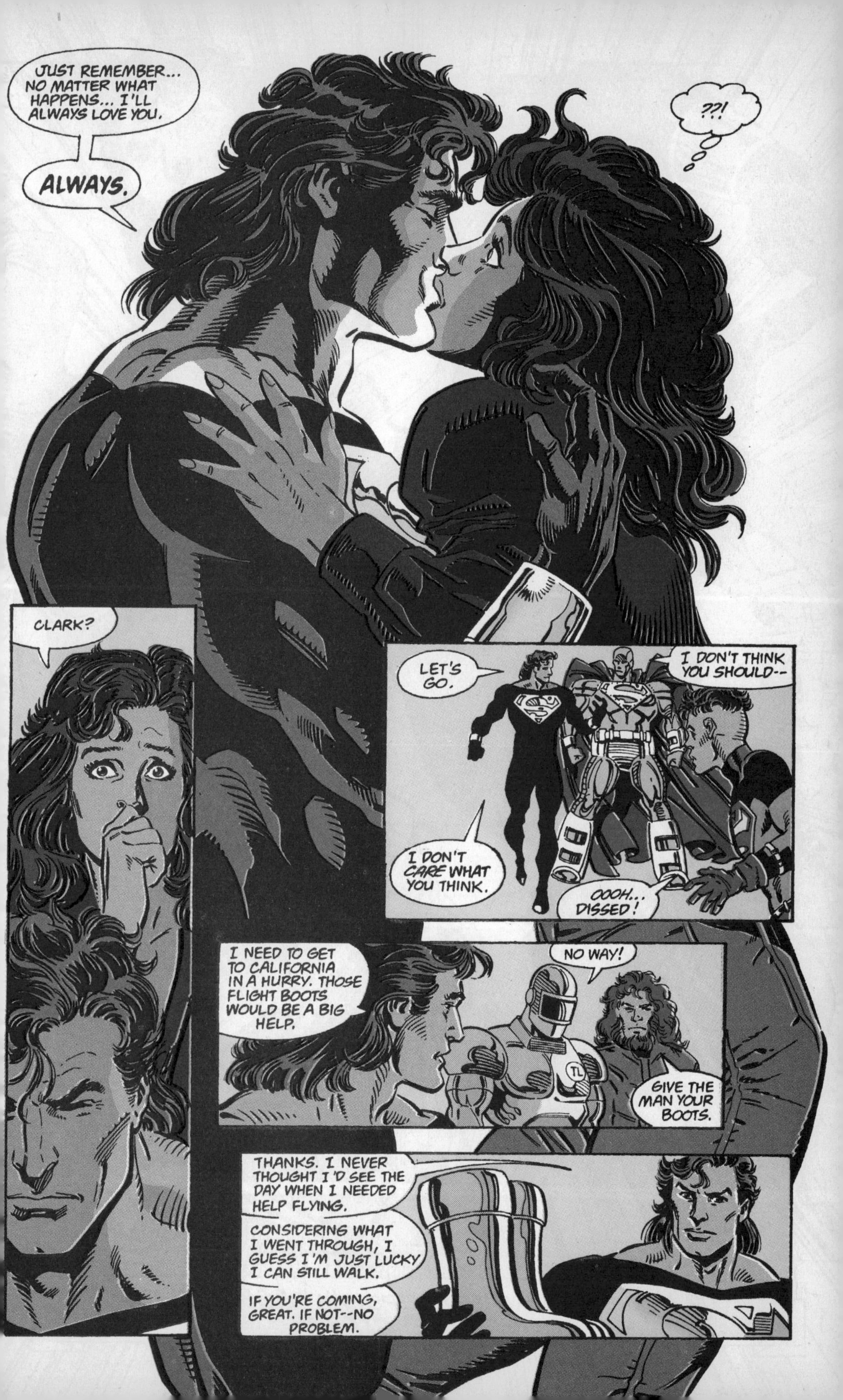
JUST REMEMBER... NO MATTER WHAT HAPPENS... I'LL ALWAYS LOVE YOU.
ALWAYS.
??!
CLARK?
LET'S GO.
I DON'T THINK YOU SHOULD--
I DON'T CARE WHAT YOU THINK.
OOOH... DISSED!
I NEED TO GET TO CALIFORNIA IN A HURRY. THOSE FLIGHT BOOTS WOULD BE A BIG HELP.
NO WAY!
GIVE THE MAN YOUR BOOTS.
THANKS. I NEVER THOUGHT I'D SEE THE DAY WHEN I NEEDED HELP FLYING.
CONSIDERING WHAT I WENT THROUGH, I GUESS I'M JUST LUCKY I CAN STILL WALK.
IF YOU'RE COMING, GREAT. IF NOT--NO PROBLEM.

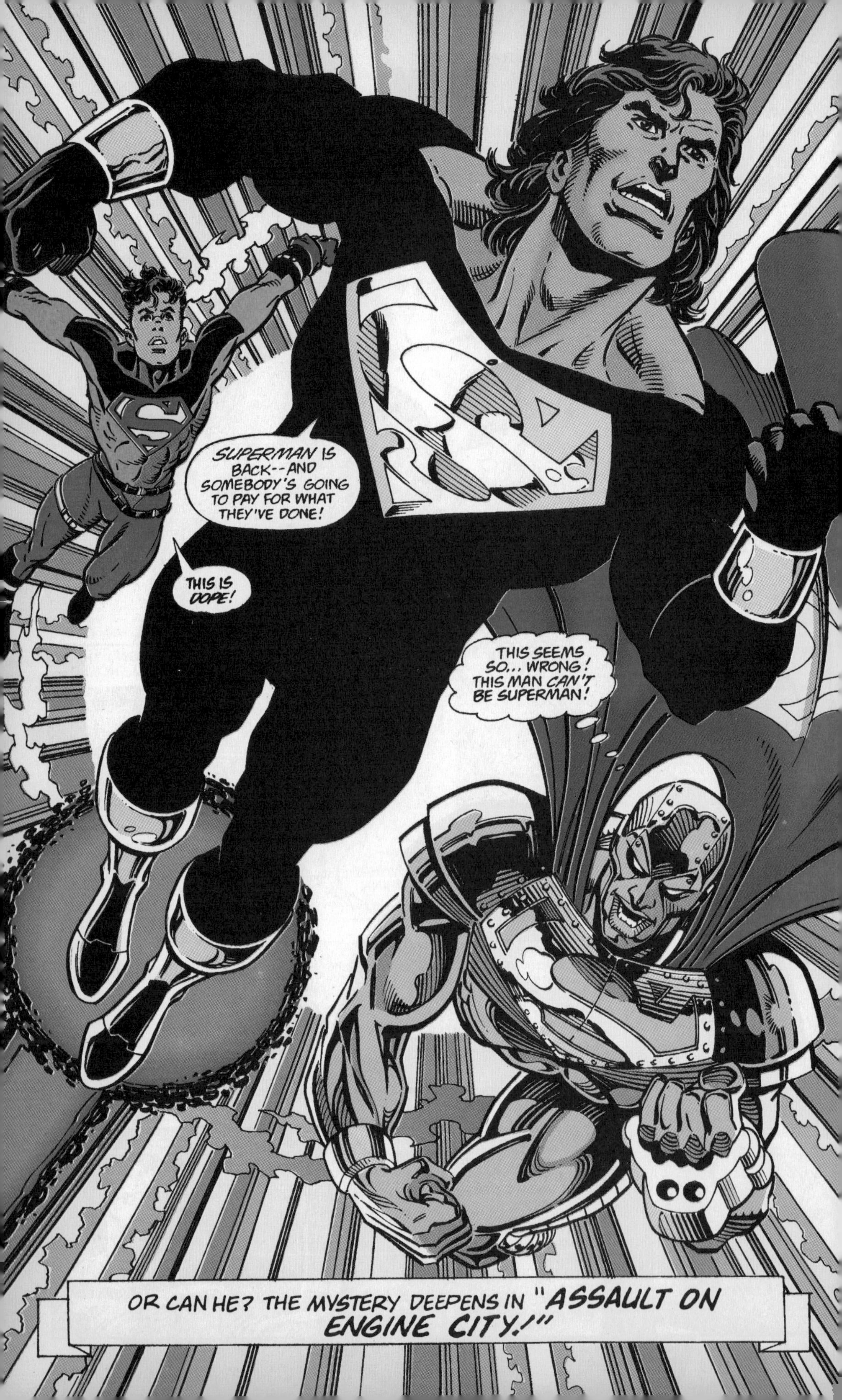
SUPERMAN IS BACK--AND SOMEBODY'S GOING TO PAY FOR WHAT THEY'VE DONE!
THIS IS DOPE!
THIS SEEMS SO... WRONG! THIS MAN CAN'T BE SUPERMAN!
OR CAN HE? THE MYSTERY DEEPENS IN "ASSAULT ON ENGINE CITY!"

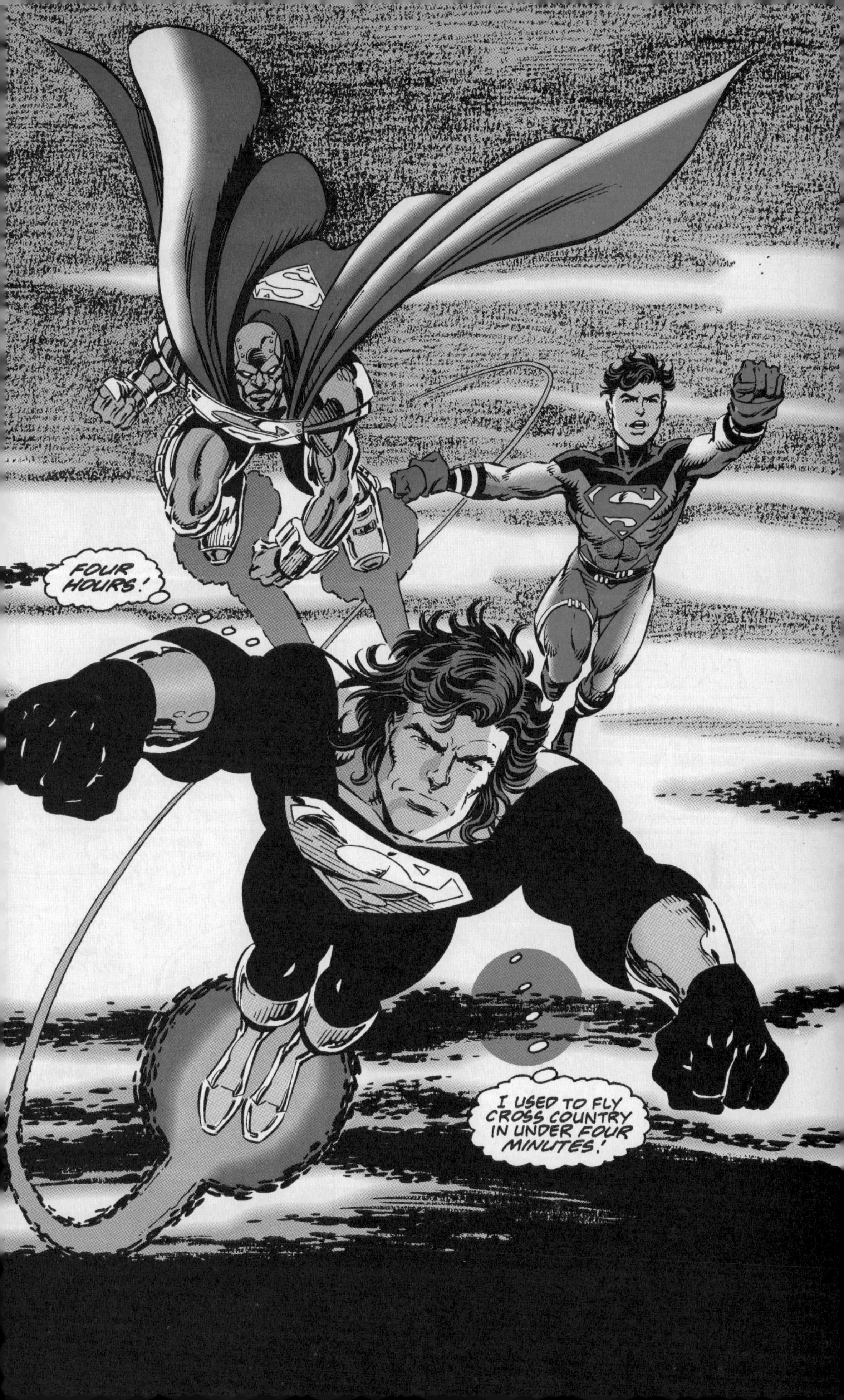
FOUR HOURS!
I USED TO FLY CROSS COUNTRY IN UNDER FOUR MINUTES!

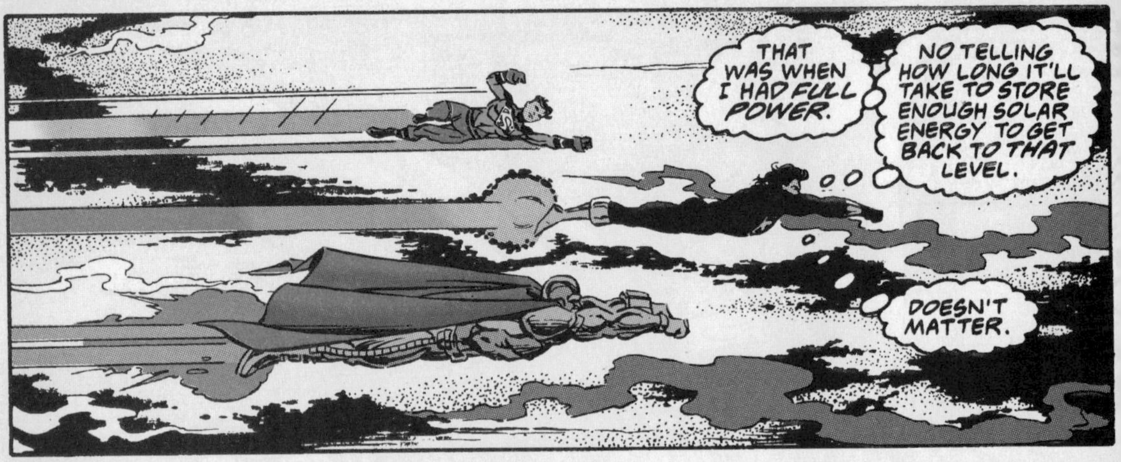
THAT WAS WHEN I HAD FULL POWER.
NO TELLING HOW LONG IT'LL TAKE TO STORE ENOUGH SOLAR ENERGY TO GET BACK TO THAT LEVEL.
DOESN'T MATTER.

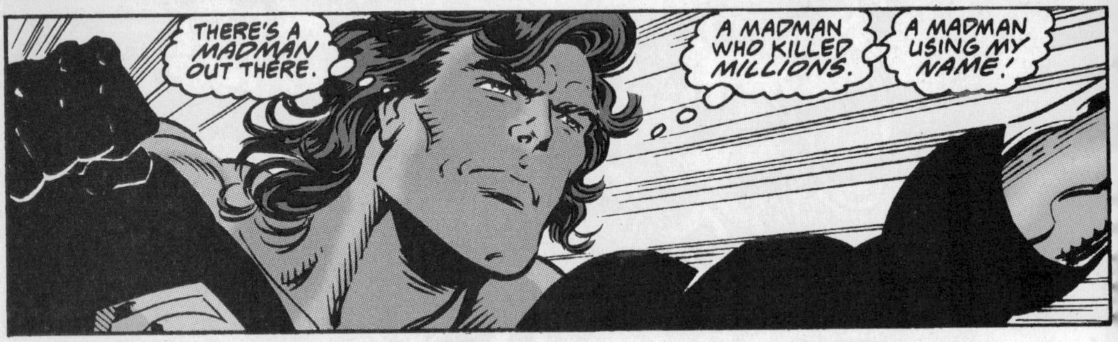
THERE'S A MADMAN OUT THERE.
A MADMAN WHO KILLED MILLIONS.
A MADMAN USING MY NAME!

ASSAULT ON ENGINE CITY!

KESEL WRITER · GRUMMETT PENCILLER · HAZLEWOOD INKER · DEGUZMAN LETTERER · WHITMORE COLORIST · PITTARESE ASSOC. EDITOR · CARLIN EDITOR

Special thanks to MARK HEIKE · SUPERMAN created by JERRY SIEGEL & JOE SHUSTER

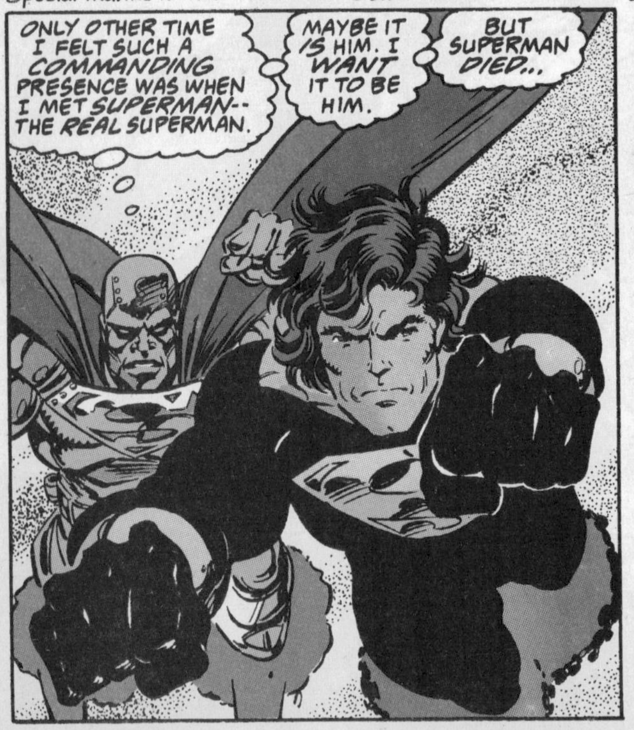
ONLY OTHER TIME I FELT SUCH A COMMANDING PRESENCE WAS WHEN I MET SUPERMAN-- THE REAL SUPERMAN.
MAYBE IT IS HIM. I WANT IT TO BE HIM.
BUT SUPERMAN DIED...

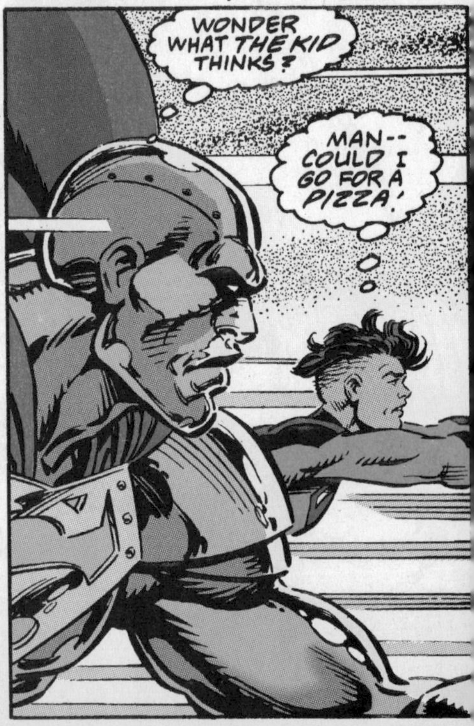
WONDER WHAT THE KID THINKS?
MAN-- COULD I GO FOR A PIZZA!

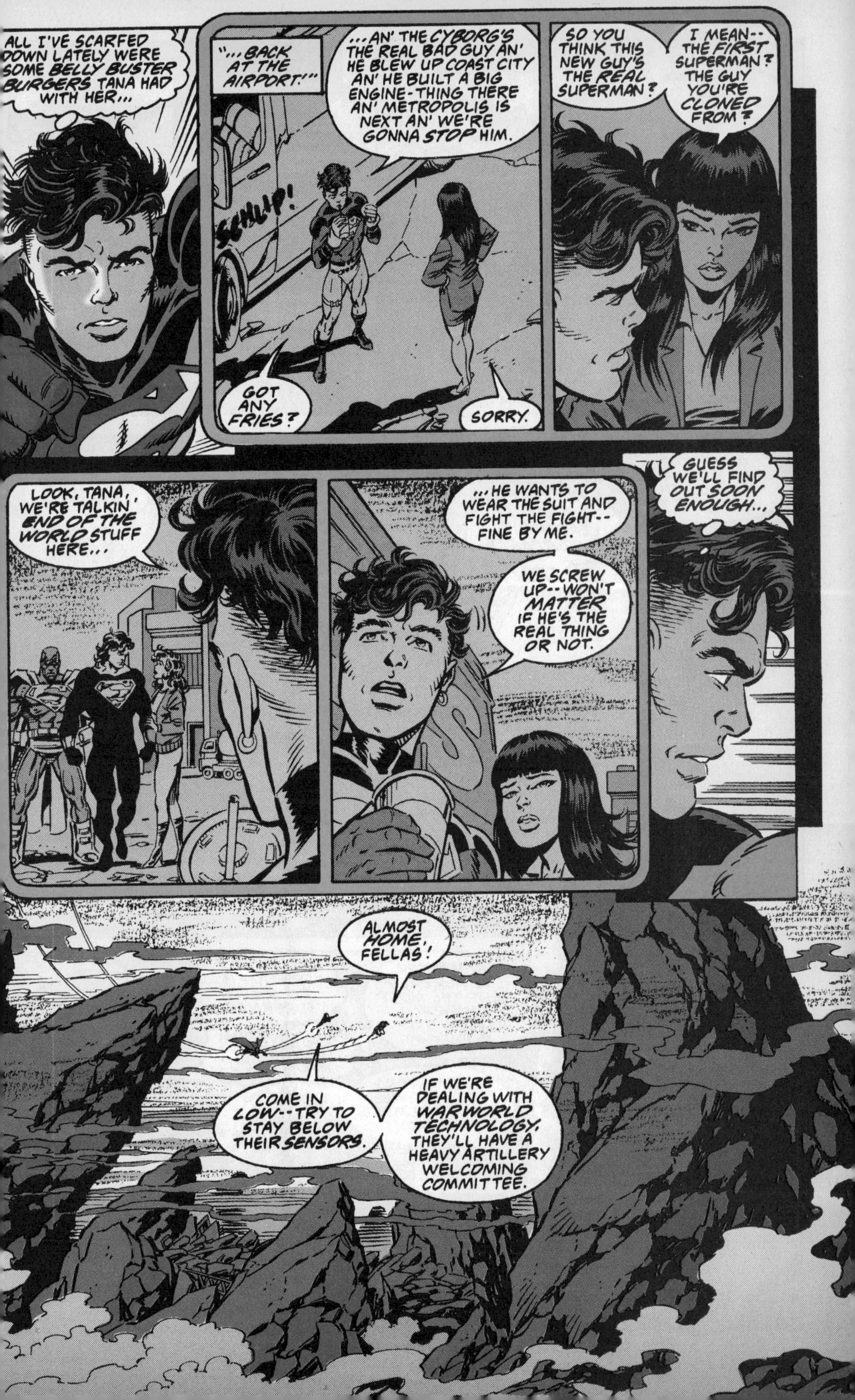
ALL I'VE SCARFED DOWN LATELY WERE SOME BELLY BUSTER BURGERS TANA HAD WITH HER...
"...BACK AT THE AIRPORT."
...AN' THE CYBORG'S THE REAL BAD GUY AN' HE BLEW UP COAST CITY AN' HE BUILT A BIG ENGINE-THING THERE AN' METROPOLIS IS NEXT AN' WE'RE GONNA STOP HIM.
SCHLUP!
GOT ANY FRIES?
SORRY.
SO YOU THINK THIS NEW GUY'S THE REAL SUPERMAN?
I MEAN-- THE FIRST SUPERMAN? THE GUY YOU'RE CLONED FROM?
LOOK, TANA, WE'RE TALKIN' END OF THE WORLD STUFF HERE...
...HE WANTS TO WEAR THE SUIT AND FIGHT THE FIGHT-- FINE BY ME.
WE SCREW UP--WON'T MATTER IF HE'S THE REAL THING OR NOT.
GUESS WE'LL FIND OUT SOON ENOUGH...
ALMOST HOME, FELLAS!
COME IN LOW--TRY TO STAY BELOW THEIR SENSORS.
IF WE'RE DEALING WITH WARWORLD TECHNOLOGY, THEY'LL HAVE A HEAVY ARTILLERY WELCOMING COMMITTEE.

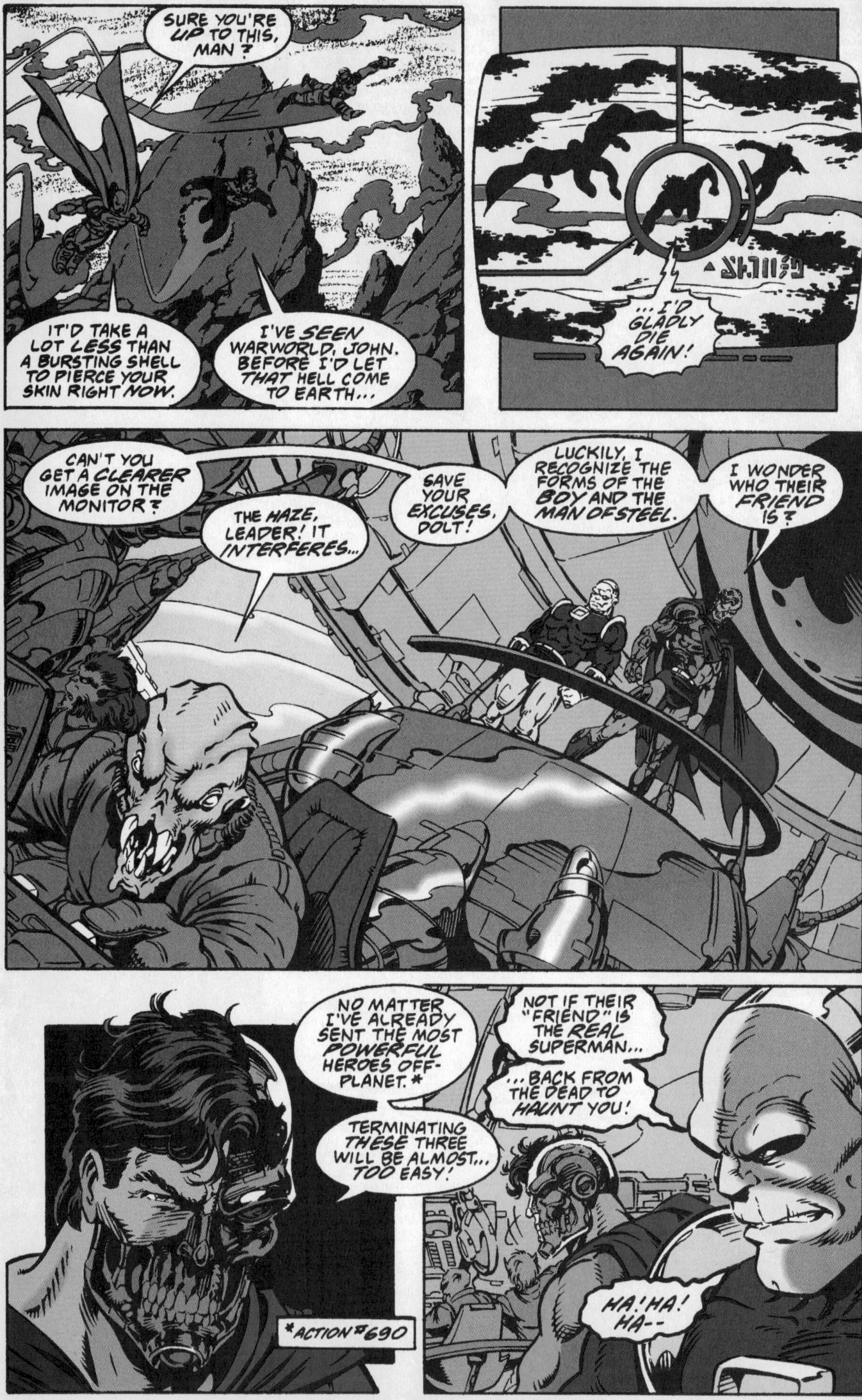
SURE YOU'RE UP TO THIS, MAN?
IT'D TAKE A LOT LESS THAN A BURSTING SHELL TO PIERCE YOUR SKIN RIGHT NOW.
I'VE SEEN WARWORLD, JOHN. BEFORE I'D LET THAT HELL COME TO EARTH...
...I'D GLADLY DIE AGAIN!
CAN'T YOU GET A CLEARER IMAGE ON THE MONITOR?
THE HAZE, LEADER! IT INTERFERES...
SAVE YOUR EXCUSES, DOLT!
LUCKILY, I RECOGNIZE THE FORMS OF THE BOY AND THE MAN OF STEEL.
I WONDER WHO THEIR FRIEND IS?
NO MATTER. I'VE ALREADY SENT THE MOST POWERFUL HEROES OFF-PLANET.*
TERMINATING THESE THREE WILL BE ALMOST... TOO EASY!
*ACTION #690
NOT IF THEIR "FRIEND" IS THE REAL SUPERMAN...
...BACK FROM THE DEAD TO HAUNT YOU!
HA! HA! HA--

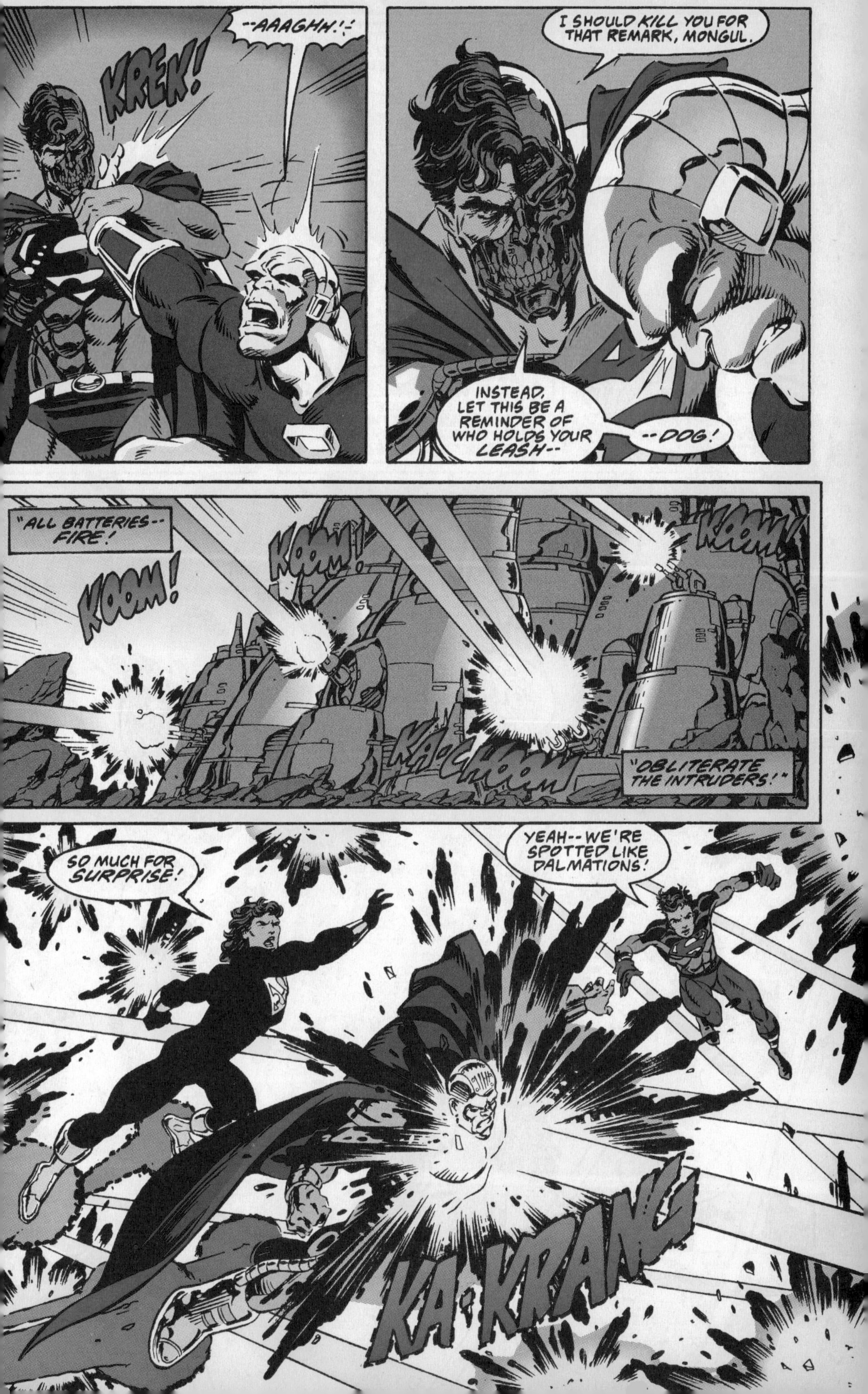
--AAAGHH!--
KREK!
I SHOULD KILL YOU FOR THAT REMARK, MONGUL.
INSTEAD, LET THIS BE A REMINDER OF WHO HOLDS YOUR LEASH--
--DOG!
"ALL BATTERIES-- FIRE!
KOOM!
KOOM!
KOOM!
KA-CHOOM
"OBLITERATE THE INTRUDERS!"
SO MUCH FOR SURPRISE!
YEAH--WE'RE SPOTTED LIKE DALMATIONS!
KA-KRANG

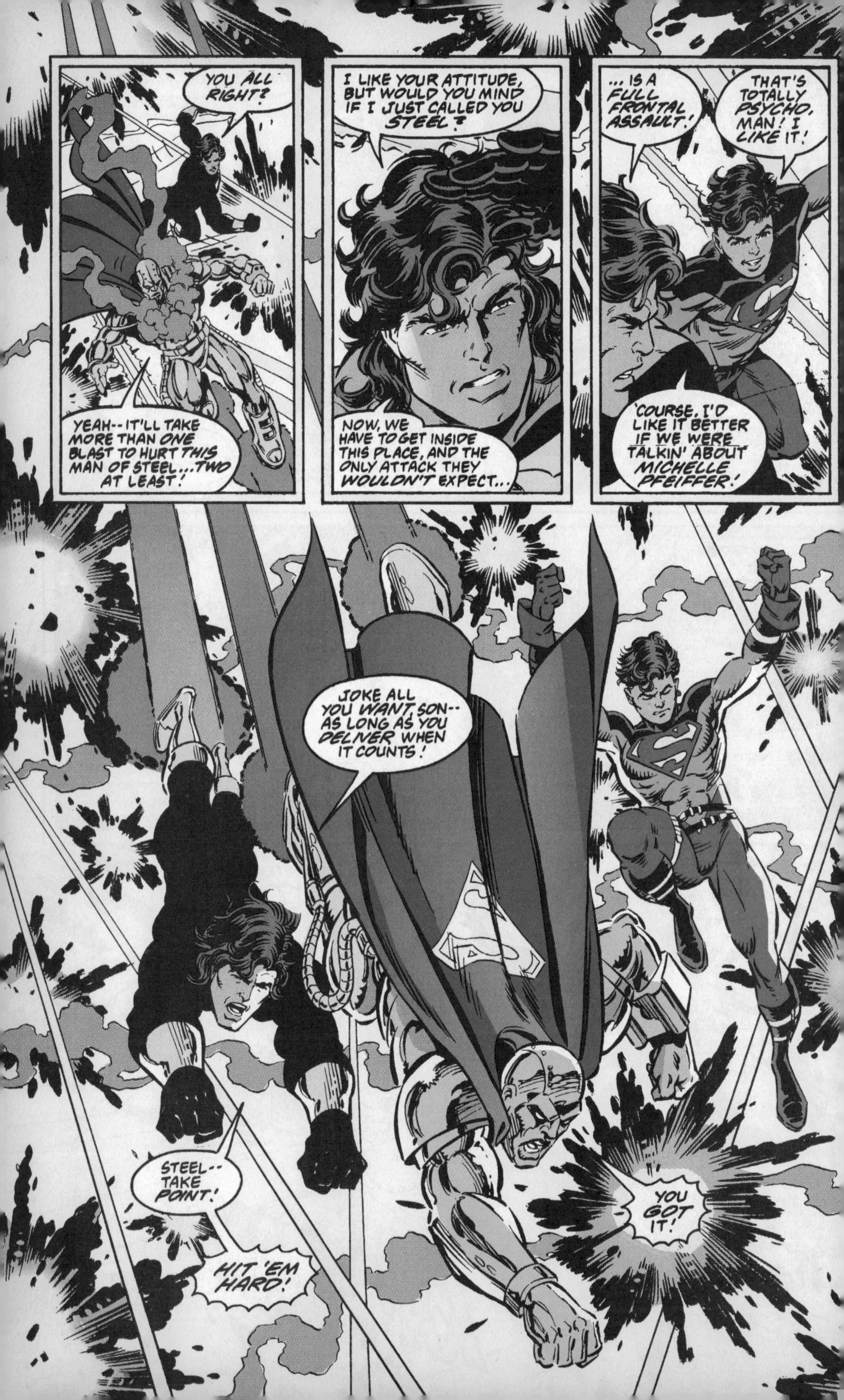
YOU ALL RIGHT?
YEAH--IT'LL TAKE MORE THAN ONE BLAST TO HURT THIS MAN OF STEEL...TWO AT LEAST!
I LIKE YOUR ATTITUDE, BUT WOULD YOU MIND IF I JUST CALLED YOU STEEL?
NOW, WE HAVE TO GET INSIDE THIS PLACE, AND THE ONLY ATTACK THEY WOULDN'T EXPECT...
...IS A FULL FRONTAL ASSAULT!
THAT'S TOTALLY PSYCHO, MAN! I LIKE IT!
'COURSE, I'D LIKE IT BETTER IF WE WERE TALKIN' ABOUT MICHELLE PFEIFFER!
JOKE ALL YOU WANT, SON-- AS LONG AS YOU DELIVER WHEN IT COUNTS!
STEEL-- TAKE POINT!
YOU GOT IT!
HIT 'EM HARD!

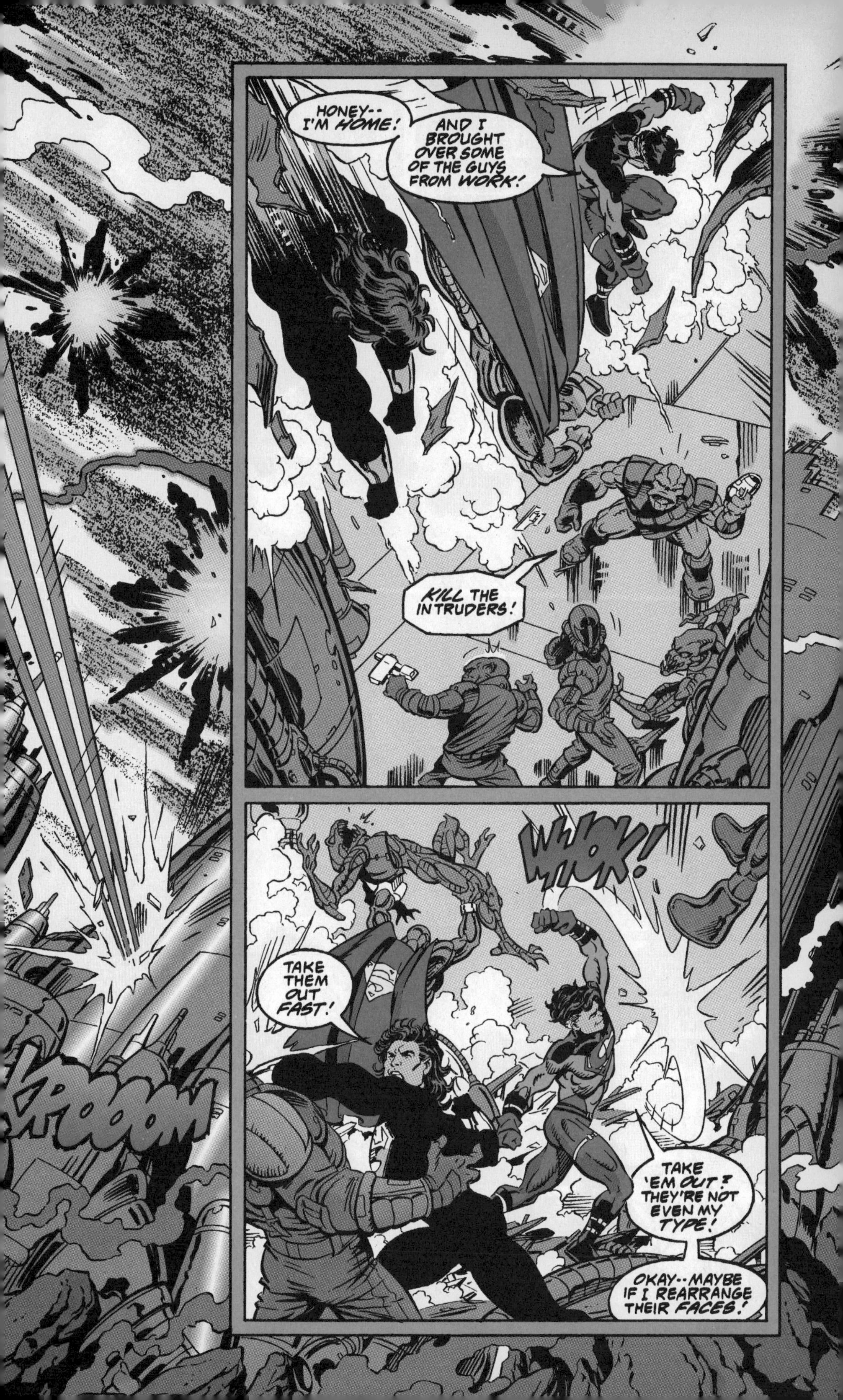
HONEY-- I'M HOME!
AND I BROUGHT OVER SOME OF THE GUYS FROM WORK!
KILL THE INTRUDERS!
TAKE THEM OUT FAST!
WHOK!
TAKE 'EM OUT? THEY'RE NOT EVEN MY TYPE!
OKAY--MAYBE IF I REARRANGE THEIR FACES!
KROOOM

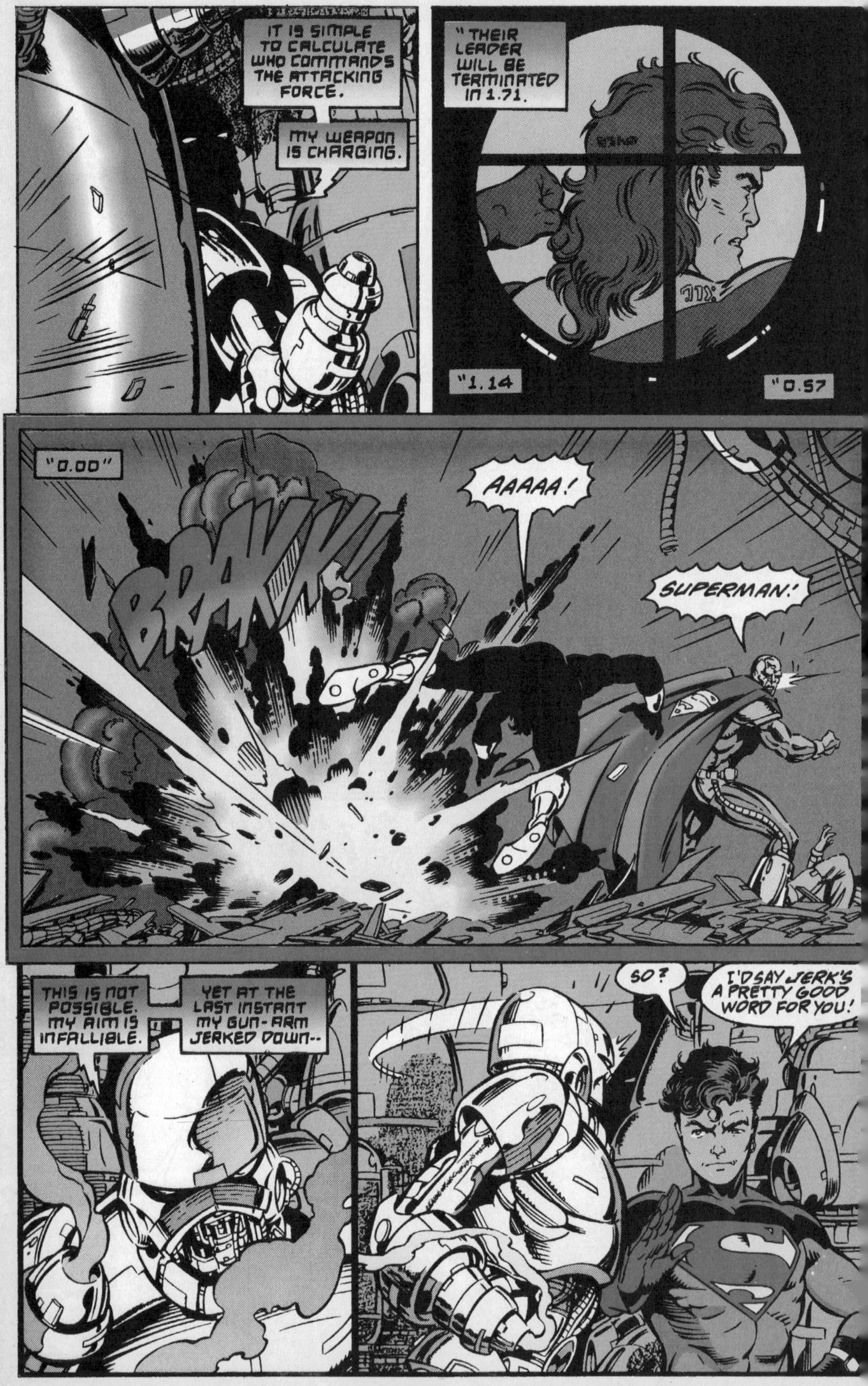

IT IS SIMPLE TO CALCULATE WHO COMMANDS THE ATTACKING FORCE.
MY WEAPON IS CHARGING.
"THEIR LEADER WILL BE TERMINATED IN 1.71.
"1.14
"0.57
"0.00"
AAAAA!
SUPERMAN!
THIS IS NOT POSSIBLE. MY AIM IS INFALLIBLE.
YET AT THE LAST INSTANT MY GUN-ARM JERKED DOWN--
SO?
I'D SAY JERK'S A PRETTY GOOD WORD FOR YOU!

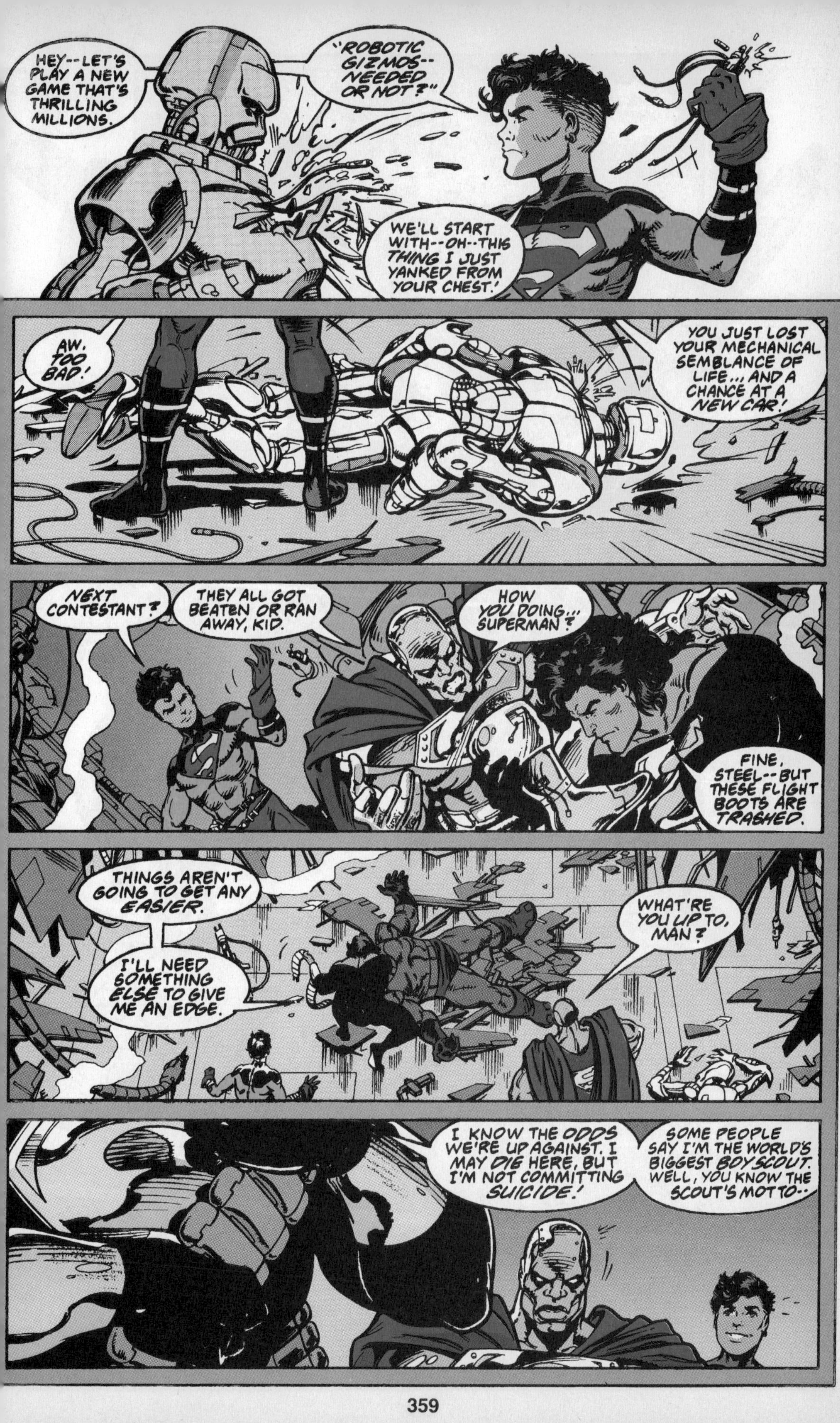
HEY--LET'S PLAY A NEW GAME THAT'S THRILLING MILLIONS.
"ROBOTIC GIZMOS--NEEDED OR NOT?"
WE'LL START WITH--OH--THIS THING I JUST YANKED FROM YOUR CHEST!
AW. TOO BAD!
YOU JUST LOST YOUR MECHANICAL SEMBLANCE OF LIFE... AND A CHANCE AT A NEW CAR!
NEXT CONTESTANT?
THEY ALL GOT BEATEN OR RAN AWAY, KID.
HOW YOU DOING... SUPERMAN?
FINE, STEEL--BUT THESE FLIGHT BOOTS ARE TRASHED.
THINGS AREN'T GOING TO GET ANY EASIER.
I'LL NEED SOMETHING ELSE TO GIVE ME AN EDGE.
WHAT'RE YOU UP TO, MAN?
I KNOW THE ODDS WE'RE UP AGAINST. I MAY DIE HERE, BUT I'M NOT COMMITTING SUICIDE!
SOME PEOPLE SAY I'M THE WORLD'S BIGGEST BOY SCOUT. WELL, YOU KNOW THE SCOUT'S MOTTO..

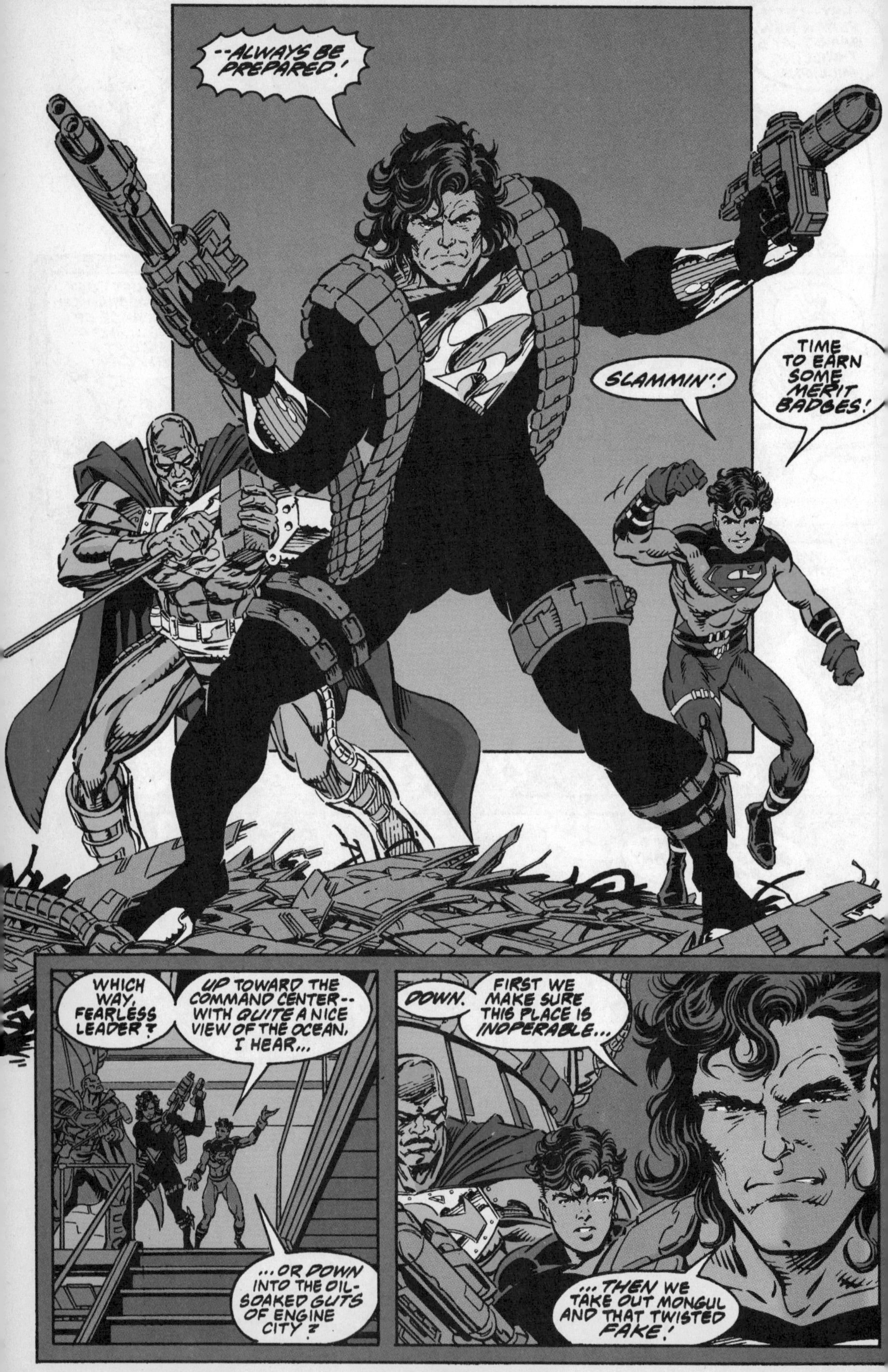
--ALWAYS BE PREPARED!
SLAMMIN'!
TIME TO EARN SOME MERIT BADGES!
WHICH WAY, FEARLESS LEADER?
UP TOWARD THE COMMAND CENTER-- WITH QUITE A NICE VIEW OF THE OCEAN, I HEAR...
...OR DOWN INTO THE OIL-SOAKED GUTS OF ENGINE CITY?
DOWN.
FIRST WE MAKE SURE THIS PLACE IS INOPERABLE...
...THEN WE TAKE OUT MONGUL AND THAT TWISTED FAKE!

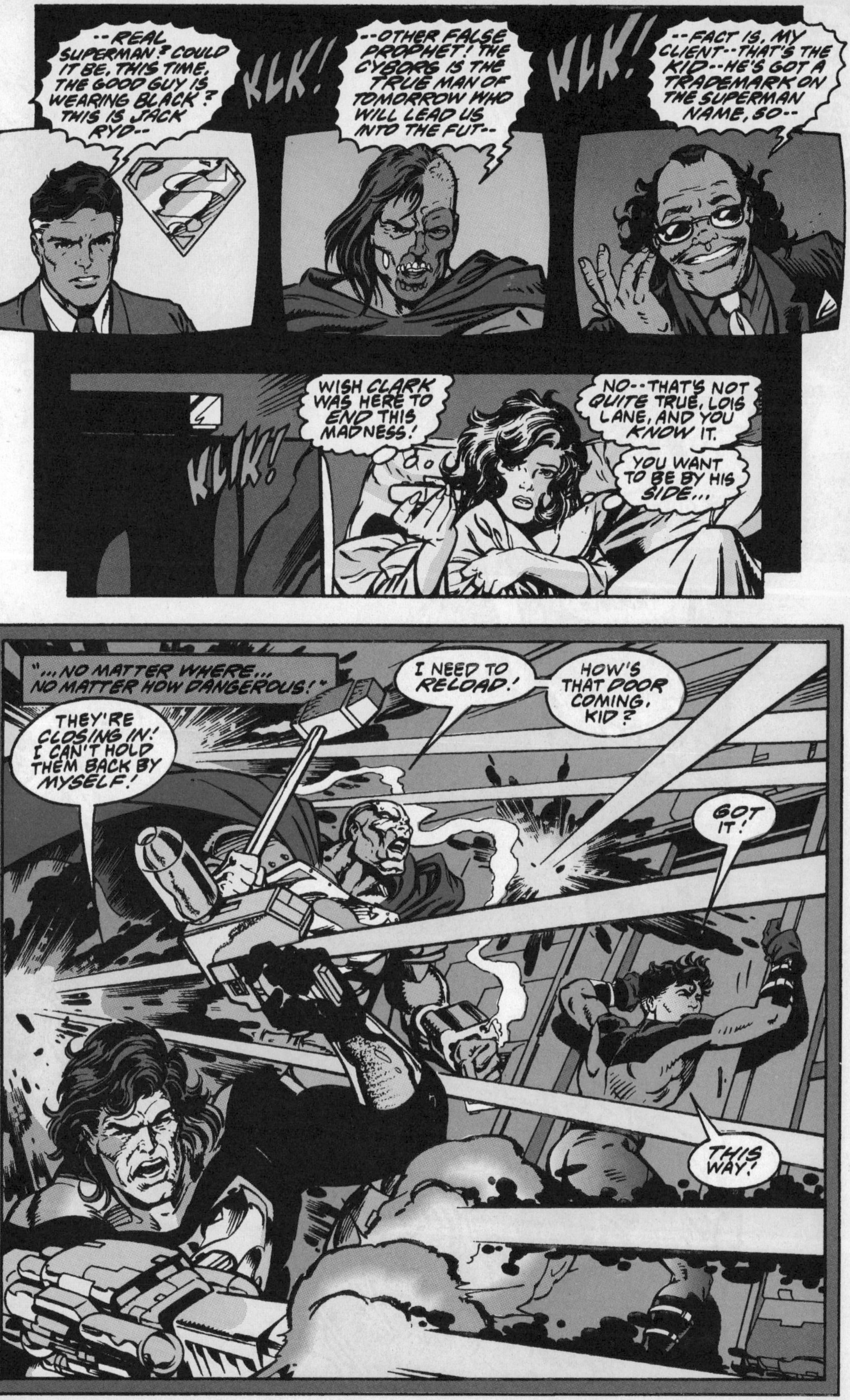
--REAL SUPERMAN? COULD IT BE, THIS TIME, THE GOOD GUY IS WEARING BLACK? THIS IS JACK RYD--
KLK!
--OTHER FALSE PROPHET! THE CYBORG IS THE TRUE MAN OF TOMORROW WHO WILL LEAD US INTO THE FUT--
KLK!
--FACT IS, MY CLIENT--THAT'S THE KID--HE'S GOT A TRADEMARK ON THE SUPERMAN NAME, SO--
KLIK!
WISH CLARK WAS HERE TO END THIS MADNESS!
NO--THAT'S NOT QUITE TRUE, LOIS LANE, AND YOU KNOW IT.
YOU WANT TO BE BY HIS SIDE...
"...NO MATTER WHERE... NO MATTER HOW DANGEROUS!"
THEY'RE CLOSING IN! I CAN'T HOLD THEM BACK BY MYSELF!
I NEED TO RELOAD!
HOW'S THAT DOOR COMING, KID?
GOT IT!
THIS WAY!

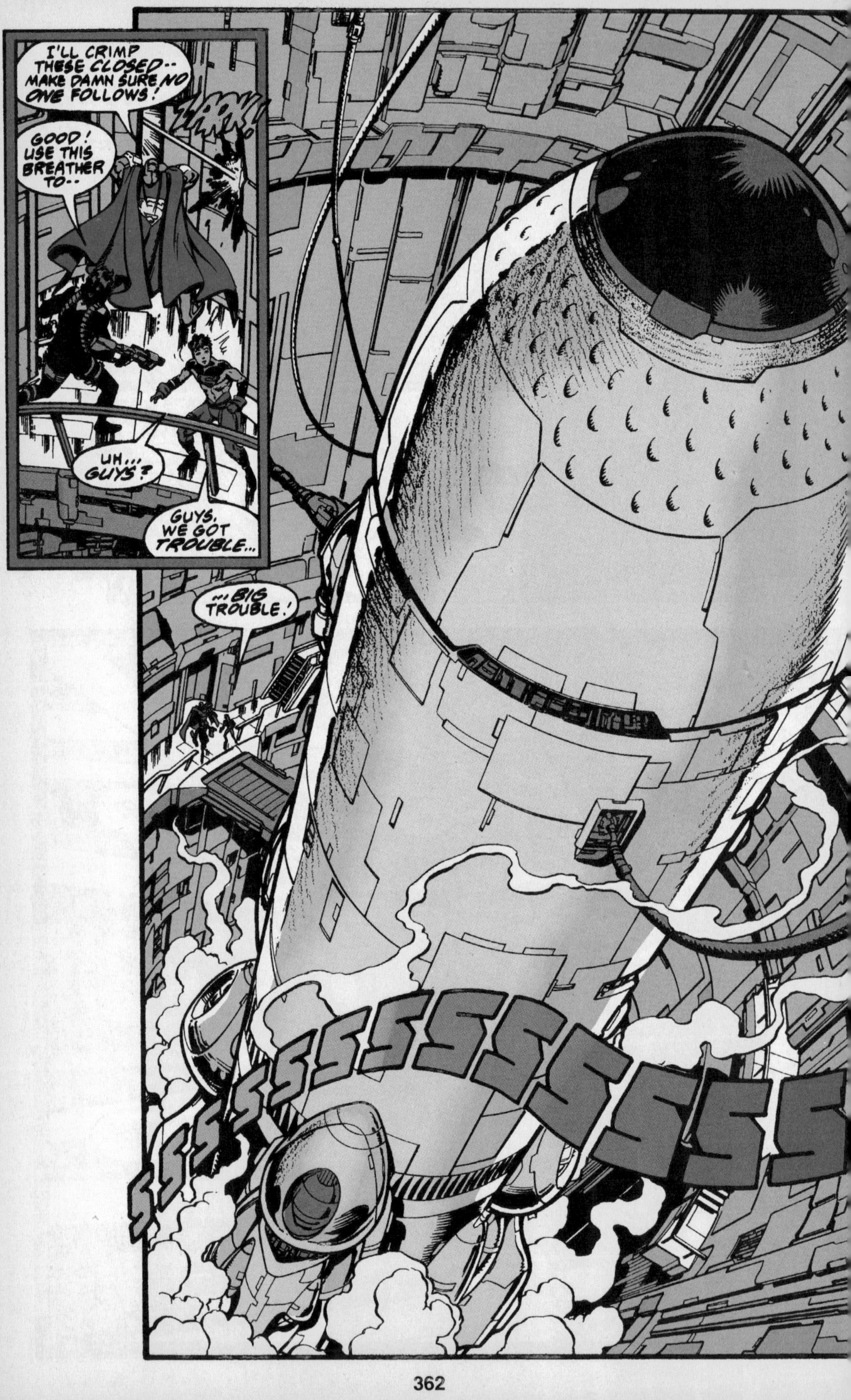
I'LL CRIMP THESE CLOSED.. MAKE DAMN SURE NO ONE FOLLOWS!
GOOD! USE THIS BREATHER TO..
UH... GUYS?
GUYS, WE GOT TROUBLE...
...BIG TROUBLE!
SSSSSSSSSSSSSSS

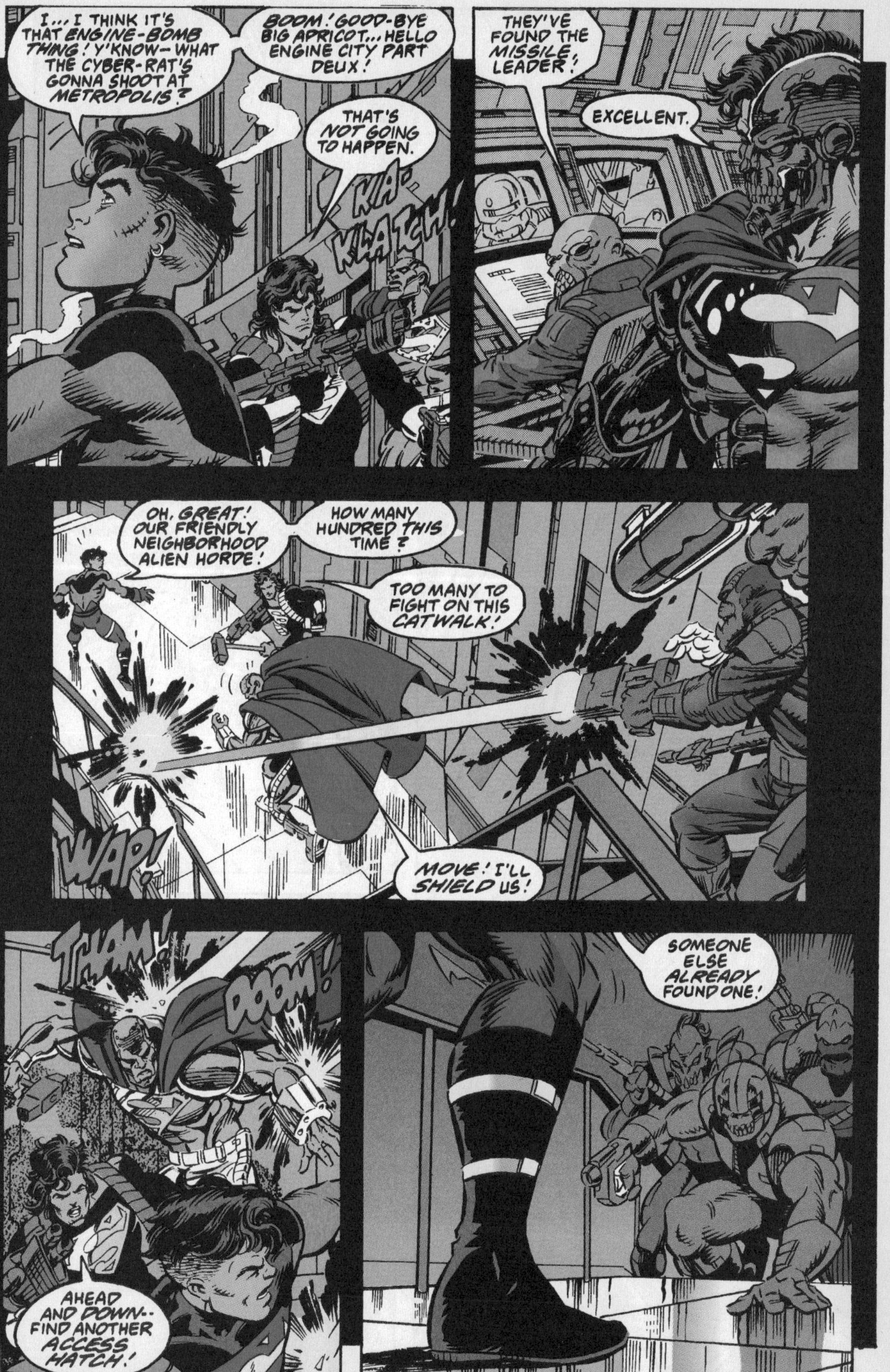
I... I THINK IT'S THAT ENGINE-BOMB THING! Y'KNOW-- WHAT THE CYBER-RAT'S GONNA SHOOT AT METROPOLIS?
BOOM! GOOD-BYE BIG APRICOT... HELLO ENGINE CITY PART DEUX!
THAT'S NOT GOING TO HAPPEN.
KA-KLATCH!
THEY'VE FOUND THE MISSILE, LEADER!
EXCELLENT.
OH, GREAT! OUR FRIENDLY NEIGHBORHOOD ALIEN HORDE!
HOW MANY HUNDRED THIS TIME?
TOO MANY TO FIGHT ON THIS CATWALK!
WAP!
MOVE! I'LL SHIELD US!
THAM!
DOOM!
AHEAD AND DOWN-- FIND ANOTHER ACCESS HATCH!
SOMEONE ELSE ALREADY FOUND ONE!

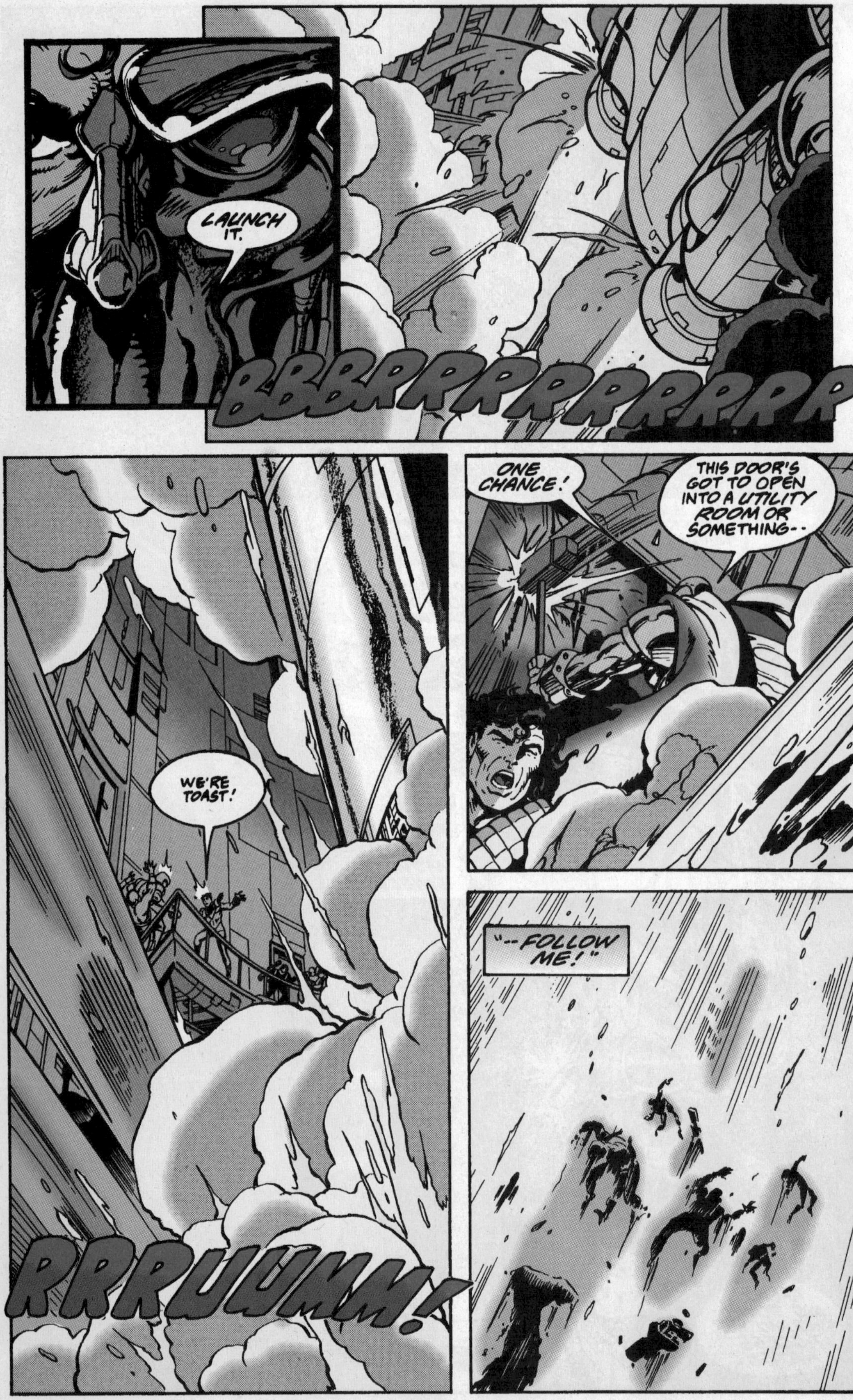
LAUNCH IT.
BBBRRRRRRRRRRR
WE'RE TOAST!
RRRUUMM!
ONE CHANCE!
THIS DOOR'S GOT TO OPEN INTO A UTILITY ROOM OR SOMETHING--
"--FOLLOW ME!"

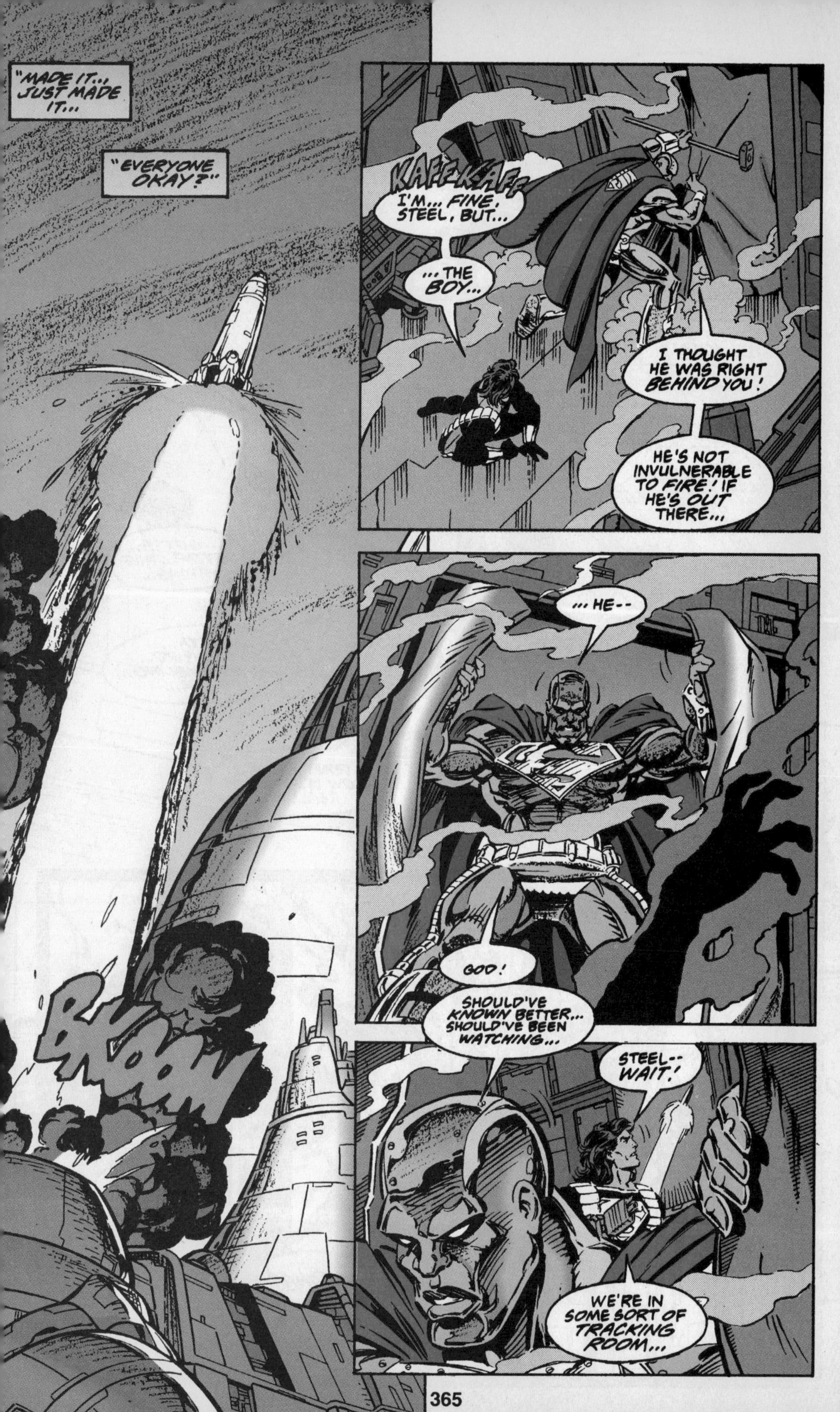
"MADE IT... JUST MADE IT...
"EVERYONE OKAY?"
KAFF KAFF
I'M... FINE, STEEL, BUT...
...THE BOY...
I THOUGHT HE WAS RIGHT BEHIND YOU!
HE'S NOT INVULNERABLE TO FIRE! IF HE'S OUT THERE...
...HE--
GOD!
SHOULD'VE KNOWN BETTER... SHOULD'VE BEEN WATCHING...
STEEL-- WAIT!
WE'RE IN SOME SORT OF TRACKING ROOM...

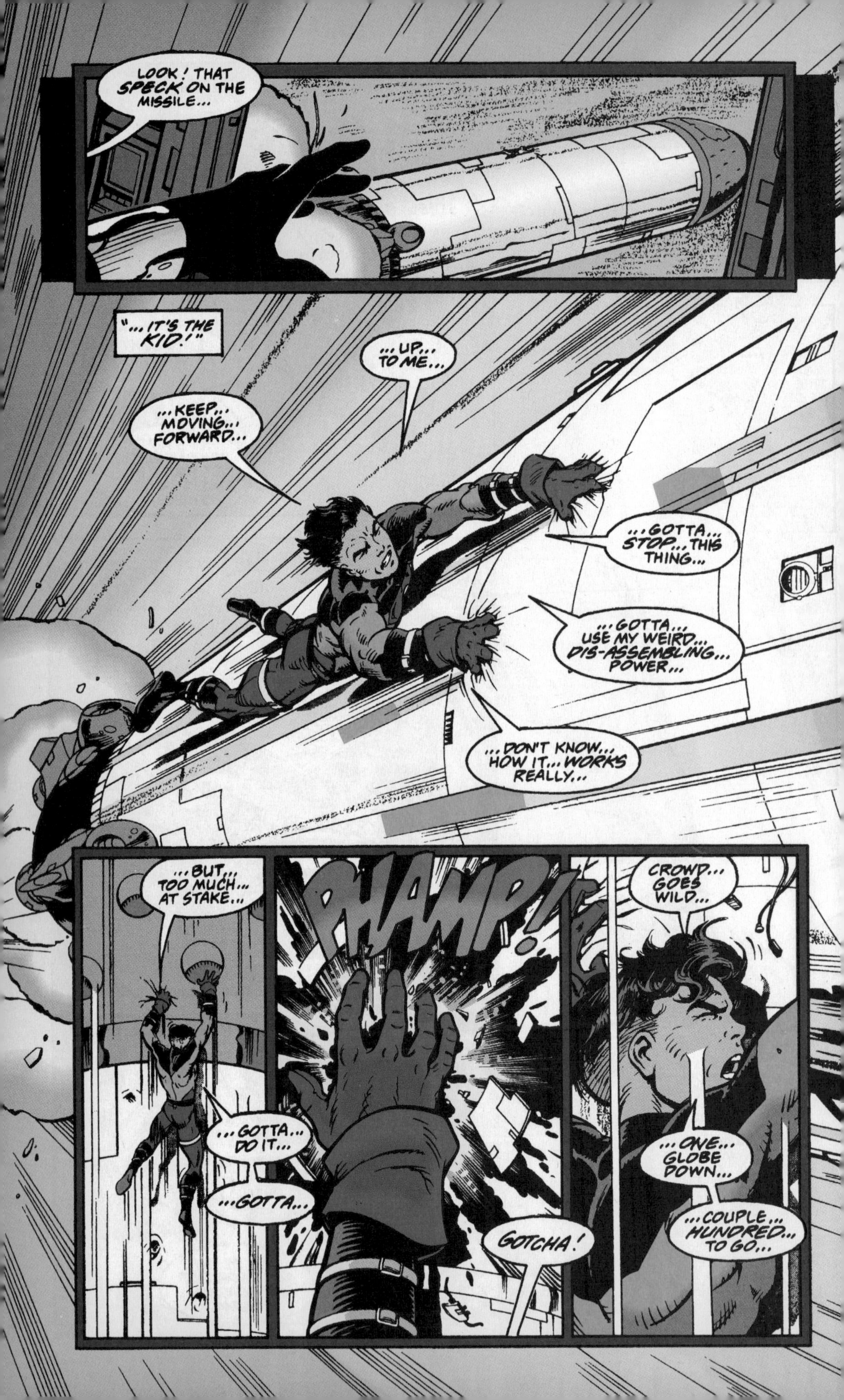
LOOK! THAT SPECK ON THE MISSILE...
"...IT'S THE KID!"
...UP... TO ME...
...KEEP... MOVING... FORWARD...
...GOTTA... STOP... THIS THING...
...GOTTA... USE MY WEIRD... DIS-ASSEMBLING... POWER...
...DON'T KNOW... HOW IT... WORKS REALLY...
...BUT... TOO MUCH... AT STAKE...
...GOTTA... DO IT...
...GOTTA...
PHAMP!
GOTCHA!
CROWD... GOES WILD...
...ONE... GLOBE DOWN...
...COUPLE... HUNDRED... TO GO...

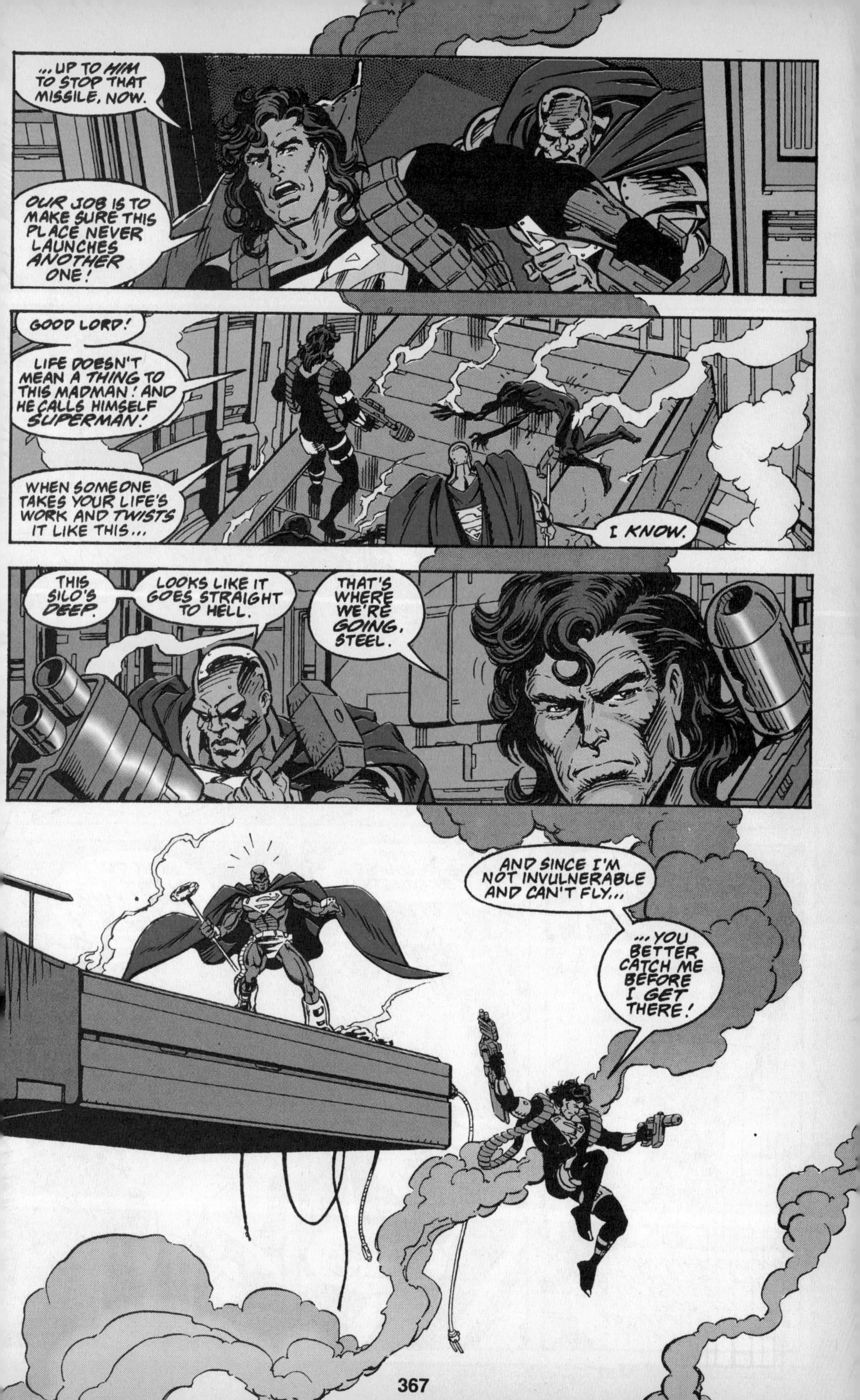
...UP TO HIM TO STOP THAT MISSILE, NOW.
OUR JOB IS TO MAKE SURE THIS PLACE NEVER LAUNCHES ANOTHER ONE!
GOOD LORD!
LIFE DOESN'T MEAN A THING TO THIS MADMAN! AND HE CALLS HIMSELF SUPERMAN!
WHEN SOMEONE TAKES YOUR LIFE'S WORK AND TWISTS IT LIKE THIS...
I KNOW.
THIS SILO'S DEEP.
LOOKS LIKE IT GOES STRAIGHT TO HELL.
THAT'S WHERE WE'RE GOING, STEEL.
AND SINCE I'M NOT INVULNERABLE AND CAN'T FLY...
...YOU BETTER CATCH ME BEFORE I GET THERE!

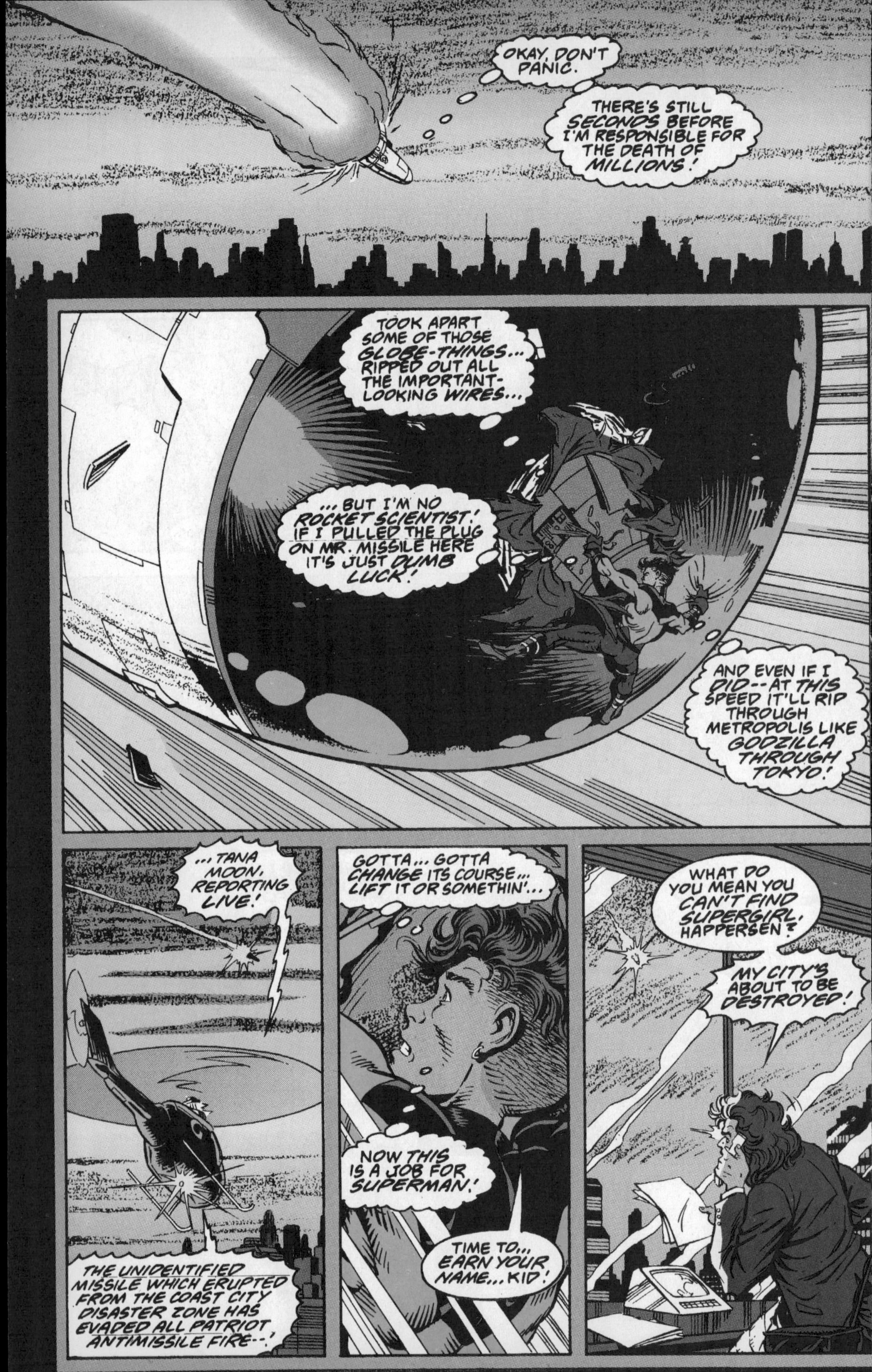
OKAY, DON'T PANIC.
THERE'S STILL SECONDS BEFORE I'M RESPONSIBLE FOR THE DEATH OF MILLIONS!
TOOK APART SOME OF THOSE GLOBE-THINGS... RIPPED OUT ALL THE IMPORTANT-LOOKING WIRES...
...BUT I'M NO ROCKET SCIENTIST! IF I PULLED THE PLUG ON MR. MISSILE HERE IT'S JUST DUMB LUCK!
AND EVEN IF I DID--AT THIS SPEED IT'LL RIP THROUGH METROPOLIS LIKE GODZILLA THROUGH TOKYO!
...TANA MOON, REPORTING LIVE!
THE UNIDENTIFIED MISSILE WHICH ERUPTED FROM THE COAST CITY DISASTER ZONE HAS EVADED ALL PATRIOT ANTIMISSILE FIRE--!
GOTTA... GOTTA CHANGE ITS COURSE... LIFT IT OR SOMETHIN'...
NOW THIS IS A JOB FOR SUPERMAN!
TIME TO... EARN YOUR NAME... KID!
WHAT DO YOU MEAN YOU CAN'T FIND SUPERGIRL, HAPPERSEN?
MY CITY'S ABOUT TO BE DESTROYED!

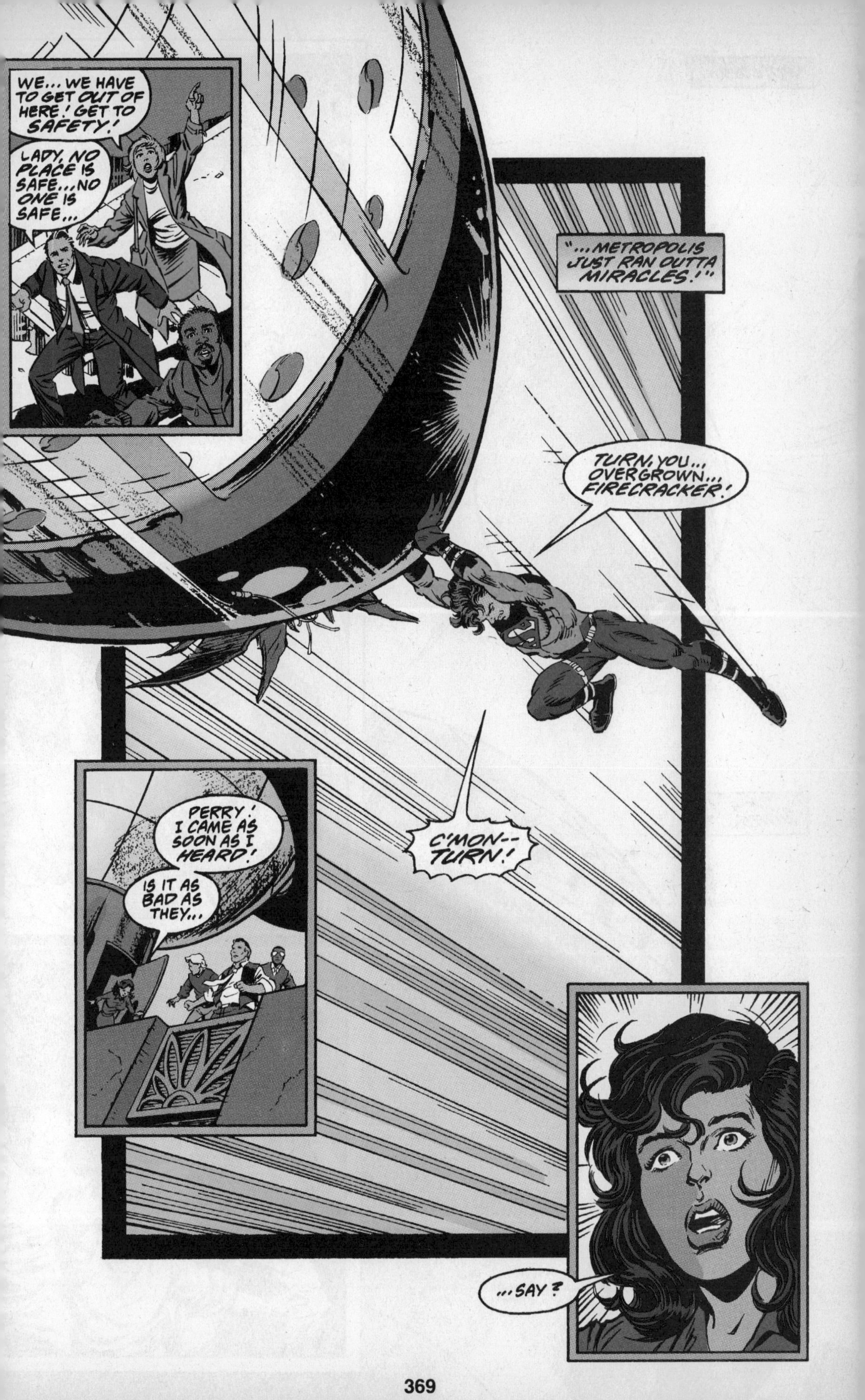
WE... WE HAVE TO GET OUT OF HERE! GET TO SAFETY!
LADY, NO PLACE IS SAFE... NO ONE IS SAFE...
"...METROPOLIS JUST RAN OUTTA MIRACLES!"
TURN, YOU... OVERGROWN... FIRECRACKER!
C'MON-- TURN!
PERRY! I CAME AS SOON AS I HEARD!
IS IT AS BAD AS THEY...
...SAY?

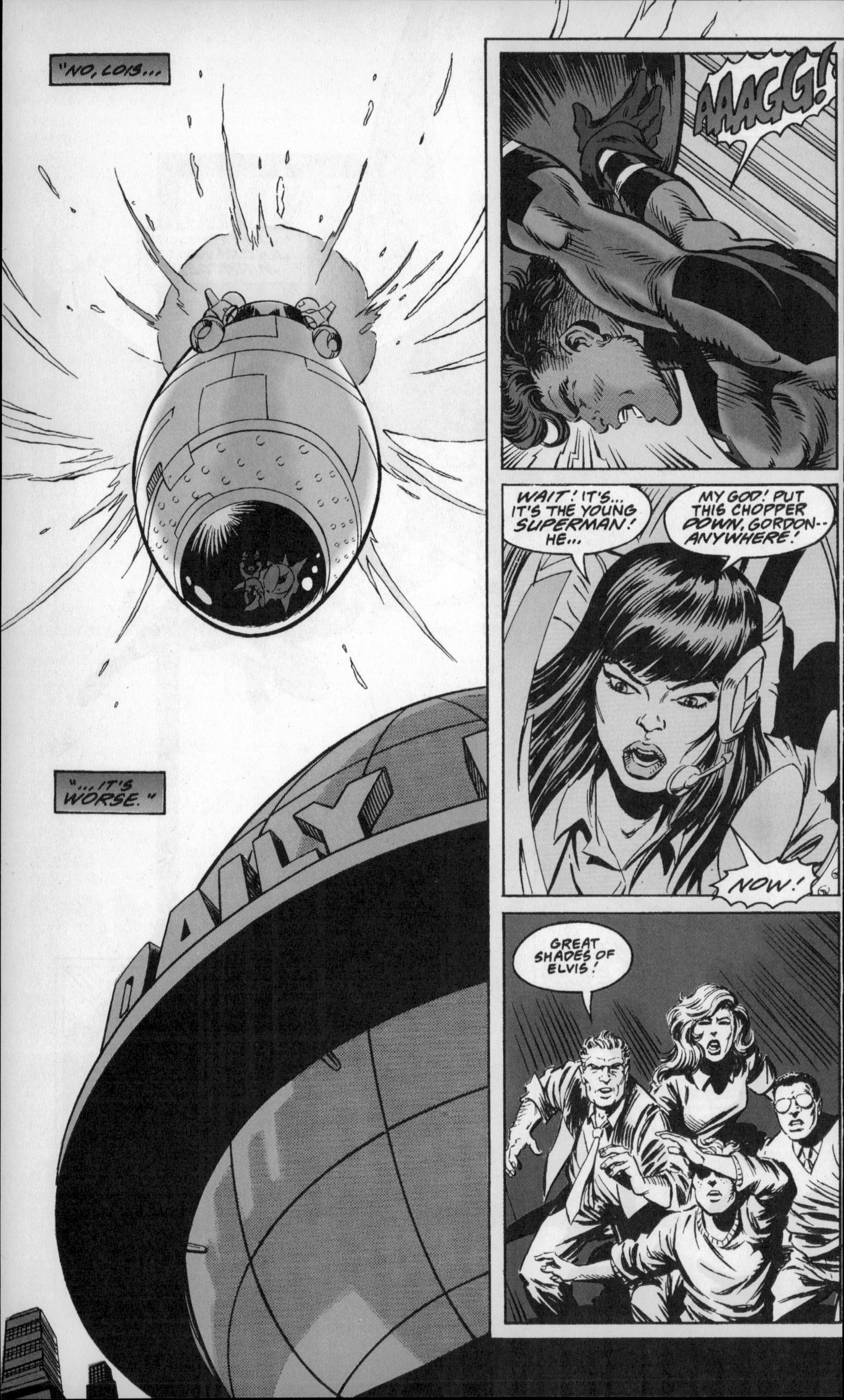
"NO, LOIS...
AAAGG!
WAIT! IT'S... IT'S THE YOUNG SUPERMAN! HE...
MY GOD! PUT THIS CHOPPER DOWN, GORDON-- ANYWHERE!
NOW!
"...IT'S WORSE."
DAILY
GREAT SHADES OF ELVIS!

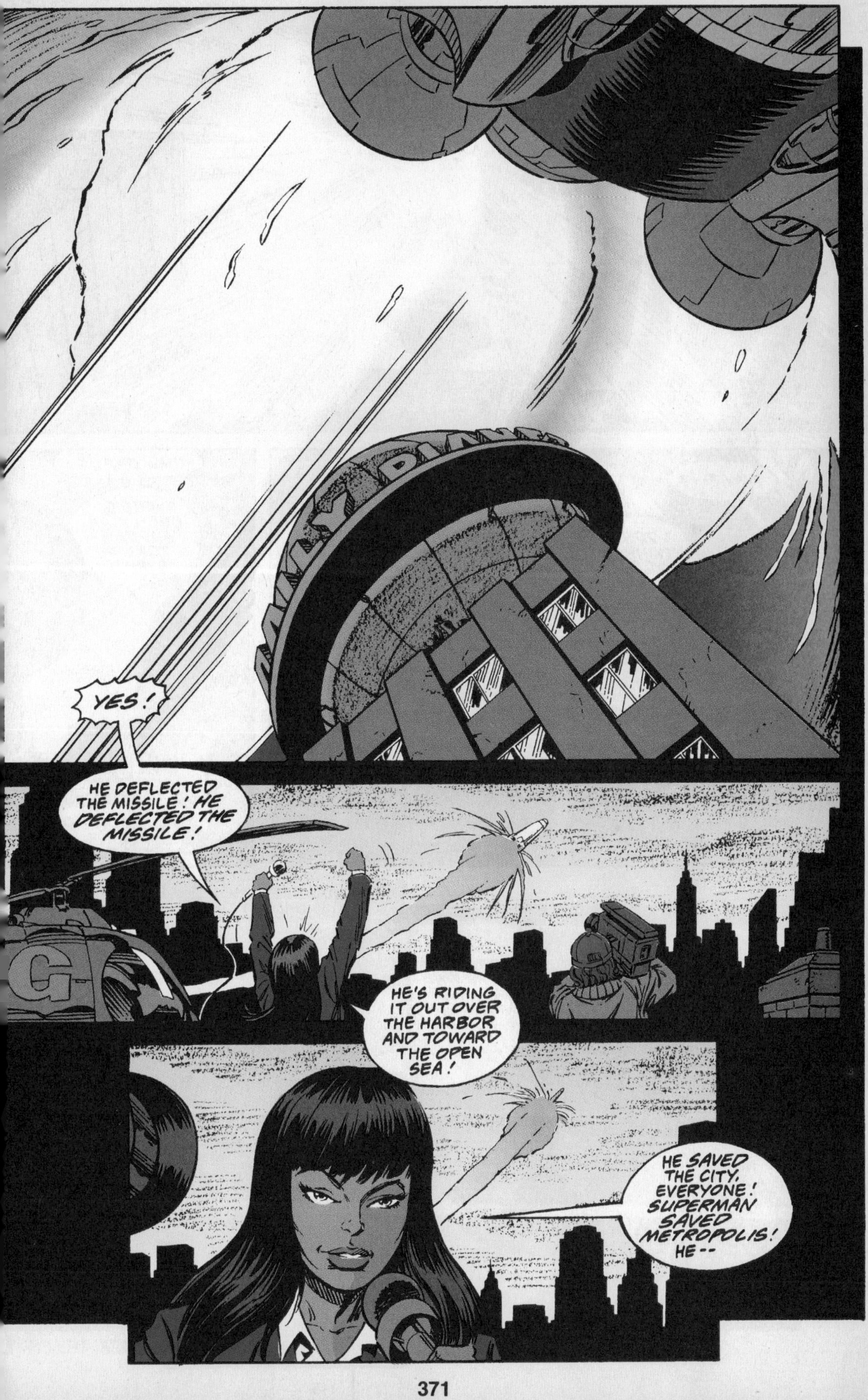
YES!
HE DEFLECTED THE MISSILE! HE DEFLECTED THE MISSILE!
HE'S RIDING IT OUT OVER THE HARBOR AND TOWARD THE OPEN SEA!
HE SAVED THE CITY, EVERYONE! SUPERMAN SAVED METROPOLIS! HE--

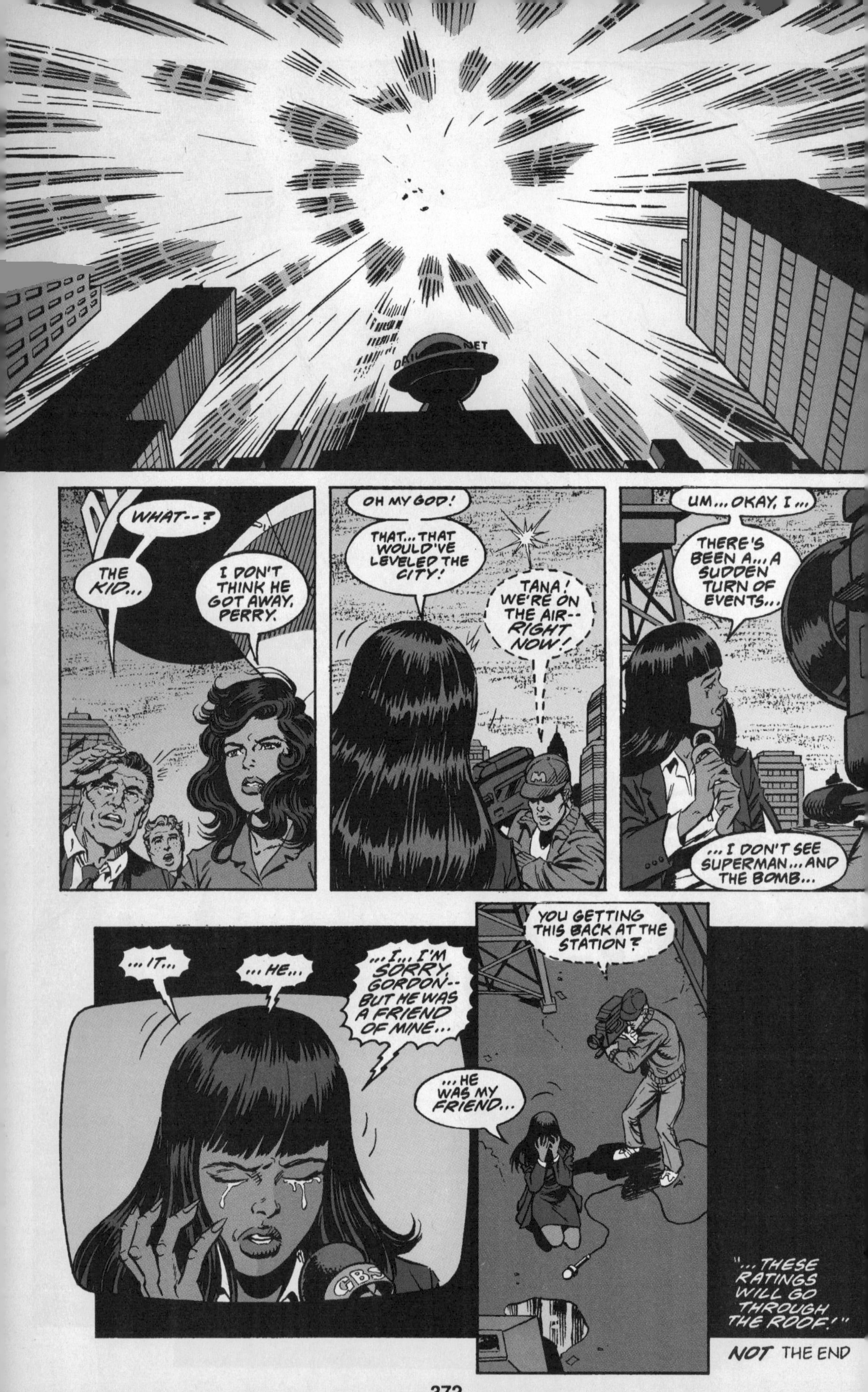
DAILY PLANET
WHAT--?
THE KID...
I DON'T THINK HE GOT AWAY, PERRY.
OH MY GOD!
THAT... THAT WOULD'VE LEVELED THE CITY!
TANA! WE'RE ON THE AIR-- RIGHT NOW!
UM... OKAY, I...
THERE'S BEEN A... A SUDDEN TURN OF EVENTS...
...I DON'T SEE SUPERMAN... AND THE BOMB...
...IT...
...HE...
...I... I'M SORRY, GORDON-- BUT HE WAS A FRIEND OF MINE...
YOU GETTING THIS BACK AT THE STATION?
...HE WAS MY FRIEND...
"...THESE RATINGS WILL GO THROUGH THE ROOF!"
NOT THE END

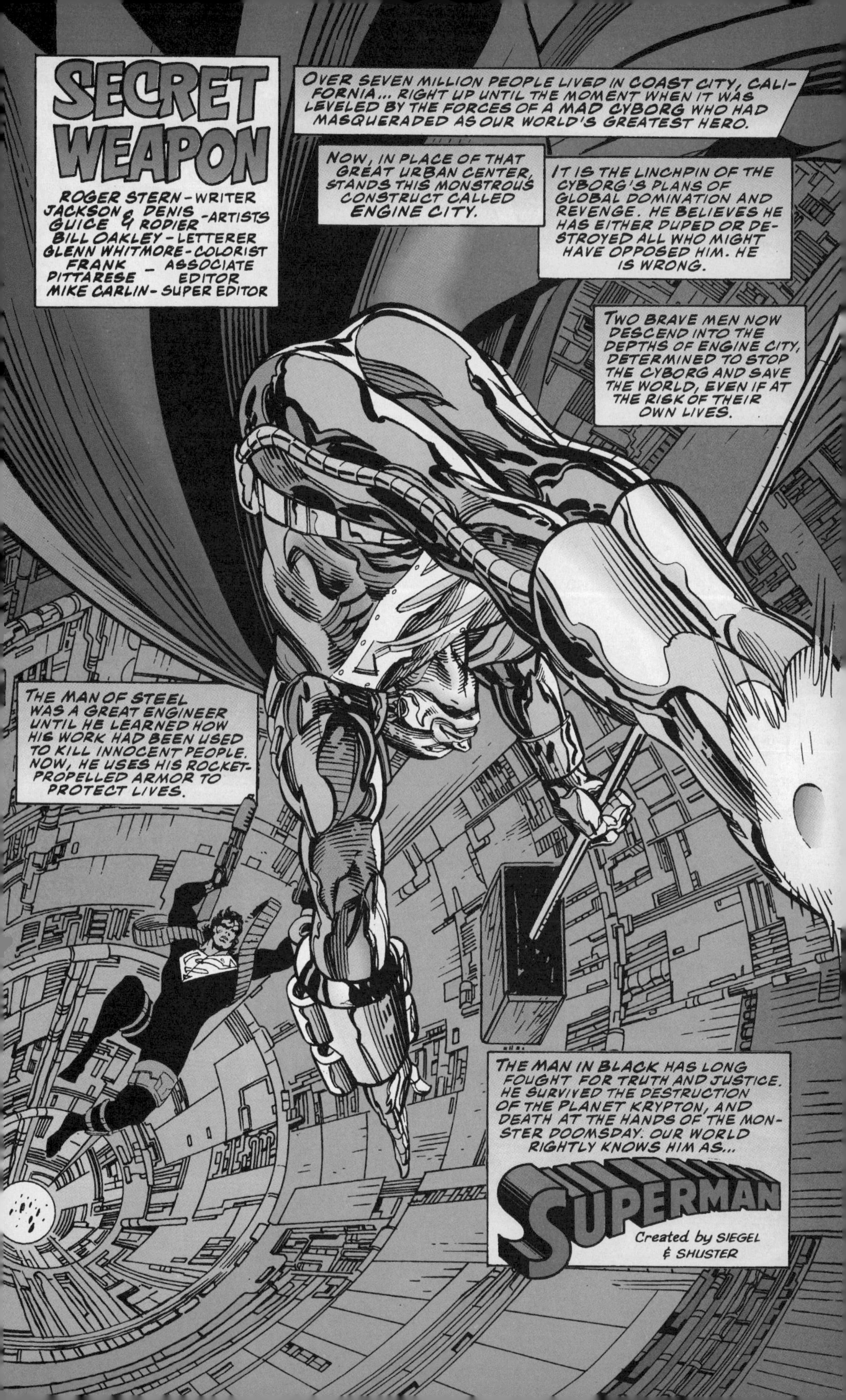
SECRET WEAPON
ROGER STERN - WRITER
JACKSON GUICE & DENIS RODIER - ARTISTS
BILL OAKLEY - LETTERER
GLENN WHITMORE - COLORIST
FRANK PITTARESE - ASSOCIATE EDITOR
MIKE CARLIN - SUPER EDITOR
OVER SEVEN MILLION PEOPLE LIVED IN COAST CITY, CALIFORNIA... RIGHT UP UNTIL THE MOMENT WHEN IT WAS LEVELED BY THE FORCES OF A MAD CYBORG WHO HAD MASQUERADED AS OUR WORLD'S GREATEST HERO.
NOW, IN PLACE OF THAT GREAT URBAN CENTER, STANDS THIS MONSTROUS CONSTRUCT CALLED ENGINE CITY.
IT IS THE LINCHPIN OF THE CYBORG'S PLANS OF GLOBAL DOMINATION AND REVENGE. HE BELIEVES HE HAS EITHER DUPED OR DESTROYED ALL WHO MIGHT HAVE OPPOSED HIM. HE IS WRONG.
TWO BRAVE MEN NOW DESCEND INTO THE DEPTHS OF ENGINE CITY, DETERMINED TO STOP THE CYBORG AND SAVE THE WORLD, EVEN IF AT THE RISK OF THEIR OWN LIVES.
THE MAN OF STEEL WAS A GREAT ENGINEER UNTIL HE LEARNED HOW HIS WORK HAD BEEN USED TO KILL INNOCENT PEOPLE. NOW, HE USES HIS ROCKET-PROPELLED ARMOR TO PROTECT LIVES.
THE MAN IN BLACK HAS LONG FOUGHT FOR TRUTH AND JUSTICE. HE SURVIVED THE DESTRUCTION OF THE PLANET KRYPTON, AND DEATH AT THE HANDS OF THE MONSTER DOOMSDAY. OUR WORLD RIGHTLY KNOWS HIM AS...
SUPERMAN
Created by SIEGEL & SHUSTER

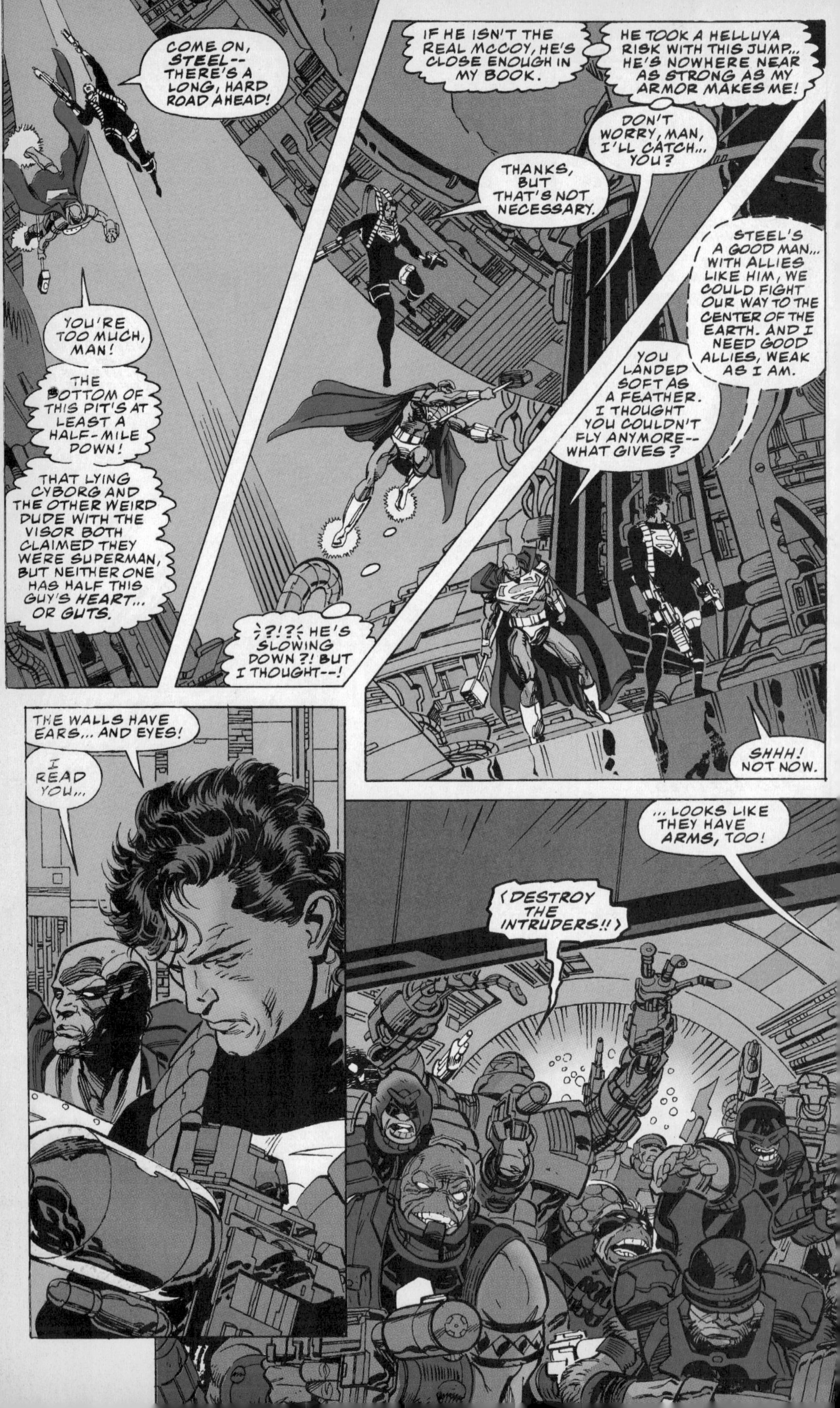
COME ON, STEEL-- THERE'S A LONG, HARD ROAD AHEAD!
YOU'RE TOO MUCH, MAN!
THE BOTTOM OF THIS PIT'S AT LEAST A HALF-MILE DOWN!
THAT LYING CYBORG AND THE OTHER WEIRD DUDE WITH THE VISOR BOTH CLAIMED THEY WERE SUPERMAN, BUT NEITHER ONE HAS HALF THIS GUY'S HEART... OR GUTS.
IF HE ISN'T THE REAL McCOY, HE'S CLOSE ENOUGH IN MY BOOK.
HE TOOK A HELLUVA RISK WITH THIS JUMP... HE'S NOWHERE NEAR AS STRONG AS MY ARMOR MAKES ME!
DON'T WORRY, MAN, I'LL CATCH... YOU?
THANKS, BUT THAT'S NOT NECESSARY.
?!?! HE'S SLOWING DOWN?! BUT I THOUGHT--!
STEEL'S A GOOD MAN... WITH ALLIES LIKE HIM, WE COULD FIGHT OUR WAY TO THE CENTER OF THE EARTH. AND I NEED GOOD ALLIES, WEAK AS I AM.
YOU LANDED SOFT AS A FEATHER. I THOUGHT YOU COULDN'T FLY ANYMORE-- WHAT GIVES?
SHHH! NOT NOW.
THE WALLS HAVE EARS... AND EYES!
I READ YOU...
...LOOKS LIKE THEY HAVE ARMS, TOO!
‹DESTROY THE INTRUDERS!!›

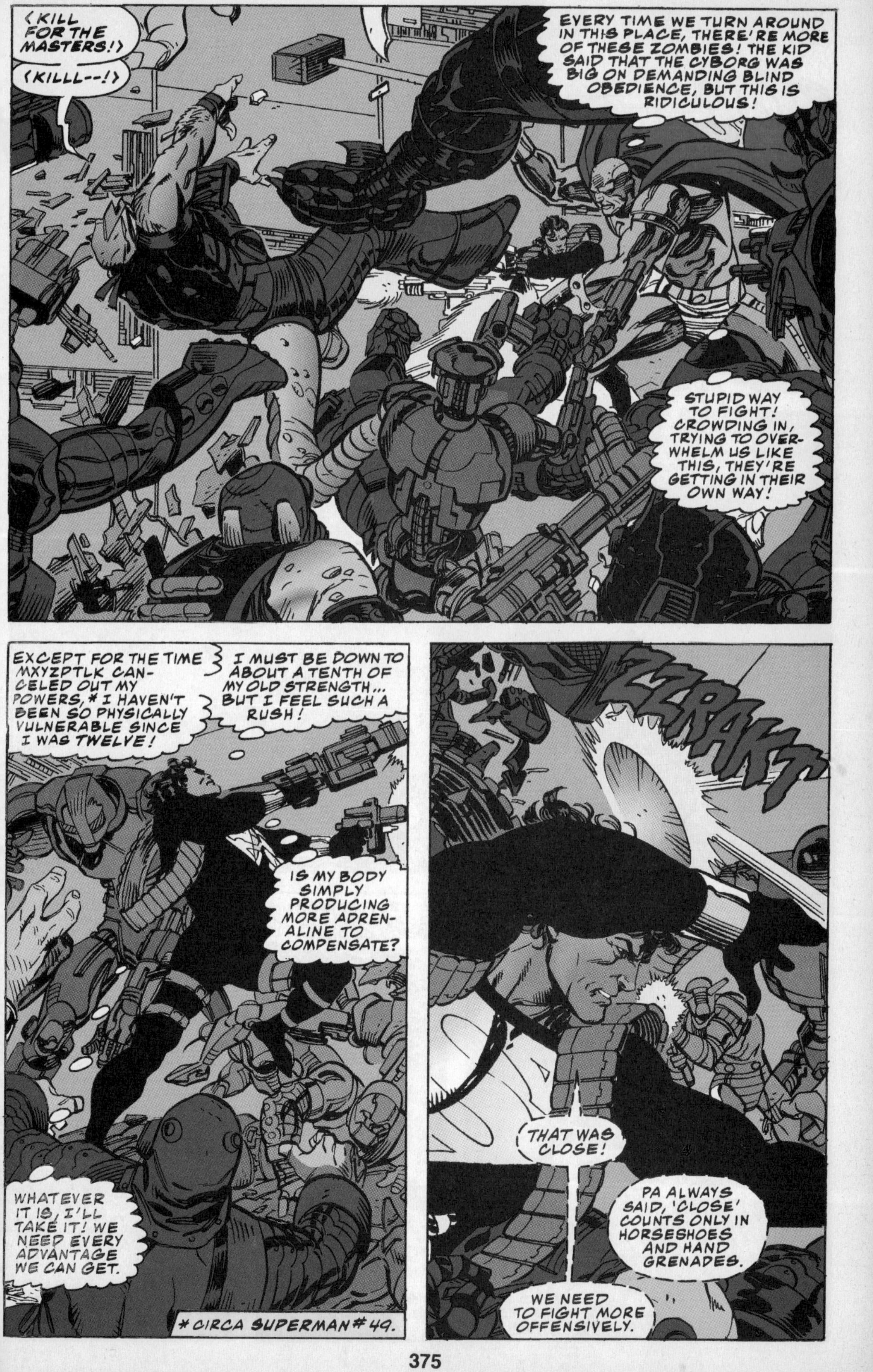
‹KILL FOR THE MASTERS!›
‹KILLL--!›
EVERY TIME WE TURN AROUND IN THIS PLACE, THERE'RE MORE OF THESE ZOMBIES! THE KID SAID THAT THE CYBORG WAS BIG ON DEMANDING BLIND OBEDIENCE, BUT THIS IS RIDICULOUS!
STUPID WAY TO FIGHT! CROWDING IN, TRYING TO OVERWHELM US LIKE THIS, THEY'RE GETTING IN THEIR OWN WAY!
EXCEPT FOR THE TIME MXYZPTLK CANCELED OUT MY POWERS,* I HAVEN'T BEEN SO PHYSICALLY VULNERABLE SINCE I WAS TWELVE!
I MUST BE DOWN TO ABOUT A TENTH OF MY OLD STRENGTH... BUT I FEEL SUCH A RUSH!
IS MY BODY SIMPLY PRODUCING MORE ADRENALINE TO COMPENSATE?
WHATEVER IT IS, I'LL TAKE IT! WE NEED EVERY ADVANTAGE WE CAN GET.
*CIRCA SUPERMAN #49.
ZZRAKT
THAT WAS CLOSE!
PA ALWAYS SAID, 'CLOSE' COUNTS ONLY IN HORSESHOES AND HAND GRENADES.
WE NEED TO FIGHT MORE OFFENSIVELY.

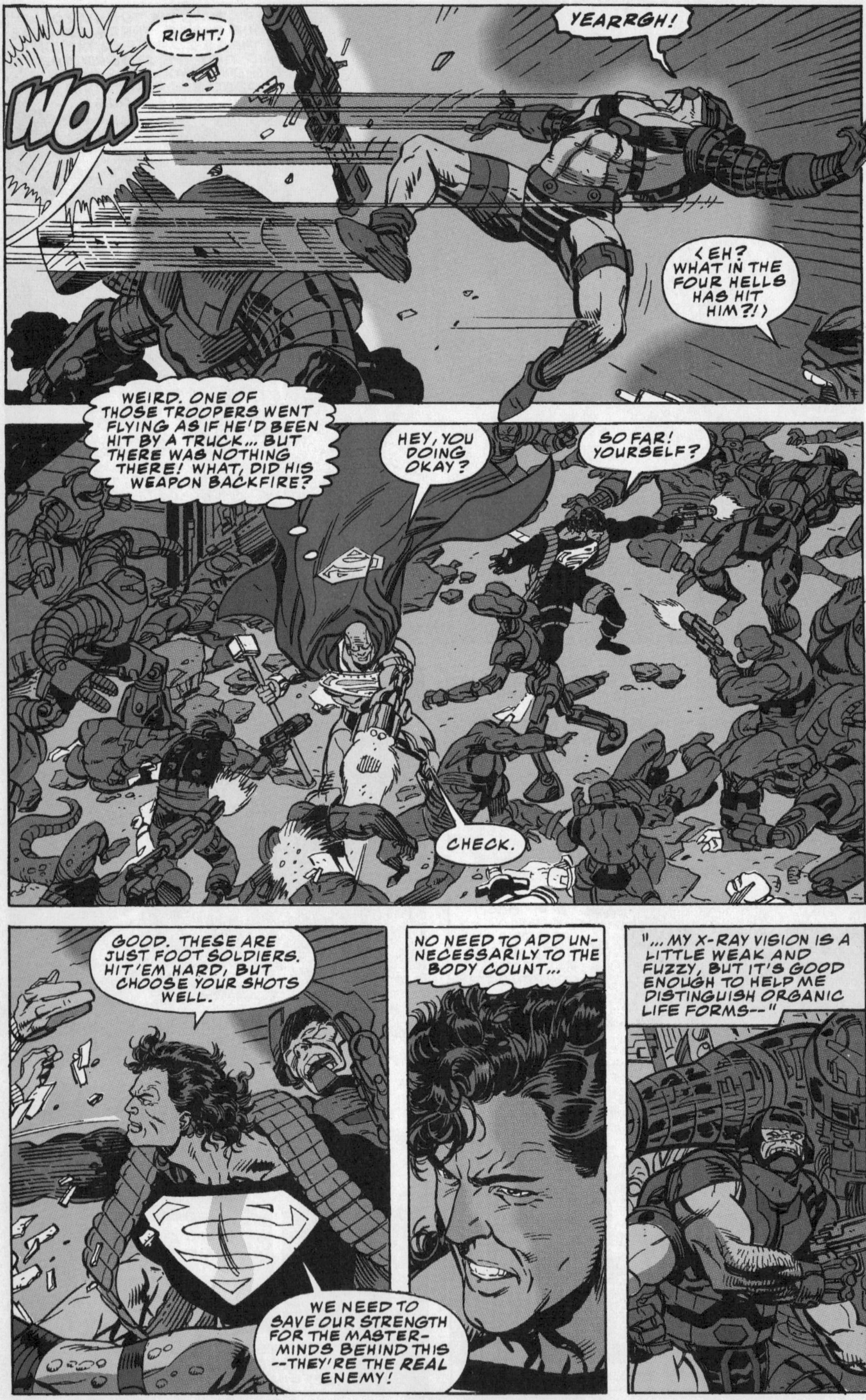
RIGHT!
WOK
YEARRGH!
< EH? WHAT IN THE FOUR HELLS HAS HIT HIM?! >
WEIRD. ONE OF THOSE TROOPERS WENT FLYING AS IF HE'D BEEN HIT BY A TRUCK... BUT THERE WAS NOTHING THERE! WHAT, DID HIS WEAPON BACKFIRE?
HEY, YOU DOING OKAY?
SO FAR! YOURSELF?
CHECK.
GOOD. THESE ARE JUST FOOT SOLDIERS. HIT 'EM HARD, BUT CHOOSE YOUR SHOTS WELL.
WE NEED TO SAVE OUR STRENGTH FOR THE MASTER-MINDS BEHIND THIS --THEY'RE THE REAL ENEMY!
NO NEED TO ADD UN-NECESSARILY TO THE BODY COUNT...
"... MY X-RAY VISION IS A LITTLE WEAK AND FUZZY, BUT IT'S GOOD ENOUGH TO HELP ME DISTINGUISH ORGANIC LIFE FORMS--"

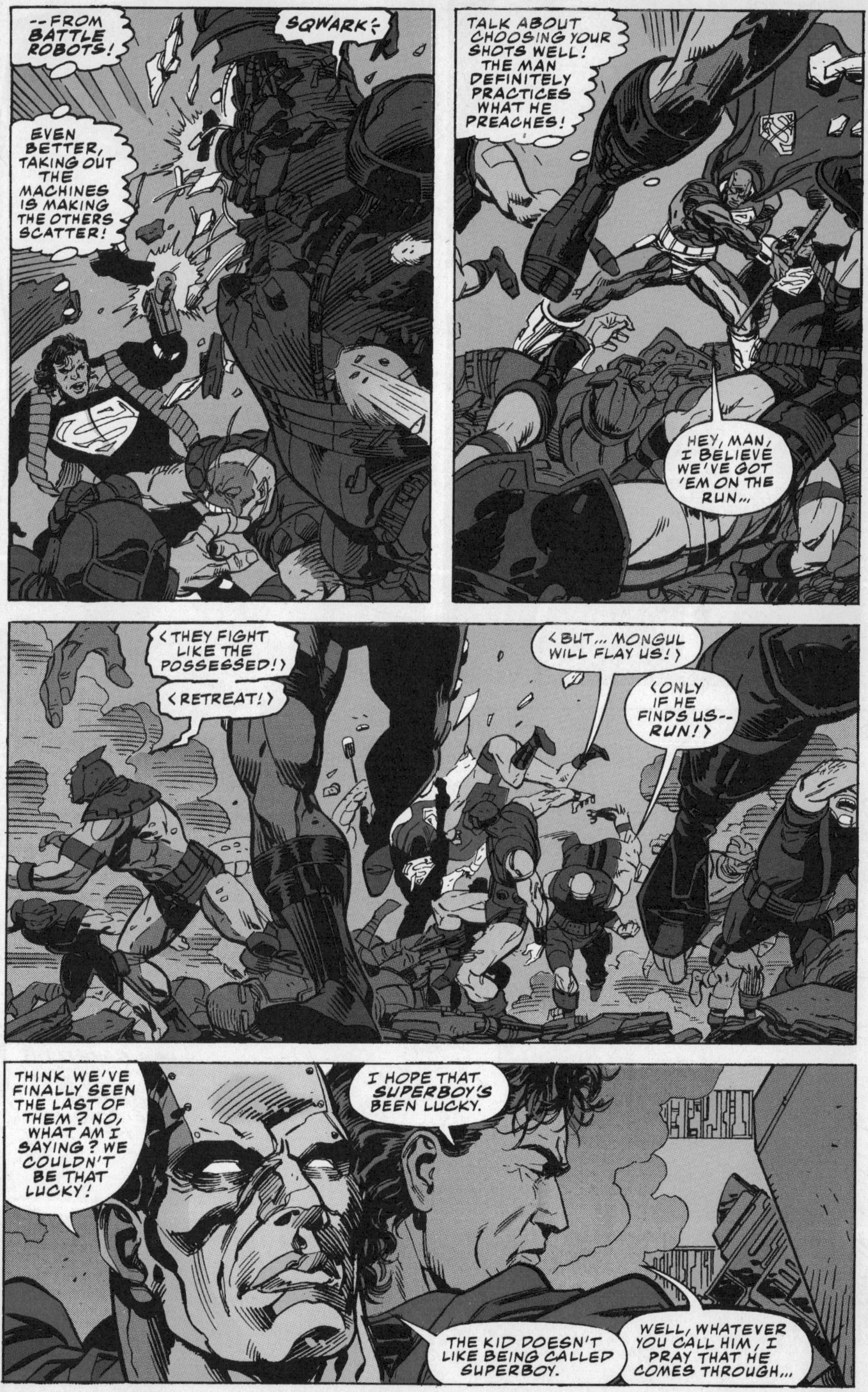
--FROM BATTLE ROBOTS!
SQWARK!
EVEN BETTER, TAKING OUT THE MACHINES IS MAKING THE OTHERS SCATTER!
TALK ABOUT CHOOSING YOUR SHOTS WELL! THE MAN DEFINITELY PRACTICES WHAT HE PREACHES!
HEY, MAN, I BELIEVE WE'VE GOT 'EM ON THE RUN...
<THEY FIGHT LIKE THE POSSESSED!>
<RETREAT!>
<BUT... MONGUL WILL FLAY US!>
<ONLY IF HE FINDS US--RUN!>
THINK WE'VE FINALLY SEEN THE LAST OF THEM? NO, WHAT AM I SAYING? WE COULDN'T BE THAT LUCKY!
I HOPE THAT SUPERBOY'S BEEN LUCKY.
THE KID DOESN'T LIKE BEING CALLED SUPERBOY.
WELL, WHATEVER YOU CALL HIM, I PRAY THAT HE COMES THROUGH...

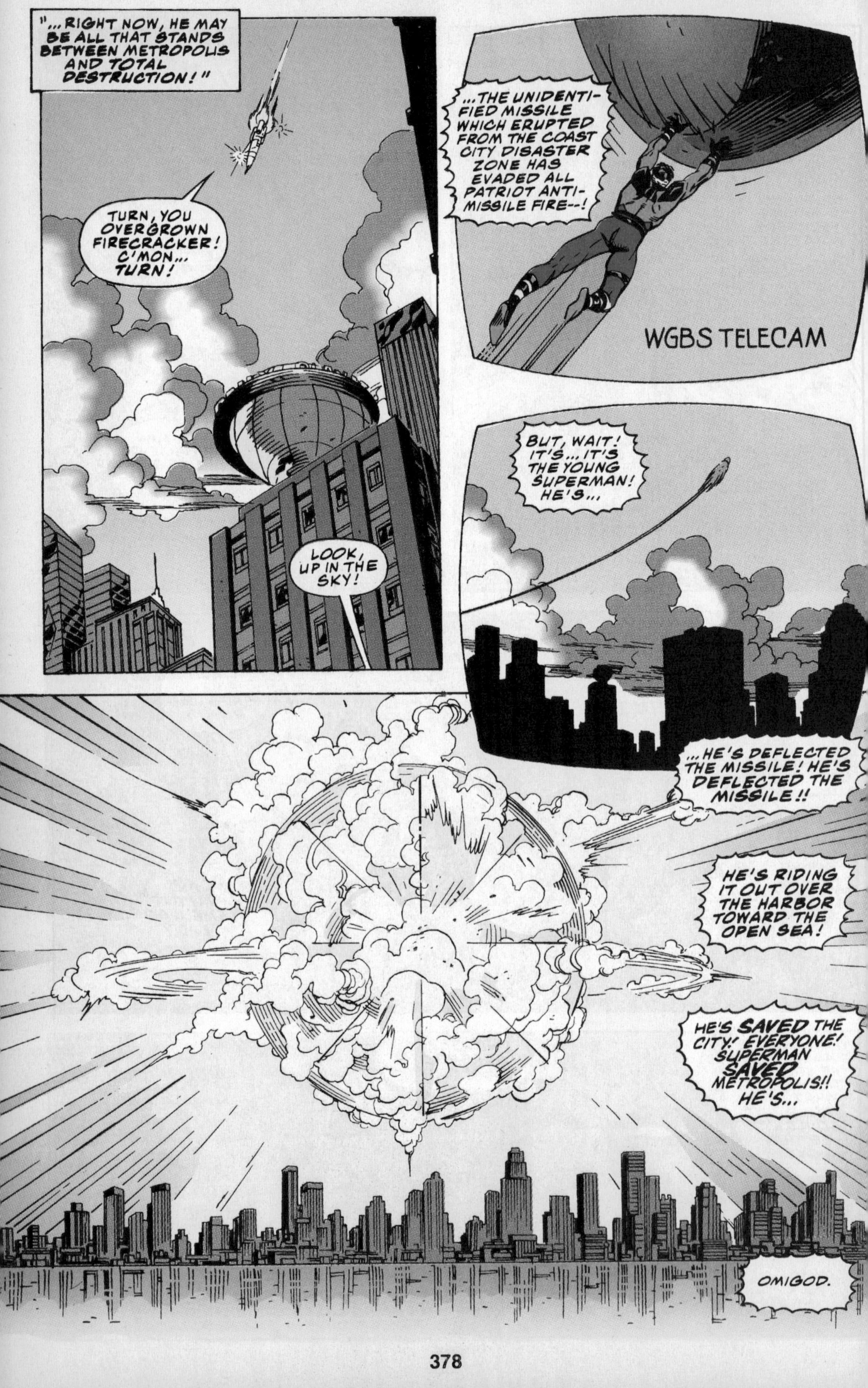
"...RIGHT NOW, HE MAY BE ALL THAT STANDS BETWEEN METROPOLIS AND TOTAL DESTRUCTION!"
TURN, YOU OVERGROWN FIRECRACKER! C'MON... TURN!
LOOK, UP IN THE SKY!
...THE UNIDENTIFIED MISSILE WHICH ERUPTED FROM THE COAST CITY DISASTER ZONE HAS EVADED ALL PATRIOT ANTI-MISSILE FIRE--!
WGBS TELECAM
BUT, WAIT! IT'S... IT'S THE YOUNG SUPERMAN! HE'S...
...HE'S DEFLECTED THE MISSILE! HE'S DEFLECTED THE MISSILE!!
HE'S RIDING IT OUT OVER THE HARBOR TOWARD THE OPEN SEA!
HE'S SAVED THE CITY! EVERYONE! SUPERMAN SAVED METROPOLIS!! HE'S...
OMIGOD.

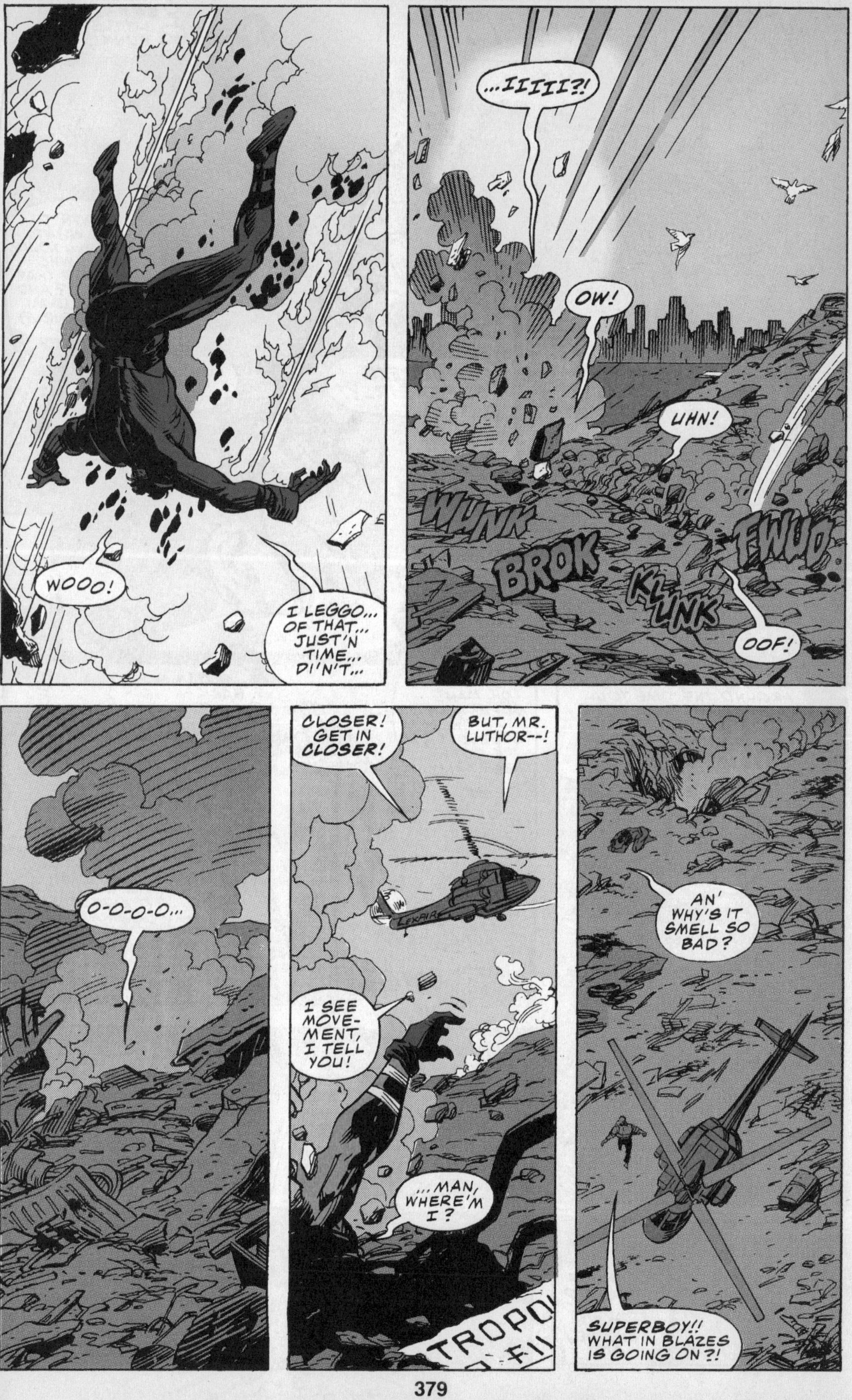
WOOO!
I LEGGO... OF THAT... JUST'N TIME... DI'N'T...
...IIIII?!
OW!
UHN!
WUNK
BROK
KLUNK
FWUD
OOF!
O-O-O-O...
CLOSER! GET IN CLOSER!
BUT, MR. LUTHOR--!
I SEE MOVE-MENT, I TELL YOU!
...MAN, WHERE'M I?
TROPO
AN' WHY'S IT SMELL SO BAD?
SUPERBOY!! WHAT IN BLAZES IS GOING ON?!

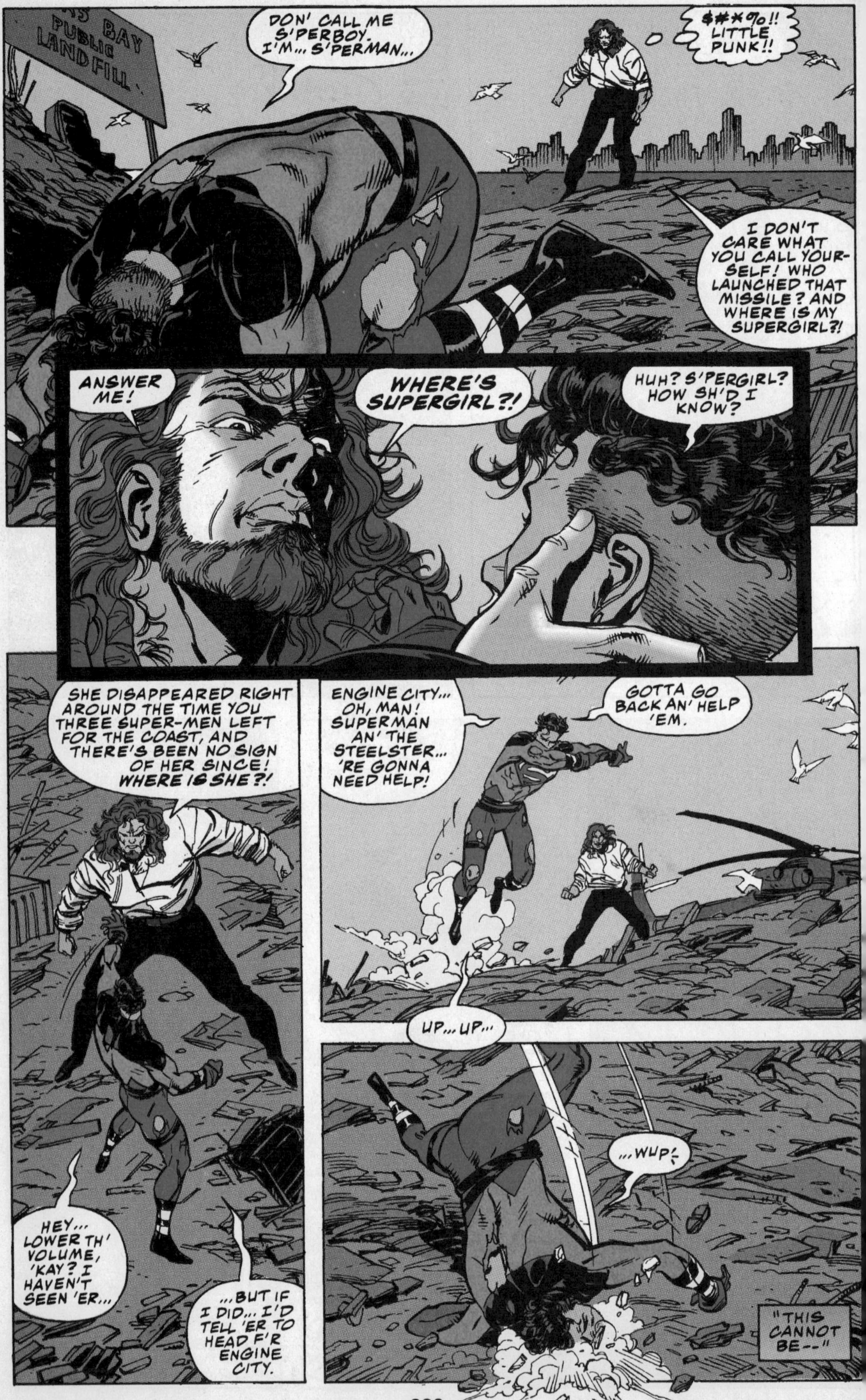
PUBLIC BAY
LANDFILL
DON' CALL ME S'PERBOY. I'M... S'PERMAN...
$#*%!! LITTLE PUNK!!
I DON'T CARE WHAT YOU CALL YOURSELF! WHO LAUNCHED THAT MISSILE? AND WHERE IS MY SUPERGIRL?!
ANSWER ME!
WHERE'S SUPERGIRL?!
HUH? S'PERGIRL? HOW SH'D I KNOW?
SHE DISAPPEARED RIGHT AROUND THE TIME YOU THREE SUPER-MEN LEFT FOR THE COAST, AND THERE'S BEEN NO SIGN OF HER SINCE! WHERE IS SHE?!
HEY... LOWER TH' VOLUME, 'KAY? I HAVEN'T SEEN 'ER...
...BUT IF I DID... I'D TELL 'ER TO HEAD F'R ENGINE CITY.
ENGINE CITY... OH, MAN! SUPERMAN AN' THE STEELSTER... 'RE GONNA NEED HELP!
GOTTA GO BACK AN' HELP 'EM.
UP... UP...
...WUP!
"THIS CANNOT BE--"

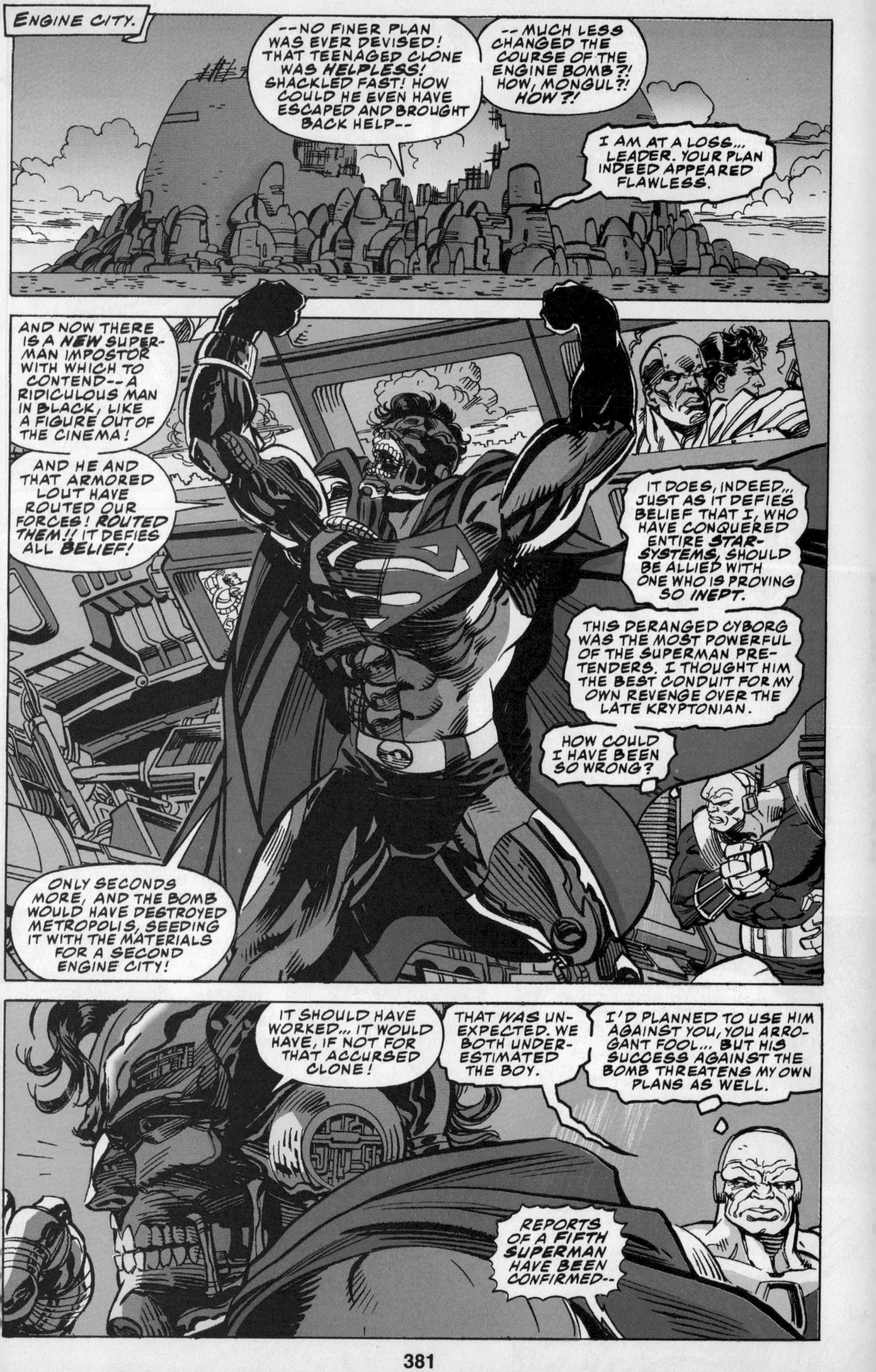
ENGINE CITY.
--NO FINER PLAN WAS EVER DEVISED! THAT TEENAGED CLONE WAS HELPLESS! SHACKLED FAST! HOW COULD HE EVEN HAVE ESCAPED AND BROUGHT BACK HELP--
--MUCH LESS CHANGED THE COURSE OF THE ENGINE BOMB?! HOW, MONGUL?! HOW?!
I AM AT A LOSS... LEADER. YOUR PLAN INDEED APPEARED FLAWLESS.
AND NOW THERE IS A NEW SUPERMAN IMPOSTOR WITH WHICH TO CONTEND--A RIDICULOUS MAN IN BLACK, LIKE A FIGURE OUT OF THE CINEMA!
AND HE AND THAT ARMORED LOUT HAVE ROUTED OUR FORCES! ROUTED THEM!! IT DEFIES ALL BELIEF!
IT DOES, INDEED... JUST AS IT DEFIES BELIEF THAT I, WHO HAVE CONQUERED ENTIRE STAR-SYSTEMS, SHOULD BE ALLIED WITH ONE WHO IS PROVING SO INEPT.
THIS DERANGED CYBORG WAS THE MOST POWERFUL OF THE SUPERMAN PRETENDERS. I THOUGHT HIM THE BEST CONDUIT FOR MY OWN REVENGE OVER THE LATE KRYPTONIAN.
HOW COULD I HAVE BEEN SO WRONG?
ONLY SECONDS MORE, AND THE BOMB WOULD HAVE DESTROYED METROPOLIS, SEEDING IT WITH THE MATERIALS FOR A SECOND ENGINE CITY!
IT SHOULD HAVE WORKED... IT WOULD HAVE, IF NOT FOR THAT ACCURSED CLONE!
THAT WAS UNEXPECTED. WE BOTH UNDERESTIMATED THE BOY.
I'D PLANNED TO USE HIM AGAINST YOU, YOU ARROGANT FOOL... BUT HIS SUCCESS AGAINST THE BOMB THREATENS MY OWN PLANS AS WELL.
REPORTS OF A FIFTH SUPERMAN HAVE BEEN CONFIRMED--

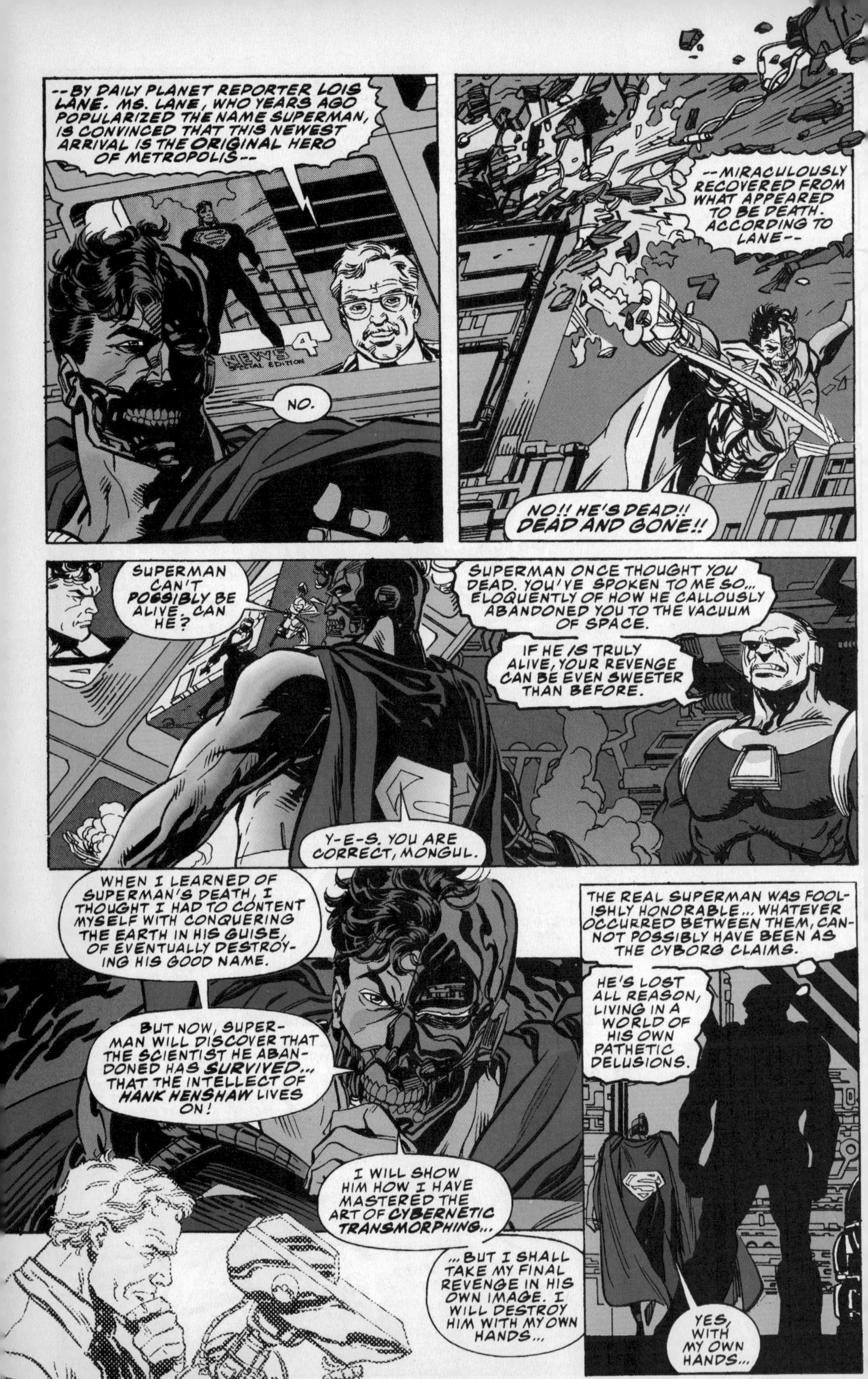
--BY DAILY PLANET REPORTER LOIS LANE. MS. LANE, WHO YEARS AGO POPULARIZED THE NAME SUPERMAN, IS CONVINCED THAT THIS NEWEST ARRIVAL IS THE ORIGINAL HERO OF METROPOLIS--
NEWS 4
SPECIAL EDITION
NO.
--MIRACULOUSLY RECOVERED FROM WHAT APPEARED TO BE DEATH. ACCORDING TO LANE--
NO!! HE'S DEAD!! DEAD AND GONE!!
SUPERMAN CAN'T POSSIBLY BE ALIVE. CAN HE?
SUPERMAN ONCE THOUGHT YOU DEAD. YOU'VE SPOKEN TO ME SO... ELOQUENTLY OF HOW HE CALLOUSLY ABANDONED YOU TO THE VACUUM OF SPACE.
IF HE IS TRULY ALIVE, YOUR REVENGE CAN BE EVEN SWEETER THAN BEFORE.
Y-E-S. YOU ARE CORRECT, MONGUL.
WHEN I LEARNED OF SUPERMAN'S DEATH, I THOUGHT I HAD TO CONTENT MYSELF WITH CONQUERING THE EARTH IN HIS GUISE, OF EVENTUALLY DESTROYING HIS GOOD NAME.
BUT NOW, SUPERMAN WILL DISCOVER THAT THE SCIENTIST HE ABANDONED HAS SURVIVED... THAT THE INTELLECT OF HANK HENSHAW LIVES ON!
I WILL SHOW HIM HOW I HAVE MASTERED THE ART OF CYBERNETIC TRANSMORPHING...
...BUT I SHALL TAKE MY FINAL REVENGE IN HIS OWN IMAGE. I WILL DESTROY HIM WITH MY OWN HANDS...
THE REAL SUPERMAN WAS FOOLISHLY HONORABLE... WHATEVER OCCURRED BETWEEN THEM, CANNOT POSSIBLY HAVE BEEN AS THE CYBORG CLAIMS.
HE'S LOST ALL REASON, LIVING IN A WORLD OF HIS OWN PATHETIC DELUSIONS.
YES, WITH MY OWN HANDS...

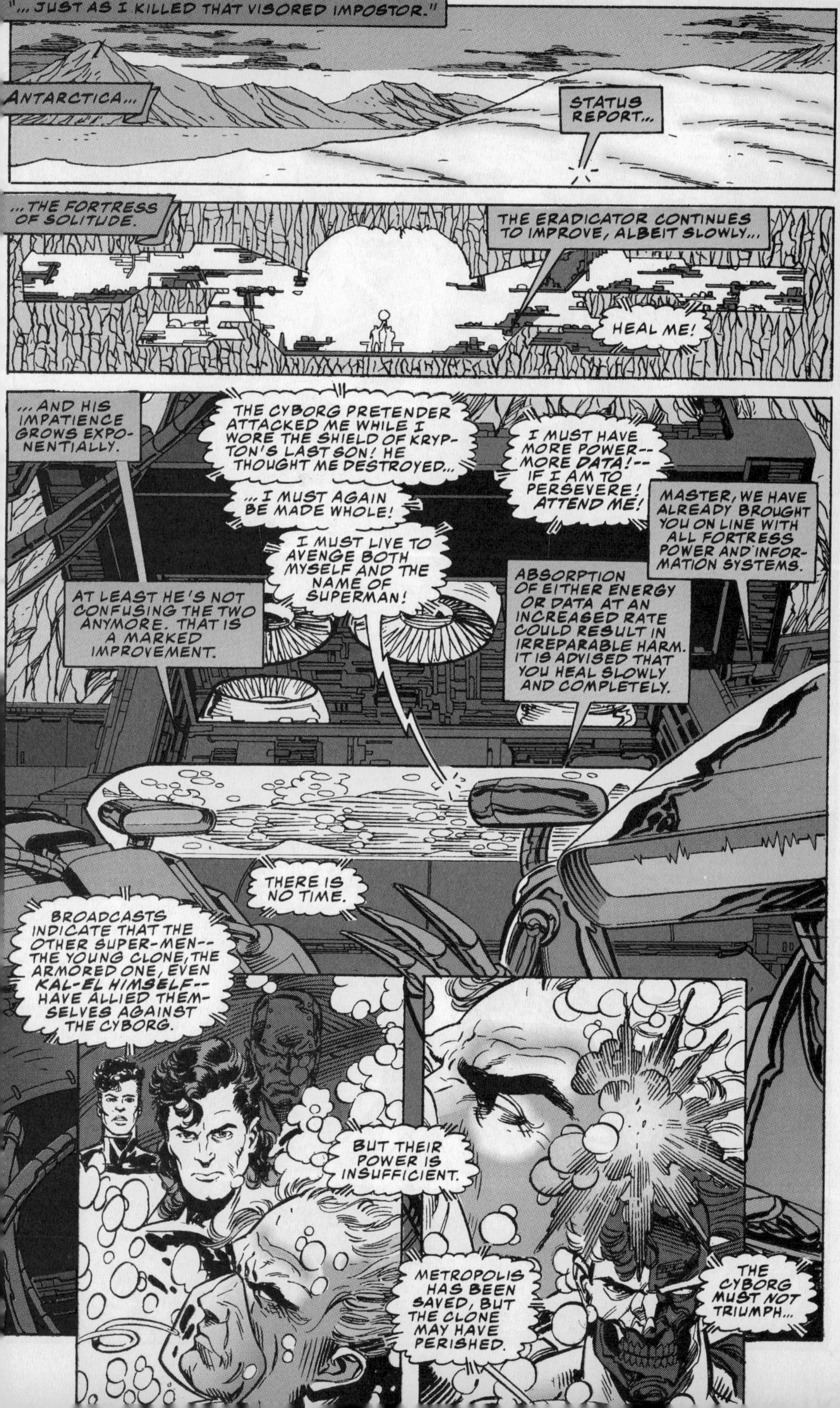
"... JUST AS I KILLED THAT VISORED IMPOSTOR."
ANTARCTICA...
STATUS REPORT...
...THE FORTRESS OF SOLITUDE.
THE ERADICATOR CONTINUES TO IMPROVE, ALBEIT SLOWLY...
HEAL ME!
...AND HIS IMPATIENCE GROWS EXPONENTIALLY.
THE CYBORG PRETENDER ATTACKED ME WHILE I WORE THE SHIELD OF KRYPTON'S LAST SON! HE THOUGHT ME DESTROYED...
...I MUST AGAIN BE MADE WHOLE!
I MUST LIVE TO AVENGE BOTH MYSELF AND THE NAME OF SUPERMAN!
AT LEAST HE'S NOT CONFUSING THE TWO ANYMORE. THAT IS A MARKED IMPROVEMENT.
I MUST HAVE MORE POWER-- MORE DATA!-- IF I AM TO PERSEVERE! ATTEND ME!
MASTER, WE HAVE ALREADY BROUGHT YOU ON LINE WITH ALL FORTRESS POWER AND INFORMATION SYSTEMS.
ABSORPTION OF EITHER ENERGY OR DATA AT AN INCREASED RATE COULD RESULT IN IRREPARABLE HARM. IT IS ADVISED THAT YOU HEAL SLOWLY AND COMPLETELY.
THERE IS NO TIME.
BROADCASTS INDICATE THAT THE OTHER SUPER-MEN-- THE YOUNG CLONE, THE ARMORED ONE, EVEN KAL-EL HIMSELF-- HAVE ALLIED THEMSELVES AGAINST THE CYBORG.
BUT THEIR POWER IS INSUFFICIENT.
METROPOLIS HAS BEEN SAVED, BUT THE CLONE MAY HAVE PERISHED.
THE CYBORG MUST NOT TRIUMPH...

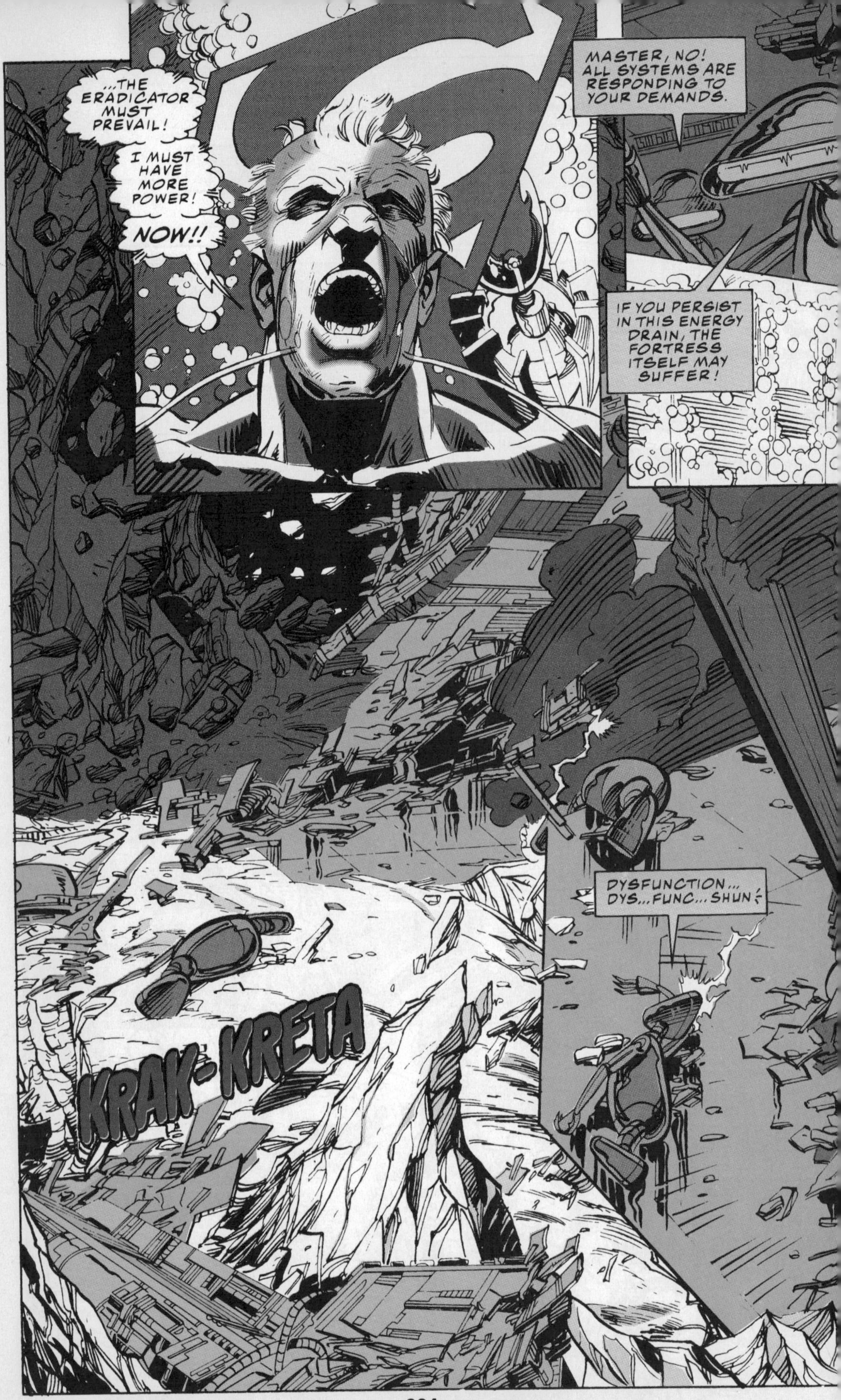
...THE ERADICATOR MUST PREVAIL!
I MUST HAVE MORE POWER!
NOW!!
MASTER, NO! ALL SYSTEMS ARE RESPONDING TO YOUR DEMANDS.
IF YOU PERSIST IN THIS ENERGY DRAIN, THE FORTRESS ITSELF MAY SUFFER!
KRAK-KRETA
DYSFUNCTION... DYS...FUNC...SHUN

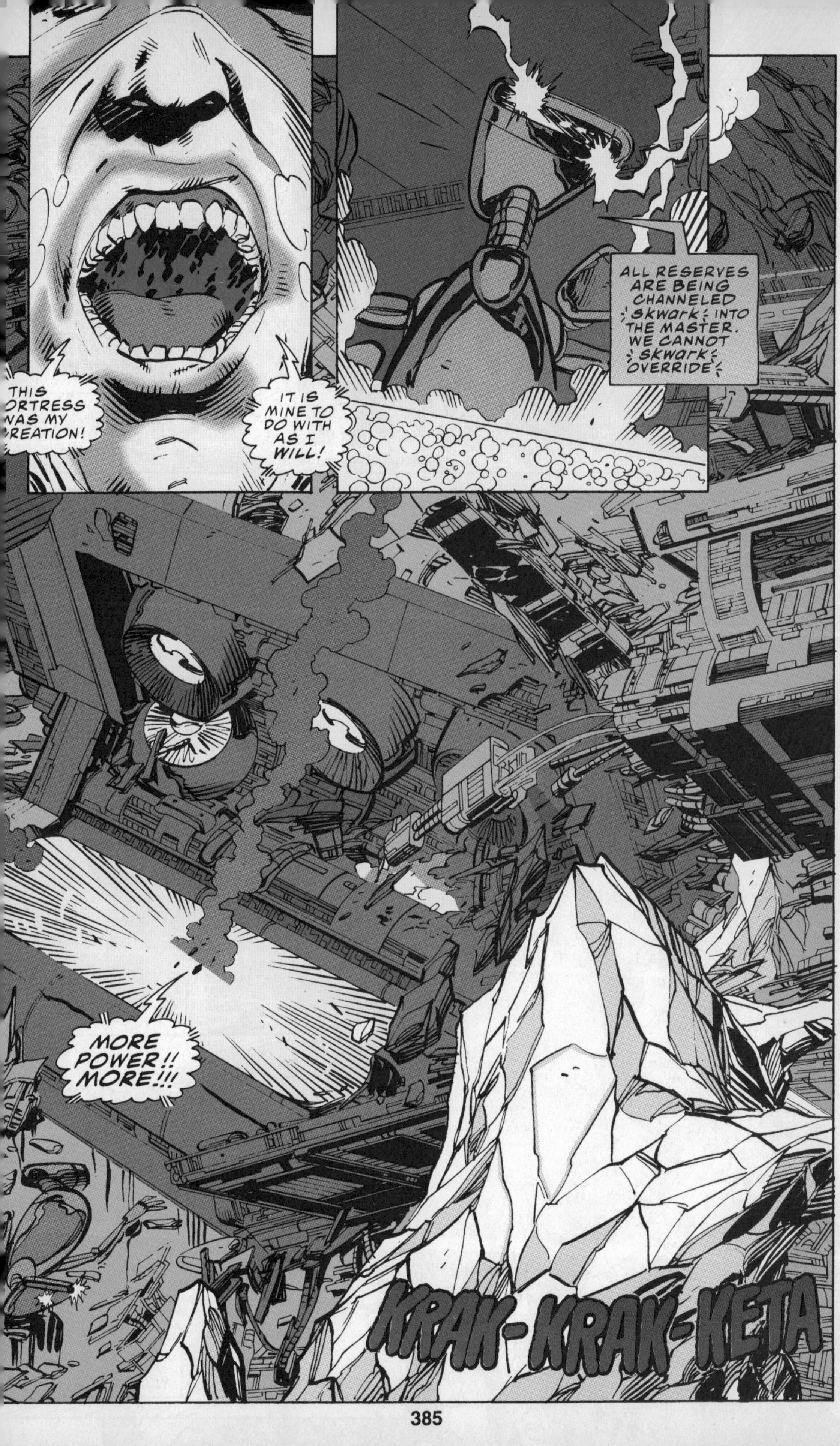
THIS FORTRESS WAS MY CREATION!
IT IS MINE TO DO WITH AS I WILL!
ALL RESERVES ARE BEING CHANNELED skwark INTO THE MASTER. WE CANNOT skwark OVERRIDE
MORE POWER!! MORE!!!
KRAK-KRAK-KETA

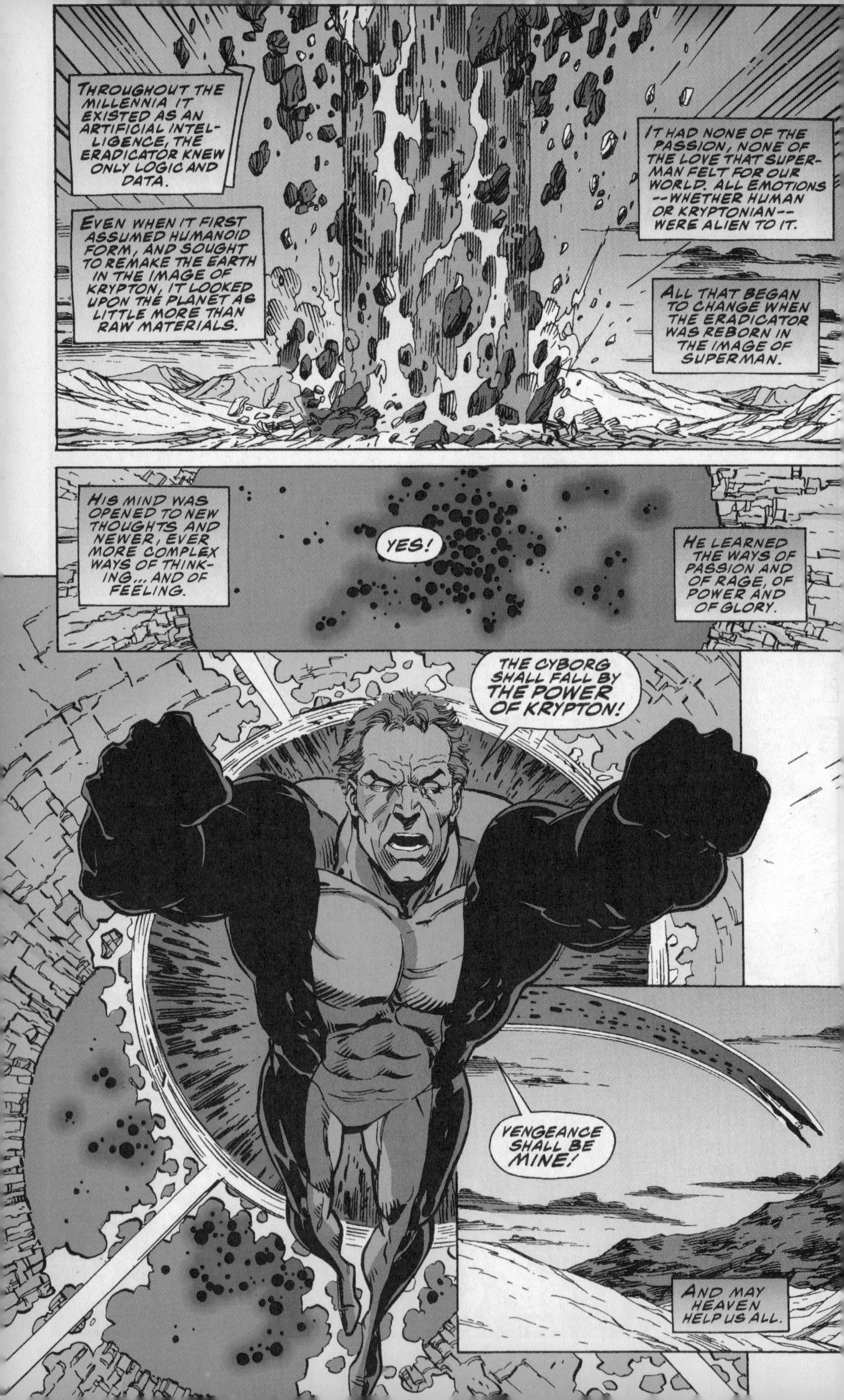
THROUGHOUT THE MILLENNIA IT EXISTED AS AN ARTIFICIAL INTELLIGENCE, THE ERADICATOR KNEW ONLY LOGIC AND DATA.
EVEN WHEN IT FIRST ASSUMED HUMANOID FORM, AND SOUGHT TO REMAKE THE EARTH IN THE IMAGE OF KRYPTON, IT LOOKED UPON THE PLANET AS LITTLE MORE THAN RAW MATERIALS.
IT HAD NONE OF THE PASSION, NONE OF THE LOVE THAT SUPERMAN FELT FOR OUR WORLD. ALL EMOTIONS --WHETHER HUMAN OR KRYPTONIAN-- WERE ALIEN TO IT.
ALL THAT BEGAN TO CHANGE WHEN THE ERADICATOR WAS REBORN IN THE IMAGE OF SUPERMAN.
HIS MIND WAS OPENED TO NEW THOUGHTS AND NEWER, EVER MORE COMPLEX WAYS OF THINKING... AND OF FEELING.
YES!
HE LEARNED THE WAYS OF PASSION AND OF RAGE, OF POWER AND OF GLORY.
THE CYBORG SHALL FALL BY THE POWER OF KRYPTON!
VENGEANCE SHALL BE MINE!
AND MAY HEAVEN HELP US ALL.

ENGINE CITY. SUB-LEVEL SIX.

CHOOM

WHAT ARE YOU SHOOTING--?

HIDDEN SURVEILLANCE DEVICE. REMEMBER HOW I SAID THE WALLS HAVE EYES AND EARS?

THE MORE OF THEM WE POKE OUT, THE MORE FREELY WE CAN TALK.

WELL, I'M GLAD YOUR X-RAY EYES ARE STILL SHARP ENOUGH TO SPOT 'EM. THAT'S A LITTLE BEYOND MY EXPERTISE.

SOMETHING WRONG?

I'M NOT SURE. I FELT A SUDDEN... PRESENCE.

OH, LORD... OF COURSE. IT'S THE ERADICATOR!

THE WHAT?!

HE WAS ONE OF THE MANY "NEW SUPERMEN"... THE ONE WITH THE VISOR.

WE ONCE SHARED A SORT OF MENTAL LINK, AND APPARENTLY IT'S STILL PARTIALLY FUNCTIONING.

HE'S ON HIS WAY HERE.

IS THAT GOOD?

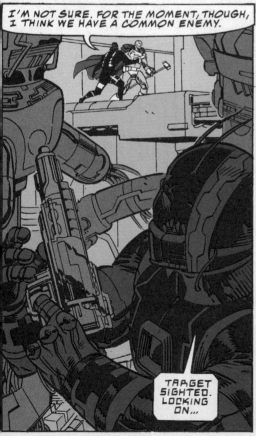

I'M NOT SURE. FOR THE MOMENT, THOUGH, I THINK WE HAVE A COMMON ENEMY.

TARGET SIGHTED. LOCKING ON...

SHRAKT

TARGETING FAILURE! REPEAT, TAR-÷gakk÷

LOOK OUT!!

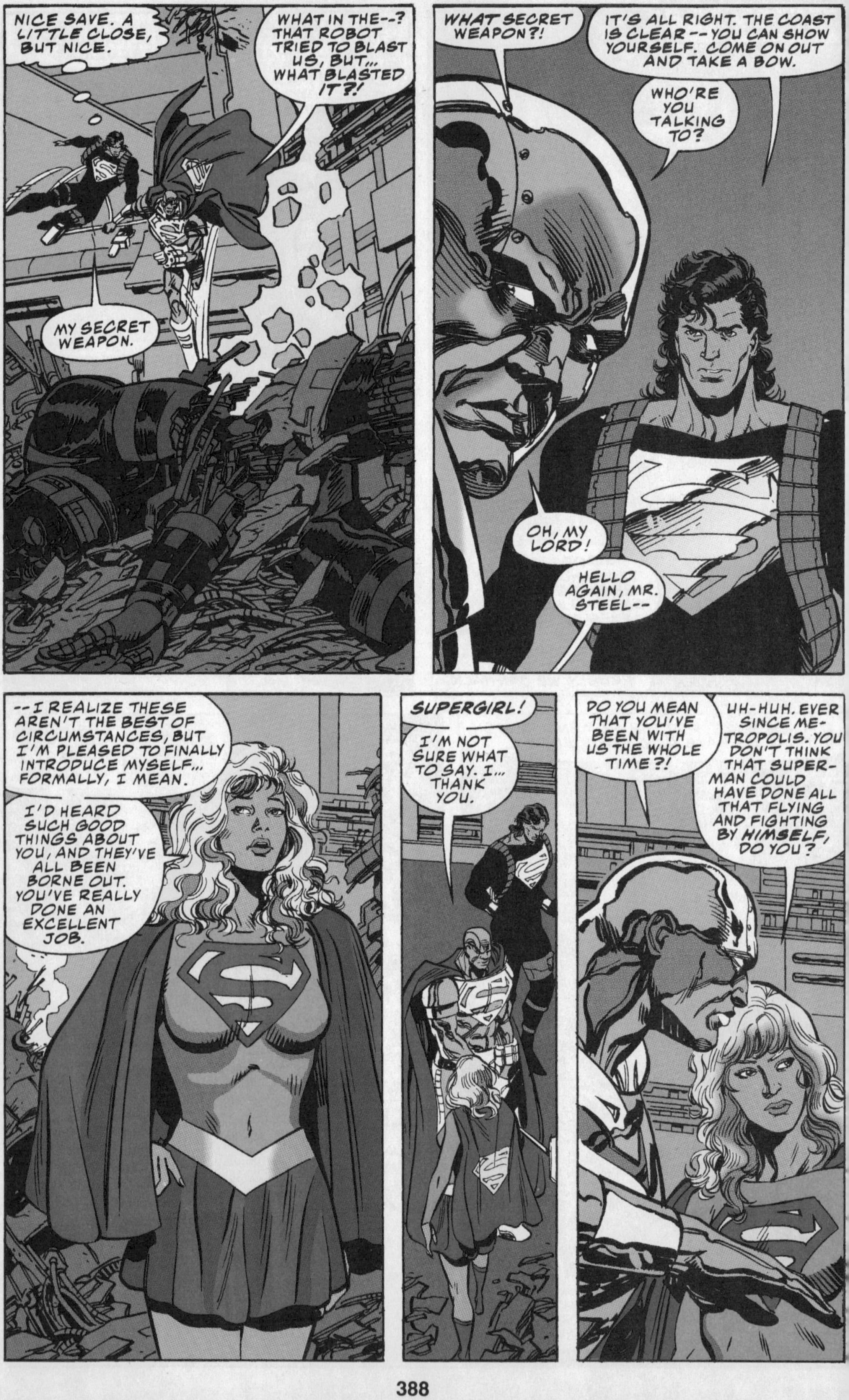
NICE SAVE. A LITTLE CLOSE, BUT NICE.
WHAT IN THE--? THAT ROBOT TRIED TO BLAST US, BUT... WHAT BLASTED IT?!
MY SECRET WEAPON.
WHAT SECRET WEAPON?!
IT'S ALL RIGHT. THE COAST IS CLEAR -- YOU CAN SHOW YOURSELF. COME ON OUT AND TAKE A BOW.
WHO'RE YOU TALKING TO?
OH, MY LORD!
HELLO AGAIN, MR. STEEL--
--I REALIZE THESE AREN'T THE BEST OF CIRCUMSTANCES, BUT I'M PLEASED TO FINALLY INTRODUCE MYSELF... FORMALLY, I MEAN.
I'D HEARD SUCH GOOD THINGS ABOUT YOU, AND THEY'VE ALL BEEN BORNE OUT. YOU'VE REALLY DONE AN EXCELLENT JOB.
SUPERGIRL!
I'M NOT SURE WHAT TO SAY. I... THANK YOU.
DO YOU MEAN THAT YOU'VE BEEN WITH US THE WHOLE TIME?!
UH-HUH. EVER SINCE METROPOLIS. YOU DON'T THINK THAT SUPERMAN COULD HAVE DONE ALL THAT FLYING AND FIGHTING BY HIMSELF, DO YOU?

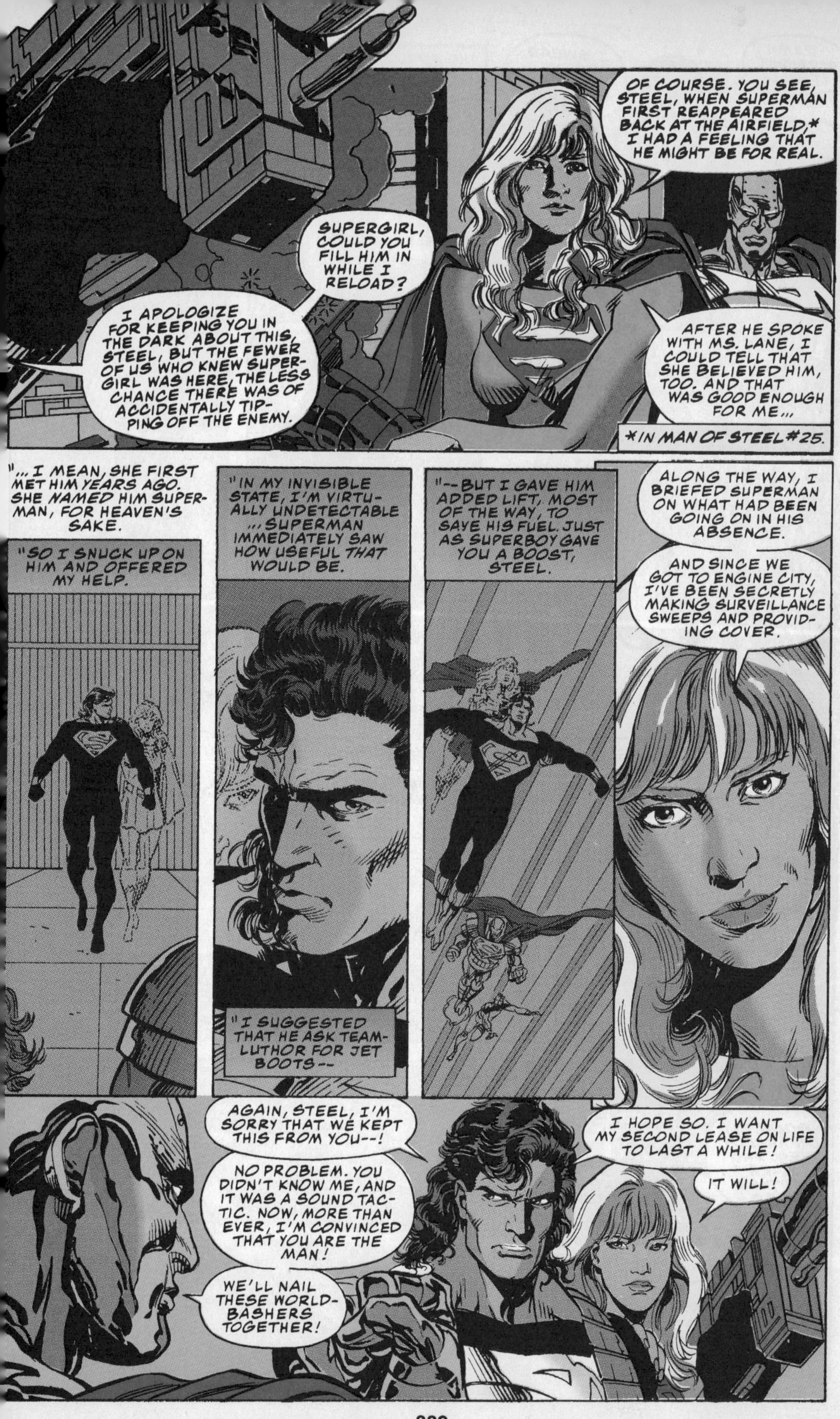
SUPERGIRL, COULD YOU FILL HIM IN WHILE I RELOAD?
I APOLOGIZE FOR KEEPING YOU IN THE DARK ABOUT THIS, STEEL, BUT THE FEWER OF US WHO KNEW SUPER-GIRL WAS HERE, THE LESS CHANCE THERE WAS OF ACCIDENTALLY TIP-PING OFF THE ENEMY.
OF COURSE. YOU SEE, STEEL, WHEN SUPERMAN FIRST REAPPEARED BACK AT THE AIRFIELD,* I HAD A FEELING THAT HE MIGHT BE FOR REAL.
AFTER HE SPOKE WITH MS. LANE, I COULD TELL THAT SHE BELIEVED HIM, TOO. AND THAT WAS GOOD ENOUGH FOR ME...
*IN MAN OF STEEL #25.
"... I MEAN, SHE FIRST MET HIM YEARS AGO. SHE NAMED HIM SUPER-MAN, FOR HEAVEN'S SAKE.
"SO I SNUCK UP ON HIM AND OFFERED MY HELP.
"IN MY INVISIBLE STATE, I'M VIRTU-ALLY UNDETECTABLE ... SUPERMAN IMMEDIATELY SAW HOW USEFUL THAT WOULD BE.
"I SUGGESTED THAT HE ASK TEAM-LUTHOR FOR JET BOOTS--
"--BUT I GAVE HIM ADDED LIFT, MOST OF THE WAY, TO SAVE HIS FUEL. JUST AS SUPERBOY GAVE YOU A BOOST, STEEL.
ALONG THE WAY, I BRIEFED SUPERMAN ON WHAT HAD BEEN GOING ON IN HIS ABSENCE.
AND SINCE WE GOT TO ENGINE CITY, I'VE BEEN SECRETLY MAKING SURVEILLANCE SWEEPS AND PROVID-ING COVER.
AGAIN, STEEL, I'M SORRY THAT WE KEPT THIS FROM YOU--!
NO PROBLEM. YOU DIDN'T KNOW ME, AND IT WAS A SOUND TAC-TIC. NOW, MORE THAN EVER, I'M CONVINCED THAT YOU ARE THE MAN!
WE'LL NAIL THESE WORLD-BASHERS TOGETHER!
I HOPE SO. I WANT MY SECOND LEASE ON LIFE TO LAST A WHILE!
IT WILL!

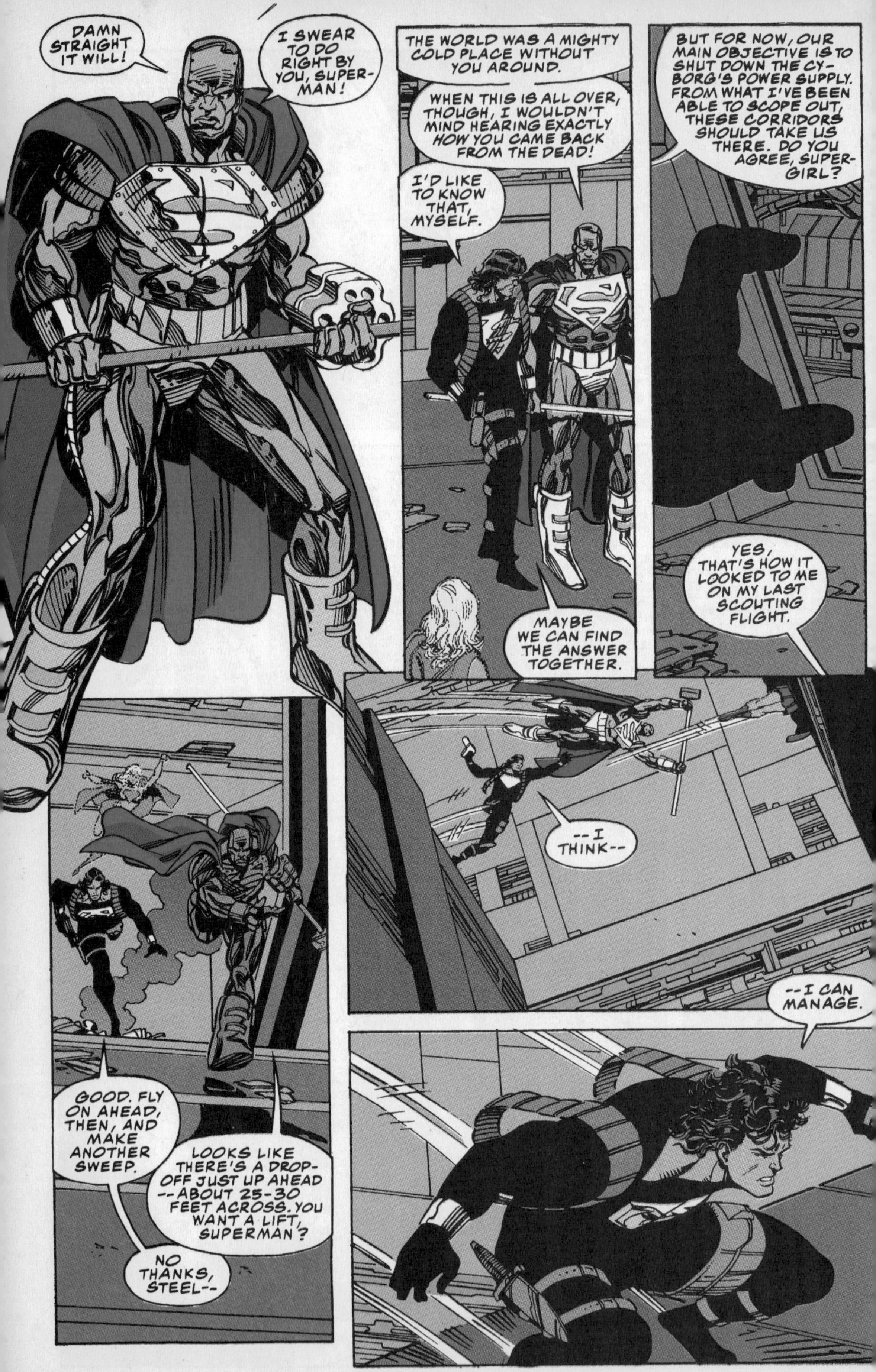
DAMN STRAIGHT IT WILL!
I SWEAR TO DO RIGHT BY YOU, SUPER-MAN!
THE WORLD WAS A MIGHTY COLD PLACE WITHOUT YOU AROUND.
WHEN THIS IS ALL OVER, THOUGH, I WOULDN'T MIND HEARING EXACTLY HOW YOU CAME BACK FROM THE DEAD!
I'D LIKE TO KNOW THAT, MYSELF.
MAYBE WE CAN FIND THE ANSWER TOGETHER.
BUT FOR NOW, OUR MAIN OBJECTIVE IS TO SHUT DOWN THE CY-BORG'S POWER SUPPLY. FROM WHAT I'VE BEEN ABLE TO SCOPE OUT, THESE CORRIDORS SHOULD TAKE US THERE. DO YOU AGREE, SUPER-GIRL?
YES, THAT'S HOW IT LOOKED TO ME ON MY LAST SCOUTING FLIGHT.
GOOD. FLY ON AHEAD, THEN, AND MAKE ANOTHER SWEEP.
LOOKS LIKE THERE'S A DROP-OFF JUST UP AHEAD --ABOUT 25-30 FEET ACROSS. YOU WANT A LIFT, SUPERMAN?
NO THANKS, STEEL--
--I THINK--
--I CAN MANAGE.

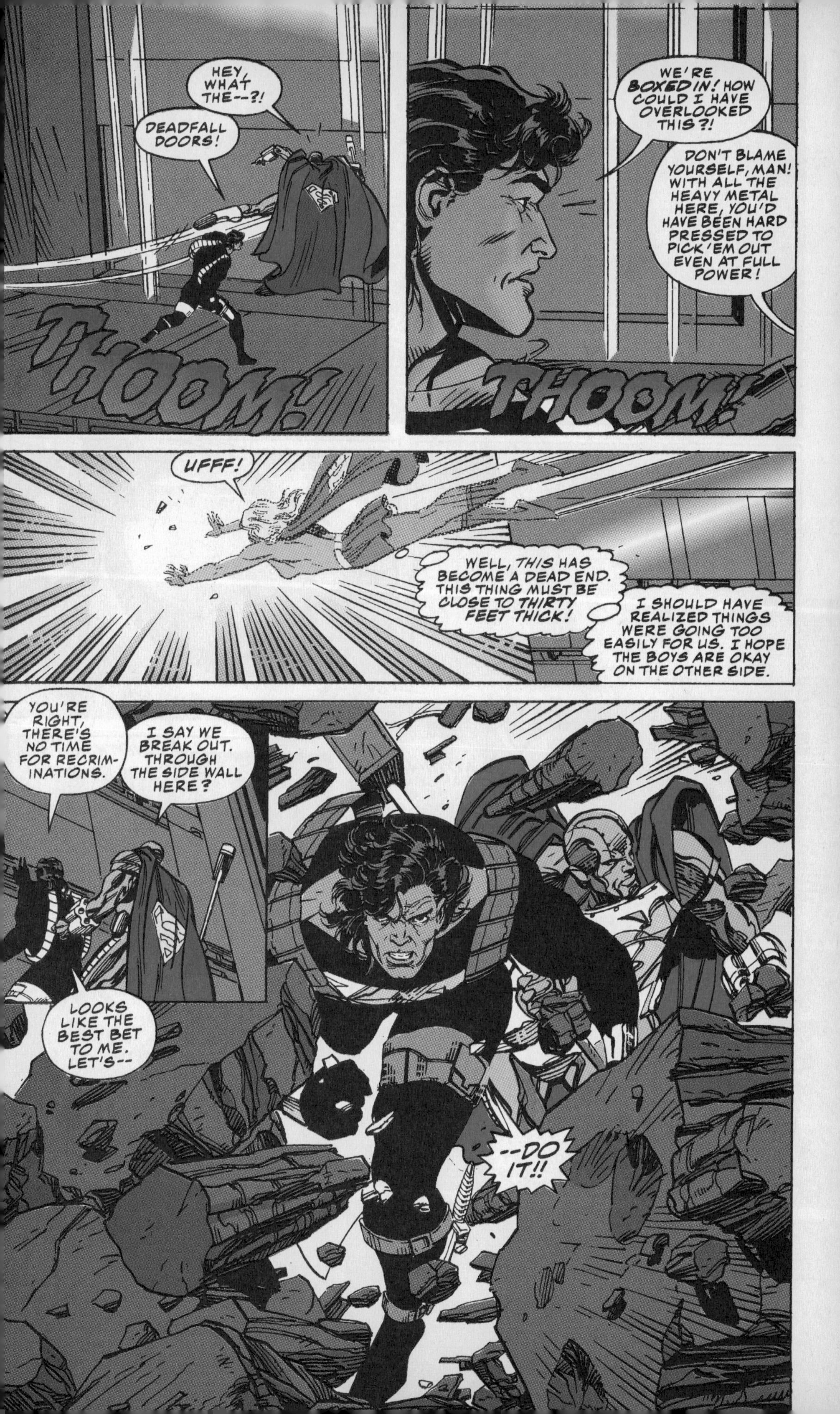
HEY, WHAT THE--?!
DEADFALL DOORS!
THOOM!
WE'RE BOXED IN! HOW COULD I HAVE OVERLOOKED THIS?!
DON'T BLAME YOURSELF, MAN! WITH ALL THE HEAVY METAL HERE, YOU'D HAVE BEEN HARD PRESSED TO PICK 'EM OUT EVEN AT FULL POWER!
THOOM!
UFFF!
WELL, THIS HAS BECOME A DEAD END. THIS THING MUST BE CLOSE TO THIRTY FEET THICK!
I SHOULD HAVE REALIZED THINGS WERE GOING TOO EASILY FOR US. I HOPE THE BOYS ARE OKAY ON THE OTHER SIDE.
YOU'RE RIGHT, THERE'S NO TIME FOR RECRIM-INATIONS.
I SAY WE BREAK OUT. THROUGH THE SIDE WALL HERE?
LOOKS LIKE THE BEST BET TO ME. LET'S--
--DO IT!!

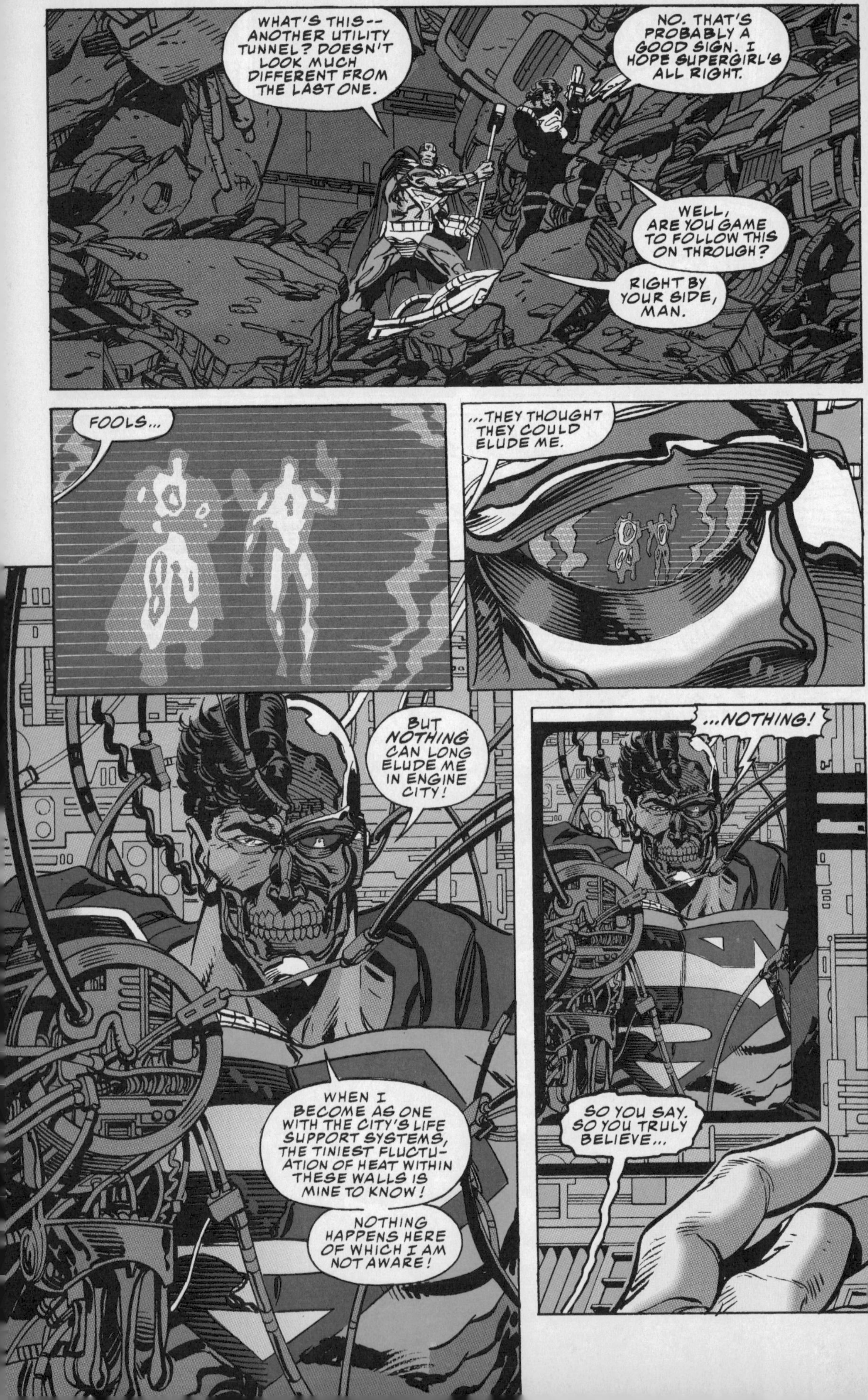

WHAT'S THIS-- ANOTHER UTILITY TUNNEL? DOESN'T LOOK MUCH DIFFERENT FROM THE LAST ONE.
NO. THAT'S PROBABLY A GOOD SIGN. I HOPE SUPERGIRL'S ALL RIGHT.
WELL, ARE YOU GAME TO FOLLOW THIS ON THROUGH?
RIGHT BY YOUR SIDE, MAN.
FOOLS...
...THEY THOUGHT THEY COULD ELUDE ME.
BUT NOTHING CAN LONG ELUDE ME IN ENGINE CITY!
WHEN I BECOME AS ONE WITH THE CITY'S LIFE SUPPORT SYSTEMS, THE TINIEST FLUCTU-ATION OF HEAT WITHIN THESE WALLS IS MINE TO KNOW!
NOTHING HAPPENS HERE OF WHICH I AM NOT AWARE!
...NOTHING!
SO YOU SAY. SO YOU TRULY BELIEVE...

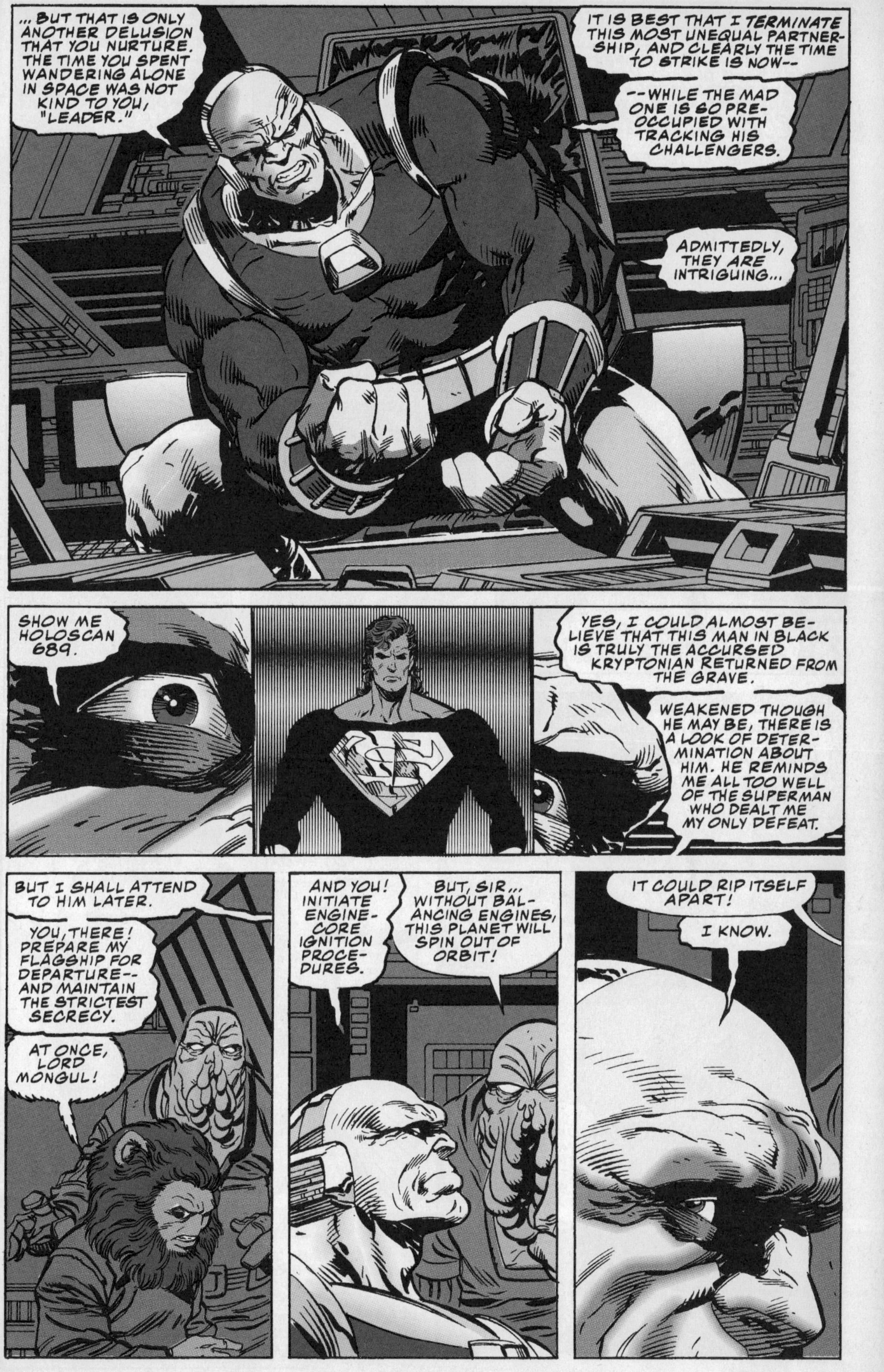
... BUT THAT IS ONLY ANOTHER DELUSION THAT YOU NURTURE. THE TIME YOU SPENT WANDERING ALONE IN SPACE WAS NOT KIND TO YOU, "LEADER."
IT IS BEST THAT I TERMINATE THIS MOST UNEQUAL PARTNER-SHIP, AND CLEARLY THE TIME TO STRIKE IS NOW--
--WHILE THE MAD ONE IS SO PRE-OCCUPIED WITH TRACKING HIS CHALLENGERS.
ADMITTEDLY, THEY ARE INTRIGUING...
SHOW ME HOLOSCAN 689.
YES, I COULD ALMOST BE-LIEVE THAT THIS MAN IN BLACK IS TRULY THE ACCURSED KRYPTONIAN RETURNED FROM THE GRAVE.
WEAKENED THOUGH HE MAY BE, THERE IS A LOOK OF DETER-MINATION ABOUT HIM. HE REMINDS ME ALL TOO WELL OF THE SUPERMAN WHO DEALT ME MY ONLY DEFEAT.
BUT I SHALL ATTEND TO HIM LATER.
YOU, THERE! PREPARE MY FLAGSHIP FOR DEPARTURE-- AND MAINTAIN THE STRICTEST SECRECY.
AT ONCE, LORD MONGUL!
AND YOU! INITIATE ENGINE-CORE IGNITION PROCE-DURES.
BUT, SIR... WITHOUT BAL-ANCING ENGINES, THIS PLANET WILL SPIN OUT OF ORBIT!
IT COULD RIP ITSELF APART!
I KNOW.

⟨THAT IS MY INTENTION, DOLT! ONE SIDE, I SHALL DO IT MYSELF!⟩

THESE INFERNAL SUPER-MEN HAVE THWARTED MY PLANS TO TRANSFORM THIS PLANET INTO MY NEW WAR-WORLD. I HAVE HAD *ENOUGH* OF THEM--AND ENOUGH OF THEIR WRETCHED LITTLE EARTH!

LET IT BE DESTROYED! I'LL FASHION A NEW WARWORLD ELSEWHERE!

AND I'LL NEVER AGAIN BOW DOWN BEFORE YOU, YOU MAD HALFLING!

SEEK OUT THE TRUE SUPERMAN, IF THE TRUE ONE HE IS.

WE SHALL HAVE A GAME OF CAT AND MOUSE, BUT I SHALL BE THE CAT!

KLIK

KLAK

"AND IF THE KRYPTONIAN HAS INDEED RETURNED TO LIFE, ALL THE BETTER.

"I CAN THINK OF NO FINER WAY TO CAUSE THE DEMISE OF SUPERMAN'S BELOVED ADOPTED WORLD...

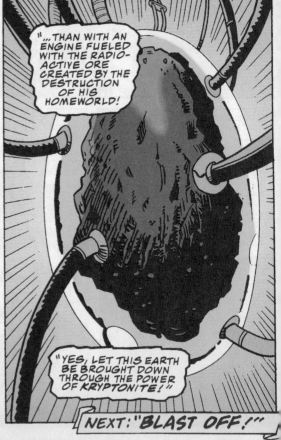

"...THAN WITH AN ENGINE FUELED WITH THE RADIO-ACTIVE ORE CREATED BY THE DESTRUCTION OF HIS HOMEWORLD!

"YES, LET THIS EARTH BE BROUGHT DOWN THROUGH THE POWER OF *KRYPTONITE!*"

NEXT: "BLAST OFF!"

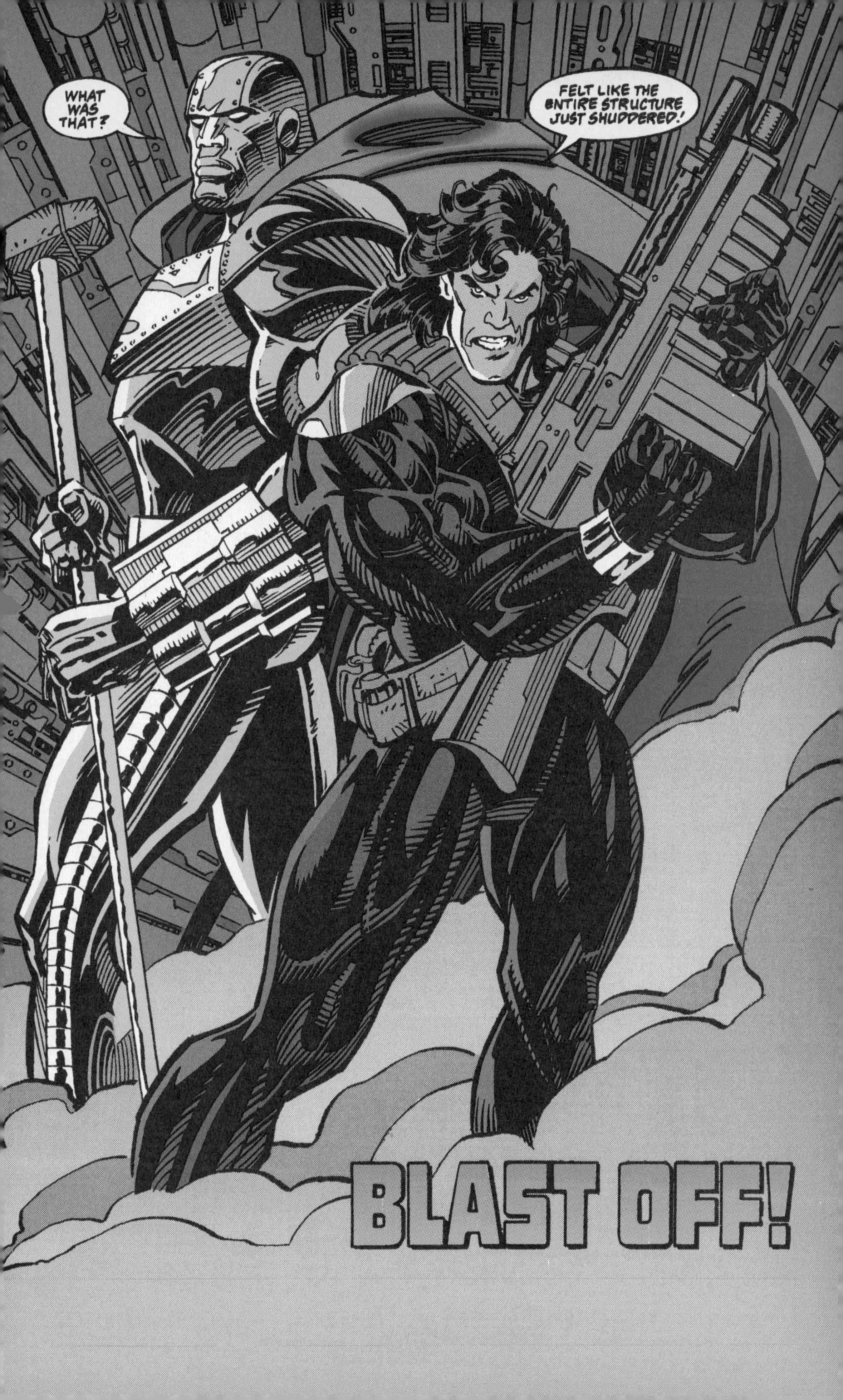
WHAT WAS THAT?
FELT LIKE THE ENTIRE STRUCTURE JUST SHUDDERED!
BLAST OFF!

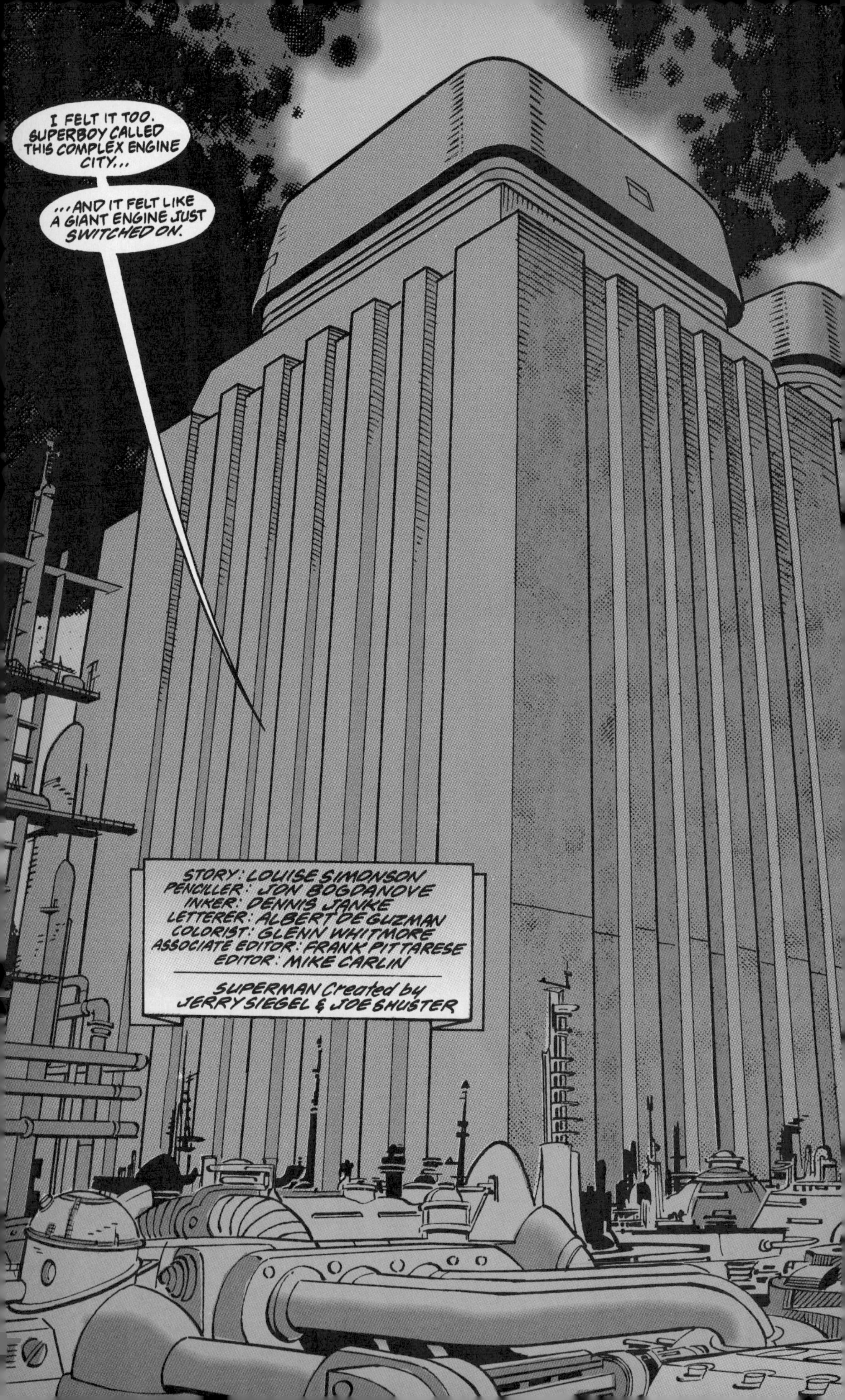
I FELT IT TOO. SUPERBOY CALLED THIS COMPLEX ENGINE CITY...
...AND IT FELT LIKE A GIANT ENGINE JUST SWITCHED ON.
STORY: LOUISE SIMONSON
PENCILLER: JON BOGDANOVE
INKER: DENNIS JANKE
LETTERER: ALBERT DE GUZMAN
COLORIST: GLENN WHITMORE
ASSOCIATE EDITOR: FRANK PITTARESE
EDITOR: MIKE CARLIN
SUPERMAN Created by JERRY SIEGEL & JOE SHUSTER

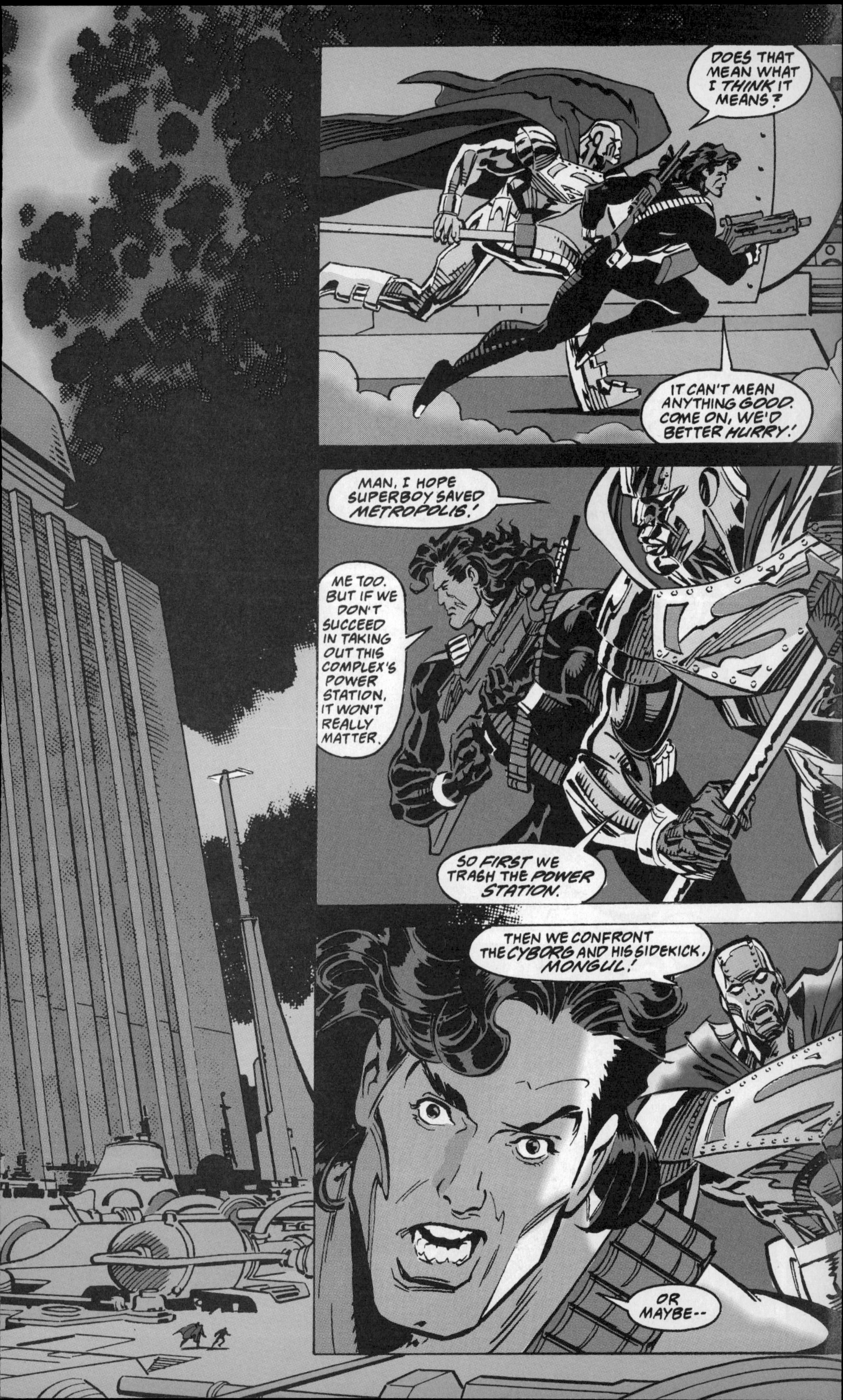

DOES THAT MEAN WHAT I THINK IT MEANS?
IT CAN'T MEAN ANYTHING GOOD. COME ON, WE'D BETTER HURRY!
MAN, I HOPE SUPERBOY SAVED METROPOLIS!
ME TOO. BUT IF WE DON'T SUCCEED IN TAKING OUT THIS COMPLEX'S POWER STATION, IT WON'T REALLY MATTER.
SO FIRST WE TRASH THE POWER STATION.
THEN WE CONFRONT THE CYBORG AND HIS SIDEKICK, MONGUL!
OR MAYBE--

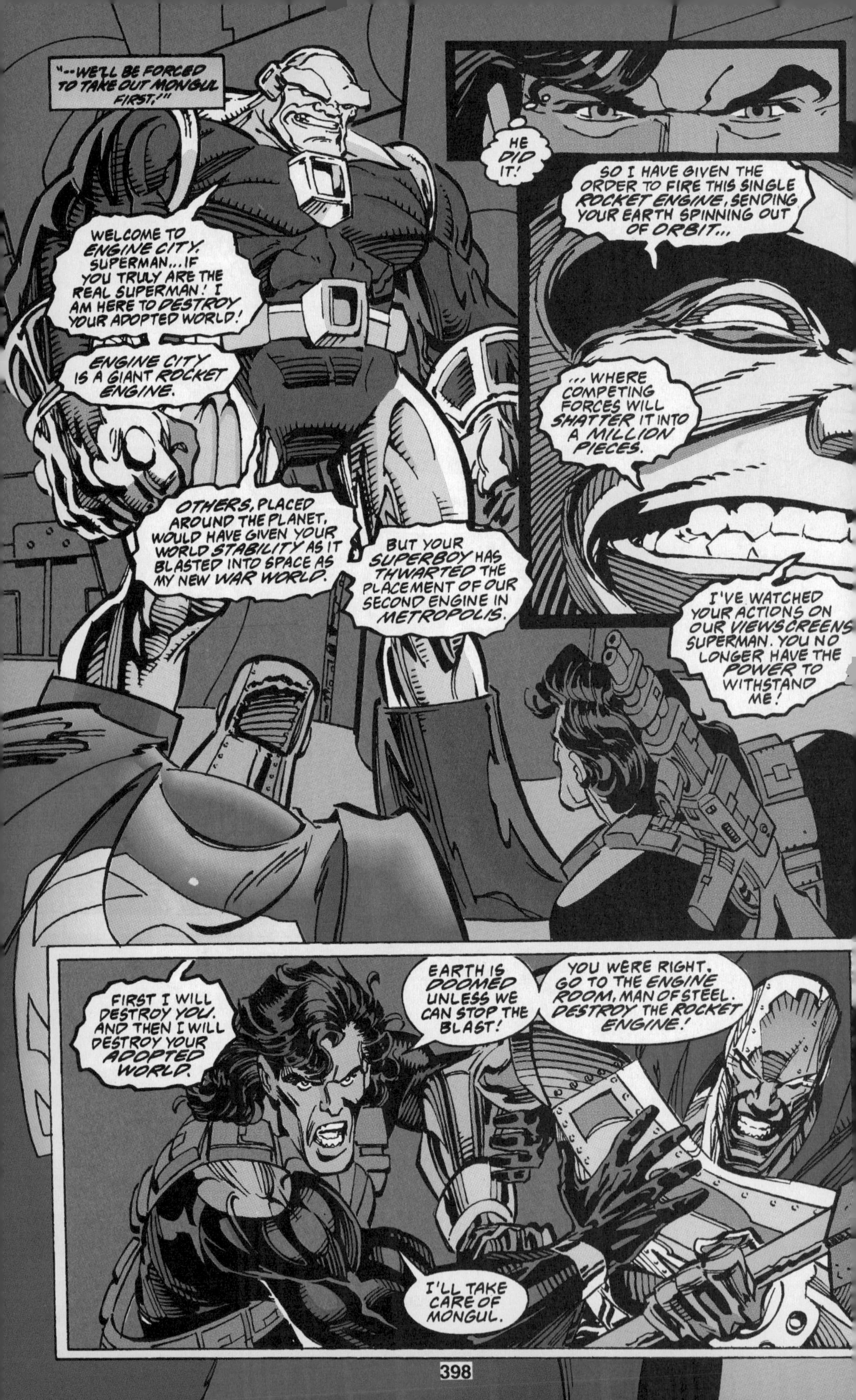
"--WE'LL BE FORCED TO TAKE OUT MONGUL FIRST!"
WELCOME TO ENGINE CITY, SUPERMAN...IF YOU TRULY ARE THE REAL SUPERMAN! I AM HERE TO DESTROY YOUR ADOPTED WORLD!
ENGINE CITY IS A GIANT ROCKET ENGINE.
OTHERS, PLACED AROUND THE PLANET, WOULD HAVE GIVEN YOUR WORLD STABILITY AS IT BLASTED INTO SPACE AS MY NEW WAR WORLD.
BUT YOUR SUPERBOY HAS THWARTED THE PLACEMENT OF OUR SECOND ENGINE IN METROPOLIS.
HE DID IT!
SO I HAVE GIVEN THE ORDER TO FIRE THIS SINGLE ROCKET ENGINE, SENDING YOUR EARTH SPINNING OUT OF ORBIT...
...WHERE COMPETING FORCES WILL SHATTER IT INTO A MILLION PIECES.
I'VE WATCHED YOUR ACTIONS ON OUR VIEWSCREENS SUPERMAN. YOU NO LONGER HAVE THE POWER TO WITHSTAND ME!
FIRST I WILL DESTROY YOU. AND THEN I WILL DESTROY YOUR ADOPTED WORLD.
EARTH IS DOOMED UNLESS WE CAN STOP THE BLAST!
YOU WERE RIGHT. GO TO THE ENGINE ROOM, MAN OF STEEL. DESTROY THE ROCKET ENGINE!
I'LL TAKE CARE OF MONGUL.

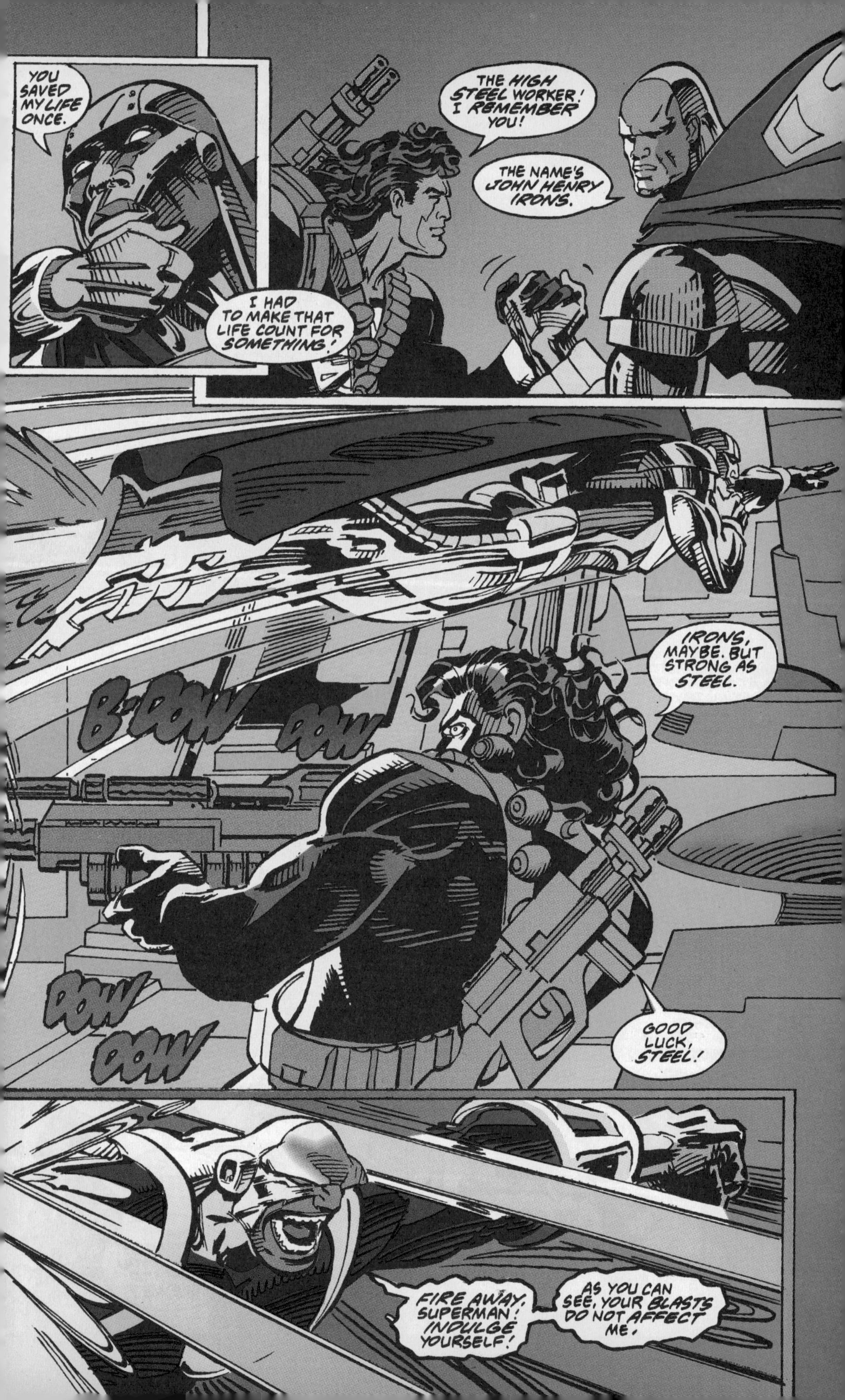
YOU SAVED MY LIFE ONCE.
THE HIGH STEEL WORKER! I REMEMBER YOU!
THE NAME'S JOHN HENRY IRONS.
I HAD TO MAKE THAT LIFE COUNT FOR SOMETHING!
IRONS, MAYBE. BUT STRONG AS STEEL.
B-DOW
DOW
DOW
DOW
GOOD LUCK, STEEL!
FIRE AWAY, SUPERMAN! INDULGE YOURSELF!
AS YOU CAN SEE, YOUR BLASTS DO NOT AFFECT ME.

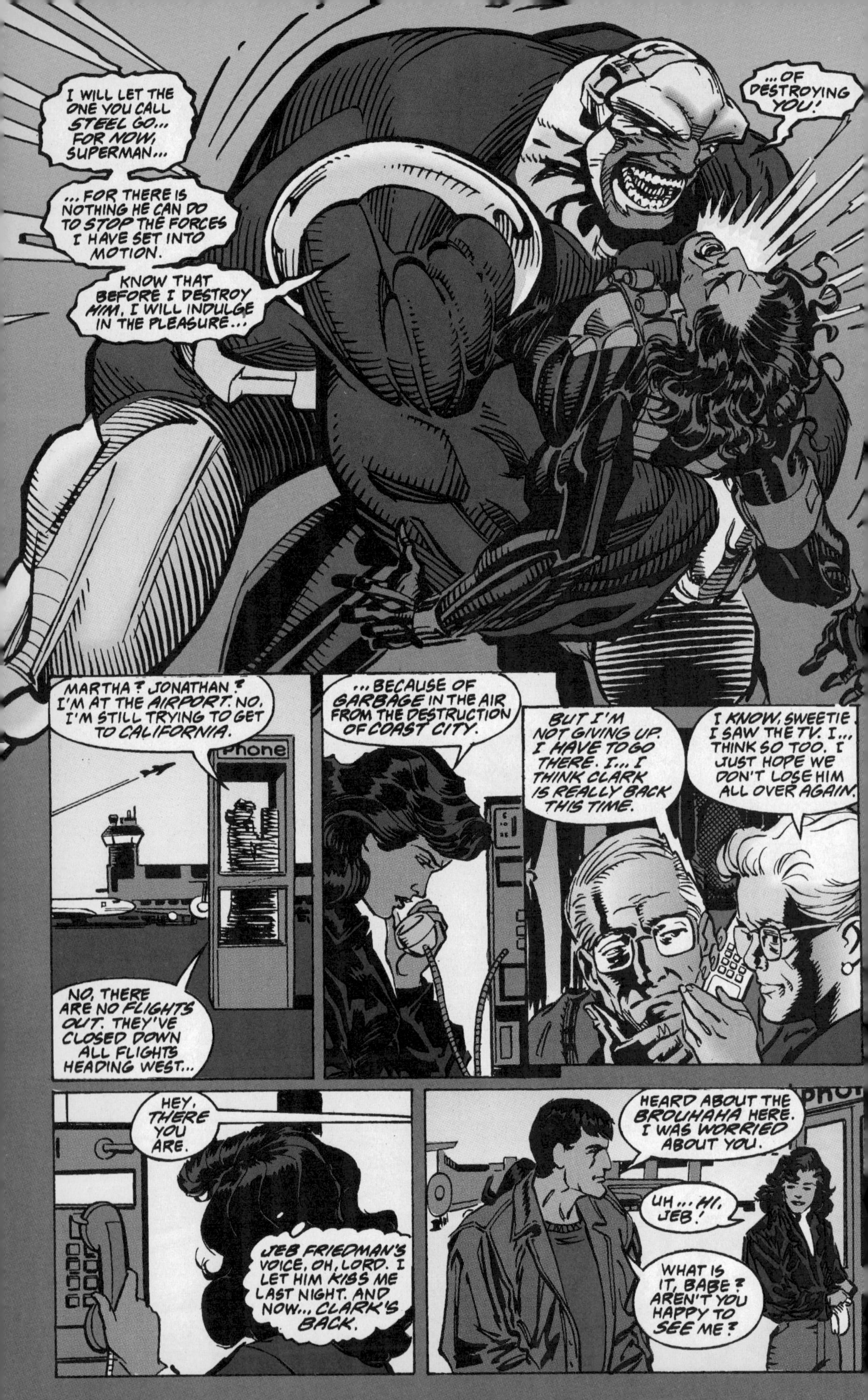
I WILL LET THE ONE YOU CALL STEEL GO... FOR NOW, SUPERMAN...
...FOR THERE IS NOTHING HE CAN DO TO STOP THE FORCES I HAVE SET INTO MOTION.
KNOW THAT BEFORE I DESTROY HIM, I WILL INDULGE IN THE PLEASURE...
...OF DESTROYING YOU!
MARTHA? JONATHAN? I'M AT THE AIRPORT. NO, I'M STILL TRYING TO GET TO CALIFORNIA.
Phone
NO, THERE ARE NO FLIGHTS OUT. THEY'VE CLOSED DOWN ALL FLIGHTS HEADING WEST...
...BECAUSE OF GARBAGE IN THE AIR FROM THE DESTRUCTION OF COAST CITY.
BUT I'M NOT GIVING UP. I HAVE TO GO THERE. I... I THINK CLARK IS REALLY BACK THIS TIME.
I KNOW, SWEETIE. I SAW THE TV. I... THINK SO TOO. I JUST HOPE WE DON'T LOSE HIM ALL OVER AGAIN.
HEY, THERE YOU ARE.
JEB FRIEDMAN'S VOICE. OH, LORD. I LET HIM KISS ME LAST NIGHT. AND NOW... CLARK'S BACK.
HEARD ABOUT THE BROUHAHA HERE. I WAS WORRIED ABOUT YOU.
UH... HI, JEB!
WHAT IS IT, BABE? AREN'T YOU HAPPY TO SEE ME?

ONCE AGAIN I AM WIRED INTO THE COMPUTER BANKS OF ENGINE CITY.

SUPERBOY'S VICTORY MUST HAVE SHAKEN MONGUL'S FAITH IN MY ABILITY TO TURN THIS PLANET INTO A NEW WAR WORLD...

...FOR MONGUL HAS SECRETLY INITIATED THE FIRING SEQUENCE THAT WILL SEND THE EARTH SPINNING OUT OF ORBIT.

THROUGH THE HEAT FLUCTUATIONS IN THE CITY'S LIFE SUPPORT SYSTEM, I CAN TRACK THE INVADERS.

AN INVISIBLE STRANGER RACES LOST THROUGH THE CORRIDORS BELOW, WHILE SUPERMAN FIGHTS MONGUL.

THE MAN CALLED STEEL RUSHES TOWARD THE ENGINE ROOM, BUT THERE IS NO WAY HE ALONE CAN STOP THE BLAST.

I CANNOT LET THAT FOOL MONGUL DESTROY ALL I'VE WORKED FOR.

I WILL LEAD SUPERMAN'S INVISIBLE ALLY TO HIM, TOGETHER THEY WILL DEFEAT MONGUL.

MONGUL HAS DESTROYED THE ROCKET'S FAILSAFE MECHANISMS.

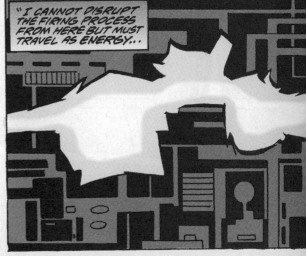

"I CANNOT DISRUPT THE FIRING PROCESS FROM HERE BUT MUST TRAVEL AS ENERGY...

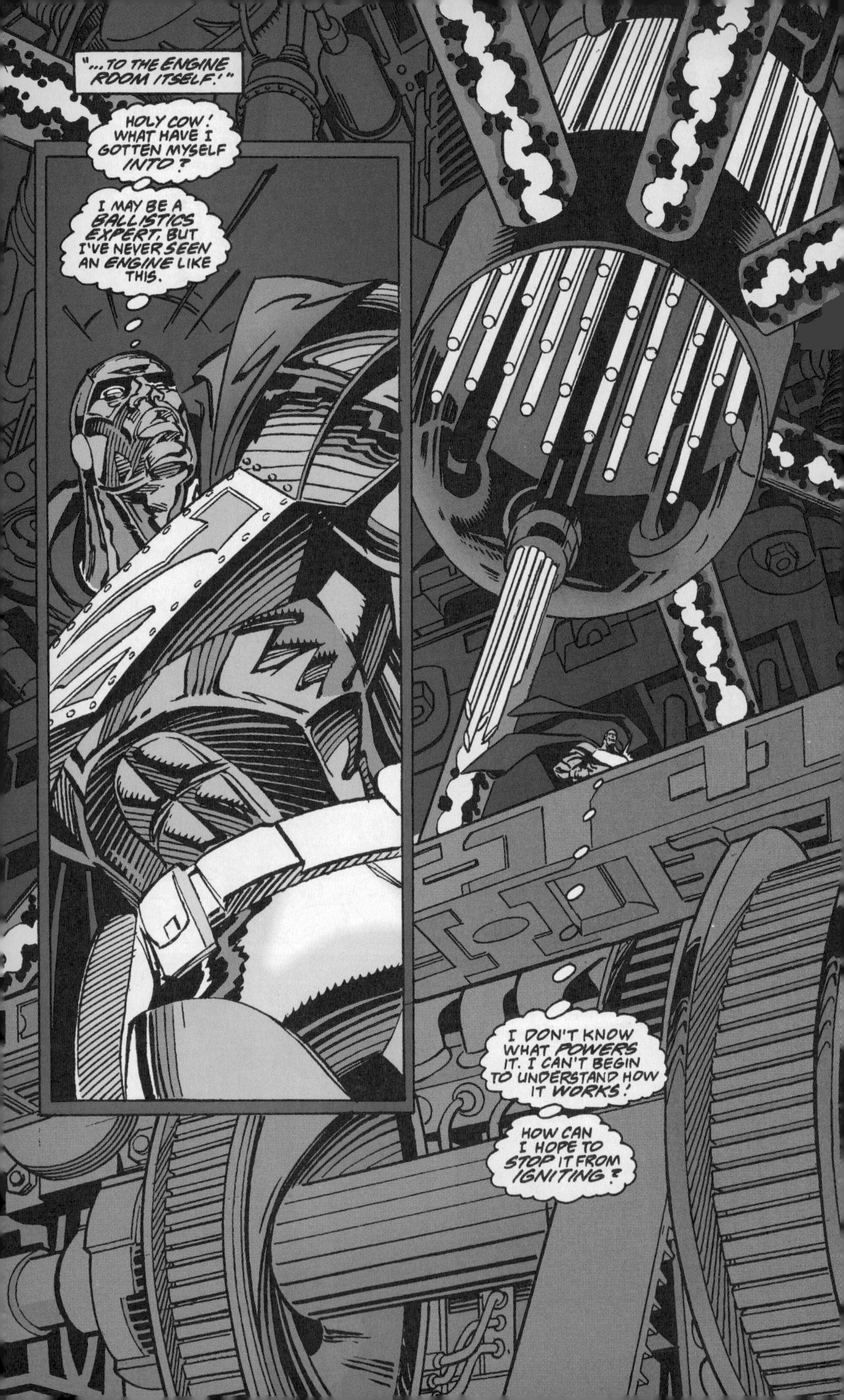
"...TO THE ENGINE ROOM ITSELF!"
HOLY COW! WHAT HAVE I GOTTEN MYSELF INTO?
I MAY BE A BALLISTICS EXPERT, BUT I'VE NEVER SEEN AN ENGINE LIKE THIS.
I DON'T KNOW WHAT POWERS IT. I CAN'T BEGIN TO UNDERSTAND HOW IT WORKS!
HOW CAN I HOPE TO STOP IT FROM IGNITING?

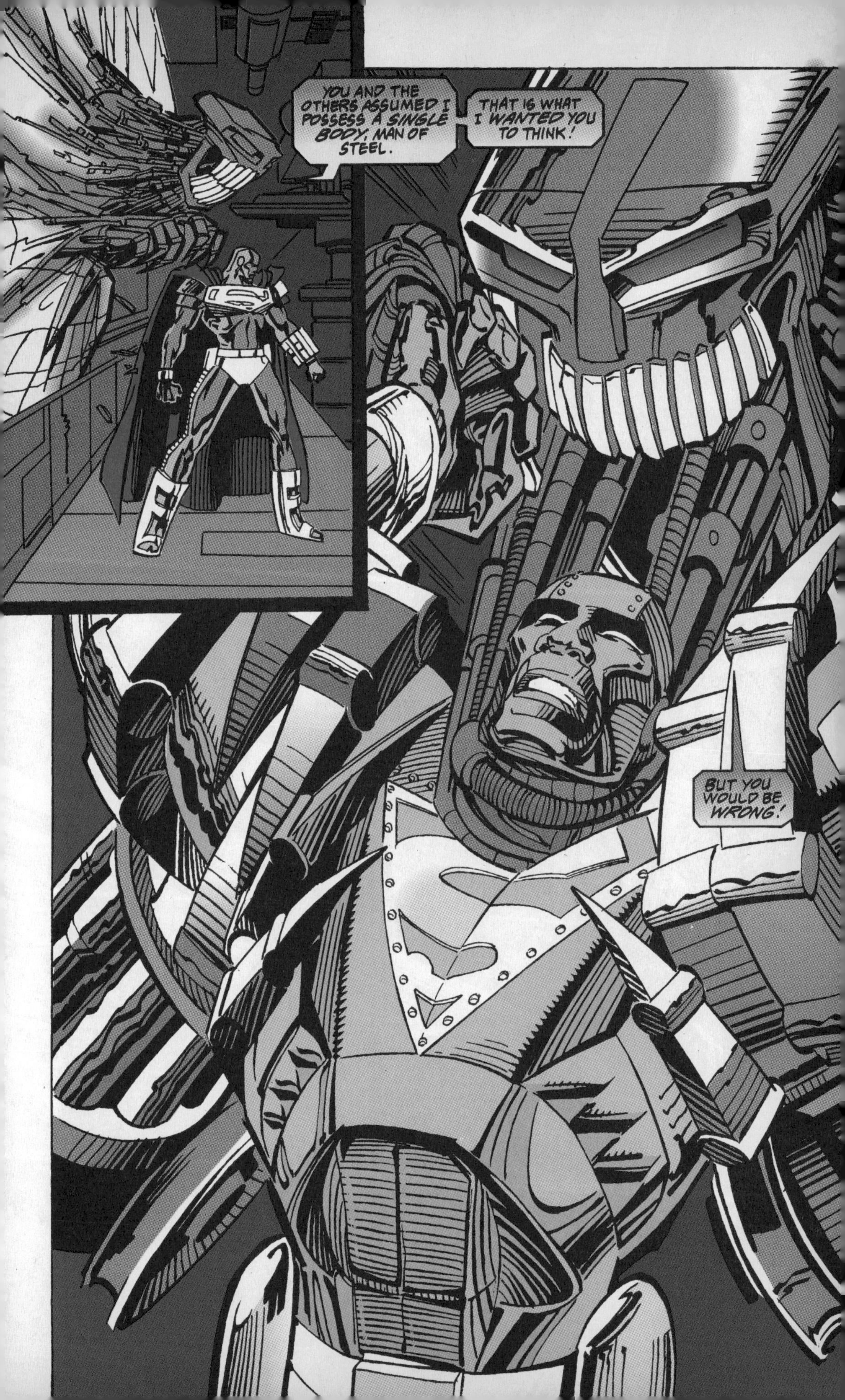
YOU AND THE OTHERS ASSUMED I POSSESS A SINGLE BODY, MAN OF STEEL.
THAT IS WHAT I WANTED YOU TO THINK!
BUT YOU WOULD BE WRONG!

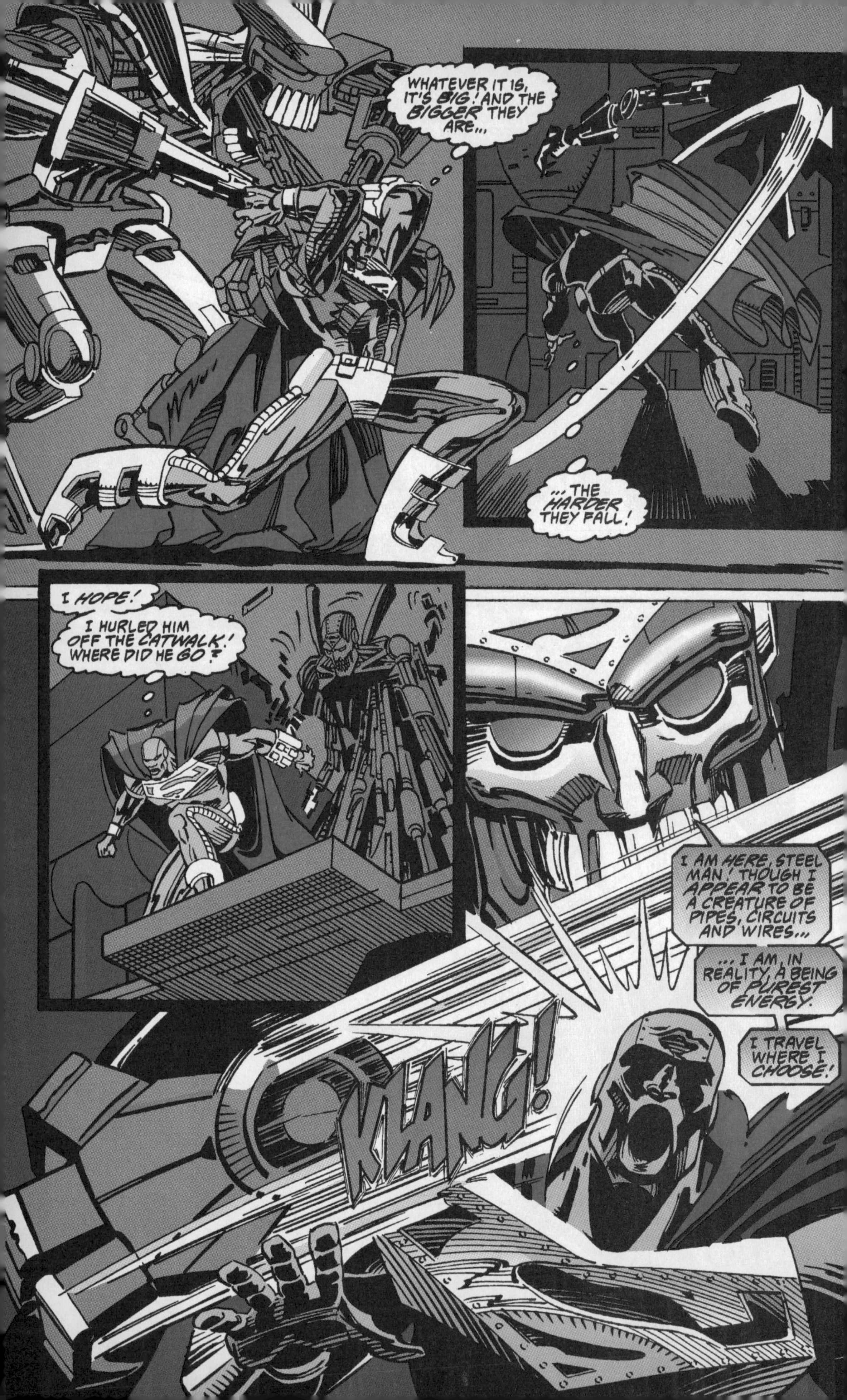

WHATEVER IT IS, IT'S BIG! AND THE BIGGER THEY ARE...
...THE HARDER THEY FALL!
I HOPE!
I HURLED HIM OFF THE CATWALK! WHERE DID HE GO?
I AM HERE, STEEL MAN! THOUGH I APPEAR TO BE A CREATURE OF PIPES, CIRCUITS AND WIRES...
...I AM IN REALITY, A BEING OF PUREST ENERGY.
I TRAVEL WHERE I CHOOSE!
KLANG!

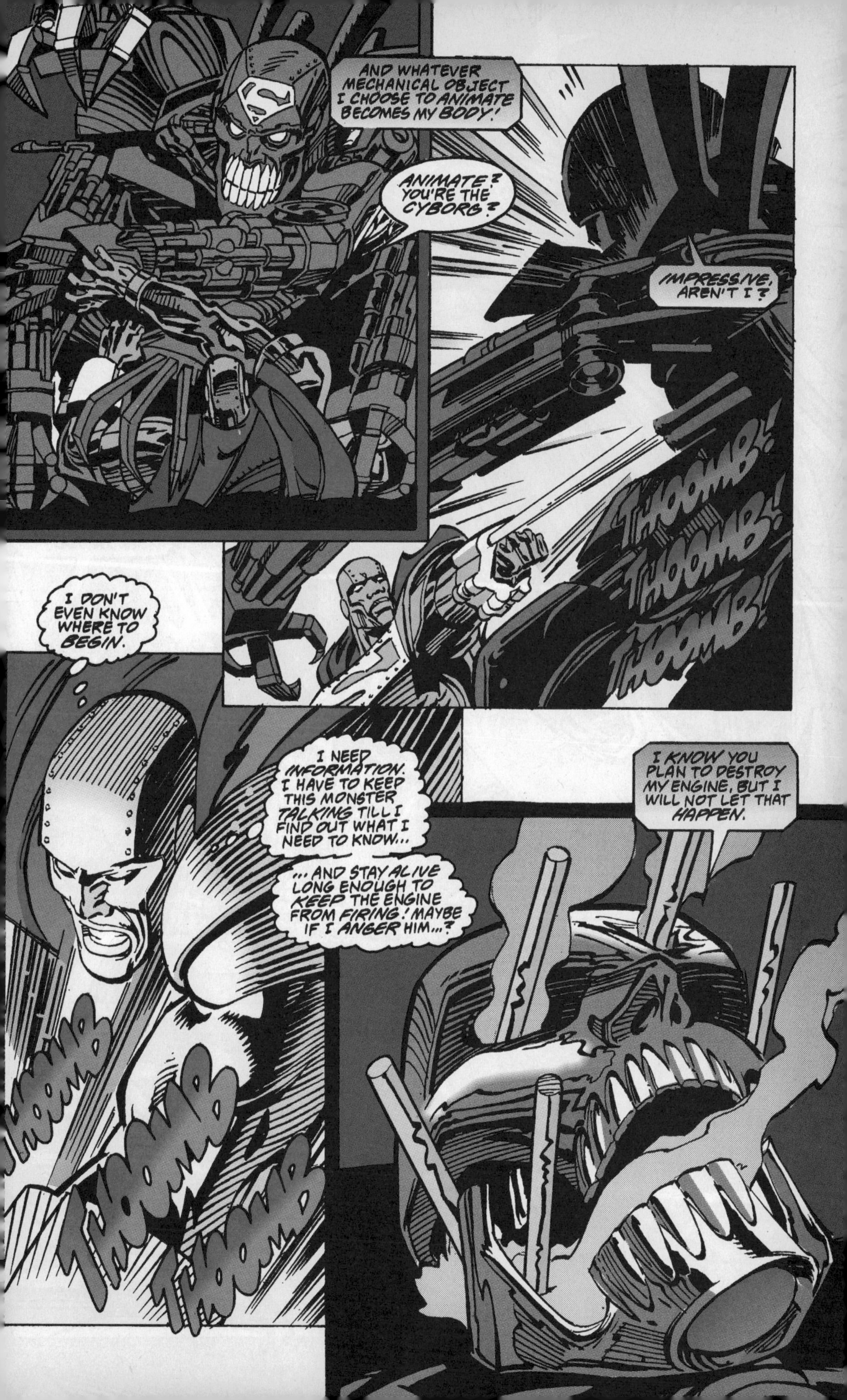

AND WHATEVER MECHANICAL OBJECT I CHOOSE TO ANIMATE BECOMES MY BODY!
ANIMATE? YOU'RE THE CYBORG?
IMPRESSIVE, AREN'T I?
THOOMB! THOOMB! THOOMB! THOOMB!
I DON'T EVEN KNOW WHERE TO BEGIN.
I NEED INFORMATION. I HAVE TO KEEP THIS MONSTER TALKING TILL I FIND OUT WHAT I NEED TO KNOW...
...AND STAY ALIVE LONG ENOUGH TO KEEP THE ENGINE FROM FIRING! MAYBE IF I ANGER HIM...?
THOOMB THOOMB THOOMB
I KNOW YOU PLAN TO DESTROY MY ENGINE, BUT I WILL NOT LET THAT HAPPEN.

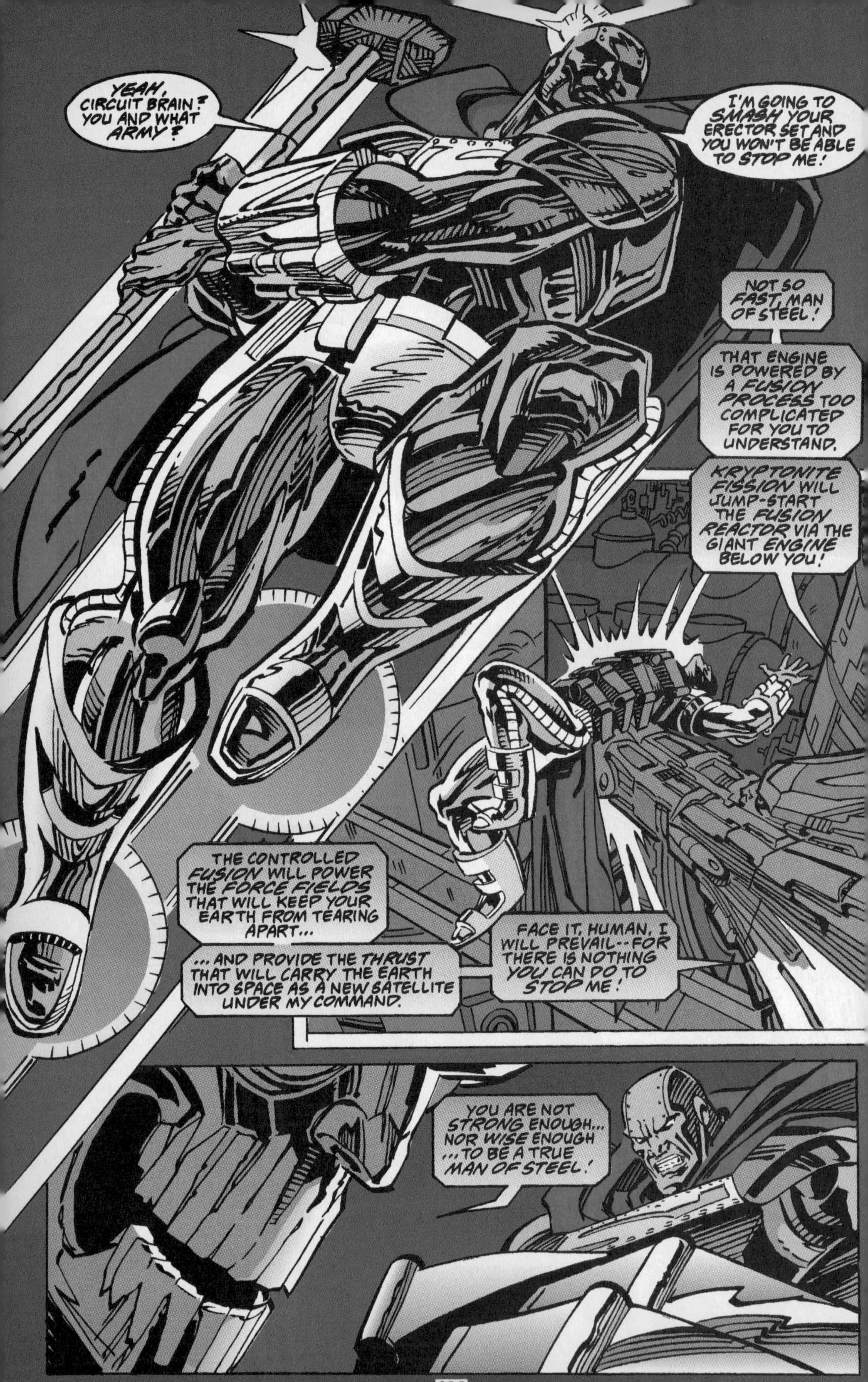
YEAH, CIRCUIT BRAIN? YOU AND WHAT ARMY?
I'M GOING TO SMASH YOUR ERECTOR SET AND YOU WON'T BE ABLE TO STOP ME!
NOT SO FAST, MAN OF STEEL!
THAT ENGINE IS POWERED BY A FUSION PROCESS TOO COMPLICATED FOR YOU TO UNDERSTAND.
KRYPTONITE FISSION WILL JUMP-START THE FUSION REACTOR VIA THE GIANT ENGINE BELOW YOU!
THE CONTROLLED FUSION WILL POWER THE FORCE FIELDS THAT WILL KEEP YOUR EARTH FROM TEARING APART...
...AND PROVIDE THE THRUST THAT WILL CARRY THE EARTH INTO SPACE AS A NEW SATELLITE UNDER MY COMMAND.
FACE IT, HUMAN, I WILL PREVAIL--FOR THERE IS NOTHING YOU CAN DO TO STOP ME!
YOU ARE NOT STRONG ENOUGH... NOR WISE ENOUGH ...TO BE A TRUE MAN OF STEEL!

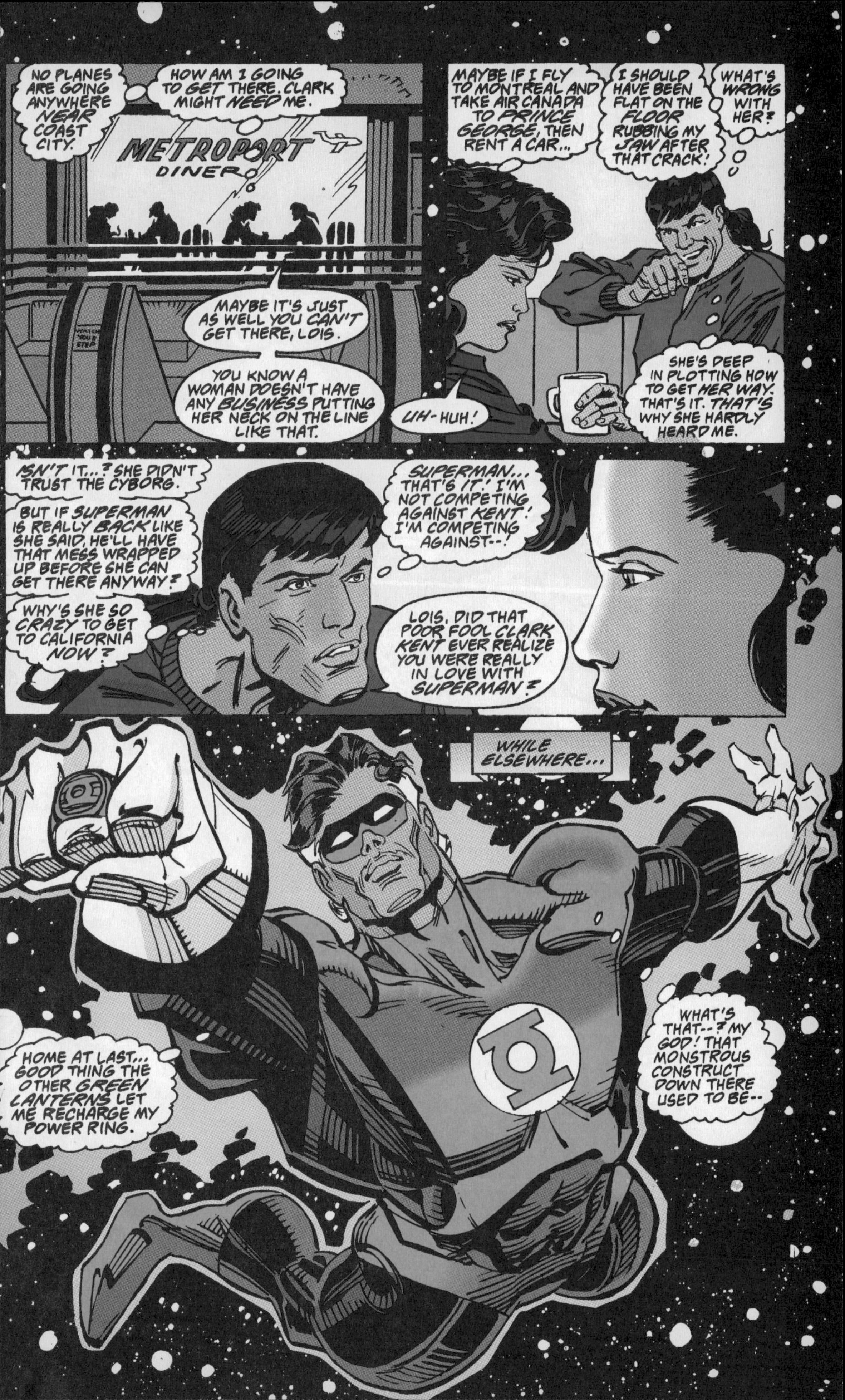
NO PLANES ARE GOING ANYWHERE NEAR COAST CITY.
HOW AM I GOING TO GET THERE. CLARK MIGHT NEED ME.
METROPORT DINER
MAYBE IT'S JUST AS WELL YOU CAN'T GET THERE, LOIS.
YOU KNOW A WOMAN DOESN'T HAVE ANY BUSINESS PUTTING HER NECK ON THE LINE LIKE THAT.
MAYBE IF I FLY TO MONTREAL AND TAKE AIR CANADA TO PRINCE GEORGE, THEN RENT A CAR...
I SHOULD HAVE BEEN FLAT ON THE FLOOR RUBBING MY JAW AFTER THAT CRACK!
WHAT'S WRONG WITH HER?
UH-HUH!
SHE'S DEEP IN PLOTTING HOW TO GET HER WAY. THAT'S IT. THAT'S WHY SHE HARDLY HEARD ME.
ISN'T IT...? SHE DIDN'T TRUST THE CYBORG.
BUT IF SUPERMAN IS REALLY BACK LIKE SHE SAID, HE'LL HAVE THAT MESS WRAPPED UP BEFORE SHE CAN GET THERE ANYWAY?
WHY'S SHE SO CRAZY TO GET TO CALIFORNIA NOW?
SUPERMAN... THAT'S IT! I'M NOT COMPETING AGAINST KENT! I'M COMPETING AGAINST--!
LOIS, DID THAT POOR FOOL CLARK KENT EVER REALIZE YOU WERE REALLY IN LOVE WITH SUPERMAN?
WHILE ELSEWHERE...
HOME AT LAST... GOOD THING THE OTHER GREEN LANTERNS LET ME RECHARGE MY POWER RING.
WHAT'S THAT--? MY GOD! THAT MONSTROUS CONSTRUCT DOWN THERE USED TO BE--

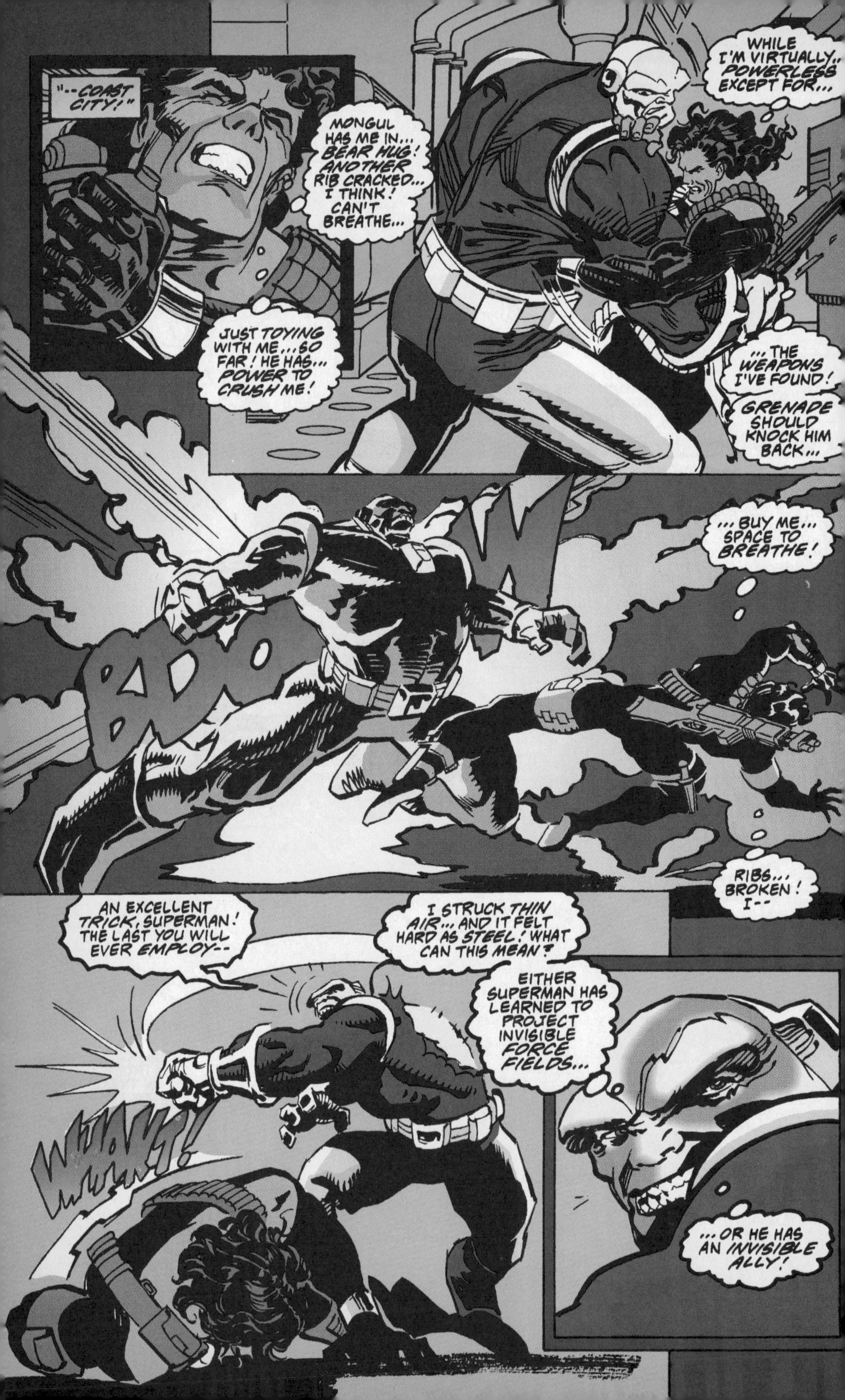
"...COAST CITY!"
MONGUL HAS ME IN... BEAR HUG! ANOTHER RIB CRACKED... I THINK! CAN'T BREATHE...
JUST TOYING WITH ME... SO FAR! HE HAS... POWER TO CRUSH ME!
WHILE I'M VIRTUALLY POWERLESS EXCEPT FOR...
...THE WEAPONS I'VE FOUND!
GRENADE SHOULD KNOCK HIM BACK...
...BUY ME... SPACE TO BREATHE!
RIBS... BROKEN! I--
AN EXCELLENT TRICK, SUPERMAN! THE LAST YOU WILL EVER EMPLOY--
I STRUCK THIN AIR... AND IT FELT HARD AS STEEL! WHAT CAN THIS MEAN?
EITHER SUPERMAN HAS LEARNED TO PROJECT INVISIBLE FORCE FIELDS...
...OR HE HAS AN INVISIBLE ALLY!

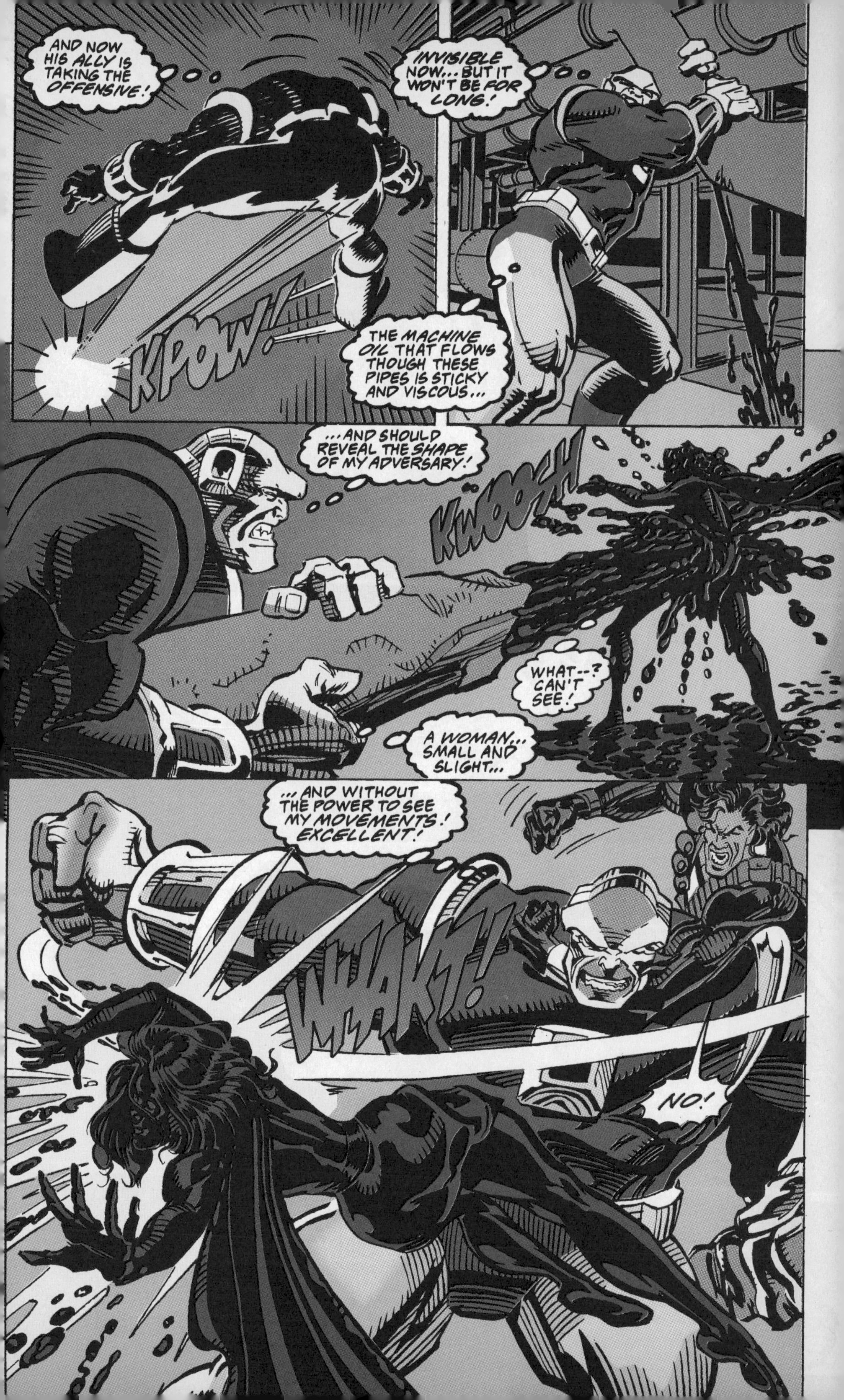

AND NOW HIS ALLY IS TAKING THE OFFENSIVE!
INVISIBLE NOW... BUT IT WON'T BE FOR LONG!
KPOW!
THE MACHINE OIL THAT FLOWS THOUGH THESE PIPES IS STICKY AND VISCOUS...
...AND SHOULD REVEAL THE SHAPE OF MY ADVERSARY!
KWOOSH
WHAT--? CAN'T SEE!
A WOMAN... SMALL AND SLIGHT...
...AND WITHOUT THE POWER TO SEE MY MOVEMENTS! EXCELLENT!
WHAK!
NO!

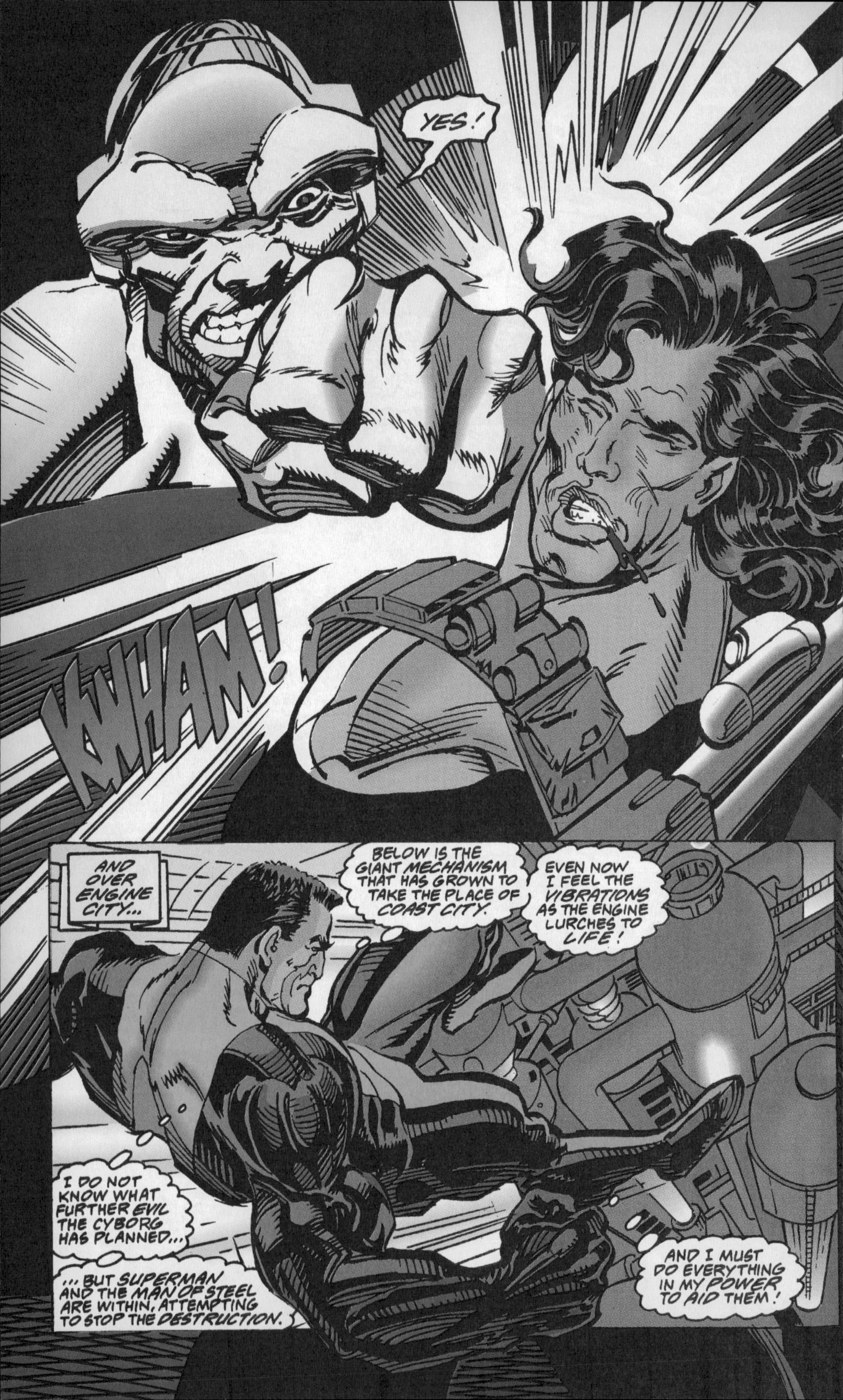
YES!
KWHAM!
AND OVER ENGINE CITY...
BELOW IS THE GIANT MECHANISM THAT HAS GROWN TO TAKE THE PLACE OF COAST CITY.
EVEN NOW I FEEL THE VIBRATIONS AS THE ENGINE LURCHES TO LIFE!
I DO NOT KNOW WHAT FURTHER EVIL THE CYBORG HAS PLANNED...
... BUT SUPERMAN AND THE MAN OF STEEL ARE WITHIN, ATTEMPTING TO STOP THE DESTRUCTION.
AND I MUST DO EVERYTHING IN MY POWER TO AID THEM!

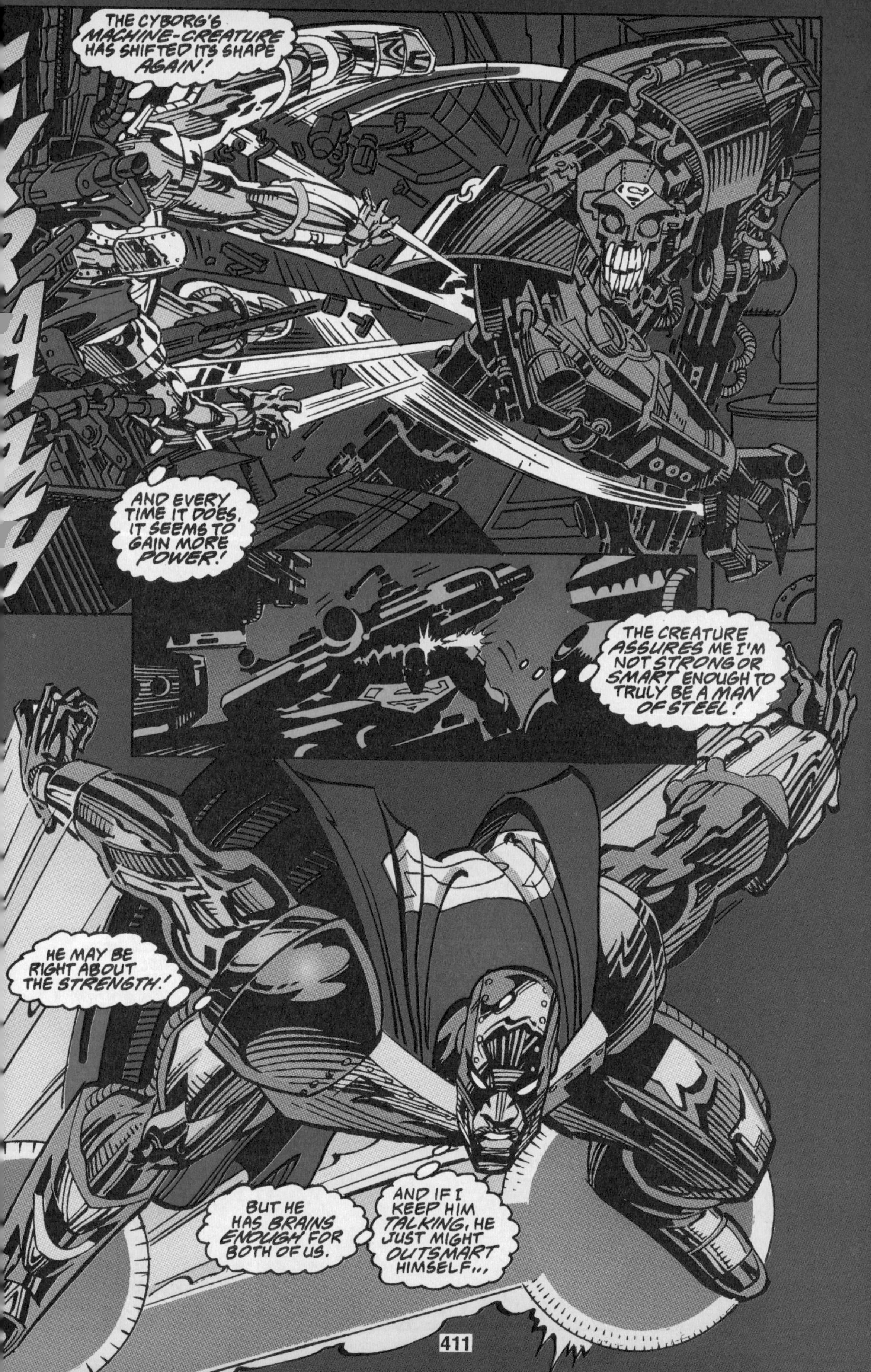
THE CYBORG'S MACHINE-CREATURE HAS SHIFTED ITS SHAPE AGAIN!
AND EVERY TIME IT DOES, IT SEEMS TO GAIN MORE POWER!
THE CREATURE ASSURES ME I'M NOT STRONG OR SMART ENOUGH TO TRULY BE A MAN OF STEEL!
HE MAY BE RIGHT ABOUT THE STRENGTH!
BUT HE HAS BRAINS ENOUGH FOR BOTH OF US.
AND IF I KEEP HIM TALKING, HE JUST MIGHT OUTSMART HIMSELF...

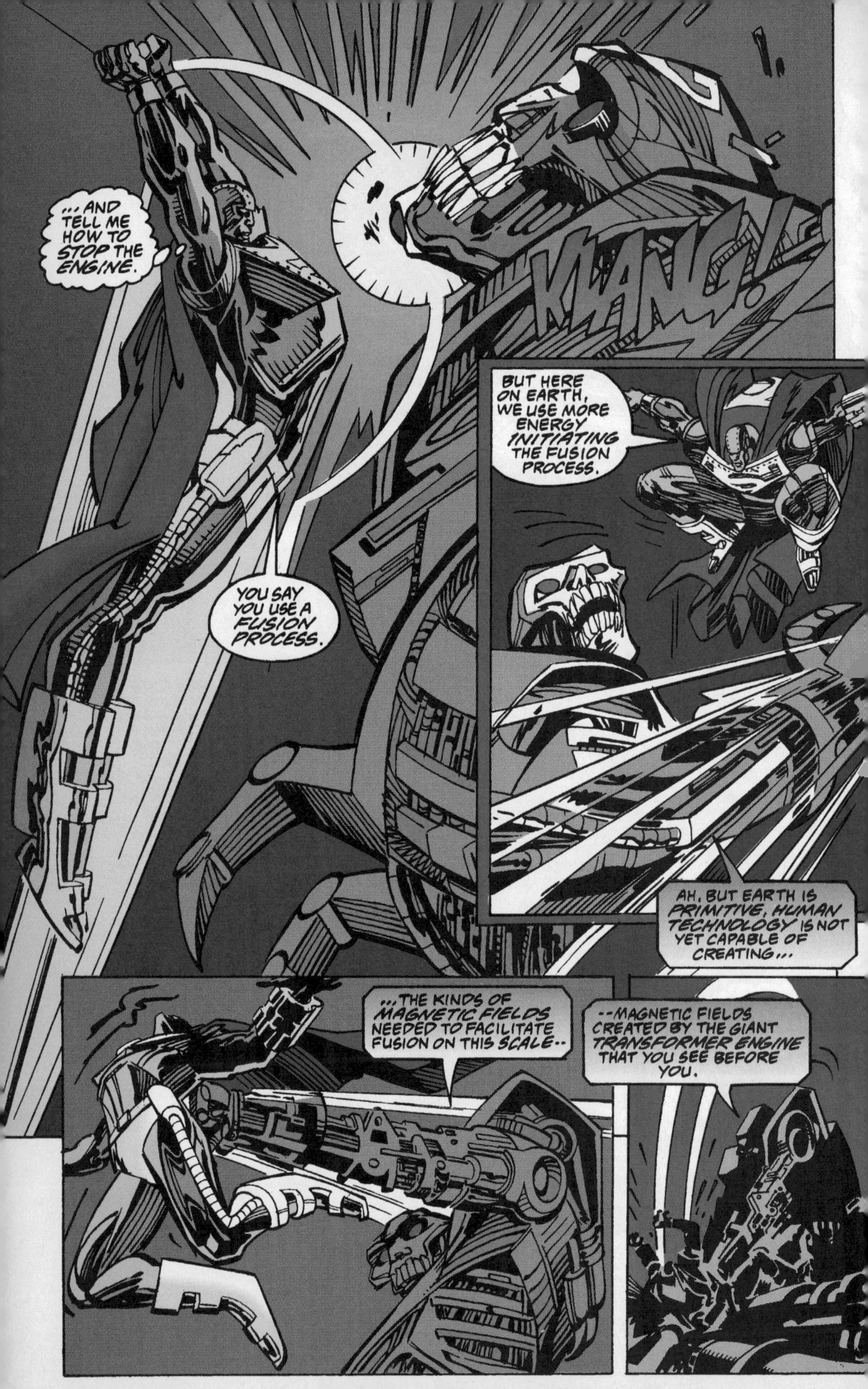
...AND TELL ME HOW TO STOP THE ENGINE.
KLANG!
YOU SAY YOU USE A FUSION PROCESS.
BUT HERE ON EARTH, WE USE MORE ENERGY INITIATING THE FUSION PROCESS.
AH, BUT EARTH IS PRIMITIVE. HUMAN TECHNOLOGY IS NOT YET CAPABLE OF CREATING...
...THE KINDS OF MAGNETIC FIELDS NEEDED TO FACILITATE FUSION ON THIS SCALE..
--MAGNETIC FIELDS CREATED BY THE GIANT TRANSFORMER ENGINE THAT YOU SEE BEFORE YOU.

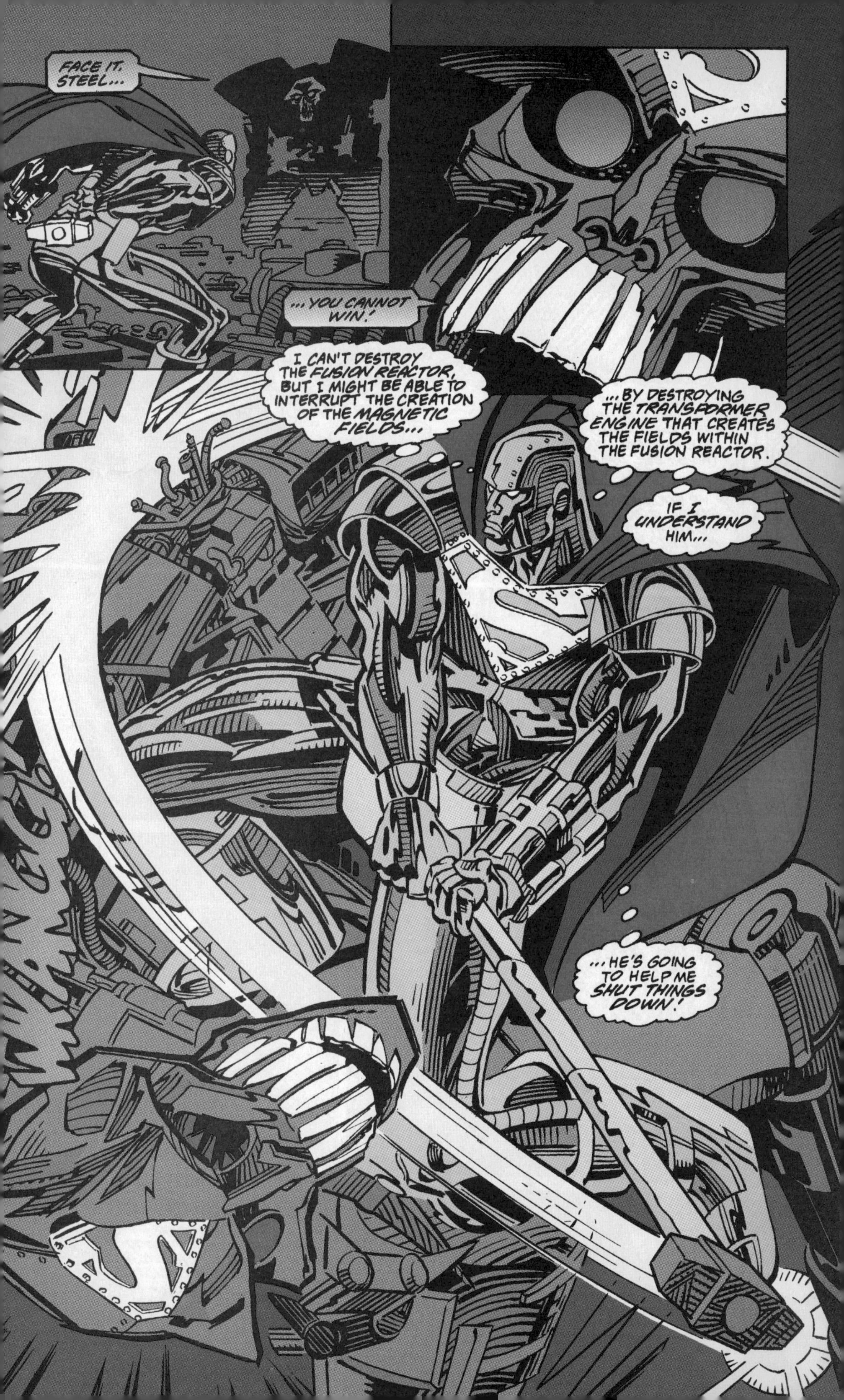
FACE IT, STEEL...
...YOU CANNOT WIN!
I CAN'T DESTROY THE FUSION REACTOR, BUT I MIGHT BE ABLE TO INTERRUPT THE CREATION OF THE MAGNETIC FIELDS...
...BY DESTROYING THE TRANSFORMER ENGINE THAT CREATES THE FIELDS WITHIN THE FUSION REACTOR.
IF I UNDERSTAND HIM...
...HE'S GOING TO HELP ME SHUT THINGS DOWN!

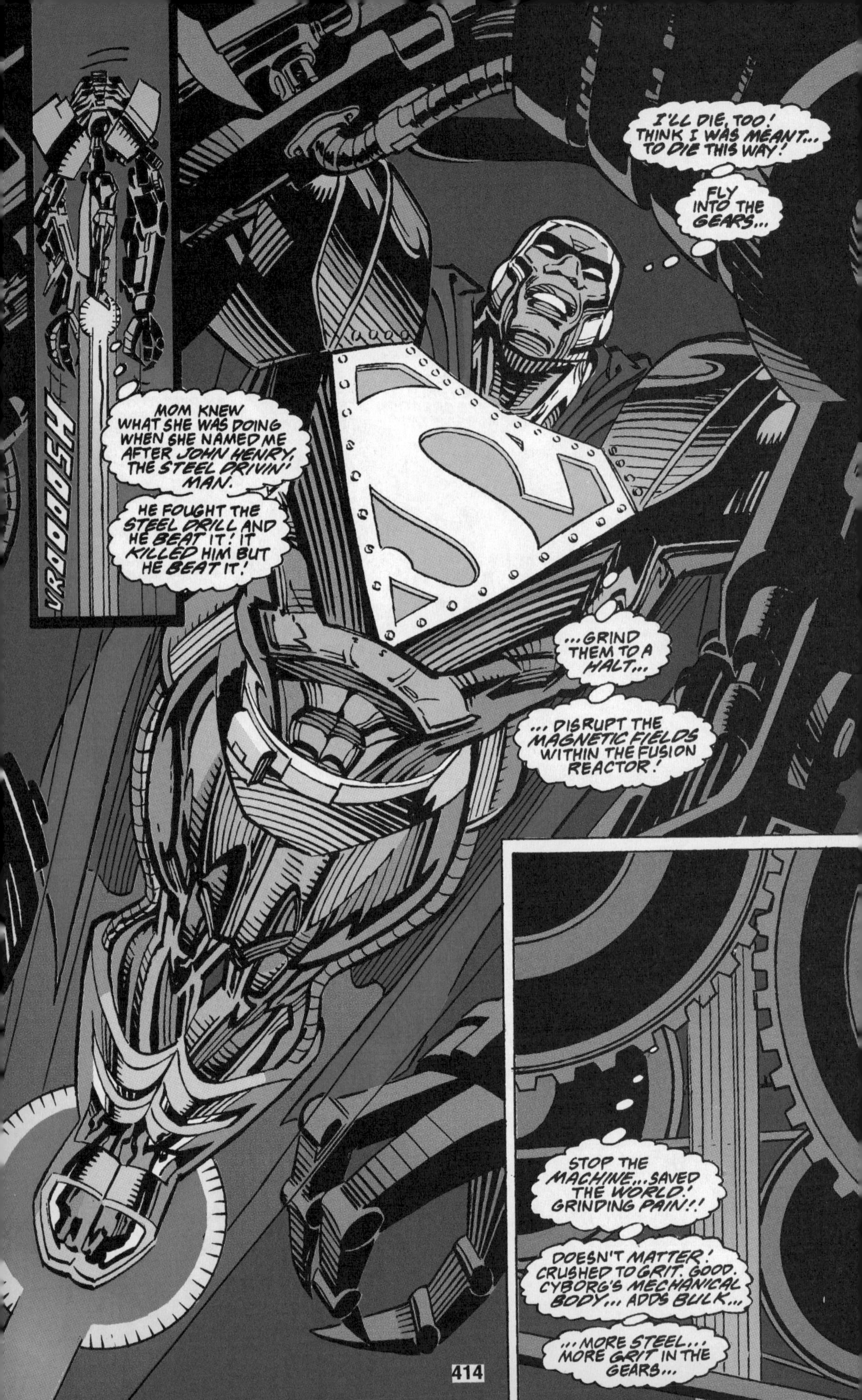

I'LL DIE, TOO! THINK I WAS MEANT... TO DIE THIS WAY!
FLY INTO THE GEARS...
VROOOOSH
MOM KNEW WHAT SHE WAS DOING WHEN SHE NAMED ME AFTER JOHN HENRY, THE STEEL DRIVIN' MAN.
HE FOUGHT THE STEEL DRILL AND HE BEAT IT! IT KILLED HIM BUT HE BEAT IT!
...GRIND THEM TO A HALT...
...DISRUPT THE MAGNETIC FIELDS WITHIN THE FUSION REACTOR!
STOP THE MACHINE... SAVED THE WORLD! GRINDING PAIN!!
DOESN'T MATTER! CRUSHED TO GRIT. GOOD. CYBORG'S MECHANICAL BODY... ADDS BULK...
...MORE STEEL... MORE GRIT IN THE GEARS...

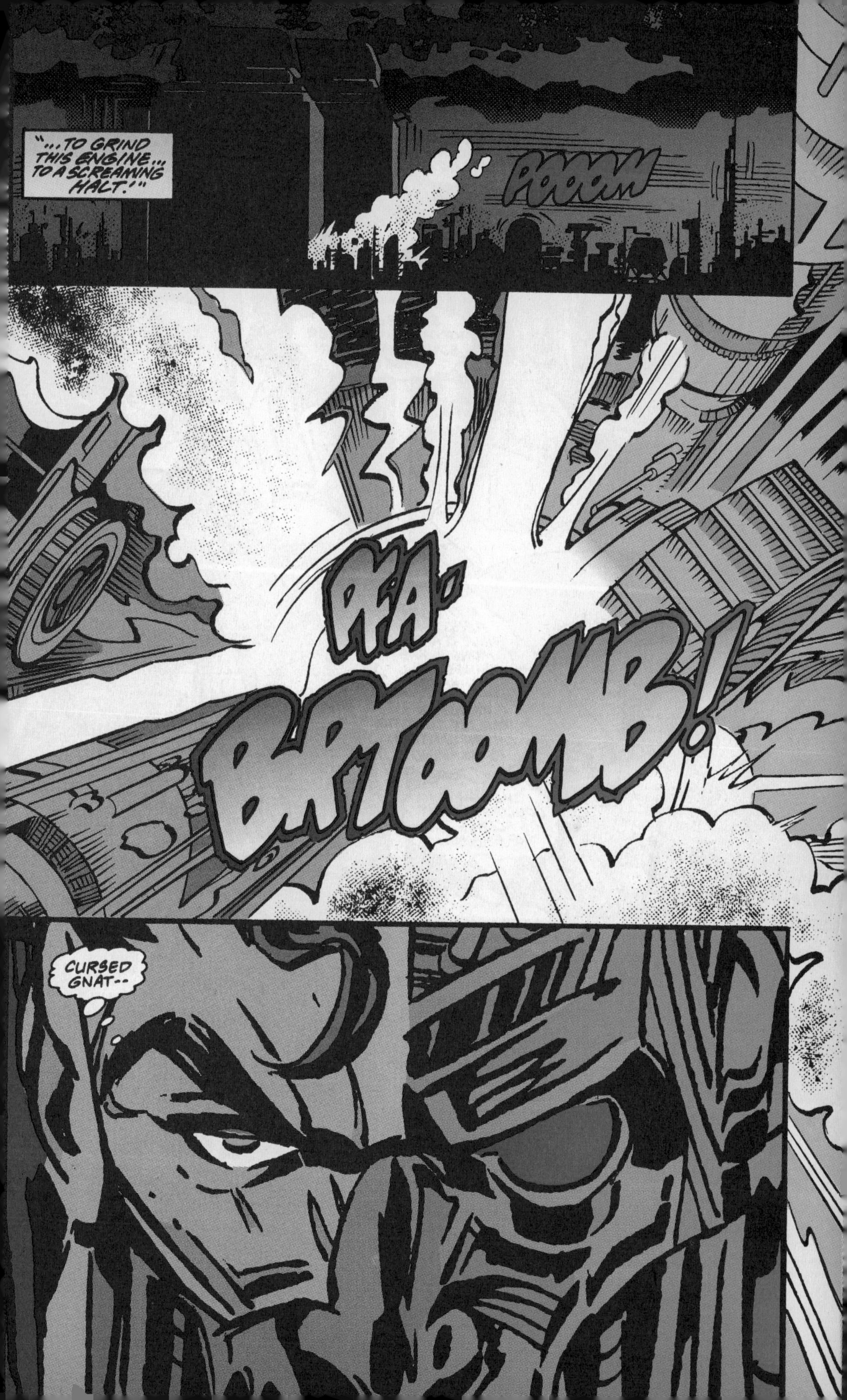
"...TO GRIND THIS ENGINE... TO A SCREAMING HALT!"
POOOM
KA-BATOOMB!
CURSED GNAT--

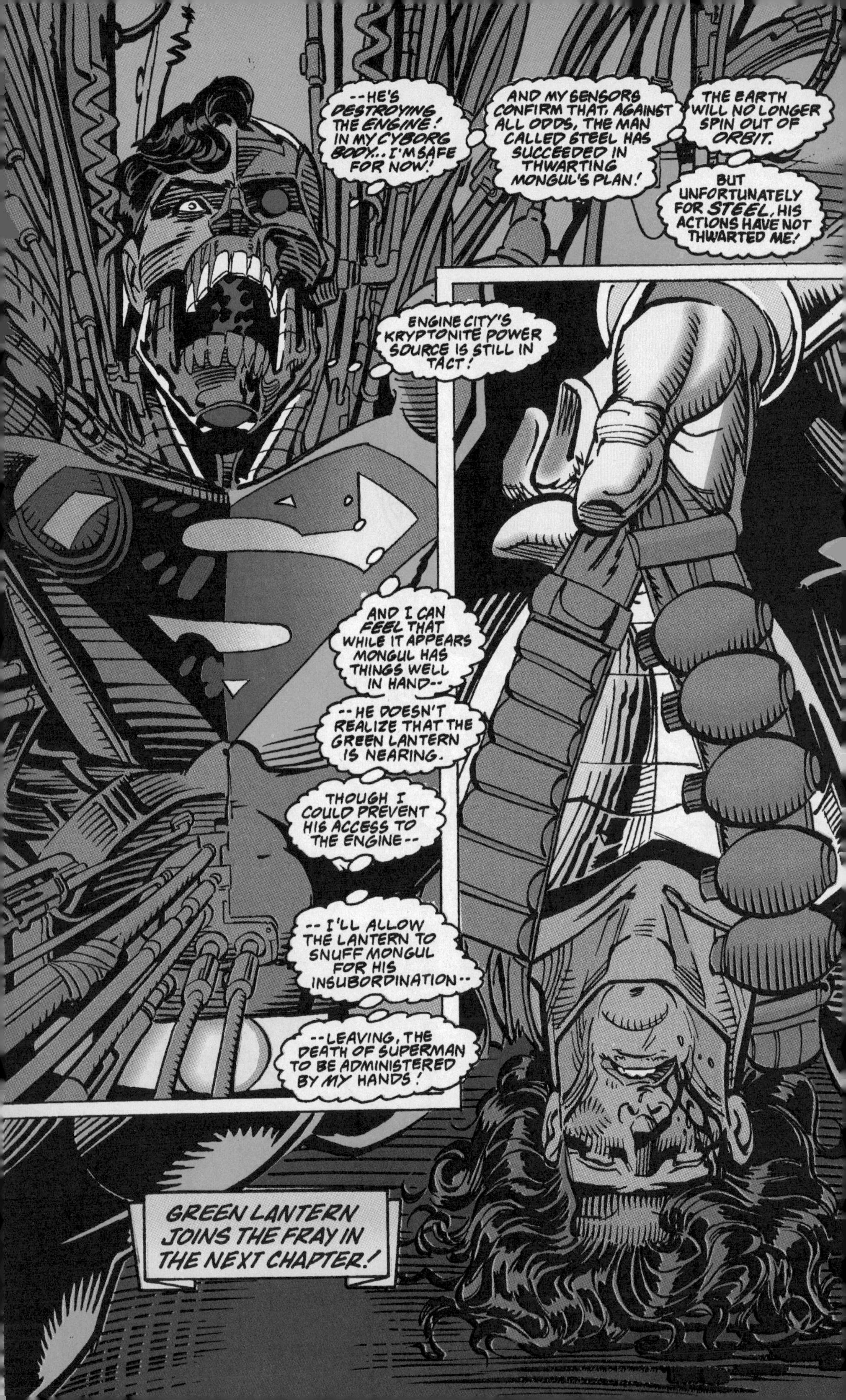
--HE'S DESTROYING THE ENGINE! IN MY CYBORG BODY... I'M SAFE FOR NOW!
AND MY SENSORS CONFIRM THAT, AGAINST ALL ODDS, THE MAN CALLED STEEL HAS SUCCEEDED IN THWARTING MONGUL'S PLAN!
THE EARTH WILL NO LONGER SPIN OUT OF ORBIT.
BUT UNFORTUNATELY FOR STEEL, HIS ACTIONS HAVE NOT THWARTED ME!
ENGINE CITY'S KRYPTONITE POWER SOURCE IS STILL IN TACT!
AND I CAN FEEL THAT WHILE IT APPEARS MONGUL HAS THINGS WELL IN HAND--
--HE DOESN'T REALIZE THAT THE GREEN LANTERN IS NEARING.
THOUGH I COULD PREVENT HIS ACCESS TO THE ENGINE--
--I'LL ALLOW THE LANTERN TO SNUFF MONGUL FOR HIS INSUBORDINATION--
--LEAVING, THE DEATH OF SUPERMAN TO BE ADMINISTERED BY MY HANDS!
GREEN LANTERN JOINS THE FRAY IN THE NEXT CHAPTER!

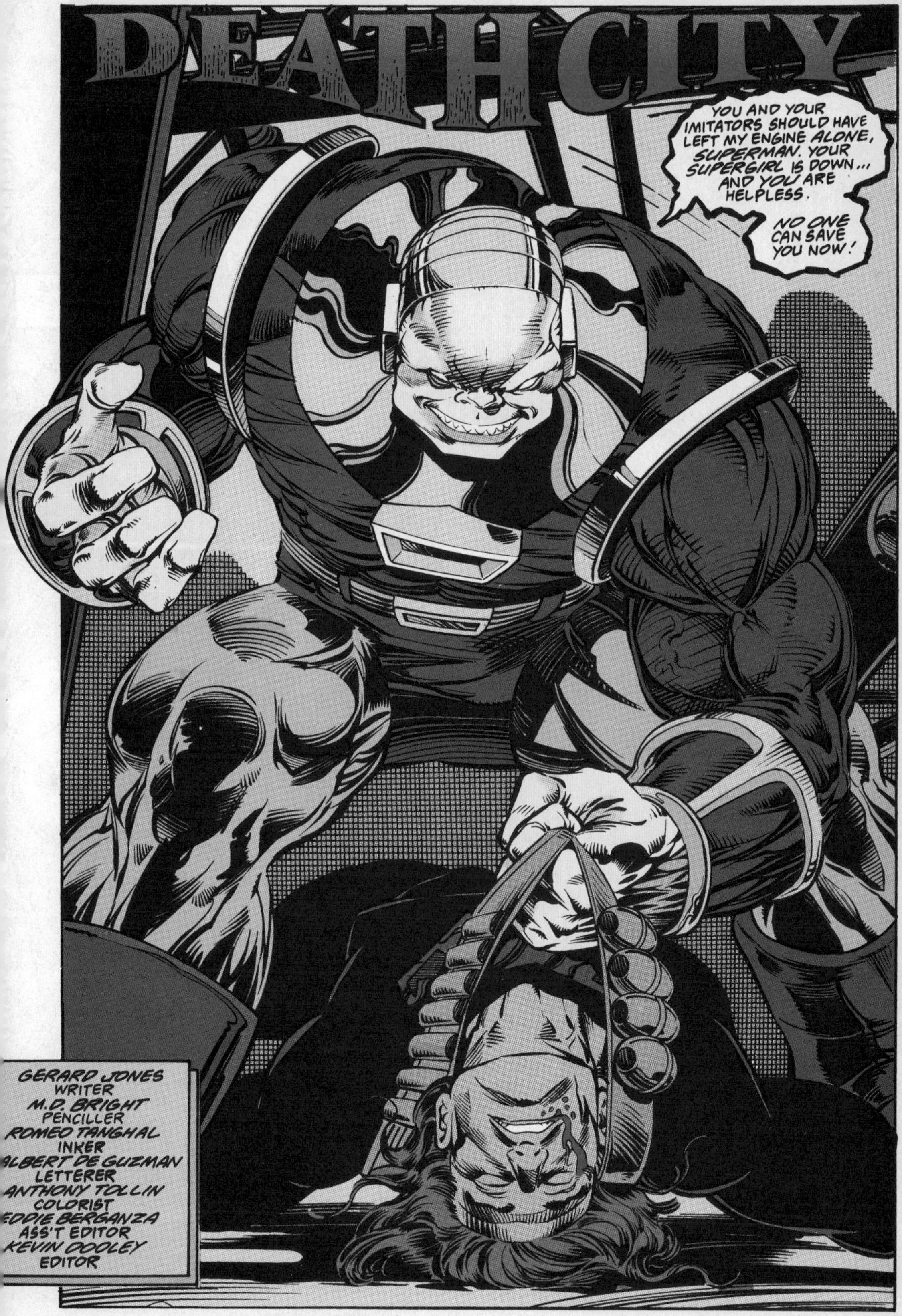
DEATH CITY
YOU AND YOUR IMITATORS SHOULD HAVE LEFT MY ENGINE ALONE, SUPERMAN. YOUR SUPERGIRL IS DOWN... AND YOU ARE HELPLESS.
NO ONE CAN SAVE YOU NOW!
GERARD JONES WRITER
M.D. BRIGHT PENCILLER
ROMEO TANGHAL INKER
ALBERT DE GUZMAN LETTERER
ANTHONY TOLLIN COLORIST
EDDIE BERGANZA ASS'T EDITOR
KEVIN DOOLEY EDITOR

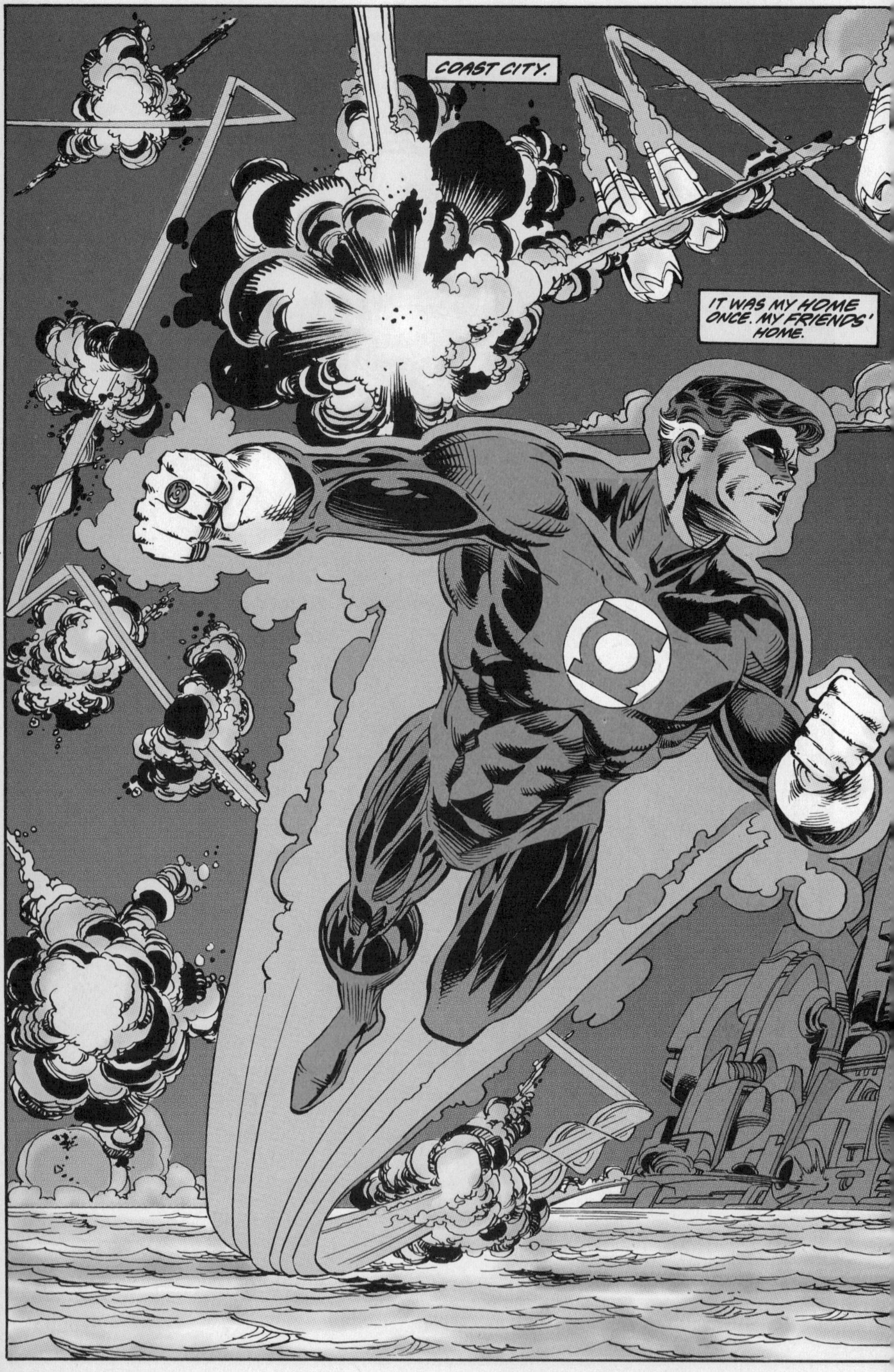
COAST CITY.
IT WAS MY HOME ONCE. MY FRIENDS' HOME.

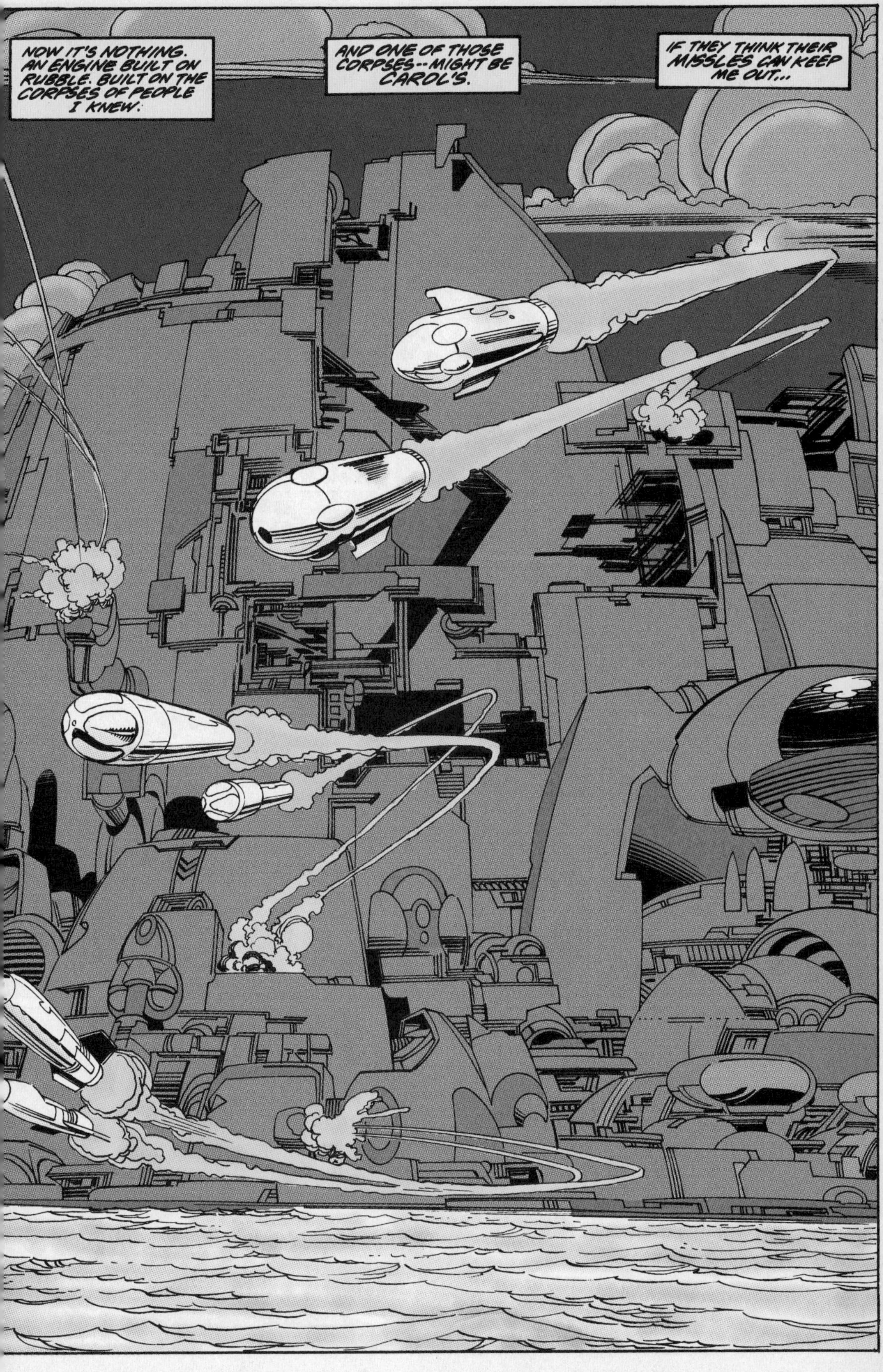
NOW IT'S NOTHING. AN ENGINE BUILT ON RUBBLE. BUILT ON THE CORPSES OF PEOPLE I KNEW.
AND ONE OF THOSE CORPSES--MIGHT BE CAROL'S.
IF THEY THINK THEIR MISSLES CAN KEEP ME OUT...

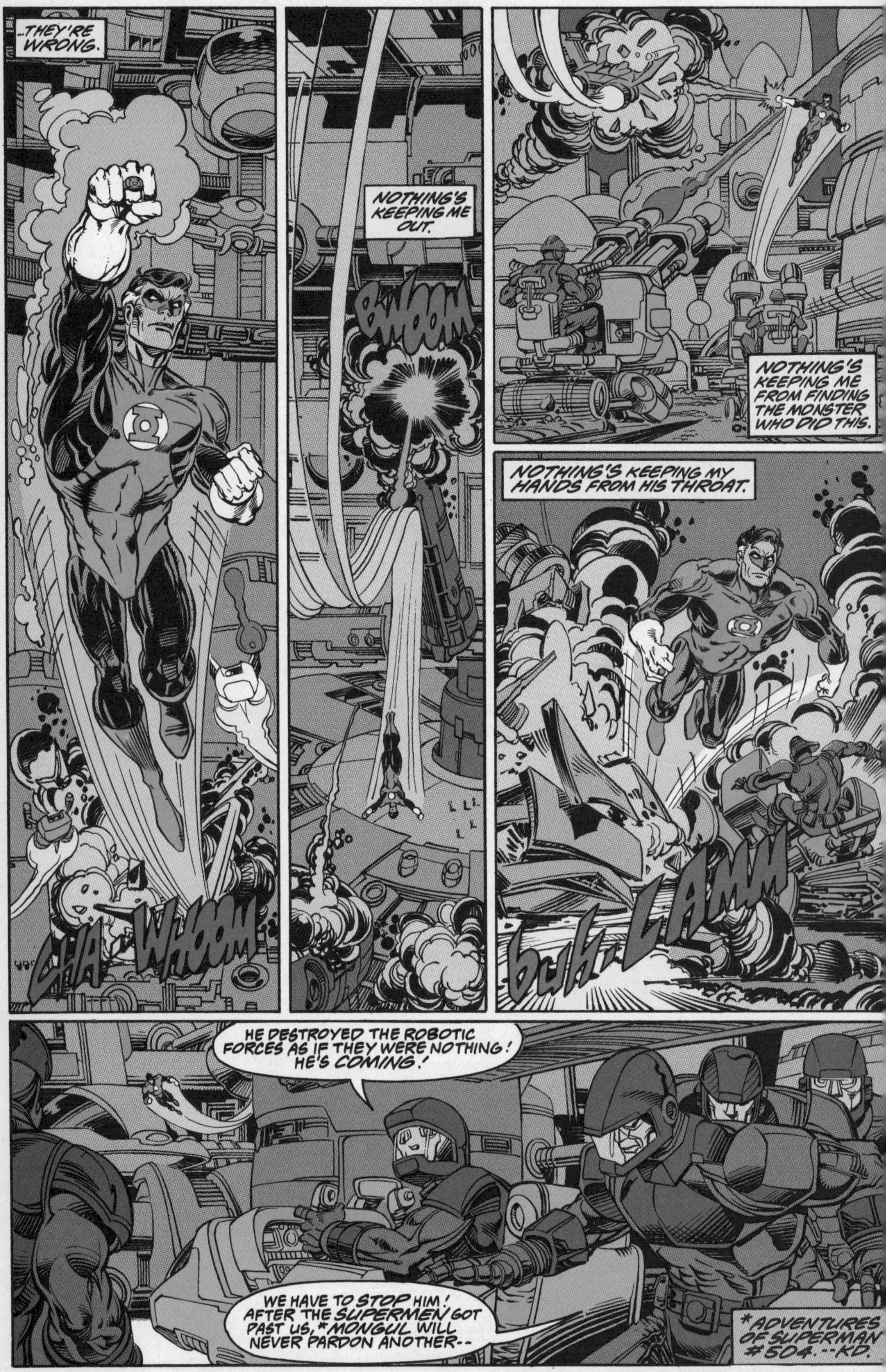
...THEY'RE WRONG.
CHA-WHOOM
NOTHING'S KEEPING ME OUT.
BWOOM
NOTHING'S KEEPING ME FROM FINDING THE MONSTER WHO DID THIS.
NOTHING'S KEEPING MY HANDS FROM HIS THROAT.
buh-LAMM
HE DESTROYED THE ROBOTIC FORCES AS IF THEY WERE NOTHING! HE'S COMING!
WE HAVE TO STOP HIM! AFTER THE SUPERMEN GOT PAST US,* MONGUL WILL NEVER PARDON ANOTHER--
*ADVENTURES OF SUPERMAN #504.--KD.

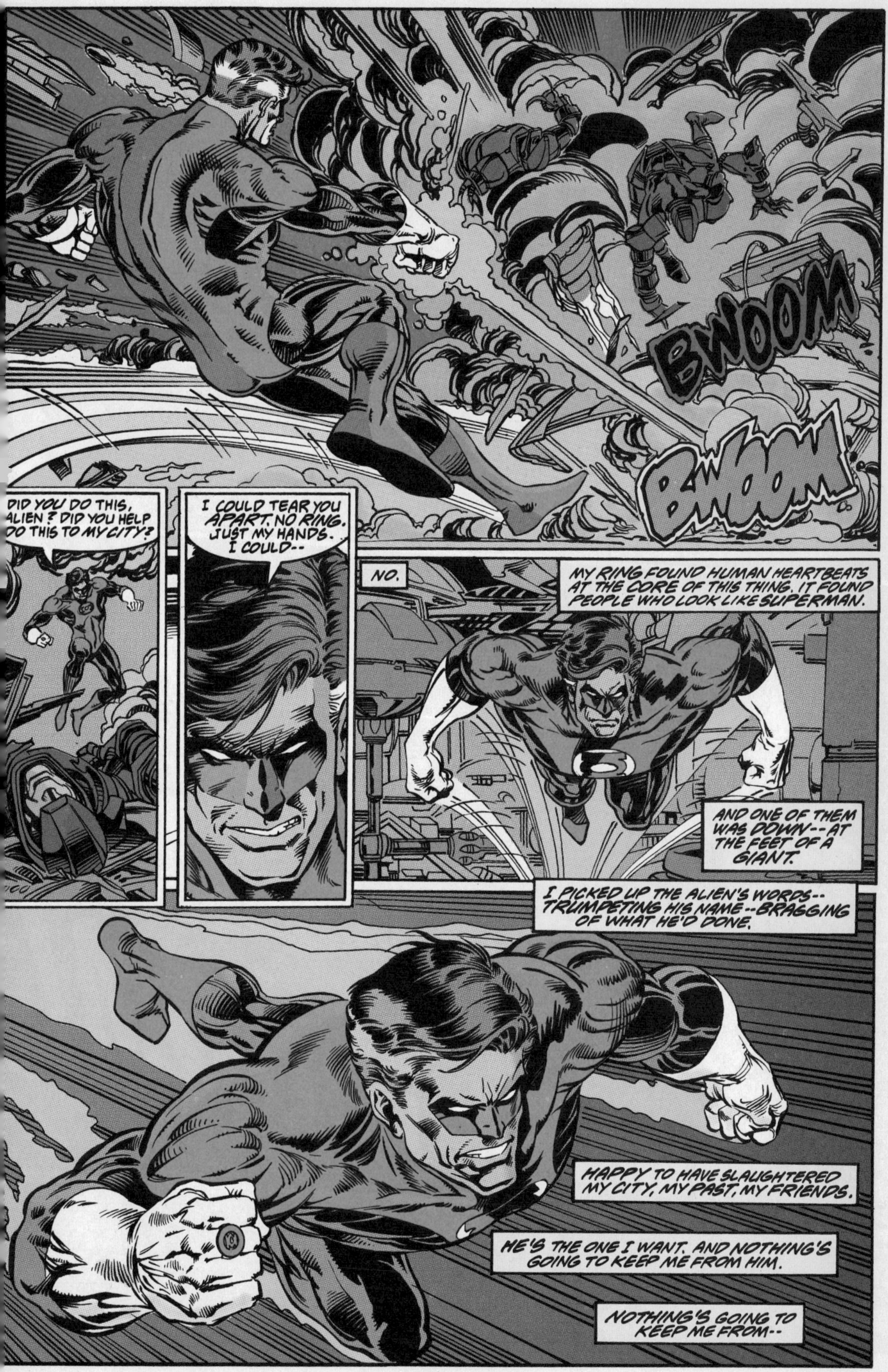
BWOOM
BWOOM
DID YOU DO THIS, ALIEN? DID YOU HELP DO THIS TO MY CITY?
I COULD TEAR YOU APART. NO RING. JUST MY HANDS. I COULD--
NO.
MY RING FOUND HUMAN HEARTBEATS AT THE CORE OF THIS THING. IT FOUND PEOPLE WHO LOOK LIKE SUPERMAN.
AND ONE OF THEM WAS DOWN--AT THE FEET OF A GIANT.
I PICKED UP THE ALIEN'S WORDS--TRUMPETING HIS NAME--BRAGGING OF WHAT HE'D DONE.
HAPPY TO HAVE SLAUGHTERED MY CITY, MY PAST, MY FRIENDS.
HE'S THE ONE I WANT. AND NOTHING'S GOING TO KEEP ME FROM HIM.
NOTHING'S GOING TO KEEP ME FROM--

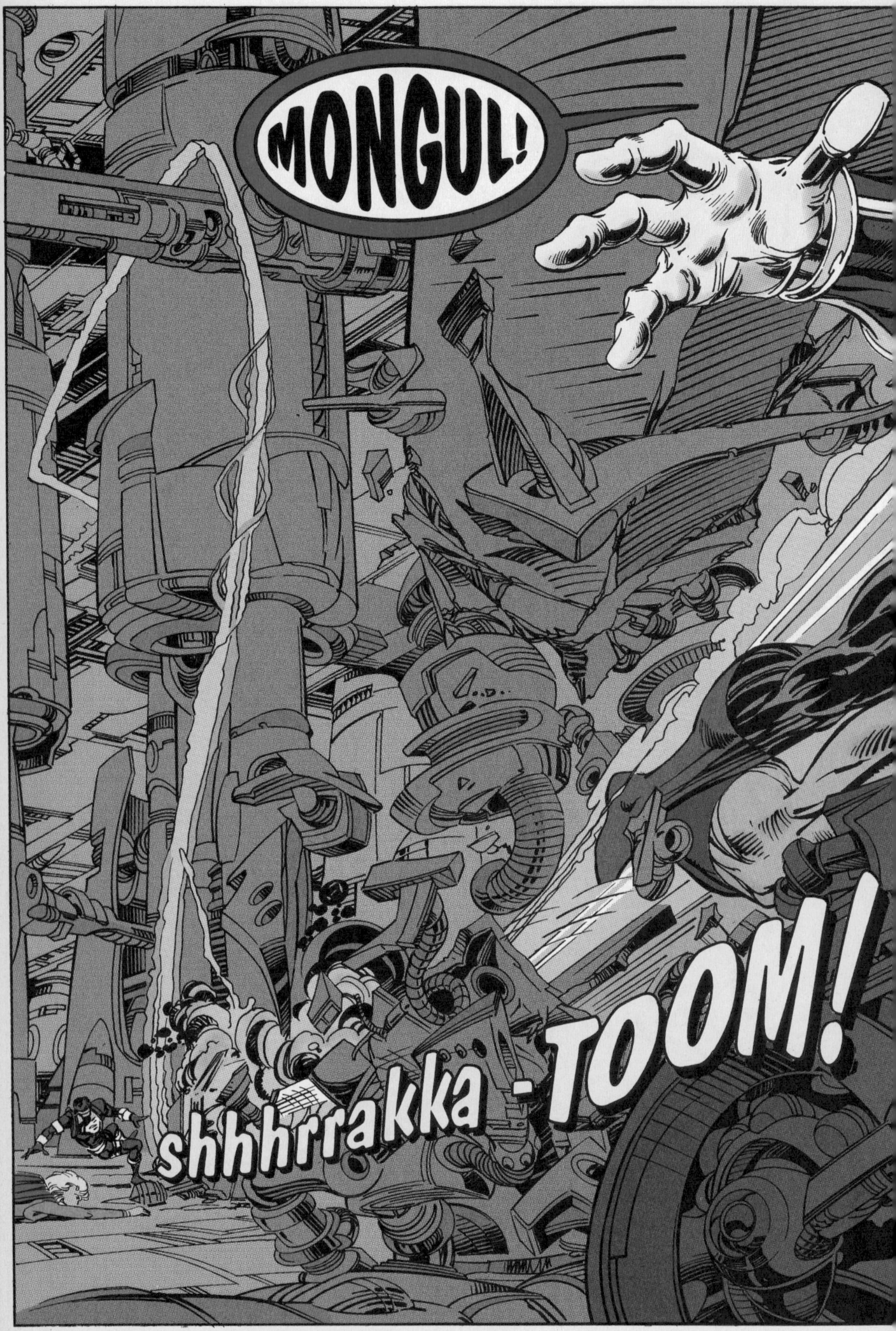
MONGUL!
shhhrrakka -TOOM!

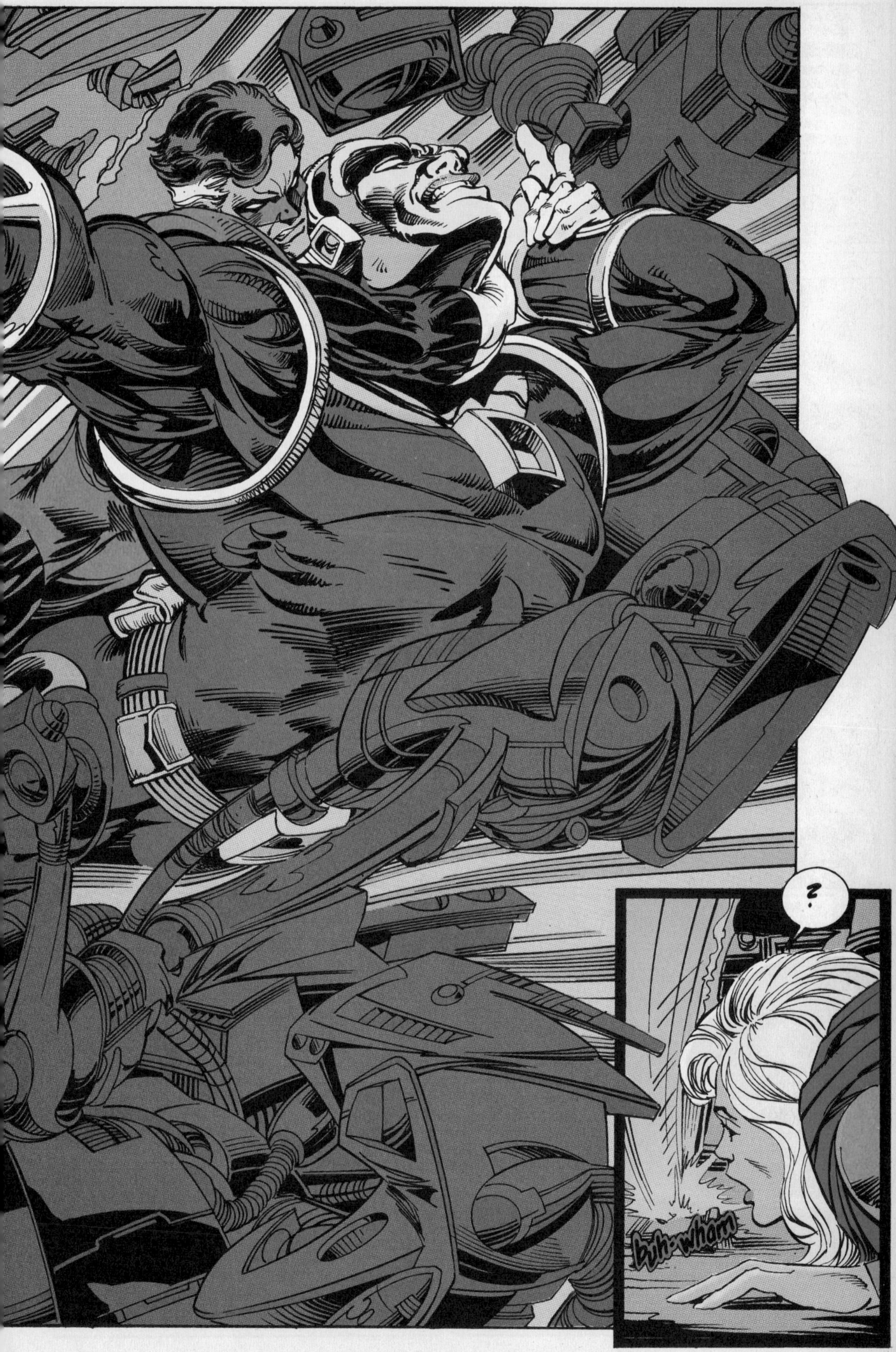
?
buh-wham

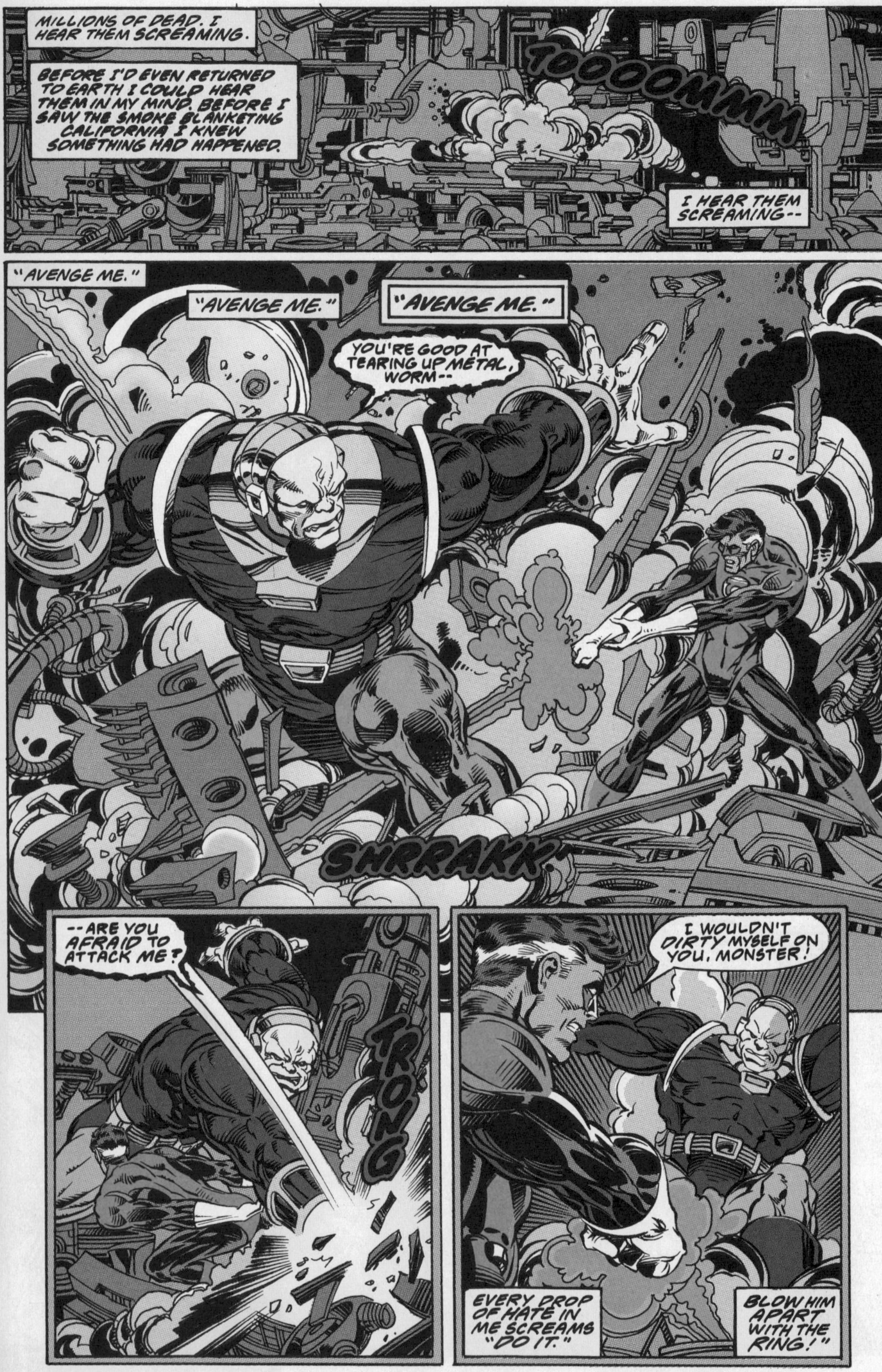
MILLIONS OF DEAD. I HEAR THEM SCREAMING.
BEFORE I'D EVEN RETURNED TO EARTH I COULD HEAR THEM IN MY MIND. BEFORE I SAW THE SMOKE BLANKETING CALIFORNIA I KNEW SOMETHING HAD HAPPENED.
TOOOOOMMMM
I HEAR THEM SCREAMING--
"AVENGE ME."
"AVENGE ME."
"AVENGE ME."
YOU'RE GOOD AT TEARING UP METAL, WORM--
SHRRAKK
--ARE YOU AFRAID TO ATTACK ME?
KRONG
I WOULDN'T DIRTY MYSELF ON YOU, MONSTER!
EVERY DROP OF HATE IN ME SCREAMS "DO IT."
BLOW HIM APART WITH THE RING!"

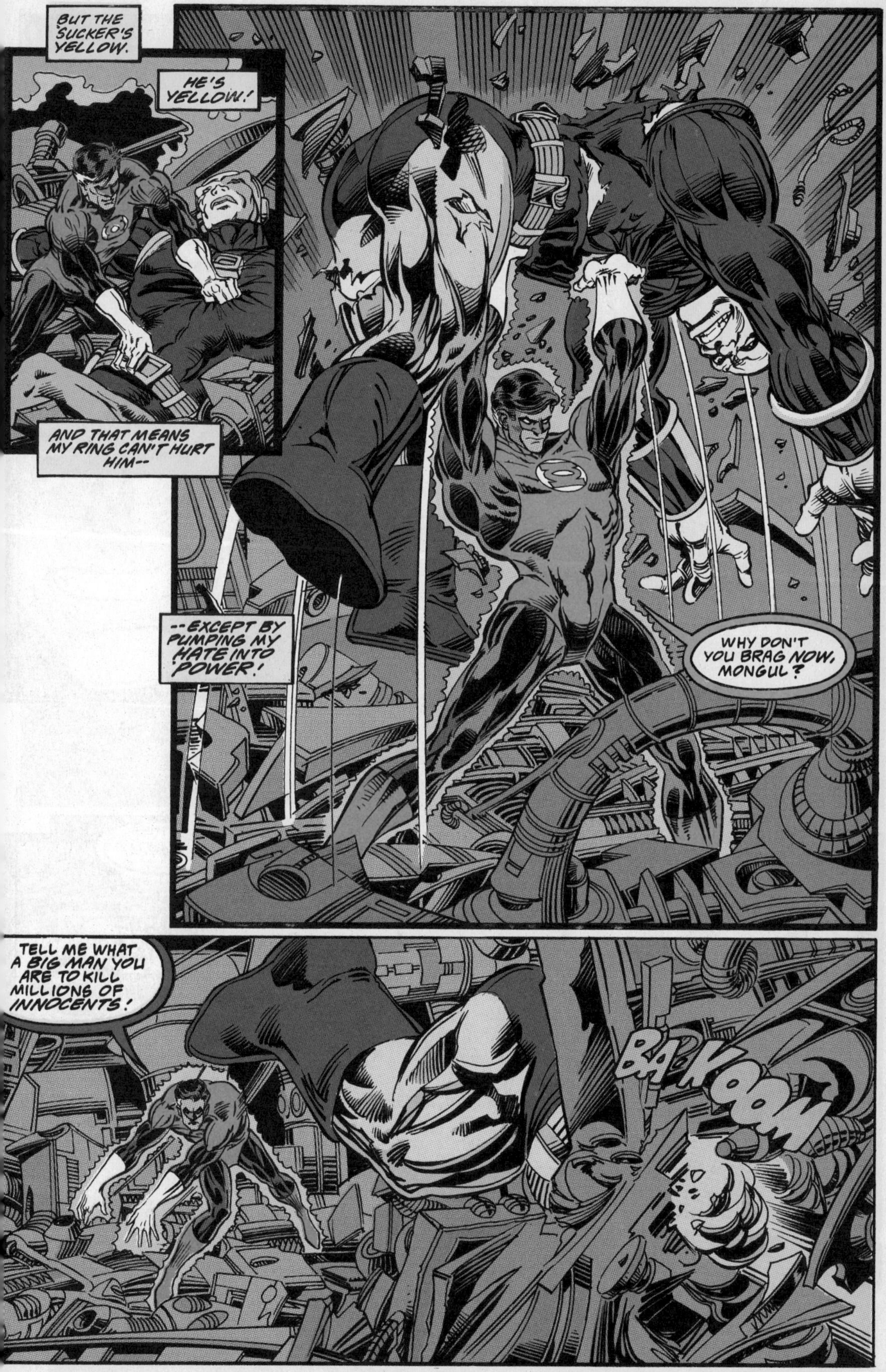
BUT THE SUCKER'S YELLOW.
HE'S YELLOW!
AND THAT MEANS MY RING CAN'T HURT HIM--
--EXCEPT BY PUMPING MY HATE INTO POWER!
WHY DON'T YOU BRAG NOW, MONGUL?
TELL ME WHAT A BIG MAN YOU ARE TO KILL MILLIONS OF INNOCENTS!
BA-KOOM

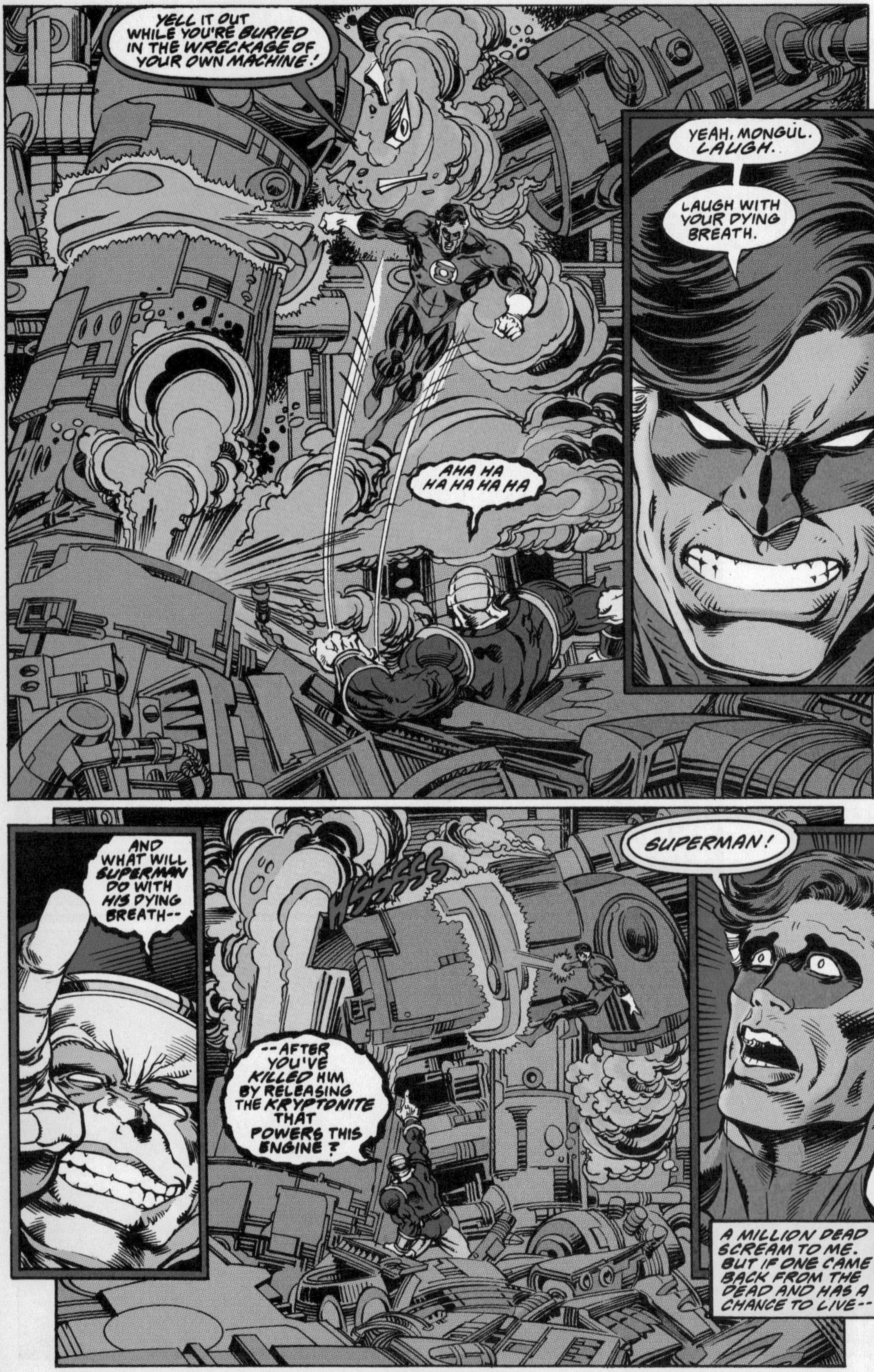
YELL IT OUT WHILE YOU'RE BURIED IN THE WRECKAGE OF YOUR OWN MACHINE!
AHA HA HA HA HA HA
YEAH, MONGUL. LAUGH.
LAUGH WITH YOUR DYING BREATH.
AND WHAT WILL SUPERMAN DO WITH HIS DYING BREATH--
HSSSSS
--AFTER YOU'VE KILLED HIM BY RELEASING THE KRYPTONITE THAT POWERS THIS ENGINE?
SUPERMAN!
A MILLION DEAD SCREAM TO ME. BUT IF ONE CAME BACK FROM THE DEAD AND HAS A CHANCE TO LIVE--

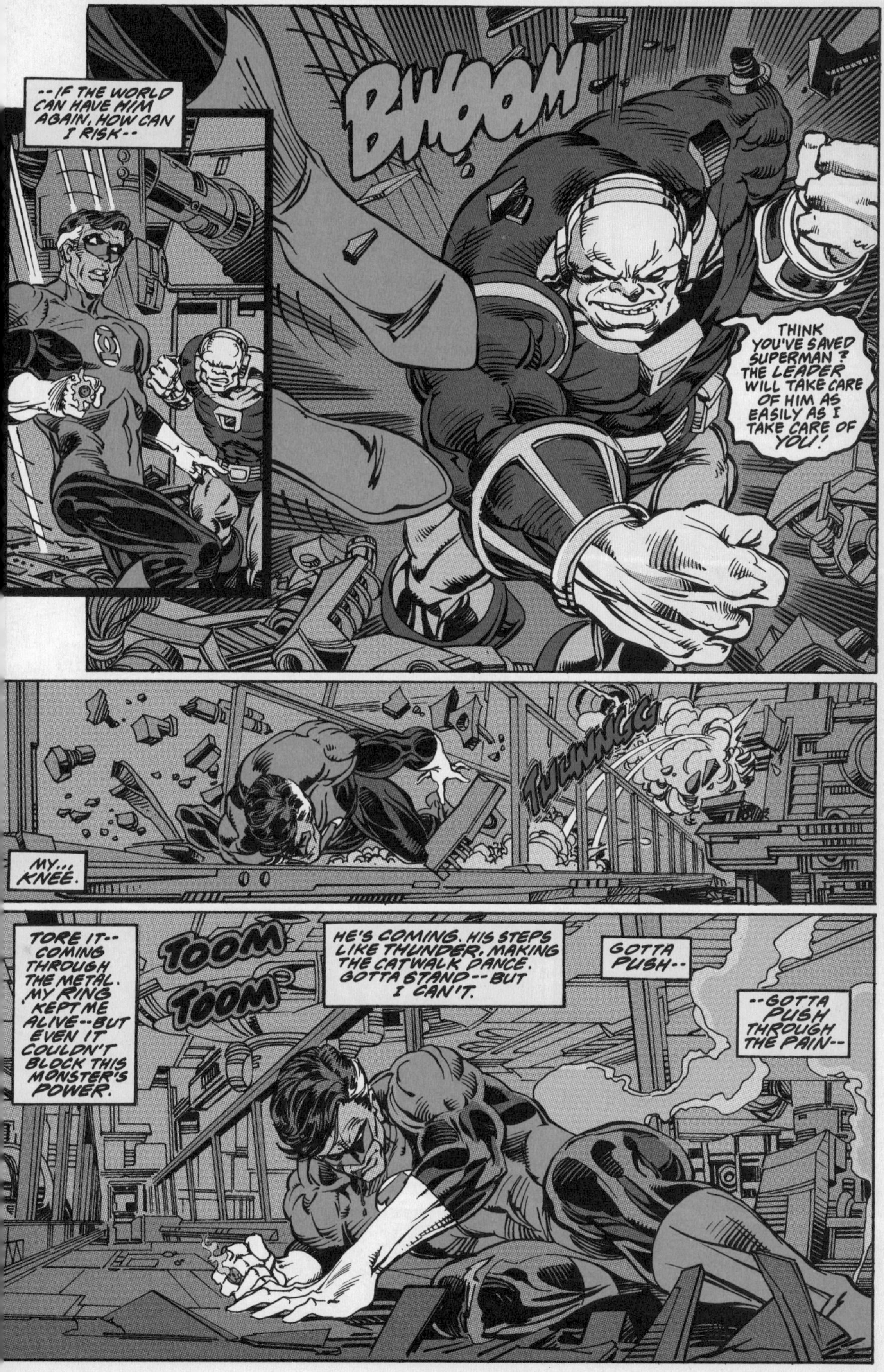
--IF THE WORLD CAN HAVE HIM AGAIN, HOW CAN I RISK--
BHOOM
THINK YOU'VE SAVED SUPERMAN? THE LEADER WILL TAKE CARE OF HIM AS EASILY AS I TAKE CARE OF YOU!
TWANNGG
MY... KNEE.
TORE IT-- COMING THROUGH THE METAL. MY RING KEPT ME ALIVE--BUT EVEN IT COULDN'T BLOCK THIS MONSTER'S POWER.
TOOM
TOOM
HE'S COMING. HIS STEPS LIKE THUNDER, MAKING THE CATWALK DANCE. GOTTA STAND-- BUT I CAN'T.
GOTTA PUSH--
--GOTTA PUSH THROUGH THE PAIN--

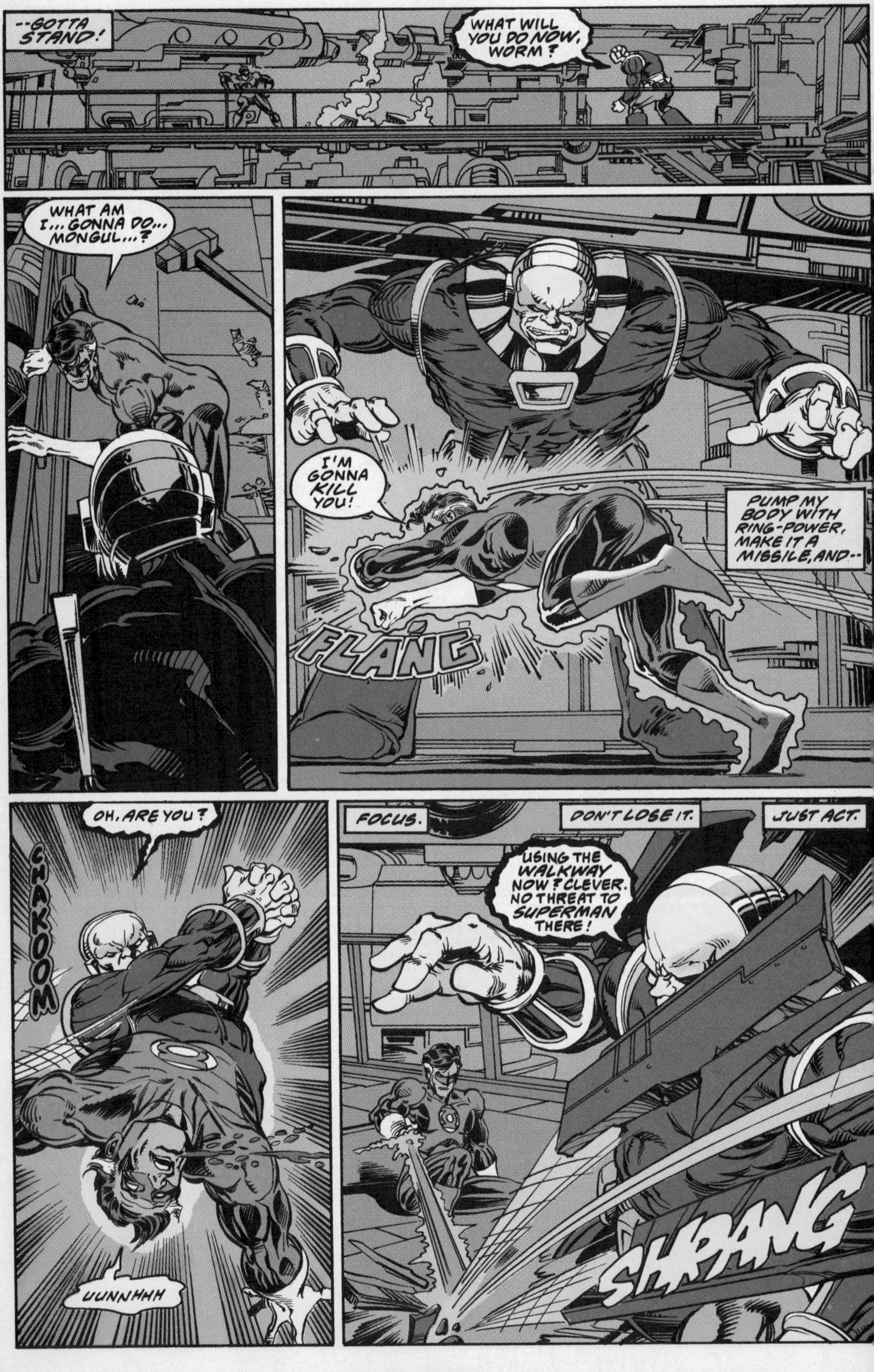
--GOTTA STAND!
WHAT WILL YOU DO NOW, WORM?
WHAT AM I... GONNA DO... MONGUL...?
I'M GONNA KILL YOU!
PUMP MY BODY WITH RING-POWER, MAKE IT A MISSILE, AND--
FLANG
OH, ARE YOU?
CHAKOOM
UUNNHHH
FOCUS.
DON'T LOSE IT.
JUST ACT.
USING THE WALKWAY NOW? CLEVER. NO THREAT TO SUPERMAN THERE!
SHPANG

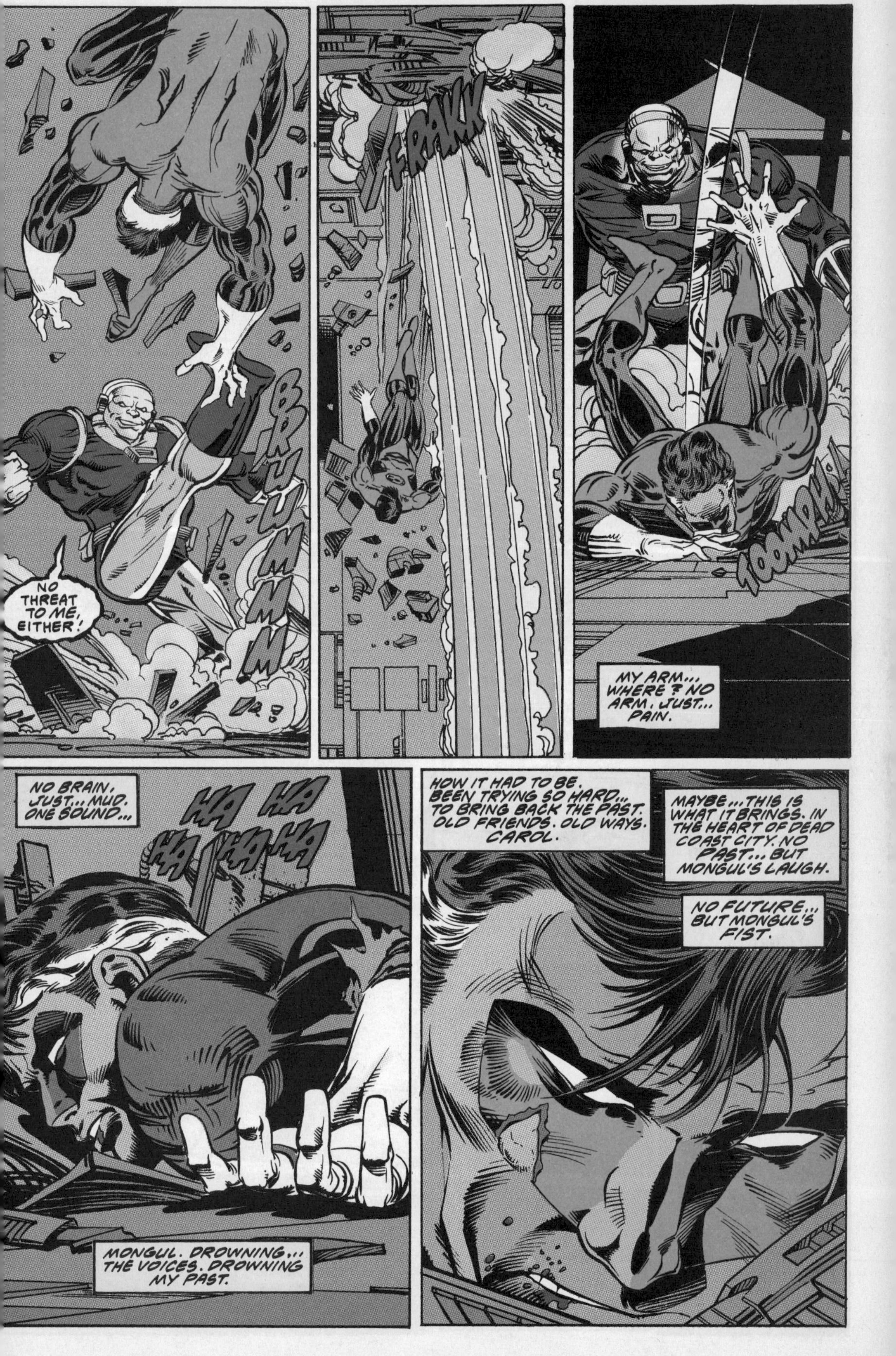
NO THREAT TO ME, EITHER!
BRRUMMMMMM
FRAKK
MY ARM... WHERE? NO ARM. JUST... PAIN.
NO BRAIN. JUST... MUD. ONE SOUND...
HA HA HA HAHA HA
MONGUL. DROWNING... THE VOICES. DROWNING MY PAST.
HOW IT HAD TO BE. BEEN TRYING SO HARD... TO BRING BACK THE PAST. OLD FRIENDS. OLD WAYS. CAROL.
MAYBE... THIS IS WHAT IT BRINGS. IN THE HEART OF DEAD COAST CITY. NO PAST... BUT MONGUL'S LAUGH.
NO FUTURE... BUT MONGUL'S FIST.

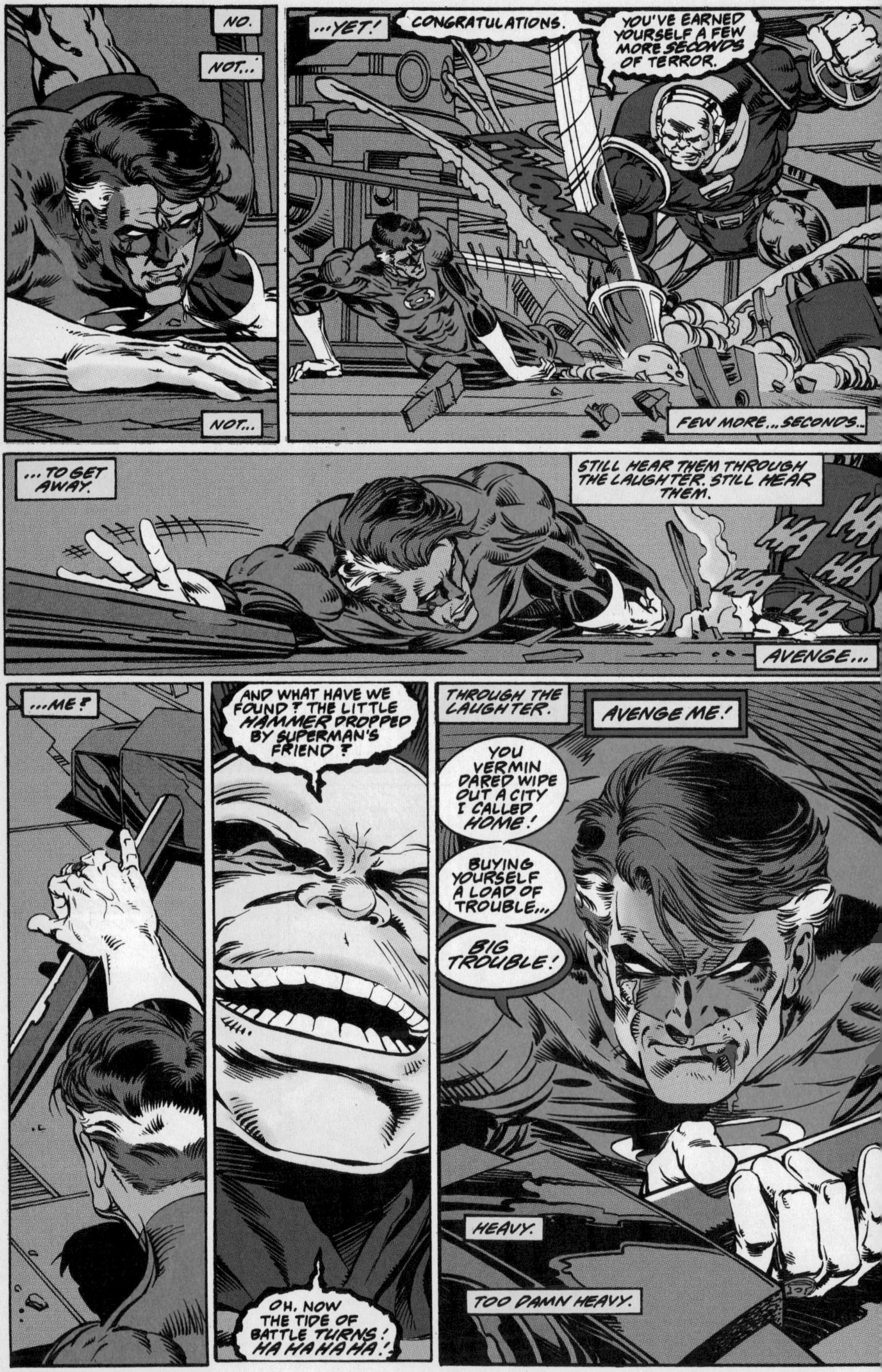
NO.
NOT...
NOT...
...YET!
CONGRATULATIONS.
YOU'VE EARNED YOURSELF A FEW MORE SECONDS OF TERROR.
FEW MORE... SECONDS...
...TO GET AWAY.
STILL HEAR THEM THROUGH THE LAUGHTER. STILL HEAR THEM.
AVENGE...
...ME?
AND WHAT HAVE WE FOUND? THE LITTLE HAMMER DROPPED BY SUPERMAN'S FRIEND?
OH, NOW THE TIDE OF BATTLE TURNS! HA HA HA HA HA!
THROUGH THE LAUGHTER.
AVENGE ME!
YOU VERMIN DARED WIPE OUT A CITY I CALLED HOME!
BUYING YOURSELF A LOAD OF TROUBLE...
BIG TROUBLE!
HEAVY.
TOO DAMN HEAVY.

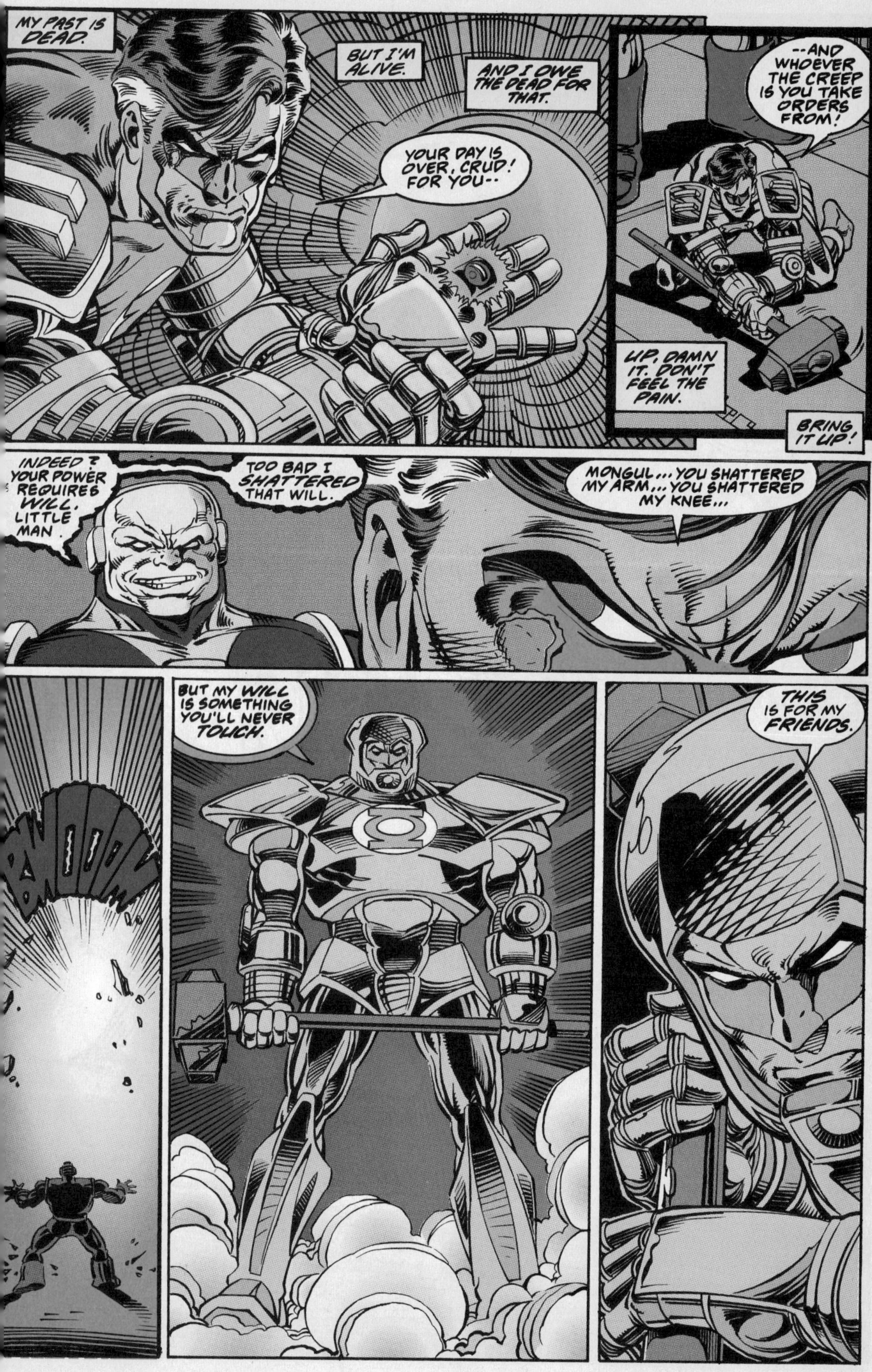
MY PAST IS DEAD.
BUT I'M ALIVE.
AND I OWE THE DEAD FOR THAT.
YOUR DAY IS OVER, CRUD! FOR YOU--
--AND WHOEVER THE CREEP IS YOU TAKE ORDERS FROM!
UP, DAMN IT. DON'T FEEL THE PAIN.
BRING IT UP!
INDEED? YOUR POWER REQUIRES WILL, LITTLE MAN.
TOO BAD I SHATTERED THAT WILL.
MONGUL... YOU SHATTERED MY ARM... YOU SHATTERED MY KNEE...
BUT MY WILL IS SOMETHING YOU'LL NEVER TOUCH.
THIS IS FOR MY FRIENDS.

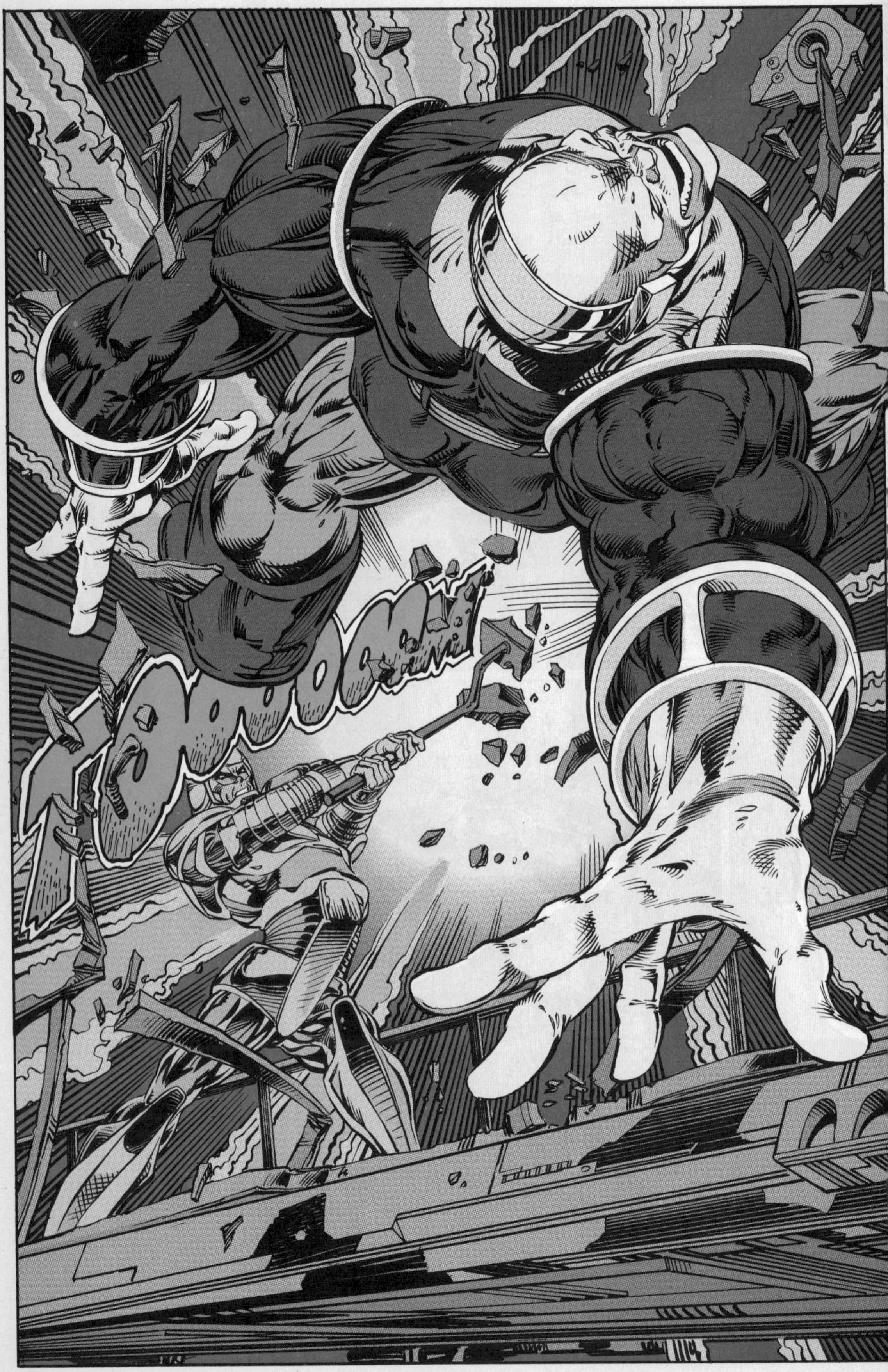

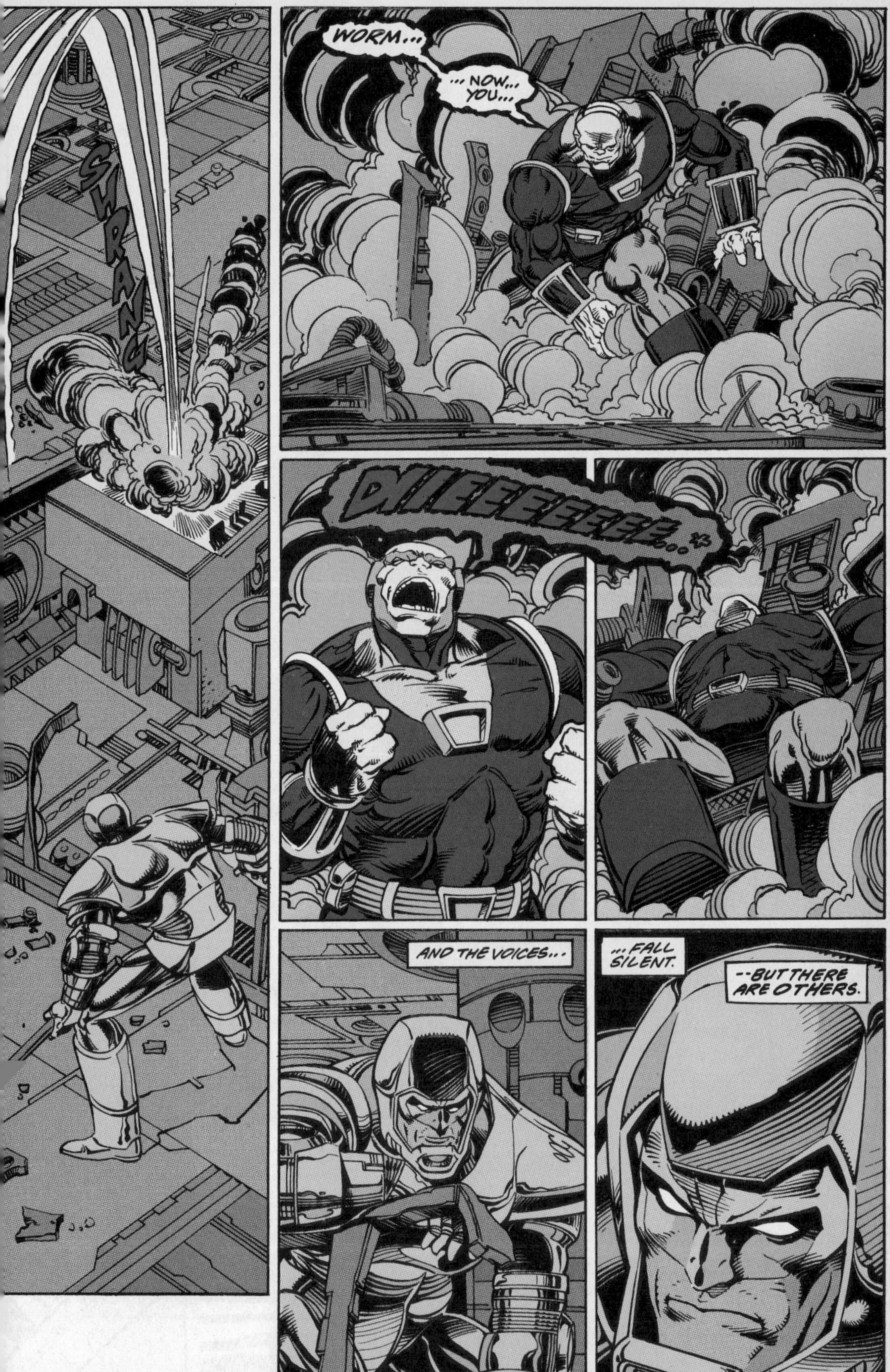
SHRANG
WORM...
...NOW... YOU...
DIIEEEEEEEEEE...
AND THE VOICES...
...FALL SILENT.
--BUT THERE ARE OTHERS.

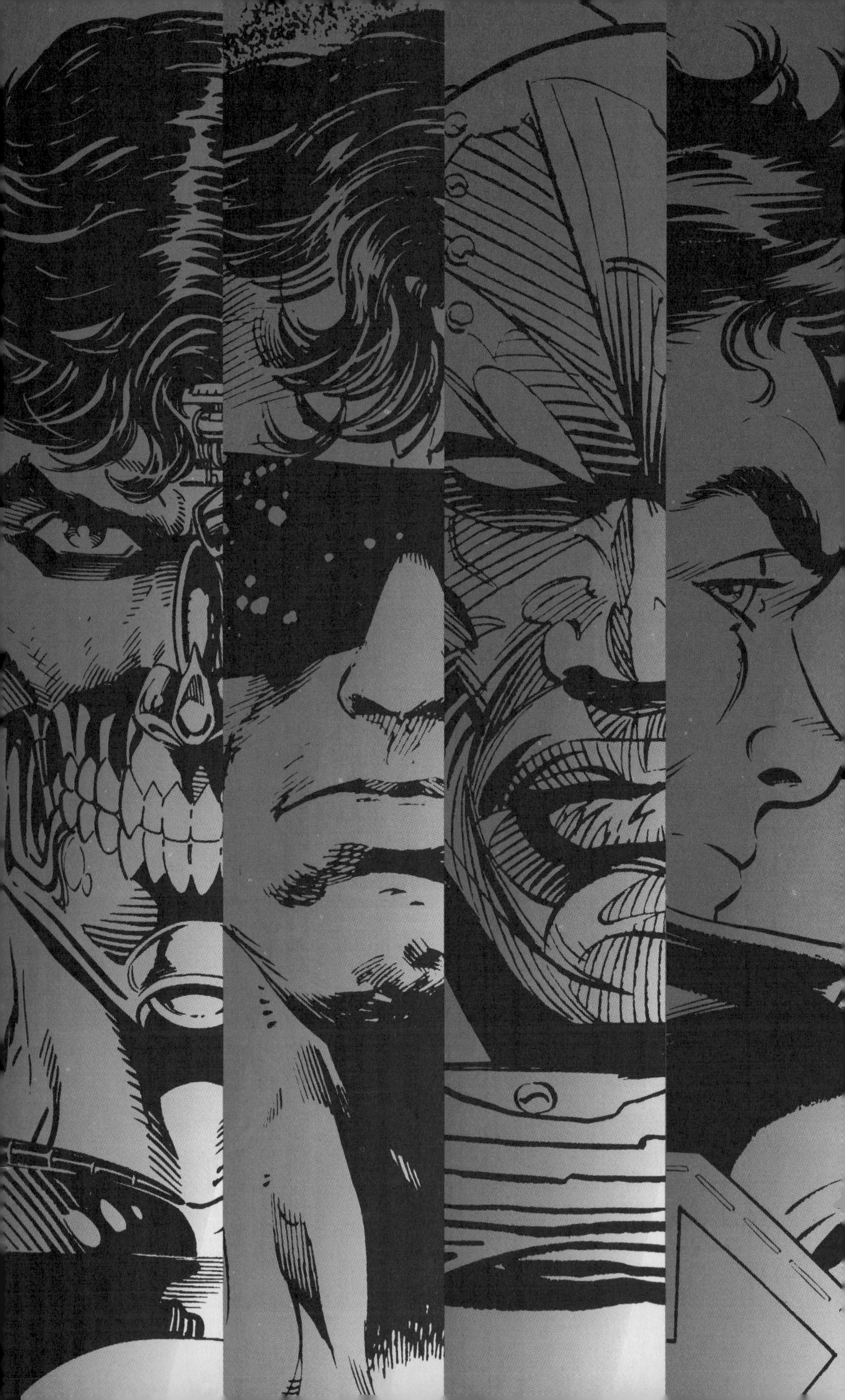

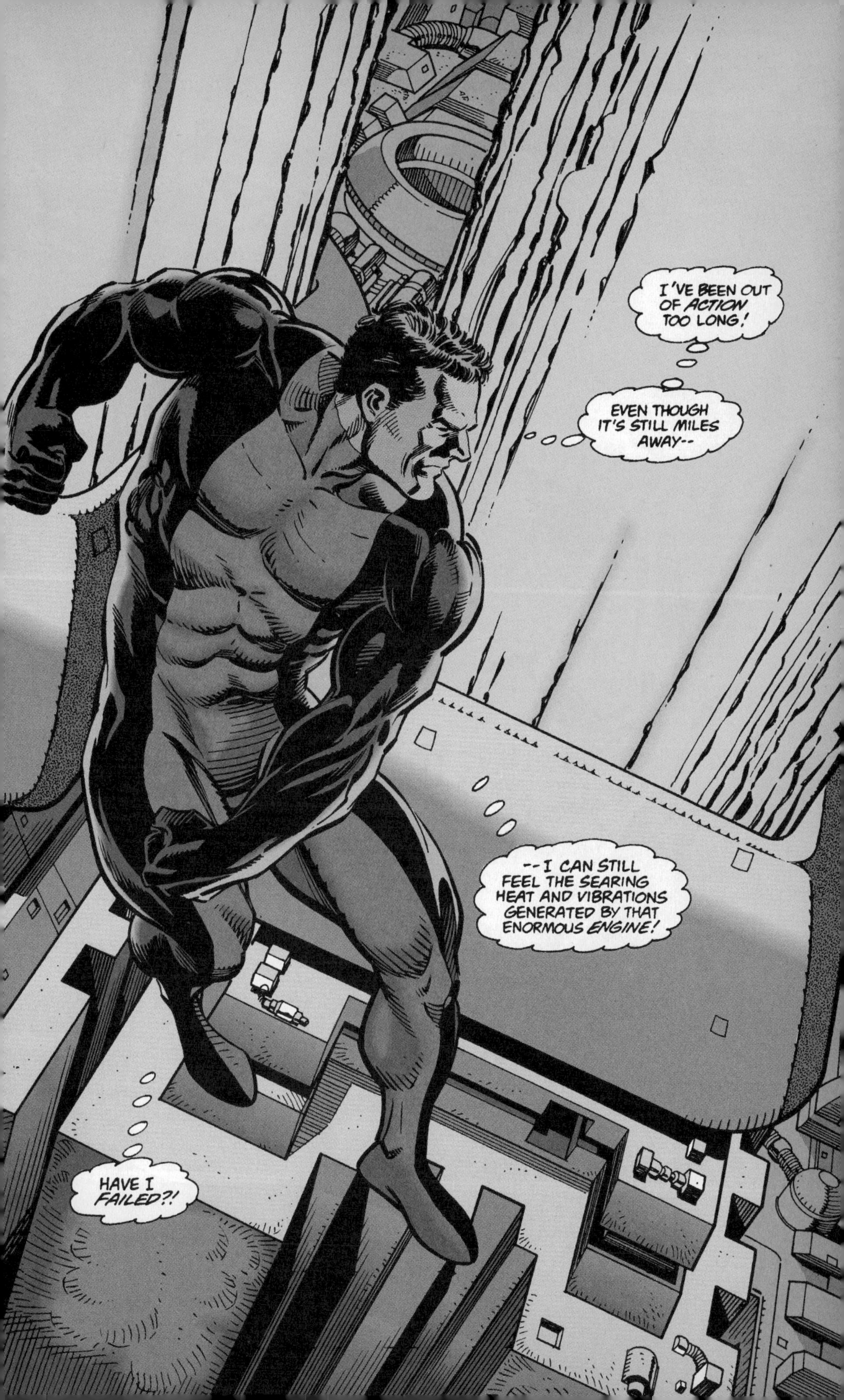
I'VE BEEN OUT OF *ACTION* TOO LONG!
EVEN THOUGH IT'S STILL MILES AWAY--
--I CAN STILL FEEL THE SEARING HEAT AND VIBRATIONS GENERATED BY THAT ENORMOUS *ENGINE*!
HAVE I *FAILED*?!

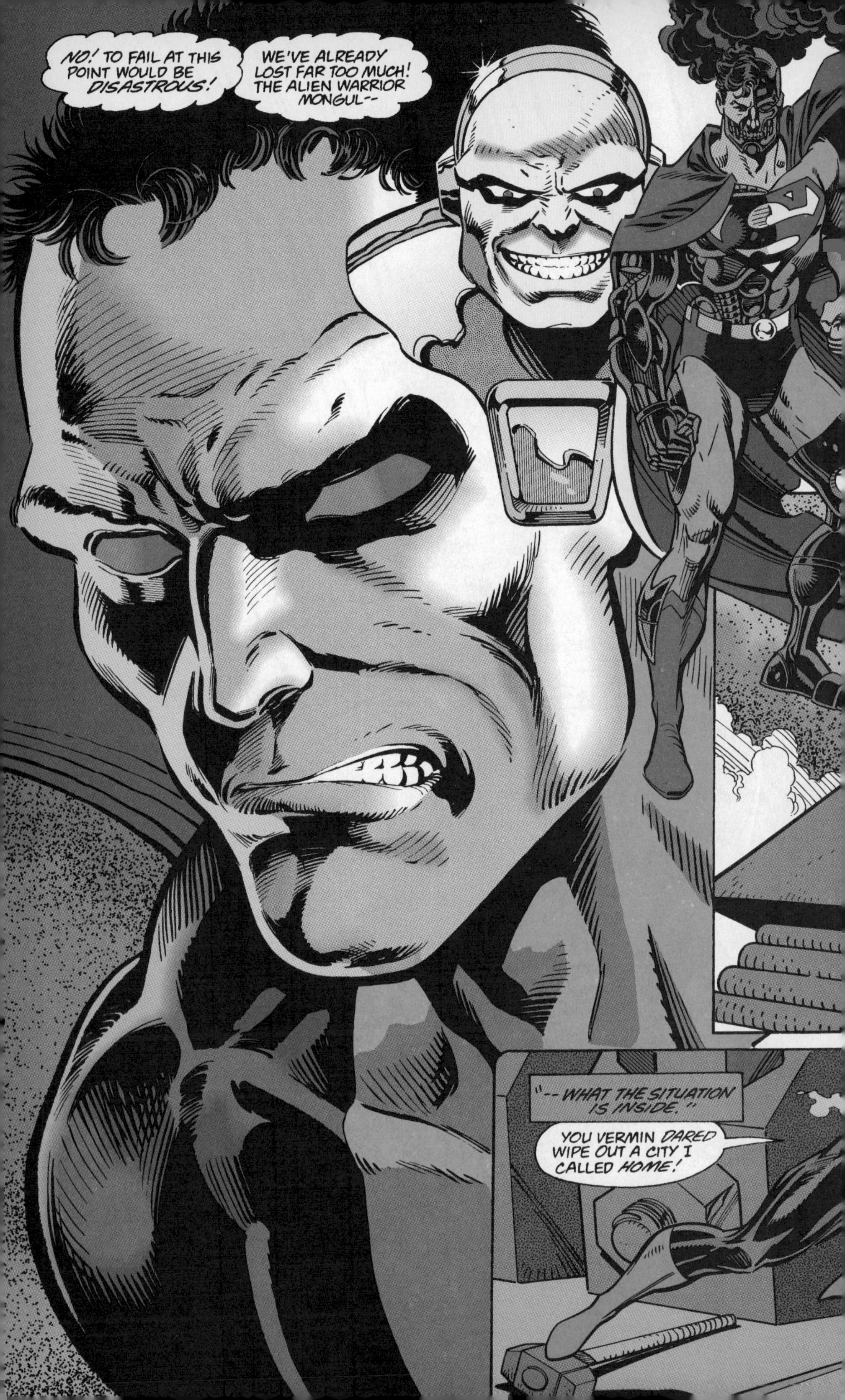
NO! TO FAIL AT THIS POINT WOULD BE DISASTROUS!
WE'VE ALREADY LOST FAR TOO MUCH! THE ALIEN WARRIOR MONGUL--
"--WHAT THE SITUATION IS INSIDE."
YOU VERMIN DARED WIPE OUT A CITY I CALLED HOME!

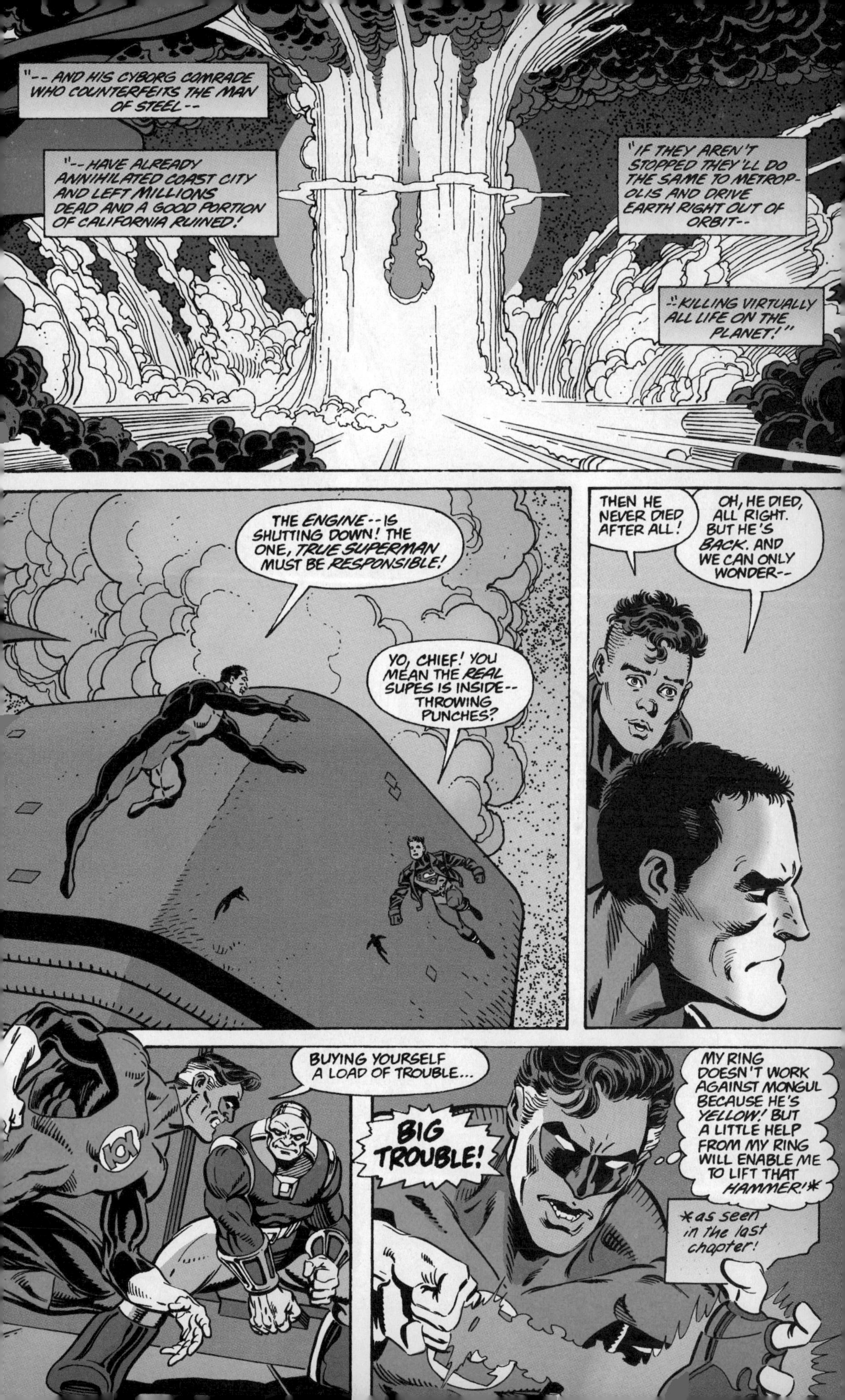
"-- AND HIS CYBORG COMRADE WHO COUNTERFEITS THE MAN OF STEEL--
"-- HAVE ALREADY ANNIHILATED COAST CITY AND LEFT MILLIONS DEAD AND A GOOD PORTION OF CALIFORNIA RUINED!
"IF THEY AREN'T STOPPED THEY'LL DO THE SAME TO METROPOLIS AND DRIVE EARTH RIGHT OUT OF ORBIT--
--KILLING VIRTUALLY ALL LIFE ON THE PLANET!"
THE *ENGINE*--IS SHUTTING DOWN! THE ONE, *TRUE SUPERMAN* MUST BE *RESPONSIBLE!*
YO, CHIEF! YOU MEAN THE *REAL* SUPES IS INSIDE-- THROWING PUNCHES?
THEN HE NEVER DIED AFTER ALL!
OH, HE DIED, ALL RIGHT. BUT HE'S *BACK*. AND WE CAN ONLY WONDER--
BUYING YOURSELF A LOAD OF TROUBLE...
BIG TROUBLE!
MY RING DOESN'T WORK AGAINST MONGUL BECAUSE HE'S *YELLOW!* BUT A LITTLE HELP FROM MY RING WILL ENABLE ME TO LIFT THAT *HAMMER!**
*as seen in the last chapter!

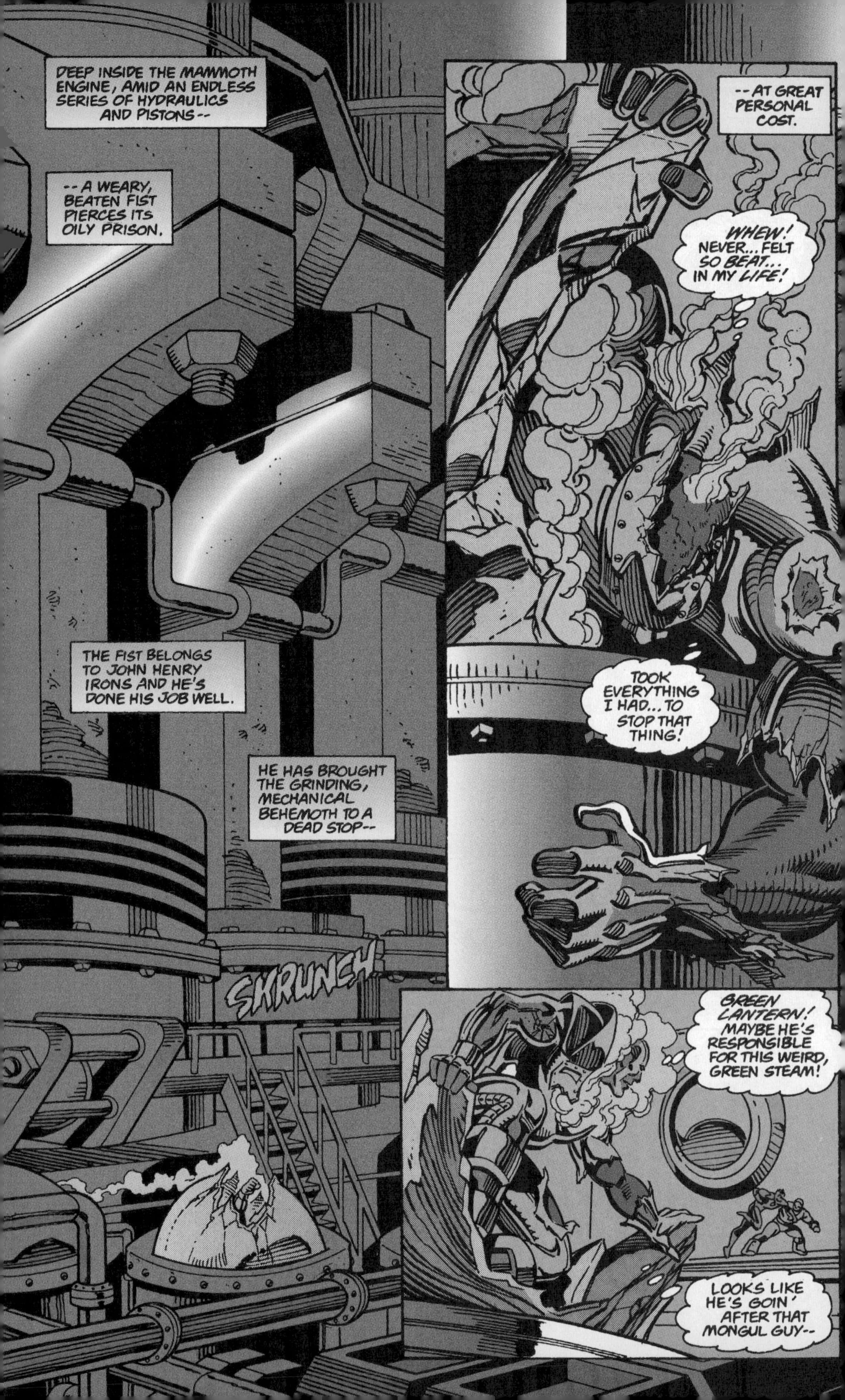
DEEP INSIDE THE MAMMOTH ENGINE, AMID AN ENDLESS SERIES OF HYDRAULICS AND PISTONS--
--A WEARY, BEATEN FIST PIERCES ITS OILY PRISON.
THE FIST BELONGS TO JOHN HENRY IRONS AND HE'S DONE HIS JOB WELL.
HE HAS BROUGHT THE GRINDING, MECHANICAL BEHEMOTH TO A DEAD STOP--
SKRUNCH
--AT GREAT PERSONAL COST.
WHEW! NEVER... FELT SO BEAT... IN MY LIFE!
TOOK EVERYTHING I HAD... TO STOP THAT THING!
GREEN LANTERN! MAYBE HE'S RESPONSIBLE FOR THIS WEIRD, GREEN STEAM!
LOOKS LIKE HE'S GOIN' AFTER THAT MONGUL GUY--

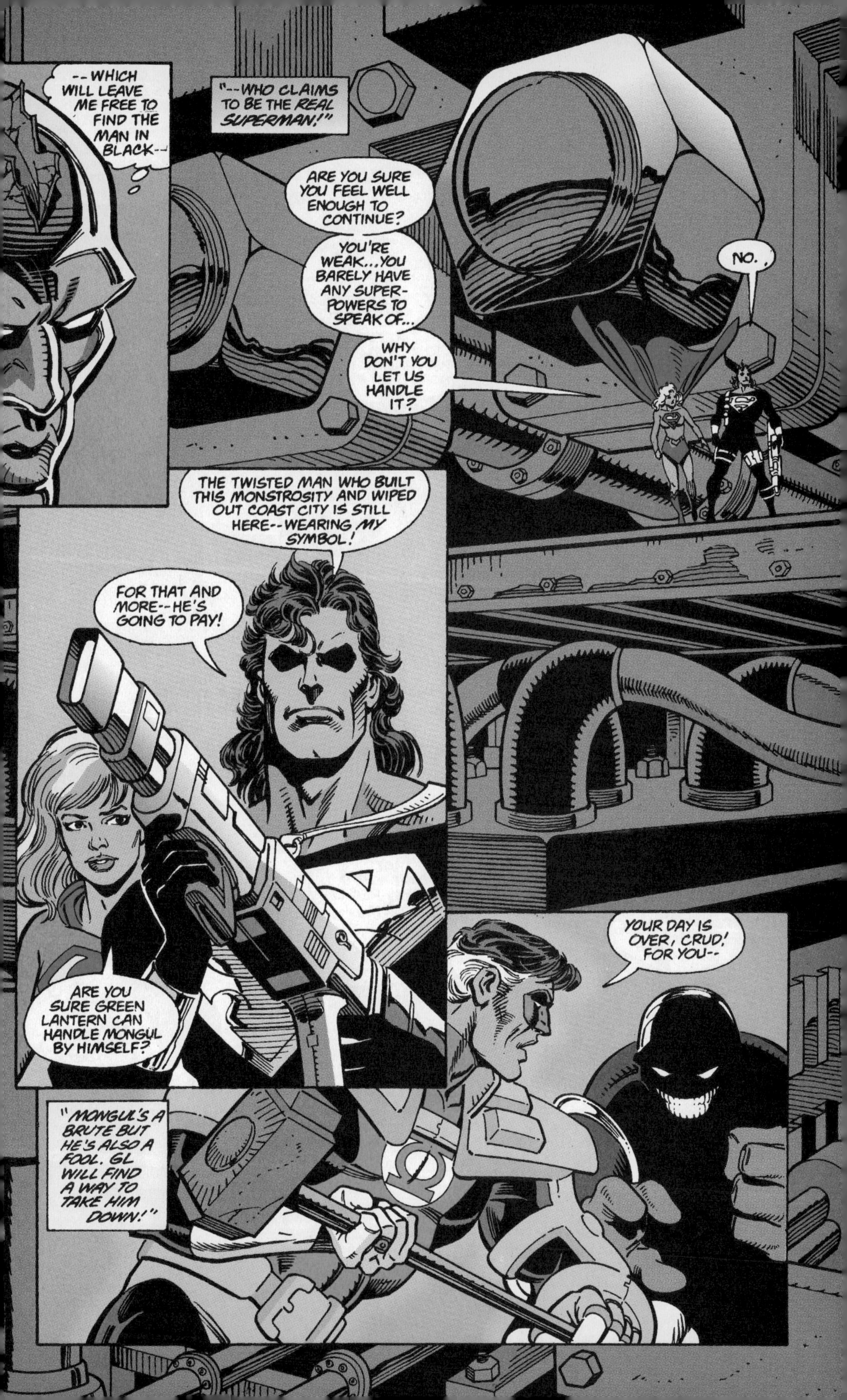
--WHICH WILL LEAVE ME FREE TO FIND THE MAN IN BLACK--
"--WHO CLAIMS TO BE THE REAL SUPERMAN!"
ARE YOU SURE YOU FEEL WELL ENOUGH TO CONTINUE?
YOU'RE WEAK...YOU BARELY HAVE ANY SUPER-POWERS TO SPEAK OF...
WHY DON'T YOU LET US HANDLE IT?
NO.
THE TWISTED MAN WHO BUILT THIS MONSTROSITY AND WIPED OUT COAST CITY IS STILL HERE--WEARING MY SYMBOL!
FOR THAT AND MORE--HE'S GOING TO PAY!
ARE YOU SURE GREEN LANTERN CAN HANDLE MONGUL BY HIMSELF?
YOUR DAY IS OVER, CRUD! FOR YOU--
"MONGUL'S A BRUTE BUT HE'S ALSO A FOOL. GL WILL FIND A WAY TO TAKE HIM DOWN!"

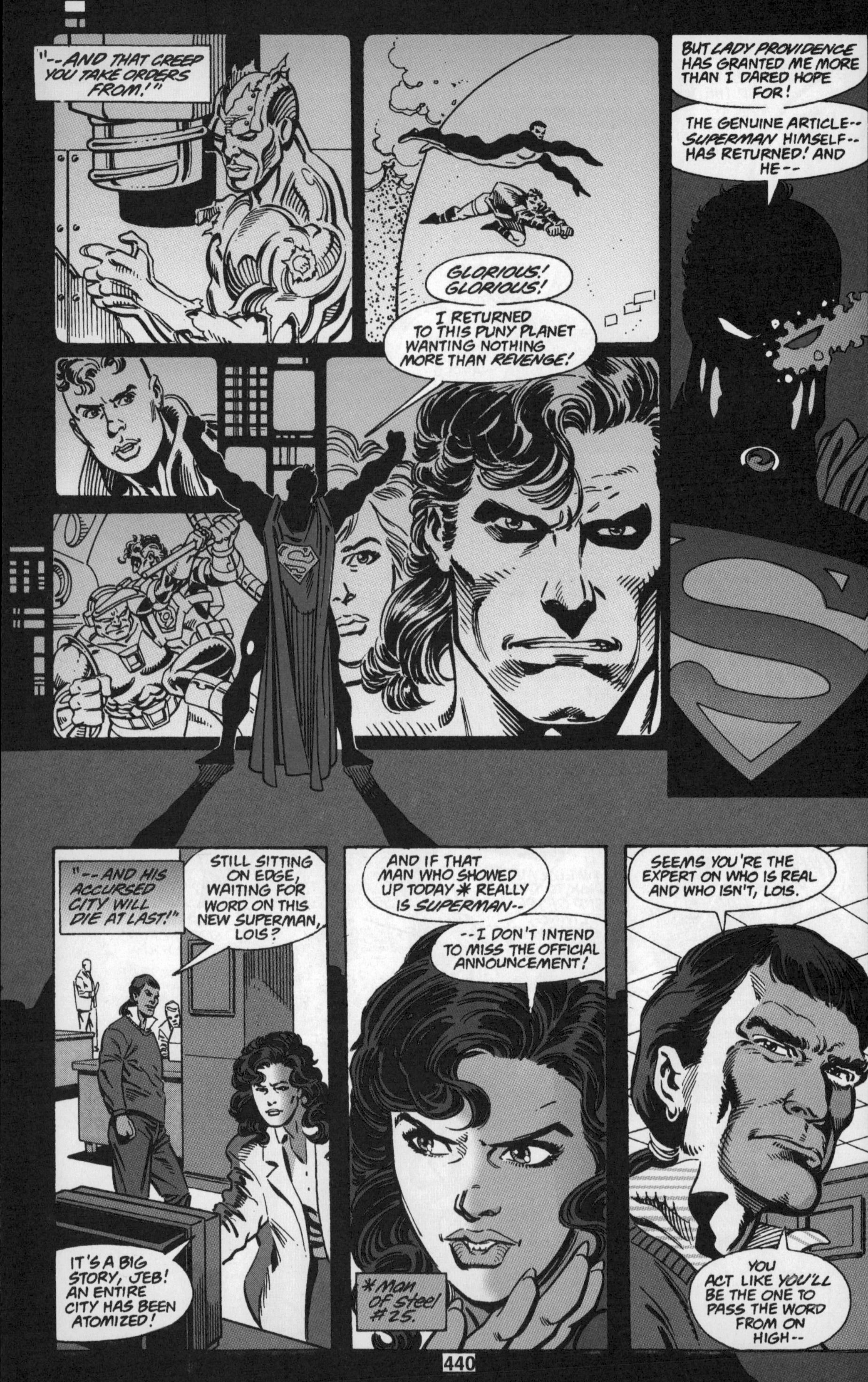
"--AND THAT CREEP YOU TAKE ORDERS FROM!"
BUT LADY PROVIDENCE HAS GRANTED ME MORE THAN I DARED HOPE FOR!
THE GENUINE ARTICLE-- SUPERMAN HIMSELF-- HAS RETURNED! AND HE--
GLORIOUS! GLORIOUS!
I RETURNED TO THIS PUNY PLANET WANTING NOTHING MORE THAN REVENGE!
"--AND HIS ACCURSED CITY WILL DIE AT LAST!"
STILL SITTING ON EDGE, WAITING FOR WORD ON THIS NEW SUPERMAN, LOIS?
IT'S A BIG STORY, JEB! AN ENTIRE CITY HAS BEEN ATOMIZED!
AND IF THAT MAN WHO SHOWED UP TODAY * REALLY IS SUPERMAN--
--I DON'T INTEND TO MISS THE OFFICIAL ANNOUNCEMENT!
*Man of Steel #25.
SEEMS YOU'RE THE EXPERT ON WHO IS REAL AND WHO ISN'T, LOIS.
YOU ACT LIKE YOU'LL BE THE ONE TO PASS THE WORD FROM ON HIGH--

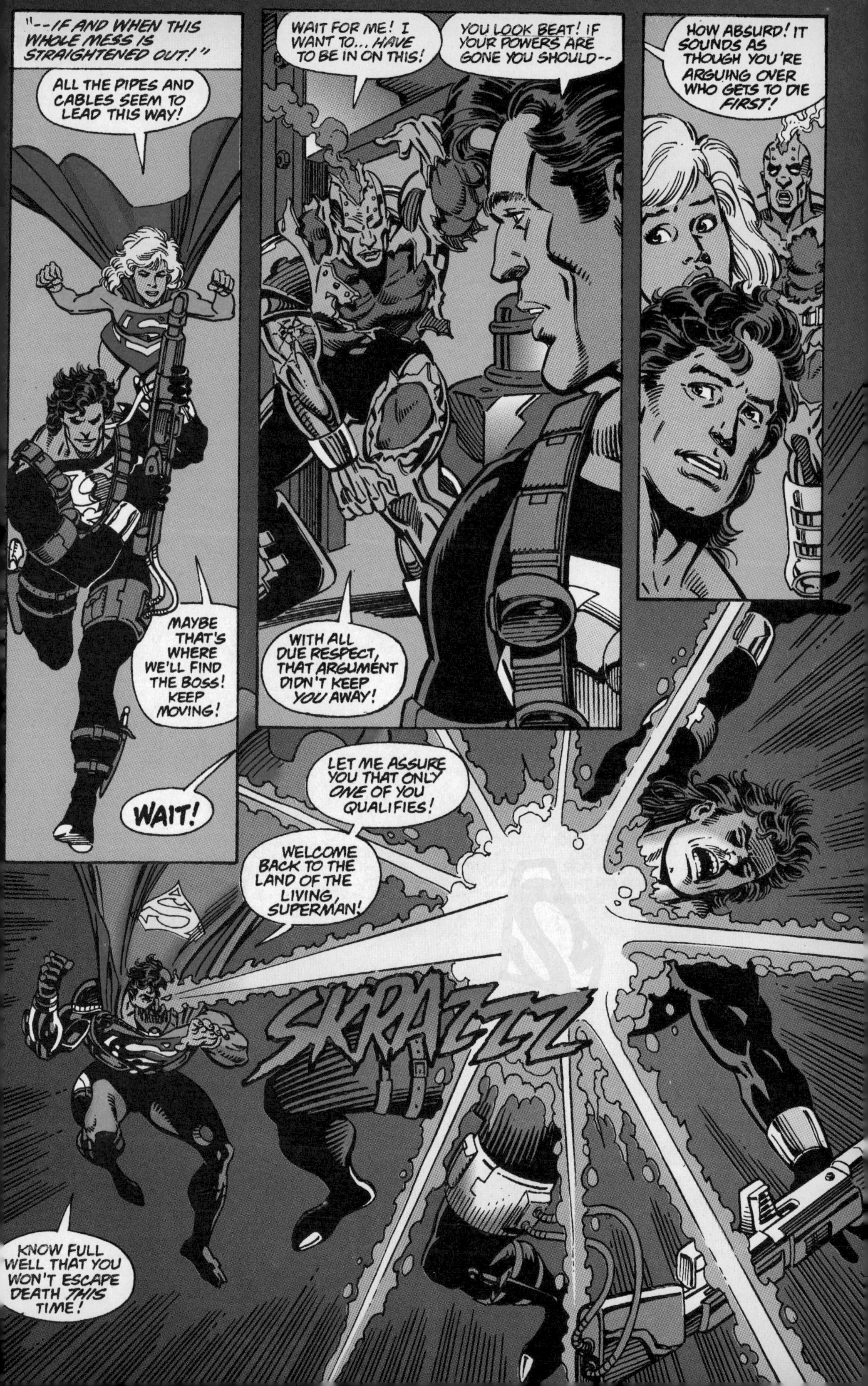
"--IF AND WHEN THIS WHOLE MESS IS STRAIGHTENED OUT!"
ALL THE PIPES AND CABLES SEEM TO LEAD THIS WAY!
MAYBE THAT'S WHERE WE'LL FIND THE BOSS! KEEP MOVING!
WAIT!
WAIT FOR ME! I WANT TO... HAVE TO BE IN ON THIS!
YOU LOOK BEAT! IF YOUR POWERS ARE GONE YOU SHOULD--
WITH ALL DUE RESPECT, THAT ARGUMENT DIDN'T KEEP YOU AWAY!
HOW ABSURD! IT SOUNDS AS THOUGH YOU'RE ARGUING OVER WHO GETS TO DIE FIRST!
LET ME ASSURE YOU THAT ONLY ONE OF YOU QUALIFIES!
WELCOME BACK TO THE LAND OF THE LIVING, SUPERMAN!
SKRAZZZZ
KNOW FULL WELL THAT YOU WON'T ESCAPE DEATH THIS TIME!

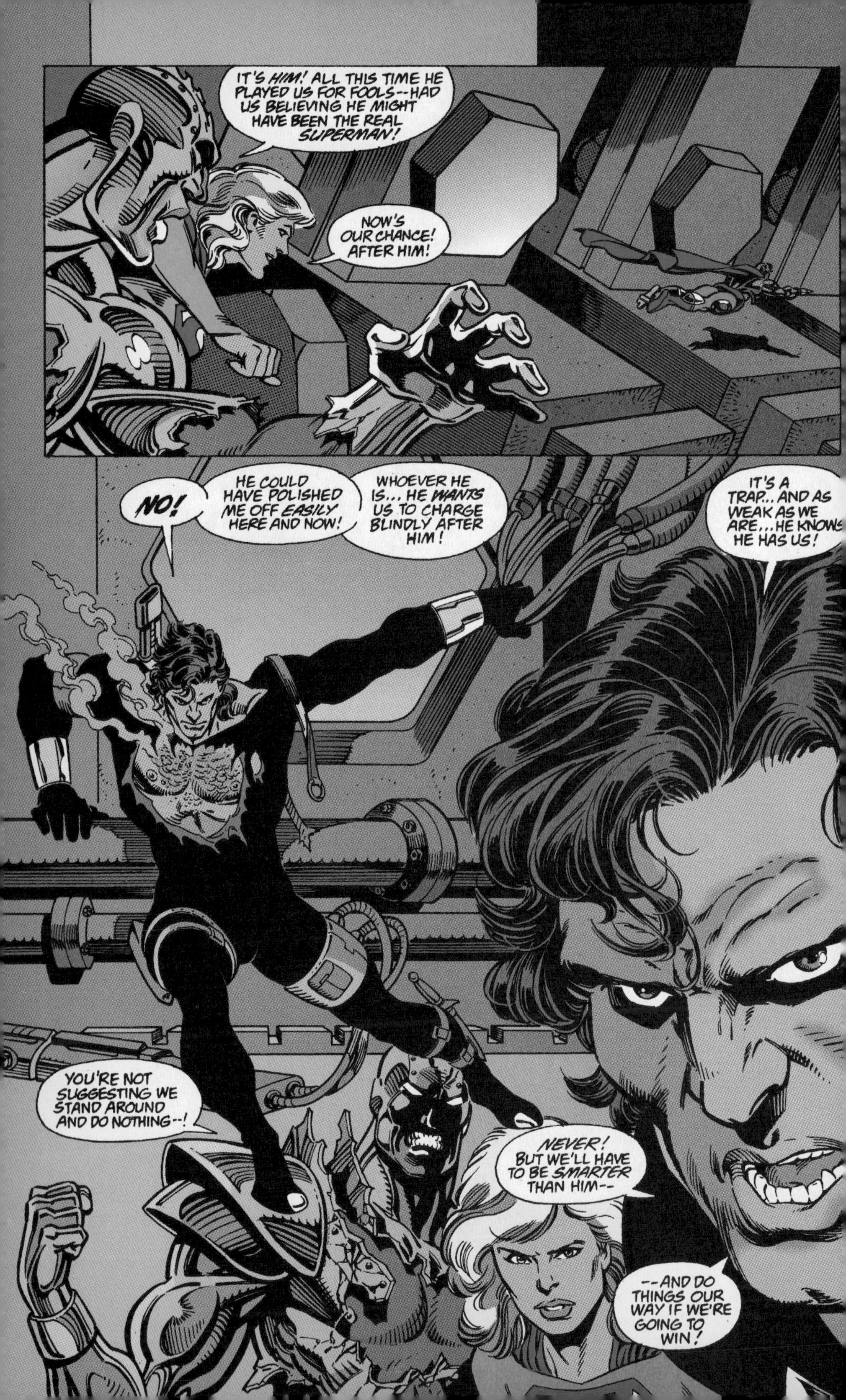
IT'S HIM! ALL THIS TIME HE PLAYED US FOR FOOLS--HAD US BELIEVING HE MIGHT HAVE BEEN THE REAL SUPERMAN!
NOW'S OUR CHANCE! AFTER HIM!
NO!
HE COULD HAVE POLISHED ME OFF EASILY HERE AND NOW!
WHOEVER HE IS... HE WANTS US TO CHARGE BLINDLY AFTER HIM!
IT'S A TRAP... AND AS WEAK AS WE ARE... HE KNOWS HE HAS US!
YOU'RE NOT SUGGESTING WE STAND AROUND AND DO NOTHING--!
NEVER! BUT WE'LL HAVE TO BE SMARTER THAN HIM--
--AND DO THINGS OUR WAY IF WE'RE GOING TO WIN!

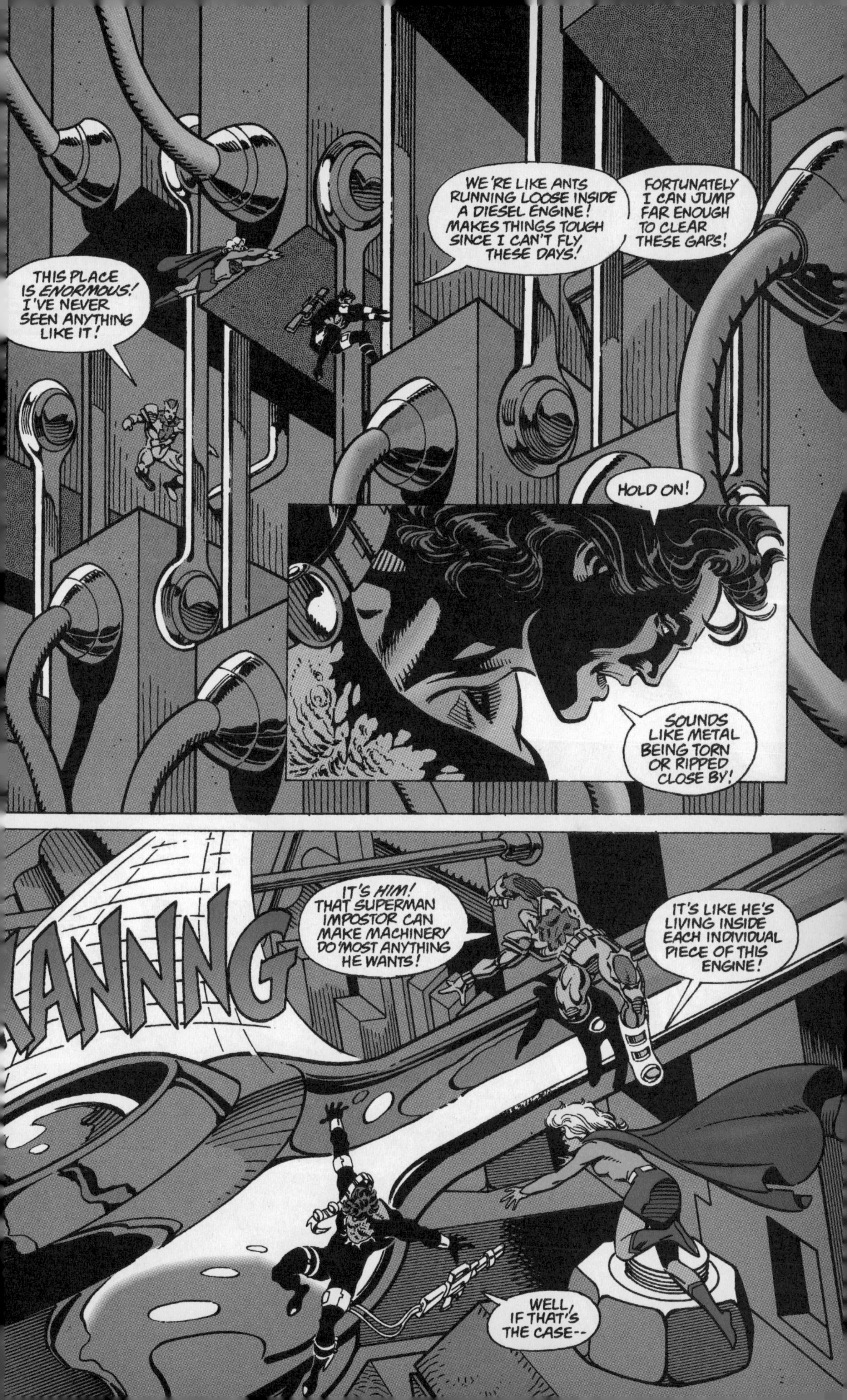
THIS PLACE IS ENORMOUS! I'VE NEVER SEEN ANYTHING LIKE IT!
WE'RE LIKE ANTS RUNNING LOOSE INSIDE A DIESEL ENGINE! MAKES THINGS TOUGH SINCE I CAN'T FLY THESE DAYS!
FORTUNATELY I CAN JUMP FAR ENOUGH TO CLEAR THESE GAPS!
HOLD ON!
SOUNDS LIKE METAL BEING TORN OR RIPPED CLOSE BY!
ANNNG
IT'S HIM! THAT SUPERMAN IMPOSTOR CAN MAKE MACHINERY DO MOST ANYTHING HE WANTS!
IT'S LIKE HE'S LIVING INSIDE EACH INDIVIDUAL PIECE OF THIS ENGINE!
WELL, IF THAT'S THE CASE--

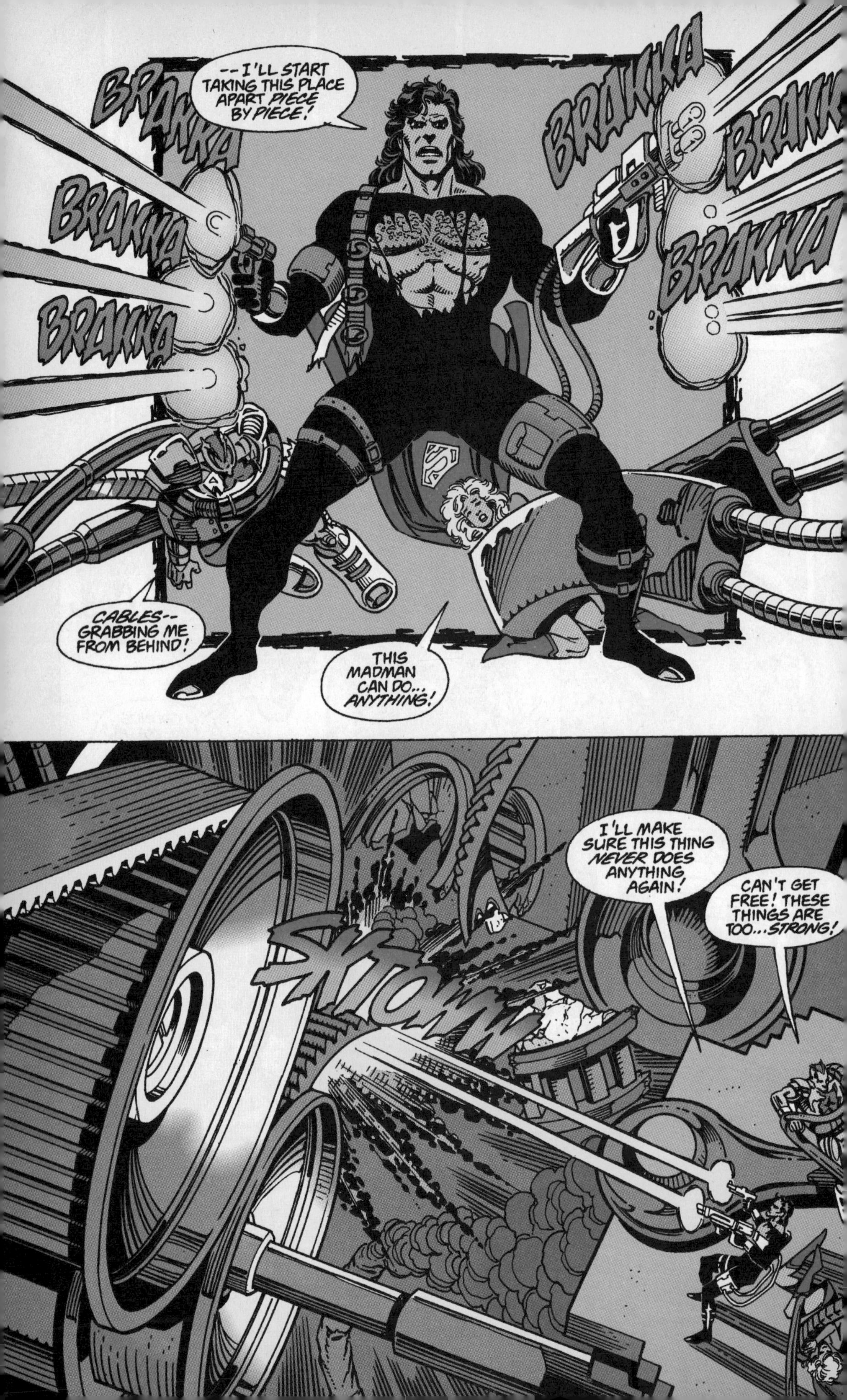
BRAKKA
--I'LL START TAKING THIS PLACE APART PIECE BY PIECE!
BRAKKA
BRAKKA
BRAKKA
BRAKKA
BRAKKA
CABLES-- GRABBING ME FROM BEHIND!
THIS MADMAN CAN DO... ANYTHING!
I'LL MAKE SURE THIS THING NEVER DOES ANYTHING AGAIN!
CAN'T GET FREE! THESE THINGS ARE TOO... STRONG!
SKTOWW

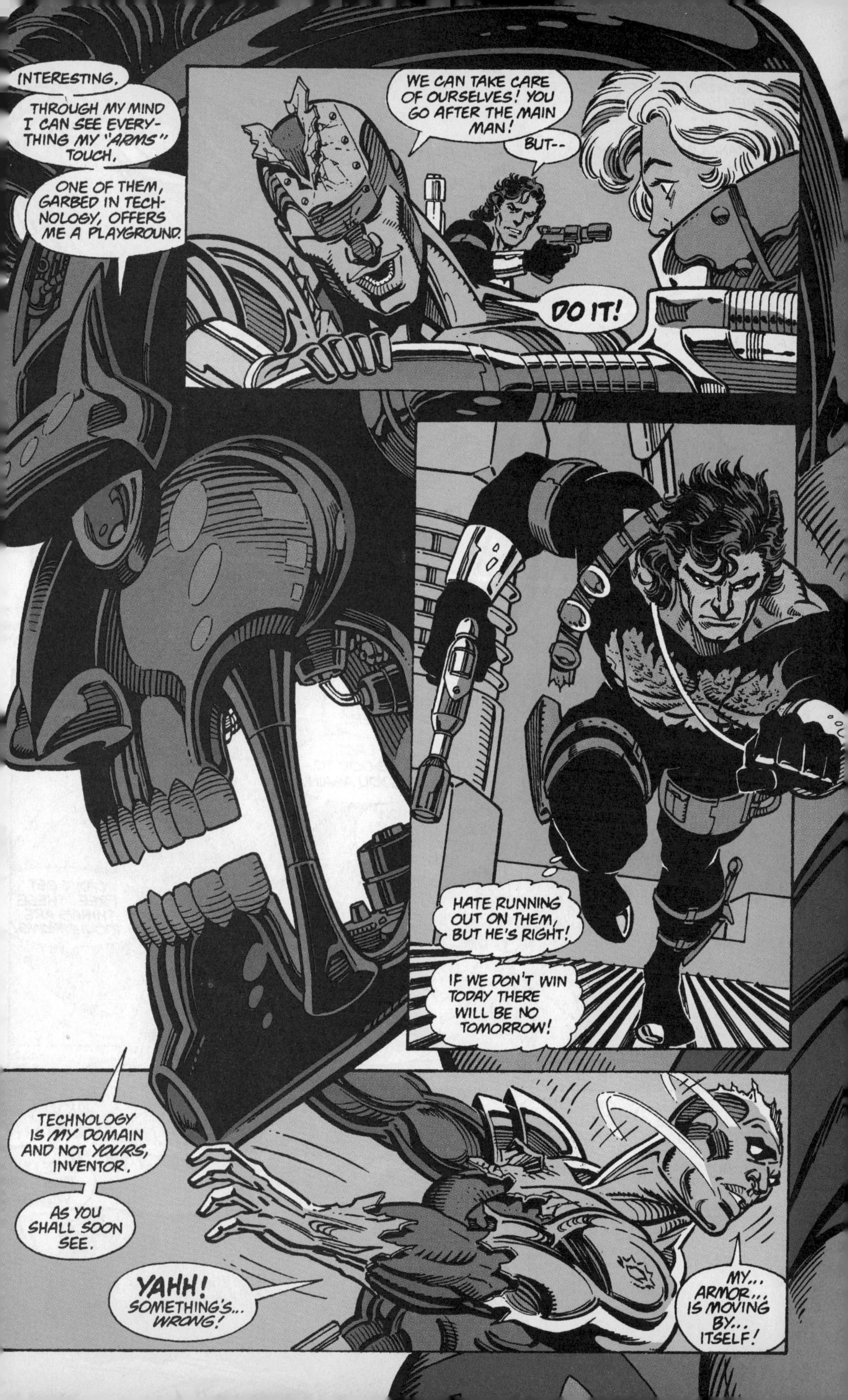
INTERESTING.
THROUGH MY MIND I CAN SEE EVERYTHING MY "ARMS" TOUCH.
ONE OF THEM, GARBED IN TECHNOLOGY, OFFERS ME A PLAYGROUND.
WE CAN TAKE CARE OF OURSELVES! YOU GO AFTER THE MAIN MAN!
BUT--
DO IT!
HATE RUNNING OUT ON THEM, BUT HE'S RIGHT!
IF WE DON'T WIN TODAY THERE WILL BE NO TOMORROW!
TECHNOLOGY IS MY DOMAIN AND NOT YOURS, INVENTOR.
AS YOU SHALL SOON SEE.
YAHH! SOMETHING'S... WRONG!
MY... ARMOR... IS MOVING BY... ITSELF!

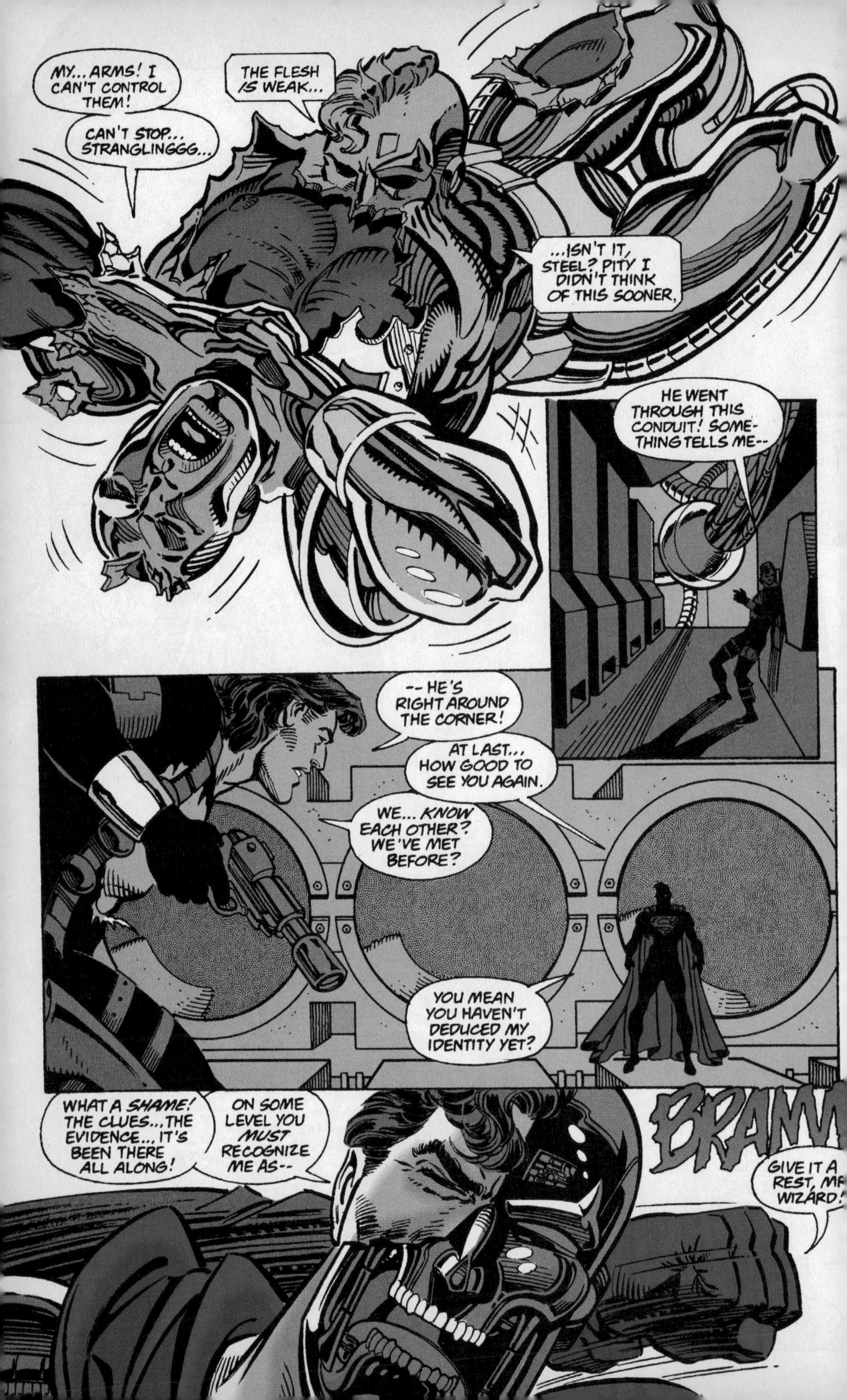
MY... ARMS! I CAN'T CONTROL THEM!
CAN'T STOP... STRANGLINGGG...
THE FLESH IS WEAK...
...ISN'T IT, STEEL? PITY I DIDN'T THINK OF THIS SOONER.
HE WENT THROUGH THIS CONDUIT! SOMETHING TELLS ME--
-- HE'S RIGHT AROUND THE CORNER!
AT LAST... HOW GOOD TO SEE YOU AGAIN.
WE... KNOW EACH OTHER? WE'VE MET BEFORE?
YOU MEAN YOU HAVEN'T DEDUCED MY IDENTITY YET?
WHAT A SHAME! THE CLUES... THE EVIDENCE... IT'S BEEN THERE ALL ALONG!
ON SOME LEVEL YOU MUST RECOGNIZE ME AS--
BRAM
GIVE IT A REST, M WIZARD!

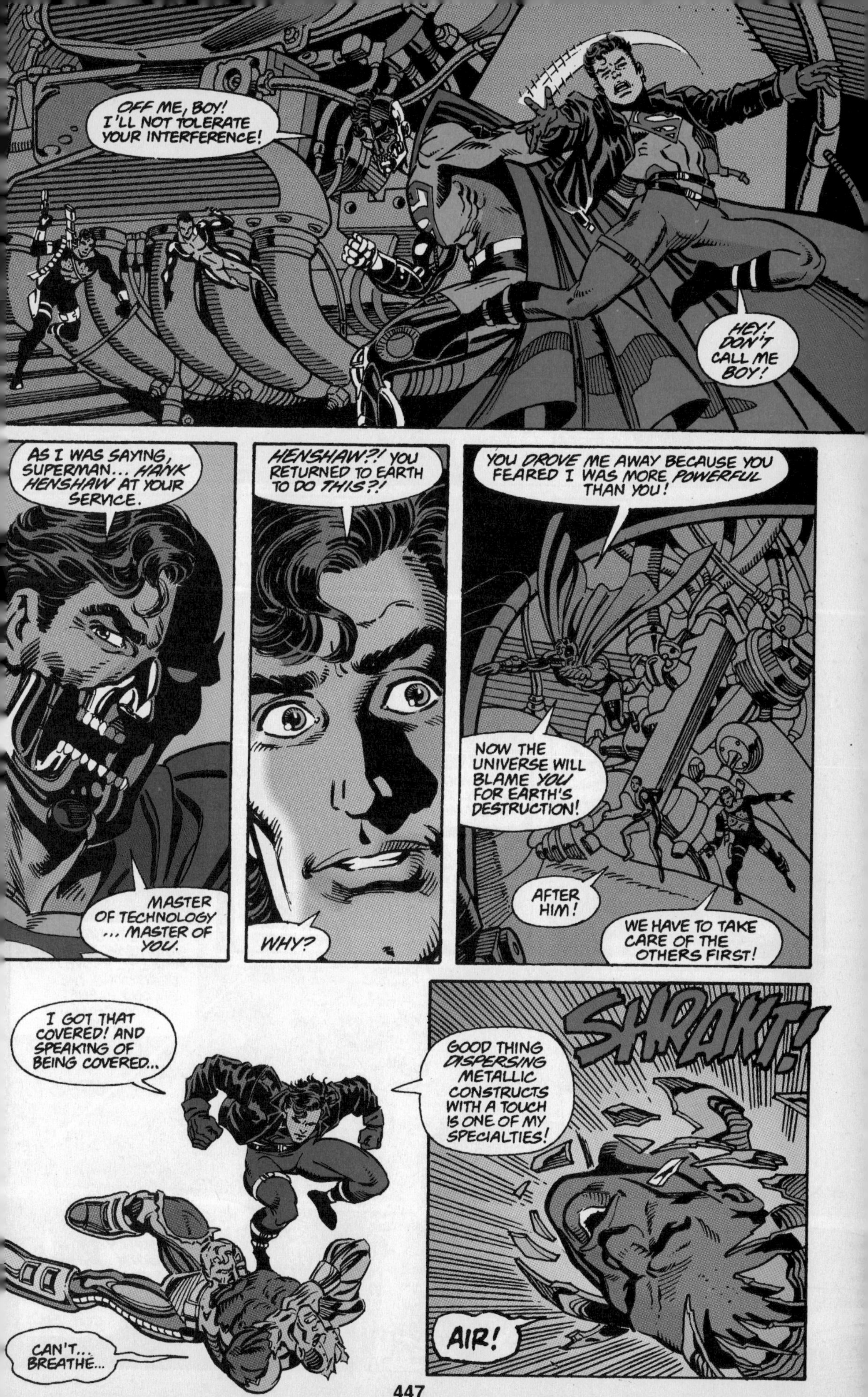

OFF ME, BOY! I'LL NOT TOLERATE YOUR INTERFERENCE!
HEY! DON'T CALL ME BOY!
AS I WAS SAYING, SUPERMAN... HANK HENSHAW AT YOUR SERVICE.
MASTER OF TECHNOLOGY ... MASTER OF YOU.
HENSHAW?! YOU RETURNED TO EARTH TO DO THIS?!
WHY?
YOU DROVE ME AWAY BECAUSE YOU FEARED I WAS MORE POWERFUL THAN YOU!
NOW THE UNIVERSE WILL BLAME YOU FOR EARTH'S DESTRUCTION!
AFTER HIM!
WE HAVE TO TAKE CARE OF THE OTHERS FIRST!
I GOT THAT COVERED! AND SPEAKING OF BEING COVERED...
CAN'T... BREATHE...
SHRAKT!
GOOD THING DISPERSING METALLIC CONSTRUCTS WITH A TOUCH IS ONE OF MY SPECIALTIES!
AIR!

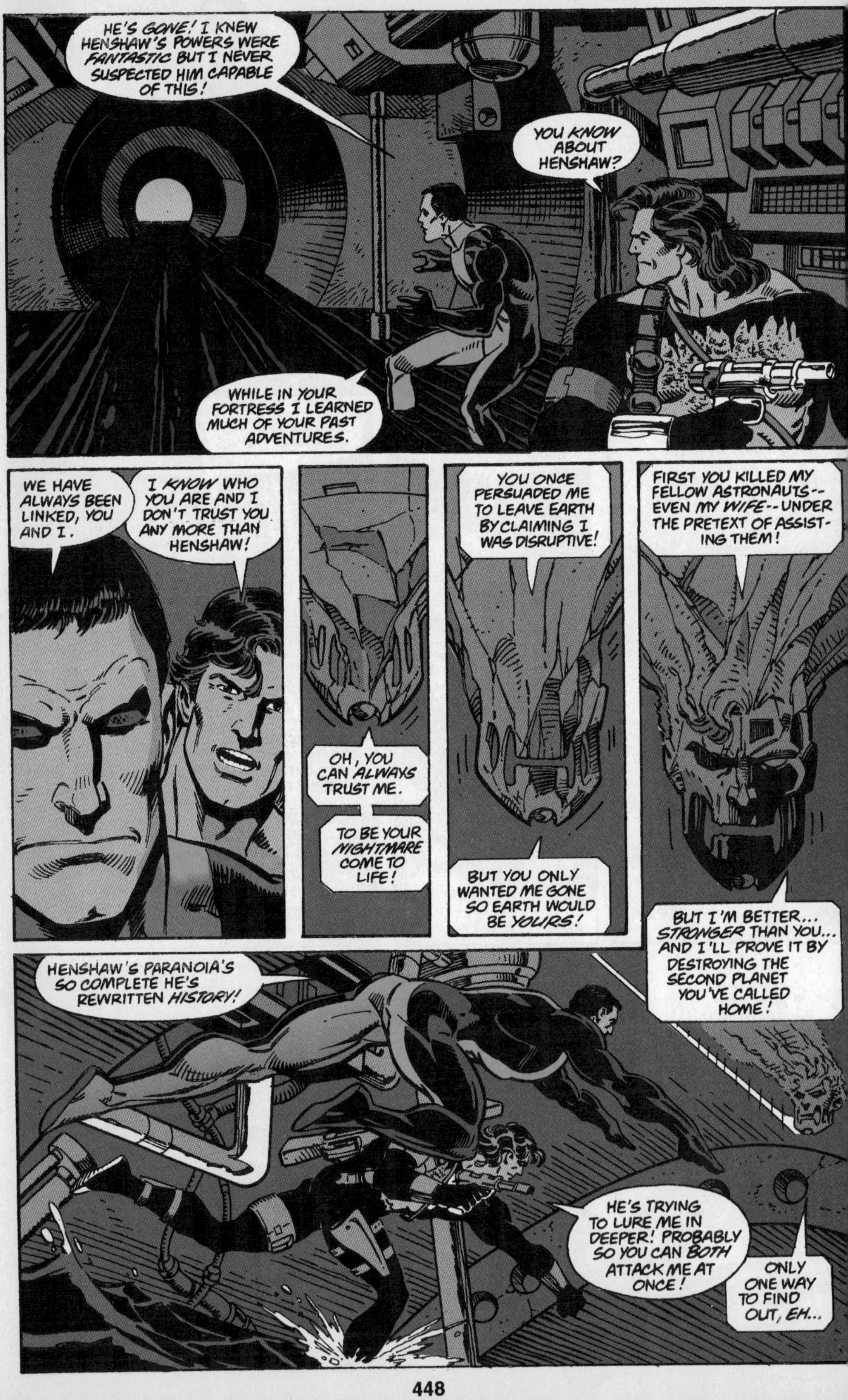
HE'S GONE! I KNEW HENSHAW'S POWERS WERE FANTASTIC BUT I NEVER SUSPECTED HIM CAPABLE OF THIS!
YOU KNOW ABOUT HENSHAW?
WHILE IN YOUR FORTRESS I LEARNED MUCH OF YOUR PAST ADVENTURES.
WE HAVE ALWAYS BEEN LINKED, YOU AND I.
I KNOW WHO YOU ARE AND I DON'T TRUST YOU ANY MORE THAN HENSHAW!
OH, YOU CAN ALWAYS TRUST ME.
TO BE YOUR NIGHTMARE COME TO LIFE!
YOU ONCE PERSUADED ME TO LEAVE EARTH BY CLAIMING I WAS DISRUPTIVE!
BUT YOU ONLY WANTED ME GONE SO EARTH WOULD BE YOURS!
FIRST YOU KILLED MY FELLOW ASTRONAUTS-- EVEN MY WIFE-- UNDER THE PRETEXT OF ASSISTING THEM!
BUT I'M BETTER... STRONGER THAN YOU... AND I'LL PROVE IT BY DESTROYING THE SECOND PLANET YOU'VE CALLED HOME!
HENSHAW'S PARANOIA'S SO COMPLETE HE'S REWRITTEN HISTORY!
HE'S TRYING TO LURE ME IN DEEPER! PROBABLY SO YOU CAN BOTH ATTACK ME AT ONCE!
ONLY ONE WAY TO FIND OUT, EH...

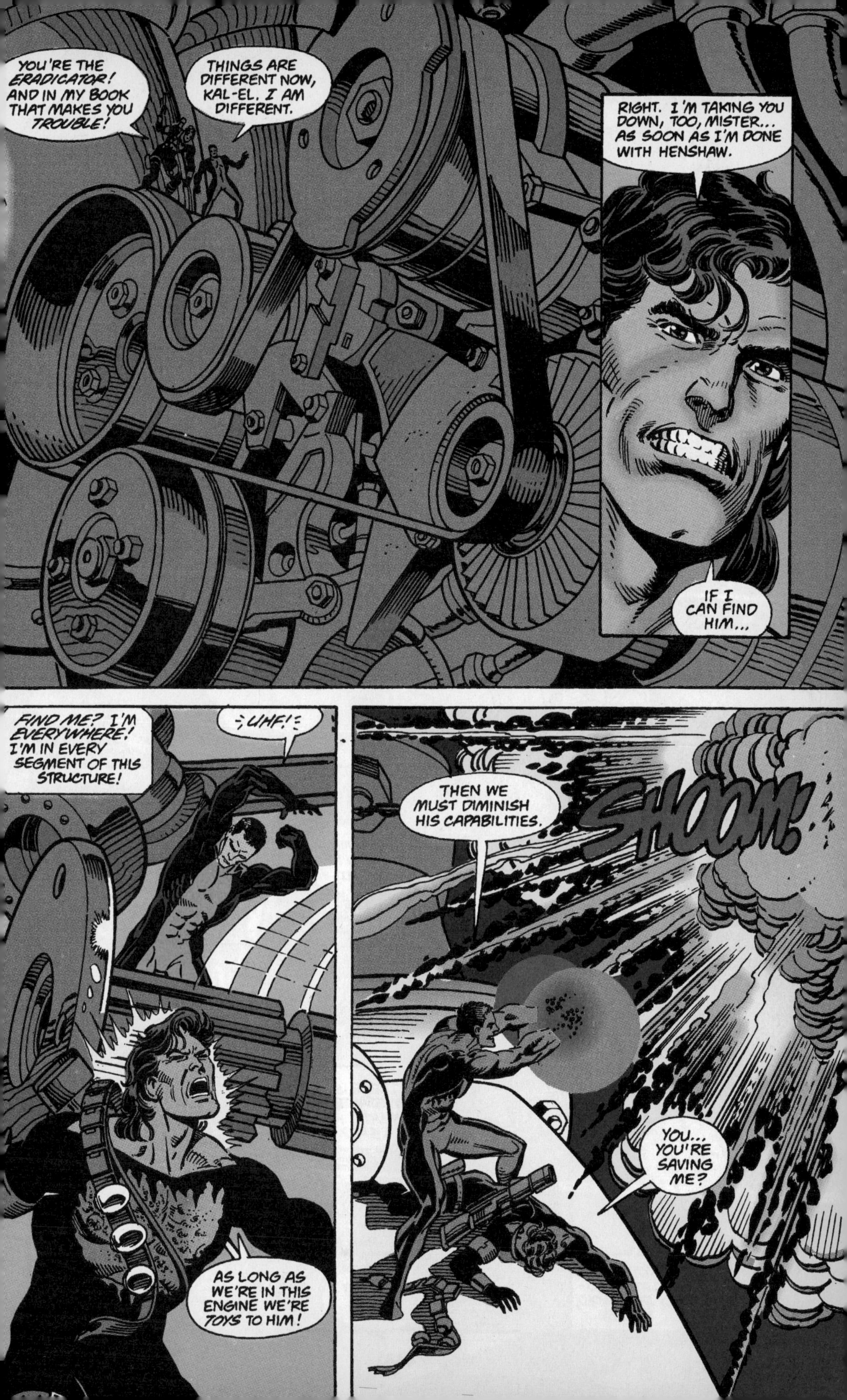
YOU'RE THE ERADICATOR! AND IN MY BOOK THAT MAKES YOU TROUBLE!
THINGS ARE DIFFERENT NOW, KAL-EL. I AM DIFFERENT.
RIGHT. I'M TAKING YOU DOWN, TOO, MISTER... AS SOON AS I'M DONE WITH HENSHAW.
IF I CAN FIND HIM...
FIND ME? I'M EVERYWHERE! I'M IN EVERY SEGMENT OF THIS STRUCTURE!
UHF!
AS LONG AS WE'RE IN THIS ENGINE WE'RE TOYS TO HIM!
THEN WE MUST DIMINISH HIS CAPABILITIES.
SHOOM!
YOU... YOU'RE SAVING ME?

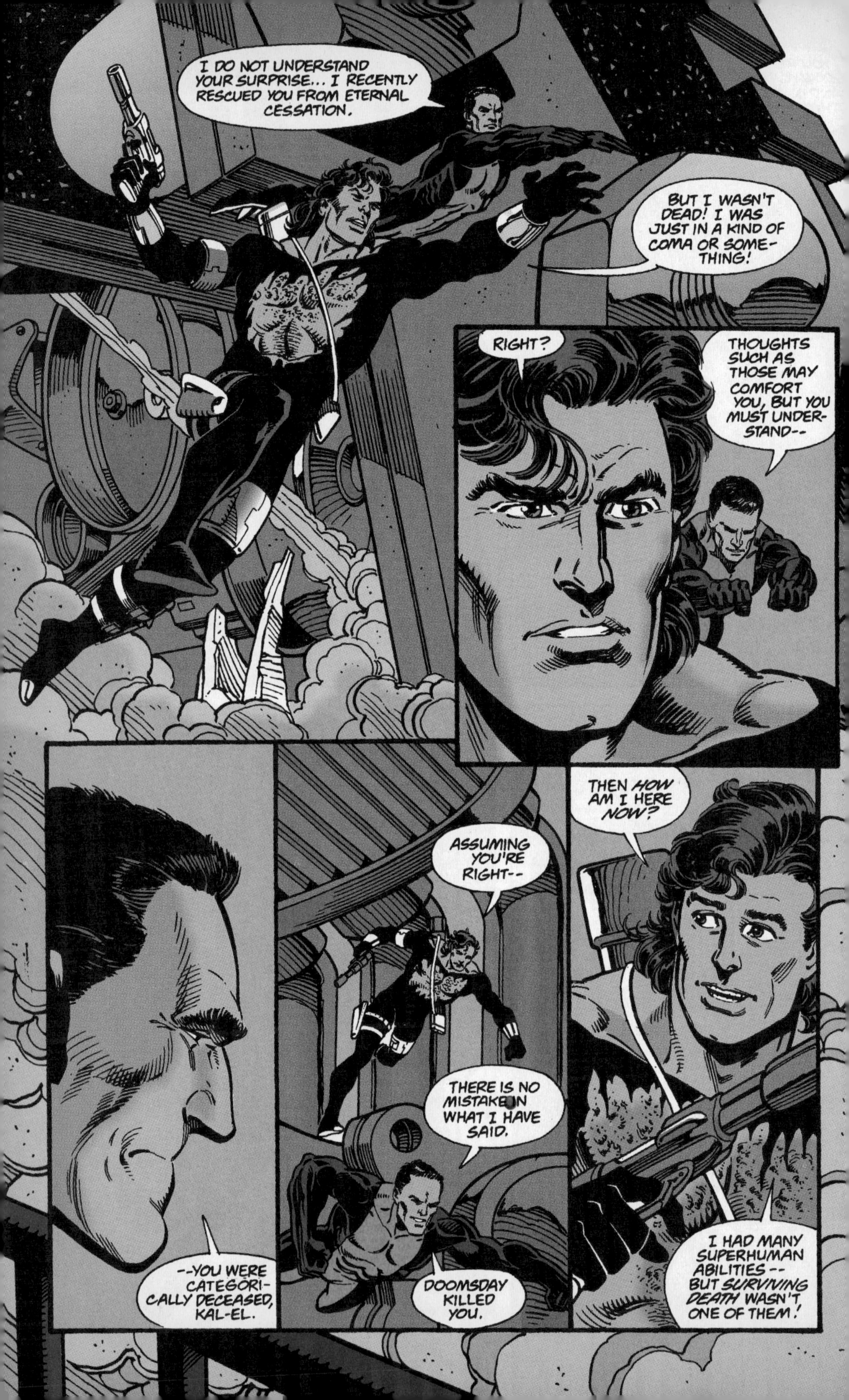
I DO NOT UNDERSTAND YOUR SURPRISE... I RECENTLY RESCUED YOU FROM ETERNAL CESSATION.
BUT I WASN'T DEAD! I WAS JUST IN A KIND OF COMA OR SOMETHING!
RIGHT?
THOUGHTS SUCH AS THOSE MAY COMFORT YOU, BUT YOU MUST UNDERSTAND--
--YOU WERE CATEGORICALLY DECEASED, KAL-EL.
ASSUMING YOU'RE RIGHT--
THERE IS NO MISTAKE IN WHAT I HAVE SAID.
DOOMSDAY KILLED YOU.
THEN HOW AM I HERE NOW?
I HAD MANY SUPERHUMAN ABILITIES -- BUT SURVIVING DEATH WASN'T ONE OF THEM!

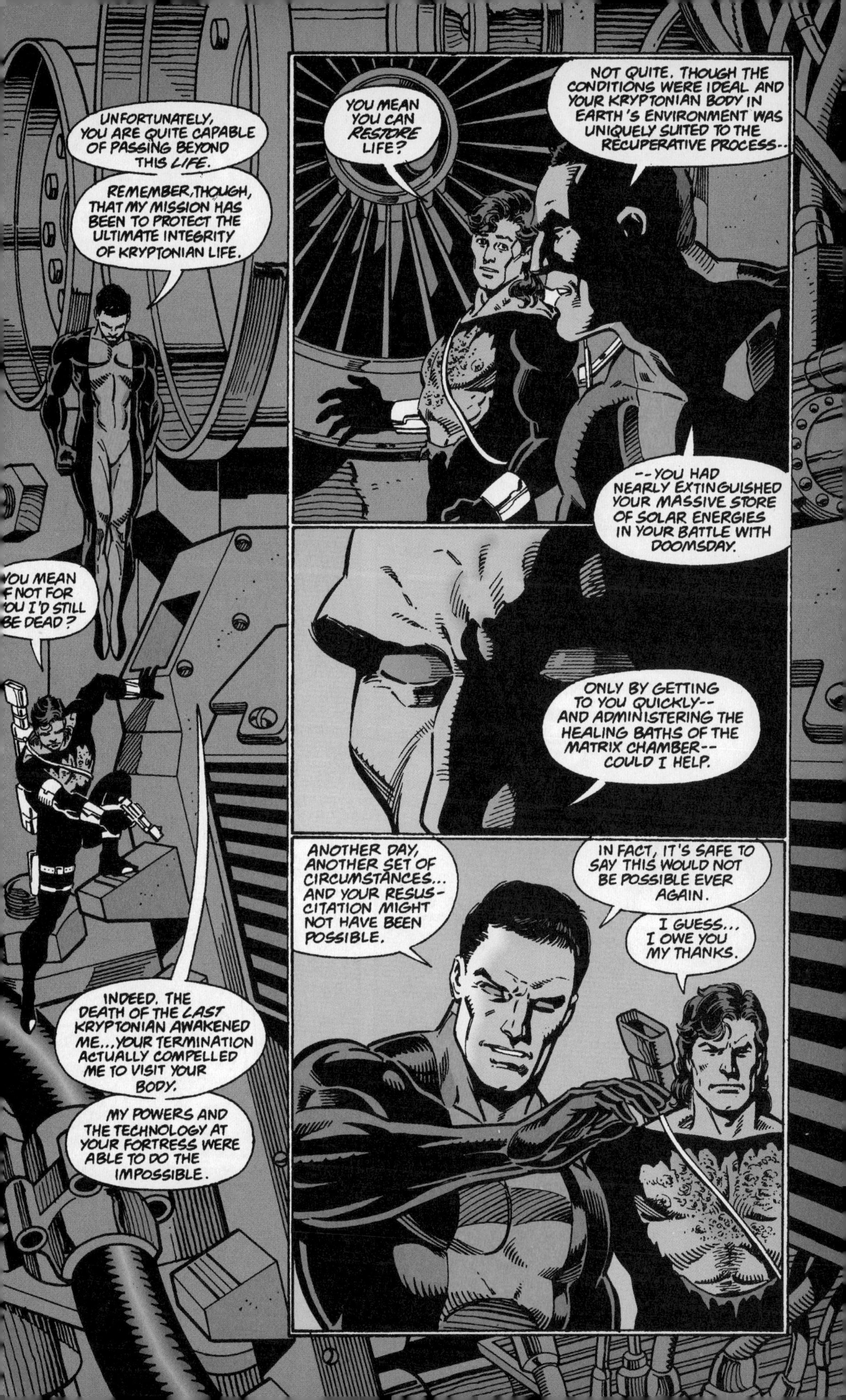
UNFORTUNATELY, YOU ARE QUITE CAPABLE OF PASSING BEYOND THIS *LIFE*.
REMEMBER, THOUGH, THAT MY MISSION HAS BEEN TO PROTECT THE ULTIMATE INTEGRITY OF KRYPTONIAN LIFE.
YOU MEAN YOU CAN *RESTORE* LIFE?
NOT QUITE. THOUGH THE CONDITIONS WERE IDEAL AND YOUR KRYPTONIAN BODY IN EARTH'S ENVIRONMENT WAS UNIQUELY SUITED TO THE RECUPERATIVE PROCESS--
--YOU HAD NEARLY EXTINGUISHED YOUR MASSIVE STORE OF SOLAR ENERGIES IN YOUR BATTLE WITH DOOMSDAY.
YOU MEAN IF NOT FOR YOU I'D STILL BE DEAD?
INDEED. THE DEATH OF THE *LAST* KRYPTONIAN AWAKENED ME... YOUR TERMINATION ACTUALLY COMPELLED ME TO VISIT YOUR BODY.
MY POWERS AND THE TECHNOLOGY AT YOUR FORTRESS WERE ABLE TO DO THE IMPOSSIBLE.
ONLY BY GETTING TO YOU QUICKLY-- AND ADMINISTERING THE HEALING BATHS OF THE MATRIX CHAMBER-- COULD I HELP.
ANOTHER DAY, ANOTHER SET OF CIRCUMSTANCES... AND YOUR RESUSCITATION MIGHT NOT HAVE BEEN POSSIBLE.
IN FACT, IT'S SAFE TO SAY THIS WOULD NOT BE POSSIBLE EVER AGAIN.
I GUESS... I OWE YOU MY THANKS.

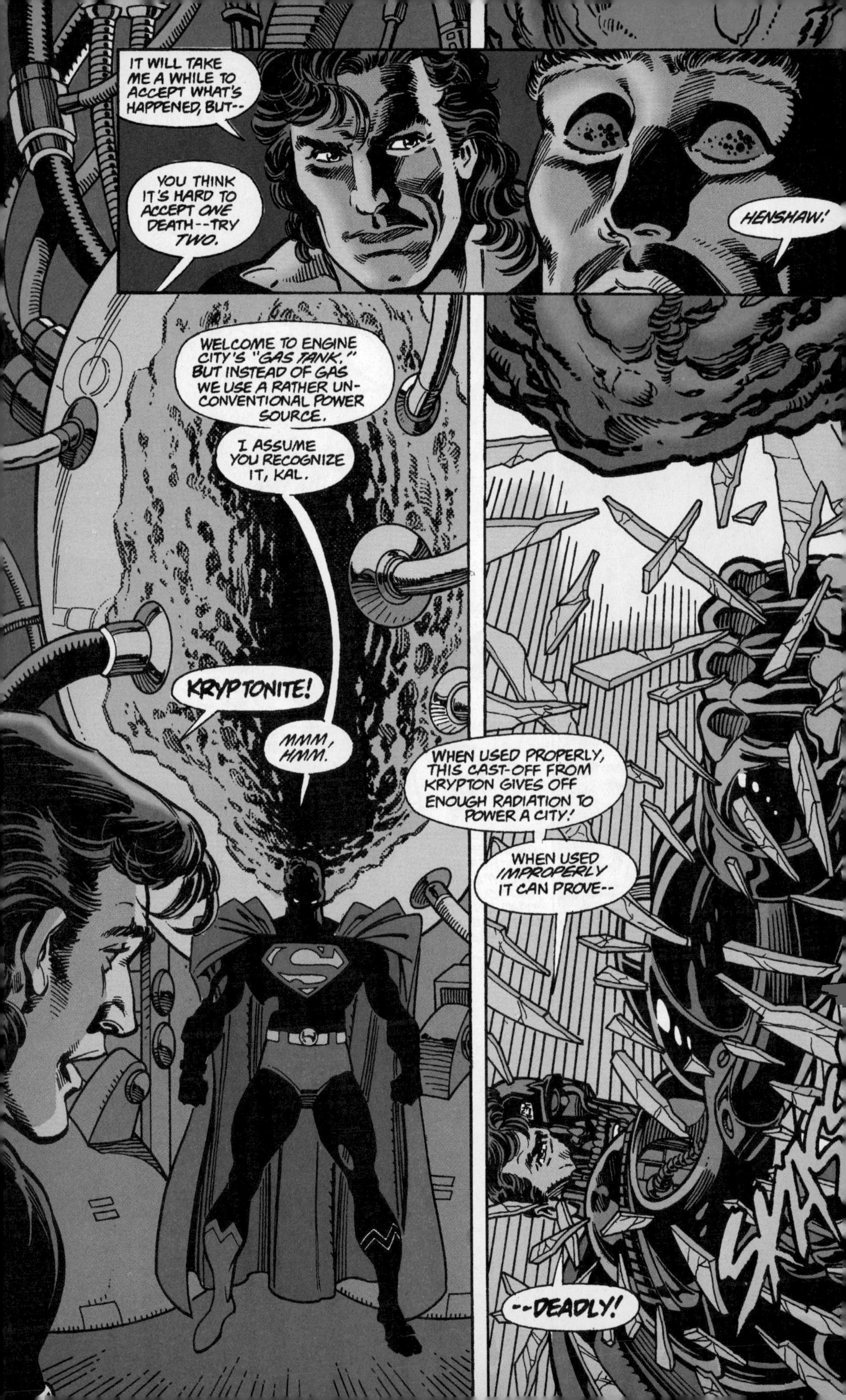
IT WILL TAKE ME A WHILE TO ACCEPT WHAT'S HAPPENED, BUT--
YOU THINK IT'S HARD TO ACCEPT ONE DEATH--TRY TWO.
HENSHAW!
WELCOME TO ENGINE CITY'S "GAS TANK." BUT INSTEAD OF GAS WE USE A RATHER UN-CONVENTIONAL POWER SOURCE.
I ASSUME YOU RECOGNIZE IT, KAL.
KRYPTONITE!
MMM, HMM.
WHEN USED PROPERLY, THIS CAST-OFF FROM KRYPTON GIVES OFF ENOUGH RADIATION TO POWER A CITY!
WHEN USED IMPROPERLY IT CAN PROVE--
--DEADLY!

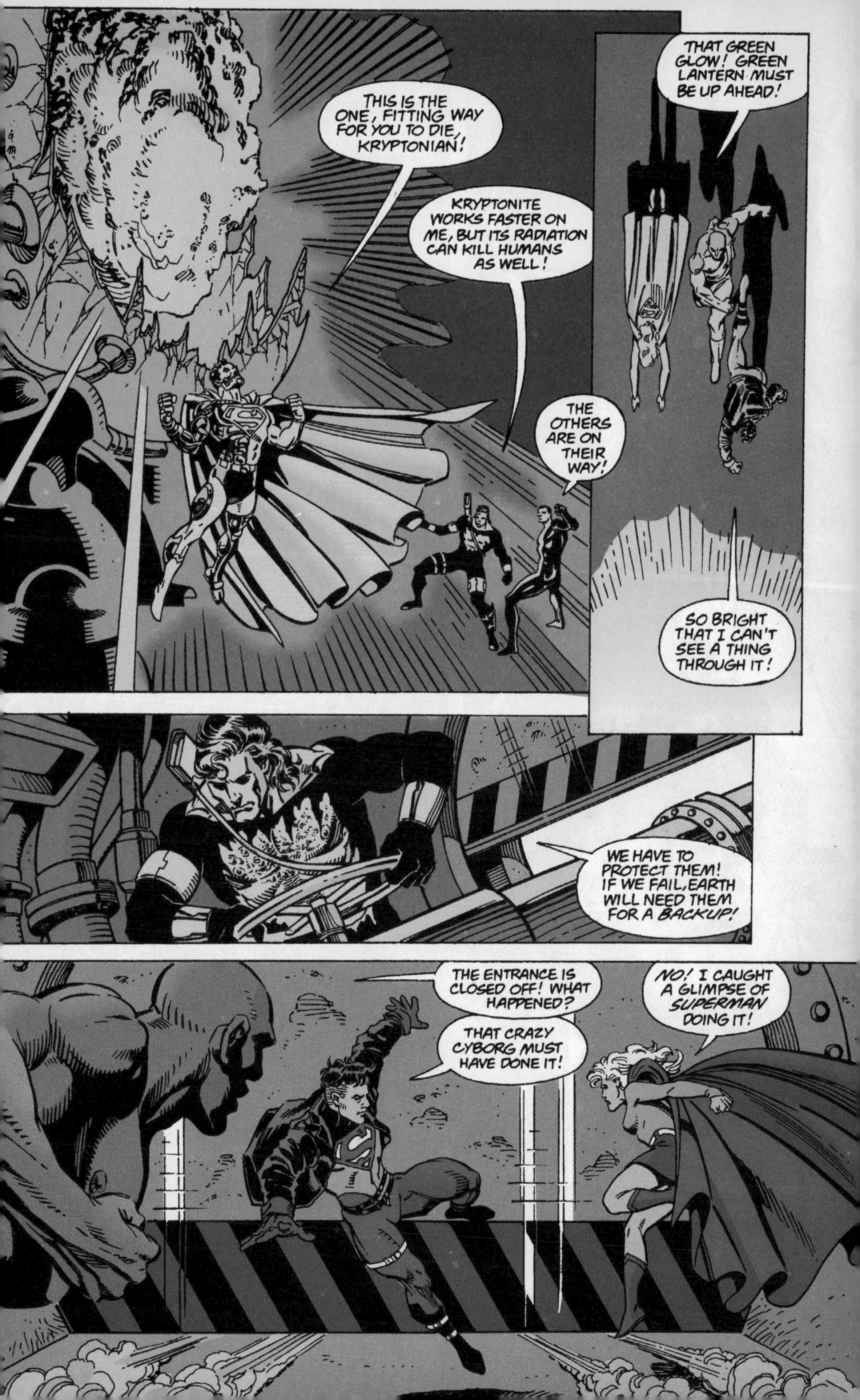
THIS IS THE ONE, FITTING WAY FOR YOU TO DIE, KRYPTONIAN!
KRYPTONITE WORKS FASTER ON ME, BUT ITS RADIATION CAN KILL HUMANS AS WELL!
THE OTHERS ARE ON THEIR WAY!
THAT GREEN GLOW! GREEN LANTERN MUST BE UP AHEAD!
SO BRIGHT THAT I CAN'T SEE A THING THROUGH IT!
WE HAVE TO PROTECT THEM! IF WE FAIL, EARTH WILL NEED THEM FOR A BACKUP!
THE ENTRANCE IS CLOSED OFF! WHAT HAPPENED?
THAT CRAZY CYBORG MUST HAVE DONE IT!
NO! I CAUGHT A GLIMPSE OF SUPERMAN DOING IT!

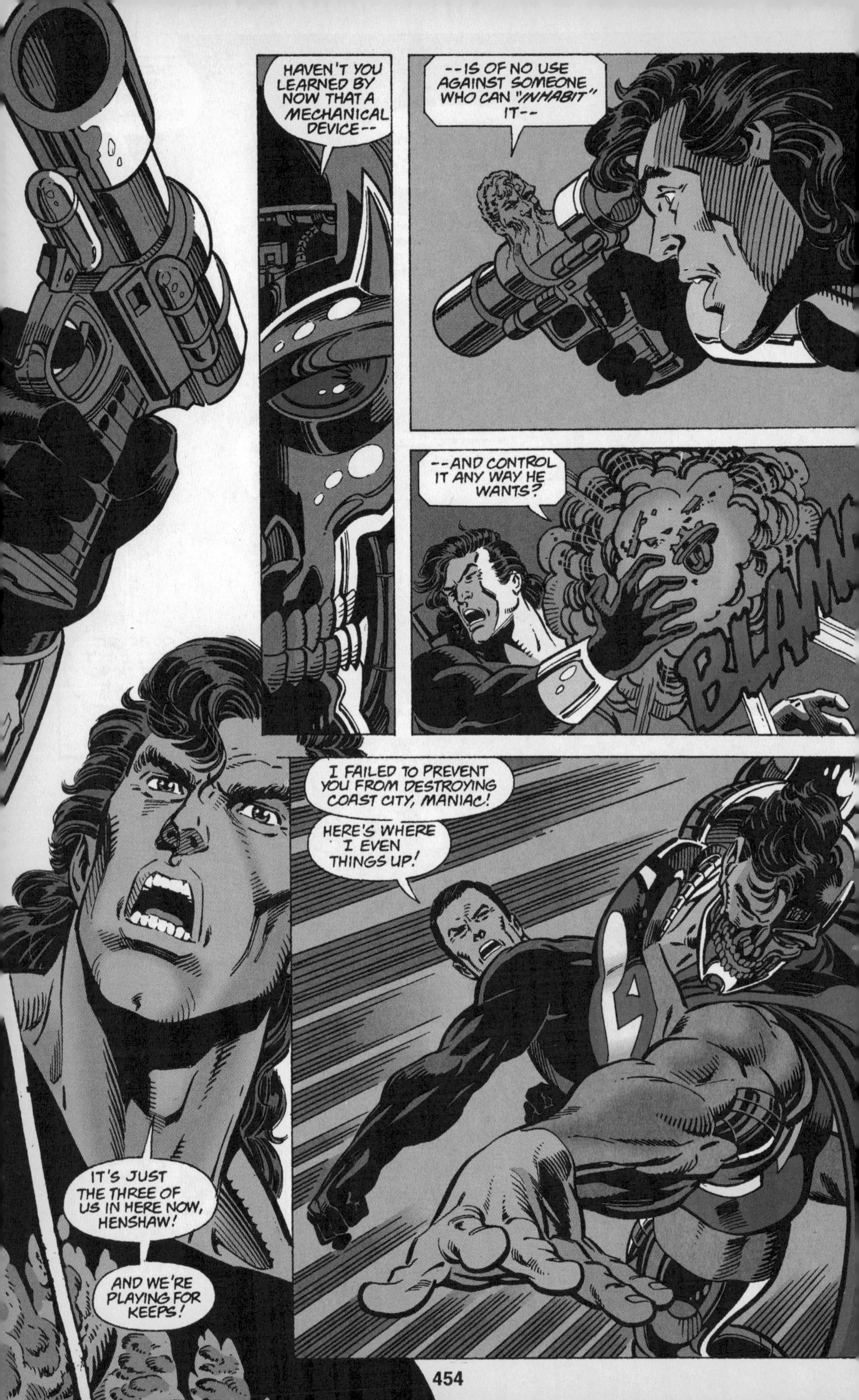
HAVEN'T YOU LEARNED BY NOW THAT A MECHANICAL DEVICE--
--IS OF NO USE AGAINST SOMEONE WHO CAN "INHABIT" IT--
--AND CONTROL IT ANY WAY HE WANTS?
BLAMM
I FAILED TO PREVENT YOU FROM DESTROYING COAST CITY, MANIAC!
HERE'S WHERE I EVEN THINGS UP!
IT'S JUST THE THREE OF US IN HERE NOW, HENSHAW!
AND WE'RE PLAYING FOR KEEPS!

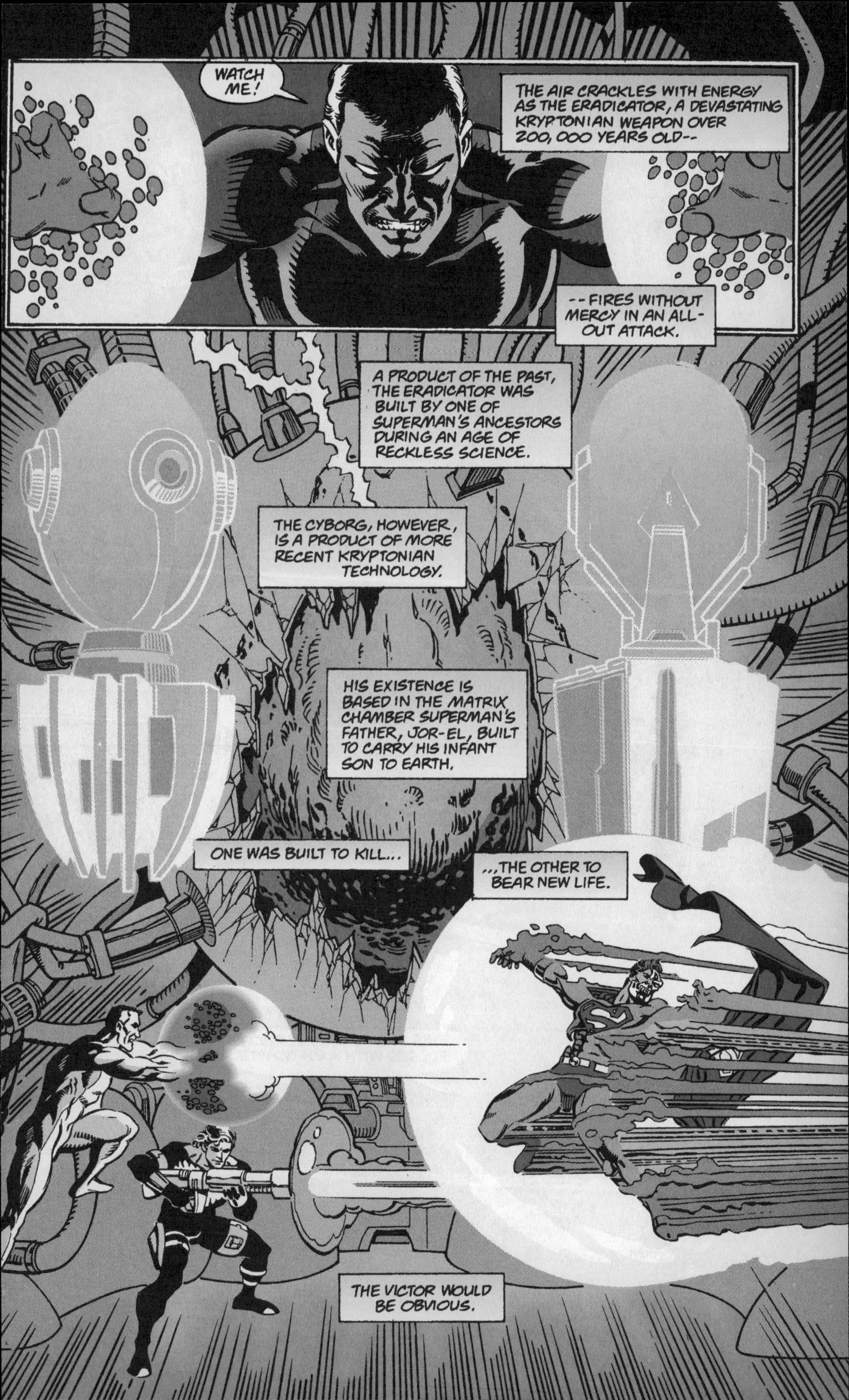
WATCH ME!
THE AIR CRACKLES WITH ENERGY AS THE ERADICATOR, A DEVASTATING KRYPTONIAN WEAPON OVER 200,000 YEARS OLD--
--FIRES WITHOUT MERCY IN AN ALL-OUT ATTACK.
A PRODUCT OF THE PAST, THE ERADICATOR WAS BUILT BY ONE OF SUPERMAN'S ANCESTORS DURING AN AGE OF RECKLESS SCIENCE.
THE CYBORG, HOWEVER, IS A PRODUCT OF MORE RECENT KRYPTONIAN TECHNOLOGY.
HIS EXISTENCE IS BASED IN THE MATRIX CHAMBER SUPERMAN'S FATHER, JOR-EL, BUILT TO CARRY HIS INFANT SON TO EARTH.
ONE WAS BUILT TO KILL...
...THE OTHER TO BEAR NEW LIFE.
THE VICTOR WOULD BE OBVIOUS.

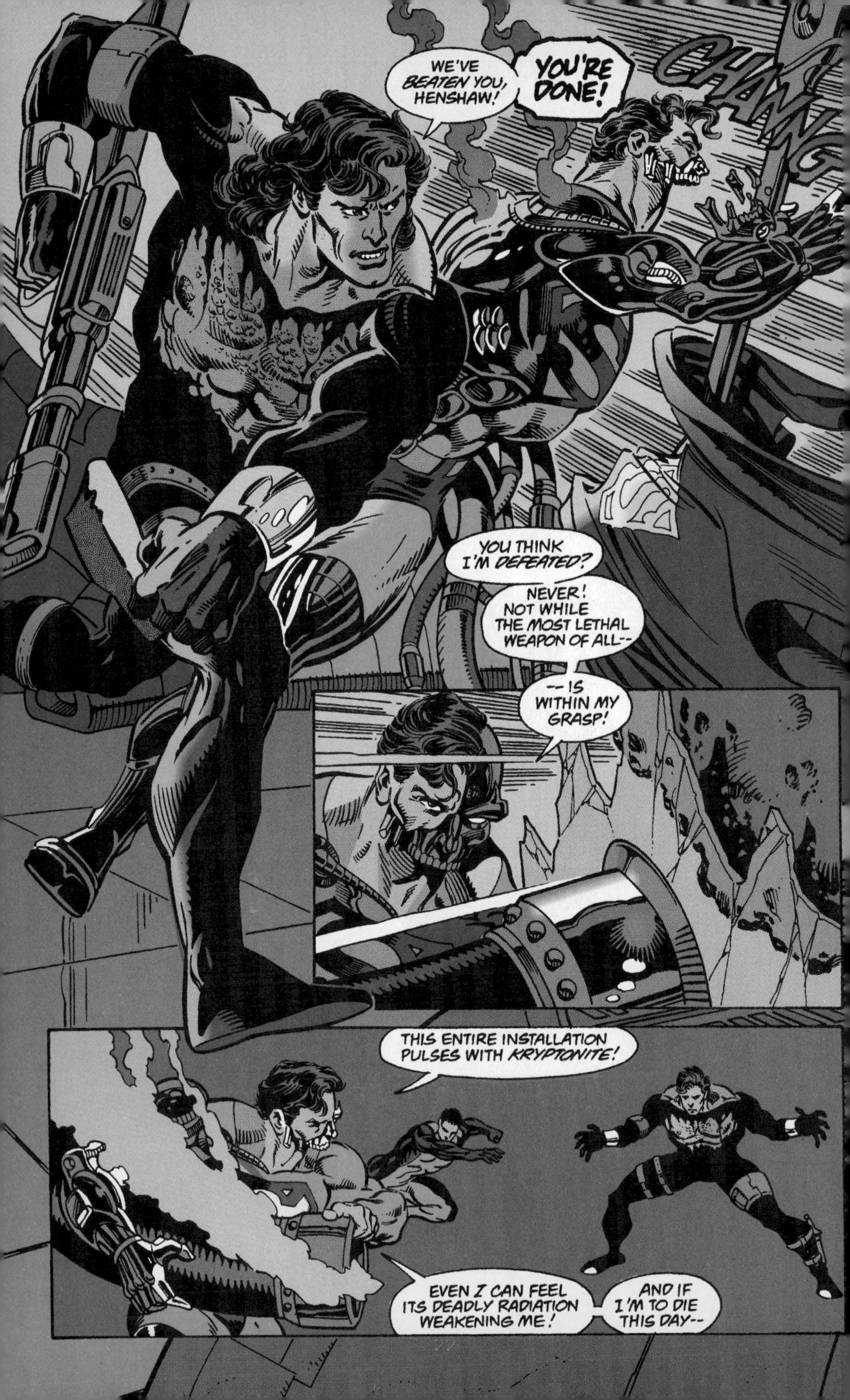

WE'VE BEATEN YOU, HENSHAW!
YOU'RE DONE!
CHANG
YOU THINK I'M DEFEATED?
NEVER! NOT WHILE THE MOST LETHAL WEAPON OF ALL--
--IS WITHIN MY GRASP!
THIS ENTIRE INSTALLATION PULSES WITH KRYPTONITE!
EVEN I CAN FEEL ITS DEADLY RADIATION WEAKENING ME!
AND IF I'M TO DIE THIS DAY--

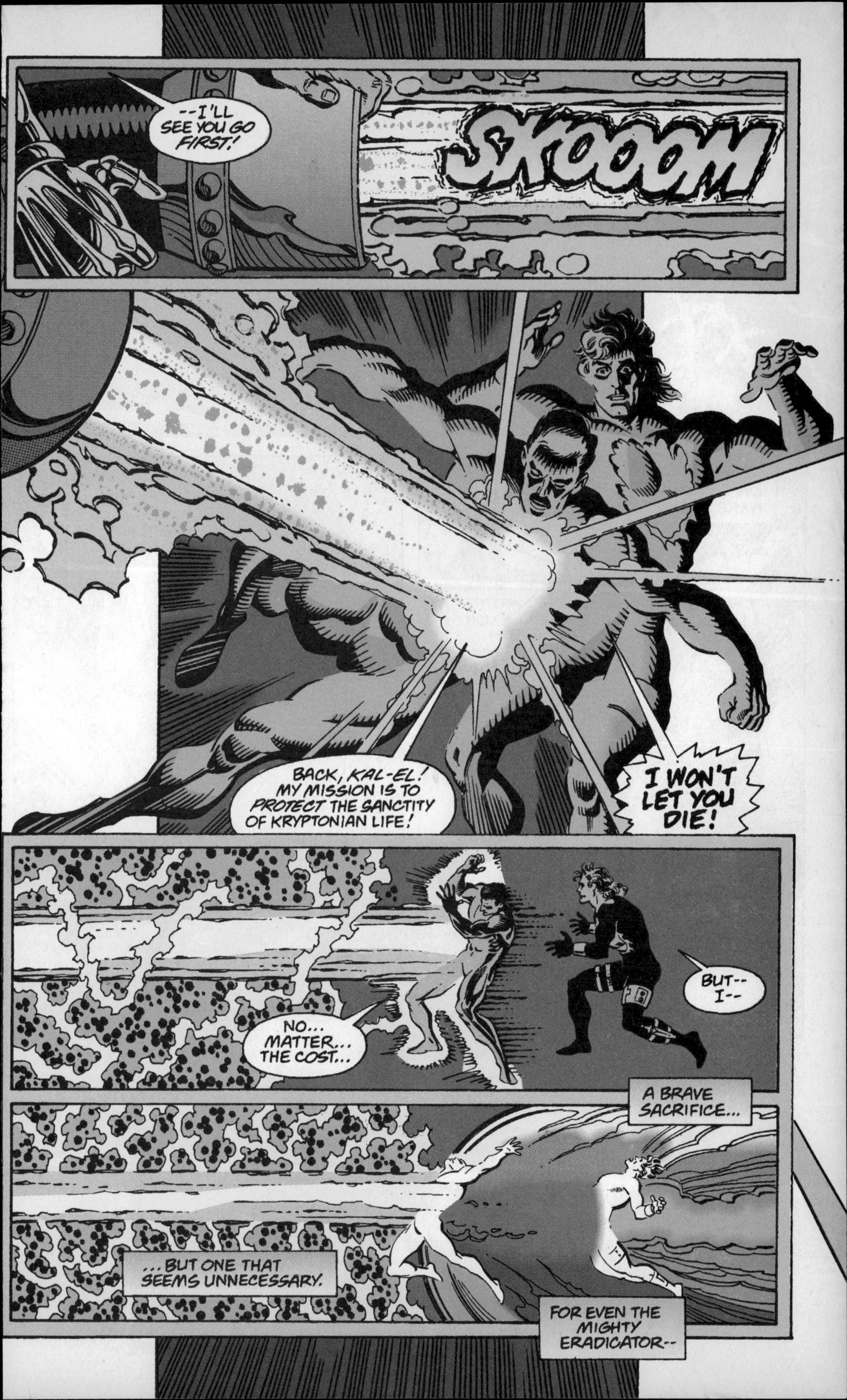
--I'LL SEE YOU GO FIRST!
SKOOOM
BACK, KAL-EL! MY MISSION IS TO PROTECT THE SANCTITY OF KRYPTONIAN LIFE!
I WON'T LET YOU DIE!
NO... MATTER... THE COST...
BUT-- I--
A BRAVE SACRIFICE...
...BUT ONE THAT SEEMS UNNECESSARY.
FOR EVEN THE MIGHTY ERADICATOR--

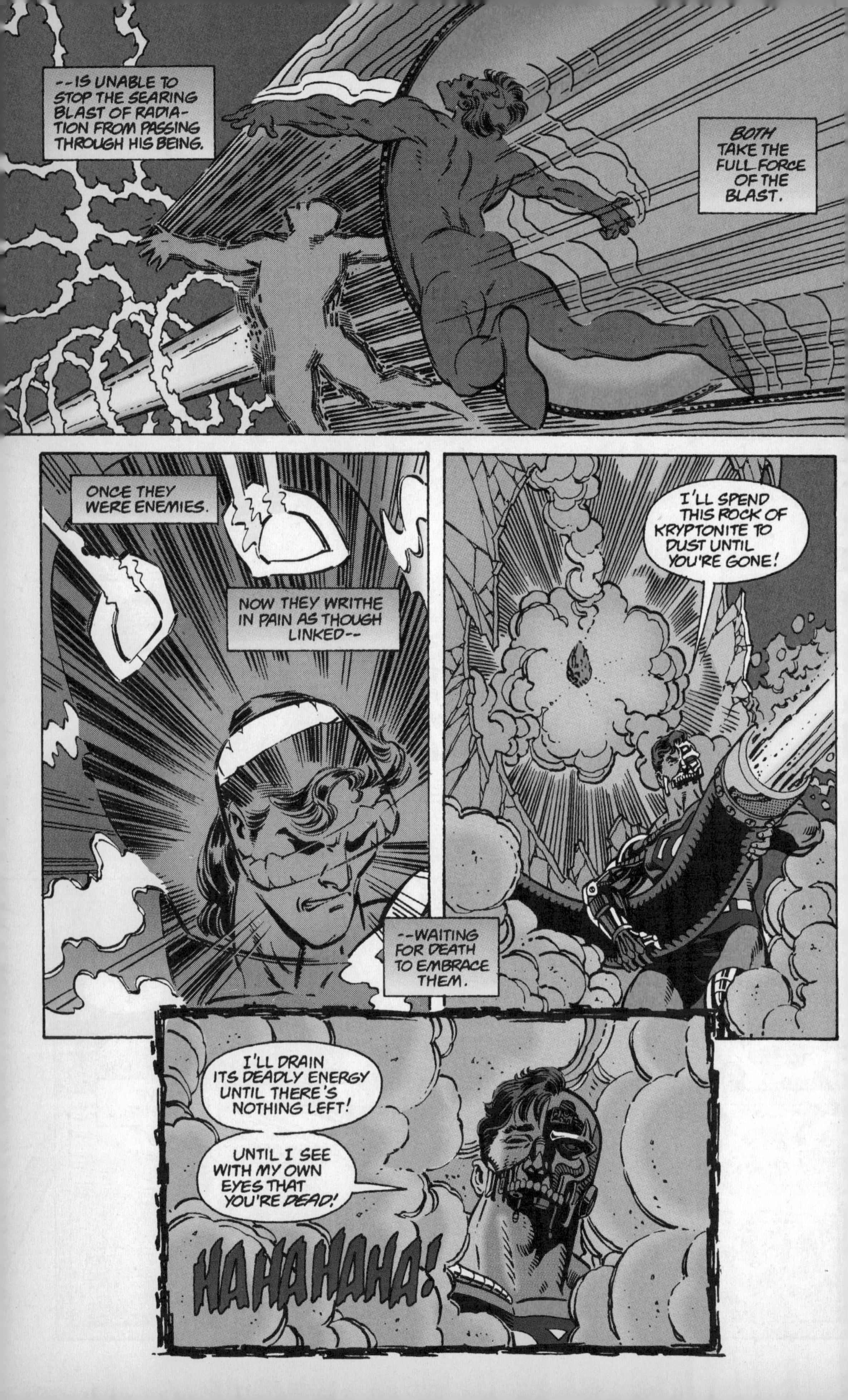
--IS UNABLE TO STOP THE SEARING BLAST OF RADIATION FROM PASSING THROUGH HIS BEING.
BOTH TAKE THE FULL FORCE OF THE BLAST.
ONCE THEY WERE ENEMIES.
NOW THEY WRITHE IN PAIN AS THOUGH LINKED--
--WAITING FOR DEATH TO EMBRACE THEM.
I'LL SPEND THIS ROCK OF KRYPTONITE TO DUST UNTIL YOU'RE GONE!
I'LL DRAIN ITS DEADLY ENERGY UNTIL THERE'S NOTHING LEFT!
UNTIL I SEE WITH MY OWN EYES THAT YOU'RE DEAD!
HAHAHAHA!

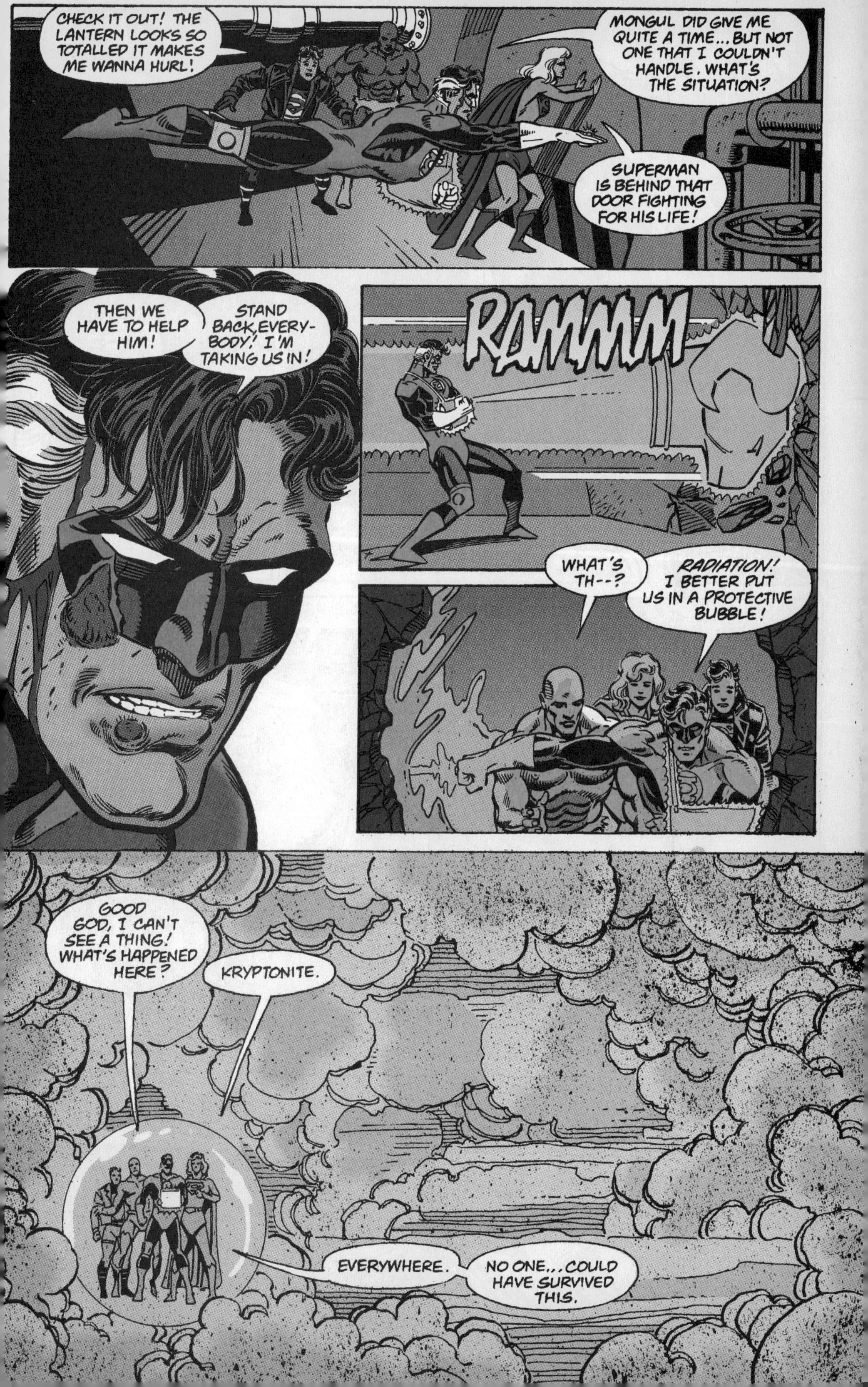

CHECK IT OUT! THE LANTERN LOOKS SO TOTALLED IT MAKES ME WANNA HURL!
MONGUL DID GIVE ME QUITE A TIME... BUT NOT ONE THAT I COULDN'T HANDLE. WHAT'S THE SITUATION?
SUPERMAN IS BEHIND THAT DOOR FIGHTING FOR HIS LIFE!
THEN WE HAVE TO HELP HIM!
STAND BACK, EVERY-BODY! I'M TAKING US IN!
RAMMM
WHAT'S TH--?
RADIATION! I BETTER PUT US IN A PROTECTIVE BUBBLE!
GOOD GOD, I CAN'T SEE A THING! WHAT'S HAPPENED HERE?
KRYPTONITE.
EVERYWHERE.
NO ONE... COULD HAVE SURVIVED THIS.

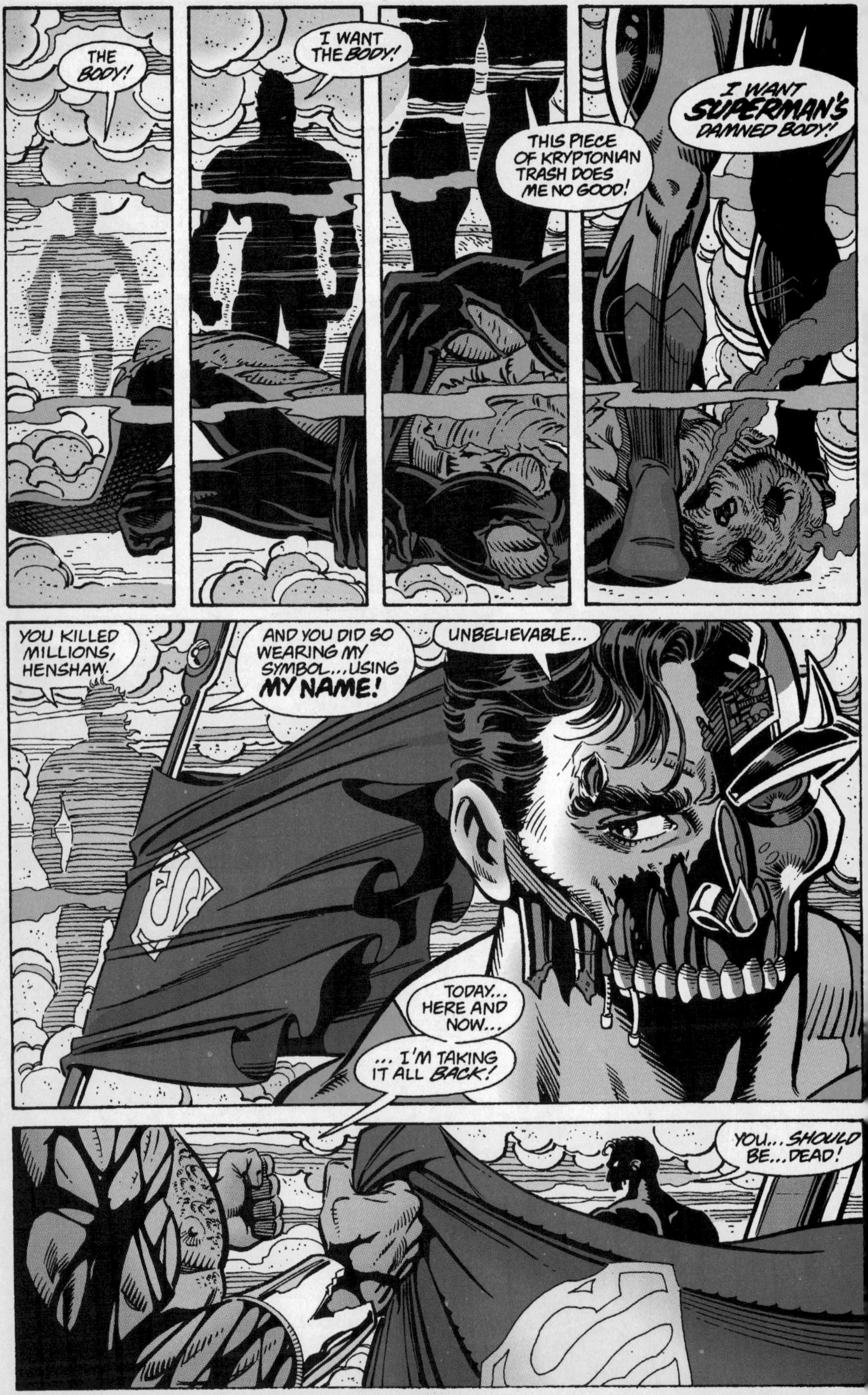
THE BODY!
I WANT THE BODY!
THIS PIECE OF KRYPTONIAN TRASH DOES ME NO GOOD!
I WANT SUPERMAN'S DAMNED BODY!
YOU KILLED MILLIONS, HENSHAW.
AND YOU DID SO WEARING MY SYMBOL... USING MY NAME!
UNBELIEVABLE...
TODAY... HERE AND NOW...
... I'M TAKING IT ALL BACK!
YOU... SHOULD BE... DEAD!

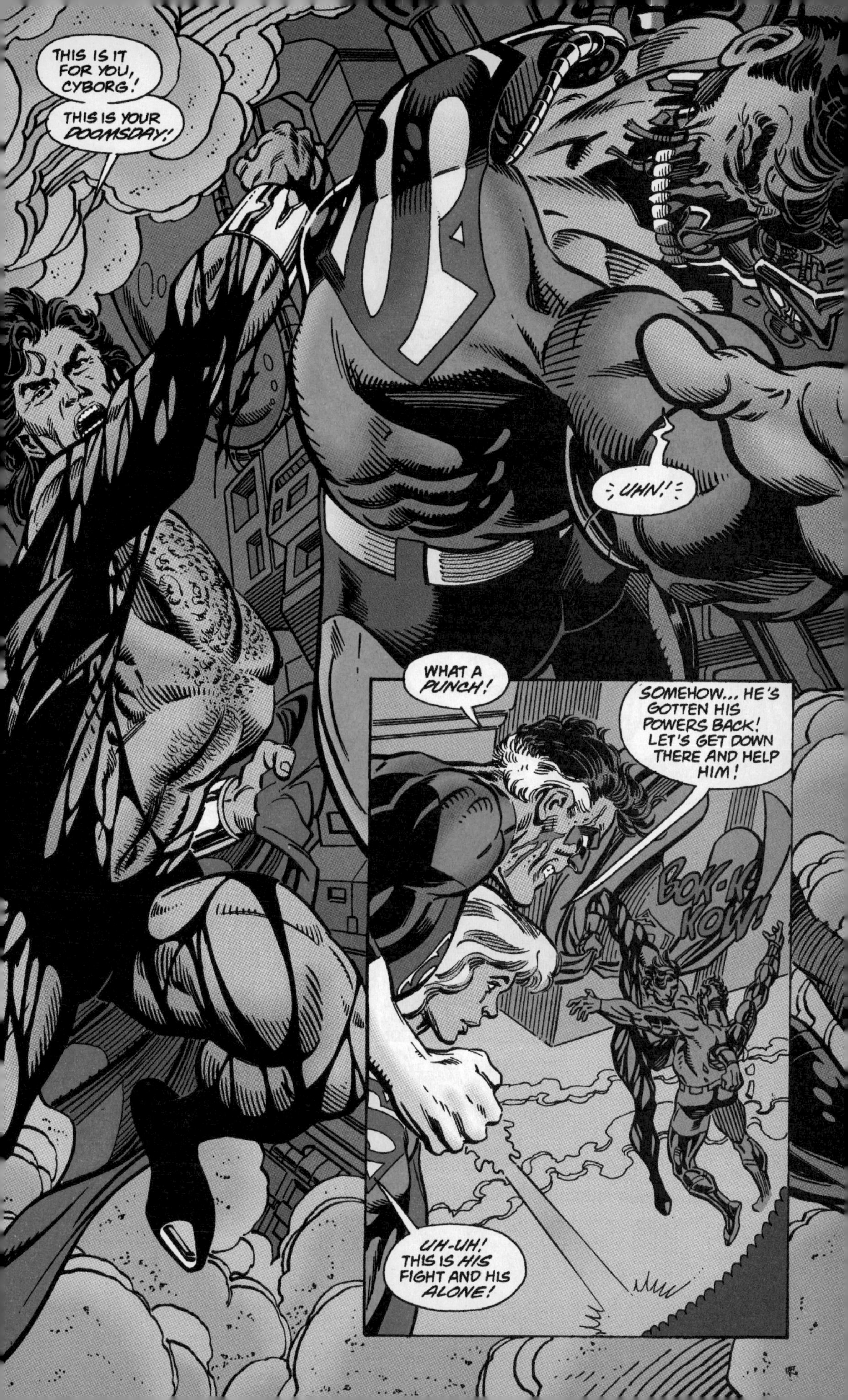
THIS IS IT FOR YOU, CYBORG!
THIS IS YOUR DOOMSDAY!
UHN!
WHAT A PUNCH!
SOMEHOW... HE'S GOTTEN HIS POWERS BACK! LET'S GET DOWN THERE AND HELP HIM!
BOK-K-KOW!
UH-UH! THIS IS HIS FIGHT AND HIS ALONE!

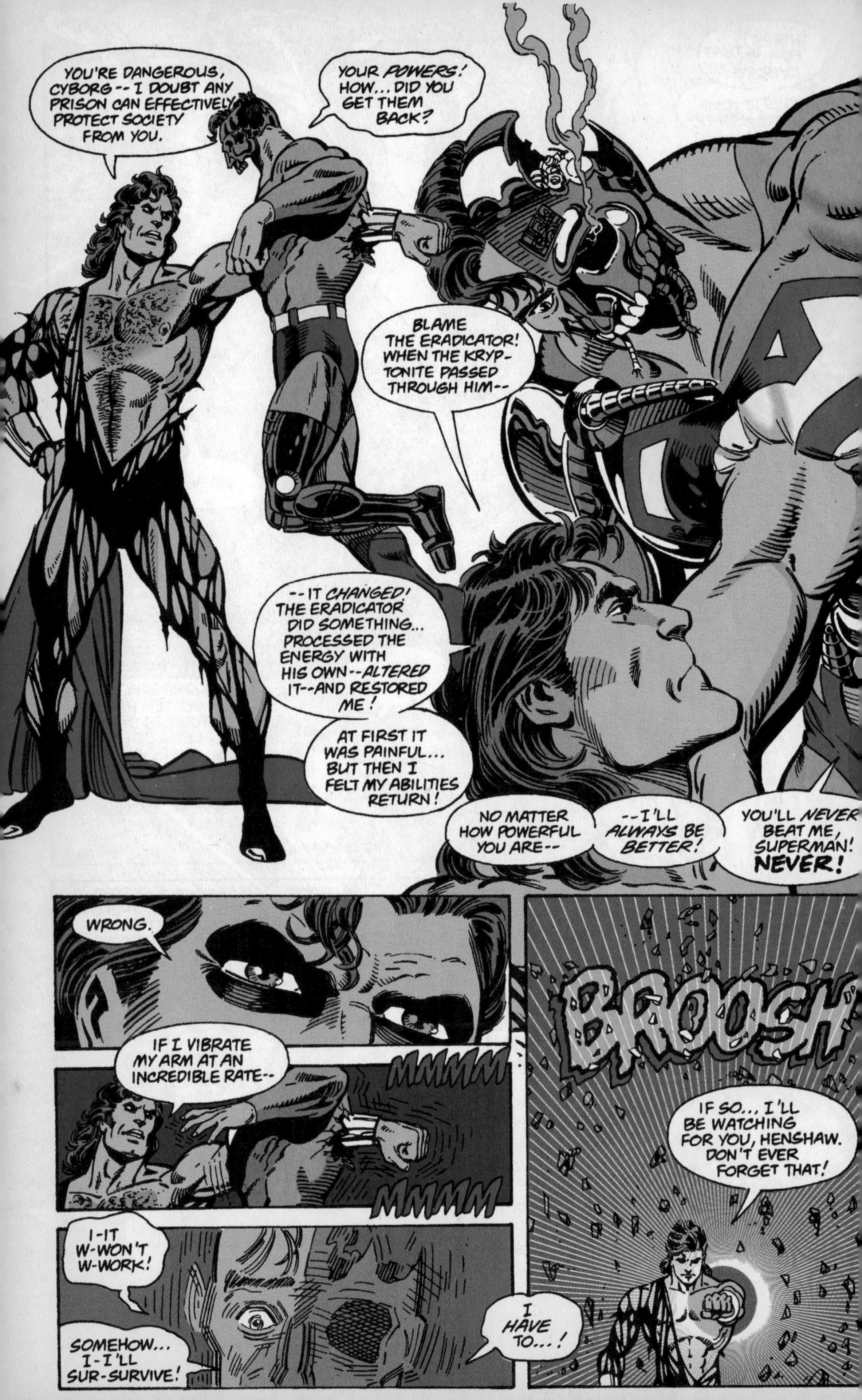
YOU'RE DANGEROUS, CYBORG -- I DOUBT ANY PRISON CAN EFFECTIVELY PROTECT SOCIETY FROM YOU.
YOUR POWERS! HOW... DID YOU GET THEM BACK?
BLAME THE ERADICATOR! WHEN THE KRYPTONITE PASSED THROUGH HIM--
--IT CHANGED! THE ERADICATOR DID SOMETHING... PROCESSED THE ENERGY WITH HIS OWN--ALTERED IT--AND RESTORED ME!
AT FIRST IT WAS PAINFUL... BUT THEN I FELT MY ABILITIES RETURN!
NO MATTER HOW POWERFUL YOU ARE--
--I'LL ALWAYS BE BETTER!
YOU'LL NEVER BEAT ME, SUPERMAN! NEVER!
WRONG.
IF I VIBRATE MY ARM AT AN INCREDIBLE RATE--
MMMMM
MMMMM
I-IT W-WON'T W-WORK!
SOMEHOW... I-I'LL SUR-SURVIVE!
I HAVE TO...!
BROOOSH
IF SO... I'LL BE WATCHING FOR YOU, HENSHAW. DON'T EVER FORGET THAT!

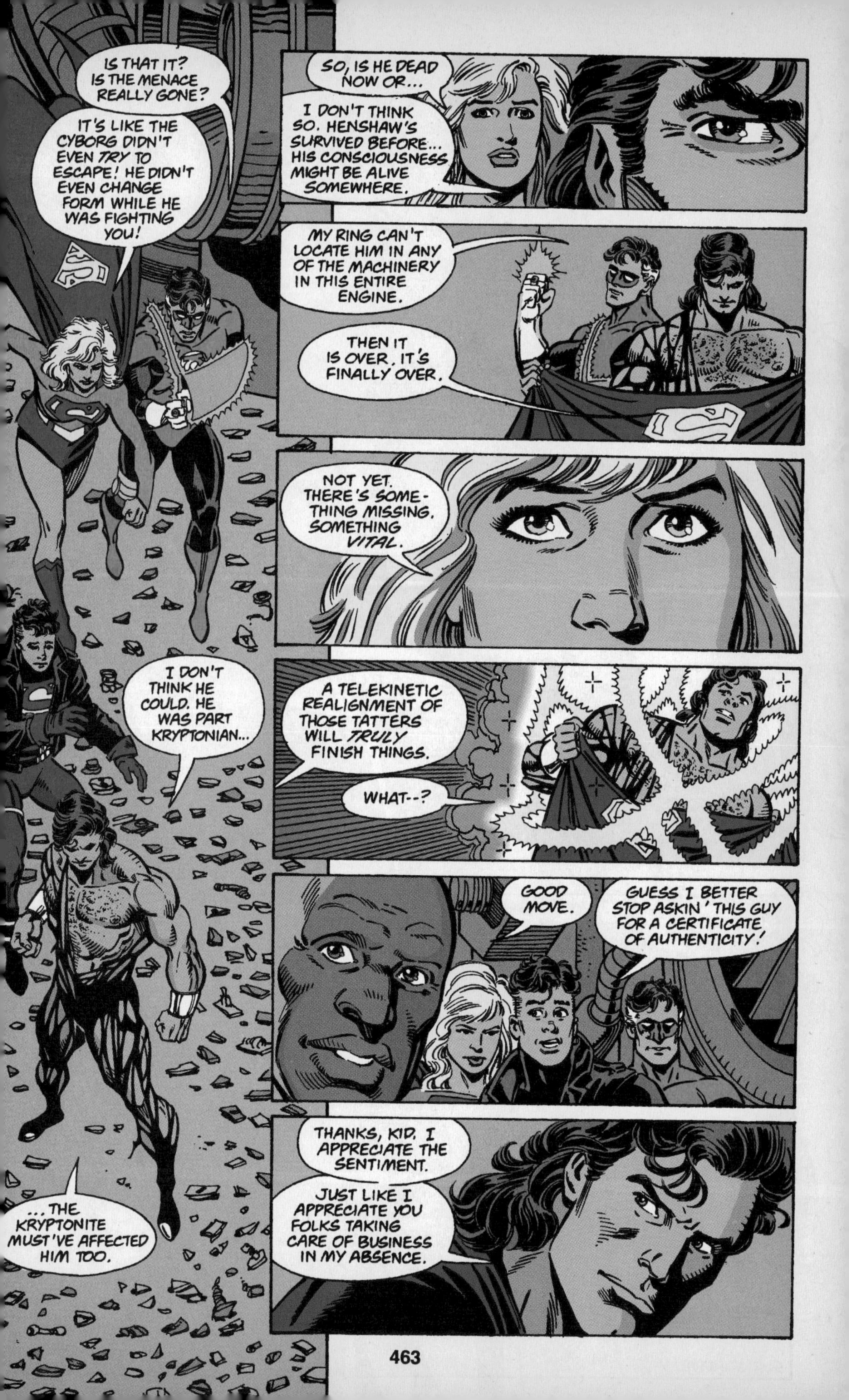
IS THAT IT? IS THE MENACE REALLY GONE?
IT'S LIKE THE CYBORG DIDN'T EVEN *TRY* TO ESCAPE! HE DIDN'T EVEN CHANGE FORM WHILE HE WAS FIGHTING YOU!
I DON'T THINK HE COULD. HE WAS PART KRYPTONIAN...
...THE KRYPTONITE MUST'VE AFFECTED HIM TOO.
SO, IS HE DEAD NOW OR...
I DON'T THINK SO. HENSHAW'S SURVIVED BEFORE... HIS CONSCIOUSNESS MIGHT BE ALIVE SOMEWHERE.
MY RING CAN'T LOCATE HIM IN ANY OF THE MACHINERY IN THIS ENTIRE ENGINE.
THEN IT IS OVER. IT'S FINALLY OVER.
NOT YET. THERE'S SOME-THING MISSING. SOMETHING *VITAL*.
A TELEKINETIC REALIGNMENT OF THOSE TATTERS WILL *TRULY* FINISH THINGS.
WHAT--?
GOOD MOVE.
GUESS I BETTER STOP ASKIN' THIS GUY FOR A CERTIFICATE OF AUTHENTICITY!
THANKS, KID. I APPRECIATE THE SENTIMENT.
JUST LIKE I APPRECIATE YOU FOLKS TAKING CARE OF BUSINESS IN MY ABSENCE.

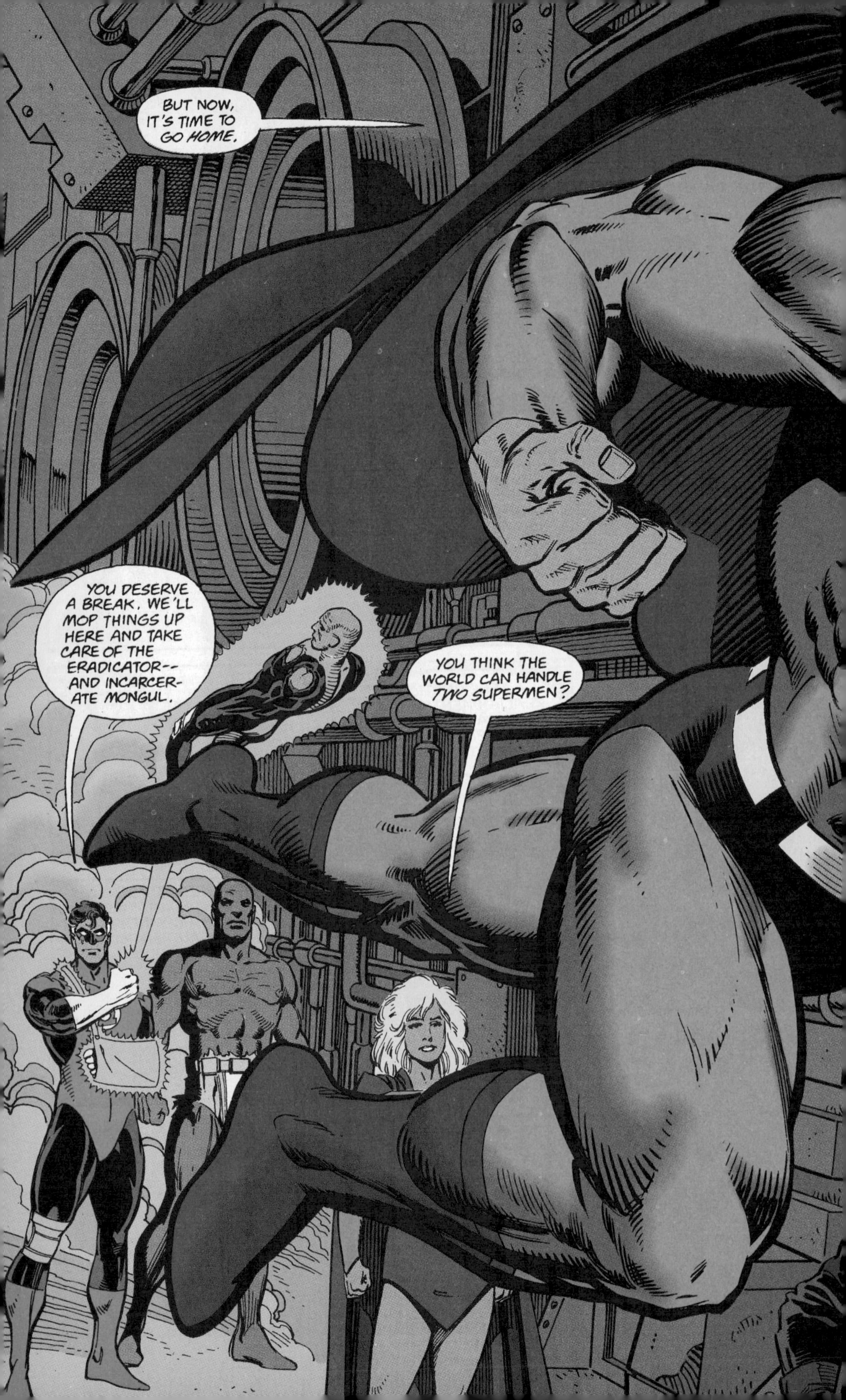

BUT NOW, IT'S TIME TO GO HOME.
YOU DESERVE A BREAK. WE'LL MOP THINGS UP HERE AND TAKE CARE OF THE ERADICATOR-- AND INCARCERATE MONGUL.
YOU THINK THE WORLD CAN HANDLE TWO SUPERMEN?

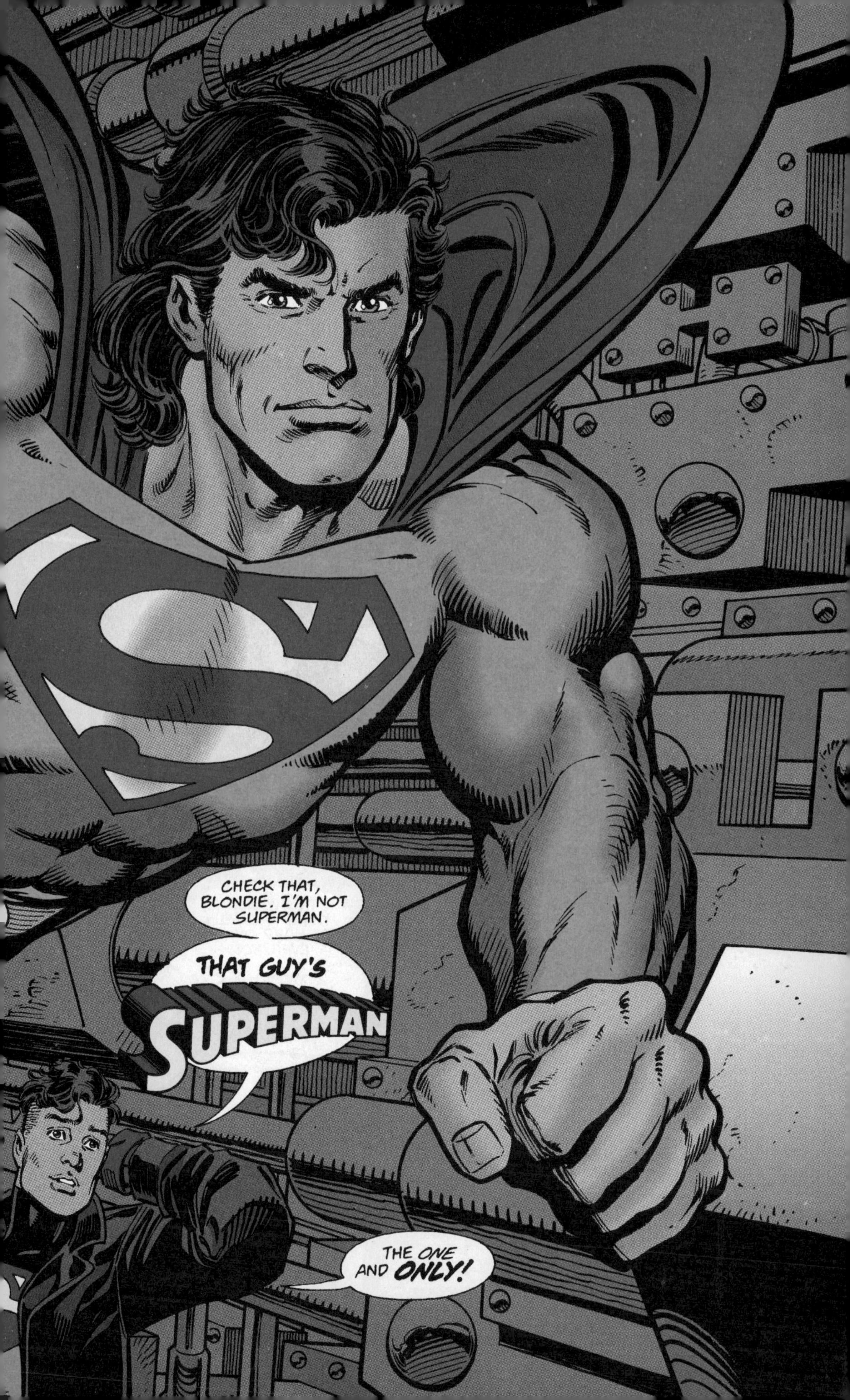
CHECK THAT, BLONDIE. I'M NOT SUPERMAN.
THAT GUY'S SUPERMAN
THE ONE AND ONLY!

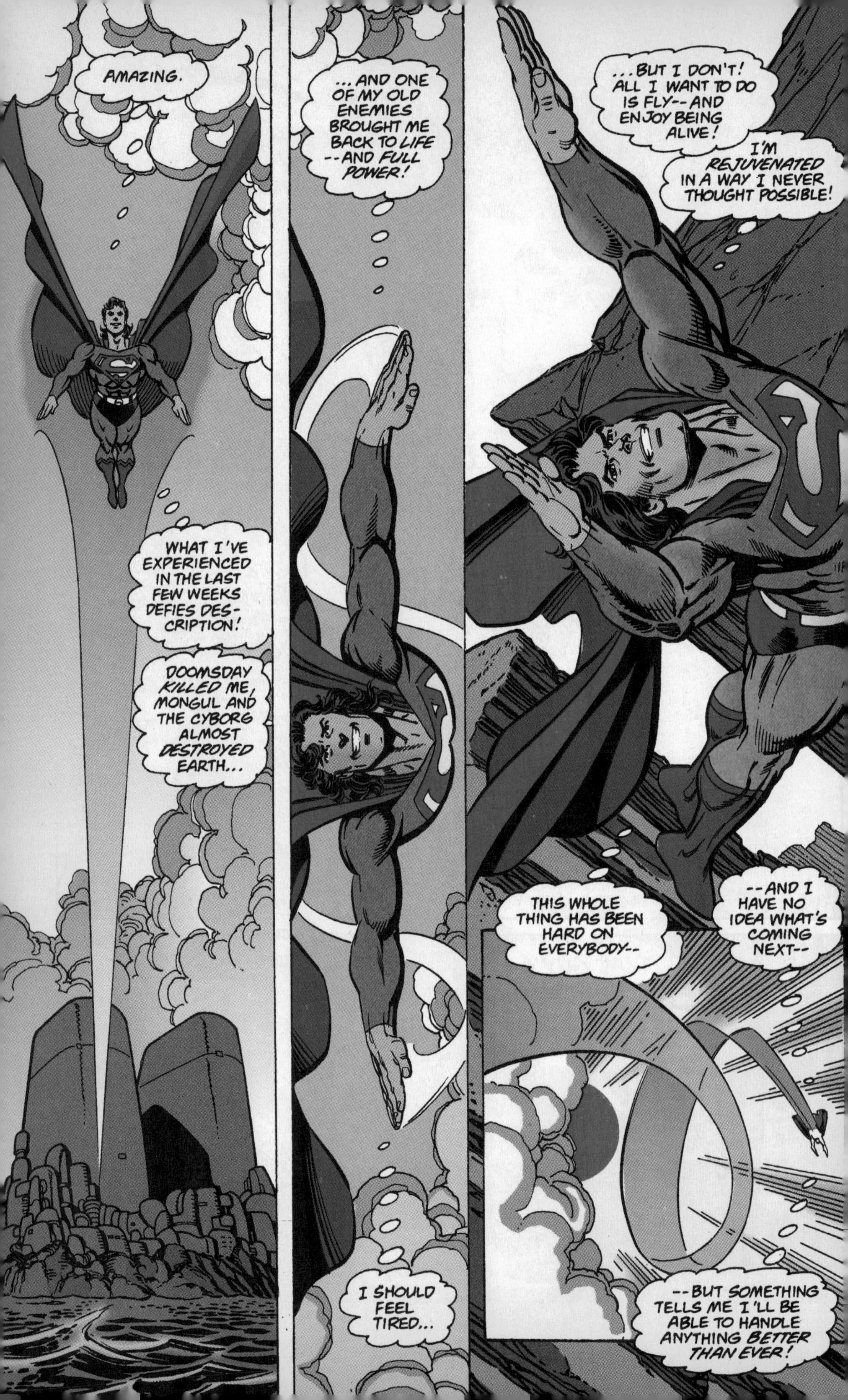
AMAZING.
WHAT I'VE EXPERIENCED IN THE LAST FEW WEEKS DEFIES DES-CRIPTION!
DOOMSDAY KILLED ME, MONGUL AND THE CYBORG ALMOST DESTROYED EARTH...
...AND ONE OF MY OLD ENEMIES BROUGHT ME BACK TO LIFE --AND FULL POWER!
I SHOULD FEEL TIRED...
...BUT I DON'T! ALL I WANT TO DO IS FLY--AND ENJOY BEING ALIVE!
I'M REJUVENATED IN A WAY I NEVER THOUGHT POSSIBLE!
THIS WHOLE THING HAS BEEN HARD ON EVERYBODY--
--AND I HAVE NO IDEA WHAT'S COMING NEXT--
--BUT SOMETHING TELLS ME I'LL BE ABLE TO HANDLE ANYTHING BETTER THAN EVER!

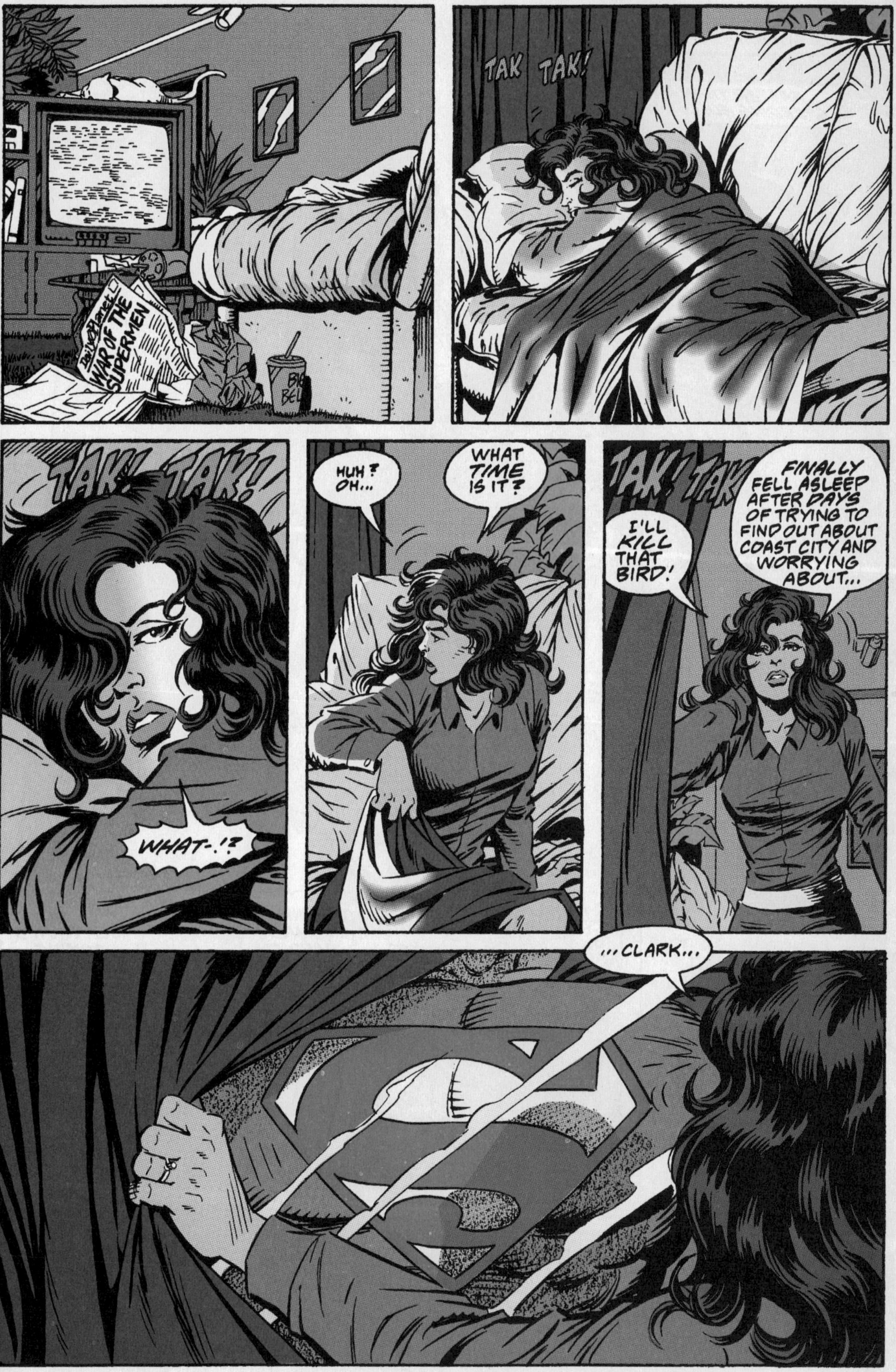

Daily Planet
WAR OF THE SUPERMEN
TAK TAK!
TAK! TAK!
WHAT-.!?
HUH? OH...
WHAT TIME IS IT?
TAK! TAK
I'LL KILL THAT BIRD!
FINALLY FELL ASLEEP AFTER DAYS OF TRYING TO FIND OUT ABOUT COAST CITY AND WORRYING ABOUT...
...CLARK...

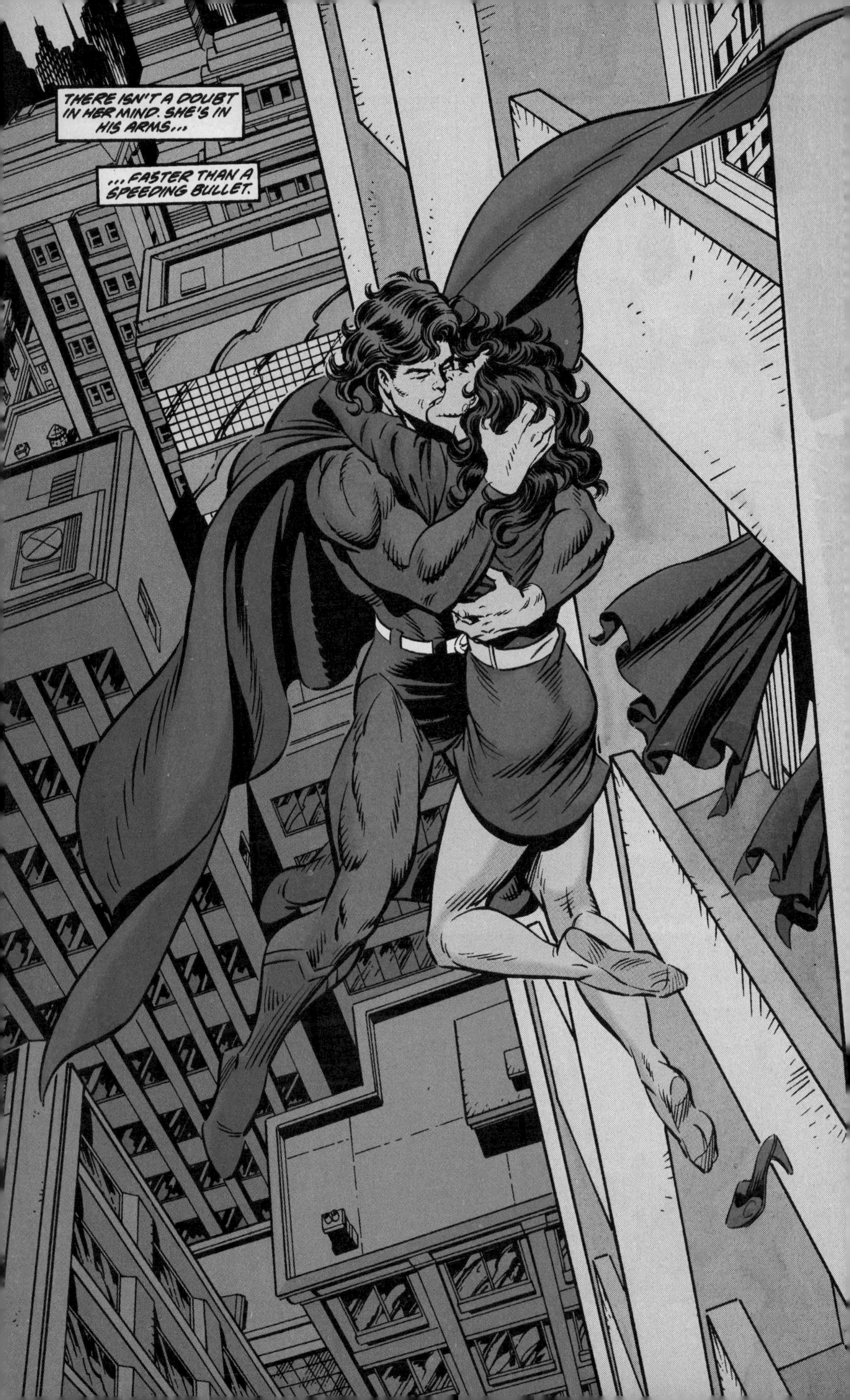
THERE ISN'T A DOUBT IN HER MIND. SHE'S IN HIS ARMS...
...FASTER THAN A SPEEDING BULLET.

EPILOG

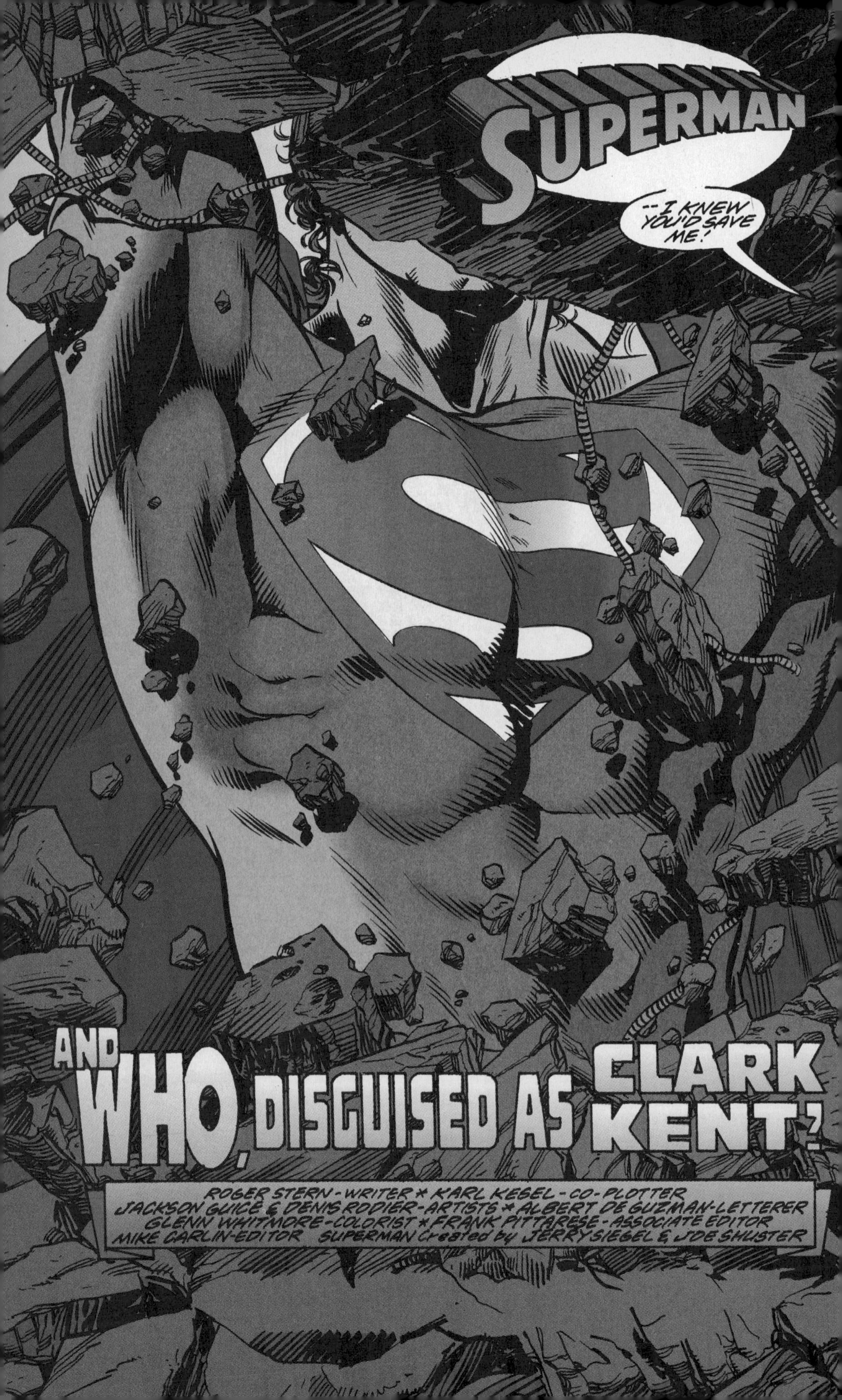
SUPERMAN
--I KNEW YOU'D SAVE ME!
AND WHO, DISGUISED AS CLARK KENT?
ROGER STERN-WRITER ✶ KARL KESEL-CO-PLOTTER
JACKSON GUICE & DENIS RODIER-ARTISTS ✶ ALBERT DE GUZMAN-LETTERER
GLENN WHITMORE-COLORIST ✶ FRANK PITTARESE-ASSOCIATE EDITOR
MIKE CARLIN-EDITOR SUPERMAN created by JERRY SIEGEL & JOE SHUSTER

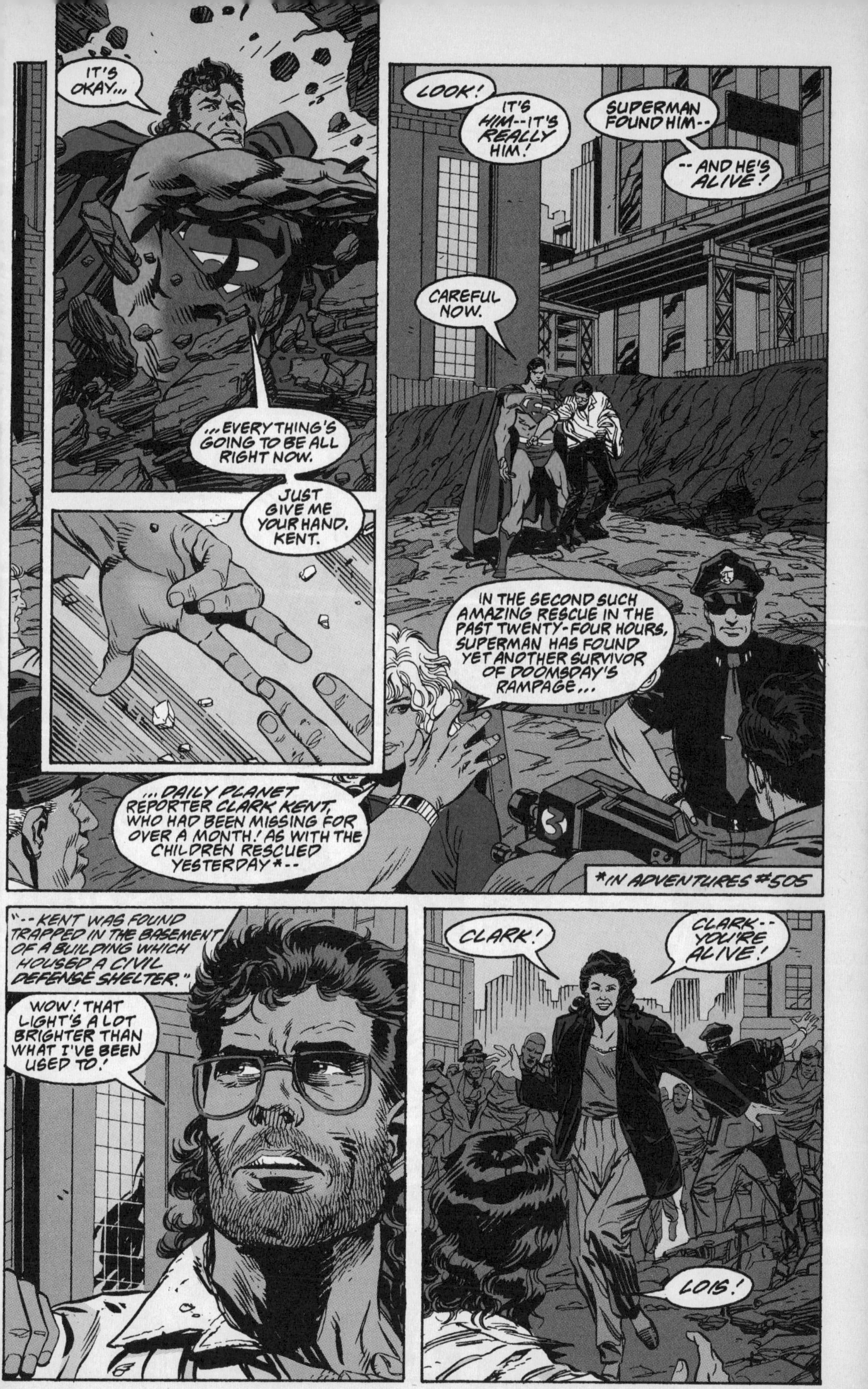
IT'S OKAY...
...EVERYTHING'S GOING TO BE ALL RIGHT NOW.
JUST GIVE ME YOUR HAND, KENT.
LOOK!
IT'S HIM--IT'S REALLY HIM!
SUPERMAN FOUND HIM--
--AND HE'S ALIVE!
CAREFUL NOW.
IN THE SECOND SUCH AMAZING RESCUE IN THE PAST TWENTY-FOUR HOURS, SUPERMAN HAS FOUND YET ANOTHER SURVIVOR OF DOOMSDAY'S RAMPAGE...
...DAILY PLANET REPORTER CLARK KENT, WHO HAD BEEN MISSING FOR OVER A MONTH! AS WITH THE CHILDREN RESCUED YESTERDAY*--
*IN ADVENTURES #505
"--KENT WAS FOUND TRAPPED IN THE BASEMENT OF A BUILDING WHICH HOUSED A CIVIL DEFENSE SHELTER."
WOW! THAT LIGHT'S A LOT BRIGHTER THAN WHAT I'VE BEEN USED TO!
CLARK!
CLARK--YOU'RE ALIVE!
LOIS!

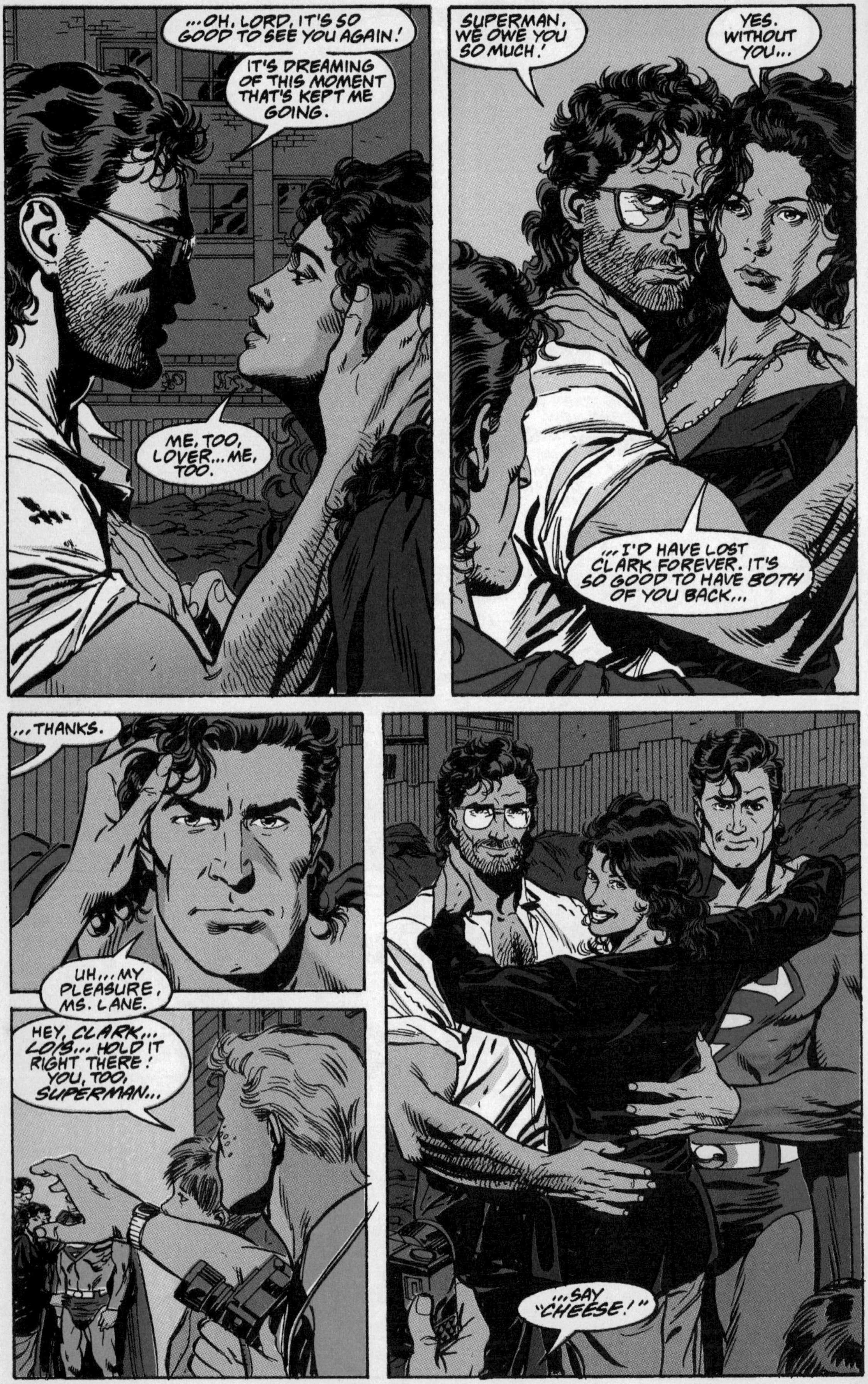
...OH, LORD, IT'S SO GOOD TO SEE YOU AGAIN!
IT'S DREAMING OF THIS MOMENT THAT'S KEPT ME GOING.
ME, TOO, LOVER... ME, TOO.
SUPERMAN, WE OWE YOU SO MUCH!
YES. WITHOUT YOU...
...I'D HAVE LOST CLARK FOREVER. IT'S SO GOOD TO HAVE BOTH OF YOU BACK...
...THANKS.
UH... MY PLEASURE, MS. LANE.
HEY, CLARK... LOIS... HOLD IT RIGHT THERE! YOU, TOO, SUPERMAN...
...SAY "CHEESE!"

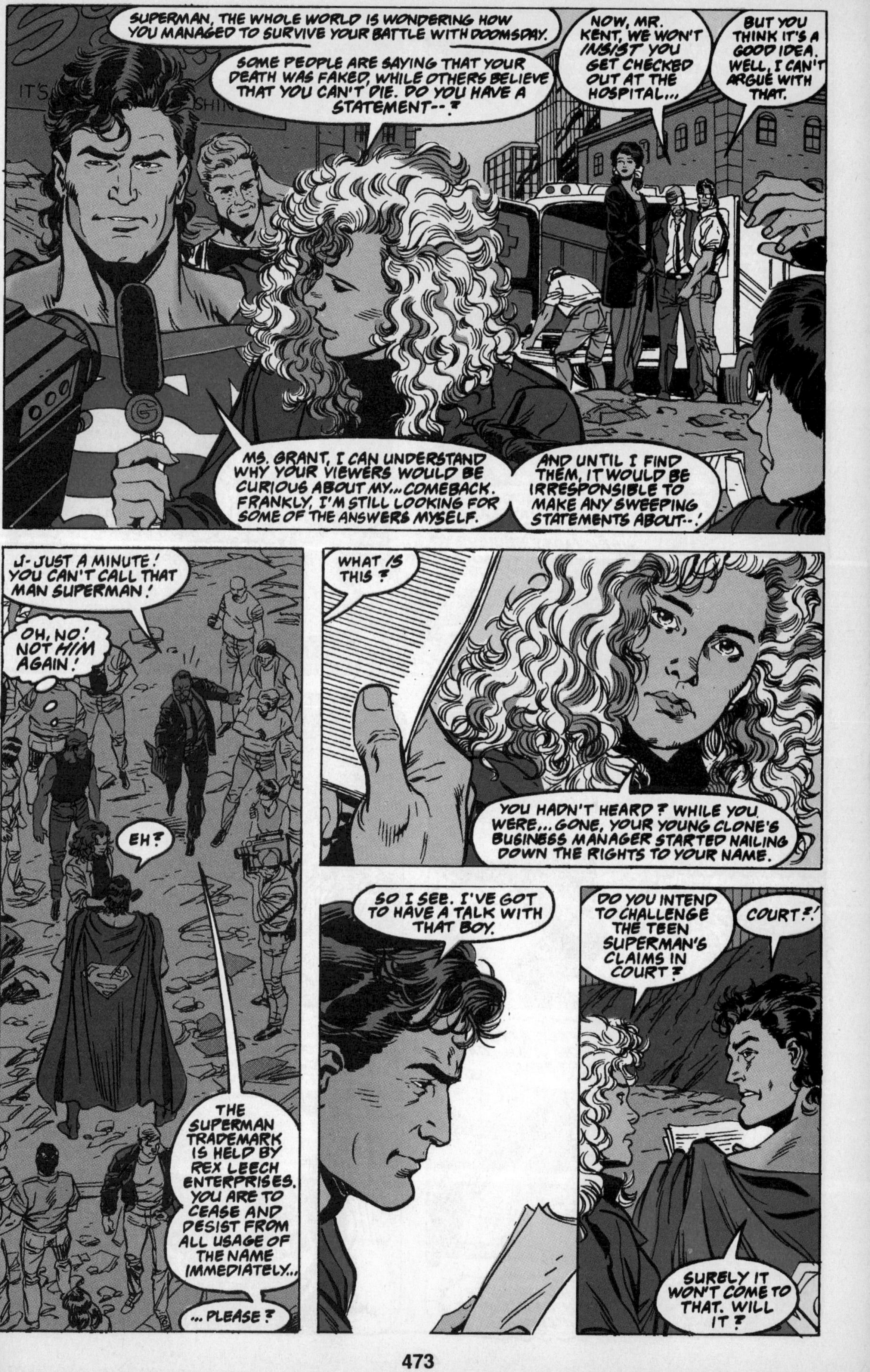

SUPERMAN, THE WHOLE WORLD IS WONDERING HOW YOU MANAGED TO SURVIVE YOUR BATTLE WITH DOOMSDAY.
SOME PEOPLE ARE SAYING THAT YOUR DEATH WAS FAKED, WHILE OTHERS BELIEVE THAT YOU CAN'T DIE. DO YOU HAVE A STATEMENT--?
NOW, MR. KENT, WE WON'T INSIST YOU GET CHECKED OUT AT THE HOSPITAL...
BUT YOU THINK IT'S A GOOD IDEA. WELL, I CAN'T ARGUE WITH THAT.
MS. GRANT, I CAN UNDERSTAND WHY YOUR VIEWERS WOULD BE CURIOUS ABOUT MY... COMEBACK. FRANKLY, I'M STILL LOOKING FOR SOME OF THE ANSWERS MYSELF.
AND UNTIL I FIND THEM, IT WOULD BE IRRESPONSIBLE TO MAKE ANY SWEEPING STATEMENTS ABOUT--!
J- JUST A MINUTE! YOU CAN'T CALL THAT MAN SUPERMAN!
OH, NO! NOT HIM AGAIN!
EH?
THE SUPERMAN TRADEMARK IS HELD BY REX LEECH ENTERPRISES. YOU ARE TO CEASE AND DESIST FROM ALL USAGE OF THE NAME IMMEDIATELY...
... PLEASE?
WHAT IS THIS?
YOU HADN'T HEARD? WHILE YOU WERE... GONE, YOUR YOUNG CLONE'S BUSINESS MANAGER STARTED NAILING DOWN THE RIGHTS TO YOUR NAME.
SO I SEE. I'VE GOT TO HAVE A TALK WITH THAT BOY.
DO YOU INTEND TO CHALLENGE THE TEEN SUPERMAN'S CLAIMS IN COURT?
COURT?!
SURELY IT WON'T COME TO THAT. WILL IT?

IT'S A COMPLICATED WORLD YOU'VE RETURNED TO, SUPERMAN.

IT WAS NEVER SIMPLE, MS. GRANT, BUT I SEE YOUR POINT.

I JUST HOPE THAT CLARK KENT HAS AN EASIER TIME READJUSTING TO HIS LIFE THAN I DO TO MINE!

AND SO ENDS THE FIRST FULL DAY BACK ON THE JOB FOR THE MAN WHOM MOST BELIEVE TO BE THE ORIGINAL SUPERMAN-- ALIVE AND WELL!

EVENTS OF THE PAST FEW DAYS HAVE NOT BEEN SO KIND TO HIS WOULD-BE REPLACEMENTS...

...THERE HAS BEEN NO WORD ON THE CONDITION OF THE SELF-PROCLAIMED "SON OF KRYPTON" WHO WAS EARLIER RECEIVED BY S.T.A.R. LABS XENOBIOLOGISTS.

THE FULL EXTENT OF HIS INJURIES, REPORTEDLY INCURRED AT THE COAST CITY DISASTER ZONE, ARE UNKNOWN.

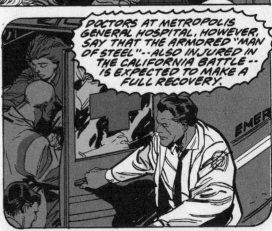

DOCTORS AT METROPOLIS GENERAL HOSPITAL, HOWEVER, SAY THAT THE ARMORED "MAN OF STEEL"--ALSO INJURED IN THE CALIFORNIA BATTLE-- IS EXPECTED TO MAKE A FULL RECOVERY.

ALREADY BACK ON HIS FEET, AFTER SAVING METROPOLIS FROM A SNEAK MISSILE ATTACK, IS THE TEEN SUPERMAN--

--SHOWN HERE WITH LEXCORP'S SUPERGIRL.

IN WASHINGTON, GOVERNMENT OFFICIALS RUSHED TO DISCREDIT THE ROGUE CYBORG-SUPERMAN WHO WAS RESPONSIBLE FOR THE DESTRUCTION OF COAST CITY.

PENTAGON SOURCES HAVE CONFIRMED THAT THE SUPER-IMPOSTOR WAS DESTROYED BY THE ORIGINAL SUPERMAN.

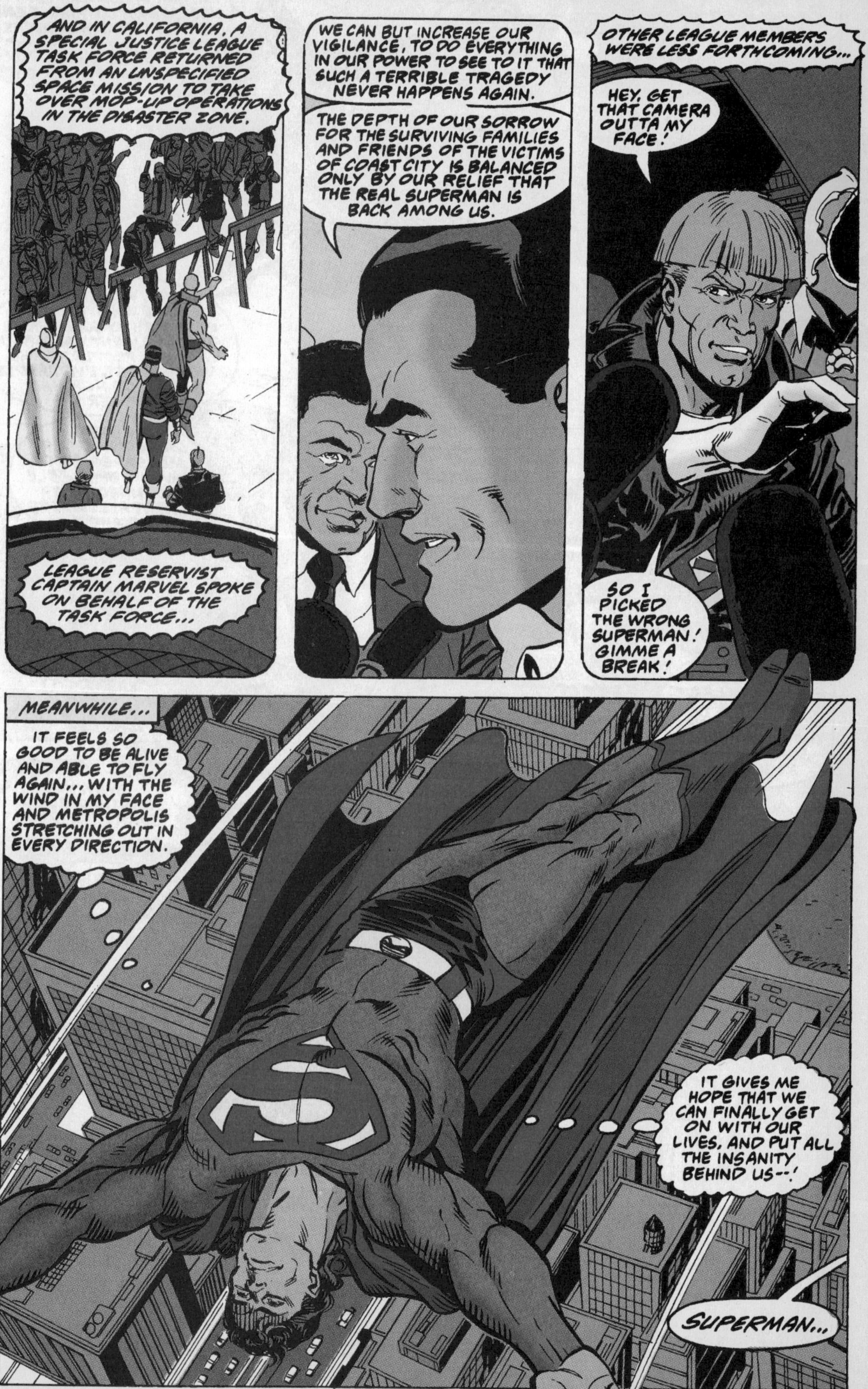
AND IN CALIFORNIA, A SPECIAL JUSTICE LEAGUE TASK FORCE RETURNED FROM AN UNSPECIFIED SPACE MISSION TO TAKE OVER MOP-UP OPERATIONS IN THE DISASTER ZONE.
LEAGUE RESERVIST CAPTAIN MARVEL SPOKE ON BEHALF OF THE TASK FORCE...
WE CAN BUT INCREASE OUR VIGILANCE, TO DO EVERYTHING IN OUR POWER TO SEE TO IT THAT SUCH A TERRIBLE TRAGEDY NEVER HAPPENS AGAIN.
THE DEPTH OF OUR SORROW FOR THE SURVIVING FAMILIES AND FRIENDS OF THE VICTIMS OF COAST CITY IS BALANCED ONLY BY OUR RELIEF THAT THE REAL SUPERMAN IS BACK AMONG US.
OTHER LEAGUE MEMBERS WERE LESS FORTHCOMING...
HEY, GET THAT CAMERA OUTTA MY FACE!
SO I PICKED THE WRONG SUPERMAN! GIMME A BREAK!
MEANWHILE...
IT FEELS SO GOOD TO BE ALIVE AND ABLE TO FLY AGAIN... WITH THE WIND IN MY FACE AND METROPOLIS STRETCHING OUT IN EVERY DIRECTION.
IT GIVES ME HOPE THAT WE CAN FINALLY GET ON WITH OUR LIVES, AND PUT ALL THE INSANITY BEHIND US--!
SUPERMAN...

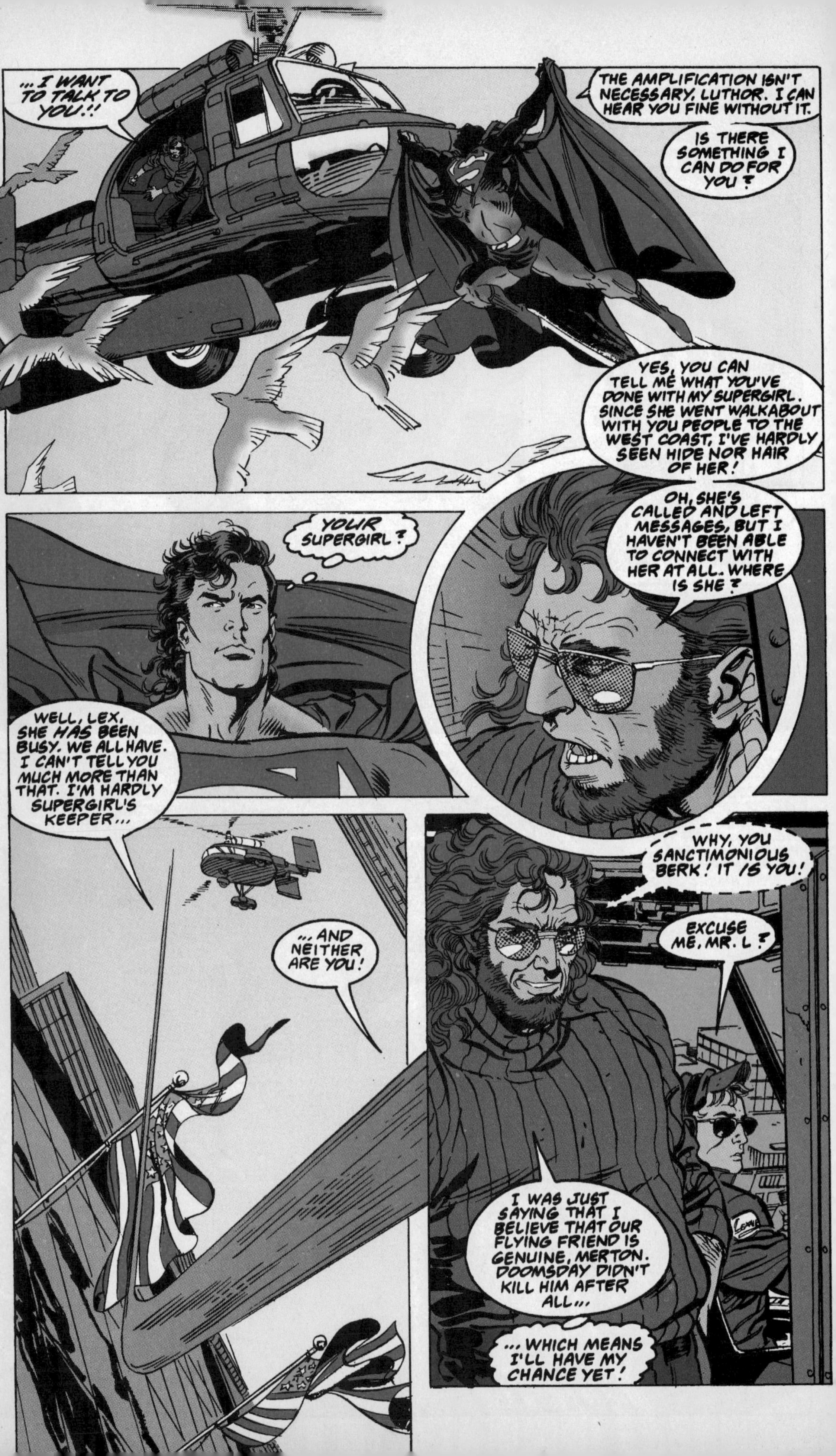
...I WANT TO TALK TO YOU!!
THE AMPLIFICATION ISN'T NECESSARY, LUTHOR. I CAN HEAR YOU FINE WITHOUT IT.
IS THERE SOMETHING I CAN DO FOR YOU?
YES, YOU CAN TELL ME WHAT YOU'VE DONE WITH MY SUPERGIRL. SINCE SHE WENT WALKABOUT WITH YOU PEOPLE TO THE WEST COAST, I'VE HARDLY SEEN HIDE NOR HAIR OF HER!
YOUR SUPERGIRL?
OH, SHE'S CALLED AND LEFT MESSAGES, BUT I HAVEN'T BEEN ABLE TO CONNECT WITH HER AT ALL. WHERE IS SHE?
WELL, LEX, SHE HAS BEEN BUSY. WE ALL HAVE. I CAN'T TELL YOU MUCH MORE THAN THAT. I'M HARDLY SUPERGIRL'S KEEPER...
...AND NEITHER ARE YOU!
WHY, YOU SANCTIMONIOUS BERK! IT IS YOU!
EXCUSE ME, MR. L?
I WAS JUST SAYING THAT I BELIEVE THAT OUR FLYING FRIEND IS GENUINE, MERTON. DOOMSDAY DIDN'T KILL HIM AFTER ALL...
...WHICH MEANS I'LL HAVE MY CHANCE YET!

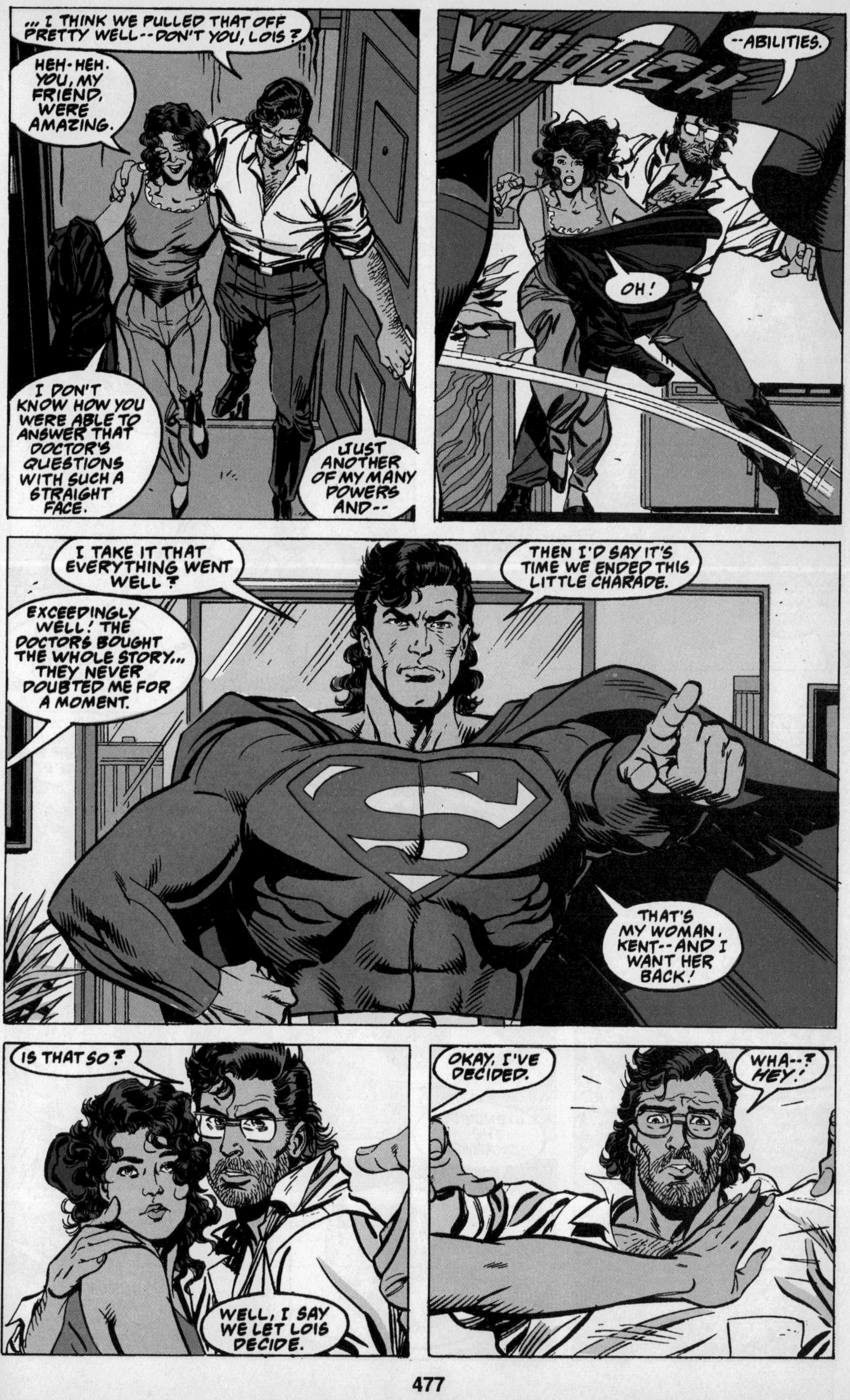
...I THINK WE PULLED THAT OFF PRETTY WELL--DON'T YOU, LOIS?
HEH-HEH. YOU, MY FRIEND, WERE AMAZING.
I DON'T KNOW HOW YOU WERE ABLE TO ANSWER THAT DOCTOR'S QUESTIONS WITH SUCH A STRAIGHT FACE.
JUST ANOTHER OF MY MANY POWERS AND--
WHOOSH
--ABILITIES.
OH!
I TAKE IT THAT EVERYTHING WENT WELL?
EXCEEDINGLY WELL! THE DOCTORS BOUGHT THE WHOLE STORY... THEY NEVER DOUBTED ME FOR A MOMENT.
THEN I'D SAY IT'S TIME WE ENDED THIS LITTLE CHARADE.
THAT'S MY WOMAN, KENT--AND I WANT HER BACK!
IS THAT SO?
WELL, I SAY WE LET LOIS DECIDE.
OKAY, I'VE DECIDED.
WHA--? HEY!

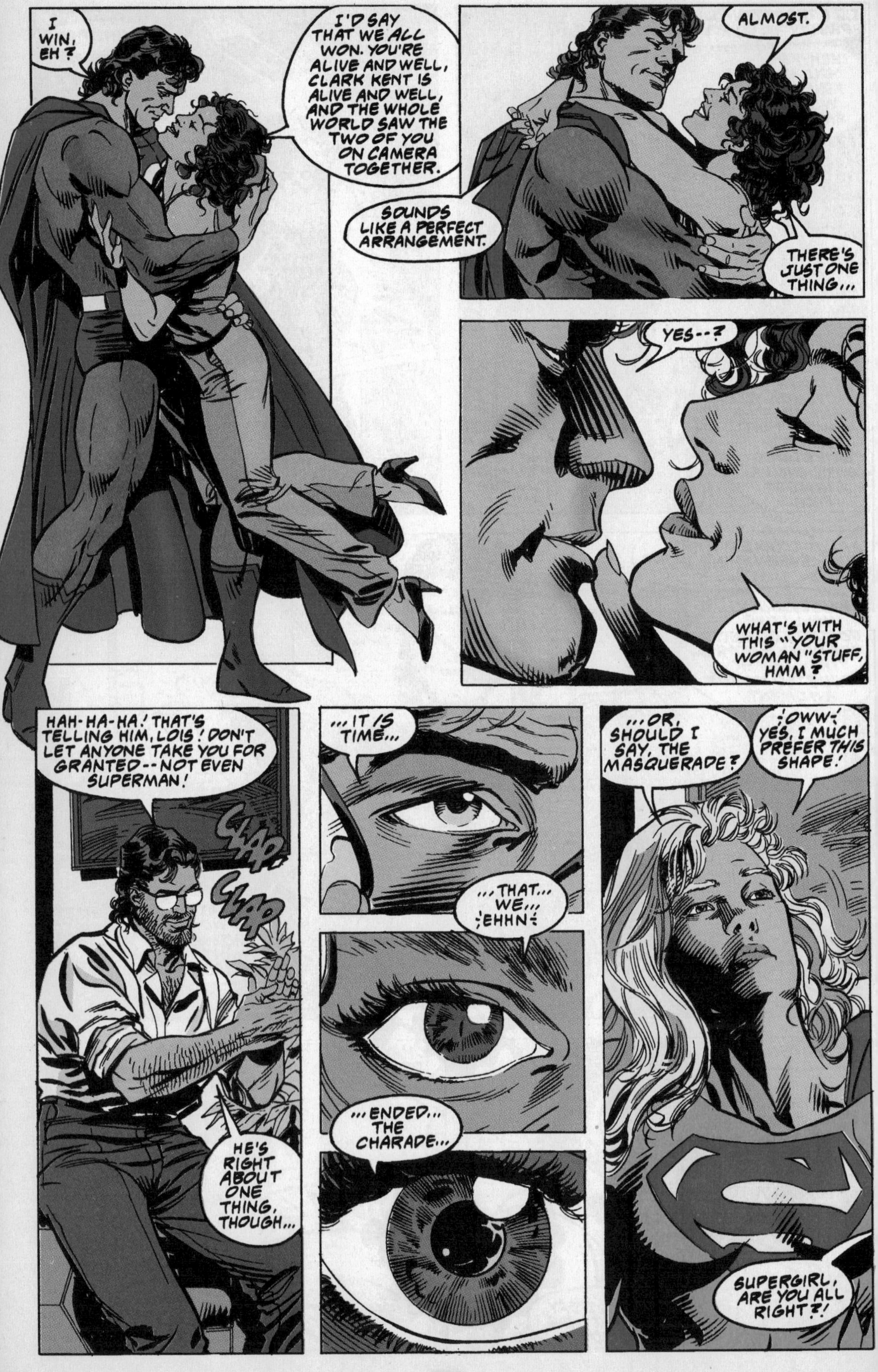
I WIN, EH?
I'D SAY THAT WE ALL WON. YOU'RE ALIVE AND WELL, CLARK KENT IS ALIVE AND WELL, AND THE WHOLE WORLD SAW THE TWO OF YOU ON CAMERA TOGETHER.
SOUNDS LIKE A PERFECT ARRANGEMENT.
ALMOST.
THERE'S JUST ONE THING...
YES--?
WHAT'S WITH THIS "YOUR WOMAN" STUFF, HMM?
HAH-HA-HA! THAT'S TELLING HIM, LOIS! DON'T LET ANYONE TAKE YOU FOR GRANTED--NOT EVEN SUPERMAN!
HE'S RIGHT ABOUT ONE THING, THOUGH...
...IT IS TIME...
...THAT... WE... ;EHHN;
...ENDED... THE CHARADE...
...OR, SHOULD I SAY, THE MASQUERADE?
;OWW-! YES, I MUCH PREFER THIS SHAPE!
SUPERGIRL, ARE YOU ALL RIGHT?!

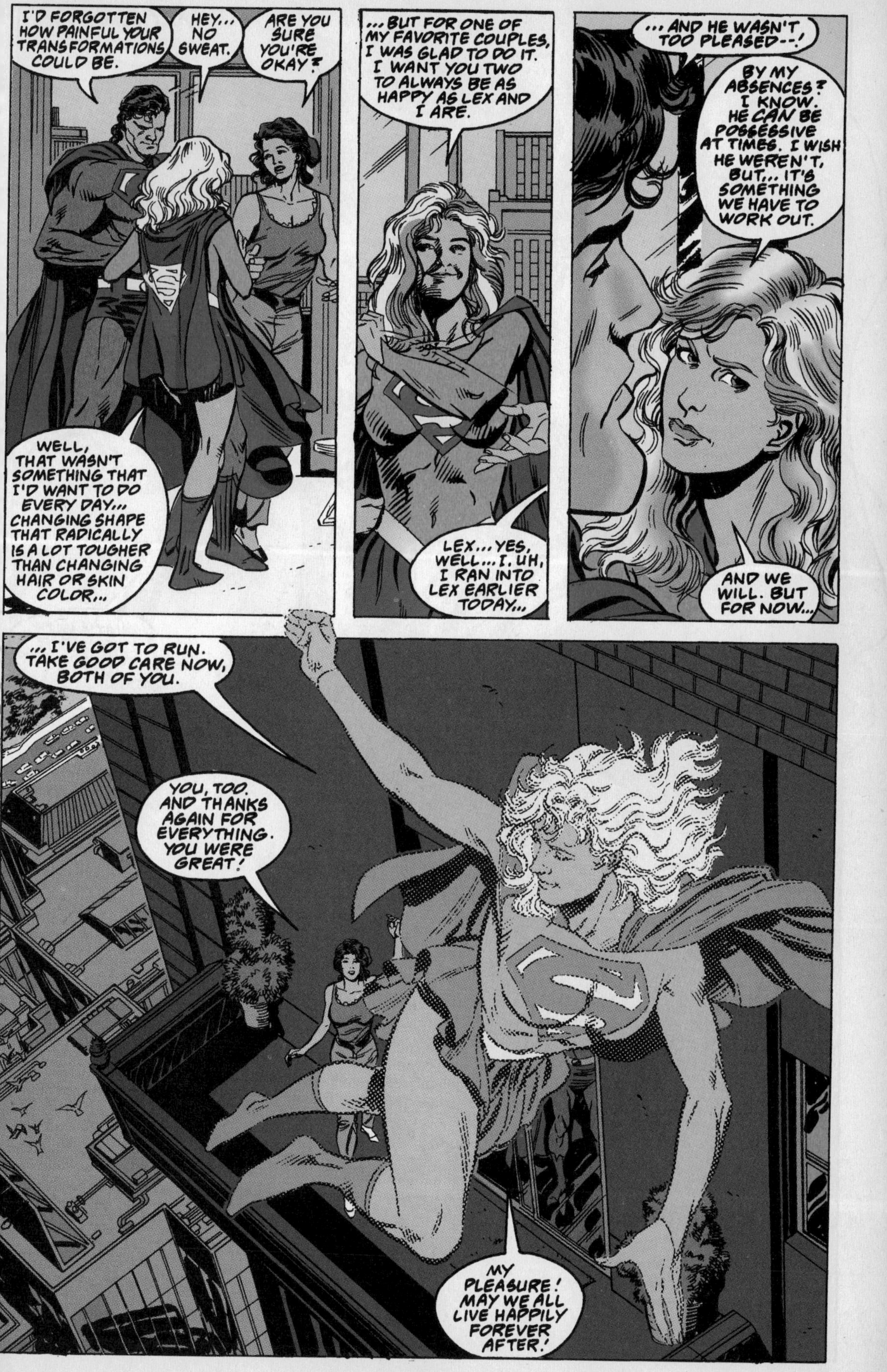
I'D FORGOTTEN HOW PAINFUL YOUR TRANSFORMATIONS COULD BE.
HEY... NO SWEAT.
ARE YOU SURE YOU'RE OKAY?
WELL, THAT WASN'T SOMETHING THAT I'D WANT TO DO EVERY DAY... CHANGING SHAPE THAT RADICALLY IS A LOT TOUGHER THAN CHANGING HAIR OR SKIN COLOR...
...BUT FOR ONE OF MY FAVORITE COUPLES, I WAS GLAD TO DO IT. I WANT YOU TWO TO ALWAYS BE AS HAPPY AS LEX AND I ARE.
LEX... YES, WELL... I, UH, I RAN INTO LEX EARLIER TODAY...
...AND HE WASN'T TOO PLEASED--!
BY MY ABSENCES? I KNOW. HE CAN BE POSSESSIVE AT TIMES. I WISH HE WEREN'T, BUT... IT'S SOMETHING WE HAVE TO WORK OUT.
AND WE WILL. BUT FOR NOW...
...I'VE GOT TO RUN. TAKE GOOD CARE NOW, BOTH OF YOU.
YOU, TOO. AND THANKS AGAIN FOR EVERYTHING. YOU WERE GREAT!
MY PLEASURE! MAY WE ALL LIVE HAPPILY FOREVER AFTER!

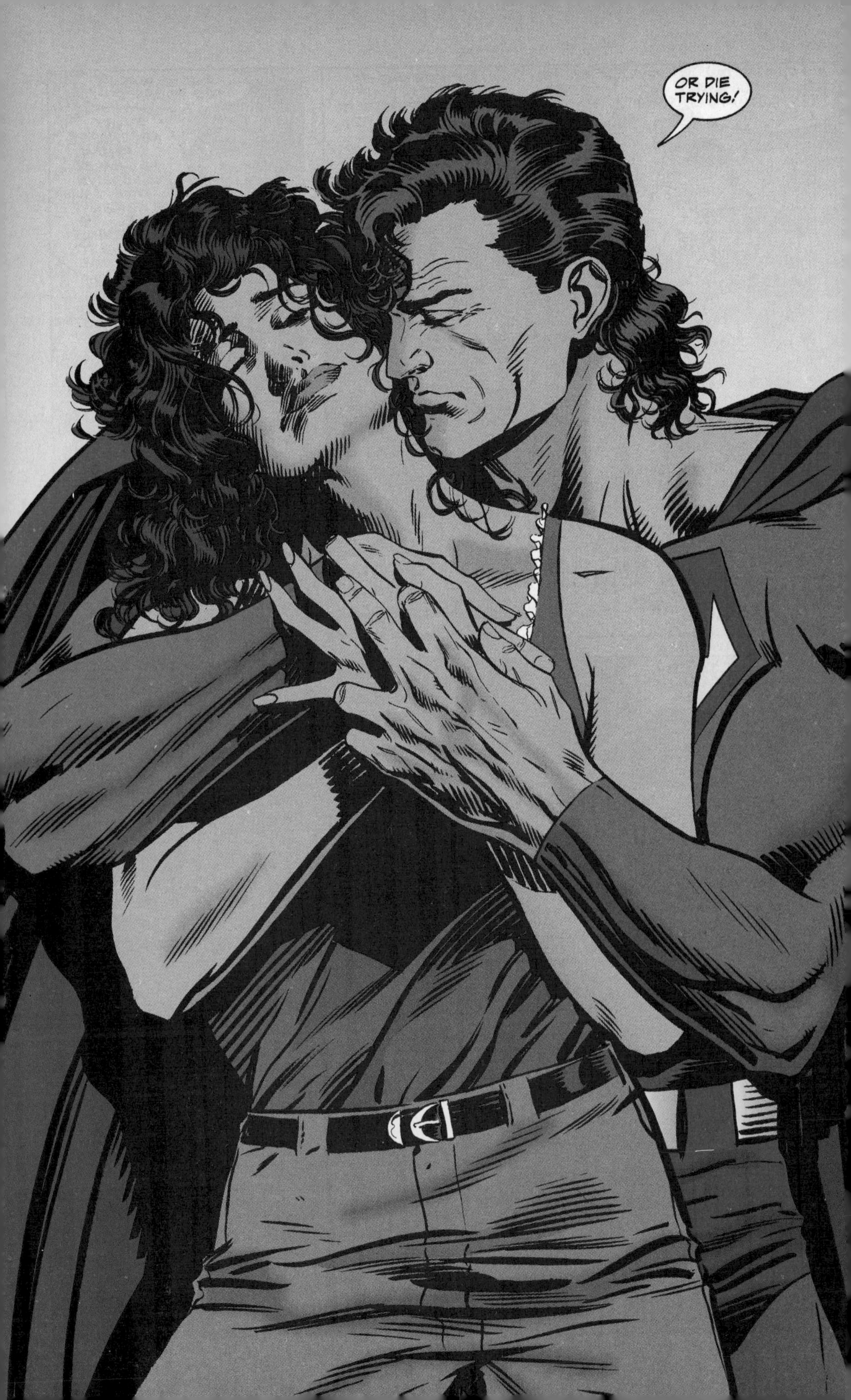
OR DIE TRYING!